EIGHTH EDITION

The
Encyclopedia of
Careers
and
Vocational Guidance

WILLIAM E. HOPKE

Editor-in-Chief

VOLUME 3

General and Special Careers

J.G. FERGUSON PUBLISHING COMPANY

Chicago, Illinois

Library of Congress Cataloging-in-Publication Data

The Encyclopedia of careers and vocational guidance/ William E. Hopke, editor-in-chief. 8th ed.
    p. cm.
    Contents: v.1 Industry profiles — v.2. Professional careers — v.3. General and special careers —v.4. Technicians' careers. Includes indexes.
    ISBN 0-89434-117-0 (set). —ISBN 0-89434-113-8 (v.1). —ISBN 0-89434-114-6 (v.2). —ISBN 0-89434-115-4 (V.3).
— ISBN 0-89434-116-2 (v.4)
    1. Vocational guidance—Handbooks, manuals, etc. 2. Occupations—Handbooks, manuals, etc. I. Hopke, William E.
HF5381.E52 1990
331.7'02—dc20

90-3743
CIP

ISBN 0-89434-117-0 (set)
       0-89434-113-8 (volume 1)
       0-89434-114-6 (volume 2)
       0-89434-115-4 (volume 3)
       0-89434-116-2 (volume 4)

Printed in the United States of America
N-8

Editorial Staff

Editorial Director: C.J. Summerfield

Assistant Editor: Amy I. Brown

Contributing Editors: Susan Ashby, John Morse, Nancy Parsegian, Mark Toch, James Unland

Writers: Pamela Dell, Lillian Flowers, Jim Garner, Phyllis Miller, Jeanne Rattenbury, Fran Sherman

Photo Editor: Carol Parden

Indexer: Carol Nielson

Designer: Shawn M. Biner, Biner Design

Copyeditors and Proofreaders: Wordsmiths

Production Manager: Tom Myles

Contents

Volume 3: General and Special Careers

KEY TO OCCUPATIONAL CATEGORIES

 Industry Profiles. This represents the articles that outline descriptions of industries in Volume 1.

 Professional, Administrative, and Managerial Occupations. Covering careers that involve extensive academic training or practical training, these occupations include many of the jobs that require undergraduate or graduate school education. Volume 2

 Clerical Occupations. Clerical occupations are those involved with handling the records, communications, and general office duties required in every business. Volume 3

 Sales Occupations. This section includes sales careers for goods, services, and property, and careers for sales-related business. Volume 3

 Service Occupations. Careers in service comprise occupations that assist people in various aspects of life, from protection by law enforcement to physical care. Volume 3

 Agriculture, Forestry, and Conservation Occupations. Encompassing the occupations that work with various elements of nature, this category includes skilled and technicians' work related to farm production, mining, animal care, and wildlife services. Volume 3 and 4

 Processing Occupations. These are occupations that involve the mixing, treating, and recomposition of materials, chemicals, and products, normally through the use of machinery or tools. Volume 3

 Machine Trades Occupations. Careers in machine trades are those that work with machine assembly, maintenance, and repair. They work with metals, plastics, wood, paper, and stone in construction and repair. Volume 3

 Bench Work Occupations. With an emphasis on hand tools and dexterity skills, bench workers make and repair products that require manual deftness, such as jewelry or optical equipment. Volume 3

Structural Work Occupations. This category details the occupations involved in construction and repair of all large structures from bridges to homes. Volume 3

 Emerging Technician Occupations. Falling mainly into the fields of science and technology, these technicians occupations are either not yet catalogued into one of the sections following or will not be catalogued into an existing field. Volume 4

 Engineering and Science Technician Occupations. These technicians work with scientists and engineers as part of a team trained in the technical aspects of the work performed. Volume 4

 Broadcast, Media, and Arts Technicians Occupations. The technicians who operate, maintain, and repair the equipment involved in broadcasting and the arts are trained to run electronic, electrical, and mechanical equipment. Volume 4

 Medical and Health Technician Occupations. Responsible for the technical equipment used in medical fields, these technicians run the sophisticated machinery used by medical specialists. Volume 4

 Miscellaneous Occupations. In this section are the occupations that require skilled or semi-skilled levels of training. This includes a diverse range of job categories, including graphics arts, transportation and technicians in information services as well as other fields. Volume 3 and 4

Clerical Occupations

This occupational group includes all those workers who have various types of clerical duties to perform in their jobs. In the early 1990s, some 20 million persons were employed in clerical jobs or in closely related positions. Generally speaking, the majority of clerical employees serve business and industry by handling the great volume of communication and record keeping necessary for operation. They may also assume responsibility for forms of communication, such as mail, telephone, telegraph, and messenger service, or they may be involved with the shipping and receiving of products and merchandise. Other clerical personnel may work as cashiers, bank tellers, air traffic agents, or operate clerical types of equipment, such as computers and many kinds of office machines. Numerous skills are reflected in this occupational group.

Approximately one of every five clerical workers is employed as a secretary, a typist, or a stenographer. Tens of thousands are employed as telephone operators, bookkeepers, cashiers, shipping and receiving clerks, or mail carriers. Fewer persons work as airline ticket agents, railroad clerks, station agents, and bank tellers.

The skill, education, and training needed for these clerical positions vary with the type of work performed. For the majority of positions, regardless of the individual's degree of formal education, on-the-job training is given to acquaint new employees with the work routine of specific job situations.

Applicants frequently enter these jobs by taking related jobs in firms, businesses, or industry in which they wish to be employed. Aptitudes for reading comprehension, grammar, spelling, arithmetic, business mathematics, and a good memory are assets for these employees. Other factors that may be considered include advanced formal educational training, years of experience, seniority, and the work performance record of the employee. Some promo-tions may be to jobs of greater responsibility, to higher pay, or to managerial and supervisory positions as heads of departments.

The employment outlook for this occupational group and for related occupations is expected to be good through the mid-1990s. Numbers of these jobs will come about as the result of the country's growing business economy, and as new businesses and industries are developed to serve the nation's needs.

Between now and 2000, although automation and technology may have some effect on the number of workers needed, employment in clerical occupations is expected to grow from 19 to 22.8 million workers. The number of new positions that will be created as a result of business expansion and a growing economy is expected to be greater than the number of clerical jobs eliminated by computers.

In the early 1990s the average salaries of clerical workers ranged from $8,740 a year for beginning file clerks to about $19,200 a year for executive secretaries. Rather wide differences were found among individuals' salaries within each occupation. Men generally earned higher salaries than women although they were employed in similar jobs. Highest salary schedules were reported in the western part of the country. Employees of public utility and manufacturing firms earned higher salaries than those working in non-manufacturing industries and retail businesses.

Fringe benefits for these workers may include paid legal holidays; paid vacation time; group life, hospitalization, surgical, and medical insurance benefits; retirement and pension benefits; and other benefits as determined by individual company policy.

These employees perform many jobs to help turn the wheels of progress in industry, manufacturing, and in all types of businesses. The entire clerical occupational group is important to the economy of the country and to the individual public profiting from their services.

Billing clerks

Definition

Billing clerks make entries in business ledgers and verify invoices and purchase orders to maintain and update records of a company's business transactions. They are responsible for posting items in accounts payable or receivable, making out bills and invoices, and verifying the company's rates for certain products and services. Billing clerks perform much of their work with the aid of adding machines and calculators.

History

As long as people have engaged in trade and commerce, there has been the need to record business transactions. Wealthy traders during the early Egyptian and Babylonian civilizations often used slaves to make markings on clay tablets to keep track of purchases and sales.

With the rise of monarchies in Europe, billing clerks were needed to record the business transactions of kings, queens, and other wealthy individuals, and also to monitor the status of the royal treasury. The Industrial Revolution, with its increase in the level of commercial transactions, intensified the need for billing clerks in all areas of business.

Today, although modern technology has changed the way they record transactions, billing clerks continue to occupy a central role in the business world.

Nature of the work

Billing clerks are responsible for keeping records and up-to-date accounts of all business transactions. This entails a variety of duties, such as typing and mailing bills for services or products provided and updating files to reflect the payment of these fees when they arrive. Billing clerks also check invoices that come from other companies to ensure that the products or services specified on the invoice have in fact been delivered and there are no overcharges or other errors. Billing clerks ensure that invoices are paid in a timely manner.

The billing clerk is responsible for entering all transaction information onto an account ledger that reflects the items bought or sold in a transaction as well as the credit terms and the date of the transactions. For example, if a billing clerk works for an insurance company, the transaction sheet will reflect when bills are payable and the amount due. As payments come in, credit is applied to this overall figure and any discounts are applied. Summary statements are prepared for periodic review by management officials. All correspondence is carefully filed for future reference. Calculators are a billing clerk's primary tool, and increasingly computers are being utilized to process and store information.

Billing clerks are also often responsible for working on the preparation of summary statements of financial status, profit and loss statements, and payroll lists and deductions. Clerks also write company checks, compute federal tax reports, and tabulate personnel profit shares.

Billing clerks set up shipping and receiving dates and are also troubleshooters; they contact suppliers or clients when payments are past due or incorrect and help solve the minor problems that invariably occur when two or more companies interact.

Billing clerks may have a specific role within a company. These areas of specialization include: *invoice-control clerks*, who post items in accounts payable or receivable ledgers and verify the accuracy of billing data; *passenger rate clerks*, who compute fare information for business trips and then provide this information to business personnel; *C.O.D. (cash-on-delivery) clerks*, who calculate and record the amount of money collected on C.O.D. delivery routes; *interline clerks*, who compute and pay freight charges for airlines or other transportation agencies that carry freight or passengers as part of a business transaction; *settlement clerks*, who compute and pay shippers for materials forwarded to a company; *billing-control clerks*, who compute and pay utility companies for services provided; *rate reviewers*, who compile data relating to utility costs for management officials; *services clerks*, who compute and pay tariff charges for boats or ships used in transportation of materials; *foreign clerks*, who compute duties, tariffs, and price conversions of products imported to or exported from foreign countries; *billing-machine operators*, who prepare bills and statements through the use of billing machines; *deposit-refund clerks*, who prepare bills for utility customers; *raters*, who calculate premiums to be paid by customers of insurance companies; and *telegraph-service raters*, who compute costs for sending telegrams. Billing clerks may work in one specific area or they may be responsible for two or more of the aforementioned jobs.

Requirements

A high-school diploma is usually sufficient for a beginning billing clerk, although business courses in the operation of office machinery and bookkeeping are also helpful. Prospective billing clerks should have some mechanical ability (for operating business machines), the ability to concentrate for long periods of time on repetitive tasks, and mathematical ability. Legible handwriting is a necessity.

High-school students should take courses in English, mathematics, and as many business-related courses such as typing and bookkeeping as possible.

Community colleges and vocational schools often offer business education courses that will provide training for file clerks.

Special requirements

No licenses or certificates are needed for employment in this field. Billing clerks who work for the federal government may need to pass a civil service examination. Some billing clerks (as well as other office personnel) may join a professional union such as the American Federation of State, County, and Municipal Employees.

Opportunities for experience and exploration

Students may get experience in this field by taking on clerical or bookkeeping responsibilities with a school club or other organization. In addition, some school work-study programs may have opportunities with businesses for part-time, practical on-the-job training. Individuals may have the opportunity to get training in the operation of business machinery (calculators, word processors, and so on) through evening courses offered by business schools. Another way of gaining insight into the responsibilities of a billing clerk is to talk to someone already working in the field.

These billing clerks are verifying invoices and completing purchase orders. Large companies require several billing clerks to process their invoices.

Related occupations

Other workers who prepare bills and invoices and calculate business transactions include insurance workers, bank tellers, general office clerks, and accountants.

Methods of entering

Those interested in securing an entry-level position should contact an appropriate company directly. Major employers of billing clerks include hospitals, insurance companies, and any other large company. Jobs may also be located through "help wanted" advertisements.

High schools sometimes have job placement services to help qualified graduates find employment. Most companies provide entry-level billing clerks with about one month of on-the-job training during which time company policy and procedures are explained. Billing clerks work with experienced personnel during this period.

Advancement

Billing clerks usually begin their employment in the more routine types of tasks such as the simple recording of transactions by hand or machine. With experience, they may advance to more complicated assignments and assume a greater responsibility for the total work to be completed. With additional training, billing clerks may be promoted to the position of bookkeeper or accountant. Billing clerks with good leadership skills may become group managers or supervisors.

The high turnover rate in the billing clerk position increases promotional opportunities. The number and kind of opportunities, however, may be dependent on the place of employment, and the ability, training, and experience of the employee.

Employment outlook

Although the increased use of data-processing equipment and other types of automated equipment may reduce the number of billing clerks needed at any one location, the growing volume of business transactions should lead to growth in employment opportunities for billing clerks through the year 2000. The federal government should continue to be a good source of job opportunities, and private companies should also have numerous openings. Employment opportunities should be especially good for those trained to operate modern office machinery.

Earnings

Beginning billing clerks should average between $10,500 and $14,000 a year, depending on the size and geographic location of the company and the skills of the worker. Experienced clerks should average between $15,000 and $23,000 per year; the higher wages will be paid to those with the greatest number of job responsibilities. Full-time workers should also receive paid vacation, health insurance, and other benefits.

Conditions of work

As is the case with most office workers, billing clerks work an average thirty-seven to forty-hour week, with most of their time spent seated at a desk. The working environment is usually well ventilated and well lighted but the job itself can be fairly routine and repetitive. Clerks spend the majority of their time entering business transactions on ledgers and then handling billing and related correspondence.

Billing clerks often interact with accountants and other office personnel and may work under close supervision.

Social and psychological factors

Billing clerks should have an even temperament and the ability to work well with others. They should find systematic and orderly work appealing and they should like to work on detailed tasks. Other personal qualifications include dependability, trustworthiness, and a neat personal appearance. The advantages of this type of work include regular work hours and no major physical or occupational hazards.

Billing clerks and other office personnel may find opportunities to learn more about the business world in general and this experience may open doors for advancement to higher positions in related fields.

GOE: 07.02.04; SIC: Any industry; SOC: 4715, 4718

◇ **SOURCES OF ADDITIONAL INFORMATION**

Career information is available from local business schools and from:

Office and Professional Employees International Union
265 West 14th Street, Suite 610
New York, NY 10011

◇ **RELATED ARTICLES**

Volume 1: Banking and Financial Services; See Table of Contents for other areas of specific interest
Volume 3: Accounting and bookkeeping workers; Cashiers; Financial institution clerks and related workers; General office clerks

Bookkeeping and accounting clerks

Definition

Bookkeeping workers have the responsibility for the systematic recording and summarizing of the financial business transactions of a business, industry, or institutional agency. Bookkeeping is a division of the broad field of accounting and the job duties of bookkeeping workers depend on the specific type of record keeping they are employed to do and the nature of the business in which they work. Nearly all bookkeeping workers, however, use calculating machines; many use computers.

History

The history of bookkeeping has developed along with the growth of business and industrial enterprise. Encyclopedias point out that the first known records of bookkeeping date back to about 3000 B.C. and the people of the Middle East, such as the Egyptians. These people employed a system of numbers to keep a record of the transactions of merchants and of the grain and farm products that were sold from the storage warehouses. Selling and trading brought about the necessity of bookkeeping systems.

Sometime after the start of the thirteenth century the decimal numeration system came into being throughout Europe, simplifying bookkeeping record systems. The merchants of Venice are credited with the invention of the double-entry bookkeeping method that is so widely used today.

An industrial United States, which has been ever-expanding in size and growing in its complexity, has continued to seek simplified modifications and quicker methods in bookkeeping procedures. Through technological developments, such as bookkeeping machines, electronic computers, and electronic data-processing equipment, many improvements have come about in the field.

Nature of the work

Bookkeeping workers are employed in keeping systematic records and up-to-date accounts of financial transactions in business and institutional firms. They may record these business transactions daily on ledger sheets, in journals, or on other types of accounting forms. Periodically, they may prepare summary statements of the financial transactions of funds received and those paid out.

The bookkeeping records of a firm or business are a vital part of its operational procedures. These records reflect the assets and the liabilities, as well as loss or profit in business operation. The records are also necessary in making income tax reports and in knowing how the different departments or areas are operating. Management relies heavily on the bookkeeping records for information on which to base many of its important decisions.

Many bookkeeping workers are either employed in general bookkeeping jobs or as *accounting clerks* or as *account information clerks*. Places of employment may be in small retail businesses, manufacturing firms of all sizes, and educational and other types of institutional agencies. Many clerks are classified as *financial institution bookkeeping and accounting clerks, insurance firm bookkeeping and accounting clerks, hotel bookkeeping and accounting clerks,* and *railroad bookkeeping and accounting clerks.*

The *general bookkeepers* and *general-ledger bookkeepers* are usually employed in the smaller business operation. This type of worker may perform all the analysis work, recording of the financial records, and any other tasks that are involved in keeping a complete set of bookkeeping records. A general bookkeeper usually performs most of the work by hand with the aid of such office equipment as typewriters, adding machines, and calculators. These employees may have other general duties in an office such as mailing statements, answering telephone calls, and filing work. *Audit clerks* verify figures and can be responsible for sending them on to an *audit clerk supervisor*, who may oversee several audit clerks.

In large business operations, an accountant may supervise a department of bookkeeping workers and bookkeeping machine operators. In these situations employees usually perform specialized tasks. *Billing and rate clerks* and *fixed capital clerks* may be responsible for posting items in accounts payable or receivable ledgers, making out bills and invoices, or verifying the company's rates for certain products and services. *Account information clerks* are responsible for preparing reports, payroll lists and deductions, writing company checks, computing federal tax reports or personnel profit shares.

A bookkeeper shows a questionable entry on a computer-generated ledger to her supervisor. Bookkeepers must be able to locate any errors and correct them.

Large companies may employ workers to systematize, record, and compute many other types of information, as well.

Accounting clerks usually perform many of their work operations by hand; however, they generally use adding machines or calculators for computational work. Accountants may be responsible for setting up the bookkeeping system that is to be used in a business organization and for interpreting facts disclosed in bookkeeping. These workers often perform both accounting and bookkeeping tasks.

In large business organizations, bookkeepers and accountants may be classified by grades, such as Bookkeeper I or II. The job classification determines the duties the worker will perform.

Requirements

Education is an important asset to the individual seeking a position as a bookkeeping worker. Employers require a high-school diploma and give preference to those who have included in their training business subjects such as business arithmetic, business machine operations, typing, and bookkeeping. Some employers seek those persons who have completed a junior college curriculum or those who have attended a post–high-school business training program. In many instances, employers offer on-the-job training in machine operations and for various types of beginning workers. School work-study programs are available in some areas where schools in cooperation with business are able to offer part-time, practical on-the-job training in combination with academic study. These programs often assist students in being able to gain more immediate employment in similar types of work after graduation. Individuals may often have the opportunity to obtain some training through evening courses offered by business schools.

A major criticism made by business executives over the past years has been the lack of training and ability on the part of employees to use correct grammar, spelling, and punctuation in their job performance. Individuals interested in bookkeeping and accounting work should pay particular attention to their academic course work in high school, placing a heavy emphasis on all aspects of English and business mathematics.

Aptitudes necessary to successful job performance in this work may include good manual dexterity, a degree of mechanical ability (for operating business machines), a strong power of concentration, and mathematical ability.

Bookkeeping workers need to have an even temperament, congenial disposition, and the ability to work well with others. These individuals should find systematic, neat, and orderly work appealing to them and they should like to work on detailed tasks. Accuracy and legible handwriting are necessities. Other personal qualifications of bookkeeping workers should include dependability, trustworthiness, and a neat personal appearance.

Potential employees need to have good vision or corrective eyeglasses and to be able to sit for long hours in this type of work. In general, relatively little walking or physical movement is required other than the use of the hands, so that people with some types of physical handicaps can be employed in these positions.

Special requirements

There are no special requirements for these positions in the way of imposed certification or licensure. Good vision is perhaps the major physical requirement. Other requirements have been stressed in the preceding section.

Opportunities for experience and exploration

Individuals who are interested in gaining experience in bookkeeping work may do so through participating in high-school work-study programs or by obtaining part-time or summer work in beginning bookkeeping jobs or in office work that is closely related in job duties.

A general exploration of what bookkeeping workers do can be pursued by talking with individuals employed in this type of work or with high-school guidance counselors, or by visiting schools that offer business training courses.

Related occupations

People with an interest in numbers and accounting can find many other occupations that require skills similar to those needed by bookkeeping and accounting clerks. These include accountants, auditors, mathematicians, actuaries, bank and savings and loan tellers, statisticians, tax preparers, and many other clerical specialists.

Methods of entering

Interested applicants may locate work opportunities by applying directly to firms they know have openings, or to those in which they would like to work if positions will open in the future. Jobs may also be located through reading newspaper "help wanted" advertisements or by listing one's availability in "situation wanted" advertisements.

High schools sometimes have job placement services or contacts with business firms that are interested in interviewing their graduates, especially those applicants who have followed a business curriculum. Business schools and junior colleges will generally assist their graduates in locating employment. Other sources of aid can be found through state employment agencies or through private employment bureaus.

Advancement

Industrious and well-trained bookkeeping workers may find promotional opportunities open in this field. Bookkeeping workers generally begin their employment in the more routine type of work tasks such as the simple recording of transactions by hand or machine. With experience, they may advance to the more complicated assignments and assume a greater responsibility for the total work tasks to be completed.

Beginning workers may start in jobs as bookkeeping clerks, typists, machine operators, cashiers, or sometimes as office assistants performing general office duties. Advancement

may be to positions as office or division manager, department head, accountant, auditor, or from Bookkeeper II to Bookkeeper I, when job positions are graded.

The high turnover rate in these occupations increases promotional opportunities; however, the number and kinds of opportunities may be dependent on the place of employment and the ability, training, experience, and initiative of the employee.

Employment outlook

In the early 1990s, more than 2 million worked in bookkeeping jobs. Positions for bookkeeping workers will be numerous, even though employment in the occupation is expected to grow slowly. The United States Department of Labor predicts that through 1995 between 390,000 and 420,000 job openings per year will be available for these workers. The turnover rate in these occupations is high, and it is expected that many persons will leave the field because of retirement, marriage, or to enter other fields. Some new job opportunities are expected as business and industry continue to expand and business operations become more complex.

The overall increase in the need for these workers is expected to rise at a moderate rate. Technological developments are increasing the use of electronic bookkeeping machines, computers, and other electronic processing equipment and decreasing the number of employees formerly needed to perform the same tasks.

Job opportunities in the future are likely to continue to be good for bookkeepers who are trained and capable of keeping complete sets of books for a business, but the bulk of the jobs are apt to be for bookkeeping and accounting clerks and others who will perform routine work assignments.

Earnings

In the early 1990s beginning accounting clerks in private business made an average of $14,000 a year. Experienced bookkeepers averaged $20,700. The average starting salary for accounting clerks in government jobs was $15,160; experienced workers earned an average of $19,496 a year. Most full-time bookkeepers and accounting clerks earned between $13,440 and $21,240 a year.

Conditions of work

The majority of office workers, including book-keeping workers, usually work a forty-hour week, although some employees in the Northeast may work a thirty-five to thirty-seven-hour week. These employees usually receive six to eight paid holidays yearly and in most places of employment one week paid vacation after six months to one year of service. Paid vacations may increase to four weeks or more, depending on length of service and place of employment. Fringe benefits may include hospitalization and life insurance, sick leave, and retirement plans.

The working conditions for these employees are usually in pleasant surroundings that are well ventilated, lighted, and provided with comfortable furnishings. The work is usually at a steady pace and of a repetitive nature; the latter is especially true for employees of large companies, who often work at only one or two specialized job duties.

Physically, the work can produce eyestrain and nervousness. Bookkeepers usually work with other people and sometimes under close supervision.

Social and psychological factors

In considering any negative factors associated with the work, one may wish to think of the confining nature of the jobs and the constant attention that is required to detail and the accuracy that places considerable responsibility on the worker. Advantages to be considered may include good working conditions, steady employment, regular work hours, and no major physical or occupational hazards.

Employees in these positions may find opportunities to learn more about the business world in general and that experience in book-keeping work can open doors for advancement to higher positions in related fields.

GOE: 07.02.01; SIC: Any industry; SOC: 4712

◇ **SOURCES OF ADDITIONAL INFORMATION**

American Institute of Certified Public Accountants
1211 Avenue of the Americas
New York, NY 10036

National Society of Public Accountants
1010 North Fairfax Street
Alexandria, VA 22314

National Association of Accountants
10 Parson Drive
Montvale, NJ 07645

◇ **RELATED ARTICLES**

Cashiers

Definition

Cashiers are employed in many different businesses and perform a variety of duties depending on their job titles and places of employment. In general, cashiers are responsible for the handling of money received from customers for products sold or services rendered.

The major task for cashiers is the operation of a cash register. The cash register records all transactions of money going into or out of that station, including credit card charges and personal checks, and, for inventory control, it often tallies the specific products sold. Many registers are computer- or calculator-assisted.

History

The history of the employment of cashiers has developed along with the economic growth and expansion of business and industry.

In earlier times, when many businesses were small, merchants were usually able to take care of most of the aspects of their own business, including receiving money from customers. As businesses expanded and supermarkets and self-service stores came into common usage, more and more businesses employed cashiers to receive customers' money, make change, provide customer receipts, and often to wrap the merchandise purchased.

Nature of the work

The job title of a cashier is usually dependent on the type of place of employment. In supermarkets they may be called *check-out clerks* or *grocery checkers*; in utility companies they may be called *bill clerks* or *tellers*; and in theater employment they may be called *ticket sellers* or *box office cashiers*. Cafeterias may title the job *cashier-checker, food checker,* or *food tabulator.* Special job titles may be given to those employed as cashiers in large business firms; these may include such titles as *disbursement clerk, credit cashier,* or *cash accounting clerk.*

In any of these jobs the employee usually receives the money paid by customers, makes change, provides customers with payment receipts when requested or when such receipts are a matter of routine. If employed in some drug or department stores, they may package or bag any merchandise purchased. Cashiers must usually keep very accurate records of amounts of money transacted during their work shifts so that end-of-the-day balances can be computed. In some places of employment cashiers prepare the bank deposits for the management. In large businesses, where cashiers are often employed in very responsible positions, employees may receive and record cash payments made to the firm, and they may be responsible for payment of the firm's bills by cash or by check. In some instances, cashiers prepare sales tax reports, compute income tax deductions for employees' pay rates, and may prepare paychecks and payroll envelopes. In currency exchanges and other businesses, cashiers cash checks, receive utility bill payments, and sell certain licenses. Other general duties may be performed, depending on the type of place of employment.

Cashiers usually operate some type of business-machine cash register in their work.

These machines may be very simple in their operation, printing on paper tape the amount of the purchase, automatically adding the total amount, and at the same time providing a paper receipt stub for the customer and opening the cash drawer for the cashier. Other machines, such as those used in hotels and very large department stores and supermarkets, may record other types of transactions, as well as compute the amount of change to be given to a customer. Frequently these more complex machines will give itemized bills of a customer's purchases or services rendered. Other machines used by cashiers may include adding machines, change-dispensing machines, and others which aid in the performance of their work.

Theater box office cashiers and *information clerk-cashiers* may also answer telephone inquiries and operate machines that dispense tickets and change. *Restaurant cashiers* may receive telephone calls for meal reservations and for special parties, type the menu, stock and keep in good order a sales counter of candies and smoking supplies, and they may sometimes seat customers. *Department store* or *supermarket cashiers* may bag or wrap purchases and during slack periods price the merchandise, restock shelves, make out order forms, and perform other duties much like *food and beverage order clerks.* Those employed as hotel cashiers usually keep accurate records of customers' telephone charges to go on the customer's account. They may also be in charge of customers' safe deposit boxes, receiving money or customers' bills, handling credit charge billing, and for notifying room clerks of customer check-outs.

Cashier supervisors, money-room supervisors, and *money counters* may act as cashiers for other cashiers—receiving and recording cash and sales slips from other cashiers and making sure their cash registers contain enough cash to make change for customers. Other cashier positions include *gambling cashiers,* who may buy and sell chips for cash; *parimutuel ticket cashiers and sellers,* who buy and sell betting tickets at race tracks; *paymasters of purses,* who are responsible for the collection and payment of monies to racehorse owners; and *auction clerks,* who are responsible for the collection of monies from final bidders at auctions.

Requirements

Individuals who are interested in becoming cashiers should recognize that some employers will require that potential employees be a minimum of eighteen years of age and a high-

Cashiers are trained to be courteous to their clients. They must also be efficient in their work.

school graduate. Some employers seek applicants with previous job experiences, sometimes giving preference to those who possess special skills in typing, elementary accounting, or selling. High-school students may find that courses in bookkeeping, typing, business machine operations, business arithmetic, and related areas are assets in developing specific job skills. Students may frequently be able to gain both the needed academic training and practical job experience through diversified cooperative training programs, sometimes called "distributive education," in their high schools. These programs are also offered in two-year community colleges.

Business schools in many cities offer special training programs for cashiers and often business organizations will operate brief training courses. Some businesses and firms require all new cashiers to take special training programs offered by them because of the nature of their work. In many instances, in both large and small firms, cashiers are given on-the-job training and often experienced cashiers will work with and supervise the trainee. Not infrequently, firms will fill cashier positions by promoting employees from within their own ranks, for example, clerk-typists, baggers, ushers, and others, who may move into cashier jobs.

The majority of cashiers are employed in positions in which they must be in constant personal contact with the public. Personal ap-

pearance and attitude are very important in a cashier's work. A pleasant and congenial disposition and a desire to serve the public are needed. Tact and diplomacy, accompanied by a smile, are real personal assets.

Cashiers should possess aptitudes for accuracy in mathematical computational work, hand-eye coordination, and finger dexterity in order to be able to work rapidly. In the job duties of the cashier, accuracy is of the greatest importance.

The work of the cashier is usually not too strenuous; employees usually, however, need to stand during most of their working hours. The amount of physical movement required is dependent upon the type of cashiering job and the place of employment.

Special requirements

The nature of the work of some cashiers demands that they handle large sums of money. Therefore, some cashiers must be able to meet the standards set up by bonding companies. Bonding companies evaluate applicants for risks, and frequently fingerprint applicants for registration and background checks. Not all cashiers will be required to be bonded, however.

In some areas cashiers may join a union. Fewer than 20 percent of cashiers are union members, however.

Opportunities for experience and exploration

Students are frequently able to find part-time employment in cashiering positions that will enable them to explore their interests and aptitudes for this type of work. Related job experiences can sometimes be obtained while in high school by working in the school bookstore or cafeteria, or by participating in community activities that require selling and the transacting of money.

High-school guidance counselors are usually able to supply students with information about careers, and students may find it helpful to discuss their job interests, personal aptitudes, and qualities with a counselor.

Other methods of job exploration may include visiting business schools that have programs for training cashiers and talking with persons already employed in cashier positions.

Related occupations

Cashiers need excellent mathematical skills, strong interpersonal skills, and an interest in business and retail trades. Other jobs that require the same types of interests and skills include bank and savings and loan tellers, accounting and bookkeeping clerks, bank managers, retail managers, food service managers, and retail clerks.

Methods of entering

Individuals may enter this occupational field by making direct application to the personnel directors of large business firms or to the management in small businesses for possible job openings. Applicants may learn of job openings through newspaper "help wanted" columns, through friends and business associates, or sometimes they may receive aid in job placement through their high school or the placement agency of business schools they have attended. Private or state employment agencies can also aid in the location of job possibilities.

For these jobs, employers may require that applicants be able to furnish personal references from educational institutions they have attended, or from former employers, to attest to their character and personal qualifications.

Advancement

Individuals employed as cashiers usually have some opportunities open to them for advancement, depending on the size and type of place of employment, personal initiative, experience, and special training and skills.

Cashiering positions often provide a person with the business experience, training, and skills to move into other types of clerical jobs or sometimes into managerial positions. Opportunities for promotion are greater within the larger businesses or firms than in the small business or store. Cashiers sometimes advance to department store heads, division managers, or to store managers. In hotels, they may be able to advance to room clerks or related positions.

The job turnover rate in this occupational group is high; the competition for the open positions, however, may continue to be keen because many of the positions can be filled by part-time employees or by those with relatively little specialized training.

Employment outlook

In the early 1990s, cashiers in the United States numbered nearly 2 million, most employed in supermarkets and grocery stores. Large numbers of cashiers also worked in department, drug, shoe, and other retail stores, and many were employed in restaurants, hotels, theaters, and hospitals.

Through the late 1990s job openings for cashiers will be more plentiful than for any other occupation.

The large number of openings anticipated can be related to the high job turnover rate in this occupational group: almost one-third leave their jobs annually, to assume family responsibilities, retire, return to school, or take different jobs. Many new openings will result from the continually expanding economic growth of business in the country with many new suburban shopping centers developing across the nation. Job openings increased greatly in the 1970s and 1980s as business turned more and more to self-service operations, supermarket buying, and to other modern merchandising methods. Most businesses likely to turn to self-service, however, have already done so, and the growth in opportunities resulting from this change is expected to moderate.

Factors that may somewhat limit the number of positions open in the future will be the increased installation of automatic change-making machines, vending machines, and other types of automatic and electronic equipment that will decrease the number of cashiers needed in some business operations.

Future job opportunities will probably be more readily available to those individuals who have obtained specialized training in bookkeeping, typing, business machine operations, and general office skills. Many part-time job opportunities should also be available.

Earnings

The minimum salary established by state and federal laws is often the starting salary for inexperienced cashiers. In the early 1990s, the median weekly salary for cashiers was about $10,500 a year. Most cashiers earned between $8,600 and $15,600 a year. Wages are generally higher for union workers, however. Experienced, full-time cashiers belonging to the United Food and Commercial Workers International Union averaged about $27,900 a year. Beginners made much less, averaging about $5.90 per hour.

Clerical supervisors and managers
Clerical Occupations

In general, cashiers employed in restaurants often earn less than those employed in other types of cashiering work in this occupational group.

In general, the fringe benefits available to these employees are somewhat limited. Depending on the size and type of place of employment, they may sometimes participate in group plans for life and hospitalization insurance, and receive one- to two-week paid vacations or longer, depending on the length of employment. They sometimes have the benefit of an employee retirement program. The majority of these benefits are available to employees paid on a weekly salary basis, who are working in large businesses or in department stores.

Conditions of work

Cashiers are usually employed on a five-day, forty-hour workweek in the majority of large retail businesses and supermarkets. In some cases, cashiers are expected to work on Saturdays because of heavy business. Their hours may differ considerably from those of other clerical workers in that many cashiers must work split shifts to cover rush hour periods and on weekends when many people shop and go out for entertainment.

Working conditions are usually pleasant and many times in attractively decorated surroundings. Large numbers of business firms today are air-conditioned and most of them are well ventilated and lighted; the work area itself, however, may be rather small and confining because many cashiers work behind counters, in cages or booths, or in other small spaces. Work spaces for cashiers are frequently located near the entrances and exits in business firms, and cashiers may be exposed to drafts.

Cashiers must be able to work rapidly and sometimes under pressure during rush hours. During many of their working hours they are

required to stand, and they must be alert at all times.

Social and psychological factors

The job of cashier can be a very responsible one and such an employee must know that a business or firm has vested in you its trust, relying upon your personal integrity. Real job satisfaction may also come from personal contacts and service to the public.

Cashiers must have patience, a pleasant and congenial disposition, and enjoy dealing with the public. Their personal appearance can also be very important to their job.

GOE: 07.03.01; SIC: Any industry; SOC: 4364

◇ **SOURCES OF ADDITIONAL INFORMATION**

For information about job opportunities in this field, contact the local office of your state employment service.

◇ **RELATED ARTICLES**

Volume 1: Food Service; Retailing
Volume 2: Buyers, wholesale and retail; Hotel and motel managers; Restaurant and food service managers; Retail managers
Volume 3: Bookkeeping and accounting clerks; Financial institution clerks and related workers; Financial institution tellers; Retail sales workers

---

Clerical supervisors and managers

Definition

Clerical supervisors and managers direct and coordinate the work activities of clerks within an

office. They supervise office workers in their tasks and confer with other supervisory personnel in the planning of department activities. Clerical supervisors and managers often define job duties and develop training programs for new workers. They evaluate the progress of subordinates and work with upper management officials to ensure that the office staff meets productivity and quality goals. Clerical supervisors and managers often meet with office personnel to discuss job-related issues or problems, and they are responsible for maintaining a positive environment within the office setting.

History

As modern technology and an increased volume of business correspondence become a normal part of daily business, offices are becoming more and more complicated places to work. By directing and coordinating the activities of file clerks and other office workers, clerical supervisors and managers are an integral part of an efficient and effective organization.

Every business and administrative office needs a clerical supervisor or manager to oversee the daily operations of the clerical support team. As offices continue to evolve and workers become more specialized, skilled supervisors and managers will be needed to effectively assign the work load and ensure that job responsibilities are completed in a timely and professional manner.

Nature of the work

The day-to-day work of clerical supervisors and managers involves the organizing and management of many varied activities. Although specific duties vary as to the type of work done in a particular office, all supervisors and managers have several basic job responsibilities.

Supervisors and managers are usually responsible for interviewing prospective employees and making recommendations on hiring. They train workers, explain office policies, and spell out performance criteria. Supervisors are also responsible for delegating work responsibilities. This requires a keen sense as to the strengths and weaknesses of individual workers and an ability to organize what needs to get done and when it must be completed. For example, if a supervisor knows that one worker is especially good at filing business correspondence, that worker will probably be assigned to any important filing tasks.

Supervisors not only train clerical workers and assign them job duties, they also recommend increases in salaries, promote workers

when indicated, and, if necessary, terminate them. Therefore, supervisors must carefully observe clerical workers perform their job responsibilities (whether they are answering the telephones, opening and sorting mail, or a variety of other tasks) and make suggestions on any necessary improvements. Managers who can communicate sensitively and effectively both in writing and speaking will be better able to carry out this kind of leadership. Motivating employees to do their best work is another important component of a manager's responsibility.

Supervisors and managers must be very good at human relations. Differences of opinion and personality clashes among employees are inevitable, and the manager or supervisor must be able to deal with grievances and restore good feelings among the staff. Supervisors and managers meet regularly with their staff to discuss progress and solve any problems.

Planning is a vital and time-consuming portion of a supervisor's job responsibilities. Not only does a supervisor plan the work of subordinates, he or she also assists in planning current and future office space needs, planning what types of office equipment and supplies need to be purchased, and planning future work schedules.

Supervisors and managers must always keep their superiors informed as to the overall situation in the clerical area. If there is a delay on an important project, for example, upper management must know why and also what steps are being taken to expedite the matter.

When necessary, supervisory personnel must relieve their subordinates and do some clerical work themselves.

Requirements

Although there are no specific educational requirements for this position, a college degree is highly recommended and a high-school diploma is essential. Many offices promote supervisors and managers from clerical workers within their organization, and therefore relevant work experience is also helpful. Prospective clerical managers and supervisors must have good leadership and communications skills, including the ability to set priorities, organize work schedules and motivate others. Experience with computers is becoming increasingly important.

High-school students should take courses in English, speech arts, mathematics, history, and as many business-related courses such as typing and bookkeeping as possible.

In college a student should pursue a degree in business administration or at least take several courses in office policies and procedures and business management. In some cases, an associates degree is considered sufficient for a supervisory position.

Community colleges and vocational schools often provide business education courses that help train clerical supervisors and managers.

Special requirements

No licenses or certificates are needed for employment in this field. Supervisory personnel who work for the federal government may need to pass a civil service examination.

Opportunities for experience and exploration

Before gaining experience in a supervisory capacity, students should get experience in fulfilling clerical responsibilities such as opening and sorting mail, answering telephones, and filing business documents. Interested persons may get this type of experience by taking on clerical or bookkeeping responsibilities with a school club or other organization. In addition, some school work-study programs may have opportunities with businesses for part-time, practical on-the-job training.

Individuals may have the opportunity to get training in the operation of business machinery (calculators, word processors, and so on) through evening courses offered by business schools. Another way of gaining insight into the responsibilities of clerical supervisors and managers is to talk to someone already working in the field.

Related occupations

Other professionals who coordinate and manage the activities of clerical workers include hotel managers, retail managers, and food services managers.

Methods of entering

Qualified persons should contact business offices directly. This is especially appropriate if the candidate already has previous clerical experience. College placement offices or other job placement offices may also know of job openings. Jobs may also be located through "help wanted" advertisements.

Often, clerical supervisors are recruited from the clerical staff. A clerk with potential supervisory abilities may be given periodic supervisory responsibilities, and, when an opening occurs for a manager or supervisor, that person may be promoted to a full-time position.

Advancement

Often, becoming a clerical supervisor or manager is the result of being promoted from a receptionist, file clerk, or other clerical position. With experience, skilled supervisory personnel may be promoted to a group manager position. Promotions, however, are often dependent on the supervisor getting a college degree or other appropriate training.

Employment outlook

Although the increased use of data-processing equipment and other types of automated equipment may reduce the number of supervisory personnel needed at any one location, the growing economy should greatly expand the number of clerical workers needed in new retail stores throughout the country. Therefore, employment of clerical supervisors and managers is expected to grow about as fast as average through the early 1990s. The federal government should continue to be a good source of job opportunities and private companies, particularly those with large clerical staffs such as hospitals, banks, and telecommunications companies, should also have numerous openings. Employment opportunities should be especially good for those trained to operate computers, word processors, and other types of modern office machinery.

Earnings

In the early 1990s beginning clerical supervisors and managers should average between $14,500 and $22,000 a year, depending on the size and geographic location of the company and the skills of the worker. Experienced supervisory personnel should average between $20,000 and $32,000 per year; the higher wages will be paid to those who work with the larger private companies located in and around major metropolitan areas. Full-time workers should also receive paid vacation, health insurance, and other benefits.

Conditions of work

As is the case with most office workers, clerical supervisors and managers work an average thirty-seven to forty-hour week, although overtime is not unusual. The work environment is usually well ventilated and well lighted but the job itself can be stressful as it entails supervising a variety of employees with a variety of temperaments.

Although many clerical supervisors and managers work a standard nine-to-five shift, the fact that many workplaces operate around the clock means that some supervisory personnel may have to work evenings as well as weekends and holidays.

Social and psychological factors

Supervisory personnel must constantly juggle the demands of their superiors with the demands of their subordinates. Deadlines on major projects could create tension, especially if several office workers are sick or otherwise unable to perform up to expectations. Communications skills and the ability to organize effectively are extremely important. Attention to detail is critical. Clerical supervisors and managers should have an even temperament and the ability to work well with others. They should find systematic and orderly work appealing and they should like to work on detailed tasks. Other personal qualifications include dependability, trustworthiness, and a neat personal appearance. The advantages of this type of work include fairly regular work hours and no major physical or occupational hazards.

GOE: 07.01.02; SIC: Any industry; SOC: 71

◇ **SOURCES OF ADDITIONAL INFORMATION**

Career information is available from:

American Management Association
135 West 50th Street
New York, NY 10020

National Management Association
2210 Arbor Boulevard
Dayton, OH 45439

◇ **RELATED ARTICLES**

Volume 1: Business Administration
Volume 3: Retail managers; General office clerks

Collection workers

Definition

Collection workers, often known as *bill collectors* or *collection agents*, are individuals employed to persuade people to pay their overdue bills, thereby maintaining the financial well-being of a company. Collection workers may work for companies independent of the one to whom the money is owed. Their obligation is for collection of money owed or repossession of property and returning either to the company for a fee.

History

Debt collection is one of the world's oldest vocations. In literature, the most famous—and unsuccessful—attempt to retrieve an overdue debt occurred in Shakespeare's *Merchant of Venice*, featuring the character Shylock as the collector. Debt collection also figures prominently in the works of Charles Dickens.

In the past, those people unable to pay their debts were sent to prison, indentured as servants or slaves until the amount owed was paid off, or forcefully recruited as colonists for new lands.

Today, debtors face less harsh consequences, but the proliferation of credit opportunities has expanded the field of debt collection. Stores offer charge accounts, as do gasoline stations. Many people buy furniture or some other commodity "on time," meaning they place a small sum down and pay off the balance plus interest over an agreed upon period of time. Mortgages are the principal means of financing the purchase of a house. Credit cards have created even greater credit opportunities, sometimes replacing cash and checks as the preferred method of payment. As a result, a credit line has become as much a part of many people's lives as a driver's license.

Nature of the work

A collection worker's main job is to persuade people to pay bills that are past due. The procedure is generally the same in firms that employ collection workers, although the duties of the various workers may overlap, depending on the size and nature of the company.

When normal billing methods—monthly statements and collection letters—fail to secure payment, the collection worker receives a bad-debt file. This file contains information about the debtor, the nature and the amount of the unpaid bill, the last charge incurred, and the date of the last payment. The collection worker then contacts the debtors by phone or by mail to inquire why the bill is unpaid and to review the terms of the sales, service, or credit contract. At that time, an attempt is made to obtain full or partial payment or to arrange a new pay schedule.

If the bill has not been paid because the customer believes it is incorrect, the merchandise purchased was faulty, or the service billed for was not performed, the collector recommends that the customer contact the original seller to settle the matter. If the problem remains unresolved, the collector again tries to secure payment.

In cases where a financial emergency or mismanagement of money has caused the lack of payment, a new schedule is arranged. In instances of fraudulent avoidance of payment, the collector may recommend that the file be turned over to an attorney.

When all efforts to obtain payment fail, collection workers known as *repossessors* are assigned to locate the merchandise not paid for and return it to the seller. Goods such as fur-niture or appliances are picked up in a truck. To reclaim automobile and other motor vehicles, the repossessor may enter and start the vehicle with special tools if the buyer does not return the key.

In large agencies, some collection workers specialize as *skip tracers*. Skip tracers are assigned to locate debtors who skip out on their debts; that is, who move without notifying their creditors to evade payment of their bills. Skip tracers search telephone directories and street listings and make inquiries at the post office in an effort to locate the missing debtor. They try to elicit information about the whereabouts of that person by interviewing, writing to, or phoning former neighbors and employers, local merchants, friends and relatives of the delinquent customer, and references listed on the original credit application. Skip tracers follow up every lead and prepare a report of the entire investigation.

Collection workers also perform clerical duties, such as reading and answering correspondence, filing, or posting amounts paid. In some small companies, they may offer financial advice to customers or contact them to inquire about their satisfaction with the handling of the account. In larger companies, *credit and loan collection supervisors* may oversee the activities of several other collection workers.

Requirements

This is a people-oriented job that requires someone who can get along with others. It involves much phone communication on a touchy subject. Collection workers need a pleasing manner and voice. They must be sympathetic and tactful, yet assertive and persuasive enough to overcome any reluctance on the part of the debtor to pay the overdue account. In addition, collectors must be alert, quick-witted, and imaginative to handle the potentially awkward situations that are encountered in this type of work. A high-school education is usually sufficient for this occupation, and courses in psychology and speech are particularly helpful. Collection procedures and telephone techniques are learned on the job in a training period spent under the guidance of a supervisor or an experienced collector. Special seminars also are available through the American Collectors Association to assist collectors in improving their collection and skip-tracing skills. A basic knowledge of legal proceedings is helpful for supervisors.

Special requirements

There are no other requirements for this occupation.

Opportunities for experience and exploration

The best way to explore collection work is to secure part-time or summer employment in a collection or credit office. Students may wish to interview a collection worker to obtain first-hand information about the practical aspects of this occupation.

Related occupations

Many other occupations require the same interests and skills as collection workers. Some of these include financial institution clerks and related workers, bookkeeping and accounting clerks, financial institution tellers, tax preparers, accountants and auditors, and statisticians.

Methods of entering

The usual way of entering the collection field is to apply directly to an employer. A "help wanted" newspaper advertisement may provide information on job openings, as will a visit to the local office of the state employment service.

Advancement

Advancement opportunities are good, though limited. Workers with above-average ability can become supervisors or collection managers. A few progress to other credit positions, such as credit authorizer, credit manager, or bank loan officer. Some may branch out to open their own collection agency.

Employment outlook

The development of a credit economy has created a larger number of bad debts, necessitating expanded collection services. In the early 1990s,

approximately 138,000 collection workers were employed in commercial banks, finance companies, credit unions, and collection agencies, as well as in retail and wholesale businesses and public utilities.

Jobs in this occupation are expected to grow faster than the national average for all occupations through the late 1990s. This will be a result of the increasing volume of credit purchases as well as the high turnover rate that characterizes this occupation.

The continued growth of retail stores coupled with the extension of credit cards to greater numbers of people will result in an increased demand for collection workers. A system that relies more and more on credit for the purchase of goods and services must expect an increasing number of delinquent accounts, and additional collectors will be required to service the accounts on an individual basis. Automation has had some impact on the field, however, eliminating the need for people to perform several functions previously handled by collectors.

Periods of recession in the economy increase the amount of personal debt that goes unpaid. Therefore, collectors find increased employment during economic slumps.

Of more significance than the creation of new jobs are the openings that will occur as collectors transfer to other occupations. Some will leave because of the stress involved in persuading people to pay their bills; others, because they do not collect enough debts to earn an adequate salary. For the same reasons, employers have difficulty recruiting applicants for collection work. On the plus side, however, this creates a promising employment situation for persons with the proper aptitudes and temperament.

Job opportunities exist throughout the United States and especially in heavily populated urban areas. Companies that have branch offices in rural communities often locate their collection departments in nearby cities. Competition for positions will be strongest in large metropolitan banks, which generally offer higher salaries and better advancement opportunities.

Earnings

Collection workers may receive a salary plus a bonus or commission on the debt amounts collected. Others work for a salary, with no commission received from income collected. The pay system varies among different companies. Incomes, therefore, vary substantially. While

While speaking with a debtor on the telephone, a collection worker refers to computer files for verification of unpaid bills.

the information is limited, it appears that in the early 1990s beginning collectors could earn between $14,500 and $28,800 a year. Those with experience could earn as much as $36,000, depending on how much they were able to collect. The income average for all bill collectors was $16,600 in 1988.

Conditions of work

Most of the time, collectors work in pleasant offices, seated at a desk, doing a job that requires heavy telephone contact. Because of the large quantity of work done over the phone, many companies use phone headsets and program-operated dialing systems such as speed-dial or automatic redial. Companies with complicated phone programs usually train their employees on the system.

Rarely does a collector have to make a personal visit to a customer. Repossession pro-ceedings are undertaken only in more extreme cases. The legal aspects must be understood when repossession is required.

These workers put in forty hours a week but often stagger their schedules. They may start late in the morning and work into the evening, or they may take a weekday off and work on Saturday. The ability to find debtors at home determines their schedule. The job may also involve receiving verbal abuse from hostile customers.

Social and psychological factors

Collection work is emotionally taxing, involving listening either to bill payers' problems or to verbal attacks made on both the collector and the company. Therefore, the job is potentially stressful.

A collector's most valuable social skill is to be able to get along with people and not antagonize them while attempting to collect payment on unpaid bills.

GOE: 07.02.02, 07.04.02; SIC: 6021, 6141; SOC: 4712, 4786

◇ **SOURCES OF ADDITIONAL INFORMATION**

American Collection Association
Lockbox 72726
Las Vegas, NV 89170

American Collectors Association
4040 West 70th Street
Minneapolis, MN 55435

◇ **RELATED ARTICLES**

Volume 1: Banking and Financial Services
Volume 2: Credit analysts, banking
Volume 3: Financial institution clerks and related workers; Financial institution officers and managers

Computer and peripheral equipment operators

Definition

Computer operating personnel perform the job of operating several kinds of equipment used in the field of data processing in which electronic machines process information and perform high-speed calculations. The *computer operator* or *console operator* puts the programmer's instructions to work on the computer, loading the machine with the correct disk or magnetic tape and monitoring the program's run. *Data entry workers* transfer information to forms the computer can read, and *peripheral equipment operators* and *data processing auxiliary equipment operators* run other machines that help computers do their work.

History

Electronic computer operating personnel is one of the newest occupations in the United States and Canada.

World War II brought into plain focus the need for a vastly different system for speed in information processing. Machines such as calculators, adding machines, and typewriters were no longer any match for the jobs to be done that required thousands of hours of manpower production.

It was during World War II that the electronic computer was developed as a means of solving engineering and scientific problems of warfare. The usefulness and adaptability of the computer were quickly recognized, and in 1951, the federal government put a computer into use in the Bureau of the Census for the 1950 population census. In 1954, the first computer to be used in a business firm was installed. By 1958, both business and government were making use of great numbers of large and small computers.

From the 1960s, computer technology has progressed. Computers have become more advanced, yet smaller and less expensive, allowing more and more businesses to put them to work. Today, almost every large business either has its own computers or buys the services of one. Computers are also indispensable to hospitals, schools, and government agencies.

Many people now have computers in their homes, as well.

Basically, computers are calculating machines that are capable of operating at tremendously high rates of speed. They can, when programmed (instructed), add, subtract, multiply, divide, and compute square roots. Mathematical computations that would require hours of brain and hand work can be performed by an electronic digital computer in seconds. Computers can perform other operations such as choosing between alternatives when different sets of data are brought together, storing information until it is needed, making comparisons, and acting upon data.

Computers, however, along with the other peripheral equipment in electronic data processing, cannot think (even though they are frequently referred to as "electronic brains"); operators and programmers are needed to tell these machines what to do and to run their operation. These individuals, performing new jobs in a new occupational world of automation and technology, are the electronic computer operating personnel.

Nature of the work

Electronic computer operating personnel operate computers and other types of machines used in electronic data processing. Depending on the size and complexity of the operation and the computer system, one or two persons may be able to perform all the necessary work operations; or a very large system may require that a number of personnel be employed, each performing a specialized task.

Computer operators, or *console operators*, start the computers, feed them programmed instructions, observe that they operate correctly, remove completed work, and see to their overall functioning.

Computer operators operate central control units or the console of the computers for "run" of data processing. Programmed instructions provide operating procedures and, although some systems have fairly standardized operating procedures, other systems may require a great deal more knowledge and skill. Panels of lights and switches are before the operator to

Operators of a mainframe computer system assess a malfunction. With such large systems, diagnoses often require more than one person.

indicate the proper functioning of the computer, when an error has been made, and the data run stopped. Console operators must then try to locate the source of error or difficulty. The supervision of the other computer operating personnel is often the responsibility of *computer operations supervisors*. Other related types of computer operating personnel include: *tabulating-machine operators* and *sorting-machine operators*, who operate the machines that take data from card systems and transfer it to the printed materials; and *digitizer operators,* who operate the equipment that encodes and decodes coordinate data for the transfer of images (such as maps and drawings) from one medium to another.

Peripheral equipment operators run the machines that work with the computers. The most common peripheral equipment is the printer. Others are disk drives and tape readers, which the operators load, unload, and monitor.

Programmers are not included among the electronic computing operating personnel; it seems appropriate, however, to point out that programmers work out the proper instructions or "programs" for the computers so that the machines will perform the correct and necessary computational steps in the proper sequence. (*See also* the separate article titled "Programmers" in Volume 2.)

Personnel in these positions may be employed in government, business and industry, research bureaus and firms, and in educational institutions. Depending on the type of computer operation (analog or digital) and the size and complexity of the operation, individuals may train for specialization or perform more than one type of duty in computer operations.

Requirements

The educational training required for these positions is almost always at least a high-school diploma and, in some instances, a college degree. Some employers, however, who install electronic data-processing equipment will transfer their present employees from related machine-operating jobs that are no longer needed to the operation of the new equipment. Some on-the-job training may be given these employees, while others with needed special abilities and training may be hired from outside the firm.

College training may be required for computer or console operators. These individuals in government positions must have a college education or its equivalent in work experience or be able to qualify on the basis of previous experience in computer work and demonstrate a general aptitude for such work on special tests. Many business firms are also using special aptitude tests to screen employees for these types of jobs. Console operators are sometimes trained in a period of approximately two to six months or longer. In training classes, these individuals are usually also taught the fundamentals of programming, as well as the operation of the console.

The federal government requires that operators of peripheral equipment be high-school graduates unless they have specialized training or previous experience in related work. Business employers also favor hiring the high-school graduate in these positions. Peripheral equipment operators may be trained in a period of approximately two weeks or longer once they are hired on the job. Periods of formal training for both console operators and peripheral equipment operators are usually followed by additional on-the-job training.

Individuals who are interested in becoming electronic computer operating personnel need to possess aptitudes for this type of work including manual and finger dexterity, mathematical ability in some cases, and in every instance the ability to think and reason logically. These personnel must be alert, able to work with extreme accuracy, and pay attention to the smallest details. Patience is a valued asset for these jobs, and individuals need to be able to work in close cooperation with others as a part of a team.

The nature of the work may be tiring because extreme concentration is required, as well as a constant use of the eyes and, depending on the type of work, a constant use of the hands. The continual stress for exactness and accuracy may produce a strain on the individual who does not easily adapt to such working conditions. Some duties may require lifting, reaching, and moving with boxes of cards, tapes, and other materials used in the work. Depending on the job, some employees, such as keypunch operators, may sit for long hours to perform their work.

Special requirements

There are no special requirements, such as licensure or certification, required of these employees. Individuals who enter these occupations, however, should realize that they may be continually required to study and learn the new methods and techniques being developed daily in the field of electronic data processing. There is a need to keep up and constantly seek out what is new in this evolving technological field. This may include taking continuing education courses and computer courses given through training, secondary, or post-secondary schools. The technology is likely to change considerably in the next years.

Opportunities for experience and exploration

Individuals interested in careers as electronic computer operators may explore the field by talking with their high-school guidance counselor and with people already employed in these jobs. High-school counselors may also be able to make available to the individual interest inventories and academic and special aptitude tests. A visit to a firm where computer services are in operation, and talks with personnel in plants and schools where technical training is offered, may provide additional information.

Students interested in the peripheral equipment operating jobs may wish to take as many high-school courses as possible in business subjects and in the operation of business machines to explore their aptitudes, likes, and dislikes for this closely related field. Computer operators and coders may wish to follow a more academic program geared to college entrance; they might obtain part-time jobs, however, in computing centers to help them explore the field. Other possible work experiences that would be related to this field would be found in business offices and firms where the working conditions are similar to those in computing centers. Students who are able typists may find part-time employment as keypunch operators.

Related occupations

The range of work available for people interested in computers, their programming, and their operations is wide and diverse. Workers are needed to develop both hardware and software as well as programmers, systems analysts, data base managers, information scientists, and data entry clerks.

Methods of entering

Electronic computer operating personnel may find the greatest number of job openings to be in the metropolitan areas in government agencies, insurance, transportation and utility companies, banks, manufacturing firms, and educational institutions. Some job opportunities may be available in service centers that process statistical data for businesses on a fee basis.

Classified advertisement in newspapers may list job openings, or individuals may contact those firms that they believe might have openings or in which they would like to work. Local and state employment offices are also sources of employment information. The federal government operates its own training program for these jobs and applications for such positions may be made through the Office of Personnel Management centers. Manufacturing firms of computers often operate training programs for their own personnel and to assist in training personnel for the companies who have bought or leased their equipment. In other instances, individuals may enter this field by receiving training in the armed forces.

In this occupational field, interested persons are often trained on the job they have obtained, which seems to indicate that job entry and training, except in the case of the experienced worker, are often closely related issues.

Advancement

Individuals employed in these jobs may, with experience, be advanced to operate the more complex equipment. In time, promotions may be made to supervisory positions or to jobs that combine supervisory responsibilities with the operation of a console unit. In some instances, computer operators are able to acquire an adequate basic understanding of programming while working and gaining in experience, and employers sometimes select these individuals for additional training so that they may assume positions as programmers.

Promotions are possible, with the necessary formal education, training, and experience, to positions as computer center manager, or programming manager.

Employment outlook

About 260,000 computer operators and 83,000 peripheral equipment operators were employed in the early 1990s. Data entry personnel occupied about 340,000 jobs. The use of electronic data-processing equipment has expanded greatly in the last fifteen or twenty years, and jobs for operators are expected to increase through the late 1990s. Some job opportunities are expected to occur as individuals transfer to other types of jobs or leave the field for family responsibilities, ill health, or for other reasons. Some of these positions and new ones will be filled from within business firms by the transfer of workers from other jobs. Where more employees are needed, however, or the firm needs to hire persons with special aptitudes, individuals will be hired from outside the firm.

Computers are commonplace in all big business operations and smaller scale equipment is found in smaller offices. Thousands of operators will be needed to fill jobs in firms having their own computer installations and in service centers that rent computer time to businesses.

Earnings

Keypunch operators in private businesses averaged around $15,600 a year in the early 1990s. Console operators had salaries averaging about $18,720 a year. Peripheral equipment operators earned approximately $16,900 a year. Experienced workers earned more than $20,280 annually, and experienced lead operators had average salaries of about $26,000 a year. These salaries are expected to rise considerably by the mid-1990s; however, salaries for these employees may be expected to vary greatly depending on the place of employment, locality in the country, complexity of job performance demanded, job experience, and the training of the worker. The job survey revealed that some employees earn more than twice as much as others, depending on these factors.

In the federal government, salaries were found to be somewhat comparable to those earned in private industry.

Government employees usually enjoy the same fringe benefits of paid vacations, holidays, and hospitalization and life insurance as do the other employees working in private industry. Exact benefits will vary with the place of employment. Both men and women are employed in these positions.

Conditions of work

Individuals employed in these jobs usually work the same number of hours weekly as do most office employees. Workweeks may range in general from thirty-five to forty hours, depending on the place of employment and locale in the country. Computer systems operate on a 24 hour schedule and employees may be asked to work on rotating shifts that would involve late-evening or night work. Tape librarians usually work only day shifts.

Working conditions are usually comfortable in air-conditioned or heated offices that are well lighted. These jobs are not considered hazardous occupations and the only physical strains that may be experienced are those usually associated with the constant use of the eyes and sometimes hands, and often the mental tiredness that comes when one must constantly give great detailed attention and remain continually alert for accuracy in work performance. Some equipment operators may need to sit for long hours to run the equipment; however, most employers allow employees work breaks, as well as regularly scheduled lunch periods to rest and enable them to continue with renewed accuracy.

Social and psychological factors

Employees in these positions usually work in close cooperation with each other, often as a team, and in most instances their work is under close supervision. The ability to work in harmony with others with a pleasant disposition and patience is an asset for these jobs. Individuals must be able to take orders and work willingly and cooperatively with management.

Individuals who are interested in the types of work performed by computer operating personnel and who find their abilities and aptitudes are compatible to those required for successful work performance in the field, may find that employment in this area will bring them personal and real job satisfactions. These employees have the opportunity to gain in new job experiences as science and technology evolve new developments in electronic data processing.

GOE: 07.06.01; SIC: Any industry; SOC: 4612

◇ **SOURCES OF ADDITIONAL INFORMATION**

Association for Computing Machinery
11 West 42nd Street, 3rd Floor
New York, NY 10036

Data Processing Management Association
505 Busse Highway
Park Ridge, IL 60068

◇ **RELATED ARTICLES**

Volume 1: Computer Hardware; Computer Software; Electronics
Volume 2: Computer programmers; Data base managers; Systems analysts
Volume 3: Secretaries and stenographers; Typists
Volume 4: Data-processing technicians; Robotics technicians; Semiconductor-development technicians; Software technicians

Counter and retail clerks

Definition

Counter and retail clerks work as intermediaries between the general public and service providers by taking orders and receiving payments for services such as video tape rentals, automobile rentals, and laundry and dry cleaning services. They often assist customers with purchasing or rental decisions, especially when sales personnel are not available.

History

The first retail outlets in the United States sold food staples, farm necessities, and clothing. These stores also often served as the post office and became the social and economic center of the community.

A number of changes occurred in the retail field during the mid- and late–nineteenth century. The growth of retail stores selling specific products such as hardware items and groceries reflected the growing diversity of available products and customer tastes.

This growth of retail outlets has continued at a steady pace, with today's society featuring such diverse stores as bicycle shops, watch repair shops, computer shops, and video rental establishments. All these outlets need qualified counter and retail clerks to assist customers and receive payment for services or products provided.

Nature of the work

The specific nature of the work varies as to the type of business being operated. In a service establishment such as a shoe repair shop, for example, the clerk receives the shoes to be repaired or cleaned from the customer, examines the shoes, gives a price quote to the customer, and then sends the shoes to the work department for necessary repairs or cleaning. The shoes are sent to the work department with a tag specifying what work should be done. This tag also serves to identify who the shoes belong to. After the work is completed, the clerk returns the shoes to the customer and collects payment.

In a rental establishment such as a bicycle store, *bicycle-rental clerks* prepare rental forms and quote rates to customers. The clerks answer customer questions regarding operation of the bikes and they may take a deposit. Clerks also check the bicycles to make sure they are in good working order and the clerks may make minor adjustments, if necessary. With long-term rentals, such as storage-facility rentals, clerks notify the customers when the rental period is about to expire and when rent is overdue. *Film-rental clerks* greet customers, check out tapes, and accept rental payment. Upon return of the tapes, the clerks check the condition of the tapes and then put them back on the shelves.

In smaller shops where there may not be sales personnel or in situations when the sales

23

Counter and retail clerks
Clerical Occupations

Counter clerks must have knowledge of the items they sell. In this case, the clerk must be familiar with the several different types of cheese.

personnel is unavailable, counter and retail clerks assist customers with purchases or rentals by demonstrating the merchandise, answering the customers' questions, recording sales, and wrapping their purchase or arranging for its delivery.

In addition to selling supplies or facilitating rental transactions, clerks may also prepare billing statements to be sent to customers. They may keep records of receipts and sales throughout the day. In supermarkets and grocery stores, clerks stock shelves and put food products into packages for the customers.

Service-establishment attendants, such as those in a laundry, take clothes to be cleaned or repaired, and enter identification data. *Watch-and-clock-repair clerks* receive clocks and watches for repair and examine the timepieces to estimate repair costs. They may make minor repairs, such as replacing a watch band; otherwise the timepiece is forwarded to the repair shop with notification of needed repairs.

Many clerks have job titles that describe what they do and where they work. These include: *laundry-pricing clerks; telegraph-counter clerks; photo-finishing counter clerks; tool-and-equipment-rental clerks; airplane-charter clerks; baby-stroller and wheelchair rental clerks; storage-facility rental clerks; boat-rental clerks; hospital-television-rental clerks; trailer-rental clerks; automobile-rental clerks; fur-storage clerks;* and *self-service-laundry-and-dry-cleaning attendants.*

Requirements

Although there are no specific educational requirements, most employers prefer workers to have a high-school diploma.

High-school students should take courses in English, speech arts, mathematics, and history. Any business-related courses such as typing and those covering principles in retailing should also be taken. Legible handwriting and the ability to add and subtract numbers quickly are a necessity.

Counter and retail clerks should have a pleasant personality and an ability to interact with a variety of people. They should also be neat and well-groomed.

Special requirements

No licenses or certificates are needed for employment in this field. In some instances, counter and retail clerks may be unionized.

Opportunities for experience and exploration

There are numerous opportunities for part-time or temporary work as a clerk, especially during the holiday season. Many high schools have developed work-study programs that combine courses in retailing with part-time work in the field. Store owners cooperating in these programs often hire these students as full-time workers after completion of the course.

Those interested in securing a position as a counter or retail clerk are encouraged to talk to someone already working in the field to get a better idea of the rewards and responsibilities of this occupation.

Related occupations

Other workers that assist customers and receive payment for services or products include sales personnel, bank tellers, cashiers, and postal service clerks.

Methods of entering

Those interested in securing an entry-level position should contact stores directly. Workers with some experience, such as those who completed a work-study program in high school, should have the greatest success, but most entry level positions do not require any previous experience. Jobs are often listed in help wanted" advertisements.

Most stores provide new workers with on-the-job training during which time experienced clerks explain company policy and procedures and teach new employees how to operate the cash register and other necessary equipment. This training usually continues for several weeks until the new employee feels comfortable on the job.

Advancement

Counter and retail clerks usually begin their employment doing the more routine tasks such as checking stock and operating the cash register. With experience, they may advance to more complicated assignments and assume some sales responsibilities. Those with the skill and aptitude may become store managers, although further education is normally required for management positions.

The high turnover rate in the clerk position increases promotional opportunities. The number and kind of opportunities, however, may be dependent on the place of employment, and the ability, training, and experience of the employee.

Employment outlook

Because of the increase in retail outlets, job opportunities for counter and retail clerks are expected to grow faster than average through the early 1990s. As is currently the case, major employers will be laundry or dry cleaning establishments, automobile rental firms, and supermarkets and grocery stores. The continued growth in video rental stores and other rental services will also increase the need for skilled clerks.

There should also be an increase in the number of opportunities for temporary or part-time work, especially during busy business periods.

Earnings

Beginning counter and retail clerks in the early 1990s generally earn near the minimum wage, which in 1989 was $3.35 an hour. Experienced clerks should average between $3.75 an hour and $9.00 an hour; the higher wages will be paid to those with the greatest number of job

responsibilities. Full-time clerks should average between $150 and $220 a week, with some clerks earning somewhat more. Those workers who have union affiliation (usually those who work for supermarkets) may earn considerably more than their nonunionized counterparts.

Full-time workers, especially those who are union members, may also receive benefits such as a paid vacation and health insurance, but this is not an industry norm.

Conditions of work

Although a forty-hour workweek is common, many stores operate on a forty-four to forty-eight-hour workweek. Most stores are open on Saturday and many on Sunday. Most stores are also open one or more weekday evenings, so working hours may vary from week to week and will inevitably include evening and weekend hours. Most counter and retail clerks work overtime during Christmas and other rush seasons. Part-time clerks generally work during peak business periods.

Most clerks work indoors in well-ventilated and well-lighted environments. The job itself can be fairly routine and repetitive. Clerks often spend much of their time on their feet.

Social and psychological factors

Counter and retail clerks should have an even temperament and the ability to work well with others. They should find systematic and orderly work appealing and they should like to work on detailed tasks. Clerks should be able to work under close supervision and also be able to work independently if supervisory personnel leave the premises. Other personal qualifications include dependability, trustworthiness, and a neat personal appearance. The advantages of this type of work include no major physical or occupational hazards.

The counter and retail clerk must be able to adjust to alternating periods of heavy and light activity. No two days—or even customers—are alike. Because some customers can be rude or even hostile, clerks must exercise tact and patience at all times. Clerks must also be prepared to work many evening and weekend shifts.

GOE: 07.03.01, 08.02.02, 08.02.03; SIC: Any industry; SOC: 4363

Court reporters

Definition

Court reporters are stenographers who record the testimony given at hearings, trials, and other legal proceedings. They use stenotype machines to take shorthand notes of public testimony, judicial opinions, sentences of the court, and other courtroom proceedings. Court reporters may transcribe the notes of the proceedings through the use of typewriters or by dictating the notes into tape recorders.

History

To record legal proceedings, court reporters use shorthand, a system of abbreviated writing that has its beginnings in forms developed more than 2,000 years ago. Ancient Greeks and Romans used symbols and letters to record poems, speeches, and political meetings.

Europeans, such as the Englishman Timothy Bright, began to develop systems of shorthand in the fifteenth and sixteenth centuries. These systems were refined throughout the seventeenth and eighteenth centuries. Shorthand was used primarily in personal correspondence and for copying or creating literary works.

Shorthand began to be applied to business communications with the invention of the typewriter. The stenotype, the first shorthand machine, was invented by an American court reporter in 1910.

Nature of the work

Court reporters are responsible for accurately recording all testimony by witnesses, lawyers, and other participants at legal proceedings. They use symbols or shorthand forms of words to rapidly record what is said. Witnesses or other persons may give testimony at between 250 and 300 words a minute, and court reporters must record this testimony word for word.

The tool used by court reporters to record proceedings is a stenotype machine. The stenotype has twenty-four keys on its keyboard. On a stenotype machine, each symbol or combination of symbols represents a sound, word, or phrase. As testimony is given, reporters strike one or more keys to create a phonetic representation of the testimony on a strip of paper. These strips of paper are then used for transcription or reference purposes.

Accurate recording of a trial is vital because the court reporter's record becomes the official transcript for the entire proceeding. If a legal case is appealed, for example, the court reporter's transcript will become the foundation for any further legal action. The next judge will refer to the court reporter's transcript to see what transpired in the trial and how the evidence was presented. Therefore, if a court reporter misses a word or phrase, the reporter must interrupt the proceedings to have the words repeated. By the same token, the court reporter may be asked by the judge to read aloud a portion of recorded testimony during the trial for clarification.

Court reporters must be comfortable recording testimony on a wide range of legal issues, from medical malpractice to income-tax evasion. In some cases, a court reporter may record testimony at a murder trial or a child-custody case. For this reason, court reporters may be subjected to tense situations and complicated arguments. The court reporter must stay as detached as possible from the hearings while faithfully recording all that is said.

Court reporters must pay close attention to all the proceedings and be able to hear and understand all that is said. Sometimes it may be difficult to understand a particular witness or attorney due to poor diction, a strong accent, or a soft speaking voice.

Computers are beginning to play a large role in helping court reporters fulfill their job responsibilities. Computer programs help a reporter convert the symbols and words of a stenotype machine into standard English. This process requires the use of a specially constructed stenotype machine and a magnetic tape to record the symbols that are then fed into the computer. The computer-based system is not only more efficient, it is also more time-effective because the computer can print out a transcript of the trial rather than have the court reporter type a transcript of the proceedings on a typewriter. These transcripts may be used by a judge or jury before rendering a decision or after a trial for review purposes.

Although the majority of court reporters work in city, county, state, or federal courts, they are also employed by private companies. Court reporters may be called on to record business meetings, large conventions, or similar events. They may also work in smaller meetings and thereby allow staff personnel to handle other responsibilities.

Court reporters must listen attentively to each word spoken during trials and simultaneously record them on a machine.

Requirements

Court reporters must have a high-school diploma or its equivalent. Those interested in this profession should take English, typing, and other related business courses in high school. Aspiring court reporters should have comprehensive training in grammar and spelling. Training in Latin would be of great benefit as it would increase a court reporter's understanding of the many medical and legal terms that often are a part of legal proceedings. Knowledge of other foreign languages is also helpful.

Court reporters are required to complete a specialized training program in shorthand reporting. These programs are usually two years in duration and include instruction on how to write at least 225 words a minute on a stenotype machine. Other topics covered include typing, transcription methods, English, and principles of law. Students must also take courses designed to make them familiar with basic anatomy and physiology. Medical and legal terms are also explained.

Degree programs in shorthand reporting are offered at various community colleges, business and vocational schools, and some universities, although university programs are rare.

Special requirements

Some states require court reporters to be certified as proficient by the National Shorthand Reporters Association (NSRA) or to be licensed by state officials. Information on certification procedures is available from the NSRA at the address given at the end of this article. It may also be necessary for court reporters who are employed by the federal government to pass a civil service examination. When working in a legal proceeding, court reporters are considered officials of the court.

Opportunities for experience and exploration

High-school students or others interested in pursuing a career as a court reporter are encouraged to talk with professionals already working in the field to learn more about the rewards and responsibilities of this profession. Attending court session is also informative. Because only those with the appropriate credentials are allowed to work as court reporters, it is impossible to get any hands-on experience before completing the required training. Part-time work as a secretary or stenographer may also help interested persons learn more about the job responsibilities of a court reporter.

Court reporters

Related occupations

Court reporters have similar recording and transcribing responsibilities as stenographers, data entry clerks, legal secretaries, and foreign language interpreters and translators.

Methods of entering

After completing the required training, court reporters usually work for a free-lance reporting company that provides court reporters for business meetings and courtroom proceedings on a temporary basis. Job placement counselors at schools offering training programs often are helpful in locating employment opportunities for qualified applicants. Qualified reporters can also contact these free-lance reporting companies directly.

Occasionally a court reporter will be hired directly out of school as a courtroom official, but ordinarily only those with several years experience are hired for full-time judiciary work.

Advancement

Skilled court reporters may be promoted to a larger court system or to an otherwise more demanding position, with an accompanying increase in pay and prestige. Those working for a free-lance company may be hired by a city, county, state, or federal court. Those with experience working in a government position may choose to become a free-lance court reporter and thereby have greater job flexibility and perhaps earn more money. Those with the necessary education, training, and experience may decide to open their own free-lance reporting company.

Employment outlook

Because of the growth in both civil and criminal judicial proceedings, employment opportunities for skilled court reporters should continue to expand through the early 1990s. There will also be job openings resulting from retirement or from those leaving the field. Job opportunities should be greatest in and around large metropolitan areas, but qualified court reporters should be able to find work anywhere in the country.

As always, job prospects will be best for those with the most training and experience. In the future, computer technology should play a greater role in transcription procedures and those trained in computer applications should have the greatest access to well-paying jobs.

Earnings

Earnings vary according to the skill and experience of the court reporter, as well as the geographic location of the court. Those just out of school may earn between $21,000 and $23,000 a year, with those employed by larger court systems generally earning more than their counterparts in smaller communities. Experienced court reporters can expect to earn between $25,000 and $33,000 a year, with those with a great deal of experience earning even more. Federal court reporters may earn between $35,000 and $41,000 a year.

Court reporters that work in small communities or as free-lancers may not work full-time. Free-lancers are usually not paid a yearly salary but rather earn an hourly rate ranging between $15 and $35 an hour, depending on experience, location of the court, and the type of work being done. Successful court reporters with jobs in business environments may earn more than those in courtroom settings, but there is less job security.

Those working for the government or full-time for a private company usually receive health insurance and other benefits, such as paid vacation and retirement pensions. Free-lancers may not receive health insurance or other benefits.

Conditions of work

Offices and courtrooms are usually pleasant surroundings. Under normal conditions, a court reporter can expect to work a standard thirty-seven- to forty-hour week. But during some trials or other complicated proceedings, court reporters often work much longer hours. They must be on hand before and after legal proceedings and must also wait while a jury is deliberating. Although weekend work is not that frequent, a court reporter must be willing to work irregular hours, including evenings. Court reporters must be able to spend long hours transcribing testimony. There may be some travel involved, especially for federal district court reporters who are usually assigned to a particular judge and travel with the judge to various trial locations. Usually those court reporters working in a large metropolitan area are also assigned to the same courtroom and judge.

Court reporters must be able to understand a variety of accents and speaking styles. They must faithfully record what they hear in the grammatical manner in which it is spoken. Court reporters must be able to ask the judge to get a witness, lawyer, or other official to repeat a word or phrase if needed. Similarly, the court reporter must be able to repeat words or phrases to clarify previous testimony. Freelance court reporters may work in a variety of situations, such as business meetings and conferences.

Social and psychological factors

The court reporter's job is vital to the integrity of the judicial system. Court reporters must be able to quickly and accurately record what is said in court. They must be attentive to detail and should be able to understand a wide variety of people, some of whom may speak with an accent or extremely quickly or slowly. Court reporters must be familiar with a wide range of medical and legal terms and must be assertive enough to ask for clarification if a term or phrase goes by without the reporter understanding it. Court reporters must be as unbi-

ased as possible and accurately record what is said, not what the court reporter believes to be true. Patience is a vital characteristic, as is the ability to work closely with the judge and other court officials.

GOE: 07.05.03; SIC: 7339, 9211; SOC: 4623

◇ SOURCES OF ADDITIONAL INFORMATION

Career and certification information is available from:

National Shorthand Reporters Association
118 Park Street, SE
Vienna, VA 22180

◇ RELATED ARTICLES

Volume 1: Law
Volume 2: Judges; Lawyers; Legal assistants
Volume 3: Secretaries; Stenographers

Data entry clerks

Definition

Data entry clerks transfer information from source documents into a computer system in a form that the computer can accept. They transcribe data (information) onto a typewriter-like keyboard that converts the information into magnetic impulses or other forms that the computer can read and process electronically.

History

Following World War II, electronic technology that was utilized to solve scientific problems during the war was transferred to peacetime government and business applications.

In 1954, the first commercial computer was built. It used machine languages. By the 1970s a computer specifically for home use was introduced.

Although the computers were not as sophisticated as they are today, their efficiency and adaptability in processing data were quickly recognized and by the 1970s computers were indispensable to private companies, schools, hospitals, and government agencies.

As computer technology advanced and computers became quicker, smaller, and less expensive, more and more businesses put them to use. Today, most large and small businesses utilize computers to process and organize mathematical data and other types of information. The boom in computer usage has led to the need for qualified computer operating personnel, including data entry clerks.

A data entry clerk inserts a cartridge of data in a computer system.

Nature of the work

Data entry clerks are responsible for entering data into computer systems so that the information can be processed to produce such documents as billing invoices, mailing lists, and other material that requires organization and compilation. Specific job responsibilities vary according to the type of computer system being utilized and the type of company in which the work takes place. For example, a data entry clerk may enter financial information for use at a bank, merchandising information for use at a store, or scientific information for use at a research laboratory.

Data entry clerks type in a series of alphabetic, numeric, or symbolic data gathered from a source document, such as a financial statement. The information from the source material is entered on a typewriter-like keyboard. Coding information (the alphabetic, numeric, or symbolic data) is converted by the entry machine to either electronic impulses or a series of holes in a tape that the computer can read and process electronically. Newer, more sophisticated computers can have data input directly without having it recorded on a tape. Sometimes, data entry clerks do not type in actual information for the computer, but type in instructions that tell the computer what functions to perform.

In small companies data entry clerks may combine data entry responsibilities on several types of computer systems with general office work. Larger companies tend to assign data entry clerks to one type of entry machinery.

Data entry clerks are responsible for adapting their entry machines for the type of data being keyed in. For example, clerks that handle vast amounts of financial data can set their machines to handle dollar amounts or transaction dates. Entry clerks are also responsible for load-ing their machines with the appropriate tape or other coding material and selecting the correct coding system (the alphabetic, numeric or symbolic representations).

Data entry clerks must always verify the accuracy of their work, either by checking the screen on which the work is displayed or by checking the data against the source document. In the case of *verifier operators* it is their job to verify the accuracy of previously punched data cards and correct those that are inaccurate. Other specialties in the data entry clerk field include:

Data typists and *keypunch operators* prepare data for input into the computer by punching data into special coding cards or into paper tapes. The cards may be punched on machines that resemble typewriters; or, if information is to be punched into tapes the work is done by machines such as bookkeeping or adding machines that have special attachments to perforate paper tape. Data typists and keypunch operators must be able to recognize any errors in the inputing process.

Data-coder operators examine codes and symbols on source material to determine how it should be entered into the computer. They may make up the operating instructions for the computer operators and assist the programmer in checking out and revising computer programs. Data-coder operators assist programmers in preparing the detailed flow charts for the computers and in translating details into coded instructions for the computer.

Terminal operators use coding systems to input information from the source document into a series of alphabetic or numeric data that can be read by the computer. After checking the entry to ensure its accuracy, they may transmit data to the computer system via telephone lines or other remote methods.

Requirements

Although there are no specific educational requirements for data entry clerks, a high-school diploma or its equivalent is usually required, and, in some cases, some college training is desirable. Some on-the-job training may be given to employees, but data entry clerks should have the ability to type and quickly scan source documents before beginning their first job.

High-school students interested in becoming data entry clerks should take English, typing, and other business courses that focus on the operations of office machinery.

Many aspiring data entry clerks now complete data-processing courses that instruct students on proper inputing methods and other skills needed for the job. Technical schools, community colleges, business schools, and some adult education courses are among the avenues available to those who want to study data processing. Data-processing courses generally run anywhere from six months to two years. Secretarial or business schools may also offer data entry courses.

Many companies test new data entry clerks to determine entry and mathematical competency levels. These companies often offer on-the-job training to instruct workers in the operation of specific data entry machinery.

Special requirements

No licenses or certificates are needed for employees in this profession. There may, however, be the need to learn new methods and techniques as the field of data processing continues to evolve.

Opportunities for experience and exploration

High-school students interested in pursuing a career in the data entry field are encouraged to talk with those already working as clerks. A visit to an office that utilizes data processing systems may be a good way of learning about the rewards and responsibilities of a career as a data entry clerk. Secretarial work or other similar office work may also be helpful in providing insight into this field. Students who are skilled typists may find part-time employment as keypunch operators.

Related occupations

Data entry clerks have similar clerical responsibilities as secretaries, court reporters, telegraph operators, typesetters, and typists.

Methods of entering

Many people entering the field have completed an educational program at a technical school or other institution that provides data-processing training. Job placement counselors at these schools often are helpful in locating employment opportunities for qualified applicants.

Classified advertisements in newspapers may list job openings, or skilled individuals may contact those firms that they believe might have openings. Major employers include insurance and utility companies, banks, and manufacturing firms. Local and state employment offices are also sources of employment information. The federal government operates its own training program for data entry clerks and applications for such positions may be made through the office of Personnel Management.

Advancement

Skilled data entry clerks may be promoted to become computer programmers or peripheral equipment operators. Competition for these positions, however, may be keen and advancement to these positions usually requires additional training and experience. In some instances, promotions may be made to supervisory positions or to jobs that combine supervisory positions with the operation of a computer. With the necessary education, training, and experience, data entry clerks may sometimes become computer center managers or programming managers.

Employment outlook

Because of improvements in data-processing technology that enables businesses to process greater volumes of information with fewer workers, employment opportunities for data entry clerks are expected to decline through the early 1990s. Jobs are becoming limited, for example, because many computer systems can now send information directly to another computer system without the need for a data entry clerk to input the information a second time. In addition, the increased use of personal computers, which allow for direct data entry and thereby bypass the necessity of an entry clerk, will also lessen the need for skilled entry personnel.

Despite the slowdown in new job openings for data entry clerks, the computer industry as a whole will remain very strong, and there should be continued employment opportunities because of retirement or job promotions. Those with the most advanced skills and the ability to adapt to the changing needs of the computer processing field will stand the best chance for continued employment. Job opportunities figure to be best in and around large metropolitan areas where most banks, insurance and utility companies, and government agencies are located.

Knowledge of different computer languages enhances a data entry clerk's employment opportunities. The ability to work on different systems, particularly specialty systems like page layout programs and typesetting programs, offers the clerk greater job flexibility.

Earnings

Beginning data entry clerks can expect to earn anywhere between $13,000 and $15,000 a year, depending on the place of employment, complexity of the job performance, and the training of the employee. Experienced clerks can expect to earn between $15,500 and $18,000, with those working for manufacturing and utility companies earning slightly more than their counterparts in banking and other service areas. Salaries for federal government employees are comparable to those earned in the private sector.

Full-time employees can expect to receive health insurance and other benefits, such as paid vacations and holidays.

Conditions of work

Most data entry clerks work a standard thirty-seven- to forty-hour week with work space usually located in comfortable, well-lighted areas. Because the work may be tiring and demands the constant use of the eyes and hands, data entry clerks must have patience and good concentration. The continual need for exactness and accuracy may produce a strain on the individual who does not easily adapt to such working conditions. Some duties may require lifting, reaching, and moving with boxes of card, tapes, and other materials. Keypunch operators and other entry personnel may sit for long hours at a time.

Social and psychological factors

Data entry clerks must be able to work in tandem with other employees and in most cases their work is under close supervision. Patience and attention to detail are vital characteristics. Workers in this profession must be able to spend long hours entering data into a machine and must be diligent and accurate in checking their work.

GOE: 07.06.02; SIC: Any industry; SOC: 4793

◇ **SOURCES OF ADDITIONAL INFORMATION**

Career information is available from:

American Federation of Information Processing Societies
1899 Preston White Drive
Reston, VA 22091

Association for Computing Machinery
11 West 42nd Street
3rd Floor
New York, NY 10036

Data Processing Management Association
505 Busse Highway
Park Ridge, IL 60068

National Association of Professional Word Processing Technicians
110 West Byberry Road
Philadelphia, PA 19116

Women in Information Processing
Lock Box 39173
Washington, DC 20016

◇ **RELATED ARTICLES**

Volume 1: Computer Hardware; Computer Software; Electronics
Volume 2: Computer programmers; Data base managers; Information scientists; Systems analysts
Volume 3: Computer and peripheral equipment operators
Volume 4: Scientific and business data-processing technicians

File clerks

Definition

File clerks review and classify articles, letters, and other types of business information and then file this material according to subject matter or by using an alphabetical or numerical system. They usually file the material in a folder and put it in a filing cabinet or other appropriate location. File clerks retrieve this material as needed and then ensure that it is returned after use.

History

File clerks and other office workers have become increasingly important as computers, word processors, and other technological advances have increased both the volume of business information available and the speed in which administrative decisions are made. File clerks play a vital role in the efficient organization and rapid retrieval of information and thus are important components of a company's organizational structure.

Today, businesses and governmental agencies are dependent on file clerks to properly file and sort business communications and cooperate with other office workers to develop a system that can accurately distribute information.

Nature of the work

File clerks carefully arrange all office information so that it can be located and retrieved quickly. One of their primary job responsibilities is to examine incoming material and file it according to a numerical system, by letter of the alphabet, or by subject matter. For example, if a magazine article dealing with advances in farming was deemed important, the file clerk would probably place the article in the "f" file folder. This information would then be available to those interested in the subject at a later date.

File clerks must be sure that the information is kept up-to-date. They add new information to existing files as it becomes available and, periodically, they throw out outdated material or transfer it to an inactive file. File clerks regularly check the files to make sure that all the material is in order, and if a piece of informa-

tion can not be found, file clerks search for the missing record.

When someone requests information, file clerks locate the appropriate file or files for the borrower. This is usually done by locating the item in an index and then finding it in the specified location. File clerks must make sure that all files are returned in a timely manner. In some cases, the file clerk will make copies of the files so that the borrower can use the material at his or her own convenience.

Although a growing number of file clerks are using computerized filing and retrieval systems, most file clerks still place paper files in file cabinets. Some clerks operate mechanized files that rotate to bring the needed records to them. Other methods include using microfilm, microfiche, or optical disks as storage mediums. In most cases, file clerks working with computerized systems or other forms of automated filing systems are responsible for coding and inputing the material into the system.

File clerks may be asked to do other clerical duties, such as operating photocopy machines or sorting mail when they are not busy with filing responsibilities.

Morgue librarians maintain and update files of news articles, encyclopedia entries, or other information for reference use by news reporters or other staff in the preparation of material for publication. *Record clerks* file sample pads of yarn and other textiles used in making cloth. These pads are needed for color comparison and stock reference; *record custodians* classify and store financial records of a bank and retrieve the information as requested by bank officials; *tape librarians* classify and store magnetic tapes that have computer programs punched into them. These magnetic tapes are used for company payroll computations and other purposes and can be reused for different sets of figures each time the same information is needed.

Requirements

A high-school diploma is usually sufficient for beginning file clerk positions, although typing skills and knowledge of office practices are also helpful. Prospective file clerks should have some mechanical ability (for operating business machines), the ability to concentrate for long periods of time on repetitious tasks, and

File clerks
Clerical Occupations

File clerks must be well-organized so that they can retrieve records quickly.

mathematical ability. Legible handwriting is a necessity.

High-school students should take courses in English, mathematics, and as many business-related courses such as typing and bookkeeping as possible.

Community colleges and vocational schools often offer business education courses that provide training for file clerks. Library cataloguing skills and documentation cataloguing skills may be offered through classroom or work-study opportunities.

Special requirements

No licenses or certificates are needed for employment in this field. File clerks who work for the federal government may need to pass a civil service examination. Some clerks (as well as other office personnel) may join a professional union such as the American Federation of State, County, and Municipal Employees.

Opportunities for experience and exploration

Students may get experience in this field by taking on clerical responsibilities with a school club or other organization. In addition, some school work-study programs may have opportunities with businesses for part-time, practical on-the-job training. It may also be possible to get a part-time or summer job in a business office by contacting offices on your own. Individuals may have the opportunity to get training in typing and office practices and procedures through evening courses offered by business schools. Another way of gaining insight into the responsibilities of a file clerk is to talk to someone already working in the field.

Related occupations

Other workers who file and sort business documents and perform assorted other clerical tasks include secretaries, general office clerks, mail clerks, and sorters.

Methods of entering

Those interested in securing an entry-level position should contact businesses or governmental agencies directly. Major employers include banks, insurance agencies, real estate companies and other large businesses. Smaller companies also often hire file clerks. Jobs may also be located through "help wanted" advertisements.

Because each company has its own filing system, most companies provide entry-level file clerks with several weeks of on-the-job training during which time company policy and procedures are explained. File clerks work with experienced personnel during this period.

Advancement

With experience, file workers may advance to more complicated filing assignments and assume supervisory responsibilities over other clerks. Those who show the desire and aptitude may be trained as a secretary, a receptionist, or an office machine operator. To be promoted to a professional position such as accountant, it is usually necessary to get a college degree or have other specialized training.

The high turnover rate in the file clerk position increases promotional opportunities. The number and kind of opportunities, however, may be dependent on the place of employment, and the ability, training, and experience of the employee.

Employment outlook

As more and more companies automate their record-keeping systems, employment opportunities for file clerks are expected to diminish. The spread of personal computers and other forms of automated filing and retrieval systems will eliminate many opportunities for file clerks. Nevertheless, numerous job opportunities will be available as people leave the field. The federal government should continue to be a good source of job opportunities and private companies throughout the country should also have openings. Employment opportunities should be especially good for those who are skilled typists and are trained to operate computers and other types of automated equipment.

There should also be an increase in the number of opportunities for temporary or part-time work, especially during busy business periods.

Earnings

Beginning file clerks should average between $9,000 and $14,000 a year, depending on the size and geographic location of the company and the skills of the worker. Experienced clerks should average between $15,000 and $21,000 per year; the higher wages will be paid to those with the greatest number of job responsibilities. The highest wages should be found with utility companies, while those in real estate, insurance, and construction should receive somewhat lower salaries. The federal government generally offers salaries competitive with those in the private sector.

Full-time workers should also receive paid vacation, health insurance, and other benefits.

Conditions of work

As is the case with most office workers, file clerks work an average thirty-seven- to forty-hour week. The working environment is usually well-ventilated and well-lighted, but the job itself can be fairly routine and repetitive. Clerks often interact with other office personnel and may work under close supervision. They may do a lot of bending and reaching, although heavy lifting is a rarity.

Many file clerks only work part-time or on a temporary basis during peak business periods.

Social and psychological factors

File clerks should have an even temperament and the ability to work well with others. They should find systematic and orderly work appealing and they should like to work on detailed tasks. Other personal qualifications include dependability, trustworthiness, and a neat personal appearance. The advantages of this type of work include regular work hours and no major physical or occupational hazards.

File clerks and other office personnel may find opportunities to learn more about the business world in general and this experience may open doors for advancement to higher positions in related fields.

GOE: 07.05.03, 07.07.01; SIC: Any industry; SOC: 4696

◇ **SOURCES OF ADDITIONAL INFORMATION**

Career information is available from local business schools and from:

Office and Professional Employees International Union
265 West 14th Street, Suite 610
New York, NY 10011

◇ **RELATED ARTICLES**

Financial institution clerks and related workers

Definition

Financial institution clerks and related workers perform many tasks in banks and other thrift institutions. Job duties vary with the size of the bank. In small banks, a clerk or related worker may perform a combination of tasks, while in the larger banks a worker may be assigned to one specialized duty, depending on the job title. All banking activities are concerned with the safekeeping, exchange transactions, and credit use of money.

History

Banking is nearly as old as civilization. Literature makes reference to "money-lenders" and "money-changers" as ancient writers describe how they bought money of other countries and in exchange gave their own local coins.

The term "banking" derives from the Italian "banco" meaning bench. Encyclopedias relate that in the early days of Italy, bankers carried on their business from benches on the streets. As Italian cities established banks, the growth gradually spread north throughout Europe and during the seventeenth century important banking developments took place in England. In 1694, the Bank of England was founded in London.

In the United States, the Continental Congress chartered the Bank of North America, which opened in Philadelphia in 1782. The first state bank was chartered in Boston in 1784 as the Bank of Massachusetts.

Although the development of banking in the United States experienced a slow growth and numerous failures, Congress and the federal government have done a great deal to make the banking system safer and more effective.

Today, banking, like many other industrial enterprise systems, has turned to the use of automation, mechanization, television, computers, and many modern methods of bookkeeping and record systems. The American people today have available to them the most modern of banking conveniences. Thousands of employees fill the positions in banks so that these services might be offered.

Nature of the work

The nature of the work for financial institution clerks and related workers is, in general, somewhat similar in the duties performed. All such workers assist in processing vast amounts of paper work that may consist of currency, deposit slips, checks, financial statements to customers, correspondence, record transactions, or indexing and filing work. In addition, they may talk with customers, take telephone calls, and perform other general office duties.

Depending on the size of the financial institution, the employee's duties may be more generalized in smaller facilities and very specialized in the larger facilities. The nature of business handled and the expanse of services offered may also help to determine a clerk's duties. Services may differ somewhat in a commercial bank from those in a savings bank, trust company or savings and loan.

Many *trust clerks* work in banks' and other financial institutions' trust departments, where they compile, record, and disseminate information about estates, stock transfers, trust department savings accounts, and the transactions and values of trust accounts. *Trust-securities clerks* keep records of investments made by the bank's trust officers for customers.

Some workers called *account analysts* and *fee clerks* are engaged in computing and supplying data about fees that banks charge for services, while others called *new accounts clerks* and *loan interviewers* interview and compile data about customers wishing to open new accounts or apply for loans.

Clerks involved with safeguarding money, securities, and other valuables include *securities vault supervisors*, *trust-vault clerks*, and *vault attendants*. Some clerks called *reconcilement clerks*, *clearing-house clerks*, and *routing clerks* process information and items received from other banks. Other clerks called *foreign-exchange-position clerks* and *exchange clerks* deal with information about monetary systems of other countries, including data about the bank's foreign investments and the value of foreign currencies.

Head stock-transfer clerks, bond clerks, advice clerks, margin clerks, trust-evaluation supervisors, securities clerks, brokerage clerks, coupon clerks, and *credit-card-control clerks* keep track of other bond, security, and credit transactions and information. Others, called *currency sorters* and *coin-machine operators*, sort and count currency using special machines. Other clerks include *insurance clerks*, *check-processing clerks* and *return-item clerks*, all at whom process checks. Some clerks called *statement-request clerks* and *telephone-quotation clerks* provide information about the status of loan applications or stock prices.

Duties for some of the more specific types of bank clerks are the following: *Collection clerks* process checks, coupons, and drafts that are presented to the financial institution for special handling. *Trust-mail clerks* keep track of mail in trust departments.

Commodity-loan clerks keep track of commodities (usually farm products) used as collateral by a large bank's foreign department. Duties may include typing of correspondence and traveling to warehouses to check on the commodities.

Bookkeeping clerks file checks, alphabetize paper work to assist senior bookkeepers, and sort and list various other kinds of material. Banks employ *bookkeepers* to keep track of countless types of financial and administrative information.

Mortgage clerks type the legal papers necessary for real estate titles, record the transactions, and maintain record card files. Many of these clerks work in savings-and-loan associations. Other clerks called *mortgage-loan-computation clerks* and *mortgage-processing clerks* involved with mortgages keep track of how much is paid and owed or prepare paper work when customers apply for loans. *Loan closers* perform duties related to obtaining loans to finance new construction projects.

Proof machine operators handle a machine which, in one single operation, sorts checks and other papers, and adds and records amounts involved.

Transit clerks sort and list checks and drafts on other banks and prepare them for mailing back to those banks.

Bookkeeping machine operators maintain records of the various deposits, checks, and other items that are credited to or charged against customers' accounts. Often they cancel checks and file them, provide customers with information about account balances, and prepare customers' statements for mailing.

Messengers deliver checks, drafts, letters, and other business papers to other financial institutions, business firms, and sometimes to local government agencies. Messengers who work only within the bank are often known as pages.

Much of the work performed by financial institution clerks involves organizing and filing bank slips. In this case, a woman is compiling canceled checks.

Statement clerks send customers' statements of withdrawals and deposits on their accounts.

Other clerks, *collateral-and-safekeeping clerks*, *reserves clerks*, and *interest clerks*, keep information about collateral, reserves, and interest rates and payments. Others called *letter-of-credit clerks* keep track of letters of credit for export and import purposes. *Wire-transfer clerks* take care of operating machines that direct the transfer of funds from one account to another.

Many banks now use computers to perform the routine tasks that formerly were done by workers by hand. To operate these new machines, banks employ *computer operators*, *tabulating machine operators*, *microfilming machine operators*, *electronic reader-sorter operators*, *check inscribers* or *encoder operators* who run machines that print information on checks and other papers in magnetic ink for machine reading, and *control clerks* who keep track of all the data and paper work transacted through the electronic data-processing divisions.

The majority of all business and industry incorporates aspects of banking in one form or another. Those persons employed in banking are usually exposed to a great deal of knowledge of how the world of business operates in general, and how the stock market operates and influences banking. The work setting is usually pleasant and employees have modern equipment with which to work. Their business associations are usually with people of good character and reputation and banking atmospheres are, in general, those of friendliness and congeniality.

Requirements

Most banks today are giving preference in their employment practices to individuals who have completed a high-school education. They are, of course, interested in applicants who have taken bookkeeping, shorthand, typing, business arithmetic, and business machines while in high school. Some banks are interested in hiring college graduates who can eventually move into managerial positions or those who have completed at least two years of college training. Exchange clerks may need to know foreign languages.

Banks are especially interested in those individuals who have an aptitude for accuracy in their work, and employers often consider this one of the prime requirements for bank work. Even the slightest error can cause untold extra hours of work and inconvenience.

A pleasing and congenial personality and the ability to get along well with fellow workers are necessary in this employment. Often an employee will be required to work closely with others in completing some tasks and, in some cases, one is in contact with the public.

The physical requirements of the work are not very demanding, although good eyesight and hearing and manual finger dexterity are needed in most positions. Applicants for jobs as bank clerks are expected to be neat, clean, and appropriately dressed for business.

Banks occasionally require lie detector tests of applicants as well as fingerprint and background investigations if finances and money will be handled on the job. Some banks are now requiring pre-employment drug testing, and random testing for drugs while under employment is becoming more acceptable.

Special requirements

No special licensure or certification is required for bank clerks and related workers; however, those employees handling money may have to qualify for bonding. Many banks now require applicants to make satisfactory scores on general intelligence and clerical aptitude tests before employment.

Although integrity and honesty are traits desired in any employee for any type of work, they are absolutely necessary for those persons employed in banks and other financial institutions where large sums of money are handled hourly. Workers must also exhibit sound judgment and good intelligence in their job performance.

Opportunities for experience and exploration

Individuals interested in these positions may explore them further by talking with their high-school guidance counselor or by visiting financial institutions and talking with the directors of personnel or with personnel actually employed in these jobs. Information on jobs with the federal government may be obtained by writing to the Office of Personnel Management, 1900 E Street, NW, Washington, DC 20415.

Sometimes banks are open to part-time employment for young people who feel they have a definite interest in pursuing a career in banking or for those with business and clerical skills. Individuals would need to make local inquiries to locate such opportunities. Other types of part-time employment where business skills are learned may also be valuable training for those planning to enter into these occupations.

Related occupations

Many careers in financial institutions require the same interests and skills as those of the clerks described in this article. Other occupations that might be of interest include bank and savings-and-loan managers, financial institution tellers, and bookkeeping and accounting clerks.

Methods of entering

Applicants for positions as financial institution clerks or related jobs should apply in person to the director of personnel. It is best to arrange an appointment first by telephone or mail so that the interview time is scheduled.

Applicants who have an acquaintance who is willing to give them a personal introduction to the director of personnel or to the officers of the institution may find this an advantage in securing employment. Personal and business references can be important to bank employers in hiring new personnel. The majority of institutions now require personal interviews with applicants before they will consider employment. In many cases the general intelligence and clerical aptitude tests that were previously mentioned under Special Requirements are also required.

Employment agencies, public and state, frequently list positions open for financial institution clerks and related workers, and newspaper "help wanted" advertisements sometimes carry listings for such employees. Large financial institutions frequently visit schools and colleges seeking qualified applicants to fill positions on their staffs.

Advancement

Many financial institution clerks begin their employment as trainees in certain types of work such as business machines operation or in general or specialized clerical duties. Employees may start out as file clerks, transit clerks, or bookkeeping clerks, and in some cases as pages or messengers. In general, beginning jobs are sometimes determined by the size of the institution and the nature of its operations. In banking work, employees sometimes learn related job tasks for possible promotion positions.

Financial institution clerks performing routine clerical tasks may receive promotions to minor supervisory positions or they may move up to tellers' or to credit analysts' positions. Sometimes their promotions may be to senior supervisory positions. Some few of these employees are promoted to jobs as bank officers; the main opportunities for these positions, however, are usually open to those employees with college degrees.

Financial institutions clerks may receive promotions as they gain in job experience through advanced educational training while on the job. The American Institute of Banking offers courses in some localities that employees may take advantage of to aid them in preparing for promotions.

In some cases, financial institution clerks may change jobs, moving into larger or different types of banks and gain salary increases or job status in this way. Other factors that influence promotional opportunities are length of service, extent of educational or specialized training, and job performance.

Employment outlook

In the early 1990s, about 41,000 statement clerks and 80,000 new-account clerks were employed nationwide. The U.S. Department of Labor predicts average growth for these positions through 2000, and thousands of job opportunities for bank clerks and related workers can be anticipated yearly during the coming years. Many of these opportunities will result from the high turnover rate that exists for these occupations because many workers resign for marital and home responsibilities.

Many financial institutions are opening branch operations to expand their services for the growing urbanization in the cities. Additionally, many new banks, trust companies, and savings-and-loan associations are being built over the country to meet the needs of an ever-expanding population. A number of older banks are also expanding and modernizing their services. This overall expansion pattern of growth in banking services is creating an even greater need for bank clerks and related workers. Employees who leave the occupation and those who retire also contribute to the opportunities available for new workers.

It seems likely that the increasing use of computers that perform many formerly routine tasks in one operation and the use of electronic data-processing methods decrease the need for some employees such as check sorters, index filers, and bookkeeping machine operators. Financial institutions now face the problem of moving their displaced workers into other jobs through training on the job or educating employees to the operation of electronic data processing and computers.

Earnings

Bank clerical workers earned from $8,550 to $12,040 per year in the early 1990s. Safe deposit clerks earned somewhat higher salaries, ranging from $9,960 to $12,700 per year. In general, salaries for all bank workers tend to be lower in smaller cities than in cities with large banking operations.

Conditions of work

The majority of financial institution workers are employed on a forty-hour workweek; bank clerks and accounting department employees, however, may have to work overtime at least once weekly and many times at the close of each month's banking operations. Check processing workers employed in large financial institutions located in urban areas may work late evening or night shifts. Those employees engaged in electronic computer operations may also work nights or evening shifts because this equipment is usually run on a two- or three-shift basis. Pay for overtime work is usually straight pay compensation.

Financial institution clerks and related workers may receive on the average five paid holidays yearly; however, in some cities the number of paid holidays may increase to twelve or more. A two-week paid vacation is common practice after one year of service, and in some financial institutions paid vacations increase to three weeks after ten or fifteen years of service. Fringe benefits usually include group life insurance, hospitalization, and sometimes surgical benefits. Jointly financed retirement plans are available to employees in some companies. Fringe benefits are generally comparable to those offered by other businesses.

Working conditions are usually in air-conditioned, pleasantly decorated and furnished surroundings. Some of the larger financial institutions in metropolitan areas, and even in some of the smaller cities, are now luxuriously furnished and heavily carpeted. Financial institutions have excellent alarm systems and many built-in features that offer protection to workers and facilities.

The job duties are not of a strenuous nature so that some types of physically handicapped people can be employed successfully in these jobs. In many tasks, very little physical movement is required.

Social and psychological factors

Many opportunities are open for men and women who are interested in jobs as financial institution clerks and in related work. Promotional opportunities usually come from within the ranks and employees who show initiative and ability may move with experience and length of service into minor or major supervisory positions.

Although the work may be in pleasant and congenial surroundings, interested persons should realize that the work performed is usually of a very repetitive nature and the duties are very similar from day to day. Most of the work is paperwork, computer entry, data processing, and other mechanical processes. It does not frequently involve customer or client contact as the teller position does. Individuals must be able to accept working in close relationship with each other, sometimes on joint tasks, as well as working under supervision. In some instances they must be flexible enough to accept working night or evening shifts.

Jobs as financial institution clerks or related workers may offer personal job satisfaction to those who find their personal interests, aptitudes, and abilities compatible with the work.

GOE: 07.02.01; SIC: 60; SOC: 471

SOURCES OF ADDITIONAL INFORMATION

American Bankers Association
1120 Connecticut Avenue, NW
Washington, DC 20036

Bank Administration Institute
60 Gould Center
Rolling Meadows, IL 60008

Institute of Financial Education
111 East Wacker Drive
Chicago, IL 60601

National Association of Bank Women
500 North Michigan Avenue
Suite 1400
Chicago, IL 60611

For information on scholarships, employment opportunities and technical assistance for minorities interested in the banking industry, please contact:

National Bankers Association
122 C Street, NW
Suite 580
Washington, DC 20001

RELATED ARTICLES

Volume 1: Banking and Financial Services; Business Administration
Volume 2: Accountants and auditors; Financial institution officers and managers; Mathematicians; Statisticians
Volume 3: Accounting and bookkeeping clerks; Cashiers; Collection workers; Financial institution tellers

Financial institution tellers

Definition

Tellers are employees of banks and other financial institutions who handle certain types of customer account transactions. They may receive and pay out monies, record customer transactions, cash checks, and perform other banking duties. Most people are familiar with commercial tellers who cash checks and handle deposits and withdrawals from customers. There are many specialized tellers, too, especially in large financial institutions.

History

Through the centuries various methods of banking have been used. Although history does not record with certainty when banking first started in the world, Babylonian records reflect that their people had a rather complex system of lending, borrowing, and depositing monies even before 2500 B.C.

In ancient times men would sit at low benches or tables to transact financial business and for the exchange of money with customers. Today, the work of the teller is in essence quite similar to that performed in ancient times—receiving and paying out money. The teller remains the initial contact between bank and customer, working from behind a service counter even as customers were served from behind a "banco" or bench in the ancient public squares.

Nature of the work

Tellers may perform a variety of related duties in their jobs. The *commercial* or *paying and receiving tellers* are primarily responsible for serving the public directly by accepting customers' deposits and providing them with receipts, paying out withdrawals, and recording the transactions, cashing checks, exchanging money for customers to provide them with certain kinds of change or currency, and accepting savings account deposits. In cashing checks, tellers are responsible for verifying signatures, identifying the person cashing the check, and for verifying that the amount for which the check is to be cashed is covered by the account against which it is to be drawn. Tellers must also be careful that deposit slips, deposit receipts, and

the amount entered in passbooks are correctly recorded. Caution must be exercised in counting amounts of money for deposit or payout. Machines are often used today to add and subtract, to make change, to print records and receipts for customers' records, and to post transactions on ledgers. Some large institutions with many branches depend on computer transactions with the main office. A teller then types in information and waits for the balance.

Tellers are usually required to keep around a certain amount of cash in their cash drawer. If they exceed the amount, they are expected to deposit the excess in the bank vault. If they are short, they request currency from the vault.

After business hours, tellers must count their cash on hand and balance the day's account on a settlement sheet by listing the money transactions of the day. They may be responsible for sorting checks and deposit slips, counting and wrapping money by hand or machine, filing new-account cards, and removing closed-account cards from the files. These tellers are supervised by *head tellers* and *teller supervisors*, who train them, arrange their schedules, and examine and reconcile their records of the day's transactions.

In large financial institutions, tellers may perform and be identified by the specialized types of transactions that they handle. *Note tellers* are responsible for receiving and issuing receipts or payments on promissory notes and for keeping these transactions correctly recorded. *Discount tellers* are responsible for the issuance and collection of customers' notes. *Foreign banknote tellers* work in the exchange department, where they buy and sell foreign currency. When customers need to trade their foreign currency for United States currency, or vice versa, these tellers determine the current value of the foreign currency in U.S. dollars, count out the requested currency and make change. These tellers may also sell travelers checks. *Collection and exchange tellers* accept payments in forms other than cash—contracts, mortgages, and bonds, for example.

Tellers may be employed in types of financial institutions other than banks. Such institutions might include various types of savings and loan associations, personal finance companies, government agencies, and large businesses operating credit offices. Tellers make up the largest specialized occupational group among bank employees.

Financial institution tellers
Clerical Occupations

With the increasing use of automatic banking machines, bank tellers perform complex tasks that the machine cannot handle.

Requirements

The majority of banks and financial institutions require that applicants have at least the minimum of a high-school education. Many bank employees today have a college education or they have taken specialized training courses offered by the banking industry. Numbers of individuals who have attained a college education work as tellers to gain experience in this aspect of banking with the anticipation of qualifying by promotion for positions as bank officers. Large numbers of individuals, however, apply for jobs in banking immediately after high-school graduation. Then, through the specific training program of the bank in which they are employed and sometimes by taking college night courses or others offered through the banking institute training programs, they continue to prepare themselves for better jobs.

Training opportunities for this occupational group are numerous. Many business schools, junior colleges, and universities offer programs in business administration or special course programs in banking.

The educational division of the American Banking Association, the American Institute of Banking, has in operation a vast program of adult education in business fields and offers training courses in numerous parts of the country that enable individuals to earn standard or graduate certificates in bank training. Individuals may also enroll for correspondence study with this institute.

Other educational institutions, such as the New York Institute of Finance and the Stonier Graduate School of Banking, offer opportuni-

ties for experienced bankers to study in specialized fields of banking or various other aspects of banking in which individuals may wish to gain additional or specific kinds of training.

Aptitudes considered to be strong assets in the work of a bank teller are accuracy, speed, a good memory, the ability to work with figures, manual dexterity so that money may be handled quickly, and neatness and orderliness in the performance of work. A prime requisite for tellers is that their honesty be above reproach, reflecting absolute trustworthiness.

Tellers must be able to present a record of references that will show good character, acceptable personal associates, and high standards of moral conduct. In personal qualities, the teller must be able to work cooperatively with others and possess a pleasing personality and friendly manner. The nature of the work of the teller and the responsibility of a financial institution to its customers demand that banking business be treated as confidential and not discussed outside the place of work.

The teller must always take the responsibilities of the work seriously and recognize that carelessness cannot be allowed in this occupation. A temperament for calmness, emotional stability, and patience for routine are positive assets to the teller who sometimes must work under pressure at busy rush hour periods.

Physically, the work of the teller is not strenuous other than that it requires standing for long periods of time.

Special requirements

The nature of the work of the teller demands that one handle large sums of money. Therefore, bank tellers must be able to meet the standards set up by bonding companies to be bonded as employees. Other than this special requirement, tellers are not required to meet special licensure or certification imposed by law or official organizations.

Opportunities for experience and exploration

Individuals may explore their interests in this occupation in numerous ways. They may talk with their high-school guidance counselor to obtain additional job information and request that they be administered interest and aptitude tests that may be discussed in the light of their abilities. Summer or part-time work experiences are frequently available, depending on the locality, through which students can work in clerical jobs, as messengers, or in other duties to observe the work of the tellers. Interested persons may also visit banks and other financial institutions to talk with persons employed in banking positions. An academic high-school program, as well as participation in school clubs and activities that will enable the student to gain experience in working with people and in developing poise and a pleasant manner, are considered assets to future employees in banking positions. Commercial courses in high school may also be helpful, such as business arithmetic, business law, typing, and the operation of general business machines.

Related occupations

Banking and financial services offer many career opportunities for those interested in numbers, finances, and customer contact. Other jobs include bank managers and officers, accounting and bookkeeping clerks, statisticians, and tax preparers.

Methods of entering

The majority of tellers are promoted into these positions from beginning jobs as bookkeeping clerks, or from various other types of clerical positions. The seniority and ability that has been demonstrated in these beginning jobs are considered in the "promotion-from-within" policy in filling teller positions.

It is sometimes possible for applicants to obtain beginning jobs as tellers, especially in large city financial institutions that offer on-the-job training programs where formal training supplants the experience one would gain by first working in related clerical type positions.

Job opportunities, open to both men and women, may sometimes be located by direct personal application to the institution or firm in which an individual would like to be employed or in which one has heard there is an opening, by reading newspaper jobs advertisements and "help wanted" ads, through private or state employment agencies, or by using the placement service in a school or college an individual has attended.

Advancement

The "promotion-from-within" policy is followed in many financial and other business institutions in promoting employees. Advancements are usually given on the basis of past job performance considering the employee's seniority, ability, and general personal qualities. Tellers may be promoted to head teller or to other types of supervisory positions such as to department head. In small branch facilities, an individual who has been transferred there as head teller from a large facility may eventually earn promotion to assistant manager or even manager.

Employees who have shown initiative in accepting their job responsibilities, in seeking additional formal education and job training, and who have evidenced their ability to assume degrees of leadership may in time be promoted to junior bank officer positions. These positions might include such jobs as assistant cashier, assistant trust officer, or assistant departmental vice president. Such advancements reflect a recognition of the individual's potential for even greater future job responsibilities.

Employment outlook

Of the more than 1.5 million people working in banks, 493,000 were tellers. About 377,000 worked in banks, and 116,000 worked in other types of financial institutions, including savings and loans and personal credit agencies. The employment outlook for tellers is predicted to be good for the foreseeable future, although growth in this occupation will probably be slower than average through the mid-1990s. As more and more banks begin using automated teller machines, automated branches, and drive-up windows, the number of tellers needed will decrease.

Banks are expanding their facilities, however, to meet the growing business needs of the public and the ever-increasing population figures. New banks are also being built and branch banks opening to provide services for urban and suburban areas. In addition, numerous employment opportunities will be available to replace those workers who have retired, moved into other job fields, or who are deceased. Thousands of job openings are also anticipated to replace those workers who will quit their positions for marital and family responsibilities.

The increased use of computers and automation technology may reduce tellers' work hours, allowing each teller to serve an in-

Financial institution tellers
Clerical Occupations

creased number of customers and raising the number of part-time workers needed. Many banks now employ part-time workers.

The field of banking is one that offers a greater degree of stability in employment than some other fields because it is less likely to be affected by low levels in the general economy.

Earnings

Yearly salaries and hourly wages paid to tellers vary over the country and may depend on the size of the bank, geographic location, experience, formal education, specialized training, ability, and initiative of the employee in seeking advancement.

In the early 1990s tellers earned an average of about $12,960 a year. The type of position makes a difference in pay. The highest paid tellers earned about $20,640 a year, while those with fewer responsibilities in lower-paying areas of the country earned as little as $9,600.

Applicants who are college graduates and who obtain employment as executive trainees may earn $12,000 to $14,500 annually. Junior officers who have gained some years of banking experience may earn substantially higher salaries than executive trainees.

Fringe benefits for these workers are, in the majority of cases, exceptionally satisfactory. Paid holidays may range from five to twelve, depending on the geographic location of employment. Paid vacation periods vary, but many employees now receive a two-week paid vacation after one year of service, three weeks after ten to fifteen years, and four weeks after twenty-five years. Group life, hospitalization, and surgical insurance plans are usually available and employees frequently have the benefits of a shared employer–employee retirement plan. In some banks profit-sharing plans are open to employee enrollment.

Conditions of work

The majority of bank employees work a forty-hour week; however, in some Northeastern geographic areas the workweek may average thirty-five to thirty-seven hours. Tellers may sometimes be required to work rather irregular hours and overtime may be necessary perhaps once a week. Many banks today stay open until 8:00 P.M. on Friday nights to accommodate workers who receive weekly salaries on that day but find it necessary to bank after 5:00 P.M. The number of persons employed as part-

time tellers seems to be increasing in financial institutions.

Working conditions are usually favorable in pleasant and attractive physical surroundings. Office equipment and furnishings in many facilities today are very modern and efforts are made to create a relaxed but efficient work atmosphere.

Social and psychological factors

Individuals employed as tellers may enjoy the satisfaction of job stability and security offered in banking work. Seasonality and economic trends do not seem to affect this occupational group to any great extent. Tellers also enjoy membership in an occupational group that carries community respect and social acceptance. Pleasant physical surroundings, congenial working relationships, clean work, satisfactory fringe benefits, and salaries comparable to those in similar occupational groups, as well as opportunities for advancement for the employee with initiative and adequate formal training are all assets for this occupation.

Those persons who do not desire to continue to learn and improve themselves through on-the-job, specialized, or formal educational training and those who find it an emotional strain to handle and be responsible for large sums of money may find the job unappealing. The teller must also sometimes work under the pressure of busy rush hours.

The potential employee who enjoys working in harmony with others and enjoys meeting and serving the public and who feels that the keen competition to be faced in seeking advancement will be a challenge may well find many satisfactions in the job of financial institution teller.

GOE: 07.02.02, 07.03.01; SIC: 60; SOC: 4364, 4791

◇ **SOURCES OF ADDITIONAL INFORMATION**

American Bankers Association
1120 Connecticut Avenue, NW
Washington, DC 20036

Bank Administration Institute
60 Gould Center
Rolling Meadows, IL 60008

Institute of Financial Education
111 East Wacker Drive
Chicago, IL 60601

National Association of Bank Women
500 North Michigan Avenue
Suite 1400
Chicago, IL 60611

◇ **RELATED ARTICLES**

Volume 1: Banking and Financial Services
Volume 2: Accountants and auditors; Financial institution officers and managers
Volume 3: Cashiers; Financial institution clerks and related workers

General office clerks

Definition

General office clerks maintain files, sort mail, and perform other clerical tasks that help an office run smoothly. In large companies, office clerks might have specialized tasks such as opening and sorting mail, but in most cases clerks must be flexible and do a variety of tasks, including typing, answering telephones, and making photocopies. General office clerks usually work under close supervision, and experienced clerks may direct the activities of those with less experience.

History

With the development of the Industrial Revolution, business occupations became specialized. Before the eighteenth century, many business people did their own office work. After, office clerks were brought in to handle increased clerical duties.

General office workers have become more important as computers, word processors, and other technological advances have increased both the volume of business information available and the speed in which administrative decisions can be made. The number of general office workers in the United States has grown to close to three million as more and more trained personnel are needed to handle the volume of business communication and information that come into an office.

Businesses and governmental agencies are dependent on skilled office workers to file and sort business communications, operate office equipment, and cooperate with other personnel to ensure the smooth flow of information.

Nature of the work

General office clerks usually perform a variety of tasks as part of their overall responsibility of helping a business or administrative operation run smoothly. They may type or file bills, statements, and business correspondence, or they may stuff envelopes, answer telephones, and sort mail. General office clerks also enter data at computer terminals, run errands, and operate photocopiers or other office equipment. Usually an office clerk performs a combination of these and other clerical tasks throughout the day, spending an hour or so on one task and then moving onto another task as an office manager or other supervisory personnel so decides.

A general office clerk may work with other office personnel such as a bookkeeper or accountant to maintain a company's financial records. Clerks might type and mail invoices and, as they gain experience, may be asked to update business files to reflect receipt of payments and verify records for accuracy.

General office clerks often deliver messages from one office worker to another. This responsibility is especially important in larger companies where office clerks play a vital role in the smooth flow of information. Clerks may relay questions and answers from one department head to another and similarly, office clerks may also relay messages from those outside the company to those working on staff.

General office clerks may also work with other office personnel on individual projects, such as preparing a yearly budget or making sure a mass mailing gets off on time.

Administrative clerks assist in the smooth operations of an office by compiling business

A general office clerk verifies data from a computer with the assistance of her supervisor.

ery and bookkeeping are also helpful. Prospective office clerks should have some mechanical ability (for operating business machines), the ability to concentrate for long periods of time on repetitive tasks, and mathematical ability. Legible handwriting is a necessity.

High-school students should take courses in English, mathematics, and as many business-related courses such as typing and bookkeeping as possible.

Community colleges and vocational schools often offer business education courses that provide training for general office workers.

Special requirements

No licenses or certificates are needed for employment in this field. General office clerks who work for the federal government may need to pass a civil service examination. Some clerks (as well as other office personnel) may join a professional union such as the American Federation of State, County, and Municipal Employees.

Opportunities for experience and exploration

Students may get experience in this field by taking on clerical or bookkeeping responsibilities with a school club or other organization. In addition, some school work-study programs may have opportunities with businesses for part-time, practical on-the-job training. It may also be possible to get a part-time or summer job in a business office by contacting offices on your own. Individuals may have the opportunity to get training in the operation of business machinery (calculators, word processors, and so on) through evening courses offered by business schools. Another way of gaining insight into the responsibilities of a general office clerk is to talk to someone already working in the field.

records, providing information to sales personnel and customers, and preparing and sending out bills, policies, invoices, and other business correspondence. Administrative clerks may also keep financial records and prepare the payroll.

Office clerks perform many of the same clerical tasks as general office clerks (sorting and filing mail, answering the telephones, and so on), but office clerks do not have any typing responsibilities.

Some general office clerks have titles that describe where they work and the jobs they do. *Congressional-district aides* work with their district's elected officials. *Police clerks* are employed in the police stations, and *concrete products dispatchers* work with construction firms on building projects.

Related occupations

Other workers who answer telephones, file and sort business correspondence, and perform assorted other clerical tasks include secretaries, file clerks, messengers, and mail clerks.

Requirements

A high-school diploma is usually sufficient for beginning general office clerks, although business courses in the operation of office machin-

Methods of entering

Those interested in securing an entry-level position should contact businesses or governmental agencies directly. Major employers include utility companies, insurance agencies, and many other large companies. Smaller companies also hire general office workers and sometimes smaller companies offer a greater opportunity to gain experience in a variety of clerical tasks. Jobs may also be located through "help wanted" advertisements.

Most companies provide entry-level general office clerks with on-the-job training during which time company policy and procedures are explained. General office clerks work with experienced personnel during this period.

Advancement

General office clerks usually begin their employment in the more routine types of tasks such as delivering messages and sorting and filing mail. With experience, they may advance to more complicated assignments and assume a greater responsibility for the total work to be completed. Those who show the desire and ability may move to other clerical positions, such as secretary or receptionist. General office clerks with good leadership skills may become group managers or supervisors. To be promoted to a professional occupation such as an accountant, it is usually necessary to get a college degree or have other specialized training.

The high turnover rate in the general office clerk position increases promotional opportunities. The number and kind of opportunities, however, may be dependent on the place of employment, and the ability, training, and experience of the employee.

Employment outlook

With the increased use of data processing equipment and other types of automated equipment, more and more employers are hiring people they feel can do a variety of office tasks. Therefore, employment opportunities for general office workers are expected to grow about as fast as average through the early 1990s. The federal government should continue to be a good source of job opportunities and private companies throughout the country should also have numerous openings. Employment opportunities should be especially good for those trained to operate automated office machinery.

There should also be an increased number of opportunities for temporary or part-time work, especially during busy business periods.

Earnings

Beginning general office clerks should average between $10,000 and $14,000 a year, depending on the size and geographic location of the company and the skills of the worker. Experienced clerks should average between $15,000 and $21,000 per year; the higher wages will be paid to those with the greatest number of job responsibilities. The highest wages should be found with utility and mining companies, while those in real estate, insurance, and construction should receive somewhat lower salaries. The federal government generally offers salaries competitive with those in the private sector.

Full-time workers should also receive paid vacation, health insurance, and other benefits.

Conditions of work

As is the case with most office workers, general office clerks work an average thirty-seven- to forty-hour week. The working environment is usually well-ventilated and well-lighted and although general office clerks have a variety of tasks, the job itself can be fairly routine and repetitive. Clerks often interact with accountants and other office personnel and may work under close supervision.

Many general office workers are employed part-time or on a temporary basis during peak business periods.

Social and psychological factors

General office clerks should have an even temperament and the ability to work well with others. They should find systematic and orderly work appealing and they should like to work on detailed tasks. Other personal qualifications include dependability, trustworthiness, and a neat personal appearance. The advantages of this type of work include regular work hours and no major physical or occupational hazards.

General office clerks and other office personnel may find opportunities to learn more about the business world in general, and this experience may open doors for advancement to higher positions in related fields.

GOE: 07.07.03; SIC: Any industry; SOC: 4632

◇ **SOURCES OF ADDITIONAL INFORMATION**

Career information is available from local business schools and from:

Office and Professional Employees International Union
265 West 14th Street, Suite 610
New York, NY 10011

◇ **RELATED ARTICLES**

Volume 1: See Table of Contents for areas of specific interest
Volume 3: Bookkeeping workers; Billing clerks; Cashiers; Clerical supervisors and managers; File clerks; Financial institution clerks and related workers

Hotel clerks

Definition

Hotel clerks are employed by hotels and similar establishments to work at desks or counters in lobbies and guest reception centers to deal directly with the public. The work involves services to guests in providing room assignments and related duties.

History

Travelers in early American days found few conveniences or comfort in the colonial inns that were located along the stagecoach routes. Weary travelers in those days were provided with beds and food, but the conveniences known to us today were unheard of then.

Innkeepers and their families ran the inns and took care of all the chores and business except for the night watch, for which a person was hired to ring a bell in the event of trouble. Thus, the first room or service clerks were probably servants who worked for the family or members of the family themselves.

In the early nineteenth century, hotels began opening their doors to guests with many new conveniences and services. The famous Tremont House opened in Boston in 1829 and provided locks on hotel doors with separate keys for the guests. In New York, the Astor House opened in 1836 and boasted of the newest of innovations—hot running water on the first floor.

Uniformed bellhops and doormen swung wide the doors of the Gilsey House, which began operation in New York in 1877. This new standard was soon to be followed by the majority of first class hotels in the country.

As hotel operations have expanded to keep pace with the growing needs of the nation, so has the need for more specialized personnel to perform the services hotel managers wish to extend to their guests and to handle all the responsibilities of hotel work. Hotel clerks have been employed as a part of this ever-expanding growth.

Nature of the work

Individuals employed as front office clerks help to build good public relations for the hotels and motels in which they are employed by providing efficient, courteous service to the public.

These clerks greet guests, assign rooms, issue keys, sort mail, provide information for guests, and perform other job duties related to room assignment work. In large hotels and motels, the job assignments of these employees may be more specialized, designated by specific titles.

Room or *desk clerks* usually are the first of a hotel or motel's clerical staff to greet guests. They are generally responsible for filling the establishment's vacant rooms by selling its services and making the guest assignments. These employees assist guests in the proper registration procedures and talk with them regarding any preferences they may have in room assignments. They may discuss the room rates, location and floor preferences, provide information regarding the services that guests may expect in the hotel, and answer any general questions the guests may have. Room or desk clerks also have the responsibility of considering the hotel's financial interests and of obtaining maximum revenues in making room assignments. They verify the customer's credit and establish how the customer will pay for the hotel room and services. Once a guest has completed registration, the clerk signals a bellhop to carry the guest's luggage and to escort him or her to the assigned rooms.

Reservation clerks have the responsibility of acknowledging room reservations either by mail or by telephone and for writing or typing out the reservation forms. Once a reservation is completed, this clerk notifies the room clerk of the expected time of arrival of the guests.

Rack clerks keep room assignment records current on forms that indicate whether rooms are occupied or vacant or when they are closed for needed repairs. These employees may also keep telephone operators, housekeepers, and other personnel informed about any changes in room occupancy.

Floor supervisors or *floor clerks* are employed only in the very large hotels and they are assigned to a specific floor to take care of the distribution of guest mail and packages in addition to other general duties.

Mail and information clerks may be employed at the front desk in hotels, motels, and other lodging facilities.

The responsibilities of any of these employees may consist of a combination of duties, depending on the organization and size of the establishment. People on late evening shifts (night room clerks, for example) may be responsible for some bookkeeping or cashiering duties or may assist in other types of clerical work.

Requirements

The majority of employers prefer to hire high-school graduates for these positions; however,

Front office clerks in hotels are often trained in public relations skills. Courtesy and consideration are essential in dealing with the public.

today, many employers are giving increasing attention to the hiring of college-trained personnel whom they may later advance to managerial positions. Those high-school graduates who have clerical aptitudes and training, particularly in typing, bookkeeping, and office machines, may be given preference for opening positions in this field. Mature individuals beyond high-school age may improve their chances for employment by enrolling in home study or evening courses such as those sponsored by the Educational Institute of the American Hotel and Motel Association.

Clerical aptitudes, a pleasing personality, and a friendly disposition are definite assets for these employees. Other personal traits to be considered are neatness in dress and grooming habits, a courteous manner, patience, and a desire to deal directly with the public and with the many types of personalities met in this work.

Special requirements

The nature of the work of some hotel clerks demands that they handle large sums of money. Therefore, some cashiers must be able to meet the standards set up by bonding companies.

In some areas clerks may join a union.

Hotel clerks
Clerical Occupations

Opportunities for experience and exploration

Individuals who are interested in exploring the occupation of hotel clerk or related job opportunities may do so in several ways. They may talk with the high-school guidance counselor who may provide them with occupational literature and information and may provide the opportunity to take interest inventories and aptitude tests for greater self-exploration. Visits to hotels and motels will allow individuals to observe the work of the front office clerks and may provide the opportunity to talk with hotel personnel managers regarding the work of these and related employees.

Students who meet the minimum age requirements for employment may wish to seek part-time or summer employment in resort areas and in hotels as bellhops or elevator operators to try to explore the occupational field. Part-time clerical positions are also sometimes available.

Related occupations

There are several occupations related to hotel clerks. Please refer to the listing at the end of this article.

Methods of entering

The majority of hotels follow a "promotion-from-within" policy in securing front office clerks. Beginning workers may find better job opportunities open to them as key clerks, mail clerks, or in other routine jobs. Bellhops and elevator operators are sometimes promoted to these front office positions, depending on their experience, ability, and work performance.

Hotels and motels that hire individuals from the outside usually provide some type of on-the-job training for these new employees. During this initial period of employment, beginning employees learn their job duties, acquire background information regarding the operation of the establishment, the location of the rooms, the types of services offered to the guests, and other general routine work duties. Experienced workers or hotel managers usually continue to assist the new employees as they gain in job experience.

Information on employment opportunities may often be obtained through local public or state employment agencies or through advertisements in the newspaper. Individuals may also apply directly to the personnel managers of hotels and motels in which they are interested in working. Job opportunities may sometimes be located through educational institutions which have training programs in hotel and institutional management.

Advancement

The majority of hotels have a promotion-from-within policy for positions in front office work. Advancements are often dependent upon an employee's experience, work performance, education and training, and the possession of the desired personal characteristics. An employee might, for example, be promoted from the job of reservation or rack clerk to room clerk. Successful job performance as a room clerk could lead to further promotions such as to assistant front office manager or to front office manager. Opportunities for promotion may be improved by taking home study courses, such as those sponsored by the Educational Institute of the American Hotel and Motel Association.

After many years of successful experience in various hotel jobs and diligent application to one's work, promotions are possible to top managerial positions. These positions might include assistant hotel manager or other managerial positions.

Employment outlook

In general, hotel clerks make up a relatively small occupational group. In the early 1990s, hotels and motels in the United States employed approximately 114,000 of these workers. The employment outlook for this occupational group for the near future points to a moderate increase in the number of job openings. The majority of opportunities are expected to be in beginning jobs that are open because of promotions from within the ranks.

Other job opportunities may be available in the metropolitan areas where new hotels and motels are being built or expanded. The great number of very large hotels or motels that have been built throughout the country, and those that are predicted to be built in the future, will undoubtedly provide some job opportunities for front office clerks in the future.

There is relatively good stability among these workers in their jobs and the employment turnover is not great. The number of workers who are employed in this occupation tends to remain rather stable in spite of general economic fluctuations, which is not a characteristic of many of the other hotel occupations and industries.

Earnings

Limited information is available on the earnings of these employees. It is estimated, however, that in the early 1990s, room clerks' average salaries ranged from $9,300 to $15,600 a year, largely depending on the location of the hotel. Large hotels in big cities generally pay the highest rates to all types of hotel clerks. Salaries for reservation, mail, and information clerks are estimated to be lower than those earned by room clerks. Clerks who had been promoted to front office managers earned an average of $25,000 a year.

Fringe benefits for these employees may include somewhat higher salaries for night-duty work, free meals while on duty, and group life and health insurance. The majority of these workers usually receive one week of paid vacation after one year of service, and two weeks after three or more years. Most establishments allow these employees four to six paid holidays a year.

Conditions of work

Hotels and motels are usually open round the clock on a twenty-four-hour, seven-day-week operation. Employees may be asked to work any one of three shifts or to work on a rotation shift plan. Staffs for night duty are usually smaller than those needed in the day and early evening shifts, so that night-duty shifts may come around less frequently for employees. Holiday and Sunday shifts may also be rotated among these personnel; however, they may frequently be asked to work overtime hours.

The majority of hotels and motels are clean, comfortable, well ventilated, and well lighted, providing pleasant working surroundings. The work is not hazardous or of a physically strenuous nature, although these employees may perform most of their duties by standing the majority of their work hours.

Social and psychological factors

Individuals employed in these jobs need to be able to live with rotating work shifts and often irregular work hours resulting from overtime duty. Flexibility and adaptability are necessary traits for these employees.

Depending on the location, the clerk may work in remote or isolated areas. Clerks at resorts may live at the facilities. These situations require that breaks, meals, and other off-duty activities normally be done at the hotel site. For those employees living at the site, it will also mean much of one's socialization be with other employees.

The work of hotel clerks and of the employees in related positions is often under the supervision of the assistant hotel manager or the hotel manager. Individuals need to be able to work cooperatively with others in these jobs and be willing to be under the supervision of management. In some areas, depending upon the locality, hotel front office clerks belong to local unions that are affiliated with the Hotel and Restaurant Employees and Bartenders International Union or the Building Service Employees' International Union.

Occasions may arise when hotel clerks must work under more than the routine job pressures, when the hotel or motel accommodates convention or tour groups or when local attractions bring in large numbers of people to the hotel. Potential employees should realize that it can sometimes be very trying and difficult to remain pleasant, calm, and patient in all their face-to-face contact with the public. Some clientele can be very difficult to please, no matter how courteously services are extended. The employee must keep in mind at all times that one of the prime responsibilities of a front office clerk is the building of good public relations for the hotel or motel.

Individuals who enjoy dealing with the public and performing public services, and who possess the necessary ability and aptitude, may find the work of hotel clerk or the work of the related positions to offer a satisfying career.

GOE: 07.04.03; SIC: 701; SOC: 4643

◇ **SOURCES OF ADDITIONAL INFORMATION**

American Hotel and Motel Association
1201 New York Avenue, NW
Washington, DC 20005

Council on Hotel, Restaurant, and Institutional Education
1200 17th Street, NW
Washington, DC 20036

For educational information, contact:

**Educational Institute of the American
Hotel and Motel Association**
1407 South Harrison Road
PO Box 1240
East Lansing, MI 48826

◇ **RELATED ARTICLES**

Volume 1: Hospitality
Volume 2: Cashiers; Hotel and motel industry
workers; Hotel housekeepers and assistants

Insurance policy processing occupations

Definition

Insurance policy processing personnel do a variety of clerical and administrative tasks that ensure that insurance applications and claims are handled in an efficient and timely manner. They review new applications, make adjustments to existing policies, work on policies that are to be reinstated, check the accuracy of company records, verify client information, and compile information used in the settlement of claims. Insurance policy processing personnel also handle business correspondence relating to any of the above duties. They use computer processors, calculators, and other office equipment in the course of their work.

History

Organized insurance was first developed in the shipping industry during the 1600s as a means of sharing the risks of commercial voyages. Underwriters received a fee for the portion of the financial responsibility they covered.

As the need for further protection developed, other types of insurance were created. After the London Fire of 1666, fire insurance became available in England. Life insurance first appeared in the United States in 1759; accident insurance followed in 1863; and automobile insurance was instituted in 1898.

Now, millions of dollars worth of insurance policies are written every day. Skilled claim examiners, medical-voucher clerks, and other insurance workers are needed to process applications and claims accurately and efficiently, to provide insurance and claim adjustments to clients.

Nature of the work

Insurance policy processing workers are involved in all aspects of handling applications and settling claims. Sometimes a policy processing worker will be assigned a variety of tasks but increasingly insurance companies are relying on specialists to do specific tasks. These specialists include: *Claim examiners* who review settled insurance claims to verify that payments have been made according to company procedures and are in line with the information provided in the claims form. They report any overpayments or other irregularities. Claim examiners are also responsible for meeting with company lawyers on any claims that involve litigation.

Cancellation clerks cancel insurance policies as directed by insurance agents. They compute any refund due and mail any appropriate refund and the cancellation notice to the policyholder. Clerks also notify the bookkeeping department of the cancellation and send a notice to the insurance agent.

Claims clerks review insurance claim forms for accuracy and completeness. Frequently, this involves calling or writing the insured party or other people involved to secure missing information. After placing this data in a claims file, the clerk reviews the insurance policy to determine the coverage. Routine claims are transmitted for payment; if further investigation is needed, the clerk informs the claims supervisor.

Claims supervisors not only direct the work of claims clerks but are also responsible for informing policy owners and beneficiaries of the procedures for filing claims. They submit claim liability statements for review by the actuarial department and inform departmental supervisors of the status of claims.

Reviewers review completed insurance applications to ensure that all questions have been answered. They contact insurance agents to inform them of any problems with the applications, and if none are found the reviewers suggest that policies be delivered to policyholders. Reviewers may collect premiums from new policyholders and provide management with updates on new business.

Policy-change clerks compile information on changes in insurance policies, such as a change in beneficiaries, and determine if the proposed changes conform to company policy and state law. Using rate books and a knowledge of specific types of policies, they calculate new premiums and make appropriate adjustments to accounts. Policy-change clerks may help write a new policy with the specified changes or prepare a rider to an existing policy.

Revival clerks approve reinstatement of insurance policies if the reason for the lapse in service, such as an overdue premium, is corrected within a specified time limit. They compare answers given by the policyholder on the reinstatement application with those previously approved by the company and examine company records to see if there are any circumstances that make reinstatement impossible. Revival clerks calculate the irregular premium and the reinstatement penalty due when reinstatement is approved, type notices of company action (approval or denial of reinstatement), and send this notification to the policyholder.

Insurance checkers verify the accuracy and completeness of insurance company records by comparing the computations on premiums paid and dividends due on individual forms and checking that information against similar information on other applications. They also verify personal information on applications, such as the name, age, address, and value of property of the policyholder, and proofread all material concerning insurance coverage before it is sent to policyholders.

Agent-contract clerks evaluate the ability and character of prospective insurance agents and approve or reject their contracts to sell insurance for a company. They review the prospective agent's application for relevant work experience and other qualifications and check the applicants' personal references to see if they meet company standards. Agent-contract clerks correspond with both the prospective agent and company officials to explain their decision to accept or reject individual applications.

Medical-voucher clerks analyze vouchers sent by doctors who have completed medical exam-

An insurance claims representative inspects damage to a car that was involved in an accident. He must place a dollar value on the damage.

inations of insurance applicants and approve payment of these vouchers based on standard rates. They note the doctor's fee on a form and forward the form and the voucher to the bookkeeper or other appropriate personnel for further approval and payment.

Requirements

A high-school diploma is usually sufficient for beginning insurance policy processing workers, although business courses in the operation of office machinery and bookkeeping are also helpful. Prospective workers should have some mechanical ability (for operating business machines), the ability to concentrate for long periods of time on repetitious tasks, and mathematical ability. Legible handwriting is a necessity. Because they often work with policyholders and other insurance workers, insurance policy processing personnel must communicate effectively.

High-school students should take courses in English, mathematics, and as many business-related courses such as typing and bookkeeping as possible.

Community colleges and vocational schools often offer business education courses that provide training for insurance policy processing workers.

Special requirements

Although no licenses or certificates are needed for employment in this field, it is important that insurance policy processing workers are familiar with state and federal insurance laws and regulations. Insurance policy processing personnel who work for the federal government may need to pass a civil service examination.

Opportunities for experience and exploration

Students may get experience in this field by taking on clerical or bookkeeping responsibilities with a school club or other organization. In addition, some school work-study programs may have opportunities with insurance companies for part-time, practical on-the-job training. It may also be possible to get a part-time or summer job with an insurance company on your own.

Individuals may have the opportunity to get training in office procedures and the operation of business machinery through evening courses offered by business schools. Another way of gaining insight into the responsibilities of insurance policy processing workers is to talk to someone already working in the field.

Related occupations

Other workers who compile, review, and maintain business records include secretaries, file clerks, reservation clerks, and auditors.

Methods of entering

Those interested in securing an entry-level position should contact insurance agencies directly. Jobs may also be located through "help wanted" advertisements or by using the local office of the U.S. Employment Service.

Some insurance companies may give potential employees an aptitude test to determine their ability to work quickly and accurately. Work assignments may be made on the basis of the results of this test.

Advancement

Insurance policy processing workers usually begin their employment in the more routine types of tasks such as reviewing insurance applications to ensure that all the questions have been answered. With experience, they may advance to more complicated assignments and as-

sume a greater responsibility for the total work to be completed. Those who show the desire and ability may be promoted to clerical supervisory positions, with a corresponding increase in pay and work responsibilities. To become a claim representative or an underwriter, it is usually necessary to have a college degree or have taken specialized courses in insurance.

The high turnover rate among insurance policy processing workers increases promotional opportunities. The number and kind of opportunities, however, may be dependent on the place of employment, and the ability, training, and experience of the employee.

Employment outlook

Because of the increased use of data processing machines and other types of automated equipment, little or no change is expected in the rate of employment of insurance policy processing workers through the early 1990s. Many jobs will result from workers retiring or otherwise leaving the field. Employment opportunities should be best in and around large metropolitan areas, where the majority of large insurance companies are located.

There should also be an increase in the number of opportunities for temporary or part-time work, especially during busy business periods.

Earnings

Based on limited information, beginning insurance policy processing workers should average between $11,000 and $13,500 a year, depending on the size and geographic location of the insurance company and the skills of the worker. Experienced workers should average between $14,000 and $20,000 per year.

Full-time workers should also receive paid vacation, health insurance, and other benefits.

Conditions of work

As is the case with most office workers, insurance policy processing employees work an average thirty-seven to forty-hour week. Although the working environment is usually well ventilated and well lighted, the job itself can be fairly routine and repetitive, with most of the work taking place at a desk. Policy processing workers often interact with other insurance professionals and policyholders, and may work under close supervision.

Because many insurance companies offer twenty-four-hour claims service to their policyholders, some claims clerks work evenings and weekends. Many insurance workers are employed part-time or on a temporary basis.

Social and psychological factors

Insurance policy processing workers should have an even temperament and the ability to work well with others. They should find systematic and orderly work appealing and they should like to work on detailed tasks. Other personal qualifications include dependability, trustworthiness, and a neat personal appearance. The advantages of this type of work include regular work hours and no major physical or occupational hazards.

Insurance workers may find opportunities to learn more about the business world in general and this experience may open doors for advancement to higher positions in related fields.

GOE: 07.05.03; SIC: 63; SOC: 4692, 4699, 4784

◇ **SOURCES OF ADDITIONAL INFORMATION**

Career information is available from:

Alliance of American Insurers
1501 Woodfield Road, Suite 400 West
Schaumburg, IL 60173

American Council of Life Insurance
1011 Pennsylvania Avenue, NW
Washington, DC 20004

Insurance Information Institute
110 William Street
New York, NY 10038

◇ **RELATED ARTICLES**

Volume 1: Insurance
Volume 2: Insurance claims representatives
Volume 3: Insurance agents and brokers, life; Insurance agents and brokers, property and casualty

Mail carriers

Definition

Mail carriers are responsible for the delivery and collection of mail on routes assigned to them. They are employees of the U.S. Postal Service. Residential carriers deliver the mail on foot to people in cities and suburbs. Rural carriers drive their routes to reach people in rural areas.

History

Down through the ages, people have found ways to communicate with each other by transmitting the written word through space and time. Even in the sixth century B.C. people would carve words into bronze tablets and then have them delivered by horseback.

Eventually, letters, written on paper were carried by unending circuits of horseback riders. Along the routes fresh horses and new riders would be waiting so that the mail would go through as rapidly as possible.

In 1775, Benjamin Franklin was appointed as the first Postmaster General by the Continental Congress and had under his jurisdiction some fifty colonial post offices. Franklin was able to bring about many improvements in the postal services including faster mail deliveries and better service.

Airmail delivery on a regular route began in 1918. Mail was flown daily between New York City and Washington, D.C.

From the days of the stagecoach and pony express to the fast-moving trains, trucks, and jets of today, the postal services of the nation have always been a highly respected occupational group, providing services to millions of people.

Rural mail carriers often drive great distances to deliver mail. Certain routes may cover more than 100 miles.

Nature of the work

The mail carriers are probably the most familiar of the postal employees to the general public. With the exception of legal holidays and Sunday, they are seen daily delivering and collecting mail along their routes. Many of these carriers work in the evenings or late afternoons, after the majority of businesses are closed. They often drive mail trucks to the mail box depositories, unlock the boxes, collect the mail, put it in the truck, and move on to the next box.

The majority of mail carriers begin their days rather early in the morning. In large cities, they report to the post office or substation in which they work, where they must arrange the mail to be delivered. Their sorting is done by using "mail cases" or upright boxes that are labeled with names of streets and house numbers or buildings. The mail carrier must also prepare and place in the route case reminders for special mail, such as registered letters or packages, C.O.D. (collect on delivery) mail, and insured mail, all of which involve special collection procedures such as money or personal receipt signatures. The carrier must also sign for mail he or she takes on a route that has postage due on it or for C.O.D. mail.

Carriers make up relay bundles that trucks will carry and place in storage in mail depositories along the route for them to pick up during the day. Many mail carriers today drive "mailsters," which are small motor-driven vehicles that enable them to store the bundles of

mail in the back of the vehicle. This eliminates some of the need for trucks to handle relay bundles. Some carriers who walk their routes use a push-type mail cart that enables them to carry more mail at a time; others use the large leather bags carried over the shoulder, limiting their loads to thirty-five pounds and using the relay pick-up system.

Rural routes are usually outside the city limits and deliveries are made by motor vehicle. Mail is generally placed in post mail boxes and outgoing mail picked up from them. These carriers may also sell stamps and money orders, and accept parcel post for mailing, as well as mail that is to be sent insured or registered. These carriers may cover routes of one hundred miles or more.

City mail carriers who work small, concentrated routes may cover them twice or more times daily, while residential carriers usually cover their daily routes only once.

Parcel post mail carriers usually drive trucks and deliver package mail not handled by the carrier who works a route on foot or with a pushcart. The parcels are sorted by postal clerks and put into sacks, each sack carrying a parcel post carrier's route number and a second number that indicates the order of delivery along a route.

Supervisors of both rural and city carriers are responsible for scheduling carriers' work hours, assuring the efficiency of their routes, and investigating and resolving any complaints the public makes about a carrier's performance.

Substitute carriers usually have a combination of duties. They may deliver mail on foot or with a pushcart for part of the day and finish out their hours by driving mail trucks in the afternoons and evenings, collecting mail from street letter boxes. They may also fill in on other types of route work when employees are sick or on vacation or assist regular carriers when the mail load is exceptionally heavy.

Other types of carriers who drive motor vehicles may deliver mail from a main post office building to substations, picking up outgoing mail that is to be sorted in the main post office for dispatch. Many of these carriers are found in large metropolitan and city operations. Their duties may often include delivering the relay mail bundles" to storage boxes for the carriers.

All types of mail carriers must be able to answer the public's questions regarding postal regulations and service and to provide postal forms when requested. The majority of work hours for all carriers are spent outdoors.

Letter carriers and *package deliverers* work for private companies, delivering millions of pieces each day. See Volume 1: Letter and Package Delivery.

Requirements

There are no specific formal education requirements for mail carriers. Those individuals who have completed a high-school education, however, may find it a real asset in being able to perform successfully on the job. Civil service examinations are given to applicants for the jobs of postal clerks and mail carriers. The written examination is composed of three parts, the longest of which is a test of general intelligence including questions on simple arithmetic, spelling, vocabulary, and reading comprehension. The applicant also has to pass another test section that includes reading accuracy, in which one compares addresses arranged in pairs and indicates differences or likenesses. The third test section examines the applicant's ability to follow instructions carefully in making changes on a mailing scheme and in routing mail.

Prospective mail carriers may also need to successfully pass a road test in which they must show their ability to handle, under various driving conditions, vehicles of the type and size they may be required to drive as carriers. These applicants must possess a driver's license at the time of their appointment.

Individuals who wish to be considered as applicants for these positions must be U.S. citizens, meet the minimum age requirement, which is usually eighteen years, and successfully pass the previously described civil service examination and the road test, if necessary. Because much mail is delivered on foot and carried in heavy shoulder sacks, applicants must also pass rigorous physical examinations to assure that they are capable of withstanding the strenuous demands of the job. Although easily maneuverable wheeled mail carts are being increasingly used in many urban areas, eliminating the need for heavy physical labor, carriers must still be able to stand for long periods and walk considerable distances. Their corrected vision should be within normal limits both for reading and for distance, because they must be able to read names and addresses accurately, and are often required to drive postal vehicles.

A good memory is a definite asset to the mail carrier. He or she must be able to rely on memory in knowing many postal regulations and rules and in arranging the mail for the route and the order for correct delivery. Desirable personal qualities include the ability to work cooperatively with others, to follow instructions, and to have some degree of flexibility to perform more than one kind of job duty.

Lifting and loading heavy sacks of mail is often strenuous. Foot carriers in suburban and rural areas may have to carry up to thirty pounds of mail in a shoulder bag. Carriers must be able to adhere to the postal regulations for carriers and yet use diplomacy in handling the public. Approximately once a year, carriers are checked out on how well they are performing their jobs.

Special requirements

There are no special requirements for these employees other than those described in the preceding section. Applicants need to keep in mind the civil service requirements for these positions, which may be changed in the future.

Opportunities for experience and exploration

Individuals may explore this occupational field by observing the work of the mail carrier, talking with postal service employees and by seeking information through high-school guidance counselors or through local U.S. Postal Service offices.

Opportunities are sometimes available to older high-school students to work part-time in post offices during Christmas holiday rush periods without taking any examinations, although preference is given to those who have taken the necessary examination and are listed on the eligibility lists.

Part-time work experience in the mail room of an office or large store may help interested applicants in determining related aptitudes for this type of work. Although no previous training is required for these positions, a business or academic high-school program is a definite asset to job success.

Related occupations

There are several occupations related to mail carriers. Please refer to the listing at the end of this article.

Methods of entering

Individuals who are interested in becoming mail carriers must now enter this field as applicants through civil service examinations. Interested individuals should contact their local post offices to find out the date and time at which the next test will be offered in their areas. Permanent jobs are granted only to those persons who have taken and successfully passed these competitive examinations. Examinations may be taken for the different types of carrier jobs. These tests are scored numerically and applicants who have passing scores or above are then listed on registers in order of their scores. When postmasters have a vacancy, they examine the rosters for those who are eligible to fill the position and may select any of the top three available persons for appointment. Those names still on the roster are returned to a list for later consideration when other vacancies occur. Appointments are made on the basis of ratings and without regard for race or religion.

In postal service work, employees must usually satisfactorily complete a probationary period of one year's work. Carriers enter their jobs, in most instances, as substitute carriers and as vacancies occur and work performance proves satisfactory, move into full-time carrier jobs. New carriers are taught how to "case" or arrange their mail on the job and they often learn their routes while working as substitute carriers or by working with full-time carriers.

Advancement

Almost all mail carriers begin as substitutes, especially city carriers, and advance to positions as regular carriers as vacancies occur. In general, the opportunities for promotions for these workers are very limited. Carriers employed in city delivery service may sometimes be advanced to types of special nonsupervisory jobs, such as carrier-technicians, carrier foreman, or route examiner; however, it should be realized that these opportunities are rather limited. In most cases, carriers may anticipate earning the privilege of preferred routes through seniority of service and to regular periodic pay increases. Large city post offices undoubtedly have more vacancies offering promotional opportunities than do the smaller offices.

Employment outlook

In the early 1990s, about 281,000 mail carriers worked for the U.S. Postal Service, 36,000 of them in rural areas. Although mail volume is expected to continue growing with the increasing number of U.S. households and businesses, applicants will outnumber open mail carrier positions for the foreseeable future. Automation advances in sorting mail are expected to somewhat decrease the number of positions open to mail carriers. On the other hand, thousands of job opportunities are anticipated yearly for mail carriers to replace those who retire or transfer to other types of work, or those who die. Competition for openings is expected to remain keen, however.

Earnings

In the early 1990s, experienced full-time carriers were paid an annual average salary of about $29,430. Part-time carriers began at about $11.25 an hour, with provision for periodic increases of up to about $15.00 an hour after ten and one-half years of satisfactory service. Base pay for full-time beginning carriers was $22,000 a year. After ten and one-half years carriers could earn as much as $30,140.

Rural carriers receive salaries that are based on a combination of fixed annual compensation and an evaluation of the amount of work required to service their particular routes. They also receive a maintenance allowance if required to use their automobiles. Rural carriers' average base salary was $29,654. Substitute rural carriers receive a base pay for the days worked and the same mileage and automobile maintenance allowance as do regular rural carriers.

Regular city carriers who work overtime hours receive time-and-a-half pay for daily overtime. Carriers also receive time-and-a-half overtime pay if they work more than forty hours in one week.

Fringe benefits usually include thirteen days of vacation annually during each of the first three years of service, and twenty days thereafter until fifteen years of service have been completed. After this, twenty-six days are given annually. Thirteen days of sick leave are also given yearly. Other fringe benefits include retirement plans, survivorship annuities, optional participation in low-cost group life and health insurance programs that are partially supported by the federal government, and workers' compensation for injuries received on duty.

Conditions of work

The conditions of work for mail carriers are often strenuous. They must perform their jobs in all types of weather, either on foot carrying a heavy mail bag or pushing a mail cart, or by driving in all kinds of traffic and under many types of road conditions. The hours worked in the post office buildings, though few, may be in well lighted and well ventilated surroundings. Even here, however, carriers must lift heavy bags of mail and be on their feet. The type of carrier work performed and the part of the country in which the worker is employed determine to some degree the conditions of work. The majority of all mail carriers must do a great deal of walking, even those who operate the motor vehicles, and they must be able to lift heavy bags, stretch, and reach in their work.

Regular city mail carriers usually work an eight-hour day, five-day week. Rural carriers work a six-day week. Most of these employees begin work very early, in some cities at 6:00 A.M. Carriers must cover their routes within specified time limits and when mail loads are exceptionally heavy, workers may feel some pressure to meet the time schedules.

Social and psychological factors

Individuals may consider the maximum job securities available to them under the Postal Service a definite advantage in being employed as a mail carrier. The fringe benefits for these employees compare most favorably with any received in other types of employment. For example, the retirement plan benefits and shared employer/employee-supported life and health insurance plans are good.

Stability is also offered to regular mail carriers by their knowledge that their work is steady employment. A disadvantage for this type of postal employee may be the limited op-portunities for advancement, as well as the need to work under all types of weather conditions or night duty when necessary.

The majority of these workers are members of unions that represent postal employees. In actual job performance, the employees are primarily on their own while delivering mail and responsible for adhering to postal codes and regulations and meeting specific time schedules. Individuals, while working as mail carriers, do frequently have the opportunity to meet and briefly talk with those to whom they make their deliveries and they may enjoy filling a responsible job and serving the public.

GOE: 07.05.04; SIC: 431; SOC: 4743

◇ **SOURCES OF ADDITIONAL INFORMATION**

National Association of Letter Carriers of the U.S.A.
100 Indiana Avenue, NW
Washington, DC 20001

◇ **RELATED ARTICLES**

Volume 1: Civil Service; Letter and Package Delivery
Volume 2: Postal clerks; Shipping and receiving clerks

Meter readers, utilities

Definition

Meter readers check the level of gas, water, steam, or electricity use in homes and businesses by going from building to building and reading meters that measure the usage level. They then record the usage level in a route book. Meter readers are also responsible for checking the meters and connection lines for damage or signs of tampering, and turning on and shutting off utility service.

History

The use of gas, water, electricity, and steam has increased dramatically over the last several de-

A meter reader determines the number of kilowatt hours of electricity that a household has consumed. He performs this task each month.

cades as our society has increasingly relied on these sources of power to run the lights, appliances, and large machinery that fill our homes and factories.

With the increased demand for utility services there has been a corresponding need for trained professionals to monitor and maintain these services. Meter readers are part of the crew that keeps these power sources running smoothly.

Nature of the work

Meter readers spend a lot of time on the go, moving from house to house, reading the meters that record the usage levels of gas, water, electricity, and steam. A meter reader may only monitor the usage of one particular utility (electricity, for example) or the meter reader may record the usage of more than one type of service. Meter readers work in a specified neighborhood and go from building to building recording the consumption level as measured by a meter located either near the back of the building or sometimes in the building itself (usually in the basement area). Meter readers may need to use a flashlight or other equipment to see the dial that shows the amount of power usage. This information is recorded in a route book that is used by the utility company to bill correctly customers for the amount of electricity or other energy source that they used. Meter readers may use a pencil and paper to record this information or, as is becoming increasingly popular, they may use a hand-held computer or other automatic machine that records the consumption use.

Because meter readers are often the only utility company representatives that have constant contact with customers, they keep an eye out for any readings that may be unusually high or low and they also check for gas leaks. They are also responsible for checking the meter and connecting equipment to make sure everything is in working order. Any evidence of damage, defects, or unauthorized tampering is noted so that the service department can act accordingly. Meter readers also are responsible for connecting and disconnecting utility service.

Chief meter readers supervise and direct meter readers in the performance of their job duties. They review the reports of the meter readers, noting any discrepancies from normal usage. They oversee the disconnection or reconnection of utility service and investigate any customer complaints concerning utility service.

Requirements

Although there are no specific educational requirements, most meter readers are high-school graduates, and some may have some college training. Meter readers should have a solid background in mathematics and be able to clearly and accurately fill out reports and other forms.

High-school students interested in pursuing a career as a meter reader should take English, mathematics, typing, and other business-related courses. In addition, aspiring meter readers should have good manual dexterity to be able to get at hard-to-reach equipment.

Special requirements

Meter readers do not need any licenses or certificates to fulfill their job responsibilities. Those employed by municipal utility companies may have to pass a civil service examination. Some meter readers may choose to pursue additional educational training or join a union in order to advance their career goals.

Opportunities for experience and exploration

Because many utility companies hire temporary meter readers during the peak summer months, it may be possible for high-school students to gain hands-on experience during this period. High-school students and others interested in pursuing a career as a meter reader are encouraged to talk with those already working in the field to learn more about the rewards and responsibilities of this occupation.

Related occupations

Meter readers share many of the same tabulating and clerical responsibilities as coding and routing clerks and mail room personnel.

Methods of entering

High-school graduates should apply directly to the appropriate utility company. Contacts can also be made as a result of summer employment or by contacting utility companies listed in the phone book.

Many utility companies provide new employees with several weeks of on-the-job training covering specific metering and safety procedures.

Advancement

Skilled meter readers often need to have some college training to qualify for promotions to the position of chief meter reader or other supervisory post. Experienced meter readers may also branch off into related work and become a service representative or part of the repair crew. They may also choose to become a bill collector or take another office position within the utility company.

Employment outlook

Job opportunities figure to remain at about their current levels through the early 1990s. Many positions will open because of retirement or those leaving the field for other reasons, but employment will be limited because of automated methods of reading meters and other technological changes. Job opportunities figure to be best in and around large metropolitan areas because the greatest number of utility companies are located in these areas. This is, however, also where job competition will be keenest.

Earnings

Salaries vary widely depending on the skill and experience of the worker and the geographic location of the utility company. Beginning meter readers can expect to earn between $11,000 and $12,000 a year, with those employed in large metropolitan areas tending to receive higher wages than others in the field. Those working for municipal utility companies may earn slightly more than their counterparts in the private sector. Experienced meter readers can expect to earn between $14,000 and $21,000 per year, with those employed in heavily populated regions sometimes earning even more.

Some meter readers are employed part-time and are paid an hourly rate ranging from $5.50 and $8.00 per hour.

Most full-time employees receive the usual health and vacation benefits, with some employees receiving pension benefits. Hourly employees may not receive as comprehensive a benefits package.

Conditions of work

Because meter readers deal with the public, they must have a neat appearance and a courteous, pleasant personality. Meter readers must be able to adapt to a variety of working conditions. They may have to read meters in dingy basements or modern office buildings. They must be able to work outdoors in all types of weather and, when necessary, they must be able to drive a truck in a variety of weather conditions. Although the work is not that strenuous, meter readers spend much of their time bending and stooping in cramped quarters. They may have to move objects around or lift meter covers to get at the meters.

Meter readers usually have a regular thirty-seven to forty-hour workweek, with extra pay for overtime. They work with a minimum of supervision. They sometimes have to go into people's homes and may, on occasion, encounter unfriendly pets. Meter readers usually wear uniforms and carry identification cards to be easily recognizable when entering a home or walking around in backyards.

Social and psychological factors

Despite the fact that the work is quite repetitive, meter readers must also be able to pay attention to detail and accurately note usage information. Mathematical errors could cause the customer a great deal of aggravation and the utility company a great deal of embarrassment. Meter readers must be able to successfully interact with a wide range of people and be able to adapt to cramped working spaces. Although meter readers usually wear company uniforms to be easily identified, some people may be uncomfortable letting the meter reader into their home. Meter readers should be able to handle such situations with patience and tact. They should also be able to handle an occasional unfriendly pet.

Many meter readers enjoy the fact that they do not work in an office setting and they enjoy the opportunity of meeting a wide range of people.

GOE: 05.09.03; SIC: 49; SOC: 4755

◇ **SOURCES OF ADDITIONAL INFORMATION**

Career information is available from local utility companies and from:

International Brotherhood of Electrical Workers,
1125 15th Street, NW
Washington, DC 20005

American Public Power Association
2301 M Street, NW
Washington, DC 20037

American Federation of State, County, and Municipal Employees
1625 L Street, NW
Washington, DC 20036

Institute of Public Utilities
113 Olds Hall
Michigan State University
East Lansing, MI 48824

National Association of Regulatory Utility Commissioners
PO Box 684
1102 ICC Building
Constitution Avenue and 12th Street, NW
Washington, DC 20044

◇ **RELATED ARTICLES**

Volume 1: Energy; Public Utilities
Volume 3: Line installers and cable splicers; Transmission and distribution occupations
Volume 4: Electrical technicians

Postal clerks

Definition

Postal clerks are employees of the United States Postal Service (USPS). Their job duties may be diversified, depending upon the size of the post office in which they are employed. Some postal clerks serve the public directly by working at the public service windows in post offices, while others work behind the scenes as distribution clerks sorting incoming and outgoing mail. Similar duties are performed by *mail clerks* in the mail rooms of business firms.

With the rise of private mail delivery services, mail clerks are also employed by letter and package delivery services. They take payment, label packages, assist customers in packing, and route mail to the delivery system.

History

Communication is as ancient as the history of humans; however, the public mail system really had its beginning during the 1400s when King Edward IV of England established a series of post houses for transporting official mail.

The American postal system dates back to 1639 when Richard Fairbanks was granted permission to receive and dispatch mail at his home for the Massachusetts Bay Colony.

In 1775, the Second Continental Congress appointed Benjamin Franklin as the first Postmaster General, establishing, to Franklin's credit, the postal system in the American colonies at the same time. Franklin was responsible for a complete reorganization of the postal system and many improvements in efficiency, speed, and service.

From the days of the early American colonies through those of the colorful history of the Pony Express, the United States Postal Service has moved forward to utilize automation, technology, and the speed of the jet age. The ZIP coding and use of computer sorting, coding, and canceled stamps have been a few of the innovations in the last decade.

Today, the United States Postal Service is a federal corporation similar to the Tennessee Valley Administration (TVA). The Postmaster General is no longer a member of the president's cabinet.

Nature of the work

Employees who are postal clerks may perform numerous kinds of duties; those who work in large city post offices, however, usually perform more specialized duties as either public window clerks or distribution clerks. In small post offices, employees may work in both types of duties, sorting mail for distribution when business at the windows is slack. In any case, all postal clerks must know how to sort mail.

Window clerks, dealing directly with the public at the post office service windows, sell stamps, accept and weigh parcel post packages, and advise customers regarding parcel post regulations and foreign mail postal fees, sell and cash money orders, register mail, distribute general delivery letter mail and packages, rent post office boxes, accept deposits for postal savings accounts, and sell U.S. Savings Bonds.

In addition, they may answer numerous customer questions about postal rates and rules. In the large city post offices, postal window clerks may specialize in only one or two of these services, such as working a window for money orders, savings bonds, and registered mail only, or working at a window at which only stamps are sold and parcel post accepted. Still another clerk may work a general delivery window.

Distribution clerks begin their work as the carriers who have collected mail, bring it into the post office, and dump it on long work tables.

Usually the new distribution clerks (or *mail handlers*) perform the task of the first rough separation of the mail into parcel post, paper mail, and letter mail. The mail is then faced (stamps down and facing the same direction) so that it may be fed into canceling machines for date, time, city, and state in which the post office is located. New types of canceling machines perform this total operation in some of the larger post offices. Once the mail is canceled, it is removed to different work sections where distribution clerks begin a sorting operation according to mail destination.

A primary distribution may be made first where mail is sorted into boxes containing compartments for local, distant states, nearby states, and for the largest cities, such as New York.

Secondary distributions may follow in which the mail is further sorted in greater detail. Local mail may be sorted by zones or streets and further separated by sections within postal zones. Some distribution clerks perform their work while traveling with the mail in buses or trains, which speeds delivery.

Parcel post sorting is performed in a similar manner; however, conveyor belts, slides, and chutes are used for the sorting and an even finer distribution is made in separating this mail.

Automation, new equipment, and electronic sorting systems have greatly facilitated the separation and distribution of mail in today's large modern post offices.

Transfer clerks are responsible for the mail being moved to and from the trains and airports with the greatest speed, efficiency, and economy possible.

All distribution clerks must be able to perform their duties quickly and efficiently with great accuracy so that the mail may be moved to correct destinations as soon as possible. Related occupations include *mail censors* who inspect incoming and outgoing prison mail.

Requirements

Applicants for postal clerk positions must be citizens of the United States, and meet the necessary minimum age requirements. The general minimum age requirement for postal jobs is eighteen years.

Although a high-school education or other special training is not required for the majority of post office entry positions, the trend in recent years seems to be more favorable for the high-school graduate to receive beginning postal job appointments.

The civil service examination was the traditional exam for postal clerk applicants. Since the department became a federal corporation, new hiring procedures, including testing, have gone into effect. For up-to-date information, contact a local post office.

Job appointments are made without regard to race, sex, or religion. Those who have scored

Postal clerks sort mail for delivery to various destinations throughout the world.

congenial manner and need to be able to deal with all types of people.

The training for these employees varies, depending on the size of the post office and the complexity of their operational procedures. All new postal employees serve a one-year probationary period during which time their job performance and general conduct are closely observed. New employees generally spend a considerable amount of time on their own memorizing postal rules and regulations, and sorting schemes and distributions so that they may become proficient, accurate workers as rapidly as possible.

Special requirements

There are no special requirements for these employees, such as licensure or certification, imposed by law or official organizations. All other special requirements, such as civil service examinations, physical traits, citizenship and age requirements, have been discussed in the preceding section.

Opportunities for experience and exploration

Young people who are interested in postal clerk positions may explore their aptitudes and interests for this type of work by seeking part-time post office work during vacation and summer periods, especially the rush holiday periods, such as Christmas. Related jobs, such as store or office clerk, stock, shipping or parts clerk, or others requiring sorting and distribution or dealing with the public, might also be assets in job experience.

Individuals may also explore these career opportunities by talking with their high-school guidance counselors for additional information and to explore their aptitudes and interests through special tests. Visits to local postal departments and talks with those employed as postal clerks can also provide some very valuable information.

successfully on the examinations are listed on a register in order of their scores. Positions are filled by selecting one of the top three available candidates. All federal employees are subject to some kind of investigation of their loyalty and moral character.

Individuals need the aptitude of a good memory, because they must memorize many postal regulations and rules and many distribution schemes. They must also be able to read rapidly and accurately and they must possess good hand-eye coordination.

Physical stamina is required for both window and distribution clerks. Window clerks must stand for long hours at a time on their feet, while distribution clerks must do a great deal of reaching, lifting, walking, standing, bending, stretching, and handling and throwing parcel post and heavy sacks of mail.

Postal clerks need to possess an even temperament and a pleasant disposition. They must frequently work under tension to meet time and schedule deadlines and often their work is performed in teams with others in close physical work space. Window clerks, who are constantly dealing directly with the public, need to have a neat appearance and a pleasant,

Related occupations

Many other occupations require the same interests and skills as those of postal clerks. Within the U.S. Postal Service there are a variety of jobs that involve the delivery of mail to homes and offices. Other jobs that may be of interest include clerical supervisors and managers, shipping and receiving clerks, and traffic agents and clerks.

Methods of entering

Most postal employees begin their careers as substitutes once they have met the general job requirements and received a job appointment. Substitutes, listed on a roster in rank order of examination scores, or veterans' preference, may be called as replacements for regular workers or to supplement a work force. Vacancies are filled in the regular staff by converting the substitutes to regulars by order of seniority.

The number of vacancies that occur depends on the size of the post office and the number of employees needed, as well as on the economic growth and population increases in the postal area served.

Advancement

Opportunities for advancement for postal clerks are considered better than those for mail carriers; they are, however, still rather limited. The number of vacancies for special postal clerks at higher levels, including jobs such as supervisor, mail dispatch expediter, and scheme examiner are not too frequently available, usually depending on the size of the post office operation.

Large numbers of postal clerks do not move up to higher level positions; however, in these jobs, as seniority accrues, individuals may bid (by written request) for the more preferred assignments, such as window jobs or other day shift work. Assignments to any higher level positions are based on merit, and consideration is given to the employee's education, experience, training, and aptitudes on written examinations.

Employment outlook

About 370,000 postal clerks worked for the United States Postal Service in the early 1990s. Most of them worked in mail processing centers rather than in local post offices, and about three-fourths worked full time.

Some new workers will be needed through the late 1990s as replacements for workers who retire or die. The number of actual positions, however, is expected to decline because technological developments, including automation and electronic sorting and canceling devices, will allow clerks to handle more mail than is possible by hand. Therefore, employment for postal clerks who sort mail will decline through the late 1990s, while employment of window clerks will probably change little.

Earnings

The majority of all postal employees are paid under the Postal Field Service Compensation Act and the grade levels of jobs depend upon duties, responsibilities, knowledge, experience, and skill required.

In the early 1990s, full-time postal clerks began at an average annual base salary of $22,238 and could advance to $30,140 after ten and one-half years. Part-time clerks earned from $11.40 to $14.90 an hour, depending on the working schedule and experience in the job. Clerks working night shifts received 10 percent more than base pay. Those who work more than eight hours a day or forty hours a week receive one-and-one-half times base pay.

When substitute workers receive appointments as regulars they are given credit for their years of work as substitutes.

Those postal clerks who work in post-offices-on-wheels are paid higher salaries than those employed in the large post offices, and clerks who work in the large city post offices receive higher salaries than those employed in small postal operations.

Fringe benefits for postal clerks, substitutes, and regulars are generally the same as for all postal employees. Thirteen days of annual vacation are given for each of the first three years of service and twenty days each year thereafter until fifteen years of service are completed. Thereafter, twenty-six days are given yearly.

Additional fringe benefits include retirement benefits, disability benefits, health and life insurance, and paid sick leave.

Conditions of work

Window clerks are considered, in most instances, to have the preferred working conditions in these jobs. The work may seem more interesting and varied than that of the distribution clerk since there is continual direct contact with the public, more mental activity, and less physical exertion.

65

Distribution clerks must do considerable walking, throwing, lifting, and other types of physical labor. Most of the job tasks are repetitive and routine and there is little or no contact with the public. In work areas behind the scenes, these employees work in close contact with each other, many times in teamwork operations. To increase one's speed, accuracy, and overall efficiency is the primary challenge for these clerks.

As departments within the Postal Service adopt new automatic and electronic equipment and as greater technological advances continue to come on the scene, the work of the distribution clerks continues to change with more labor-saving techniques. Working conditions vary with the equipment used, size of the postal operations, and specialization of the type of clerk.

The majority of regular postal employees work eight-hour days, five-day weeks. The physical surroundings are usually pleasant and the close work areas afford employees the opportunity to develop a spirit of cooperation and friendliness among themselves.

Social and psychological factors

Job satisfaction is experienced by many postal clerks through the close, cooperative working relationships enjoyed in their jobs and in the responsibility assumed for speed and work accuracy.

Postal clerks may sometimes work under a certain degree of tension and strain when time schedules must be met, especially during rush seasons; however, in general, employees become accustomed to the importance of speed in this type of work.

The majority of postal employees are members of the American Postal Workers Union, National Association of Letter Carriers, National Post Office Mail Handlers, or National Rural Letter Carriers Association.

GOE: 07.05.04; SIC: 431; SOC: 4742

◇ **SOURCES OF ADDITIONAL INFORMATION**

Write or visit a local post office for more information about careers as postal clerks.

◇ **RELATED ARTICLES**

Volume 1: Civil Service; Letter and Package Delivery
Volume 3: Cashiers; Mail carriers; Shipping and receiving clerks; Traffic agents and clerks; Typists and word processors

---

Public opinion researchers

Definition

Public opinion researchers help measure public sentiment concerning various products, services, or politics by gathering information via questionnaires and interviews. They collect, analyze, and interpret data and opinions to forecast trends and help business people, politicians, and other decision makers determine what the public wants.

Public opinion is gauged by using a percentage of the population in which there is a variety of people, who closely parallel the larger population in terms of age, race, income and other factors.

History

Everybody has opinions, and it is the role of the public opinion researcher to conduct interviews that accurately reflect those opinions so that decision makers in the business and political communities have a good idea of what people want on a wide range of issues.

Public opinion research was started in a rudimentary way in the 1830s and 1840s when local newspapers asked their readers to fill out straw ballots noting who they had voted for in an election. And, although political opinion research remains popular, public opinion research is most widely used by businesses to determine what products or services consumers like or dislike.

As questionnaires and interviewing techniques have become more refined, public opinion research has been used increasingly effectively to reflect individual attitudes and opinions. Companies like the Gallup Poll and the Harris Survey conduct surveys that are used for a wide range of political and economic purposes. Some people continue to question the accuracy and importance of polls, but they have become an integral part of our social fabric and skilled researchers play an important role in analyzing public opinion.

A public opinion researcher interviews a person outside of a hardware store. Shopping centers are often good places to seek those who are willing to answer questions.

Nature of the work

Researchers utilize a variety of methods to collect and analyze public opinion. The particular method depends on the target audience and the type of information desired. If a shopping mall owner is interested in gauging the opinions of shoppers, for example, the research company will most likely station interviewers in selected areas around the shopping mall so that they can question the shoppers. On the other hand, an advertising firm may be interested in the opinions of a particular demographic group, and the research firm would then plan a procedure, perhaps a telephone survey, that provided access to that selected group. Other field collection methods include interviews in the home and at work. The use of questionnaires that are filled out by respondents and then returned through the mail is another popular survey technique.

Planning is an important ingredient in developing a questionnaire or other survey technique. Researchers decide what portion of the population they will survey and develop questions that allow for an accurate gauging of opinion. Researchers investigate whether previous surveys have been done on a particular topic and, if so, what the results were.

The actual collection of information takes place in one of the methods described above. It is important that the same procedures are used in the collection process so that the survey is not influenced by the individual styles of the interviewers. For this reason, the collection process is closely monitored by supervisory personnel.

Research assistants assist in training survey interviewers, in preparing survey questionnaires and related materials, and in tabulating and coding survey results. Other specialists within the field include:

Market research analysts collect, analyze, and interpret data to determine potential sales of a product or service. They prepare reports and make recommendations on subjects ranging from preferences of prospective customers to future sales trends. A working knowledge of statistics is needed because mathematical models are utilized in the analysis of the research. Market research analysts research available data and accumulate new data through personal interviews and questionnaires. Research analysts pay close attention to screen out unimportant or invalid information and chart relevant data. Some marketing analysts specialize in one industry or area. For example, agricultural marketing analysts prepare sales forecasts for food businesses, which use the information in their advertising and sales programs.

Survey workers interview people to determine their buying habits or opinions on public issues. Survey workers contact people in their homes, at work, at random in public places, or via the telephone and question them in a specified manner, usually following a questionnaire format.

Public opinion workers are primarily employed by private companies, but they are also employed by the government and colleges and universities, often in research and teaching capacities. They may help a company implement a new marketing strategy or help a political candidate decide what campaign issues that the public feels are important.

Requirements

Prospective public opinion researchers should be interested in dealing with problem-solving situations involving data-collection and data-analysis processes. Because the ability to communicate both verbally and in written form is crucial, high-school students interested in becoming public opinion researchers should take courses in English, speech arts, and social studies. In addition, students should take mathematics, especially statistics, and any courses in journalism or psychology that are available. Knowledge of a foreign language and word processing are also helpful.

A college degree in economics or business administration provides a good background for public opinion researchers. A degree in sociology or psychology is very helpful for those interested in studying consumer demand or opinion research, whereas work in statistics or engineering might be helpful for those who lean toward certain types of industrial or analytical research.

A master's degree in business administration and a familiarity with computer applications are frequently expected, because of the increasingly sophisticated techniques employed in public opinion research. A master's degree in sociology or political science is also helpful.

A doctorate is not necessary for most researchers but is highly desirable for those who plan to become involved with complex research studies or work in an academic environment.

Special requirements

No certificates or licenses are needed to work as a public opinion researcher. Those working for the federal government may have to pass a civil service examination. As a means of professional enrichment, many researchers belong to organizations such as the American Marketing Association and the American Association for Public Opinion Research. Further information on these and other groups is available by contacting individual organizations at the addresses given at the end of this article.

Opportunities for experience and exploration

It is often possible for high-school students to work as survey workers for a telemarketing firm or other consumer research company. There may also be work opportunities where one can learn about the coding and tabulation of survey data. Actual participation in a consumer survey also offers interested persons

contact with a marketing research project and therefore an insight into the processes involved in the field. In addition to these work experiences, high-school students or others interested in pursuing a career as a public opinion researcher are encouraged to talk with professionals already working in the field to learn more about the rewards and responsibilities of this profession.

Related occupations

Public opinion researchers have many of the same research and interpretive job responsibilities as economists, urban planners, interviewing clerks, and census takers.

Methods of entering

Many people enter the field as survey workers, research assistants, or coders and tabulators, and with experience become interviewers or work in data analysis. Those with the necessary education, training, and experience may begin as interviewers or in data analysis. College placement counselors can often help qualified students find an appropriate position in public opinion research. Contacts can also be made as a result of summer employment or by locating public and private research companies in the yellow pages of the phone book.

Advancement

Opportunities for advancement are numerous and often follow the pattern of a research assistant becoming an interviewer or data analyst and, after sufficient experience in these or other aspects of research project development, becoming involved in a supervisory or planning capacity. With the proper educational training (a master's degree or doctorate), a person can become a manager of a large private research organization or a marketing research director for an industrial or business firm. It is also possible for public opinion researchers to become involved in university teaching or research and development. Those with extended work experience in public opinion research and with sufficient credentials may choose to start their own company.

Employment outlook

With a growing awareness of the value of public opinion research among business and political decision makers, employment opportunities are expected to expand through the early l990s. Although it is estimated that there are fewer than 100,000 full-time employees currently in the field, there should be ample job opportunities for those trained in public opinion research. Major employers include public and private research firms, advertising agencies, and universities. The federal government also hires public opinion researchers.

As is usually the case, those with the most experience and education should find the greatest number of job opportunities.

Earnings

Starting salaries vary according to the skill and experience of the applicant, the nature of the position, and the size of the company. A college graduate can expect to earn between $17,000 and $19,000 a year, depending on the geographic location of the firm. Those with a graduate degree can expect to earn between $19,000 and $24,000 a year to start. Experienced public opinion researchers in positions involving supervisory or planning responsibilities may earn between $25,000 and $33,000 a year, with some highly skilled professionals working for large firms earning even more. Managers may also receive bonuses based on the company's performance. Those in academic positions may earn somewhat less than their counterparts in the business community. Federal government salaries are competitive with those in the private sector.

Most full-time public opinion researchers receive the usual medical, pension, vacation, and other benefits.

Conditions of work

Public opinion researchers usually work a standard thirty-seven- to forty-hour week, although occasionally they may have to work overtime if a project is on deadline. Those in a supervisory position may work especially long hours overseeing the collection and interpretation of information.

When conducting telephone interviews or organizing or analyzing data, researchers work in comfortable offices, with typewriters, calculators, and data processing equipment close at hand. When collecting information via personal interview or questionnaire, it is not unusual to spend time outside in shopping malls, on the street, or in private homes. There may be some evening and weekend work because that is a time when people are most readily available to be interviewed.

Some research positions may include assignments that include some travel, but these are generally short assignments.

Social and psychological factors

Those who work interviewing people must be outgoing and enjoy interacting with a wide variety of people. Because much of the work entails getting people to reveal their opinions and beliefs, public opinion researchers must be good listeners and as nonjudgmental as possible. Researchers must be patient and be able to handle rejection as some people may be uncooperative during the interviewing process. Interviewers must be able to spend time in people's homes, in shopping malls, and in a variety of other work environments.

Those who work in data analysis should be able to pay close attention to detail and spend long hours analyzing complex data. There may be some pressure when forced to collect data or solve a problem within a specified period of time.

Those who plan the questionnaires should have good analytical skills and be able to design a questionnaire that allows interviewers to collect relevant information.

Despite a sometimes strenuous working environment, many people find the work of conducting public information research to be exciting and rewarding.

GOE: 07.04.01; SIC: 7392, 7399; SOC: 4642

◇ SOURCES OF ADDITIONAL INFORMATION

Career and membership information are available from:

American Marketing Association
250 South Wacker Drive
Suite 200
Chicago, IL 60606

American Association for Public Opinion Research
PO Box 17
Princeton, NJ 08542

Society for Marketing Professional Services
801 North Fairfax Street, Suite 215
Alexandria, VA 22314

Women in Advertising and Marketing
4200 Wisconsin Avenue, NW
Suite 106-238
Washington, DC 20016

◇ **RELATED ARTICLES**

Volume 1: Advertising; Marketing
Volume 2: Marketing research personnel;
Public relations workers

Railroad clerks

Definition

Railroad clerks perform clerical job duties in transacting and keeping records of railroad business. Their jobs may involve many kinds of clerical work or only one or two specialized duties, depending on the size and type of railroad business location in which they are employed. Job duties also vary with the level, responsibility, and job title of the railroad clerk.

History

The railroad system in the United States has become more and more complex with each passing decade as the interconnecting network of some 200,000 miles of railroad lines has been laid to serve all parts of this country. As the systems of freight, express, and passenger service have expanded and become more complex with an increasing volume of business, more clerical employees have been needed to keep accurate records, compile statistics, and transact railroad business.

Nature of the work

Reams and volumes of paperwork are necessary to keep accurate records and to provide information on the business transactions of railroad companies. Railroad clerks perform the clerical job duties necessary to efficient business operations.

Railroad clerks may be employed in railroad yards, terminals, freight houses, railroad stations, and company offices. The clerk employed in a one-person station or small office may have a variety of clerical job duties; in the larger yards, terminals, and offices, however, the clerk may perform only one or two specialized tasks.

Railroad clerks employed on class I "line-haul" railroads perform such clerical duties as selling tickets, bookkeeping, compiling statistics, collecting bills, investigating complaints and adjusting claims, and tracing lost or misdirected shipments. *Yard clerks* use information from records or other personnel to prepare orders for railroad yard switching crews. They also keep records about cars moving into or out of the yard. *Demurrage clerks* compute charges for delays in loading or unloading freight, prepare bills for these charges, and send the bills to the shippers or receivers responsible for the delays. They also communicate with shippers and receivers about time and place of arrival of shipments and time allowed for unloading freight before any charges are levied. *Documentation-billing clerks* prepare the billing documents that list a shipper's name, the type and weight of cargo, destination, charges, and so on. They total the charges, check for accuracy, and resolve discrepancies. *Tariff inspectors* visit railroad freight and ticket offices, where they examine records to make sure that current tariff rates are being used. They tell agents how to correct errors and they prepare reports for the railroad's management. *Interline clerks* examine waybills and ticket sales records to compute the charges payable to the various carriers involved in interline business. *Revising clerks* verify and revise freight and tariff charges on shipment bills. *Accounts adjustable clerks* compute corrected freight charges from waybill data. *Pullman car clerks* assign and dispatch sleeping cars to railroad companies that request them and assign Pullman conductors to trains. *Dispatcher clerks* schedule train crews for work, notify them of their assignments, and record the time and distance they work. *Callers* notify crew members to report for work and keep records about absenteeism. *Voucher clerks* receive claims for lost or damaged goods and prorate the cost of the goods to the various carriers involved in an interline shipment. *Train clerks* record the exact time each train arrives at or leaves the station, compare those times with schedules, and inquire about reasons for delays. They also process other data about train movements. *Railroad-maintenance clerks* keep records about repairs being made in tracks or rights-of-way, including the location and type of repair and the materials and time involved. *Locomotive lubricating-systems clerks* review records to identify and locate locomotives that need oil changes or lubricating-system repairs and notify repair shop personnel of the work that needs to be done. *Express clerks* receive packages from customers, compute charges, write bills, receive payments, issue receipts and release packages to receivers. *Car checkers* make sure that trains are complete when they arrive at the railroad yard, ensure that seals on cars have not been tampered with, and mark cars to show the switching crew where they should go.

Secretaries, typists, stenographers, bookkeepers and operators of business and computing machines comprise a second group of railroad clerical workers. All of these employees perform job duties descriptive of their job titles, similar to those they would perform in other types of business and industry.

Thousands of railroad clerks are employed in higher level senior jobs that require technical skills and knowledge and a commensurate degree of job responsibility. Such workers might include cashiers who must deal with the public on uncollected bills, accountants who are concerned with company financial transactions, and records and statistical clerks responsible for statistical compilations on railroad traffic, employees, and other business details. These employees are also frequently responsible for compiling periodic reports for the federal

A key responsibility of railroad clerks involves keeping accurate records of railroad traffic.

government on railroad business, transactions, and operational traffic.

Supervisory and chief clerks in railroad operations are responsible for supervising the work of other railroad clerks and for departmental clerical operations. Personnel at this clerical level may also be required to work with complicated problems in business operations.

Job duties performed by these railroad clerical workers enable the companies to account accurately for their every business transaction.

Requirements

A high-school education is usually required of applicants for these jobs. In many instances companies also require that potential employees successfully pass clerical aptitude tests. Some railroad companies prefer to hire employees who have had experience in working with figures for certain clerical jobs. In jobs where a special knowledge is required, such as accounting or statistics, employees must usually have advanced formal educational training, either in colleges or business schools. Computers are commonplace in most large offices so it would be to the potential clerk's advantage to receive some computer training.

Clerical and mathematical aptitudes are clearly indicated as assets for the potential railroad clerk. Physical traits should include good eyesight and hearing and overall good physical health to assure regular job attendance. Finger and hand dexterity can be important to the clerical worker who must type, file, use business machines, or do much writing and figuring.

A temperament for patience and detail, and sometimes for repetitive job tasks, may be required of the clerical worker. The amount of contact the worker has with the public or with other employees will depend on the type of clerical work performed and the size of the place of employment; a congenial disposition and the ability to get along well with others, however, are valued assets to job success.

Clerical jobs are not considered strenuous in nature or physically demanding, although there may be occasions when the employee must work under a certain amount of pressure to turn out a job on time. Other clerical workers perform all of their job duties in station or terminal office settings. Offices are usually well-lighted and furnished with the necessary office equipment. Large company offices may be more elaborately furnished and equipped than those of smaller stations.

Special requirements

There are no special requirements for these employees such as licensure or certification imposed by law or official organizations; the majority of railroad clerical employees, however, are members of the Brotherhood of Railway and Steamship Clerks, Freight Handlers, Express and Station Employees. This union represents railroad clerks on all major railroads.

Opportunities for experience and exploration

Individuals who obtain employment with railroad companies as messengers or office assistants may use this opportunity to observe the work performed by persons in clerical positions. Part-time office work, as office assistants or helpers, in other industries and companies

may frequently be available to high-school students who are interested in observing the work of secretaries, typists, stenographers, bookkeepers, and business machine operators.

Students may talk with the high-school guidance counselor to obtain additional job information and to request tests that will enable them to explore and appraise further their interests, aptitudes, and abilities.

Related occupations

Nearly every industry or business has a need for clerks, and the skills and interests of people working in the railroad industry can easily be transferred to other clerical positions. Other jobs of interest might include billing clerks, bookkeeping and accounting clerks, clerical supervisors and managers, general office clerks, shipping and receiving clerks, and traffic agents and clerks. Other office related work includes secretaries, receptionists, telephone operators, typists and word processor operators, and file clerks.

Methods of entering

Railroad companies frequently fill railroad clerical positions by employing new applicants or by promoting workers already employed as office assistants or messengers. Once an applicant is accepted for employment with a railroad company this person may be given a temporary appointment as an "extra" and listed for "extra board" work until such time as a regular job appointment becomes available and is made.

Individuals interested in railroad clerical jobs may make direct application to the railroad companies or inquire about job application procedures through the union representing this group of employees. Newspaper advertisements may sometimes list openings for clerical employees.

Advancement

Railroad clerks may sometimes advance to assistant chief clerks or to positions of higher administrative status. Clerks who continue their formal education and training in some field of specialization, such as accounting or statistics, may have opportunities for promotions into jobs as auditors or statisticians.

Other promotional opportunities may include advancement to traffic agent, buyer, storekeeper, or ticket and station agent. The records kept by bookkeepers reflect assets, liabilities, profits, and losses in the operation of a particular business. Cashiers are expected to be courteous, efficient, and accurate in extremely busy, high-energy situations.

Employment outlook

Various types of railroad clerical workers now make up the largest single group of railroad employees. In the early 1990s, class I "line-haul" railroads employed more than 75,000 of these workers, and thousands more were working for short line railways. There has been a decline in employment for this occupational group.

Electronic data processing and computers are expected to play a part in the predicted continual employment decline for these workers, as more and more of the processing of freight bills and the recording of information on freight movements and yard operations is done by machines. Although a decline in employment is the trend that is expected to continue, several thousand job opportunities are expected to become available yearly for these workers. Job turnover in this occupational group is relatively high as the result of retirements, deaths, and employees' transferring to other fields or industries.

Earnings

In the early 1990s, employees of class I "line-haul" railroads who were working in clerical jobs which involved billing, operations, filing, and inventory control, were earning average straight-time pay of about $14,100 a year. Those employed as secretaries, stenographers, typists, and office machine operators received an average of $14,040 yearly, while senior clerks and specialists averaged $15,600 yearly. Salaries vary depending on union agreements, training, experience, job responsibilities, and the type of operation in which the employee works.

Railroad employees are usually paid time-and-a-half for overtime worked over eight hours a day. Most railroad employees are given a one-week paid vacation after one year on the job, two weeks after three years, and three weeks beyond fifteen years. Nonoperating employees usually receive seven paid holidays yearly in most companies.

The Railroad Retirement Act, administered by the federal government, provides for all railroad employees with more than ten years of service to receive pensions upon retirement. Other stipulations in this act provide certain pension provisions for the disabled and for dependents of all railroad employees.

Unemployment compensation benefits granted to railroad workers for specified periods of time when they become unemployed are provided for through the Federal Railroad Unemployment Insurance Act. The Act also gives the worker compensation for work days lost because of illness or injury. Other fringe benefits include several types of insurance programs operated under trade union agreements. These may include group life insurance and comprehensive medical and hospital insurance coverage for employees and their dependents.

Conditions of work

A forty-hour work week is the usual schedule for railroad clerical employees in nonsupervisory positions. Individuals who have temporary appointments may have an irregular work schedule, depending on the type of railroad setting in which they are employed. Clerical workers who sell tickets, among their other duties, may also work night hours.

The work for this group of railroad employees is not considered hazardous or physically strenuous; in some types of clerical work, however, eyestrain can result. Some clerical employees, such as those that check freight shipments in the yards, may perform some duties outdoors in all kinds of weather. The majority of these workers perform their duties in offices or stations.

Social and psychological factors

Individuals who like to work with detail and who do not tire of repetitive tasks may find the jobs of clerical railroad employees interesting. The employee in the large company office may have more opportunity for congenial and sociable relationships with the other workers than the employee in the small terminal station. The amount of supervision given the employee usually depends on the skill, training, and ability of the worker, as well as years of experience.

Clerical employees may find satisfaction in realizing the importance of their jobs to efficient business operations.

Receptionists
Clerical Occupations

GOE: 07.05, 07.07; SIC: 401; SOC: 4759

◇ SOURCES OF ADDITIONAL INFORMATION

Association of American Railroads
American Railroads Building
50 F Street, NW
Washington, DC 20001

Transportation Communications International
Three Research Place
Rockville, MD 20850

◇ RELATED ARTICLES

Volume 1: Transportation
Volume 3: Bookkeeping and accounting workers; Cashiers; Insurance policy processing occupations; Conductors, railroad; Reservation and transportation ticket agents; Secretaries; Stenographers; Traffic agents and clerks; Typists

Receptionists

Definition

Receptionists, so named because they receive callers to places of business, have the important job of giving a business's clients and visitors a positive first impression of the business. These workers greet clients and visitors, answer their questions, and direct them to the people in the office they wish to see. Receptionists also answer telephones, take and distribute messages for other employees, and make sure no one enters their place of business unescorted or unauthorized. Many receptionists also perform other clerical duties.

History

Centuries ago, as businesses began to compete with each other for customers, merchants and other business people began to recognize the importance of treating customers well, making sure they were comfortable, and giving them the immediate impression that the business was friendly, efficient, and trustworthy. These businesses began to employ hosts and hostesses—workers who would greet customers, make them comfortable, and often serve them refreshments while they waited or while they did business with the owner. As businesses grew larger and more diverse, these hosts and hostesses—only recently renamed receptionists—took on the additional duties of keeping track of a business's many workers and directing callers to the employee they needed to see. Receptionists also began to be valuable as information dispensers, answering growing numbers of inquiries from the public as businesses became more complex. As medical services expanded, more receptionists were needed to direct patients to physicians and clinical services and to keep track of appointments and payment information.

Soon receptionists became indispensable to business and service establishments both large and small. Today it is hard to imagine most businesses functioning without a receptionist to greet visitors, answer calls, and direct clients and customers. The smile of a friendly receptionist buys instant goodwill for almost any place of business.

Nature of the work

The first person a client or customer usually meets when visiting a business is the receptionist. Consequently, the receptionist is responsible for making sure the first impression that the caller receives of that business is a good one. The receptionist is a specialist in human contact—the most important part of a receptionist's job is dealing pleasantly and effectively with people. Receptionists greet customers, clients, patients, and salespeople, take their names, and determine their business and the person they wish to see. The receptionist then either directs the caller to that person's office or location, or makes an appointment for a later visit. Receptionists often keep records of all visits, writing down the caller's name, the purpose of the visit, the person visited, and the date and time.

Receptionists are frequently responsible for answering inquiries from the public about a business's nature and operations. To answer these questions efficiently and in a manner that conveys a favorable impression of the business, a receptionist must be as knowledgeable as possible about the business's products, services, policies, and practices, and must be familiar with the names and responsibilities of all other employees. This part of a receptionist's job is so important that some businesses call their receptionists *information clerks*.

Almost all types of employers hire receptionists—they work in industry, manufacturing, wholesale, retail, real estate, insurance, medicine, government, banking, church administration, and law. Their day-to-day duties depend almost entirely on the nature of the place at which they work.

Most receptionists answer the telephone at their place of employment; many operate switchboards or call directors. These workers usually take and distribute messages for other employees and may also receive and distribute mail. In small businesses especially, receptionists may also perform a variety of other clerical duties, including typing and filing correspondence and other paperwork, proofreading, taking dictation, preparing travel vouchers, and simple bookkeeping. In some businesses receptionists are responsible for monitoring the attendance of other employees, and in businesses where employees are frequently out of the office on assignments, receptionists may keep track of their whereabouts to assure they receive important phone calls and messages. Today's receptionists are using word processors more and more frequently in performing their clerical duties.

In large firms especially, receptionists are partially responsible for maintaining office security. They may require all visitors to sign in and out and carry visitors' passes during their stay. Since visitors may not enter most offices unescorted, receptionists are frequently responsible for accepting and signing for mail, parcels, and other deliveries. Receptionists must usually follow strict security rules in providing information and admitting people to the office.

A large number of receptionists work in physicians' and dentists' offices, hospitals, clinics, and other medical services establishments. Workers in medical offices receive patients, take their names, and escort them to examination rooms. They also make future appointments for patients and may prepare statements and collect bill payments. In hospitals, receptionists obtain information from patients, including name, address, doctor's name, and insurance coverage or other method of payment. They assign patients to rooms and keep records on the dates patients are admitted and discharged.

Receptionists in beauty shops arrange appointments for clients and escort them to operators' booths or chairs. Workers in bus or train companies answer inquiries about departures, arrivals, and stops. Other related occupations may include *in-file operators*. These workers collect and distribute credit information to clients for credit purposes. *Registrars, park aides,* and *tourist-information assistants* may be employed as receptionists to public or private facilities. Their duties can include keeping a record of the visitors entering and leaving the facility, as well as providing information as to what services the facility provides. *Information clerks, automobile club information clerks,* and *referral-and-information aides* provide answers to questions by telephone or in person from both clients and potential clients. They may also keep a record of all inquiries. *Land-leasing examiners* provide information to the general public about the status of government owned lands. These workers may examine documents in order to process and collect fees. They may also keep a record of all transactions and inquiries. *Schedulers* and *space schedulers* may provide customers with information regarding the availability of staff and facilities.

Requirements

Most employees require receptionists to have a high-school diploma. Because most receptionist positions are entry level, however, business or office experience is usually not required. Some businesses prefer to hire workers who have completed post–high-school courses at a junior college or business school. Applicants need a friendly, outgoing personality, excellent people skills, and a neat appearance. A good grasp of English and grammar is helpful, and some employers require typing, switchboard, and other clerical skills.

High-school students may prepare for receptionist positions by taking courses in busi-

A receptionist must maintain a professional and pleasant manner on the telphone and in person at all times.

ness procedures, office machine operation, typing, shorthand, business arithmetic, English, and public speaking. Participation in such extracurricular activities as debating, drama, and scouting provide valuable experience in working and talking with others. Students interested in post–high-school education may find that courses in basic bookkeeping and principles of accounting help them find higher-paying receptionist jobs with greater chance for advancement.

Special requirements

There are no special requirements for this type of position.

Opportunities for experience and exploration

A good way to obtain experience in working as a receptionist is through a high-school work/study program. Students participating in such programs spend part of their school day in classes and the rest working for local businesses. This arrangement helps students gain valuable practical experience before they look for their first job. High-school guidance counselors can provide information about work/study opportunities.

Related occupations

People who enjoy meeting with the public and have the same skills as those required of receptionists might also enjoy the work of financial institution clerks or tellers, secretaries, retail sales workers, hotel clerks, counter clerks, teachers aides, and telemarketers.

Methods of entering

High-school students may contact their school guidance counselors, who often work with local businesses to find employment for students. Local state employment offices frequently have information about receptionist work, and newspaper want ads list openings as well. Workers should also check listings for state, city, and federal openings and canvass local firms to find out about unadvertised positions.

Advancement

Advancement opportunities are limited for receptionists, especially in small offices. Large offices may provide more opportunities. The more clerical skills workers have, the greater their chances for promotion to such better-paying jobs as secretary, administrative assistant, or bookkeeper. College or business school training can help receptionists advance to higher-level positions. Many companies also provide training for their employees, including receptionists, helping workers gain skills for advancement on the job.

Employment outlook

According to the Association of Independent Colleges and Schools, about 660,000 workers will be employed as receptionists by the mid-1990s. Factories, wholesale and retail stores, and service providers employ a large percentage of these workers. Nearly one-half of the receptionists in the United States work in health-care settings, including offices, hospitals, nursing homes, urgent care centers, and clinics. Almost one-third work part-time.

Growth in this field should be about as fast as average through the early 1990s with many openings resulting from the occupation's high turnover rate. Growth in jobs for receptionists will probably be greater than for other clerical positions because increasing office automation will have little effect on the receptionist's largely interpersonal duties and because the growth in the number of businesses providing services means many more receptionists will be needed. In addition, more and more businesses are learning how valuable a receptionist can be in the firm's public relations efforts—helping businesses convey a positive image.

Earnings

Earnings for receptionists may vary widely with the education and experience of the worker and the type, size, and geographic location of the business. According to a survey conducted by the Executive Compensation Service, receptionists earned an average of $16,540 per year in the early 1990s. Receptionists who operated switchboards or call directors, or performed other office work received higher pay.

The federal government paid receptionists a starting salary of $12,501 a year; the average annual salary for receptionists in the federal government was $16,560.

Conditions of work

Because receptionists usually work near or at the main entrance to the business, their work area is one of the first places a caller sees. Therefore, these areas are usually pleasant and clean and are often carefully furnished and decorated to make a favorable, businesslike impression. Work areas are almost always air-conditioned, well lighted, and relatively quiet, although a receptionist's phone rings frequently. Receptionists work behind a desk or counter and spend most of their work day sitting, although some standing and walking is required when filing or escorting visitors to their destinations. The job may be stressful at times, especially when a worker must be polite to rude or uncooperative callers.

Most receptionists work five days, thirty-five to forty hours a week. Some work some weekend and evening hours, especially those in medical offices. Employers usually provide

paid holidays and vacations, sick leave, medical and life insurance coverage, and a retirement plan of some kind.

Social and psychological factors

Desire and ability to work well with people are essential for a receptionist. A receptionist must enjoy meeting new people and must want to be helpful. Good receptionists need to be well groomed, have pleasant voices, and possess the ability to express themselves clearly. Because receptionists sometimes deal with demanding people, an even, patient disposition and good judgment are very important. All receptionists should know how to be courteous and tactful. A good memory for faces and names also comes in handy. Most important are good listening and communication skills and an understanding of human nature.

GOE: 09.01.01; SIC: Any industry; SOC: 4645

◇ **SOURCES OF ADDITIONAL INFORMATION**

Association of Independent Colleges and Schools
One Dupont Circle, Suite 350
Washington, DC 20036

Professional Secretaries International
301 East Armour Boulevard
Kansas City, MO 64111

◇ **RELATED ARTICLES**

Reservation and transportation ticket agents

Definition

Reservation and transportation ticket agents are employed by airlines, bus companies, railroads, and steamship lines to help customers in several ways. *Reservation agents* make and confirm reservations for passengers; use timetables, manuals, reference guides, and tariff books to plan the reservations and routing; and may maintain an inventory of passenger space available.

Ticket agents sell tickets at ticket counters in the terminal or in ticket offices. They use schedules and rate books to plan routes and compute ticket costs; ensure that seating is available; answer inquiries; check baggage and direct passengers to proper places for boarding; announce arrivals and departures; and assist passengers in boarding.

History

Since the earliest days of commercial passenger transportation, by boat and overland stagecoach, someone has had to be responsible for making sure that space is available for all passengers and that all passengers pay their way. As transportation grew into a major industry over the years, with railroads and ocean liners beginning to flourish in the 1800s, the job of making reservations and selling tickets became a specialty.

Since the introduction of passenger-carrying jet planes in 1958, the number of people who choose to travel by air has multiplied many times over. Today the airlines handle more than 85 percent of all public travel within the United States and an even larger percentage to cities overseas. They employ about three-fourths of all reservation and ticket agents.

Like other service industries, the transportation industry depends on the goodwill of its customers. Automation has increased the speed and ease with which passengers' reservations are made, confirmed, or changed, but the passengers expect more than efficiency. They expect friendly and courteous service, clearly stated information, guidance through the terminals, and willing assistance with all the details and problems involved in their travel plans.

Nature of the work

Airline reservation agents are telephone-sales agents who work in large central offices of airline companies. Their primary job is to book and confirm reservations for passengers on scheduled airline flights. At the request of the customer or a ticket agent, they plan the routing and other arrangements, using timetables, airline manuals, reference guides, and a tariff book.

After finding out where the passenger wants to go, when, and from which airport, the reservation agents type instructions on a computer keyboard and very quickly obtain information on flight schedules and the availability of seating. If the plane is full, the agents may suggest an alternate flight or check to see if space is available on another airline that flies to the same destination. They may even book seats on the other airline, especially if their own line can provide service on the return trip. The computers are used to make, confirm, change, or cancel reservations.

Reservation agents also answer telephone inquiries about such things as schedules, fares, arrival and departure times, and cities serviced by their airline. They may maintain an inventory of passenger space available so they can notify other personnel and stations of changes and try to utilize the full capacity of all flights. The work of these personnel is supervised and coordinated by *senior reservation agents*.

In the railroad industry, *reservation clerks* perform similar tasks. They receive requests for and assign seats or compartments to passengers, keep station agents and information clerks informed about available space, and communicate with reservation clerks in other towns or on other railroads.

Ticket agents for any transportation—air, bus, rail, or ship—sell tickets to customers at terminals or at downtown ticket offices. Like reservation agents, they book space for customers. In addition, they prepare the tickets, calculate fares, and collect payment. At the terminals they check and place tags on luggage, direct passengers to the proper areas for boarding, keep records of passengers on each departure, help with customer problems such as lost baggage or missed connections, and may sell travel insurance.

In airports, *gate agents* assign seats, issue boarding passes, make public address announcements of departures and arrivals, and help passengers board the planes. They also make sure the flight attendants have all the equipment they need and sometimes provide information to disembarking passengers about ground transportation and local hotels.

The work of airline ticket agents is supervised by *ticket sales supervisors*, who may also perform the same duties as ticket agents. In airline central offices, *ticketing clerks* compile and record the information needed to assemble tickets that are mailed or otherwise sent to customers.

Requirements

Airlines generally require a high-school diploma. Some college is preferred, though not essential. Job applicants should be able to type. Because reservation and ticket agents are in contact with the public, appearance, personality, and a good speaking voice are important. Previous experience working with the public is helpful.

New reservation agents are given about a month of classroom instruction. They are taught to read schedules, calculate fares, and plan itineraries. They learn how to use the computer to get information and to reserve space. They also learn about company policy and government regulations that apply to the industry.

Ticket agents receive about one week of classroom instruction. They learn how to read tickets and schedules, to assign seats, and to tag baggage. This is followed by one week of on-the-job training, working alongside an experienced agent. After mastering the simpler tasks, the new ticket agents are trained to reserve space, make out tickets, and handle the boarding gate.

Special requirements

Because agents are in constant contact with the public, they need to be pleasant, tactful, and outgoing. It is important, for example, to keep calls to a minimum time without alienating customers. A knowledge of foreign languages

Reservation and ticket agents answer telephone inquiries about schedules and fares. Computers provide immediate access to the most recent information.

would be useful for agents of an international transportation company.

No other special requirements are demanded for this occupation.

Opportunities for experience and exploration

High-school students may wish to apply for part-time or summer work with transportation companies in their central offices or at terminals. Even if the duties are only vaguely related, the students will at least have the opportunity to become familiar with operations. Any job or volunteer activity that involves serving and working with the public would be helpful. Jobs providing information or assisting people, such as information clerk, receptionist, or guide, would be especially meaningful.

Through school counselors or teachers, field trips to an airport or other type of terminal can be arranged. Learning how to operate a computer while still in school will make the later job training easier. Students can become active in their school's computer club.

Related occupations

Young people interested in sales positions might also wish to consider work as a retail sales worker, a wholesale sales worker, counter clerks, brokerage sales workers, or real estate sales workers or brokers.

Clerks interested can be utilized in almost any industry and in a wide variety of ways. Some of these include general office clerks, shipping and receiving clerks, court reporters, and telemarketers.

Methods of entering

Students who want to continue their education beyond high school may consult with teachers or guidance counselors for advice about courses of study that would be relevant. Some junior colleges offer courses specifically designed for those wanting to become ticket agents. College placement services may be able to provide information or listings of jobs in this field.

Job applicants may apply directly to the personnel or employment offices of the transportation companies for up-to-date information about job openings, requirements, and possible training programs.

Advancement

With experience and a good work record, some reservation and ticket agents are promoted to supervisory positions. A few may become city and district sales managers for ticket offices. Beyond this, opportunities for advancement are limited.

Employment outlook

In the early 1990s, about 112,000 people in the United States were employed as reservation and transportation ticket agents; three out of four worked for airlines. Employment for these workers will grow more slowly than average through the early 1990s. Although demand for transportation will increase, the increased use of computers will limit the number of agents required. Most openings will occur as experienced, older agents transfer, retire, or die. Competition for these jobs, however, is heavy because of the glamour of working for an airline and because of the attractive travel benefits.

Transportation companies are affected by economic conditions: when recessions cause a decrease in travel, many agents are laid off and no new agents are hired until business picks up again.

Earnings

In the early 1990s, on the average, airline reservation agents earned $28,017, gate agents earned $30,076, and ticket agents earned $31,824. In the railroad industry, AMTRAK reservation clerks earned between $22,089 and $27,600, and ticket agents earned from $23,238 to $29,452. Bus company ticket agents earned about $21,240. Agents often receive free or reduced-fare transportation for themselves and their families.

Conditions of work

Reservation and ticket agents generally work forty hours a week. Their schedules may be irregular because most types of transportation companies operate at all hours, seven days a week. Until agents acquire seniority, they may have to work nights or on weekends. The work is very hectic during holidays and other busy periods, also during severe weather, when passengers may become difficult.

Many agents belong to such labor unions as the Air Line Employees Association; the Transport Workers Union of America; the Brotherhood of Railway and Steamship Clerks, Freight Handlers, Express and Station Employees; and the International Brotherhood of Teamsters, Chauffeurs, Warehousemen and Helpers of America.

Social and psychological factors

Agents must be able to deal well with all types of people, especially under adverse conditions, such as severe weather when airline flights are delayed or canceled and passengers become irritated and angry. As representatives of their employers, agents need to remain calm and cheerful despite annoyances, the pressures of work, or personal difficulties. A thorough knowledge of industry procedures will help them to be resourceful in solving whatever problems the traveler may encounter.

GOE: 07.03.01; SIC: 401, 413, 451; SOC: 4644

◇ **SOURCES OF ADDITIONAL INFORMATION**

For a pamphlet describing the duties of reservation and ticket agents, write to:

Air Line Employees Association, International
5600 South Central Avenue
Chicago, IL 60638

Information about employment on particular airlines may be obtained by writing to the personnel manager of each company. Addresses of companies are available from:

Air Transport Association of America
1709 New York Avenue, NW
Washington, DC 20006

◇ **RELATED ARTICLES**

Volume 1: Transportation; Travel and Tourism
Volume 2: Conductors, railroad; Hotel and motel managers
Volume 3: Hotel clerks; Shipping and receiving clerks; Travel agents

Secretaries

Definition

Secretaries perform a wide range of jobs that vary greatly from business to business. Most secretaries, however, type, keep records and files, answer telephones, handle correspondence, schedule appointments, make travel arrangements, and sort mail. The amount of time secretaries spend on these duties depends on the size and type of the office as well as on their own job training. Secretaries may specialize by working in law firms or medical offices, or may spend much of their day working with computers or in foreign languages.

History

People have always needed to communicate with one another for societies to function efficiently. Secretaries play an important role in keeping lines of communication open. Before there were telephones, messages were transmitted by hand, often from the secretary of one party to the secretary of the receiving party. In medieval times the way a secretary was able to help his or her boss was quite different than today, but certain elements have remained the same. A secretary today must understand the needs of the business where he or she is employed just as a secretary in days past.

In the ancient world, early secretaries developed methods of taking abbreviated notes so that they would be able to capture as much as possible of their superiors' words. In sixteenth-century England the modern precursors of the shorthand methods we know today were developed. In the nineteenth century, Isaac Pitman and John Robert Gregg developed the shorthand systems that are still used in offices and courtrooms in the United States. Although many office executives use dictating machines in composing letters and memoranda today, secretaries who can write shorthand are often at a great advantage in the job market.

The equipment secretaries use in their work has changed drastically in recent years. Almost every office, from the smallest to the largest, is automated in some way. Familiarity with machines including switchboards, photocopiers, and personal computers has become an integral part of the secretary's day-to-day work.

Nature of the work

Secretaries perform a variety of administrative and clerical duties. Their work includes processing and transmitting information to the staff and to other organizations. Sometimes a secretary is the only worker in a small office. They may not only operate the office machines, but also arrange for their repair or servicing. These machines include computers, dictating machines, photocopiers, switchboards, and calculators. These secretaries also order office supplies, and make trips to the local post office or bank as is required, while performing regular duties such as answering phones, sorting mail, keeping files, taking dictation, and typing letters.

Some offices have word processing centers where all of the firm's typing is handled. In this case, *administrative secretaries* handle all secretarial duties except for typing and dictation. This leaves them free to respond to office correspondence, prepare reports, do research and present the results to employers, and otherwise assist the professional staff. Often these secretaries work in groups of three or four so that they can relieve each other if one secretary has a heavier than normal load of work.

In many offices, secretaries make appointments for their bosses and keep track of the office schedule. They make travel arrangements for the professional staff or for clients, and occasionally are asked to travel with the staff members to assist while they are out of town. Some secretaries, on the other hand, are left to take charge of the office while the employer is away.

Secretaries take minutes at meetings and write up reports, and compose and type letters. Often, secretaries who have spent many years at one firm will find their responsibilities growing as they learn the business. Some are responsible for finding speakers for conferences, planning receptions, and arranging public relations programs. Some write and proofread copy to be printed before making the arrangements to have it printed or microfilmed. They greet clients and deal with them, and often are asked to supervise other staff members and newer secretaries.

Many secretaries do very specialized work. *Legal secretaries* prepare legal papers including wills, mortgages, contracts, deeds, motions, complaints, and summonses. They often work under the direct supervision of an attorney. They assist with legal research by reviewing legal journals and preparing legal briefs for their employers. They must learn an entire legal vocabulary that is used in legal papers and documents. *Medical secretaries* make appointments, type and send bills to patients, maintain medical files, and pursue correspondence with patients, hospitals, associations. They assist medical scientists or physicians with articles, reports, speeches, and conference proceedings. They, too, need to learn an entire vocabulary of medical terms and be familiar with laboratory or hospital procedures. *Technical secretaries* work for engineers and scientists preparing reports and papers that often include graphics and mathematical equations that are difficult to type. The secretaries maintain a technical library and help with scientific papers by gathering and editing materials.

Social secretaries are often called *personal secretaries,* and they arrange all of the social activities of their employers. They handle private as well as business social affairs, and may plan parties, send out invitations, or write speeches for their employers. Social secretaries are often hired by celebrities or high-level executives who have busy social calendars to maintain. Many associations and clubs have *membership secretaries* to compile and send out newsletters or promotional materials while maintaining membership lists, dues records, and directories. Depending on the type of club, the secretary may be the one who gives out information to prospective members and who keeps current members and related organizations informed of upcoming events.

Educational secretaries work in elementary or secondary schools or on college campuses. They take care of all clerical duties at the school. Their responsibilities may include preparing bulletins and reports for teachers, parents, or students, keeping track of budgets for school supplies or student activities, and maintaining the school's calendar of events. They may work for school administrators, principals, or groups of teachers or professors depending on the position. Other educational secretaries work in administration offices, state education departments, or service departments.

In recent years, all kinds of secretaries have been performing tasks previously left for professional staff members and managers. The ease of personal computers has enabled secretaries to use complex word-processing, graphics, database, and spreadsheet programs to help their businesses. Secretaries' jobs are changing, but they are becoming even more important in their positions as information managers in today's fast-paced working world.

Requirements

For the most part, secretaries must have high-school diplomas to qualify for positions. They need good office skills that include rapid and accurate typing, and good spelling and grammar. Some positions require a minimum number of words per minute as well as shorthand. Some of these skills can be learned in business education courses that are taught in many local vocational and business schools. Courses that are helpful include business English, typing and shorthand. Increasingly, some experience with word processing is helpful.

Personal qualities are also important in secretaries. They often are the first members of a firm that clients meet, and therefore must be friendly, poised, and properly dressed. Because they must work closely with others in the office, they should be easy to get along with and tactful. Besides their interpersonal skills, secretaries must be well organized. These skills, as well as planning skills, will not only get them hired, but also help them advance in their careers.

The work done by most secretaries is not physically strenuous, but there are often deadlines to be met, and the secretary needs to adapt himself or herself to the business. Employers are interested in speed, but they insist on accuracy and neatness. Mistakes cost a business money, so businesses often test prospective secretaries for their aptitude both in typing and in other skills.

Special requirements

Licensure is not officially required for secretarial positions. Most office employees do not belong to unions, although some belong to the Office and Professional Employees' Union, depending on the business. The National Secretaries Association sponsors a program of professional certification. The program allows secretaries over the age of twenty-five who have worked as secretaries for three to seven years to take a difficult series of examinations in various subject areas. A secretary who can complete these examinations successfully receives a Professional Secretary Certificate.

Some employers encourage their secretaries to take certain courses and to be trained to use

Secretaries must be able to operate several types of business machines including the typewriter, word processing program, photocopier, and fax machine. Required knowledge of other equipment varies with each company.

any new piece of equipment in the office. Requirements vary widely from firm to firm.

Opportunities for experience and exploration

High-school guidance counselors have interest and aptitude tests to help students assess their suitability to a career as a secretary. Local business schools often welcome visitors, and sometimes offer courses that can be taken in conjunction with a high-school business course. Work/study programs provide students with an opportunity to work in a business setting to get a sense of the work secretaries do.

Part-time or summer jobs as switchboard operators, file clerks, and receptionists are often available. These jobs are the best indicator of future satisfaction in the secretarial field. Summer camps may pay students to help run simple office machines or type. Students who are accurate, speedy typists can occasionally find part-time jobs typing. Any job that teaches basic office skills is helpful.

Related occupations

Those doing paperwork, typing, and information recording include bookkeepers, receptionists, stenographers, administrative assistants, office managers, personnel clerks, and medical record technicians.

Methods of entering

Most people looking to work as secretaries find jobs through want ads in local newspapers or by applying directly to businesses. Both private employment offices and local state employment services place secretaries, and business schools help their graduates find suitable jobs.

Advancement

Secretaries often begin by assisting executive secretaries and can work their way up by learning the way their business operates. College courses in business, accounting, or marketing can help the ambitious secretary enter higher management areas. First-step promotions from secretary are usually to positions such as secretarial supervisor, office manager, or administrative assistant. Training in computer skills can also lead to advancement. Secretaries who become proficient in word processing, for instance, can get jobs as instructors or as sales representatives for software manufacturers.

Qualifying for the designation Certified Professional Secretary (CPS) is increasingly recognized in business and industry as a consideration for promotion. The examinations required for this certification are given by a department of Professional Secretaries International. Legal secretaries can become similarly certified by the National Association of Legal Secretaries.

Employment outlook

Secretaries have an excellent job outlook. All kinds of businesses employ secretaries, and despite the increasing trend toward automation, skilled secretaries are expected to be able to find jobs without great difficulty through the early 1990s. Automated equipment may mean that more professionals are doing some of their own typing on personal computers, but some administrative duties will still need to be handled by secretaries. The personal aspects of the job and responsibilities such as making travel arrangements, scheduling conferences and transmitting staff instructions have not changed.

Increasingly, secretaries who keep their skills current and learn to use the new computerized equipment, will be the ones to get the best jobs.

Earnings

The salaries that secretaries earn vary widely by geographic location, type of office, and the skill, experience, and level of responsibility of the secretary. In the early 1990s secretaries earned average annual salaries ranging from $16,000 to $28,000.

Beginning salaries in the federal government are on the low side, while beginning salaries in the mining and public utilities industries are quite high. In large northern and western cities, secretaries are likely to earn more money than in the south.

Most secretaries receive paid holidays and two weeks vacation time after a year of work in addition to sick leave. Many offices provide benefits including health and life insurance and pension plans. Secretaries who specialize and those with computer skills and other experience are likely to command higher salaries.

Conditions of work

Most secretaries work in pleasant offices with modern equipment. Offices vary widely, however, and while some secretaries have their own offices and work for one or two executives, other secretaries share crowded rooms with other secretaries and office workers. Most office workers work forty-hour weeks, with some working a little less. Very few secretaries work on the weekends on a regular basis, although some may be asked to work overtime if a particular project demands it. The work is not physically strenuous or hazardous, although deadline pressure is occasionally a factor and sitting for long periods of time can be uncomfortable. Most secretaries are not required to travel. Part-time and flexible schedules are easily adaptable to secretarial work.

Social and psychological factors

In almost every secretarial job, the work involves other people. Secretaries can find office environments to suit almost any taste—large, small, modern, or traditional. Days are filled with work that is varied in content and detail, and a motivated secretary will find challenges in learning the office routine, improving technical skills, and meeting deadlines. It can be a gratifying career in itself, or lead to a variety of other careers.

GOE: 07.01.03; SIC: Any industry; SOC: 4622

◇ **SOURCES OF ADDITIONAL INFORMATION**

Professional Secretaries International
301 East Armour Boulevard, Suite 200
Kansas City, MO 64111

National Association of Secretarial Services
100 Second Avenue, South, Suite 604
St. Petersburg, FL 33701

National Association of Legal Secretaries (International)
2250 East 73rd Street, Suite 550
Tulsa, OK 74136

◇ **RELATED ARTICLES**

Volume 1: See Table of Contents for specific industries
Volume 2: Computer and peripheral equipment operators; Receptionists; Typists
Volume 3: Legal assistants; Medical record administrators

Shipping and receiving clerks

Definition

Shipping and receiving clerks are employed in many businesses and industries involved in shipping and receiving merchandise, materials, and products.

History

The jobs of shipping and receiving clerks have emerged to meet the demands created by the rapid industrialization reflected in this nation's history. The development of modes of transportation to move industrial products has resulted in the need for these workers.

In the early days of the nation, when transportation was limited and people invented, made, and sold within their own colony many of the materials and products needed, a general store was sufficient to handle all merchandise. As people moved to all corners of the nation and as they continued to invent, sell, and buy, goods were transported all over the country.

Today, hundreds of thousands of types of materials, merchandise, and products travel around the globe.

Workers to handle the movement, shipping, and receiving of commercial products are now hired all over the world in all kinds of businesses, manufacturing plants, and industries.

Nature of the work

In numbers of large firms, the shipping and receiving departments are separated and employees work as either shipping or receiving clerks under the supervision of a head receiving or shipping clerk. In some small stores or firms, one or two persons may handle all shipping and all receiving.

Individuals employed as shipping and receiving clerks are responsible for the proper shipping of merchandise and products, as well as their being received in good condition. They must keep accurate records of all shipments made and received.

Clerks employed in shipping must check to be sure that an order has been filled correctly before it is shipped, and they must sometimes request, in written form, the merchandise from a supply room. Depending on the kind of merchandise and the type and size of the place of employment, shipping clerks either pack and wrap the goods for shipment, or direct how this is to be done by other workers. In some places of employment, shipping clerks must order the kind and size of trucks needed for shipments and supervise the weight distribution and packing of the shipments in the trucks. Safe handling is a part of their job responsibilities. These clerks are also responsible for determining the best methods of transportation for shipment, as well as the least expensive and quickest method.

Among other duties, shipping clerks must prepare the bills of lading and any other shipping forms needed, make records of the weight and cost of each shipment, check each shipment for correct address, and be informed on postal information and regulations regarding shipment. Accurate records must be kept on every shipment, such as records that can later be used to check back on dates and method of shipment, and records for accounting, inventory, and delivery purposes.

The work of receiving clerks is quite similar to that of shipping clerks. As orders are received these clerks check them in by using shipping invoices and bills of lading to make sure the merchandise or products have been shipped as ordered and to verify that the order arrived at the intended destination in good condition. Claims must be processed by these clerks on any part of an order that was damaged in shipment. These clerks are usually responsible for tracing lost shipments, signing freight bills that all merchandise was received, and for any other clerical details involved in receiving orders. The accuracy of records kept by receiving departments is most important for inventory, accounting, and pricing purposes.

Receiving clerks sometimes price merchandise as it is received and then route it to the proper department, storage area, or warehouse division. In some large firms and industries, receiving clerks do not price merchandise and products, but forward shipments, after they have been checked by them, to the marking rooms. Specific routines vary with individual company policies.

In different industries, shipping and receiving clerks may have various titles and specialized duties. In water transportation, *cargo checkers* calculate the amount of space needed for a particular cargo, prepare plans to show where cargo is stowed on the ship, and keep records about the amount, type, and condition of cargo being loaded or unloaded. Similarly, *booking clerks* use information about type, weight, and destination of cargo shipments to book them in such a way that space is used to a maximum. *Ship runners* locate space for cargo on the decks. *Incoming-freight clerks* arrange with recipients to remove their cargo from decks and prepare bills for shipping and storage charges for the packages received.

In rail transportation, *reconsignment clerks* reroute freight to new destinations according to shippers' instructions. *Car checkers* make sure that freight trains are complete when they arrive at the railroad yard, report missing or tampered-with cars, and prepare instructions for switching crews.

In the construction industry, *truckload checkers* examine and keep records about materials being transported by truck to and from construction sites. *Aircraft-shipping checkers* compare newly-built aircraft with blueprints to make sure that all spare parts and accessories are included for delivery to the purchaser. *Fuel-oil clerks* keep records about the amount and value of fuel oil bought, received, stored, and used at electric generating plants. *Grain elevator clerks* keep records about weight, type, location, grade, temperature, and destination of grain that is received, stored, and shipped at grain elevators.

Checkers at stockyards count livestock as they are unloaded from trucks, issue receipts to the shippers, and herd livestock into pens according to markings that identify who will receive them. *Vault workers* receive, sort, and route sealed money bags at the vaults of armored car companies, deliver bags to armored car guards, and keep records of these exchanges.

Shipping-order clerks receive orders to ship a plant's products, decide what kind of transportation is needed, and arrange the transportation and give instructions to the carrier. *Shipping checkers* make sure that the quantity, quality, labeling, and addressing of merchandise to be shipped are correct. *Route-delivery clerks* prepare the itemized delivery sheets that tell truck drivers where to deliver particular items of merchandise. *Routers* mark the merchandise to indicate its route. *Stubbers* on the loading dock remove sales-slip stubs from packages and use them to keep records of deliveries. *Receiving checkers* compare the contents of received shipments against bills of lading, invoices, or receipts and watch for defective items.

Requirements

The job requirements for these workers generally include a high-school education, even in beginning jobs. Some individuals may qualify without having finished high school; employers today, however, seek the high-school graduate as the preferred employee. Students who have taken such subjects in high school as business arithmetic, geography, typing, bookkeeping, and related business subjects may find this type of training to be a particular asset.

Aptitudes for mathematical computation, for performing detailed work, for good memory, and for systematic order in carrying out one's work responsibilities are especially valuable. Clerks in these jobs must be able to read well and to write legibly. An even temperament, patience, and the ability to work well and get along in a congenial manner with others are important qualities.

Physical traits should include good eyesight and hearing, and normal physical strength. However, in some shipping departments where clerks are required to pack goods for shipment and assist in loading them for transportation, more than the normal amount of physical strength may be required. This requirement depends on the place, size, and type of place of employment. These clerks must usually stand most of their working hours and some of these jobs require a great deal of reaching, bending, stretching, and stooping.

A shipping clerk carefully seals a package that will be shipped out later in the day.

Special requirements

There are no special requirements, such as licensure or certification imposed by law or official organizations. Some shipping and receiving clerks do belong to a teamsters' union, The International Brotherhood of Teamsters, Chauffeurs, Warehousemen and Helpers of America. Union–company agreements may stipulate specific working conditions, such as hours and wages.

Opportunities for experience and exploration

Students sometimes find the opportunity to explore these jobs by obtaining part-time work during summer vacations and Christmas holidays. If jobs as shipping and receiving clerks are not available on a part-time basis, jobs as errand runners and stockroom helpers may provide an opportunity to observe the work that is actually done in shipping and receiving departments.

Visits to personnel departments that hire shipping and receiving clerks, and to business and industry to observe these employees at work may provide interested persons with first-hand information. High-school students may wish to talk with the high-school guidance counselor to obtain additional occupational information on these jobs and to further explore their interests, aptitudes, and ability for this type of work.

Related occupations

Persons who have the interests and aptitude to work as shipping and receiving clerks will also most probably be qualified to work in the clerical jobs such as billing clerks, traffic clerks, stock clerks, postal clerks, mail clerks, and general office clerks.

Methods of entering

Individuals interested in entering this field usually do so by making direct application to the personnel departments of the companies, businesses, or industries in which they wish to be employed. Job opportunities are sometimes located through friends, newspaper want ads, and through state and private employment agencies. Union offices may sometimes have employment information, depending on the type of industry.

Interested persons should keep in mind that small retail stores, small shipping firms, and other small businesses hire shipping and receiving clerks, as well as large industry and big warehouses. In these situations, the work of shipping and receiving clerks may be combined with other jobs, such as checking stock, filling orders, and the pricing of merchandise.

Job applicants who can supply employers with good high-school and personal references have an additional asset in their favor when making work applications.

Advancement

Opportunities for advancement for these workers depend a great deal upon the personal initiative, interest, and accuracy of the worker. Individuals employed as shipping and receiving clerks usually have many roads open to them for advancement, but it is up to them to make the most of these opportunities.

Within shipping and receiving departments, these clerks may have the opportunity to advance to receiving or shipping superintendent, traffic manager, supervisor, or to head shipping and receiving clerks.

Clerks who have shown initiative in really learning about a company's or firm's products and who have shown ambition in their jobs, performing with accuracy, dependability, and excellent work records, may have other opportunities for advancement, especially if they have acquired additional formal course or college training. They may advance to positions as purchasing agents, industrial traffic managers, or warehouse managers.

Employment outlook

In the early 1990s, approximately 729,000 workers were employed as shipping and receiving clerks. One out of three worked in manufacturing firms, about half worked in wholesale houses and retail stores, while others were employed by transportation and freight firms that handled freight to be sent out, or they were working in many and varied kinds of business firms. The work setting for shipping and receiving clerks is primarily in the metropolitan areas where large factories, industry, big business firms, and warehouse centers tend to be located. Mostly male workers have been employed.

Employment of shipping and receiving clerks will probably increase more slowly than average through the mid-1990s because of automation and because of the slow growth expected in the manufacturing and wholesale trades where they are mostly employed. The majority of these job openings will occur as the result of individuals retiring, leaving the field, or replacing the deceased.

Beginners may find keen competition for job openings since the nature of the work requires little specialized training and many persons are usually available for the entry jobs.

It should be recognized, also, that in the future automation and the striving for methods of increased efficiency, such as containerized shipping, may also affect the number of these workers that will be needed. The rate of employment may lag behind the volume of products and merchandise distributed if increased efficiency methods are found and if receiving and shipping operations are simplified by computerized record keeping and greatly improved mechanical equipment to move orders. Even with such improvements, however, the number of these clerks needed is expected to increase gradually.

Earnings

Overall, shipping and receiving clerks in the early 1990s were receiving an average salary of $17,470 a year; half earned between $13,728 and $23,700. Clerks working for wholesale houses averaged $20,210, and those employed by public utilities were earning $22,089.

Overtime work, which may frequently be required of these employees, is generally compensated by time-and-a-half pay. Fringe benefits may include a company–employee shared insurance program, paid vacations, retirement benefits, and company discounts on any merchandise purchased in the place of employment. These benefits will vary with the place of employment and are usually determined by individual company policy.

Conditions of work

These clerks usually work a forty-hour week; however, when products, merchandise, or other materials are urgently needed or have been delayed for shipment they may work overtime at night, on Saturdays, Sundays, and holidays. An average workday is usually an eight-hour shift, and Saturday work is common for those employees who work in department stores or other retail businesses.

Working conditions will vary, depending on where the employee works. Employment in some of the retail businesses in the newer shipping centers or in some large department stores may be in comfortable basement areas that are air-conditioned, well heated, and well lighted. Other locations of employment may be in large warehouses that are cold, somewhat open, poorly lighted, and dusty.

These occupations are not considered to be hazardous; however, workers in industry who ship and receive large, heavy merchandise and products must be cautious in handling the orders to avoid excessive physical strain on the back and legs and to prevent falls, crushing their fingers, and other types of accidents.

During certain periods of the year, such as Christmas holiday rush periods, these employees, in some industries and businesses, may work under pressure to get merchandise in or out on time schedules. In other instances, manufacturing firms may demand a rush order on certain raw material products or a shipment that has been delayed. Although most of these employees may perform their work indoors the majority of the time, some are required to work outside on loading platforms in all kinds of weather, at least during a part of each of their workdays.

Social and psychological factors

Shipping and receiving clerks who demonstrate personal initiative, interest in their jobs, and in the firm by which they are employed, and who perform their work with accuracy, order, and care, may have a number of good opportunities for job advancement and often times in terms of their own interests.

GOE: 05.09.01; SIC: Any industry; SOC: 4753

◇ **SOURCES OF ADDITIONAL INFORMATION**

American Society of Transportation and Logistics
PO Box 33095
Louisville, KY 40232

International Brotherhood of Teamsters, Chauffeurs, Warehousemen and Helpers of America
25 Louisiana Avenue, NW
Washington, DC 20001

◇ **RELATED ARTICLES**

Volume 1: Retailing; or see Table of Contents for areas of specific interest
Volume 2: Industrial traffic managers
Volume 3: Accounting and bookkeeping workers; Postal clerks; Traffic agents and clerks

Statistical clerks

Definition

Statistical clerks collect and analyze numerical records such as sales records and survey sheets and then assemble and clarify these records following set procedures. They tabulate results and may present findings in the way of graphs and charts.

History

The collection and interpretation of business data are important tools in the running of an efficient organization. Statistical clerks help develop such information by putting together numerical records that are used for record keeping and other functions.

As business decisions become increasingly dependent on demographics and other types of information that can be tabulated, statistical clerks will continue to play an important role in the compilation of relevant data.

Nature of the work

Statistical clerks are involved in record keeping, data retrieval, and analysis. They compile numerical information (such as questionnaire results and production records) and tabulate it so that it can be used for further study. Statistical clerks must carefully review the raw data and their results for accuracy. They perform many of their clerical functions by hand; however, they generally use adding machines or calculators for computational work. Statistical clerks either record information by manually transcribing it in a business ledger or by entering the data into a computer terminal or personal computer. With quality statistical software programs now available, more and more statistical clerks are using computers in their work. Statistical clerks in a variety of fields are involved with handling and analyzing data. These include: *Compilers,* who analyze raw data gathered from surveys, census data, and the like, and organize and arrange this information into specified categories or groupings. These statistics are compiled into survey findings or census reports. Compilers may prepare graphs or charts to illustrate their findings.

Chart calculators work for power companies and compute the power factor and net amount of electric power used by the company's customers and determine the peak load demand to verify that the correct rates are being charged. They enter this information on record forms so that customers are billed at the appropriate rates.

Advertising statistical clerks tabulate statistical records for companies on the cost, volume, and effectiveness of their advertising. They often compare the amount of their customers' merchandise that is sold before an advertising campaign to that sold after the advertising campaign.

Planimeter operators use a special measuring tool to trace the boundaries of specified land areas. They usually use aerial photographs to help identify the boundary lines of individual plots of land.

Chart clerks compile records measuring the quantity of natural or manufactured gas produced, transported, and sold to calculate the volume of gas and petroleum used on specific pipelines.

Chart changers change charts and record data from industrial recording instruments. They are also responsible for maintaining the recording instruments, such as pyrometers and flowmeters.

Medical-record clerks tabulate statistics for use in reports and surveys to help medical researchers illustrate their findings. They also compile, verify, and file the medical records of hospital or clinic patients and make sure that these records are complete and up-to-date. Medical-record clerks may assist in compiling the necessary information used in completing hospital insurance billing forms.

Requirements

A high-school diploma is usually sufficient for beginning statistical clerks. Prospective clerks should have some mechanical ability (for operating business machines), the ability to concentrate for long periods of time on repetitious tasks, and mathematical ability. Legible handwriting is a necessity.

High-school students should take courses in English, mathematics, and as many business-related courses such as typing and bookkeeping as possible.

Community colleges and vocational schools often offer business education courses that provide additional training for statistical clerks in the areas of data processing and office procedures.

Special requirements

No licenses or certificates are needed for employment in this field. Statistical clerks who work for the federal government may need to pass a civil service examination. Some clerks (as well as other office personnel) may join a professional union such as the American Federation of State, County, and Municipal Employees.

Opportunities for experience and exploration

Students may get experience in this field by taking on clerical or bookkeeping responsibilities with a school club or other organization. In addition, some school work-study programs may have opportunities with businesses for part-time, practical on-the-job training. It may also be possible to get a part-time or summer job in a business office by contacting offices on your own. Individuals may have the opportunity to get training in the operation of business machinery (calculators, word processors, and so on) through evening courses offered by business schools. Another way of gaining insight into the responsibilities of a statistical clerk is to talk to someone already working in the field.

Related occupations

Other workers who perform calculations and prepare statistical reports include accounting and bookkeeping clerks, personnel clerks, auditors, accountants, and insurance clerks.

Methods of entering

Those interested in securing an entry-level position should contact businesses or governmental agencies directly. Major employers include insurance agencies, utility companies, and many other large businesses. Jobs may also be located through "help wanted" advertisements.

Most companies provide entry-level statistical clerks with on-the-job training during which time company policy and procedures are explained. Beginning clerks work with experienced personnel during this period.

Advancement

In many instances, statistical clerks begin their employment as general office clerks and, with experience and further training, they become statistical clerks. With experience, they may advance to more complicated assignments and assume a greater responsibility for the total statistical work to be completed. Those with good leadership skills may become group managers or supervisors. In order to become an accountant or bookkeeper, it is usually necessary to get a college degree or have other specialized training.

The high turnover rate in the clerk position increases promotional opportunities. The number and kind of opportunities, however, may be dependent on the place of employment, and the ability, training, and experience of the employee.

A statistics clerk asks her supervisor to confirm data that she has entered on the computer.

Employment outlook

Although the amount of statistical data to be processed is expected to increase over the next ten to fifteen years, job opportunities for statistical clerks are expected to decline over this same period. This is a result of data-processing equipment that can now do many of the record-keeping and data retrieval functions previously performed by statistical clerks. Despite the drop in employment opportunities, there should continue to be openings caused by people retiring or otherwise leaving the field. Employment opportunities should be especially good for those trained in the use of computers and other types of automated office machinery.

Earnings

Salaries of statistical clerks vary widely, depending on skill, experience, level of responsibility, and geographic location. Beginning clerks with private companies should earn an average of about $15,000 per year in the early 1990s; experienced stenographers should earn about $21,500 annually. Clerks who work for public utility companies should fare the best in terms of wages, while those in the insurance or real estate industries may earn somewhat lower salaries. Statistical clerks working for the federal government should average about $13,500 per year to start; those with experience should earn about $17,000 annually.

Full-time workers should also receive paid vacation, health insurance, and other benefits.

Conditions of work

As is the case with most office workers, statistical clerks work an average thirty-seven to forty-hour week. The work environment is usually well ventilated and well lighted, and although statistical clerks have a variety of tasks, the job itself can be fairly routine and repetitive. Clerks often interact with accountants and other office personnel and may work under close supervision.

Statistical clerks who work at video display terminals for long periods of time may experience some eye and neck strain.

Social and psychological factors

Statistical clerks should have an even temperament and the ability to work well with others. They should find systematic and orderly work appealing and they should like to work on detailed tasks. Other personal qualifications include dependability, trustworthiness, and a neat personal appearance. The advantages of this type of work include regular work hours and no major physical or occupational hazards.

Statistical clerks and other office personnel may find opportunities to learn more about the business world in general and this experience may open doors for advancement to higher positions in related fields.

GOE: 07.02.03; SIC: Any industry; SOC: 4794

◇ **SOURCES OF ADDITIONAL INFORMATION**

Career information is available from local business schools and from:

American Statistical Association
1429 Duke Street
Alexandria, VA 22314

◇ **RELATED ARTICLES**

Volume 1: Mathematics
Volume 2: Accountants and auditors; Statisticians
Volume 3: Bookkeeping and accounting clerks; General office clerks

---

Stenographers

Definition

Stenographers use either shorthand or a stenotype machine to take dictation and later transcribe their notes into memoranda, letters, or other business documents. Stenographers may take down remarks at meetings or other proceedings and later give a summary report or a word-for-word record of the proceedings. They may also do such office tasks as typing, filing, and operating office machines.

History

Although businesses and other types of organizations have not always been as complex as they are today, precise written records of spoken communications, such as that provided by stenographers, have contributed greatly to overall efficiency in the communications process. Even in the Stone Age, people had means of keeping records of verbal interactions, and people have continually experimented with methods and symbols for abbreviating spoken communications.

In 1837, Isaac Pitman introduced the first modern method of shorthand (called the Pitman Method). Later, in 1880, John Gregg introduced the Gregg Method, and today both of these methods are still widely used. A symbol used to represent a sound is the phonetic principle that gives us modern-day shorthand.

Shorthand began to be applied to business communications with the invention of the typewriter. The stenotype, the first shorthand machine, was invented by an American in 1910.

Nature of the work

In addition to taking dictation and transcribing and writing business correspondence, stenographers may also have a variety of other office duties, such as typing, operating photocopy and other office machines, answering telephones, and performing receptionists' duties. They may sit in on staff meetings and later transcribe a summary report of the proceedings for use by management. In some situations, stenographers may be responsible for answering routine office mail by composing the letter.

Some *stenographers*, called *stenotype operators*, take dictation of business correspondence on a machine that prints symbols for full words. They later transcribe this material through the use of a typewriter or word processor. *Steno pool supervisors* supervise and coordinate the work of stenographers by assigning them to people who have documents to dictate or by giving them manuscripts, rolls of tape, or recordings to transcribe. They also check final typed copy for accuracy. Other areas of specialization for stenographers include the following:

Print shop stenographers take dictation and operate a special typewriter that produces metal printing plates for use by addressing machines.

Transcribing-machine operators listen to recordings (often through earphones or earplugs) and use a typewriter or word processor to transcribe the material. They can control the speed of the tape so that they can comfortably type every word they hear. Transcribing-machine operators may also have various clerical duties, such as answering the telephones and filing correspondence.

Technical stenographers may specialize in medical, legal, foreign language, or other technical areas of preparation. They should be familiar with the terminology and the practice of the appropriate subject.

Requirements

Although there are no specific educational requirements, most stenographers should have a high-school diploma and in many instances they should have advanced technical training from a private business school or college.

Stenographers should have good reading comprehension and spelling skills, as well as good finger and hand dexterity. A pleasant personality and the ability to get along with others is also important.

Some high-school students follow a business education curriculum and take courses in typing, shorthand, and business procedures. These students may later enter a business school or college for more advanced technical training. Other high-school students may follow a general education program and take courses in English, history, mathematics, and the sciences. These students will seek all of their technical training beyond high school. Although some students who have followed a business curriculum are able to obtain jobs immediately after high-school graduation, the preferred job opportunities and higher salaries may be more readily available to those who have sought advanced technical training or some degree of specialization.

There are numerous opportunities for advanced training. Hundreds of business schools and colleges throughout the country offer technical or degree programs and many have both day and evening classes. A list of accredited business schools and accreditation standards is available from the Accrediting Commission for Business Schools at the address given at the end of this article.

Special requirements

No licenses or certificates are needed to work in this field. Some stenographers, especially those who work for the federal government, may belong to a union such as the Office and Professional Employees' International Union.

To work for the federal government, stenographers must usually pass a civil service test and be able to take dictation at the rate of eighty words per minute and type approximately forty words per minute. Tests of verbal and mathematical ability are also required. Employers in the private sector may require similar tests. Court reporters are required to complete a course in shorthand before being hired. Some are certified by the National Shorthand Reporters Association.

Stenographers must be able to listen and write simultaneously.

Opportunities for experience and exploration

Students may get experience in this field by taking on clerical or typing responsibilities with a school club or other organization. In addition, some school work-study programs may have opportunities with businesses for part-time, practical on-the-job training. It may also be possible to get a part-time or summer job in a business office by contacting offices on your own. Individuals may have the opportunity to get training in the operation of word processors and other office machinery through evening courses offered by business schools. Another way of gaining insight into the responsibilities of a stenographer is to talk to someone already working in the field.

Related occupations

Other workers who record and type information include secretaries, bookkeepers, typists, and administrative assistants.

Methods of entering

High-school guidance counselors and business education teachers may be helpful in locating job opportunities. In addition, business schools and colleges frequently have a placement program to help their trainees and graduates find employment. Those interested in securing an entry-level position can also contact businesses or governmental agencies directly. Jobs may also be located through "help wanted" advertisements.

Many companies have aptitude tests administered to potential employees before they are hired. Employers are interested in the speed and accuracy with which a worker can perform. Some individuals who are initially unable to meet the job requirements may take entry jobs as typists or clerks and, as they gain experience and technical training, may be promoted to the position of stenographer.

Advancement

Skilled stenographers can advance to secretarial positions, especially if they develop their interpersonal communications skills. They may also become heads of stenographic departments or in some cases they may be promoted to the position of office manager. In a few instances, experienced stenographers may go into business for themselves as public stenographers. Those who take the necessary training can become shorthand reporters.

Employment outlook

Job opportunities for stenographers should fall off sharply through the early 1990s, largely because of the use of dictation machines. Despite this decline, some jobs will become available as people retire or otherwise leave the profession. As always, those with the most skill and experience, and those with a particular area of expertise (such as legal or medical stenographers) should have the best employment possibilities.

Earnings

Salaries for stenographers vary widely, depending on skill, experience, level of responsibility, and geographic location. Beginning stenographers with private companies should earn an average of about $18,000 per year in the early 1990s; experienced stenographers should earn about $21,500 annually. Stenographers working for the federal government should average about $14,500 per year to start; those with experience should earn about $17,000 per year.

Full-time workers should also receive paid vacation, health insurance, and other benefits.

Conditions of work

As is the case with most office workers, stenographers work an average thirty-seven to forty-hour week. Relatively few stenographers work in the evenings or on weekends.

The physical work environment is usually well ventilated and well lighted. Although stenographers may sometimes have to work under the pressure of deadlines, the job itself is not hazardous or physically strenuous, and much of it is performed while seated.

The amount of supervision a stenographer receives will depend on the job level, such as junior or senior stenographer, and the nature of the work. Some firms offer more supervision than others.

The majority of stenographers are not required to travel; however, some may accompany their employer on business trips in order to take dictation.

Some stenographers are employed part-time or on a temporary basis during peak business periods.

Social and psychological factors

Stenographers should have an even temperament and the ability to work well with others. They should find systematic and orderly work appealing, and they should like to work on detailed tasks. Other personal qualifications include dependability, trustworthiness, and a neat personal appearance. The advantages of this type of work include regular work hours and no major physical or occupational hazards.

Stenographers and other office personnel may find opportunities to learn more about the business world in general and this experience may open doors for advancement to higher positions in related fields.

GOE: 07.05.03; SIC: Any industry; SOC: 4623

◇ **SOURCES OF ADDITIONAL INFORMATION**

Office and Professional Employees International Union
265 West 14th Street, Suite 610
New York, NY 10011

◇ **RELATED ARTICLES**

Volume 1: See Table of Contents for areas of specific interest
Volume 3: Court reporters; General office clerks; Receptionists; Secretaries; Typists and word processors

Stock clerks

Definition

Stock clerks receive, store, distribute, and record the inventory for materials or products used by a company, institution, or store.

History

Almost every type of business establishment imaginable—shoe store, restaurant, hotel, auto repair shop, hospital, insurance office, supermarket, or steel mill—buys materials or products from outside distributors and uses these materials in its operations. A large part of the company's money is tied up in these inventory stocks, but without them, operations would come to a standstill. Stores would run out of merchandise to sell, mechanics would be unable to repair cars until new parts were shipped in, factories would be unable to operate once their basic supplies of raw material ran out.

To avoid these problems, businesses develop systems to store enough goods and raw materials to ensure smooth operations, to get these materials to the place they are needed, and to know when it is time to order more.

These inventory control systems are the responsibility of stock clerks.

Nature of the work

Stock clerks work in just about every industry, their titles sometimes varying with their responsibilities. No matter what kind of storage or stock room they work in—food, clothing, merchandise, medicine or raw materials—the work of stock clerks is essentially the same. They receive, sort, put away, distribute and keep track of the items a business sells or uses.

When goods are received in the stockroom, stock clerks unpack the shipment and check the contents against documents such as the invoice, purchase order and bill of lading, which lists the contents of the shipment. The shipment is inspected, and any damaged goods are set aside. Stock clerks may reject or send back damaged items, or call distributors to complain about the condition of the shipment. In larger companies, this work may be done by the *shipping and receiving clerk.*

Once the goods are received, stock clerks organize them and sometimes mark them with identifying codes or prices so that they can be placed in storage according to the existing inventory system. In this way, the material or goods can be found quickly and easily when it is needed. Inventory control is also easier to maintain this way. In many firms, stock clerks use hand-held scanners and readers and computers to keep inventory records up to date.

In retail stores and supermarkets, stock clerks may bring merchandise to the sales floor and stock shelves and racks. In stockrooms and warehouses, they store materials according to plan in bins, on the floor, or on shelves. In other settings, such as restaurants, hotels and factories, stock clerks deliver goods when they are needed, usually following a regular schedule or at the request of other employees or supervisors. Although many stock clerks use mechanical equipment such as fork lifts to move heavy items, some may perform strenuous and laborious work. Most stock clerk jobs involve much standing, bending, walking, stretching, lifting and carrying.

When items are removed from the inventory, records must be adjusted to reflect the products' use. These records are constantly kept current, and goods inventories are periodically checked against these records. Every item or material is counted and the totals compared with the records on hand or the records from the sales, shipping, production, or purchasing departments. This will help to identify how fast items are being used, when other items must be ordered from outside suppliers, or even whether items are disappearing from the stockrooms. New types of cash registers are now used in maintaining an inventory count, as they record the sale of each type of item and amount automatically.

The duties of stock clerks often vary depending on the place of employment. Stock clerks working in small firms perform many different tasks, including shipping and receiving, inventory control, and purchasing. In larger firms, responsibilities may be more narrow, and people's work may be more specialized. More specific job categories include *inventory clerks, stock-control clerks, material clerks, merchandise distributors,* and *shipping and receiving clerks.*

At a construction site or factory which uses many types of raw and finished materials when in operation, there are many different types of specialized work for stock clerks. *Tool-crib attendants* receive, store, and issue the various hand tools, machine tools, dies, and other equipment used in an industrial establishment. *Parts-order-and-stock clerks* purchase, store, and distribute the spare parts needed for motor vehicles and other industrial equipment. *Metal-control coordinators* oversee the movement of metal stock and supplies used in producing nonferrous metal sheets, bars, tubing, and alloys. In mining and other industries that regularly use explosives, *magazine keepers* store explosive materials and components safely and distribute them to authorized personnel. In the military, *space-and-storage clerks* keep track of the weights and amounts of ammunition and explosive components stored in the magazines of an arsenal, and check their storage condition.

Many types of stock clerks can be found in other industries. At newspapers, *cut-file clerks* collect, store, and hand out the layout cuts, ads, mats, and electrotypes used in the printing process. *Parts clerks* handle and distribute spare and replacement parts in repair and maintenance shops. In eyeglass centers, *prescription clerks* select the lens blanks and frames for making eyeglasses according to the optometrists' specifications, and keep stock inventory at a preset level. In motion pictures, *property custodians* receive, store, and distribute the props needed for shooting. In hotels and hospitals, *linen-room attendants* issue and keep track of inventories of bed linen, table cloths, and uniforms, while *kitchen clerks* verify the quantity and quality of food products being taken from the storeroom to the kitchen. Aboard ships, the clerk in charge of receiving and issuing supplies and keeping track of inventory is known as the *storekeeper.*

Requirements

Although there are no specific educational requirements for beginning stock clerks, employers prefer to hire high-school graduates. Reading and writing skills and a basic knowledge of mathematics are necessary; typing and filing skills are also useful. Good health is important, especially good eyesight.

Special requirements

Depending on where they work, some stock clerks may be required to join a union. This is especially true of stock clerks who are employed in industry and who work in large cities where the percentage of union membership is high.

When a stock clerk handles certain types of materials, extra training or certification may be required. Generally, those who handle jewelry, liquor, or drugs must be bonded.

Opportunities for experience and exploration

The best way to learn about the responsibilities of a stock clerk is to get a part-time or summer job as a salesclerk, stockroom helper, stockroom clerk or, in some factories, stock chaser. A job like this is relatively easy to get, and it can show a student about stock work as well as the duties of workers in related positions. This sort of part-time work can also lead to a full-time job.

Related occupations

Stock clerks have many of the same interests and aptitudes as other specialized clerks including general office clerks, accounting and bookkeeping clerks, shipping and receiving clerks, file clerks, data entry clerks, and billing clerks.

Methods of entering

Job openings for stock clerks are often listed in the want ads. School counselors, parents, relatives, and friends can also be good sources for job leads, and may also be able to give personal references if an employer requires them. Job

A stock clerk operates an elevation machine so that he can place bulky packages at many levels in the warehouse.

seekers should then contact the personnel office of the firm looking for stock clerks and fill out an application for employment.

Stock clerks usually receive on-the-job training. New workers start with simple tasks such as counting and marking stock. The basic responsibilities of the job are usually learned within the first few weeks. As they progress, stock clerks learn to keep records of incoming and outgoing materials, take inventories, and place orders. As more wholesale and warehousing establishments convert to automated inventory systems, training and retraining on this equipment may take longer. Stock clerks who bring merchandise to the sales floor, stock shelves, and sales racks need little training.

Advancement

Stock clerks with ability and determination have a good chance of being promoted to jobs with greater responsibility. In small firms, stock clerks may advance to sales positions or become assistant buyers or purchasing agents. In large firms, stock clerks can advance to more responsible stock handling jobs such as invoice clerk, stock control clerk, or procurement clerk.

Furthering one's education can lead to more opportunities for advancement. By studying at a technical or business school or taking home-study courses, stock clerks can prove to their employer that they have the intelligence and ambition to take on more important tasks.

More advanced positions, such as warehouse manager or purchasing agent, are usually given to experienced people who continue with their education beyond high school.

Employment outlook

In the early 1990s nearly 2 million people worked as stock clerks. Of these, 60 percent worked as stockroom, warehouse, or yard clerks, while 40 percent worked as sales floor stock clerks. Many sales floor clerks worked part-time. Almost 60 percent of stockroom, warehouse, and yard stock clerks worked in retail and wholesale firms; about 20 percent were in factories; and the remainder worked in hospitals, government agencies, schools, and other organizations. Nearly all sales floor stock clerks were employed in retail establishments, with about two-thirds working in supermarkets.

Although the volume of inventory transactions is expected to increase significantly in the coming years, little change in employment for stock clerks is expected through the early 1990s. This is a result of increased automation and other productivity improvements that will enable clerks to handle more stock. Sales floor stock clerks will probably be less affected by automation because most of their work is done on the sales floor, where it is difficult to locate or operate complicated machinery.

Because this occupation employs a large number of people, many job openings will occur each year to replace stock clerks who transfer to other jobs and leave the labor force. Many stock clerk jobs are entry level, and so the majority of vacancies are created by normal career progression to other occupations.

Earnings

Beginning stock clerks usually earn the minimum wage or slightly more. Experienced stock clerks can earn anywhere from $5 to $10 per hour, with time-and-a-half for overtime. Average earnings will vary with the type of industry and geographic location. Stock clerks working in the retail trade generally earn wages in the middle range. In transportation, utilities, and wholesale businesses, earnings are usually higher; in finance, insurance, real estate and other types of office services, earnings are usually lower.

Stock clerks usually can find steady, year-round work. Those working for large compa-

nies or national chains may receive excellent benefits. After one year of employment, stock clerks are generally given one to two weeks of paid vacations each year, as well as health and medical insurance and retirement plan options, depending on the company.

Conditions

Stock clerks usually work in relatively clean, comfortable, and well lighted areas. Working conditions may vary considerably, however, depending on the industry and the type of merchandise being handled. For example, stock clerks who handle refrigerated goods must spend some time in cold storage rooms; those who handle construction materials such as bricks and lumber may occasionally work outside in harsh weather. Most stock clerk jobs involve much standing, bending, walking, stretching, lifting, and carrying. Some may be required to operate machinery to lift and move stock.

Because stock clerks are employed in so many different types of industries, the amount of hours worked every week depends on the type of employer. Usually, stock clerks in retail stores work a five-day, forty-hour week, while those in industry may work forty-four hours, or five-and-one-half days, a week. Many others are able to find part-time work. Overtime can be common, especially when large shipments arrive or during peak times like the holiday season.

Social and psychological factors

Stock clerks should be alert and careful workers, and they should be able to perform highly detailed work. The operations of their entire company depend on their ability to perform their jobs accurately and quickly.

This may require a good memory if the storage facility is large. The stock clerk may also need counting and inventory skills. Precision work is important, as is efficiency. Because they work constantly with other people, stock clerks should also have strong interpersonal skills and the ability to communicate well. For the ambitious and conscientious person, a position as a stock clerk with a good employer could be the door to many career opportunities.

GOE: 05.09.02; SIC: Any industry; SOC: 4754

◇ **SOURCES OF ADDITIONAL INFORMATION**

Distributive Education Clubs of America
1908 Association Drive
Reston, VA 22091

Food Marketing Institute
1750 K Street, NW
Washington, DC 20006

National Retail Merchants Association
100 West 31st Street
New York, NY 10001

◇ **RELATED ARTICLES**

Volume 1: Construction; Food Service; Retailing; Wholesaling
Volume 2: Buyers, wholesale and retail; Purchasing agents; Retail managers
Volume 3: Billing clerks; Cashiers; Clerical supervisors and managers; Counter and retail clerks; Food service workers; Hotel and motel industry workers; Manufacturers' sales workers; Retail sales workers; Shipping and receiving clerks; Traffic agents and clerks; Wholesale trade sales workers

Switchboard operators

Definition

Switchboard operators work the equipment that handles telephone calls coming in and going out of a corporation or telephone company.

History

In the 115 years since Alexander Graham Bell was granted a patent for his invention, the telephone evolved from being a novelty gadget to an indispensable part of our daily lives. Now it is possible to talk to virtually any corner of the world on the telephone. Technological breakthroughs have allowed us to replace exposed, inefficient telephone cables with fibre optic lines and satellites for transmitting signals. Some phone features that we take for granted, such as conference calls, call waiting, and automatic call forwarding, have only been developed in the past few years. Today, even computers "talk" to one another over the telephone.

Technology has also changed the job of the telephone switchboard operator. In the past, operators had to connect every phone call manually, wrestling with hundreds of different cables and phone jacks and trying to match the person making the call to the number being dialed. Today, however, most telephone switchboards are electronic, and the operator can connect many more calls by merely pushing buttons or dialing the proper code or number. Computers have replaced many of the old duties of switchboard operators, such as directory assistance and "automatic intercept" of non-operating numbers. Still, switchboard operators are needed to keep the machinery working properly and to perform special duties.

Nature of the work

Despite advances in technology, many situations still exist where the assistance of the switchboard operator is needed. When a caller wants to reverse long-distance charges, find a telephone number in another city, or know the cost of completing a call, the operator needs be consulted. Operators also help contact the police or fire department in an emergency, and arrange conference calls for business or professional people.

Two groups of switchboard operators provide these services. The first of these, *central-office operators*, work for the telephone company. They help customers with calls that require assistance, such as person-to-person calls, collect calls, overseas calls, and special request calls from public pay phones. When a call comes into the phone company, a signal lights up on the switchboard, and the central-office operator makes the connection for it by pressing the proper pushbuttons, dialing the proper numbers or, in some older systems, plugging

Switchboard operators must have a pleasant demeanor when answering telephones.

the phone cord into the proper jack on the switchboard console. The operator obtains the information needed to complete the call and records the details for billing. The operator may consult charts to determine the charges for pay phone calls and ask the caller to deposit the correct amount to complete the call. If the customer requests a long-distance connection, the operator will calculate and quote the charges and then make the connection.

Directory assistance operators answer customer inquiries for local telephone numbers by using computerized alphabetical and geographical directories. The directory assistance operator will type the spelling of the name requested and the possible location on a keyboard, then scan a directory or microfilm viewer to find the number. If the number can't be found, the operator may suggest alternate spellings of the name and look for those. When the name is located, the operator often doesn't need to read the number. Instead, a computerized recording will provide the answer while the operator handles another call.

The other group of switchboard operators are in charge of directing the internal and incoming calls of an individual company or corporation. These *telephone operators* are often called *PBX operators*, which stands for "private branch exchange" operator. They connect interoffice or house calls, answer and relay outside calls, assist company employees in making outside calls, supply information to callers, and

record messages for employees. The equipment they operate is very much like that of central-office operators, although new systems for the most part make electronic, not manual, connections. When not handling calls, these switchboard operators may perform other office tasks, such as typing, sorting mail and receiving visitors.

There are many other specialized types of switchboard operators. *Police district switchboard operators* run switchboards to receive and transmit police communications, such as calls from citizens for assistance or from police officers in the field. They may also make calls for ambulances or fire-fighting equipment.

Communication-center operators handle airport communication systems, such as public address paging systems, telephone switchboards, courtesy telephones, and internal radio systems between divisions of the airport. They also monitor electronic alarm systems that will detect any serious malfunctions in equipment such as elevators, fire alarm systems, emergency doors, and heating and ventilation systems.

Telephone-answering-service operators manage the switchboards to provide answering services to clients who at times cannot be reached by phone. They record and deliver messages, furnish information, accept phone orders, and relay calls. They may also place phone calls at the client's request or locate the client in case of emergencies.

Other types of switchboard supervisors perform advisory services for clients to show them how to get the most out of their phone system. *Private-branch-exchange advisers* conduct training classes to demonstrate the operation of switchboard and teletype equipment, either at the telephone company's training school or on the customer's premises. They may analyze a company's telephone traffic loads and recommend the type of equipment and services that best fit the company's needs. *Service observers* monitor the telephone conversations between central-office operators and customers to observe the operators' behavior, technical skills, and adherence to phone company policies. Both of these types of workers may give advice on how operators can improve their handling of calls and their personal demeanor on the phone.

Requirements

Some employers require a high-school diploma for switchboard operators, although most training takes place on the job. Prospective operators should have good reading, spelling, and arithmetic skills. In addition, a clear, pleasant speaking voice and good hearing are important. High-school courses in speech, office practices, and business math provide a solid background for persons interested in this occupation.

People may also find it useful to enroll in courses at a business or professional college. Such colleges usually have placement offices that can be helpful in finding jobs. Taking extra classes, such as word processing or data entry, might make a person more attractive to a potential employer.

Special requirements

Other skills that are useful for switchboard operators include good hand-eye coordination and manual dexterity. The ability to work well under pressure is also a plus, because work environments can become stressful at peak times. Many telephone companies and business firms require operators to pass a physical examination.

Switchboard operators do not need to be licensed. Many operators, however, belong to the unions that represent the other workers at their company. The Communications Workers of America and the International Brotherhood of Electrical Workers are two unions that have switchboard operators from both private corporations and phone companies as members.

Opportunities for experience and exploration

Students who wish to learn more about the job of a switchboard operator should look for part-time or summer jobs with companies that need receptionists and switchboard operators. Many for-profit and nonprofit companies have openings for office help where employees can learn to operate advanced phone systems. These part-time positions could also lead to full-time employment.

Related occupations

The variety and scope of occupations available in the telecommunications industry is enormous. Some other jobs that might be of interest include systems analysts, computer program-

mers, telephone and PBX installers and repairers, line installers and cable splicers, and electrical repairers.

Methods of entering

Job openings for switchboard operators can be found in "want ads," through private or public employment agencies, through school placement offices, and through relatives and friends who know about firms that are hiring. To begin work as a switchboard operator, a person should first contact the place where he or she would like to be employed and make an appointment with the personnel office. After filling out a job application, a person usually goes through an interview and may have to take a written test.

Once a new operator manages to land a job, he or she is taught how to use the equipment and keep records of calls. Once the trainee has learned the procedure, he or she will put through practice calls. In the telephone companies, classroom instruction usually lasts up to three weeks and is followed by on-the-job training. Classroom instruction covers the times zones and geography so that central-office operators can understand rates and know where major cities are located. Tapes are used to familiarize trainees with the various signals and tones of the phone system, and to give them the chance to hear their own phone voices and improve their diction and courtesy. Close supervision continues after training is completed.

PBX operators who handle routine calls usually have a shorter training period than telephone company operators. These workers are usually trained informally by experienced personnel, although in large businesses an instructor from the local telephone company may train new employees.

Advancement

After gaining one or two years of experience, central office operators may be promoted to junior service assistant, service observer, supervisor or PBX service advisor. Some people even move to craft jobs such as telephone installer or repairer. Large private companies may advance their switchboard operators to more responsible clerical positions, if they have the necessary office skills. Some companies may offer tuition reimbursement plans that allow employees like switchboard operators to take classes and gain the skills necessary for jobs with higher pay and more responsibility. Many small businesses, however, may have limited advancement opportunities.

Employment outlook

Government figures show that switchboard operators held more than 353,000 jobs in the early 1990s. More than half of these worked as PBX operators in manufacturing plants, hospitals, businesses, and department stores, while the remainder were employed by various phone companies. Roughly 20 percent of all operators worked part-time, although relatively few of those employed by telephone companies were part-time workers.

Through the early 1990s, employment of switchboard operators is expected to grow faster than the average for all occupations. Employment growth, however, will vary among the different types of operators. Employment of PBX operators is expected to grow at a rate equal to that of all occupations, as businesses expand to meet the changing needs of their customers.

Switchboard operator/receptionists have the greatest prospects for growth because their flexibility and multiple job skills appeal to employers. Handling incoming calls and visitors to a company combined two jobs for one employee.

On the other hand, employment prospects for telephone company operators are poor. Employment of these workers has been declining for the past twenty-five years, as automation and technological advances improve productivity and reduce the requirements of human labor. This trend is expected to continue. As new equipment replaces the need for human workers, however, unions have tried to make sure that companies reduce employment either through attrition or through the retraining and reassignment of workers.

Telephone use is expected to grow in the coming years, as the number of households continues to grow and as more uses are found for phone transmissions in business and industry. Any anticipated labor growth, however, will be offset by improvements and innovations in technology. New developments such as electronic switching, computerized billing, direct dialing, and voice recognition technology, combined with cost-cutting measures and increased productivity programs, will keep a downward pressure on the growth of switchboard operator jobs with the nation's phone companies.

Earnings

In the early 1990s, switchboard operators earned a median annual salary of $16,400, with the middle 50 percent of all operators earning between $11,600 and $22,000. The top ten percent of all operators earned upwards of $24,400 a year. According to a survey by the Administrative Management Society, PBX operators nationwide earned an average annual salary of $13,364.

Telephone company operators generally earn more than PBX operators. Telephone operators employed by AT&T and the various Bell Operating Companies, who are represented by the Communications Workers of America, earned an average annual salary of more than $22,500 in the early 1990s.

Insurance, pensions, holidays, vacations, and other benefits for PBX operators are the same as those for other clerical employees of a firm. Operators belonging to unions are given generous vacation plans, as well as overtime pay for work beyond the length of a normal workday or workweek, as well as Sundays and holidays. Additional provisions include paid sick leave; group life, medical and dental insurance; sickness and accident benefits; retirement and disability pensions; savings plans; and employee stock ownership plans.

Conditions

Switchboard operators generally work in bright, pleasant, air-conditioned surroundings. For most of their work, they must sit at their work station, and they need permission from supervisors to leave their desks. Many telephone company operators work at video display terminals, which may cause eyestrain and muscle strain if not properly designed.

The work of a switchboard operator can be very repetitive and, in telephone companies, is closely supervised. There are many times when the atmosphere may become stressful and hectic, especially at peak calling times and during drives to increase efficiency. Switchboard operators, however, must strive at all times to be pleasant and helpful with the public, both callers and people that are visiting the company.

Telephone company operators generally work thirty-two-and-one-half to thirty-seven-and-one-half-hours per week. Switchboard operators who work for private businesses generally have the same hours as other clerical workers. In telephone companies, however, as well as in hotels, hospitals and other places where phone service is needed on a twenty-four-hour basis, operators work in shifts, even on holidays and weekends. Some operators work split shifts, handling the switchboards during the peak calling times in the late morning and early evening and taking time off in between. The assignment of shifts is usually determined by seniority.

Social and psychological factors

Switchboard operators should enjoy dealing with the public and be able to listen carefully to what they need. Of course, they should also enjoy spending long periods of time talking on the phone. Operators for private businesses are expected to project a positive image for their company, so they must be helpful, competent, and courteous at all times with all callers and visitors. Telephone company operators must also be helpful and competent, as their supervisors occasionally monitor their work on the phone. Switchboard operators need to be dependable and punctual. They should also be able to withstand the tedium that the job entails, and stay ready to respond to emergencies whenever they arise.

GOE: 07.04.06; SIC: Any industry; SOC: 6932

◇ SOURCES OF ADDITIONAL INFORMATION

Communications Workers of America
1925 K Street, NW
Washington, DC 20006

International Brotherhood of Electrical Workers
1125 15th Street, NW
Washington, DC 20005

International PBX/Telecommunicators
c/o Judy Kay Roberts
151 White Cedar Drive
Houston, TX 77015

National Association of Temporary Services
119 South St. Asaph Street
Alexandria, VA 22314

United States Telephone Association
900 19th Street, NW
Suite 800
Washington, DC 20006

United Telegraph Workers
20525 Center Ridge Road
Suite 420
Cleveland, OH 44116

◇ RELATED ARTICLES

Volume 1: Telecommunications
Volume 3: General office clerks; Line installers and cable splicers; Receptionists; Reservation and transportation ticket agents; Secretaries; Splicers; Telephone and PBX installers and repairers; Telephone operators

Tax preparers

Definition

Tax preparers prepare the income tax returns for individuals and small businesses for a fee, either for quarterly or yearly filings. They assist in establishing and maintaining business files and records to expedite tax preparations. They may also provide guidance for methods to increase future savings from tax payments.

History

Franklin D. Roosevelt once said, "Taxes are the dues that we pay for the privileges of membership in an organized society." It is sometimes difficult, however, for taxpayers to keep such high-minded views, especially around the time that taxes are due. The one thing people might like even less than paying taxes is filling out tax forms. But because everyone carries the burden of taxation, it is still possible to keep a sense of humor about income taxes. As Benjamin Franklin succinctly put it, "In this world nothing can be said to be certain, except death and taxes."

While the personal income tax may be the most familiar type of taxation, it is actually a relatively recent method for raising revenue. To raise funds for the Napoleonic Wars between 1799 and 1816, Britain became the first nation to collect income taxes, but a permanent income tax was not established there until 1874. In the same manner, the United States first imposed a temporary income tax during the Civil War. It wasn't until 1913, however, with the adoption of the 16th Amendment to the Constitution, that a tax on personal income became the law of the nation. In addition to the federal income tax, many states and cities have adopted income tax laws since 1919. Income taxes are an example of a "progressive tax," one that charges higher percentages of income as people earn more money.

Nature of the work

Tax preparers help individual taxpayers and small businesses keep the proper records and file the proper forms to pay their legally required tax. Tax preparers may work for tax service firms, such as H & R Block and other firms that advertise heavily in the weeks prior to April 15. Other tax preparers may be self-employed, working full-time or part-time to earn extra money. However they are employed, tax preparers must be well acquainted with federal, state, and local tax laws, and use their knowledge and skills to help taxpayers take the maximum number of legally allowable deductions and pay the minimum amount of tax they owe.

The first step in preparing tax forms is to collect all the data and documents that will be needed to calculate the client's tax liability. The client may have to hand over such documents as tax returns from previous years, wage and income statements from employers, records of other sources of income, statements of interest and dividends earned, records of expenses, property tax records, and so on. The tax preparer then interviews the client for further information that may have a bearing on the amount of taxes owed. If the client is an individual, the tax preparer will ask about any important investments, extra expenses that may be deductible, contributions to charity, insurance payments and other information. If the cli-

ent is a business, the tax preparer may have to find out about capital gains and losses, taxes already paid, payroll expenses, and miscellaneous business expenses, and tax credits.

Once the tax preparer has a complete picture of the income and expenses a client has experienced in the past year, he or she identifies which tax forms and schedules will be needed to file the tax return properly. While some taxpayers have very complex income and expenses that take a long time to document and calculate, other individuals have typical, straightforward returns that take less time. The tax preparer often can calculate the amount a taxpayer owes during a single interview, filling out the proper forms, and preparing the complete return right then. At other times, when the return will be more complicated, the tax preparer may have to collect all the data at the interview and perform the mathematical calculations later. If a client's taxes are unusual or very complex, there are many tax law handbooks and bulletins that a tax preparer may consult.

Calculators and computers are used in the preparation of tax returns. If the tax preparer uses a calculator, he or she will write the figures on the tax form directly. If a computer is used, the tax preparer will type in the necessary information on a preset grid or work sheet, then make the calculations or allow the computer program to make them, and print out the final tax form with all the proper information. New computer programs can be very versatile, and may even print up data summary sheets for the tax preparer and the client that can serve as checklists and references for the next tax filing.

Tax preparers very often have another tax expert or preparer check their work. This is especially true if the preparer works for a tax service firm. The second tax preparer will check to make sure the allowances and deductions taken were all proper, and that no others were overlooked. They also make certain that the tax laws were interpreted properly and that calculations were correct. It is very important that a tax preparer's work is free of errors. Tax preparers are required by law to sign every return they complete for a client, along with providing their social security number or federal identification number. They must also provide the client with a copy of the tax return and keep a copy in their own personal files.

Federal taxes in the United States are collected yearly, usually on April 15, for those filing against withheld taxes from paychecks. Others, such as the self-employed, as required by law to file every three months.

Requirements

A high-school diploma is a basic necessity for tax preparers. Useful courses for students interested in tax work include business, accounting, mathematics, communications, and psychology. Students can also gain an advantage by learning how to use computers early. While employers do not always require computer knowledge of tax preparers, and while computers cannot replace human judgment and understanding of basic tax laws, computers can save much time and effort in calculations and record keeping.

For those students who wish to go on to college, many colleges and universities now offer courses and complete majors in the area of taxation. Students might elect to earn a bachelor's degree or a master's degree in business administration while earning a minor in taxation. Some universities offer a master's degree in taxation.

In addition to formal education, tax preparers are responsible for continuing professional education. Both federal and state tax laws are revised every year, and the tax preparer has a duty to know these new laws thoroughly by January 1 of each year. This can mean up to sixty hours of extra study in a single month. Major tax reform legislation can increase this amount of study even further. A federal tax reform bill can total more than 3,000 pages, and the tax preparer needs to know all the intricacies and implications of the new laws. To help tax preparers keep up with new developments, the National Association of Tax Practitioners offers some 130 continuing education classes every year. Tax service firms also offer classes that explain tax preparation both for professionals and for individual taxpayers.

Special requirements

Few licensing requirements exist for tax preparers in the United States. Since 1983, tax preparers in California have been required to register with the state Department of Consumers. Tax preparers who apply for registration there must be at least eighteen years old and have a high-school diploma or the equivalent. In addition, they need to have undergone sixty hours of formal, approved instruction in basic income tax law, theory, and practice, or two years of professional experience in preparing personal income tax returns.

The Internal Revenue Service offers an examination for tax preparers. Those who complete the test successfully are called *enrolled*

A tax preparer reviews a completed tax form with her client. With the client's approval, the tax form can then be mailed to the government.

agents, and are entitled to represent any taxpayer in any type of audit before the IRS or a state tax board. (Those with five years' experience working for the IRS as an auditor or in a higher position can become enrolled agents without taking the test.) The test, which is in four parts, is offered annually and takes two days to complete. There are no education or experience requirements for taking this examination, but the questions it contains are roughly equivalent to those asked in a college course. Study materials for the exam and applications may be obtained from local IRS offices.

Opportunities for experience and exploration

If a career in tax preparation sounds interesting, students should first gain some experience by completing income tax returns for themselves and, if possible, for their families and friends. Of course, these returns should be double-checked by the actual taxpayers, because they will be liable for any fees and extra taxes that may need to be paid if the return is prepared incorrectly. Students might also look for internships or part-time jobs in the offices of tax service and tax preparation firms. Many of these firms exist around the country, and extra office help might be needed as tax deadlines approach and the office becomes hectic.

The IRS also trains people to answer tax questions for an 800-number telephone service. These people are employed during the early spring of each year.

Methods of entering

Want ads in the newspaper and school guidance offices are two good places for students to look for openings with tax service firms. Private and state employment agencies may also have information and job listings. Because tax work is very seasonal, most tax firms begin hiring tax preparers in December for the upcoming tax season. Some tax service firms will hire tax preparers from among the graduates of their own training courses.

For those who want to open their own tax service business, either part-time or full-time, an interview with another self-employed tax preparer is essential. These practitioners will have invaluable knowledge and experience to draw from, and can offer advice on how to get a private practice started and what dangers to avoid. This is normally advised only for tax preparers with some experiencing though.

Advancement

One path to advancement for experienced tax preparers is to open their own businesses. Some tax preparers may wish to continue their professional education and work toward becoming certified public accountants. Others may want to specialize in certain areas of taxation, such as real estate taxation, corporate taxation, or taxes for nonprofit organizations. Tax preparers who specialize in certain fields are able to charge higher fees for their services. (*See* Volume 2: Accountants and auditors, for further information on certification.)

Employment outlook

Because tax laws grow more complex every year and are constantly changing, the demand for services of tax preparers and other tax professionals is high. Many people are taking even the simplest tax forms to tax preparers because of the frustration and time required to complete them. The increased demand, however, is expected to be met by the tax preparers already working, because of the increasing use of computers for tabulating data and storing records. Recent surveys of employers in large metropolitan areas have found that there is an adequate supply of tax preparers already available. In less populated areas, the prospects for employment may be better.

Earnings

Tax preparers generally charge a fee per tax return, which may range from $50 to $200, depending on the complexity of the return and the preparation time required. Fees vary widely in different parts of the country, however. Tax preparers in large cities and in the western U.S. generally charge more. Higher fees can usually be charged by tax preparers who offer year-round financial advice and services. Another factor in setting fees is the amount of time spent studying new tax laws and keeping up with new developments.

Conditions

For the most part, tax preparers work in comfortable, efficient, well-lighted areas. Those who work for tax service firms may work at storefront desks or in cubicles during the three months preceding April 15. Tax preparation offices are located in many different areas, from downtown offices to neighborhood shopping malls. In addition, many tax preparers work at home to earn extra money while they hold a full-time job.

The hours and schedules that tax preparers work vary greatly, depending on the time of year and the manner in which they are employed. The three months before April 15 are the busiest time, and even part-time tax preparers may find themselves working very long hours. Workweeks can range from as little as twelve hours to forty or fifty or more, as tax preparers work late into the evening and on weekends. Tax service firms are usually open seven days a week and twelve hours a day during the first three months of the year. Because of the changes in tax laws that occur every year, tax preparers often advise their clients throughout the year about possible ways to reduce their tax obligations, such as investing in tax shelters and contributions to IRAs.

Social and psychological factors

Tax preparers carry great responsibility. Their clients expect them to know all the ins and outs of the tax laws and ways to take advantage of tax loopholes. Pressures can mount as the tax deadline approaches, but tax preparers must do a complete and honest job when preparing each client's tax return. In addition to possible fines or loss of customers, their professional reputation is on the line if any errors are made.

At the same time, tax preparers can earn a great deal of satisfaction from their work. Easing people's concerns about taxes and finding ways that they can save money can bring a great deal of pleasure. People who like to work independently and set their own hours will enjoy being self-employed. Tax preparers should like dealing with people and be skillful in setting their clients at ease during interviews. Tax preparers also have many opportunities to meet other people in the tax field by attending seminars, courses and meetings of professional societies.

GOE: 07.02.04; SIC: 7291; SOC: None

◇ **SOURCES OF ADDITIONAL INFORMATION**

National Association of Tax Practitioners
1015 West Wisconsin Avenue
Kaukauna, WI 54130

National Association of Tax Consultors
454 North 13th Street
San Jose, CA 95112

American Institute of Certified Public Accountants
1211 Avenue of the Americas
New York, NY 10036

◇ **RELATED ARTICLES**

Volume 1: Accounting; Banking and Financial Services; Insurance
Volume 2: Accountants and auditors; Actuaries; Assessors and appraisers; Credit analysts, banking; Insurance claims representatives; Underwriters
Volume 3: Bookkeeping and accounting clerks; Insurance policy processing occupations; Insurance agents and brokers, life; Insurance agents and brokers, property and casualty

Teacher aides

Definition

By taking care of some of the more routine tasks involved in education, *teacher aides* free teachers' time so they can spend more of it teaching. Teacher aides prepare some instructional materials, help students with classroom work, and supervise students in school areas other than the classroom. Some aides prepare administrative paperwork, grade tests, and operate audiovisual teaching equipment. In some school districts teacher aides also help teach academic and vocational subjects.

History

Elementary education began as early as 100 A.D. when the people of Judah set up schools within their synagogues to contribute to the religious training of young children. Secondary education probably began in ancient Greece. From that time until the eighteenth century, in both

Europe and America, formal secondary education existed mainly to train clergy and was reserved for the wealthy. Benjamin Franklin pioneered the idea of broader secondary education with the creation of the academy, which offered a flexible curriculum and a wide variety of academic subjects.

Not until the nineteenth century, however, did children of other than wealthy parents commonly attend school into the secondary grades, and not until the twentieth century was secondary school attendance made mandatory in the United States. In addition, until the nineteenth century in the United States, teachers were rarely required to have been educated beyond the highest grade level at which they taught. In 1823, after people began to believe that teachers should have further education to prepare them for teaching children, the first post-secondary school for teachers opened in Vermont.

While teachers throughout history may have had helpers, it is reasonable to assume that the teacher aide as we know it today began

Teachers aides gain valuable experience when assisting young students in a classroom. Many of their tasks involve giving individual students special attention that the teacher has no time to give.

to be necessary in the twentieth century, as more and more students attended school and as teachers began to be required to have specialized training. As formal elementary and secondary education became more widely available, teachers' jobs became more complex. Teachers began to be required to teach more students in each class. An increasingly bureaucratic society demanded that more records be kept of students' achievements and teachers' activities. Advancements in technology, changes in teaching theory, and a great increase in the amount and variety of teaching materials available all contributed to making the job of preparing to teach and assessing the results of teaching more time-consuming—leaving teachers less and less time for the teaching they had been trained for.

Possibly to remedy this problem, teacher aids began to be employed to take care of the more routine aspects of running an instructional program—aspects that did not require a teacher's special skills. Because teacher aides command lower salaries than teachers, school districts may have seen the hiring of teacher aides as a way to increase the amount taught in schools without having to hire more teachers. Today, many school districts employ teacher aides, to the great benefit of hard-working teachers and of students in large classrooms where personal attention can otherwise be very limited.

Nature of the work

Teacher aides work in both public and private elementary and secondary schools. Depending on the school district in which they work, they may perform a variety of administrative, clerical, and instructional duties. Teacher aides often take attendance in classrooms and distribute materials such as books, handouts, and writing supplies. They may keep health records on students. Teacher aides often set up and operate equipment such as slide and film projectors, and may help teachers by typing, filing, and duplicating records and teaching materials. Sometimes teacher aides prepare requisition forms to obtain supplies or library materials for classroom use. Many teacher aides are in charge of keeping order in classrooms, school cafeterias, libraries, hallways, and playgrounds. They may help make sure students get on the correct school bus.

Another responsibility of the teacher aide is correcting and grading homework and tests, usually for "objective" work—that is, assignments and tests that require definite right answers. Teacher aides often use answer sheets to mark students' papers and examinations and keep records of the scores students receive. In some schools, especially large ones and colleges or universities, an aide may be called a *grading clerk* and be responsible only for scoring objective tests and computing and recording test scores. Often using an electronic grading machine or computer, the grading clerk totals errors found and computes the percentage of questions answered correctly. The worker then records this grade and averages students' test grades to determine their grade for the course.

Some school districts, however, use teacher aides to help with actual classroom teaching. After consultation with the teacher, a teacher aide prepares a lesson plan and develops such teaching aids as bibliographies, charts, and maps. Through lecture, group discussion, and other techniques, a teacher aide presents subject matter. Aides may give students assignments, listen to elementary children read in small groups, or take charge of special projects such as science fairs. They may even participate in parent–teacher conferences to discuss students' progress. These teacher aides work under the direct supervision and guidance of certified teachers. They may or may not specialize in one subject area.

Some teacher aides help teachers who work with mentally, physically, or emotionally handicapped children. They conduct the same type of work in the classroom that other teacher aides do.

Requirements

Requirements for teacher aides depend on the school district and the kinds of responsibilities the aide will have. In districts where aides perform mostly clerical duties, applicants may not need to have finished high school. Aides usually receive training on the job, and newly hired aides also participate in orientation sessions and formal training. In these sessions, aides learn about the school's organization and operation. They also learn how to prepare instructional materials such as charts and bulletin boards, and how to keep records, operate audiovisual equipment, and administer first aid.

In districts that give aides teaching responsibilities, aides usually need more training, often including some college work. A number of junior and community colleges offer associate degree programs that prepare teacher aides.

Many schools prefer to hire teacher aides who have some form of experience in working with children; others prefer to hire workers who live within the school district. Teacher aide applicants may be required to pass a physical examination.

All teacher aides must be able to work and communicate effectively with both children and adults, and should have good verbal and written skills.

Special requirements

According to the U.S. Department of Labor, ten states certify teacher aides. Some require a high-school diploma or general equivalency degree (GED), while others require some college training. Aides working in special education need paraprofessional permits in Kansas, Louisiana, Texas, and Wisconsin.

Opportunities for experience and exploration

High-school students who wish to become teacher aides may obtain experience in working with children by volunteering to help with religious education classes at their church, synagogue, or other place of worship. They may volunteer to help with scouting troops or work as counselors or helpers at summer camps. College students may obtain work experience by working in a college-related—or laboratory—school where aspiring teacher aides can help with real classes while earning course credit.

Related occupations

Careers in education are many and diverse. These can include preschool teacher, day-school owner or teacher, kindergarten teacher, dean, university and college faculty member, high-school teacher, elementary school teacher, counselors, librarians, and principals.

Methods of entering

Once they have fulfilled any certification requirements, most workers apply directly to school district superintendents for teacher aide positions. Students in college-level programs may contact their school placement offices for information about openings. Newspapers may advertise openings in the want-ads section.

Advancement

Teacher aides usually advance only in terms of increases in salary or responsibility, which come with experience. Aides in some districts may receive time off to take college courses. If they earn bachelor's degrees they may become certified teachers.

Employment outlook

About 650,000 people worked as teacher aides in the early 1990s. Most aides work in elementary and secondary schools throughout the country with most in the lower grades.

Growth in this occupation should be about as fast as average through the late 1990s, because of the expected increase in elementary school enrollments. Enrollment increases and thus opportunities for teacher aides are likely to be greater in the South and West than in the Northeast and North Central states. Most openings will be for workers to replace aides who leave the work force or change careers. The field has a very high turnover rate.

Positions for aides, however, are highly dependent on the economy and the budgets of states, municipalities, and the federal government. When governments are forced to cut education expenditures, teacher aides may be among the first to be laid off.

Earnings

Earnings also vary with location, responsibility, and the aide's academic qualifications. Teacher aides performing nonteaching activities earn an average of about $6.50 an hour. Aides involved in teaching earned about $7.00 an hour on the average. Many aides work part-time. Many have health and pension benefits similar to those of teachers in their school districts, and many are covered under collective bargaining agreements.

Conditions of work

Teacher aides generally work in pleasant surroundings. Newer schools tend to be clean, well lighted, and well heated. Some have air conditioning. Some older schools may not be as comfortable—they may need painting or have unpredictable heating systems. Teacher aides may work outdoors when weather permits. Those in elementary schools may spend some time kneeling, while all aides may do a great deal of standing and walking. Although such a job is usually not physically strenuous, working closely with children can be stressful and fatiguing. Because schools close in the summer months, most aides work about ten months out of the year. Aides are not paid during the vacation period.

Social and psychological factors

Above all, teacher aides must enjoy working with children, and be able to handle their de-mands, problems, and questions with patience and fairness. A teacher aide must be willing and able to follow instructions, but should also be able to take the initiative in projects. Flexibility, creativity, and a cheerful outlook on life are definite assets when working with children. A career as a teacher aide can be very compatible with home and family responsibilities, or in combination with part-time or freelance work.

GOE: 07.01.02, 11.02.01; SIC: 8211; SOC: 399, 4795

◇ **SOURCES OF ADDITIONAL INFORMATION**

American Federation of Teachers
555 New Jersey Avenue, NW
Washington, DC 20001

◇ **RELATED ARTICLES**

Volume 1: Education
Volume 2: Recreation workers; School administrators; Teachers, kindergarten and elementary school; Teachers, preschool; Teachers, secondary school
Volume 3: Child care workers; Nannies

Telemarketers

Definition

Telemarketers, or *telephone solicitors,* make and receive phone calls for a company to sell its goods, market its services, gather information, receive orders and complaints, and handle other miscellaneous business. They may work directly for one company, for several companies who use the same service, or for a telemarketing firm.

History

It is not an exaggeration to say that the telephone has become an indispensable part of our daily lives. The speed of communicating by phone and the ability to reach the exact person we want to speak with have drastically changed the way business is conducted over the past one hundred years. This applies to all the areas of business—investing, growing, buying, and selling.

Business activities and theories of business practice have also developed over the past century, to the point where business administration is now a serious academic pursuit. One area of business that has developed and continues to grow is marketing, which involves finding the most likely customers for a product or service and then targeting that customer for sales and other business activity. Marketing has boomed in the years since World War II and continues to grow as companies look for ways to expand their customer base. One of the most important activities in marketing is telemarketing, or the use of phone calls to find out more about potential customers, to stay in touch with current customers, and to keep consumers informed of the advantages of a particular product or service.

Nature of the work

Telemarketers generally work for two different types of businesses. Some telemarketers are part of the in-house staff of a company or corporation, and all their calls are made or taken on behalf of that company. Others work for telemarketing service agencies and make or receive their calls for the clients of the agency. Agencies are useful for companies that don't want to or can't keep a full-time telemarketing staff on the payroll, or that need telemarketing services only intermittently. Both large corporations and small firms employ telemarketing agencies, which sometimes specialize in certain fields such as fundraising, product sales, insurance, or finance.

Whether working for a company or a telemarketing agency, telemarketers are responsible for handling incoming calls and placing calls to outside numbers. Incoming calls might include requests for information or an order for a product that has been advertised on television, through direct mail marketing or in catalogs. Telemarketers also staff the phones that handle toll-free, "800" numbers, on which customers can ask questions about the use of a product or make complaints. Airline reservations, concert and sports tickets, and credit card problems can all be taken care of by telemarketers. Newspapers often employ *classified ad clerks* to transcribe classified ads from callers. A person whose sole job is taking orders from callers over the phone is called an *order clerk*.

Telemarketers make outside calls for a great number of purposes as well. One of their most important jobs is to sell products and services to consumers. The names of the people they call may come from a prepared list of previous customers, the phone book, reply cards from magazines, a list purchased from another source, or randomly dialed "cold calls." Once made, these calls often serve as a source of leads for the regular sales staff of a company. A wide range of products can be successfully sold in this way, everything from newspaper subscriptions and aluminum siding to charity fund drive contributions.

Cultural organization such as ballet and opera companies, public television, and theater companies use telemarketers to solicit subscriptions and to get donations. Fundraising relies heavily on telemarketing.

Telemarketers place outbound calls for other reasons besides selling. They may conduct marketing surveys among consumers to find out the reasons behind their buying habits, or what they like and dislike about a certain product. They may call to endorse a candidate in an upcoming election or to tell citizens about an important vote in their city council. When making calls business-to-business, telemarketers may try to solicit attendance at important meetings, assist a company in recruiting and job placement, or collect demographic information for use in an advertising campaign.

Once the sale is made, the telemarketer will enter it into a computer or fill out a form, so that order fillers can get the product ready for shipment. When making outbound calls, telemarketers usually work from a prepared script whose words they are not allowed to change. This is especially true of market research surveys, because people need to be asked and need to respond to the exact same questions if the data from the survey is to be valid at all. Often when a customer tries to object to or turn down a sales pitch, the telemarketer will read a standard response that has been prepared to anticipate the customer's objections. At other times, the telemarketer must rely on persuasive sales skills and quick thinking to win over the customer and make the sale. Telemarketers have to be a little more skillful when selling business-to-business, because the customer usually has a very clear idea of the needs of his or her business and will ask very pertinent questions.

Many federal, state, and local laws govern the sort of language and sales tactics that can be used in phone soliciting. These are intended to protect consumers from unscrupulous telemarketers operating phone scams. Telemarketers should be aware of the letter and intent of these laws and conduct their phone sales in an honest and unambiguous manner.

A telemarketer solicits magazine subscriptions over the phone. Much of the work is done in the evenings when more potential buyers are at home.

Requirements

The type of skills and education a person needs to become a telemarketer depends in part on the firm for which they are trying to work. A high-school diploma is usually required for any type of position, while some employers only hire people who have earned college degrees. If the phone calls will involve a complex product, as is the case in many business-to-business calls, people trained in that field may be hired and then instructed in telephone and sales techniques.

Because they must be able to talk persuasively and listen to customers carefully, telemarketers will find classes in communications, speech, drama, and broadcasting particularly useful. Business and sales classes, as well as psychology and sociology, are also valuable.

Special requirements

Several professional organizations exist to further the cause of ethical and effective telemarketing. Two of the biggest are the American Telemarketing Association and the Direct Marketing Association, which have chapters in most large cities. Membership in these societies is entirely voluntary, however, and the groups usually recruit telemarketing agencies and firms rather than individuals. The ATA offers many educational programs that help people improve their telemarketing skills.

While some states are considering guidelines or legislation to regulate the activities of telemarketers, California is the only state to actually have done so. Certain types of telemarketing agencies must register with the State of California annually, although most business-to-business telemarketing is exempted because sales are usually not the main goal.

Opportunities for experience and exploration

There are many ways for people to gain practice and poise in telemarketing. Many organizations use volunteer phone workers during campaigns and fund drives. One of the most visible of these is public television stations, which conduct fundraising drives several times a year and are always looking for volunteer help to staff the phone banks. Other groups that routinely need volunteer telemarketers include local political campaigns, churches, schools and nonprofit social organizations such as crisis centers and inner-city recreation programs.

Related occupations

Telemarketing combines sales work with telephone skills. Other similar occupations include telephone operators, switchboard operators, retail sales workers, wholesale trade sales workers, door-to-door sales workers, manufacturers' sales workers, and route drivers.

Methods of entering

Agencies that hire telemarketers usually advertise for new employees in the classified section of the newspaper. Another possible source of job leads is temporary employment agencies, many of which specialize in placing telemarketers with firms. A person who wishes to become an in-house telemarketer for a specific firm should call or write to the personnel office of that firm to find out about job openings. Employers make it a practice at some point to interview job applicants over the phone, judging a person's telephone voice, personality, demeanor, and assertiveness.

Once hired, the employee goes through a great deal of on-the-job training. Trainers instruct the novice telemarketers on the use of equipment, the characteristics of the product or service that they will be selling, and proper sales techniques and listening skills. They rehearse the trainees on the script that has been prepared and guide them through some practice calls.

Advancement

People who are successful as telemarketers will find that many different opportunities for advancement can arise. Telemarketing is a rapidly growing field, with many new developments still ahead. A telemarketer learns quite a lot about products and services while on the job, so one path to advancement might be moving into a job in advertising or marketing, or as a sales representative for those products and services.

Within telemarketing agencies, employees may advance to jobs as assistant managers, managers, and supervisors. Salaries can increase rapidly, because sometimes managers and supervisors earn a commission on the net sales rung up by the agency. Other telemarketers may move into telephone sales training, either with an agency or as an independent consultant. Very often, experienced telemarketers can find new jobs with higher-paying firms, or even start their own telemarketing agency.

Employment outlook

Because of the phenomenal growth of the telemarketing industry, job prospects for telemarketers are excellent in the early 1990s. People who are already involved in the telemarketing industry believe that it is a field with an unlimited future because of advances in telephone technology and, more importantly, the cost effectiveness of phone sales. The increased competition for the consumer dollar makes the added savings of telemarketing even more important. For example, a regular sales representative can make an average of five sales calls a day, at a cost of about $225 each when all costs are factored in. In the course of one hour, an experienced telemarketer can make ten to fifteen phone calls.

Innovations in marketing also allow firms to pinpoint their target markets more accurately, which increases the chances of successful sales calls.

Many firms that had previously employed telemarketing agencies are now establishing their own telemarketing work forces because of the advantages of having a well informed sales staff. Many other firms cannot afford to keep telemarketing staffs or are only beginning to explore the ways they can use telemarketing. These firms still employ independent telemarketing agencies.

Experts estimate that almost 275,000 firms are now using telemarketing. According to a report by a private telemarketing company, this means full- and part-time jobs for nearly four million telemarketers. Because of rapid growth in the field and high turnover among telemarketers, there are many opportunities for entering the field.

Earnings

The pay of telemarketers varies with the type of work they do. For part-time phone solicitors making basic calls to consumers, the pay can range from the minimum wage to around $8.00 per hour. The pay may be higher for those telemarketers who deliver more elaborate sales presentations or who make business-to-business calls. As telemarketers gain more experience and skills, pay scales rise. Seasoned telemarketers can earn from $17,000 to $30,000 per year. Those telemarketers who start their own companies have the chance to earn even higher amounts.

Conditions of work

The offices in which telemarketers work can range from the very basic, with standard phones and desks, to very highly advanced, with computer terminals, the latest in phone technology, and even machines that automatically dial numbers from a database. The number of employees may range from four or five to more than a hundred in a single office. While the work is not strenuous, it can become very repetitive. The amount of supervision depends on the employer and the region of the country. California and a few other states have laws that prohibit the monitoring of calls by supervisors unless both the telemarketer and the person being called are aware of it. In other states, some telemarketing firms may have stricter supervision.

Telemarketing requires many hours of sitting and talking on the phone. Customer rejections, which can range from polite to very rude, can cause a great deal of stress. Because of this, many telemarketers only work four- and five-hour shifts. Telemarketing is an ideal job for people looking for part-time work because workweeks generally run from twenty-four to thirty hours. Because many agencies need staff at unusual hours, telemarketers are able to find positions in which the work hours match their own lifestyles. Many agencies require staffing twenty-four hours a day to handle calls such as airline reservations and reports of credit card thefts. Telemarketers who make business-to-business calls work during normal business hours, while those who call consumers make most of their calls in the evening and on weekends, when more people are at home.

Social and psychological factors

Even though their work is done over the phone, telemarketers must be able to deal with people well. The work requires the ability to sense how the person on the other end of the line is reacting, how to keep them interested in the sales pitch, how to listen carefully to their responses and complaints, and how to react tactfully to impatient and sometimes hostile people. Telemarketers should be able to think quickly and answer questions with confidence. They have to balance a sensitivity to the concerns of their company on one hand, and the needs of the person called on the other.

Telemarketers must also have a warm, pleasant voice on the phone that conveys sincerity as well as confidence. They should also be able to work well with details. While on the phone, they have to take orders, get other important information and fill out complete sales records, all of which require an accurate, alert mind.

Working in phone sales exposes a person to many rejections and rebuffs. This can produce stress, especially when sales commissions are at stake, but a good telemarketer will be able to take the rejections in stride and not lose confidence. It is essential to the success of the telemarketer to not take rejection personally. For most telemarketing jobs, it is expected that most calls will not result in a successful response. Like any other salesperson, a telemarketer can gain a great deal of satisfaction in overcoming a customer's hesitation and making the final sale.

GOE: 08.02.08; SIC: Any industry; SOC: 4366

◇ **SOURCES OF ADDITIONAL INFORMATION**

American Marketing Association
250 South Wacker Drive
Chicago, IL 60606

American Telemarketing Association
5000 Van Nuys Boulevard
Suite 400
Sherman Oaks, CA 91403

Direct Marketing Association
6 East 43rd Street
New York, NY 10017

Society for Marketing Professional Services
801 North Fairfax Street
Suite 215
Alexandria, VA 22314

Women in Advertising and Marketing
4200 Wisconsin Avenue, NW
Suite 106-238
Washington, DC 20016

◇ **RELATED ARTICLES**

Volume 1: Advertising; Marketing
Volume 2: Demographers; Fundraisers; Marketing, advertising and public relations managers; Marketing research personnel
Volume 3: Public opinion researchers; Manufacturers' sales workers; Radio, television, and print advertising sales workers; Securities and financial services sales representatives; Service sales representatives

Telephone operators

Definition

Telephone operators aid persons using telephone services, as well as other telephone operators, to place calls and to make telephone connections.

History

The invention of the telephone is perhaps one of the most important accidents recorded in our technological history. In 1875, Alexander Graham Bell, through experimenting with a method of sending telegraph messages, accidentally discovered the basic mechanics of the telephone. In 1876, he was successful in speaking over the telephone and in August of that same year, the first long distance call, covering a distance of eight miles, was completed by him.

Today, there is a vast complex of telephone communication systems, over land and sea, across continents, in industry, and among vehicles of travel, such as airplanes, ships, trucks, and cars.

In this system of telephone communications, the telephone operator plays an important role. Around the clock these individuals aid the public in placing calls, and often the quick action of the telephone operator can save a life, lead to an arrest or a rescue, or be vital in avoiding some type of catastrophe.

Nature of the work

Automation and technology have now made it possible for telephone customers to dial direct on local and long distance station-to-station calls. But for other calls, such as reverse charge, person-to-person, and credit card calls, *central-office operators* provide assistance. They may also help customers who have difficulty in dialing or those in emergency situations. They may also assume the duty of recording the necessary information on long distance calls for customer billing, although now this is usually done automatically by computer. These operators wear a headset that contains both an earphone and a microphone, leaving their hands free to operate the switchboard or, more often now, the computer terminal at which they are seated. They are supervised by *central-office-operator supervisors.*

Directory assistance operators assist customers and long distance operators by answering inquiries for telephone numbers that are not listed in the most recent directories, that have been changed, or that customers are unable to locate for themselves. These operators usually work seated at the console of a computerized directory.

PBX operators work on private branch exchange (PBX) systems for large companies. They transfer incoming calls, give information to callers, assist employees in making calls, and record charges for outgoing calls. In small business establishments and in offices with equipment that allows direct inward dialing, these operators sometimes serve as office receptionists, sort mail, greet customers, and perform other general office duties as their job demands and time allows. They are trained by *PBX-service advisers*, who also analyze telephone traffic to determine the business's equipment needs and recommend ways to improve service. *Chief telephone operators* supervise other operators, notify maintenance workers of equipment problems, and compile office directories.

Communication-center operators work in large airports to answer calls, page travelers, monitor electronic alarm systems, and operate a two-way radio system among far-flung departments.

Telephone-answering-service operators work individually or for a small business, contracting to answer your phone and take clear, accurate messages for a fee.

Police district switchboard operators transmit and receive police communications. Still other types of specialized telephone operators include overseas and marine operators, rate and route operators, and mobile operators. In many cases, however, operators perform more than one type of telephone service.

Industry predicts that with continued technological developments much of the old switchboard equipment will be replaced with many push-button operated and automatic features, and this trend is well under way.

Requirements

Although a high-school education is not a requirement for telephone operators, people who

During training sessions, student operators practice using push-button consoles while they consult instruction booklets.

Personal qualifications should include tact, patience, a desire to work with people and to be of service to others, a pleasing voice, even disposition, and the ability for good judgment in job performance. Operators must also have legible handwriting and they must be punctual and dependable in job attendance. Of prime importance is emotional stability and a courteous manner in dealing with the public.

Special requirements

Telephone operators are morally and legally bound not to repeat any conversations overheard through the switchboards in their work. The majority of telephone operator jobs have traditionally been filled by women, but in recent years a significant number of men have become telephone operators. The minimum age requirement for this job is usually between sixteen and eighteen years.

International operations usually speak at least one foreign language. Therefore, language study is helpful.

No other special requirements are demanded for this occupation, such as licensure or certification imposed by law or official organizations.

Opportunities for experience and exploration

Students who are considering becoming telephone operators may explore this career by arranging for a visit to a local or long distance telephone company to observe the operators at work and by talking with operators. They may also talk with their high-school guidance counselor to gain career information and assistance in exploring their occupational abilities, interests, and aptitudes.

Part-time jobs are frequently available in switchboard work or sometimes in a combination of switchboard and office duties. Actual job experience is perhaps one of the best methods of determining one's interest in a career.

While in high school, students may find that participation in public speaking and dramatics can be an asset in the development of clear speech, a well-modulated voice, tact, and poise. Participation in clubs and other group activities can help students learn how to work effectively with others. Students should apply themselves in English, arithmetic, and public speaking.

have completed high school are preferred as employees. The majority of companies also prefer to hire the high-school graduate or experienced operator for part-time positions.

New employees are usually given one to three weeks of individual training under the supervision of a service assistant. During this time they are taught and they practice how to handle the more difficult types of calls. Once the new employees have progressed in their speed and "know-how" in handling calls on their own, they are assigned a regular position on the switchboard.

New employees continue to receive on-the-job training throughout their careers as offices are installed with more modern and automatic equipment and as the methods of working with the equipment continue to change. Service assistants are responsible for instructing the new operators in various other types of operating services, such as that of figuring rate charges and supplying rate information.

Manual dexterity is an aptitude that is an asset to the telephone operator; however, the degree of dexterity needed is about the same as that required for the operation of any type of office equipment. These employees must have a clear voice for speaking, without any heavy accents of speech impediments, as well as good hearing and eyesight. The majority of employers now require that all applicants satisfactorily pass a physical examination, and many firms require the potential employee to perform successfully on pre-employment tests in spelling, arithmetic, and learning ability.

Related occupations

Telephone operators are skilled in interpersonal communications. They are polite and considerate and have a desire to work with the public and to help others, whether the needs are large or small. Other occupations that might be of interest include retail or wholesale sales workers, counter or retail clerks, public opinion researchers, telemarketers, and travel agents.

Methods of entering

Individuals may enter this occupation by direct application to employing companies and firms. In some cities, telephone offices maintain an employment office, while in other localities, employment interviews are conducted by a chief operator or personnel manager.

Employment opportunities may be located by visiting employing firms, by using the services of state or private employment agencies, through newspaper advertisements, or sometimes, through high-school placement offices.

Jobs may be found with telephone companies in the offices of business and industry, factories, airports, hospitals, public buildings, large city schools, colleges, or in firms providing telephone answering service, or wherever there is a switchboard operation.

Advancement

Telephone operators may have opportunities for advancement to positions as service assistants and next to group or assistant chief operators. A top position is that of chief operator. Chief operators are responsible for the planning and directing of the activities of a central office, as well as personnel functions and the performance of the employees. Supervisory positions have become increasingly available to women in recent years.

Service assistants may sometimes advance to PBX service advisors, who have the responsibility for instructing and helping customers' employees in the correct use and operation of PBX equipment.

Opportunities for advancement are usually dependent upon the employee's initiative, ability, experience, length of employment, and job performance, as well as the size of the place of employment and the number of supervisors needed.

Some telephone and switchboard operators find employment and advancement opportunities in related fields in jobs such as telephone order taker, telephone solicitor for business and product firms, or as a telephone-quotation clerk who quotes current stock quotations to customers.

Employment outlook

About 547,000 telephone operators were employed in the early 1990s. More than half were PBX operators.

Through the late 1990s, overall employment of telephone operators will grow about as fast as average. Employment of directory assistance and central office operators in telephone companies will decline, as it has for the past twenty-five years, because of new technology. But employment of PBX operators should grow faster than average as businesses expand.

Earnings

The wages paid to telephone operators vary from state to state, from one section of the country to another, and even from city to city. The types of duties performed by the employee also affect the salary earned. For example, those employees who perform clerical or receptionist duties may be paid at different levels from those employees who perform only switchboard operator duties.

Telephone operators in the early 1990s earned an average yearly salary of $18,096; half earned between $14,000 and $23,400, while one in ten earned less than $10,600 and another one-tenth earned more than $28,080. Those in the federal government earned an average of $16,272. PBX operators averaged $15,000.

Operators are usually paid at the rate of time-and-a-half for Sunday work and they may receive an extra day's pay for working on legal holidays. Some additional remuneration is usually paid when employees work split shifts or shifts that end after 6:00 P.M. Time-and-a-half pay is generally given if operators work beyond a five-day week. Choice of work hours is usually determined on the basis of seniority of the operator. Pay increases are, in most instances, determined on the basis of periodic pay scales.

Fringe benefits for these employees usually include paid vacations of one week after one year's service, two weeks yearly up to ten years, three weeks up to twenty years, and four weeks thereafter. The majority of companies give six or more paid holidays yearly.

Most telephone company employees are covered by group insurance plans for sickness, accident, and death, and the majority have retirement and disability pension plans available to them. Sick leave is usually given, with the days allotted determined by the number of years of service.

Conditions of work

The telephone industry operates around the clock giving the public twenty-four-hour daily service. Operators may, therefore, be required to work night shifts, evening hours, and on Sundays and holidays. Some operators are asked to work split shifts to cover rush-hour periods and they may be called for emergency duty when telephone lines are heavily loaded with calls. In general, telephone operators work a forty-hour, five-day week.

The telephone operator's job demands good physical health for punctual and regular job attendance; the work, however, is not physically strenuous or demanding. Operators are seated to perform their work at the switchboard and are allowed to take periodic rest breaks.

General working conditions are usually in pleasant surroundings, comfortably air-conditioned and ventilated, with relatively little noise or confusion.

Social and psychological factors.

Telephone operators generally continue to work under some type of supervision during their entire careers. The majority of companies use the technique of "service observing" in which all operators are periodically observed for the quality of service that is being rendered to the public. Former operators specially trained for these observations listen to calls and are alert to courtesy rendered, speed of answering, voice clarity, and other factors involved in operating services.

Telephone operators must be patient and courteous at all times. Customers can be very demanding and impatient and it is part of the telephone operator's job to be calm and helpful as in any job dealing with the public.

Individuals who have the desire to serve the public, to work in close cooperation and harmony with others, and who can realize the important part they will play as one link in a vast system of communications may find the career of telephone operator to provide valuable and satisfying job experiences.

GOE: 07.04.06; SIC: 4813; SOC: 4732

◇ **SOURCES OF ADDITIONAL INFORMATION**

Communications Workers of America
1925 K Street, NW
Washington, DC 20006

United States Telephone Association
900 19th Street, NW, Suite 800
Washington, DC 20006

◇ **RELATED ARTICLES**

Volume 1: Telecommunications
Volume 2: Radio and telegraph operators
Volume 3: Receptionists; Telemarketers

Title searchers and examiners

Definition

Title searchers and examiners conduct searches of public and private records to determine the legal title of ownership for a piece of real estate.

History

A person who owns real estate has many options in improving his or her investment. To do anything with the land—mortgage it, sell it, build on it, or even give it away—the person's complete or partial ownership to the land must be proven and documented. This ownership is known as a title. This, however, is not an easy task. Land changes hands so frequently that often questions arise as to who is really the rightful owner of the property.

In the United States, most major real estate dealings are publicly recorded, usually with the county recorder or registrar. This system began in colonial Massachusetts and has spread throughout the rest of the country, giving us a unique method for keeping track of real estate transactions. In some areas of the country, a title can be traced as far back as 200 years or more. Over that length of time, a parcel of land may have been in the hands of many different owners. Large pieces of land can be sectioned into smaller parcels, and certain rights, such as the right to mine beneath a property or run roads and irrigation ditches over it, can be sold or leased separately from the land itself. Official records can become confused, contradictory, or incomplete. Because of the profitability of the real estate business, many new methods of leasing and selling property are certain to be devised in the future, making the task of identifying proper ownership even more complicated and important.

Nature of the work

Clients hire title searchers and examiners to make certain the ownership of all parts and privileges of a piece of property. The client may need to have these questions answered for many reasons: in addition to land sales and purchases, a lawyer might need a title search to fulfill the terms of someone's will, a bank might need it to repossess property used as collateral on a loan, a company might need it when acquiring or merging with another company, or an accountant might need it when preparing tax returns.

The work of the title searcher is the first step in the process. When a request for a title search is received, the title searcher first determines the type of title evidence that will have to be gathered, the purpose for which it will be used, the people involved, and the legal description of the property. The searcher then compares this description with the legal description contained in public and private records to verify such factors as the deed of ownership, tax codes, tax parcel number, and description of property boundaries.

The task can take title searchers to a variety of places, including the offices of the county tax assessor, the recorder or registrar of deeds, the clerk of the city or state court, and other city, county, and state officials. Title searchers consult legal records, surveyors' maps, and tax rolls. The clients who hire title searchers may also keep records called indexes. These indexes are kept up to date for use by their own staff and outside searchers, and contain important information on mortgages, deeds, contracts and judgments. For example, a law firm specializing in real estate and contract law would probably keep extensive indexes, using information gathered both in its own work and from outside sources.

As the title searcher examines the legal documents, the important information is recorded on a standardized work sheet. This information can include judgments, deeds, mortgages (loans made using the property as collateral), liens (charges against the property when it has been used as for the payment of a debt), taxes, special assessments for streets and sewers, and easements. The searcher must also carefully record from which records this information is taken, where they are located, the date on which any action took place, and the names and addresses of the people involved.

Using the data gathered by the title searcher, the title examiner determines the legal condition of the property title. Title examiners will study all the relevant documents for a property to determine the chain of ownership, plus records of marriages, births, divorces, adoptions, and other important legal proceedings. To verify certain facts, they may need to interview judges, clerks, lawyers, bankers, real estate brokers, and other professional people. They may also summarize the legal documents they have found and used, and use these abstracts as references in later work.

From all this information, title examiners will prepare reports that describe the full extent of a person's title to a property; the right to sell, buy, use, or improve it; any restrictions that exist; and the actions that would be required to clear the title. If the title examiner works in a title insurance agency, he or she will prepare and issue a policy that guarantees the legality of the title, with whatever restrictions have been found. The client can then proceed to use the property as he or she sees fit, insured against any losses that might arise if questions of title are raised in the future.

Title searchers and examiners work in a variety of settings. Some work for law firms, title insurance companies, or companies that write title abstracts. Others work for various branches of government at the city, county, or state level. In larger offices, a *title supervisor* may direct and coordinate the activities of other searchers and examiners. Generally, title searchers and examiners can find consistent work in any area of the country with an active real estate market.

Requirements

A high-school diploma is necessary to begin a career as a title searcher. Classes that will be helpful on the job include business, business law, English, social studies, real estate, real estate law, and typing. Skills in reading, writing, and research methods are important to title searchers.

Because their work is more complex, title examiners should take at least some college course work. Pertinent courses include business administration, office management, and real estate law and other types of law.

Special requirements

A few states require that title searchers and examiners be licensed or certified. Also, some title search firms may belong to the American Land Title Association, or regional or state title associations. These groups maintain codes of ethics and standards of practice among their members. Title searchers and examiners who work for a state, county, or municipal government may belong to a union representing other government workers.

Opportunities for experience and exploration

Some law firms, real estate brokerages, and title companies may have internships for students interested in work as a title searcher or examiner. Information on the availability of such internships can usually be gotten by contacting the regional or local land title association or school guidance offices.

Related occupations

Title examiners and searchers are required to be patient, organized, and have good communications skills. Other jobs with similar requirements include general office clerks, file clerks, billing clerks, and accounting and bookkeeping clerks.

Methods of entering

Those students and graduates interested in a career as a title searcher or examiner should send resumes and letters of application to firms in their area who need these types of workers, including abstract companies, title insurance companies, and law firms. Other leads for employment opportunities are local real estate agents or brokers, government employment offices, and local or state land title associations. Graduates from two- or four-year colleges can consult their college placement office for additional information on job openings.

Advancement

For title searchers and examiners, most skills are learned on the job. A basic understanding of title search can be gained in a few months, as employees first use the indexes which their employers maintain. As time goes on, however, it becomes more important for these employees to gain a broader understanding of the intricacies of land title evidence and record-keeping systems. This knowledge and a number of years of experience are the keys to advancement.

With experience, title searchers can move up to become tax examiners, special assessment searchers, or abstractors. With enough experience, a searcher or examiner might be promoted to title supervisor or head clerk. Other paths for ambitious title searchers and examiners include other types of paralegal work or, with further study, a law degree.

Employment outlook

The health of the title insurance business is directly tied to the strength of the real estate market. In prosperous times, more real estate activity is transacted, and more title searches are needed. While the real estate business in America is cyclical—that is, it has successive periods of growth and recession—in general the employment outlook for title searchers and examiners is excellent.

Earnings

Depending on their employer and the area of the country, title searchers can earn anywhere from $10,000 to $13,750 per year in the early 1990s. Title examiners generally earn more, with salaries ranging from $14,850 to $19,250. Title searchers and examiners may also receive such fringe benefits as vacations, hospital and life insurance, profit sharing, and pensions, depending on the policies of their employer.

Conditions

Title searchers and examiners generally work a forty-hour week. Because most public records offices are only open during regular business hours, there might not be much overtime work for searchers and examiners, except when working on private indexes and writing abstracts.

The offices in which title searchers and examiners work can be very different in terms of comfort, space, and modern equipment. Searchers and examiners spend much of their day poring over the fine print of legal documents and records, so they may be afflicted occasionally by eyestrain and back fatigue. Generally, however, offices are pleasant and the work is not strenuous.

Social and psychological factors

Title searchers must be very methodical, analytical, and detail-oriented in their work. As they study the many hundreds of documents that may contain important data, they must also be thorough. Overlooking important points will damage the accuracy of the final report, and may inflict heavy financial costs to

the client or the firm. It is important not to lose sight of the reason for the title search, in addition to remembering the intricacies of real estate law.

In addition to their very detailed work, title examiners also have to deal with clients, lawyers, judges, brokers, and others. This requires good communication skills, poise, patience, and courtesy.

GOE: 07.01.05, 07.05.02; SIC: 6541; SOC: 396

◇ SOURCES OF ADDITIONAL INFORMATION

American Land Title Association
1828 L Street, NW, Suite 705
Washington, DC 20036

Insurance Information Institute
110 William Street
New York, NY 10038

National Association of Legal Assistants
1601 South Main Street, Suite 300
Tulsa, OK 74119

◇ RELATED ARTICLES

Volume 1: Civil Service; Insurance; Law; Real Estate
Volume 2: Assessors and appraisers; Insurance claims representatives; Lawyers and judges; Legal assistants; Underwriters
Volume 3: Clerical supervisors and managers; Insurance policy processing occupations

Traffic agents and clerks

Definition

Traffic agents and clerks handle the booking, billing, claims, and related paper work for the safe and efficient movement of cargo by air, water, truck, or rail. They analyze the costs of different forms of transport and calculate the shipping rates for the customers. Traffic agents are responsible for knowing the rules and restrictions of each type of transport.

Traffic agents and clerks
Clerical Occupations

History

As the modes of passenger transportation have increased, so have the means of transporting freight from place to place. Businesses gradually had the choice of sending their goods by air, water, truck, or rail. Then arose the problem of finding the means that would be the most efficient, economical, and safest arrangement for the type of cargo in question. Water transportation is the cheapest but the slowest. Air is the fastest but the most expensive. Rail is cheaper than motor transportation but is, of course, limited to the track network. All these transportation methods together, however, have provided the United States with the greatest physical distribution system in the world.

Nature of the work

Traffic agents and clerks are employed by individual transportation companies and their work differs greatly from one kind of carrier to another.

All commercial carriers are highly regulated because of their interstate and international activities. They are controlled by such laws as the Interstate Commerce Act, Bill of Lading Act, Federal Trade Commission Act, Federal Maritime Commission Regulations, and the Railways Labor Act. It is, therefore, essential that traffic agents and clerks be constantly aware of how legislation affects their work. Source of the various positions held by traffic agents and clerks are the following:

Rate supervisors analyze rates and routes in an effort to find ways to reduce transportation costs. They supervise the work of *traffic-rate clerks* who determine the rates a transportation company will charge for shipping cargo of various kinds.

Freight rate analysts also analyze rates, along with current and proposed government regulations, to determine how the transportation company should revise its rates and practices. They also compile the company's rate manual.

Traffic managers direct and coordinate other workers who document, classify, route, and schedule outgoing freight and who verify and reship incoming freight at the warehouse. Other traffic managers quote rates and give other information to customers and handle customer complaints about damaged, missing, or overcharged goods.

Traffic agents contact industrial and commercial firms to solicit freight business and travel agencies and other organizations to solicit passenger business. These workers call on prospective shippers to explain the advantages of using their company's services. They quote tariff rates, schedules, and operating conditions such as loading or unloading practices. When an agreement is reached, the sales worker, also called solicitor, might also serve as liaison between the shipper and carrier, help to settle complaints, or follow up on the handling of special goods such as live animals, delicate equipment, or perishable goods. Traffic clerks keep records of freight, incoming and outgoing, by recording the destination, routing, weight, and tariffs. These workers may also be required to keep records of both damaged freight and clients claims of overcharge. *Shipping services sales representatives* do similar work for parcel-delivery businesses.

Requirements

Traffic agents and clerks put into effect the plans or programs others have developed or organized. They must be responsible, dependable, and exacting. They must also be able to work with numerical data.

One or two years of college is generally preferred by most companies for entrance into this field. High-school students aspiring to the position of traffic agent or clerk should take courses in economics, mathematics, science, and business administration.

Many community and junior colleges offer traffic and transportation curriculums to prepare students for employment as traffic agents and clerks. Some institutions combine course work and on-the-job experience leading to an associate degree or a certificate of completion. The traffic agent and clerk, regardless of the specific aspect of traffic being considered, should take courses in the following: the economics of transportation; transportation laws and regulations at the federal, state, and local level; mathematics and statistics of passenger, vehicle, and cargo flows; principles of traffic safety; physics; communications; and psychology.

Special requirements

Students who are interested in pursuing careers in any aspect of traffic should explore the requirements for license or certification of their freight specialty in their state or with specific employers they may be considering.

Opportunities for experience and exploration

The best opportunity for experience in this field would be a summer job with a transportation company or a local moving company in a clerical capacity or as a truck helper.

Related occupations

Communication and organization skills are very important in traffic management. These same skills are valuable in many other career areas. Most clerical jobs, such as shipping and receiving clerks, general office clerks, and statistical clerks, require these abilities as do professional occupations.

Traffic agents monitor the flow of cargo through the use of sophisticated computer systems.

agents and clerks contribute their knowledge of tariffs, carriers, and routes.

Methods of entering

The person interested in becoming a traffic agent or clerk can do so by applying to one's college placement service or a state employment service. In addition, work-experience programs provided by many companies permit the student to get established with an employer as well as to obtain valuable experience. You could also contact employers by letters of application.

Advancement

There is room for advancement in this field. For example, someone entering the field as a rate and claims clerk might eventually become a rate analyst. A routing clerk could be promoted to terminal cargo manager, and a company representative could be elevated to the position of traffic manager.

Employment outlook

Traffic management is a small but growing occupation and is expected to continue to grow as fast as other occupations through the early 1990s. Openings will continue to occur with the development of new businesses and with the retirement, death, and movement of experienced agents and clerks. Whether shipping foodstuffs, steel, books, or machinery, traffic

Earnings

Beginning salaries for traffic agents and clerks averaged about $17,470 per year in the early 1990s, depending upon the particular field of traffic entered. The starting salary is also dependent upon the applicant's level of education, college-coordinated experience, and other relevant work experience.

Fringe benefits usually include vacations and health insurance plans and possible tuition reimbursement plans.

Conditions of work

Because of the diverse characteristics of each mode of transportation, it is difficult to give a general statement of working conditions that would be accurate in all cases. Some positions consist of outdoor work, others are almost exclusively indoors, and some are combinations of the two. Hours may be long or shift work may be required, since some terminals operate around the clock. Some positions, however, require regular hours with weekends off.

Social and psychological factors

Traffic agents and clerks analyze and translate instructions given to them by others. They must carry these instructions out or interpret them for others under their direction. In the field of traffic, special attention is placed on this

123

quality. What a traffic agent or clerk does, if not done well, may mean that someone—a customer, an employee, a shipper, a truck driver, or a property owner—may suffer needless damage to life or to property, or may be unnecessarily inconvenienced. Responsibility is essential in this field.

GOE: 07.02.04; SIC: Any industry; SOC: 4152

◇ **SOURCES OF ADDITIONAL INFORMATION**

National Association of Freight Transportation Consultants
PO Box 21418
Albuquerque, NM 87154

National Freight Transportation Association
PO Box 21856
Roanoke, VA 24018

◇ **RELATED ARTICLES**

Volume 1: Letter and Package Delivery; Transportation; Wholesaling
Volume 2: Industrial traffic managers
Volume 3: Postal clerks; Railroad clerks; Shipping and receiving clerks

Typists and word processors

Definition

Using typewriters, word processors, and other office machines, *typists* convert handwritten or otherwise unfinished material into clean, readable, typewritten copies. Typists type reports, letters, forms, tables, charts, and other materials for all types of businesses and services. Word-processing operators type information using a computer that stores material electronically instead of printing it directly onto paper. Other typists use special machines that convert manuscripts into Braille, coded, or typeset copy. Many typists also perform routine clerical functions.

History

The invention of the typewriter in 1829 by W. A. Burt eventually created the occupation of typist, as typewriters went on the market in the United States between 1847 and 1856. This tool greatly increased business efficiency and productivity, and these benefits grew as typists became skilled at quickly and accurately transforming messy handwritten documents into neat, consistent typed copies. Today's type-writer is the product of many years of refining, redesigning, and improving the practicality, speed, and efficiency of the machine. The size, the shape, and the positions of the letter keys changed many times.

The introduction of word processors to the workplace revolutionized typing. These machines have typewriter keyboards but computers for brains. As typists type, the words appear on a video display terminal screen. Typists can correct errors and make any necessary changes right on the screen, before a copy is printed on paper, eliminating the need for retyping whole pages to correct mistakes. The word processor stores the information in its memory or on tape, so the typist can go back to it again and again for copies or changes.

The term word processing entered the English language in 1965, when International Business Machines (IBM) introduced a typewriter that put information onto magnetic tape instead of paper. Corrections could be made on this tape before running the tape through a machine that converted the signals on the tape to characters on a printed page. Today, word processors are quickly replacing typewriters in the office. Both, however, are still being used to prepare the written communications business depends upon. Typists have the important job of producing those communications as quickly and efficiently as possible.

Nature of the work

Typists are used in almost every kind of workplace. They work in banks, law firms, factories, schools, hospitals, publishing firms, and department stores. Newspapers and television stations need typists, as do light and power companies, real estate agencies, insurance companies, and airlines. Typists may work in large groups in large offices, or may work with only one or two other people in small offices such as doctors', lawyers', and employment agencies. They also work for government, law enforcement agencies, and the armed forces.

Some typists perform few duties other than typing. These typists spend approximately 75 percent of their time typing. They may type statistical data, medical reports, legal briefs, addresses, letters, and other documents from handwritten copies. They may work in pools, dividing the work of an entire large office among many workers and under the supervision of a *typing section chief*. These typists may also be responsible for making photocopies of typewritten materials for distribution.

Beginning typists may start with typing address labels, headings on form letters, and documents from legible handwritten copy. More experienced typists may work from copy that is more difficult to read or may be expected to set up complicated data in tabular form. *Billing typists* work in businesses that sell products or services, where they type invoices, shipping labels, and bills of lading. *Bordereau clerks* type applications for insurance coverage at insurance companies.

Clerk-typists spend up to 50 percent of their time typing, usually using electric and electronic typewriters to type reports, bills, and forms. They also perform a variety of clerical tasks, however, such as filing, answering the phone, acting as office receptionist, and running copy machines.

Many typists type from recorded tapes instead of written or printed copy. *Transcribing-machine operators* and their *supervisors* sit at keyboards and wear headsets, through which they hear spoken contents of letters, reports, and meetings. Typists can control the speed of the tape so they can comfortably type every word they hear. They proofread their finished documents and may erase dictated tapes for future use.

Certain typists use special machines to create copy. *Perforator typists* type on machines that punch holes in tape, which is used to automatically create typewritten copy. *Telegraphic-typewriter operators* and their *supervisors* receive and transmit telegraphs by typing messages using typewriter-like keyboards. In publishing and printing, *photocomposing-perforator-machine operators*, *photocomposing-keyboard operators*, *veritype operators*, and *typesetter-perforator operators* type on special machines that directly or indirectly produce typeset or other printed copy. Some of these typists must also code copy to show what size and style of letters and characters should be used. They may also be required to actually design and lay out pages of printed publications.

Braille typists and *braille operators* use special typewriter-like machines to transcribe written or spoken English into braille. *Cryptographic-machine operators* operate typewriter-like equipment that codes, transmits, and decodes secret messages for the armed forces, law enforcement agencies, and business organizations. These typists select a code card from a code book, insert the card into the machine, and type the message in English on the machine, which converts it to coded copy. A decoding card is used to follow the same process for decoding.

Many typists work at computer terminals. *Magnetic-tape-typewriter operators* enter information from written materials on a computer console to produce magnetic disks or tapes for storage and later retrieval. *In-file operators* use a terminal to post or receive information about individuals' credit records for credit-reporting agencies. When an agency subscriber calls with a question about a subject's credit, the typist calls that person's record up on the video screen and reads the information. *Terminal operators* and *terminal-system operators* enter numerical or alphabetical characters using the keyboard of an on-line computer as it is running to exchange information with another computer as many as thousands of miles away. (*See also* the separate article titled "Data entry clerks" elsewhere in this volume.)

Most common of the computer typists, however, are the *word-processing operators* and their *supervisors*. A word processor keyboard is much like a typewriter's except letters and numbers show up as electronic lights on a video display terminal (VDT). Word-processing operators put documents into proper formats by entering codes into the word processor, telling it which lines to center, which words to underline, where the margins should be set, and how the document should be stored and printed. Word-processing operators can edit, change, and insert materials just by pressing keys, which make errors disappear instanta-

A word processor must be familiar with a computer keyboard and several brands of word processing software.

neously. Word processors are particularly efficient for form letters, in which only certain parts of a document change on each copy. When a word-processing operator has finished formatting and typing a document, it is electronically sent to a printer, which produces what looks like typewritten copy. The document is often saved on a tape cassette or disk so that any subsequent changes to it can be made easily and any new copies produced immediately.

Requirements

Most employees require that typists have completed high school and be able to type neatly and correctly at least forty or fifty words per minute. More and more employers are looking for typists with word-processing experience. Typists also need a good knowledge of spelling, grammar, and punctuation, and may be required to be familiar with standard office equipment.

Word-processing operators must be able to type forty-five to eighty words per minute, and should know how to organize documents such as letters, reports, and financial statements.

All typists need manual dexterity and the ability to concentrate. They should be attentive to detail, alert, and efficient. Because typists must frequently work directly with the people whose documents they type, they need good interpersonal skills, including a courteous and cheerful demeanor.

Typing skills are taught in high schools, colleges, business schools, and home-study courses. Some people learn typing through self-teaching materials such as books, records, and computer programs. Business schools and community colleges often offer certificates or associate degrees for typists and word processors.

Word-processing courses are offered in community colleges and business schools. High schools are just beginning to offer word-processing training. Workers who want to become word-processing specialists should enroll in a business school or two-year college word-processing program. For those who do not pursue such formal education, employers frequently provide word-processing training to new employees and current typists. Word-processor manufacturers also offer sessions to introduce users to the basics of operating their equipment. In general, it takes a minimum of three to six months of hands-on experience to become a skilled word-processing operator.

Special requirements

There are no special requirements for typists.

Opportunities for experience and exploration

As with many clerical occupations, a good way to gain experience as a typist is through high-school work/study programs. Students in these programs work part-time for local businesses and attend classes part-time. Another way to gain typing experience is to do volunteer typing for friends, church, or other organizations. Persons working as typists using typewriters may be able to explore using word-processing equipment if the office has both types of machines.

Related occupations

Typists and word processors require manual dexterity, attention to detail, and good language skills. Other occupations that might be of interest include data entry clerks, clerical supervisors, programmers, and computer equipment and peripheral equipment operators.

Methods of entering

Business school and college students may learn of typist positions through their school placement offices. Some large businesses recruit typists at these schools. High-school guidance counselors may know of local openings for typists. Persons interested in typist positions should check newspaper and business journal advertisements. Typists should also apply directly to the personnel departments of large companies that hire many typists; they may also wish to register with an agency that finds part-time employment for typists. To apply for typist positions with the federal government, job seekers should apply at the nearest regional Office of Personnel Management, the address of which may be found in the telephone book under United States Government. State, county, and city governments may also have listings for typist positions.

Persons studying word processing in a business school or college may find that many companies actively recruit word-processing operators at school. School placement offices provide information about recruiting.

Advancement

Typists usually receive salary increases as they qualify and are promoted from junior to senior typing positions, which are often given a classification or pay scale, such as Typist I or II. They may also advance from clerk typists to technical typists or from a job in a typing pool to a private office typing job.

Magnetic-tape-typewriter operators, often called mag-tape typists or terminal-system operators, may be promoted to word-processing supervisor or selected for in-house professional training programs in data processing.

A degree in business management or executive secretarial skills increases a typist's chances for advancement. In addition, many large companies and governments provide training programs allowing typists to upgrade their skills and move to other jobs, such as secretary, statistical clerk, or stenographer.

Some typists, once they have acquired enough experience, go into business for themselves, providing typing services to business clients, or free-lance from their homes, typing

reports, manuscripts, and papers for professors, authors, business people, and students.

The more word-processing experience a typist has the better the opportunities to move up. Word-processing operators often begin working as word-processing trainees. They may to be promoted word-processing operators, then word-processing specialist I, word-processing specialist II, and word-processing supervisors. They may also move into related fields and work as word-processing equipment salespeople or servicers, or word-processing teachers or consultants. With further education, they could eventually become computer programmers or systems analysts.

Employment outlook

About one million people worked as typists in the early 1990s. Business employed one-third of these people; education, medicine, and services employed another third. About one-quarter worked in government.

Growth in the typing field will show little or no change through the late 1990s, largely because improved technology has greatly increased typists' productivity. Many jobs will be available for typists, especially for workers to replace typists who change careers or leave the work force. The Association of Independent Colleges and Schools predicts that 12.3 percent more typist jobs will be held in 2000 than were in the mid-1990s. When and if voice data entry systems become commercially viable (probably not until the early 2000s at the earliest), there may be a sharp decline in the number of typists needed.

For the foreseeable future, however, the demand for word-processing specialists will remain very high—far exceeding the supply. Workers with the best technical skills and knowledge of several word-processing languages have the best chances of getting hired.

Earnings

Salaries for typists vary with the industry. They are highest in public utilities and manufacturing. Workers in finance, insurance, and real estate received the least pay. Workers with word-processing experience generally receive higher salaries than those without.

In the early 1990s, entry-level typists earned an average annual salary of $14,150, while experienced workers earned $18,180 on average. Most typists earned between $13,080

127

and $19,800 a year, although about ten percent earned more than $24,840 and another ten percent less than $10,680.

The federal government paid typists a starting salary of between $12,601 and $13,749. The most experienced workers earned as much as $17,875.

According to the Administrative Management Society, salaries for word-processing operators are increasing faster than those for other office workers. Operators in the private sector earned between $16,910 and $20,900, depending on the job's complexity and level of responsibility.

Conditions of work

Typists and word processors usually work at desks or terminals in clean, well-lighted, and well-ventilated offices. They usually sit most of the day and may spend the day in a fairly small space. Offices with electronic equipment are usually temperature and humidity controlled to protect the machines. Typing and word-processing equipment can be noisy, and typists may work near frequently ringing phones. In general, however, offices are modern, pleasant, and comfortable. The work is detailed and often repetitious.

Recent years have seen the development of controversy over the effect of working at video display terminals can have on workers' health. Working with these screens in improper lighting can cause eyestrain. Sitting at these terminals all day can cause musculoskeletal stress and pain, and research suggests that pregnant women working at VDTs may have miscarriages or babies with birth defects. Recently, the industry began to pay closer attention to these problems and to improve health and safety standards in VDT-equipped offices.

The other common ailment for typists is carpal tunnel syndrome. CTS is an ailment of the tendons in the wrist, triggered by repetitive movement. If left unchecked, it can require surgery to correct. However, proper placement of the typing keyboard at almost lap level can prevent injury. Several companies have designed desks, chairs and working spaces to accommodate in the best physical manner the needs of typists and word processors. This also includes keeping video display terminals at two feet distance and slightly below eye level.

Screens are now available that are placed over the video display to block ultra-violet light. The UV light is now believed to be harmful. Eyeglasses can also be coated with a UV protective layer to block harmful rays.

Typists usually work thirty-five to forty hours per week, five days per week. They may work overtime occasionally to finish special projects and may receive overtime pay. In large cities workers usually receive about seven paid holidays, two weeks' vacation after one year of employment, sick leave, health and life insurance, and a pension plan. Some large companies also provide dental insurance, profit sharing opportunities, and bonuses.

The nature of a typist's work lends itself to flexible work arrangements. Many typists work in temporary positions, which provide variety and great flexibility in hours and days worked. Many work part-time. Some offices are also experimenting with the concept of home-based offices, in which typists receive and send work on home word processors through telephone hook-ups. These jobs may be especially convenient for workers with disabilities or family responsibilities, but they often do not provide a full range of benefits or the social benefits of interacting with coworkers.

Social and psychological factors

People who like to pay attention to detail and do not mind a certain amount of repetition in their work may be well suited to typing jobs.

The continued repetition may become boring for word processors and typists. At the other end of the spectrum, the pressure of deadlines for many creates stress and anxiety. Much typing and typesetting work is deadline oriented. Typists and word-processor operators need to be tactful, patient people, who are willing to take direction and able to deal with the stress of tight deadlines and changing priorities. These workers may find satisfaction in knowing that their work is vital to the operation of today's fast-paced business world. Typist jobs may be suitable for workers with physical disabilities, because workers sit almost all the time. These jobs offer flexibility and opportunity—jobs are available all over the country, and the abailability of part-time work makes these jobs highly compatible with family and home responsibilities.

Word-processor operators need some mechanical aptitude and logical minds. Working in front of VDTs may be physically harmful, especially for pregnant women.

GOE: 07.06.02; SIC: Any industry; SOC: 4624

◇ **SOURCES OF ADDITIONAL INFORMATION**

Association of Information Systems Professionals
104 Wilmot Road
Suite 201
Deerfield, IL 60015

Executive Women International
Administrative Services
Spring Run Office Plaza
965 East 4800 Street
Suite 1
Salt Lake City, UT 84117

International Data Base Management Association
10675 Treena Street
Suite 103
San Diego, CA 92131

Professional Secretaries International
301 East Armour Boulevard
Kansas City, MO 64111

◇ **RELATED ARTICLES**

Volume 1: See Table of Contents for areas of specific interest
Volume 2: Data base managers
Volume 3: Computer and peripheral equipment operators; Receptionists; Secretaries and stenographers

Sales Occupations

This has been called the age of distribution. Certainly one of the most significant economic revolutions of the past one hundred years has been the rapid growth in the field of sales. Today, more Americans are employed in sales and sales service than in any other occupation.

Distribution is the middle step in a three-stage economic process that begins with the production of goods and ends with their consumption. Most consumers are also producers or distributors and their income provides purchasing power to aid the economic cycle. Sales is the key to successful distribution.

The level of skill required for varied sales positions differs widely and ranges from the minimal training of a variety store worker to the highly specialized knowledge of the electronics sales worker.

Regardless of the type of sales activity, the sales worker must be able to locate prospective customers or, in the case of retail sales, must successfully capitalize on the initial sales inclination of customers. The sales worker frequently works independently and has many of the advantages and problems of the self-employed person in business.

Never before have so many workers been involved in sales activities. Today, more people are employed in distributing and servicing products than are required to produce them.

More than 8 million people were employed in sales occupations in the early 1990s. One-fourth of these were part-time employees who worked less than thirty-five hours per week. Women held about 40 percent of all sales positions and were particularly prominent in retailing where they sold to the consumer. Men held most of the positions in sales outside retail stores, such as insurance, real estate, and wholesale products sold to retail merchants.

The successful sales worker finds numerous opportunities for advancement. The highest testimony to the values of a sales background may be seen in the increasing trend to select company presidents out of sales departments.

The sales management network, including branch sales manager, regional sales manager, product sales manager, general sales manager, director of marketing, and vice-president of sales and marketing, also offers opportunities for personal growth.

College education enhances opportunities for advancement. Studies show that more than 25 percent of all sales workers hold a college degree.

The long-range trend is for a greater percentage of our population to enter sales and related service occupations each year. This growth appears selective. For example, in the past ten years the percentage of sales workers employed in wholesale trade, life and casualty insurance, real estate, and manufacturing trade showed a greater than average increase. The percentage of direct-to-consumer sales workers showed some increase. The slowest growing field was retail sales—which is the largest field of sales.

Growth of the sales field will be aided by improvements in methods of doing business. Orders will be processed more rapidly and accurately with the help of electronic equipment. New demonstration techniques will improve sales presentations and enable the purchaser to order more carefully. While automation may reduce employment in many areas of our economy, competition for sales and the importance of personal contact should maintain the role of the sales worker. Only in certain lines (retail sales of groceries, drugs, quick lunches, and commonly sold variety items) should the effect of automation become significant.

Conditions in the field of sales should encourage the recruitment of increasingly more skilled sales workers. The size and complexity of orders should increase.

Auctioneers

Definition

Auctioneers appraise, assemble, and sell articles to the highest bidder during an auction. Auctioneers coordinate the pace of the auction and evaluate the items to be sold first. Sometimes to engage more interest an auctioneer may save the most popular items for last. An auctioneer acts as salesperson for the family or agency selling the items to be auctioned.

History

Prior to the development of department stores, rural families had their own methods for dispensing and acquiring needed items and machinery. For small or individual items a barter or trade might be made to exchange a needed tool or other possession. When many different items were being sold, however, the family would hold an auction. An auctioneer would assist the family in dispensing of their property for the purpose of acquiring needed cash, or if the family was moving and could not bring with them all of their possessions.

As time wears on, auctions have become popular ways to buy farm equipment, artwork, livestock, or personal property from estates. An auction dispenses of many varied items in a fairly quick manner by selling one item and moving through the list of goods from start to finish. Auctions have also a become popular way to raise money for charity or other fundraising events. They are fun as well as functional and have grown in occurrence in rural areas as well as cities.

Nature of the work

There are two main facets of an auctioneer's work: the selling itself and the preliminary preparation and evaluation. It is the latter aspect that takes more time and skill and is less familiar to people. Prior to the auction itself, the auctioneer will meet with the sellers and determine the objects to be sold. An auctioneer will make note of the lowest bid, called the "reserved bid," that the sellers will accept for each item. If there are legal aspects to be discussed, an auctioneer will confer with the sellers.

Appraisal of the goods may take the most time. The auctioneer determines the value of each and compares it to the reserve bid established by the sellers. The auctioneer may make notes as to where they will begin bidding and may set prices they anticipate receiving for certain special items. The auctioneer will also make notes on the type of item being sold, its history, or any unique qualities the item might have. This information can encourage higher bids and interest more buyers.

Once the evaluation has taken place, an auctioneer must organize the items out in the lot or area the auction will be held. Sometimes the auctioneer might put out a booklet or guide listing describing the items for sale for that particular auction. It may also list the sequence that the items might be sold so that buyers will know when the items they are most interested in will be up for sale. In addition to the booklet, auctioneers organize any advertising to promote the sale. Newspaper and magazine ads, flyers, signs, and pictures can reach people from many different areas and bring in a good crowd. Some rural areas have auctions as special attractions for tourists around summer holidays such as the Fourth of July and Labor Day or to commemorate town events and local celebrations.

Usually the auctioneer will organize and set up the auction far enough in advance for people to peruse the area and gain an idea of what the auction might be specializing in. Antique furniture and clothing, farm equipment, and artwork are some of the things sold by auctions. Other auctions concentrate on large machinery or cars, as well as livestock, stamps, coins, and books.

The auctioneer services the buyer as well as the seller. An auctioneer is familiar enough with the potential value of the items to encourage prices or begin bids at a certain price. The encouragement and stimulation an auctioneer provides, however, is offset by the excitement and competition among the buyers. Auctioneers must be quick-thinking and comfortable addressing crowds, not only offering them information about the items for sale but acting at times as an entertainer.

It is common for auctioneers to enlist the help of assistants who bring the items to the auctioneer and keep a steady flow of goods being passed on. In addition, another assistant may be in charge of collecting money, issuing

Auctioneers
Sales Occupations

While standing on the flat-bed of a pickup truck, an auctioneer sells farm equipment which is displayed in the background.

receipts, and keeping track to whom each item was sold.

Most auctions run according to a similar plan: The items for sale are made available to the buyers in a catalog or by being put on display. In the case of real estate auctions, however, photographs may be circulated and in some instances, land that is miles away can be sold, though the auctioneer will mention some history and description of the area. Often these types of auctions take less time, but the preparation is more detailed. Auctioneers must know the dimensions of the buildings they are selling, boundary lines for lots and farms, and if there is any money owed on the property, as well as information on terms of payment and zoning laws.

Requirements

Auctioneers must be effective speakers and entertainers. They are commanding attention and interest in the items with the power of their voice and their good humor and manner. Auctioneers should have good stamina as auctions often take place outdoors in warmer weather and can last for quite a few hours at a stretch. Auctioneers must also be alert to be able to keep track of the crowd activity, the progress of the assistants as well as the selling of the goods.

They should also like working with people, as much deliberation goes into the preparation of an auction. A keen sense of evaluation and an absolutely honest nature will make for a successful auctioneer.

Special requirements

Training for auctioneers is available at the National Auctioneers Association in Kansas, the Certified Auctioneers Institute at Indiana University in Bloomington, Indiana, as well as the Missouri Auction School. In addition, there are other schools located in various areas of the country and these may be researched through the *American Trade Schools Directory*.

Auctioneer training can involve appraising, presentation, and, of course, speech classes so that an auctioneer does not strain his or her voice while working long hours. Auctioneers who intend to concentrate on specific areas may take classes to complement the selling of livestock or real estate. Some auctioneers have a background in art or antiques.

Though most auctioneers are bonded because they handle large sums of money, licensing for auctioneers varies from state to state. Some auctioneers are required to pass examinations and pay licensing fees. Auctioneers who work in specialized areas, such as real estate or livestock have other requirements. Auctioneers who sell land must be licensed real estate sales agent or brokers. For selling livestock for human consumption, auctioneers find many states require additional licensing. Auctioneers should be familiar with laws and regulations in the states in which they practice.

Opportunities for experience and exploration

Persons wishing to explore the field of auctioneers would do well to attend some of them and see firsthand what the responsibilities involve. Also, classes in speech, drama, and communication are helpful as auctioneers rely heavily on their voices, not only for speaking and presentation, but also to get the buyer's attention through style and performance.

Charities and other social organizations occasionally use nonprofessionals for fund raising auctions.

Related occupations

Other occupations that require some of the same interests and aptitudes as those of auctioneers include appraisers, retail sales workers, real estate brokers and agents, antiques dealers, and art dealers.

Methods of entering

Beginning auctioneers may work as assistants, handling money and receipts or bringing over the sale items to the experienced auctioneer. They may also begin by working local and county fairs or smaller auctions.

Sometimes professional trade schools offer placement or internships that link beginners with established workers. Beginners may have to work part time until they gain more experience and become well known. Auctioneers who work for large auction houses may receive more assignments as they get more experience and complete any training the firm offers them.

Advancement

Experienced auctioneers can make a good reputation for themselves. As most auctioneers get paid by commission, they may decide to specialize in selling real estate, farm equipment, or artwork, items that are likely to bring in more revenue for less preparation and shorter presentations.

Auctioneers who work with auction houses may move up in the ranks and get the more prestigious assignments. Auctioneers also may advance as they develop their individual knowledge on areas such as art and antiques, real estate, or farm equipment.

Working as an auctioneer may also turn into more of a hobby or side job for people who branch off into different lines of work, but enjoy conducting auctions.

Employment outlook

Many beginners work part time as auctioneers, or gain experience as assistants. Some auctioneers get exposure working charity or fundraising events. The areas of interest and expertise an auctioneer follows may also have an influence on their employment possibilities. Often times livestock, farm equipment, and farm land is sold in more rural areas. Because many auctioneers get jobs based on their reputation and familiarity within a town, some auctioneers may need to live in or near that town, or travel through frequently enough for people to know their abilities.

Artwork is often sold in urban areas and may take a more specialized background as well. Auctioneers with good skills and personality as well as a good style of delivery, however, often have success finding work. For an ambitious auctioneer who is willing to travel to various jobs and invest time gaining experience, regular jobs are possible, as is the case for auctioneers employed by firms who invest time gaining more knowledge from the better-known auctioneers.

Earnings

Auctioneers have an above average wage earning potential. Wages for part time auctioneers in the early 1990s are close to $10,000 and full-time auctioneers may earn more than $20,000. On a daily basis, the wages range between $100 and $2,000.

Often auctioneers get paid on commission. This may occur once an auctioneer has gained suitable experience or has specialized in selling certain goods, such as real estate or livestock. Part-time auctioneers may supplement their income by assisting more experienced workers acting as cashiers or helping with publicity or organization of the items.

Conditions of work

Because auctioneers sometimes travel to where their assignment is, this can provide for a range of working conditions. Auctions are held year round. They are held in cities as well as small towns and occur in all types of weather. Auctioneers may work outside during a state fair or inside in a large hall. The type of goods being sold may also dictate their working conditions; for instance, farm equipment is commonly sold in rural areas.

Auctioneers are often set up with a podium and microphone, as certain auctions may draw more than two thousand people. This assists the auctioneer in keeping the crowds' attention, as the noise and activity can be stressful.

Social and psychological factors

Auctioneers have the opportunity to travel to different areas, earn considerable wages without the restriction of traditional working hours and work independently. Some auctioneers are good performers as well, and as such have the chance to "entertain" good-sized audiences.

An auctioneer who is motivated and experienced can learn about many different subjects and often enjoys meeting different people.

133

Automobile sales workers
Sales Occupations

GOE: 08.02.03; SIC: 7389; SOC: 447

National Auctioneers Association
8880 Ballentine
Overland Park, KS 66214

◇ **SOURCES OF ADDITIONAL INFORMATION**

Livestock Marketing Association
7509 Tiffany Springs Parkway
PO Box 901402
Kansas City, MO 64190

Missouri Auctioneer School
1600 Genesee
Kansas City, MO 64102

◇ **RELATED ARTICLES**

Volume 1: Retailing; Wholesaling
Volume 2: Buyers, wholesale and retail; Retail managers
Volume 3: Counter and retail clerks; Retail sales workers; Wholesale trade sales workers

Automobile sales workers

Definition

Automobile sales workers help a customer in selecting a new or used car. They are familiar with the type and model of the car they are selling. They know the features of the car and can provide a valuable service to the customer in assisting him in his choice. Automobile sales workers also perform a service to the dealer they are employed by in making sure the dealer's customers are happy with their purchase.

History

There have been automobile sales workers since the first line of automobiles was produced for sale. In the 1870s when the first steamer vehicles were designed, they were usually designed by and belonged to the owner. When larger scale production began, however, the designer had no time left to sell his product. The designer was found in the shop supervising the production. It became necessary to hire a person who knew how the vehicle operated.

Nature of the work

An automobile sales worker usually sells either used cars or new cars. The sales worker is em-

ployed by a dealer who frequently specializes in one particular automobile make.

Usually the customers come to the showroom and this is the first contact the sales worker has with the customer. In slow seasons, however, it may be necessary for the sales worker to go looking for customers. He or she can do this through newspaper advertising, advertising cards placed on automobiles mentioning a trade-in price, telephone soliciting, and various other methods of prospective customer contact.

The automobile sales worker must use psychology in understanding customers. Some customers may be interested only in the appearance of the car and the ease of handling it. Other customers may be more concerned with the performance and engine specifications. The sales worker must be able to figure out specifically what it is the customer wants and point out these features of the automobile to customers to aid them in deciding to buy. An automobile represents a large investment and customers may hesitate taking the final step. Sales workers must be able to convince the customer that he or she is doing the right thing and getting a good automobile. The sales worker must be convinced that the product is good and reasonable in price.

Once the customer has decided on a particular automobile the sales worker places the order and draws up the necessary papers. This may include financing and insurance. The sales worker checks the automobile before it is delivered to the customer and explains the conditions of the warranty. If the customer is pleased with the service of the sales worker, he or she will come back with future business and will also recommend the sales worker to any friends who are looking for a car.

One of the elements of car sales that differs from other retailing is that some bartering takes place between customer and salesperson. The price of the car is determined through negotiations.

With so many brands of automobiles on the market, a salesperson must actively convince a customer to purchase an automobile from him.

Requirements

A pleasing personality is necessary to be a successful sales worker. An automobile sales worker must be able to influence people and must be able to overcome sales resistance. They must also have a thorough knowledge of the product offered for sale. A good personal appearance and manners are important requirements. An automobile sales worker must be familiar with finance and insurance rates.

Special requirements

There are no special requirements for this field.

Opportunities for experience and exploration

It is important to know how an automobile runs. There are books available in libraries that explain the principle of automobile mechanization. Any type of sales experience could help people decide if they have the personality for sales work. New and used car dealers frequently hire students to wash cars after school hours. There are also small jobs such as changing tires, batteries, and lights available to students.

Related occupations

Sales work is available in many different fields. Other areas of interest might include travel agent, route drivers, retail sales workers, wholesale trade sales workers, securities and financial services sales representatives, and service sales representatives.

Methods of entering

There are several ways to become an automobile sales worker. Naturally the more experience a person has, the sooner he or she will be able to enter sales. A high-school graduate who has some experience and has shown initiative can be given further on-the-job training. Some large dealers provide special classes on sales training. Some automobile manufacturers provide training manuals and other educational materials.

A dealer usually has weekly sales meetings. Dealers prefer their sales workers to have had such courses as psychology, business law, public speaking, math, and English.

Advancement

A successful automobile sales worker who can manage other people in addition to selling automobiles may advance to assistant sales manager, sales manager, or general manager.

Employment outlook

The U.S. automobile industry experienced a severe decline in sales in the 1970s and early 1980s, partly because of competition from foreign cars and partly because of a general recession that prompted many prospective buyers to postpone their purchases. Employment opportunities in the auto industry were therefore extremely limited. By the early 1990s, however, the automobile industry was showing signs of recovery, so job opportunities improved, too.

About 160,000 people were employed as new and used automobile sales workers.

Earnings

Earnings depend on the area of the country in which the sales worker is employed. In a rural area there will be fewer car sales. In urban and suburban areas there is a greater turnover in the car market. Some automobile agencies pay on a straight salary basis and others pay a commission.

Automobile sales workers made an average salary of more than $26,000 a year in the early 1990s. Those working for dealers who sold fewer than 200 autos annually averaged less, while those who worked for dealers selling more than 1,000 cars a year averaged more.

Conditions of work

Showrooms are usually clean and light. New cars are always clean. Used cars are normally outside on a lot. Most used cars are cleaned thoroughly before being put on the lot for sale.

Most dealers provide paid vacations and many provide life insurance, hospitalization, and medical plans.

Most automobile sales workers must work some evenings. Families frequently shop for a car after regular working hours. Some automobile dealers are open on Sunday. There will be some evening and weekend work for an automobile sales worker.

Social and psychological factors

Because automobile sales workers are constantly in competition there can be a resulting strain on a person. It is important that the sales worker be pleasant and get along well with people.

There may be a discouraging period of days when sales workers make no sales, so they must be able to maintain a sense of self-confidence and determination to overcome these slack periods. This is particularly true during periods of a slow economy in auto sales overall.

GOE: 08.02.02; SIC: 5511; SOC: 4342

◇ **SOURCES OF ADDITIONAL INFORMATION**

National Automobile Dealers Association
8400 Westpark Drive
McLean, VA 22102

National Independent Automobile Dealers Association
600 Las Colinas Boulevard
Suite 314
Irving, TX 75039

◇ **RELATED ARTICLES**

Volume 1: Automotives; Business Administration; Retailing; Wholesaling
Volume 2: Retail managers
Volume 3: Manufacturers' sales representatives; Retail sales workers; Wholesale trade sales workers

Car-rental agents

Definition

Car-rental agents, also known as *car-rental clerks*, take orders for customers wishing to reserve automobiles. They service customers in person as well as over the phone. Sometimes car-rental clerks work closely with travel agencies, hotels, and corporate accounts. Car-rental agents may make suggestions as to the type and size car customers may need for the distance they are travelling or for their specific purpose.

History

Because advances in transportation have made it possible to travel across countries and oceans, adjunct services have developed for the convenience of travelers. More sophisticated modes of transportation take travelers further and to more remote areas. This ability, however, has created new needs and luxuries for travelers at the other end of the line. Travelers formerly relied on friends and relatives, as well as public transportation for local shuttling. Some even borrowed cars belonging to friends and business associates. As the need increased, car-rental agencies sprang up in key locations and afforded the traveler an economic and convenient way for maneuvering around a strange city. Vacationers and business travelers now find it possible to cover an expanse of ground independently and in a manner suited to their own schedule.

Nature of the work

Car-rental clerks may work at agencies located at airports, marinas, bus, and train terminals. They act as salespeople and take orders and reservations from clients who wish to rent an automobile. They sell not only the availability of the automobiles that the agency carries, but additional services such as insurance and collision coverage. They inform the customer as to the different options and makes of cars they may choose from. Rental agents are also expected to know information regarding the details of the vehicles, for instance, how the air conditioning works, whether the car has an automatic or manual transmission, and if it has power seats and windows. The agents may take reservations in person or over the phone. They may receive requests through the mail as well. Clerks make note of all the reservations they receive either entering them on a computer or filling out a special form that the company keeps on file. The agent is responsible for making sure the details of the reservation are correct. Details such as the type of car requested, the dates a car is to be in use, anticipated mileage, or destinations are examples of the information a clerk might need to know when handling a reservation. Also, it should be clear if the customer is planning to return the car to the original or different branch location of that particular rental agency.

Clerks accept preliminary payment for the reservations by credit card. In rare cases, transactions involve cash, and that is usually done for in-person requests or if someone mails in a check accompanying their reservation. Rental agencies also accept travelers' checks as payment. Agents will run credit checks to ensure that payment will be approved. If there is a problem or error, clerks must have a phone number in which to contact the customer in hopes of rectifying it. Many car-rental agencies accept all major credit cards to better service their customers and give them varied options for payment.

When customers come in to pick up their car, the rental agent checks to make sure that particular vehicle is available and is in good condition. The car should be clean and running well. The agent should know the condition the car is in and often check the vehicles themselves and make note of any damages to the exterior of the car. Agents also make sure the terms in the rental contract have been carried out, and that the customer is receiving the automobile or type of automobile he or she originally requested. In situations where a car is no longer available for the customer, many times the agent will offer them a larger, nicer car at no additional cost.

Once the car has been returned by the customer, the agent must calculate mileage and the duration of the rental and is also responsible for adding any tax, handling, or additional fees. The agent enters this information into a computer and presents the customer with an itemized invoice. In addition, the clerk assesses the condition of the returned car to ensure that there has not been any damage while it has been out of the agency.

Agents may work with a number of different people within the rental firm. They may delegate certain tasks to others and oversee their completion, acting as a kind of coordinator. Agents from different branches of the same firm may assist each other and coordinate efforts for pick-ups and returns that occur at different locations.

Requirements

Car-rental agents should understand that in dealing with the public, courtesy, and thoroughness are important qualities. Good car-rental clerks should be patient, have good organizational skills, and neat work habits. A

Car-rental agents
Sales Occupations

A car rental agent at an airport prepares the necessary forms for a client.

cheerful manner and good speaking voice will make a customer feel at ease.

Car-rental clerks are not required to have any specific education, however, many agencies prefer the employee to have a high-school diploma or GED certificate. In addition, courses in communication, data processing, mathematics, and general business are often helpful.

Special requirements

Many car-rental agencies offer on-the-job training to their clerks. The instruction is most likely to include taking reservations, working with the telephone and computer system and guidelines in evaluating the condition of the automobiles. Basics of sales techniques such as offering additional services and suggesting certain vehicles to match the customer's need may also be included.

Agents will also become more familiar with the cars the firm rents, and may be required to drive certain cars and make note of special features and options the cars contain. Additional skills such as car maintenance and courses in sales are also helpful. Foreign languages are helpful, particularly for rental agents at airports with international flights. Languages that are frequently needed include Spanish, Japanese, French, and German; different locations will have different needs, though.

Rental agents often belong to one of the unions in the industry. Organizations such as the International Brotherhood of Teamsters and the Automotive, Allied, and Industrial Workers Union provide guidelines for improvement of performance and development of skills.

Opportunities for experience and exploration

Those wishing to explore the field of car-rental agents may gain useful experience in a variety of sales or customer service jobs. Previous job history working with automobiles, computers, or record keeping is also useful. Job experiences that require workers to be detail oriented, courteous, and focus on communication offer skill development that is highly sought after in the rental agent profession.

Related occupations

Car-rental agents are but a small part of the vast travel, tourism, and hospitality industry in the United States. Other occupations that might be of interest include flight attendants, travel agents, hotel and motel clerks, and hotel and motel managers, and other occupations that cater to travelers.

Methods of entering

Applicants should contact the human resource departments of car-rental agencies and request an application. They may also inquire as to job prerequisites and interview openings. Applicants should be prepared to list their job history or make note of any previous training and classes that might highlight their strengths and skills. Some new employees are hired on a part-time basis and given more hours and responsibilities as their familiarity with the job improves.

Advancement

Rental agents may be promoted to supervisory and management positions. Experienced clerks may be asked to oversee training of new employees, create work schedules, and assign shifts or be responsible for recruiting additional manpower for busy periods. Some employees may take management or business training classes for additional preparation for advancement or may transfer to the corporate offices of the agency and work in the areas of personnel or administration.

Employment outlook

As travel continues to be a necessity as well as a luxury, related services continue to benefit and grow. The number of car-rental clerks is expected to increase 33 percent by the early 1990s. The high number of part-time employees in this field coupled with a significant separation rate of 36 percent keep a steady availability of jobs open. Many car-rental agencies are likely to hire new employees prior to their peak season in the summer and for temporary help during holidays. A temporary employee who has demonstrated good performance, however, may be offered a full-time position in the agency.

Earnings

Because there is such a need for rental cars, clerks are in demand to fill the ongoing shifts that agencies operate. Wages for car-rental agents are favorable compared to related customer service types of jobs. Though there are not any stringent guidelines for salaries, car-rental agents without any prior experience can earn almost $6.00 per hour. Clerks with more experience may earn as much as $10.00. Wages may be more if the agent works the less popular shifts.

Employees who belong to a union may be eligible for regular salary increases and good benefits packages. Often benefits such as sick pay, paid vacations, and health insurance are available through union memberships. Some agencies pay bonuses for incentives and hold contests to boost sales.

Conditions of work

Car-rental agents may work at airports, hotel courtesy desks, or other transportation terminals. They may also be employed at office locations in downtown sections of large cities. They may work at the front counter handling customers in person or operate telephones and computers and enter reservations that are called in by clients. Often car-rental agents work in a secretarial pool, typesetting where there are rows of desks equipped with phones, computers, or order sheets. Some facilities may be crowded and noisy and in some environments the pace can be very hectic.

Because airports, train, and bus stations are open all-year round, car-rental agencies can expect being busy everyday. A car-rental clerk may have to work nights and possibly put in overtime during holidays and summers when travel is especially high.

Social and psychological factors

Car-rental clerks may handle a high volume of reservations each day, whether over the phone or in-person. They are often asked to fulfill specific needs for automobiles that may not be available. These factors can contribute to stress and expose the employee to interaction with difficult customers. Car-rental clerks must be detail oriented and know how to solve problems that arise. Assistant managers also have the added responsibility of overseeing the work of their staff.

GOE: 09.04.02; SIC: 7514; SOC: 4363

◇ **SOURCES OF ADDITIONAL INFORMATION**

American Automotive Leasing Association
1001 Connecticut Avenue, NW
Suite 1201
Washington, DC 20036

American Car Rental Association
2011 I Street, NW
5th Floor
Washington, DC 20006

◇ **RELATED ARTICLES**

Volume 1: Automotives; Hospitality; Retailing; Transportation; Travel and Tourism
Volume 2: Hotel and motel managers; Retail managers; Travel agents
Volume 3: Automobile sales workers; Cashiers; Counter and retail clerks; Travel agents

Door-to-door sales workers

Definition

Door-to-door selling is a means of marketing goods and services by direct, personal contact with the ultimate consumer—usually, but not always, in the consumer's home. The distinguishing characteristic of this method of marketing is that the *door-to-door sales worker* arranges to contact the buyer to create a sale, instead of waiting for a buyer to come into a store or other permanent place of business. This kind of selling is also known as direct-to-consumer selling. This type of sales also includes *peddlers* and *vendors*. These last two types of workers make their products available in public places.

History

Direct selling in North America goes back to the storied "Yankee Peddler" of colonial times who traveled by wagon, on horseback, and sometimes afoot, bringing to isolated settlers many products not easily available otherwise. This forerunner of the modern direct salesperson created a demand, satisfied a need, and was always a welcome visitor.

Over the years, direct selling has launched many products, now found in almost every household, for which there was little or no demand when first introduced. It has, therefore, created mass markets that support many important industries.

Today, direct selling is one of four principal distribution channels for consumer goods and services, along with the retail store, direct-by-mail solicitation, and the mail order catalog. It is a multibillion dollar industry, and the thousands of companies engaged in direct selling market a wide variety of merchandise, including appliances and housewares, such as vacuum cleaners, cookware, china, tableware and linens, foods, drugs, cosmetics and toiletries, costume jewelry, clothing, nursery stock, and greeting cards. Direct selling is an important method of securing subscriptions to many newspapers and magazines.

Direct selling makes a contribution to education because it is basic to the production and marketing of encyclopedias and other educational publications and materials. It is often said that encyclopedia sets cannot be successfully demonstrated by the retail bookstore clerk. The customer wants to know more about the product and needs a specialist to demonstrate it and answer questions.

Nature of the work

Direct selling requires the salesperson to go into an available sales territory, find prospective buyers, introduce, explain, demonstrate, and take orders for the product or product line that he or she represents. Although there is a wide variation in types of direct selling plans, most fall into one or more of the major categories described below.

The Direct Company Representative. Such a representative may be an employee or an independent contractor, authorized to take orders for a product and compensated by a commission paid on such orders. The independent contractor type of direct company representative has the advantage of deciding when and how much time he or she will devote to selling the company's product. Direct company representatives are most often very well trained in presenting their product. Most encyclopedias are sold by sales people in this category. Workers who sell magazine subscriptions in this way may be hired, trained, and supervised by a *subscription crew leader*, who assigns crew members to a specific area, reviews the orders they take, and compiles sales records.

The Exhibit Plan. Sometimes the direct salesperson, with approval and cooperation of the company, will set up an exhibit booth at a place where large numbers of people can be expected to pass, such as a state fair. Here the salesperson sells to interested prospects and makes contacts for later demonstrations at home.

The Dealer Plan. This plan allows the direct salesperson to function as the proprietor of a small business, purchasing the product wholesale and reselling it at the retail price, mainly through house-to-house contacts.

The Group Plan. Under this arrangement, an individual purchaser is given the opportunity to sponsor further sales. For example, under a "Party Plan," the sales representative arranges with an interested sales prospect to invite a group of friends to his or her home for a display and demonstration of the products for sale. The host or hostess receives merchandise or a discount for the use of the home and for assembling the potential customers.

The C.O.D. Plan. In this case the direct seller carries sample merchandise or a sample book and sells for a specific direct-selling company at established list prices. The salesperson takes the order, perhaps collects an advance deposit, and sends the order to the company, which ships the merchandise direct to the customer on a C.O.D. basis, or to the direct seller who delivers and collects.

Whatever the sales plan, the direct seller has some unique advantages over the retailer counterpart. Direct sellers do not have to wait passively for the customer to come to them; the sellers go out and get a customer for their product. The direct seller often carries only one product or a limited line of products, and thus is much more familiar with the features, benefits, and advantages of the merchandise. As a rule, he or she gets the chance to demonstrate the product where it will most likely be used—in the home.

On the other hand, to be highly successful, the direct seller must develop strong selling skills and a persuasive selling formula. In a brief visit, the direct seller must gain acceptance and win the confidence of the prospect, develop an interest in the product or service offered, create a desire to buy, and close the sale.

To help those selling their products, the companies provide training programs, make available appropriate gifts and premiums that can be used to further the sales effort, and increasingly invest in advertising to make the selling job easier.

Requirements

Direct selling is, perhaps, the most wide-open of all occupational fields insofar as education, experience, and background skills are concerned.

Most door-to-door sellers have high-school diplomas, and approximately three out of ten have attended college. There seems to be little correlation, however, between courses taken in school and direct selling success, although English, public speaking, and psychology are undoubtedly helpful.

The basic requirement apparently is a desire to earn money while enjoying the freedom and independence of organizing one's own time and effort. A few personal traits, however, seem to be common to the more successful direct salesperson, including drive, attitude, and discipline.

A door-to-door salesman offers a variety of aluminum sidings to a homeowner. Many door-to-door salespeople call ahead for appointments.

Regarding discipline, the direct sales worker is usually independent, with no boss standing over him or her and prodding. It takes a substantial amount of self-discipline to organize one's own work and persevere in the face of turndowns.

Finally, it helps if the direct seller has a genuine liking for people and a friendly personality. Direct selling officials emphasize, however, that a person need not be a hearty extrovert to succeed. Shyer, more introverted persons often possess a sensitivity that is a decided plus in winning customer confidence.

Special requirements

The direct-to-consumer sales worker sometimes encounters local regulations designed to give the community some control over the activities of sales. For example, some municipalities and villages require licenses before house-to-house solicitations are allowed.

Opportunities for experience and exploration

Few career fields offer so many opportunities for acquiring experience and background that can be most helpful should an individual later decide to enter some other type of employment. It is possible to test direct selling on a part-time basis during vacation periods, while going to school, or on weekends while holding another job before deciding on it as a career. The only real investment is time and effort. Young people in Junior Achievement or in the

Door-to-door sales workers
Sales Occupations

Junior Sales Clubs of America, or those who take part in community benefit sales drives, all have developed some experience in direct selling.

Related occupations

Many other opportunities exist in the sales arena for those persons who find direct selling of interest and who possess the necessary talents and personal qualities. Some of these other jobs include route drivers, retail sales workers, automobile sales workers, retail managers, and wholesale trade sales workers.

Methods of entering

Direct selling is an easy field to enter. Almost all direct selling companies are continually on the lookout for new salespeople to meet the requirements of a market that is constantly expanding as population and family incomes increase. These companies advertise for representatives in the metropolitan dailies, in community newspapers, and in sales workers' specialty magazines. Also, interested people can contact the company of their choice by mail, phone, or personal visit. Most firms have district or area representatives whose jobs are to interview applicants and arrange for the necessary training of those who show promise. A student starting on a part-time basis may stay on full time.

Many people enter direct selling through contacts they have had with other direct sales representatives.

Advancement

All important companies in the direct-selling field present opportunities for advancement to those who can qualify. Because direct selling offers the chance to earn the extra money needed in an emergency, many temporary and part-time people are added to the ranks each year. This increases the number of career direct sellers required in recruiting, training, and management capacities.

Sales representatives who demonstrate administrative and business skills, as well as the ability to train others in sound selling techniques, can be promoted to area, branch, or district manager positions. A high percentage of the men and women now responsible for management and direction of the most successful firms in the field got their start as sales workers. Advancement opportunity is not limited to the sales end alone. Successful direct sales workers can move into non-sales executive positions with their companies—in marketing, merchandising, advertising and promotions, and even purchasing, helped by their understanding of selling and sales problems.

Employment outlook

About 5 million people currently work as direct sales workers in the United States and Canada. Of these almost half are women.

Thoughtful men and women connected with direct selling look on their industry as a stable one with excellent growth possibilities. As new products are developed for the consumer, the need increases for direct salespeople to introduce, demonstrate, and create a demand for these products.

The number of direct selling companies seems to have remained fairly constant over the past few years, and the growth in sales volume has generally followed the statistical up-curve of other types of retailing. The limiting factor in direct selling has been the lack of enough good salespeople to tap the potential. This industry, incidentally, has also been an important source of jobs for people displaced during periods of economic decline or by changing technology.

Earnings

Direct salespeople usually earn a straight commission on their sales, ranging from 10 percent to 40 percent of an item's suggested retail price. Therefore their typical or average income is hard to estimate as it is so completely governed by each individual's desire to succeed, time and effort put into the job, training and ability, and capacity to analyze thoughtfully a failure to secure an order and so improve the performance the next time a call is made.

A realistic, average annual income figure for good, full-time direct sales workers in the early 1990s is between $11,000 and $16,000 a year. It can be more and it can, of course, be less. It is safe to say that incomes of direct sellers compare favorably with those in the selling profession generally. Frequently, to earn more income, sales workers work more than 40-hour weeks.

142

Conditions of work

The direct salesperson has been called the world's smallest independent business person. Some direct sellers work in their own or nearby communities. Some travel more widely to cover additional territory made available to them by the companies with which they are associated.

When selling items that represent a considerable investment on the part of the customer or family, it is necessary to do the selling when both the husband and wife are at home and can, together, make the buying decision. For many items sold directly regular business hours are most suitable.

Some direct salespeople set a certain minimum weekly income goal and put in just enough hours each week to achieve it. There is certainly nothing wrong with this, although it is obviously not the best way for an ambitious person to advance in a direct selling career. This work, of course, involves being outdoors in all kinds of weather, and may also involve carrying a sometimes heavy sample case.

Direct selling requires the stamina to endure periods of discouragement and the resilience that makes this sales worker respond to discouragement by giving a better sales performance at the next opportunity. The good salesperson must also learn to expect a certain amount of rudeness and still maintain tact and patience.

Direct selling may not appeal to the young man or woman who seeks the security of a weekly paycheck of fixed amount. Those who go into business for themselves must be willing to risk their livelihood on the ability to perform and dispense with security guarantees in favor of greater monetary and personal rewards. So it is with the successful direct seller, whose income may fluctuate from week to week, but who generally winds up with a far-above-average annual income.

Social and psychological factors

Direct selling is a satisfying occupation for the person who likes a constant challenge and enjoys responding to it.

As in any business or occupation, there have been some undesirable people in direct selling. The overwhelming majority, however, are men and women who are respected in their communities and by their customers. The direct selling companies are aware that they are judged by the calibre of people who represent them and, over the years, have been increasingly selective in their choice of field representatives.

The enhanced status of the direct salesperson in the business community, as an important cog in consumer distribution of goods and services, and the increasingly valuable nature of direct selling services, are primarily responsible for growing public acceptance.

GOE: 08.02.05; SIC: Any industry; SOC: 4366

◇ **SOURCES OF ADDITIONAL INFORMATION**

Direct Selling Association
1776 K Street, NW
Suite 600
Washington, DC 20006

National Association for Professional Saleswomen
PO Box 2606
Novato, CA 94948

Professional Salespersons of America
3801 Monaco, NE
Albuquerque, NM 87211

World Federation of Direct Selling Associations
1776 K Street, NW
Suite 600
Washington, DC 20006

◇ **RELATED ARTICLES**

Volume 1: Apparel; Book Publishing; Magazine Publishing; Retailing
Volume 2: Advertising workers; Buyers; Retail managers
Volume 3: Manufacturers' sales workers; Retail sales workers; Services sales representatives

Insurance agents and brokers, life

Definition

An *insurance agent* sells policies that provide life, retirement income, and various other types of insurance to new clients or to regular customers. Sometimes, the agent may be referred to as a life underwriter, since he or she may be required to estimate insurance risks on some policies.

History

For several centuries people have tried to minimize the financial effect of death by pooling their risk with that of others. As hundreds or thousands of people purchase policies, insurance companies build up cash reserves from which death benefits may be paid as needed.

The first life insurance company in the United States was founded in Philadelphia in 1759 and was known as A Corporation for the Relief of Poor and Distressed Presbyterian Ministers and of Poor and Distressed Widows and Children of Presbyterian Ministers. The company still exists, although its name has been shortened to the Presbyterian Ministers Fund.

In the middle of the nineteenth century, companies similar to today's life insurance firms began to develop. Two types of organizations grew: mutual companies, which the policyholders own, and stock companies, which the stockholders own. The emergence of the full-time agent, who was paid a commission on the basis of what was sold, contributed greatly to the growth of life insurance.

Despite depressions, wars, and other catastrophes, the total amount of life insurance held has shown a remarkably consistent upward growth. In the early 1990s, about 1,800 companies sold life insurance. Their policyholders own more than six trillion dollars worth of protection.

Nature of the work

Life insurance sales agents act as field representatives for the companies to which they are under contract. They may be under direct contract or work through a general agent who holds a contract. Others are insurance brokers who act as independent operators and purchase insurance at their client's request from one of several companies. Some brokers carry, in addition, types of insurance (automobile, household, medical) to provide a more complete service package for their clients. All life insurance agents and brokers engage in a number of social and study activities designed to improve the volume and quality of sales.

The work of the agent may be divided into five functions: identifying and soliciting prospects, explaining services, developing insurance plans, closing the transaction, and follow-up. These will be explained in turn.

The life insurance agent must use initiative in identifying and soliciting prospects. Few agents can survive in the life insurance field through normal business and social contacts. One company, for example, asks that each week each agent make between twenty and thirty personal contacts with prospective customers, through which eight to twelve interviews may be obtained, resulting in from zero to three sales. Naturally, many days or weeks may pass without any sales. Then, suddenly, several sales in a row may quickly develop.

To identify prospects, some agents obtain leads by following newspaper reports to learn of newcomers to the community, birth of children, or business promotions. Other agents specialize in occupational groups, selling to doctors, farmers, or small businesses. Many agents use general telephone or mail solicitation to help identify prospects. All agents hope that satisfied customers may suggest future sales.

Successful contact with prospective clients may be a difficult process. Many potential customers may already have been solicited by a number of life insurance agents or may assume that they are not interested in buying insurance at this time. Agents, therefore, are often hard-pressed to obtain their initial goal—a personal interview to sit down and talk about insurance with the potential customer.

Agents usually travel to the customer's home or place of business for the sales interview. During this meeting, the agents seek to explain their services. Following sound sales techniques, this explanation must be adapted to the needs that the client outlines or faces. A new father, for example, may wish to ensure his child's college education. An older person may be most interested in provisions dealing with retirement income. With experience, agents learn how best to answer questions or objections raised by potential customers. The agents must be able to describe the coverage offered by their company in clear, nontechnical language.

With the approval of the prospective client, the agent develops an insurance plan. In some cases, this will involve only a single standard life insurance policy. In other instances, the agent will review the client's complete financial status and develop a comprehensive plan for death benefits, payment of the balance due on a home mortgage if the insured dies, creation of a fund for college education for children, and retirement income. Such plans usually take into account several factors: the insured's personal savings, mortgage and other obligations, social security benefits, and existing insurance coverage.

To best satisfy the customer's insurance needs, and in keeping with the customer's ability to pay, the agent draws upon a variety of insurance alternatives. The agent may, for example, recommend term insurance (the cheapest form of insurance as it may only be used as a death benefit) or ordinary life (which may be maintained by premium payments throughout the life of the insured, but which might be converted to aid in retirement living). In some cases, the agent may suggest a limited payment plan, such as twenty-payment life, which provides a completely paid-for policy upon the completion of a given number of annual premiums. Many agents develop comprehensive plans for life insurance to protect a business enterprise (such as the loss that will result from the death of a key partner); employee group insurance plans; or the creation and distribution of wealth through estates. The skill of the agent and the variety of plans offered by the company are combined to develop the best possible insurance proposal for customers.

Closing the transaction is the climax and probably the most difficult part of the insurance process. At this point, the customer must decide whether to purchase the recommended insurance plan, ask for a modified version of it, or conclude that no additional insurance is needed or financially possible.

Assuming that the customer decides to purchase a policy, the agent must arrange for the client to take a physical examination; company policies require that only good health risks be insured at standard rates. The agent also must obtain a completed insurance application and the first premium, and send them with other supporting papers to the company for its approval and for the formal issuance of a policy to the customer.

The final phase of the insurance process is follow-up, both to provide service to the poli-

A life insurance agent uses a computer to access information about a client's prospective policy. The computer is linked to a mainframe at the company's administrative offices.

cyholder or his beneficiaries and to sense the opportunity for additional sales.

The successful life insurance salesperson works hard at his or her job. A Census Bureau report revealed that 88 percent of all insurance agents (including both life and other types of insurance) averaged over forty hours of work a week. To fit into the free time of clients, many of the hours worked by the insurance salesperson are in the evenings or on weekends. In addition to the time spent with customers, agents must spend time in their home or office preparing insurance programs for customer approval, developing new sources of business, and writing reports for the company.

Requirements

Formal requirements for the life insurance field are few. Because more mature individuals are better able to master the complexities of the business and inspire customer confidence, most companies prefer to hire persons at least twenty-one years of age. Many new agents are more than thirty years of age. Most companies insist on at least a high-school education; many strongly prefer college training. College courses in English, economics, business law, sociology, psychology, and insurance are particularly helpful.

Of greater importance are the required personal characteristics. While no agent possesses all of them, the following traits are most helpful: genuine liking and appreciation for people; a positive attitude toward others and sympathy for their problems; personal belief in the values of life insurance coverage; willingness to spend

145

several years learning the business and becoming established; persistence, hard work, and patience. The salesperson should also be resourceful and organized to make the most effective use of his or her time.

The requirements for success in life insurance are high; in fact, so high that most who enter the field fail to succeed in it. A study made some years ago revealed that among all sales agents hired, only 45 percent were still employed by their company after one year. After a period of five years, only 14 percent were still with the same company. While some agents switched employers and remained in the field, it is obvious that most persons hired as life insurance salespeople leave for other occupations.

Despite the high rate of failure, life insurance sales offers a rewarding career for those who meet its exacting requirements. One authority says that life insurance offers the easiest way to earn $1,000 to $2,000 a month, but the most difficult to earn $300 or $400. This means that persons with strong qualifications may readily develop a successful insurance career, but the poorly qualified person finds it a very difficult field.

Special requirements

The life insurance salesperson must obtain a license in each state in which he or she sells insurance. In applying for this license, agents must be sponsored by the company which they represent. The company usually pays the license fee.

In most states, before the license is issued, the agent must pass a written test on insurance fundamentals and state insurance laws. Company training programs are usually directed toward preparation for these examinations. Often, the new agent may sell on a temporary certificate while preparing for the written examination. When no formal examination is required (as is the case in a few states), the license is awarded on the basis of the applicant's place of residence and character. Information on state life insurance licensing requirements can be easily obtained from the state commissioner of insurance.

For full professional status, many companies recommend that their sales workers become a Chartered Life Underwriter. To be designated "C.L.U.," salespeople must have successfully completed at least three years in the field and must have passed a series of examinations conducted by the American College, Bryn Mawr, Pennsylvania, which test the candidate's ability to apply to insurance problems their knowledge of life insurance, fundamentals, economics, business law, taxation, trusts, and finance. Only a small percentage of all sales workers are C.L.U.s.

Opportunities for experience and exploration

Because of state licensing requirements, it is difficult for young people to obtain actual part-time experience in life insurance sales. The most notable exceptions are the student-agency programs developed by several companies to provide college students with practical sales experience and a trial exposure to the field.

Persons wishing to learn about life insurance may supplement their readings and discussions in three practical ways: sales experience of any sort provides a measure of aptitude for life insurance sales (keep in mind, however, that many people can sell tangibles such as clothes in a retail store or advertisements in a program for a school play, but are unable to sell intangibles such as insurance); any part-time or summer work in an insurance company office will provide background information on the requirements for the field and an understanding of its problems, people, and prospects for the future; formal college or evening school courses in insurance provide a clearer picture of its techniques and its opportunities.

Related occupations

The selling of insurance requires many of the same interests and aptitudes in individuals as those required for real estate agents and brokers, retail sales workers, wholesale trade sales workers, and automobile sales workers.

Methods of entering

Applications for employment may be directed to personnel directors of insurance companies or to managers of branches or agencies. In either event, the new agent affiliates almost immediately with a local sales office. Prospective life insurance agents should discuss their career interests with representatives of several companies to select wisely the best employer. To increase the sales volume and income of the agency, the typical insurance office manager is prepared to hire all candidates who may be readily recruited and properly trained.

Potential employers should be carefully evaluated to select an organization that offers sound training, personal and intelligent supervision, resources to assist sales, adequate financial support, and a company name that will be well-received by customers. Students graduating from college should be able to arrange campus interviews with recruiting representatives of insurance companies. Persons with work experience in other fields usually find life insurance managers pleased to discuss opportunities in sales.

In addition to discussing personal interests and requirements for success in the field, employer representatives usually give prospective agents aptitude tests developed by their company or by the Life Insurance Marketing and Research Association.

Formal training usually involves three phases: precontract orientation summarizing the field, using excerpts from training manuals or other materials, which are designed to provide candidates with a clearer picture of the field; on-the-job training to present insurance fundamentals, techniques of developing sales prospects, principles of selling and establishment of a work schedule; intermediate instruction which may include company training of an advanced nature. More than 25,000 agents annually take the insurance courses prepared by the Life Underwriter Training Council (LUTC) and sponsored in most cities by local member associations of the National Association of Life Underwriters (NALU). After completing a specified number of courses, an agent may apply for the professional educational designation of Life Underwriter Training Council Fellow, sponsored by LUTC and conferred by NALU.

Advancement

Unlike some occupations, many of the ablest people in the field are not interested in advancement into management. In some cases, for example, a successful agent may earn more than the president of the company. An experienced agent often grows in the area of volume of business and quality of service rather than in responsibility for the work of others. Other agents develop professionally by specializing in various phases of insurance.

Many successful agents, however, aspire to positions in sales management. At first, they may begin by helping train newcomers to the field. Later, they may be made assistant managers of their office. Top agents are often asked by their company to take over as managers of an existing branch or to develop a new one. (In some cases, persons entering management must take a temporary salary cut as managers, particularly at the beginning, and may earn less than successful agents.) Often an experienced agent may be invited by a rival company to become a branch manager.

There are several types of life insurance sales office arrangements. Branch office managers are salaried employees who act for their company in a geographical region. General agency managers are given franchises by a company and develop and finance their own sales and service office in a given area. While general agents are not directly affiliated with their company, they must operate in a responsible manner to maintain their right to represent the company. General insurance brokers are self-employed persons who place insurance coverage with more than one life insurance company.

The highest management positions in the life insurance field are in company headquarters. Persons with sales and field management experience may be invited to accept a home office position.

Employment outlook

In the early 1990s, there were about 250,000 life insurance agents and brokers in the United States.

A number of factors should encourage moderate growth of employment in the life insurance field. Since 1900, the percentage of our citizens older than sixty-five has grown at a rate twice that of the general population. To meet the special needs of this group, many insurance policies can be converted from a death benefit to retirement income. Also, the twenty-five to fifty-four age group is growing, and it is this age group that has the greatest need for insurance.

Expanded social security programs, "G.I." insurance policies, and group insurance contracts have not reduced the tendency for Americans to purchase life insurance. Rather, they seem to have increased people's appreciation for insurance protection, and made the agent's job more complex in planning financial protection.

Employment opportunities for life insurance agents will also be aided by the general increase in our population, the heavy turnover among new agents, and the thousands of openings created by death and retirement alone.

Insurance agents and brokers, life
Sales Occupations

Despite these factors, growth will be slower than average for all occupations, as some life insurance business is taken over by "multiline" insurance agents, as department stores and other businesses outside the insurance industry begin to offer insurance and other financial services, and as computers make individual agents more efficient.

Earnings

The beginning agent usually receives some form of financial assistance from the company. He or she may be placed on a moderate salary for a year or two; often the amount of salary support declines each month on the assumption that commission income on sales will increase. Eventually, the straight salary is replaced by a drawing account—a fixed dollar amount advanced each month against anticipated commissions. This account helps agents balance out high and low earning periods.

Life insurance companies also usually assist their agents with office expenses such as desk space, supplies, stationery, postage, and secretarial assistance. Most agents, however, pay their own travel, telephone, entertainment, and other expenses.

Agents receive commissions on two bases: a first-year commission for making the sale (usually 55 percent of the total first-year premium); and a series of smaller commissions paid when the insured pays his annual premium (usually five percent of the yearly payments for nine years). Most companies will not pay renewal commissions to agents who resign.

Annual earnings of agents vary widely, from the beginning agent who may sell a policy a month up to the approximately 20,000 agents each year who qualify for the "Million Dollar Round Table" by selling policies with a face value of more than $1 million. The typical agent with five to ten years' experience earned about $42,000 in the early 1990s. Those with ten or more years' experience averaged $65,000.

Conditions of work

The job of the life insurance agent is marked by extensive contact with others. Most agents are active participants in groups (churches, community activities, service clubs) through which they will be exposed to prospective clients. Similarly, life insurance agents make strong personal contacts with individuals.

As they are essentially self-employed, the agents must be capable of operating on their own. In return, the life insurance field offers the chance to go into business for oneself without the need for capital investment, long-term debt, and personal liability.

Commenting on what they liked least about the life insurance field, a group of experienced agents listed: the amount of detail work required of an agent; the ignorance of the public concerning life insurance; the uncertainty of earnings while becoming established in the field; and the amount of night and weekend work. The last point is particularly important. Some agents begin by working four nights a week and both days of the weekend. After becoming established, this may be cut down to three or two evenings and only one day of the weekend. Agents are often torn between the desire to spend more time with their families and the reality that reducing evening and weekend work may handicap their income.

Social and psychological factors

Life insurance agents can readily sense their contribution to society as they see that they have provided financial protection for the family of a breadwinner whose life may end any time, for young people who might otherwise not be able to attend college, or for a couple who will be able to afford retirement.

Successful agents enjoy the company of people they meet through life insurance contacts. The independent nature of the life insurance field means that abilities and effort will be directly related to earnings.

On the negative side, the policies sold by most companies are very similar. To make a sale, the agent must rely heavily on personal sincerity, persuasive abilities, and the offer of continued service.

GOE: 08.01.02; SIC: 63; SOC: 4122

◇ **SOURCES OF ADDITIONAL INFORMATION**

Life Insurance Marketing and Research Association
PO Box 208
Hartford, CT 06141

For information on insurance companies, programs, and publications, write:

American Council of Life Insurance
1001 Pennsylvania Avenue, NW
Washington, DC 20004

National Association of Life Underwriters
1922 F Street, NW
Washington, DC 20006

◇ **RELATED ARTICLES**

Volume 1: Insurance
Volume 2: Insurance claims representatives; Underwriters
Volume 3: Insurance agents and brokers, property and casualty; Manufacturers' sales representatives; Securities and financial services sales representatives

Insurance agents and brokers, property and casualty

Definition

Property and casualty insurance agents and brokers sell policies that help individuals and companies cover expenses and losses from such risks as fire, burglary, traffic accidents, and other emergencies. These salespeople also may be known as *fire, casualty, or marine insurance agents or brokers.* Sometimes, they are called *property and casualty underwriters.*

History

The story of the development of property and casualty insurance parallels the history of human economic development. This insurance was first found in the marine field. A single shipwreck could put a shipowner out of business. It became essential to share this risk. Organized maritime insurance began in the seventeenth century at Lloyd's coffeehouse in London. Descriptions of individual ships, their cargoes, and their destinations were posted. Persons willing to share the possible loss, in return for a fee, signed their names below these descriptions indicating what percentage of the financial responsibility they were willing to assume. Those who signed were known as underwriters.

As experience was acquired, predictions of loss became more accurate and rates standardized. To provide protection for larger risks, individuals organized companies. The first ma-

rine insurance company in the United States, the Insurance Company of North America, was founded in Philadelphia in 1792. This company still survives.

Other types of insurance developed in response to people's need for protection. Insurance against loss by fire became available after the disastrous lesson of the London Fire of 1666. The first accident insurance policy in the United States was sold in 1863. Burglary insurance, protection against property taken by forced entrance, was offered soon thereafter. Theft insurance, which covers other forms of stealing, was first written in 1899.

Around the turn of the century the development of the horseless carriage" led to the automobile insurance industry. The first automobile policy was sold in 1898. This area of the insurance field grew rapidly. In the early 1990s private and passenger auto liability totaled more than 33 billion dollars.

Growth of business and industrial organizations necessitated protection for employees injured on the job. The first workers' compensation insurance was sold in 1910.

Insurance companies have always been alert to new marketing possibilities. In the last few decades, increasing emphasis has been placed upon "package" policies offering comprehensive coverage. Typical is the homeowner's policy which, in addition to fire protection, covers losses from explosions, windstorms, hail, smoke, aircraft and other vehicles, riots, and civil commotion. In the mid-1950s, a group of private firms provided the

Business partners discuss the prospects of insuring their company's cars with an insurance agent's company.

first insurance on the multimillion dollar reactors used in atomic energy plants.

Recently, however, certain social changes have brought about major shifts in the policies of property and casualty companies. Because of the rising rate of vandalism, burglaries, and thefts, such as shoplifting, many companies either refuse to insure against these occurrences or else have raised rates to a prohibitive level. Theft, fire, and burglary insurance have become financial impossibilities for many small merchants in urban areas. Universities and large corporations must pay very high premiums to obtain protection against increasing vandalism.

In the field of automobile insurance, the increasing incidence of theft and road accidents has also taken a tremendous toll. In a recent year the auto insurance companies lost close to $1,200,000,000 in claims, and over the past decade claims exceeded premiums by almost $2 billion.

Nature of the work

Property and casualty insurance salespersons work under one of three types of contracts. An agent serves as the authorized representative of one or several companies. In general, the policies the agent writes are limited to those offered by these companies. A broker has no connection with a company but orders policies for customers through several agents or directly

from the companies. Special agents or office agents represent the company that employs them. They write only policies offered by their company. In many cases, special agents work out of a regional office that handles other insurance functions such as claims investigation or claims adjusting. Where special or office agents are salaried employees of a company, agents and brokers are self-employed. Often agents or brokers will employ additional salespeople or solicitors on a salary or on a commission.

All three types of sales workers operate in a similar fashion. Each one orders or issues policies, collects premiums, renews and changes existing coverage, and assists clients with reports of losses and settlement of claims. Backed by the resources of the companies that they represent, individual agents may issue policies insuring for loss or damage for everything from furs and automobiles to ocean liners or factories.

Agents are authorized to issue a "binder" to provide complete protection for customers between the time they sign the policy application and its approval by the granting company. Naturally, the agent must be selective in the risks accepted under a binder. When a risk is refused by a company or its agent, the customer may become hostile to the broker.

Some agents or brokers specialize in one type of insurance such as automobile. All agents or brokers, however, must have a knowledge of the kind of protection required and the exact differences offered by each company they represent.

Requirements

An agent or broker must thoroughly understand insurance fundamentals and recognize the differences between the many options provided by various policies. The salesperson who reflects such knowledge in conversations with clients usually gains their respect and confidence. To provide greater service to customers and to increase volume of sales, beginning agents usually study and enter new areas of insurance protection. The process of obtaining this knowledge requires an analytical mind, the ability to teach oneself how to use standard manuals, and the capacity for hard work.

The agent or broker must be able to meet strangers easily and to talk readily with a wide range of persons such as teenagers with their first cars, business executives faced with heavy responsibilities, and widows confronted for the first time with financial management of a home. Agents must be resourceful, self-confident, conscientious, and cheerfully buoyant. As in other types of sales, a strong belief in the service being sold helps agents to be more convincing in their sales presentations. As they spend so much of their time with others, agents must have a genuine liking for people. Equally important is the desire to serve others through insurance sales. To be successful, the agent must be able to present insurance information in a clear, nontechnical fashion. He or she must be able to develop a logical sales sequence to present information in a successful style.

Successful agents usually participate in a number of community group activities. They find that people respond positively to them. They often have an unusual facility for recalling names of people and past conversations.

Because they work in small organizations, agents must possess both personal sales and management abilities. Many insurance offices consist of the agent and a single secretary. The freedom enjoyed by the agent necessitates careful self-planning.

Minimum educational requirements include a high-school degree. Although college training is not a prerequisite, an increasing number of agents and brokers hold a college degree. Many have taken insurance courses, which are offered in hundreds of colleges and universities in the United States. Others find a general background in business administration, accounting, economics, or business law helpful. For some phases of property insurance, such as fire protection on commercial establishments, an engineering background may prove helpful.

Special requirements

All agents and most brokers must obtain licenses in each state in which they sell insurance. Most states require that the agent pass a written examination dealing with the insurance laws of the state and fundamentals of property and casualty insurance. Often, candidates for licenses must show evidence of some formal study in the field of insurance. Where a written examination is not required, the state insurance commission reviews references dealing with the agent's residence and character before granting the license.

For the highest professional status, agents may seek to qualify for the designation Chartered Property Casualty Underwriter (C.P.C.U.). The C.P.C.U. requires that the agent must have successfully completed at least three years in the field, have demonstrated

high ethical practices in all work, and passed a series of ten examinations offered by the American Institute for Property and Casualty Underwriters. Agents and brokers may prepare for these examinations through home study or by taking courses offered by colleges, insurance societies, or individual companies. As an intermediate step, many agents complete a study and examination program conducted by the Insurance Institute of America. Successful completion of this program means the agent receives a certificate and is ready for final study before taking the first parts of the C.P.C.U. examinations.

Opportunities for experience and exploration

Because of state licensing requirements, it is difficult for young people to obtain part-time experience in this field. Summer employment, of any sort, in a property and casualty insurance office should provide a helpful view of the field. As many offices are small and must be attended at all times, students have often found summer positions with individual agencies or brokerage firms.

Colleges with work-study programs may offer the opportunity for practical experience in an insurance agency.

Related occupations

The insurance industry offers an enormous range of occupational opportunities. Among the many careers available to persons with interests and abilities similar to insurance agents are insurance policy processing occupations, top managers and executives, underwriters, life insurance agents and brokers, and claims representatives.

Methods of entering

College graduates are frequently hired through campus interviews for salaried sales positions with major companies. Other graduates secure positions directly with agents or brokers through placement services, employment offices, or classified advertisements in newspapers. Many high-school and college graduates apply directly to insurance companies or to local agents. Sometimes, persons employed in other fields take evening or home-study courses in insurance to prepare for employment in property and casualty insurance.

Once hired, the new agent or salesperson uses training materials prepared by a company or by the industry. In smaller agencies, newcomers may be expected to assume major responsibility for their own training using written resources placed at their disposal and working directly with experienced agents. In larger organizations, initial training may include formal classroom instruction. Sometimes, insurance societies sponsor courses designed to help the beginning agent. Almost all agents receive directed, on-the-job sales supervision.

Advancement

Salaried sales agents may advance in one of several ways. They may decide to establish their own agency or brokerage firm. They may join or buy out an established agency. Or they may advance into branch or home office management with an insurance company.

Self-employed agents or brokers usually remain with the organization that they have developed. Often, they grow professionally by expanding the scope of their insurance activities. Many agents expand their responsibilities and the size of their office volume by hiring additional salespeople. Occasionally, an established agent may enter related areas of activity. Typical is the property insurance agent who branches out into real estate sales. Many agents and brokers devote an increasing amount of their time to worthwhile community projects, which helps to build goodwill and probable future clients.

Employment outlook

More than 375,000 people worked as insurance agents and brokers in the United States in the early 1990s. About eight percent of them worked exclusively in fire, marine, and casualty insurance.

The overall demand for insurance should increase as the general population grows and the level of personal and corporate possessions rises. Most homeowners and business executives budget insurance as a necessary expense. Their dependence is reflected in the fact that insurance premium rates have gone up almost 600 percent in the last twenty years. Laws that require businesses to provide workers' compensation insurance and require car owners to obtain automobile liability protection help to create an expanding insurance market.

Despite increasing sales, however, employment of insurance agents will probably grow more slowly than average through the mid-1990s. There are many reasons for this trend. Computers are making agents more efficient in performing routine clerical tasks, and more policies are being sold by mail and through retail stores. Also, as insurance becomes more and more crucial, many large businesses are hiring their own risk managers, who analyze their insurance needs and select the policies best for them.

Earnings

The employed sales agent is usually paid a moderate salary while learning the business. After becoming established, however, most agents are paid on the basis of a commission on sales. Agents who work directly for an insurance company often receive a base salary in addition to some commission on sales production. Salespersons employed by companies often receive fringe benefits (retirement income, sick leave, paid vacations) not enjoyed in the same form or in the same amount by the self-employed agent or broker.

In the early 1990s, new sales workers received an average of $1,440 per month during their six-week training period and for about thirty months thereafter, depending on performance. Thereafter, they usually received a commission. Agents with five to ten years of experience earned, on the average, more than $42,000 a year. Those with more than ten years of experience earned an average of more than $66,000; many earned more than $100,000.

Unlike life insurance, which features a high first-year commission, the property and casualty agent receives the same rate each time the annual premium is paid.

Conditions of work

One of the most significant aspects of the work of the property and casualty agent is the variety of the job. An agent's working day may begin with an important conference with a group of executives seeking protection for a new industrial plant and its related business activities. Following this meeting, the agent may proceed to the office to spend several hours studying the needs of the customer and drafting an insurance plan. The proposal must be good because several other local agents will be competing for the contract. While working at the office, the agent receives several calls and visits from prospective or current clients asking questions about protection and policy conditions, changes, or new developments.

At noon, the agent may attend a meeting of a service club or lunch with a policyholder. After lunch, the agent may visit a garage with a customer to discuss the car repairs needed as the result of an automobile accident. Back at the office, the agent may talk on the telephone with an adjuster of the insurance company involved.

In the late afternoon, the agent may call on a superintendent of schools to discuss insurance protection for both participants and spectators at athletic events and other public meetings. The school may have no protection, and the agent should evaluate the insurance needs.

Again returning to the office, the agent may telephone several customers, dictate responses to the day's mail, and handle other matters that have developed during the day. In the evening, the agent may call on a family to discuss insurance protection for a new home.

Social and psychological factors

The property casualty agent can sense a key role in selling for an industry that provides employment for thousands of people, invests $30 billion in our economy, and provides protection that in one form or another assists almost every American.

Property and casualty insurance permits businesses to expand without fear of unexpected financial reverses that would occur if each company had to set aside sufficient funds to anticipate possible property and casualty losses. Business expansion would thus be seriously curtailed.

GOE: 08.01.02; SIC: 63; SOC: 4122

◇ **SOURCES OF ADDITIONAL INFORMATION**

Independent Insurance Agents of America
100 Church Street, Suite 1901
New York, NY 10007

Insurance Information Institute
110 William Street
New York, NY 10033

Insurance Institute of America
720 Providence Road
Malvern, PA 19355

◇ **RELATED ARTICLES**

Volume 1: Banking and Financial Services; Insurance; Real Estate
Volume 2: Insurance claims representatives; Real estate agents and brokers; Underwriters
Volume 3: Insurance agents and brokers, life; Securities and financial services sales workers

Manufacturers' sales workers

Definition

The *manufacturer's sales worker* displays, demonstrates, or describes products made by the company that employs him or her to sell the products to potential customers. The representative usually calls on these customers (wholesale houses, retail merchants, business concerns, and institutions) at their places of business.

History

The role of the manufacturer's sales worker evolved along with the industrialization of our economy. Mass production of products demanded mass distribution. When retail store owners, for example, found that they could purchase merchandise without having to travel to its place of manufacture, they eagerly welcomed the traveling representative.

At first, these traveling representatives used all the tricky devices at their disposal to make a sale and then quickly left town before complaints of overselling or poor quality developed. It soon became evident, however, that the long-range interests of both the manufacturer and the representatives required a more factual sales description and, eventually, service to make sure that the product provided maximum satisfaction to the customer. Today's customer, in addition, often receives the security of a written guarantee from the manufacturer.

As their occupation developed, the manufacturers' representatives benefited from the transportation revolution that has altered our country in the last one hundred years. The improved railroad networks of the late nineteenth century permitted the representative to move effectively from town to town. The advent of the automobile further enabled people to travel quickly to many more communities and to more easily transport a sizeable quantity of product samples and descriptive catalogs. The growth of commercial aviation made it possible for a highly specialized representative to sell directly to accounts in New York, Atlanta, Los Angeles, and Minneapolis—all during the course of a single week.

The food products industry is the largest employer of manufacturers' representatives. Other fields with large numbers include printing, publishing, fabricated metal products, chemicals and dyes, electrical and other machinery, and transportation equipment.

Nature of the work

The particular products sold by manufacturers' representatives directly affect the nature of their work. Some salespeople, for example, may represent a sporting goods manufacturer. They may spend most of their time driving from town to town calling on retail stores that carry sporting equipment and visiting with high-school and college coaches and athletic directors. Often the representative in this line is a former athlete or coach who feels very much at home in this kind of environment.

Other representatives may sell food products for a major processor. They usually know the grocery stores and major chains that will carry their products. Their main concern, therefore, is to ensure the maximum volume of sales. The representative may negotiate with the retail merchant to obtain the most advantageous store and shelf position for display of his or her firm's products. Salespeople will en-courage the store or chain to advertise their products—sometimes by offering to pay part of the advertising costs or by reducing the selling price to the merchant so that the latter may be able to offer a special sale price on certain items. The sales worker may check to make sure that shelf items are neatly arranged and that reserve stocks are still fresh.

The salesperson for a major steel producer makes individual sales that may run into millions of dollars. In a single transaction, this worker may arrange for terms under which a washing machine manufacturer, a construction company, or a toy company will purchase all the steel products needed for a period of time. Because of the significance of such sales to the company that employs the sales worker, the steel salesperson has a particularly long period of training and preparation before assuming complete responsibility for a set of customers. When not selling to manufacturing or construction firms, the steel salesperson may sell to jobbers who handle smaller amounts of metal considered too impractical for the steel companies themselves to distribute. The steel sales workers may do much of their business by long distance telephone as they sell a product that is standardized and that, to the usual customer, requires no particular description or demonstration.

Sales workers who sell highly technical machinery or complex office equipment are often referred to as sales engineers or industrial salespeople. They frequently must begin by analyzing the customer's production process or flow of clerical materials. They usually prepare an extensive sales presentation that includes precise information on the equipment recommended for purchase or long-term rental, the cost of this equipment, and the total effect upon the customer's profits or quality of service. Sales engineers often work with the research and development departments of their own companies on methods of adapting products to a customer's specialized needs. In many cases, the salesperson also provides initial instruction on the new equipment or works with installation experts who provide this service. Technical sales workers are often backed up with a sales assistance staff designed to provide specific information to support sales activities and permit the salespeople to devote a greater percentage of their time to direct sales contact.

The work of manufacturer's representatives may be summed up under these varied functions: They make periodic calls on regular customers and occasional contact with customers having specialized needs; inform customers of old and new products, availability of supply, and prices; help with ordering and inventory control; arrange for delivery and installation; handle customer complaints on the spot or refer them to the company for settlement; check on the activity and products of competitors and perhaps attempt to lure customers away from other companies; and, in general, do all that they can to most effectively represent their company in an assigned area.

To provide background for their sales activities, the manufacturers' salespersons must study new products; write up orders, maintain expense records, plan future calls, schedule appointments, make travel plans, and perform similar activities; and follow-up on pending business. Sometimes salespeople attend trade conferences or set up displays in hotel rooms to promote sales to local buyers.

Sometimes, the sales worker does not engage in direct selling activities but strives to create a better general market for his products. Typical is the sales representative for a drug company who calls on physicians and hospitals to inform them of the availability of new products and to distribute samples. This worker is usually a trained pharmacist, and is called a detail person.

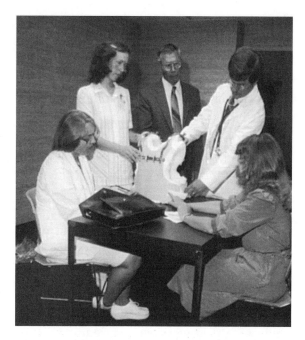

A medical supplies salesman demonstrates new equipment to a few hospital staff members.

Requirements

While many high-school graduates (well qualified in other respects) are now serving as manufacturers' representatives, an increasingly higher percentage of those employed in this field have a college degree. The more complex a product, the greater the likelihood of its being sold by a college-trained person. This could be a four-year or two-year college program.

Those in engineering sales usually have a college degree in an appropriate engineering field. Other fields that demand specific college majors include chemical sales (chemistry or chemical engineering training), office systems (accounting or business administration), and pharmaceuticals and drugs (biology, chemistry, or life science).

Manufacturers of less technical products prefer college persons with general educational backgrounds. A survey of members of a sales executives' organization asked what courses should be recommended for prospective salespeople. The subjects were listed in this order: English, speech, psychology, marketing, public relations, economics, advertising, finance, accounting, personnel administration, and business law.

When hiring sales workers, employers rely heavily upon personality factors. Sometimes they are measured by psychological tests. At other times, a single or a series of interviews are used to identify the extent to which a candidate possesses the requisite personal skills for success in selling. The successful salesperson usually is cheerful, optimistic, buoyant in the face of setbacks, sociable with both acquaintances and strangers, sincere, and tactful. This person must be able both to make a good initial impression and to maintain it in working repeatedly with the same customers.

The good salesperson must be able to work independently for much of the time. He or she must have sufficient self-motivation to aggressively seek out the maximum amount of business possible from each contact. The successful sales worker usually has above-average verbal skills. He or she must also be able to develop an appreciation for public standards of style, design, and taste.

Special requirements

There are no formal licenses or other requirements for the position of manufacturers' representative. The only special requirement is the knowledge dictated as necessary by employers in accordance with the complexities of the products to be sold. This may include work experience and higher educational training.

Opportunities for experience and exploration

Many students are able to measure their abilities and interests through part-time and summer vacation sales work. Because many products require specialized sales approaches, the manufacturer is not likely to offer much opportunity for exploratory sales experience. Actual sales work in any field, however, provides an indication of sales potential.

Occasionally, a manufacturer may hire college students for summer tryout assignments. These positions provide an opportunity for the prospective employer and employee to appraise each other. Statistics show that a high percentage of students hired for these specialized summer programs eventually become career employees after graduation. Some high schools and junior colleges offer distributive education courses that combine classroom study with paid work experience in sales.

Related occupations

There are as many types of sales workers as there are different industries in the United States. Other occupations that will appeal to those young people who have the abilities and interests necessary to work as manufacturers' sales representatives are retail sales workers, wholesale trade sales workers, retail managers, route drivers, door-to-door sales workers, and automobile sales workers.

Methods of entering

Many sales employers will list openings with high-school and college guidance placement offices, and public and private employment agencies. In many areas, sales associations refer persons to suitable openings. Occasionally, a regular customer may recommend a candidate to the manufacturer.

High-school graduates may be hired directly for sales positions or may join an organization in a nonselling capacity (office or stock or shipping clerk) with the eventual goal of transferring to sales. This experience provides good background on the company and its products, problems, and policies.

Almost every newcomer must complete a training period before receiving a sales assignment. In some cases, the new salesperson rotates through several departments of the manufacturing organization. The largest companies may use formal training classes that may last two years or more; the smallest organizations may emphasize supervised sales experience.

Advancement

As in the case of sales workers in many lines, the top manufacturers' representative often prefers to remain at the basic sales level rather than to seek advancement into management. For those who seek promotions, however, the manufacturers' salesperson has usually good opportunities for advancement. Some companies offer promotion to the sales staff to numerous positions at the management level.

As an initial step, the experienced worker may be asked to assist in the training of new salespersons. Later, one may become a sales supervisor or assistant branch manager in charge of the work of other salesmen. Persons who prove themselves in these preliminary assignments may progress to become branch manager, district manager, or regional manager. Sometimes, experienced salespersons may specialize in management of a particular product, such as directing the sales of a company's data-processing systems that will go to public institutions. The most successful sales managers may become executives at company headquarters.

It is not unusual for people who began their career as sales workers to enter related positions with their company. They might, for example, become a purchasing agent—buying from other salespersons and using their knowledge of the sales field to better cope with their presentations. Often persons with sales experience enter market research—attempting to measure what motivates customers to buy and what products might sell and how to market them. Actual sales experience is so useful in market research that many firms insist on it as a prerequisite.

Because salespeople are in constant touch with other firms, they may have frequent opportunities to switch employers. Sometimes sales workers may go into business for themselves. They often become a manufacturer's representative, selling similar products made by several companies.

Employment outlook

More than 550,000 people in the United States worked as manufacturers' representatives in the early 1990s. Future opportunities will, obviously, vary greatly depending upon the product involved. For example, relatively fewer salespersons may be needed to sell groceries as giant food chains replace individual grocers. The manufacturer's salesperson in this field may need a higher level of skill as he will handle larger and more complex orders on a group-buying basis.

By contrast, look at the prospects for the salesperson in the air-conditioning field. Ninety percent of all homes in the United States are potential customers for central air conditioning. Office buildings need air conditioning to attract tenants and their prospective employees. Complex manufacturing processes may demand rigid temperature control. Space vehicles must manufacture or process their own air.

In general, however, employment of manufacturers' representatives will probably grow more slowly than average through the late 1990s. The number of positions resulting from retirement, death, and transfer of current salespersons to other occupations is estimated at thousands per year. The turnover rate for these workers, like that for other sales workers, is high.

Earnings

Full-time manufacturers' representatives in the early 1990s earned an average of $23,400. Half earned between $19,000 and $38,800, while one in ten earned less than $15,000 and another one-tenth earned more than $53,000.

Because individual performance may be readily identified, total earnings of salespersons are directly related to job performance. Some companies adjust salaries to reflect total volume of sales. Other manufacturers pay a straight commission, while others pay a combination of salary, commission, and bonuses. The amount that salespeople earn depends upon their sales skill, the quality of the merchandise that they carry, geographic location, the number of potential customers and their demand for the workers' products, and the general economic situation. The aircraft and automotive industries and manufacturers of electrical machinery and equipment usually pay the highest starting salaries. The stability of employment in these industries, however, is dependent on the general condition of the economy.

In addition to salary or commission, travel and on-the-road expenses are usually paid by the employer. Some companies also provide a car or pay an allowance to those who use their own cars.

The typical manufacturer's representative receives a two- to four-week annual vacation, depending upon his or her period of service. Many employers also offer retirement income, sick leave, medical expense insurance, and other benefits.

Conditions of work

The sales representative often works long and irregular hours. Some workers have large territories. They must travel in the evening to be available for the next day's activities. Sometimes weeks or months elapse between visits to the home office.

Even when at home, sales workers will spend many evenings entertaining customers, attending sales conferences, and writing up orders and reports.

In the early years in the business, the salesperson may be transferred frequently by the company to different territories, both as a deliberate attempt to diversify experience and to provide increasingly more difficult assignments.

Because of these factors, a worker with a family might find that the combination of a disrupted home life, extensive traveling, and intense business competition could affect his or her physical and emotional health.

Manufacturers' representatives tend to work for larger organizations. Smaller companies may sell their products through a wholesaler.

The sales job requires good physical stamina. Much of the day is spent standing or traveling. The salesperson may carry bulky samples or product catalogs. Occasionally, sales workers will assist a customer to arrange a display of the company's products or help move stock items or even help take inventory.

Social and psychological factors

The salesperson should sense the importance of his or her role in the distribution of manufactured goods and its effect upon both the producer and the customer. The role of the salesperson is varied. Travel is an important aspect of most jobs in this field. Improved technology will create many new products to be mastered and sold.

GOE: 08.02.01; SIC: Any industry; SOC: 4249

◇ **SOURCES OF ADDITIONAL INFORMATION**

Professional Salespersons of America
3801 Monaco, NE
Albuquerque, NM 87111

Sales and Marketing Executives International
Statler Office Tower, Suite 458
Cleveland, OH 44115

◇ **RELATED ARTICLES**

Volume 1: See Table of Contents for areas of specific interest
Volume 2: Marketing, advertising, and public relations managers; Marketing research personnel; Purchasing agents; Retail managers;
Volume 3: Door-to-door sales workers; Retail sales workers; Wholesale trade sales workers

Radio, television, and print advertising sales workers

Definition

Radio and television advertising workers work for local and national media stations to sell air time to advertising agencies or companies so that their goods and services are brought to the eyes and ears of consumers.

Print advertising workers are the sales staff for the space that is sold in a newspaper, magazine, or periodical to businesses wishing to advertise their services.

History

Print advertising began with newspapers in the late 19th century. Newspapers enticed advertisers through the practice of writing favorable articles about companies that bought space in the publication. In 1909, however, the practice was halted, and a newspaper watchdog organization was founded to keep track of potential abuse of advertisers influencing journals.

Radio and television have always relied on sponsors to assist them in bringing programs into peoples homes for entertainment and education. The assistance that these sponsors offered, however, was in the form of financial revenue in exchange for air time that would mention or promote their business, products, or services. Early television programs were sometimes named not for the host or star of the program, but for the sponsoring company that was paying for that particular show to be presented on television.

During these beginning times of radio and television, however, it was possible for there to be only one sponsor for most programs. A thirty-minute program of entertainment was considered lengthy. Today, however, television airs hour-long dramas, two-hour movies, and mini-series or specials that may air two hours for four consecutive nights. Likewise, radio personalities may have shows three or four hours in duration, and it now takes many sponsors to support the cost of airing a program whether on radio or television. The phenomenal popularity of television and the accessibility to radio—in our homes, cars and headphone sets we wear to work—make both mediums successful, though potentially expensive outlets for advertising.

Since the middle of the twentieth century, most broadcasters and publications have tried to remain independent of their sponsors, although sponsors who object to a certain broadcast or article have the choice of withdrawing their financial support from companies who air views that differ from the advertisers.

Nature of the work

Radio and television time salespeople may have a wide variety of clients. Restaurants, hotel chains, beverage companies, food product manufacturers, and automobile dealers have a need to advertise to attract potential customers. Radio and television time salespeople are also known as *broadcast time salespeople* or *account executives* and contact these and other potential clients and interest them in buying media time for the purpose of advertising. The commercials broadcast on radio or television consist of short spots and are aired for ten, thirty, or sixty seconds.

Print sales workers are responsible for selling space in a publication to an advertiser for a fee. The sales staff must keep track of the amount of space available for advertisers, how much space has been sold, and what the rates are for quarter, half, three–quarter and full-page ads. For color printing there will be a whole other range of fees. In magazines, special advertising gimmicks, such as pop-ups and scented panels, are available through negotiations with the sales staff.

Advertising a business's goods and services is an excellent way for the company to increase sales. *Account executives* for both air and print advertising know this and plan strategies and contact prospective clients through telephone calls or office visits to present ideas and proposals to advertise and showcase their particular products. Salespeople also try to coordinate the best air times for the consumers that a business wishes to reach or target.

Salespeople take into consideration the client's budget, image, and characteristics of their product. Results of market research firms, surveys, and other research sources make information available about the viewing and reading habits of children, college students, adolescents, housewives, and working men and women, and whether they are single or married. By knowing which groups of people watch certain shows, listen to specific radio stations, or read a certain magazine or newspaper, salespeople can help a business select air time or print space for the consumers they most want to reach. For instance, Saturday morning television attracts a young audience; a late night movie attracts an older audience. Prime time television viewing hours, however, often attract family audiences and the commercials may reflect family-oriented products.

For magazines, there are specific publications that have a predominantly female audience between the ages of 18-30; other magazines target men, or older women, or working women, or parents. For practically any group, there is at least one publication or show that reaches a large number of them.

Radio and television time salespeople often work for advertising agencies in large cities. The advertising agencies represent clients who make their products known through radio and television spots, as well as magazine ads. Other broadcast time salespeople work directly for radio and television networks.

Prospective customers are cultivated through business leads that may come from supervisors, research, or lists kept by the sales departments. Salespeople are sensitive to clients' budgets and resources and often go to great lengths to convince a client to buy air time or advertising space with their organization. They have brochures that explain their viewing or reading market, the average income of those individuals, the number of people that see those ads, and any other information that may be likely to encourage a potential advertiser to choose their organization as a valuable tool for promoting a product. Inviting clients to meetings, presentations, and educating them to certain marketing strategies can encourage contracts. Salespeople not only have to pursue new clients but also service current ones, making sure they are happy with the results of the relationship and advertising package. It is the main objective for salespeople to sell as much air time or ad space to their clients as possible. If there are current clients who are interested in buying more time, or expanding their contracts, a salesperson must try and fill those needs.

The revenue brought in by selling advertising space or time comes from local, national, and network advertising. Local advertising may come from an area health club that wishes to announce a special membership drive or a retail store promoting a sale. A commercial would not be seen by people outside of a certain area, and the cost of this time would reflect that limitation. A print ad is purchased for larger regions in magazines but can still be targeted to a few states. With magazine binding in different locations, it is possible to have the same magazine sell with completely different advertisers in New York than it has in Chicago.

National advertisers are often huge companies that may manufacture soft drinks, major airlines, vacation resorts, or hotel chains. Network advertising is compensation paid by the networks to individual stations for airing network programs. The right to show these programs was purchased by other network sponsors.

Radio and television time salespeople do considerable research and make critical evaluations as to what kind of advertising is best suited for each client. In addition, they might recommend how long a spot will be, as well as supply information on the cost, who it will reach and target it to those consumers most likely to desire that product or service.

159

A salesman for a radio station makes appointments to meet with advertisers. At the meeting, the salesman will try to convince the advertiser to purchase some air time.

Requirements

To work in sales of any kind takes persuasiveness, an outgoing personality, and motivation. Radio and television time salespeople however, should have a keen understanding of programming trends as well as an understanding of each potential client's business so that they may arrange the most beneficial time slot to showcase their business or product.

Print salespeople need to be capable of maintaining a good relationship with current clients as well as pursuing new clients on a continual basis. The work is very independent and the advertising worker has to be disciplined at pursuing potential clients, meeting with customers on a regular basis, having a very flexible schedule for client meetings and interviews, and keeping track of all the information that is needed to keep both client and company happy.

The ability to get along well with others and personal drive are additional qualities that salespeople should have. A friendly and professional business manner and tact will help them know when to evaluate the progress of a deal. In this field it is also helpful to have a broad understanding of buying trends, because so much of advertising is creative, encouraging the consumer to buy while entertaining them or informing them.

Special requirements

Many radio and television salespeople have previous experience in sales or broadcasting. Both areas provide useful knowledge in approaching and servicing clients and the specifics of programming and its relation to selling air time. It is possible to obtain an entry level position in broadcasting and through hard work and ability be promoted to sales.

Print sales workers often start with smaller publications as in-house sales staff members, answering the phones and taking orders from phone-in customers. This may include handling classified ads for newspapers or small print ads that are designed by in-house artists and typesetters.

An increasing number of salespeople have college degrees. Despite any prior experience or formal training, students select classes that will give them a good balance of business education, broadcast and print knowledge, and liberal arts. Business classes may include studies in economics, marketing and sales, and advertising. Additional courses in radio and television, journalism, writing, English, and speech prove helpful as well. Salespeople must represent themselves to clients in a knowledgeable and professional way and can supplement their studies with any number of part time jobs or extra curricular activities.

In addition, many radio and television time salespeople find it useful to belong to a professional organization or society. Among those organizations are the Broadcast Promotion and Marketing Executives, which welcomes members of public relations and advertising firms that work with both radio and television networks; the Television Bureau of Advertising for professionals in the television industry; and the Radio Advertising Bureau whose members promote selling radio time. Addresses for these associations appear at the end of this article.

Opportunities for experience and exploration

Many high-schools and two-year colleges, and most four-year colleges have media departments that may include radio stations and public access or cable television channels. Students may work as aides, production assistants, programmers, or writers for these departments and gain worthwhile experience in media. Likewise, school newspapers and yearbooks often need people to sell advertising to local merchants, and theater departments often look for people to sell ads for performance programs.

Community publications often hire part-time and summer help for sales and clerical positions for the classified advertising department. Other publications may also hire students for part-time posts.

Related occupations

Persons working in advertising sales combine an interest in sales with interests in advertising, printing, and broadcasting. These latter two industries offer a wide range of similar and related occupations including creative directors, program directors or copy editors, art directors, sales managers, copy writers, and station managers.

Methods of entering

Radio and television stations do not usually advertise job openings in newspapers, so it may be best to do preliminary research on the local networks. Find out the type of programming a specific radio station does, if its market is geared for younger adults, or if the format is predominantly news-oriented. Get the names of the general manager and personnel director so any correspondence sent to them is personalized and reflects attention to detail.

Advertising agencies, however, may advertise job openings. The competition is quite fierce for entry level jobs with most agencies, particularly large agencies in big cities, so it may take several tries before a job is found.

Publications do advertise for the lower level positions on occasion, but the best method of finding work in advertising of any form is to send resumes to as many agencies, publications, or broadcasting offices as possible in the location where employment is desired. It is possible that the resume will arrive as an opening becomes available. More than half of the jobs do not remain open long enough to take out an ad. Follow up letters with a phone call to the person in charge of hiring, so that he or she realizes there is a genuine interest in the company.

For students in education programs, investigate the possibility of internships or on-campus employment in related areas. Previous experience is often a head start in a new career.

Advancement

Larger agencies and networks often look to hire people with experience, so it is common for new salespeople to begin at smaller companies. These opportunities offer sales people experience and confidence that they can bring to more advanced positions. There is also the possibility for more rapid promotion at smaller stations.

Radio and television time salespeople may get promoted to management executive level positions; however, advancement can also come in the way of bigger clients and network positions.

Employment outlook

More and more people rely on the mediums of radio and television for their entertainment and information. Cable and local channels also provide more diversity for programming and as such increase the opportunity for advertisers to get exposure. In addition, many smaller towns have radio stations, and some even have local television stations. These increase market opportunities and do not limit job prospects solely to large cities.

The number of publications in the United States continues to grow, although there is a large failure rate in new publications. The possibility for finding employment is far greater in larger cities such as New York, Los Angeles, and Chicago, where most magazines have headquarters, but smaller publications may be located elsewhere, and large national publications have sales offices in several cities. Most towns and cities have some form of newspaper that will also require an advertising sales staff, and that is unlikely to change any time in the near future.

Earnings

Though is it common for television time salespeople to have higher pay scales than salespeople in radio, both areas have good salary ranges. Beginning broadcasting salespeople in the early 1990s may earn between $18,000 to $35,000 per year and advance to as much as $46,000 after acquiring a few years' experience.

Advertising sales workers' starting salaries range from $17,500 to $33,000 a year. Experienced workers may earn salaries up to $44,200 a year, on average. Some salespeople draw straight salary, some receive bonuses that reflect their sales achievement, and still other salespeople earn their entire wage based on commissions.

Salespeople can put in a full forty-hour week, though it is likely that it will not be a strict nine-to-five workday. Service calls, presentations, and client entertainment are an active part of a salesperson's job. Also keeping current with programming and competitive advertising may require a salesperson to watch different programs, listen to the radio or read other publications.

GOE: 08.01.02; SIC: 7311; SOC: 4662

Conditions of work

The widespread opportunities for advertising salespeople reflect the diversity in working conditions. Larger advertising agencies, publications, and networks may have more modern and comfortable working facilities. Sometimes salespeople are out of the office entirely and must call in to keep in touch with their home office. Smaller markets may have more modest working environments. Travel is a large part of a salesperson's responsibility to his or her clients, and it is possible to have many different clients in various types of businesses and services as well as in different areas of the country.

Social and psychological factors

There can be quite a hectic pace in working in the advertising sales profession. Clients can be demanding and competition can be high. There is, however, much potential for earnings and advancement for good salespeople and for interaction with other people. The profession also provides an interesting balance of business and creative environments.

◇ **SOURCES OF ADDITIONAL INFORMATION**

Broadcast Promotion and Marketing Executives
6255 Sunset Boulevard, Suite 624
Los Angeles, CA 90028

Television Bureau of Advertising
477 Madison Avenue
New York, NY 10022

Radio Advertising Bureau
304 Park Avenue South
New York, NY 10010

◇ **RELATED ARTICLES**

Volume 1: Advertising; Broadcasting; Magazine Publishing; Newspaper Publishing
Volume 2: Advertising workers; Commercial artists; Marketing, advertising, and public relations managers; Radio and television program directors
Volume 3: Billing clerks; Telemarketers

Real estate agents and brokers

Definition

The *real estate broker* executes orders from buyers or sellers for the sale or rental of property and receives a commission for these services. The agent is employed by a broker in renting or selling property for clients on a commission basis. Both are sometimes called *real estate agents*. A Realtor is an agent who is a member of the National Association of Realtors.

Normally there is one broker for each piece of property being sold; there may be more than one agent showing the property to potential buyers. The broker schedules viewing times for the property.

History

Humans have always valued property. Next to food and clothing, real estate has been their most cherished possession. Real estate may be defined as land and all things permanently attached to it, such as buildings, trees, and minerals.

Until the last few centuries, property ownership was concentrated in the hands of a few people and was traditionally passed down from father to son. Three factors contributed to the rise of the real estate business. First, the growing portion of the society owning property. Second, the general increase in the total population and in the number of pieces of real estate; as the number of property sellers and purchasers grew, the need for real estate agents developed. Third, the laws regarding real estate transfer are exacting; both sellers and buyers place increasing reliance upon specialists in this field.

Professionalization of the real estate field developed rapidly in the twentieth century. In 1908, the National Association of Real Estate Boards (N.A.R.E.B.)—now called the National Association of Realtors—was founded and has encouraged the highest ethical standards for the field.

Nature of the work

The work of real estate brokers varies. They receive listings of residential, commercial, or agricultural property for sale or rent. Brokers usually visit each property so that they may be able to describe it accurately. The visits are particularly important as no two pieces of property are alike. Unlike other fields of sales, real estate brokers must analyze individually each item they sell to best present it to prospective customers. It is frequently their duty to actively solicit listings for their agency.

Frequently, the broker counsels the owner concerning the asking price for the property. The owners usually sign a contract agreeing that if they sell the property, they will pay the broker a percentage of the selling price. Commission on commercial property is higher than private homes.

If the property is ready to be shown, an agent reviews his or her files to identify prospective customers. Other agents in the same office may have good prospects for the property also. Frequently, after a week or two of exclusive listing by one broker, the sale property is shared with other local real estate firms through a multiple-listing agreement so that other firms may show the property to their customers. To stimulate activity, the broker advertises the house in local newspapers.

As potential purchasers are located, the agent arranges a convenient time for them to be shown the property. When the property is vacant, the broker is usually the person who retains the key. To adjust to the free times of potential customers, the agent frequently shows property in the late afternoon, during weekday evenings, and on weekends. In many areas, Sunday afternoon "Open Houses" are used to encourage visits through available property. As a representative of the broker's firm is usually available in each house, open houses make maximum use of part-time agents.

When not showing properties, real estate agents spend the rest of their time on the telephone, contacting prospective buyers and sellers.

In showing property, the successful agent emphasizes points that might be of particular interest to prospective purchasers. To some people, the agent may emphasize the convenient floor plan or the proximity of schools and shopping centers. To other people, the agent may stress the soundness of the home construction, available financing arrangements, and factors that may contribute to the long-range value of the property. Acting as a real estate counselor, the agent points out features that should be weighed in considering alternative purchases. The agent also must be familiar with tax rates, zoning regulations, and insurance needs.

Finally, to capitulate the transaction the agent must bring the buyer and seller together at terms agreeable to both. Where the two parties differ on price, the agent must rely on his or her talents as a skilled negotiator. The agent prepares or completes the formal sales contract, advises the new owner regarding title search and title insurance, assists in other legal procedures, and may help arrange for a loan as a mortgage against the property itself.

The specialist in commercial or agricultural real estate operates in much the same fashion. The specialist, however, usually makes fewer sales, often conducts extensive searches for property meeting specifications set by clients, and studies property more carefully.

In addition to real estate management, brokers with the necessary qualifications often combine other work, such as selling insurance or practicing law, with their real estate business.

163

Requirements

There is no ideal educational requirement for the real estate field. As a minimum, most employers expect at least a high-school diploma. An increasing percentage of real estate agents and brokers have some college training. A good general education provides background helpful in working with the many different types of people encountered by the agent. College courses in psychology, economics, sociology, marketing finance, business administration, architecture, and engineering are helpful. Many agents and brokers have taken formal college courses in real estate. Hundreds of colleges and universities offer courses in real estate; a complete list is available from the National Association of Realtors, 430 North Michigan Avenue, Chicago, IL 60611.

Successful brokers and agents must be willing to study the field constantly. In a rural district, for example, they may need to keep abreast of the latest developments in fertilizers, farm marketing, erosion, and water supplies.

The job of the agent requires a general liking for people. Agents must work successfully with many different types of people and inspire their trust and confidence. They must be able to express themselves well, and enthusiasm is helpful in all types of sales.

The agent must have good judgment to combine sound knowledge of current real estate market values with intelligent predictions of future developments in the communities that they serve.

Maturity is an asset. In fact, many successful agents enter the field in their middle-age years. Wide acquaintanceship in a geographical area facilitates entering the field. The agent must be willing to participate in local civic and social organizations.

The agent must be tactful. Frequently, one receives a listing that exactly meets the specifications established by a customer. Unfortunately, when the property is shown the customer may be indecisive about what he or she really wants. The agent must be patient and may show one customer through dozens of pieces of property without closing a sale.

Special requirements

Every state and the District of Columbia requires that real estate agents and brokers be licensed. Most states ask prospective agents to pass written examinations on real estate fundamentals and state real estate laws. Brokers must pass more extensive examinations and in some states must have credits for college courses in real estate or sales experience of usually one to three years.

State licenses are usually renewed annually without examination. Agents who move to another state must qualify under the licensing laws of that state.

To supplement minimum state requirements, many agents take courses in real estate principles, laws, financing, appraisal, and property development and management. These courses are often sponsored by local real estate boards that are members of the National Association of Realtors or its affiliates, such as the American Institute of Real Estate Appraisers.

Opportunities for experience and exploration

Calling on local real estate brokers and agents should provide useful information on the field. Information on licensing requirements may be obtained from local real estate boards or from the real estate departments of each state. State licensing requirements prohibit the opportunity for preliminary sales experience. Part-time and summer employment in a real estate office, however, may provide a clearer picture of the field.

Related occupations

Other occupations also require interests similar to those possessed by real estate agents and brokers. Other jobs include property and real estate managers, appraisers and assessors, insurance agents and brokers, and underwriters.

Methods of entering

The typical entry position is as an agent working for a broker with an established office. The beginner usually applies directly to local real estate firms, or may be referred through public and private employment services. Brokers seeking agents may run newspaper advertisements. Local real estate boards may be able to suggest which offices may be hiring.

Because agents are paid solely on a commission basis, individual brokers may decide to take under contract all the capable agents they can train and retain, without dividing their business to the point where agents make so little they are tempted to leave.

The beginning agent must choose between the advantages of a small or large organization. In a small office, the newcomer will train informally under an experienced agent. The newcomer's duties will be broad and varied, and as the junior member of a small organization, they may often be menial. In a larger firm, the new agent may proceed through a more standardized training process and may specialize in one phase of the real estate field—commercial, mortgage financing, and so forth.

The first months are usually difficult for the beginning agent. He or she needs to develop a reputation for service and a clientele of satisfied customers. Persons who have successfully purchased or sold a home through an agent are inclined to turn to that person for help with future real estate transactions.

The beginner spends much time on the telephone seeking listings of property to sell and answering calls in response to advertisements.

Advancement

While many successful agents develop professionally by expanding the quality and quantity of their services, others seek advancement by entering management or by specializing in residential or commercial real estate.

The agent may enter management by becoming the head of a major division of a large real estate firm. Other agents purchase an established real estate business, join one as a partner, or set up their own offices. The self-employed agent must meet the requirements for a broker's license.

The agent wishing to specialize has a number of available options. A major decision is the selection between residential and commercial sales. The real estate broker may develop a property management business. In return for approximately five percent of the gross receipts, the property manager operates apartment houses or multiple-tenant business properties for their owners. The property manager is in charge of renting (including advertising, tenant relations, and collecting rents); building maintenance (heating, lighting, cleaning, and decorating); and accounting (financial recording and filing tax returns). (*See also* the separate article title "Property and real estate managers" in Volume 2.)

A limited number of agents may qualify for the complex role of the appraiser, who estimates the current market value of lands and buildings. Appraisers play a key role in the settlement of estates and in the placement of all types of mortgages. (*See also* the separate article titled "Appraisers and assessors" in Volume 2.) Highly experienced agents may serve as real estate counselors, advising clients on the suitability of available property. Other agents may enter mortgage financing, placing real estate loans with interested financial institutions or private lenders.

Real estate brokers may play a key role in land development through cooperating in plans for cities, subdivisions, housing tracts, shopping centers, and industrial sites.

Some brokers engage in the business of buying and selling homes for their own account. Anticipating metropolitan expansion, brokers may buy up lands that may appreciate in value and thus may facilitate development.

Occasionally, experienced brokers may join real estate departments maintained by major corporations and large governmental agencies.

Employment outlook

About 400,000 people worked as real estate agents and brokers, many of them part-time, in the early 1990s. Through the late 1990s, employment of these workers will probably grow about as fast as average for all occupations. Our expanding population will probably create additional demand for real estate services. The housing developments that are springing up in ever-widening spirals around metropolitan areas reflect the increasing demand by Americans for private housing. Growing affluence suggests that the percentage of Americans owning their own homes will increase. Increased mobility indicates a continued high volume of real estate transactions. People are buying their first home later in life, but as the general age of the population increases, the overall number of owners should continue to rise.

A downturn in the general economy, however, usually results in a diminishing of mortgage financing and decreased construction of new homes. Problems with the savings and loan industry will also adversely affect mortgages. Entry into the field at such times is more difficult.

As the average age of real estate agents and brokers is considerably higher than for workers in many other occupations, the majority of opportunities for new agents will be made available through retirement and death, in addition to the openings made available by agents who transfer to other types of work.

Real estate agents and brokers
Sales Occupations

Earnings

Compensation in the real estate field is almost entirely upon a commission basis. In the early 1990s, commissions ranged from five to ten percent of selling price, averaging about seven percent. Agents usually split commissions with the brokers who employ them. The broker may take half the commission in return for providing the agent with the office space, advertising support, sales supervision, and the broker's good name. When two or more agents are involved in a transaction (for example, one agent listing the property for sale and another selling it), the commission is usually divided between the two on the basis of an established formula.

Full-time real estate agents earned an average of about $22,800 a year in the early 1990s. Brokers may advance their agents a stated amount each month on a drawing account against future commissions on sales. Brokers earned an average salary of about $37,900. Many made much more. Brokers have a much higher gross salary, but they have to pay staff and office expenses, heavy advertising costs, travel and entertainment expenses, and other costs of doing business. Agents may have to pay their own travel expenses.

Agents and brokers may supplement their income by appraising property, placing mortgages with private lenders, or by selling property or casualty insurance. Since earnings are irregular and economic conditions unpredictable, agents and brokers should maintain sufficient cash reserves for slack periods.

Conditions of work

A glance at the real estate advertisements in the classified section of any newspaper presents the picture of a highly competitive field. It is relatively simple to enter the real estate field. Any person who qualifies for a license needs only a telephone number to be in business. The existence of many part-time agents provides competition for those making their entire living from the field.

The beginner must accept the frustration inherent in the early months in the business. All agents must begin by accepting modest listings—and work hard to get them.

After he or she becomes established, the agent may expect to work many evenings and weekends. Unlike some other areas of sales, real estate agents do little overnight travel. In some areas, real estate brokers do much of their work out of their own homes.

Most real estate agents and brokers work in small business establishments. Only in metropolitan areas do agents have the option of joining larger organizations. Real estate positions are found in every part of the country, but are concentrated in large urban areas and in smaller, rapidly growing communities.

Regardless of the size of the community in which they work, good agents know its economic life, the personal preferences of its citizens, and the demand for real estate.

Qualified agents and brokers are usually affiliated with the National Association of Realtors through membership in one of the over 1,300 local boards and associations that belong to N.A.R. Active members who subscribe to the N.A.R. Code of Ethics may use the term "Realtor." This designation may not lawfully be used by others.

Qualified specialists may join such N.A.R. affiliates as the American Institute of Real Estate Appraisers, the National Institute of Real Estate Management, or the National Institute of Farm and Land Brokers.

Social and psychological factors

The real estate agent plays a significant role in helping families with what is usually their largest single investment and in helping businesses with acquisitions vital to their continued growth and to the communities in which they are located. The agent's reputation for integrity and service will be a key factor in determining his or her success.

Real estate workers render a unique service matching millions of pieces of property available for sale each year with interested purchasers. The fact that property can readily be sold, should the need arise, encourages many Americans to purchase real estate. Some transactions are made solely as an investment.

GOE: 08.02.04; SIC: 6531; SOC: 1353

◇ **SOURCES OF ADDITIONAL INFORMATION**

National Association of Realtors
430 North Michigan Avenue
Chicago, IL 60611

Realtors National Marketing Institution
430 North Michigan Avenue
Suite 500
Chicago, IL 60611

Society of Industrial and Office Realtors
777 14th Street, NW
Suite 400
Washington, DC 20005

◇ **RELATED ARTICLES**

Retail sales workers

Definition

Sales workers in retail trade assist customers with purchases by identifying their needs, demonstrating merchandise, receiving payment, recording sales, and wrapping their purchase or arranging for its delivery. They may also be called *sales clerks, retail clerks,* or *salespersons.*

History

The development of retailing paralleled the growth of civilization. In planning their cities, the Greeks and Romans provided large market places where individual merchants could display and sell their wares.

As Europe emerged from the Middle Ages, organized trade began again with the development of medieval fairs. During the thirteenth century, more than 3,000 fairs were held on a regular basis. By the fifteenth century, weekly markets began to replace the fairs.

As specialization in manufacture developed, the medieval artisan appeared. The artisans were craft workers who sold what they produced. Most of the goods were made after they received a specific order from the customer.

The Industrial Revolution, and its techniques of mass production in anticipation of customer needs, encouraged the development of specialized retail establishments.

The first retail outlets in the United States were trading posts and general stores. At trading posts, goods obtained from Indians were exchanged for items imported from Europe or manufactured in the East. Trading posts had to be located on the fringes of settlements, and relocated to follow the westward movement of the frontier. As villages and towns grew, what had been trading posts frequently developed into general stores. General stores sold food staples, farm necessities, and clothing. They often served as the post office and became the social and economic center of their community. They were sometimes known as dry goods stores.

A number of changes occurred in the retail field during the mid- and late nineteenth century. The growth of specialized retail stores (hardware, feed, grocery, drug) reflected the growing sophistication of available products and customer tastes.

The first grocery chain store, which started in the city of New York in 1859, led to a new concept in retailing. In the late nineteenth century, merchants such as Marshall Field developed huge stores that were named after their large number of separate departments. Their variety of merchandise, wide ability to advertise their products, and low selling prices contributed to their rapid growth and good success.

The twentieth century has witnessed the creation of supermarket and suburban shopping centers, the emergence of discount houses, and the expansion of credit buying. Today, retailing is the second largest industry in the United States. Grocery stores and chains have the highest annual sales in the retail field, followed (in order of size) by automobile dealers, department stores, restaurants and cafeterias, lumber and building suppliers, drug and proprietary stores, furniture stores, variety stores, liquor stores, hardware stores, and jewelry stores.

Retail sales workers
Sales Occupations

Most retail salesworkers operate on a commission, prompting them to use aggressive sales techniques.

Nature of the work

Salespersons work in more than one hundred different types of retail establishments and in a variety of roles. One salesperson for example, may work in a small specialty shop where, while waiting on customers, he or she may check inventory, order stock from traveling sales workers or by telephone or mail, place newspaper display advertisements, prepare window displays, and rearrange merchandise for sale.

Another salesperson may work in the furniture department of a large department store. The workers in this department alternate periods of work to provide six long days of available service to customers. Staff meetings help improve sales effectiveness and knowledge of merchandise. The work of the salesperson is supported by advertising, window decorating, sales promotion, buying, and market research specialists.

Some retail sales workers must have specialized knowledge. This is especially true of those who sell expensive, complicated products such as stereos, appliances, and personal computers.

Farm equipment sales workers must stock the latest equipment and machinery to meet the needs of farmers in their area. Agricultural chemical sales workers sell pesticides, herbicides, and fertilizers to farmers in their area and must know in detail what each product does.

Regardless of the type of store in which salespersons work, each one performs basic functions including creating in customers the desire to buy merchandise; answering questions concerning the store and its products; fitting, demonstrating, or measuring items for customers; completing transactions by wrapping goods, receiving payment, and making change; preparing sales slips to facilitate inventory control, store auditing, and customer charging; accepting customer exchanges and returns of goods; and maintaining, in a neat fashion, product and display cases.

Requirements

Employers generally prefer to hire high-school graduates for most sales positions. Subjects such as English, sales, and commercial arithmetic provide good background. Many high schools and two-year colleges have distributive education programs that include courses in merchandising, principles of retailing, and retail selling.

In retail sales, as in other fields, the level of opportunity tends to coincide with the level of education. In many stores, college graduates enter immediately into an on-the-job training program to prepare them for management assignments. Successful and experienced non-college graduates may also qualify for these programs. Useful college courses include economics, business administration, marketing, and home economics. Many colleges offer a major in retailing. Many executives express a strong preference for liberal arts graduates, especially those with some business courses or a master's degree in business administration.

The sales worker in retail trade must be in good health. Many selling positions require standing most of the day. The sales worker must have stamina to face the grueling pace of Christmas business without loss of physical vigor or personal sales impact. Personal appearance is important. Salespeople should be neat and well-groomed and have a pleasing personality.

A pleasant speaking voice, a natural outgoing friendliness, tact, and patience are helpful personal characteristics. The sales worker must be able to converse easily with strangers of all ages. In addition to qualities that make for success with people, the sales worker must be equally at home with figures. He or she should be able to add and subtract accurately and quickly.

Requirements vary depending upon the type of sales involved. In every phase of the business, salespersons advance faster if they have a natural flair for retailing—the strong desire to sell products through creative merchandising techniques, good sales presentations, and an appreciation of current fashion and taste.

Special requirements

While no special licenses are required, most states have established minimum standards that govern retail employment. Some states set a minimum age of fourteen, or may require at least a high-school diploma, and prohibit more than eight hours of work a day or forty-eight hours in any six days. These requirements are often relaxed for employment during the Christmas season.

Opportunities for experience and exploration

Because of its seasonal nature, retailing offers numerous opportunities for temporary or part-time sales experience. Most stores add extra personnel for the Christmas season. Summer vacation centers hire sales employees, usually high-school or college students. Fewer sales positions are available during the summer in metropolitan areas, as this is frequently the slowest time of the year.

Many high schools and junior colleges have developed distributive education programs that combine courses in retailing with part-time work in the field. The distributive education student may receive academic credit for this work experience in addition to pay at regular wages. Store owners cooperating in these programs often hire students who complete the courses as full-time personnel.

Many specialized retail programs offered by schools or colleges require their students to obtain actual sales experience.

Related occupations

Other occupations utilize the same interests and skills that retail sales workers possess. Some of these include wholesale trade sales workers, automobile sales workers, real estate agents and brokers, insurance agents and brokers, door-to-door sales workers, and restaurant managers.

Methods of entering

Beginning salespersons are usually hired as the result of direct application to retail stores. Major department stores maintain extensive personnel departments. In smaller stores, the manager may do the hiring. Occasionally, sales applicants are given aptitude tests.

Young people may be hired immediately for sales positions. Often, however, they begin with work in the stockroom as clerks, help to set up merchandise displays, or assist in the receiving or shipping departments. After a year of such experience, the young person may be advanced to a sales assignment.

Training varies with the type and size of the store. In large stores, the beginner may benefit from formal training courses. These courses discuss sales techniques, store policies, mechanics of recording sales, and provide an overview of the entire store. This program is usually followed by on-the-job sales supervision. The beginner in a small store may receive personal instruction from the manager or a senior sales worker, followed by directed sales experience.

College graduates may be hired through visits to college placement offices. Such visits are a part of the recruiting programs of most large retail and chain stores.

College graduates and noncollege persons with successful sales experience often enter executive training programs (sometimes referred to as "flying squads" because they move rapidly through different parts of the store). As they rotate through various departments, the trainees are exposed to merchandising methods, stock and inventory control, advertising, buying, credit, and personnel. By spending from several days to several months in each of these areas, trainees receive a broad background of knowledge designed to help them as they advance into the ranks of management.

Advancement

Retailing offers unusual opportunities for advancement. Obviously, larger stores have more numerous opportunities for promotion. Retailing, however, is a mobile field and successful and experienced persons may readily change employment. This is one of the few fields where advancement to executive positions is possible regardless of education, if the salesperson has the necessary initiative and ability.

The beginning sales worker first develops by specializing in a particular line of merchandise. The person becomes an authority on a product line, such as sporting equipment, women's suits, or building materials. Many good sales workers prefer the role of the senior sales worker and remain at this level. Others may be asked to become supervisor of a section. Eventually, they may develop into a de-

169

partment manager, floor manager, division or branch manager, or general manager.

Persons with sales experience often enter related areas, such as buying. The entry here is as an assistant buyer, moving with experience into a buyer's position. Other retail store workers advance into support areas, such as personnel, accounting, public relations, or credit.

Employment outlook

In the early 1990s, about four million people were employed as sales workers in retail stores of all types and sizes.

Retailing reflects in direct proportion the health of the general economy. The employment of retail sales personnel should grow about as fast as average for all occupations during the next decade.

Thousands of job openings will occur in newly built shopping centers. Other positions will result from existing stores staffing for longer business hours or reducing the length of the workweek. Many new sales workers in retail trade will use retail sales as a stepping stone to another sales or business career. Because of all of these factors, it is estimated that there will be thousands of job openings for retail sales workers each year through the late 1990s—more than in almost any other occupation.

Several factors, the full effects of which have yet to be measured, may reduce the long-range demand for sales personnel. The continued growth of self-service stores may reduce the demand. Drug, variety, grocery, and other stores are rapidly converting to self-service. The rising standard of personal income suggests that consumers may spend less of their new-found funds for additional goods, and much of the surplus will go rather into education, travel, and personal services.

At the same time, however, many products (such as stereo components, electrical appliances, computers, and sporting goods) require extremely skilled sales workers. On balance, one might conclude that sales employment will rise more slowly than the volume of sales. As easy-to-sell goods may be marketed in self-service stores, the demand in the future will be strongest for particularly skilled sales workers.

There should continue to be good opportunities for temporary and part-time workers, such as before Christmas and during special sales. Stores are especially interested in persons who, as they return year after year, develop good sales backgrounds.

Earnings

In the early 1990s, most beginning sales workers started at the federal minimum wage. Hourly wages throughout the retail trade ranged up to more than $10 an hour. Wages vary greatly, depending primarily on the type of store and the degree of skill required.

Department stores or retail chains may pay more than smaller stores. Obviously, higher wages are paid for positions requiring a high degree of skill. Many sales workers also receive a commission (often four to eight percent) on their sales. Full-time retail sales workers earned an average of $18,096 in the early 1990s. Half earned between $10,800 and $22,440, and one in ten earned more than $31,800. Another one-tenth, however, earned less than $8,120.

Salespersons in many retail stores are allowed a discount on their own purchases, ranging from 10 to 25 percent. This privilege is sometimes extended to the worker's family. Meals in the employee restaurants maintained by large stores may be served at below cost. Many stores provide sick leave, surgical and medical insurance, life insurance, and retirement benefits. Most stores give paid vacations.

Conditions of work

Sales workers with seniority have reasonably good job security. When business is slow, stores may curtail hiring and not fill vacancies that occur. Most stores, however, are able to weather mild business recessions without having to release experienced sales workers. During periods of economic depression, keen competition exists among salespersons for job openings.

There are nearly two million retail stores in this country, and sales positions are found in every region. The experienced salesperson may find employment in almost any state. The vast majority of positions, however, are located in large cities or suburban areas.

Although a forty-hour workweek is common, many stores operate on a forty-four or forty-eight-hour workweek. Most stores are open Saturday and many on Sunday. Most are open one or more weekday evenings so working hours may vary from week to week. Most sales workers receive overtime pay during Christmas and other rush seasons. Part-time salespersons generally work at peak hours of business.

As competition is keen, many retailers work under pressure. The sales worker may not be directly involved but will feel the pressures in turn.

The sales worker must be able to adjust to alternating periods of high activity and dull monotony. No two days—or even customers—are alike. Because some customers are hostile and rude, salespersons must learn to exercise tact and patience at all times.

Young people with ability find that retailing offers the opportunity for unusually rapid advancement. One study revealed that half of all retail executives were under thirty-five years of age. It is not uncommon for a young person under thirty-five to be in charge of a retail store or department with an annual sales volume of over $1 million. Conversely, the retail executive who makes bad merchandising judgments may quickly be out of a job.

Social and psychological factors

America's capacity for manufacturing would be meaningless without the help of the retailer. Retailers bring goods to places where customers want to buy them. Retailers divide large amounts of goods into units that customers buy.

The retail industry stimulates business by guaranteeing markets to manufacturers and by extending credit to permit customers to buy more goods than they might otherwise purchase.

Sales workers directly affect the success of a retail establishment. They and their stores play an important role in developing standards of style and taste acceptable to the public.

GOE: 08.02.02; SIC: Any industry; SOC: 43

◇ SOURCES OF ADDITIONAL INFORMATION

National Retail Merchants Association
100 West 31st Street
New York, NY 10001

Professional Salespersons of America
3801 Monaco NE
Albuquerque, NM 87111

◇ RELATED ARTICLES

Volume 1: Retailing; or see Table of Contents for areas of specific interest
Volume 2: Buyers; Retail managers
Volume 3: Door-to-door sales workers; Manufacturers' sales workers; Wholesale trade sales workers

---

Route drivers

Definition

The *route driver* drives a truck over an established route to deliver products such as milk, soft drinks, laundry, dry cleaning, or ice cream to regular customers. The driver usually collects payments from customers and attempts to interest them in new products or services offered by the company.

Route drivers may use their own truck and operate as an independent business, as food vendors often do. They may also be drivers for a business which purchases the vehicles. Newspaper deliverers have vehicles supplied by the company.

History

In the United States, there have always been individuals who earned their livelihoods by selling materials and goods from door to door. The frontier peddler, for example, has become legend. The products sold and the manner in which they were delivered were, of course, influenced by important developments in society. Automobiles replaced horse-drawn vans in providing transportation for sales workers on their routes. New roads made it possible for one sales worker to serve more people. New products created new demands from an expanding population. Most route drivers today are much

Route drivers
Sales Occupations

A route driver interacts with people all day as he stops at several businesses and residences to pick up and deliver parcels.

more specialized than their predecessors. They sell fewer things (milk, bakery products, and so forth) and services (such as dry cleaning) to more people than did the all-purpose peddler.

Nature of the work

Route drivers spend the major portion of their time driving panel or light trucks and selling items ranging from dry-cleaning services to pastries. For this reason, route drivers are sometimes called *driver-sales workers* or *route-sales workers*. Their duties vary with the kinds of items or services they are selling, the size of the company they work for, and the kind of route that they service. There are two kinds of route drivers: those who sell, collect, or deliver to retail establishments (*wholesale route drivers*), and those who perform similar functions directly to the public (*retail route drivers*). Most route drivers are employed by dairies, bakeries, and laundry and dry-cleaning plants located in large cities. A route driver is often required to know the location of streets in certain sections of a city. Route drivers are often known by the kind of product they sell. The term route driver includes those who provide bakery, milk, dry cleaning, laundry, newspapers, and other goods and services.

Among the duties performed by route drivers are the following: loading or supervising the loading of the delivery truck; delivering previously ordered material to stops or assigned routes; obtaining new orders; attempting to improve the route by soliciting new customers; collecting payments and keeping records of the transactions; emptying the truck and turning in collections. Retail route drivers make five to ten times as many stops as do wholesale route drivers.

Newspaper-delivery drivers deliver newspapers and magazines to dealers and vending machines; *newspaper carriers* deliver them directly to subscribers. Both types of workers collect money and keep records. *Lunch-truck drivers* sell sandwiches, box lunches, drinks, and similar items to factory and office workers, students, and people attending outdoor events. *Coin collectors* collect and distribute coins to vending machines.

Sales route-driver helpers assist the route driver in various ways, such as loading and unloading the truck, carrying goods from the truck to the customer's office, store, or house, and driving. *Route sales-delivery drivers supervisors* supervise and coordinate the work of route drivers; they plan routes and schedules, collect cash receipts, handle customer complaints, keep records, and solicit new business.

Requirements

Route drivers must be able to get along well with people, especially those route drivers who work directly with the public. They must know how to deal with people who have complaints about products or services that the route driver handles. Route drivers must be neat in appearance and pleasant in manner. They must have orderly work habits because they prepare instructions for others who are to fill the orders they take, and they also must keep records of the payments to be made by their customers. The success of route drivers is dependent upon the extent to which they keep their present customers happy, and the extent to which they get new customers. To meet these requirements, route drivers must have self-confidence, initiative, and tact. They must be able to work without direct supervision. Above all, they must be honest and have personal integrity.

In addition to these personal qualities, route drivers must be good drivers. In most states they must qualify for a chauffeur's license (commercial driver's permit). State motor vehicle departments can provide information on this license.

Most newly employed route drivers are high-school graduates. Employers prefer applicants who have taken high-school courses in the following areas: sales, public speaking, driver training, bookkeeping, and business arithmetic. Courses in merchandising and retailing are also helpful.

Employers generally prefer individuals who are twenty-five years of age or older. Upon high-school graduation, a person interested in eventually becoming a route driver can gain valuable experience by accepting a position as a sales worker or as a retail trade sales worker.

Special requirements

There are no special requirements for these positions, although many employers give psychological tests to applicants to determine if they are or can possibly become safe drivers and good sales workers.

Opportunities for experience and exploration

High-school students may obtain a part-time or summer job as a route driver's helper. They can visit laundries, bakeries, dry-cleaning plants, and other establishments to observe route drivers preparing their trucks for route deliveries. Most simply, they can talk to the dry-cleaner route driver who comes to their house and ask any questions about the particular kind of work of the route driver.

Related occupations

Other occupations combine the sales and the driving aspects of a route driver's job. These include door-to-door sales workers, appliance repairers, vending machine mechanics, taxi drivers, and bus drivers.

Methods of entering

Route drivers gain their positions in several ways. Some have held jobs as retail sales workers or other sales workers. Others started out as a route driver's helper upon graduation from high school or during summer vacations and accepted positions as route drivers when openings developed. Still others waited for a proper opportunity and accepted jobs in plants that employ route drivers. Many large companies

have on-the-job training programs. They sometimes identify people in their plants who they feel would become good route drivers and train them in a knowledge of the products they are to sell on their route, as well as assigning them to work a route with an experienced route driver or supervisor for a brief period of time.

Advancement

Sales supervisor and route supervisor are positions to which many route drivers look forward, but these positions are relatively scarce. Most retail route drivers advance themselves by moving to positions as wholesale route drivers because there is usually more money attached to a wholesale route. Other route drivers use the experience they have gained on their routes as a means of accepting sales positions in other fields in which earnings are higher.

Employment outlook

More than 200,000 sales route drivers were employed in the early 1990s.

There has been a decline in the number of retail route drivers since 1940. This decline was a result of a number of factors. In World War II, the shortage of workers and gasoline made it necessary to cut sharply the number of home deliveries of products. Delivery was never fully resumed after the war. Also, many people now have large refrigerators and home freezers—items that have reduced the need for bakery and dairy route drivers. These changes may have run their course, and it is expected that the number of route drivers will change little in the foreseeable future. Because of retirements, deaths, and transfers, there will continue to be a need for large numbers of retail route drivers each year. In addition, the population of the nation continues to move toward the suburbs, where there will be an increased need for these services.

Many wholesale route drivers have been replaced by sales workers because a number of large companies have developed so many products that one route driver cannot handle all of them. These sales workers take orders, and the goods are delivered by truck drivers. This is especially true in areas where large supermarkets have replaced small grocery stores. New products, however, have also increased the need for wholesale route drivers in order to introduce these products in food stores throughout the country.

Route drivers
Sales Occupations

Earnings

Most route drivers work for a salary plus a commission on their sales. There are great differences in the amount of money made by different route drivers. Wholesale route drivers generally make more money than retail route drivers because they sell items in large quantities and get larger commissions. The earnings of route drivers are closely related to their effectiveness as persuasive sales workers. There are also differences related to the section of the country in which route drivers work and the kind of product that they deliver. On the average, sales route drivers earned between $12,000 and $25,000 in the early 1990s.

Most route drivers wear uniforms. In some cases the companies pay for these uniforms and for their cleaning. The fringe benefits enjoyed by route drivers vary. Some have paid vacations ranging from one to four weeks and some, paid holidays. Some route drivers are provided with hospitalization and medical benefits and are covered by pension plans.

Conditions of work

There are great differences in the number of hours route drivers work. Some route drivers work more than sixty hours a week; others work only thirty hours. The number of hours that route drivers work is determined by a number of factors: the season of the year, the ambition of the individual route driver, union regulations, and the nature of the route.

The retail route driver has to make deliveries in all kinds of weather and has to do a good deal of lifting, carrying, and climbing. Some route drivers, such as those delivering milk or newspapers, have to work unusual hours.

Route drivers have to be aware of road restrictions. Some have size and weight limitations; others have commercial vehicles restrictions. Some communities have barred vehicles such as ice cream trucks because of potential dangers of children running into the road.

Social and psychological factors

Route drivers are given a great deal of freedom. They seldom work under any strict supervision. They are provided with the opportunity, in general, to decide how fast they will work and when they will take breaks for rests or for meals. This freedom means that route drivers must exercise considerable self-discipline. If they abuse this freedom, they will lose customers and their employer will suffer. Since retail route drivers meet many people, they must enjoy working with people and be able to adapt to different kinds of personalities.

The union to which many route drivers belong is the International Brotherhood of Teamsters, Chauffeurs, Warehousemen and Helpers of America (Ind.). Some other route drivers are members of unions representing plant workers or their employers.

GOE: 08.02.07; SIC: Any industry; SOC: 4753

◇ SOURCES OF ADDITIONAL INFORMATION

Commission of Accredited Truck Driving Schools
1155 21st Street, NW
4th Floor
Washington, DC 20036

International Brotherhood of Teamsters, Chauffeurs, Warehousemen and Helpers of America (Ind.)
25 Louisiana Avenue, NW
Washington, DC 20001

National Association of Truck Driving Schools
PO Box 21433
Billings, MT 59104

◇ RELATED ARTICLES

Volume 1: Franchising; Transportation
Volume 3: Bus drivers, intercity and local transit; Collection workers; Door-to-door sales workers; Furniture Movers; Manufacturers' sales workers; Truck drivers, local and over-the-road

Securities and financial services sales representatives

Definition

Securities sales workers, sometimes called *registered representatives, account executives,* or *brokers,* work to represent both individuals and organizations in the buying and selling of stocks, bonds, or other securities. *Broker's floor representatives* are responsible for the buying and selling of securities on the floor of a stock exchange. *Securities traders* also buy and sell securities but usually as a representative of a private firm. *Financial services sales agents* assist clients in developing sound financial plans for continuing their business.

History

Raising capital to finance the needs of government and commerce was, and often still is, an arduous task. European monarchies, particularly during the eighteenth and nineteenth centuries, relied heavily upon bankers to meet the costs incurred by the interminable wars that devastated the Continent, and to help in the industrial expansion that was in its infancy. This source was not sufficient, though, and governments, banks, and industry turned to the burgeoning middle class, offering them securities and stocks—a fractional ownership—in exchange for their money. In London, dealers in these shares organized in 1773, and in the United States the New York Stock Exchange was officially formed in 1817, from its forerunner established in 1792.

The stock exchange functions as a marketplace, where stockbrokers buy and sell securities for individuals or institutions. Stock prices can fluctuate from minute to minute, and the price at any given time is determined by the demand. The Federal Securities Act of 1934 set up a federal commission to control the handling of securities, and rendered illegal any manipulation of prices on stock exchanges. This was a direct result of the disastrous stock market crash of 1929. Today the public is protected by regulations that set standards for listing, require public disclosure of financial condition, and prohibit the manipulation rampant in the 1920s, which led to the crash.

Nature of the work

The duties of securities sales workers, also called *account executives* or *registered representatives,* are varied and interesting. They open accounts for new customers, obtaining from them all the information required to permit the customers to buy and sell securities through their brokerage firm. They execute buy and sell orders for customers by relaying the information to the floor of the exchange where the order is actually put into effect. They obtain information on a company's prospects from their research department, at the request of a customer, and are often called upon to advise a customer on the wisdom of a purchase or sale. They must be prepared to answer all questions on the technical aspects of stock market operations and also be informed on current economic conditions. They are expected to have sufficient knowledge to anticipate certain trends, and to counsel customers accordingly in terms of their particular stock holdings.

Some securities sales workers specialize in specific areas such as handling only institutional accounts, bond issues, or mutual funds such as *securities traders.* Whatever area in which they may operate, securities sales workers must keep abreast of all significant political and economic conditions, maintain very accurate records of all transactions, and continually solicit new customers.

Requirements

Because of the background of knowledge necessary to handle this job properly, most brokerage houses will only hire those people who possess college degrees, particularly in business administration and finance. The ability to read and understand financial reports, and to properly evaluate statistics are essential to intelligent judgments. Because of the continual public contact, interested individuals should be well groomed, have a pleasant manner, and large reserves of tact and patience. Above all, they must have a well-developed sense of responsibility, because in many instances they will be handling funds that represent the life savings of clients.

175

Securities and financial services sales representatives
Sales Occupations

A financial planner examines a couple's portfolio and proposes new ways of investing their money. His confidence, honesty, and knowledge of the market are the main selling points of his service.

Special requirements

Almost all states require the licensing of securities sales workers. Written examinations are sometimes administered, and in some instances it is necessary to post a personal bond.

Securities sales workers must also register as representatives of their firm in accordance with the regulations set forth by the securities exchange dealt with, or with the National Association of Securities Dealers. An examination must be passed to qualify as a registered representative.

Opportunities for experience and exploration

Selling experience of any kind provides a good background for the securities sales worker. Occasionally, young people can find summer employment in a brokerage house. A visit to a local investment office or the New York Stock Exchange will provide a valuable opportunity to observe how transactions are handled and what is required of people in the field.

Related occupations

Other occupations that require financial skills and interests include financial and savings institution tellers, financial and savings institutions clerks, banking credit analysts, bank managers and officers, and securities sales workers.

Method of entering

Many brokerage concerns hire beginning securities sales workers, provide a training program for them, and then retain them for a probationary period to determine their capacities. The training period lasts about six months and includes both intensive classroom instruction and on-the-job training. Application may be made directly to the personnel office of the concern.

Advancement

Depending upon aptitudes and ambitions, workers may advance rapidly in this field. Accomplished sales workers find that the size and number of accounts that they service increase to the point where it is no longer necessary to solicit new customers. Others become branch managers, research analysts, or partners in their own firms.

Employment outlook

About 97,000 people were employed as securities sales workers in the early 1990s. Opportunities are expected to be good through the late 1990s, growing much faster than the average for all occupations, because of the continual growth of interest in the stock market because of economic growth and rising personal incomes. People with limited means can invest small amounts of money through a variety of methods such as investment clubs, mutual funds, and monthly payment plans; and the expansion of business activities together with new technological breakthroughs will create increased demand for the sale of stock to meet capital requirements.

Demand for securities sales workers fluctuates with the economy. Turnover among beginners is high, because they have a hard time getting enough clients. Because of potential high earnings, competition is intense.

Earnings

The salaries of trainees and beginners range from $1,080 to $1,440 per month although larger firms pay a somewhat higher starting wage. Once the securities sales worker has acquired a sufficient number of accounts, he or she works solely on a commission basis, with fees resulting from the size and type of security bought or sold. Some firms pay annual bonuses to their sales workers when business warrants it.

Experienced securities sales workers dealing with individual investors made an average of about $76,000 annually in the early 1990s. Those who handled institutional accounts made about $187,000 a year as an average.

Conditions of work

Securities sales workers have offices that are generally clean and well lighted. The work week is somewhat more flexible than in other fields, with overtime spent in paper work during heightened activity, and comparably fewer hours during dull trading periods. It is sedentary work, requiring little physical effort.

Social and psychological factors

The atmosphere of a brokerage firm is frequently highly charged, and the peaks and drops of market activity can be tension-producing. Earnings can fluctuate greatly depending on the condition of the market, and some securities sales workers have found it necessary to supplement their income through other means during times of extended market inactivity. Watching fortunes being made is exciting, but the reverse occurs frequently, too, and it requires much responsibility and maturity to weather the setbacks that one inevitably encounters. It is, however, one of the more interesting, challenging, and rewarding fields in which to work.

GOE: 11.06.03; SIC: 6211; SOC: 4124

◇ **SOURCES OF ADDITIONAL INFORMATION**

National Association of Securities Dealers
1735 K Street, NW
Washington, DC 20006

New York Stock Exchange
11 Wall Street
New York, NY 10005

American Stock Exchange
86 Trinity Place
New York, NY 10005

Securities Industries Association
120 Broadway
New York, NY 10271

◇ **RELATED ARTICLES**

Volume 1: Banking and Financial Services
Volume 2: Economists; Financial institution officers and managers
Volume 3: Financial institution clerks and related workers; Insurance agents and brokers, life; Insurance agents and brokers, property and casualty; Real estate agents and brokers

Services sales representatives

Definition

Services sales representatives sell a variety of services, from furniture upholstery and graphic arts to pest control and telephone communications systems. Depending on their particular line of work, they may demonstrate or describe their services to potential customers. Services sales representatives usually call on custom-

ers by phone or go to their homes or places of business.

History

The direct selling of services has developed along the same lines as the direct selling of

Services sales representatives
Sales Occupations

products; the sales representative is the key to the successful interaction between those who need services and those who provide them. Services sales representatives contact prospective clients, determine their needs, and outline the types and prices of services that can help the customer.

Although word-of-mouth recommendations are still important, services sales representatives increasingly rely on telecommunications and computer technology to identify potential customers and their needs.

Nature of the work

Although specific job responsibilities depend on the type of service being sold, all services sales representatives have a variety of duties in common. First, it is vital that sales representatives understand and be able to discuss the services their company provides. For example, a shipping service sales representative must be familiar with shipping rates, import and export regulations, and a host of other factors involving packaging and handling.

The sales procedure follows a similar pattern regardless of the particular service being sold. The sales representative develops lists of prospective clients through the use of selected telephone and business directories, by asking customers and other business associates for leads, by looking for new customers as they cover their assigned territories, and by receiving inquiries from potential customers. Sales representatives then meet with prospective customers and explain how the services being offered can meet their needs. This often requires using literature or demonstrations to describe their company's products. Sales representatives then answer customer questions and try to persuade them to purchase the services.

Keeping in constant touch with customers and potential customers is another important component of a services sales representative's job. If they fail to make a sale to a potential customer, for example, sales workers may follow up with more visits, letters, and phone calls. By the same token, constant contact with current customers encourages the continued use of services and increases the likelihood that the satisfied customer will recommend the services to friends or business acquaintances.

A sales representative's job can vary with the size of the company. Those working for larger companies, for example, generally are more specialized and are assigned to specific territorial boundaries and specific accounts. Those who work for smaller companies may

have public relations duties and administrative tasks in addition to their sales functions.

There are many specialists within the services sales representatives' field. These include: *sales-service promoters,* who create goodwill for companies by attending appropriate conventions and calling on sales representatives to advise on ways of increasing sales of a particular service; *telegraph personal service representatives,* who call on telegraph agents and customers to demonstrate how to use telegraph equipment, explain operating procedures, discuss rates and services, and make recommendations for meeting the customer's needs; and *sales representatives,* who sell warehouse space and services to manufacturers and others who need it.

Psychological tests and industrial relations sales agents sell programs of psychological, intelligence, and aptitude testing to businesses and schools. They aid in integrating the programs into the school or business operation and help in the administration, scoring, and interpretation of the tests.

Data-processing services sales representatives sell complex services such as inventory control and payroll processing to companies utilizing computers in their business operations; *travelers' checks sales representatives* visit banks, consumer groups, and travel agencies to explain benefits of travelers' checks; *business services sales agents* sell business services, such as linen supply and extermination services, usually within a specified territory.

Financial-report service sales agents sell services such as credit and insurance investigation reports to stores and other business establishments. *Communications consultants* discuss communications needs with residential and commercial customers. They suggest services, such as telephone, teletypewriter or ticker tape machines that would help clients meet their communications needs

Telephone services sales representatives visit commercial customers to review their telephone systems, analyze their communications needs, and recommend additional telecommunication services, if necessary.

Public utilities sales representatives visit commercial and residential customers to promote the increased or more economical use of gas, electricity, or telephone service. They quote rates for changes in service and installation charges.

Advertising sales representatives sell advertising space or broadcast time to advertising companies that maintain their own advertising departments; *hotel services sales representatives* contact business, government, and social groups to solicit conference and convention business for the hotel.

Education courses sales representatives recruit students for technical or commercial training schools. They inform prospective applicants of enrollment requirements and tuition fees. *Group-sales representatives* work for sports teams or other entertainment organizations and promote group ticket sales or season ticket sales. They may also arrange for group seating and special activities on the day of the event. *Sales-promotion representatives* visit retail outlets and encourage the use of display items such as posters, napkins, and other promotional material to increase retail sales.

Other sales representatives have job titles that define who they work for and what services they sell. These include: *pest control service sales agents; franchise sales representatives; herbicide service sales representatives; shipping services sales representatives; graphic art sales representatives; signs and displays sales representatives; printing sales representatives; signs sales representatives; audiovisual program productions sales representatives; electroplating sales representatives; elevators, escalators, and dumbwaiters sales representatives; dancing instruction sales representatives; television cable service sales representatives; upholstery and furniture sales representatives; automotive-leasing sales representatives;* and *burial needs salespersons.*

A service sales representative offers a variety of telephone services and maintenance options to a customer.

Requirements

While some high-school graduates are now serving as services sales representatives, an increasingly large number of those employed in this field have a college degree. The more complex a service, the greater the likelihood of it being sold by a college-trained person. For example, a company that markets advertising services would most likely seek a sales representative with an undergraduate degree in advertising or a masters' degree in business administration.

High-school students should take college-preparatory courses including English, speech arts, mathematics, and history. College programs will vary as to the particular area of interest, but should include course work in psychology, marketing, public relations, finance, and business law.

It is very important for a potential salesperson to have a good personality. The successful salesperson usually is cheerful, optimistic, sociable with both acquaintances and strangers, sincere, and tactful. The person must be able to both make a good initial impression and to maintain it while working repeatedly with the same customer. Good verbal skills are a necessity.

The good salesperson must also be able to work independently for much of the time. He or she must have sufficient self-motivation to continue to seek customers even after a long day or a series of setbacks.

Special requirements

In general, there are no licenses or certificates needed to work in this field. The only special requirement is the necessary knowledge and training dictated by employers in accordance with the complexities of the services being sold. This may include advanced educational degrees and work experience in the field in which one will sell.

Opportunities for experience and exploration

Because many services require specialized knowledge and sales approaches, it is unlikely that an untrained worker will be given much opportunity for exploratory sales experience. Many students, however, are able to measure their abilities and interest through part-time sales work in a store or other similar sales environment. In addition, some school work-study programs may have opportunities with businesses for part-time, practical on-the-job training. Another way of gaining insight into the responsibilities of a services sales representative is to talk to somebody already working in the field.

Related occupations

Other occupations that require sales ability and knowledge of the service they sell include travel agents, real estate agents, securities sales representatives, and wholesale and retail trade sales representatives.

Methods of entering

Because maturity and the ability to work independently are so important, many employees prefer to hire people who have achieved success in other jobs, either in sales or in a related field. For those entering the job market just out of college, school placement offices may be helpful in supplying job leads. In addition, those interested in securing an entry-level position can contact appropriate companies directly. Jobs may also be located through "help wanted" advertisements.

Almost every new sales representative must complete a training period before receiving a sales assignment. The larger companies may use formal training classes that last several months; the smaller organizations may emphasize supervised sales experience. Selling highly technical services such as communications systems usually involves more complex and lengthy sales training. In these situations, sales representatives usually work as part of a team and receive technical assistance from support personnel. For example, those who sell telecommunications equipment might work with a communications consultant.

Advancement

The primary form of advancement for services sales representatives is an increase in the number and size of the accounts they handle and, possibly, an increase in their sales territory. Some experienced representatives with leadership abilities may become branch office managers and supervise other sales representatives. A few representatives advance to top management positions or become partners in their companies. Some may go into business for themselves.

It is not unusual for someone to begin as a sales representative and then enter a related position with a company. For example, a successful sales representative may become a purchasing agent or a marketing executive.

Employment outlook

As a result of the continued demand for services in general, employment opportunities for services sales representatives as a whole are expected to grow much faster than the average through the early 1990s. Future opportunities, however, will vary greatly depending on the service involved. For example, the continued growth in office automation should lead to increased opportunities for data-processing services sales representatives and the growth in the advertising field should similarly increase opportunities for sales representatives in that field. Opportunities for education courses sales representatives, on the other hand, should only be about average with others involved with the school-age population.

As with other sales occupations, the high turnover among services sales representatives will lead to many new opportunities each year. As always, those with the most education, training, and sales experience will have the best job opportunities.

Earnings

Earnings of individual sales workers are, obviously, dependent on sales skills, the quality of the services that they represent, geographic location, the number of potential customers and their need for the workers' services, and the general economic situation. A beginning services sales representative in the early 1990s can expect to earn between $19,500 to $25,000, depending on the above factors; experienced sales representatives can earn anywhere between $25,000 and $75,000, with extremely successful sales representatives (especially those who sell technical services) earning even more. Experienced sales workers often earn more than their branch managers. It is important to realize however that because sales can go up and down frequently, earnings can fluctuate widely.

Sales representatives work on different types of compensation plans. Some get a straight salary; others are paid commissions based on the total volume of sales. Most sales representatives are paid a combination of salary, commission, and bonuses.

Bonuses may be based on the increase in number of new clients brought into the company, or an increase in overall sales, or some other measure of gain. Bonuses may be several thousand dollars at some companies.

In addition to salary or commission, travel and on-the-road expenses are usually paid by the employer. Some companies also provide a car or pay a transportation allowance for those who travel. Most employers also offer full-time sales representatives a two- to four-week annual vacation, medical insurance, and other benefits.

Conditions of work

The services sales representative works long and irregular hours. Sales workers with large territories frequently spend all day calling on customers in one city and then travel to another city to make calls the next day. Many sales representatives spend at least several nights a month away from home. The sales worker with a limited territory may have less overnight travel, but like all sales workers, will have to spend many evenings preparing reports, writing up orders, and entertaining customers and potential customers. Some representatives who sell primarily by phone spend the majority of their time in the office.

Although most sales representatives work long hours and must make appointments to fit the convenience of customers, they are able to have a degree of flexibility and variety in their workdays. They can set their own schedules as long as they meet their company's goals.

Sales work is physically demanding. Sales representatives may spend most of the day on their feet. They are constantly traveling from one place to another. Sales workers also face competition from other representatives and the possibility that their customers may switch their business to another organization.

Social and psychological factors

A successful sales worker should be able to handle irregular working hours, the possibility of lengthy travel, and the competitive demands of the job. For those with a family, these demands may be especially difficult.

Sales workers, because of the nature of their job, require outgoing personalities. The ability to take interest in, communicate to, and listen to customers is important. For individuals who are not comfortable interacting with strangers or large groups of people, sales work can be extremely stressful. For the successful salesperson interaction with other people is one of the enjoyable parts of the job.

Sales representatives should have good communications skills and the ability to interact well with others. They should also be able to work independently and spend long periods of time alone. Other personal qualifications include dependability, trustworthiness, and a neat personal appearance.

The role of the sales worker is varied. The salesperson should sense the important of his or her role in the distribution of services and its effect upon both the provider and the customer.

Because sales are affected by changing economic conditions and other variables, services sales representatives must be able to adjust to fluctuating earnings.

GOE: 05.05.09; SIC: Any industry; SOC: 4783

◇ **SOURCES OF ADDITIONAL INFORMATION**

Professional Salespersons of America
3801 Monaco NE
Albuquerque, NM 87111

Sales and Marketing Executives International
Statler Office Tower
Suite 458
Cleveland OH 44115

National Association for Professional Saleswomen
PO Box 2606
Novato, CA 94948

◇ **RELATED ARTICLES**

Volume 1: See Table of Contents for areas of specific interest
Volume 3: Door-to-door workers; Insurance agents and brokers, life; Insurance agents and brokers, property and casualty; Manufacturing representatives; Real estate agents and brokers; Retail sales workers; Security sales workers; Wholesale trade sales workers

Toll collectors

Definition

Toll collectors receive payments from private motorists or commercial drivers for use of highways, tunnels, bridges, or ferries. Toll collectors accept toll and fare tickets previously purchased. When collecting money, toll collectors check that the proper amount has been received and give drivers correct change when necessary. Toll collectors act as cashiers and provide necessary cash reports and daily revenue received and provide service and support to motorists and commercial drivers.

History

The development of roads and passageways was a by-product of usage, as many of the more popular, well-traveled thoroughfares were those that led to key cities and destinations. Our early highway system, however, lacked continuity and adequate planning. The 1956 Federal Aid Highway Act was Congress' answer to a highway system that was comprised of individual roads and needed to be developed with accessibility and consistency throughout the country.

As the quality and efficiency of our highway system developed, however, additional revenue was needed to offset the cost of new roads being built as well as the maintenance of existing ones. Tariffs or tolls started being collected to gain the additional revenue necessary to develop roads and interstate systems that could in fact span the nation.

Nature of the work

The responsibilities of toll collectors focus on two areas of concentration. Primarily, they are cashiers who collect revenue from motorists to use designated roads, tunnels or ferries. Even more than acting as cashiers, however, toll collectors have a wide range of administrative duties that provide service and guidance to motorists as well.

When handling money, toll collectors begin with a change bank containing currency and change so that they may make change for motorists paying their fares, but who do not have exact change. Toll collectors keep these monies organized and separate as to denomination, so they may change quickly and accurately, especially during rush hour traffic. At the end of their eight-hour shift, the toll collectors calculate the amount of revenue received for that day by subtracting the original bank amount from the total amount of money they now have. Toll collectors also prepare cash reports, commutation ticket reports, and deposit slips that report the day's tallies. Toll collectors have keen perception and are often able to spot counterfeits of any kind.

The administrative duties that toll collectors may be responsible for include filling out traffic reports and facility inspections to make sure that the general area is clean of litter and ticket stubs and that toll gates and automatic lanes are working properly. Toll collectors notify their supervisors or support agencies concerning hazardous roads, weather conditions, or vehicles in distress. They also may be requested to give directions, supply maps, and estimate destinations to the nearest rest stop or service station. Toll collectors are sometimes the only link on a particular long stretch of highway, and as such may need to assist in certain emergencies or contact police or ambulance support in case of an emergency.

Sometimes toll collectors provide supervisory tasks like monitoring automatic and nonrevenue lanes, relieving fellow employees for lunch or coffee breaks, or complete violation reports. Toll collectors are able to classify vehicles according to size and toll rates. Ferry operators may direct boarding vehicles and monitor capacity as well collect fares. Toll operators at tunnels must enforce any regulations regarding usage, such as that of tank trucks carrying glass bottles, and maintain any other safety precautions.

Requirements

Toll collectors fulfill a variety of responsibilities and as such should have certain abilities. Toll collectors must have good eyesight and hearing. These sensory abilities are important to determine the class of vehicles so that they know what toll fare to charge as well as being able to hear motorists requests or certain instructions from a supervisor in the midst of heavy traffic. Manual dexterity in handling and organizing money and fare tickets, as well as giving change, is also important.

Toll collectors are often required to be at least eighteen years of age, but all employees should be in generally good health and have reasonable stamina. Some collectors must stand for hours at a time and have the mental concentration to work efficiently during high traffic times. Toll collectors must be able to maneuver successfully over the traffic lanes and booth platforms. Toll collectors sometimes work near exhaust fumes, and this also should be taken into consideration.

Toll collectors should be considerate and helpful to motorists. They should also be perceptive and have neat work habits. Honesty in a toll collector is imperative.

A toll collector gives a driver her change.

Special requirements

Toll collectors usually do not require any additional training other than what the highway department supplies its new employees. Certain abilities, however, can assist collectors in performing their job well. Communication skills, listening as well as speaking, are important. Lost or confused motorists rely on the guidance of toll collectors. Sometimes the working conditions can be noisy. Adequate mathematical abilities, receiving payment, counting change, and calculating daily totals are tasks that require concentration and detail. Workers should know the importance of having these skills or developing them further, as they are an important part of the job.

Opportunities for experience and exploration

Students interested in careers as toll collectors should contact state and local departments of transportation as well as state highway departments. Some counseling professionals may have additional information on such careers or related agencies to contact to inquire in more depth about the nature of the work and the necessary requirements.

Related occupations

Being responsible for the collection and balancing of monies received and returned is an important facet of several other occupations.

These include financial and savings institution tellers and clerks, counter and retail clerks, cashiers, retail sales workers, and route drivers.

Methods of entering

Applicants interested in becoming toll collectors may write to their state and local departments of transportation, highway agencies, or civil service organizations for appropriate information on education requirements, job prerequisites, and application materials. For states that require qualification testing, information on test dates as well as preparation materials may also be requested.

Advancement

Sometimes advancement for toll collectors may result in promotion from part-time to full-time employment, or from the late evening shift to daytime work. Supervisory and operations positions often result in more money or better benefits packages. Promotions that require additional responsibilities may also require further training. Some training may be handled on-the-job; certain management education, however, is best learned in the classroom of an accredited college or training program. Workers with aspirations for promotions may consider taking courses in advance so that when openings exist they already have some additional training and show initiative.

Toll collectors
Sales Occupations

Employment outlook

Employment opportunities for toll collectors often hinge on economic factors such as automobile sales, gas prices, and trends in consumer spending for luxury items like travel. In the early 1990s, opportunities are good for toll collectors. The fact that highway toll booths are open twenty-four hours a day does much to augment the need for employees. As the highway system continues to develop, compensating revenue will also be needed and some form of collection will have to occur. Automation cannot readily take the place of personal service and assistance.

Earnings

Wages for full-time toll collectors vary with the area and state the collector is employed. Salaries in the early 1990s, however, begin at approximately $12,000 per year and increase to possibly $20,000 with additional experience and good employment record. Part-time employees are usually paid by the hour and may begin earning the minimum hourly wage. Collectors who work the later shifts may earn more, and most employees earn time and a half or double time for overtime or holiday hours.

Toll collectors receive vacation time calculated on the number of hours worked in conjunction with years of employment. Employees with one to five years of service may receive eighty hours of vacation. This scale can increase to possibly 136 six hours of vacation for seasoned workers with nine to fourteen years of employment.

Benefits packages usually include health insurance coverage for the employee and their family as well as pension and retirement plans. Toll workers often enjoy the generous employee benefits of working in government service.

Conditions of work

Toll collectors may either stand or sit on stools in the booths they occupy. Toll booths are stationed along highways, bridges, tunnels, or rivers or other waterway passages where ferries operate. Usually, full-time toll collectors work an eight-hour shift; the shifts, however, may operate around the clock, with the first shift running from 7:00 A.M. to 3:00 P.M. Other shifts may run from 3:00 P.M. to 11:00 P.M. and 11:00 P.M. to 7:00 A.M.

Most toll booth complexes have rest room and shower facilities. Some may have kitchen and break room accommodations as well. Some workers have assigned lockers or share lockers with workers on different shifts. Usually the facilities are better when there are not any oasis or service stations adjacent. Toll stations have communications equipment so that they may notify state police or the department of transportation of any emergencies or hazardous conditions.

Social and psychological factors

Toll collectors have important responsibilities. They collect the needed revenue for the further development of state highways and provide vital services and assistance to motorists and commercial drivers. Toll collectors may work very busy shifts that coordinate with rush hour or holiday travel. Sometimes, they are requested to work weekends, evenings, and holidays, or put in additional time to compensate for ill or vacationing employees. Much of the overall success of our highway administration can be attributed to toll collectors.

GOE: 07.03.01; SIC: 4785; SOC: 4364

◇ **SOURCES OF ADDITIONAL INFORMATION**

American Association of State Highway and Transportation Officials
444 North Capitol Street, NW, Suite 225
Washington, DC 20001

◇ **RELATED ARTICLES**

Volume 1: Transportation
Volume 3: Cashiers; Counter and retail clerks; Retail sales workers

---

Travel agents

Definition

The *travel agent* assists individuals or groups wishing to take trips by planning itineraries; making transportation, hotel, and tour reservations; obtaining or preparing tickets; and performing related services.

History

The first travel agency in the United States was established in 1872. Before this time, wars and international barriers, inadequate transportation and hotels, lack of leisure, and minimum standards of living inhibited travel. Despite the glamour attached to such early travelers as Marco Polo, people of the Middle Ages and the seventeenth and eighteenth centuries were not accustomed to travel.

The Industrial Revolution created products that were more and more involved in international trade. Commercial traffic between countries stimulated both business and personal travel. Yet until the twentieth century travel was rigorous and most areas were unprepared for tourists.

The travel business began with Thomas Cook, an Englishman who first popularized the guided tour. In 1841, Cook arranged his first excursion—a special Midland Counties Railroad Company train to carry passengers from Leicester to a temperance meeting in Loughborough. His business grew rapidly. He helped 165,000 visitors attend the Great Exhibition of 1851. The following year, he organized the first "Cook's Tour." Earnest groups of tourists were soon seen traveling by camel to view the Pyramids and the Sphinx, gliding past historic castles on the Rhine, and riding by carriage to view the wonders of Paris.

The development of the railroads, the substitution of faster steam for sailing ships, the advent of the automobile and the bus, and the arrival of the airplane provided a quality of transportation that encouraged travel. At the same time, cities, regions, and countries began to appreciate the economic aspects of travel. Promotional campaigns were organized to attract and accommodate tourists.

Formal organization of the travel industry was reflected in the establishment in 1931 of the American Society of Travel Agents (A.S.T.A.) and the National Association of Travel Organizations.

In the past decade, travel agents have noted great increases in family travel. This is in part a result of increased leisure time. With some business firms now utilizing the four-day work week, there is even greater need for travel agents to help people in planning their vacations wisely.

Nature of the work

The travel agent may be a salesperson, travel consultant, tour organizer, travel guide, bookkeeper, and small business executive. If he or she works in a one-person office, the agent combines all of these functions. Others work in offices with dozens of employees and specialization is possible. In some cases, travel agents are employed by national or international firms and draw upon very extensive resources.

As a salesperson the travel agent must be able to motivate clients to take advantage of one's services. The travel agent studies the interests of travel customers, learns where they have traveled, appraises their financial resources and available time, and presents alternative plans in the most effective fashion.

As a travel consultant, agents give clients suggestions regarding travel plans and itineraries, information on transportation alternatives, and advice on class and rates of hotels and motels. They also help with passport and visa regulations, foreign currency and exchange, climate and wardrobe, health requirements, customs regulations, baggage and accident insurance, travelers checks or letters of credit, car rentals, sightseeing, and welcome or escort services.

Many travel agents only sell tours developed by other organizations. The most skilled agents, however, often organize tours on a wholesale basis. This involves developing an itinerary; arranging tour leadership; making tentative reservations for transportation, hotels, and even for side trips; publicizing the tour through a descriptive brochure and other travel agents; scheduling reservations; and handling last-minute problems. Sometimes tours are arranged at the specific request of a group or to meet a particular need.

In addition to other duties, travel agents may serve as tour guides, leading trips ranging

185

Travel agents
Sales Occupations

A travel agent gives a client the plane ticket he ordered over the phone. Before he leaves, she goes over the ticket to ensure that all of the information is as he originally ordered.

from one week in a local area to six months around the world. Agents often find tour leadership a useful way to gain personal travel experience and to become thoroughly acquainted with persons who may represent potential customers for additional trips. Tour leaders usually receive all their expenses. Most travel agents, however, must arrange for coverage of work during their absence, which often prohibits tour leadership for small, self-employed agents.

The agent serves as a bookkeeper to handle the complex pattern of transportation and hotel reservations that characterize each trip. He or she works directly with airline, steamship, railroad, and bus companies. He or she makes direct contact with hotels and sightseeing organizations or works indirectly through a correspondent agency in the city involved. These arrangements demand exacting standards of accuracy. After reservations are made, the agent must write up or obtain tickets, develop itineraries, and send out bills for the reservations involved.

In larger agencies, one staff member may become an authority on sea cruises, another on trips to the Far East, and a third may develop an extensive knowledge of either low-budget or luxury trips.

In addition to the regular travel business, a number of travel jobs are offered by oil companies, automobile clubs, and transportation companies. Some jobs in travel are on the staffs of state and local governments seeking to encourage and expedite tourism.

Requirements

The prime requisite for success in the travel field is a sincere interest in travel. Certainly the agent's own background of travel experience and knowledge of major tourist centers, the

merits of various hotels, local points of interest, and climate make that person a more effective and convincing source of assistance. Yet the work of the travel agent is not one long vacation. He or she operates in a highly competitive industry.

The travel agent must be able to make quick and accurate use of transportation schedules and tariffs. The agent must be able to quickly handle addition and subtraction.

Most travel agents work with a wide range of personalities. They must also be able to generate enthusiasm. Age is of little importance, but good appearance and grooming are required.

A knowledge of foreign languages is useful, as many customers come from other countries and the agent frequently must write foreign hotels or agencies to make reservations.

Private vocational schools, adult education programs in public high schools, and colleges offer travel courses, and some colleges and universities grant bachelor's and master's degrees in travel and tourism. College training is helpful, but not required for work as a travel agent. Yet, college training will become increasingly important and eventually, most agents will be college graduates. A liberal arts or business administration background is recommended. Useful liberal arts courses include foreign languages, geography, English, history, political science, art and music appreciation, and literature. Pertinent business courses are transportation, business law, hotel management, marketing, office management, and accounting. As in many other fields, computer skills are increasingly important.

High-school students desiring to enter the field of travel should study English, social studies, commercial mathematics, typing, and foreign languages.

Special requirements

To be able to sell various types of transportation, the travel agent must be approved by the conferences of carriers involved. These are the Air Traffic Conference, the International Air Transport Association, the Trans-Atlantic Passenger Steamship Conference, the Trans-Pacific Passenger Conference, and the Rail Travel Promotion Agency.

To sell tickets for these individual conferences, the agent must be clearly established in the travel business, have a good personal and business background, and demonstrate a degree of permanency in the travel field. Not all agents are authorized to sell by all the above conferences. Naturally, those who wish to sell the widest range of services seek an affiliation with all five.

In California, travel agents not approved by a conference must be licensed by the state. All agents must have state registrations in Hawaii, Ohio, and Rhode Island.

Opportunities for experience and exploration

Actual travel experience provides useful knowledge of the expectations, merits, and problems of travel.

Any type of part-time experience with a travel agency would be helpful. The one-person agency may welcome help during peak periods of the year or when the agent must be away from the office. If your high school or junior college has career conferences or talks, it may be appropriate to suggest that a speaker from a travel industry be included. Visits to local travel agents may be welcome and provide a fund of very helpful information.

Examination of the various travel magazines should provide a broader picture of the field and some of its current issues and newest developments.

Related occupations

The hospitality and travel and tourism industries are immense and offer innumerable employment options for those with a strong interest in travel and working with people. Other careers include hotel and motel managers, hotel and motel clerks, airline flight attendants, travel and reservation agents, and cruise line personnel.

Methods of entering

Young people seeking careers in the travel field usually begin by working for a transportation company. Fortunately, a number of suitable positions exist, and they are particularly appropriate for young people. Airlines, for example, hire flight attendants, reservation agents, and ticket clerks. Railroads and steamship companies also have clerical positions, although their slow growth in recent years has restricted the hiring for entry-level assignments. Persons with travel experience may secure positions as

tour conductors. Organizations with extensive travel operations may employ travel agents.

As travel agencies tend to have relatively few employees, most openings are filled as a result of direct application and personal contact. In evaluating the merits of various travel agencies, employment candidates may wish to note whether or not the owner belongs to A.S.T.A. That group also may help in several additional ways. It sponsors adult night school courses in travel agency operation which are available in some metropolitan areas. It offers a fifteen-lesson travel agency correspondence course that is open to anyone for a fee. Also available, for a modest charge, is a travel agency management kit containing information particularly helpful to a person considering setting up his or her own agency. Its publication, *Travel News*, includes a classified advertising section listing positions open and agencies to sell or buy.

Advancement

Usual advancement opportunities within the travel field are limited to growth in terms of travel volume or extent of specialization. The agent, for example, may hire additional employees, or set up branch offices.

Travel bureau employees may decide to go into business for themselves. Prospective agents should take the correspondence course offered by the American Society of Travel Agents.

Agents may show their professional status by belonging to A.S.T.A., which requires three years of satisfactory travel agent experience and approval by at least two carrier conferences.

Employment outlook

About 100,000 people were employed as travel agents in the early 1990s.

Although future prospects in the travel field will depend to some degree on the state of the economy, the travel industry is expected to expand rapidly in the next ten years as more Americans travel for pleasure and business. New travel agencies will open and existing ones will expand, causing employment of these workers to grow much faster than the average for all occupations through the late 1990s. Much of the travel done in the United States will continue to be business related.

187

Travel agents
Sales Occupations

Earnings

Their rate of commission varies, depending on the type of sale, from 8 to 10 percent of the cost to the individual. Air travel commissions vary on domestic flights and on international trips. Steamship companies pay a commission on a sliding scale depending upon the season. Bus tours, sightseeing trips, and resort hotels often pay a commission of 10 percent or higher.

The enterprising agent will supplement transportation and hotel sales by also offering automobile rentals, travel books, baggage forwarding, currency exchange, gift services, house rentals, insurance, letters of credit, prepaid meals, travelers checks, and transfers.

The travel agent's commission is not paid by the client (the traveler) but by the transportation companies, hotels, and other organizations from which the traveler receives services and accommodations.

Employed travel agents may be hired either on a regular salary, paid entirely on a commissioned basis, or receive a salary plus a modified commission or bonus. Salaries of travel agents overall in the early 1990s averaged from $12,000 to $24,000. Small travel agencies provide less than an average amount of fringe benefits such as retirement, medical, and life insurance plans. Self-employed agents tend to earn more than those who work for others although, of course, the business risk is greater.

In addition to income, travel agents receive a number of attractive opportunities for personal travel. Major airlines and steamship companies, knowing that agents who have used their services may recommend them more highly, offer some trips to agents at only 25 percent of the usual cost. Occasionally, the opening of a new hotel, airline route, or resort area leads to free trips to agents to promote their recommending these companies for travel. If they organize tours, agents may be able to take advantage of the fact that transportation carriers and hotels usually offer one free trip for each fifteen to twenty paid members of a travel group.

Conditions of work

While an interesting and appealing occupation, the job of the travel agent is not as simple or glamorous as might be expected.

Travel is a highly competitive field. Almost every travel agent can offer the client the same service. Agents must depend upon repeat customers for much of their business. Their reliability, courtesy, and effectiveness in past transactions will determine whether this repeat business will come to them.

The agent also works in an atmosphere of keen competition for referrals. The travel agent must resist direct pressure or indirect pressure from organizations that have provided favors (free trips, for example) and book on the basis of the client's best interests.

Most agents work a forty-hour week, although this frequently includes working a half-day on Saturday or an occasional evening. During rush times of the year (from January through June) overtime may be necessary. Agents may receive additional salary from this work or be given compensatory time off.

The agent usually works in pleasant physical surroundings, designed to prove attractive to the clients.

As they gain experience, agents become more effective. One study revealed that 98 percent of all agents had more than three years' experience in some form of the travel field. Almost half had twenty years or more in this area.

Social and psychological factors

The travel agent should sense the many contributions made by this field. Travel performs a vital role in promoting international understanding and world peace.

Travel also plays an important role in education. Today, more than 100,000 American students travel abroad each year.

Travel also plays a significant economic role. The approximately $10 billion spent on foreign travel by citizens of all countries makes travel a major contributor to international trade.

The pressures that come with being a travel agent are associated with arranging immediate travel plans for someone, dealing with impatient or unpleasant customers, and problems that arise through computer failure, airline cancellations and delays, and lack of correct information from other sources.

GOE: 08.02.06; SIC: 4724; SOC: 4369

◇ **SOURCES OF ADDITIONAL INFORMATION**

American Guides Association
8909 Dorrington Avenue
West Hollywood, CA 90048

American Society of Travel Agents
1101 King Street
Alexandria, VA 22314

Travel Industry Association of America
1133 21st Street, NW
Washington, DC 20036

◇ **RELATED ARTICLES**

Volume 1: Hospitality; Transportation; Travel
and Tourism
Volume 3: Reservation and transportation
ticket agents

Wholesale trade sales workers

Definition

The *wholesale trade sales worker* calls regularly on
retailers and buyers for industrial and commercial concerns and institutions, seeking their orders for a number of products. The sales
worker represents a wholesaler organization
that does not manufacture products but purchases them for resale.

History

The wholesale industry in the United States began approximately more than one hundred
years ago. Before that time, retail stores purchased their goods directly from the manufacturers. Once or twice a year, merchants would
travel to major seaports and manufacturing
centers to purchase new products for resale. Industrial concerns usually made, or purchased
locally, components for the goods that they
produced. Institutions were able to solve their
relatively simple needs by going directly to
producers.

For contrast, consider today's complex
problems of supply faced by a modern hospital,
an electronics firm, and a retail chain. The hospital needs thousands of items ranging from
specialized surgical instruments to a complete
supply of drugs. The electronics firm produces
many of its own parts, but finds that it can
much more reasonably purchase some items
than to set up its own production facility. The
retail chain wishes to sell the largest possible
variety of products which its customers will
buy.

Between these two areas, the role of the
wholesale salesperson developed. The earliest
wholesalers in the United States were probably

the ship chandlers of New England who assembled goods required by merchant and military
ships. Shipowners found that a specialized and
centralized supply source enabled them to
equip vessels quickly and send them back out
to sea.

The need for wholesalers grew as industrialization changed U.S. manufacturing capacities, distribution problems, consumer tastes,
and as more complex retail establishments replaced general stores. Individual manufacturers
found they could sell more reasonably through
use of a wholesaler. Purchasers of goods found
it more convenient to deal with a few sources of
supply rather than hundreds of organizations.

Improved transportation enabled wholesale
firms to ship goods to almost any part of the
country. The traveling salesperson emerged
complete with illustrated product catalogs, special promotional deals, and financial support
for local advertising. Competition between
wholesalers helped develop more highly skilled
salespeople. As a related function, the traveling
sales worker often would check on the financial
condition of prospective customers and might
help collect delinquent accounts that they
owed.

Nature of the work

The work of wholesale salespeople will vary
greatly depending upon the products they
carry, the customers to whom they sell, and the
geographical area in which they operate. Every
good salesperson, however, attempts to sell
goods by providing maximum service to the
customers.

Major wholesale houses cover a region or
the entire country with a network of sales

Wholesale trade salesworkers spend much of their day on the road. For that reason, they equip their cars with portable office equipment such as desktop computers and cellular telephones.

workers. Generally, these workers are responsible for an assigned geographical area. Salespersons periodically call on all regular customers in this territory and, occasionally, call on any other potential customers in an attempt to develop new business for themselves.

In their calls, salespeople show each customer the widest possible variety of merchandise in which he or she may be interested. Sales workers bring along samples, pictures, or specifications of available products and talk about their salability, utility, economy, and quality.

Some sales workers concentrate on a few products. The electrical appliance wholesale sales worker may carry from ten to thirty items, ranging from food freezers and air-conditioners to waffle irons and portable heaters. Others, such as representatives of drug wholesalers, may catalog as many as 50,000 individual items.

The wholesale sales worker may help the retailer with merchandise display, advertising plans, and provide general information on styles and trends. The sales worker knows that the successful retailer will be a better customer.

When working with regular customers, the sales worker may check stock and prepare orders for items that will be needed before the next visit. Sales workers write up orders and forward them to the wholesaler's office. As special problems develop, such as the speed with which a product may be delivered, the sales worker may telephone the office.

Sales workers also try to arrange terms of credit under which purchases are made. Some sales workers help collect for products sold. Sales workers also prepare their expense account records and reports, plan their work schedule, arrange general travel plans, and schedule appointments in advance.

To create customer goodwill, sales workers may entertain customers at lunch or in the evening. Both wholesale sales workers and their customers attend sales conferences and trade or professional conventions to learn of new developments in their field and to make or maintain personal contacts.

Requirements

When hiring sales workers, most employers prefer at least a high-school education. Useful courses include English, bookkeeping, economics, typing, office practice, and sales theory. Junior college training is highly desirable.

Each year, a higher percentage of sales workers are selected from the ranks of college graduates. The scope of wholesaling is so broad that college training in many different fields is useful. Biological science majors are desired by wholesalers in the pharmaceutical field. Engineering training is useful in sales of complex technical equipment. Among the many useful college courses are English, economics, marketing, credit, wholesaling, retailing, advertising, and accounting.

Desirable personal traits include self-confidence, enthusiasm for the job, and an understanding of human nature. The salesperson works constantly with people and so must enjoy them and get along well with them.

While some high-school graduates become sales trainees, the typical beginner works as a receiving clerk, stock clerk, order filler, packer, or shipping clerk. Through work in these nonselling positions, the newcomer gains knowledge of the many items carried by the wholesaler and obtains valuable information on the operations of the company office. As an intermediate step, the prospective sales worker may serve as an order clerk—accepting telephone and written inquiries from customers or from sales workers in the field.

As a final step in training, the new sales worker often accompanies an experienced sales worker to learn sales techniques, observe conditions of work in the field, and become acquainted with customers. It usually takes two years or more to prepare the trainee for outside selling. At such time the sales worker is assigned a territory.

Special requirements

There are no licenses required or other special requirements. The only requirements are established by individual wholesale employers concerned with matching the sales worker's background qualifications with the complexity of products to be sold.

Opportunities for experience and exploration

As employers require highly skilled sales workers, it is difficult for an inexperienced person to obtain exploratory work experience. Occasionally, a young person interested in this field may serve as a sales assistant helping a sales worker arrange product displays, carrying samples, and making emergency deliveries.

Summer employment in a wholesale warehouse or office would be helpful. Processing, shipping, or checking on orders from sales workers in the field would provide an excellent view of the work.

Related occupations

Young people with an aptitude and interest in selling and sales can find opportunities in other fields and other specialties such as automobile sales, retail sales, door-to-door sales, and route sales.

Methods of entering

High-school graduates often apply directly for entry positions. A list of local wholesale employees may be found in the classified section of the telephone directory. Public employment services often have listings for many entry-level positions.

Sales workers with experience in other lines, or other experienced mature persons, may learn of sales openings through public and private employment services, and through sales associations. College graduates may learn of sales openings through these same sources, as well as through college placement offices. They usually enter directly into supervised sales activities.

Advancement

Because of the high level of experience required for success in the field, newcomers spend their early years improving their sales ability and developing a knowledge of products. As sales workers mature, they are shifted to increasingly large territories or more difficult types of customers. In some wholesale organizations, an experienced sales worker may be taken off a geographical territory and be made a product specialist. Typical is the general furniture sales worker who may specialize in sales to motel developers or the office equipment sales worker who is assigned responsibility for dealing with a state government.

Within the wholesale field itself, there are several lines of advancement. The sales worker may become a regional sales supervisor and, eventually, a sales manager. Experienced sales workers may transfer to such related wholesale functions as buying (buyer, merchandise manager), finance (accountant, credit manager, auditor, or controller), personnel (recruitment, trainer, wage and salary administrator), and operations (warehouse manager, inventory control administrator, and operations manager). Other sales workers may enter public relations, advertising, and new business development.

An estimated one-sixth of all employees in the wholesale field are in managerial or supervisory positions.

Occasionally a wholesale sales worker may go into business independently. Often this is as a manufacturer's representative, handling the sale of products from a number of organizations. Manufacturers' representatives perform many of the same functions as the wholesaler, but on a more modest scale. Sometimes experienced wholesale sales workers are asked by a company to head up or serve on a sales force. It is not unusual for a company that has marketed its products through wholesalers to decide that it wants direct marketing.

Employment outlook

In the early 1990s, there were about 1.4 million wholesale sales workers. Most sold machinery to industry and business. Other large employers of these workers are wholesalers dealing in food, drugs, electrical goods, hardware, and clothing.

The number of wholesale sales workers required through the late 1990s should rise faster than the average in the labor force as a whole.

Wholesale trade sales workers
Sales Occupations

Population expansion, economic growth, and the continued development of additional products should encourage the wholesale industry. Centralization of purchasing through retail chains, consolidation of existing separate organizations, and the concentration of business in fewer companies, however, will tend to reduce the number of customers and, consequently, the need for sales workers.

The net result is that the wholesale sales worker of the future must be qualified to handle larger average orders. The wholesaler whom the worker represents will be able to provide more efficient service through improvements in automatic materials handling equipment and the installation of data-processing and record-keeping systems.

To better meet competition (both from other wholesalers and from other sales sources), the wholesale sales worker may have to provide additional special services to customers, which may occupy an increasing amount of the sales worker's time.

Thousands of openings probably occur each year because of the retirement or death of experienced sales workers. Other vacancies will result as successful wholesale sales workers transfer to other marketing and business positions and as unsuccessful sales workers leave.

Earnings

Beginning sales workers usually are on a salary basis or a combination salary and commission plan, dependent upon the company's policy regarding wages.

As they assume direct responsibility for a sales territory, wholesale sales workers may be shifted to a straight commission basis (receiving a fixed percentage of each dollar sold) or a modified commission scale (receiving a low base salary plus a lower rate of commission on sales).

In the early 1990s, average yearly earnings for wholesale sales workers were about $28,080. Half earned between $19,960 and $40,500. One in ten earned less than $14,950, and another one in ten earned more than $53,000.

Practically all wholesale sales workers have steady year-round work. However, as many sales workers experience wide seasonal fluctuations in income, they may receive a weekly or monthly drawing account that will eventually be balanced against the commissions earned annually. To help with the extensive travel required, many companies provide the sales worker with a car and travel expenses and also cover the worker's living expenses while on the road.

An increasing number of wholesale organizations provide paid vacations of two to four weeks depending on length of service, medical and life insurance, and retirement benefits.

Conditions of work

The wholesale salesperson works long and irregular hours. Sales workers with large territories (such as a portion of a state) frequently spend all day calling on customers in one city and much of the night traveling to the place in which they will make calls the next day. The sales worker with limited territory may have little overnight travel, but like all sales workers, will have to spend many evenings preparing reports, writing up orders, and entertaining customers.

Several times a year, the sales workers may travel to a company meeting and participate in trade conventions and conferences.

Sales work is physically demanding. They may spend most of the day on their feet. They are constantly traveling from one place to another. Frequently, they must carry a heavy sample case or catalogs. In the case of a person with a family, the home life may be affected by the irregular working hours and the competitive demands of the job.

The sales worker constantly faces the threat that the customers (many of whom are key in terms of the volume of their purchases) may switch their business to another competitive organization. By contrast, the retail merchant sells to many customers and the loss of one is relatively unimportant.

Social and psychological factors

The wholesale sales worker should take pride in playing a key role in an industry that contributes to our economy by serving the customers to whom it sells and the manufacturers from whom it buys.

The wholesale firm assembles hundreds or thousands of products from many sources of manufacture and permits the retailer or other user to purchase many items from a single source.

In today's buyer's market, the wholesale sales worker provides a service that permits customers to keep inventories lower by purchasing goods as they are needed, buying on credit, and receiving suggestions for better use or more effective marketing.

Use of wholesale houses and their sales workers permits manufacturers to specialize on production rather than attempt to maintain a nationwide sales force, develop an aggressive consumer-oriented advertising program, and create a shipping and distribution program. Keenly interested in making more sales, the wholesale representative provides more than adequate coverage of potential customers. As one often sells items similarly produced by competing manufacturers, the wholesale sales worker should assume a neutral position.

GOE: 11.05.04; SIC: Any industry; SOC: 402

◇ **SOURCES OF ADDITIONAL INFORMATION**

National Association of Wholesaler-Distributors
1725 K Street, NW
Washington, DC 20006

Professions Salespersons of America
3801 Monaco NE
Albuquerque, NM 87111

Sales and Marketing Executives International
Statler Office Tower
Suite 458
Cleveland, OH 44115

◇ **RELATED ARTICLES**

Volume 1: Wholesaling; See Table of Contents for areas of specific interest
Volume 2: Advertising workers; Buyers, wholesale and retail; Retail managers
Volume 3: Manufacturers' sales workers; Retail sales workers; Shipping and receiving workers

Service Occupations

Service occupations form the fastest growing occupational group. Persons employed in these jobs render various types of service that aid in the protection of people's lives and property. They also provide services that add to personal comfort, pleasure, and enjoyment. In the early 1990s, more than 18.5 million persons were employed in service occupations.

More than 1.2 million of all persons employed in service occupations work in private households and homes. Their job duties as domestic service workers may include preparing and serving meals, laundry and ironing chores, general cleaning, and sometimes caring for the very young or the aged. The great majority of these workers are women.

Approximately 7.6 million other service workers are employed as waiters, bartenders, cooks, or in other types of work in hotels, restaurants, and other food establishments.

Another large service group consists of those people who clean and service hotels, motels, and other buildings. This group numbers more than 2.9 million and includes janitors, chambermaids, and porters.

About 2 million people were police officers, FBI agents, and fire fighters, who are employed in the protection of life and property. Service workers who render personal services numbered about 2.1 million persons, also. In the latter group are workers such as barbers, beauty operators, bellhops and bell captains, hotel housekeepers and assistants, flight attendants, waiters and waitresses, hospital attendants and nurse's aides.

For some of the service occupations the skill, education, and training required are greater than for others. Waiters and waitresses are required to have no specific educational preparation; neither are bell captains, many cooks and chefs, or hotel housekeepers and assistants; for each of these occupations, however, special training can be obtained.

Individuals interested in the service occupations should realize, however, that although employers may not require a high-school, college, or special vocational education, it is considered a distinct personal asset to obtain the greatest amount of education possible. In many of the service occupations, competition for the top positions is keen and educational training and personal initiative are important factors to advancement opportunities.

The employment trend for the service occupations through the late 1990s is expected to be good, with employment on the rise at an even greater rate than in the past. More service workers will be employed to meet rising demands created by increased income, leisure,and health needs. The anticipated increase in employment will enable some service occupations to expand more rapidly than others, while still others may decrease or remain about the same depending on the general economy.

Among the factors affecting the anticipated rise in employment for certain service occupations are the ever-increasing population, the mobility of the population, the urbanization patterns that continue to grow, and the greater emphasis on and accessibility to medical and health services. Adversely, automation may be the contributing factor in the decline in employment in some service occupations as more time- and labor-saving devices come on the market and into the homes and industrial life of America. It is expected, however, that the number of service jobs that might decline will be far fewer than those increasing through the demands for new workers and replacements.

The service occupational group performs many necessary and personal services for U.S. society. This entire occupational group is primarily comprised of those individuals who desire to protect and serve the public and who find real and personal job satisfaction in services rendered.

Barbers

Definition

A *barber* performs the services of cutting, trimming, shampooing, coloring, and bleaching hair and of trimming and shaping beards and mustaches. The barber may fit and groom artificial hair pieces, such as wigs.

History

The history of barbering may be traced far beyond the turn of the century when the "Barber Shop Quartet" became so well known. One of the ancient trades, barbering is described by writers of ancient Greek history. Relics of types of razors have been found dating to the Bronze Age and drawings of people in early Chinese and Egyptian cultures showed men with shaven heads.

Treatment of illnesses by bloodletting, originally done by monks, was appointed as a task for the barbers in 1163 by the pope. The pope had decided that bloodletting by monks was inappropriate. Trained physicians were an established group by 1163, but they supported the use of barbers for the simple tasks of wound and abscess treatment.

From the twelfth century to the eighteenth century, barbers were known as barber-surgeons. They performed medical and surgical services such as extracting teeth, treating disease, and cauterizing wounds.

Barbers began to form guilds in the fourteenth century. In France, a barber's guild was formed in 1361. In 1383, the French king's barber was decreed to be the head of the barbers' guild. In 1462, the Barbers of London became a trade guild.

Barbers distinguished themselves from surgeons and physicians by their title; they were referred to as the doctor of the short robe and the university-trained doctors were doctors of the long robe. In England during the first part of the sixteenth century, laws were established that began to limit the medical activities of barbers. They were allowed to bloodlet and to perform tooth extractions. Surgeons were also banned from performing activities relegated to barbers, such as shaving.

Surgeons separated from the barbers' guild in England in 1745, and in 1800 established their own guild—the Royal College of Surgeons. Laws were passed that restricted the activities of the barbers to non-medical practices. Barbers continued to be trained through apprenticeships until the establishment of barber training schools at the turn of the twentieth century. From that era on, barbers were used for shaving and haircuts.

The barber emerged as a respected tradesperson. Today, the red and white striped barber poles still remain, not only as a symbol of the barber shop, but of the barber-surgeon; the white depicting bandages that were used and the red symbolizing the patient's blood.

Women did not patronize babershops until the 1920s. The bob cut, where women had their hair cut above the shoulders or neck, was the first hairstyle for women that used a razor for cutting. Women regularly used barbers for hair styling and cutting when the bob became widespread and accepted in mainstream society. This opened the door for women to become haircutters, trained to work with women's hair styles.

Nature of the work

In general, the duties of the barber are well defined. Barbers cut, trim, shape and style, tint or bleach, and shampoo hair. They give shaves, facials, scalp treatments, and massages and advise customers on grooming habits and cosmetic aids. They also trim and style beards and mustaches, fit and style wigs, and perform for customers other personal services incidental to good grooming.

Barbers use, with trained skill, certain tools in their services, such as scissors, clippers, razors, combs, brushes, vibrators, hot towels, tweezers, and razor sharpeners. Tools and equipment and working surroundings must be kept in aseptic and sterile condition.

In training, barbers learn some aspects of physiology and anatomy, including the bone structure of the head and elementary facts about the nervous system. Barbers either cut hair as the customers request them to, or they decide how to cut it by studying the head contour, quality and texture of the hair, and personal features of the customer. Each customer is an individual and no two possess the same types of personal and physical characteristics.

Barbers may be employed in shops that have as few as one or two operators, or in large

Barbers
Service Occupations

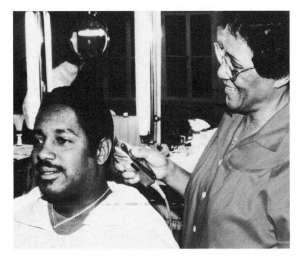

Barbers are often good conversationalists, which keeps a client at ease while the barber cuts hair.

all states they must be graduates of a barber school that is state-approved.

In most states barbers must first be licensed as barber apprentices. After a specified period of employment, usually one to two years, the barber apprentice may take another written and practical examination to qualify for a license as a journeyman barber. When barbers move from one state into another, they must satisfy the license requirements of the state into which they are moving. Some states will recognize the license from another state, so the barber does not require retesting.

Training opportunities are available in about 400 private barber colleges and public vocational training schools. Periods of training are generally nine months to one year. Most training institutions require approximately 1,000 to 1,800 hours of formal instruction including courses in hygiene, anatomy, skin and scalp diseases, and sanitation. Other course work includes lectures, demonstrations, and practice in the art of barbering, and the use and care of tools and equipment. Some schools give training in business policies and practices, the psychology of sales and advertising, professional ethics, unionism, and business management. Some states have schools that offer advanced course work for barbers who wish to specialize in such techniques as hair coloring and/or styling. Students should be careful to select barber schools that have training programs that meet at least the minimum requirements of that state. Some schools require students to purchase their basic barbering instruments at a cost of about $430.

A barber needs certain aptitudes to be successful. Finger dexterity is important for it is needed in all aspects of a barber's work. Hand and eye coordination are equally necessary.

Acceptable personal qualities are most important to the successful barber. The public looks for the tactful, pleasant, courteous, friendly barber who likes people and is skilled. A barber needs to present a neat, clean, and well-groomed appearance. At all times barbers must be in control of their temper and try to give the best service possible.

Hazards in the trade include nicks and cuts from scissors and razors, minor burns when care is not used in handling hot towels, or perhaps skin irritations that may arise from the constant use of grooming aids that contain forms of chemicals.

Some of the chemicals used in hair dyes can be quite abrasive and plastic gloves are usually required for handling and contact. Pregnant women are advised to avoid contact with many of those chemicals present in hair products.

cities, in shops employing ten or more. Some barbers work in combination barber and beauty shops while others are employed in shops in hotels, hospitals, and resort areas. Those who own their own shops must also take care of the details of business operations. Bills must be paid, orders, invoices, and supplies checked, equipment serviced, records and books kept, and time must be spent with salespeople. The selecting, hiring, and discharging of other workers are also the owner's responsibilities. Barber shop employees may include manicurists, shoe shine boys, assistant barbers, and custodial help. Shop owners are likely to have demands made upon them to participate in civic and community projects and activities as do other responsible businesspeople.

Requirements

States vary in the educational and training requirements for barbers. Some states require potential barbers to have the minimum of an eighth-grade education; other states require a high-school education. Nearly all states now require barbers to be licensed or to be certified by a state board of examiners for barbers. To obtain a license or to be certified, the individual, in nearly all states, must pass a practical examination demonstrating his skills and ability and a written test reflecting his knowledge of the trade. The great majority of states will not examine persons applying under the ages of sixteen or eighteen years. Applicants must also be able to obtain health certificates, and in almost

196

Special requirements

Barbers in most states must pass written and practical examinations to be licensed as apprentice barbers and more advanced examinations to be licensed as journeymen barbers. The cost of licenses, examinations, and annual renewals varies from state to state. Usually, fees for these examinations range from $15 to $85. Health certificates are required in most states. Information on special requirements may be obtained from each of the state boards of barber examiners.

Opportunities for experience and exploration

Those who are interested in becoming barbers may explore this occupation in a number of ways. They may visit barber colleges and talk to the administration, teachers, and students and request permission to visit a class in barbering instruction. Potential students may observe and talk with licensed barbers who are practicing the trade. They may wish to seek summer employment in barber shops as clean-up and errand workers so that they may observe first-hand the work of the barber.

Related occupations

Other occupations that require an interest in style and personal service include electrologists, nail technicians, and cosmetologists.

Methods of entering

Barbering jobs are most frequently obtained through personal application or with the aid of barbering unions. The largest union for barbers is the United Food and Commercial Workers International Union. Most barber colleges assist their graduates in locating employment opportunities. Applicants also use placement services of state or private placement agencies. Employment and employees are sometimes located through newspaper advertisements. Community acquaintances may also assist the beginning barber in making business contacts. Some salons have their own training programs from which they hire new employees.

Advancement

Barbers usually begin as licensed barber apprentices and through experience, written, and practical examinations advance to journeymen barbers. Within barber shops there is little opportunity for advancement except by seniority and skill to the assignment of the "first chair," which is the chair nearest the shop entrance. Barbers can change their place of employment and move to bigger, more attractive, and better-equipped shops. Self-employment and shop-ownership are the highest attainment by many barbers. Experience and financial capital are usually obtained before seeking a shop ownership. The cost of equipping a one-chair shop can be very expensive. Some barbers aspire to owning a large shop or a chain of barber shops.

Employment outlook

Approximately 94,000 persons were employed as barbers in the United States in the early 1990s. About two out of three owned their own shops.

Future employment opportunities for barbers are not as predictable as the opportunities that might be available in other occupations. Most openings that present themselves will be replacements for those who leave the trade for other work, retire, or die.

Employment may rise in the coming years, as new shopping centers and suburban areas continue to open and grow with the expanding population. Opportunities as hairstylists are also increasing.

The competent and well-trained barber should find employment without too much difficulty, but it may not always be in the geographic locality or in the shop desired.

Earnings

Tips from customers must be considered an important factor in determining a barber's salary. The amount to be earned in tips is unpredictable and depends on the locale of employment, the personality and skill of the barber, individual shop policies, and the income levels of the customers.

In the early 1990s, barbers with some experience were earning about $16,500 to $21,500 a year. Hairstylists and some barbers who owned their own shops had incomes of $24,000 a year or more. Most barbers work on a commission basis, receiving from 60 to 70 percent of what they are paid by customers. Others work for set salaries plus a percentage commission. Only a small number of barbers work for a salary without commission.

Paid vacations, medical insurance, and death benefits are available to some employees and more likely to those belonging to a union.

Conditions of work

Barbers usually work a five- or six-day workweek, which averages approximately forty to fifty hours. Weekends and days preceding holiday seasons may be unusually busy workdays. Some employers allow barbers to have extra days off when trade is down and slack periods occur.

Working hours vary but are usually from 8:00 A.M. to 6:00 P.M. or 9:00 A.M. to 6:00 P.M. In some cities employees work alternate shifts; for example, they work from 8:00 A.M. to 3:00 P.M. or from 3:00 P.M. to 9:00 P.M.

Barbers work in shops that must, by law, meet and maintain strict state sanitation codes. Shops are usually comfortably heated, ventilated, and well lighted. Barbers are usually assigned a chair position and their own work area in a shop. They are required to be on their feet most of their working hours but little walking is involved. In general, they work in a small space. The barber stands most of the workday.

Social and psychological factors

A barber must perform services for all types of people and yet remain pleasant and congenial, even though some customers are difficult to satisfy. Patience and an even temperament are qualities to be desired by barbers.

The nature of the work requires a repetition of the services performed and a barber must like the work and be interested in people in order to find job satisfaction.

If customers are in a hurry, the barber may feel the need to work with both speed and skill to satisfy customers. Striving always to please the public may create psychological tensions.

Usually, only apprentice barbers work under close supervision. Many barbers belong to labor unions and work under union agreements.

GOE: 09.02.02; SIC: 7241; SOC: 5252

⬦ **SOURCES OF ADDITIONAL INFORMATION**

Hair International/Associated Master Barbers and Beauticians of America
1318 Starbrook Drive
Charlotte, NC 28210

National Association of Barber Styling Schools
304 South 11th Street
Lincoln, NE 68508

National Barber Career Center
3839 White Plains Road
Bronx, NY 10467

⬦ **RELATED ARTICLES**

Volume 3: Cosmetologists, Electrologists

Bartenders

Definition

Bartenders mix and dispense alcoholic and nonalcoholic drinks in hotels, restaurants, cocktail lounges, and taverns. Besides mixing ingredients to prepare cocktails and other drinks, they serve wine and beer, collect payment from customers, order supplies, and arrange displays of bar stock and glassware. Bartenders or their helpers may prepare fruit for garnishes, serve simple appetizers, wash glasses, and clean the bar area.

History

Tending bar was only one of the duties of yesteryear's innkeeper. When inns and small hotels were a family affair, and when the drinks dispensed were no more complicated than a tankard of ale or a mug of mulled wine, bartending specialists were not required. Today's large hotels and restaurants call for a variety of experts, not the least of which are the bartenders. Even in the average neighborhood cocktail lounge or tavern, they may have to cope with requests for such exotic concoctions as Screaming Zombies, Harvey Wallbangers, Golden Cadillacs, and Singapore Slings. A growing number of larger establishments use equipment to mix drinks automatically, but the bartenders must still be knowledgeable to handle unusual orders and to work efficiently when the automatic equipment may not be operating.

At peak business times such as happy hours and weekend evenings, bartenders must be able to take orders and serve drinks quickly.

Nature of the work

Bartenders take orders from waiters and waitresses for customers seated in the restaurant or lounge; they also take orders from customers seated at the bar. They mix drinks by combining exactly the right proportion of liquor, wines, mixes, and other ingredients. Bartenders must know dozens of drink recipes and be able to measure accurately by sight so they can prepare drinks quickly, without wasting anything, even during the busiest periods. They may be asked to mix drinks to suit a customer's taste, and they also serve beer, wine, and nonalcoholic beverages. Besides mixing and serving drinks, bartenders collect payment, operate a cash register, clean up after patrons, and may serve snacks or light food items to persons seated at the bar.

A well-stocked bar has dozens of types and brands of liquors and wines, as well as beer, soft drinks, soda and tonic water, fruits and fruit juices, and cream. Bartenders are responsible for maintaining this inventory and ordering supplies before they run out. They arrange bottles and glassware in attractive displays and often wash the glassware. In some of these duties they may be assisted by *bartender helpers*.

Bartenders who own their businesses must also keep records and hire, train, and direct the people who work for them.

Today there are machines that automatically mix and dispense drinks. They are generally found in larger operations. But even if they became more prevalent, they would not replace bartenders. Bartenders still need the knowl-

edge and expertise to be able to fill unusual orders or to do the work manually in case the automatic equipment breaks down or does not function properly.

In combination taverns and packaged-goods stores, *bar attendants* also sell unopened bottles of alcoholic and nonalcoholic beverages to be taken from the premises. *Taproom attendants* prepare and serve glasses or pitchers of draft beer.

Requirements

Bartenders must know a variety of cocktail recipes, how to stock a bar, and how to dress and conduct themselves properly. They must be familiar with state and local laws concerning the sale of alcoholic beverages. Many vocational and technical schools offer short courses in bartending, but most bartenders learn their trade on the job. They may have had previous experience as bartender helpers, waiters' assistants, or waiters or waitresses.

Bartenders must be in good physical condition to stand long hours while working and to lift heavy cases of beverages or kegs of beer. Because they deal with the public, they must have a pleasant personality and a clean, neat appearance.

Special requirements

Generally, bartenders must be at least twenty-one years of age, although some employers prefer those who are older than twenty-five. In some states, bartenders must have health certificates assuring that they are free of contagious diseases. And sometimes they must be bonded.

The principal union for bartenders is the Hotel Employees and Restaurant Employees International Union (AFL-CIO), but membership is not a requirement.

Related occupations

Bartenders are congenial, outgoing people who enjoy working with people and who can remain calm in sometimes hectic conditions. Other workers in food service include waiters, waitresses, restaurant managers, waiters' and waitresses' assistants, cooks, chefs, and bakers.

Opportunities for experience and exploration

Because of the age requirement, students under the age of twenty-one will find it impossible to get actual bartending experience. Part-time or summer jobs as waiters' assistants or waiters or waitresses, however, will put them in a position where they can watch a bartender at work and in that way learn how to mix drinks and do other bartending tasks. Preparing drinks at home is good experience, although in itself it does not qualify a person to become a bartender. Any part-time or summer job that involves serving food and beverages to the public will give students the opportunity to see if they have the right temperament for this occupation.

Further exploration may include talking with school counselors, visiting vocational schools that offer bartending courses, interviewing bartenders, and reading bar guides and manuals.

Methods of entering

Persons who are interested in becoming bartenders often begin by working as bartender helpers, waiters' assistants, or waiters or waitresses. Small restaurants, neighborhood bars, and vacation resorts usually offer a beginner the best opportunity. Many people tend bar part-time while working at other jobs or attending college, often serving at banquets and private parties at restaurants, hotels, or in private homes. Vocational schools that offer bartending courses sometimes help their graduates find jobs.

Application may be made directly to hotels, restaurants, cocktail lounges, and other businesses that serve alcoholic beverages. Some employment agencies specialize in hotel and restaurant personnel. Information about job opportunities may also be obtained from the local offices of the state employment service.

Advancement

With experience, a bartender may find employment in a large restaurant or cocktail lounge where the pay is higher. Opportunities for advancement in this field, however, are limited. A few persons may earn promotions to head bartender, wine steward, or beverage manager. Some bartenders open their own businesses.

Employment outlook

Approximately 500,000 bartenders were employed in the early 1990s, about 70 percent of them in restaurants and bars. Most others worked in hotels and private clubs, and less than 10 percent were self-employed.

Employment of bartenders is expected to increase faster than the occupational average through the late 1990s. New restaurants, hotels, and bars will open as the population grows and as spending for food and beverage outside the home increases. People with higher incomes and more leisure time will go out for dinner and cocktails more frequently and take more vacations. As large numbers of women join the work force, families will dine out more often. All of this means more jobs for bartenders.

Openings regularly occur as older bartenders retire, die, or leave the occupation. There is a high turnover rate, too, because many bartenders are students or others who do not plan to make bartending a career.

Earnings

Earnings for this occupation cover a broad range. With tips, full-time bartenders in the early 1990s earned an average of about $12,720 a year. About 10 percent earned more than $21,700. Besides wages and tips, bartenders usually get free meals at work and may be furnished bar jackets or complete uniforms.

GOE: 09.04.01; SIC: 5813; SOC: 5212

Conditions of work

Many bartenders work more than forty hours a week. They work nights, weekends, and holidays, and split shifts are common. They have to work quickly and under pressure during busy periods. Also, they need more strength than average to lift heavy cases of liquor and mixes.

Many bartenders feel the difficulties of the job are more than offset by the opportunity to talk to friendly customers, by the possibility of one day managing or owning a bar or restaurant, or by the need for good part-time work.

Social and psychological factors

It is important that persons entering this field like people, since they will be in constant contact with the public. Even when the work is hardest and the most hectic, bartenders are expected to engage in friendly conversation with customers. Patrons of a bar will often use the bartender as a sounding board, a psychiatrist, a confessor. All they really want is a sympathetic ear. Good bartenders will appear interested without getting personally involved.

The success of a restaurant or cocktail lounge depends on having satisfied customers. For this reason, teamwork among the employees is crucial. Often working in cramped quarters, bartenders must cooperate quickly and willingly with other food and beverage service workers.

◇ **SOURCES OF ADDITIONAL INFORMATION**

A directory of colleges and other schools that offer programs and courses in hospitality education is available from:

Council on Hotel, Restaurant, and Institutional Education
1200 17th Street, NW
Washington, DC 20036
General information about bartenders is available from:

American Bartenders Association
PO Box 15527
Sarasota, FL 34277

Educational Foundation of the National Restaurant Association
250 South Wacker Drive
Chicago, IL 60606

◇ **RELATED ARTICLES**

Volume 1: Food Service; Hospitality
Volume 2: Restaurant managers
Volume 3: Cooks, chefs, and bakers; Fast food workers; Food service workers

Child care workers

Definition

Child care workers care for groups of children housed in various kinds of institutions funded by the city, county, or private organizations. These children may be institutionalized because of neglect or disability. The relationship between child care workers and their charges is important and often focuses on providing guidance and encouraging suitable life skills so that the children may lead active and productive lives on their own. The position of child care worker offers one the challenges of working with groups of children who have different backgrounds and needs, and maintaining the role of group supervisor while being able to es-

Child care workers
Service Occupations

Child care workers entertain children through educational means. In this case, he engages them with playful songs.

tablish one-on-one relationships with each child in the work environment.

Nature of the work

The responsibilities of the child care worker cover many of the tasks found in a traditional home environment. Child care workers have such duties as waking the children up in the morning and making sure they have a nutritious breakfast. It is also necessary for the child care worker to see that the children are properly dressed and ready for their daily activities, which may include school (or other types of instruction), therapy, or planned daily tasks. Furthermore, a child care worker may be counted on to assist children with homework and studies, and develop daily living abilities such as hygiene or manners. A child care worker may also be responsible for formal instruction, whether it be a class or part of a child's therapy program. Household tasks—cooking, laundry, or other chores—may be delegated to some of the older, more capable children to encourage participation and independence. Such direction can benefit the group and establish a healthy sense of cooperation and community.

A child care worker's accountability to the children does not end with the roles of teacher and disciplinarian, however. In the evenings or on weekends the child care worker may be expected to engage in recreational activities with the children. Planning outings, holiday activities, such as baking and making crafts, and participating in sports and games allows both the children and child care worker to develop a more open and friendly relationship.

Continual quality interaction with all the children is a significant part of the day-to-day routine. It is the amount of time that a child

care worker invests in the children that suggests that this job is most closely related to parenthood. In addition, it is in the diversity of these duties that child care workers find their greatest challenges and most positive rewards.

The child care worker may find a significant number of children in these institutions who have been abused, mentally or emotionally disturbed, delinquent, or handicapped. The child care worker must be resourceful and patient, quick-thinking to handle small crises and disagreements, and firm to reinforce house rules and impart discipline. It is also important for the child care worker to be strong-willed and adaptable to a variety of needs, whether physical or emotional, and understand the inherent challenges that certain limitations and diverse backgrounds provide.

Requirements

An advantage in the field of child care workers is that there is no special training or education required for entry level positions. Because personal maturity and reliability are vital qualities though, the majority of institutions list only a high-school degree as essential. Child care workers often receive training on the job to become familiar with the rules and regulations specific to that institution.

Despite the basic requirement of a high-school diploma, there are many possibilities for education and development. Most two-year college programs offer courses that a child care worker would find beneficial, such as classes in child or behavioral psychology, as well as sociology studies. In addition, arts and crafts, cooking, sewing, metal- and woodcraft, and other skill-oriented courses can be considered as children in these institutions can learn from any number of activities and projects.

Those interested in pursuing a four-year college degree may want to consider fields of study in psychology, early childhood or special education, and course work in physical or occupational therapy. Earning a degree in areas such as these may direct the type of institution in which you will pursue employment.

In addition to any formal education however, the child care worker must have certain personal qualifications for this particular line of work. Patience, compassion, a sense of fairness, and resourcefulness are characteristics that the child care worker will find necessary in handling small groups of children. As this is an area where service to others and attention to their needs creates the base of the child care worker's activities, an even temper and personal strength are imperative.

Special requirements

Depending on the avenue of educational development a child care worker pursues, certain special requirements may be necessary. For instance, therapists and teachers are required to have state and professional certification. Also, the child care worker may choose to pursue workshops and seminars to support a specific area of interest or specialization.

Opportunities for experience and exploration

For someone interested in becoming a child care worker there are ample opportunities for exposure to this field. Presently, part-time employment possibilities comprise more than 40 percent of the total number of jobs, and many institutions welcome volunteer assistance as well. In these capacities one may be allowed to work in a variety of departments and receive reasonable introduction to a particular institution and the field of child care worker in general.

Most neighborhoods have suitable outlets for exploration including community centers, day care institutions, and local agencies for the handicapped and disabled. Such opportunities can serve to help focus any further career and education.

Related occupations

Many careers are available to people with a skill and interest for children, including preschool teachers, elementary and kindergarten teachers, nannies, nurses, pediatricians, and child psychologists.

Methods of entering

As mentioned previously, formal training is not always a requirement of employers in this field of work. Many people who work as child care workers have informal experience in child care gained from their personal experiences as parents.

People with educational experience in child care or child development should check with their school placement offices for information on job openings in their area.

Advancement

As in many cases, continued service and training help pave the way for advancement. A child care worker may receive promotions and additional responsibilities after some months on the job and after demonstrating good performance. After becoming acquainted with the field in general the child care worker may choose to pursue additional education to support an area of specialization. There is also significant turnover in this profession. This can help workers advance more readily, either within their current institution or at another one.

Employment outlook

The number of child care workers in the early 1990s were estimated to be more than 600,000. By the year 2000 government projections estimate the number in this field to be more than 700,000. Religious organizations and special interest groups for the needy are providing more services for children, thereby increasing the size of institutions and their number. This reflects a continued need for workers in the child care field. In addition, because of the high employee turnover rate, most child care workers can find suitable employment.

Earnings

Entry level child care workers with no prior experience can expect to earn the minimum hourly wage at most institutions. Salaries for full-time child care workers though, range from $11,000 to $15,000. For institutions where the child care worker lives on the premises with the children, however, the employee's room and board is often figured into their salary.

Fringe benefits are offered to child care workers as a part of their employment package. Though the benefits vary, they may include health and life insurance benefits, paid holidays, and sometimes up to three weeks' vacation. In addition, some of the larger institutions may offer some kind of pension or retirement benefit.

Conditions of work

Because the purpose and facilities of institutions vary, the living conditions of the child care worker and the children are also diverse. Most institutions offer clean but simple apartments or cottages for their on-campus staff, or separate areas of the dormitories if the workers live in group housing with the children.

The hours that child care workers put in are often long, as there is much unpredictability in caring for children. There are always a few hours set aside each day, however, for the child care worker to have some individual time for relaxation, to accomplish personal tasks, attend seminars or workshops, and meet with co-workers.

Often there are child care workers—individuals or couples who function as dorm parents—who report to a group leader for supervision and direction.

Social and psychological factors

There is great achievement in knowing that you have had a positive influence on somebody's life, and it is this experience that often encourages people to pursue the career of child care worker.

The diverse facilities of some institutions, the long hours, and relatively modest pay for time invested, does not hold people to this occupation for their entire work history. The turn-over rate is high, and many people leave this field when they feel that they have contributed all they could.

GOE: 10.03.03; SIC: 835; SOC: 5264

◇ **SOURCES OF ADDITIONAL INFORMATION**

National Association for Family Day Care
815 15th Street, NW, Suite 928
Washington, DC 20005

Play Schools Association
19 West 44th Street, Suite 615
New York, NY 10036

◇ **RELATED ARTICLES**

Cooks, chefs, and bakers

Definition

Cooks, chefs, and *bakers* are employed in the preparation and cooking of food, usually in large quantities, in hotels, restaurants, cafeterias, and other establishments and institutions. Some of these type of cooks are *sandwich makers, coffee makers, fountain servers,* and *pantry goods makers.*

Cooks plan menus, estimate requirements, and order food from suppliers, measure and mix ingredients and season foods, test food being cooked, and apportion and arrange it on serving plates. They may wash and prepare vegetables and fruits. Butchers are often classified by the types of meat they prepare: *meat butchers, poultry butchers* and *fish butchers.* Other workers bake breads, cakes, and pastries, and supervise other cooks and kitchen employees. Cooks may be specialists in one particular type of food preparation, such as baker, sauce cook, or vegetable cook. Others work in specialized places, such as *railroad train cooks, passenger and cargo ship cooks,* or *psychiatric hospital cooks.*

Chefs participate in many of the tasks of cooks and other kitchen personnel, but their primary responsibility is to supervise and coordinate the activities of the specialists engaged in preparing and cooking foods. In addition to many of the same duties assigned to cooks, chefs select and develop recipes; may hire, train, and dismiss workers, and keep time and payroll records. Some chefs specialize by type of cuisine, such as French, German, or Italian.

The duties of bakers are in many ways similar to those of cooks and chefs, but they specialize in the preparation of breads, rolls, muffins, biscuits, pies, cakes, cookies, and pastries.

History

The art of cookery is as ancient as the history of humankind. The early Greeks, Egyptians, and Romans valued cooks as highly respected members of society.

France has offered to the world some of the finest cooks and chefs. Historical records reflect the interest of the French people in the art of cookery. Even today, cooks and chefs who know the art of French cuisine are valued in some of the world's most luxurious hotels and restaurants.

The hostelries of early American days provided food and rest for the weary traveler. Although these inns and taverns employed cooks, it was not until hotels were built in the large cities that the occupation of cook was really developed.

The pleasure of dining out has become big business in the United States. The public has its choice from the simplest, most inexpensive meal to the most expensive and elaborate. Whether a restaurant prides itself on "home cooking" or on exotic foreign cuisine, its cooks and chefs are largely responsible for the reputation it acquires.

Nature of the work

Cooks and chefs are primarily responsible for the preparation and cooking of foods. Chefs usually supervise the work of cooks; however, the skills required and the job duties performed may vary depending upon the size and type of food service offered.

Cooks and chefs begin the preparation of food by planning menus in advance. They estimate the amount of food that will be required for a specified period of time, order it from various suppliers, and check it for quantity and quality when it is received. Following recipes, they measure and mix ingredients for soups, salads, gravies, sauces, casseroles, and desserts; and prepare meats, poultry, fish, vegeta-

bles, and other foods for baking, roasting, broiling, and steaming. The utensils and equipment used in the food preparation may include blenders, mixers, grinders, slicers, and tenderizers; the large cooking equipment consists of ovens, broilers, grills, roasters, and steam kettles, all with thermostatic controls that must be adjusted to regulate temperatures. During the mixing and cooking, cooks and chefs rely on their personal judgment and experience to add seasonings; they constantly taste and smell food being cooked and pierce it with a fork to test it for doneness. To fill orders, they carve meats, arrange food portions on serving plates, and add appropriate gravies, sauces, or garnishes.

Some larger establishments employ specialized cooks, such as *pie makers*, *pastry cooks*, and *pastry cook helpers*. The *Chef de Froid* designs and prepares buffets, and *larder cooks* prepare cold dishes for luncheon and dinner serving. Other specialists are *raw shellfish preparers*, *carvers*, and the *garde manger* who specializes in preparing cold meats and dishes made from leftovers.

In smaller establishments that do not employ many specialized cooks or kitchen helpers, the general cooks may have to do some of the preliminary work themselves, such as washing, peeling, cutting, and shredding vegetables and fruits; cutting, trimming, and boning meat; cleaning and preparing poultry, fish, and shellfish; and baking bread, rolls, cakes, and pastries.

Commercial cookery is usually in large quantities, and many cooks, including *school cafeteria cooks*, *mess cooks*, and *school cafeteria head cooks* are trained in "quantity cookery" methods. Numerous establishments today are noted for specialties in foods, and some cooks specialize in the preparation and cooking of exotic dishes, very elaborate dishes, or some particular creation of their own for which they have become famous. Restaurants that feature national cuisines may employ *foreign food specialty cooks*.

In the larger commercial kitchens, the chefs may be responsible for the work of a number of cooks, each preparing and cooking food in specialized areas. They may, for example, employ expert cooks who are specialized in frying, baking roasting, broiling, or in sauce cookery. Cooks are usually titled by the specialized kinds of cooking they do, such as fry, vegetable, or pastry. Chefs have the major responsibility for supervising the overall preparation and cooking of the food.

Additional duties of chefs may include training other cooks on the job, planning menus, pricing food for menus, purchasing food, and estimating quantity of consumption

A chef proudly displays the food he has prepared for a banquet. The presentation of food on such occasions is very important.

in daily operations. Chefs may be responsible for determining portion weights to be prepared and served, and among their other duties they may supervise the work of all the kitchen staff who assist in the preparation of food. The kitchen staff may assist by washing, cleaning, and preparing foods for cooking; cleaning utensils, dishes and silver; and assisting in many ways with the overall cleanliness and sanitation of the kitchen. The majority of chefs spend a part of their time in striving to create new recipes to win the praises of customers and build reputations as experts. Many, like *pastry chefs* and *ice-cream chefs* focus their attention on particular kinds of food.

Expert chefs who have a number of years of experience behind them may be employed as *executive chefs*. These chefs do little cooking or food preparation. Their main responsibilities are management and supervision. Executive chefs interview, hire, and fire all kitchen personnel, and sometimes they are responsible for the dining room waiters, waitresses, and other dining room employees. These chefs consult with the managers regarding the profit and loss of the food service and ways to increase business and cut costs. A part of their time is spent

inspecting equipment. Executive chefs are in charge of all food services for special functions such as banquets and parties, and many hours are spent in the coordination of the work for these activities. They may supervise the special chefs and assist them in planning elaborate arrangements and creations in food preparation. Executive chefs may be assisted by *sous chefs*.

Smaller food establishments may employ only one or two cooks and kitchen helpers to assist them. In these jobs, the cook or cooks prepare all the food with the aid of the helpers in getting food ready for cooking, and with their assistance keep the kitchen in a sanitary condition. Smaller restaurants and public eating places usually offer standard menus with little variation, so that the cook's job itself becomes rather standardized and does not involve the preparation of a wide variety of dishes. Such establishments may employ *specialty cooks, barbecue cooks, pizza bakers, automatcar attendants, food order expediters, kitchen food assemblers,* or *counter supply workers.* In some restaurants food is cooked as it is ordered and cooks preparing food in this manner are known as *short-order cooks.*

Regardless of the duties performed, cooks and chefs are largely responsible for the profit or loss and reputation of the eating establishment in which they are employed.

Bakers perform the work of cooks and chefs specifically in the preparation of breads, rolls, muffins, biscuits, pies, cakes, cookies, and pastries. Bakers may be supervised by a *head baker.* In large establishments, *second bakers* may supervise other bakers who work with a particular type of baked goods. Bakers are often assisted by *baker helpers.*

Requirements

The occupation of chef, cook, or baker has specific training requirements. Many cooks start out as kitchen helpers and acquire their skills on the job, but the trend today is to obtain training through high schools, vocational schools, or community colleges. Professional associations and trade unions offer apprenticeship programs, and there is a three-year apprenticeship program administered by local offices of the American Culinary Federation in cooperation with local employers and junior colleges or vocational schools. Some large hotels and restaurants have their own training programs for new employees. It takes only a short time to become an assistant or a fry cook, for example, but it requires many years of training and experience to acquire the skills necessary to become an executive chef or cook in a fine restaurant. The armed forces also offer good training and experience.

Although a high-school diploma is not required, it is an asset to job applicants who want to increase their chances for job opportunities and success. For those planning a career as a chef or head cook, courses in business arithmetic and business administration are useful.

Culinary students spend most of their time learning to prepare food through actual practice. At the same time, they learn how to use and care for kitchen equipment. Training programs often include courses in menu planning, determination of portion size, food cost control, purchasing food supplies in quantity, selection and storage of food, and use of leftovers. Students also learn hotel and restaurant sanitation and public health rules for handling food. Courses offered by private vocational schools, professional associations, and university programs often emphasize training in supervisory and management skills.

A successful chef or cook should demonstrate a keen interest in food preparation and cooking and have a desire to experiment in developing new food combinations and new recipes. Possessing these interests and the necessary technical knowledge, skills, and training, chefs and cooks can find genuine satisfaction in the trade.

Special requirements

Chefs, cooks, and bakers are required by law in most states to possess a health certificate and to be examined periodically as a form of protection to the public in food handling. These examinations, usually given by state boards of health, assure the public that the individual is free from communicable diseases and skin infections.

Immaculate personal cleanliness and good health are necessities in this trade. Applicants should possess physical stamina and be without serious physical impairments for the mobility and activity required in the work. Many working hours require standing, walking, and moving about.

Chefs, cooks, and bakers must possess a keen sense of taste and smell. Hand and finger agility, hand-eye coordination, and good memory are aptitudes that are helpful. An artistic flair and creative talents in working with food are definitely strengths for the trade. A knowledge of business skills and a proficiency in mathematics can prove valuable to cooks and to chefs in particular.

Chefs are known for their specialties. Often the success of a restaurant depends on the quality and the uniqueness of the cuisine.

The principal union for cooks and chefs is the Hotel Employees and Restaurant Employees International Union (AFL-CIO).

Opportunities for experience and exploration

Students may explore their interests in this occupation by obtaining part-time and summer jobs in related work experiences. Employment may be available in fast-food or other restaurants, or in institutional kitchens as sandwich or salad maker, soda-fountain attendant, or kitchen helper.

Jobs as waiters or waiters' assistants may be available in larger hotels or in summer resorts, which will provide the opportunity to observe firsthand the work of chefs and cooks.

Practicing and experimenting with cooking at home and taking high-school home economics courses in cooking are other ways of testing one's interest in becoming a cook or a chef. Many department stores, specialty food stores, and cookware shops regularly schedule cooking demonstrations.

Related occupations

People engaged in cooking not only have a good sense for food and its presentation but also need an artistic spirit and a strong technical background. Other occupations in food service include waiters, waitresses, maitre d's, wine stewards, and waiters' and waitresses' assistants.

Methods of entering

Apprenticeship programs are one method of entering the trade. These programs usually offer sound basic training and the apprentice is able to earn a salary while being trained. Upon completion of the apprenticeship, cooks may be hired full time in their place of training or assisted in finding employment with another establishment. Cooks are hired as chefs only after they have acquired a number of years of experience. Cooks who have been formally trained through public or private trade or vocational schools and in culinary institutes may have school placement services available to them.

In many cases, a cook begins as a *kitchen helper* or as a *cook's helper* and, through experience gained in on-the-job training, is able to work into the job of cook. To do this, the person sometimes starts out in a small restaurant, perhaps as short-order or grill cook or as sandwich or salad maker, and transfers to larger places of employment as experience is gained.

School cafeteria workers who want to become cooks may have an opportunity to receive school food–services training. Many school districts, with the cooperation of school food–services divisions of the state departments of education, provide on-the-job training and sometimes summer workshops for interested cafeteria employees. Similar programs are offered by some junior colleges, state departments of education, and school associations. Cafeteria workers who have completed these training programs are often selected to fill positions as cooks.

Job opportunities may be located through employment bureaus, trade associations, unions, contacts with friends, newspaper want ads, local offices of the state employment service, or by direct application to places of employment in which the individual would like to work.

Advancement

Advancements in this trade depend on the personal qualifications, skill, training, experience, originality, and ambition of the individual. They are also somewhat dependent upon the general business and economic trends of employment in the labor market.

Cooks with experience may advance themselves by moving to other places of employment for higher wages or to establishments that desire some specialized skill in preparing a particular kind of food.

Cooks who have a number of successful years of job experience may find positions open to them as chefs; however, in some cases it may require fifteen or twenty years to obtain such a position, depending on personal qualifications and employment factors.

Expert cooks who have obtained supervisory responsibilities as head cooks or chefs may advance to positions as executive chefs or to other types of managerial work. Some go into business for themselves as caterers or restaurant owners; others may become instructors in vocational programs in high schools, colleges, or other academic institutions.

Employment outlook

In the early 1990s, there were about 1,680,000 cooks, chefs, and bakers in the United States. Most worked in hotels and restaurants, but many worked in schools, colleges, airports, and hospitals. Still others were employed by government agencies, factories, private clubs, and other organizations.

When compared with all occupations, there will be an average increase in the employment of chefs, cooks, and bakers through the early 1990s. The demand will grow with the population. People with higher incomes and more leisure time will dine out more often and take more vacations. The families of working women will dine out more frequently as a convenience. Many job openings occur annually as older, experienced workers retire, die, or transfer to other occupations.

Small restaurants, school cafeterias, and other eating places with simple food preparation will provide the greatest number of starting jobs for cooks. Job applicants who have had courses in commercial food preparation will have an advantage in large restaurants and hotels, where hiring standards are often high.

Earnings

The salaries earned by chefs and cooks are widely divergent and depend on many factors, such as size, type, and location of employment, and skill, experience, training, and specialization of the worker. Salaries are usually closely in line with the type of place of employment. For example, restaurants and diners serving inexpensive meals and a sandwich-type menu generally pay cooks less than establishments with medium-priced or expensive menus. The highest wages are earned in the West and in large, well-known restaurants and hotels.

In the early 1990s, cooks, chefs, and bakers (excluding short-order and fast-food workers) earned an average of $11,260 a year. Half earned between $9,120 and $14,760, and one-tenth earned $20,520 or more. Cooks and chefs in famous restaurants, of course, earn much more than the above rates; they may be paid $48,000 a year or more.

Chefs and cooks usually receive their meals free during working hours and have the necessary job uniforms furnished, laundry free, for them.

Conditions of work

Chefs, cooks, and bakers may work a forty or forty-eight-hour week, depending on the type of food service offered and union agreements affecting local geographic areas. Some food establishments are open twenty-four hours a day, while others may be open only during the day, but begin work in the very early morning and close late in the evening. Hours depend on the type of business and food service available. Establishments open long hours may have two or three work shifts, with some chefs and cooks working day schedules while others work evenings.

Overtime hours are frequently worked, depending on the amount of business and rush-hour trade. These employees work many weekends and holidays, although they may have a day off weekly or rotate with other employees to have alternate weekends free.

Working conditions vary. Many kitchens are modern, well lighted, well equipped, and air-conditioned, but some older, smaller eating places may be only marginally equipped. The work of cooks can be strenuous, with long hours of standing, lifting heavy pots, and working near hot ovens and ranges. Possible hazards include falls, cuts, and burns, although serious injury is uncommon. Even in the most modern kitchens, cooks, chefs, and bakers usually work amid considerable noise from the operation of equipment and machinery.

Social and psychological factors

Cooks, chefs, and bakers should be able to work as part of a team and to work under pressure during rush hours, in close quarters and with a certain amount of noise and confusion. They may find some customers difficult to please and on occasion have to recook or replace food orders because of individual demands. These employees need a mild temperament and patience to contend with the public daily and also to work closely with many other kinds of employees in a congenial manner.

Experienced cooks may work with little or no supervision, depending on the size of the food service and where employed. Less experienced cooks may work under much more direct supervision from expert cooks or chefs.

Many cooks are required to work early morning or midnight shifts. Doughnuts, breads, and muffins for morning service, such as breakfast, must be baked by 6 or 7 a.m. This requires night shift bakers to produce. Some people find working late hours very difficult to adjust to.

The art of cookery provides many opportunities for self-expression and the expression of creative talents. Many chefs have earned fame for themselves and the restaurants and hotels where they work because of their skill in artfully preparing the traditional favorites, creating new dishes, and improving familiar ones. They may become as famous as the restaurant in which they work.

GOE: 05.05.17; SIC: 5812; SOC: 5214

◇ **SOURCES OF ADDITIONAL INFORMATION**

American Culinary Federation
10 San Bartola Road
PO Box 3466
St. Augustine, FL 32084

American Institute of Baking
1213 Bakers Way
Manhattan, KS 66502

Chefs de Cuisine Association of America
830 8th Avenue
New York, NY 10019

Council on Hotel, Restaurant, and Institutional Education
1200 17th Street, NW
Washington, DC 20036

Educational Foundation of the National Restaurant Association
250 South Wacker Drive
Chicago, IL 60606

For publications listing the educational training available in post–secondary schools for culinary skills, please write for:

Programs in Hotel, Restaurant, Institutional Management in the United States: Junior Colleges and Culinary Schools
American Hotel and Motel Association
Education Information Office
1021 New York Avenue, NW
Washington, DC 20005

◇ **RELATED ARTICLES**

Volume 1: Baking; Food Processing; Food Service
Volume 2: Dietitians; Food technologists; Restaurant managers
Volume 3: Bakery products workers; Canning and preserving industry workers; Confectionery industry workers; Dairy products manufacturing workers; Meat packing production workers

Correction officers

Definition

Correction officers guard persons who have been arrested and are awaiting trial or who have been tried, convicted, and sentenced to serve time in a penal institution. They search prisoners and their cells for weapons, drugs, and other contraband; inspect windows, doors, locks, and gates for signs of tampering; observe the conduct and behavior of inmates to prevent disturbances or escape; assign work to inmates and supervise their activities; guard prisoners being transported between jail, courthouse, prison, mental institution, or other destinations; and make verbal or written reports to a superior officer. When necessary, these workers may use weapons or force to maintain discipline and order.

Correction officers are responsible for the physical needs of the prisoners, such as providing or obtaining meals and medical aid and assuring the cleanliness of the cells. In addition, they often counsel inmates informally, supplementing the treatment of psychologists and other mental-health professionals.

History

At one time the punishment for criminal behavior was left in the hands of the injured individual, or the blood relatives if the person had been murdered. This resulted in blood feuds, which in time were resolved by the payment of money to the victim or the victim's family. With the development of kingdoms, certain actions came to be regarded as an affront to the king or the peace of his domain, and the king assumed the responsibility for punishing the wrongs committed by a subject or his clan. Thus, crime became a public offense.

Early criminals were treated inhumanely, often put to death for minor offenses, exiled, forced into hard labor, turned into slaves, or left to rot in dungeons. Eventually the belief that punishment deters crime weakened, and the custom of imprisonment grew. Houses of correction were designed in the hope of rehabilitating prisoners through a simple life and hard work. The earliest of the penitentiaries was Bridewell, established in London in 1553. Out of these institutions came the prison reform movement, which gained impetus in the eighteenth century and continues today.

Nature of the work

This occupation is concerned with the safekeeping of persons who have been arrested and are awaiting trial or who have been tried and found guilty and are serving time in a correctional institution. They maintain order in accordance with the institution's policies, regulations, and procedures and often offer informal counseling to prisoners.

To prevent disturbances or escape, correction officers carefully observe the conduct and behavior of the inmates at all times. They watch for forbidden activities and infractions of the rules, as well as poor attitudes or unsatisfactory adjustment on the part of the prisoners. They settle disputes before violence can erupt. They may search the inmates or their living quarters for weapons or drugs and inspect locks, bars on windows and doors, and gates for any evidence of tampering. The inmates are under guard constantly—while eating, sleeping, exercising, bathing, working. They are counted periodically to be sure they are all present. Some officers are stationed on towers and at gates to prevent escapes. All rule violations and anything out of the ordinary are reported to a superior officer such as a *chief jailer*. In case of a major disturbance, correction officers may use weapons or force to return order.

Correction officers give work assignments to prisoners, supervise them as they carry out their duties, and instruct them in unfamiliar tasks. Officers assure the health and safety of the inmates by checking the cells for unsanitary conditions and fire hazards and administering first aid for illness or injury.

These workers may escort prisoners from their cells to the visiting room, medical office, or religious services. Certain officers called *patrol conductors* guard prisoners who are being transported between jail, courthouse, prison, mental institution, or other destinations, either by van, car, or public transportation. Officers at a penal institution may also screen visitors at the entrance and accompany them to other areas within the facility. From time to time, they may inspect mail addressed to the prisoners, checking for contraband; help investigate crimes committed within the prison; or aid in the search for escapees. Some *police officers* specialize in guarding juvenile offenders being held at a police station house or detention room pending a hearing, return to their parents, or transfer to a correctional institution, often investigating the background of first offenders to determine the reason for the crime and to make a recommendation to the magistrate regarding disposition of the case. Lost or runaway children are also placed in the care of these officers until parents or guardians can be located and notified.

Immigration guards guard aliens held by the immigration service awaiting investigation, deportation, or release. *Gate tenders* check the identification of all persons entering and leaving the institution.

In most correctional institutions, psychologists and social workers are employed to counsel inmates with problems. It is an important part of a correction officer's job, however, to supplement this with informal counseling. Officers may help inmates adjust to prison life, to prepare for return to civilian life, and to avoid committing crimes in the future. On a more immediate level, they may arrange for an inmate to visit the library, help inmates get in touch with their families, suggest where to look for a job after release from prison, or discuss personal problems. In some institutions, correction officers may lead more formal group counseling sessions.

Correction officers usually keep a daily record of their activities and make regular reports, either verbal or written, to their supervisors. The reports concern the behavior of the inmates and the quality and quantity of work they do, as well as any disturbances, rule violations, and unusual occurrences that may have taken place.

Head correction officers supervise and coordinate the activities of correction officers during an assigned watch or in an assigned area. They perform roll call and assign duties to the officers; direct the activities of a group of inmates and the release and transfer of prisoners in accordance with the instructions of a court order; maintain security and investigate disturbances among the inmates; maintain prison records and prepare reports; and review and evaluate the performance of their subordinates.

In small communities, *correction officers* (sometimes called *jailers*) may also act as deputy sheriffs or police officers when they are not occupied with guard duties.

Requirements

Candidates for the occupation of correction officer generally must be 21 years of age and have a high-school diploma or its equivalent. Individuals with less than a high-school education may be considered for employment if they have qualifying work experience. Other requirements include good health, strength, sound judgment, and the ability to think and act quickly.

Training of correction officers varies from the special academy instruction provided by the federal government and some states to the informal on-the-job training furnished by most states and some local governments. The training academies have programs lasting from four to eight weeks and instruct trainees on institutional policies, regulations, and procedures; the behavior and custody of inmates; security; and report writing. On-the-job trainees spend two to six months under the supervision of an experienced officer; during that time, they receive similar training while gaining actual experience. Correction officers may be given addi-

A prison guard observes the actions of inmates while they venture out of their cells for a brief period.

tional training periodically as new ideas and procedures are developed.

States may begin to require random or comprehensive drug testing of their officers, either during hiring procedures or while employed at the facility.

Special requirements

In many states, applicants may be asked to pass a physical exam in which their physical fitness, eyesight, and hearing are checked against specific standards. Some states require one or two years of previous experience in corrections or related police work, and a few have a mandatory written examination.

Correction officers who work for the federal government and most state governments are covered by civil service systems or merit boards and may be required to pass a competitive exam for employment.

Opportunities for experience and exploration

High-school students interested in a career as correction officer may explore the occupation further by talking with school guidance counselors and interviewing officers from local correctional institutions.

Because of the age requirement and the nature of the work, there are no opportunities for young people to gain actual experience while still in school. Between the ages of eighteen and twenty-one, however, individuals may prepare for employment by taking college courses in criminal justice or police science. They may also investigate the possibility of obtaining a civilian job as clerk or other worker for the police department or other protective service organization.

Related occupations

Criminal justice is a broad field offering those people with interests in this area's occupations such as police officers, state police officers, security consultants, security guards, and police radio dispatchers.

Methods of entering

To apply for a job as correction officer, individuals should contact federal or state civil service commissions, state departments of correction, or local correctional institutions and facilities and ask for information about entrance requirements, training, and job opportunities.

Advancement

With additional education and training, experienced officers may qualify for promotion to head correction officer or advancement to some other supervisory or administrative position. Some officers transfer to related areas, such as probation and parole.

Employment outlook

As the general population has increased, so has the jail and prison population—and the necessity for correction officers to guard the inmates.

In the early 1990s, there were approximately 150,000 of these workers employed in the United States. Almost half of them worked in such state-run correctional facilities as prisons, prison camps, and reformatories. Most of the rest were employed at city and county jails or other institutions, while a few thousand worked for the federal government.

The extremely crowded conditions in today's correctional institutions have created a need for more correction officers to guard the inmates more closely and relieve the tensions. A greater number of officers will also be required as a result of the expansion or new construction of facilities. As prison sentences become longer through mandatory minimum sentences set by state law, the number of prisons required will increase. In addition, many job openings will occur from a characteristically high turnover rate, as well as from the normal need to fill vacancies caused by the death or retirement of older workers. All in all, the employment of correction officers should increase through the late 1990s at a faster rate than the average for all occupations.

Because security must be maintained at correctional facilities at all times, correction officers can depend on steady employment. They are not usually affected by poor economic conditions or changes in government spending. Correction officers are rarely laid off, even when budgets need to be trimmed. Instead, because of the high turnover, staffs can be cut quickly simply by not replacing those officers who leave.

Most jobs will be found in relatively large institutions located near metropolitan areas, although opportunities for correction officers exist in jails and other smaller facilities in cities and towns throughout the country.

Earnings

There was a wide variation in wages for correction officers in the early 1990s, depending on the level of government.

Local governments paid an average starting salary of $18,700 a year, and top earnings averaged $24,300. Median earnings were $20,600.

State governments paid correction officers an average starting salary of $17,760 per year, with a maximum that averaged $24,300. The median was $20,000.

The federal government paid a starting salary of $15,280 a year, with maximum salaries in excess of $41,000 for sergeants and other supervisors. The average for all federal correction officers and sergeants was $21,600 per year.

Benefits for correction officers may include uniforms or a cash allowance to buy their own; hospitalization and major medical insurance, either wholly or partially paid for; and disability and life insurance. Officers who work for the federal government and for most state governments are covered by civil service systems or merit boards.

Conditions of work

Work schedules for correction officers may include nights, weekends, and holidays, because prison security must be maintained around the clock. The workweek, however, generally consists of five eight-hour days, except during emergencies, when many officers work overtime.

Correction officers may work in- or outdoors, depending on their duties. Conditions can vary even within an institution: some areas are well lighted, ventilated, and temperature-controlled, while others are overcrowded, hot, and noisy. Officers who work outdoors, of course, are subject to all kinds of weather. Correctional institutions occasionally present hazardous situations. If violence erupts among the inmates, correction officers may be in danger of injury or death. Although this risk is higher than for most other occupations, correction work is usually routine.

Social and psychological factors

An understanding of human behavior is an important quality for correction officers to possess. If they are to be effective counselors, they must be able to inspire the prisoners' confidence and develop a reputation for being fair. They must report all violations of the rules without showing any favoritism.

Physical and emotional strength are needed to cope with the stress inherent in dealing with criminals, many of whom may be dangerous or incapable of change.

A correctional officer has to remain alert and aware of the surroundings, the prisoners' movements and attitudes and any potential for danger or violence. This continual heightened level of alertness may create psychological stress for some employees.

GOE: 04.01.01; SIC: 9223; SOC: 5133

◇ **SOURCES OF ADDITIONAL INFORMATION**

For information on a career in the correction field and about schools that offer programs in criminal justice, financial aid, and job listings, write to:

Contact Center
PO Box 81826
Lincoln, NE 68501

Additional information on correction careers is available from:

The American Correctional Association
4321 Hartwick Road, Suite L208
College Park, MD 20740

◇ **RELATED ARTICLES**

Volume 1: Civil Service; Politics and Public Service
Volume 2: Recreational therapists; Recreation workers; Social workers
Volume 3: Security guards; Social workers; State police officers

Cosmetologists

Definition

Cosmetologists, often called *beauty operators, beauticians,* or *hairdressers,* perform professional personal services for customers to aid them in the improvement of their personal appearance. Primarily, the personal services rendered are concerned with the care and treatment of hair, skin, and nails.

History

A desire to improve personal appearance is not a recent vogue in U.S. culture. Neolithic cave wall drawings, writers of ancient times, and historical excavations depict the interest of the people in hairstyles and in oils, perfumes, and other articles that would aid beauty grooming. Egyptian women of 8,000 years ago, especially those of wealth and nobility, demanded great care of their hair and used cosmetic aids. People of royalty in the Middle Ages had servants who styled and cared for their hair. Portraits and paintings from Colonial American days recall the high-fashion hair designs and colored powdered wigs worn by men and women alike.

Until about seventy years ago the services of the beautician were performed in customers' homes. The beauty salons or shops now known

to the U.S. public have emerged as public businesses only in relatively recent years.

Today, beauty shops are prevalent everywhere and their services are available to almost everyone. The public now regards the services of beauty shops as more than luxury; psychologically, the services are viewed as important to personal morale, feelings of confidence, and to a person's general well-being. In the United States, beauty shops number among the largest of the personal service industries.

Nature of the work

A cosmetologist performs personal services for customers that may include hairstyling, cutting, trimming, straightening, permanent waving, coloring, tinting, bleaching, and shampooing. A cosmetologist may also give facials, massages, manicures, pedicures, and scalp treatments, and may shape and tint eyelashes and eyebrows. They sometimes do makeup analysis, suggest cosmetic aids, and advise customers regarding what products to use and how to use them with the greatest benefits. Many specialize as *hairstylists.* Today, numbers of cosmetologists called *wig dressers* are trained in the styling and care of wigs. Through advanced training, cosmetologists may specialize in some aspect of their work, such as permanent waving, cutting hair, or setting only the more difficult high-fashion hairstyles.

In small shops the job duties may include making appointments for customers, cleaning equipment, sterilizing instruments, and keeping a pleasing decor in the shop.

Cosmetologists use certain tools and equipment in their work, such as scissors, razors, brushes, clippers, cosmetic aids, massage and manicure equipment, hair dryers, towels, and reclining chairs. Most of the equipment and tools are provided by the shop owners.

The work of barbers and that of cosmetologists are closely associated, and both barbers and cosmetologists perform their services in the same type of surroundings, although beauty shops may be more attractively decorated to appeal to the female clientele. Cosmetologists are employed in privately owned shops throughout the country, many of them small businesses. They may also be employed in beauty shops in large city department stores, drugstores, hospitals, and hotels. Cosmetologists may be employed to demonstrate hairstyles in various stores, fashion centers, photographic centers, and in television studios. Still others, with advanced training, may qualify to teach in beauty culture colleges and vocational training schools.

In some shops, *manicurists* tend customers' nails, filing and polishing them, and tending the cuticles. Cosmetologists work in close personal contact with the public. They may have customers at any age level and some specialize in children's haircuts, for example.

Cosmetologists serving the public must have pleasant, friendly, yet professional, attitudes, as well as skill, ability, and interest if they are to build a following of customers as a steady clientele. The nature of the work demands that cosmetologists be aware of the psychological aspects of dealing with all types of customers.

Requirements

The National Association of Cosmetology Schools estimated in the early 1990s that there were more than 3,900 public vocational and private training schools for cosmetologists.

Although a high-school education strengthens any applicant's chances of success, personally and vocationally, the minimum education entrance requirement for most training schools is the completion of the eighth grade. Some schools require applicants to have a high-school

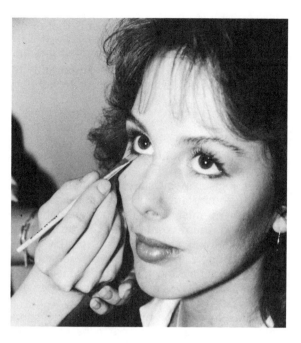

Cosmetologists often give their customers make overs. Such work requires a steady hand and a delicate touch.

diploma. This requirement varies with the state.

Applicants who anticipate that they may desire to teach beauty culture at some future time will need a high-school education and, quite likely, from two to four years of college training.

The majority of private schools offer training programs of six to nine months; in some states, however, courses require from twelve to fifteen months for completion. Public vocational school programs may cover a span of two or three years equal to the last three years of high school, because academic subjects are also a part of the curriculum.

Training courses in public and private schools may include lectures, demonstrations, and practical work. In practical training, students usually begin to practice on mannequins and on each other. As students gain experience, they may work on public customers who patronize the training clinics for their lower prices. Classroom training may include such subjects as anatomy, elementary physiology, hygiene, sanitation, applied chemistry, shop planning, applied electricity, and cosmetology.

The cost of beauty culture training programs varies with factors such as the adequacies of the school's physical plant, training facilities, staff, location, and length of formal training. Tuition may also be affected by requirements of the state board of examiners.

215

The work of the cosmetologist is that of offering to the public skilled professional services. A pleasant personality and a genuine liking for people are extremely important to success in this occupation.

Special requirements

Cosmetologists in all states must obtain a license. In some states applicants (at least sixteen years of age) must first pass an examination to qualify as a junior cosmetologist. After passing this examination and practicing for one year, they are eligible to take a second examination for senior cosmetologist. Fees for license examinations and yearly renewals of the license vary from state to state.

States vary in the number of hours of formal course training required to be eligible to apply for a cosmetologist's license with a state board of examiners. States may require from 1,000 hours (six months) to 2,500 hours (fifteen months) of combined practical and classroom training. Some states allow applicants for a state license to complete the requirement in apprenticeship programs. Apprenticeship programs, however, are gradually decreasing in number as state boards of examiners are realizing that applicants need more formal and technical training.

Applicants must meet other criteria to be eligible to take the state board examinations for licenses. The minimum age requirement is sixteen for the majority of states. Because requirements vary from state to state, applicants are urged to inquire at the licensing board of the state in which they plan to be employed.

The major union is the United Food and Commercial Workers International Union.

Opportunities for experience and exploration

The occupation of cosmetologist may be explored by visiting the various training institutions, such as public vocational high schools and private beauty colleges. Some schools may permit visits and observations in the training classes. Observing and talking with licensed cosmetologists may provide additional information. There is little opportunity to explore this occupation by part-time work experience; however, some individuals obtain summer or weekend jobs as general shop helpers.

Related occupations

Cosmetologists have a strong sense of style and color and enjoy working closely with people. Other occupations that offer these challenges include barbers, nail technicians, interior designers, interior decorators, and electrologists.

Methods of entering

Cosmetologists secure their first jobs in various ways. The majority of beauty colleges and private and public vocational training schools aid their graduates in locating job opportunities. Many schools have formal placement services.

Applicants may apply directly to beauty shops in which they would like to work. Newspaper want ads may be used or applicants may use city or state employment services.

Advancement

The majority of cosmetologists begin their careers as general beauticians performing a variety of services. In some states one must begin as a junior operator and, after a year of experience at this level, the individual is eligible to take an examination to become licensed as a senior cosmetologist. Some seek advanced educational training to become specialized in one aspect of beauty culture, such as hairstyling or coloring.

A hairdresser in some cases may advance by skill, training, and seniority to shop manager, and some may aspire to shop ownership. After cosmetologists have obtained some years of practical experience and, in many cases, additional academic training, they may wish to become teachers in schools of beauty culture. These opportunities, however, are usually open only to those who possess exceptionally good skills and abilities.

The cosmetologist with experience and skill may advance by moving to beauty shops that are located in areas of higher financial income.

Cosmetologists may move into positions such as representatives of cosmetic companies, equipment firms, beauty editors for publishing firms, makeup artists in motion picture and television studios, or into jobs as inspectors on state licensing examination boards of beauty culture. Other related job opportunities include *body makeup artists*, who work with photographers and models, *mortuary beauticians*, and *scalp treatment operators*.

Employment outlook

Thousands of job opportunities are expected to be available yearly for cosmetologists through the early 1990s. Many opportunities are occurring as the general population increases, as more shops are opened in suburban shopping centers, and as working women want the professional services of the cosmetologist more frequently.

Increasingly, good employment opportunities are available to the part-time cosmetologist.

An estimated 600,000 people were employed as cosmetologists in the early 1990s. The number of male workers is increasing steadily. Currently, it is estimated that the demands for cosmetologists far outnumber the supply.

Earnings

Salaries of cosmetologists depend on a number of influencing factors, such as experience, ability, speed of performance, socioeconomic level of the shop's clientele, shop location (suburban or urban), and the salary arrangement on which the operator agrees to work. Most cosmetologists are employed on a commission basis; others receive a base salary plus 40 to 50 percent commission.

Customers' tips are an important factor in the cosmetologist's earnings. Considering all of these factors, it is difficult to estimate actual salary figures. Estimates have been made that the salaries for experienced operators in the early 1990s ranged from $15,600 to $25,000. Beginning cosmetologists with average skill earned from $7,800 to $9,980. In exclusive city salons, expert operators, those who are specialized, and top hair stylists earned more.

Fringe benefits in this occupation may include group health and life insurance, one- to two-week paid vacations, and other employee benefits, depending on the employer. The availability of fringe benefits varies widely and these benefits, except for paid vacations, are usually available only to those employed in large establishments, such as department stores, or to those employed in the operation of a chain of beauty salons.

Conditions of work

Most cosmetologists work a forty-hour week, although some may work forty-four to forty-eight hours weekly. Working hours usually include Saturdays and, very frequently, evening appointments. They may sometimes work a shift schedule. Holiday seasons and special community events may cause increased business, which would involve overtime work.

Cosmetologists usually work in well-lighted and comfortably ventilated shops. Surroundings are generally pleasant.

The nature of the cosmetologist's work demands standing the majority of the work day. The continual use of water, shampoos, lotions, and other solutions with chemical contents may cause irritations of the skin for some hairdressers.

Cosmetologist must at all times be tactful, courteous, and in control of their emotions in rendering their professional services to the public, especially to those customers who are difficult to satisfy or disagreeable.

Social and psychological factors

Although many of the services performed by cosmetologists are repetitive in nature, the individual personalities of the public add to the interest, satisfaction, and challenge of the occupation. Cosmetologists have a continual challenge for creativity and artistic flair in their jobs through hair styling, fashion creation, and makeup work for customers.

The cosmetologist may find it trying to work constantly in such close personal contact with the public at large, especially in striving to satisfy the more difficult-to-please customers. The work demands an even temperament, pleasant disposition, and patience. For some individuals these constant demands may create nervous strain and tension.

Cosmetologists usually work in attractive, well lighted and comfortably ventilated shops. Surroundings and place of employment, the attitude of the employer, and the skill and experience of the operator will determine the degree of supervision under which the cosmetologist must work.

GOE: 09.02.01; SIC: 7231; SOC: 5253

◇ **SOURCES OF ADDITIONAL INFORMATION**

National Association of Accredited Cosmetology Schools
5201 Leesburg Pike, Suite 205
Falls Church, VA 22041

National Beauty Career Center
3839 White Plains Road
Bronx, NY 10467

National Cosmetology Association
3510 Olive Street
St. Louis, MO 63103

◇ **RELATED ARTICLES**

Volume 1: Personal and Consulting Services
Volume 3: Barbers; Electrologists

Dental assistants

Definition

Dental assistants work in dentists' offices, helping dentists treat and examine patients. They also perform administrative and clerical tasks that make the office run smoothly and free the dentist's time for working with patients.

History

The job of a dentist is one that has always required more than two hands. Drilling, pulling, cleaning, and operating on teeth requires one pair of hands to operate the instruments and another pair to hold the patient's mouth open and keep it clear of liquids and debris. So dentists have probably always had assistants to help them when they physically could not perform a dental operation or examination alone.

But the job of the dental assistant as we know it today is a creation of the twentieth century. Techniques in dentistry and the care of teeth underwent a revolution as discoveries in chemistry and industry made possible dental radiography and more precise and effective dental instruments. In addition, the discovery that fluoride helped prevent tooth decay led to more work for dentists because people were in many cases able to keep their teeth throughout their lives, provided they visited their dentists for quick remedial action once cavities began. Recently, public awareness of the importance of dental care began to grow, and more and more companies began providing dental insurance to employees.

As a result, dentists became busier. As they took in more patients and performed more different kinds of dental services, they had less time for performing more routine tasks such as keeping patients' files and instructing them on techniques of oral hygiene. With a little training, other workers learned to take on these duties, and the dental assistant became indispensable to the modern, busy dental office.

Nature of the work

Dental assistants help dentists examine patients in the dentist's chair. They usually greet patients, escort them to the examining room, and prepare them for examining by covering their clothing with paper or cloth to protect it from water and stains. They also adjust the head rest of the chair and raise it to the proper height. Many dental assistants take X rays of patients' teeth and process the film for the dentist to view. They also obtain patients' dental records from the office files, so the dentist can review them before the examination. During examinations and dental operations, dental assistants use suction devices to keep the patient's mouth dry and hand the dentist instruments as they are needed. When the examination or procedure is over, the assistant may give the patient instructions for taking care of the mouth while it heals. They also provide instructions on preventing plaque build-up and keeping the mouth clean and healthy between office visits.

Dental assistants also help with a variety of other clinical tasks. When a dentist needs a cast of a patient's mouth—a device used for diagnosing and planning correction of dental problems—assistants may mix the materials necessary for this procedure. They may also pour, trim, and polish these study casts. Some assistants prepare materials for making dental restorations, and many polish and clean patients' dentures. Dental assistants may perform laboratory work required to make temporary dental replacements. Some states allow dental assistants to apply medications to teeth and gums, isolate individual teeth for treatment using rubber dams, and remove excess cement after cavities have been filled.

Dental assistants may also check patients' vital signs during office visits and help dentists with any medical emergencies that arise during dental procedures.

Many dental assistants also perform clerical and administrative tasks. When they are not helping the dentist, they may sit at a desk and greet patients, type records, and answer the telephone. They often set up appointments for patients, prepare bills for services rendered, collect payment, and issue receipts. They may also keep inventory of dental supplies and order them when necessary.

Dental assistants are not the same as dental hygienists, who are licensed to scale and polish teeth.

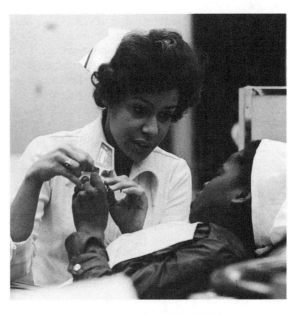

A dental assistant prepares a young patient for dental treatment.

Requirements

Most dental assistant positions are entry level. They usually require little or no experience and no education beyond high school, because many assistants learn their skills on the job.

Many assistants, however, do go on to receive training after high school, at the many trade schools, technical institutes, and community and junior colleges that offer dental assisting programs. Armed Forces schools also train some dental assistants. Students who attend the two-year college programs receive associate degrees, while those who attend trade and technical school programs finish after one year and earn a certificate or diploma. To enter these post–high-school programs, candidates must have a high-school diploma. Some schools require that applicants have received good grades in science, typing, and English in high school; some require an interview or written examination; and some require that applicants pass physical and dental examinations. In the early 1990s about 290 of these programs were accredited by the American Dental Association's Commission on Dental Accreditation. Some four- to six-month nonaccredited courses in dental assisting are available from private vocational schools.

The University of North Carolina School of Dentistry also offers a correspondence course for assistants who cannot participate full-time in an accredited formal program. The course generally takes two years to complete, but is equivalent to one year of full-time formal study.

Accredited programs instruct students in dental assisting skills and theory through classroom lecture and laboratory and preclinical experience. Students take courses in English, speech, and psychology, as well as biomedical sciences including anatomy, microbiology, and nutrition. Courses in dental sciences cover oral anatomy, oral pathology, and dental radiography, to name just a few. Students learn chairside assisting and price-management, through practical experience obtained in affiliated dental schools and local dental clinics and offices.

Graduates of accredited programs may be allowed to perform more different kinds of duties when they begin work and may receive higher salaries than assistants with high-school diplomas alone.

High-school students who wish to work as dental assistants may prepare by taking courses in general science, biology, health, chemistry, and office practices. Typing is also an important skill for dental assistants.

Because they are primarily responsible for making patients comfortable in the dentist's office, dental assistants need a clean, well-groomed appearance and a pleasant personality. Manual dexterity and the ability to follow directions are also important in this field.

Special requirements

Dental assistants may wish to obtain certification from the Dental Assisting National Board, but this is usually not required for employment. Certified Dental Assistant (CDA) accreditation shows that an assistant meets certain standards of professional competence. To take the certification examination, assistants must be high-school graduates who have taken a course in cardiopulmonary resuscitation and must fulfill one of the following requirements: they must have graduated from a formal training program accredited by the Commission on Dental Accreditation; one year of postsecondary training and two years experience as a full-time dental assistant; or worked full-time as a dental assistant for five years.

Dental assistants in twenty-one states may take X rays under a dentist's direction only after completing a precise training program and passing a test. Persons who receive CDA credentials have fulfilled this requirement. To keep their CDA credentials, however, assistants must prove their skills through retesting or acquire further education.

Opportunities for experience and exploration

Students in formal training programs receive dental assisting experience as part of their training. High-school students can learn more about the field by talking with assistants in local dentists' offices. Part-time, summer, and temporary work may be available as office clerical help.

Related occupations

Persons who work in providing dental care are but one small segment of those workers in the health care industry. People with the skill and interest to help others include physical therapists, dental hygienists, dentists, prosthetists and orthotists, dental laboratory workers, and registered nurses.

Methods of entering

High-school guidance counselors, family dentists, dental schools, and dental associations may provide workers with leads about job openings. Students in formal training programs often learn of jobs through school placement services.

Advancement

Dental assistants may advance in their field by moving to larger offices or clinics, where they may take on more responsibility and earn more money. In small offices they may receive higher pay by upgrading their skills through education.

Further schooling is also required for advancing into dental assisting education positions. Dental assistants who wish to become dental hygienists must enroll in a dental hygiene program. Because many of these schools do not allow students to apply dental assisting courses toward graduation, assistants who think they would like to move into hygienist positions should plan their training carefully.

In some cases, dental assistants move into sales jobs with companies that sell dental industry supplies and materials.

Employment outlook

According to the U.S. Department of Labor, in the early 1990s dental assistants held more than 169,000 jobs in private dental offices, group practices, dental schools, hospitals, public health departments, private clinics, and U.S. Veterans Administration and Public Health Service hospitals.

With private practices tending toward larger offices, and with the number of small- to medium-sized offices increasing, the growth in opportunities for dental assistants should be faster than average through the early 1990s. As the population continues to increase and dental insurance becomes more widely available, assistants will find increased job opportunities. Many openings will occur as workers change careers or leave the work force to assume family responsibilities.

The employment outlook for dental assistants could be adversely affected by a drop in individual dentists' patient loads, a situation that is possible because of recent improvements in preventive dentistry and a growing supply of dentists. Nevertheless, through the foreseeable future, qualified dental assistants should have little trouble finding jobs.

Earnings

Dental assistants' salaries are highly dependent on their particular responsibilities, the policies of the office in which they work, and the geographic location of the employer. According to the National Association of Dental Assistants, salaries were highest on the West Coast and lowest in the Southeast, with the average dental assistant earning around $15,000 annually in the early 1990s. The American Dental Association reported that median annual earnings for full-time dental assistants were about $14,500.

Federal starting salaries for dental assistants vary with the educational background of the employee. Beginning assistants with a high-school diploma earned $13,100 a year to start, while graduates of a one-year accredited post–high-school program with one year of experience started at nearly $13,900. The average federal salary for dental assistants was $16,400.

Conditions of work

The offices in which dental assistants work are generally clean, modern, quiet, and pleasant. They are also well lighted and well ventilated. In small offices, dental assistants may work solely with dentists, while in larger offices and clinics they may work with dentists, other dental assistants, dental hygienists, and laboratory technicians. Although dental assistants may sit at desks to do office work, they frequently spend a large part of the day standing beside the dentist's chair where they can reach instruments and materials.

Making X rays poses some danger, but most offices have lead shielding and safety procedures that minimize the risk of exposure to radioactivity.

About one-third of all dental assistants work forty-hour weeks, often including some Saturday hours. About one-half work between thirty-one and thirty-eight hours a week. The remainder work less.

Social and psychological factors

Persons interested in becoming dental assistants need to practice the techniques they teach their patients to use. This means they will have to follow a solid oral hygiene regimen, including regular brushing, flossing, and dental check ups. They also need a willingness to help other people and the ability to deal with people who are frightened of dental procedures. Even more than doctor's appointments, some people fear dentist appointments. It can be difficult for the employees in dentistry to overcome patient anxiety; it is important, however, to make every effort to try. It requires patience and understanding on the part of the dental worker. Energetic and resourceful people make good dental assistants who enjoy their work.

GOE: 10.03.02; SIC: 8021; SOC: 5232

◇ **SOURCES OF ADDITIONAL INFORMATION**

American Dental Assistants Association
919 North Michigan Avenue
Suite 3400
Chicago, IL 60611

Commission on Dental Accreditation
American Dental Association
211 East Chicago Avenue
Chicago, IL 60611

Dental Assisting National Board
216 East Ontario Street
Chicago, IL 60611

◇ **RELATED ARTICLES**

Volume 1: Health Care
Volume 2: Dentists; Medical technologists; Physician assistants
Volume 3: Dental hygienists
Volume 4: Dental laboratory technicians; Laboratory technicians

Display workers

Definition

Merchandise displayers design and install displays of clothing, accessories, furniture, and other merchandise in windows, showcases, and on the sales floors of retail stores to attract the attention of prospective customers. Display workers who specialize in dressing mannequins are known as model dressers. Others are named according to the area they decorate: showcase trimmers and window dressers.

History

Eye-catching displays of merchandise attract customers and encourage them to buy. This effective form of advertising has been used down through the ages by anyone with something to sell. Farmers who displayed their produce at market were careful to place their largest, most unblemished, most tempting fruits and vegetables at the top of the baskets. Peddlers opened their bags and cases and arranged their wares in attractive patterns. Store owners decorated their windows with collections of articles they hoped to sell. Their success was often a matter of chance and depended heavily on the persuasiveness of the seller.

As glass windows became less expensive, store fronts were able to accommodate larger window frames. This exposed more of the store to the passerby, and the more decorative displays were found to be effective in drawing customers in.

With the advent of self-service stores, the personal touch was minimized and the merchandise had to sell itself. Displays became the most important inducement for the customers to buy. Advertising will bring people into the stores, but an appealing display may make the difference between a customer who merely browses and one who buys.

Small retail stores generally depend on the owner or manager to create the merchandise displays, or they may hire a free-lance window dresser for a modest fee on a part-time basis. Large retail operations, such as department stores, retain a permanent staff of specialists. Competition among these stores is strong, and whether they are successful or marginal depends on capturing a good portion of the market; therefore, a large share of their publicity budget is allotted to creating unique, captivating displays.

Nature of the work

Using their imagination and creative ability, as well as their knowledge of color harmony, composition, and other fundamentals of art and interior design, merchandise displayers in retail establishments create an idea for a setting designed to show off merchandise and attract the attention of customers. Often the display is planned around a theme. With the approval of the display manager, the display workers then construct backdrops, using hammers, saws, spray guns, and other hand tools; install background settings, such as carpeting, wallpaper, and lighting; gather props and other accessories; arrange the mannequins and the merchandise; and place price and descriptive signs where they are needed.

They may be assisted in some of these tasks by carpenters, painters, or store maintenance workers. They may use merchandise from various departments of the store or props from previous displays. The displays are dismantled and new ones installed every week or two. In very large stores that employ many display workers, each may specialize, for example, in carpentry, painting, making signs, or setting up interior or window displays. A display director usually supervises and coordinates the activities and confers with other managers to select the merchandise to be featured.

Commercial decorators prepare and install displays and decorations for trade and industrial shows, exhibitions, festivals, and other special events.

Working from blueprints, drawings, and floor plans, commercial decorators use woodworking power tools to construct installations at exhibition halls and convention centers for trade shows, festivals, and other special events. They install booths, exhibits, carpeting, drapes, and other decorations, such as flags, banners, and lights; and they arrange furniture and accessories.

Requirements

Display workers must at least have graduated high school, preferably with such helpful courses as art, woodworking, mechanical drawing, and merchandising. Some employers require college courses in art, interior decorating, fashion design, advertising, or related subjects.

High schools and community and junior colleges that offer distributive education and marketing programs often include display work in the curriculum. Courses useful to display workers are also offered by fashion merchandising schools and fine arts institutes.

Much of the training for display workers is received on the job. They generally start as helpers for routine tasks such as carrying props and dismantling sets. Gradually they are permitted to build simple props, working up to constructing more difficult displays. As they become more experienced, display workers who show artistic talent will be assigned to plan simple designs. The total training time varies depending on the beginner's ability and the variety and complexity of the displays.

Special requirements

There are no special requirements other than the personal qualifications of creative ability, imagination, manual dexterity, and mechanical aptitude. Display workers should be in good physical condition to be able to carry equipment and climb ladders. They also need agility to work in close quarters without upsetting the props.

Display workers are needed year-round, but during the Christmas season, they often execute their most elaborate work.

Related occupations

Those people with strong interests in design and art can explore other careers such as art directors, advertising workers, television and radio set designers, theater lighting designers, book designers, and graphic designers.

Opportunities for experience and exploration

Display work is included in many of the marketing programs taught in high schools and in community and junior colleges. Fashion merchandising schools and fine arts institutes offer courses that would be useful for this occupation.

Part-time and summer jobs in department stores and other retail stores or at convention halls and exhibition centers will provide an overview of those operations. Photographers and theater groups need helpers to work with props and sets, although they may require some experience or knowledge related to their

work. Otherwise, students may become active in school drama and photo clubs.

Field trips may be arranged to large retail stores and trade centers, and interviews set up with display directors, sales promotion managers, or other merchandising experts.

Methods of entering

School vocational counselors are sources of guidance and information, and school placement offices may have listings of jobs in this and related fields.

Persons wishing to become display workers may apply directly to retail stores, decorating firms, or exhibition centers. A number of display workers choose to seek free-lance work. Competition in this area, however, is intense, and it will take time to establish a reputation, build a list of clients, and earn an adequate income. Part-time free-lancing while holding another job would be more feasible. It would also give beginners a chance to develop a portfolio of photographs of their best designs, which can then be used to sell their services to additional stores.

Advancement

Display workers with supervisory ability may become display directors of a large store, then sales promotion directors or heads of store planning.

Another way to advance is to start a free-lance business in the design field, which requires very little financial investment but will need time to generate a good income, as discussed above.

The skills developed in this occupation may lead to other art-related fields, such as interior design or photography, although these will require additional formal training.

Employment outlook

There were about 30,000 display workers employed in the early 1990s. Most of them worked in department and clothing stores, but many were employed in other retail stores such as variety, drug, and shoe stores, and book and gift shops. Some had their own businesses, and some were employed by design firms that handle professional window dressing for small stores. Employment of display workers was distributed throughout the country along the lines of the population, with most of the jobs concentrated in large towns and cities.

The employment of display workers throughout the early 1990s is expected to keep pace with the average for all occupations. Any growth will be the result of an expanding retail trade and the increasing popularity of visual merchandising. Openings will occur normally as older, experienced workers retire, die, or leave the occupation for any number of reasons.

The fluctuation of the economy affects the volume of sales in retailing, as people buy less in hard times. This may be reflected in lay-offs or a freeze on hiring. Opportunities for display workers are better in large stores, particularly in metropolitan areas.

Earnings

In the early 1990s, large employers paid beginning display workers about $5.25 an hour, more for beginners with some college courses. Experienced workers earned about $450 per week. Display managers received around $30,000 per year, with some managers in large metropolitan stores earning even more. It is possible for free-lancers to earn upwards of $30,000 a year, but their income depends entirely on their talent, reputation, the number of their clients, and the amount of time they work.

Conditions of work

Display workers generally put in thirty-five to forty hours a week, except during busy seasons such as Christmas and Easter, when they may have to work evenings and weekends as well.

The work of constructing and installing displays requires prolonged standing, bending, stooping, or working in an awkward position. There is some risk of falling off ladders or being injured from handling sharp or rough materials or power tools, but serious injuries are uncommon.

Social and psychological factors

This occupation will appeal to imaginative, artistic persons, who will find it a rewarding experience to use their creative ability to visualize a design concept and then use their mechanical aptitude to transform it into reality. Although displayers work with inanimate objects such as props and materials, an understanding of human motivations will help them create displays with strong customer appeal. Also, original, creative displays grow out of an awareness of current design trends and popular themes.

GOE: 01.02.03; SIC: 7319; SOC: 322

◇ **SOURCES OF ADDITIONAL INFORMATION**

For more information, contact the local retailers and local offices of the state employment service. The following associations may be of some assistance.

National Associaton of Display Industries
470 Park Avenue, South, 17th Floor
New York, NY 10016

National Retail Merchants Association
100 West 31st Street
New York, NY 10001

International Exhibitors Association
5103-B Backlick Road
Annandale, VA 22003

◇ **RELATED ARTICLES**

Volume 1: Advertising; Apparel; Retailing
Volume 2: Advertising workers; Commercial artists; Designers; Photographers
Volume 4: Exhibit technicians

Dry cleaning and laundry workers

Definition

Dry cleaning and laundry workers dry clean, wash, dry and press clothing, linens, curtains, rugs, and other articles for families, industry, hospitals, schools, and other institutions.

History

As early as the Stone Age, people learned to weave fibers into cloth. The four natural fibers—cotton, linen, wool, and silk—were the world's only sources of fabric from then until the late nineteenth century. As soon as people learned to use fabric for clothing and other articles, they began to devise ways of cleaning it once it became soiled. Ancient peoples scrubbed their clothing in streams and rivers, using rocks and sticks to loosen and remove stains and dirt. In later centuries they learned to use soaps and other cleaning agents derived from natural sources. People washed their clothing and other fabric items by hand until the nineteenth century, when machines to agitate and wring out clothes were invented. With the industrial revolution came automatic washing and drying machines. With the growing population and increasing numbers of hospitals, schools, factories, and other businesses, came the need for a huge supply of textile items that needed to be cleaned continually. Institutional laundries sprang up to fulfill institutions' needs for fresh sheets, towels, uniforms, and other articles.

Also in the late nineteenth century, the first synthetic, nitrocellulose rayon, was invented. Today, fabrics are made from hundreds of different synthetic fabrics, derived from such sources as coal, wood, ammonia, and petroleum. New fabrics called for new cleaning techniques. Items that lost their shape or color in water began to be cleaned with chemical solvents. Some natural fibers were found to last longer and retain better appearance when cleaned with chemicals. Dry cleaning establishments were developed to clean articles that could not be washed.

Nature of the work

All regions of the country have laundries and dry cleaners. Some institutions such as hotels, schools, and prisons have their own laundries. Many schools, hospitals, and other institutions use linen supplies, which launder linens, uniforms, and other articles and rent these items to their customers. Customers who own their washable articles may take them to commercial laundries. Other laundries may supply and launder work uniforms, gloves, rugs, mats, and other items to businesses and other industries.

Dry cleaners clean, repair, and press items that cannot be laundered with water, although some large dry-cleaning plants also wash and press shirts and other clothing. Dry-cleaning operations are set up in various ways. One large plant may receive business through several of its own retail stores. A wholesale plant does cleaning for several independent stores. In addition, a single retail store may have its own plant.

In smaller laundries and dry cleaning plants, an individual worker may perform sev-

A launderer steam presses a cotton shirt for a customer.

eral different cleaning tasks. In larger plants, workers may be more specialized.

Sales route drivers drive trucks to pick up and deliver garments and other laundry. They turn in bundles of soiled items to other workers at the plant. They also stop in at businesses and homes along the route to drum up business for the firm. *Dry-cleaning branch store managers* and sales clerks receive items from customers, add up the cost of cleaning them, write the customer a slip stating the charges and the day the items may be picked up, bundle and mark the clothing to identify the customer to whom it belongs, and inspect the items for rips and stains. They also retrieve the cleaned items for the customer and receive payment. Some businesses have *curb attendants* who retrieve and deliver cleaned articles to customers remaining in cars outside the store or plant. *Laundry pricing clerks* work in laundries where they compute the cost of a customer's laundry, keep inventory of customers' articles, and prepare statements to be sent to customers.

Businesses that use industrial laundries may employ *laundry workers* to assemble bundles of soiled items for delivery to the laundry and to check and verify the contents of laundered bundles returned to the business. At linen-supply establishments, *linen-supply load-builders* assemble bundles of laundered linens and uniforms to give to the sales route driver for delivery. *Linen-room supervisors*, *linen controllers*, and *linen graders* are involved with keeping track of the number, type, and condition of items in a linen supplier and making sure customers receive and properly care for linens they order.

Once soiled items reach a laundry or dry cleaner, *markers* put tags on articles so they will not be lost and send the articles to rooms where they will be cleaned. There, *classifiers* sort articles into lots according to the treatment they need: different colors, fabrics, and types of gar-

ments go into different lots. *Sorters* in laundries may weigh laundry and put individual customers' items into net bags to keep them together, or sort items using machines.

Laundry spotters identify spots on articles and brush them with chemicals or other cleaners until the stain dissolves. In dry cleaners, spotters may be designated according to the type of material spotted, because different fabrics require different chemicals for safe spot removal. Establishments that wash or clean rugs may employ *rug measurers* to record the sizes of rugs so that after washing, the rugs can be restored to their original measurements.

When articles are ready to be cleaned, *laundry laborers and loaders* take laundry to the washing machines. Some machines can hold more than 1,000 pounds. *Washing machine operators* load articles into washing machines and start them. They pull levers or throw switches to add bleach, soap, or starch. When the washing cycle is complete, they remove the articles and load them into extractors—machines that remove about 50 percent of the water from the laundry. Machines in modern laundries may both wash and extract water from the articles. One worker may tend several machines. Workers then remove the damp laundry and put it on conveyor belts that take it to driers, conditioners, or other machines for further processing. In other laundries, workers may wash delicate articles in small machines or by hand.

Dry cleaners operate machines that clean garments, drapes, and other materials using solvents. Dry cleaners must know how different fabrics react to different chemicals and heat and select treatments for articles accordingly. They or their *assistants* place articles into the drum of a dry-cleaning machine, fasten its cover, and start the drum rotating. They then add cleaning solution to the drum. When the cleaning cycle is complete, they extract the solvent from the articles and later follow procedures to drain, filter, and reclaim the solvent for reuse. They put cleaned items into tumblers, which dry and deodorize them. *Hand dry cleaners* clean delicate items or those needing individual attention by hand.

Some workers specialize by cleaning rugs, furs, leather, pillows, or gloves using special processes. Fur cleaners put furs into special machines that use sawdust to clean. They then remove the sawdust with forced air or a tumbler drum. *Fur-lining scrubbers* clean linings with chemicals using sponges or pads. Some furs are cleaned by hand.

Conditioner-tumbler operators put damp laundry into a machine that semi-dries and untangles flatwork. *Tumbler operators* operate drying machines. *Operators of continuous towel rollers* put dry towels onto a machine that winds them into rolls before they are ironed or packaged. *Assemblers in wet-wash laundries* put customers' clothes together after washing and before finishing by comparing pinned-on tag numbers with numbers on customers' orders. *Dry-cleaning assemblers* assemble customers' orders after garments are finished.

When items are dry or semi-dry they are ready for pressing or finishing. *Pressers* or *finishers* use heat and steam to press items with machines that look like two padded ironing boards hinged together. A presser places a garment on the bottom board and activates a mechanism that lowers the top board and applies heat and steam. Finishers are often designated by the type of garment or fabric they work on, and those who hand press delicates are called *hand ironers*. *Silk finishers* work on delicate items, pleats, velvet, and so on. *Flatwork finishers* feed linens into automatic pressing machines. *Puff ironers* pull portions of garments, such as sleeves, ruffles, or trim, over heated ball-shaped metal forms to press places that cannot be ironed with a flat press. Other types of finishers include *fur ironers, handkerchief pressers,* and *shirt pressers.*

Items that lose their shape during cleaning or laundering need to be blocked. *Blockers* measure knitted garments before and after cleaning. They then shrink and stretch the garment to its original shape and size, pin it to a machine, and apply steam to make it retain its shape. *Form pressers* operate pressing-blocking machines. *Hatters* and *hat blockers* use steam and special forms to clean, reshape, and stiffen hats. *Glove formers* and *sock ironers* use heated forms to reshape and dry articles.

If items are damaged during cleaning, they may be repaired. Table cloths, sheets, and uniforms are patched by *patching machine operators.* Menders repair rips and tears in garments. *Hat trimmers* replace and repair trim on cleaned hats by hand or machine. In dry-cleaning plants, *rug repairers* repair damaged rugs.

Other kinds of finishers include *shavers,* who brush cleaned suede to raise nap, and *fur glazers* and *polishers,* who operate machines that restore luster and shine to cleaned furs. Some workers operate machines that fold items such as linens and shirts; some fold items by hand. *Flatwork tiers* tie finished linens into bundles and package them for delivery.

Operators and *workers* in small laundries may sort, spot, wash, dry, finish, and package laundry themselves.

Laundries and dry cleaners also employ *checkers,* who verify the number and type of cleaned articles by checking against customer lists, and *inspectors,* who check to make sure items have been cleaned and finished in line with company standards. They return articles to be redone if they find wrinkles, spots, tears, and so on.

Management personnel in the field include *laundry superintendents* and *supervisors,* and *dry cleaning and rug cleaning supervisors.* These workers oversee the operations of plants and the activities of employees. *Sales managers* manage sales functions of dry cleaning establishments.

Some laundries also employ *laundry-machine mechanics* to maintain and repair machines.

Requirements

In most shops, laundry and dry-cleaning workers learn their skills on the job—the only requirement is usually a high-school diploma or its equivalent. Large plants may offer more formal training programs than smaller ones. Spotters, because they must learn how different chemicals react with different fabrics and dyes, may take as many as two years to fully learn their trade. Finishers can learn to do their jobs skillfully in under a year, as can dry cleaners.

Depending on the job, high-school courses that might be helpful to these workers include chemistry, textiles, and machine shop. Courses in sewing, clothing construction, and textiles would be useful for inspectors, repairers, and finishers.

Another way to learn dry cleaning and laundry skills is through trade associations, which provide newsletters and seminars. The International Fabricare Institute, Textile Rental Services Association of America, and the Neighborhood Cleaners Association, which operates the New York School of Drycleaning, offer many courses and seminars and publish journals, newsletters, and bulletins to help workers learn new skills and techniques.

Workers need to be in good health at plants. They should enjoy working with their hands and machines, and should have good eyesight and manual dexterity. They must be dependable, fast workers who can follow order and withstand repetition.

Special requirements

There are no special requirements for this type of work.

Opportunities for experience and exploration

To find out more about laundry and dry cleaning work, students may arrange to visit a plant and talk with workers. Students may try obtaining part-time or summer employment in the field to further these types of jobs.

Related occupations

Other jobs that might be of interest include hotel and motel industry workers, janitors and cleaners, private household workers, and hotel housekeepers and assistants.

Methods of entering

Persons interested in laundry or dry cleaning positions may contact state or local employment offices or read newspaper want ads to find job leads. The best way to find work, however, is to apply to dry cleaning or laundry plants.

Advancement

Workers in dry cleaning and laundry jobs generally advance by learning and moving to more skilled tasks. Employers may send promising employees to programs offered by trade associations. Advancement in these jobs is generally limited, however.

Motivated workers may become plant managers after several years of experience. Many businesses, however, prefer to hire college graduates with degrees in management for these positions.

Employment outlook

More than 340,000 dry cleaning laundry workers were employed in the early 1990s, most in institutional, industrial, and commercial plants in large cities. Many worked in hotel and hospital laundries and many in small family laundries.

The employment outlook for these positions is generally favorable, because the growth in the country's population and in the number of working people promises a continuing demand for laundry and cleaning services. In the next 10 years, however, automation advances will cut the numbers of unskilled and semi-skilled workers needed, and most openings will be for skilled workers, drivers, and managers. In the dry-cleaning industry, many opportunities exist for workers to learn pressing and spotting. Job prospects look best for workers who are versatile, who can do many of the jobs in the industry and have a good knowledge about textiles.

Earnings

The geographic location of the plant and the type of jobs individuals perform greatly affect their wages. Skilled employees earned more than unskilled. Skilled spotters and dry cleaners may earn $20,500 a year or more. Finishers can often earn more than $18,000 a year, working for a piecework rate with a guaranteed minimum wage. However, the average for all dry cleaning and laundry employees was about $13,000 a year in the early 1990s.

Working thirty-five hours a week, beginning laundry workers earned between $7,800 and $8,600 a year in the early 1990s. The more skilled a worker becomes, the higher the pay, and the laundry workers in the early 1990s earned as much as $11,830. Workers receive time-and-a-half for working overtime and may receive slightly higher regular wages for working night shifts. Some plants award bonuses to fast workers, and many route sales workers earn a commission.

Conditions of work

Dry cleaning and laundry workers work in clean, well-lighted plants that are ventilated to remove fumes. Most workers stand for long hours near machines whose noise and heat may be annoying. Workers occasionally suffer burns from hot equipment, and working with toxic chemical solvents requires caution. These chemicals may cause allergic reactions in some people.

These workers generally work thirty-five to forty hours a week, although the number of hours available may fluctuate with the amount of work. Many plants are open Saturdays. Dry cleaners often arrive at work early to ready garments for other workers to begin on. Many workers work overtime during spring and fall rush periods.

Social and psychological factors

Laundry and dry cleaning workers must be able to work and get along well with others. Since different jobs in a plant depend on each other, teamwork is essential. Workers who do not tire of repetitious tasks and who can take directions and follow instructions will do well in this field.

GOE: 06.02.16; SIC: 7216; SOC: 7659

◇ **SOURCES OF ADDITIONAL INFORMATION**

International Fabricare Institute
12251 Tech Road
Silver Spring, MD 20904

Institute of Industrial Launderers
1730 M Street, NW, Suite 610
Washington, DC 20036

International Drycleaners Congress
PO Box 1
Cupertino, CA 95015

◇ **RELATED ARTICLES**

Volume 1: Hospitality
Volume 2: Hotel and motel managers
Volume 3: Hotel and motel industry workers; Janitors and cleaners; Private household workers

Electrologists

Definition

Electrologists are trained workers who remove unwanted hair from the skin of patrons. Electrologists remove hair and retard further hair growth from the area by inserting sterilized needles that conduct electricity into hair follicle and deaden the hair root using small charges of electricity. They use forceps to gently remove the loosened hair.

History

Different cultures dictate concepts of beauty that are often assimilated and imitated by men and women. Beauty treatments are used for ritual or ornamentation or simply attracting a member of the opposite sex. In modern societies many people find unwanted or excess facial hair unappealing and unattractive. This has particularly been a problem among young girls and women. Sometimes chemicals to dissolve the hair have been used, but there is the potential problem of the product being a skin irritant. Sometimes shaving, waxing, or tweezing has been used as a temporary relief from the problem.

Technological advances and research in skin treatment have made possible the permanent relief from unwanted hair through the use of electrolysis. Electrolysis treatments can be used on women and men to remove unwanted hair from almost any area of their bodies. In addition, electrolysis is safer than many chemical products and treatments when performed in professional settings.

Nature of the work

Electrologists work with only one patron at a time. This enables them to give their complete attention and concentration on the delicate treatment they offer. Electrolysis can sometimes be painful or uncomfortable, and it offers a patron reassurance to know that all the practitioner's focus is on them and their needs.

The first task in the treatment is the sterilization of the patch of skin that will be worked on. Rubbing alcohol or an antiseptic is often used. Electrologists use round-tipped needles to enter the opening of the skin fold, also known as the "hair follicle." The papilla is the organ beneath the hair root and is also probed by the needle. The electrologist sets in advance

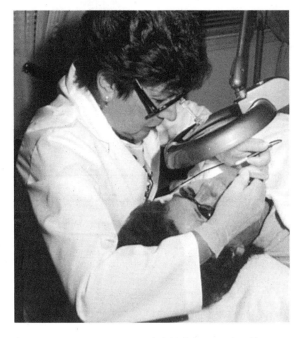

An electrologist removes unwanted facial hair from a patient. The patient must wear eye protection to shield herself from the intense light.

the amount and duration of the electrical current and presses gently on a floor pedal to distribute that current through the needle. The electrical current helps deaden the tissue, and the hair can be lifted off with a pair of forceps.

Electrologists remove hair from almost any area of the body. The most common areas they treat are the arms, legs, chest, and portions of the face such as upper or lower lip, chin, or cheek. It is not permitted for an electrologist to remove hair from inside the ears or nose or from the eyelids. Also, electrologists must have written consent of a physician as well as legitimate malpractice insurance coverage to remove hair from a mole or birthmark.

Electrologists determine the extent of a patron's treatments that will be necessary for complete removal of the unwanted hair. They may schedule weekly appointments that last fifteen, thirty, forty-five, or even sixty minutes long. The length of the individual appointments is determined by the amount of hair to be removed as well as thickness and depth of the hair. If a patient is sensitive to the treatments, the electrologist may set up shorter appointments so as not to put the patron in undue discomfort.

Electrolysis is mainly performed for aesthetic reasons. As with cosmetic surgery, the procedure can be fairly expensive. The electrologist should consult with a client to see what is desired and why and then discuss the cost of the procedure.

Requirements

Students with high-school diplomas or equivalency certificates may enroll in trade schools or professional schools that offer electrologist training. Some states require licensing for their graduates of this profession, and this may reflect on the length and depth of training that the schools offer.

Students study microbiology, dermatology, neurology, and electricity. They also learn about sterilization and sanitation to avoid infections or injury. Cell composition, the endocrine system, and anatomy may also be covered along with the vascular-pulmonary system.

Though the training offered is designed to educate students about the theory of electrolysis and its relation and effect to the skin and tissue, usually the larger concentration is of a practical nature. Focus on the different types of equipment, how they function, their purpose, and the development of confidence in running certain machines can require hours of the student's training. In addition, hands-on experience with patrons needing different treatments gives students confidence and quality preparation.

Programs may be offered on a full-time or part-time basis. Though tuition varies, some schools offer financial assistance or payment plans to make their programs more affordable. Sometimes lab and materials fees are charged. Applicants should research whether the school is accredited or associated with any professional organizations. In addition, students should also become familiar with their state's licensing laws.

Special requirements

States that require licensing offer examinations through that state's health department. The examination or state board may vary in focus and range from health, related health or cosmetology. Students should be familiar with their state's licensing requirements prior to their training so they can be sure their education provides them with the information necessary for completion of training and licensing.

Electrologists have many professional organizations that provide information on new equipment, special seminars, and networking and employment opportunities. The American Electrolysis Association, the International Guild of Professional Electrologists and the Society of Clinical and Medical Electrologists can offer vital information for developing professionals and guidelines for certification and advanced study.

Opportunities for experience and exploration

Students interested in finding out more about the field of electrologists may wish to write for information from local trade schools. Also, some two-year colleges that offer course work in medical-technician careers may be able to supply literature on programs and training in that field.

Cosmetology schools are located in many different areas and may also prove to be a helpful resource for investigating this profession. Some schools and training programs allow interested students to speak with faculty and guidance counselors for additional information.

Related occupations

Those people with interests and aptitudes for work as an electrologist might also find interesting the work of barbers, beauty operators, EEG technicians, EKG technicians, and X-ray technologists.

Methods of entering

Newly licensed electrologists may begin as assistants to an already practicing technician. They may handle extra patrons from overbookings or have new patrons referred to them. Beginning electrologists can build up a clientele in this way without having to cover the costs of equipment and supplies themselves.

Some electrologists may open their own business in a medical office complex and receive referrals from their neighboring health care professionals. Others may be employed by clinics or hospitals before deciding to pursue their own office space.

Advancement

Advancement for electrologists usually comes in building up the various aspects of their practices. Experience and reputation often supplies more and repeat patients. Some electrologists who work as part of a clinic staff may move on

to open their own shop or to move in a more visible and accessible location, or a well-known office complex.

Employment outlook

A moderate increase is expected to continue for electrologists. Hospital and clinics often strive to develop new services and technologies, and this can result in more jobs for electrologists. In addition, the trend toward large group practices to pool resources and offset joint costs, such as common supplies, support staff, and so on, may make it more feasible for beginning electrologists to open their own practice right out of school.

The development of more out-patient care facilities as well as some increasing benefits in health insurance packages indicate that electrologists may always be in significant demand.

Earnings

Because electrologists schedule treatments that vary in length, often their fees are based on quarter-hour appointments. Rates for a fifteen-minute treatment may begin at $10.00 in some cities, while electrologists in large urban regions may begin at $20.00. Thirty-minute and sixty-minute treatments in large cities may begin at $50 and $100, respectively. Though rates in smaller towns are often less, electrologists may still earn a competitive wage for their work.

Electrologists who are employed by a medical practice or clinic may charge more if a portion of their fee must help cover office space, utilities, and support staff like receptionists and bookkeepers.

Conditions of work

Whether the electrologist works in a beauty salon, a medical center, or has a private shop, the nature of the work requires the environment to be clean, comfortable, and professional. Electrologists perform delicate work and may work in spaces that are quiet to allow for greater concentration, or perhaps will have music playing in the background to help put their patients at ease.

A neat appearance is important, so often electrologists wear uniforms or lab coats. This decision may also allow for more comfort and less distraction to the patient as well as the electrologist.

Social and psychological factors

Electrologists perform personal and sometimes painful treatments for their clients, so it is important that the electrologist be patient and caring and develop a good bedside manner. Electrologists help people feel good about themselves by improving aspects of their physical appearance and sometimes feel the pressure of a patient who is impatient or unrealistic about the results, or is nervous and feels ill at ease.

Electrologists, however, enjoy the flexibility and independence that their career can provide for them as well as take pride in their skills. Electrologists feel a sense of accomplishment for the various stages of progress a patient experiences.

GOE: 09.05.01; SIC: 7299; SOC: 5253

◇ **SOURCES OF ADDITIONAL INFORMATION**

American Electrology Association
47 Wilson Avenue
Englishtown, NJ 07726

National Commission for Electrologist Certification
1327 Jones Drive, Suite 107A
Ann Arbor, MI 48105

Society of Clinical and Medical Electrologists
PO Box 52
Killeen, TX 76540

◇ **RELATED ARTICLES**

Volume 1: Health Care

Fast food workers

Definition

Whether the menu lists pizza, tacos, hamburgers or fried chicken, a *fast food worker* is responsible for serving the customer the correct order in an efficient, professional, and courteous manner. Fast food workers may be employed in large chain restaurants or privately owned food stands. Though usually these restaurants serve one kind of food, even in establishments with a wide selection of dishes, the fast food worker should be familiar with the menu, including price, size of the portion, or any side dish or condiments included and how something is prepared.

History

As transportation means developed, allowing people to travel away from their homes and subsequently from their home-cooked meals,

alternative dining facilities multiplied. On shorter carriage and train trips, many travelers opted to bring packaged meals from home. Early travel routes often followed main passageways through towns. Train layovers sometimes allowed for meal breaks, and food carts offering stews and quick dinners could sometimes be found near train depots. Many of the scheduled stops provided passengers with the opportunity to enjoy a more leisurely meal at local inns and diners.

After the turn of the century train travel became more popular and efficient; passengers could now go from state to state, rather than being limited to only the neighboring cities. Along with these developments, trains offered travelers good, reasonably priced meals in a relatively short time. When automobile travel became popular, small independent stands offered meals and sandwiches, prepared and served quickly so as not to tie up the hurried traveler. With the development of highways and limited access roads, restaurants were built right off the road.

Today, strings of well-known fast food franchises can be found in metropolitan areas as well as dotted along highways throughout the United States. The most famous is probably McDonald's, though for history, it is only third oldest.

In 1930, fried chicken was the specialty in a small Kentucky restaurant opened by Colonel Sanders. By 1956 Sanders was promoting his own recipe throughout the area, and eventually his one-restaurant business became the nationally known Kentucky Fried Chicken. The second-oldest fast food restaurant is Burger King, opened by the Burger King Corporation of Miami, Florida, in 1954.

Fast food has become increasingly popular because it compliments the busy schedules of working families. In addition, the restaurants are conveniently located, offer moderately priced meals, and have a consistent food product. In addition, many fast food restaurants offer certain price specials or discounts, such as a "two-for-the-price-of-one" deal. Others offer prizes or hold contests that encourage repeat business. There is also a fairly recent trend for more restaurants to offer more healthy food, such as salads and soups.

Nature of the work

Fast food workers may have a variety of duties. Some fast food establishments may require employees to be familiar with all aspects of the restaurant: greeting and serving customers, light cleanup and maintenance, as well as preparation of some of the simpler food items. Smaller restaurants may encourage this out of necessity, not having enough staff to specialize. Larger chain restaurants may incorporate this practice as a way of familiarizing the fast food worker with the restaurant's needs as a whole, which may lead to specialization at a later date.

Fast food workers who are part of the kitchen staff may begin as assistants to the trained cooks. These assistants may work with the setup of supplies, refilling condiment containers or doing prep work such as slicing meats or garnishes. Workers in this category may be relied upon to do general clean up in the kitchen area to promote sanitation as well as a safety.

Kitchen staff employees who cook the food are responsible for preparing the food to meet the company's standards. In this regard, the meal must be made consistently and neatly. Cooks must be agile and quick in their handling of food.

The cashier in a fast food restaurant may be responsible for taking the customer's order as well as entering the order into the computer or cash register, taking payment and returning required change for the meal. In some fast food establishments the cashier may act as counter worker and have additional tasks. These added duties could include filling the customer's order, selecting the various sandwiches, side orders, or beverages from those stations and serving it to the customer on a tray or assembling it in a carry out container. It is often the duty of a cashier to greet customers, welcoming them to the restaurant in a friendly and courteous way. While those employees are mostly responsible for interacting with customers and filling their order, they may also be required to keep their immediate work station clean and neat.

In addition to customer interaction, the counter worker also needs to communicate effectively with the kitchen and managerial staff. The counter worker may have a special order for a sandwich or alert them to any shortages of food items. The counter worker may need to notify the manager about a disgruntled customer.

In the different areas of fast food work, employees must be able to keep up the pace, exhibit motivation, and be willing to work as part of the team.

Requirements

For an entry level position at a fast food restaurant, a worker should be motivated, cheerful, and cooperative. The fast food business requires a quick pace at breakfast and lunch rushes. A motivated employee is willing to work extra hard or offer to help a fellow employee during these times. Quick thinking in accepting money or counting back change is as necessary as it is for the handling of food when the restaurant is busy.

The fast food worker should be neat in appearance as well as have neat work habits. Some fast food restaurants require that their employees wear uniforms or follow a dress code. They also may have rules of behavior and manner. Employees must respect these guidelines as sometimes failure to do so results in the employee being sent home or docking their pay. Good qualities and work habits found in a reliable fast food worker also reflect the professional attitude that managers and franchise owners strive for in their restaurants.

A fast food worker prepares a milk shake for a customer. In most franchised fast food restaurants, employees must wear designated uniforms.

Special requirements

As fast food worker makes their way up the ranks of the restaurant, they may decide to pursue special training or education. If they are working at a part-time job and are still in high school, courses such as home economics, advanced cooking, or other food service courses may be helpful. Likewise, study in health and sanitation can be beneficial.

If a fast food employee is already at a large franchise, is making plans to apply to one, or is interested in pursuing management training, there are many outlets for preparation. Many franchises have their own "university" training programs. McDonald's, Dunkin Donuts, and Burger King offer serious course work in such areas as maintenance of restaurant equipment; hiring, training, and motivating employees; and purchasing supplies.

Most other chain franchises offer instruction as well, so that the restaurant product and image is kept consistent and so that they may offer new franchise owners assistance in getting started in the business.

Opportunities for experience and exploration

Course work in home economics courses and other classes that develop cooking skills are good preparation for the fast food worker. In addition, general business or management courses provide a solid basis for entry level workers.

If there are opportunities for employment in the school cafeteria or other food service area, a student may look into that. Neighborhood restaurants, local hot dog, or hamburger stands may also hire summer help.

Also, certain high schools offer work-study cooperative programs to students to assist them to gain job experience. Such programs may have an area that concentrates on food service occupations or may host lectures from community members already involved in the field.

Related occupations

Individuals interested in food service are offered a wide array of work environments and many levels of employment. These include restaurant managers, food service managers, waiters and waitresses, table staff, cooks, chefs, bakers, dietitians, and dietitian technicians.

Methods of entering

The number of part-time positions at fast food restaurants is very high—often fifty percent. These restaurants rely heavily on their part-time employees and are accustomed to planning their work schedules accordingly. Applying at restaurants that utilize part-time or student help is a good start for entry level workers. Even at smaller, privately owned establishments, the fast food worker will be introduced to some of the common factors of the industry: working with a variety of people, keeping up at a quick pace, being friendly, cooking, as well as packaging and serving food.

Local papers often advertise for help in neighborhood restaurants, and some establishments contact the school counseling department to post job openings. However, the majority of positions may be obtained by walking in and filling out an application. Entry level positions open up quickly so re-application is recommended if no openings are available immediately.

Advancement

Because of the diversity in the fast food business, there is ample opportunity for workers to find an area of interest or specialization. Employees may take advantage of manager-trainee opportunities or tuition assistance to progress higher up within the company. Some fast food workers use their experience to go on to other areas of food service: waiting tables or working as a restaurant hostess or manager. Others may decide to go to a vocational cooking school or pursue hotel and restaurant management.

Employment outlook

Because of the quality of training and preparation that parent companies offer to franchise owners, fast food restaurant businesses boast a significant success rate of 95 percent. More than 550,000 people were employed at fast food restaurants in the early 1990s, and a 31 percent increase is projected for the year 2000, bringing that total to more than 775,000.

Owning a franchise is a popular business venture and one that demands the recruitment and promotion of reliable and capable staff.

Entry level jobs are not difficult to come by. Submitting an application and keeping in touch for openings can lead to the beginning of a career in the fast food industry.

Earnings

The expected earnings for fast food workers are comparable to many other part time jobs with most entry level workers beginning at the minimum hourly wage. Larger franchises often offer annual and bonus raises. Restaurants that have late evening or all-night hours may compensate employees working those shifts with higher hourly wages. Sometimes employees earn additional compensation or time-and-a-half for working overtime (more than eight hours for one shift), or working on holidays.

Some restaurants and individually owned franchises offer bonuses for tuition assistance and holiday and anniversary bonuses.

Conditions of work

Fast food restaurants should meet safety and sanitary standards enforced by local and state health departments. These agencies require an establishment to be well ventilated and to have proper lighting and adequate heating and cooling systems so employees can work in a comfortable environment.

Large fast food restaurant franchises are often decorated pleasantly and incorporate the logo, company color schemes, or characters of their parent companies. They supply adequate and comfortable seating facilities, as well as rest rooms and water fountains, all of which are maintained according to corporate standard.

Fast food employees may work shifts of five to nine hours in length, receiving appropriate coffee and lunch breaks. Often these establishments have private rooms, separated from the main dining rooms, for employees to eat lunches and relax.

Fast food workers may have regular work hours, for instance mornings only, or floating schedules that require them to work a combination of evenings, afternoons or weekends. Fast food workers may be called in by their managers to work an extra shift or work overtime if another employee is ill, or if the restaurant is very busy. Fast food workers should be fairly flexible because there is no way to determine in advance how busy or understaffed the restaurant will be.

Social and psychological factors

Fast food employees meet many nice people and develop professional and marketable work skills. They learn to work under pressure and to meet the work standards presented to them. A fast food worker learns tangible skills like working a cash register or computer, cooking, and good communication.

Unlike some other types of work, however, the fast food business is a no-nonsense job. A cashier or counter worker may handle hundreds of dollars a day. Cooks work over fryers and grills and handle knives and meat slicers. The work requires concentration and a professional attitude.

GOE: None; SIC: 5812; SOC: None

◇ **SOURCES OF ADDITIONAL INFORMATION**

National Restaurant Association
1200 17th Street
Washington, DC 20036

235

National Soft Serve and Fast Food Association
516 South Front Street
Chesaning, MI 48616

Educational Foundation of the National Restaurant Association
250 South Wacker Drive, 14th Floor
Chicago, IL 60606

◇ **RELATED ARTICLES**

FBI agents

Definition

Special agents of the Federal Bureau of Investigation are employees of the federal government. The FBI, a division of the U.S. Department of Justice, investigates violations of many different federal laws. The FBI has jurisdiction over some 185 federal investigative matters.

History

The history of the Federal Bureau of Investigation began in 1908 when it was founded as the investigative branch of the U.S. Department of Justice. Until 1924, when J. Edgar Hoover was appointed its director, the FBI experienced a rather slow development. Under Hoover's direction, and with increased responsibilities for the enforcement of a number of federal laws, the FBI began its growth towards becoming internationally famous and the largest scientific crime detection laboratory in the world.

As a part of its growth, the FBI in 1934 was given the general authority to handle federal crime investigation and through its work, within three years, more than 11,000 criminals were convicted. In 1939, the FBI was established as the clearing house for all matters pertaining to internal security. During the war, the FBI rendered many security services for war production plants and worked to gather evidence on spy and espionage activities within the plants.

The FBI criminal laboratory today is composed of numerous sections to carry out effectively the Bureau's scientific fact-finding and investigative reports. From these sections, such as fingerprinting, ballistics, documents, and photography, law enforcement agencies all over the nation are able to receive and compile factual scientific evidence to use in the trials of individuals that may clear the innocent or convict the guilty. The fingerprinting section of the FBI laboratory is the largest in the world, containing millions of sets of fingerprints.

Nature of the work

The headquarters of the FBI is located in Washington, D.C., and from this location the work of some fifty-nine field divisions is supervised. Agents are assigned to perform the investigation of any case, irrespective of its nature, unless they are agents who have specialized in some particular field. In the latter instance, agents are most likely to work on those cases that demand their specialized talents. For any case, the responsibility of the FBI agent is to investigate violations that involve federal laws. Violations may include such crimes as bank robbery, extortion, kidnapping, frauds, and thefts against the federal government, espionage, interstate transportation of stolen property, mail fraud, sabotage, and Atomic Energy Act investigations. FBI special agents are responsible for protecting the security of the United States and for investigating any subversive acts that might be threatening to security. In performing investigative work, agents have at their disposal a vast network of communication systems and the crime detection laboratory in Washington. When cases are completed, FBI agents submit full reports to the Bureau's headquarters.

FBI agents usually carry special identification to properly identify themselves as employees of the Bureau. They usually wear ordinary business suits, and not special uniforms such as police wear. Agents involved in potentially dangerous work may be permitted to carry firearms on their person for self-protection during investigations.

FBI agents usually work as individuals unless potential danger is present or the nature of the case demands two or more persons. The work of the agent is always confidential and may not be discussed beyond other authorized Bureau members. This precludes any discussion of work assignments, even with the agent's immediate family or friends. The Bureau and its agents work in close cooperation with law enforcement agencies all over the world though the FBI does not function as a law enforcement agency. FBI agents function strictly as investigators.

Agents perform their work in various ways, depending upon the nature of cases. They may need to travel for periods of time or live in various cities. Agents may talk with people to gather information, spend time searching various types of records, and observe people, especially those persons who are suspect of criminal intentions or acts. FBI agents participate in carrying out arrests, and may take part in or lead raids of various kinds. On occasion, they are summoned to testify in court cases; it is not the agent's role, however, to express judgments or opinions regarding the innocence or guilt of those involved in violations and tried in court. The agent's work is to gather facts and report them. Sometimes in court they are asked to describe their investigative actions.

Requirements

To qualify for the occupation of FBI special agent, an applicant must have been graduated from an accredited four-year college with a major in accounting or a physical science, or from a state-accredited resident law school. Law school training must have been preceded by a minimum of two years of resident undergraduate work in college.

Every applicant must successfully pass very rigid examinations to qualify as an agent. These examinations include a rigorous physical test, and oral and written tests that examine the applicant's knowledge of law or accounting and his ability and aptitude for meeting the public and conducting investigations. The FBI administers all of its own examinations except the one for physical fitness.

This FBI employee analyses specimens of suspected narcotics. Her experiments render evidence that help solve crimes.

Extremely thorough and exhaustive investigations are made into the applicant's background and character. When appointments are made, they are on a temporary, probationary basis. After one year of successful service, the appointments become permanent.

When a special agent applicant receives an appointment to the FBI, a period of intensive and extensive training is required of the candidate at the FBI Academy at the Quantico, Virginia, U.S. Marine Base. The period of training lasts fifteen weeks, after which the agent is assigned to one of the field offices. A part of the training is given at the FBI headquarters in Washington, D.C. During training, the candidate is taught FBI rules and regulations, fingerprinting, firearms that are generally used by the FBI, defensive tactics, and federal criminal law.

The education and training of the FBI agent is virtually never-ending. New techniques, better methods, and new knowledge are continually taught throughout the career, either through experience on the job, advanced study courses, in-service training, or special conferences.

Potential candidates must be in excellent physical health to pass the rigid physical examination. They must have very good eyesight, and hearing must be unimpaired so that one is capable of hearing a normal conversation from at least fifteen feet with each ear. Applicants cannot have any physical defects that would interfere with their job performance, which may demand participating in raids, climbing, running, the use of firearms, and the ability to use defensive tactics in self-protection or the protection of others. All applicants must be able to stand rigorous physical strain and exertion.

FBI agents must assume grave responsibilities as a normal part of their jobs. Their reputation and character must be above reproach, as must their dependability and integrity. Bravery and courage must be in the temperament of the individual interested in this type of work. Agents must be able to accept continual challenge in their jobs, realizing that no two days of work assignments may be exactly alike. A stable and personally secure person who can work daily with challenge, change, danger, and who has great flexibility may find an FBI career satisfying.

Special requirements

Persons interested in this occupation must be citizens of the United States. They must be at least five feet, seven inches tall and between the ages of twenty-three and thirty-five. Applicants must be willing to serve anywhere in the geographic boundaries of the United States or in Puerto Rico. The educational and physical requirements listed above may be considered special qualifications for this occupation.

Opportunities for experience and exploration

There is almost no opportunity for summer or part-time work experience in this occupation because of the education and training required and because of the nature of the work.

Those persons who are interested in the FBI, however, may explore the occupation by reading, talking with their guidance counselor, or by visiting and taking a conducted tour of the FBI headquarters in Washington, D.C., which is open to the public.

Related occupations

The skills required of FBI agents are very similar in education and training as those needed for police officers, security guards, security consultants, and state police officers.

Methods of entering

Persons interested in the occupation of FBI special agent should write directly to the Director of the Federal Bureau of Investigation, U.S. Department of Justice, Washington, DC 20535. The Bureau will supply information on existing vacancies, give requirements for the positions, state how to file applications, and inform applicants of locations where examinations will be given.

Applicants may be interviewed and tested in FBI field offices. Although the FBI has its own methods of selecting employees, the examinations given are similar in administration to those given by the office of Personnel Management. Periodically, the FBI sends out announcements concerning examinations to be given and possible vacancies to be filled.

Advancement

Although FBI special agents are not appointed under the Federal Civil Service Regulations, as are other federal workers, they are eligible to receive salary raises periodically within the grade set up for their positions. These within-grade increases are, of course, dependent upon a satisfactory job performance. Advancements in grade may be earned as experience is gained through satisfactory job performance.

Higher-grade administrative and supervisory positions in the FBI are filled by advancement from within the ranks. Positions open to advancement may include special agent in charge of a field office, inspector, and field supervisor.

Employment outlook

Approximately 9,000 agents worked in the fifty-nine field offices of the FBI in the early 1990s.

The FBI has always enjoyed a traditionally low turnover of employees. As a lifetime service career field, the FBI makes most job appointments to fill vacancies occurring because of retirement or death, or to fill positions that have been left open as a result of promotions from within the ranks. Some appointments are made to fill new positions created through the expansion of the Bureau. During World War II, there were approximately 5,000 FBI agents. By the early 1990s the number had increased to about 9,000 agents.

In spite of the somewhat limited number of positions available because of low employment turnover, the FBI encourages well-qualified and interested persons to submit applications. Competition is keen for openings that come available, but there are openings for candidates on a regular basis.

Earnings

FBI agents were earning approximately $26,000 as an entrance salary in the early 1990s. This wage was slightly above the beginning salary for the entry employment of college graduates in other federal agencies. In the early 1990s, experienced field agents earned up to $51,600 in annual salary, and supervisory agents earned more.

Under certain circumstances, agents may work overtime and receive overtime pay up to approximately $6,120 a year.

Conditions of work

FBI agents may work a very strenuous and flexible schedule, frequently more than the customary forty-hour week. They are on call for possible assignment twenty-four hours a day. Assignments may be given for any location at any time. Agents may work under potentially dangerous circumstances in carrying out their assignments. Every aspect of the agent's work is of a confidential nature. Agents must retire at age fifty-five if they have served twenty years.

FBI agents receive fringe benefits of paid vacations, annuities on retirement, and sick leave. Although conditions of work for some case assignments may possibly be hazardous, the career of FBI agent offers responsibility and adventure.

Social and psychological factors

FBI agents must work with many kinds of people and under varied circumstances in performing their jobs. It is necessary that agents possess the ability for self-control and self-discipline and always demonstrate sound judgment, tact, and diplomacy in accepting their responsibilities. Both physical and psychological strains are present in this occupation.

The work of agents, although not performed under close personal supervision but more often independently, is still carried out with agents being in continual contact with their superiors.

FBI agents may find personal satisfaction in a career of service to their government.

GOE: 04.02; SIC: 9221; SOC: None

◇ **SOURCES OF ADDITIONAL INFORMATION**

The Federal Bureau of Investigation
U.S. Department of Justice
Washington, DC 20535

Friends of the FBI
1001 Connecticut Avenue, NW, Room 1135
Washington, DC 20036

◇ **RELATED ARTICLES**

Volume 1: Civil Service; Political and Public Service
Volume 2: Crime laboratory technologists; Lawyers and judges
Volume 3: Police officers; Private investigators; State police officers

Fingerprint classifiers

Definition

Fingerprint classifiers catalog and compare fingerprints of unknown persons or suspected criminals with records to determine if the persons who left the fingerprints at the scene of a crime were involved in previous crimes.

History

Although it is commonly accepted that we are all unique individuals, our fingerprints actually verify this fact. Even though personal appearances may change during adolescence and adulthood, fingerprints remain intact and unchanging throughout our lives. Even if injured and scarred, enough of the distinguishing marks are maintained for fingerprint classifiers to have astonishing success in making a positive identification.

Fingerprints are not only used as a means of identification, but may serve as signatures for contracts. Some of us had our palm prints put on our birth certificates as newborns. One of the first organized fingerprint files dates back to 1897 when the International Association of Chiefs of Police began the National Police Bureau of Identification. This association was a breakthrough in the documentation of fingerprints, in addition to making these records accessible to the police and investigators. The Identification Division of the Federal Bureau of Investigation (FBI) was established by Congress in 1924. Currently, the FBI has nearly 200 million fingerprints on file.

as well as in a single impression of all fingers at once.

Fingerprint classifiers work in laboratories and offices, as well as traveling to other areas such as crime scenes. Outside fingerprint retrieval may be more difficult and require more specialized processes, such as dusting glassware, windows, or walls with a fine powder. This powder contrasts with many different surfaces and will highlight any fingerprints that remain. Another method of retrieving fingerprints is to lift them off with a flexible tape. This tape can be brought back to the laboratory for further evaluation and matching.

Fingerprint classifiers have a challenging profession that brings them in contact with a variety of circumstances. It involves work that requires dedication, patience, and the ability to perform in some very difficult conditions. Sometimes fingerprint classifiers work with corpses and weapons used in violent crimes.

Nature of the work

Fingerprinting is meticulous, detailed work. A clear print can be more easily evaluated and identified than one where not enough or too much ink has been used. Other factors, such as scarred fingertips or other flaws resulting in accidents or sickness may alter the original print in some way so it is necessary for the classifier to be familiar with basic patterns and sequences of fingerprints.

Fingerprints retrieved from crime scenes may appear on personal affects such as watches, books, or wallets. In addition, weapons or tools, such as screwdrivers or drills, may bear fingerprints. Sometimes classifiers travel to a crime scene to inspect various sites for fingerprints, such as the entryways of a house or building, and check windows and doors.

Fingerprint classifiers compare new prints against those found after the commission of similar crimes. The classifier documents this information and transfers it to the main record-keeping system, often times a large mainframe computer system. A fingerprint classifier may keep individual files on current crimes and note any corresponding similarities between them.

To collect the print, a person's fingers and thumb are cleaned. The fingers are then rolled across a plate wet with printer's ink, making sure the entire surface of the finger is inked. Then the finger is placed over the fingerprint card in a rolling motion away from the person's body. The thumb print is placed in the ink and rolled across the print card toward the direction of the body. Each finger is recorded separately

Requirements

Fingerprint classifiers must have remarkable powers of observation and detail. They must be persistent and have the temperament to work under pressure. Fingerprint classifiers have skills of logic and have neat and precise work habits. Good eyesight and memory are also crucial.

Fingerprint classifiers come in contact with catalogs of similar looking material. They must be patient and clear thinking and enjoy working independently. Some classifiers work with computers that can provide groups of fingerprints or prints having similar composition. A background in computers may be necessary.

Fingerprint classifiers must be prepared for different experiences while working on a case. Some classifiers must take fingerprints off corpses or travel to unpleasant crime scenes. They sometimes work with criminals or have difficulty retrieving fingerprints from items such as doorknobs, guns, telephones, or tools.

Special requirements

Two-year and four-year colleges often offer course work in criminology and law enforcement. Police training schools usually offer classes in fingerprint classification, and sometimes students find it useful to supplement their studies with photography courses. Such classes help develop a student's abilities of perception and detail as well as offer training in the skill of classifying fingerprints.

Professional organizations such as the International Association for Identification provide certification for voice print examiners and latent print examiners. Membership for this association is more than 2,000 persons and promotes research and training in the forensic sciences.

Opportunities for experience and exploration

Students interested in the work of fingerprint classifiers should take political science courses and law enforcement courses. They may also decide to write to local police departments, branches of the FBI, and other government agencies requesting information on training and job preparation. Because many more fingerprinting bureaus rely on the assistance of computers for classification and record keeping, courses in data processing or computer graphics can provide skills in researching and electronic record keeping.

A fingerprint classifier examines a fingerprint and registers it on a computerized database. The computer helps match fingerprints that are lifted from the scene of a crime with those that are on the computer file.

Related occupations

Work in this field combines an excellent eye for details, an interest in police work, and knowledge of record-keeping and computer science. Other jobs that include some or all of these skills include police officers, FBI agents, private detectives, investigators, data-base managers, medical record administrators, and systems analysts.

Methods of entering

Fingerprint classifiers who work with the FBI often begin work as fingerprint clerks or assistants. Clerks are able to show their ability to become classifiers through hard work, attention to detail, and motivation and commitment. Clerks pursuing status as a fingerprint classifier take a battery of tests that includes a written spelling test, a physical examination, and an aptitude test. Fingerprint classifiers undergo a serious investigation by the FBI that examines their character and background. This investigation may consist of contacting previous employers, instructors, and sometimes friends and

relatives. Fingerprint classifiers must be U.S. citizens.

Advancement

Fingerprint classifiers who begin as security clerks may pursue police training or positions at fingerprinting bureaus. Some may become security supervisors. Fingerprint classifiers who already work with police departments may pursue advancement with a different government agency or apply for positions with the FBI.

Employment outlook

The continued need for security for businesses and the efforts of police and law enforcement agencies to deter criminals make employment opportunities for fingerprint classifiers good for the early 1990s.

Earnings

Fingerprint classifiers are employed by various government agencies as well as the security divisions of companies. Some find employment at fingerprint bureaus in towns and cities of different sizes. As the opportunity for employment differs, so does the wage scale.

Beginning fingerprint classifiers in the early 1990s earned approximately $12,000 a year. Annual raises may be between $2,000 and $3,000, and classifiers can earn $20,000 with a few years' experience.

Fingerprint classifiers who work with security departments can earn more than $12,000 in a few years. Classifiers who are employed by the FBI may begin at $12,000 and receive almost two weeks vacation for their first year. Supervisors may earn as much as $50,000.

Conditions of work

Fingerprint classifiers must review stacks of records and other data. This type of work is slow moving. They work in laboratories equipped with their tools and chemicals or in offices that hold record and documents. They work alone, sometimes for long hours at a time and must work quickly and skillfully. Often the progress of solving a certain crime rests on the information that a classifier is able to uncover. There is considerable stress and no margin for error.

Some fingerprint classifiers travel to crime scenes and bring carrying cases of chemicals and tools with them so that they may perform some functions outside of their normal working environment. Sometimes the places the classifiers travel to are rough and unpleasant. They must be adaptable and able to work in a variety of environments.

Social and psychological factors

Fingerprint classifiers are a vital part of the justice system. They work independently and are detail oriented. They must also be accepting of the fact that their job may put them in contact with criminals or crime scenes, as well as difficult situations involving law enforcement. There can be considerable stress and frustration as sometimes progress and success in matching fingerprints of a criminal is slow in coming.

GOE: 02.04.01; SIC: 9221; SOC: 399

◇ **SOURCES OF ADDITIONAL INFORMATION**

A career kit about occupations in the FBI, titled FBI Career Opportunities, is available by writing to:

Federal Bureau of Investigation
U.S. Department of Justice
Washington, DC 20535

◇ **RELATED ARTICLES**

Fire fighters

Definition

Fire fighters have the responsibility of protecting life and property from the hazards of fire. This protection is offered by fighting fires to prevent property damage, by saving lives through rescue from fire, and through safety inspections and safety education to prevent fires. Fire fighters assist in other types of emergencies and disasters in community life. This article is mainly concerned with full-time professional fire fighters.

History

For centuries people have fought fire to protect life and property. In biblical times, people would group themselves into brigades to form fire-fighting lines, and even into the early colonial days, the settlers used the bucket brigade lines to pass water buckets from hand to hand in combating fires.

Many U.S. museums today house some of the old-time fire-fighting equipment that was first invented in this country, such as hand-pulled vehicles with tanks to hold water that could be hand pumped through a hose to direct a stream of water onto fire. In those days, the tanks were filled and refilled by the bucket brigades. Many of these vehicles were themselves destroyed by fire, since the hand-pumped force of the water was weak, the hoses short and stiff, and the vehicles, of necessity, had to be drawn close to fires to be used by those men who operated the pumps and handled the hoses.

As automobiles, trucks, and machinery were invented and improved upon in industry, new and better fire-fighting equipment also appeared. Other scientific advancements have also made contributions, such as the invention of the fire extinguisher.

Today, huge fire trucks roll with great speed and blasting sirens, carrying terrifically powerful mechanized pumps, scientifically designed rescue equipment, and trained workers who know their jobs of protecting the public from the many perils of fire.

Nature of the work

The range of duties of a professional fire fighter varies with the size of the fire department and the population of the city in which one is employed. However, each fire fighter's particular responsibilities are well defined and clear-cut. In every fire department there are divisions of labor or job duties. For example, fire fighters know, when their department goes into action, whether they are to raise the life nets; try to rescue persons caught in fires; raise ladders; connect hoses to water hydrants; or attempt to break down doors, windows, or walls with fire axes so that other fire fighters can enter the area with the water hoses. Fire fighters are often known by the job duties they perform. They may frequently be referred to as hose handlers, ladder handlers, truck drivers, inspectors, or tiller handlers who steer the rear wheels on very long fire trucks that carry aerial ladders.

Fire fighters may fight the fire of a massive burning building giving off intense heat or they may be called to extinguish nothing more than a slight brush fire or a blazing garbage can. Fire fighters on duty at fire stations must be prepared and able to go on alarm call at any moment. Time may save or cost a life in fighting fire. Some fire fighters wear protective suits to prevent their hands and bodies from being burned in their work or, if not suits, protective gloves, hats, boots, and coats. Because of the mass confusion that may result at the area of a

fire and the dangerous nature of the work, the workers are well organized into details and units and they work under the supervision of commanding officers, such as *fire captains, battalion chiefs,* or the *fire chief.* These officers may reassign the fire fighters' duties at any time, depending on the needs of a particular situation.

Once fire fighters have extinguished a fire, they often remain at the site for a certain length of time to make sure that fires are completely out. The causes of the fire, especially if it resulted in injury or death or if it may have been set intentionally, may be examined by *fire-investigation lieutenants* or *fire marshals,* who report to the district attorney, testify in court, or arrest suspected arsonists.

Sometimes fire fighters answer calls requesting help in rescuing pets from high and unreachable places, aid in giving artificial respiration in cases of drownings or waterfront accidents, or emergency aid for heart attack victims on public streets. They may also administer first aid in other types of situations.

Some fire fighters are assigned as *fire inspectors,* and their work is to prevent fires. They may inspect buildings and their storage contents for trash, rubbish, and other materials that would easily ignite; for poor, worn-out, or exposed wiring; and for other conditions that are considered to be fire hazards. These conditions are usually reported to the owners of the property for correction; if not corrected, these conditions must be reported to the proper authorities for correction. Fire inspectors also check to see that public buildings are operated in accordance with fire restrictions and city ordinances and that the management complies with the safety regulations and fire precautions. Often fire fighters are called upon to give speeches on fire prevention before school and civic groups. A *fire prevention bureau captain* may be in charge of these and other fire-prevention efforts.

While fire fighters are on station duty and between alarm calls, they perform varied but regular duties. They must keep all fire-fighting equipment in first-class condition for immediate use. This includes polishing and lubricating mechanical equipment, keeping water hoses dry and stretched into shape, and their own personal protective gear in good repair. They must hold practice drills for timing and procedure, verify and record fire alarms, and stand watch at the fire alarm instrument stations.

Many fire fighters study while on duty to improve their skills and knowledge of fire-fighting techniques and to prepare themselves for examinations that may partially determine

Fire fighters aim high-pressure water hoses on a flaming warehouse. It takes two strong people to control the hose.

their opportunities for promotion. Often they are required to participate in training programs.

Housekeeping duties and cleaning chores are performed by the fire fighters on duty on a rotation basis since many fire fighters must live at the fire stations for duty periods of twenty-four hours at a time. In small towns, some fire fighters are only employed on a part-time basis and are on alarm call only from their homes, except perhaps for practice drills. In such instances, usually only a fire chief and assistant live at the station and are employed full time.

Fire fighters work in other settings, too. Many industrial plants employ *fire marshals* who take charge of fire-prevention and fire-fighting efforts and personnel. At airports, potential or actual airplane crashes bring out crash, fire, and *rescue workers* who prevent or put out fires and save passengers and crew members.

The work of fire fighters is very dangerous, and the occupation is considered a hazardous one. The nature of the work demands training, practice, courage, and teamwork; however, fire fighting is more than alert physical activity—it

is a science that demands continued study and learning.

Requirements

The majority of job opportunities open to fire fighters today requires that the applicants have a high-school education; in smaller communities, however, applicants may not have to be high-school graduates. In most cases, applicants are required to pass written tests on intelligence; in some municipalities, there may be civil service examinations. Formal education is an asset to potential fire fighters because their career training involves a continuous education program, and the progress made may affect the individual's future opportunities for advancement.

Two-year post–high-school fire technology programs, available at many junior and community colleges, emphasize the mastery of skills and technical information necessary in the development of expert judgment in fire department administration and fire fighting. Courses involve the study of the laws of physics and hydraulics as they apply to pump and nozzle pressures. Fundamentals of chemistry are taught to provide an understanding of chemical methods of extinguishing fires. Skill in communications, both written and spoken, is also emphasized.

Very rigid physical examinations are usually required for the job of fire fighter, as well as physical performance tests, which may include running, climbing, and jumping. These examinations are clearly defined by local civil service regulations but may vary.

In most cases, fire fighters must meet an age requirement of at least twenty-one but not more than thirty-one years of age. Candidates must also meet height and weight requirements. The applicant is required to have good vision (20/20 vision is required in some departments), no hindering physical impairments, and strong physical stamina.

Usually the individuals who score the highest on the tests administered have the best chances of receiving job appointments as fire fighters. Those who have had fire-fighting experience in the military service or who have served as volunteer community fire fighters may receive preferential consideration on their job applications.

Beginning fire fighters may receive several weeks of intensive training, either as on-the-job training or through formal fire department training schools. In these training periods, basic fundamentals are learned regarding city laws and ordinances, fire prevention, ventilation, first aid, the use and care of equipment, and general duties. After this period of time, the fire fighter usually starts out on the job as ladder handler or hose handler and is given additional responsibilities with training and experience.

A mechanical aptitude is an asset to this career. A congenial temperament and the ability to adapt to situations calling for teamwork or leadership are highly desirable traits. Fire fighters must also be willing to obey orders and to follow in good form the orders given. Fire fighters need sound judgment and the ability to reason and think logically with constant mental alertness in situations demanding courage and bravery.

Special requirements

Other than the mental and physical examinations, the physical agility and stamina, and the height and weight requirements previously discussed, there are no special requirements, such as licensure by law. It should be realized, however, that this is a highly organized occupational group and that many professional fire fighters, as well as volunteer and "call" fire fighters, belong to the International Association of Fire Fighters (AFL-CIO).

Opportunities for experience and exploration

Individuals interested in the occupation of fire fighter may explore their interest in the work by talking with local persons who are employed as fire fighters and by talking with their high-school guidance counselors. They may also gain permission to attend some of the formal fire fighters' training classes offered by city fire departments.

In some cases, depending on the size of the town or city department and age requirements, young people may be able to gain experience by working as volunteer fire fighters.

Courses in lifesaving and first aid offer experience in these aspects of possible future job responsibilities. Exploration in these areas can be done through community training courses and sometimes through the training offered in the Boy Scouts. In the military service, interested individuals may request their training and assignment in fire-fighting units to gain experience.

Summer job experiences as aides are sometimes available to students with the federal government in park and forest service work. In these jobs, an individual may find the opportunity to learn about fire prevention, control, and detection. Information may be obtained from the National Park Service, United States Department of Interior, Washington, DC 20013.

Related occupations

Public service in local communities can be performed in other careers such as ambulance drivers, emergency medical technicians, police officers, and civil defense officers.

Methods of entering

Applicants may enter this occupation by applying to take the local civil service examinations which usually include passing the physical health, physical performance, and written general intelligence examinations.

Applicants who successfully pass all of the required tests and receive a job appointment may serve a probationary period in which they receive intensive training for a period of time. After the completion of such training, if they have progressed satisfactorily, they may be assigned to a fire department for specific duties. The probationary period may extend beyond the basic training period in some situations.

In some very small towns and communities, applicants may enter through on-the-job training as volunteer fire fighters or by direct application for such a city government appointment.

Advancement

Promotions for fire fighters are generally from within the department. Fire fighters are usually promoted to "fire fighter first grade." As successful job performance is demonstrated and experience gained, fire fighters may be promoted to lieutenants, captains, deputies, battalion chiefs, assistant chiefs, and, finally, to fire chief. Fire fighters may sometimes work three to five years or more to receive a promotion to lieutenant. Promotions are usually dependent upon the fire fighter's position rating, which is determined by scores made on the periodic written examinations, seniority, and the previously mentioned factors of job performance and years of experience. By continuous study and in-service course work, fire fighters try to prepare themselves to take the competitive examinations that may enhance their ratings for future job promotions.

Employment outlook

There were more than 310,000 fire fighters in the early 1990s, with most employed by municipal fire departments.

The outlook for job opportunities as fire fighters through the early 1990s is relatively good, with several thousand openings anticipated yearly. The majority of job opportunities are likely to occur to fill replacements of the deceased, retired, or those positions left open when fire fighters have resigned from the occupation. A larger number of replacements is usually required in this occupation than in some others because fire fighters may have the opportunity to retire at an early age.

Most new jobs will be created as small communities expand and replace their volunteer fire services with organized city fire departments.

In some fire departments, the hours to be worked have been shortened and two persons may be employed to cover a shift normally worked by one person.

Employment of fire fighters is usually rather stable with a low turnover ratio of workers. As fire departments expand to keep pace with growing city populations, however, the number of positions available may increase accordingly. Competition for jobs is keen in most cities. Large cities' and urban fire departments will remain stable in the number of fire fighters employed. Smaller cities will be required to expand the size of their force as the population increases. Because the occupation is a rather stable one, and the number of unemployed people desiring such work may be high, competition in times of recession may be especially keen.

The development of new and well-functioning scientific fire-fighting equipment and techniques has somewhat limited the immediate need for increased numbers of fire fighters in our society. Automation has entered the picture of the fire fighter's occupational world. This factor, however, does not offset the number of fire inspectors needed in growing congested metropolitan areas or the number needed to educate the public in fire prevention techniques.

Earnings

In the early 1990s, average beginning salaries for full-time fire fighters were about $20,000 a year. Maximum salaries averaged $27,000. Fire lieutenants, captains, and fire chiefs made more. Earnings vary greatly with the size of the fire department and the geographical location.

Volunteer fire fighters are not paid, but they do earn the satisfaction of serving their communities. Experience as a volunteer fire fighter is also valuable to a person applying to a city department.

Fringe benefits for these employees usually include free protective fire-fighting clothing or salary allowance to cover the cost of the clothing equipment; compensatory time off or overtime pay for additional hours worked beyond the regular work schedule, which is usually straight pay or time-and-a-half pay; liberal pension plans providing for disability benefits and early retirement options; paid vacations; paid sick leave; and in some cases, paid holidays or compensatory time off for holidays worked.

Conditions of work

The work of the fire fighter is often thought of as exciting and "action geared"; the job, however, is one of grave responsibilities, and life or death is often dependent upon the fire fighter.

The working conditions are frequently hazardous and dangerous and involve risking one's life in many situations. Floors, walls, or even entire buildings can cave in on fire fighters as they work to save lives and property in raging fires. Exposure to smoke, fumes, chemicals, and gases can end a fire fighter's life or permanently injure him or her.

In many fire departments, fire fighters may be on duty, living at fire stations for long hours. They may work twenty-four-hour shifts and then have equal time off and periodically have seventy-two hours off after a certain number of days of duty. In large cities and metropolitan areas, the hours worked are usually shorter and shifts may vary between eight and fourteen hours, depending on whether day or night shifts are worked and the rotation of the shifts. Workweeks may range from forty to approximately ninety-six hours, usually averaging fifty to sixty hours. While on duty, fire fighters generally have some time to follow leisure interests that will not interfere with their alertness to active call of duty. The nature of the work and the hours on duty at fire stations may mean the fire fighter can spend less time at home and in family-life interests and activities than many other occupations might allow.

The occupation requires a great deal of physical strength and stamina and fire fighters must work to keep themselves physically fit and conditioned. They must be mentally alert at all times. Fire fighters may be called into action at any time of the day or night and be required to work in all types of weather conditions, sometimes for long hours.

The protective services offered to the public by fire fighters are vitally needed, but interested individuals should recognize the dangerous nature of the work.

Social and psychological factors

Fire fighters, while on active call, usually work under the close supervision of commanding officers such as battalion or assistant fire chiefs. Their work must be accomplished by highly organized team efforts in order to be effective, since there is usually a great deal of excitement and public confusion at the site of the fire. Fire fighters must be cooperative in following orders. Some fire fighters, in the ever present anticipation of being called on active duty, can never fully relax and find the occupation creates a state of nervous tension for them.

The occupation of fire fighter is one that demands bravery and courage and constant mental alertness. A desire to be of service to others is perhaps one of the principle motivating factors influencing a person in becoming a fire fighter.

GOE: 04.02.04; SIC: 9224; SOC: 5123

◇ SOURCES OF ADDITIONAL INFORMATION

International Association of Fire Chiefs
1329 18th Street, NW
Washington, DC 20036

National Fire Protection Association
Batterymarch Park
Quincy, MA 02269

◇ RELATED ARTICLES

Volume 1: Civil Service; Politics and Public Service
Volume 2: Health and regulatory inspectors; Occupational safety and health workers
Volume 3: Park rangers
Volume 4: Fire control and safety technicians

Flight attendants

Definition

Flight attendants, formerly referred to as *stewardesses* and *stewards*, render a variety of personal services to passengers of airlines to make their traveling as comfortable and enjoyable as possible. Flight attendants are employed by commercial airlines on almost all passenger flights, both national and international.

Flight attendants are responsible for the safety and comfort of the passengers from the moment the plane is boarded until the final disembarkment. Although rarely called for while on duty, they are trained for air emergencies.

History

In December 1903, the Wright brothers made aeronautical history with the first airplane flight. As time passed, inventors improved air transportation, and by 1930 air travel was on the way to becoming commercialized. It was in 1930 that the occupation of airline stewardess came into being with the hiring of some graduate nurses by United Air Lines to care for the comfort and convenience of their passengers. Many other airlines followed this trend, believing that stewardesses could render a real service in passenger welfare and company public relations.

It is the flight attendant's responsibility to make the passengers as comfortable as possible.

Today, uniformed flight attendants fly the skies for the commercial airline firms of the world. They now comprise a well-established occupational group that has grown rapidly in the last fifty years.

Nature of the work

Flight attendants perform a variety of preflight and in-flight duties. Prior to takeoff, they must attend the briefing session of the flight crew; carefully check flight supplies, emergency life jackets, oxygen masks, and other passenger safety equipment; and see that the passenger cabins are neat, furnished with pillows and blankets, and in good order. They must also check the plane galley to see that food and beverages to be served in flight are on board and that the galley is secure for takeoff.

The attendants welcome passengers and check their tickets as they board the plane, show them where to store briefcases and other small parcels, direct them to their cabin section for seating, and assist them in putting their coats and hats in overhead compartments.

On many flight takeoffs, a flight attendant speaks to the passengers as a group, sometimes over a loudspeaker, giving the names of the crew and the flight attendants; welcoming passengers; and explaining weather, altitude, and safety information. The use of lifesaving equipment and safety procedures are also demonstrated.

Flight attendants check the safety belts of passengers routinely at takeoff and on landing,

and during any rough weather encountered during flight time. They may distribute stationery and reading materials to passengers and answer any questions regarding flight schedules, weather, or the geographic terrain that is being covered on the trip. Sometimes they call passengers' attention to places of interest en route. They observe passengers during flight to assure their personal comfort, and assist anyone who becomes airsick or nervous.

During some flights, attendants serve prepared breakfasts, lunches, dinners, or between-meal refreshments. They are responsible for certain clerical duties, such as passenger reports and reboarding passes. They keep the passenger cabins clean and comfortable during plane flights. If attendants are serving on international flights, they may provide customs and airport information and sometimes translate some flight information or instructions for passengers into any one of several foreign languages.

The majority of flight attendants are stationed at home bases in large metropolitan areas where airlines maintain their main base operations. A few who work on international lines may be based in a foreign country.

Requirements

Airline companies are very selective in accepting applicants for employment as flight attendants. These employees play a major role in promoting good public relations for airline companies with the public. They are in constant contact with the public, and the impressions they make and the quality of service they render represent a type of advertisement for the airline. The companies are particularly interested in employing young people who are attractive, intelligent, courteous, poised, and able to work in a congenial and tactful manner with the public. Applicants must also have pleasant speaking voices.

Flight attendants need to have at least a high-school education. Applicants who have additional college education are often given preference in employment. Business training and experience are also considered assets. Attendants employed by international airlines usually are required to have the ability to converse in a foreign language.

The majority of airline companies maintain their own training schools for attendants. Training programs may last from four to six weeks. There are also some private schools that train flight attendants. Interested applicants should first contact airline companies, however, to learn of their training programs and any other special requirements.

Airline company training schools usually include in their programs classes in company operations and schedules, first aid, grooming, emergency operations, flight regulations and duties, and other types of job-related instruction that usually includes public relations courses, baby care, and flight terminology. The training period also includes practice flights during which flight attendants perform their duties on the job under supervision.

An on-the-job probationary period, usually six months, follows training school. During this time, experienced attendants give close attention to the performance, aptitudes, and abilities of the new attendants. After this time, new attendants may serve as reserve personnel and replace attendants who are ill or on vacation.

Most airline companies have set physical requirements that applicants must meet regardless of training. In general, applicants must be at least nineteen-years-old and in excellent physical condition, with no visual or hearing impairments. They may be between five feet, two inches and six feet tall, with weight in proportion to height.

Young people who are interested in this occupation need to have a congenial temperament, pleasant personality, and the desire to serve the public. They must have the ability to think clearly and logically, even in emergency situations, and they must be able to follow instructions working as team members of flight crews.

Each year airline companies have thousands of applicants desiring to be flight attendants, but only a small number of applicants are able to meet the requirements for these positions.

Special requirements

Special requirements for this occupation have been discussed in the preceding section; however, it should be pointed out that under the physical qualifications, applicants are generally required to pass an airline physical examination. Regarding vision, glasses or contact lenses are sometimes acceptable, but in most cases the applicant's vision must be 20/20 corrected, or 20/50 or better uncorrected.

The majority of flight attendants are members of the Transport Workers Union of America or Association of Flight Attendants. At the present time no specific licensure or other type of certification is imposed by law.

Opportunities for experience and exploration

Opportunities for experience in this occupation are almost nil until the individual has completed flight training school. Interested persons may explore the occupational requirements by talking with their high-school guidance counselor, visiting with flight attendants employed by airline companies, or talking with those employed in airline company personnel offices. Airline companies and private training schools publish numbers of brochures describing the work of flight attendants. These materials are available upon request.

Related occupations

The duties of airline flight attendants are broad. In scope of job responsibilities the job is similar to those of waiters and waitresses, emergency medical technicians, maitre d's, safety consultants, and hosts.

Methods of entering

Individuals who are interested in becoming flight attendants should make direct application to the personnel divisions of the airline companies. Information regarding the names of the companies and their locations can be obtained by writing to the Air Transport Association of America. Addresses of airline personnel division offices can also be obtained from almost any airline office or ticket agency. Some of the major airlines have personnel recruiting teams that travel throughout the country interviewing prospective flight attendant applicants. Airline company offices can provide interested persons with information regarding recruitment visits. Sometimes city newspaper advertisements announce the scheduled visits of airline personnel.

Advancement

There are a number of advancement opportunities open to flight attendants. They may advance to positions as first flight attendant, sometimes known as flight purser, to supervising flight attendant, instructor, or recruitment representative. They may also have the opportunity to move up to chief attendant in a particular division or area.

There once was a high rate of turnover in this field; now, however, turnover is low. Many people compete for available supervisory jobs.

Numbers of flight attendants who can no longer qualify for flight duty because of health or other factors move into other airline department jobs. These jobs may include those of reservation agent, ticket agent, clerk, secretary, or stenographer. They may also work in public relations, sales, air transportation, dispatch, or communications divisions.

Trained flight attendants may also find similar employment in other transportation industries, such as interstate bus companies or luxury cruise ship lines.

Employment outlook

Some 72,000 professionally trained flight attendants were employed in the early 1990s in the United States.

Employment opportunities for flight attendants are predicted to be greater than average in the next decade. Air travel has become an accepted mode of travel for an increasing percentage of the population. Speed and convenience have added to the demand. To meet the needs of the traveling public, airline companies are turning to the use of larger planes that require more attendants to service the passengers.

Interested applicants should realize, however, that regardless of the number of job opportunities predicted yearly, the occupation of flight attendant is one that attracts thousands of young people with its glamour appeal. Competition may be keen and the occupational requirements are strict. Not every qualified applicant will be accepted.

Earnings

In the early 1990s, the average income of beginning flight attendants was $15,600 a year. Experienced flight attendants averaged about $27,600. The basic pay of attendants on all flights is based on a schedule of eighty hours of flying time a month. Salaries in this occupation are somewhat dependent on individual company pay scales, number of flying hours permitted, experience, rank, and whether the flight route is domestic or international. Most airlines give periodic salary increases until a maximum pay ceiling is reached.

Flight attendants are limited in their jobs to a specific number of flying hours. In general, they may work each month approximately eighty hours of scheduled flying time and an additional average of thirty-five hours on ground duties.

Flight attendants in training are usually paid (by the airline company) either living expenses or a remuneration training salary. Expenses incurred while on duty in flight schedules and away from the home base are usually paid by the company. Such expenses might include food, ground transportation, and overnight sleeping accommodations. Some airlines may require first-year flight attendants to furnish their own uniforms; however, most companies supply the airline uniform.

Fringe benefits for these employees usually include paid sick leave and vacation time, free or reduced air travel rates for attendants and their families, and, in some cases, group hospitalization and life insurance plans and retirement benefits.

Conditions of work

Flight attendants are usually assigned to a home base in a major city or large metropolitan area. Home-base locations might include New York, Chicago, Boston, Miami, Los Angeles, San Francisco, Saint Louis, or others. Some airline companies assign attendants on a rotation system to home bases, or they may give preference to the requests of those with rank and seniority on bids for certain home bases. Attendants who have attained the longest records of service may be given the most desirable flights.

Flight attendants need to be able to accept flexibility in their work schedules, since commercial airlines maintain operations twenty-four hours a day throughout the entire year. They may be scheduled to work nights, weekends, and on holidays, and they may find some of their allotted time off occurs away from home between flights. Attendants usually have approximately fifteen days off each month.

The work performed by flight attendants may be physically demanding in some respects. They are usually on their feet the majority of the flight time servicing passengers' needs, checking safety precautions, and, in many cases, serving meals in flight. The occupation is not considered a hazardous one; however, there is a certain degree of risk in any type of flight work.

Social and psychological factors

Many individuals find the job of flight attendant to offer rewarding job satisfaction. There are opportunities to travel, to meet and converse with many types of people, and, in international work, to observe foreign cultures. The flight attendant often has a chance to meet celebrities aboard a flight or to witness historic events in distant places. A sense of satisfaction may also come from serving the public and in being part of a highly respected occupational group.

Individuals might consider disadvantages involved in the occupation as a matter of personal taste. Factors that might be considered are the irregular work hours and workdays, which include weekends and holidays, and the likelihood of being based in a geographic area far from home.

Those individuals who see their interests aptitudes, training, and physical qualifications as compatible with the requirements of this occupation may wish to apply for training in this field, and may find that the occupation offers them personal career satisfaction.

GOE: 09.01.04; SIC: 4512; SOC: 5211

◇ **SOURCES OF ADDITIONAL INFORMATION**

Airline Flight Attendants Association
PO Box 158
Buelton, CA 93427

Independent Federation of Flight Attendants
630 Third Avenue
5th Floor
New York, NY 10017

◇ **RELATED ARTICLES**

Volume 1: Aviation and Aerospace; Transportation
Volume 2: Pilots
Volume 3: Reservation and transportation ticket agents; Travel agents
Volume 4: Avionics technicians

Food service workers

Definition

Food service workers, including *waiters and waitresses* of many different types, take customers' orders, serve food and beverages, make out checks, and sometimes take payments. These basic duties, however, may vary greatly depending on the specific kind of food service establishment.

History

As towns and cities have grown up all over the world, so has the work food service workers grown into an exceedingly large and respected occupational group.

It is only in comparatively recent times, however, that waiting on customers in public eating places has become recognized as a separate occupation. In ancient and medieval times, inns were established along main highways to provide food and lodging for travelers. Usually, the innkeeper and his family, and perhaps a few servants, were able to look after all the traveler's needs. Wealthy people did almost all their entertaining in their own homes, where they had large staffs of servants to wait on their guests.

Improved roads and means of transportation in the eighteenth and nineteenth centuries led to an increase in travel, especially for pleasure. Inns near large cities, no longer merely havens for weary travelers, became pleasant places to dine on day excursions into the country. The rise of an urban middle class created a demand for restaurants where one could enjoy good food and socialize in a convivial atmosphere. More and more waiters and waitresses were needed to serve the growing number of customers. In the great hotels and restaurants of Europe in the nineteenth century, the skills of serving elegantly prepared food in a polished and gracious manner were raised to a high art.

In the United States, the increasing ease and speed of travel has contributed to a very mobile population, which has increased the great demand for commercial food service. People are eating out more and more for a variety of reasons. Today, the food service industry is one of the largest and most active sectors of the economy.

Nature of the work

Food service workers have varied job duties depending on the size and kind of food establishment in which they are employed. In small restaurants, sandwich shops, and grills, and at food counters in drugstores, diners, fast-food outlets, and cafeterias, customers usually demand quick service. *Informal waiters and waitresses* and *lunchroom or coffee-shop counter attendants* give their attention to meeting this expectation. They take customers' orders, serve food and beverages, make out bills, and sometimes collect the money, as well as clear and clean tables and counters. Between serving customers, waiters and waitresses in small establishments may prepare salads and beverages, replenish supplies, and set up table service for future customers, and spend some time cleaning equipment and the surroundings. Counter attendants often do some simple cooking; make sandwiches, salads, and cold drinks; and prepare ice cream dishes. They also may have to help with such tasks as cleaning kitchen equipment, sweeping and mopping floors, and carrying out trash. Other workers in this category include *cafeteria counter attendants* and *supervisors, canteen operators,* and *fountain servers.*

In large restaurants and in those where dining takes on a more formal atmosphere, *formal waiters and waitresses* may perform essentially the same services as in the smaller establishments; however, the service may be extended to include other courtesies. These may include presenting menus to the customers after they are seated, assisting in suggesting choices from the menu, informing the customers of special preparations and seasonings of food, and sometimes suggesting beverages that would be complementary to the meal. They check to see that the correct silver service is on the table and try to attend to any special requests the customers may have to make their dining more pleasurable. Waiters and waitresses in these es-

tablishments follow the more formal and correct protocol procedures for serving food. *Captains, headwaiters,* or *head waitresses* may greet and seat the guests and supervise the service of the waiters and waitresses. *Wine stewards* assist the customer in selecting wines from the restaurants available stock.

Dining room attendants, once called *bus boys and bus girls,* are waiters' and waitresses' assistants. They may clear and reset tables, carry soiled dishes to the dishwashing area, bring in trays of food, and clean up spilled food and broken dishes, thus giving waiters and waitresses more time to serve customers. In some restaurants, they also serve water, bread, and butter to customers. During slow periods, they may also fill salt and pepper shakers, clean coffee pots, and do various other tasks. *Cafeteria attendants* clear, wash, and set tables; carry trays of dirty dishes to the kitchen; and may serve coffee to customers.

While the dining room and cafeteria attendants assure clean and attractive table settings in the dining areas, *kitchen helpers* maintain an efficient and hygienic kitchen by cleaning food preparation and storage areas, sweeping and scrubbing floors, removing garbage, and separating trash. They may also move supplies and equipment from storage to work areas, perform some easy food preparation functions, and wash the pots and pans used in cooking. They furnish support for the dining room staff by scraping food from plates, stacking them in the dishwasher, cleaning flatware, and removing water spots from glasses.

In addition to small restaurants such as grills, sandwich shops, tearooms, soda shops, and diners, and the larger or more formal restaurant and hotel dining rooms, food service workers may be employed aboard ships and trains, in hospitals, schools, factories, and many other establishments where food is served. Some specialized waiters and waitresses may be designated by the place in which they work or the type of service they perform, such as *bar, dining car, room service, take-out, buffet, club waiters and waitresses,* or *carhops.*

Requirements

Applicants for jobs as waiters, waitresses, or food counter workers are usually not required to have a high-school diploma; most employers, however, favor applicants with some high-school training, preferably those who have completed from two to three years of high-school work. Graduation from high school is generally considered a personal asset. There are no educational requirements for waiters' assistants, kitchen helpers, and cafeteria counter workers.

Vocational schools may offer special training courses for waiters and waitresses, and sometimes special course training is offered by restaurant associations in conjunction with schools or food agencies. Many employers seek persons who have had such training.

The smaller, more informal type of restaurant may hire waiters and waitresses without special training or previous experience. The needed job skills, in these cases, are learned on the job. Larger restaurants and those with more formal dining atmospheres may demand experienced waiters or waitresses and favor hiring those who have had some special course training. Food counter workers, waiters' assistants, and kitchen helpers, almost without exception, learn their skills on the job.

Food service workers must be free from physical defects that would impair their movements of work, and possess good physical stamina. The work performed requires many long hours of standing and walking. It may also require lifting heavy trays of food, dishes, and water glasses as well as bending and stooping. In some cases, employees may work near steam tables or hot ovens.

Regarding personal requirements, waiters, waitresses, and food counter workers need to possess a congenial temperament, patience, and the desire to please and be of service to the public. All food service workers must be neat and immaculately clean in their personal hygiene and dress. Those who serve the public should present a pleasing appearance to the public, be able to speak English reasonably well, and be able to use the basic skills of arithmetic in order to compute customers' food checks. In some restaurants that specialize in the foods of a certain country, waiters and waitresses might need to speak a foreign language, most frequently French or German. A good memory and sales techniques are additional personal assets.

A baker measures flour and other ingredients to make bread. Much of the food preparation in a restaurant occurs well before it opens that day for business.

Special requirements

Food service workers, in almost all cases, are required to obtain health certificates that certify they are free from communicable diseases, as shown by physical examination and blood tests. This is required for food handlers in protection of the general public.

The principal union for waiters and waitresses, food counter workers, waiters' assistants, and kitchen helpers is the Hotel Employees and Restaurant Employees International Union (AFL-CIO); however, not all employees are union members.

Opportunities for experience and exploration

Opportunities are especially good in the food service field for persons with limited skills or education. Those interested in becoming waiters and waitresses often gain experience by doing part-time or summer work in drugstore soda fountain shops, theater refreshment centers, and fast-food establishments, as well as in small restaurants, grills, and sandwich shops. Many waiters and waitresses had their start as dining room attendants, carhops, or food counter workers.

Further exploration may be through observing waiters and waitresses at work, visiting vocational schools that offer special training courses, and by talking with high-school guidance counselors.

Related occupations

Many workers are employed in food service. Other occupations of interest might be cooks, chefs, bakers, bakery products workers, butchers, and fast-food workers.

Methods of entering

Individuals interested in entering this occupational field generally do so by applying in person for any positions open or help needed. Job openings are frequently listed in newspaper advertisements, or they may be located through local offices of the state employment service or private employment agencies. The private agencies may charge a percentage fee for their placement services.

In some localities where food service workers are unionized, potential employees may seek job placement assistance through union offices.

Advancement

Employees may advance to better-paying jobs by transferring their place of employment to larger and more formal food establishments, or they may gain better positions as they obtain more training and experience.

In general, advancement is limited in this field. Nevertheless, waiters and waitresses may find promotions open for positions as headwaiter, hostess, captain, or other supervisory position, eventually even to restaurant manager, depending on their training, experience, and work performance record, as well as on the size and type of food establishment for which they work. Food counter workers have the opportunity to advance to cashier, cook, waiter or waitress, counter or fountain supervisor, or line supervisor in a cafeteria. Large organizations, such as hamburger chains, may have management training programs or less formal on-the-job training for dependable workers who have leadership ability. Promotion opportunities are much more limited for waiters' assistants and kitchen helpers. Some of them become waiters

or waitresses, cooks' helpers, or short-order cooks; these promotions, however, are more likely in large restaurants and institutions. It should be remembered that some of these positions require that the individual possess reading, writing, and arithmetic skills.

Advancement may, in some cases, mean that the employee has the opportunity to earn more in service tips than in actual salary increases, depending again on the size, type, and location of the food service.

Some individuals may aspire to establishing and owning their own business or to entering into an owner partnership after they have earned and reserved some capital and gained the necessary training and experience.

Employment outlook

In the early 1990s an estimated 4.5 million people held jobs as food service workers.

The employment outlook for food service workers is expected to be relatively good through the late 1990s, especially in large cities and tourist areas. Thousands of new job opportunities will be available with the building of more restaurants, hotels, motels, and combination business-eating establishments. Contributing to the great demand for public food services are a growing population and an increase in spending for food and beverage outside the home. Higher incomes and more leisure time encourage frequent dining out and more travel. Also, greater numbers of working women and their families find it a convenience to take many of their meals out.

As in other occupations where many people regularly leave for a variety of reasons, the need for replacement employees offers numerous opportunities. Jobs for beginning workers will be more plentiful in lower-priced restaurants, where the turnover rate is high, particularly among students and other part-time workers. Higher-priced and more formal restaurants tend to demand experienced workers and the job turnover rate is lower in these establishments, which increases the job competition.

Food service workers may find many temporary job opportunities open to them in summer or winter resort areas, and some workers like to move with the seasonal trade. Because food services are frequently used as a short-term employment source, many of the people hired do not intend to make it their career choice for life. This provides frequent openings throughout the industry.

Earnings

The earnings of food service workers are determined by a number of factors, such as the type, size, and location of the food establishment, geographic locality, union membership, experience and training of the workers, basic wages paid, and, in some cases, tips earned. To estimate the average wage scale would be a difficult and questionable task.

Waiters and waitresses depend a great deal on tips to supplement their basic wages, which in general are relatively small. According to limited data, in the early 1990s waiters and waitresses earned an average of $11,300 yearly; half earned between $7,900 and $14,400, and one-tenth earned more than $18,600, excluding tips. Tips, usually ranging from 10 to 20 percent of the customers' checks, often amount to more than the wages paid, especially in the larger metropolitan areas. Food counter workers earned comparable wages. Some of these employees receive tips of 10 to 20 percent, but tips are not customarily given to counter workers in such places as fast-food restaurants and cafeterias.

Dining room attendants earned slightly higher basic wages; they also receive a percentage of the waiters' or waitresses' tips. Kitchen helpers earned still higher basic wages, but they are not in a position to receive tips.

Benefits for food service workers usually include free meals during the hours when they work, and uniforms are often furnished for them by the food establishment.

Conditions of work

Although working conditions have improved greatly with the air conditioning and modernization of restaurant buildings and equipment, and many labor-saving techniques are now available, this occupational group is still subject to certain work hazards. These may include burns from heat and steam; cuts and injuries from knives, glassware, and other equipment; and sometimes hard falls from rushing on slippery floors.

In some of the more formal and finer restaurants, the dining room may have deep-carpeted floors and a rather luxurious decor.

The hours worked will vary with the place of employment. The majority of waiters and waitresses work forty- to forty-eight-hour work weeks, while food counter workers, waiters' assistants, and kitchen helpers generally work fewer than thirty hours a week. Split shifts are common to cover the rush hours of business; some employees may work the lunch and dinner shifts, for example, with a few hours off in between. This is a benefit, of course, for students, who can then plan their courses around work schedules.

Most food service workers have to work evenings, weekends, and holidays. Some holiday work may be rotated among all the employees. One day off per week is usually in the schedule for these workers.

Work in this field is strenuous, requiring long hours of standing and walking, carrying heavy trays or pots and pans, and lifting other types of equipment. Rush hours are hectic for these employees, particularly for those who serve the public, attending to several tables or customers at the same time.

Social and psychological factors

Food service workers may find real personal satisfaction in their jobs, but people interested in this work should realize that regardless of their desire to please and serve the public, the public is not always easily pleased. They may encounter customers who are discourteous and those who cannot be satisfied. In public food service, the employee must meet and deal with all types of people, using tact and courtesy and maintaining a pleasant personality.

The operation of a restaurant or other food service depends on the teamwork of its employees. An even disposition and a sense of humor, especially under pressure, contribute greatly to efficiency and the creation of pleasant working relationships. The ability to converse easily with customers is a major asset for those working directly with the public.

The work performed is usually under the direct supervision of a superior; however, the sincere, hardworking employee should be able to earn the respect of his or her employer and co-workers.

GOE: 09.04.01; SIC: 5812; SOC: 5213

◇ SOURCES OF ADDITIONAL INFORMATION

Educational Foundation of the National Restaurant Association
250 South Wacker Drive
Chicago, IL 60606

For information on schools and colleges that provide training on food service, contact the council on Hotel, Restaurant, and Institutional Education at the:

National Restaurant Association
1200 17th Street, NW
Washington, DC 20036

Gaming occupations

Definition

Employees in the gaming industry are often categorized under the general heading of *gambling dealer*. These workers conduct gambling tables such as dice, roulette, or cards in gambling halls or casinos. Employees may have duties that include exchanging real currency for playing chips of varying denominations, or playing coins for slot machines, for instance. Workers stipulate that all bets must be placed prior to the beginning of the games and collect these bets. Workers announce winning colors or numbers to players and pay out winning bets according to odds and collect losing bets. Many employees specialize in one type of game that they conduct.

History

Certain gambling pastimes share histories in different countries and are reasonably similar to games played today. Keno was played in China more than 2,000 years ago. The Chinese name for the game was then "pak kop fiu," which means white pigeon ticket. These birds were trained to fly the tickets and winning numbers back and forth. The game of blackjack is commonly referred to as "twenty-one" and has roots in the fifteenth century. The French, Spanish, and Italian people all had their own version of this counting game played with cards, though the total winning number was different for each country.

Gambling became a way to pass time in the United States beginning late in the nineteenth century. In 1869 Nevada attempted to control illegal gambling by making it legal. For more than forty years, from 1869 to 1919, gambling in that state was legal. However, a reform movement banned gambling for the next twenty-one years until 1931 when Nevada made gambling legal once again.

Currently, many states have legal lotteries, and often a percentage of the earnings are earmarked for special programs or state development projects. Churches, schools, and social organizations often run "Las Vegas Night" type fund-raisers to earn money for programs, and many churches have weekly bingo games. The serious, high-stakes games, however, are played in Las Vegas, Nevada, and Atlantic City, New Jersey.

Large industries have grown and developed in these two cities to accommodate the gambler and his needs and desires. Now many large hotel chains have opened resorts and casinos to benefit from the gambling trade as well as to further develop the facilities of these vacation areas.

Nature of the work

The gaming industry is comprised of a variety of workers in specific service tasks or employees who train to conduct certain games. One example of a service position is that of cashier. Cashiers may be separated into *coin cashiers* or *change persons*. Basically, these employees may work in a cage or at a station and make change and sell coins to patrons for slot machines. They may pay off slot machine jackpots and keep records of all transactions, as well as balance the money drawer after each shift. Cashiers also provide information to guests, call for cocktail waitresses to visit the slot area, or provide other required services. Cashiers in this capacity may perform duties similar to that of a host.

Cage cashiers may provide the *slot cashiers* with additional change or sell chips to patrons. These workers operate the main cashier cage in the casino and act much like a banker. They may accept checks, credit cards for currency advances, and check credit references to discourage fraud. Likewise, these workers must balance their cash drawers and keep cash records.

Dealers may conduct game tables for baccarat, blackjack, dice, poker, and roulette. These workers exchange real currency for casino currency, whether in the form of chips or coins, ask for bets prior to the game, and make appropriate payoffs and/or collect losing bets. In the case of games like blackjack, cards are also dealt to the dealer who tries to win money from the regular players for the "house," or the casino. Poker dealers, however, only shuffle and deal cards to guest players, and the casino's winnings are a percentage of the pot.

Games such as baccarat, dice or craps, and roulette, are conducted by more than one employee. In baccarat there are three dealers, two of whom collect money for bets and the third who calls the game rules. Dice dealers also collect money for bets at the game table and exchange money for chips. A manager called a *box person* supervises the exchange and another assistant, called the *stick handler*, collects the dice after they have been thrown and passes the dice to the next shooter. Because dice is one of the fastest games and there is potential for cheating, three people work this particular table. Roulette dealers sell chips, take bets, spin the roulette wheel, toss the ball in, and announce the winners. Chips are collected and passed as well as sorted by color by the *chip mucker*.

Other game attendants include *keno runners*, who pick up tickets, money, and bets from patrons who are in the lounge or playing at another gaming table and deliver these to the keno writer. Runners take winning tickets to the payoff window and return winnings to the player.

Shift supervisors and *pit bosses* oversee the performance of the game attendants. Sometimes these workers monitor one or more game tables, other times this work is performed by staff dealers.

Requirements

Employees in this industry must be able to work in hectic environments and enjoy meeting and working with a variety of people. Workers

A croupier offers a thrower his choice of dice at a craps table.

should understand the importance of giving good service to guests and be able to handle the situation of coping with frustrated players.

Workers should have good communication skills, be pleasant, and enjoy the work. Employees must be responsible, alert, and totally trustworthy, as large sums of money are exchanged which requires quick thinking and calculating skills.

Special requirements

For many positions in the gaming industry, education requirements are minimal. However, personal and performance requirements such as speaking clear, correct English, reliability, and motivation are necessary. Good mathematical skills for making change or calculating odds are also important.

Schools in resort areas sometimes offer classes to train workers in specific games and skills. Dealer schools hold classes that last as long as ten weeks to train students how to deal cards for one specific game. Classes in dice, blackjack, or poker may be offered. Tuition can be as much as $400. Other schools may offer certification to students who have learned all the games. This award is called a Certificate of Professional Casino Croupier and can prepare an employee for nearly any game table position.

Although some positions offer on-the-job training, competition for the better jobs can be intense. Most dealer jobs require a certificate or suitable training from a dealer school, though sometimes experience from another casino can take the place of this requirement. College programs may include training in hotel and restaurant management or schooling in the casino industry. Often management trainee positions are open to these graduates.

Licensing and certification requirements may vary from one casino or location to another. For instance, in Atlantic City all gaming employees must be licensed for their specific job position. Nevada, however, has the requirement that dealers have a degree from a dealer's school or considerable experience. Dealer licenses are renewable every two years and cost approximately $275.

Union support is very strong in Las Vegas, though not as much so in Atlantic City. Work permits are required in both areas with a minimum age of twenty-one-years old. Work cards cost about $14, and some casinos require FBI fingerprint clearance.

Opportunities for experience and exploration

Contacting area casinos as well as the state's departments for tourism, hotel and motel associations, and recreation are all potential sources for information. Casinos can offer information about the types of jobs available for skilled or unskilled workers. Also, library books on the gaming industry or different gambling games can also be a fine resource.

Related occupations

The work of persons in gaming establishments is often similar in responsibility and interest to cashiers, counter clerks, and bank and savings and loan tellers and clerks.

Game workers such as dealers need many of the same interpersonal skills that waiters, waitresses, and bartenders have.

Methods of entering

Applicants should contact casinos, hotels, and resorts that are located in areas where gambling is legal. Personnel officers may also be contacted for information on openings and entry level requirements. Previous experience may be difficult to acquire if the applicant lives in an area other than Las Vegas or Atlantic City. Previous work experience, however, is often a big advantage as are personal maturity and good references from other jobs. Applicants may want to contact casinos prior to the heavy vacation season or be willing to accept part-time employment and work their way up.

Advancement

Advancement most often comes to employees who demonstrate professionalism, get along with the players, have self-confidence, and establish good work records. Part-time employees may be offered full-time positions as cashiers, keno runners, or keno writers. Some dealers may get better shift schedules or a promotion to a higher wage table. Most supervisory positions require additional education and training as well as experience in the casino. For these positions, leadership and managerial skills are necessary as well as keen perception.

Employment outlook

Many casinos are open late in the evening, and some are open twenty-four hours. The number of games and tables in the casinos, as well as additional service staff make the employment opportunities for gaming workers fairly promising in the early 1990s. Many casinos take on additional employees during the busy season, and many opportunities are available for part-time as well as full-time employees.

Earnings

Most gaming employees work eight hour shifts, five days per week. Unlike some other occupations, weekend and evening hours can be highly sought after, as often they bring in more tips and are the busiest time for players. In Nevada shifts operate all day long, though in Atlantic City, casino hours are from 10:00 A.M. to 4:00 A.M. on Sundays through Thursdays and

10:00 A.M. to 6:00 A.M. Fridays, Saturdays, and holidays.

Wages for entry workers may be as much as $800 per month. In addition to that workers receive tips from players for various services performed. Cashiers can earn up to $9 per hour and blackjack dealers and craps (dice) dealers may earn an hourly wage of $5.50. Game supervisors and casino managers on the other hand may earn up to $4,000 per month, which does not include tips or bonuses.

Workers often get two breaks and a lunch period per day. Benefits may include health insurance, paid vacations, additional compensation for working holidays, and pension plans.

Conditions of work

While the casinos may be pleasant, comfortable, and nice looking, the activity may bring considerable noise and potential distraction. Many of the gamblers are friendly and easy going. They appreciate the professional attitude of the workers and often compensate them with tips.

Employees must concentrate for long periods of time, work quickly, and often have little opportunity to talk with the gamblers. Many games rely on hand signals or short phrases for communication. Evening hours are the busiest, and may remain busy until early hours of the morning.

Social and psychological factors

The gaming industry appears to be fun and recreational, but this is only an appearance. The work is fast-paced, and close work with the people may be stressful, depending on their moods.

In much the same position that bartenders are, gaming workers will deal with customers who are unable to maintain a sense of moderation over their participation. Employees must be able to handle unruly, or disturbed, patrons with tact and be able to alert management to any potential problem without creating a disturbance in the casino. Gaming employees must be able to work with all levels of experienced and inexperienced gamblers.

GOE: 09.04.01; SIC: 7999; SOC: 5254

◇ **SOURCES OF ADDITIONAL INFORMATION**

North American Simulation and Gaming Association
c/o Dr. Bahram Farzanegan
University of North Carolina—Asheville
Asheville, NC 28804

◇ **RELATED ARTICLES**

Volume 1: Hospitality, Recreation and Park Services
Volume 2: Hotel and motel managers; Recreation workers
Volume 3: Bartenders; Security guards

Homemaker-home health aides

Definition

A *homemaker-home health aide*, also known as a *home attendant*, serves elderly or infirm persons by visiting them in their homes and caring for them by doing various household chores, which the patients are unable to perform for themselves, or attending to their personal needs. They are sometimes considered a part of the nursing or medical assistance category because the tasks of the homemaker-home health aide can include carrying out certain instructions regarding prescriptions or therapies set forth by the patient's physician or nurse.

History

At one time, whenever people were unable to take care of themselves because of their advanced age and accompanying limitations, or someone suffered from a serious handicap requiring specialized medical treatment that might include a program of physical therapy or specialized diet or medications, people were confined to hospitals or sanitoriums to ensure that they would receive proper, professional care. In addition, people inflicted with contagious diseases or disabilities that required constant supervision and attention were also cared for away from their homes in institutions that were better able to provide adequate care and monitoring. Although years ago it was more likely that one parent, usually the mother, stayed home to tend the house, the needs of the infirm person often outweighed the facilities, time, and energy that one person had to offer. The "business" of running a household that did not have modern appliances and conveniences left little time for the family to tend to the needs of the terminally or seriously ill.

Rural areas often made available "visiting nurses" to check up on patients who lived far from town and lacked regular transportation for medical visits. These nurses, however, eventually discovered that the needs of the patients were more far-reaching. Patients were happy to receive the company of another person in their home, someone to read their mail to them, or help them write letters. Sometimes their needs revolved around having a few grocery items picked up from the local store. As the demand for this kind of home care advanced, home attendants found that there was a need for their services, and the profession of homemaker-home health aides began to flourish. Now, it is not only rural areas that benefit from this type of care. Cities and towns of all sizes have homemaker-home health aides attending to the diverse needs of people who for many different reasons are not self-sufficient, but particularly for aging population in general.

Furthermore, advances in modern medicine have made it possible for treatments to be taken at home for any number of illnesses. Hospitals and stores now rent items such as wheelchairs and oxygen tanks, enabling people to have medical equipment available to them in their own homes. It is also more common for people who are ill to find personal and emotional comfort in being able to recover or receive treatment in their home environment. The homemaker-home health aide is a service occupation that has benefitted from these changes and advances.

Nature of the work

The people who require the services of a homemaker-home health aide fall into many categories. The most significant group of people requiring such assistance, however, is the elderly. As people live longer, even if they are not suffering from a specific illness or handicap, the limitations of old age can make it difficult for a person to meet the daily challenges of living, especially if the person lives alone and does not have any friends or family nearby to attend to his or her needs. Visits to the grocery store or pharmacy are a necessity for everyone; however, it can be more difficult for the elderly to attend to these tasks. Likewise, the isolation that advanced age sometimes brings makes the homemaker-home health aide a vital service to the needy.

Though the elderly comprise one major group of people who rely on the help of a homemaker-home health aide, patients of any age who are recovering at home following hospitalization and children whose parent or parents are ill or neglectful are also in need of this type of assistance. Aides may be trained to supply care to people suffering from specific illnesses such as AIDS, Alzheimer's disease, or cancer, or patients who are developmentally disadvantaged and lack sufficient daily living skills.

As in many service occupations, especially those that focus on personal care and attention, the homemaker-home health aide has a variety of patients who require his or her care. County or city health agencies, departments on aging, and community-based service organizations all have patients who need assistance in life management. Because of this, aides may also find that there is a diversity of tasks they may be asked to perform. Patients who are unable to feed or dress themselves may depend on the services of a homemaker-home health aide to prepare their meal trays, feed them, and clean up after mealtime. Likewise, the homemaker-home health aide may offer assistance in dressing and grooming, including washing and bathing, cleaning teeth and nails, and shampooing the patient's hair. Massages, alcohol rubs, whirlpool baths, and other therapies and treatments may also be a part of a patient's required care. A homemaker-home health aide may also work closely with the patient's physician or home nurse in carrying out such duties as giving prescribed medications or dietary supplements.

Household chores may be another aspect of the homemaker-home health aide's responsibilities. Light housekeeping such as changing and washing bed linens, doing the laundry and ironing, and dusting may be necessary. When a homemaker-home health aide is required to look after the children of a disabled or neglectful parent, the tasks may include making lunches for the children, assisting them with their homework, or providing company and supervision in the evening hours. Personal attention and comfort is also a necessary aspect of an aide's care. Reading to children, playing games, or visiting with an elderly patient can also be a suitable way for a homemaker-home health aide to provide support. Because elderly persons do not always have the means to venture out alone to the store or for a walk, a homemaker-home health aide may accompany an ambulatory patient to the park for an afternoon or to the physician's office for an appointment.

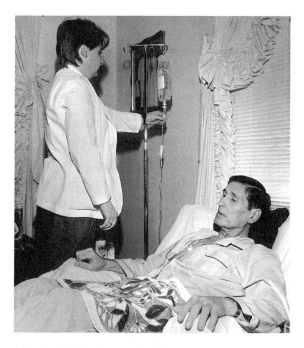

A home health aide adjusts a patient's intravenous device.

Requirements

An even temperament and a willingness to serve others are important characteristics for a homemaker-home health aide. Aides should be friendly, patient, sensitive to a patient's needs, and tactful. At times an aide will also have to be stern in dealing with people who may not be very cooperative or in the best spirits because they are uncomfortable or in pain. Genuine warmth and respect are also attributes that can make the responsibilities of caring for others an enjoyable and rewarding profession.

Because the tasks of the homemaker-home health aide vary so greatly, and the range of potential responsibilities is great, aides should be in good physical condition themselves. Many times an aide will have to assist patients in and out of chairs, up and down stairs, or help them get up from their beds. This can be very strenuous work and requires a fair amount of strength.

Most agencies will offer training to homemaker-home health aides if they have no previous experience in caring for others. Such training may include instruction on how to deal with a depressed or reluctant patient, how to prepare easy and nutritious meals, and tips on housekeeping. Specific course work on health and sanitation may also be required.

A homemaker-home health aide must be willing to follow instructions and abide by the health plan created for each individual patient. Aides provide an important outreach service, supporting the care administered by the patient's physician, therapist, or social worker.

Special requirements

In 1982, the National Homecaring Council developed *A Model Curriculum and Teaching Guide for the Instruction of the Homemaker-Home Health Aide.* The training set forth in this curriculum proposed instruction that combined classroom study and hands-on experience. Sixty hours of classroom instruction is supplemented by an additional fifteen hours of field work. Though this curriculum is still in the proposal stage, it reflects the widespread desire to upgrade training and curriculum for people in the homemaker-home health aide field. Advanced training would ensure a higher quality of preparation and performance on the part of the workers.

Local hospitals may offer their own programs for training in the field of homemaker-home health aide, or in conjunction with the health service agencies in the area. County and city sponsored agencies and programs may also have specific course work required prior to their employees entering the field. Required training for homemaker-home health aides, however, varies between agencies. Many programs require only a high-school diploma for entry level positions. Previous or additional course work in home economics, cooking, sewing, and meal planning are very helpful. Also, courses that focus on family living and home nursing are a plus.

Agencies are most likely to focus their training on first aid, hygiene, and principals of health care. Cooking and nutrition, including meal preparation for patients with specific dietary needs, are often an aspect of instruction. Homemaker-home health aides are often offered course work in psychology and child development, as well as family living. Hands-on experience can be a vital area of training. Aides may learn how to bathe, dress, and feed patients, as well as learning how to help them walk upstairs or get up from bed. The more specific the skill required for certain patients, the more an agency is likely to have more comprehensive instruction.

Opportunities for experience and exploration

Because there are many different areas in which homemaker-home health aides are employed, a person interested in finding out more about this line of work could contact any number of local agencies and programs and request information on the organization's employment guidelines or training programs. Visiting the county or city health department and asking to speak to a personnel director may provide useful information as well. Often, local organizations sponsor "open house" type events to enlighten the community to the services they provide. This could serve as an excellent opportunity to meet the staff people involved in hiring and program development.

Related occupations

The health care field is large and offers many opportunities for people with interests similar to those required of homemaker-home health aides. Other occupations that might be suitable include nursing and psychiatric aides, licensed practical nurses, food service workers, dietitians, dietetic technicians, medical laboratory technologists, physicians, and podiatrists.

Methods of entering

Some social services enlist the assistance of volunteers. By contacting the agencies and inquiring about such openings, a person pursuing the homemaker-home health aide field could get an early introduction to the type of work this profession requires.

Checking the local yellow pages for agencies that provide health care to the aged or disabled or organizations that focus on family services can provide a list of employment prospects. Nursing homes, public and private health care facilities, and local chapters of the Red Cross and United Way are likely to hire entry-level employees. The National Homecaring Council can also send information on reputable agencies and departments who employ homemaker-home health aides.

Advancement

As homemaker-home health aides develop their skills and deepen their experience they may find advancement into management or supervisory positions. Those who find the most enjoyment working with their patients may branch off to more specialized care and pursue additional training. Additional experience and education can often bring higher pay and increased responsibility.

Aides may wish to work in a clinic or hospital setting, and will return to school to complete a nursing degree. Social workers, therapists, and registered dietitians are also related fields in which a homemaker-home health aide may wish to move. Along with a desire for advancement, however, must come the willingness to meet any additional education requirements.

Employment outlook

As government and private agencies develop more programs to assist the dependent, the need for homemaker-home health aides continues to grow. In the early 1990s approximately 1.3 million persons worked in health care. Government statistics indicate an anticipated increase of 35 percent through the mid-1990s.

Because the purpose of the services provided is to help as many people as possible, the need for such professionals may continue such growth for some time. People are living to more advanced ages, and many employment benefits packages are including home health care options. Hospital and nursing home facilities attempt to balance increases in staff and limitations in physical facilities. The availability of homemaker-home health aides can allow such institutions to augment personnel without overcrowding.

Earnings

Earnings for homemaker-home health aides are commensurate with salaries in related health care positions. There can be considerable flexibility in working hours depending on the agency as well as the patient load an aide carries. For many aides who begin as part time employees, their starting salary is usually the minimum hourly wage. For full-time aides who have significant training or experience, their earning scale may be around $6 per hour. Larger agencies, however, can pay as much as $8 per hour for a forty-hour week.

There are no set guidelines for vacations and benefits packages, as these vary with the type and size of the employing agency. Many full-time homemaker-home health aides, however, receive one week paid vacation following their first year of employment, and often receive two weeks paid vacation for the following years of service. Full-time aides can also be eligible for health insurance and retirement benefit. Though the hours that an aide may work can vary depending on their patients' needs, there is the possibility for employees to receive holiday or overtime compensation.

Conditions of work

Because homemaker-home health aides may have more than one patient, the hours an aide works can fluctuate with the tasks required. Many of the patients an aide cares for may be ill or disabled, some may be elderly and have no one else to assist them with light housekeeping or daily errands. These differences can dictate the type of responsibilities a homemaker-home health aide may have for each patient.

Working with the infirm or disabled can be a rewarding experience, as an aide enhances the quality of their lives with their help and company. However, the personal strains, on the patients as well as the aides, can make the work challenging and at times frustrating. There is considerable physical activity involved in this line of work, either helping patients to walk or dress, not to mention travelling from one home to another and running various errands for them.

Social and psychological factors

In some instances, a homemaker-home health aide is a patient's only company, comfort, and assistance in their lives. The potential for deep appreciation and friendship is very high in this service profession. Some aides may find it difficult balancing the needs of many different patients, each with their own set of needs. There is little consistency in the home environments that a homemaker-home health aide may work, and there can be significant stress in trying to care for people who may be quite dependent.

GOE: 11.02.03; SIC: 8082; SOC: 5263

◇ **SOURCES OF ADDITIONAL INFORMATION**

National Homecaring Council
Division of the Foundation for Hospice and Home Care
519 C Street, NE
Washington, DC 20002

◇ **RELATED ARTICLES**

Volume 1: Health Care; Personal Services
Volume 2: Dental hygienists; Dentists; Dietitians; Health services administrators; Human services workers; Occupational therapists; Physicians; Physician assistants; Podiatrists; Psychologists; Social workers
Volume 3: Nursing and psychiatric aides
Volume 4: Medical and health technician occupations

Hotel and motel industry workers

Definition

Hotel and motel industry workers provide a variety of services to their guests to keep them comfortable. Some workers perform housekeeping duties such as laundering linens, cleaning rooms, and providing extra pillows or blankets for the guests. Other employees handle reservations and accommodations. Employees who work in the coffee shops and restaurants of the lodge may purchase food and supplies, cook, or serve the guests or prepare trays to be brought up by room service or bellpersons. The hotel and motel industry is very developed, but managers and owners still work hard to improve services and accommodations and give people a reason to return.

History

The hotel and motel industry has experienced a phenomenal development because the first public inn was built in Jamestown, Virginia, in 1607. Lodging houses no longer offer only a roof over one's head, a bed, and a meal. Hotels now cater to political fund-raising events, weddings and other formal parties, meetings and sales seminars. One area where the hotel industry has gained reputation and increased revenue is hosting conventions. Large conventions can bring nearly one thousand people into a city. Hotels benefit by providing rooms, meals, meeting centers, and hospitality suites to the executives, teachers, and tradespeople who attend conventions annually. Some larger hotels accept convention bookings prior to accepting reservations for any other significant event or party. For this and other reasons, it is no wonder that the hotel and motel industry employs over one million people.

Nature of the work

It takes a considerable staff to run a hotel or even a medium-sized motel. There are many services to provide, and even with certain work categories overlapping, there is much work to be done to ensure the comfort and enjoyment of the guests. Basically, most hotel employees fall into one of the following categories: managers and executives, department heads and assistants, customer-assistance workers, and service employees.

Manager positions are often broken up into *manager* and *assistant manager* roles. Managers oversee the other departments and have leaders or department heads who report to them or initiate changes or developments the manager introduces. Managers may set room rates and rates for fees and services, such as room service or phone calls. Managers also keep track of profit margins for individual categories as well as for the entire hotel. Assistant managers may be in charge in the absence of the manager and are expected to carry out procedures and regulations according to the manager's guidelines.

Hotel executives function in the business end of the industry. While managers work to ensure quality service and realize a profit, executives often perform duties that focus on the hotel as a product to be sold. Advertising campaigns, getaway specials, image improvement, and name recognition are some of the areas of concentration for hotel executives. Often, executives may work with advertising agencies, departments of tourism, or travel agents to continue to get exposure and plan advertising campaigns. In chain hotels, executives from different cities may meet and discuss other ways to promote the hotel to travellers.

Department heads are supervisors that are often in charge of staff or related services. These workers may be assigned for such areas as reservations, housekeeping, food and beverage, personnel, or other categories.

The employee who acts as supervisor for housekeeping may train *housekeepers* and *maids* to clean and inspect rooms, stock linens and toiletries, and provide additional services such as picking up and delivering dry cleaning, or supplying rooms with irons or additional hangers. Housekeeping supervisors may make up work schedules for maids, assign rooms to be cleaned, and keep current records on which rooms are clean and available to incoming guests.

Reservation managers may also train new reservations clerks how to use office computers to enter arrival and departure dates, credit card information, and instruct them in the proper way to handle difficult phone calls or requests. These employees may also be in charge of room clerks or other front office workers who assist guests in registering and perform other information services for hotel guests. Reservation managers keep records of guests, how many rooms are available for busy holiday weekends and report these figures to the hotel manager. Reservation managers must be prepared to handle such crises as overbooking or a lost reservation. An error or oversight such as this may damage the reputation of the establishment.

Many times *food and beverage department heads* will work with kitchen or lounge staff in larger restaurants. They purchase liquor and soft drink supplies, as well as food items and groceries. They often receive visits from manufacturers' representatives who supply them with their products. They may try a new brand of coffee or barbecue sauce and introduce it to the kitchen staff. Sometimes the supervisor of this department works in conjunction with the chef or executive chef. In addition, the food and beverage supervisor may keep track of sales and record inventory stock for reordering purposes. Sometimes they train waiters, waitresses, bus boys, and bartenders. Food quality and production is also monitored and evaluated.

Executive chefs are in charge of the hotel kitchen and has such duties as developing the menu, setting prices, hiring or training cooks and chefs, buying supplies, and handling inventory. The executive chef may also buy some of the finer wines that are recommended with dinner or work with the hotel's wine steward to plan appropriate combinations.

Doorkeepers, bell captains, and *bellpersons* perform various duties that center around greeting guests, assisting with transportation such as cabs or courtesy vans. They may also park cars, assist guests with luggage, and act as general customer service employees. Security personnel work with the general safety and well-being of the guests and employees. They may be asked to visit a room where the guests are making too much noise, work undercover to watch for pickpockets or thieves during hectic summer months, or discourage nonguests from loitering in the hotel for no apparent reason.

Requirements

Persons who work in the hotel and motel industry should enjoy working with people. For some positions, such as maids and room cleaners, cooks, and certain clerical or support staff jobs, even though the employees may not have direct contact with guests, they must work with possibly hundreds of other employees to offer the best possible service and accommodations possible. Workers should be responsive to a

The manager of customer relations at a hotel organizes the accommodations for a large party with the assistance of her colleague.

hectic pace and respectful of the image and reputation the hotel strives to maintain.

Most positions require a high-school diploma or equivalency certificate. More sophisticated jobs may require some college training or technical–high-school training. Course work in English, communications, data processing, or business may provide a good background for entering into one of the beginning service positions in this industry.

Special requirements

Different positions in the hotel and motel industry require different training and preparation. Many opportunities are available to graduates of hotel and motel management schools. Many two-year colleges have programs in cooking and food service as well as reservations services and tourism. Four-year colleges may provide course work in management, accounting, public relations, and home economics.

Additional information on employment opportunities and necessary training may be available from numerous organizations associated with the industry. The Educational Institute of the American Hotel and Motel Association and the Council on Hotel, Restaurant, and Institutional Education offer information on education and training. The American Culinary Federation supports workers in the food service industry. Union affiliations include the Hotel Employees and Restaurant Employees International Union.

By becoming more familiar with the types of positions available, students may be able to research and plan the training and education accordingly.

Opportunities for experience and exploration

Magazines on travel and tourism, newspaper travel supplements, and the Yellow Pages section of phone books can supply information on area hotels and their addresses. Requesting application materials may offer additional guidelines on positions currently available and necessary preparation. Human resource departments may conduct general interviews for service staff and place applicants where they might fit best or interview for specific positions. Most any type of position in the industry will teach new and valuable skills and offer experience for job advancement.

Related occupations

The travel and tourism industry is an enormous multinational industry that offers a wide variety of occupational opportunities. Other jobs that might be of interest include hotel and motel managers, travel agents, airline flight attendants, and transportation ticket clerks and agents.

Methods of entering

Many hotels seek additional help during the summer months when travel and vacation seasons are high. Some hotel positions require on-the-job training, however, previous course work in computer science or data processing, home economics, or bookkeeping may provide skills to land an entry-level position. Interested applicants should contact motels or hotels to inquire about availabilities and application materials. College or technical school graduates may contact their placement offices for information on interviews or send resumes and cover letters to the human resource department of the hotels they wish to apply at.

Advancement

Hotel and motel employees may seek advancement in a number of ways. Some employees in entry level positions may take on additional responsibilities after gaining adequate experience. Many hotels post open positions at the personnel office, and some establishments make it a policy to promote from within when possible. For instance, room clerks may be promoted to reservations clerks, bellpersons may become bell captains, and so on.

Working in the hotel industry can educate employees to the kinds of opportunities available in that business. Interested people should also consider classes that will give them the appropriate skills for advancement. Of course, experience and good performance are always a path toward a better position; however, some employees may realize that additional education and training are necessary.

Employment outlook

Because larger hotels are pursuing other types of business besides tourism, such as conventions, sales seminars, and so on, they often stay busy all year long and require the additional staff members for support. Opportunities may be best with larger hotels and chains, as they can offer more avenues for advancement as well as more job security.

There are considerable opportunities, however, at smaller hotels and motels. Some establishments are not large in size or do not have nationwide accommodations, but are, rather, small and exclusive. The travel industry continues to grow, and more than half the employees in the hotel industry are part-time and nearly half are younger than twenty-four years old. The industry can have many openings for trained, full-time employees.

Earnings

Wages for hotel and motel employees vary with the kind of work, training, and shifts assigned. Entry-level general service employees often start with the minimum wage. For employees scheduled on night shifts, the hourly wage or overall salaries are higher.

Service employees, such as waitresses, waiters, and bartenders, may earn between $4 and $7 per hour. A significant portion of their income, however, comes from tips and gratuities.

College graduates with degrees or certification in hotel and motel management may earn annual salaries between $13,000 and $20,000 as managers in training. General managers may average salaries of $36,000, depending on the size and location of the hotel. Experience, too, is a big factor as managers in exclusive hotels may earn more than $60,000 per year.

Executive chef positions are in demand in this industry and can command more than $90,000 per year, though many earn closer to $35,000. Cooks may earn up to $10 per hour in some areas and general kitchen helpers may earn close to $4 per hour.

Raises are typically given annually and are sometimes accompanied by an employee review, conducted by the department head or supervisor. Increases may be based on years of service, merit, promotion, or additional education or training pursued.

Conditions of work

Employees in most any area of the hotel and motel industry enjoy pleasant, clean, and comfortable working conditions. Many hotels have modern kitchens that provide good ventilation and adequate work space. Many establishments have modern electronic equipment, whether for security purposes or office automation, to create a more efficient work flow.

The hotel and motel industry, however, may be quite fast paced. The staff's primary responsibility is to ensure the comfort of the guests, and that can be a challenge to cater to hundreds of individual needs. The employees, however, can take great pride in knowing that they have made a particular trip enjoyable for the hotel patrons by offering them warmth and good service.

Social and psychological factors

There are considerable opportunities in the hotel and motel industry for people who enjoy working with others and who can provide courtesy and service to travellers. Hours and shifts can be varied to accommodate personal schedules or school careers. There is a significant opportunity for advancement and often the salaries and fringe benefits are good. The hectic pace and the responsibility of working holidays, however, can be difficult to manage as well as catering to difficult or demanding guests.

GOE: 07.04.03; SIC: 7011; SOC: 4643

◇ **SOURCES OF ADDITIONAL INFORMATION**

American Hotel & Motel Association
1201 New York Avenue, NW
Washington, DC 20005

Educational Institute of the American Hotel & Motel Association
PO Box 1240
East Lansing, MI 48826

◇ **RELATED ARTICLES**

Volume 1: Hospitality; Travel and Tourism
Volume 2: Hotel and motel managers
Volume 3: Cooks, chefs, and bakers; Hotel clerks; Hotel housekeepers and assistants; Reservation and transportation ticket agents

Hotel housekeepers and assistants

Definition

Hotel housekeepers and *assistants* perform the many kinds of jobs necessary in keeping a hotel neat, clean, and attractive to the public and hotel guests. Hotel housekeepers are responsible for the assistants such as maids and other employees. In the very large hotels, they may be assisted in their supervisory duties by floor housekeepers.

Their major role is supervising workers who clean the guest rooms. This includes laundry duties as well as maid service. Housekeepers may also be responsible for physical maintenance of rooms and furniture, for which they supervise repainting and repair work.

History

The colonial inns of early American days, located along the stagecoach routes, provided places where tired travelers could stop and rest overnight. Travelers in those days found few conveniences beyond beds and plain food.

Innkeepers took care of most of the inn's business and often the innkeeper's family saw to the housekeeping chores, or there was a "hired helper" who earned room and board and a small wage by taking care of the housework.

In 1829, the famous Tremont House Hotel in Boston was opened to traveling guests, and in 1836, the Astor House in New York opened. As new hotels were built, the conveniences for guests increased, as well as the size of the hotel and the number of guests to be accommodated. More help was needed to keep the hotel and guest rooms clean, neat, and comfortable. As hotels continued to expand in size, hotel housekeepers were employed to supervise, organize, and train the employees in the work of hotel housekeeping.

Nature of the work

Individuals employed as hotel housekeepers hold responsible jobs. They must see that the hotel is kept neat, clean, and attractive in appearance at all times. In some very large hotels, these workers are given the job title of executive housekeeper. Their duties usually entail hiring, training, organizing, and supervising the work of cleaning assistants, linen room attendants, and sometimes repairers and other service employees. They may also have the responsibility for discharging employees in their department. Hotel housekeepers are often charged with the responsibility of keeping employee records; purchasing and ordering supplies, hotel furniture, and housekeeping equipment; and reporting needed repairs and the condition of the rooms and furnishings to the hotel manager. In some hotels, they may have varied responsibilities in suggesting or overseeing interior decorating work. Hotel housekeepers in very large hotels may be responsible for supervising staffs of sometimes several hundred people and in such a situation their job is primarily one of administrative duty. In smaller hotels, they must sometimes perform some of the work themselves, such as the job duties carried out by house cleaning assistants or other employees.

Very large hotels may have housekeeper floor supervisors to assist the executive housekeepers in supervisory work.

Assistant workers, formerly called *maids*, perform job duties in general cleaning around the hotel and guest rooms. The job duties may include emptying trash, making beds, collecting soiled linen and replacing it with fresh supplies, dusting, vacuuming, keeping furniture polished and properly arranged, and cleaning and supplying bathrooms. Some of the larger hotels employ assistants whose only duties are keeping guest room baths in immaculate and polished order.

Cleaning assistants sometimes keep utility and linen rooms orderly, stocked, and inventoried, or these responsibilities may be carried out by linen room attendants or other service employees.

Seamstresses are usually employed to repair hotel linens, drapes, bed spreads, employee uniforms, and other items that are subject to wear and tear in hotel operation.

Other assistant workers usually perform routine cleaning and heavy lifting duties. They may clean rugs, upholster furniture, clean rooms, lobbies, and lounges, set up furniture in meeting rooms, or make ready areas for special banquets or other functions.

Housekeepers and some types of assistant workers may also be employed in motels throughout the nation today. Unless the place of employment is a very large motel, however, housekeepers in charge of other employees usually perform some of the same work duties as the assistant employees.

Requirements

Hotel housekeepers and assistants are not required to have any special degree of formal educational preparation; as in any occupation, however, the minimum of a high-school education enhances the individual's chances for advancement to jobs of greater responsibility and opportunity. This would hold true especially for the housekeepers and executive housekeepers.

The job of hotel housekeeper or executive housekeeper often requires former job experience either in hotel work as floor supervisor or in other comparable situations, such as in hospital settings. Some type of formal training or specialized preparation may be required for these positions. The National Executive Housekeepers Association requires a minimum of seventy-seven hours of course training to hold a certified membership in their organization.

An institution such as Kellogg Center at Michigan State University in East Lansing, Michigan, provides educational opportunities for accumulating course hours in this type of training. Many individuals who enter such training are already employed in some type of hotel housekeeping work.

Some colleges and universities offer short-period training courses, evening or extension division courses where employees may learn some of the skills of hotel and personnel management in housekeeping. Cooperative courses are sometimes set up with the assistance of the National Executive Housekeepers Association. Four universities currently offer the degree of bachelor of science in administrative housekeeping. The first of the four schools to offer such a program was the University of Washington in Seattle, Washington. Other course work may be offered by colleges and universities having hotel housekeeping divisions in schools of home economics and in those having departments of hotel, restaurant, and institutional management.

Some hotels provide on-the-job training for assistant workers. With employees who have held one or more of the assistant positions, the hotel may choose to promote from within for training into the housekeeper post. They may also hire new employees to train for the position.

No specific aptitudes are of special importance for maids; a congenial, friendly, and patient temperament, however, is a definite asset because these employees work in a public setting among many people. For these jobs, initiative and integrity are important qualities.

Individuals need to possess good physical stamina to keep up with the usual rigorous pace of this type of service work. Workers might be hampered in performing their job duties if they possess any serious physical impairments restricting physical movement.

Working conditions in hotels are usually in pleasant surroundings; the job duties, however, performed by some assistant workers may not be thought of as the most desirable in that the work may be physically strenuous and involve primarily cleaning duties.

Special requirements

There are no special requirements, such as licensure or certification, demanded of individuals for these occupations. Many hotel housekeepers belong to the National Executive Housekeepers Association, but this is not a requirement for this job.

A hotel housekeeper straightens up a room and makes the bed while the customer is out. In hotels and motels, such tasks must be completed daily.

Opportunities for experience and exploration

Individuals who are interested in hotel housekeeping jobs may further explore the occupation by talking with their high-school guidance counselors and by visiting and talking with persons employed in this work in hotels.

A part-time summer job as an assistant in the service department of a hotel might enable students to explore interest in this type of work and also allow for observation of the hotel housekeeper's job duties. Persons interested in executive hotel housekeeping through college degree or formal educational training might write or visit institutions offering such programs.

Related occupations

The hotel and motel industry, as well as travel and tourism more broadly, offer a wide range of career opportunities. Other jobs that might be of interest include hotel and motel managers, hotel clerks, bellhops, waiters and waitresses, travel agents, tour guides, janitors and cleaners, and clerks.

Hotel housekeepers and assistants
Service Occupations

Methods of entering

The majority of jobs obtained by assistants are by direct personal application to the personnel managers of hotels and motels. Many times these jobs are also located through state employment offices, through newspaper advertisements, or through friends who know that jobs are open. Former work experience and good character references are important to assistant hotel workers when seeking this kind of employment.

Hotel housekeepers may also seek employment by direct application to the hotel personnel manager. These jobs, however, are more frequently located through job listings with employment bureaus, training school placement offices, or through newspapers or professional hotel magazine publications. Experience, formal training, and personal recommendations may weigh heavily in obtaining these jobs.

Advancement

Assistant workers do not have many opportunities open to them for advancement. They may move in job location to larger and better hotels and sometimes receive higher wages, depending on their training and experience. Some assistants may be considered for jobs as floor or assistant housekeepers.

Hotel housekeepers may be promoted to executive housekeepers in the very large hotels or first to assistant executive housekeepers. These jobs are usually the top-ranking ones in a hotel's service department. Some advancement may be gained through regular wage advances or by moving to jobs in larger hotels.

Employment outlook

In the early 1990s, about 23,000 persons were employed by hotels and motels as housekeepers and assistants. Many openings for housekeepers and their assistants are expected each year through the late 1990s. The majority of the openings will occur to meet the need for replacing retired workers or to replace those who have changed occupations.

The expanding number of hotels and large motels are creating some new jobs, especially in large cities.

Jobs as hotel housekeepers are somewhat limited, as are jobs as executive housekeepers, by the fact that there is usually just one position of this type in a hotel. More vacancies,

however, are reported than there are qualified people to fill them. Job turnover for these positions may be rather low, and it sometimes takes years for a vacancy to occur in one hotel. Comparable positions may be open in hospitals, college and university residence halls, and in some state schools or hospitals.

Job openings for assistant hotel workers, such as maids, are expected to be in the thousands through the early 1990s. Most of these openings will occur as a result of deceased or retired workers or to replace those who have taken jobs in other fields.

Many temporary job openings occur for assistant workers in resort hotels and motels that are open on a seasonal basis, or have a seasonal rush period. The job-turnover rate among these assistant workers is high.

Earnings

The earnings of hotel housekeepers and assistants depend on a number of factors, such as the size, location, and type of hotel and, for assistant workers, the additional amount that may accrue from tips. Duties and responsibilities may also help to determine salary ranges.

For hotel housekeepers and executive housekeepers the additional factors of former experience and formal education, particularly a college degree, help to determine the wages to be earned. Sometimes wages are partly determined by the number of workers to be supervised and in proportion to the approximate operating hotel budget. Because of these factors, housekeepers' annual salaries range from $9,000 to $48,000 a year, with $24,000 as the average.

Wages are generally lower for housekeepers and assistants in southern cities than in other parts of the country. Some hotels provide assistant workers with one free meal while on duty.

Conditions of work

The working conditions for hotel housekeepers and executive housekeepers are usually in pleasant surroundings. These workers are sometimes given free living accommodations in the hotel and, although they have regularly scheduled work hours, they may also be on call twenty-four hours a day.

The work hours for all of these employees, including the assistants, is usually a forty- to forty-eight-hour workweek. In some few cities, employees work less than a forty-hour work-week. Hotels are open twenty-four hours daily and the assistant workers, especially, may work three rotating shifts, morning, afternoon, or evening. Skeleton crews are usually on duty throughout the night. Some hotels pay a slightly higher wage for employees who work the "graveyard" (all-night) shift.

These employees usually receive paid vacations of one or more weeks depending upon their years of service. Some hotels give certain holidays off with pay and other fringe benefits may include group life and hospitalization insurance, laundry-free uniforms, and some free meals.

The work of hotel housekeepers or executive housekeepers may not be as physically strenuous as that of the assistant workers. Many of the former's duties are supervisory and administrative in nature, and yet they may be required to be on their feet many hours a day, overseeing work performed.

Assistant workers, however, usually perform many physically strenuous tasks that require stooping, lifting, reaching, pushing, and pulling. The occupation, however, is not considered a hazardous one.

Social and psychological factors

Hotel housekeepers and assistants need to be able to get along with all types of people. A congenial, friendly attitude is an asset as there may be occasional contact with the hotel guests.

The hotel housekeepers need some talent and ability in organizing and directing the work of others and in giving work orders in a manner acceptable to others. Assistant workers must be able and willing to follow the directions of their supervisors and also satisfied to perform many routine and repetitive tasks in their jobs.

GOE: 05.12.18; SIC: 7011; SOC: 5241

◇ **SOURCES OF ADDITIONAL INFORMATION**

American Hotel & Motel Association
1201 New York Avenue
Washington, DC 20005

National Executive Housekeepers Association, Inc.
1001 Eastwind Drive, Suite 301
Westerville, OH 43081

◇ **RELATED ARTICLES**

Volume 1: Hospitality; Travel and Tourism
Volume 2: Hotel and motel managers
Volume 3: Hotel clerks; Private household workers

Janitors and cleaners

Definition

Building custodians, or *janitors,* are responsible for the care and maintenance of a variety of buildings, such as apartment houses, hospitals, office buildings, manufacturing plants and other public structures.

Care of the building includes daily maintenance work, and some repair work when needed. Daily maintenance includes cleaning, washing, and other janitorial functions. It also may include monitoring heating and cooling systems.

History

Prior to the Industrial Revolution, individual entrepreneurs assigned the maintenance of business premises to a servant or an employee, or did the work themselves. The development of big business, of towering skyscrapers and vast plants required the services of a special person or persons to assume this task. The postwar population explosion and resultant building upsurge, from hospitals to apartment houses, spurred the demand for more janitors.

While the offices of a library are being remodeled, a janitor takes the opportunity to clean the light fixtures.

Nature of the work

Janitors perform a wide range of jobs, using materials that vary from simple mops for washing floors, to power tools for making minor repairs. They are responsible for selecting the proper methods and equipment that will enable them to clean and maintain the structure in which they work. They clean offices and hallways; tend to furnaces so that heating needs are adequate; maintain plumbing facilities; eliminate insects and rodents, or arrange for an exterminator to do the job; remove refuse; repair minor damages to the building; and handle complaints, directing them to the proper authority.

In specific settings they may be called *commercial* or *institutional cleaners* or *industrial cleaners*. Those known as *wall cleaners* and *floor waxers* perform the specific duties suggested by their job titles. *Central supply workers* clean, sterilize, and assemble hospital equipment, supplies, and instruments. Similar duties are performed by *laboratory equipment cleaners* in other industries.

Janitors who direct the work of others include *building superintendents*, *janitorial services supervisors*, and *maintenance supervisors*.

Requirements

No special educational requirements exist. Those seeking entry, however, should be able to do simple arithmetic and follow instructions. Tact and courtesy in dealing with people are assets, along with physical strength and manual agility.

Special requirements

There are no special requirements other than those already mentioned.

Opportunities for experience and exploration

High-school shop courses may help custodians perform the variety of tasks required in their jobs. In some cities, unions and government agencies offer training programs, some of which include remedial courses in reading, writing, and arithmetic. Familiarity with cleaning tools and materials, whether gained through part-time employment or in maintaining personal premises, will prove helpful.

Related occupations

Other jobs with similar skill requirements and interests include hotel housekeepers and assistants and private household workers.

Methods of entering

Entry into jobs may be obtained through filing application with state employment offices or companies, or by responding to want ads. Skills are usually learned through on-the-job training.

Advancement

More complex tasks are usually assigned beginners who have gained experience with the various cleaners and tools. If the custodian is the only maintenance employee in a building, advancement opportunities are limited. Supervisory positions are possible, however, for those who work on a large maintenance staff, especially for those who hold a high-school diploma. Some custodians go into their own business and provide building maintenance to a number of clients on a fee basis. Some administrative skill is necessary to do this.

Employment outlook

In the early 1990s, more than 3.1 million janitors were employed in the United States.

Population growth, general affluence, and the upsurge in building augur a favorable outlook for building custodian jobs through the late 1990s. This promising trend will be somewhat offset, however, by innovations in cleaning and maintenance technology that have reduced the physical effort involved in custodial work.

Earnings

Earnings vary widely, depending on industry and geographical location. Full-time janitors earned an average of $13,100 in the early 1990s. Most earned between $10,900 and $24,050.

Conditions of work

The use of hazardous tools and machines may result in a variety of minor cuts, bruises, and burns. Indoor and outdoor work may be required, as well as evening work. Custodians who are required to move a great deal of furniture, or are continually bending and lifting, may develop physical problems.

Social and psychological factors

Limited paths to advancement may create a sense of frustration. However, custodians set

their own hours and pace of work. Some are required to work night or early morning shifts. The work is physically strenuous, and janitors who work with machinery maintenance and heating systems need to adjust to the noise, grease, and general physical strain. In addition, the variety of jobs, whether dealing with tenants or the building, rarely results in boredom.

GOE: 05.12.18; SIC: 7349; SOC: 5244

◇ **SOURCES OF ADDITIONAL INFORMATION**

Cleaning Management Institute
15550-D Rockfield Boulevard
Irvine, CA 92718

National Executive Housekeepers Association
1001 Eastwind Drive
Suite 301
Westerville, OH 43081

◇ **RELATED ARTICLES**

Volume 1: Hospitality
Volume 3: Hotel housekeepers and assistants; Security guards; Stationary engineers
Volume 4: Air-conditioning, heating, and refrigeration technicians

Meatcutters

Definition

Meatcutters are concerned with cutting animal carcasses into smaller portions and preparing

meat, poultry, and fish for sale in food outlets or for cooking in hotels and restaurants. Meatcutters are also known as butchers when they are employed in or run retail stores.

A meat cutter in a slaughterhouse slices a pig into marketable slabs of meat. Nearly all parts of a pig can be processed and consumed.

History

In early America, one person often performed the entire procedure of slaughtering, cutting up, and marketing meat. Refrigeration, rapid mass transportation, population growth, affluence, and increased emphasis upon good nutrition sparked the phenomenal expansion of the meat industry in the post–Civil War period.

Automation and supermarket requirements are rapidly changing the character of this job. Power tools and machines have already displaced some meatcutters, and the growing tendency to centralize the cutting and distribution of meat in a given area will eliminate still more positions.

Nature of the work

Meatcutters use special tools such as band saws, power cutters, butcher knives, cleavers, and electric grinders to divide animal carcasses into smaller portions and prepare the meat for sale in a wholesale or retail food outlet or for cooking in hotels and restaurants. For easier handling, the carcasses are cut into quarters before shipment from a meat packing plant or central distribution center. Meatcutters first divide the quarters into rounds, loins, and ribs, and then into serving-size portions such as roasts, steaks, and chops. Less expensive cuts and meat trimmings are cut into stewing pieces or ground into hamburger. Meats cut for sale in food outlets must then be weighed, priced, labeled, and graded according to government standards. Some meatcutters specialize as *chicken and fish butchers.*

In retail stores, *meatcutters,* often called *butchers,* are responsible for displaying the food properly, waiting on customers, and cutting or-ders to meet special needs. They may also filet fish, dress poultry, make sausage, and pickle meats. Selection of meats from wholesale distributors, record keeping, and inventory maintenance are also important aspects of the job.

In hotels and restaurants, *meatcutters* are usually referred to as meat butchers. Their duties involve both large quantities and individual portions and may include estimating requirements and ordering meat supplies, inspecting and storing meat upon delivery, and keeping records. A head butcher has the responsibility of supervising the work of other butchers. Other related occupations include *schactors, all around butchers,* and *meat dressers,* whose work is concerned with the slaughter and preparation of carcasses.

Requirements

Most employers prefer applicants who have a high-school diploma and the potential to develop into managers. The majority of meatcutters acquire their skills on the job, many through apprentice programs. A few attend schools specializing in the trade, but they still require additional training and experience after graduation before they can work as meatcutters.

Trainees begin by doing odd jobs such as removing bones and fat from retail cuts. Gradually they are taught to use power tools and equipment; how to prepare various cuts of meat, poultry, and fish; and how to make sausage and cure meats. Later they may learn such things as inventory control, meat buying, and record keeping. Those in an apprentice program must pass a meatcutting test at the end of their apprenticeship.

Meatcutters who wait on customers need a pleasant personality, neat appearance, and the ability to communicate clearly. Above-average strength is needed to lift large, heavy pieces of meat.

Special requirements

Important skills for this occupation are manual dexterity, good depth perception, color discrimination, and good eye-hand coordination.

A health certificate may be required, and many cutters are members of the United Food and Commercial Workers International Union.

Opportunities for experience and exploration

Summer or part-time employment in retail food stores, wholesale food outlets, or restaurant and institutional kitchens is one means of acquiring experience. Some vocational schools offer courses in meatcutting. School counselors may be a source of guidance. Interviews with meatcutters and field trips to meat packing plants may prove useful.

Related occupations

Other people whose work includes skills and aptitudes similar to meatcutters include fast-food workers, food service workers, restaurant managers, and supermarket managers.

Methods of entering

The usual path of entry to meatcutting is to apply for a job with a retail or wholesale food company that has an apprenticeship program. After about two years of on-the-job training, sometimes coupled with classroom work, apprentices are given a meatcutting test in the presence of their employer and, in a union shop, a union member. Those who fail the exam may take it again at a later time. In some areas, apprentices who can pass the test may not have to complete the training program. Information about work opportunities may be obtained from local employers or local offices of the state employment service.

Advancement

Experienced meatcutters may be promoted to supervisory positions, such as meat department manager in a supermarket. A few become buyers for wholesalers and supermarket chains. Some become grocery store managers or open their own meat markets.

Employment outlook

Meatcutters held 222,000 jobs in the early 1990s, mostly in retail stores but also in wholesale stores, restaurants, hotels, hospitals, and other institutions. The number of meatcutters is expected to decline slightly through the late 1990s. One reason is the growing practice of central cutting—that is, the cutting and wrapping of meat in one location for distribution to other outlets—by supermarket chains and meat packing plants. Central cutting increases efficiency by permitting cutters to specialize in type of meat and type of cut. Nevertheless, many entry jobs will become available as older workers retire, die, or leave the profession.

Earnings

In the early 1990s, meatcutters earned between $13 and $19 an hour, the cutters in urban areas being paid more than those in smaller cities. Assuming a 40-hour week, these workers earn from $27,450 to $39,900 a year. Beginning apprentices usually earn between 60 and 70 percent of an experienced cutter's wage, with increases every 6 months. Among grocery store occupations, meatcutters earn the highest wages.

Conditions of work

Health and safety standards require clean and sanitary work areas. Places of employment are usually comfortable, but physical hazards are posed by the use of machinery and sharp instruments. Proper safety habits and protective garments eliminate much of the danger. Care in the workplace with the use of protective gloves, and resting when fatigued, help avoid serious injuries. Constant access to refrigerated areas involves exposure to sudden temperature changes. Meatcutters stand almost continuously and must also carry heavy sides of meat.

Social and psychological factors

In addition to the physical dangers involved, meatcutters must also display tact in their dealings with customers. Technological advances will reduce the amount of training required as well as the demand for meatcutters in the future, and those who hold these jobs will tend to become specialists instead of generalists.

GOE: 05.10.08; SIC: 2011; SOC: 5217

◇ **SOURCES OF ADDITIONAL INFORMATION**

American Meat Institute
PO Box 3556
Washington, DC 20007

American Association of Meat Processors
PO Box 269
Elizabethtown, PA 17022

United Food and Commercial Workers International Union
1775 K Street, NW
Washington, DC 20006

◇ **RELATED ARTICLES**

Volume 1: Food Processing; Food Service
Volume 2: Restaurant managers
Volume 3: Cooks, chefs, and bakers; Food service workers

Medical assistants

Definition

Medical assistants assist physicians in offices, hospitals, and clinics. They keep medical records, help examine and treat patients, and perform routine office duties to free physicians' time for working directly with patients and to make sure the office runs efficiently.

History

Health care has made its most rapid progress during this century. New surgical techniques, new drugs, new treatments, and new disease-prevention methods have helped save millions and millions of lives. In addition, the population in this country has grown rapidly, and hospitals, clinics, and health care centers have become more plentiful and more crowded.

In the face of these explosions in available services and people who need them, physicians who once could run a small private practice with perhaps one nurse as an assistant, need more help. The amount of supplies, the number of patient records, and the new and complex forms of insurance and payment that health care providers must deal with make medical assistants essential in any busy medical office. Medical assistants were a recognized, registered group by 1950.

Nature of the work

Medical assistants may perform mostly clerical or mostly clinical duties or both, depending on the size of the office. The larger the office, the greater the chance that the assistant will specialize in one type of work or the other.

For their clinical duties, medical assistants help physicians by preparing patients for examination or treatment. They may check and record patients' blood pressure, pulse, temperature, height, and weight. Medical assistants often ask patients questions about their medical histories and record the answers for the patient's file. In the examining room the medical assistant may be responsible for arranging medical instruments and handing them to the physician as requested during the examination. Medical assistants may prepare patients for X rays and laboratory examinations, and administer electrocardiograms. They may apply dressings, draw blood, administer treatments, and give injections. It may also be the medical assistant's responsibility to give patients instructions about taking their medications or otherwise treating themselves. In addition, medical assistants may collect specimens such as Pap smears for laboratory tests and may be responsible for sterilizing examining room instruments and equipment.

Very often medical assistants are also responsible for preparing examining rooms for patients and keeping examining and waiting rooms clean and orderly. Sometimes medical assistants also monitor office medical supply inventories and order new supplies when necessary. They may also deal with representatives from pharmaceutical and medical supply companies, when they come to take orders for or try to sell products.

Medical assistants often also perform a wide range of administrative tasks. Medical secretaries and medical receptionists perform administrative activities in medical offices, but are distinguished from medical assistants by the fact that they rarely perform clinical functions. Administrative and clerical tasks medical assistants may fulfill include typing case histories and operation reports; keeping office files, X rays, and other medical records up to date; keeping the office's financial records; preparing and sending bills and receiving payment; and transcribing dictation. Assistants may also answer the telephone, greet patients, fill out insurance forms, schedule appointments, take care of correspondence, and arrange for patients to be admitted to the hospital. Word processors and computers are becoming more important to the medical assistant's record-keeping functions.

Some medical assistants work in ophthalmologists' offices, where their clinical duties involve helping these physicians examine and treat patients' eyes. They use special equipment to test and measure eyes and check for disease. They administer eye drops and dressings and teach patients how to insert and care for contact lenses. They may also maintain surgical instruments and help physicians during eye surgery. Other medical assistants may work as *optometric assistants*, who may be required to prepare patients for examination and assist them in eyewear selection or as *chiropractor assistants*, who duties may include treatment and examination.

Requirements

Medical assistants usually need a high-school diploma, but in many cases they receive their specific training on the job. High-school courses in the sciences, especially biology, are helpful, as are courses in typing, computers, and office practices.

Formal training for medical assistants is available in some high schools and at a number of trade schools, community and junior colleges, and universities. Programs at colleges generally award an associate degree and take two years to complete. Other programs last as long as a year and award a diploma or certifi-

After a medical assistant has consulted with a patient, she relays the relevant information to the physician. This intermediate step saves the physician much time.

cate. Schools for medical assistants can be accredited by either of two agencies—the Committee on Allied Health Education and Accreditation, which has approved seventy-three medical and ophthalmic programs, and the Accrediting Bureau of Health Education Schools, which accredits 134 medical assisting programs. Students in these programs do course work in biology, anatomy, physiology, and medical terminology, as well as typing, transcribing, shorthand, and record keeping. Some learn computer skills. These programs also give students supervised hands-on clinical experience in which they learn laboratory techniques, first-aid procedures, use of medical equipment, and clinical procedures. They also learn about administrative duties and procedures in medical offices, and receive training in interpersonal communication and medical ethics.

Medical assistants must be well-groomed, courteous, and able to follow directions. They must be able to deal with people who are frequently under stress and be able to make them feel at ease.

Special requirements

Medical assistants need not be licensed, but they may voluntarily take examinations for credentials awarded by professional organizations. Ophthalmic assistants can be certified at 3 levels by the Joint Commission on Allied Health Personnel in Ophthalmology: Certified Ophthalmic Assistant, Certified Ophthalmic Technician, and Certified Ophthalmic Technologist. For medical assistants, the Registered Medical Assistant (RMA) credential is awarded by the American Medical Technologists, and the American Association of Medical Assistants (AAMA) awards a credential for Certified Medical Assistant (CMA).

Opportunities for experience and exploration

Students in post–high-school medical assistant programs will be able to explore the field through the required supervised clinical experience. Others may wish to volunteer at hospitals, nursing homes, or clinics to get a feel for working with people in a medical environment. All workers interested in this field may want to talk with the medical assistants in their own or other local physicians' offices to find out about this occupation.

Related occupations

Other occupations that entail work with patients within health care include physicians, laboratory technicians, X-ray technicians, registered nurses, nurse anesthetists, nurse practitioners, nursing and psychiatric aides, and dental assistants.

Methods of entering

Students enrolled in college or other post–high-school medical assistant programs can learn of positions through their school placement offices. High-school guidance counselors may have information about positions for students about to graduate. Newspapers and state employment offices are other good places to look for leads. Workers may also wish to call local medical offices to find out about unadvertised openings.

Advancement

To advance, many medical assistants must change occupations. Medical assistants may be able to move into managerial or administrative positions without further education, but mov-

ing into a more advanced clinical field such as nursing requires more schooling. As more and more clinics and group practices open, more and more office managers will be needed, positions that well-qualified, experienced medical assistants may be able to move into. As with most occupations, today's job market gives medical assistants with computer skills better chances for advancement in any direction.

Employment outlook

About 160,000 medical assistants worked in physicians' offices, clinics, hospitals, health maintenance organizations, and other medical facilities in the early 1990s. Nearly 70 percent worked in private practitioners' offices. The ratio of medical assistant personnel to physicians was seven to one in 1990.

The employment outlook for medical assistants is exceptionally good through the early 1990s. Most openings will be to replace workers who leave their jobs, but many will be the result of a predicted surge in the number of physicians and outpatient care facilities. In addition, new and more complex paperwork falls on the medical profession continually, creating a growing need for assistants in medical offices.

Experienced and formally trained medical assistants are preferred by many physicians, so these workers have the best employment outlook. Word-processing skills, other computer skills, and formal certification are all definite assets.

Earnings

According to the American Medical Association, beginning medical assistants earn about $8,400 a year in the early 1990s. The average medical assistant earned about $12,360 and experienced workers earned as much as $18,000. Salaries were, however, as in many occupations, dependent on the size and location of the workplace and the qualifications of the employee.

Conditions of work

Most medical assistants work in pleasant, modern surroundings, although older hospitals and clinics may have ventilation peculiarities. Sterilizing equipment may require caution, and working with people who are ill may be upsetting at times. Most assistants work forty hours per week, frequently including some Saturday hours.

Social and psychological factors

People who enjoy helping and comforting others are well suited to the position of medical assistant. Medical assistants must also be conscientious, dependable, and able to respect patients' privacy by keeping medical information confidential. The job takes good vision and manual dexterity and a mature attitude toward the human body. Overall, the position of medical assistant is important to helping patients feel at ease in the doctor's office, and people with good communication skills and a desire to serve should do well as medical assistants.

GOE: 10.03.02; SIC: 8011; SOC: 5233

◇ **SOURCES OF ADDITIONAL INFORMATION**

American Association of Medical Assistants
20 North Wacker Drive, Suite 1575
Chicago, IL 60606

American Association for Medical Transcription
PO Box 6187
Modesto, CA 95355

American Registry of Medical Assistants
59 1/2 Southwick Road
Westfield, MA 01085

Registered Medical Assistants
710 Higgins Road
Park Ridge, IL 60068

◇ **RELATED ARTICLES**

Volume 1: Health Care
Volume 2: Dental assistants; Medical technologists; Medical-record administrators; Physician assistants
Volume 4: Biomedical equipment technicians; Medical laboratory technicians; Medical-record technicians

Models

Definition

Models pose for artists and photographers, and display wearing apparel for fashion designers, clothing manufacturers, and retail stores. They include: the artist's model, who poses for paintings, sculptures, and other types of art; the photographer's model, who poses for commercial advertisements; and the fashion model, who models clothing live. Fashion modeling includes runway modeling, which is where the model is up on a platform, or runway, and presents an outfit to the audience by walking across the platform. This is the method of presentation for most haute-couture fashion designers selling clothing to retailers.

History

Since there have been artists, there have been models who posed for them. In earlier times, many of these models were, in fact, the friends or family of the artists.

The history of the photographer's model is comparatively recent. Although the modern camera was invented by George Eastman in 1889, its possible uses in commercial advertising were not realized for more than twenty years. Shortly after the turn of the century, businesses discovered that a pretty picture could sell more products than 1,000 words. Consequently, advertisements began to feature pictures of young women who seemed to endorse a manufacturer's product. As commercial photography continued to grow and develop so did the career of the photographers' model, who may be male or female these days.

The story of fashion models begins in Paris, where they were first employed to display the exclusive clothing that had been designed by French dressmakers for wealthy women. Before 1900, U.S. fashions were, for the most part, copies of the French originals, and it was seldom considered necessary for copied clothing to be shown by live models. Shortly after World War I, the U.S. garment industry created some original designs and began to mass produce clothing. Fashion modeling developed concurrently with the U.S. garment industry. As these fashion houses slowly multiplied, so did the number of models who were needed to show clothing to prospective buyers. In the past forty years, the U.S. garment industry has assumed world leadership in the production of clothing and increasing numbers of models have been needed to display these garments.

Nature of the work

Although the basic duty of each type of model is to pose, there are significant differences in the work done in the three classifications.

The work of the *artist's model* is to pose for an individual artist or for a class of art students. In posing, he or she must stand or sit in one position for several hours at a time. Permission to relax is usually given once during each hour. Often the model must pose on a platform under hot and bright lights, and sometimes wear little or no clothing. One job may last a day; another for several weeks.

Photographer's models pose for photographs or illustrations. Their job is to lend attractiveness to an advertisement to enhance the product to be sold. There is great variety in the work of this type of model. One photograph may be taken in a studio under hot lights with the model wearing a heavy fur coat. Another may be taken outdoors in midwinter with the model wearing only a bathing suit. One job may last only an hour, while another may require an entire day. In their work, models may travel to other states or even to other countries to be photographed in beautiful, unusual, or exotic settings.

Rarely does the photographer's model work full time. Weeks may pass from one job to the next, especially if they work on a free-lance basis. If they sign a contract with a modeling agency, however, their schedule may be fuller,

because the agency will be able to secure modeling jobs for them.

The photographer's model who has some acting ability may secure a job in a television commercial. This work is usually videotaped or filmed, as opposed to the still photograph. Although television modeling is a very lucrative field, it is very difficult to break into for the average model.

Fashion modeling differs from the other types in three basic ways. First, the models usually work for clothing manufacturers, fashion designers, or department stores on a full-time basis; second, they do not merely pose in one position, but walk about assuming a variety of poses in their display of the clothing; third, they often speak to prospective purchasers to inform them of the model number and price of each garment.

Some fashion models may be employed by clothing manufacturers as showroom or fitting models. During regular business hours, they are called on to model garments whenever the employer requests, or whenever a buyer comes in to see the "line" of the manufacturer or wholesale house. At certain peak seasons of the year, models may be on duty constantly in the showroom. Toward the end of a season, however, there may be many hours when the showroom is empty. During these times the fashion model may perform other duties, such as routine filing, answering the telephone, and acting as a receptionist.

In many large department stores, a staff of full-time models is employed to promote the sale of various garments or accessories. The store may have a regularly scheduled style show during the daily lunch hour; at other times, models may walk throughout the store showing apparel and talking with customers about the garments and accessories being worn. Models may be hired by a perfume distributor to hand out free samples in a store.

All fashion models employ certain techniques to effectively exhibit the clothing they display. Immaculate grooming is basic, from the proper application of makeup and hair care to the smallest personal details. They must walk gracefully with an erect carriage; they must properly pivot, turn backwards and to the side. They must know how to carry their hands and arms gracefully, and the positions needed to emphasize certain details of their costume. They must also know how to call attention to accessories, such as purses, jewelry, or gloves.

Some fashion models do not work regularly, but are called only for special style shows, or for certain buyers' showings. Some prefer to free-lance, since they may have other jobs or responsibilities. Some models devote part of their time to fashion modeling and part to modeling for commercial photographers.

Requirements

There are significant differences in the requirements necessary for each type of model.

Least demanding are those for the position of artist's model, where physical stamina is most important. This model simply must be able to sit or stand in one position in front of one or many artists for long periods of time without moving.

There are no standard educational requirements for models. Most employers of photographer's models prefer at least a high-school education. Many employers of fashion models state a preference for college graduates with the ability to communicate well and with a general cultural background.

The basic requirement for photographer's models is that they photograph well. It must be emphasized, however, that not all attractive people have the qualities that are acceptable to commercial photographers. Often characteristics such as wholesomeness and sincerity, as well as freshness of face or manner, are as important in this field as good looks.

The major requirement for the fashion model is, of course, physical appearance. Although most people think of all models as being young and slender, this is not necessarily the case. There is no set standard for a model's physical description, because many different types are needed. Many garment manufacturers seek fashion models who are between the ages of sixteen and thirty and between five feet, five inches and five feet, eleven inches in height. Male models generally must be between six feet and six feet, two inches and wear a size 40 or 42 suit. But persons failing to meet these specifications should not feel that there is no possibility for them in this career.

Because some fashion houses create styles for persons of middle years who are above-average weight, they need models who are more mature looking. Other firms that specialize in evening clothes often require models of above-average height to display their garments. Companies that produce junior sizes require models who can wear those sizes without alterations. Those that manufacture misses' or womens' sizes may seek models who can wear sizes 10 or 12.

Modeling is a particularly fatiguing occupation because it requires many hours of standing and walking, or of sitting or standing still in

Fashion models can work in a variety of environments. Some of the most lucrative and consistent jobs often involve catalogue work.

uncomfortable positions. Thus, an important requirement is good health and physical stamina. In addition, both the prospective fashion and photographer's models must be prepared to give up most of their social life and to limit their diets. They will have to have many extra hours of sleep each night and to avoid rich foods and beverages in order to maintain their figures and appearances.

Another important requirement is immaculate grooming. The photographer's and fashion models will have to spend more hours than the average person on care of skin, hair, nails, and general physical fitness. Especially important to the fashion model is the ability to walk gracefully, carrying hands, arms, and torso in a poised and chic manner.

Most fashion and photographers' models must have special training to meet all of the above requirements. They may attend a reputable modeling school where they learn the skills and techniques of modeling. Or they may enter a good charm school in order to learn the application of makeup, appropriate clothing, and the proper ways to walk and stand. Some models take special courses in dancing or physical fitness in order to achieve suppleness and grace of carriage.

Special requirements

To work in television, the model must join the appropriate union. Other than this, there are no special requirements for employment in this field unless an agency would specify its own. Courses in acting may prove helpful.

Opportunities for experience and exploration

The high-school counselor may help a student aspiring to be a model by providing books, articles, and pamphlets about this career and by recommending modeling schools and agencies. Experience in fashion modeling may be obtained in home economics courses as well as from local fashion shows and beauty contests.

Young people interested in becoming models should try to obtain professional opinions concerning their chances for success. They may ask the buyer or fashion director of a large local store. They may seek the advice of a commercial photographer. Or they may travel to a large city in which there are model agencies and ask the opinions of staff members.

Related occupations

Other occupations that will allow persons with an interest in photography and art to express their skills include painters, sculptors, photographers, graphic designers, muralists, and art directors.

Methods of entering

To gain employment as an artist's model, a young man or woman may apply directly at various art schools, check newspaper want ads, or apply at the state employment office.

It is not nearly as simple to enter the other two modeling fields, because competition is much keener and a high priority is placed on previous experience.

Graduates of modeling schools may be aided by the school's placement office in securing their first job. Another possibility for the prospective model is to register at a modeling agency. Many agencies, however, select only those people with qualities that they feel will be acceptable to employers. If accepted by an agency, the future model's registration card and photographs will be placed on file and he or she will be called for a job when the agency feels they have one for which this person is qualified. In return for the agency's services, models pay 10 percent of their earnings.

The aspiring model may wish to contact employers directly. This procedure, however, may entail many long hours of traveling from place to place, and of waiting in reception rooms for interviews with employers, photographers, or advertising personnel.

Prospective photographer's models are encouraged to have professional photographs made of themselves to show employers how well they photograph. This type of model must have many copies of such photographs to leave them with potential employers. On the back of each picture should be the model's name, address, phone number, height, weight, and coloring, along with clothing, shoe, and glove sizes. This picture will be placed in a file along with pictures of many other models. When someone of this type and size is needed for a picture, the model may be called to pose.

Many photographer's models keep portfolios of their work that they may carry with them to show employers the kinds of jobs they have had. The larger and more impressive the model's portfolio, the greater the possibility that the agency will call him or her for an assignment.

Aspiring models who plan to seek work in a large, unfamiliar city should go there prepared to look for a job for at least three months. They should have enough money to support themselves in relative comfort and to pay for such modeling necessities as a fashionable wardrobe, professional hair and beauty care, adequate diet, and such incidentals as additional photographs or special short-term schooling.

Any young person who hopes to become a model should approach the career with an understanding that the chances of success are small. Many thousands of young people with good qualifications attempt a modeling career each year and only a very limited number are able to succeed.

Advancement

There is no usual line of advancement in the modeling profession. It is a rarity indeed for the artist's model to advance in the usual sense of the word. It is to be expected, however, that the better art schools and the more successful artists may pay higher hourly wages to an experienced model.

Fashion or photographer's models have advanced in their profession if they receive an increasing income and are in greater demand. Their career, however, is usually a short one because the model who works in the field for longer than eight years is considered to have been highly successful. Certain facial and figure changes often make it difficult for most older people to compete with younger, fresher, and more slender models.

Even the high degree of success with which a photographer's model may meet can lead to the shortening of a modeling career. When people have been on the covers of many magazines and have appeared in many magazine features, the novelty appeal begins to wear thin, and they are passed by in favor of models who have not received such wide coverage. Also, models who become identified with one particular product may find it difficult to qualify for jobs with other sponsors or photographers.

Most fashion and photographers' models, therefore must learn a skill to which they may turn when it is no longer possible for them to continue modeling. Many fashion models have gained enough knowledge to move into fashion designing, advertising, public relations, or retailing. Others attend special schools between modeling assignments in order to learn business, technical, or vocational skills. Still others go to work for model agencies or open agencies of their own.

Employment outlook

Although there will always be a need for well-qualified models, there are probably entry positions for no more than 500 each year. Because at least ten times that number try to become models each year, chances for success are only about one in ten. For artists' models there are a greater number of openings but it is almost never enough income to live on.

There are increasing employment possibilities for men in the modeling field. Mature men are equally as well qualified as young men to become photographers' models.

Earnings

A model's earnings vary according to experience and depend on the number, length, and type of assignments he or she receives. In the early 1990s, top fashion models working full time for wholesalers or retailers earned approximately $40,000 a year and more. Models working retail shows earned between $15,000 and $18,000 or more. Female models working for agencies in the early 1990s made $100 to $125 an hour. Models who appeared in television commercials could earn at least $180 a day for a job as an extra and $275 and more as a principal character. In addition, they receive a fee whenever the commercial is aired.

Fashion models who are employed by department stores earn approximately the same salary as salespersons. The rate of pay is generally between $8 and $12 an hour, depending on the size and location of the store and the quality and cost of the merchandise involved. The more versatile the model, the greater the opportunity he or she has for employment. But much time is spent auditioning for assignments, and models must usually provide their own accessories and often must buy a complete outfit to obtain a particular assignment.

Modeling can be a gateway to consultant jobs in the fashion and merchandising field, and some models become actors and actresses.

Conditions of work

Models work under a variety of conditions depending upon their classification.

The artist's model usually works indoors in a loft, a studio, or a classroom. These rooms may be large and drafty with high ceilings and inadequate heating or cooling facilities. The more modern art schools, however, will be well heated, well ventilated, and well lighted. This model may wear ordinary street clothing, some exotic costume, or pose in the nude.

The photographer's model, on the other hand, may work either indoors or outdoors. There may be times when models are asked to pose in a bathing suit outside in chilly weather. At other times, they may model wool clothing in midsummer on hot city pavements. In the photographer's studio, models are often asked to hold a pose for a long period of time while lights and background details are adjusted. Much patience is required for models to wait while problems are solved and many different persons offer opinions about any one photograph. Because they are seldom employed full time, photographers' models may not always have enough money to maintain themselves between jobs. Therefore, they may find it necessary to seek other kinds of work on a temporary basis. Because it is essential that they have extensive wardrobes, they may frequently work at part-time jobs to buy the necessary clothes for their assignments.

Fashion models usually work indoors in well-lighted and well-ventilated showrooms. They must stand and walk a great deal during busy seasons. During slack seasons, there may be little for them to do and time may pass slowly. If they are employed in a department store, models are able to walk about the store and talk with many persons. They work indoors in usually pleasant surroundings. Although they are standing or walking for most of the working day, they have the advantage of a great deal of variety of location and people in their work.

Social and psychological factors

Models must enjoy their work thoroughly and not allow themselves to become impatient or exasperated by delays or disappointments. Many young persons who enter a modeling career do so because they anticipate that it will be glamorous. Once embarked upon the career, they find little glamour and much hard work. Nevertheless, there are many satisfactions to be found in achieving success in this difficult field. Most models enjoy dressing well and looking trim and chic. They enjoy the excitement of the fashion and advertising worlds. They find that

the people with whom they work are interesting. Often, they have an opportunity to meet or to work with famous or successful persons. Although their careers as models may be short, they often find that they have taken a first and important step toward a worthwhile career in fashion or advertising.

GOE: 01.08.01; SIC: 7363; SOC: 445

◇ SOURCES OF ADDITIONAL INFORMATION

Modeling Association of America International
2110 Central Park South, Suite 14-C
New York, NY 10019

World Modeling Association
PO Box 100
Croton-on-Hudson, NY 10520

◇ RELATED ARTICLES

Volume 1: Apparel; Retailing
Volume 2: Actors and actresses; Fashion designers; Radio, TV, and motion picture occupations

Nannies

Definition

Nannies are trained child monitors who attend to children's needs and perform various combinations of tasks. Nannies care for small groups of children in the same family and the children's ages may range from infant to eleven years old. Their skills may include supervising the nursery, amusing children by organizing play activities, and keeping the children's quarters clean and intact. They may be responsible for supervision for part of or all of the day.

History

Though nannies have been a staple of British house staffs for many years, they are a relatively new service to the United States. In recent years as there has been an increased demand for highly skilled, reliable, private child care, nannies no longer have to be imported from England to the United States, as was previously done. Now nannies are trained in this country in one of the nanny schools that are scattered across the United States.

Many more mothers are opting for part-time work, and still others run businesses out of their homes. Although this allows mothers to be with their children more than if they worked a traditional forty hour week, there is still the unpredictability of children's needs. A nanny can be part of a support staff that assists the family in completing work tasks as well as caring for those needs. Having a trained child monitor in the home to oversee activities and meals, as well as help with certain domestic chores balances the demands of a two income household.

Women training to be nannies assist a young boy on the swings. Nanny school is one the newer types of vocational training available.

Nature of the work

Nannies perform their child care duties in the homes of the children of the families who employ them. Unlike other kinds of household help, nannies are specifically concerned with the needs of the children in their charge. Nannies prepare the children's meals, making sure they are nutritious, attractive presentations and dishes the children enjoy. They may do grocery shopping specifically for the children. Nannies may accompany the children during their mealtimes and oversee such development as table manners and proper eating. Nannies will also clean up after the children's meals. If there is an infant in the family, a nannie will wash and sterilize bottles and feed the infant. In addition, a nanny will change the infant's diapers. It is not part of a nanny's regular duties to cook for the adult members of the household or do domestic chores outside of those required for assisting the children.

Nannies are responsible for keeping order in the children's quarters. They may clean up their bedrooms, the nursery and playroom, making sure beds are made with clean linens and there are enough blankets in the winter. Nannies will wash and launder the children's clothing and make any necessary repairs. Nannies will make sure that their charge's clothing is put neatly away, and if the child is older may begin instruction in order and neatness, teaching a child how to organize their possessions. Nannies bathe and dress the children and instill proper grooming skills in older charges. Children often seek the assistance of their nanny to get them ready for family parties or holidays. Children also learn how to dress themselves and take care of their appearance as they get older.

Nannies are not only responsible for the care and training of their children, but also act as companion and guardian. Nannies may plan games and learning activities for the children and supervise their play, encouraging fairness and good sportsmanship. Nannies may be responsible for planning certain activities to commemorate holidays, special events, or birthdays. Perhaps these activities center around field trips, arts and crafts, or parties and teas.

Nannies act as parent assistants because they focus so closely on the children and encourage the good behavior set down by the parents. They are responsible for carrying out the parents' directions for activities and manners. Nannies may travel with the families on trips and vacations, or they may take the children on a short excursion by themselves.

Nannies are detail oriented when it comes to the children they are looking after. They keep records of illnesses, allergies, and injuries. They also make note of learning skills and related progress as well as personal achievements, such as abilities in games or arts and crafts. Nannies encourage the children to grow up happy and capable by setting forth good examples and helping the children to follow the guidelines developed by their parents.

Requirements

Nannies are frequently required to have a high-school diploma or GED certificate. They must also have a driver's license as they may be asked to chauffeur the children to doctor's appointments, birthday parties, or other outings.

Nannies must love children and have an even and generous temperament when working with them. They must be kind and affectionate and genuinely interested in the child's well-being and development. Nannies must be able to work well independently and have good judgment to handle any small crisis which might arise or any emergency. Nannies must know how to instill discipline and carry out the parents' wishes.

Nannies are not part of the family and should not be too familiar with its members. A nanny should respect the family, be loyal and committed to the children. Nannies should be tactful and respect the family's personal business and private lives.

Nannies must be in good physical condition, have stamina and energy, and promote good health habits to the children under their care.

Special requirements

The American Council of Nanny Schools in University Center, Michigan, provides a list of its accredited schools and information on each. Nannies completing their training from one of the ACNS schools receive a certificate of completion. Training may last twelve to sixteen weeks. There are also two- and four-year programs available on subjects such as early childhood education, child development, and child care at many junior and senior colleges.

The course work involved in nanny training may focus on communication, family health, and first aid and child psychology. In addition, classes in child behavior, child growth and development, and food and nutrition may also be covered. It is also vital for nannies to study specifics on the care of infants. Classes may also include play and recreational games, children's literature as well as safety and health. Because nannies may be responsible for children of various ages, the course work is designed to give information on each stage of development and children's different needs.

Professional nanny schools may also give instruction on family management, appearance, and conduct.

Though it is not required for nannies to earn certificates, it is important that they select training that is accredited and professional so they may enter the field skilled and prepared.

Opportunities for experience and exploration

Future nannies should investigate many forms of child care. Baby sitting is an excellent way to gain experience taking care of children. Often, a baby-sitter cares for children without any su-

pervision and can learn management, responsibility, and handle small crises. Volunteer or part-time work at day care centers, nurseries, or grade schools can also be beneficial. Classes in psychology provide useful instruction, and home economics training teaches home management, sewing, and nutrition.

Methods of entering

Students applying to public or private schools should have completed their high-school education or earned a GED certificate. Many schools ask for transcripts, letters of recommendation from teachers or employers, and many wish to know what related classes or employment the applicant has had. Sometimes schools require applicants to come in for an interview or screening and undergo a physical examination to make sure they are in good health. Working as a nanny takes energy and endurance.

Some schools provide work exchange programs where a student lives with a family and handles some aspects of child care in return for room and board.

Advancement

Over half the working nannies are under the age of thirty. Many nannies work in child care as a way to support themselves through school, or may leave to have families of their own. Some nannies are hired to only take care of infants and may be employed by a new family every couple of years or so. Some nannies enter the teaching field to train future nannies or go back to school for a degree in child psychology or early childhood education.

Employment outlook

While there is still a trend for mothers to work outside the home, even at part-time jobs, there will still be a need for quality, professional child care givers. Presently, the demand for nannies outweighs the supply and graduating nannies may find themselves with several job offers. It may take years to come close to meet the growing need for nannies. This need for nannies is expected to continue its increase through the 1990s.

Earnings

A nanny's salary can range between $175 to more than $400 per week. This range is based on a five-day workweek and as much as sixty hours a week. Nannies hardly ever work only forty hours per week. This salary range also depends on such factors as how many children they are caring for, how long they have been with the family, and previous experience. Some salaries take into consideration whether or not the nanny lives in. The U.S. Department of Labor, however, put a value on room and board at almost $40 per week, and should not effect overall wages too greatly. Presently, the highest demands for nannies are in large cities on the West and East coasts. This demand can reflect higher wages.

Most nannies have weekends off, though there are ample other benefits they may receive. Some nannies are asked to travel with the family. If it is a business-oriented trip, a nanny may be compensated with wages as well as additional days off upon return. If the travel is for vacation a nanny may get a paid bonus for giving up her personal days off.

Nannies often have work contracts with the family which may designate fringe benefits and salary increases. Nannies may have health insurance supplied to them by their employer as well as worker's compensation and social security tax. and pay raises vary, 7 or 8 percent being on the high end of the scale.

Nannies are valued workers and often receive many benefits from the families who employ them.

Conditions of work

Because nannies work in the houses of their employers, their working conditions may vary. Some nannies are "live-ins," sharing the house of their employer. They may do this because it is more convenient for them and there is room, or it may be required due to the number of children in the family or if the family has a newborn that requires additional care. It is also common for a nanny to live with the family during the week and return to her own home on the weekends. When nannies live in the house of the family, they usually have their own quarters or a small apartment that is separate from the rest of the family's bedrooms and offers them some privacy. Sometimes the nanny's room may be right next to the children's room so it is possible for the nanny to hear right away if help is needed.

Nannies who do not live in may expect to stay at the house for long periods of time,

much longer than a traditional nine-to-five job would warrant. As it is often the nanny's responsibility to put the children to bed in the evening, a nanny may not return home until much later in the evening. Families rely on the assistance of a good nanny and therefore a nanny is usually very well treated and appreciated.

Social and psychological factors

Nannies are committed to the children they care for and are with them for long hours, several days at a time. Nannies may not have scheduled free time or many outside interests other than the family. This may make it difficult for nannies to have personal lives or form many outside friendships. Nannies should be comfortable in their quarters and follow family guidelines about having visitors or personal time.

Nannies are responsible for supporting the parents' ideas about raising children. There may be some matters of disagreement and a nanny should know how to discuss such ideas without offending the employer—the parents. Nannies must use good judgment in caring for the children and handle small crises in a way that reflects the views of the parents.

Nannies must be aware of their role in the family and be careful about taking on tasks and chores that are more suitably handled by another member of the house staff. Nannies should be able to communicate well with all members of the family.

For nannies who are employed for years with the same family in a successful working relationship, the most difficult task is leaving when the children no longer require daily supervision. The aspects of separation can be difficult for both nanny and child. The nanny will usually move on to work with another family, or she or he may retire and perhaps return to or start his or her own family.

GOE: 10.03.03; SIC: 8811; SOC: None

◇ SOURCES OF ADDITIONAL INFORMATION

Au Pair in America
Program for Americans Abroad
American Institute for Foreign Study Scholarship Foundation
102 Greenwich Avenue
Greenwich, CT 06830

International Nanny Association
PO Box 26522
Austin, TX 78755

National Academy of Nannies, Inc.
3300 East First Avenue
Suite 520
Denver, CO 80206

◇ **RELATED ARTICLES**

Volume 2: Teachers, kindergarten and elementary; Teachers, preschool; Teachers, secondary school
Volume 3: Child care workers; Teacher aides

Nursing and psychiatric aides

Definition

Nursing aides and *psychiatric aides* help physicians and nurses to care for people who are physically or mentally ill. They work in hospitals, nursing homes, clinics, medical labs, and physicians' offices performing a variety of tasks that are critically important in the health care field. Patients come to rely on the care they receive from aides who are also known as hospital attendants or nursing assistants.

History

From earliest times, healthy people have been called upon to care for weak, sick people. People who are sensitive to the suffering of others and who want to help comfort others have found health care fields to be very rewarding. Community life must include care of the sick, and methods for dealing with illness exist in all societies. The social and economic development of societies is closely tied to the fundamental need to care for the sick.

Early Greek, Indian, Chinese, Aztec, and other civilizations established places resembling current hospices and hospitals to care for the sick in their midst. The growth and spread of Christianity gave new importance to caring for the sick. Monasteries had infirmaries for their own sick members, and they welcomed pilgrims and travellers who were ill to use their facilities. Military and chivalric groups also tended to the sick with hospital and charity work. Two hospitals were founded in the 11th century in Jerusalem by the Knights Hospitallers of St. John, and they cared for the mentally ill as well as the physically ill.

The religious history of nursing, combined with the social desire to help others and scientific curiosity, provides the basis for what is now the career of thousands of Americans: helping nurses and physicians care for their patients.

As the practice of medicine has become more complex, the need for nursing aides has grown. In the nineteenth century a nurse named Florence Nightingale led a movement for reform in nursing. In 1873 the first school of nursing in the U.S. was established in New York City at Bellevue Hospital. But not everyone who feels the "calling" to be a nurse is able to pursue the difficult educational path to licensing. Working as a nursing aide is often the perfect first step toward becoming a licensed nurse, while providing a necessary link in the health care system.

The increased burden on trained nurses has made nursing aides irreplaceable. The aides provide basic care for those who are incapacitated, and free nurses and doctors to minister to their patients' diseases.

Nature of the work

The work done by nursing and psychiatric aides varies greatly. Much of the difference depends on the place of work, whether it is a hospital, a nursing home, a mental heath facility, or a drug rehabilitation center.

Nursing aides respond to patients' calls, deliver messages, serve meals, help feed patients who cannot feed themselves, bathe and dress patients, bring and empty bedpans, help patients in and out of bed, or move them places in wheelchairs or stretchers, assist patients to walk if they are able, give massages, and treat irritated skin on bedridden patients.

As assistants in hospitals, they may perform routine organizational tasks such as moving supplies in supply rooms or arranging the pharmacy's shelves. Besides the basics of routine care, a major function of hospital assistants is to spend time with patients. The patients count on the encouragement and support of their aides.

Practical nurses perform certain tasks that aides with less experience cannot. Under the supervision of a physician, for example, a practical nurse may check a patient's vital signs. *Birth attendants* help nurse-midwives or obstetricians to assist women in childbirth. These attendants also require special training. *First-aid attendants* have certification in the techniques of first aid and are especially helpful in emergency situations.

In the category of nursing and psychiatric aides, specialists include *psychiatric aides* who report to psychiatrists, psychologists, social workers, and therapists. They often spend time with their patients, reading, playing games, or watching television. Because they socialize more with their patients, they are able to recognize change and improvement more easily than some of the physicians who see the patients less. They thus play an invaluable role in patient care.

Mental-retardation aides specialize in patients who are mentally handicapped. *Nursing aides* can have a wide range of responsibilities. If a patient seems to be improving and needs less care from a physician, a nursing aide may be asked to step in and perform more functions.

Orderlies often have more physical responsibilities than other aides. They wheel stretchers when patients have to be transferred, help patients change beds and sometimes are asked to help restrain violent patients in mental health facilities. *Geriatric nursing aides* help care for the elderly. They work in nursing homes and hospitals as well as in patients' homes. As the life span gets longer and the elderly population in the United States grows, geriatric nursing aides are in increasingly large demand.

Requirements

The most important requirements for nursing and psychiatric aides are personal characteristics. These include a desire to help others, dependability, emotional stability, honesty, integrity, patience, understanding, an even temper and a pleasant, sympathetic manner. Orderlies also must be strong physically.

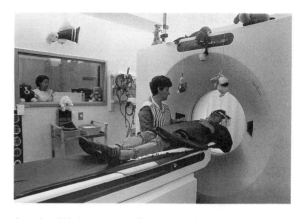
A nursing aid helps a young patient undergo chemotherapy.

Many hospitals require a high-school diploma, and courses in biology, chemistry, and English are helpful. Some high schools offer health care courses in conjunction with local nursing homes or hospitals. Community colleges and vocational schools offer courses and programs geared to the student interested in health care.

Special requirements

There are no special licensing requirements needed for nursing and psychiatric aides. Practical nurses, birth attendants, and first-aid attendants must go through training that usually lasts about a year to be certified.

Opportunities for experience and exploration

Because almost every community has a hospital, clinic, nursing home, or drug rehabilitation center, access to experience in the health care field is relatively easy. Even young students are enthusiastically welcomed as volunteers. This is a wonderful opportunity to help one's community while learning first-hand the kind of work that nursing and psychiatric aides do

Part-time jobs are sometimes available for qualified applicants as an orderlies' helper. Community or public-health services and the Red Cross are other sources of information for those interested in nursing aide jobs.

Taking health care courses is also a good way to learn about the field. Teachers at vocational schools and community colleges are often able to guide students to the kind of health care facility that best suits them.

Related occupations

The health care field is broad and diverse and offers many occupational opportunities to those with a compassion and caring for people. Other jobs include physicians, registered nurses, nurse anesthetists, nurse practitioners, physical therapists, X-ray technologists, biomedical equipment technicians, and dietitians.

Methods of entry

Those interested in being nursing or psychiatric aides can often get part-time jobs to begin with working at night or on the weekends. Entrants are often middle-aged, but many high school and college students also explore the field with part-time work.

Applications for jobs are taken at the personnel offices of most hospitals as well as at many local employment offices. Most nursing homes expect to train their new nursing or psychiatric aides on the job, but some hospitals prefer to hire aides who have had some previous experience.

In addition to classroom instruction and on-the-job supervision by licensed nurses, much training is accomplished working directly with patients. Nursing aides help make beds and feed and bathe patients soon after they are hired.

Approximately twenty states had laws requiring courses to train new nursing aides and several other states were considering such laws. Because of these regulations, some hospitals require as much as a year's experience as a home health aide or nursing aide before hiring.

Advancement

With further intensive training and exams, nursing aides and psychiatric aides can become registered or licensed practical nurses. Some hospitals grant skilled aides higher status, more pay, and fringe benefits. Some encourage currently working nursing aides to continue working part-time as they train to become licensed practical nurses.

Employment outlook

Job opportunities for nursing aides and psychiatric aides are expected to grow through the 1990s. Growth is expected to be especially high in the geriatric area, with the number of private nursing homes for the elderly on the increase. Most wage and salary jobs are currently in hospitals and nursing homes, but help is also needed in clinics and drug rehabilitation centers.

More than 1.3 million people were working as hospital assistants, nursing aides, and orderlies in the early 1990s. More than 88,000 people were working as psychiatric aides in the early 1990s. Both of these numbers were expected to grow.

Earnings

All nursing and psychiatric aides earn at least the minimum wage. The range of full-time salaries in nursing homes is from $8,300 to $11,000 while hospitals pay $9,400 to $19,000 annually depending on the aide's experience. Benefits include health insurance, sick leave, paid holidays, and paid vacation after one year of work. In the early 1990s full-time nursing aides, orderlies, mental retardation aides, and psychiatric aides earned an average of $12,700 to $15,400 annually.

Beginning aides with no experience might start at about $200 per week at Veteran's Administration hospitals, and although wages are not ideal, they are improving. Some health care centers have pension plans, and some provide inexpensive meals as well as housing and laundry service.

Conditions of work

Hospitals and nursing homes are usually clean, pleasant places to work. The average work week is thirty to forty hours long, but the work is in shifts, and some shifts are at night, on the weekend, or on holidays. The work can be strenuous both physically and emotionally, and often includes bending, stretching, and lifting. There is also the possibility of exposure to contagious diseases.

Psychiatric aides have contact with patients who can be confused, disturbed, or violent, and this work can be emotionally exhausting. Most aides spend much of their working day on their feet, and are active constantly. Although the work may involve repeated tasks, having many patients prevents it from becoming boring.

Social and psychological factors

Emotional stability and maturity play important roles in the work of nursing aides. Aides are constantly faced with the pain and suffering of their patients as well as with the inevitability of death. They counteract these sometimes depressing elements of their work with the knowledge that their work brings relief to those in pain. Providing comfort and companionship to their patients and helping the doctors and nurses to heal their illnesses, nursing aides can be satisfied knowing they are doing a service to their patients.

GOE: 10.03.02; SIC: 806; SOC: 5236

◇ **SOURCES OF ADDITIONAL INFORMATION**

ANA-NLN Committee on Nursing Careers
American Nurses' Association
2420 Pershing Road
Kansas City, MO 64108

American Hospital Association
840 North Lake Shore Drive
Chicago, IL 60611

American Health Care Association
1201 L Street NW
Washington, DC 20005

American Medical Association
535 North Dearborn Street
Chicago, IL 60610

◇ **RELATED ARTICLES**

Volume 1: Health Care
Volume 2: Licensed practical nurses; Medical assistants; Prosthetists and orthotists; Registered nurses
Volume 3: Medical and health technicians occupations

Occupational safety and health workers

Definition

Occupational safety and health workers are responsible for the prevention of work-related accidents and diseases, property losses from accidents and fires, and injuries from unsafe products.

History

For centuries, people thought that accidents and illnesses just happened, or they superstitiously blamed such unfortunate occurrences on fate, the wrath of the gods, or evil forces. Very little was done in the way of prevention other than to wear charms or offer sacrifices. At the same time, slave labor was plentiful, lives were expendable. The builders of the great structures of the ancient world gave scant thought to their human inventory, and the workers were compelled to accept their lot in life. Even in more modern times, the early history of the Industrial Revolution shows workers were considered of less importance than the machines they operated or the output of a factory or mine. Little relationship was seen between the safety and health of the workers and productivity.

In this century, however, the rapid growth of technology has made it possible to design machinery and equipment with built-in safety mechanisms; research in medicine has increased our knowledge of the effect of environment on health; psychology has made us aware of the human factors that may lead to accident or illness; and the influence of labor unions and

291

the government has led to more concern for the men and women in industry and the conditions of their workplace.

Today people are probably safer at work than anywhere else. Not only has industry instituted practical safety measures, reducing hazards by developing new machinery and devising better safeguards, but it has established work safety rules and safety education programs. And it continues to allocate large sums to research and development in this area.

Nature of the work

This occupational category is made up of four groups: safety engineers, fire protection engineers, industrial hygienists, and loss control and occupational health consultants.

Safety engineers are concerned with preventing accidents. Their specific duties depend on where they work. In large industrial plants, they may develop a safety program that covers several thousand employees. They examine plans for new machinery and equipment to see that all safety precautions have been included. They determine the weight-bearing capacity of the plant floor. They inspect existing machinery and design, build, and install safeguards where necessary. In case of accidents, safety engineers investigate the cause. If it is related to a mechanical problem, they use their technical skills to correct it and prevent a recurrence. If it is because of human error, they may educate the workers in proper safety procedures.

Safety engineers who work for trucking companies, known as *safety coordinators*, instruct truck and trailer drivers in matters pertaining to traffic and safety regulations and care of the equipment. They ride with drivers and patrol highways to detect errors in handling cargo and driving the vehicle. They also watch for violation of company regulations and observe the conditions of the vehicles and the roads. They investigate accidents and recommend measures to improve safety records and to conserve equipment.

In the mining industry the safety engineers, or *mining inspectors*, inspect underground and open-pit mines to ensure compliance with the health and safety laws. They check timber supports, electrical and mechanical equipment, storage of explosives, and other possible hazards, and test the air quality for toxic or explosive gas or dust. They may also design safety devices and protective equipment for mine workers, lead rescue activities in case of emergencies, and instruct mine workers in safety and first-aid procedures.

The light, heat, and power industry employs safety engineers, or *safety inspectors*, to ensure the safety of the workers engaged in construction and maintenance of overhead and underground power lines. The safety inspectors check safety belts, ladders, ropes, rubber goods, and tools; observe crews at work to be sure they use goggles, rubber gloves, and other safety devices; and examine the condition of tunnels and ditches. They investigate accidents, devise preventive measures, and may instruct workers in safety matters.

Many safety engineers work with design engineers to develop safe models of their company's products and then monitor the manufacturing process to ensure the safety of the finished product. *Fire protection engineers* also have different tasks depending on the place where they work. In general, their job is to safeguard life and property against fire, explosion, and related hazards. Those in design and consulting firms work with architects and other engineers to build fire safety into new buildings. They study buildings before and after completion for such factors as fire resistance, usage and contents of the buildings, water supplies, and entrance and exit facilities. Fire protection engineers who work for manufacturers of fire equipment design fire-detection equipment, alarm systems, and fire-extinguishing devices and systems. They may investigate causes of fire and may organize and train personnel to carry out fire-protection programs.

Fire-prevention research engineers conduct research to determine the cause and methods of preventing fires. They study such problems as fire in high-rise buildings and test fire retardants and the fire safety of manufactured materials and devices. The results of such research are used by fire protection engineers in the field. Fire-prevention research engineers also prepare educational materials concerning fire prevention for insurance companies.

Fire marshals supervise and coordinate the activities of the fire fighting personnel in an industrial establishment. They also inspect equipment such as sprinklers and extinguishers; inspect the premises for combustion hazards and enforcement of fire laws and ordinances; conduct fire drills; and direct fire fighting and rescue activities in case of emergencies.

While safety and fire prevention engineers see to the prevention of accidents, *industrial hygienists* are concerned with the health of the workers in an industrial plant or governmental organization. They collect and analyze samples of dust, gases, vapors, and other potentially toxic material; investigate the adequacy of ventilation, exhaust equipment, lighting, and other conditions that may affect employee health, comfort, or efficiency; evaluate the exposure to radiation and to noise; and recommend ways of eliminating or controlling such hazards. These hygienists work at the job site.

Others work in the private laboratories of insurance, industrial, or consulting companies, where they analyze air samples, research health equipment, or investigate the effects of chemicals. Health physicists are specialists in radiation. Still other hygienists specialize in the problems of air and water pollution.

Loss control and occupational health consultants are safety inspectors hired by property-liability insurance companies to perform services for their clients. They inspect insured properties and evaluate physical conditions, safety practices, and hazardous situations; determine whether the client is an acceptable risk and the amount of the insurance premium; and devise and monitor a program to eliminate or reduce all hazards. They may also help set up health programs and medical services and train safety personnel.

An occupational safety and health worker tests the city's water supply to monitor the chemical and bacterial levels.

Requirements

Occupational safety and health workers must have at least a bachelor's degree in engineering or one of the physical or biological sciences. Employers usually prefer a bachelor's or master's degree specifically related to occupational safety and health, such as safety engineering or management, industrial hygiene, fire protection engineering, public health, or health physics, or a degree in chemical or mechanical engineering. Graduates of a two-year college curriculum may be hired as technicians, particularly if they have related experience.

Workers in this field must keep abreast of the new and changing trends and technologies. For this reason, many insurance companies provide training seminars and correspondence courses for their staffs. The Occupational Safety and Health Administration (OSHA) offers courses on topics such as occupational injury investigation and radiological health hazards. The American Society of Safety Engineers, the National Safety Council, and other groups also provide continuing professional education.

Special requirements

Good physical condition may be necessary to keep up with the physical demands of some jobs in this field. A few states require that oc-

cupational safety and health professionals be licensed.

Opportunities for experience and exploration

Science teachers, teachers of technical subjects, and school vocational counselors may offer guidance to courses of study and possible work-study programs. Interviews with and lectures by occupational safety and health professionals, particularly if coupled with field trips to an industrial plant or other work site, will give students an opportunity to ask questions and get an overview of the field. Part-time and summer jobs in manufacturing plants will give them first-hand experience in observing working conditions and becoming familiar with some of the equipment that safety workers are concerned with. There may also be jobs of vaguely related interest in hospitals and insurance companies.

Related occupations

The research side of occupational safety is conducted by engineers in many different fields, including mining, construction, and pollution-control. The implementation side ranges from automotive exhaust technicians, who study and test pollution output from engines, to radiation control technicians for nuclear power plants. The jobs can be quite specific for whichever area the safety worker concerns himself or herself. The occupation can also be quite broad for government employees of departments such as the Occupational Safety and Health Administration (OSHA), who are concerned with all businesses and their potential health problems.

Methods of entering

There are no shortcuts in the educational process, but as students begin to approach their academic goals, they may seek part-time and summer jobs that are more and more closely related to their career objectives. College guidance counselors and placement offices may be a source of jobs. Persons interested in becoming occupational safety and health workers may contact engineering and technical societies, talk to company recruiters, or apply directly to the personnel or employment offices of appropriate industrial or insurance companies.

Advancement

Safety and health workers in the insurance industry may be promoted to department manager of a small branch office, then to a larger branch office, and from there to an executive position in the home office. In industrial firms, they can move up to safety and health manager for one or more plants. Technicians with the proper education and experience can advance to professional safety and health positions.

Marks of recognition in this field are the designations Certified Safety Professional; Certified Industrial Hygienist; and Member, Society of Fire Protection Engineers. The Board of Certified Safety Professionals and the American Board of Industrial Hygiene certify candidates who complete the required experience and pass an examination.

Employment outlook

Approximately 90,000 people were employed as occupational safety and health workers in the early 1990s. About half of them were safety engineers; most of the rest were fire protection engineers, industrial hygienists, or workers who combined two or more areas; and a few were engineering or industrial hygiene techni-

cians. The largest number of workers in this field is found in manufacturing, insurance, and engineering and architectural service industries. Occupational safety and health workers are concentrated in population and industrial centers. Insurance consultants usually have offices in a major city and travel to and from various sites.

Employment of occupational safety and health workers is expected to grow more slowly than the national occupational average through the 1990s, as government regulatory programs and spending grow more slowly. Casualty insurance companies will hire more safety and health workers as more small employers request the services of their loss-control and occupational health consultants. Openings will also occur as experienced workers move to other occupations, retire, or die. Prospects will be best for college graduates with degrees specifically related to occupational safety or health.

Earnings

In the early 1990s, experienced safety and health workers averaged about $33,600 per year. Starting salaries were about $24,000 a year for those with a bachelor's degree, somewhat higher for those with a graduate degree. Many safety and health supervisors earned more than $48,000 a year.

Conditions of work

Most occupational safety and health workers are based in offices but spend much of their time at work sites, inspecting safety hazards, talking to workers, or taking air or dust samples. They may have to travel a great deal, depending on their job specialty and location. For example, a safety engineer who works exclusively at one plant may travel only to an occasional seminar or conference, while an insurance consultant will spend about half the time away from the office, inspecting work sites. The work settings will vary, some being dirty, some noisy. Also, the nature of the work may require a lot of physical activity.

Social and psychological factors

Safety and health workers combine technical interests with social concerns, working both with machines and with people. To be effective in establishing safety programs and procedures, they must be able to communicate well and to motivate others. They have to be adaptable to different situations and to fit in comfortably with people on all levels, such as a union representative, the supervisor of a welding shop, or a corporate executive.

GOE: 11.10.03; SIC: 9199; SOC: 1473

◇ SOURCES OF ADDITIONAL INFORMATION

American Industrial Hygiene Association
475 Wolf Ledges Parkway
Akron, OH 44311

American Society of Safety Engineers
1800 East Oakton Street
Des Plaines, IL 60018

Society of Fire Protection Engineers
60 Batterymarch Street
Boston, MA 02110
Career information on consulting in the field of in-

surance loss control may be obtained from the home offices of many property-liability insurance companies.

National Institute for Occupational Safety and Health
Division of Training and Manpower Development
Robert A. Taft Laboratories
4676 Columbia Parkway, Cincinnati, OH

◇ RELATED ARTICLES

Volume 1: Civil Service; Health Care; Trade Unions
Volume 2: Construction inspectors, government; Engineers; Health and regulatory inspectors
Volume 4: Engineering technicians; Fire safety technicians; Industrial safety-and-health technicians; Nuclear power plant radiation control technicians; Pollution-control technicians

Pest control workers

Definition

Pest control workers use chemicals and mechanical traps to rid residential and commercial premises of rodents, insects, and other household pests.

History

Pest control as an industry is a fairly recent development. In earlier times, fumigators were often brought into houses where someone had suffered a highly contagious disease, such as smallpox. The most common method of banishing germs was to burn a large amount of some antiseptic but highly corrosive substance such as sulfur, which often damaged furniture and household goods. Twentieth-century chemical research has made possible the use of substances toxic to pests, but not harmful—in

the quantities used by exterminators—to people, pets, or household furnishings.

Nature of the work

Exterminators travel to homes, restaurants, hotels, food stores, and other places where pests are likely to gather. Chemical sprays for flies, roaches, and other household insects are applied in cracks in floors and walls, under sinks, and in other places that provide shelter for these pests. Mechanical traps are set for rodents, and poisonous bait is left for them in areas where it will not contaminate food supplies or endanger children or pets. Many commercial establishments have service contracts with an exterminating company, which sends workers on a biweekly, monthly, or quarterly basis to make sure the premises remain free of pests. Workers often advise their customers on

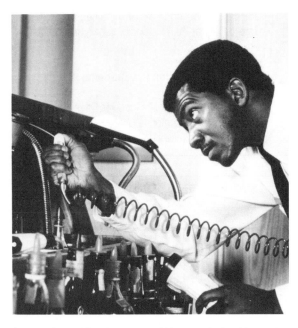

An exterminator delicately sprays pesticides around a bar. He must be careful not to touch any of the liqueur bottles with his wand.

housekeeping and home-repair methods to keep pests from returning. The work of several exterminators may be directed and coordinated by an *extermination supervisor*.

Termite exterminators perform a more extensive and complicated job to attack the termites that live in underground colonies and eat away the foundations and structural members of wooden houses. They may be assisted by *termite exterminator helpers*. A chemical barrier is laid down between the termite colony and the wooden parts of the house, usually in the soil around the foundation. This barrier traps the termites either underground, where there is no wood to eat, or in the walls, where they cannot find water. Eventually, the colony dies of starvation or dehydration.

Termite exterminators must sometimes make structural changes in the buildings they service. Holes must be drilled in basement floors to pump chemicals into the soil under the house. To keep termites from returning, treaters must sometimes raise foundations or replace infested wood. If this alteration work is very extensive, however, it is usually referred to building contractors and carpenters.

Once termites have been thoroughly eradicated from a building, they are not likely to return soon, so termite exterminators work on a one-time visit, rather than a contract basis.

Fumigators rid buildings of pests by using traps and poisonous gases.

Requirements

Pest control workers should be in good general health and able to lift fairly heavy weights. Because route workers usually make service calls alone, they need a driver's license and a safe driving record. Most employers prefer to hire high-school graduates. Those wishing to enter this field will find high-school courses in chemistry and mathematics helpful.

Manual dexterity and mechanical ability are important for pest control workers. Termite exterminators will also find a knowledge of carpentry valuable. Because pest control workers must deal with the public, good grooming and courtesy are essential.

Special requirements

Pest control workers are required to be licensed in many states. Some of these states also require the applicant to pass a written examination. In some exterminating companies, employees must be bonded.

Opportunities for experience and exploration

Students who have held part-time and summer jobs as drivers or helpers on milk, bakery, dry-cleaning, or other routes will find the experience helpful if they are interested in becoming pest control workers. An interest in chemistry as a hobby or, in the case of termite treaters, in woodworking and carpentry, is also an asset.

Related occupations

Other workers with similar interests and aptitudes as pest control workers include janitors, cleaners, housekeepers, maids, and private household workers.

Methods of entering

Pest control workers usually obtain their jobs through newspaper ads or leads from friends. Most large firms conduct informal training classes, lasting two or three weeks, for new employees. On-the-job training is gained by accompanying experienced workers or termite treaters on service calls. After a training period of two to three months, the new employee is usually ready to make routine service calls alone.

Advancement

Pest control workers with job experience and sales aptitude may become pest control salespersons, who contact prospective customers to inform them of the firm's services, or service managers. Some may advance to owning their own exterminating businesses. Termite exterminators who are skilled at structural work may become carpenters.

Employment outlook

In the early 1990s, approximately 40,000 pest control workers were employed in the United States.

The demand for exterminating services is expected to change little through the mid-1990s. New and more powerful pesticides and more frequent treatments will be needed, as rodents and insect pests reproduce rapidly and tend to develop a resistance to pesticides.

Earnings

In the early 1990s, beginning exterminators earned about $16,200 annually. More experienced employees earned about $23,400. Some workers receive commissions based on a percentage of the service charge to the customer.

Conditions of work

Most pest control workers are employed in urban areas, where older buildings provide easy access to pests. Termite exterminators tend to work in suburbs and small towns, where there are many wood frame buildings. Exterminators must often carry equipment and supplies weighing as much as fifty pounds. Termite ex-

terminators may have to crawl under buildings and work in dirty or damp cellars.

Most of the chemicals used in exterminating are not harmful to humans if handled properly, although some may be injurious if inhaled in large quantities or left on the skin.

Social and psychological factors

Pest control workers need to use good judgment in deciding what types of chemicals to use, and how much, in each service situation. They must be careful in applying these chemicals, to prevent contamination of food. People with a strong aversion to dirt or sensitivity to unpleasant odors are not well suited to this field.

Employees who have frequent contact with customers should be courteous and well-groomed. For the route worker, good driving skills are also important.

GOE: 03.04.05; SIC: 7342; SOC: 5246

◇ **SOURCES OF ADDITIONAL INFORMATION**

National Pest Control Association
8100 Oak Street
Dunn Loring, VA 22027

International Pesticide Applicators Association
PO Box 1377
Milton, WA 98354

◇ **RELATED ARTICLES**

Volume 1: Construction
Volume 2: Construction inspectors, government; Health and regulatory inspectors
Volume 3: Carpenters

Police officers

Definition

Police officers are employed in protective service work. They are charged with the responsibility of protecting the life and property of our nation by their work in community, town, and city police departments. The scope of their responsibilities demands the performance of many job duties. Basically, their major responsibilities include preserving the peace, preventing criminal acts, enforcing the law, and arresting those who are violators of the law. Police officers are under oath to uphold the law twenty-four hours a day.

This definition does not include civilian employees of police departments; state, county, or federal government police employees; or police and detectives employed by private businesses.

History

Humans have historically sought and had some form of protection for their life and property and to help preserve their welfare.

The origins of police work are virtually unknown. Looking back to the days of tribal living and the early social organizations of community life, history depicts the policing of people by some chief authority. Feudal lords had retainers who saw to it that taxes were paid and who may have attempted to gain some kind of law and order among the people. Moving with history into the fourteenth century, we find that rape, beatings, and robberies were commonplace with little organized control exerted to protect the town's citizenry.

Gradually, England began some institutions for public justice and as these institutions developed, the influence of their work spread to other parts of the world. The Anglo-Saxons and the Normans played a role in the development of a sounder philosophy of police work, and one that closely resembles the ideas expressed today by people all over the world.

Police work, as we know it today, has evolved with our complex society into a scientifically founded field based on the principles of justice and freedom inherent in a democratic society. The whole concept of police work had to wait in its development upon an evolving system of local self-government in which nonmilitary, nonsecret police, could function as responsible regulators of community life.

Nature of the work

Police officers are responsible for preserving law and order at all times.

In recent years increased drug addiction, juvenile crime, and social change have made greater demands on every police officer. Duties may be many and varied, or in large city departments, may be highly specialized. Police officers may be employed by a state, county, or municipality.

In smaller towns and communities, officers may direct traffic during the rush-hour periods and at special local events when traffic is unusually heavy or jammed; they may administer first aid in emergency situations, assist in rescue operations of various kinds, investigate cases of breaking and entering, issue tickets, or arrest offenders of traffic or parking laws or other regulations; and they may patrol public places such as parks and streets and public gatherings for purposes of law and order. Police are sometimes called upon to prevent or break up riots and to act as escorts at funerals, parades, and other public events. As part of their routine night duties, they may check the safety of locks on the doors of business firms and see that the proper lights are burning as protection to the business firms. As officers patrol their assigned beats, either on foot or in cruise cars, they must be alert for all types of actions and situations that may arise and they must be ready to go into whatever action is necessary. Many times they must be alert for the identification of stolen cars and the apprehension of the offenders, to the identification and the location of lost children, and to identify and apprehend escaped criminals and others wanted by the police and various law enforcement agencies.

In large city police departments, officers usually have more specific duties and specialized assignments. Police departments, in these instances, are usually made up of special work divisions such as the division of communications, criminal investigation, firearms identification, fingerprint identification, accident prevention, and administrative services. In very large cities, police departments may have special units of work such as the harbor patrol, canine corps, mounted police, vice squad, fraud or "bunco" squad, traffic control, records control, and rescue units. A few of the job titles that go with these specialties are *identification and records commanders and officers, narcotics and* vice detectives or investigators, homicide squad commanding officers, detective chiefs, traffic lieutenants, sergeants, parking enforcement officers, public safety officers, accident-prevention-squad officers, safety instruction police officers, and community relations lieutenants. The size of the city and the number of police needed usually determine the number of work divisions or special units in a police department.

In the largest city police departments there may be the jobs of police chiefs, precinct sergeants and captains, desk officers, booking officers, police inspectors I and II, identification officers, complaint evaluation supervisors and officers, crime prevention police officers, and internal affairs investigators. A majority of officers may perform their duties in patrol work or in traffic duties such as patrol police lieutenants or harbor police launch commanders. Some officers work as plainclothes detectives in criminal investigation divisions. Other specialized police officers are; police reserves commanders; police officer commanding officers III, who act as supervisors in missing persons and fugitive investigations and police officers III, who investigate and pursue nonpayment and fraud fugitives. Most police officers are trained in the use of firearms and carry a gun on their person. Police in special divisions, such as chemical analysis, handwriting, and fingerprint identification have special training to perform their work.

Police officers have to testify in court regarding their knowledge of cases they have worked on. Police personnel are required to make out accurate and complete case reports of their work. At all times the police work in close communication with their own headquarters and usually with their coworkers.

Requirements

As police work has become more organized to keep pace with the complexities of present day society, the requirements for entrance into the field have become more clearly defined. Today, in almost every large city, police job appointments are governed by local civil service regulations. Many smaller cities and towns are beginning to follow this same trend in their employment practices.

Where civil service appointments are made, job applicants must be at least twenty-one years of age and some municipalities stipulate the age limit shall not be more than thirty-five. Candidates must have, in most cases, 20/20 uncorrected vision, good hearing, and their weight must be in proportion to their height. Male and female applicants must meet locally

A police officer checks on the health of a hospitalized child that he rescued from a car accident. Such aspects of a police officer's job are frequently unpublicized.

prescribed weight and height rules. Most job regulations restrict applicants to those who are U.S. citizens.

Civil service appointments usually require written tests that are designed to measure the candidate's intelligence and general aptitude for police work. The physical examinations that are also required usually include tests of physical agility, dexterity, and strength. Very frequently the candidate's personal history is given close scrutiny as well as his or her character references and personality traits.

Applicants need a pleasant, congenial, and even temperament and must be able to execute sound judgment even in emergency situations. Honesty, as a character trait, must be above reproach.

The majority of police departments today require that applicants have a high-school education. Some departments will accept police recruits who have not finished high school but the completion of a high-school education is likely to open the greatest opportunities for promotion and advancement. In some cases, depending on the job, some college training may be required. College training and/or special course training may also be required by large city police departments where applicants will do specialized work. An increasing number of colleges offer two- and four-year educational programs in police work and police administration. More than 800 junior colleges and universities offer courses in law enforcement. High-school students who are interested in pursuing this line of work may find the subjects of English, business law, mathematics, U.S. government and history, psychology, sociology, and physics most helpful. Because physical stamina is most important in this work, sports and physical education are also of value. There are now police forces that require candidates to be college graduates for some or all positions.

Police officers are usually given a period of special training once they have received an appointment to their job, which must be completed before actual job assignments are given. This training, usually known as a probationary trial period, may last from three to six months. In small towns and communities, such training may be given on the job by work with an experienced officer. Large city police departments usually also give classroom instruction in laws, accident investigation, city ordinances, traffic control, and so forth. These departments generally also instruct in the handling of firearms, methods of apprehension and arrest, self-defense tactics, and first-aid techniques. Physical fitness training may be a required and continued activity in most police departments, as well as routine physical examinations. Police officers can have no physical disabilities that would prevent them from carrying out their duties.

Depending upon the type of assignment given to police personnel, their work can involve unpleasant duties and expose them to many unpleasant situations of life. They may be called on to deal with all types of people under all types of circumstances. The public with whom they are in contact in performing their duties may be under emotional stresses causing them to react with anger, hostility, or brutality and to exhibit many other types of human feelings such as pity, depression, or states of anxiety. Police work demands emotional stability of the person performing the job duties, as well as the ability to think clearly and act rationally under all types of circumstances.

Police officers generally wear special uniforms and are required to carry on their person certain equipment, such as guns, flashlights, handcuffs, and police whistles.

Special requirements

Special requirements for police work have been discussed in the preceding section, such as height, weight, vision, hearing, physical stamina and agility, and the written and physical examinations. No special licensure or certification is required or imposed by law for these personnel. Some divisions, such as forensics, may have specific requirements for the post.

Opportunities for experience and exploration

Individuals who are interested in exploring these occupations may do so by talking with their high-school guidance counselors or with police officers who are already engaged in the work. They may also wish to visit colleges offering programs of studies in police work or write them for the details of their training programs.

In some cases, persons who have finished high-school training can begin exploring this occupation by seeking employment as police cadets in large city police departments. These persons are paid employees who work part-time in clerical and other duties. They also attend training courses in police science on a part-time basis. At age twenty-one they are eligible to be considered as applicants for police work.

Related occupations

Many jobs with similar requirements to those of police officer are available in the criminal justice field. These include state police officers, private investigators, lawyers, probation officers, and security guards.

Methods of entering

Applicants interested in police positions should usually apply directly to local civil service offices or examining boards to qualify as candidates for police officer. In some locations, the written examinations may be given to groups at specified times. In smaller communities, not utilizing civil service methods, applicants should apply directly to the police departments or to city government offices in the place where they reside.

Advancement

Advancements in these occupations are determined by several factors. The eligibility of the candidate for promotion may depend on specified lengths of service, job performance, formal education and training courses, and the results of written examinations. Those who become eligible for promotion and qualify by the above criteria are listed on the promotional list along with other qualified candidates. As positions of different rank come open, candidates are promoted to fill them, according to their position on the list. Lines of promotion usually begin with officer third grade to grade two and grade one. Other possible promotional opportunities include the ranks of sergeant, lieutenant, and captain. Advancement to the very top ranking positions, such as division, bureau, or department director or chief may be made by direct appointment. The majority of these top positions are held by officers who have come up through the ranks.

Large city police departments offer the greatest number of advancement opportunities. Most of the larger departments maintain separate divisions each requiring departments of administration, line officers, and, in general, more employees at each rank level.

The majority of city police departments offer various types of in-service study and training courses to open up more promotional opportunities. At the same time, this approach allows police departments to keep up to date on the latest police science techniques that upgrade the overall standards of police work. Training courses are provided by police academies, colleges, and other educational institutions, and some of the various subjects offered are civil defense, foreign languages, and forgery detection. Some municipal police departments share the cost with their officers or pay all educational expenses if they are willing to work toward a college degree in either police work or police administration.

Intensive twelve-week administrative training courses are offered by the National Academy of the Federal Bureau of Investigation in Washington, D.C. Limited numbers of officers are selected to participate in this training program.

Advancements on police forces in small towns and communities are considerably more limited by the rank and number of police personnel needed. Other opportunities for advancement may be found in related police and protective service work in private companies, state and county agencies, and institutions.

Employment outlook

In the early 1990s, an estimated 530,000 full-time police officers were employed by local police departments.

Employment of police officers will increase about as fast as average for all occupations through the late 1990s, as population growth continues in our nation.

The future opportunities that will be available, however, may be somewhat determined by technological, scientific, and other changes occurring today in police work. A greater degree of specialization in various areas of police work seems imminent, and this will increase the amount of educational and specialized training required to perform the work. Automation in traffic control is limiting the number of officers needed in this area. New approaches through social science and psychological research are changing the methodology used in working with public offenders. These trends point to a future demand for well-educated specialized personnel.

New positions will open as a result of many retirements from police departments, to replace those who are deceased and to fill positions in expanding police departments. Retirement ages are relatively early in police work as compared to other occupations. Some openings will also be available to replace those who have left the field to enter other occupational areas.

Earnings

In the early 1990s, entrance salaries for police officers averaged $21,600 a year. Maximum earnings for police lieutenants were as much as $37,000.

Most police officers are eligible for regular periodic salary increases to the limit set for their rank and a specified length of service. Police departments in general pay special compensation to cover the cost of uniforms. They usually provide any equipment required such as firearms and handcuffs. Overtime pay may be given for certain work shifts or for emergency duty. In these instances the compensation is usually straight or time-and-a-half pay, or sometimes compensatory time off is given instead of pay.

Fringe benefits for police workers may include paid sick leave, medical and life insurance plans, and paid vacations of two weeks to one month, depending on their length of service. Retirement plans for police personnel are very good in most cases. They are sometimes able to retire after twenty or twenty-five years of service, receiving one-half their normal salary.

Conditions of work

Police officers may work under many different types of circumstances. Much of their work

Private household workers
Service Occupations

may be performed out of doors, by riding in patrol cars or walking the areas assigned to them. In emergency situations, no consideration is made of weather conditions, time of day or night, or day of the week. Police officers may be on twenty-four-hour call duty. Although regular work hours are assigned, individuals in police work must be willing to live by an unpredictable and often erratic work schedule. Personal flexibility is almost demanded in the work.

In general, police work consists of an eight-hour day and a five-day week, but in emergencies, work hours and days may extend far beyond this. The occupation is considered dangerous and hazardous. Some officers are killed or wounded in performing their duties. The routine of the assigned duties may sometimes become boring; in general, however, police work holds the anticipation of the unknown and unexpected and may offer many challenging, interesting, and exciting experiences.

The work demands a constant mental-physical alertness as well as great physical strength and stamina.

Social and psychological factors

Police officers work in close contact with all types of people and must be without prejudice. They also need to possess sound emotional stability and control themselves with an even temperament in all circumstances. They must be flexible about change, erratic work hours, and their exposure to all types of human emotion. Courage, dependability, honesty, and the willingness to accept grave responsibilities are

traits compatible to the nature of police work. Individuals in these jobs must be able to live with the tensions, strains, and problems in the lives of others and to maintain their own stability under physical and mental stresses.

GOE: 04.01.02; SIC: 9221; SOC: 5132, 5133

◇ **SOURCES OF ADDITIONAL INFORMATION**

American Federation of Police
1000 Connecticut Avenue, NW, Suite 9
Washington, DC 20036

American Police Academy
Lock Box 15350
Chevy Chase, MD 20815

National Police Officers Association of America
1316 Gardiner Lane, Suite 204
Louisville, KY 40213

◇ **RELATED ARTICLES**

Volume 1: Civil Service
Volume 2: Crime laboratory technologists; FBI agents; Lawyers and judges
Volume 3: Correction officers; Security guards; State police officers

Private household workers

Definition

The term *private household worker* includes a number of occupations, all of which are concerned with the home. Whether a cook, cleaning worker, housekeeper, or governess, the private household worker's responsibility is to tend to the well-being of either residences or the people who inhabit them.

History

For centuries, the size of a person's household staff was a measure of his or her wealth. That is still true today to some extent, but the rise in standard of living has had its effect as well. Families of modest means can afford to hire a day worker to look after children while both parents work or a maid for a half-day to help with cleaning. Household work in the United States was often considered the first step on the economic ladder for immigrant families. Now many of the agencies that hire out help for household jobs are run by the sons and daughters of those workers.

Nature of the work

The nature of the tasks performed by private household workers can best be described by function. The *general house worker,* or *day worker* is hired by the hour, fulfills numerous duties from cleaning furnishings and making beds to buying, cooking, and serving food. As the title suggests, the *personal attendant* performs personal services for the employer, such as mending, washing, and pressing garments, or seeing that these jobs are done; helping the employer dress; and keeping private quarters clean and tidy. The *child monitor* cares for children, giving them baths, supervising their play, and preparing their meals. Baby sitters may perform some or all of these tasks, but on a daily or hourly, rather than a full-time basis. Hours for baby sitters may or may not be regular.

Housekeepers usually have more responsibility and less supervision. At the pinnacle is the *home housekeeper,* who manages a household with a large staff of full-time workers. She or he directs their activities, orders food and cleaning supplies, keeps a record of expenses, and may even hire and fire. The *cook,* the *domestic laundry worker,* and the *ironer* are usually restricted to the functions of cooking and laundry, but the cook's responsibilities are broader in scope. The cook first plans menus or follows instructions; prepares the food; serves meals; and performs such duties as making preserves and fancy pastries.

Companions are on more of a par with their employers; indeed, they often are of the same social background. Their prime responsibilities are to act as aid or friend to a convalescent or a person living alone. They tend to their employer's personal needs and often look after social and business affairs. A *governess* does something of the same for children, supervising their recreation, diet, and health, according to the parents' instructions.

Although women predominate in household work, men also work in this field. *Caretakers* and *yard workers* help keep private homes in good condition. They are responsible for heavy work, tending the furnace, caring for the yard, painting fences, and the like. A *valet* performs personal services for a male employer, such as caring for clothing, mixing and serving

In addition to supervising a child's recreation, diet, and health, a household worker must also be sensitive to a child's emotional needs.

drinks, and running errands. The *butler,* like the home housekeeper, may supervise other household workers, assigning and coordinating their work. He also receives and announces guests, answers the telephone, and serves drinks. He may assign these duties to a *second butler.*

Requirements

There are no formal educational requirements for most household workers. The ability to clean, cook, sew, wash and iron, and care for children is generally acquired by young people while helping with the housework in their own homes. And whatever skills are lacking usually can be acquired with experience as an assistant to an experienced household worker. The growing number of such household devices as dishwashers, vacuum cleaners, and electric mixers, however, does make some classroom training worthwhile. The opportunities are available through home economics courses offered in high schools, vocational institutions, and by federal and state employment services. Personal appearance and demeanor are important to a person who wishes to do household work. Because of the close contact between household workers and the members of the household, employers look for agreeable, discreet, and trustworthy individuals who are neat, clean, and in good health.

Special requirements

Educational and cultural background is more important than work experience for the positions of governess and companion. The former often needs a broad background in the arts; the latter should have the same interests as her employer. Some knowledge of practical nursing is also valuable, if the employer is ill or an invalid. Some employers require cooks and infant's nurses to have a health certificate, often arranging and paying for the necessary physical examination.

Opportunities for experience and exploration

Those who enjoy housework and home repairs are likely to be successful household workers. There is no shortage of part-time, after-school work to further develop these capabilities. And the summer offers high-school students numerous opportunities to gain further experience at vacation homes.

Related occupations

Other workers that have the same skills as the private household worker include hotel housekeepers, hotel and motel maids, child care workers, day-school teachers, and nannies.

Methods of entering

Many household workers maintain jobs on a part-time basis. Some jobs will be acquired through friends or past and present employers. State employment offices can also be a way of finding part or full-time employment.

Advancement

Advancement other than a wage increase is generally not available within households with only one or two workers. To improve their positions, domestic workers must change to a home where a job requiring greater skill is available. These opportunities are limited in number.

Employment outlook

About 993,000 private household workers were employed in the United States in the early 1990s. Their employment is expected to decline through the late 1990s.

Earnings

The wages earned by household workers vary according to the size of the employer's income, kind of work performed, and local standards of pay. Generally, the money is better in larger cities, especially in the northern part of the country. Workers who live in usually receive the same wage rates as those who live out, in addition to free room and board. The latter usually receive a free meal and the cost of their transportation. According to limited data available, most private household workers earn between the minimum wage and $7 an hour.

Conditions of work

Almost all household employees spend their working hours at the family residence. The exception is the laundry worker, who may work at home. However, few household workers actually live in for any period of time. Those who do generally work more than the thirty-five hours a week of outside help. Day workers often acquire several customers for whom they do cleaning and other chores on a part-time basis at specific intervals. Duties are negotiated with each employer, sometimes on a day-to-day basis. Even though modern washing and cleaning equipment and materials have helped considerably, housework can involve hard labor, especially for day workers who usually are given the heavier tasks to do. There is some added demand for day workers during the holiday season. But work tends to fall off for them and other household workers during the summer vacation months.

Social and psychological factors

Young people in recent years have felt, in increasing numbers, that household service lacks dignity. "Live-ins" in homes with no other employees are likely to be alone most of the time and become isolated from family and friends. They usually, however, become attached to the family for whom they work. A unique factor in this kind of work is the ability of the worker to set the pace of work for the day, to decide what to do next, or how to do it without having any supervisor approve every move.

GOE: 09.01.03; SIC: 8811; SOC: 5241

◇ **SOURCES OF ADDITIONAL INFORMATION**

State or local employment agencies can provide further information on job opportunities.

National Academy of Nannies, Inc.
3300 East First Street
Suite 520
Denver, CO 80206

◇ **RELATED ARTICLES**

Volume 1: Personal and Consulting Services
Volume 2: Hotel housekeepers and assistants
Volume 3: Child care workers; Licensed practical nurses; Nannies

Private investigators

Definition

Private investigators, are also known as *private eyes* and *private detectives,* and their duties involve gathering information and evidence for the purpose of helping individual clients as well as police departments and other agencies. They may also offer protection and security for their clients. Sometimes private detectives help look for missing persons, gather information in relation to fraud or theft or investigate persons possibly involved in wrong-doing. The evidence that private investigators sometimes supply their clients can include photographs, fingerprints, and personal effects.

History

The need for private investigation can be traced as far as history itself. Kings and military leaders often benefited from secret information, whether it be a plan of attack from an enemy kingdom or corruption in their own army. Private investigators have long supplied additional support to police departments hunting for dangerous criminals. Today, however, private investigators have evolved into highly trained, perceptive, problem-solving professionals. Their skills have made them capable of assisting with a wide range of cases, and they provide important services to private individuals as well as large companies.

Nature of the work

Private investigators conduct searches and studies to gather information and evidence that will assist them, or the people they are working for, in solving their case. Not all private investigators assist in crime-solving; some work exclusively with missing persons, some with the security of a company or private individual, and some private investigators work in gathering background and history on persons involved in divorce trials. Private investigators may be independently employed or work for a

A private investigator assesses a damaged car from a hit-and-run accident. Through this inspection, he may find clues that will help locate the culprit.

communication skills are essential for private investigators, as they must be tactful when conducting an interview and be able to secure personal information about people they may be investigating.

Good memory, perception, and detailed work habits are helpful to a detective in keeping records and gathering information. Private investigators should also have good concentration as sometimes the work is routine. Good health and stamina are important, as investigators are sometimes required to work long hours in all kinds of conditions and under different circumstances.

detective agency. Some investigators are kept on retainer by insurance companies and provide regular services for them.

While the range of clients a private investigator may serve can be varied, there are common aspects in the work itself. Investigators interview people to gain information or discover witnesses to certain related events, as well as to get statements of fact regarding the case they are working on. Investigators may spend several hours, at any time of the day, in watching a building or following a criminal. Private investigators may gather clues or fingerprints from crime scenes, or take objects to a laboratory for closer examination. Most every private investigator follows up his or her actions and progress with written reports, so that clients may know the current status of the case, as well as documenting certain events for later reference.

Private investigators might use cameras or video equipment, tape recorders, or lock picks while gathering evidence for their investigation. Private investigators use these various tools in a manner that is acceptable by the law.

Requirements

Private investigators should enjoy flexible and varied working conditions and projects. A natural curiosity, problem-solving abilities, and intelligence are also important traits. Private investigators should enjoy working independently and be able to balance patience and the intrigue of mystery in performing their work.

Private investigators should be honest individuals and know how to pursue answers to their cases without breaking the law. Good

Special requirements

Because private investigators perform such valuable and sometimes personal services, they must be well-trained in methods of investigation and the parameters of the law. For this reason, formal training is necessary.

Some two- and four-year colleges offer course work in criminology and law enforcement. This may serve as an adequate background; however, the more comprehensive training programs are likely to be from detective and investigation schools. Prerequisites for these schools sometimes include a college degree. College classes in photography, communication, journalism, and social sciences such as psychology and sociology are often helpful. If offered, specialized courses in forensics, law, and investigative research are helpful.

In the private investigation schools, much of the course work offered concentrates on hands-on education. Schools may teach students how to lift and develop fingerprints, investigate robberies, pick locks, work with various types of electronic equipment, and test for human blood. Students might also be briefed on how to type up reports and how to file paperwork.

Types of instruction can vary with the school, as can the length and cost of the program. Many large cities have schools and instruction available, and it may be best to contact a number of schools to find out what their various programs have to offer.

Licensing and bonding requirements for private investigators may vary between states. Some states offer examinations or other forms of certification, and it is best to find out in advance what the requirements are. In addition, certain schools may offer specific instruction that prepares graduates for state examinations.

Opportunities for experience and exploration

Future private investigators might check the Yellow Pages of their local telephone books for information on private investigation training. Requesting application materials as well as program catalogs can give the opportunity to compare schools and decide which one might offer the best training for them.

Related occupations

Many other occupations offer persons an opportunity to employ interests in criminal justice. Other jobs include police officers, security consultants, FBI agents, military police, and security guards.

Methods of entering

Some private investigation schools offer placement for their graduates. Some schools have their graduates work at associated investigation firms for more practical experience. Security jobs or investigation work with companies may be advertised in local papers. A few private investigators may start out by opening up their own service.

Advancement

Because each case that a private investigator handles has the potential to be different from the one before, there is good opportunity to learn more and develop his or her skills. Some private investigators move on to larger agencies to advance and get experience solving different kinds of cases. Private investigators who enjoy having more independence may choose to open their own office.

The separation rate in the field of private investigation is extremely high. This work is not for everyone, and many people find out within the first five years if they have the skill and commitment that this occupation requires. The high dropout rate, however, does leave much room for other private detectives to advance to better-paying jobs and working conditions.

Employment outlook

An increasing number of companies are spending more money on security. The unfortunate rise in business crime creates more projects for investigators to explore. Insurance fraud, security in departments that handle research, development of new products or machinery, accident investigation, and property damage are situations that can require professional investigation and security maintenance. In addition, such cases as these can be handled by investigators who have their own offices, or larger firms.

Earnings

The nature of investigative work is that it can take place any time of the day or night, in any number of places. The steps a private investigator takes to gather information and solve cases can be numerous. Because of these factors, investigators most often get paid by the hour. Beginning private investigators may get salaries that range between $9 and $12 per hour. In addition, another $.20 to $.25 per mile is included for car expenses and mileage.

Private investigators have very high earning potential. Investigators with years of experience and a formidable list of contacts can command $250 per hour. The rates can be even higher than that, depending on the individual, the area, and the nature of the case.

Conditions of work

Private investigators are often drawn to their line of work because of the diversity and unpredictability. The working conditions that investigators encounter reflect this potential. Most investigators have a link to an office environment of some kind to perform their administrative and reporting duties as well as to handle client communication. Once a private investigator is on a case, however, he or she may have to travel across country, pick through garbage bins, or watch someone from his or her automobile for hours on end.

Some private investigators work undercover at department stores to watch for shoplifters, while others investigate the scene of a murder. Investigators who look for missing persons may circulate photographs of the victim to police departments and highway officials. The working conditions are as varied as the cases, as well as the investigators who solve them.

Social and psychological factors

Private investigators must be adaptable to different working conditions, a variety of cases and have good problem-solving abilities. Motivation and self-direction can be equally important traits, as private investigators must know how to gather information from different sources.

The hours an investigator works can be long and unpredictable. Often, private investigators do not have much time for themselves and their families. This kind of work can be straining in a family situation. Some private investigators do encounter dangerous circumstances, though often the work is made out to be more glamorous than it really is.

GOE: 04.01.02; SIC: 7381; SOC: 5132

◇ **SOURCES OF ADDITIONAL INFORMATION**

National Association of Investigative Specialists
PO Box 33244
Austin, TX 78764

United States Private Security and Detective Association
PO Box 6303
Corpus Christi, TX 78466

◇ **RELATED ARTICLES**

Volume 1: Civil Service; Personal and Consulting Services
Volume 2: FBI agents; Police officers
Volume 3: Security guards

Security guards

Definition

Security guards are responsible for protecting public and private property against theft, fire, and vandalism. They work in a variety of locations, including banks, industrial plants, educational institutions, department stores, airports, sports arenas, and railroad yards.

History

When people first began to live together in large settlements and to accumulate stores of personal and public property, they realized the necessity of protecting their homes and belongings. People of considerable wealth probably assigned some of their servants to the special task of protecting their property from theft. In military camps and royal households, soldiers fulfilled this function.

In towns and villages of medieval Europe, guards were hired by the community to patrol the streets at night as a protection against fire and theft. With the growth of industrialism and government services in the last century, increasing numbers of security guards have been needed to ensure the safety of valuable goods and confidential documents.

Nature of the work

Security guards may have various titles, to go with the type of work they do or the setting they work in. They may be referred to as *patrollers* or *merchant patrollers, bouncers* who eject unruly persons from places of entertainment, *bodyguards, golf-course rangers* who patrol golf courses, or *gate tenders*. They may work as *airline security representatives* in airports or as *armored-car guards* and *drivers*.

Many guards are employed during normal working hours in public and commercial buildings and other areas where there is a good deal of pedestrian traffic and public contact. Others patrol buildings and grounds outside of normal working hours, such as nights and weekends. Guards are usually uniformed.

Guards in public buildings may be assigned to a certain post, or they may patrol an area. In museums, art galleries, and other public buildings visited by many people, guards answer visitors' questions and give them directions; they also enforce rules against smoking, touching art objects, and so forth. In commercial buildings, guards may sign people in and out after hours, and inspect packages being carried out of the building. Bank guards observe customers carefully for any sign of suspicious behavior that may signal a possible robbery attempt.

Guards at large public gatherings such as sporting events and conventions keep traffic moving, direct people to their seats, and eject unruly spectators.

After-hours guards are usually employed at industrial plants, defense installations, construction sites, and transport facilities such as docks and railroad yards. They make regular rounds on foot, or, if the premises are very large, in motorized vehicles, checking to be sure that no unauthorized persons are on the premises, that doors and windows have not been tampered with, and that no property is missing. They may be equipped with walkie-talkies to report in at intervals to a central guard station. Sometimes guards perform custodial duties, such as tending furnaces and setting thermostatic controls.

Guards who work in situations where they may be called upon to apprehend criminal intruders are usually armed.

A bank security guard keeps a police officer posted on the events of the day.

Requirements

There are no specific educational requirements for guards, although most employers prefer to hire high-school graduates. General good health, alertness, emotional stability, and ability to follow directions are important traits in this job. Military service and experience in local or state police departments are assets. The prospective guard should also have no criminal record.

For some hazardous or physically demanding jobs, guards must be under a certain age and meet height and weight criteria. For top-level security positions, in facilities like nuclear power plants, or vulnerable information centers, guards may be required to complete a special training course. They may also have academic requirements.

Special requirements

Guards employed by the federal government must be armed forces veterans, have some previous experience as guards, and pass a written examination. Many positions require experience with firearms. Often, guards must be bonded.

Opportunities for experience and exploration

Because of the nature of the work, high-school students have little or no opportunity to obtain part-time experience as guards. Jobs such as lifeguard, safety patrol, and school hallway monitor, however, can provide helpful experience.

Many of the less strenuous guard positions are filled by older people who are retired officers or armed forces veterans.

Related occupations

Other workers who perform jobs similar to those of security guards include police officers, state troopers, security consultants, and private investigators.

Methods of entering

Candidates for guard positions are often required to pass written examinations and tests of their eyesight and hearing. In their first few weeks on the job, guards are often accompanied on their rounds by a more experienced worker until they have become familiar with the routine.

Armed guards are given training in firearms handling if they have had no previous experience; they may also be trained in first aid and security procedures.

Advancement

Except for periodic salary increases, there is little opportunity for advancement for guards unless they are employed in military-style guard forces in which individuals move up in rank.

Guards with outstanding ability, especially those with some college education, may move up to the position of chief guard, with responsibility for the supervision and training of an entire guard force in an industrial plant or department store.

Employment outlook

In the early 1990s, about 879,000 persons were employed as security guards in the United States.

The demand for guards is expected to be strong through the late 1990s, as the crime rate rises with population growth. Since so many guards and watchmen are older, retired, or semiretired, turnover in this field is rapid, and new personnel are always needed to fill positions.

Earnings

Security guards' earnings vary depending on their level of training and experience and on the type and location of employer. In the early 1990s, hourly wages ranged from about $3.35 to about $11.00, averaging about $6.25. Guards employed by the federal government earned between $13,800 and $15,500 a year to start. Security guards may receive overtime pay and wage differentials for second and third shifts.

Conditions of work

Guards may work indoors or outdoors; if the latter, they will inevitably be exposed to inclement weather at times. In high crime areas and in industries vulnerable to theft and vandalism, there may be considerable physical danger. Guards who work in museums and other public buildings are on their feet for long periods.

Some companies employ guards around the clock in three shifts, and assign workers to these shifts on a rotating basis.

Social and psychological factors

Guards are entrusted with the responsibility of protecting property and, often, human lives, which can be a source of great pride. They have the satisfaction of knowing that they are performing an essential service for society. Situations that encounter frequent problems or dangers may, however, be stressful to the guard.

GOE: 04.02.02; SIC: 7381; SOC: 149

◇ **SOURCES OF ADDITIONAL INFORMATION**

American Federation of Police
1000 Connecticut Avenue, NW
Suite 9
Washington, DC 20036

American Police Academy
Lock Box 15350
Chevy Chase, MD 20815

International Association of Security Service
PO Box 8202
Northfield, IL 60093

International Union of Security Officers
2404 Merced Street
San Leandro, CA 94577

◇ **RELATED ARTICLES**

Volume 2: Security consultants
Volume 3: Building custodians; Police officers; State police officers

Shoe and leather workers and repairers

Definition

Shoe repairers repair and restyle shoes and other products, such as saddles, harnesses, handbags, and luggage. More highly skilled *custom shoemakers* and *orthopedic-boot-and-shoe designers and makers* may design, construct, or repair orthopedic shoes in accordance with foot specialists' prescriptions.

History

Shoe making was mainly a hand process performed by *cobblers* until 1845, the date of the first application of machinery to shoe manufacturing. Today, shoe manufacturing is a typical mass production industry, and the work of shoe repairers has been implemented by such technological innovations as power machines and by the introduction of mass-produced replacement parts and decorative ornaments.

Nature of the work

Replacing worn heels and soles is the most frequently performed task of shoe repairers. In small shops, a single worker may perform all the tasks necessary to repair an item, but in large shops individual workers may be assigned specialized tasks—for example, sewing, trimming, buffing, dying, and so on, can all be the duties of *pad hands.*

Self-employed shoe repairers must be business-minded. In addition to actual repair work, they may have such managerial duties as making estimates of repair costs, preparing sales slips, keeping records, and receiving payments. They may also supervise employees.

A few shoe repairers are employed in the shoe repair departments of department stores, shoe stores, and cleaning plants. Other related types of workers include *leather stampers,* who imprint designs on leather goods and custom-leather-products makers such as *harness makers, luggage makers,* and *saddle makers.*

Requirements

Shoe repairers should have considerable manual dexterity, eye-hand coordination, and general physical stamina. While there are no special educational requirements, a high-school or vocational school education is preferred.

Special requirements

There are no special requirements for shoe repairers.

Opportunities for experience and exploration

Under the provisions of the Manpower Development and Training Act, training programs for shoe repairers are offered. Many vocational schools also provide courses in this area. Summer or part-time employment as a helper assisting experienced repairers will provide valuable firsthand experience.

Shoe and leather workers and repairers
Service Occupations

For simple chores such as adding heel tabs and regluing soles, shoe repairers frequently service people as they wait.

A visit to the shoe repair department of a large establishment may be arranged.

Related occupations

Other workers who deal with leather or apparel include clothes designers, fashion models, leather tanning and finishing workers, and apparel industry workers.

Method of entering

The usual method of entering this field is to be hired as a helper in a shoe repair shop that offers on-the-job training or some sort of apprenticeship programs. Placement services of vocational schools often help their students find jobs, and state employment services often list job openings.

Advancement

Helpers begin doing such simple tasks as staining, brushing, and shining shoes. As they gain experience, they progress to more complex jobs. After approximately two years of apprenticeship, helpers who demonstrate ability and initiative can become qualified shoe repairers.

Skilled crafts workers employed in large shops may advance to foremen or managers. For those who open their own shops, advancement takes the form of increased clientele and income.

Employment outlook

About 43,000 shoe and leather workers and repairers were employed in the United States in the early 1990s. Employment in this occupation is expected to decline through the late 1990s. Factors that will limit growth are the increasing popularity of footwear that cannot be repaired and of more durable, longer-wearing materials that require less frequent repair. Nevertheless, retirements and deaths of experienced repairers are expected to create numerous job openings each year.

Earnings

Shoe repairers in the early 1990s generally earned about $300 a week. One in ten earned $420 or more, and shop owners earned considerably more. Assuming a forty-hour week, these workers earned, on the average, $15,600 a year.

Conditions of work

Although some repair shops are crowded and noisy, with poor light or ventilation and characterized by unpleasant odors, working conditions in large repair shops, shoe repair departments, and in more modern shoe service stores generally tend to be good.

Most shoe repairers work a five- or six-day week, eight hours a day. Self-employed workers work considerably longer—often ten hours a day. Employees in large shops receive from one to four weeks paid vacation and at least six paid holidays a year.

Social and psychological factors

Although shoe repair work is not physically strenuous, long hours of standing and a great deal of tedious work are involved. Self-employed shoe repairers tend to work long hours, often in unpleasant working conditions.

GOE: 05.05.15; SIC: 7251; SOC: 6854

◇ **SOURCES OF ADDITIONAL INFORMATION**

Shoe Service Institute of America
5024-R Campbell Boulevard
Baltimore, MD 21236

◇ **RELATED ARTICLES**

Volume 1: Apparel
Volume 2: Fashion designers
Volume 3: Dry cleaning and laundry workers;
Leather tanning and finishing workers; Models

Ski lift operators

Definition

Ski lift operators monitor the fuel-line—diesel or electricity—for the lift that transports skiers up the slope or mountainside and collects fares or checks lift passes. In addition, they also operate the lift by pulling the levers to make it start, pause, stop, or slow down. A ski lift operator checks equipment and makes notations for, or reports any, necessary repairs. A ski lift operator may also be required to maintain the operating condition of the machine.

History

Skiing was originally a method of travel and survival as well as recreation. The sport has scattered roots throughout the world, with many historians believing it originated in ancient Sweden and citing as well Norse myths that mention sliders or skins used for this purpose. Skis have been found in bogs in Sweden and Finland which archaeologists date at 4000 to 5000 years old. Skis were used by Nordic military forces through the 1700s.

Skiing in the United States began in the 1800s in the Midwest. As the sport developed and grew in popularity, though, skiers sought the more challenging regions of the west in the states where the Rocky Mountains spread. Skiing is now enjoyed in many different areas of the country, whether it is alpine (downhill) skiing or nordic (cross country) skiing. In the 1930s the first rope tows were utilized and are now used everywhere.

Nature of the work

Ski lift operators work and monitor the lifts that take people up the hills or mountains of a ski resort. There are many different kinds of lifts that an employee may be asked to operate. Generally, the lifts fall into two basic categories: aerial lifts and surface lifts. Aerial lifts include chair lifts, jig-back trams, and gondolas, and are generally used for higher or larger slopes and mountains. Surface lifts include J-bars, platter pulls, T-bars, and rope tows. Though the lifts are different, they are all operated and maintained in much the same way. Levers, switches, or turnkeys are used to start up the machines that run on electricity, diesel, or gas fuel. There are controls to regulate speed as well as turn the lifts on and off or put them at pause. Lifts are often supported by an auxiliary motor in case of a malfunction.

It is the responsibility of the ski lift operator to make sure that the lifts are in good running order. Usually the first and last tasks of an operator as he or she begins and ends his or her shift is to conduct a thorough inspection of the lifts; starting them up to see how they run, clearing them off of any snow or fallen branches, and making notations of any machine part that is not working correctly. An operator will look over the motor, breaks, switches, and, cables, as well as clear a clean path on the unloading platform. Prior to opening the lift to the guest, an operator will ride the lift to examine its working order at a closer range. Ski lift operators are very mindful of safety and look over the lifts with a keen eye. They also encourage safe skiing and may in-

A ski lift operator assists two skiers as they prepare for a long ride up a mountain. It is not uncommon for skiers to have difficulties getting on a lift.

struct children or inexperienced skiers how to properly get off the lift.

Ski lift operators keep daily logs of the weather conditions and notations on the working order of the equipment. These records may be handed over to a supervisor or shared with the maintenance department to keep on file along with other inspection records.

Operators provide safe transportation up the slopes and offer advice and instruction for safety precautions. They are an extension of the friendly image resorts want to convey and are an asset to the staff.

Requirements

Ski lift operators should be in good physical condition to withstand the challenge of working outdoors. Ski lift operators should be dependable and enjoy working with people. Many times resorts hire employees at least eighteen years of age. Some resorts require the employee to have a high-school diploma or GED certificate. Operators should be responsible and thorough in their work habits and be able to stay alert to properly watch the condition of the lifts.

Special requirements

Most applicants for ski lift operator positions receive on-the-job training. They are taught how the various lifts work, learn the names of the parts, and sometimes are taught simple repairs. There are some classes though that may

increase one's chances for employment or advancement, such as English and communications, machine shop, sociology, psychology, and any classes in first aid and safety can be an advantage.

Opportunities for experience and exploration

Because ski lift operators spend considerable working hours outdoors and enjoy skiing and are familiar with the sport, it might be recommended to take skiing lessons or become more involved in winter sports. Part-time winter jobs with the local parks and recreation department may at least give an applicant an idea as to whether or not he or she enjoy or can withstand winter activities. Libraries often carry books on winter sports and may also have some selections on skiing.

Related occupations

Recreation occupations will continue to offer many job openings as Americans spend more and more time in pursuit of leisure. Other careers of interest include recreational therapists, recreation leaders, camp counselors, sports coaches, professional athletes, and sports instructors.

Methods of entering

Ski resort listings can be obtained through individual state departments' of recreation or tourism, libraries, and outdoor or skiing magazines. Once the names and addresses of the resorts are received, inquiries may be directed to the personnel department or the recreation supervisor. If the applicant already lives in an area where skiing is popular, there may be additional jobs through the local parks and recreation department. The best time to apply for these jobs would be in later summer to allow time for an interview to be scheduled prior to skiing season.

Advancement

Ski lift operators may become supervisors or managers, hiring and training new employees, making work schedules, and delegating duties. Some may pursue other job opportunities at the resort, perhaps becoming a reservations clerk or assistant manager. Some operators plan for advancement by taking college courses during the off season for the sport.

Employment outlook

As the travel industry in general continues to grow and people have a fair amount of dispensable income, the outlook for ski lift operators is projected to be good. With developments in the manufacturing of artificial snow and many resorts offering travel packages, the skiing seasons may become more popular.

Many operators may have better job opportunities and job security by working year-round at the resort in a related capacity.

Earnings

Though most ski lift operators work forty-hour weeks, the nature of their occupation limits them to working a portion of the year, typically from November to April. In addition, many ski lift operators can expect to work Saturdays and Sundays, and often times, holidays, unless they have seniority.

The wages are usually based on hourly rates, with beginning operators earning approximately $4.50 per hour. Some of the larger resorts may pay $10 to their more experienced operators.

Fringe benefits may include a season's pass to use the lifts or free use of some of the resorts other facilities, such as health clubs and spas. Some ski lift operators work for the resort year-round doing other tasks.

Conditions of work

Ski lift operators most often work in resorts and most definitely in the cold and snowy months. They are most often outdoors tending the ski lift except when they are finishing reports or handling other types of administrative duties.

Operators are accustomed to the cold and have learned over the years the most appropriate way to dress for this kind of outdoor work. Sometimes the weather is windy and freezing cold; however, as long as the lifts are open, the operators can expect to be at work. Most ski lift operators wear many layers of clothing, with the outermost layer of a nylon, wind-breaking material, or perhaps a finely woven wool to keep out the sleet and snow.

Ski lift operators spend a good deal of time helping skiers, answering their questions and keeping the unloading zones safe. These services provided and the friendly attitudes the operators display reflect the good image of the resort that employs them.

Social and psychological factors

While ski lift operators enjoy working with the public in the pleasant setting of a resort, there is considerable responsibility involved. Operators must be constantly alert to the conditions of the slopes and the lift, assist inexperienced skiers with getting on and off the lift, and keep current records of the day's events. Many ski lift operators, however, have the temperament for the job and know enough about skiing to be perceptive to potential problems.

GOE: 09.05.08; SIC: 7999; SOC: 5254

◇ **SOURCES OF ADDITIONAL INFORMATION**

American Ski Association
1888 Sherman, Suite 500
Denver, CO 80203

United States Ski Association
PO Box 100
Park City, UT 84060

◇ **RELATED ARTICLES**

Volume 1: Recreation and Park Services
Volume 2: Professional athletes; Recreational therapists; Recreation workers; Sports instructors; Sports occupations
Volume 3: Tour guides

State police officers

Definition

State police officers patrol highways and enforce the laws and regulations that govern the use of those highways. They are often known as state troopers or highway patrol officers.

They arrest or warn drivers who violate traffic laws, monitor passing traffic for stolen vehicles, provide assistance and information to motorists, direct traffic in congested areas, and escort motor processions and parades. In case of accident, they direct traffic around the area, render first aid to injured persons, and investigate the causes of the accident. They appear in court as witnesses in traffic or criminal cases, keep records, and make reports.

State police officers may perform general police work to enforce criminal laws, sometimes assisting law-enforcement officers who are not under state jurisdiction.

History

Police are government agents who enforce the law and maintain order. In the United States, as in England, this responsibility throughout history has been left to the local communities. As a result, our local, county, state, and federal police agencies exist almost independent of each other.

The state police are relatively new agencies. Except for the Texas Rangers, created in 1835, they have developed only in the last one hundred years. State agencies concerned with crime and safety came into being for several reasons: because local police agencies were neglecting to enforce laws pertaining to vice; because county sheriffs failed to provide effective patrols in rural areas; and because of the invention of the automobile and the growing network of highways. Also, it became clear that in times of local disturbances, governors needed someone other than the state militia to call on to enforce the laws.

Today every state has uniformed police. About one-fourth of the states restrict their police officers to the enforcement of laws and regulations governing the operation of motor vehicles and the use of highways. State police operations are customarily confined to unincorporated areas as a matter of policy, although a few states restrict them by statute.

Attempts were made in the past to place some large city police departments under the control of the state police, but without success because of the conflicts that developed. Today local and state police agencies routinely cooperate for more effective law enforcement.

Nature of the work

A major part of the work of state police officers is to patrol the highways and enforce the laws and regulations that are designed to ensure the safety of all citizens traveling thereon. Riding in patrol cars equipped with two-way radios, the highway patrol officers monitor the traffic for troublesome or dangerous situations. They write traffic tickets or issue warnings to drivers who are violating traffic laws or not observing safe driving practices. They are on the alert for stolen vehicles and may arrest drivers where ownership is questionable. They radio assistance for drivers who are stopped because of mechanical failure, a flat tire, illness, or some other reason. They also provide direction for travelers, along with information about lodgings, restaurants, or tourist attractions.

In case of a highway accident, the officers take charge of activities at the site, directing traffic, giving first aid to any injured parties, and calling for emergency equipment such as ambulances, fire trucks, or tow trucks. Then they write up a report to be used by investigating officers who will try to determine the cause of the accident.

Highway patrol officers direct traffic around congested areas caused by fires, road repairs, and other emergencies. They may provide escorts for funeral processions, military convoys, or parades. They may check the weight of commercial vehicles to see that they are within the allowable limits, conduct driver examinations, or give safety information to the public.

In addition to vehicle safety, traffic matters, and other highway responsibilities, state police officers in most states do some general police work, keeping order and apprehending criminals. The state police often are the primary law-enforcement agency in communities or counties that have no police force or large sheriff's department. In those areas, they may investigate such crimes as burglary and assault. They also may assist city or county police to capture law-breakers or control civil disturbances.

Highway patrol officers must keep accurate records and write reports. They sometimes appear in court as witnesses in traffic violation and criminal cases.

Detectives and *investigators* work in plain-clothes to investigate or try to prevent criminal activities. Often undercover, they frequent hangouts of known or suspected criminals to gather information about their habits, friends, and so forth. They examine the scene of a crime, collect evidence, question witnesses, keep records, and write reports. After they apprehend and arrest criminals, the detectives prepare the cases for court and testify before the court and grand jury. Detectives and investigators may specialize in such areas as homicide, narcotics, or vice.

Other state police officers may instruct trainees, pilot police aircraft as *highway patrol pilots,* or specialize in fingerprint classification or chemical and microscopic analysis of criminal evidence. Division and bureau chiefs, commanding officers and *motorized squad commanding officers* have administrative and supervisory duties, directing the activities of their assigned areas.

Two state police officers issue a warning to a motorcyclist on an interstate highway.

Requirements

The appointment of state police officers is governed by state civil service regulations. All candidates must be citizens of the United States and must pass a competitive examination to be eligible. Other entry requirements vary, but in most states applicants must have at least a high-school diploma, or its equivalent in a combination of education and experience, must be at least twenty-one years of age, and possess a valid driver's license. The best-prepared applicants will be those who have had high-school or college courses in English, government, psychology, sociology, American history, business law, chemistry, and physics, or those with previous military police training.

Each state also sets standards for physical and personal qualifications. Applicants usually have to submit to a physical examination to ensure that they have the strength and agility required for police work. Their background and character will undergo careful scrutiny, because complete honesty is an absolutely essential trait in law-enforcement officers. A sense of responsibility and an ability to remain calm and use good judgment in an emergency are among the other qualities that the state looks for when considering candidates for its police force.

In all states, recruits are entered in a formal training program. For several months they receive classroom instruction in state laws and jurisdictions, and they study procedures for accident investigation, patrol, and traffic control. They are drilled in self-defense, learn how to handle firearms, practice driving and maneuvering an automobile at high speeds, and learn how to give first aid. Experienced officers may take advanced training in police science, administration, law enforcement, or criminology at junior colleges, colleges and universities, or special police institutions such as the National Academy of the Federal Bureau of Investigation.

In some states, recent high-school graduates may enter state police work as paid civilian cadets. They attend classes on police work and perform clerical tasks and other nonenforcement duties until they reach the age of 21. At that time, if they qualify, they may be appointed to the state police force, when they will go through standard training.

Special requirements

The normal requirements for police work seem special when compared with those of many other occupations. There may possibly be other requirements that vary from state to state, based on standards they set for their own police officers.

State police officers
Service Occupations

Opportunities for experience and exploration

Because of the nature of police work and the requirements necessary to engage in it, actual experience is not possible for students and other persons considering a law-enforcement career prior to entering it. They can best prepare for it by taking high school and college courses in English, government, psychology, sociology, American history, business law, chemistry, and physics. Agility and strength can be built through physical education courses and involvement in sports. Driver education courses are helpful, as is military police training.

Exploring this occupation can be accomplished by talking with school guidance counselors or with state police officers, by visiting colleges that offer courses in police science or writing to them requesting information about their programs, and by researching the public library card catalog for books on the subject.

Related occupations

Other careers in criminal justice include local police officers, police detectives, security consultants, lawyers, judges, legal assistants, police radio dispatchers, and private investigators.

Methods of entering

Persons interested in becoming state police officers may apply directly to their state civil service commissions or state police headquarters, which are usually located in each state capital. These agencies can provide information about the specific entrance requirements for their states.

Advancement

Most states advance their officers on the basis of the merit system. To become eligible for promotion, police recruits must first serve a probationary period ranging from six months to three years, depending on the state.

A number of factors are considered to determine which officers are qualified for promotion. Certainly, successful completion of training courses, job performance, and personal conduct are important criteria for measuring such potential. In addition, officers must pass a competitive examination.

The usual progression up the ranks is from private to corporal, to sergeant, to first sergeant, to lieutenant, then to captain. As officers move up in grade, they will have the opportunity to specialize in such areas as accident prevention, criminal investigation, and analysis of evidence. Experienced officers prepare for the possibility of promotion by taking advanced courses in administration, police science, law enforcement, or criminology at junior or community colleges, four-year colleges and universities, or at special police training institutions such as the National Academy of the FBI.

Employment outlook

About 62,000 police officers were employed by state governments in the early 1990s.

State police employment is expected to grow about as fast as average through the late 1990s. Competition will be heavy because there are generally more applicants than there are job openings in this occupation. Women and members of minority groups will have the best opportunities.

Most openings will become available as older, experienced employees retire, die, or leave the occupation for other reasons. The greatest need will be for highway patrol officers. As record numbers of Americans use their automobiles for transportation and recreation, traffic control and highway safety become more urgent concerns and will require the attention of additional police officers.

The demand for criminal investigators will not be as great, although specialists will be needed to handle the increasingly complex work done in crime laboratories and electronic data-processing centers. In many state police departments, however, these positions will be filled by civilian employees rather than by uniformed officers.

Employment of state police officers is not particularly affected by poor economic conditions. Layoffs are rare even when state police budgets are reduced; instead, as employees leave, their jobs are left unfilled or are assigned to others already in the department.

Earnings

State police officers generally receive regular raises, based on experience and performance, until a specified maximum is reached. In the early 1990s, beginning officers earned an average salary of $21,600 a year. While maximum salaries ranged to more than $24,000 a year in some states, the average was about $24,000. Earnings were generally higher in the West and lower in the South.

Sergeants had starting salaries that averaged $27,200 a year, with a maximum of approximately $32,700. For lieutenants the starting average was $30,500 a year, with a maximum of $37,000.

State police agencies usually provide uniforms, firearms, and other special equipment, or they may give officers an allowance for their purchase. Liberal pension plans are usually part of the benefit package for state police officers.

Conditions of work

State police officers generally are required to work forty hours a week. In some states the work week may be longer, but the trend is toward forty hours. The nation's highways are never empty; traffic moves at all hours of the day and on all days of the week. So highway patrol officers must be prepared to work different shifts, including nights, weekends, and holidays. They must be ready to report at any time in case of an accident or other emergency, and to work extra hours until the situation is cleared up.

Much of state police work is routine, but it has its potential dangers. Officers often work alone while on patrol. They must be out in all kinds of weather. Accidents may happen even on a routine patrol if the roads are wet or icy or if fog reduces visibility; their likelihood increases when pursuing criminals at high speeds. There is the danger of being injured while apprehending criminals or controlling public disorders, especially if the offenders are armed. The physical activity of this occupation and the tension and stress that accompany emergency situations require more than average strength and stamina.

Social and psychological factors

Persons who are looking for a challenging, exciting, interesting career will find this occupation attractive, but it takes a special combination of traits and characteristics to be suited for such demanding work.

An even temperament is essential to be able to communicate effectively with people of all types, from all levels of society. In stressful situations, people may become confused, abusive, or hysterical, and often only the calming influence of the police officers involved can bring about order and prevent more serious trouble.

The state police officer's working hours are filled with a variety of experiences, and the officers are faced daily with events that can change in a split second. This climate of changeability calls for alertness and flexibility— the ability to think fast, act fast, and change directions easily in times of emergency. At the same time, officers need emotional stability to live constantly with the uncertainty and tensions of a job that could suddenly put their lives in danger. This element of stress also affects family members of the officer and must be considered when accepting a post.

Honesty is a trait that is important in all areas of life, but it is especially important for employees in law enforcement. More often than occurs in most other professions, police officers may be faced with illegal, immoral, or unethical temptations. The duties of their occupation demand nothing less than complete honesty.

Above all, persons who aspire to a career as police officers need a mature attitude, a willingness to accept the responsibility for the safety and welfare of people.

GOE: 04.01.02; SIC: 9221; SOC: 5132

◇ **SOURCES OF ADDITIONAL INFORMATION**

American Federation of Police
1000 Connecticut Avenue, NW
Suite 9
Washington, DC 20036

American Police Academy
Lock Box 15350
Chevy Chase, MD 20815

For scholarship and educational information, please contact:

Blacks in Law Enforcement
256 East McLemore Avenue
Memphis, TN 38106

International Association of Women Police
11 West Monument Avenue
Suite 510
PO Box 2307
Dayton, OH 45401

For general information on police work, contact:

National Police Officers Association of America
1316 Gardiner Lane
Suite 2021
Louisville, KY 40213

◇ **RELATED ARTICLES**

Volume 1: Civil Service
Volume 2: Crime laboratory technologists; FBI agents; Lawyers and judges
Volume 3: Police officers

Tour guides

Definition

Tour guides plan and oversee travel arrangements and accommodations for groups of tourists. A tour guide acts as an escort or chaperon for trips within a single area or one that includes many different stops and destinations. Tour guides assist travelers with questions or concerns and may provide travelers with itineraries regarding information on such topics as climate, points of interest, foreign currency, or local customs. Tour guides research their destinations thoroughly so that they may bridge any potential strangeness of a new area for the travelers they escort.

History

There is always a certain fascination with the unknown. Curiosity about distant cities and foreign cultures is what developed societies and nations. Traveling from one area to another was originally for the purposes of settlement, advancement, and improvement of living conditions. Today, however, travel is commonplace. People travel for business, for recreation, and for education. School children may take field trips to their state's capitol city, and college students may study in foreign countries. Recreation and vacation travel, however, account for much of people's disposable income.

Early travelers were often accompanied by guides or scouts who had become familiar with the routes because they had made earlier trips to investigate safe and comfortable passageways. Later on, young children and women were not expected to travel alone so often relatives or house servants acted as their companions. Today, tour guides act as escorts for peo-

ple visiting foreign countries or to provide additional information on interesting facets of cities or towns. Tour guides take the place of the early scouts, but still act as experts in settings and situations that other people find unfamiliar.

Nature of the work

Tour guides escort groups of tourists to different cities and countries and are knowledgeable companions and chaperons. Tour guides try to ensure that the passengers in a group tour enjoy an interesting and safe trip. Tour guides work to meet the needs of the group by finding out general interests and by directing individuals to those specific areas, whether these may be museums, nature walks, or local shops. They also make themselves aware of individual considerations such as special meals or lodging needs.

A tour guide may schedule airline flights, bus reservations, or train tickets. Some book cruises, house boats, or car rentals. Tour guides research area hotels and other lodgings for the group and plan sightseeing tours, whether by bus or walking, and stops at various points of interest.

Handling all the details of a trip prior to departure is one basic responsibility of a tour guide. Hotel reservations, special exhibits, theatrical presentations, and side trips all have to be made in advance. Itineraries and daily activities are scheduled, and alternate outings are planned in case of inclement weather conditions and to give passengers options.

The second area of focus is, of course, the tour itself. Here, the tour guide must make sure all aspects of transportation, lodging, and recreation meet the itinerary planned. A tour guide must see to it that travelers' baggage and personal effects are loaded and handled properly. Some tours include meals and trips to local establishments and a guide must be sure that each passenger is present for the various arrivals and departures of the trip's activities.

Tour guides provide interesting information on the locale to the group and alert them to special sights. Tour guides become familiar with the history and significance of places through research and previous visits. They see that the group stays together so that they do not miss their transportation arrangements or get lost. Guides also arrange free time for travelers to peruse individual interests, although time allotments and common meeting points are established in advance.

Tour guides must be resourceful to handle necessary changes in plans or unacceptable accommodations. They must know an area's resources so that they are able to offer assistance in dealing with emergencies such as an ill passenger or lost personal items. Tour guides are prepared to answer or find out answers to various questions passengers may have regarding currency, restaurants, and necessary travel identification or preparations.

A tour guide takes a group of tourists down the Salmon River in Idaho.

training may take nine to twelve months and offer job placement to graduates. Community colleges may offer programs in tour escort training. Often programs such as these may be taken on a part-time basis. Classes may include world geography, psychology, human relations, and communication courses. Sometimes students go on field trips themselves to gain experience. Travel agencies and tour companies often offer their own training so that they may coordinate the instruction to complement the tour packages they offer.

Requirements

Tour guides are outgoing, friendly, and confident people. They are aware of the travelers' needs and the kinds of questions and concerns they might have. They are sensitive to the range of activities that areas have to offer and plan sightseeing trips accordingly.

Tour guides are comfortable being in charge of large groups of people and have good time management skills. They are resourceful and are able to adapt to different environments. They are also fun loving and know how to make others feel at ease in unfamiliar surroundings.

Special requirements

Although tour guides do not need a college education, they should at least have a high-school degree. Also, humanities courses such as speech, communication, art, sociology, and history prove beneficial. Some tour guides study foreign languages and cultures as well as geography and architecture.

Some cities have professional schools that offer curriculum in the travel industry. Such

Opportunities for experience and exploration

One way to become more familiar with the responsibilities of tour guides is to accompany local tours. Many cities of all sizes have their own historical societies and museums. Signing up for lectures at the library or at community centers may illustrate some of the responsibilities involved with speaking in front of groups and the kinds of research that may be necessary in giving a presentation. Each state has information available on tours and exhibits of a historical nature, and many trips can be taken as one-day excursions.

Related occupations

The travel and tourism industry, as well as the hospitality industry, is a vast international one that offers many exciting and varied careers to people interested in working with travelers and in seeing foreign locations. Other jobs include travel agents, hotel and motel managers, cruise ship personnel, airline flight attendants, ticket reservation agents, airport personnel, and railroad occupations.

Methods of entering

A person interested in the tour guide profession may begin as a guide for a museum or state park. This would be a good introduction to handling groups of people, giving lectures on points of interest or exhibits, and developing confidence and leadership qualities. Cities with zoos, theme parks, or local walking tours through historical districts often need volunteers or part-time employees to work in their information centers and to offer directions and answer a variety of inquiries.

Travel agencies, tour bus companies, and departments of conservation often need additional help during the summer months when the travel season is high. Societies and organizations for architecture and natural history, as well as other cultural interests, often train and employ guides and provide valuable experience. Students should submit applications and make appointments for interviews.

Advancement

Tour guides gain experience by handling more and more tours, as well as more and more complicated trips. Advancement may come in the form of specialization, such as foreign countries or multiple-destination tours. Some tour guides choose to open their own travel agencies or work for wholesale tour guides, selling trip packages to individual or retail tour escorts.

Some tour guides become travel writers and report on destinations to magazines and newspapers. Other guides may decide to work in the corporate world and plan travel arrangements for company executives.

Employment outlook

Because of the many different opportunities for travel, business, recreation, and education, there is a significant need for tour guides. Travel agencies and tour companies understand the importance of repeat business and as such seek to employ knowledgeable, courteous, and capable escorts. Although certain seasons are more popular for travel than others, well-trained tour guides can be kept busy all year long.

Earnings

Tour guides may find that they have peak and slack periods of the year that correspond to vacation and travel seasons. Many tour guides, however, work eight months of the year and earn up to $13,000. Travel demand is higher in large cities, and some experienced escorts may earn almost $300 per week. Many escorts receive tips and gratuities for special services performed in addition to that amount. Guides receive their meals and accommodations free while conducting a tour, as well as a daily stipend to cover their personal expenses.

Tour guides very often receive paid vacations as part of their fringe benefits package; some may also receive sick pay and health insurance as well. Some companies may offer profit sharing and bonuses.

Conditions of work

Variety is a key element in the tour guide profession. Although most tour guides work in offices while they plan travel arrangements and handle general business, once guides are conducting trips they experience a wide range of different circumstances. Tours to distant cities involve maneuvering through airports. Side trips may involve bus rides, train transfers, or private car rentals. Package trips that encompass seeing a few different foreign countries can require the guide to speak a different language in each city.

Tour guides must know how to act as a link between hotel and lodging staff and travelers if special accommodations are needed or if the rooms are not up to the standard promised to the guide. Tour guides must help everyone else enjoy the trip and be resourceful enough to know how to handle unexpected situations such as delayed flights and overbooked hotel rooms.

Social and psychological factors

Tour guides must not be intimidated by new or foreign surroundings. They should be curious and appreciative of cultural differences and even tempered to offset the unpredictability of traveling. Tour guides should enjoy working with people as much as traveling and have good leadership abilities.

GOE: 07.05.01; SIC: 7999; SOC: 5255

◇ **SOURCES OF ADDITIONAL INFORMATION**

American Guides Association
8909 Dorrington Avenue
West Hollywood, CA 90048

American Sightseeing International
309 Fifth Avenue
New York, NY 10016

◇ **RELATED ARTICLES**

Volume 1: Hospitality; Travel and Tourism
Volume 3: Reservation and transportation
ticket agents; Hotel and motel Industry workers;
Travel agents

Agriculture, Forestry, and Conservation Occupations

The similarities among the professions of agriculture, forestry, fisheries, and conservation are twofold. They include most outdoor types of work, and they involve the special relationship of humans to living things and to their environment. Although the overall organization of this volume of occupations follows the major classifications of the *Dictionary of Occupational Titles*, fourth edition, this section has exceptions. Instead of including in this group only farming, fishery, forestry, and related occupations, some occupations are included here that the DOT included elsewhere. For example, agricultural extension workers (DOT: Professional, administrative, and managerial) is included here.

Agriculture is no longer simply a way of life—it is big business. United States' consumers spend billions for food annually. Rapid developments in technology over the past few decades have enormously increased the level of productivity and have transformed farming from an elementary way of making a living into a science. Agriculture today consists of not only production and cultivation, but also scientific research, the processing of raw materials, and distribution. It is a highly complex and interrelated industry.

The situation is changing rapidly and radically for farming. While the number of farms is steadily decreasing, the individual farm is growing much larger. Modern technology dictates that a farm must be a large operation if it is to be profitable. Spiraling costs of land, equipment, and labor have made it increasingly difficult for a young person who is without a farm background to get started in farming. The young person who is fortunate enough to own a farm must possess the skills of manager, supervisor, laborer, bookkeeper, and financier. In many instances one must also be a veterinarian and a crop and soil specialist. Above all, one must constantly keep abreast of new changes in technology and research, and be aware of the important role that the government plays in agricultural economics. Today's farmers need a much higher level of knowledge and skills than did their predecessors.

But agriculture today means more than the process of farming. It means all the fields that make up the support force for production and distribution of food and fiber. The farmer needs an ever-increasing amount of support from the technical and scientific disciplines to maintain a high-level of productivity. There is new technology at all stages, including super-sized railroad cars; unit trains; bulk shipments; computerized operations; new approaches to processing, storing, wholesaling, and retailing; and improved packaging. Farm-related jobs employed about 3 million persons in the early 1990s.

Careers in forestry can be found in the forest service, the park service, or the wildlife and outdoor recreation services of the state and federal governments.

Special research teams of wildlife specialists seek out, describe, and interpret new relationships between wild animals and their environment. They also conduct research on how to cultivate, develop, and improve forest or marginal land productivity. Programs to educate such specialists are increasing in number.

The study and understanding of marine life and its usefulness to humans is the concern of the careerist in the fisheries profession.

Implicit in the fields of agriculture, forestry, and fisheries is the role of the conservationist. Conservation programs must be carried out not only to meet the needs of today, but also to plan the course of action for tomorrow. The increasing burden placed upon our natural resources will be intolerable and ultimately destructive unless the many conservation programs are implemented and expanded. Without these programs, without the specialist in conservation, there may ultimately be neither farm nor forest, neither fish nor fowl.

Agricultural scientists

Definition

Agricultural scientists study all aspects of living organisms and the relationships of plants and animals to their environment. They may conduct basic research in laboratories or in the field to increase knowledge; apply this knowledge to such things as increasing crop yields and improving the environment; plan and administer programs for testing foods, drugs, and other products; direct activities at public exhibits like the zoo or botanical gardens; teach in colleges and universities; work as consultants to business firms or the government; write for technical publications; or work in technical sales and service jobs for manufacturers of agricultural products.

History

From his origin, man has observed and studied all living things around him. Often his early theories regarding life were incorrect. Around 600 B.C. a Greek philosopher, Anaximander, developed the theory that all living things originally came from water.

As Europe emerged from the Middle Ages, early scientists from many countries contributed to the development of biology. In 1514, Vesalius, a Belgian, became the first to dissect human bodies and founded anatomy. In the seventeenth century, an Englishman, William Harvey, discovered circulation of blood and contributed to the development of physiology. Scientific techniques were improved when Anton van Leeuwenhoek, a Dutchman, developed the microscope. In the eighteenth century, a Swedish naturalist Linnaeus, developed a classification system for scientifically categorizing plants and animals.

The term "biology" was coined 150 years ago by Jean-Baptiste Lamarck, a distinguished French naturalist. During the nineteenth century, Charles Darwin developed a theory of evolution of all biological life. Matthias Schleiden and Theodor Schwann discovered the cellular makeup of all biological life. An Austrian monk by the name of Gregor Johann Mendel used generations of garden peas to test his theories that provided the foundation for the science of genetics. Louis Pasteur of France and Robert Koch of Germany helped found the science of bacteriology.

It was only natural that the rich flora and fauna of the United States encouraged the development of American biologists. John James Audubon and Louis Agassiz were among the pioneers in zoology. Asa Gray in botany and Luther Burbank in plant breeding also made distinguished contributions to biology. The whole field was aided by the establishment in 1887 of what is now known as the National Institutes of Health.

In recent years, biologists have made spectacular contributions in many fields. In agriculture, for example, the development of hybrid corn led to a 20 to 30 percent increase in bushels grown per acre. The discovery, by Sir Alexander Fleming, of penicillin on the eve of World War II saved countless thousands of lives during that conflict and still remains one of our leading medicines.

Nature of the work

Like most other sciences, biology involves two types of research: basic and applied. Basic research is the quest for fundamental truths, while applied research is the practical application of those truths to everyday problems. The two often merge into each other, as when a scientist seeks the cause of a disease and thus is able to develop a cure for it.

Agricultural scientists who apply their knowledge of biology to agricultural matters such as food, fiber, and horticulture have many different titles and duties, some of which are described below.

Agronomists investigate large-scale food-crop problems, conduct experiments, and develop new methods of growing crops to ensure more efficient production, higher yield, and improved quality. They are concerned with the control of plant diseases, pests, and weeds, and may analyze soils to find ways to increase production and reduce soil erosion.

Animal scientists conduct research in and develop improved methods for housing, breeding, feeding, and controlling diseases of domestic farm animals and pet animals.

Horticulturists investigate the problems of fruit and nut orchards as well as garden plants such as vegetables and flowers. They conduct experiments to develop new and improved varieties to increase crop quality and yields and to improve plant culture methods for the land-

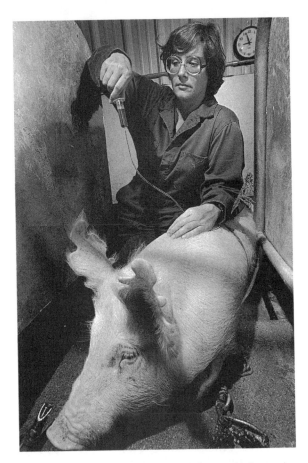

An agricultural scientist takes a blood sample from a swine for an animal stress study. The study will help determine what effects, if any, modern methods of raising livestock have on farm animals.

scaping and beautification of communities, parks, and homes.

Dairy scientists study the selection, breeding, feeding, and management of dairy cattle to find out how various types of food and environmental conditions affect milk production and quality, as well as to develop new breeding programs to improve dairy herds.

Poultry scientists similarly study the breeding, feeding, and management of poultry to improve the quantity and quality of eggs and other poultry products.

Animal breeders, using their knowledge of genetics, develop systems for breeding economically important animals to achieve desired characteristics such as strength, fast maturation, resistance to disease, and quality of meat.

Plant breeders apply genetics to improve plants' yield, quality, and resistance to harsh weather, disease, and insects.

Much of the research conducted by agricultural scientists is done in laboratories and requires a familiarity with research techniques and the use of laboratory equipment and com-

puters. Some research, however, is carried out wherever necessary; thus, a botanist may have occasion to examine the plants that grow in the volcanic valleys of Alaska, or a zoologist to study the behavior of animals on the plains of Africa.

Requirements

The educational requirements are exceptionally high for agricultural scientists, and a doctorate is usually mandatory for those who teach in colleges or universities, are involved in independent research, or hold administrative or management positions in this field. Persons with a relevant master's degree may be employed in applied research, that is, the practical application of the findings of the basic researchers to specific agricultural problems.

A bachelor's degree may be acceptable for some beginning jobs, and new graduates may be hired as testing or inspecting technicians, or as technical sales or service representatives. Promotions, however, are very limited for these employees unless they earn advanced degrees.

The type of degrees earned must relate directly to agricultural and biological science. Undergraduates should have a firm foundation in biology, with courses in chemistry, physics, and mathematics. Most colleges and universities have agricultural science curriculums, although liberal arts colleges may emphasize the biological sciences. State universities usually offer agricultural science programs, too.

Candidates for advanced degrees in agricultural science usually are required to do field-work and laboratory research along with their classroom studies and preparation of a thesis.

Special requirements

Agricultural scientists are expected to be familiar with research techniques and know how to use laboratory equipment and computers. Research in this field may be conducted independently or as part of a group; researchers should be self-motivated enough to work effectively alone, yet able to function cooperatively as a team member when that is called for. They also need the ability to communicate their findings both orally and in writing.

Personal characteristics generally shared by agricultural scientists are an abiding curiosity about the nature of living things and their environment, systematic work habits in their approach to investigation and experimentation, and the persistence to continue or start over when experiments are not immediately successful.

The work done in offices and laboratories does not require unusual strength, but physical stamina is necessary for those scientists who do field research in remote areas of the world.

Persons in this field who teach in public schools will have to satisfy the state's requirements for education and experience. Skill in communicating is also of primary importance to those who teach.

Opportunities for experience and exploration

Persons who are considering careers as agricultural scientists have a number of ways to test their interest in and acquire familiarity with the field.

Students may begin in high school to study courses such as biology, chemistry, physics, and mathematics, and to learn how to operate a computer. It may be possible for some students to act as laboratory assistants to their science teachers.

Field trips to research laboratories may be arranged, along with lectures by or interviews with agricultural scientists. School guidance counselors are a good source for information and advice. And, for inspiration, students may read books based on the lives of famous scientists.

Part-time and summer jobs may provide experience related to the students' goals, but even those jobs that have only a vague relationship can prove helpful. Students who have had college courses in biology may find work as laboratory assistants or aides. Graduate students often have the opportunity to work on research projects at their universities. Depending on their age and educational level, other students may consider possible work in such places as hospitals and veterinarian's offices; florist shops, landscape nurseries, orchards, and farms; zoos, aquariums, botanical gardens, and museums. Volunteer work is often available in hospitals and animal shelters.

Related occupations

Persons with an interest in scientific inquiry and exploration may also be interested in the work of chemists, biochemists, physicists, as-

tronomers, biomedical engineers, pharmacists, pharmacologists, and toxicologists.

Methods of entering

Agricultural scientists are often recruited prior to graduation. The college or university placement offices are a source of information about jobs and they may arrange interviews with the recruiters who visit the campus.

Direct application may be made to the personnel departments of colleges and universities, private industries, or nonprofit research foundations. Persons interested in positions with the federal government may contact the local offices of state employment services and the U.S. Office of Personnel Management, or the Federal Job Information Centers, which are located in various large cities throughout the country. Private employment agencies are another method that might be considered. Large companies sometimes conduct job fairs in major cities and will advertise them in the business sections of the local newspapers.

A less direct way but one that is frequently used by more experienced scientists is to become active in professional associations and to use the personal contacts made there for job referrals and introductions.

Advancement

Advancement in this field depends on education, experience, and quality of job performance. Agricultural scientists with advanced degrees generally start in teaching or research and advance to administrative and management positions, such as supervisor of a research program. The number of such jobs is limited, however, and often the route to advancement is through specialization. The narrower specialties are often the most valuable. The ability of certain programs to obtain financial grants and other funding help the workers involved to advance.

Persons who enter this field with only a bachelor's degree are much more restricted. After starting in testing and inspecting jobs or as technical sales and service representatives, they may progress to advanced technicians, particularly in medical research, or become high school biology teachers. In the latter case, they must have had courses in education and meet the state requirements for teachers.

Employment outlook

In the early 1990s, about 44,000 people worked as agricultural scientists in the United States. About 20,000 of them were employed in colleges and universities in both teaching and research. About half worked for the federal, state, or local government. Some worked in private industry, mostly for agricultural services, fertilizer, and seed companies. More than 2,400 worked as self-employed consultants.

The employment of agricultural scientists is expected to increase about as fast as average through the late 1990s as private industry gets more involved in such areas as applying biotechnology, including recombinant-DNA research, to agriculture. As in most other fields, openings will also occur as older, experienced employees retire, die, or leave the occupation for other reasons.

The outlook is good for persons with advanced degrees; the others will face stiff competition. Some holders of agricultural and biological degrees will enter related occupations as agricultural and biological technicians, medical laboratory technologists, or health care professionals.

The field of agricultural science is not much affected by economic fluctuations. Employees involved in teaching, long-term research projects, and agricultural activities rarely lose their jobs during a recession.

Earnings

According to a College Placement Council survey, in the early 1990s beginning agricultural scientists with a bachelor's degree earned an average of about $20,400 per year.

Beginning salaries in the federal government ranged from $17,000 to $21,400 a year with a bachelor's degree; $21,400 to $26,200 with a master's degree; and $31,600 to $38,000 with a doctorate. The average overall annual salary for agricultural scientists in the federal government was about $40,300.

Conditions of work

Agricultural scientists work regular hours, although researchers may choose to work longer when their experiments have reached a critical point.

They generally work in offices, laboratories, or classrooms where conditions are clean, healthy, and safe. Some biological scientists, such as botanists, ecologists, or zoologists, may periodically take field trips, which require strenuous physical activity and where living facilities are primitive.

Social and psychological factors

Agricultural scientists deserve and enjoy prestige and respect from their fellow citizens and colleagues. This occupation attracts a special kind of person, one whose concerns and goals extend far beyond the personal and embrace the interest and welfare of human beings throughout the world. They exhibit a dedication to solving problems on the grand scale, such as improving and increasing food production, conquering disease, and protecting the environment.

GOE: 02.02.02; SIC: 07; SOC: 1853

◇ **SOURCES FOR ADDITIONAL INFORMATION**

American Dairy Science Association
309 West Clark Street
Champaign, IL 61870

American Society for Horticultural Science
701 North St. Asaph Street
Alexandria, VA 22314

American Society of Agronomy
677 South Segoe Road
Madison, WI 53711

American Society of Plant Toxonomists
Department of Botany
University of Georgia
Athens, GA 30602

Botanical Society of America
75 North Eagleville Road
u—43 University of Connecticut
Storrs, CT 06268

Crop Science Society of America
677 South Segoe Road
Madison, WI 53711

National Association of Animal Breeders
Box 1033
Columbia, MO 65205

Phycological Society of America
Department of Botany
Louisiana State University
Baton Rouge, LA 70803

Soil Science Society of America
677 South Segoe Road
Madison, WI 53711

◇ **RELATED ARTICLES**

Volume 1: Agriculture; Biological Sciences; Chemicals and Drugs; Chemistry; Education; Health Care; Physical Sciences
Volume 2: Biochemists; Biologists; Chemists; College and university faculty; Engineers
Volume 3: See Agriculture, Forestry, Fisheries, and Conservation Occupations
Volume 4: See Agriculture, Forestry, and Conservation Technician Occupations

Agricultural extension service workers

Definition

Agricultural extension service workers distribute information and instructions concerning improved methods of agriculture and home economics to the county rural population. They advise farmers regarding farm problems, crops and their rotation, varieties of seeds, fertilization, soil conservation, farm management, livestock breeding and feeding, use of new machinery, and marketing. They also supervise the work of home demonstration agents and lead the work of young people's clubs.

History

It was in the late eighteenth century that President George Washington decided to establish some educational agency of government dedicated to the assistance of the farmers. Washington's proposal eventually developed into what is now known as the Department of Agriculture.

President Thomas Jefferson furthered the plan when he developed the concept of schools for the farmers. This responsibility was eventually delegated to the state agricultural or land-grant colleges established under the Morrill Act of 1862 and promoted by President Abraham Lincoln.

Once established, the state agricultural colleges were not at all certain what agricultural information was factual enough to teach.

Through the Hatch Act of 1887 experimental stations were created through which information regarding soils, crops, livestock, fruits, and machinery could be gathered. They became sources of information to both the agricultural colleges and the farmer.

One major difficulty was still encountered. There seemed to be no effective way of getting the information to farmers without bringing them to the college. It was decided that people who were familiar with the work of the farmer and who were educated in the agricultural sciences should go into the field and carry information to the farmers so that they could apply it to their farming programs.

Thus, the concept of today's agricultural extension work was developed and placed in operation in 1914 on a federal basis by the passage of the Smith-Lever Act. It was opened to any state that wished to join the educational project on a cooperative basis and most states accepted the opportunity. It is because of this that every state agricultural college in the nation today has an extension service as one of its major departmental classifications.

Nature of the work

Agricultural extension service workers normally are engaged in the teaching of agricultural subjects at places other than college campuses. They usually conduct these educational programs on an informal basis to help people analyze and solve agricultural problems. They cover such areas as soil and crop improvement, livestock, farm machinery, fertilizers, new methods of planting, and any other information that may be of assistance to the farmer. Much of the information is offered on an informal basis, possibly while the farmer is engaged in planting or harvesting or in small evening group meetings of five or six farmers. Other information is offered by the extension service worker speaking before larger groups on a more formal basis.

County-agricultural agents work closely with federal extension service workers in gathering information to be presented to the farmers. Information on agronomy (theory and practice of soil management and crop production), livestock, marketing, agricultural economics, home economics, horticulture (growing of fruits), and entomology (study of insects) may come either from the state agricultural college or from the federal government's Agricultural Extension Service. It is the job of the county agricultural worker to review the new information, perhaps condense it, and then present it as effectively as possible to the farmers in a particular area. The county or federal extension service agent's work is primarily educational in nature and is aimed at increasing the efficiency of agricultural production and marketing and the development of new and different market outlets.

County agricultural agents also work closely with *county home-demonstration agents,* who assist the homemakers in the county in improving their home management and nutrition. The home demonstration agent is responsible for keeping up to date in any area relating to the home and for providing this information to the people in a particular county or group of counties.

Four-H Club agents organize and direct the educational projects and activities of the 4-H Club, including analyzing needs of individuals and the community, developing teaching materials, training volunteers, and organizing exhibits at state and county fairs.

Both the home demonstration and the agricultural agents rely on mass communication for getting out information. Newspapers, radio and television broadcasts, and other types of informational sources available within the area are utilized by them in reaching the people who have the greatest use for this information.

There is a degree of specialization involved, especially on the federal level. Federal agricultural extension service workers often become program leaders responsible for the development and maintenance of relationships with various state and territorial land-grant colleges and universities and with heads of various pub-

lic and private agencies involved in agriculture. In some cases, they also become educational research and training specialists responsible for the development of research programs in all phases of extension work, and the results of these programs are shared with the various state agencies. Subject matter specialists develop programs through which new information can be presented to the farmers effectively, while educational media specialists condense information and distribute it as it becomes available to the various states for use in their local extension programs. These extension service workers may be designated as *extension service specialists.* Those at higher supervisory levels, who direct and coordinate the work of other extension service workers, are called *extension service specialists-in-charge.* An extension service worker who has charge of programs for a group of counties is a *district extension service agent.*

Federal agricultural extension service workers are employed by the U.S. Department of Agriculture to assist county extension officers and supervisors in planning, developing, and coordinating national, regional, and state extension programs. They have their headquarters in Washington, D.C. County agricultural agents are normally employed jointly by the state agricultural college in each state and the U.S. Department of Agriculture. The work of the federal extension service agent and the county agent is meant to complement and supplement one another.

County agents may also specialize, especially in those counties employing more than two or three agents. A county employing as many as ten agents may have specialists in crop production, dairying, poultry production, farm machinery, soils, and livestock. Many counties in which a number of different forms of agriculture are carried on will have five or more agents and the nature of the demands on these workers will necessitate their specialization.

Requirements

The work of the agricultural extension service worker normally requires a background of practical farming experience and a thorough knowledge of the types of problems confronting farmers. Farmers may naturally prefer to work with people who they feel have a complete understanding of their work.

Extension service workers are required to have a bachelor's degree, usually with a major in either agriculture or home economics, and those who hope to join the on-campus staff at the state agricultural college are usually expected to have at least a master's degree. The college program will normally include courses in English, history, chemistry, biology, economics, education, and speech, as well as animal science, crop production, agricultural geology, horticulture, soils, and farm management. A number of colleges have developed regular agricultural extension curriculums to be followed by those hoping to enter the field.

After graduation from college, in-service training programs are usually available through which the state agricultural college and the Department of Agriculture can keep the county agents up to date on new programs and policies affecting agriculture and on newly developed teaching techniques. Attendance at such programs may be required or may be on a voluntary basis.

The high-school student looking forward to a career as an extension service agent should take courses in English literature and composition, algebra, geometry, biology, physics, and the social sciences, including history and political science or government.

Extension agents must enjoy working with people, be aggressive without being antagonistic, have a particular feeling for farmers and their problems, and be able to teach. They must also be patient and willing to learn from farmers. They should have the ability to organize group projects, meetings, and broad educational programs for both adults and younger people involved in agriculture. Agents should have the interest that will enable them to keep up to date with the huge supply of new agricultural information constantly being made available. They must be willing to learn the newest teaching techniques to be utilized in getting the information to the residents of the particular area.

Special requirements

There are no special requirements such as licensure needed by a person in this field.

Opportunities for experience and exploration

One may explore the work of agricultural extension service agents while in high school by reading a number of pamphlets and occupational information brochures published about the occupation or by visiting with an agricul-

This agricultural extension service worker explains to a farmer how stubble mulching can protect farmland from soil deterioration.

tural extension service agent. Any of the state agricultural colleges will send materials or give interested students the names of extension service agents in a particular area, thus enabling the student to write for information. The individual may find it possible to visit the agent in the office or in the field. It may also be possible to visit with farmers or others engaged in agriculture, thus gaining their impressions of the work carried on by the agricultural extension service agent in their particular county. High-school counselors will be of assistance to the young person hoping to gather additional information regarding the field.

Related occupations

Other areas of employment that allow persons to utilize an interest in the land and in agriculture include farmers, farm operatives, farm managers, dairy ranchers, cattle ranchers, canning and preserving industry workers, and beekeepers.

Methods of entering

The person entering extension service work will normally be a college graduate and will have the assistance of the college's placement service in finding a job. Most applicants, however, will apply to the director of the extension service at the agricultural college in the state in which they hope to work. Providing a job vacancy is available, the director of the extension service will screen the qualifications of the various applicants and submit the names to a board or council that will be responsible for making the final selection.

Advancement

Competent agricultural extension agents are normally promoted fairly rapidly and early in their careers. The promotions may be in the form of assignments to more responsible positions within the same county or reassignment in a different county within the state, or the promotions may be only on a financial basis. Many agents, after moving through a succession of more responsible extension jobs, may join the staff at the state agricultural college. A number of directors of existing extension services began their careers in this way.

It is also possible to branch out into other areas. Agricultural extension service agents may often go into related jobs, especially those in industries which specialize in agricultural products. Former extension service agents can be found selling fertilizer, seed, feed, or farm machinery. The training they have received and their background in agriculture provides for ample flexibility in employment possibilities.

Employment outlook

Agricultural extension service agents are employed in nearly every agricultural county in the nation. In those counties where a number of crops are being produced by the farmers, there may be as many as ten or more agents employed. There were approximately 19,775 Extension Service agricultural agents in the United States in the early 1990s, and the number is expected to increase in the future although it will grow more slowly than the average for all occupations through the late 1990s. It is anticipated that their work will be extended to new and additional segments of the population, including the many rural but nonfarming families and various suburban residents who are coming to recognize the value of the assistance rendered by agricultural extension service workers. Then too, the farming industry is becoming more complex, and a greater degree of specialization will be needed on the part of extension service workers. Farm people will become even more aware of the need for their county agents. Extension service agents will be needed in depressed rural areas where their

services may help the residents earn better livings for their families.

In addition to this, the idea of agricultural extension service programs is spreading to many foreign countries, and there should be an increasing demand for our county and federal agents to assist their counterparts in setting up and operating agricultural extension service programs.

Earnings

The earnings of agricultural extension service agents vary from state to state and from county to county. The average annual salary of extension agents, however, was $24,000 a year in the early 1990s. Salaries for experienced home demonstration agents averaged about $22,200 a year.

Conditions of work

The work itself is often taxing both mentally and physically. Extension service agents with a heavy workload may find themselves faced with problem after problem requiring them to work in the field for long periods of time. They may be in their office handling routine matters every day for a month and then not re-enter the office for the next month and a half. (They usually have a private office where they can speak in confidence with those who seek assistance.) As a rule, agricultural extension service agents spend about half of their time in the field working with farmers on specific problems, arranging for or conducting group meetings or simply distributing new updated information. They usually drive from 500 to 1,500 miles per month while on the job.

The work may be hard on the agent's family in that a number of evening meetings will be required, and the agent will be invited to many weekend activities. Agents may conduct small informal meetings on Monday and Tuesday nights to discuss particular problems being faced by a small group of farmers in the county. They may be home on Wednesday, working with a student's 4-H club on Thursday, conducting another meeting on Friday, and then judging a livestock show at the county fair on Saturday.

The hours are not regular and the pay is not particularly high for the number of hours put into the job. Agents may often have demands from people who do not understand their function and responsibilities. It is rewarding, however, and there is an opportunity to work out-of-doors. In addition, there is the satisfaction of working with people who appreciate the assistance.

In many states the jobs of agricultural agents are under civil service retirement plans with a minimum retirement age of sixty-two and an average retirement age of sixty-five. In some states, the agents come under the teachers' retirement program. Both types of plans are usually satisfactory.

Social and psychological factors

Agricultural extension service agents may often have the feeling of being overworked, especially in areas where a number of problems are constantly being identified and demanding solutions. But they do have the satisfaction of being engaged in interesting, progressive work. The people with whom the agent works are dedicated to their vocation and anxious to have his or her assistance. It is these people who give the agent the feeling of being needed. The work is not confining, and the individual with enterprise and initiative is usually rewarded with recognition and promotions when possible.

GOE: 11.07.03; SIC: 076; SOC: 239

◇ SOURCES FOR ADDITIONAL INFORMATION

Federal Extension Service
U.S. Department of Agriculture
Washington, DC 20250

You may also want to consult your local county extension office.

◇ RELATED ARTICLES

Volume 1: Agriculture; Business Administration; Civil Service; Education; Recreation and Park Services
Volume 2: Home economists
Volume 3: See Agriculture, Forestry, Fisheries, and Conservation Occupations
Volume 4: See Agriculture, Forestry, and Conservation Technicians

Coal mining operatives

Definition

Coal mining operatives extract coal from surface mines and underground mines, using complex and expensive machinery.

History

Even before the development of agriculture or weaving, Stone Age people were mining for minerals buried in the earth: flints to make weapons, mineral pigments for ornamentation. At first they dug open pits to reach the more easily accessible ores. Then they built primitive tunnels underground, where early miners used sticks and bones to dig out soft or broken rocks. Hard rocks were broken by driving metal or wooden wedges into a crack in the surface. An early method for dealing with particularly large, stubborn rocks was to build fires alongside them until they became thoroughly heated and then to dash cold water against them: the sudden contraction would cause the rocks to fracture.

Breaking through rock barriers became less tedious when, in the seventeenth century, Europeans began to use gunpowder from China to explode them, but it was not until the invention of dynamite in 1866 that modern mining techniques were born.

The coal industry played a vital role in the rapid industrial development of the United States. Its importance increased dramatically during the 1870s with the expansion of the railroads and the development of the steel industry, and during the 1880s when steam began to

333

be used to generate electric power. The production of bituminous coal doubled each decade from 1880 to 1910, and by 1919 production was more than 500 million tons.

Coal was the primary source of energy until after 1920, when it was almost replaced by hydroelectric power and oil. Its use was further reduced after World War II, when natural gas became the fuel of choice. Oil and natural gas are preferred because they are cheaper, cleaner, and easier to handle; but today the rising price of oil and its uncertain supply are making coal a major energy source again.

Nature of the work

There are two kinds of coal mines: surface and underground. The method used is determined by the depth and location of the coal seam and the geological formation around it. In surface mining, or strip mining, the overburden—the earth above the coal seam—has to be removed before the coal can be dug out. Then, after the mining has been completed, the overburden is replaced so the land can be reclaimed. For underground mining, entries and tunnels are constructed so that workers and equipment can reach the coal.

The machinery used in coal mining is extremely complex and expensive. There are power shovels that can move 3,500 tons of earth in an hour, and continuous mining machines that can rip 12 tons of coal from an underground seam in a minute. It is the job of the coal mining operatives to operate these machines safely and efficiently. Their specific duties vary depending on the type of mine and the machinery they operate.

Some of the operatives used in surface mining are described as follows.

Bulldozer operators use a tractor equipped with a concave blade attached across the front to remove trees, rocks, soil, and other obstructions from the mining area. They push rocks and dirt within reach of the shovels and scoops of machines that remove the overburden. They also help replace the overburden when mining has been completed.

Machine drillers operate drilling machines to bore holes in the overburden at points selected by the blasters. They must be careful to avoid binding or stoppage of a drill while in operation. They may replace worn or broken parts using hand tools, change drill bits, and lubricate the equipment.

Blasters study the rock formation to determine where explosives should be placed, what type to use, and how much. They instruct the

machine drillers as to where to bore the necessary holes, then set the explosive charges in the holes and detonate them to fracture the overburden.

Stripping shovel operators and *dragline operators* control the shovels and draglines that scoop up and move the broken overburden, which is pushed within their reach by the bulldozers. With the overburden removed, the coal is exposed so that machines with smaller shovels can remove it from the seam and load it into trucks.

Underground mining uses three methods to extract coal that lies deep beneath the surface. They are continuous, longwall, and conventional mining. Following is a description of each and some of the operatives they employ.

Continuous mining produces most of the coal from underground. It is a system that uses an electric, hydraulically operated machine that mines and loads coal in one step. Cutting wheels attached to hydraulic lifts rip coal from the seam. Then mechanical arms gather the coal from the tunnel floor and dump it onto a conveyor, which moves the coal to a shuttle car or another conveyor belt for transportation out of the mine. *Continuous-mining machine operators* sit or lie in the cab of the machine, drive it into the mining area, and manipulate levers to position the cutting wheels against the coal. They and their helpers may adjust, repair, and lubricate the machine and change cutting teeth.

In longwall mining, coal is also cut and loaded in one operation. With steel canopies supporting the roof above the work area, the mining machinery moves along a wall that may be 300 to more than 700 feet long, while its plow blade or cutting wheel shears the coal from the seam and automatically loads it onto a conveyor belt for transportation out of the mine. *Longwall-mining machine operators* advance the cutting device either manually or by remote control. They monitor lights and gauges on the control panel and listen for unusual sounds that would signal or indicate a malfunction in the equipment. Their assistants, called *tailers,* help advance the plow blade, adjust the depth of the cutting tool, signal when it is in proper position, and adjust and make minor repairs to the machinery. As the wall in front of the longwall mining machine is cut away, the operator and his helper move the roof supports forward, allowing the roof behind the supports to cave in.

Conventional mining, unlike continuous or longwall mining, is done in separate steps: first the coal is blasted from the seam, and then it is picked up and loaded. Of the three underground methods, conventional mining requires the largest number of workers. *Cutter operators* work a self-propelled machine equipped with an endless chain with teeth that travels around a blade six to fifteen feet long. They drive the machine into the working area and saw a channel along the bottom and sides of the coal face, a procedure that makes the blasting more effective because it relieves some of the pressure caused by the explosion. They may adjust and repair the machine, replace dull teeth, and shovel debris from the channel. Using mobile machines, *drilling-machine operators* bore blast holes in the coal face after first determining the depth of the undercut and where to place the holes. Then *blasters* place explosive charges in the holes and detonate them to shatter the coal. After the blast, *loading-machine operators* drive electric loading machines to the area and manipulate the levers that control the mechanical arms to gather up the loose coal and load it onto shuttle cars or conveyors for transportation out of the mine.

A coal mining operative uses a specially designed piece of equipment to gather and transport recently blasted coal.

Requirements

A high-school diploma is not necessary, but coal miners must be at least eighteen years of age and in good physical condition to withstand the rigors of the work.

Coal mining operatives learn their skills on the job. New employees start as trainees, or "red hats." After the initial training period, they become general laborers and work at routine tasks that do not require much skill, such as shoveling coal onto conveyors. As they gain more experience and become familiar with the mining operations, they are put to work as helpers to experienced machine operators. In this way, they eventually learn how to operate the machines themselves. In union mines, when a vacancy occurs and a machine operator job is available, an announcement is posted so that any qualified employee may apply for the position. The job is usually given to the person with the most seniority.

Special requirements

Federal laws require that all mine workers be given safety and health training before beginning work, and they must be retrained annually thereafter. Union contracts and some states also require pre-service training and annual retraining in subjects such as health and safety regulations and first aid.

The union to which most coal miners belong is the United Mine Workers of America, although some are covered by the Southern Labor Union, the Progressive Mine Workers, or the International Union of Operating Engineers. There are also some independent unions within single firms.

Related occupations

Other jobs that are involved with the extraction or refinement of energy sources include petroleum refining workers, petroleum drilling workers, geologists, and geophysicists.

Opportunities for experience and exploration

Because of the age limitation for coal mining operatives, opportunities do not exist for most high-school students to gain actual experience. Students over the age of eighteen may possibly find summer work as laborers in a coal mine, performing routine tasks that require no previous experience. Older students may also investigate the possibility of summer or part-time employment in metal mines, quarries, oil drilling operations, heavy construction, road building, or truck driving; while the work may not be directly related to their goals, the aptitudes required are similar and the experience may prove useful.

If safety rules do not prohibit them, field trips to local mines may be arranged. Otherwise, representatives of the coal mining industry may be invited to speak at an assembly, along with a film or slide presentation. School guidance counselors may be a source of further information.

Methods of entering

The usual method of entering this field is by direct application to the employment offices of the individual coal mining companies. However, mining machine operators must "come up through the ranks," acquiring the necessary skills on the job. Therefore, persons interested in this occupation will have to start as trainees and do general labor before being permitted to assist experienced operators and learn how to operate the machinery.

Advancement

Coal mining operatives are limited in their opportunities for advancement. The usual progression is from trainee to general laborer, to machine operator's helper. After acquiring the skills needed to operate the machinery, the helpers may apply for machine operator jobs as they become available. All qualified workers, however, will be competing for those positions, and vacancies are almost always filled by workers with the most seniority.

A few coal mining operatives become supervisors, but additional training is required for the higher supervisory or management jobs.

Employment outlook

In the early 1990s the U.S. coal industry employed approximately 63,000 mining machine operatives. More than half of these were heavy-equipment operators; the rest included blasters and those classified by the machines they operate: continuous mining, drilling, loading, cutting, hoisting, and longwall mining machine operators.

Coal is mined in twenty-six states. Employment is concentrated mostly in the Appalachian area, including West Virginia, Kentucky, Pennsylvania, and Virginia, although large numbers of workers are also found in Ohio, Illinois, Alabama, and Wyoming.

The employment of coal mining operatives is expected to rise more slowly than the national occupational average through the early 1990s. The demand for individual operators depends on the type of mine opened and the methods and machinery used. Increased surface mining means that more bulldozer operators, dragline operators, and power shovel operators will be required. A growth in underground mining will call for more continuous mining machine operators and longwall mining machine operators.

Many openings for coal mining operatives will also occur as older, experienced workers retire, die, or leave the occupation.

Because coal is a major resource for the production of such products as steel and cement, it is strongly affected by changes in the economic activity. In a recession the demand for coal drops, and many miners may be laid off.

Earnings

Production workers in coal mining are paid better than those in the mining industry as a whole, and a lot better than the average for all production workers in private industry. In the early 1990s coal miners averaged $12.97 per hour, compared to $11.00 for all miners and $7.98 for workers in private industry (except farming).

Among the coal mining operatives, the average hourly rates varied. Highest-paid were the power-shovel operators at $12.80 an hour. Longwall miner operators were close behind with $12.75. Continuous mining machine operators earned $12.69, while their helpers received $12.49. Loading machine operators averaged $12.20 an hour. Cutting machine operators were paid $12.18 and their helpers $12.13. Bulldozer operators earned $12.01, blasters $11.90, and machine drillers $11.81. These hourly figures do not include overtime or incentive pay. Operatives who work the evening shift receive an additional $.24 an hour; those on the night shift an additional $.36 an hour.

Most mine workers are given ten holidays a year. Those who work in mines covered by a contract between the Bituminous Coal Operators Association and the United Mine Workers receive fourteen days of paid vacation a year. After working six years, they get one extra day a year up to a maximum of thirteen additional vacation days. There are generally three regular vacation periods during the year, and the miners must take their vacations during one of them. After one year, mine workers also are entitled to five personal/sick days and four floating vacation days that may be taken anytime. Miners not covered by a BCOA-UMW contract usually get two weeks vacation after one year.

Most coal miners also receive health and life insurance, as well as pension benefits. The insurance generally includes hospitalization, surgery, convalescent care, rehabilitation services, and maternity for the workers and their dependents. The size of the pension depends on the worker's age at retirement and the number of years of service.

The United Mine Workers of America negotiates the contracts that cover most coal miners. The Southern Labor Union, the Progressive Mine Workers, the International Union of Operating Engineers, and independent single-firm unions also have contracts with mine operators.

Conditions of work

Coal mining is hard work, under often harsh and sometimes hazardous conditions. Workers in surface mines are outdoors in all kinds of weather, while those underground work in tunnels that are cramped, dark, dusty, wet, and cold. They are all subjected to loud noise from the machinery and work that is physically demanding and dirty.

Since passage of the Coal Mine Health and Safety Act in 1969, mine operators have improved the ventilation and lighting in underground mines and have taken steps to eliminate safety hazards for all workers. Nevertheless, operators of the heavy machinery both on the surface and below ground run the risk of injury or death from accidents. Other possible hazards for underground miners include roof falls or cave-ins, poisonous and explosive gases, and long exposure to coal dust. After a number of years, workers may develop pneumoconiosis, or "black lung," which is a disabling and sometimes fatal disease.

Social and psychological factors

There is a camaraderie among workers who share heavy labor, hardship, and danger. Mine workers may be characterized by a concern for their fellow miners. There is no room for carelessness in this occupation. The safety of all de-

pends on teamwork, with everyone alert and careful to avoid accidents. Miners are not afraid of discomfort, dirt, and strenuous work.

Other workers, in related occupations, are needed to run safe and efficient mines. They include hoist operators, maintenance electricians, maintenance mechanics, rock dust sprayers, roof bolters, safety engineers, section supervisors, shuttle-car operators, stripping shovel oilers, and truck drivers.

GOE: 05.11; SIC: 12; SOC: 8319

◇ SOURCES FOR ADDITIONAL INFORMATION

General information on mining occupations is available from:

American Mining Congress
1920 N Street, NW
Suite 300
Washington, DC 20036

International Union, United Mine Workers of America
900 15th Street, NW
Washington, DC 20005

National Coal Association
1130 17th Street, NW
Washington, DC 20036

Society of Mining Engineers
PO Box 625002
Littleton, CO 80162

◇ RELATED ARTICLES

Volume 1: Energy; Metals; Mining; Physical Sciences
Volume 2: Ground water professionals; Petrologists; Surveyors
Volume 3: Electrical repairers; Industrial truck operators; Logging industry workers
Volume 4: Coal mining technicians; Electro-mechanical technicians

Dairy farmers

Definition

Dairy farmers raise milk-producing cows and sell the milk on the open market. They must maintain the barns, milking areas, and other parts of the farm and train and supervise any farm workers that assist them in their tasks. As business owners, dairy farmers are responsible for keeping financial records and making all the managerial decisions needed to keep the farm operating.

History

Raising cattle is one of the oldest of human occupations, going back before the beginnings of recorded history. Early dairy farmers probably had several cows to provide milk for their families with some additional milk to use for barter for clothing and other necessities.

In the United States, dairy farms and other types of farms increased in size during the nineteenth century as the population grew and the grazing areas of the great plains regions were opened.

Although the application of science and technology has changed dairy farming over the last fifty years, the fundamental principle of milking each cow twice a day has remained. And, although dairy farming remains a demanding and competitive occupation, each year highly educated men and women become involved in the profession.

Nature of the work

Although dairy farmers' first concern is with the production of the maximum amount of high-grade milk, they also raise corn and grain to provide feed for their animals.

The dairy farmer must be able to repair the many kinds of equipment essential to the business; keep accurate records; be part laborer and part supervisor; and be knowledgeable about disease, sanitation, and methods of improving the quantity and quality of milk.

Milking is generally done between five and six o'clock in the morning. During milking (either by hand or by machine), the cows are fed a combination of milk and grain. After milking, the milk is cooled immediately, as it spoils quickly. Records are kept of each cow's milk production to discover which cows are profitable and which should be traded or sold to livestock farmers.

After milking, when the cows are at pasture, the farmer washes, sweeps, and sterilizes the stalls and the barn with boiling water. In larger operations, this task may be done by *dairy farm workers*. This cleaning is extremely important as cows contract diseases from unsanitary conditions which, in turn, may contaminate the milk. Dairy farmers must have their herds certified free of disease by representatives of the Department of Health. The cows are milked again at around 5 o'clock in the evening, and the entire round of cleaning the barn and stalls must be repeated in preparation for the next day. These chores must be done seven days a week, fifty-two weeks a year.

The dairy farmer's responsibilities don't end with the milking of the cows. Equipment and containers must be cleaned; fences and machinery repaired; winter silage gotten ready; and new feed crops planted or harvested. Sick or calving cows must also be attended to.

Dairy farmers have many managerial responsibilities. For example, they must determine the best time to plant, fertilize, and cultivate the feed grain, keep financial records of the farm operation, and train and supervise workers in the use of equipment and the performance of the farm work. Dairy farmers also often have to secure loans from banks or other financial institutions to purchase machinery, fertilizers, farm animals, and feed.

Most dairy farms are family owned and operated, with family members the main workers. Large dairy farms, however, may employ twenty to thirty people and sometimes more. In large dairy operations, the dairy farmer may hire a *dairy farm supervisor* to oversee the day-to-day farming operations. Dairy farm supervisors coordinate and supervise the activities of the farm workers. They oversee the milking, breeding, and caring for cows, and perform some lay-veterinary duties on the animals. Supervisors assign workers to feeding, milking, and other tasks, and inspect the barn and milking parlors to ensure that they are being properly cleaned and maintained. They are also responsible for maintaining records of feed and milk production and making any appropriate dietary changes in order to increase the cows' milk productivity. Farm supervisors also schedule breeding, vaccinating, and dehorning activities and may artificially inseminate cows to produce desired offspring. All of the dairy farm supervisor's activities are reported to and okayed by the dairy farmer.

Dairy farm workers aid the dairy farmer in all aspects of work including washing the cows, cleaning the stalls, inspecting the farm animals for diseases, feeding the animals, and herding the animals from the pasture to the milking parlor. They also milk the cows either by hand or by machine, and cultivate, harvest, and store feed crops. They often maintain and repair fences and farm equipment.

Machine milkers operate machines that milk dairy cows. They disinfect the cow's teat and udder before milking and collect a sample of the milk to examine for blood or other irregularities. They attach a cup to the cow's udder and start the machine, removing the cup when the required amount of milk has been collected. Machine milkers then pump the milk into a storage tank and clean and sterilize the equipment before reusing it on other cows.

A dairy farmer hooks up a cow to a milking machine. This apparatus also gauges the amount of milk being drawn from the cow.

Requirements

Although there are no specific educational requirements, the increasingly complex scientific, business, and financial knowledge necessary to run a dairy farm usually requires completion of a two- or four-year college program in agriculture or a related field. Many farmers also seek a masters degree in agricultural science. Even people who have lived on farms must have a strong educational background in order to succeed in this highly competitive field.

Aspiring dairy farmers should have knowledge of farm management, disease control, soil preparation and cultivation, machinery maintenance, and an understanding of business practices and accounting. They should also have a basic affection for farm animals and a thorough knowledge of their special requirements. All dairy farmers (as well as other farmers) should enjoy being outdoors and be in good physical condition. Mechanical aptitude and the ability to work with tools are also important skills. Increasingly, a knowledge of computers is becoming important, since computers can be used to monitor the various farming operations.

High-school students should take courses in algebra, geometry, accounting, and English. Extension courses should also be taken to keep up on new developments in farm technology and scientific advances.

There are many colleges with two- and four-year programs in animal science or animal husbandry. Typical courses include animal hus-

bandry techniques, feeds and feeding, farm management, farm animal breeding, and animal health.

Special requirements

There are no licenses or certificates needed to work in this field. It is vital, however, that dairy farmers keep abreast of all the latest developments and technological advances that occur.

Opportunities for experience and exploration

For young people who do not belong to a farm family, there are many opportunities for part-time farm work, especially during the summer months.

In addition, organizations such as the 4-H Clubs and Future Farmers of America offer especially good opportunities for hearing about, visiting, and participating in farm and farm related activities. Agricultural colleges often have their own farms where the student can gain actual experience in farm operations as well as classroom work.

Related occupations

Other professionals concerned with operating a farm and raising farm animals include agricultural engineers, dairy scientists, extension service specialists, and feed and farm management advisors.

Methods of entering

Because of the high costs involved with starting a dairy farm, many dairy farmers get their start by managing someone else's farm. It is extremely rare for someone without some family connections to start a farm from scratch.

For those with some capital to invest, it may be possible to get started by renting property and herds on a share-of-the-profits basis with the owner. There are government lands, such as national parks, available to rent as well. Later, when the dairy farmer wants to own a farm, it may be possible to borrow up to half the estimated value of the land, buildings, and animals from a bank or other financial institution.

Advancement

Often becoming a dairy farmer represents the culmination of years of advancement from ordinary farm worker to the position of farm owner. Much training, experience, and money are needed to become a dairy farmer. Successful dairy farmers may buy more farm animals or more grazing land to increase productivity. A successful farmer may also choose to automate farming operations to increase efficiency and lower labor costs.

Employment outlook

Because of the continued trend toward fewer and larger farms, the number of opportunities for dairy farmers is expected to decline through the year 2000. The increasing complexity of running a farm and the rising costs of these operations will severely limit the number of dairy farms in operation. Most opportunities will be created when a successful dairy farmer retires or otherwise leaves the field.

Earnings

Exact earnings are hard to estimate as they fluctuate somewhat and vary as to the size of the farm. In general, larger dairy farms generate more income than smaller farms. A dairy farmer can earn less than $10,000 per year or over $70,000 per year, depending on how productive the cows are, the price of milk, and the costs of operating the farm. Sometimes, of course, a dairy farmer may actually lose money in the course of a year. Many farmers have off-farm incomes larger than their farm income.

Because dairy farmers are business owners, they have to pay for their own health insurance and other benefits.

Conditions of work

Dairy farmers work seven days a week, all year round. If they want to take a vacation, they must find someone dependable to operate the farm in their place. Farmers work long and irregular hours, making excellent health a necessity. Much of the work will be done outdoors in all types of weather. Even during the cold winter months, the cows must be milked and fed and machinery must be maintained and repaired. Unless the farm is large, a dairy farmer may spend most of the time working alone.

Farm work can be fairly dangerous. Dairy farmers may be injured or catch diseases transmitted by farm animals. In addition, they may be injured by planting and harvesting machinery and they are subject to illnesses and diseases from handling and breathing dangerous pesticides and other chemicals and from handling crops that have been sprayed with insecticides.

Social and psychological factors

Because running a farm is an economically risky proposition, a farmer must be able to work long hours under stressful conditions. Patience and good managerial skills are vital ingredients for a successful dairy farmer. The farmer should be able to work alone for long periods of time and also be able to supervise and coordinate the work of others. Good written and verbal skills are very important.

The independence one gains by owning a farm can only be fully achieved if one exercises enormous amounts of self-discipline. Unless specific guidelines are set and adhered to, it is often difficult to accomplish what needs to be done. The ability to plan effectively and follow through on those plans are skills without which a farmer can not operate.

Despite the stress and the long hours involved, farming offers an opportunity for those who enjoy working with animals and working out of doors to have an occupation that can be both financially and psychologically rewarding.

GOE: 03.01.01; SIC: 0241; SOC: 5512, 5514, 5522, 5524, 5611, 5612, 5617

◇ SOURCES OF ADDITIONAL INFORMATION

For information on career opportunities in dairy farming, contact:

American Farm Bureau Federation
225 Touhy Avenue
Park Ridge, IL 60068

Future Farmers of America
Box 15160
5632 Mt. Vernon Memorial Highway
Alexandria, VA 22309

National Council of Farmer Cooperatives
50 F Street NW, Suite 900
Washington, DC 20001

For information concerning agricultural education, contact:

National Association of State Universities and Land Grant Colleges
Division of Agriculture
One DuPont Circle, Suite 710
Washington, DC 20036

Higher Education Program
U.S. Department of Agriculture
Washington, DC 20250

◇ RELATED ARTICLES

Volume 1: Agriculture
Volume 3: Agricultural scientists; Farmers; Farm operatives and managers
Volume 4: Animal production technicians

Dog groomers

Definition

Dog groomers comb, cut, trim, and shape the fur of all types of dogs and cats.

History

The dog is one of mankind's most beloved animals. It is likely that the dog was the first animal that people ever domesticated. More than 10,000 years ago, wild dogs resembling dingoes were captured, tamed, and put to work in various ways. Today, dogs are still used for the types of work they performed centuries ago, such as herding sheep, retrieving game and guarding property. In the United States, most dogs are kept as pets and companions in more than 40 million homes. More than 200 different breeds of dog can be identified, and many dog shows hold competitions for the best pedigree, or the best family history, of different breeds. But whether a dog is a first-class pedigree or a mutt, it enjoys being bathed and groomed.

Nature of the work

Although all dogs and cats benefit from regular grooming, it is shaggy, long-haired animals that give dog groomers the bulk of their business. Some types of dogs need regular grooming for their expected appearance; among this group are poodles, schnauzers, cocker spaniels, and many types of terriers. Show dogs are also groomed very frequently. Before beginning grooming, the dog groomer will talk with the dog's owner to find out the style the dog is to have. The dog groomer also will rely on experience to determine how the particular breed of dog is supposed to look.

The dog groomer first places the animal up on a grooming table. To keep the dog steady during the clipping, a nylon collar or noose, which hangs from an adjustable pole attached to the grooming table, is slipped around its neck. The dog groomer talks to the dog or uses other techniques to keep the animal calm and gain its trust. If the dog doesn't calm down but instead snaps and bites, the groomer may muzzle it. If a dog is completely unmanageable, the dog groomer may ask the owner to have the

341

Dog groomers must develop a friendly rapport with animals so that the dogs will remain calm while getting their hair trimmed and nails cut.

dog tranquilized by a veterinarian before grooming.

After calming the dog down, the groomer brushes the dog and tries to unmat the hair. If the dog's hair is very overgrown or is very shaggy like an English sheepdog's, the groomer may have to cut away part of its coat with scissors before any real grooming begins. Brushing the coat is good for both long- and short-haired dogs because it removes shedding hair and dead skin. It also neatens the coat so the groomer can tell from the shape and proportions of the dog how to cut its hair in the most attractive way.

Once the dog is brushed, the groomer will cut and shape the dog's coat with electric clippers. Next, the dog's nails are trimmed, and its ears are cleaned. Care must be taken not to cut the nails too short because the nails may bleed and the dog will be in pain. If the nails do bleed, a special powder is applied to stop the bleeding. The comfort of the dog or cat is a very important concern for the groomer.

The dog is then given a bath, sometimes by another person known as a *dog bather*. The dog is lowered into a stainless steel tub, sprayed with warm water, scrubbed with a tearless shampoo and rinsed. This may be repeated several times if the dog is very dirty. The dog groomer has special chemicals that can be used to deodorize a dog that has had an encounter with a skunk or has gone for a swim in foul water. If a dog has fleas or ticks, the dog groomer treats them at this stage by soaking the wet coat with a solution to kill the insects.

The dog's eyes, ears, and nose are protected from this toxic solution, however, and may be cleaned more carefully with a sponge or wash cloth. A hot oil treatment may also be applied to condition the dog's coat.

The groomer dries the dog after bathing, either with a towel, a hand-held electric blower, or a drier cage with electric blow driers. Poodles and some other types of dogs have their coats fluff-dried, then scissored for the final pattern or style. Poodles, which at one time were the mainstay of the dog-grooming business, generally take the longest to groom because of their intricate clipping pattern. Most dogs can be groomed in about an hour-and-a-half, although grooming may take several hours for shaggier breeds whose coats are badly matted and overgrown.

More and more cats, especially long-haired breeds, are now being taken to pet groomers. The procedure for cats is the same as for dogs, although cats are not dipped when bathed. As the dog or cat is groomed, the groomer will check to be sure there are no unhealthy signs in the animal's eyes, ears, skin, or coat. If there are any abnormalities, such as bald patches or skin lesions, the dog groomer will tell the owner and may recommend that the animal be checked by a veterinarian. The dog groomer may also give the owner some tips on hygiene for the animal.

Requirements

There are generally three ways that a person interested in dog grooming can be trained for the field: enrollment in a dog-grooming school; working in a pet shop or kennel and learning on the job; or reading one of the many books on dog grooming and practicing on his or her own.

Probably the best way to gain a thorough knowledge of dog grooming is to take an accredited dog grooming course or enroll in dog-grooming school. The National Dog Groomers Association accredits fifty different schools of dog grooming and sends a list to people free of charge on request. Five schools of dog grooming are recognized by the National Association of Trade and Technical Schools: the Pedigree Professional School of Dog Grooming, the New York School of Dog Grooming (three branches), and the Nash Academy of Animal Arts. Many other dog-grooming schools advertise in dog and pet magazines. It is important for students to choose an accredited, licensed school, both for their employment opportunities and their own professional knowledge.

To enroll in most dog-grooming schools, a person has to be at least seventeen years old and must be fond of dogs. Previous experience in dog grooming can sometimes be applied for course credits. Students study a wide range of topics, including the basics of bathing, brushing, and clipping; the care of ears and nails; coat and skin conditions; dog anatomy; terminology; and sanitation. They also study customer relations, which can be very useful for those who operate their own shops. During training, students practice their techniques on live dogs, which people bring in for grooming at a discount.

Students can also learn dog grooming while working for a grooming shop, kennel, animal hospital, or veterinarian's office. They usually begin with tasks such as shampooing the dogs and trimming their nails, then gradually work their way up to brushing and basic cuts. With experience, they may learn more difficult cuts and use these skills to earn more pay or start their own business.

The essentials of dog grooming can also be learned from one of the several good books on grooming that are available. These books contain all the information a person needs to know to start his or her own dog-grooming business, including the basic cuts, bathing and handling techniques, and the type of equipment needed. Still, many of the finer points of grooming, such as the more complicated cuts and various safety precautions, are best learned while working under an experienced groomer.

High-school diplomas generally are not required for persons working as dog groomers. A diploma or GED certificate, however, can be a great help to persons who would like to advance within their present company or move to other careers in animal care that require more training, such as animal technicians. Courses that are useful in this career include English, business mathematics, general science, zoology, psychology, bookkeeping, office management, typing, art, and first aid.

Special requirements

State licensing or certification is not required of dog groomers at this time. To start a grooming salon or other business, a person may need to get a license from the city or town in which he or she plans to start a business.

The National Dog Groomers Association of America is a professional group that promotes dog grooming as a career and publishes a list of dog-grooming schools they recognize and accredit. Dog groomers will find many benefits from associating with this and other groups, such as the Humane Society of the United States and the United Kennel Club. Because dog groomers should be concerned with the health and safety of the animals they service, membership in groups that promote and protect animal welfare is very common.

Opportunities for experience and exploration

To find out if they are suited for a job in dog grooming, students should know or try to find out how well they work with animals. This can be done in many ways, including the proper care of the family pet. Youth organizations such as the Boy Scouts, Girl Scouts, and 4-H Clubs sponsor projects that give members the chance to raise and care for animals. Students might also try to get a part-time job working with and caring for animals at an animal hospital, kennel, pet shop, animal shelter, nature center, or zoo.

Methods of entering

Graduates from dog-grooming schools can take advantage of the job placement services that most schools offer. Generally there are more job openings than there are qualified groomers to fill them, so new graduates may have several job openings to consider. These schools can find out about job openings in all parts of the country, and are usually happy to contact prospective employers and write letters of introduction for graduates.

Other sources for job information include the want ads of the daily newspaper and listings in dog and pet magazines. Job leads may also be available from private or state employment agencies, or from referrals of salon or kennel owners. Persons looking for work should phone or send letters to prospective employers, inform them of their qualifications, and visit their establishments, if appropriate.

Advancement

Dog groomers who work for other people may advance to a more responsible position such as office manager or trainer. If a dog groomer starts his or her own shop, it might become successful enough to expand or to open branch offices or franchises around the area. Skilled groomers may want to work for a dog grooming school as an instructor, possibly advancing to a job as a school director, placement officer, or other type of administrator.

The pet industry is booming, so there are many other avenues of advancement for groomers who like to work with dogs. With more education, a groomer may get a job as an animal technician or veterinary assistant at a shelter or animal hospital. Those who like to train dogs may open obedience schools, train guide dogs, work with field and hunting dogs, or even train stunt and movie dogs. People can also open their own kennel businesses, breeder and pedigree services, gaming dog businesses, or pet supply distribution firms.

Employment outlook

The demand for skilled dog groomers has grown in recent years and is expected to continue to increase. The National Dog Groomers Association estimates that more than 30,000 dog groomers were employed in the early 1990s, and expects that more than 3,000 new groomers will be needed every year over the next decade.

Every year more people are keeping dogs and cats as pets. They are spending more money to pamper their animals, but often don't have enough free time or the inclination to groom their pets themselves. Grooming is not just a luxury for pets, however, because regular attention makes it more likely that any injury or illness will be noticed and treated.

Earnings

Groomers can charge either by the job or by the hour. Generally they earn around $7.50 an hour. If they are on the staff of a salon or work for another groomer, they get to keep 50 to 60 percent of the fees they charge. For this reason, many groomers branch off to start their own businesses. Those who own and operate their own pet-grooming service can earn anywhere from $20,000 to $50,000 annually, depending on how hard they work and the type of business they attract.

Groomers generally buy their own clipping equipment, including barber's shears, brushes, and clippers. A new set of equipment costs around $275, while used sets cost less. Groomers who work at salons, grooming schools, pet shops, animal hospitals, and kennels often get a full range of benefits, including paid vacations and holidays, medical and dental insurance, and retirement pensions.

Conditions of work

Working conditions can vary greatly, depending on the location and type of employment. Many salons and pet shops are clean and well lighted, with modern equipment and clean surroundings. Others may be cramped, dark, and smelly. Groomers need to be careful while on the job, especially when handling flea and tick killers, which are toxic to humans. When working with any sort of animal, a person may encounter bites, scratches, strong odors, and fleas and other insects. They may also have to deal with sick or bad-tempered animals. The groomer must regard every dog and cat as a unique individual.

Groomers who are self-employed can work out of their homes. Many people convert their garages into work areas so that in nice weather they can work in the fresh air and bathe and dry the dogs in their yards. Some groomers buy vans and convert them into grooming shops. They can then drive to the homes of the pets they work on, which many owners find very convenient. Those who operate these "groomobiles" can work on thirty or forty dogs a week, and factor their driving time and expenses into their fees.

Groomers usually work a five-day, thirty-five-hour week. If they work any overtime, they are compensated for it. Those who own their own shops or work out of their homes, like other self-employed people, work very long hours and can have irregular schedules. Other groomers may work only part-time. Groomers are on their feet much of the day, and their work can get very tiring when they have to lift and restrain large animals.

Social and psychological factors

The primary qualification for a person who wants to work with pets is a love of animals. Animals can sense when someone does not like them or is afraid of them. A person needs certain skills in order to work with nervous, aggressive, or fidgety animals. They must be patient with the animals, be able to gain their respect, and like to give the animals a lot of love and attention.

Persistence and endurance are also good traits for dog groomers, because grooming one dog can take three or more hours of strenuous work. They must also be able to deal with the pets' owners tactfully and gain their trust. Repeat customers and referrals are extremely important, especially for self-employed groomers. Groomers should also enjoy working with their hands and have good eyesight and manual dexterity to cut a clipping pattern accurately.

Pet owners and other people in pet care generally have respect for a dog groomer who does a good job and treats animals well. Many people, especially those who raise show dogs, grow to rely on particular dog groomers to do a perfect job each time. Dog groomers can earn a great deal of satisfaction from taking a shaggy, unkempt animal and transforming it into a beautiful creature. On the negative side, a groomer might grow to resent neglectful owners who regularly return their pets in the same sorry mess regularly. Some owners may blame the groomer if the animal becomes ill while in the groomer's care or for some malady or condition that is not the groomer's fault. Because they deal with both the pets and their owners, dog groomers can find their work both challenging and rewarding.

GOE: 03.03.02; SIC: 0752; SOC: 5624

⬦ **SOURCES OF ADDITIONAL INFORMATION**

National Dog Groomers Association of America
PO Box 101
Clark, PA 16113

New York School of Dog Grooming
248 East 34th Street
New York, NY 10016

Nash Academy of Animal Arts
595 Anderson Avenue
Cliffside Park, NJ 07010

⬦ **RELATED ARTICLES**

Volume 1: Agriculture
Volume 2: Veterinarians
Volume 3: Dairy farmers; Farmers; Farm operatives and managers; Farriers
Volume 4: Animal production technicians; Animal health technicians

Farmers

Definition

Farmers raise crops such as corn, wheat, tobacco, cotton, vegetables, and fruits; or specialize in some phase of producing animals or poultry, mainly for food; or maintain herds of dairy cattle for the production of milk. While some farmers may combine several of these activities, most specialize in one specific area. Farm laborers are either hired workers or members of farm families who perform such physical tasks as cleaning the barns and feeding the animals. Farm supervisors work on large farms where they coordinate the work of laborers and hire additional crews as needed.

Farmers own or lease the property on which they cultivate plant or animal life. Most farms are now thousands of acres for cattle and plant production. Subsistance farms produce only enough to support the farmer's family.

Farmers
Agriculture, Forestry, and Conservation Occupations

History

Farming is an ancient occupation, going back before the beginnings of recorded history. Before farming began, people were hunters, and tribes roamed from area to area, killing animals for food, clothing, and shelter, and picking whatever wild berries, nuts, and fruits might be found. As the population grew, rudimentary efforts to tame wild animals and cultivate food plants began to provide a more constant source of food. Goats and sheep were raised in mountainous or hilly lands and were moved from one grazing spot to another.

The big breakthrough in farming came when people realized that seeds saved through the winter could be planted in the spring and planned crops could be raised and harvested. There is evidence that wheat was cultivated in Mesopotamia (now Iraq) as early as 4700 B.C. and that cotton, too, was used by ancient people in producing cloth. Peas, beans, rice, and barley were also very early crops.

Farming methods and implements were crude: oxen dragged forked sticks through the ground to break up the soil; scattered seeds were pressed into the earth by having sheep driven over the land; family members often sat in the fields guarding the newly planted seeds from scavenging birds.

In colonial America almost 95 percent of the people were farmers, planting such crops as Indian corn, wheat, flax, and, further South, tobacco. With the exception of turkeys, all of the livestock raised were brought over from the Old World. Chickens were brought by the Spaniards in the sixteenth century and by the English colonists to Virginia and Massachusetts. Hogs, cattle, sheep, and goats were also imported. Hay was raised to feed livestock, and just enough other crops were raised to supply the farmer's family throughout the year. Tobacco was one of the most important crops of the Southern colonies.

The invention of farm machines in the 1800s, such as the reaper, the threshing machine, the steel plow, and the two-horse cultivator, enabled the farmer to put a great deal of land under cultivation, and the widespread sale of farm products began. In the early twentieth century, the tractor was developed, and a new and important crop, soybeans, was imported from the Orient and widely planted and processed.

Along with the introduction of many laborsaving farm machines came new and improved methods of soil conservation. The use of fertilizers, contour farming, strip cropping, and strip rotation greatly increased the productivity of the land, at the same time that it pre-

served it. The Department of Agriculture, created in 1862, and the growth of agricultural colleges, with their various extension services, combined to make the farmer more knowledgeable, productive, and efficient in the use of his land and livestock.

The result of the massive technological changes, and the enormous increase of productivity, is that today a relatively small number of farms are producing greater amounts of America's farm products. While larger numbers of workers and technicians are being employed on individual farms, particularly the corporate-run ones, the overall number of workers is decreasing.

Nature of the work

There are probably as many different types of farmers as there are different types of economically important plants and animals. In addition to *diversified crops farmers,* who grow varying combinations of fruits, grains, and vegetables depending on the market and the weather, and *general farmers,* who raise livestock as well as crops, there are *cash grain farmers,* who grow barley, corn, rice, soybeans, and wheat; *vegetable farmers; tree-fruit-and-nut crops farmers; field crops farmers,* who raise alfalfa, cotton, hops, peanuts, mint, sugarcane, and tobacco; *bonsai culturists,* who raise dwarf trees; *animal breeders; fur farmers; livestock ranchers; poultry farmers; beekeepers; reptile farmers; worm growers;* and *fish farmers.*

Corn and wheat farmers begin the growing season by breaking the soil up with plows, then harrowing, pulverizing, and leveling it. Some of these tasks may be done after the harvest, and others just before planting.

Corn is usually planted about the middle of May with machines that place the corn seeds into "hills" a few inches apart, making weed control easier. On the average a crop is cultivated three times during the season. Corn is also used in the making of silage, the process by which corn is cut, stored in silos, allowed to ferment, and when free of molds, used as a substitute for hay.

Wheat may be sown in the fall or spring, depending on the severity of winter and the variety of wheat. It is planted with a drill, close together, thus preventing cultivation once planted. Harvest for winter wheat occurs in early summer. A combine is used that harvests and threshes the wheat in one operation. The wheat is then stored in large grain storage elevators owned by private individuals, companies, or cooperatives.

346

Cotton planting is begun in March in the Southwest, and somewhat later in the southern states.

Tobacco plants require careful tending and protection from harsh weather conditions. The soil in which they are grown must also be thoroughly broken up, smoothed, and fertilized before planting, as tobacco is very hard on the soil.

The peanut crop can be managed more like other types of farm corps and is not nearly so sensitive to weather and disease, nor does it require the great care of tobacco and cotton.

Specialty crops such as fruits and vegetables are most subject to seasonal variations, so that the farmer must rely heavily on the hiring of seasonal labor. Also, this individual employs more specialized equipment than do general farmers.

The hay farmer, as an example, must be able to judge the exact time for mowing that will yield the best crop in terms of such factors as stem toughness, leaf loss, and the growing season of subsequent cuttings. All of this must be weighed in terms of weather conditions. Thus, to accomplish this harvesting task, the farmer must use specialized equipment such as mowing machines and hay rakes that are usually tractor drawn. The hay is pressed into bales by another machine for easier storage and then transported to storage facilities or to market.

Planting seasons are just as crucial as harvest. Such crops as potatoes need to be planted during a relatively short span of days in the spring. The fields must be tilled and ready for planting, and the farmer again must estimate weather conditions so his seedlings will not freeze from late winter weather.

The crop specialty farmer often uses rather elaborate irrigation systems to water the crops during those seasons of inadequate rainfall. Often these systems are portable, and it is necessary to move large sections of piping from field to field.

Livestock farmers generally buy calves from ranchers who breed and raise them. Livestock farmers feed and fatten young cattle and generally raise their own corn and hay to cut feeding costs. They must have some knowledge of the diseases of cattle and the proper methods of feeding. In addition to their crop acreage, they must also allow for fenced pasturage for their cattle and provide adequate shelter for the animals in bad weather. Some livestock farmers may specialize in breeding good stock for sale to ranchers and dairy farmers. These specialists are interested in maintaining and improving purebred animals of the particular breed they have chosen to work with. Bulls and cows are

Farmers try to offset the high cost of machinery by either increasing their yields or sharing equipment with other farmers.

then sold to ranchers and dairy farmers who want to improve their herds.

Sheep ranchers raise sheep primarily for their wool. Large herds are maintained on rangeland in the western states. Since large areas of land are needed, the sheep rancher must usually buy grazing rights on government-owned lands.

Although dairy farmers' first concern is with the production of the maximum amount of high-grade milk, they also will raise corn and grain to provide feed for their animals to reduce costs.

The dairy farmer must be able to repair the many kinds of equipment essential to their business; keep accurate records; be part laborer and part supervisor; and be knowledgeable about diseases, sanitation, and methods of improving the quantity and quality of the milk.

Milking is generally done between five and six o'clock in the morning. During milking, the cows are fed a combination of milk and grain. After milking, the milk is cooled immediately as it spoils quickly. Records are kept of each cow's production of milk to discover which cows are profitable and which should be traded or sold for meat.

After milking, when the cows are at pasture, the farmer cleans the stalls and the barn by washing, sweeping, and sterilizing with boiling water. This is extremely important as milk cows contract diseases from unsanitary conditions which, in turn, may contaminate the milk. Dairy farmers must have their herds certified free of disease by representatives of the Department of Health. Equipment and containers must also be cleaned; fences and machinery repaired; winter silage gotten ready; and new crops planted or harvested. Sick or calving cows must also be attended to. The cows are milked again at around five o'clock in the evening, and the entire round of cleaning barn and equipment must be done again in preparation for the next day. These chores must be done by the farmer seven days a week, fifty-two weeks of the year. (*See also* the separate article titled "Dairy farmers" elsewhere in this volume.)

The great majority of poultry farmers do not hatch their own chicks but buy them from commercial hatcheries. The chicks are kept in brooder houses until they are seven or eight weeks old and are then transferred to open pens or shelters. At six months the hens begin to lay eggs, and roosters are culled from the flock to be sold for meat.

The basic job of poultry farmers is to keep their flocks healthy. They must provide shelter from the chickens' natural enemies and from extreme weather conditions; the shelters must be kept extremely clean, because diseases can spread through a flock in a very short time; they must choose the food that will allow the chicken to grow or produce at its maximum, at the same time attempting to keep costs down; and they must be equipped to collect eggs, grade them by weight, and candle, pack, and ship them.

Raising chickens to be sold as broilers or fryers requires equipment to house them until they are six to thirteen weeks old. The birds then must be marketed either live or cleaned; for the latter, the poultry farmer must have equipment to kill, pluck, and clean the birds. Those farmers specializing in the production of eggs must gather eggs at least twice a day, and more often in very warm weather. The eggs must then be stored in a cool place, inspected, graded, and packed for market. The poultry farmer who specializes in producing broilers is usually not an independent producer but is under a financial contract with a backer who is often the operator of a slaughterhouse or the manufacturer of poultry feeds and supplies.

Requirements

There are no specific educational requirements, but to be successful, the farmer, whether working with crops or animals, should have a knowledge of the principles of soil preparation and cultivation, disease control, machinery maintenance, as well as a knowledge of business practices and bookkeeping. Crop farmers must also know their crops well enough to be able to choose the proper seeds for their particular soil climate. They also need experience in the evaluation of crop growth and weather cycles because a successful harvest is dependent upon their decisions. Those working with animals should have a basic affection for them, and a thorough knowledge of their special requirements. All farmers, regardless of their specialty, should enjoy being outdoors, and should be in excellent physical condition.

High-school courses should include algebra, geometry, carpentry, accounting, and English. Extension courses should also be taken to keep abreast of all new developments in farm technology and scientific advances.

Special requirements

There are no actual special requirements to become a farmers. A true love of land and animals and a tenacious spirit, however, will go a long way in helping farmers be successful.

Opportunities for experience and exploration

Because few people enter farming as a full-time occupation, unless they grew up on or around a farm, the opportunities for experience from childhood on are plentiful for those who make this their business. For young people who do not belong to a farm family, there are many opportunities for part-time farm work as a hired hand, especially during seasonal operations.

In addition, organizations such as 4-H Clubs and Future Farmers of America offer especially good opportunities for hearing about, visiting, and participating in farm and farm-like activities. Agricultural colleges often have their own farms where the student can gain actual experience in farm operations as well as classroom work.

Related occupations

Many other occupations will allow people who have an interest in farming to utilize the same skills and aptitudes. Other jobs include veterinarians, animal production technicians, meat, packing production workers, artificial insemination technicians, butchers, botanists, and agricultural scientists.

Methods of entering

In general, it is becoming increasingly difficult for a person to enter farming without either some family connection with a farm or considerable financial support from some source. The capital investment in a farm today is so great that it makes it almost impossible for anyone to start from scratch.

For cotton or tobacco farming in some sections of the country where much hand labor is used, the investment in machinery would not be very great, but labor costs would be quite high. In the sections of the country where irrigation is used and large tracts of land are planted in cotton, the capital invested in a farm frequently amounts to more than $160,000.

Because the capital outlay is so high, many wheat, corn, and specialty crop farmers start by being tenant farmers and renting land and equipment, or by sharing the cash profits with the owner of the land. These tenants thus hope to gain both the experience and cash to purchase and manage their own farms.

Generally, livestock farmers also start by renting property, and perhaps animals, on a share-of-the-profits basis with the owner. There are government lands, such as national parks, available for rent as well. Later, when the livestock farmer wants to own property, it is possible to borrow up to half the estimated value of the land, building, and animals. There is a minimum capital requirement of approximately $30,000. Dairy farmers can begin in much the same way as livestock farmers, by renting land and herds. Then they, too, can apply for a loan of approximately half the cost of land, buildings, and herd. Loans are becoming more difficult to obtain though. After several years of lenient loan policies, banks or savings and loans have tightened requirements.

The best way to get into the poultry industry is to start by working part-time on a poultry farm during summers away from school. Another possibility is to seek a job with a firm closely related to poultry farming, such as feed or equipment dealers. Many will then go to work full-time and ultimately become managers of farms, which are actually owned by larger firms such as feed producers.

Advancement

Advancement in the various kinds of crop farming would occur by buying one's own farm or additional acreage to increase production and, thus, income. The same holds true for livestock, dairy, or poultry farmers.

It is generally agreed that the more formal education a person has in any field, the better one's opportunity to advance.

Employment outlook

In the early 1990s, about 1,442,000 people were employed as farm managers or operators, and another 1,079,000 were employed as farm workers of all kinds.

The long-range forecast is for a decrease in the number of people working in agriculture as farmers and farm laborers. Large corporate farms are fast replacing the small farmer, who is being forced out of the industry by the spiralling costs of feed, grain, land, and equipment. The late 1970s and early 1980s were an especially hard time, when many small farmers were forced to give up farming, many of them losing farms that had been family property for generations, leading to widespread concern that this traditional American way of life would be wiped out.

Earnings

Farm operators and managers earned an average of $19,700 a year in the early 1990s. But farm income in general is deceptive. Because farmers use many of their own products, one can assume that published figures do not tell the complete story. Also, farm income fluctuates widely from year to year. Many farmers earn more from nonfarming jobs than from farming.

Conditions of work

The conditions of work for farmers are fairly obvious. They are outdoors a good deal of the time regardless of weather conditions. Long hours and hard manual labor make excellent health and strength a necessity. During planting and harvest seasons, farmers will work very long and irregular hours with few breaks in the routine. Even during the cold winter months they must repair machinery and buildings.

Much of the work will be done alone unless the farm is fairly large. Dairy farmers, of course, work seven days a week all year round.

In addition, many farms are often isolated, away from many conveniences and at times from some necessities such as immediate medical attention.

Social and psychological factors

There are many risks in being in a business where the net income is often dependent upon so many factors beyond the owner's control. Average, efficient business executives during normal times can expect a reasonable return on their investment. Such is not always the case, particularly in crop farming, because of the element of weather. In spite of how well farmers manage their farm and their resources, there may be times when the weather acts to undo all of their efforts. Patience and the ability to recoup resources following some crop discouragement are psychological imperatives.

In addition, the independence one gains by owning a farm can only be fully achieved if one exercises enormous amounts of self-discipline. Unless specific requirements are set and adhered to, it is often difficult to get accomplished what needs to be done.

For the young person who enjoys working out of doors and derives pleasure and satisfaction from seeing plants and animals grow, farming offers a real opportunity to work at an occupation that can be both financially and psychologically rewarding.

GOE: 03.01.01; SIC: 019, 029; SOC: 56

◇ **SOURCES FOR ADDITIONAL INFORMATION**

National Council of Farmer Cooperatives
50 F Street, NW
Suite 900
Washington, DC 20001

National Young Farmer Educational Association
5632 Mt. Vernon Memorial Highway
PO Box 15160
Alexandria, VA 22309

Farmers' Educational and Cooperative Union of America
10065 East Harvard Avenue
Denver, CO 80251

National Grange
1616 H Street, NW
Washington, DC 20006

◇ **RELATED ARTICLES**

Volume 1: Agriculture
Volume 2: See Agriculture, Forestry, Fisheries, and Conservation Occupations
Volume 3: See Agriculture, Forestry, and Conservation Technician Occupations

Farm operatives and managers

Definition

Farming is a well-mechanized, substantial business in the United States today. It has changed drastically from the earliest days of agricultural subsistence farming. *Farm owners, operators,* and *managers* in modern farms must have broad knowledge and skills that include not only an understanding of farming, but also of business.

These experts understand crop production, animal science, irrigation, soil science, and farm business management. Many small, family-owned farms have now merged to form substantial business ventures with cash flows that equal other rural businesses. Farm operatives and managers may specialize in meat, eggs, dairy products, or plant production. They may also have working knowledge in several areas.

History

The history of farming goes back as far as history itself. People have long tilled their land and been sustained by the food they produced. They have also raised animals, drunk the milk produced by their cows, and eaten the eggs from their chickens. The variety of farms today is mind boggling. Crop farmers are concerned with a huge range of crops, horticultural farmers may specialize in plants, flowers, bulbs, or shrubbery, and animal farmers raise a wide variety of animals for food and other industries.

Nature of the work

American farm operators produce enough food and fiber not only to feed the United States, but also to export huge quantities to countries all over the world. Farm operators may be the owners of their farms, as often is the case on family farms, or they may be tenant farmers who rent the land they work on. On crop and horticultural farms, *farm operators* choose the crops or plants to be harvested, till the soil, plant the crops or plants, care for them, and harvest them. Care for crops often includes cultivating, spraying and dusting, and irrigation. Then the farm operators sort and package the crops and plan their marketing or storage.

On dairy, poultry, and livestock farms, farm operators take care of the animals. They have titles such as *farm general manager* and *dairy farm manager*. They keep the animals' housing and bedding in good condition, feed the animals, and keep them healthy. Farmers must protect animals from diseases by inoculating them. They may also help in areas such as breeding, slaughtering, and marketing the animals they raise.

Farm managers are usually hired by farm owners to oversee various facets of the farm's operation. The managers usually work on larger farms that are run more like businesses. A large crop farm, for instance, may have one manager who oversees planning, one who handles planting and harvesting, and another manager who is in charge of marketing or storing the crops. Their titles can be as diverse as *seed corn production manager* and *plant propagator*.

A farm may grow several different crops and breed livestock as well, or it may specialize in one crop or animal. Almost every farm markets its own produce.

Besides the day-to-day work of farm operatives and managers, they must also plan a yearly schedule. They watch the economy and market prices and decide which crops to grow.

During the winter months, farm operators and managers review the past year's crop yield and financial status. With such information, they can forecast operation costs for the coming year.

They may store a crop for one season or keep their livestock longer until prices rise. They keep detailed records of their crops, methods of fertilization, and financial history, and keep track of new farm machinery that may help them. Jobs that used to take weeks can be accomplished in a matter of hours with some efficient irrigating, fertilizing, and harvesting machinery. Milking machines, hay balers, tractors, and combines have helped change the way farmers do their work.

Farm operators may set up and operate machinery, erect fences and sheds, and make managerial decisions. On large farms, they may oversee farm workers who do much of the physical labor. In this case they may train the workers in the use of equipment and the performance of farm work. They decide when to seed, fertilize, cultivate, harvest, and market their crops. Some farm operators secure loans from credit agencies to help the farm purchase new machinery, or pay for fertilizer, livestock, or feed.

Farm managers on large farms may oversee one activity such as feeding livestock. On small farms, the manager is responsible for everything from planning output to planting and harvesting. Professional farm managers may find jobs at farm-management firms that may manage some farm operations or oversee farm operators on several farms. In this case, the manager may monitor production and establish output goals.

Requirements

Many farm workers learn about agriculture by growing up on a farm. Others study at special agricultural colleges or major in agriculture at a large university. High-school students who are interested in farming should take agriculture courses if they are offered. Courses in mathematics, the sciences, and business are also helpful, as are courses in economics.

State land-grant colleges offer agricultural programs that lead to bachelor's degrees, as well as shorter programs in specific areas. Some universities offer advanced studies in horticulture, animal science, agronomy, and agricultural economics. Motivated students can pursue studies leading to master's degrees or doctorates.

Technical schools often have home-study courses, and evening classes are available in many areas for adult farmers. Two-year colleges often have programs leading to associate degrees in agriculture.

College graduates can take examinations in farm management to be certified as farm managers (AFM). The American Society of Farm Managers and Rural Appraisers gives the examinations. The aspects of farming that are covered in the examinations include business, financial, and legal.

Students may specialize in areas such as agricultural economics, dairy science, horticulture, animal science, soil science, or crop and fruit science. Most students in agricultural colleges also are required to take courses in farm management and in business, finance, and economics.

Special requirements

People who want to be farm managers or farm operators must have college degrees. Most have specialized in some agricultural field.

Opportunities for experience and exploration

Farming programs for young people are sponsored across the country by the National FFA Organization, formerly known as Future Farmers of America. 4-H Clubs also provide sources of training for prospective farmers. The increasingly complex world of farming, however, also requires knowledge of areas outside farming. Students interested in farming should hone their skills in science, business, and finance by taking appropriate courses. Agricultural courses will also help prospective farmers decide if this is the career for them.

Many farms need extra hands during busy harvesting seasons. Students may be hired to help out with the animals or with crops, or even with farm buildings that need tending in the off months. This kind of experience may help a student decide if farming is right for him or her.

Related occupations

Related occupations include agricultural journalists, farm broadcasters, farm equipment dealers and mechanics, veterinarians, livestock buyers and brokers, agricultural commodity graders, foresters, tree surgeons, sheep herders, beekeepers, horse trainers, and horseshoers.

Methods of entering

Most farm workers have grown up on farms. Others who enjoy working the land take up farming by buying farmland. Some start by leasing land from businesses or other farmers or by farming part of someone else's land. Farmland has become very expensive in the United States, but beginners with good backgrounds may be able to get credit from the Farm Credit System or from a bank. The U.S. Department of Agriculture also offers loans through the Farmers Home Administration.

Beginning farmers should be informed of the risks and costs of operating farms. The more practical experience and education a beginning farmer starts out with, the better are his or her chances of succeeding. Farm operatives and managers not only give initial evaluation of finances but they continue to provide financial updates.

Those who wish to work as farm operators on smaller farms must have a combination of skills. They must have the mechanical aptitude to take care of small repairs, the managerial skills to keep the farm operations smooth, and a basic knowledge of accounting and bookkeeping to keep financial records. Increasingly, a familiarity with computers is necessary on most larger farms where various computers are used to monitor farm operations.

Advancement

Farmers who cannot afford their own farms may start out as tenant farmers or farm laborers. Often farm managers learn the business of the farm before becoming farm operators, and before they are able to afford to buy their own farms. With the right skills and education, they are given more responsibility and higher pay, or can move to larger farms.

Farm operators must try new processes and keep up with modern farming advances. New technologies and methods may improve crop production or livestock-raising. Operators should also be aware of foreign agricultural policies and monetary exchange rates, because much of the material produced on U.S. farms today is exported.

Employment outlook

The trend in farming is toward large-scale farming, meaning that toward the end of the century more farmers will be working on large, mechanized farms than will be working on smaller farms. The U.S. Department of Labor predicts that the number of farm workers will continue to drop, resulting from economic forces as well as better machines and scientific farming methods.

Small specialty farms, however, seem to be increasing. Farmers growing crops such as strawberries, peaches, or other products limited by climate and geography, are becoming more successful. Many farmers have turned to nonfarm jobs during the off-season to increase their incomes, and to allow them to continue farming.

Agriculture is still one of the largest fields of employment in the U.S. The world population continues to expand, and with it the need for food and fiber. The increase in the complexity of farming is expected to propel the demand for experienced, well-trained farm managers. That demand will be even greater as the numbers of absentee farmers increase. These owners will hire farm operators and managers to run their farms for them or to oversee tenant farmers.

Earnings

In the early 1990s the average salary for farm operatives and managers was about $17,000. A farmer's earnings, however, are tied directly to the success or failure of the farm. Earnings de-

pend on the weather, growing conditions, the economy, and competition, in addition to management skills and money invested. If dairy, poultry, or livestock prices are high, or demand for a certain crop increases, earnings will be good. If a crop fails, because of a drought, for instance, the farm can lose money. Larger farms are at greater risk of losing quantities of money, but they also have the potential to earn more for the farmer. Many farmers have off-farm income that can be larger than their farm income.

Besides the variations from year to year in farm incomes, there are also differences by the type of farm. Farms that specialize in cattle, hog, sheep, and tobacco generated an average of $10,000 in the early 1990s, while similar-sized farms specializing in melon, poultry, eggs, and horticulture, generated average incomes over $90,000.

Conditions of work

Farming can be a difficult and frustrating career, but it can be very satisfying as a way of life. The hours are long and the work is physically strenuous, but working outdoors and watching things grow can be very rewarding. The changing seasons bring variety to the day-to-day work. The work is seldom five eight-hour days per week. When harvesting time comes, or the weather is right for planting or spraying, farmers work long hours to see that everything gets done. Farm managers and operators must spend part of each month planning the operation of the farm, but they also may have slow periods and rushes to accomplish certain tasks.

Farm operators who own their farms are their own bosses. Those who are hired by others often have the final say in daily decisions, especially if the farm owner does not live on the farm. Farm operators and managers must work with other farm workers as a team. Often this team consists of family members, and farmers enjoy working as a family.

Dangers to farmers include machine-related injuries, exposure to the weather, and illnesses caused by allergies or animal-related diseases. Fires and falls cause accidents at farms, but by being careful, farmers can avoid these dangers.

Farmers work in rural settings across the United States. The kind of farming depends on the size and location of the farm. In the South, where warm seasons are long, crops that grow slowly are cultivated. Hilly land provides good pasture for dairy farming, while flatlands are ideal for growing grains.

Social and psychological factors

In bad years, even good farmers may lose money. The toll on farmers in the last decade has been difficult to take. Many have lost their farms to creditors, and others have taken on nonfarm jobs to pay the bills.

Many farmers, however, have been able to keep pace with the scientific and mechanical changes, and have watched their farms grow larger and more profitable. People working as farm operators and managers share the ups and downs of agricultural life. Many say that they would never choose any other career, because working with the land or working with animals is so satisfying.

GOE: 03.01.01; SIC: 0762; SOC: 56

◇ **SOURCES OF ADDITIONAL INFORMATION**

American Farm Bureau Federation
225 Touhy Avenue
Park Ridge, IL 60068

American Society of Farm Managers and Rural Appraisers
950 South Cherry Street
Suite 106
Denver, Colorado 80222

National Council of Farmer Cooperatives
50 F Street, NW
Suite 900
Washington, DC 20001

U.S. Department of Agriculture
Higher Education Program
Washington, DC 20250

◇ **RELATED ARTICLES**

Volume 1: Agriculture
Volume 3: Agriculture, Forestry, Fisheries, and Conservation Occupations
Volume 4: Agriculture, Forestry, and Conservation Technician Occupations

---

Farriers (horseshoers)

Definition

Farriers put horseshoes on horses and mules. They replace worn shoes and trim and shape the horse's hooves to ensure that the horseshoes will fit properly. After measuring the hooves, they select the correct aluminum or steel shoes from stock, shape them using a forge and hammer, and nail the shoes to the horse's hooves.

History

Farriers are blacksmiths who specialize in making and fitting horseshoes. The word "farrier" comes from the Latin word for "iron." Long ago, farriers used a forge and anvil to mold iron and form horseshoes. These horseshoes pro-

tected the horse's hooves and helped give the horse balance.

Today, the most frequently used metal for horseshoes is aluminum and most horseshoes are made in factories. Nevertheless, skilled farriers are still needed to adapt and fit the horseshoes for each horse. Horses are used by millions of people each year (primarily for recreation), and farriers continue to play an important role in their care.

Nature of the work

Although farriers are primarily responsible for caring for the hooves of horses, to best care for the animals they must be familiar with the complete anatomy of the horse's lower legs and the variety of ailments and diseases that can affect horses.

To replace a horseshoe, the farrier must lift up the horse's leg and hold the leg between the farrier's knees, with the hoof facing upward. The farrier stands facing the animal's rear. Farriers use pinchers to take off the worn shoe and snippers to clean and trim the hooves. After shaping the new shoe to the horse's hoof, farriers nail the new shoe onto the hoof.

Up until recently, all horseshoes were made from raw metal through a process of heating the metal in a furnace or forge and then taking the metal out of the fire with tongs and hammering it into the proper shape. The ability to know the proper time to take the metal out of the furnace was crucial to this whole process. Although special corrective shoes are still often made in this fashion, the majority of horseshoes are factory-made and the farrier must only shape the horseshoe to the individual hoof measurements of the animal. This process may require heating the horseshoe, but often farriers can shape the shoes to the horse's hooves without heating the metal. They do this by using a hammer or mallet to pound the metal into the curved shape needed. The flexibility of the metal used allows rebending.

After placing the horseshoe on, the farrier files the hoof flush with the shoe and applies horseshoe borium to improve the traction of the horse. Farriers do not only replace worn shoes, they also place leather pads or oakum-pine tar mixtures on bruised or cracked hooves for protection.

The type of new shoe put on a horse is dependent on the type of horse and the purpose of the horseshoe. For example, racehorses may have a different style of horseshoes put on than horses used in jumping competitions. Similarly, horses with diseased or injured hooves must have corrective horseshoes specially fitted.

Farriers must be well acquainted with the hoof ailments and the various diseases that could affect a horse's lower leg. As they take off the old horseshoes, farriers look for any signs of disease. In many cases, a farrier may be replacing a horseshoe because a veterinarian has prescribed the replacement as a result of a disease. In other cases, the farrier may notice something wrong with a hoof while working on the horse and pass this information onto the horse's owner and a veterinarian.

The farrier uses a variety of tools while working on a horse. For example, to remove worn horseshoes, farriers use nail snippers and pinchers; calipers and steel tape are usually used to measure the hoof. Farriers utilize tongs, an anvil, and a hammer in order to shape the heated horseshoe.

Farriers must adjust factory-made horseshoes to fit each horse. This involves beating the metal and often reheating it several times.

Requirements

Most farriers graduate from schools that offer training in horse shoeing. These training programs are typically ten to sixteen weeks in duration and include course work in horse-handling techniques, anatomy of a horse's hooves and lower legs, and forging techniques. During the training program, students get experience in shoeing horses, making corrective shoes, and adjusting and fitting factory-made horseshoes.

There are many of these training schools around the country. The American Farrier's Association can provide interested students with the names and addresses of quality schools. The Association's address is given at the end of this article.

In addition to the training programs, it is also desirable that aspiring farriers have some experience handling horses or other animals. It is also helpful to have a mechanical aptitude and some business experience. Good eyesight and coordination are also important, as is being in good physical condition.

Most training programs do not require applicants to have a high-school diploma. Colleges that offer these programs, however, do require applicants to be high-school graduates.

High-school students should take courses in English, mathematics, biology, and any courses that discuss the anatomy of animals.

Special requirements

In most states, no license or certificate is needed to work in this profession. Some farriers may belong to the Union of Journeymen Horseshoers of the United States. In addition, many farriers join the American Farrier's Association as a means of professional enrichment.

Opportunities for experience and exploration

It may be possible to get a part-time or summer job as a farrier's assistant. If this is not possible, it is desirable to get a part-time or summer job on an animal farm, as this would provide an opportunity to work with horses and other animals. It may also be possible to get a job at a racetrack and in this way learn about working with horses.

In addition, organizations such as the 4-H Club and various riding clubs offer good opportunities for hearing about professional opportunities. Another good way of learning about the profession is to talk to someone already working in the field.

Related occupations

Other professionals concerned with caring for animals include dog groomers, artificial-breeding technicians, and dog bathers. People who enjoy working with animals may also be interested in becoming veterinarians or animal trainers. Those who enjoy forging metal may want to look into becoming blacksmiths or craft workers.

Methods of entering

Some farriers may be hired as apprentices and learn the craft on-the-job. These opportunities, however, are becoming more and more rare

and most farriers now get their jobs only after completing a school training program.

Farriers get work the same way most self-employed craft workers do: they advertise and use word-of-mouth contacts. Farriers must meet horse owners and others involved in the field and then prove themselves with good, fairly-priced work.

Advancement

Farriers usually stay in the field, refining and sharpening their skills. Because much of a farrier's work is repeat business, developing a good reputation is vital toward increasing job opportunities. As they develop increased skills and good reputations, farriers get more business and higher wages.

Employment outlook

As the number of horses used for riding and other purposes continues to grow, job opportunities for farriers will flourish. Jobs should be available all across the country with many opportunities at racetracks, riding stables, breeding farms, and other locations. Some opportunities will arise as farriers retire or otherwise leave the field.

Job opportunities figure to be especially bright because much of the work is repeat business. Horses should be shod every couple of months and this is a continual source of employment for skilled farriers.

Earnings

Earnings vary as to the skill and experience of the farrier, the type of work requested, and geographic location. Full-time farriers should earn between $19,000 and $27,000 a year, depending on the type of work performed. For example, a farrier may receive $40 to $65 for shoeing an unshod horse (a process that should take between one and two hours) to more than $120 for making special corrective horseshoes. Farriers that work on racehorses should earn somewhat more than those who work on other horses or mules.

As farriers develop added skills and a good reputation, their earnings should grow. As with most self-employed workers, the first few years may not be as lucrative as hoped. Because farriers usually run their own businesses (a few may be employed by large stables and the like), they usually have to provide for their own health insurance and other benefits.

Conditions of work

Although in some instances farriers may work in indoor locations, such as blacksmith shops, they usually work out of doors or in unheated stables. Many farriers work out of a truck that has their tools and all other necessary equipment.

Because farriers are usually self-employed, they usually work irregular hours. Some weeks they may work fifty or sixty hours while other weeks they may work only fifteen or twenty hours. Much of their work may be on weekends or in the evenings.

Farriers should be able to work under physically demanding conditions. Many times they may have to work on a less than cooperative animal. Farriers have to handle horses carefully and have to adjust both their position and the horse's position while they work.

In addition to the possible danger that comes from being kicked or bitten by a horse, there is also a slight possibility that farriers can catch a disease transmitted by a horse or other farm animal. They may also be injured while heating the metal or in shaping the horseshoes. It should be noted that while these dangers do exist, skilled farriers usually are very careful and face a minimum of risks.

Social and psychological factors

A farrier must be able to work well with animals and also be able to interact with horse owners. Patience and good communications skills are vital. Farriers should also be able to work alone for long periods of time and be able to handle working in a barn or similar environment. The farrier's job can be physically demanding, and, therefore, farriers should be in good physical condition and be able to adapt to a variety of working environments.

Despite the stress and the long hours involved, being a farrier offers an opportunity for those who enjoy working with animals and working out of doors to have an occupation that can be both financially and psychologically rewarding.

GOE: 03.03.02; SIC: 7699; SOC: 5624

◇ **SOURCES OF ADDITIONAL INFORMATION**

For information on school training programs as well as career opportunities, contact:

American Farrier's Association
PO Box 695
Albuquerque, NM 87107

For information on career opportunities, contact:

American Horse Council
1700 K Street, NW
Washington, DC 20006

◇ **RELATED ARTICLES**

Volume 1: Agriculture
Volume 3: Dairy farmers; Farmers; Farm operatives and managers
Volume 4: Animal health technicians; Animal production technicians

---

Fishers, commercial

Definition

Commercial fishers net, trap, and hook fish and other marine life for sale to processors, restaurants, retail fish markets, and other businesses.

History

America's lakes, streams, and thousands of miles of coastal waters have yielded a rich harvest of fish and seafood since long before the beginning of recorded history. Many native American tribes ate a diet that was largely fish. They used fish to fertilize their crops and fish bones for tools and other implements. When Europeans began to colonize North America, they made commercial fishing a major industry. At that time, the abundance of fish and other marine life was beyond comprehension. Lakes and streams teemed with trout and perch. The Gulf of Mexico offered up shrimp and oysters. In Pacific waters swam tuna and salmon, and the Atlantic Ocean shore was crowded with lobster and crab. Fleets of fishing boats and mammoth whaling vessels headed out to sea, returning with huge catches. For many communities, fishing was the way of life. Grueling and dangerous, but rugged and exciting, fishing held and still holds charm for those who want to work under the open sky.

Time has changed the fishing industry drastically. Pollution has made many waters unfishable. Increasing government regulation has restricted fishers in new ways. And technological advances have changed how people look for, catch, and process fish. The days of the family fishing boat are giving way to the days of the corporate fishing fleet. But some of the old romance about fishing lingers, and the occupation still attracts a steady stream of workers.

Nature of the work

Fishers are classified according to the type of equipment they use, the type of fish they catch, and where they go to catch them. Fishers work all over the country. Maine, Maryland, Massachusetts, Louisiana, Florida, Texas, California, Oregon, Washington, and Alaska all have major fishing industries. Northeastern states are good for lobster and sardine fishing, while fishers in the Gulf states catch shrimp and oysters. Most tuna fishers work off the California coastline. U.S. vessels also travel into the Bering Sea and to Africa and China for tuna.

Net fishers are usually deep sea fishers. Using many different kinds of nets and working either alone or as members of a fishing vessel crew, they put nets into the sea and draw them aboard when they are full of fish. Some boats go out and return the same day. Some are gone for weeks or months, keeping their catches fresh in refrigerated holds. While small boats may carry only two or three crew members, large tuna boats can carry as many as 22 and measure as much as 200 feet long.

After boats leave port, they head for fishing grounds; crew members keep track of weather reports and fishing conditions over the radio. In fishing waters, they scan for schools of fish using electronic equipment. When they have located a possible catch, they begin to lower the nets. *Purse seiners*, which mainly catch tuna, use a huge net—often a mile long and hundreds of feet deep. The net is weighted on the bottom and is held vertical by floats attached to the top. A smaller boat called a skiff, driven by a *skiff operator*, holds one end of the net while the fishing vessel circles around the school of fish to surround it with the net. That done, fishers close the bottom of the net by pulling steel cables attached to its bottom. Then they pull the net and the fish in and haul the catch on board.

Other finfish and shellfish are caught by *net fishers*. Net fishers are responsible for readying and repairing nets while the boat is moving to and from the fishing waters. To haul in the catch they often use hydraulic pumps and conveyor belts. Sometimes they sort and clean fish before or after returning to shore. Large tuna boats that stay at sea for many weeks can bring back as many as 1,200 tons of fish, which the fishers usually turn over to cannery workers at the port when they return.

Other fishers catch fish, including tuna, with poles, hooks, and lines. *Line fishers* work alone or in crews. They lay out lines and attach hooks, bait, and other equipment, depending on the type of fish they seek. This process can take several hours. They then put these lines into the water. To haul catches on board they use hands, reels, or winches. Then they take the catch off the hooks, sometimes first stunning them by hitting them with clubs, and store them in the boat's hold or in boxes packed with ice. Some of these fishers use a gaff—a long pole with a hook on the end—to help them catch fish and bring them aboard. Line fishers may also clean fish while their vessel heads to shore.

Because ships usually do not return to shore until bad weather comes, darkness falls, or the ship's hold is full of fish, net and line fishers repeat their tasks all day.

Fishers who catch marine life inland or near the shore usually use small boats and come in by nightfall. They fish for salmon, crabs, shrimp, lobsters, oysters, bass, and shad. *Pot fishers* trap crab, eel, and lobster using baited cages with funnel-shaped net openings. They lower these pots into the water, pull them in when they trap the quarry, and dump the catch onto the deck. These fishers need to measure each animal to make sure it is large enough to legally keep; those under size are thrown back. If the catch is lobster, fishers must sometimes insert pegs between the hinges of their claws to keep them from killing each other in their containers. These fishers usually sell their catches live to processors who can them, freeze them, or sell them fresh.

Other fishers include *terrapin fishers, weir fishers,* and *oyster fishers.* Terrapin fishers trap these turtles by stretching nets across marshes, creeks, or rivers, and chasing the terrapins into the nets. They may pole a skiff around in grassy waters and catch terrapins with a hand net, or may wade in mud and catch them by hand. Weir fishers make traps out of brush or netting, chase the fish into them, and remove the catch with a purse seine. Oyster fishers harvest oysters from beds in bays or river estuaries, using tongs, grabs, and dredges. They create "sea farms" to grow their catches by creating an environment suitable for growing oysters and by keeping natural predators out of the oysters' waters.

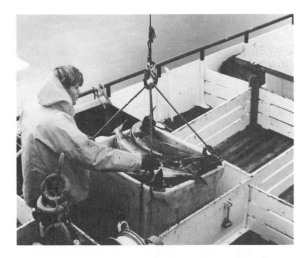

A commercial fisherman secures his catch of the day off the coast of Iceland.

Requirements

Fishers learn their skills through experience on the job. Certain academic courses, however, can help prepare workers for their first fishing job. Some high schools in port cities and some colleges and technical schools offer useful courses in handling boats and fishing equipment, biology, meteorology, navigation, and marketing. Commercial fishing programs are offered by three trade schools: Bellingham Vocational Technical Institute in Washington, Southwest Oregon Community College in Oregon, and Willmar Community College in Minnesota.

Special requirements

Commercial fishing vessels, but not crew members, need licenses. There are no other special requirements for fishing occupations.

Opportunities for experience and exploration

High-school students may try to obtain summer work on a small fishing boat or at fishing ports to explore this field. They may be able to talk to fishers and boat owners to find out more about the work and life of fishers.

Related occupations

Other workers involved in similar activities include artificial insemination technicians, farmers, dairy farmers, fish-production technicians, and trappers.

Methods of entering

Many people enter their family's fishing operation as a matter of course. Others should ask for a deckhand helper's job by applying to captains of commercial fishing vessels, which may be owned by canning and packing companies, as well as by individuals.

Advancement

Fishing has little formal structure within which workers can advance. They can, however, increase their earnings and responsibilities by becoming more skilled at vessel and net operation, by working faster, and by exploring ways of becoming involved in all aspects of the fishing industry. Enterprising fishers may save money to buy their own boats. Some run their own processing operations or catch seafood for their own restaurants. Advancement is limited only by the individual's own desire and drive. Owning one or more boats usually provides the highest profits for commercial fishers.

Employment outlook

Once a booming industry, fishing has gone through hard times in the past few decades. There are now fewer than 50,000 fishers working in the United States. A few years ago, however, the employment outlook for fishers began to look more positive. Although the industry can be affected by such variables as environmental law, ship and ship maintenance costs, and marine science developments, federal law on a 200-mile offshore boundary claim has relieved U.S. fishers from some competition with foreign vessels. More modern vessels, research on new uses of and ways to increase fish populations, and needed federal money for the industry are helping commercial fishing operations grow.

Earnings

Earnings of fishers vary with the season, the economy, the abundance of fish, market demands, and the worker's skills and willingness to stay out at sea. Few fishers receive a fixed wage. Instead, they may earn percentages of the catch; in New England, shipowners can receive 40 percent of the catch's receipts. Ten percent of this may go to the captain, and the captain and crew share the remaining 60 percent. Year-round fishers can earn about $14,400 a year, depending on the weather, the amount of fish caught, and the current demand for the catch. Seasonal fishers may earn $9,000 or less. Fishers with their own boats, however, can earn as much as $48,000 a year; those owning canneries $120,000 a year or more. Many workers earn hourly rates ranging from minimum wage to $7.20 or so an hour. Some are paid according to the number of pounds of fish they catch.

Conditions of work

Fishers often work long hours under dangerous and difficult conditions. Hauling fish takes great strength and endurance, and the work can be exhausting. Fishers work in all kinds of weather and sometimes spend months at sea in cramped quarters. Some fishers work all year; some work in certain seasons when certain fish can be caught.

Some fishers belong to unions. The crew members of vessels of the American Tunaboat Association are all members of a union, and they receive pensions, health and welfare benefits, and liberal disability benefits if they are injured while working on a vessel.

Social and psychological factors

People who enjoy risk, independence, and hard work will enjoy commercial fishing. Fishers need a disposition that enables them to work without a fixed routine and to deal with the everyday dangers of working with heavy equipment on wet decks, and in stormy seas. Because fishers live with others in close quarters on long trips, they need self-discipline. Because teamwork is essential on ships when seas are rough, fishers must stay calm in the face of trouble. Mechanical aptitude is also essential for fishers, because they spend a good deal of time setting up, repairing, and maintaining equipment. Business acumen will benefit fishers who want to be independent skippers of their own boats.

GOE: 03.04.03; SIC: 091; SOC: 583

◇ **SOURCES FOR ADDITIONAL INFORMATION**

American Tunaboat Association
One Tuna Lane
San Diego, CA 92101

National Fisheries Institute
2000 M Street, NW, Suite 400
Washington, DC 20036

◇ **RELATED ARTICLES**

Volume 1: Agriculture
Volume 3: See Agriculture, Forestry, Fisheries, and Conservation Occupations
Volume 4: See Agriculture, Forestry, and Conservation Technician

Foresters

Definition

Foresters protect and manage forests, which cover one-third of the land area of the United States. Forests are one of our greatest natural assets, providing raw materials, protection of water and wildlife resources, employment, and beauty for all people to enjoy.

History

Not so long ago, forests were considered a hindrance to farming, a barrier to settlement, and a surplus commodity of slight value to a small population of settlers. No profession existed to protect and manage the forests. But even in colonial times, the need to protect the tall pines of Maine and the live-oak forests of coastal Georgia for shipbuilding was recognized. As the population grew and land-clearing spread in the mid-nineteenth century, foresighted people realized that forests were becoming valuable, and unless protected, would become scarce. Laws enacted by the federal and state governments and rising prices for wood slowed down forest destruction, and opening the West to farming allowed forests to reclaim farms abandoned in the East. In 1900, the seven founders of the Society of American Foresters were practically the whole profession of forestry. But by 1905, the U.S. Forest Service was established in the Department of Agriculture, and, in 1907, assumed responsibility for the newly proclaimed national forest, staffed by professional foresters. The profession developed rapidly, charged with protecting the forests from fire, insects, and diseases; managing them for crops of wood, water, wildlife, and forage; preserving and making their beauty accessible; and training others to carry on the work.

Nature of the work

Many foresters do much of their work out of doors, especially during the early part of their careers. Young foresters map the locations and estimate the amounts of such resources as timber, game shelter and food, snow and water, and forage for cattle and sheep. They may also determine areas that need treatments, such as planting trees, scattering seed from helicopters,

control of disease or insects, thinning dense forest stands, or pruning trees to produce better lumber or plywood. They may lay out logging roads or roads to lakes and camp grounds, and make the plans for building camp grounds and shelters. They may supervise crews doing all these jobs and inspect the work after it is done. They may select and mark trees to be cut and check on the cutting and the removal of the logs and pulpwood. They may be in charge of the lookouts, patrols, and pilots who detect fires, and may lead crews that fight fires. They oversee the operation of camp grounds, collect fees and issue permits, give talks to groups of campers, find lost hikers, and rescue climbers and skiers.

But the work, even for younger foresters, is not all outdoors. They must record the work done in the forest on maps and in reports. Sometimes they use computers, data-processing equipment, and aerial photography. Then too, there are young foresters whose work is mostly indoors, in the technical laboratories and factories of wood-using industries, such as sawmills, plywood and hardboard plants, pulp and paper mills, wood preserving plants, and furniture factories. These foresters are specialists in wood technology or pulp and paper technology. Many foresters work in laboratories and greenhouses, as well as in the forests, to learn how trees and forests grow.

Because a forest offers many benefits, it is often possible to use the same forest for several purposes. To do this successfully, foresters must not only know a great deal about the forests, but must also be able to understand people, explain things to them, and secure their cooperation. Foresters, from the very start of their career, can expect to be called on to speak before various groups, from elementary school classes to service clubs and meetings of scientific societies. Not all foresters are in frequent contact with the public, but all foresters find that their advancement depends on their ability to work with other people.

Most of the work that a forester does involves the application of scientific knowledge. Some foresters, particularly those who work in research, specialize in a single science, but most foresters must have a broad understanding of many sciences. Foresters must have a good background in mathematics. This background is necessary also for understanding the physics involved in radio communication, aerial photography, behavior of fires, the ways of the

A forester measures the diameter of a Douglas fir. She is compiling information for a report on annual forest growth.

weather, and the mechanics of logging equipment. Foresters need to have a general grasp of the chemistry and physiology involved in the life of plants and animals, in the control of destructive insects and diseases, in the eradication of weedy trees and shrubs, the preservation of wood, and the conversion of wood to useful products.

They must know something about the rocks and soils on which forests grow and the ways of water in lakes, streams, and underground. They must be able to recognize and identify many of the trees, shrubs, and other plants; the animals of the forest; and the diseases and insects that prey on them. They must know how trees grow and reproduce.

Naturally, no one can master all these subjects, but foresters must know enough about them to be able to find expert help when the need arises. Some foresters know a great deal about one or two of the basic sciences. In fact, some foresters are engaged in research that gets deeply into the basic physical and biological sciences. They work in laboratories with many modern techniques and devices.

The scientific knowledge of how forests live is brought to bear by *silviculturists*, foresters who practice the art of establishing or reproducing forests, regulating their makeup, and influencing their growth and development along desired lines. The art of silviculture and the principles of economics and finance are the main foundations of forest preservation and management.

One branch of forestry, known as forest engineering or logging engineering, is on the borderline between forestry and engineering. Some of the work in this field is design and construction of roads, bridges, dams, and buildings in forest areas. The design, selection, and installation of equipment for moving logs and pulpwood out of the forest is the special field of the logging engineer. Logging and forest engineers may be graduates of schools of forestry that give courses in this specialty, or they may be civil, mechanical, or electrical engineers.

Another type of specialist, the *forest ecologist,* conducts research to find out how forests are affected by changes in environmental conditions, such as soil, light, climate, altitude, and animal populations.

A great deal of physical work in the woods needs to be done in most forestry organizations, and it is done by people with experience and aptitude, but with little formal education beyond high school, or by forest technicians who have graduated from one- or two-year programs in forest technicians' institutes or ranger schools. The work of a forest technician is highly skilled and requires experience, aptitude, and training, but it does not require the professional education received by foresters. Those individuals whose strongest wish is to continue to work out of doors in constant contact with the forest, may be happier as forestry technicians than as professional foresters. Moreover, individuals who prefer remaining in one locality to being transferred from place to place and to positions of increasing responsibility, may find the technician's life more attractive than the forester's.

Requirements

A professional forester is a graduate of a four-year university-level school of forestry, and generally has a bachelor's degree. Some foresters combine three years of liberal arts education with two years of professional education in forestry, and receive the degrees of bachelor of arts and master of forestry. There are approximately forty-six schools of forestry in the United States accredited by the Society of American Foresters, the professional society to which most foresters belong. Schools of forestry are found in thirty-four states, and most of them are parts of state universities.

The courses of study in all accredited schools of forestry are basically similar. Indeed, to be accredited, a school must offer a specified amount of instruction in five essential fields of forestry; silviculture (the art of tending and reproducing forests), forest management (the application of business methods and silvicultural principles to the operation of a forest property), forest protection (from fires, insects, diseases, wildlife, and weather), forest economics (the costs and returns involved in forest management enterprises, both public and private, the basis for making management decisions), and forest utilization (the harvesting and marketing of forest crops and commodities). The courses in these five subjects are generally concentrated in the junior and senior years, which make up the professional portion of the forester's schooling. To prepare for these subjects, the forestry student needs a grounding in mathematics, surveying, chemistry, physics, botany, zoology, soil science, and geology. Moreover, to help develop skills needed for self-education, the student takes basic courses in literature, social studies, economics, and writing. All these courses are organized in a program that fills the freshman and sophomore years largely with basic sciences and humanities.

Foresters do actual work in the forest as a part of their university training. Some schools of forestry are so close to forests that regular three-hour to all-day laboratory sessions are conducted in the school forest. Following the sophomore year, in many schools of forestry, there is a summer camp period of eight to eleven weeks. This is really a continuous laboratory period during which the students take part in the life of the forest, and, under guidance of the faculty, store up experience on which they will draw in their junior and senior professional courses. Often, during the latter part of their senior year, students take a field trip or spend several all-day periods working on advanced problems in forest management and silviculture. In addition, some schools of forestry require that their students work for one summer for a forestry organization such as the U.S. Forest Service, National Park Service, a state forest service, or forest industry. The employer usually reports on the student's attitude, capacity, and development.

This continuous experience in the forests and the actual practice of forestry reinforces the student's classroom work, gives the forestry school graduate a clear picture of the profession, and enables him or her to make contacts leading to employment on graduation.

In addition to the basic sciences and humanities, and the five "core" forestry subjects, elective courses are offered to enable students to specialize in such fields as forest engineering (or logging engineering), wood technology, range management, wildlife management, forest recreation, and watershed management.

The four academic years plus some summer are well filled with work and study. Indeed, many foresters are convinced that a longer program is necessary for the combined process of

education and professional training. It is a good possibility that the leading schools will lengthen their courses to at least five years in the near future.

Graduates of forestry schools who wish to specialize in research or teaching, or who wish to strengthen their education in some other special field, may take graduate work at many of the forestry schools to earn master's degrees or doctorates.

A small but growing number of junior colleges or special forest technician institutes offer six-month to two-year programs of study to train high-school graduates interested in the work of forest technicians. The courses of study include less mathematics and basic sciences than do the professional forestry school programs and place more stress on subjects such as surveying, mapping, accounting, the care and use of tools and equipment, and outdoor operations such as thinning, logging, and sawmilling. The graduates of these schools are in great demand, and have no difficulty in finding employment.

Special requirements

Forestry requires above average intelligence. Because of the nature of the work, the forester must often make decisions on the basis of incomplete knowledge. This means that the individual must be self-reliant and have a high degree of initiative. A forester should have a scientific attitude and curiosity, and should have a strong liking for the outdoors.

Because trees grow slowly and the changes in forests are gradual, foresters must have more than average patience and a firm conviction that the work they do is important. The forester often works alone, away from the scrutiny of supervisors or colleagues. If one makes mistakes or is careless, the results may not be apparent for many years. Therefore, the forester must be completely dependable and conscientious. It is not necessary that foresters have the physical attributes of athletes, but they must have more than average endurance and they should enjoy physical activity.

Opportunities for experience and exploration

Two subjects are especially important for students who wish to enter a forestry school. These are English and mathematics, the keys

Foresters
Agriculture, Forestry, and Conservation Occupations

the student needs above all others to gain admission to a good school of forestry and to succeed there. The forestry student must read widely, rapidly, and with understanding. He or she must be able to speak well. The student planning to enter a school of forestry should take all the mathematics available in high school. History, languages, chemistry, physics, art, and music are also important.

Many schools of forestry have arranged their course schedules so that junior college graduates, with the proper preparation, can transfer into the junior year of the forestry course. Junior college students who wish to enter schools of forestry should come with the best possible preparation in English, mathematics, physical and biological sciences, and chemistry.

One very good way to explore the field of forestry is by making the acquaintance of some foresters to find out whether they are the kind of people one wants to work with. They can help your school counselors advise you on the choice of a forestry school and they may even be able to help you find summer work in forestry or a related field. They may help arrange visits to forestry schools and to forests, forestry research laboratories, and forest products manufacturing plants. In some parts of the country, local chapters of the Society of American Foresters invite prospective forestry students to some of their meetings and field trips.

Related occupations

Many other workers are involved with the care and maintenance of the nation's forest wilderness areas. Others include park rangers, park technicians, range managers, and logging industry workers.

Methods of entering

Foresters gain employment with the agencies of the federal government and of many state governments on the basis of competitive civil service examinations that are open to forestry school graduates. Private companies hire foresters by recruiting at the schools of forestry. Most foresters interested in teaching must first earn advanced degrees, such as the master of science, master of forestry, or doctorate, before they are qualified for positions in schools of forestry.

Advancement

Professional foresters who have graduated from university-level schools of forestry often spend an initial period on their first job doing work that is not at a fully professional level. They may, for example, do the elementary surveying involved in forest inventory or engineering work, they may work in logging or construction crews, or they may act as supervisors of planting or insect control crews. In progressive organizations, this training period for the young professional forester is kept short and is used to provide a real understanding of operations from the bottom up. After such a training period, which many young foresters enjoy after the confinement of school days, foresters are usually moved on to more responsible positions. This almost always means an increase in "paper work" and a corresponding decrease in the time the forester spends in physical work out of doors. As foresters move on to positions of greater responsibility in a public or private forestry organization, they may choose either a line or a staff position. A line position is one in which the forester supervises technicians and other foresters. At the lower levels, the forester in a line position may have direct supervision over two to five other foresters; at higher levels one may still directly oversee only a small number of people, but each of these, in turn, is in charge of small groups of foresters. Success in a line position requires not only professional competence and knowledge, but the sort of personality that makes a leader. Progressive forestry organizations devote a great deal of effort to developing the leadership qualities of their line foresters.

In research work, the forester may begin as a laboratory assistant working gradually into detailed research activities and eventually into leadership or administrative positions in forestry research.

Employment outlook

There were more than 28,000 foresters working in the United States in the early 1990s. Of these, more than half were employed by various agencies of the federal government, including the Forest Service, Bureau of Land Management, National Park Service, and the Bureau of Indian Affairs. State governments employed one-fifth of the total, and local governments employed a few hundred. Many worked in private industry. Some foresters were managers of their own land, were in business for themselves as consultants, or were employed by consulting

364

firms. A third major group was the teachers of forestry and extension foresters.

Most estimates of future employment trends in forestry suggest that opportunities will increase slowly through the late 1990s. Budgetary limitations have led to cutbacks in federal and state programs in many instances. Some growth is expected in private industry, which may need additional personnel to improve logging and milling practices in order to reduce waste.

Earnings

Foresters with bachelor's degrees employed by the federal government earned average starting salaries of $17,280 or $21,360, depending on their college records, in the early 1990s. Whether working for private industry or federal, state, or local governments, foresters' salaries depend on the number of years of education and experience in the field. The average salary for foresters in the federal government in the early 1990s was around $37,200.

In general, the best-paid foresters were those described as self-employed—mostly private consulting foresters—the lowest pay scales were found, on the average, in state employment.

Conditions of work

The forester generally works a forty-hour week, although one must be prepared for overtime duty, particularly when emergency conditions arise.

The health of a forester is an extremely important consideration, not only as a requirement for entrance to the field, but in dealing with the often strenuous aspects of the day-to-day duties. Foresters whose work interests are more research-centered may not find the physical requirements as demanding, since they may be spending more time in laboratory work. They, too, often spend time in the field but generally under conditions where the physical activities are less rigorous. Their workweek may tend to be more regular and their routines somewhat less varied.

Foresters usually work in smaller towns or cities where they become involved in and identified with community life. Yet they are able to avoid some of the narrowing influences of small town life because of their activity in a profession with very wide geographical scope. It is traditional for the forester to go and see how

colleagues "across the mountains" are handling common problems.

Social and psychological factors

Beyond knowing how important their work is for human society, foresters have a deeper knowledge that people must live in harmony with the world of which they are a part. To achieve this harmony people must understand how their world changes, develops, and renews itself. They must become aware that the world's forests are not inexhaustible. Foresters are dedicated to the faith that, with this understanding, people can continue to use their forests for the many benefits they offer. This is, in essence, the role that the forester plays, and from this belief generally draws deep satisfaction.

GOE: 03.01.04; SIC: 08; SOC: 1852

◇ SOURCES FOR ADDITIONAL INFORMATION

American Forest Council
1250 Connecticut Avenue, NW, Suite 320
Washington, DC 20036

American Forestry Association
1516 P Street, NW
Washington, DC 20005

Society of American Foresters
5400 Grosvenor Lane
Bethesda, MD 20814

U.S. Department of Agriculture
Forest Service
PO Box 2417
Washington, DC 20013

◇ RELATED ARTICLES

Grain merchants

Definition

Grain merchants purchase grain for resale. They are involved in all aspects of buying and selling grain and are concerned with the quality, market value, shipping, processing, and storing of the grain.

History

Throughout history, grain plants have been important sources of food. The ancient Greeks and Egyptians, for example, raised wheat and barley as food crops. In the Orient, the Chinese pioneered the use of rice in a similar fashion. The Aztecs and other American Indians raised corn very successfully.

Grain merchants have played a vital role in the trading process. They buy the raw grain from the growers and then distribute it to markets all over the world. By purchasing, processing, transporting, and storing grain until another buyer can be found, grain merchants facilitate the smooth flow of the commodity all year round, both during times of shortages and surpluses.

Nature of the work

Grain merchants purchase grain when the stock on hand reaches a predetermined reorder point, when a person or organization specially orders it, or when market conditions are especially favorable. To purchase grain, the grain merchant must consider the type of grain specified, the market price of such grain, quantity discounts, freight handling or other transportation costs, and delivery time. Much of this information can be obtained by comparing listings in catalog and trade journals, interviewing supplier's representatives, keeping up with current market trends, and examining sample goods. Many merchants now also use computers to obtain up-to-date price listings, to keep track of inventory levels, and to process routine orders.

Grain merchants must be sufficiently familiar with the various qualities of grain to determine whether certain grains should be purchased. Merchants inspect samples of grain by weighing it, checking its moisture content, and examining it for the presence of insects or other signs of damage. Grain must also be classified according to type.

The U.S. government has developed grain standards and in this way ensures that grains of a certain grade all meet the same specifications. After the grain merchants make an initial appraisal of the quality of the grain, they send samples to a federal grain inspector for an official appraisal.

It is important that grain merchants develop a good working relationship with farmers and other suppliers in order to attain a good price on the grain, favorable payment terms, quick delivery on emergency orders, or help in obtaining the grain during times of scarcity. To negotiate these and other conditions, grain merchants must have good communications skills, be able to work effectively with others, and take high-pressure situations in stride.

Although grain merchants often are involved in many aspects of the buying, storing, and reselling process, there are a variety of specialists that perform different functions. These specialists include: *Grain buyers* who evaluate and purchase grain for resale and milling. They select the type of grain to order based on current demand and possible future considerations. Grain buyers arrange for the transportation and storage of the grain and also identify possible resale markets. They hope to make money by reselling the grain at a higher price than they purchased it. To minimize their risk, buyers may purchase commodity futures, which are agreements to buy or sell an amount of their crop at a future date. These futures are hedges against a change in the price of grain (or other commodity).

Grain buyers who manage grain elevators must inspect all grain that comes to these holding terminals and calculate its market value. In estimating its market value, they must not only take into account the purchase price of the grain, but also transportation, handling, and other charges. Grain elevator managers keep daily records on the kinds and grades of grain received, prices paid, amount purchased, and the amount in storage. They also supervise grain elevator workers in the unloading, loading, storing, and mixing of the grain for shipment and milling.

Grain broker-and-market operators buy and sell grain and futures contracts for investors through the commodity exchanges. They advise their customers on factors that may influence the price of grain, such as grain production and consumption. The largest commodity exchange is the Chicago Board of Trade; other large commodity exchanges include the Kansas Board of Trade and the Minneapolis Grain Exchange. Although broker-and-market operators usually never see the grain they buy and sell, they can determine its quality by virtue of the government's official appraisal. Like other types of brokers, they work on a commission basis. Their actions are regulated by the Commodity Futures Trading Commission.

Commodities brokers do the actual buying and selling of future grain contracts. These contracts call for the delivery of grain at a future date. Through an auction process, these commodities brokers provide a public forum in which the future price of grain is set. This process is not only for public speculation but also provides grain merchants and grain farmers with a mechanism to safeguard their investment. Many times merchants will sell some of their crop on the futures market as a hedge to guard against changes in the price of grain.

Clean-rice brokers coordinate rice buying and milling activities. After examining market conditions, they determine what type of clean (milled) rice to purchase, find storage facilities, and arrange for its future resale. Clean-rice brokers must keep records of purchases and shipping and handling costs and prepare sales contracts.

A grain merchant inspects a shipment of wheat before purchasing it. He checks for the presence of insects, the moisture content, and any signs of damage.

Requirements

Although there are no specific educational requirements, a high-school diploma is a necessity and at least some college training is very helpful.

High-school courses should include English, mathematics, science, and as many business and agriculture classes as possible.

To further professional opportunities, many grain merchants get an undergraduate or graduate degree in agriculture, economics, or finance; for others a two-year program in the same subjects is sufficient. Course work should include agricultural economics, accounting, purchasing, finance, and business law. As farm finances tighten with less loans available, grain merchants will probably deal with fewer, more specialized farms.

A grain merchant should have a calm temperament and be able to make decisions regarding large sums of money. He or she should also possess initiative, good judgment, an analytical mind, and the ability to work on details.

Special requirements

In general, no licenses or certificates are needed to work in this profession. Some grain merchants who deal with the public on commodities futures or in other capacities must pass a competency test and be licensed by the federal government. Those who work for the federal government may have to pass a civil service examination.

Opportunities for experience and exploration

There may be some opportunities for high-school students to get part-time jobs with a farming cooperative or other grain purchasing organization, especially if the person is located in an agricultural community with grain elevators. Many cities and towns, such as Chicago, Kansas City, St. Louis, and others in the Midwest are large centers of the grain trade and as such have numerous job opportunities.

It may also be possible to get part-time work at a commodity exchange and learn about the profession from that angle. In addition, some school work-study programs may have opportunities with grain elevators for part-time, practical on-the-job training. Another way of gaining insight into the responsibilities of a grain merchant is to talk to someone already working in the field.

Related occupations

Other professionals who negotiate contracts to purchase supplies or equipment include retail and wholesale buyers, purchasing agents, and office administrators.

Methods of entering

For those with college training, school placement services usually offer assistance in finding work. In addition, it is also possible to contact prospective employers directly. Jobs are also often listed in "help wanted" advertisements. Major employers include regional grain elevators and commodity exchanges. The Department of Agriculture and other governmental agencies also hire grain merchants.

Advancement

Often, becoming a grain merchant represents a promotion from the position of grain elevator worker, clerk at a commodity exchange, or other similar position. A skilled grain merchant may become a grain elevator manager or a grain buyer for a large company. As always, those with the most training and experience stand the best prospects of advancing to positions of higher pay and greater responsibility. There is also considerable opportunity for advancement through changing employers. Some skilled grain merchants may become consultants for the federal government or take a similar position with a bank, insurance company, or other private company.

Employment outlook

Although the global economy, the availability of grain products, and a variety of other factors will influence the job market, employment opportunities should remain fairly strong through the 1990s.

Grain merchants should continue to find work as grain buyers, commodities brokers, grain broker-and-market operators, grain elevator managers, and clean-rice brokers. There will be some job opportunities as a result of people retiring or otherwise leaving the field. Job prospects should be best in communities with a large amount of agricultural trade and in metropolitan areas such as Chicago and Kansas City that are home to many regional grain centers and trading houses. Some grain merchants will be self-employed and others may work for farm cooperatives or grain companies. They may also work for the federal government or as consultants for banks or other financial institutions that provide loans to grain establishments.

Earnings

As with other brokers, some grain merchants work on a commission basis and others work for a straight salary. Earnings vary as to the size of the employer, the experience of the employee, and the specific job responsibilities. Beginning grain merchants can expect to earn $15,500 to $22,000 per year, depending on the above factors. Experienced grain merchants should earn between $24,000 and $37,000 per year, with some experienced grain merchants earning even more. Salaries should be highest for elevator managers at large regional terminals and for successful grain buyers and brokers. A great deal of a grain merchant's success is dependent on making the proper contacts with grain suppliers and buyers. Those who work for the federal government may earn somewhat less than those in the private sector.

Full-time grain merchants usually receive paid holidays, health insurance, and other benefits. Many firms also have pension plans. Grain merchants who travel are usually reimbursed for expenses incurred for lodging, transportation, and other expenses.

Conditions of work

While much of their work is done inside in a typical office setting, grain merchants often need to inspect goods outdoors or in grain elevators. Those who work on commodity exchanges will probably work in large, noisy trading areas.

Grain merchants generally work a standard thirty-seven to forty-hour week, although overtime is a strong likelihood in situations when grain supplies are in demand or in a state of flux.

Some grain merchants, especially grain buyers, travel a great deal. These trips are necessary to buy and sell grain, make any necessary inspections, and keep in contact with current and prospective clients.

Social and psychological factors

Because grain merchants work with so many different types of people, they must have good communications skills and be diplomatic, tactful, and cooperative. Frequently it rests on the grain merchant to get "rush" orders accepted, arrange favorable payment terms, and prompt delivery service. Other personal qualifications include dependability, trustworthiness, and a neat personal appearance. Grain merchants must not only be able to work under deadline pressure but also be able to handle the stress of negotiating business deals worth millions of dollars. Although grain merchants often buy and sell grain using other people's money, the pressure to make the right decision can be great. Grain merchants must be able to make quick decisions, but more importantly they should have the analytical, mathematical, and business skills needed to ensure that those decisions are correct.

GOE: 11.06.04; SIC: 6231, 6221; SOC: 1443

 SOURCES OF ADDITIONAL INFORMATION

Career information is available from:

Grain Elevator & Processing Society
301 4th Avenue South
PO Box 15026
Commerce Station
Minneapolis, MN 55415

Terminal Elevator Grain Merchants Association
1030 15th Street, NW, Suite 1020
Washington, DC 20005

 RELATED ARTICLES

Volume 1: Retailing
Volume 2: Purchasing agents
Volume 3: Manufacturers' sales workers; Securities and financial services sales representatives; Shipping and receiving clerks

Landscapers and grounds managers

Definition

Landscapers and grounds managers plan and design gardens, parks, lawns, and other landscaped areas, and supervise the care of the trees, plants, and shrubs that are part of these areas. Specific job responsibilities depend on the type of natural area involved. Landscapers and ground managers direct projects at private homes, parks, schools, arboretums, government offices, and botanical gardens. They are involved with purchasing material and supplies, and with training, directing, and supervising employees. Grounds managers handle the maintenance of the land after the landscapers' designs are implemented. They may work alone or supervise a grounds staff.

History

The landscaping of formal gardens and the cultivation of flowers are ancient arts. The hanging gardens of Babylon, the landscaped areas of Persia and India, the smaller formal gardens of Athens, and the terraces and geometric gardens of Italy are early examples of this art. In the eighteenth century, gardens became more informal and natural, as typified by the plantings around George Washington's Mount Vernon home.

The first large landscaped area in the United States was New York's Central Park, which was done in the 1860s. While landscaped parks and gardens have not been as dominant in the United States as in Europe and elsewhere, a growing enthusiasm is creating an increasing demand for skilled landscapers and grounds managers.

Nature of the work

There are many different types of landscapers and grounds managers and specific job requirements depend on the duties involved. Specialists within the field include: *Landscape contractors,* who perform landscaping work on a contract basis for homeowners, highway departments, operators of industrial parks, and others. They confer with prospective clients and study the landscape design, drawings, and bills of material to determine the amount of landscape work required, such as the installation of lighting or sprinkler systems, erection of fences, and the types of trees, shrubs, or ornamental plants required. They inspect the grounds, and they calculate labor, equipment, and materials costs. They also prepare and submit bids, draw up contracts, and direct and coordinate the activities of *landscape laborers* as they mow lawns, plant shrubbery, dig holes, move topsoil, and perform other related landscaping tasks.

Greenskeepers I supervise and coordinate the activities of workers who are engaged in keeping the grounds and the turf of a golf course in good playing condition. They consult with the greens superintendent to plan and review work projects; they determine work assignments, such as fertilizing, irrigating, seeding, mowing, raking, and spraying; and they mix and prepare spraying and dusting solutions. They may also repair and maintain mechanical equipment. *Greenskeepers II* follow the instructions of greenskeepers I as they maintain the grounds of golf courses. They cut the turf on green and tee areas, dig and rake grounds to prepare and cultivate new greens, connect hose and sprinkler systems, plant trees and shrubs, and operate tractors as they apply fertilizer, insecticide, and other substances to the fairways or other designated areas.

Greens superintendents supervise and coordinate the activities of greenskeepers and other workers engaged in constructing new golf course areas and in preserving existing areas. They review test results of soil and turf samples, and they direct the application of fertilizer, lime, insecticide, or fungicide. Their other duties include touring the grounds to determine the need of irrigation or changes in mower height, keeping and reviewing maintenance records, and interviewing and hiring workers.

Industrial-commercial groundskeepers maintain areas in and around industrial or commercial properties by cutting the lawn, pruning trees, raking leaves, and shoveling snow. They also plant grass and flowers and are responsible for the upkeep of flower beds and public passageways. Industrial-commercial groundskeepers may repair and maintain fences and gates and also operate sprinkler systems and other equipment.

Parks-and-grounds groundskeepers maintain city, state, or national parks and playgrounds. They plant and prune trees, haul away garbage, repair driveways, walks, swings, and other equipment, and clean comfort stations.

Lawn and tree service spray supervisors supervise and direct the activities of landscape workers who are engaged in pruning trees and shrubs, caring for lawns, and performing related tasks. They coordinate work schedules, prepare job cost estimates, and answer customer questions and concerns.

Tree-trimming supervisors coordinate and direct the activities of workers engaged in cutting away tree limbs or removing trees that interfere with electric power lines. They inspect power lines and direct the placement of removal equipment. Tree-trimming supervisors answer consumer questions when trees are located on private property.

Landscape gardeners care for hedges, gardens, and other landscaped areas. They mow and trim lawns, plant trees and shrubs, apply fertilizers and other chemicals, and may repair walks and driveways. Depending on the size of the job, they may carry out or supervise the work activities. They maintain the grounds of private or business establishments.

Tree surgeons prune and treat ornamental and shade trees to improve their health and appearance. For example, they scrape decayed matter from cavities in the trees and fill the holes with cement to promote healing and to prevent further deterioration. They also spray trees with pesticides and fertilizers.

Scouts locate and exterminate plant and tree pests and diseases through the use of herbicides, insecticides, or fungicides. They inspect infested areas after treatment to determine the treatment's effectiveness. Scouts may specialize in the treatment of a particular type of infestation, such as gypsy moth or boll weevil.

Weed inspectors locate and exterminate noxious weeds. They prepare a poisonous solution based on the type of weed involved and then spray the infected area with the solution. They visit the infected area after the treatment to ensure that the treatment was effective.

Tree trimmers and *tree pruners* prune all types of trees to enhance their beauty, correct situations such as overhanging branches, or cure disease. They may apply tar or other protective substances to cut surfaces to seal out insects.

Lawn-service workers plant and maintain lawns. They remove leaves and dead grass and apply insecticides, fertilizers, and weed killers as necessary. Lawn-service workers use aerators and other tools to pierce the soil to make holes for the fertilizer and water.

Hand sprayers spray herbicides and other chemicals on trees, shrubs, and lawns. They may use a truck-mounted tank or portable spray equipment to reach affected areas.

A grounds keeper at an arboretum uses a large grass cutting machine. On vast tracks of land, such machines are helpful.

Requirements

Educational requirements obviously depend on the specific area of expertise, but in general a high-school diploma is necessary for the majority of positions, and at least some college training is needed for those with supervisory responsibilities. Aspiring landscapers and grounds managers should enjoy working out-of-doors and have an interest in preserving and maintaining natural areas. They should also be physically fit, have an aptitude for working with machines, and have good manual dexterity.

High-school students should take classes in English, mathematics, chemistry, biology, and as many courses as possible in horticulture and botany.

Those interested in receiving college training should enroll in a two- or four-year program in horticulture, landscape management, or agronomy. Course work should be selected with an area of specialization in mind and might include classes in landscape maintenance and design, turf grass management, botany, and plant pathology. Those wishing to have managerial responsibilities should take courses in personnel management, communications, and business-related courses such as accounting and economics.

Many trade and vocational schools also offer landscaping and related programs. There are also several extension programs that allow you to take courses at home.

Special requirements

Licensing and certification procedures differ from state to state and also vary according to specific job responsibilities. For example, in some states landscapers and grounds managers need a certificate to spray insecticides or other chemicals. Landscape contractors and other self-employed people may also need a license to operate their business. All managerial personnel must carefully supervise their workers to ensure that environmental regulations (as specified by the Environmental Protection Agency and other local and national governmental agencies) are adhered to.

Many landscapers and grounds managers belong to a variety of organizations for professional enrichment. These professional organizations include the Professional Grounds Management Society, the National Landscape Association, and the American Society for Horticultural Sciences. Addresses for these and other organizations are available at the end of this article.

Opportunities for experience and exploration

Part-time work at a golf course, lawn-service company, greenhouse, botanic garden, or other similar enterprise is an excellent way of learning about the responsibilities in this field. Many companies are eager to hire part-time help, especially during the busy summer months. In addition, there are numerous opportunities to get work mowing lawns, growing flowers, and tending gardens. Interested students can also join garden clubs, visit local flower shops, and attend botanical shows.

It is also possible to learn about this profession by talking to someone already working as a landscaper or grounds manager.

Related occupations

Other workers involved with maintaining natural areas include horticulturists, nursery managers, cemetery workers, and park technicians. Those interested in this profession may also wish to become florists, agronomists, or government agricultural inspectors.

Methods of entering

Work experience obtained on a part-time basis often leads to a full-time job with the same employer. Those who enroll in a college, university, or other training program should receive help in finding work from the job placement office at the school. In addition, direct application to botanical gardens, nurseries, golf courses, and other similar locations is an excellent means of obtaining employment. Jobs may also be listed in "help wanted" advertisements.

Most landscaping and other such companies provide on-the-job training for entry-level personnel during which time company policy and procedures are explained.

Advancement

In general, landscapers and grounds managers can expect to advance to more responsible and better-paying positions as they gain experience and additional educational training. For example, a greenskeeper with a high-school diploma must usually have at least some college training in order to become a greens superintendent. It is also possible to go into a related field, such as selling equipment used in maintaining lawns, parks, and other natural areas.

Those in managerial positions may wish to advance to a larger establishment or go into consulting work. In some instances, skilled landscapers and grounds managers may start their own companies.

Employment outlook

As people continue to become aware of the importance of parks and gardens in providing beauty, recreational opportunities, and a chance for relaxation, job opportunities for landscapers and grounds managers should expand. This trend should continue at least through the 1990s. Employment opportunities should be available across the country. Major employers should include landscaping companies, golf courses, and parks. Jobs should be available with local and state governmental agencies as well as the private sector. As always, those with the most training and experience should enjoy the best employment opportunities.

Earnings

Salaries depend on the experience and education level of the worker, the type of work being done, and geographic location. High-school graduates with no further training or education who start as landscape laborers can expect to earn between $10,500 and $13,000 per year to start. Those with a college degree should earn between $14,500 and $16,000 annually. Those with managerial responsibilities should earn between $17,000 and $19,000 per year to start. Landscape contractors and others who run their own businesses should earn between $22,000 and $30,000 per year, with those with a greater ability to locate customers earning even more.

Fringe benefits vary from employer to employer, but generally include medical insurance and some paid vacation.

Conditions of work

Landscapers and grounds managers spend much of their time outside. Landscape laborers and others involved with the planting and other physical work may spend all of their time outside, while those with administrative or managerial responsibilities spend at least a portion of their workday in an office. Most of the outdoor work is done during daylight hours, but work takes place all year round in all weather conditions. Most people work thirty-seven to forty hours a week, but overtime is especially likely during the summer months when landscapers and grounds managers take advantage of the warmer weather. Weekend work is highly likely.

Much of the work can be physically demanding. Workers should expect to shovel dirt, trim bushes and trees, and bend down to plant flowers and shrubbery. Managerial personnel should be willing to work overtime updating financial records and making sure the business accounts are in order.

There is a small chance that workers may be injured while using planting and pruning machinery. They are also subject to illnesses and diseases from handling and breathing pesticides and other chemicals and from handling plants that have been sprayed with insecticides. Proper precautions should limit any job-related hazards.

Social and psychological factors

Those working in landscaping and grounds management should be able to work outdoors for long periods of time and be able to closely follow instructions. Those in managerial positions should be able to supervise workers and communicate effectively, both verbally and in writing. The necessity of working in wooded or heavily planted areas might be somewhat unpleasant, especially in the hot, humid summer months.

Despite the long hours and sometimes physically demanding work schedule, those who enjoy working out-of-doors with plants and trees can find self-expression and satisfaction in a career that brings such pleasure and beauty.

GOE 03.01.03; SIC: 0781; SOC 5515, 5621, 5622

◇ SOURCES OF ADDITIONAL INFORMATION

For information on career opportunities and educational training, contact:

American Society for Horticultural Sciences
710 North Saint Asaph Street
Alexandria, VA 22314

Professional Grounds Management Society
12 Galloway Avenue
Suite 1E
Cockeysville, MD 21030

National Landscape Association
1250 I Street, NW
Suite 500
Washington, DC 20005

Associated Landscape Contractors of America
405 North Washington Street
Falls Church, VA 22046

American Society of Landscape Architects
1733 Connecticut Avenue, NW
Washington, DC 20009

For information regarding home-study programs, contact a local vocational school or the local Cooperative Extension Service.

◇ RELATED ARTICLES

Volume 2: Landscape architects
Volume 4: Ornamental horticulture technicians; Park technicians

Logging industry workers

Definition

Logging industry workers are engaged in cutting down trees and cutting them into logs. They select areas to be logged, determine the quantity to be harvested, and cut the trees. They load logs into trucks or trains, which drive the wood to sawmills and other factories, where it is processed into lumber, paper, and other wood products.

History

The vast, unsettled North American continent yielded what seemed like a limitless supply of trees for lumber to the colonists and timber merchants who began arriving as early as the sixteenth century. Settlers and lumberjacks built ships, roads, wagons, homes, churches, stores, and schools from the wood they cleared to build colonies and from the surrounding forests.

Today, conservationists worry that irresponsible logging will wipe out the country's forests, and the logging industry has had to devise ways to avoid cutting timber unnecessarily and to plant new trees to replace felled ones. The timber today's loggers fell goes into buildings, furniture, paper, poles, pilings, shingles, and many other products.

Nature of the work

The logging industry is concentrated in the Northwest, Northeast, South, and Great Lakes states. Trees are cut from designated forests or tracts in large numbers, cut into pieces for transporting and processing, conveyed to landings or loading areas, and loaded into trucks or trains for delivery to mills.

To decide where to begin cutting, a worker called a *cruiser* surveys a forest to estimate the value of a tract's marketable timber. This worker collects data for use in determining the best and safest places to fell the trees and for determining how to set up a logging camp, locating the landing, and devising routes for getting the timber to the landing.

Several methods are used for moving logs to landings. In skidding, *logging-tractor operators* drag logs to landings. In high-lead logging, workers fasten individual logs to steel cables and operate a winch to pull each one to the landings. By stretching a cable between two standing trees, loggers using skyline logging techniques hold logs aloft while they move to landings, reducing damage to young trees not ready to be cut. Using a cable-grappler, one worker picks up logs under the direction of another and sets them down at the landing. *Rafters* tie logs together and float them to the mill where *log sorters* sort and maneuver them into the mill.

Forest engineers design and direct operations for cutting and removing timber from an area. They decide how best to reach and leave areas, build campsites, and store cut timber. *Logging superintendents* oversee the entire operation of cutting in a particular area.

Fallers cut down trees, applying their knowledge of trees and cutting to control the tree's fall so as to minimize damage to young trees and danger to other workers. These skills are important in selective harvesting, but in areas where loggers cut all trees in a tract, such judgment is less crucial. Fallers look for twists, rot, kinds of limbs, and the direction in which a tree leans to determine where to place cuts and how deep to make them. Using a chain saw or ax, *fallers and brush clearing laborers* clear debris and brush from their work area and from the path they plan to take to escape when the tree begins to fall. When they are ready to begin cutting, fallers score cutting lines with an ax and begin cutting the tree along these lines with a chain saw. They saw back-cuts to weaken the tree trunk so it will fall in the right direction, leaving enough sound wood to control the tree's fall. While sawing, they insert wedges or jacks in the cut to give the saw enough room to cut. When the tree begins to tip, fallers stop their saws, pull them from the cut, and run to a predetermined location to avoid being hurt by flying debris and falling limbs as the tree falls and hits the ground.

Another way to cut trees is with hydraulic tree shears. *Tree-shear operators* can use these machines to cut trees up to two feet in diameter.

After trees are felled, *chain saw operators* trim their tops, limbs, and roots as do *tan bark operators* who harvest tree bark. These workers and others called *buckers* use chain saws to cut limbs from trunks and saw trunks into lengths. Buckers place poles or limbs under the trunks to keep them from rolling, and cut them into pieces for lumber, poles, planks, pilings, veneer blocks, or other products. *Rivers* and *tree cutters* are other kinds of workers who fell and cut trunks into pieces. *Logging markers* are sometimes employed to mark logs for cutting so as to maximize useable wood in specified lengths.

Fallers and buckers may be instructed by a *felling-bucking supervisor* who trains these workers, tells them which trees to cut first, and gives them the cutting specifications desired by the sawmill or other customer. *Logging supervisors* also oversee falling and bucking operations, as well as the loading of logs at landings.

Some wood is not cut into lengths, but is instead turned into wood chips for use in making pulp, paper, and fuel. *Pulp pilers* separate the logs that will be used for those purposes. *Log-chipper operators* use a trailer-mounted grapple loader and chipping machine to convert logs and logging waste into chips. *Woods bosses* direct workers in pulling, blasting, and transporting tree stumps to be made into turpentine.

Many workers are employed in moving logs from felling sites to landings. *Hook tenders* coordinate activities of workers who move logs using high-lead or other cable-yarding systems. *Rigging slingers,* under the hook tender's direction, tell *choke setters* how to position and secure cables around logs, and direct the *yarding engineer* in pulling the logs from the cutting area to the landing. *Riggers,* under the direction of hook tenders, install blocks or guy lines used to secure cables to stumps. *Hoisting engineers* operate powered hoists to move logs with these cables.

When logs are yarded, or brought to the landing where they will be loaded, *chasers* use hand signals to show yarding engineers or logging-tractor operators where to drop logs. There, other workers, including *jammer operators, sorting-grapple operators,* and *log loaders,* use machines to sort, stack, and load logs onto truck trailers or railroad cars.

Other workers in the industry, called *log graders, scalers, markers and pickers,* estimate the value of logs or pulpwood in sorting yards and similar locations, where they inspect the wood for defects and measure it to determine marketable volume.

A chain saw operator cuts felled trees into uniform logs that will be shipped to lumber yard for inspection and classification.

Requirements

Logging workers usually need a high-school diploma before they can be hired as full-time entry-level workers. Workers without diplomas can sometimes obtain part-time or helper positions. Because automation in this industry is continually increasing, workers skilled in using machines have the best chances for employment. Knowledge of electronics and mathematics also helps workers find and keep jobs.

Most workers learn their skills on the job, but high-school students who are interested in the field may prepare by taking courses in agricultural subjects, botany, and mathematics, as well as shop courses teaching auto mechanics and power-tool usage. Some schools in timber-producing regions offer courses in forestry and logging. Foresters need college educations.

Logging workers need to know how to drive logging vehicles and must be healthy and agile. Because machines now do most of the work, however, loggers no longer need exceptional strength. They must be alert and have stamina, however, and are frequently required to pass physical examinations before they are hired.

The ability to take directions and remain cool in emergencies or dangerous situations is essential for staying safe in the logging industry.

Special requirements

There are no special requirements for logging industry positions.

Opportunities for experience and exploration

High-school students who are at least seventeen years old may be able to get summer or part-time jobs with logging companies. They will probably first perform unskilled tasks such as clearing brush or helping on a survey crew. Such work can, however, introduce students to the occupation and conditions of work, and give them the opportunity to talk with other workers about their jobs.

Related occupations

Other workers involved in wood science forestry management are park technicians, park rangers, range managers, wood science technologists, and sawmill workers.

Methods of entering

Students who obtain summer or part-time work in logging often move into full-time jobs after they graduate. Job seekers should apply for work at the offices of logging companies in the areas where they wish to work. Although logging is concentrated in a few areas of the country, most states will have small logging companies, whose names and addresses can often be found in the telephone directory's Yellow Pages. State forester offices may keep lists of logging companies.

Timber, lumber, or pulp and paper companies may have job openings, and school guidance counselors in timber states may know of available positions. Unions to which logging workers belong also often compile job listings.

Foresters graduating from college programs may learn of opportunities through school placement centers and trade journals.

Advancement

Loggers may advance in their jobs in several ways. They may move into more skilled tasks, take on supervisory positions, move into company management, or start their own logging firms.

Logging helpers and laborers can learn more skilled tasks on the job and move into these positions if openings occur. Some skilled logging tasks can take as many as four years to learn well. Some large companies have programs to train employees in falling, bucking, skidder driving, or loading. Training is normally done by more experienced employees, so those workers who have been on the job a long time may be promoted to trainer.

Workers who move into supervisory jobs have shown leadership skills, have been with the company a long time, or have received further education. Advancement is often easier in smaller companies. To move into management positions, workers need a great deal of experience and education. Large companies may hire only college graduates as managers.

Employment outlook

According to the U.S. Department of Labor, about 135,000 workers are employed as loggers, log graders and scalers, and forest conservationists in the early 1990s. The Department of Labor expects logging employment opportunities to decline, although other sources predict employment will remain at current levels through the early 1990s. Although demand for wood products is expected to increase, improvements in machinery and other technology will make a production increase possible without hiring new workers. Some openings should be available for workers to replace those who retire or change jobs. Competition for such openings will be keen, however, and workers with mechanical skills will have the best chances. Those who have been laid off by one company will seek employment at other companies, competing with less experienced candidates.

Earnings

Logging wages vary with the logger's skills, the company's payment system, and whether the weather in the region where the logger works allows logging operations to continue year-round.

In most parts of the country, workers who cut trees into logs or bolts are paid by the piece or the volume of work they do. Others are paid hourly wages, which logging companies and independent contractors set for their employees. Union workers may be paid more than nonunionized employees.

The average logging worker, according to the U.S. Bureau of Labor Statistics, earned about $27,800 a year in the early 1990s, assuming a forty-hour workweek and year-round employment. The Oregon Employment Division reported that workers earn between $11.88 and $16.40 an hour, depending on their task, with experienced hook tenders, fallers, and buckers earning the highest wages. Yearly salaries for workers in areas other than the South are difficult to compute, because the amount of work a logger can perform depends upon the season.

Foresters and supervisors usually earn salaries instead of hourly wages. Beginning foresters working for the U.S. Forest Service receive between $12,000 and $16,800 a year. Forest Service starting salary for more experienced workers is between $16,604 and $20,565. Beginning workers in state, county, and other agencies range from $13,200 to $19,800 a year.

Conditions of work

Loggers work outdoors in all kinds of weather—hot, dry, humid, cold, snowy, wet, and sunny. Most work forty hours a week plus overtime. In the South, conditions usually permit year-round work, while workers in the West usually work only nine or ten months because of forest fires. Snow and wet stop work less frequently than they did before the introduction of rubber-tired skidders and forwarders, which make work possible even when snow is nearly three feet deep. When loggers cannot work, they repair equipment, work on their farms, take other jobs, or go on vacation.

Logging can be uncomfortable and dangerous. Insects bite workers; brambles scratch them. Working with heavy machinery, falling timber, and power saws poses many dangers. The terrain can be treacherous, with slippery mud, rocks, and vines underfoot. Of all kinds of workers, loggers have one of the highest rates of accidents on the job.

Safety in logging has been improved, however. Gloves, hard hats, ballistic nylon pants and safety boots have helped reduce injuries. Safer power tools and increased government regulation and inspection of logging operations have also decreased dangers.

Workers may belong to unions, although those in the South seldom do. Many workers in the Pacific Northwest belong to unions such as the International Woodworkers of America (AFL-CIO).

Social and psychological factors

Workers who enjoy the camaraderie of crew work and working outdoors in a rugged, unstructured atmosphere should enjoy logging. Few of today's loggers live in logging camps, as almost all did earlier in this century. Improvements in roads and vehicles have made it possible for loggers to return home at night and drive or ride a crew bus to work in the morning.

GOE: 03.04.02; SIC: 2411; SOC: 579, 8725

◇ **SOURCES FOR ADDITIONAL INFORMATION**

Society of American Foresters
5400 Grosvenor Lane
Bethesda, MD 20814

American Pulpwood Association
1025 Vermont Avenue, NW, Suite 1020
Washington, DC 20005

Pacific Logging Congress
4494 River Road, North
Salem, OR 97303

Northeastern Loggers Association
PO Box 69
Old Forge, NY 13420

◇ **RELATED ARTICLES**

Volume 1: Agriculture; Recreation and Park Services
Volume 3: See Agriculture, Forestry, Fisheries and Conservation Occupations
Volume 4: See Agriculture, Forestry, and Conservation Technicians

---

Park rangers

Definition

Park rangers enforce laws and regulations in national, state, and county parks. They help care for and maintain parks and inform, guide, and ensure the safety of park visitors.

History

The U.S. National Park System was created in the first decade of the twentieth century to preserve and protect the nation's natural and cultural resources. When created, the national park system contained less than one million acres. Today, however, the country's national parks cover more than 76 million acres of mountains, plains, deserts, swamps, historic sites, lakeshores, forests, rivers, and ocean coasts. To protect the fragile, irreplaceable resources sheltered in these parks, and to protect the millions of visitors who climb, ski, hike, boat, fish, and otherwise explore them, the National Park Service employs park rangers. State and county parks employ rangers to perform similar tasks.

Nature of the work

Park rangers have a wide variety of duties ranging far beyond their responsibility to protect the parks from visitors and visitors from parks. They have the important job of assuring that visitors are able to fully experience the natural and cultural heritage of the country in which they live.

Their first responsibility is usually, however, safety. Rangers in parks with treacherous terrain, dangerous wildlife, or severe weather must make sure hikers, campers, backpackers, and others follow outdoor safety codes. They often require that visitors register at park offices so that rangers will know when someone does not return from a hike or climb and may be hurt. Rangers often participate in search-and-rescue missions for visitors who are lost or injured in parks. In mountainous or forested regions they may use helicopters or horses on searches.

Many rangers patrol park areas to monitor visitors' use of park land. Snow rangers on skis patrol ski slopes, and rangers patrolling in air boats skim the waters of the Everglades. Rangers are trained in first aid and rescue procedures and have been responsible for saving the lives of many visitors who have been careless in the outdoors or who have been unavoidably injured or lost in bad weather or darkness.

Rangers are next concerned with protecting the parks from inappropriate use and other threats. They register vehicles and collect fees for parking and driving, which are used to help maintain roads and facilities. They enforce the laws, regulations, and policies of the parks, patrolling to prevent vandalism, theft, harm to wildlife, and fires. Rangers may arrest and evict people who violate these laws. Some of their efforts to conserve and protect park resources include keeping cars and other motorized vehicles off sand dunes and other fragile lands. They make sure visitors do not litter, pollute water, chop down trees for firewood, or start

unsafe campfires that could lead to catastrophic forest fires. When forest fires do start, rangers often help put them out—a dangerous, arduous task.

Rangers also help with conservation, research, and ecology efforts not connected to visitor use. They may study wildlife behavior patterns by tagging and following certain animals, for example, to determine whether the park should take measures to control or encourage wildlife populations. They study plants, water quality, and park air to monitor and mitigate effects of pollution and other threats emanating from sources outside park boundaries.

In addition, park rangers help visitors enjoy and experience parks. In historical and other cultural parks, rangers give lectures and provide guided tours explaining the history and significance of the site. In natural parks they may lecture on conservation topics, provide information about plants and animals in the park, and take visitors on interpretive walks, pointing out the area's flora, fauna, and geological characteristics.

Park rangers are also indispensable to the management and administration of parks. They issue permits to visitors and vehicles and help plan the recreational activities in parks. They are involved with planning and managing park budgets. They also keep records and compile statistics concerning weather conditions, resource protection activities, and the number of park visitors.

Many rangers supervise workers who build and maintain park facilities, workers who are employed part-time or seasonally, and employees who work in concession facilities. Rangers often have their own park-maintenance responsibilities, such as trail building, landscaping, and caring for visitor centers.

In some parks, rangers are specialists in certain areas of park protection, safety, or management. For example, in areas where there is a lot of snow and a high incidence of avalanches, experts in avalanche control and snow safety are designated as snow rangers. They monitor snow conditions and patrol park areas to make sure visitors are not lost in snow slides.

Requirements

Employment as a federal or state park ranger requires either a college degree or specific amounts of education and experience. In the early 1990s approximately 200 colleges and universities offered bachelor's degree programs in park management and park recreation. To meet employment requirements, students in other relevant college programs must accumulate at least twenty-four semester hours of academic credit in park recreation and management, history, behavioral sciences, forestry, botany, geology, or other applicable subject areas. High-school students who wish to prepare for such college work should take courses in science and mathematics.

Without a degree, applicants need three years of experience in parks or conservation and must show they understand park work and have good communication skills. A combination of education and experience can also fulfill requirements, with one academic year of study equalling nine months of experience.

Rangers need skills in protecting forests, parks, and wildlife or in interpreting natural or historical resources. Law enforcement and management skills are also important. Rangers who wish to move into management positions may need graduate degrees. In the early 1990s, approximately fifty universities offered master's degrees in park recreation and management, and eight had doctoral programs.

Many accidents occur in national parks. For that reason, rangers must be trained in first aid and emergency care.

Special requirements

There are no special requirements for this occupation.

Opportunities for experience and exploration

Persons interested in exploring park work may wish to apply for part-time or seasonal work in national, state, or county parks. Such workers usually perform maintenance and other un-skilled tasks, but they may have an opportunity to observe park rangers and talk with them about their work and possibly to make contacts for future employment. Many park research activities, study projects, and rehabilitation efforts are conducted by volunteer groups affiliated with universities or conservation organizations. Such volunteer work may give workers insight into the field of park service.

Related occupations

Other workers that have similar aptitudes, skills, and interests include recreation workers, range managers, conservation workers, com-

mercial fishers, park technicians, and logging industry workers.

Methods of entering

Many workers enter national park ranger jobs after working part-time or seasonally at different parks. These workers often work at information desks or in fire control or law enforcement positions. Some help maintain trails, collect trash, or perform forestry activities. Persons interested in applying for park ranger jobs with the federal government should write to their local Federal Job Information Center or the Federal Office of Personnel Management in Washington, D.C., for information on how to apply. Job seekers should write to state parks departments for information on applying for jobs in state parks. For a listing of positions available, contact the Federal Job Information Center or the regional Federal Employment offices.

Advancement

Nearly all park rangers start in entry level positions, which means that nearly all higher level openings are filled by promoting current workers. Entry level rangers may move into positions such as district ranger or park manager or may become specialists in areas such as resource management or park planning.

Rangers who show management skills and become park managers may move into district, regional, or headquarters administrative positions. With more responsibility comes higher pay. For more complete information, see Volume 1: Recreation and Park Services.

Employment outlook

Park ranger jobs are scarce and competition for them fierce. The Park Service has reported that the ratio of applicants to available positions is sometimes as high as 100 to 1. Persons who intend to compete for these positions, then, must attain the greatest number and widest variety of applicable skills possible and may wish to study subjects they can use in other fields—forestry, conservation, wildlife management, history, and natural sciences, for example. The scarcity of openings is expected to continue indefinitely.

Therefore, job seekers may wish to apply for outdoor work with agencies other than the National Park Service, including other federal land and resource management agencies and similar state and local agencies. These agencies usually have many more openings.

Earnings

Rangers in the National Park Service are employed by the U.S. Department of the Interior. Beginning rangers are usually hired at the GS-5 grade level. More experienced or educated rangers may enter the Park Service at the GS-9 level, which paid approximately $24,000 to start in the early 1990s. The government may also provide housing to rangers who work in remote areas.

Rangers in state parks work for the state government. They receive comparable salaries and benefits, including paid vacations, sick leave, paid holidays, health and life insurance, and pension plans.

Conditions of work

Rangers work in parks all over the country, from the Okefenokee Swamp in Florida to the Rocky Mountains of Colorado. They work in the mountains and forests of Hawaii, Alaska, and California, and in urban and suburban parks throughout the United States. Many historic sites are east of the Mississippi River.

National park rangers are hired to work forty-hour weeks, but their hours can be long and irregular, with much overtime. They may receive extra pay or time off for working overtime. Some rangers are on call all the time for emergencies. Rangers' work hours are generally longer during the parks' busiest tourist seasons.

Although many rangers work in offices, many also work outside in all kinds of climates and weather. Workers may be called upon to rescue injured visitors in cold, snow, rain, and darkness. Rescues can be highly dangerous. Rangers in Alaska must adapt to long daylight hours in the summer and few daylight hours in the winter. Working outdoors in often beautiful surroundings, however, can be wonderfully stimulating and rewarding for the right kind of worker.

Social and psychological factors

The right kind of worker to fill a park ranger position is one who believes in the importance of the country's park resources. People who enjoy working outdoors, independently and with others, may enjoy park ranger work. Rangers need self-confidence, patience, and a cool head in the face of emergencies. Those who participate in rescues need courage and endurance. Those who deal with visitors need tact, sincerity, and a sense of humor. A sense of camaraderie among rangers in many areas can add to the enjoyment of being a park ranger.

GOE: 04.02.03; SIC: 08; SOC: 1139

 SOURCES FOR ADDITIONAL INFORMATION

American Park Rangers Association
PO Box 1348
Homestead, FL 33090

National Recreation and Park Association
3101 Park Center Drive
12th Floor
Alexandria, VA 22303

United States Department of the Interior
National Park Service
Office of Public Affairs
PO Box 37126
Washington, DC 20013

◇ **RELATED ARTICLES**

Volume 1: Agriculture; Biological Sciences; Civil Service; Recreation and Park Services
Volume 2: Biologists; Engineers; Geologists
Volume 3: See Agriculture, Forestry, Fisheries, and Conservation Occupations
Volume 4: See Agriculture, Forestry, and Conservation Technicians Occupations

Range managers

Definition

Range managers research, develop, and carry out methods to improve and increase the production of forage plants, livestock, and wildlife without damaging the environment; develop and carry out plans for water facilities, erosion control, and soil treatments; restore rangelands that have been damaged by fire, destructive pests, and undesirable plants; and manage the upkeep of range improvements, such as fences, corrals, and reservoirs. Range managers are sometimes known as *range scientists, range ecologists,* or *range conservationists.*

History

Early in the history of the world, primitive peoples grazed their livestock wherever forage was plentiful. As the supply of grass and shrubs became depleted, they simply moved on, leaving the stripped land to suffer the effects of soil erosion. When civilization gained a foothold and the nomadic tribes began to establish settlements, they recognized the need for conservation and developed simple methods of terracing, irrigation, and the rotation of grazing lands.

Much the same thing happened in the United States. The rapid expansion across the continent in the nineteenth century was accompanied by the destruction of plant and animal life and the abuse of the soil. Our natural resources appeared inexhaustible, and the cries of alarm from a few concerned conservationists went unheeded. It was not until after 1890 that conservation became a national policy. Today several state and federal agencies are actively involved in protecting our soil, water, forests, and wildlife.

Rangelands cover more than a billion acres of the United States, mostly in the Western states and Alaska. Many natural resources are found there: grass and shrubs for animal grazing, wildlife habitats, water from vast watersheds, recreation facilities, and valuable mineral and energy resources. In addition, rangelands are used by scientists who conduct studies of the environment.

Nature of the work

Range managers are sometimes known as range scientists, range ecologists, or range conservationists. Their goal is to maximize range resources without damaging the environment. They accomplish this in a number of ways.

To help ranchers attain optimum livestock production, range managers study the rangelands to determine the number and kind of livestock that can be most profitably grazed and the best grazing seasons. The system they use must be designed to conserve the soil and vegetation for other uses, such as wildlife habitats, outdoor recreation, and timber.

Grazing lands must continually be restored and improved. Range managers study plants to determine which varieties are best suited to a particular range and to develop improved methods for reseeding. They devise biological, chemical, or mechanical ways of controlling undesirable and poisonous plants, and methods

A range manager inspects the grass on which cattle graze. The quality of the grass has a large impact on the health of the cattle.

of protecting the range from damage by fire and rodents.

Range managers also develop and help carry out plans for water facilities, structures for erosion control, and soil treatments; and they are responsible for the construction and maintenance of such improvements as fencing, corrals, and reservoirs for stock watering.

Although a great deal of range managers' time is spent outdoors, they also spend some time in an office, consulting with other conservation specialists, preparing written reports, and doing administrative work.

Rangelands have more than one use, so range managers often work in such closely related fields as wildlife and watershed management, forest management, and recreation. Other related fields include *fire wardens*, *fire lookouts*, *fire rangers*, *forest fire fighters*, and *smoke jumpers* whose work is concerned with the prevention and containment of fire on the range or in the forest. *Forest workers*, *tree planters*, *soil conservationists*, and *park naturalists* are concerned with the maintaining of ecological balance on both the range and in the forest preserves.

Requirements

The minimum educational requirement for range managers is usually a bachelor's degree in range management or range science. To be hired by the federal government, graduates will need at least 42 hours in plant, animal, or soil sciences and natural resources management courses, including at least 18 hours in range management. For teaching and research positions, graduate degrees in range management are generally mandatory. Advanced degrees may also prove helpful for advancement in other jobs.

To receive a degree in range management, students must have acquired a basic knowledge of biology, chemistry, physics, mathematics, and communication skills. Specialized courses combine plant, animal, and soil sciences with principles of ecology and resource management. Certain electives are desirable and include such courses as economics, forestry, hydrology, agronomy, wildlife, computer science, and recreation.

While a number of schools offer some courses in range management, only about eighteen colleges and universities have degree programs in range management or range science.

College students may get some training and experience prior to graduation. Summer jobs in range management are available in federal agencies, primarily the Forest Service, the Soil Conservation Service, and the Bureau of Land Management.

Along with their technical skills, range managers need the ability to speak and write effectively and to work well with others. And they should have a love for the outdoors, as well as good health and physical stamina for the strenuous activity that this occupation requires.

Special requirements

Other than those mentioned above, there are no special requirements for this occupation.

Opportunities for experience and exploration

High-school students considering a career in range management may test their interest in outdoor work by applying for summer jobs on ranches or farms. Courses in science, mathematics, English, and perhaps computer science would be good preparation for college studies. School guidance counselors may be able to offer additional suggestions. Other ways of exploring this occupation might include a field trip to a ranch, related films or slide presentations, or interviews with or lectures by range managers, ranchers, or conservationists.

College students can get more direct experience by applying for summer jobs in range management with such federal agencies as the Forest Service, the Soil Conservation Service, and the Bureau of Land Management. This experience may better qualify them for jobs when they graduate.

Related occupations

Other work that involves similar interests, aptitudes, and skills includes park rangers, park technicians, logging industry workers, soil scientists, agricultural scientists, biologists, agriculture engineers, and foresters.

Methods of entering

The usual way of entering this occupation is to apply directly to the appropriate government agencies. Persons interested in working for the federal government may contact the Forest Service and the Soil Conservation Service of the Department of Agriculture, or the Bureau of Indian Affairs and the Bureau of Land Management of the Department of the Interior. (These agencies also hire college students for summer jobs in range management.) Others may apply to local state employment offices for jobs in state land agencies, game and fish departments, or extension services.

College placement offices have listings of jobs available and may be of help to graduates seeking employment.

Advancement

Range managers may advance to administrative positions, in which they plan and supervise the work of others and write reports. Others may go into teaching, research, or consulting. It should be remembered that an advanced degree is often necessary for the higher-level jobs in this occupational field. Another way for range managers to advance themselves is to en-

ter business for themselves as range-management consultants or ranchers.

Employment outlook

In the early 1990s there were between 8,000 and 10,000 range managers. The federal government employed most of them in the Forest Service and the Soil Conservation Service of the Department of Agriculture, and in the Bureau of Indian Affairs and the Bureau of Land Management of the Department of the Interior. State governments employ range managers in game and fish departments, state land agencies, and extension services.

In private industry the number of range managers is increasing. They work for coal and oil companies to help reclaim mined areas, for banks and real estate firms to help increase the revenue from landholdings, and for private consulting firms and large ranches. Some range managers with advanced degrees teach and do research at colleges and universities. Other range managers work overseas with the U.S. and U.N. agencies and with foreign governments.

This is a small occupation, and most of the openings will arise when older, experienced range managers retire, die, or leave the occupation. Employment will grow more slowly than the average for all occupations through the late 1990s. The need for range managers should be stimulated by a growing demand for wildlife habitats, recreation, and water, as well as by an increasing concern for the environment.

An increasing number of large ranches will call for range managers. Range specialists will also be employed in larger numbers by private industry to reclaim lands damaged by oil and coal exploration.

An additional need for range managers could be created by the use of rangelands for other purposes, such as wildlife habitats and recreation. Federal employment for these activities, however, depends upon legislation concerning the management of range resources, and smaller budgets may limit employment growth in this area for a time.

Earnings

Range managers with the federal government averaged about $31,200 a year in the early 1990s. Those with a bachelor's degree started at either $17,200 or $21,300 a year, depending on their college grades.

State governments and private companies paid their range managers salaries that were about the same as those paid by the federal government.

Conditions of work

Range managers, particularly those just beginning their careers, spend a great deal of time on the range. That means they must work outdoors in all kinds of weather. They usually travel about by car or small plane, but in rough country they will use a four-wheel-drive vehicle or get around on horseback or on foot.

Range managers may work alone or under direct supervision; often they work as part of a team. In any case, they must deal constantly with people—not only their superiors and co-workers, but with the general public, ranchers, government officials, and other conservation specialists.

As range managers advance to administrative jobs, they spend more time in offices, writing reports, and planning and supervising the work of others.

When riding the range, managers may spend a considerable amount of time away from home, and the work is often quite strenuous.

Social and psychological factors

Successful range managers have a deep love for the outdoors and respect for our natural resources. They are generally persons who do not want the restrictions of an office setting and a rigid schedule. Range managers need to be self-motivated and flexible. They may spend most of their time riding the range, but they also must tend to some office work. When they are out on the range, they may not be able to get home each evening. Range managers should be able to work both alone or as part of a team, and they need the ability to communicate effectively with many different people, from the general public to high-level professionals in government and conservation.

GOE: 02.02.02; SIC: 9199; SOC: 1852

 SOURCES FOR ADDITIONAL INFORMATION

Career information and a list of schools offering range-management training may be obtained from:

National Recreation and Park Association
3101 Park Center Drive
12th Floor
Alexandria, VA 22303

Society for Range Management
1839 York Street
Denver, CO 80206

For information about career opportunities in the federal government, write to:

Bureau of Land Management
Department of the Interior
Washington, DC 20240

U.S. Department of Agriculture Forest Service
PO Box 2417
Washington, DC 20013

U.S. Department of the Interior
National Park Service
PO Box 37126
Washington, DC 20013

Soil Conservation Service
U.S. Department of Agriculture
PO Box 2890
Washington, DC 20013

 **RELATED ARTICLES**

Volume 1: Agriculture; Biological Sciences; Civil Service; Recreation and Park Services
Volume 2: Biologists; Engineers
Volume 3: See Agriculture, Forestry, Fisheries, and Conservation Occupations
Volume 4: See Agriculture, Forestry, and Conservation Technician Occupations

Soil scientists

Definition

Soil scientists are interested in physical, chemical, and biological characteristics and behaviors of soils. They attempt to determine the origin, distribution, composition, and classification of soils so that they may be put to the most productive use.

History

As recently as 200 years ago, no one suspected soil could be depleted by constant use. When crops were poor, everything was blamed except the soil that they were grown in. In some sections of the world mysterious or supernatural forces are still considered responsible.

Soil is one of our most important natural resources. Like air, it is often taken for granted. An increasing population, however, has made the U.S. conscious of the fact that its welfare is dependent upon fertile soil, capable of producing food for hundreds of millions of persons.

Soil is formed by the breaking of rocks and by the decaying of trees, plants, and animals. It may take as long as 500 years to make one inch of topsoil. Unwise and wasteful farming methods can destroy that inch of soil in just a few years. When the natural cover is removed, every rain may carry thousands of pounds of precious topsoil away. Rains also dissolve the chemicals in unprotected soils, making it more difficult to grow healthy crops. Erosion has been a problem of major proportions in the United States, but soil scientists and soil conservationists have made some progress at halting erosion.

Although farming has always been practiced more or less successfully, it was not until approximately one hundred years ago considered important enough to deserve the attention of the federal government. In May 1862, the United States Department of Agriculture was formed. Its primary purpose at the time was to give information about agriculture to farmers. Although the Department started as a small unimportant undertaking, it has become one of the largest agencies of the federal government despite the fact that there are only half as many farmers in this country as there were one hundred years ago.

The 1933 Agricultural Adjustment Act inaugurated a policy of giving direct government aid to farmers. The Soil Conservation Service was established two years later. This Service developed as a direct result of the disastrous dust storms of the mid-1930s, which blew away millions of tons of valuable topsoil and destroyed fertile crop land throughout the Midwestern states. Because of the efforts of the scientists who are employed by the Soil Conservation Service, much of this ruined land has been reclaimed.

Since 1937, the states, in cooperation with the Department of Agriculture, have organized into soil conservation districts. The Department sends soil scientists and soil conservationists to help the farmers within the district establish and maintain practices that will utilize land in the wisest possible ways.

Nature of the work

Soil scientists do much of their work outdoors. They must tramp over fields, confer with farmers, advise on crop rotation or fertilizers, assess the amount of field drainage, and take soil samples. They advise about proper cover crops to protect bare earth from the ravages of the wind and weather.

Soil scientists may also tend to specialize in one particular aspect of the work. An agrogeologist, for example, may be called a soil mapper or a soil surveyor. This specialist studies soil structure, origin, and capabilities through field observations, laboratory examinations, and controlled experimentation. His or her investigations are aimed at determining the most suitable uses for a particular soil.

Soil-fertility experts attempt to develop practices to increase or maintain productivity. They test the soils chemically and conduct field investigations to determine the relation of soil acidity to plant growth. They also relate the use of various fertilizers and other soil amendments to local soil characteristics, to tillage, crop rotation, and other farm practices, and to the requirements of particular crops.

All soil scientists work in the laboratory. They make chemical analyses of the soil, and examine soil samples under the microscope to determine bacterial and plant-food components. They write reports that are chiefly drawn from their field notes and from the samples of soil that they have analyzed.

A soil scientist who works in an agricultural greenhouse tests the effects of fertilizer on soil quality and plant growth.

Soil science is part of the science of agronomy, which also encompasses crop science. Soil and crop scientists work together in agricultural experiment stations during all seasons, doing research on crop production, soil exhaustion, and various kinds of soil management.

Soil scientists are also employed by such private business firms as fertilizer companies, where they may engage in research to improve the product, or sales work to increase the use of the product. They may be employed by private research laboratories, real estate firms, or land appraisal boards. They may work for state road departments to advise about the quality and condition of the soil over which roads will be built, or they may work as private consultants and number among their clients bankers or others who are engaged in making loans on property. Some soil consultants work for park departments or for farm management agencies. Employment other than by state or federal departments of agriculture is relatively unusual.

Some soil and crop scientists travel to remote sections of the world in search of plants and grasses that may thrive in this country and that may contribute to our food supply, to our pasture land, or to our soil replenishing efforts. A number of soil scientists with advanced degrees teach in colleges of agriculture. Many who teach also conduct research projects.

Requirements

A bachelor's degree in agronomy or soil science is required to become a soil scientist. Such courses as physics, geology, bacteriology, botany, chemistry, soil and plant morphology, soil fertility, soil classification, and soil genesis will be required of the prospective soil scientist.

Most colleges of agriculture also offer the master's and the doctoral degrees in agronomy or soil science. To direct and administer research programs, doctoral degrees are usually required. The same is true for teaching positions at the university level. Master's degrees are helpful for many research positions.

The high-school student interested in pursuing a career in agronomy or soil science should select a college preparatory course. One should take mathematics and science, as well as English and public speaking. One will have to be able to speak persuasively and effectively to become a convincing soil scientist.

The soil scientist must enjoy work and must be able to inspect small samples of soil carefully over a period of time. One must write and submit reports.

Special requirements

Some federal or state government jobs may require a civil service examination.

The prospective soil scientist must be in good general health. He or she will have to spend many hours out of doors in all kinds of weather, so must not only enjoy such a life but be able to stand up under sometimes difficult and uncomfortable physical conditions.

It is usually considered desirable for a prospective soil scientist to have had some farm experience or background. Students who reach college age without having lived or worked on a farm may be able to earn college credits for successful summer work on a farm.

Related occupations

Other careers that might be of interest to people with the same skills and aptitudes as those required of soil scientists include range managers, biological scientists, agricultural scientists, park technicians, logging industry workers, and foresters. Many farming occupations also work with soil science.

Opportunities for experience and exploration

High-school students interested in a career in soil science may explore the occupation in one of several different ways. They may work part-time, weekends, or summer vacations on a farm in their community; they may take courses in vocational agriculture in high school; they may join the 4-H Club or the Future Farmers of America.

The college graduate with a degree in agronomy or soil science should make application directly to the Soil Conservation Service of the U.S. Department of Agriculture or the appropriate state government agency. University placement services may have listings for specific openings.

Advancement

Salary increases represent the most tangible form of advancement for most soil scientists. The nature of the job may not change appreciably even after many years of service. There is, of course, always the possibility of advancement into positions of greater responsibility. Administrative and supervisory positions, however, are few in comparison with the number of jobs that must be done in the field. Those who go on to obtain graduate degrees may anticipate moving into more responsible positions, especially in soil research. For those soil scientists in college teaching, an advanced degree may well mean an advancement in academic rank and in responsibility. Many colleges and universities offer fellowships and assistantships for graduate training or employ graduate students for part-time teaching or research.

For soil scientists employed by private business firms, there may be the opportunity to advance into positions of such responsibility as head of department or research director. Advancement to supervisory positions or other positions of responsibility is also possible in such state agencies as, for example, a state road department.

Employment outlook

Initial employment opportunities for soil scientists, like other agricultural scientists, should grow about as fast as the average for all occupations during the next decade. Because those who are currently engaged in the work are

demonstrating its practical value to the economy of the nation, there may be an increasing demand for similar services. At present, the U.S. Department of Agriculture is engaged in a long-range project of surveying all the soil in all rural areas of the country. This program includes research, soil classification and correlation, interpretation of results for use by agriculturists and engineers, and training of others to use the results. Much of the work toward the accomplishment of this goal has been done, but for the next few years there will be many opportunities for those interested in assisting with this service. There will also be increasing opportunities for soil scientists in teaching and in research.

As the scientist's knowledge of the principles of food and nutrition increases, a greater awareness develops of the importance of the soil in which food is grown. Research has shown that food grown on poor soil does not nourish the body as adequately as food grown on fertile soil. As more persons comprehend the importance of this discovery, there will be greater demand for research into ways to make soil more fertile. Such public awareness may well create additional jobs for soil scientists.

Earnings

The federal government classifies soil scientists with other agricultural scientists. Beginning federal salaries for these workers in the early 1990s ranged from $17,280 to $21,300 for those with bachelor's degrees, $21,300 to $26,100 for those with master's degrees, and $31,600 to $37,900 for those with doctorates. The overall average federal salary for agricultural scientists was about $40,300. The average salary in all sectors of the field was $20,400. Salaries for college teachers were somewhat less than those for top federal employees. Private business salaries should be roughly comparable to those in federal service.

Conditions of work

Most soil scientists work forty hours a week. Their work is varied, ranging from field work to the work of examining samples of soil and constructing detailed maps that must be done in the laboratory. Some jobs may involve travel, even to foreign countries, and some may include teaching responsibilities or the supervision of training programs in the field.

Social and psychological factors

The work of soil scientists gives them the satisfaction of knowing that they are engaged in a worthwhile activity. Because of their work, farm production has increased.

GOE: 02.02.02; SIC: 071; SOC: 1853

◇ **SOURCES FOR ADDITIONAL INFORMATION**

Soil and Water Conservation Society
7515 NE Ankeny Road
Ankeny, IA 50021

Soil Science Society of America
677 South Segoe Road
Madison, WI 53711

◇ **RELATED ARTICLES**

Volume 1: Agriculture; Biological Sciences; Civil Service; Recreation and Park Services
Volume 2: Biologists; Chemists
Volume 3: See Agriculture, Forestry, Fisheries, and Conservation Occupations
Volume 4: See Agriculture, Forestry, and Conservation Technician Occupations

Processing Occupations

The field of processing concerns itself with the refining, mixing, treating, and working of materials and products. The *Dictionary of Occupational Titles*, Fourth Edition, explains that workers must be able to understand how the process works and must be able to read and follow formulas or other specifications. Vats, stills, ovens, furnaces, mixing machines, and related equipment are usually involved.

As indicated by the definition, workers in this field perform such essential jobs as shaping and molding casts for commercial and private transport; coating the surfaces of a variety of articles with protective or decorative metals; processing the foods we eat; and generally fur-

thering the production process along the steps to completion.

Experience in the processing field is most frequently acquired through on-the-job training and upgrading from a less-skilled position. Such high-school courses as mathematics, physics, and chemistry are extremely useful for anyone considering a job in this field. Advancement is limited and mainly in the form of wage increases.

Employment opportunities during the 1990s should be moderately good, despite increasing mechanization of some aspects of processing methods. Thousands of openings will occur each year because of retirements, transfers, or death.

Bakery products workers

Definition

Bakery products workers produce bread, cakes, biscuits, pies, pastries, crackers, and other baked goods in commercial and manufacturing bakeries.

History

Ovens have been used for baking since the time of the ancient Egyptians. Ovens were built throughout Europe by the Middle Ages, with usually one in each village.

Early American settlers used wood-burning stoves to bake their own bread at home. Buying

bread, cake, or pie from someone else was practically unheard of. But the beginnings of an industrial society changed the American idea of self-sufficiency. Urban workers and apartment dwellers no longer always had time or facilities to make their own baked goods. In addition, technology made possible huge ovens, mixers, and ways of controlling heat and measurements that enabled manufacturers to make mass quantities of good baked food at reasonable prices. Today, most Americans buy bread at the grocery store and rarely bake their own. And manufactured cookies and crackers are found on shelves in nearly every American kitchen. The freshness, taste, and consistency of these products are the responsibility of bakery products workers.

Nature of the work

Most bakery workers participate in only some of the stages involved in creating a baked item. All-round bakers, who develop recipes and mix, shape, bake, and finish baked goods, usually work in small businesses, hotels, or restaurants. They may, however, supervise workers in a manufacturing bakery, along with the *bakery supervisor*. Other workers are usually designated by the type of machine they operate or the stage of baking they are involved with.

In preparing the dough or batter for goods baked in a large bakery, different workers make the different components. *Blenders* tend machines that blend flour. Skilled technicians known as *broth mixers* control flour sifters and various vats to measure and mix liquid solutions for fermenting, oxidizing, and shortening. These solutions consist of such ingredients as yeast, sugar, shortening, and enriching ingredients mixed with water or milk. The broth mixer must carefully control the temperature of the broth—if it is just a few degrees too hot or cool, the dough or batter will not rise properly. The broth mixer runs these solutions through a heat regulator and into dough-mixing machines.

Dough mixers operate equipment to mix ingredients for bread using a set formula. They measure ingredients and put them into a huge mixing machine. In old two-story bakeries, ingredients were measured on the second floor and then dumped into the mixer on the first floor. Newer bakeries are all on one floor. After the flour, water, and yeast or broth are in the mixer, the worker starts the machine, setting instruments to control time, speed, and temperature. Dough mixers then push the dough into heat- and humidity-controlled ferment rooms, where the dough begins to rise into what is known as sponge. After the sponge has risen, mixers bring the batch of dough back to the mixer and mix it again. Batches can weigh as much as a ton.

Dough-mixer operators use their judgment and experience in mixing dough using semiautomatic equipment. During mixing they check the temperature of the broth, the viscosity of dough, and the speed of mixing. They feel the dough to make sure it is the right consistency and may regulate a machine that divides the dough into loaves, recording the temperature, feed rate, and viscosity of the dough.

Other workers who are involved with dividing dough into loaves are *dividing-machine operators*, who control machines that automatically divide and shape dough into units of specified size, weight, and shape before baking. *Dough-brake-machine operators* tend machines that knead bread dough before it is divided. After it is in loaf pans, dough is usually allowed to rise again, a stage called proofing. It is then sent to the ovens.

Batter mixers tend machines that mix ingredients for batters for cakes and other products. These workers must select and install mixing utensils in huge mixers, depending on the kind of batter to be mixed. They regulate the speed and time of mixing and check the consistency of the batter.

Other kinds of mixers and shapers include *unleavened-dough mixers*, who use a five-position mixer to make matzo, *sweet-goods-machine operators*, who roll and cut sweet dough to make rolls and other sweets products, and *pretzel twisters*, who form pretzel shapes out of dough by hand or machine. *Cracker-and-cookie-machine operators* roll dough into sheets and form crackers or cookies before baking. They check the machine's work and remove any malformed items before baking. *Wafer-machine operators* perform similar tasks with wafer batter. *Batter scalers* operate machines that deposit measured amounts of batter on conveyors. *Doughnut makers* and *doughnut-machine operators* mix batter for, shape, and fry doughnuts. Some workers operate machines that grease baking pans or that place pie crusts and fillings into pie plates for baking.

Bench hands perform a variety of tasks by hand. They form dough into loaves or buns by rolling it to a specified thickness with a rolling pin or machine, sprinkling flour as necessary to keep the dough from sticking. They knead the dough and cut it into loaves, weigh them, and place them in baking pans. They may use dividing machines to form buns.

When the products are ready for baking, they are sent to the ovens. *Oven tenders* tend stationery or rotary hearth ovens. They place pans of dough or batter on long wooden paddles, slide them into the oven, and regulate the heat and humidity in the oven during baking. They note the color of the goods as they bake, remove them, and place them on racks or conveyors to cool. An automatic depanner lifts loaves out of pans.

Many other workers perform jobs that finish goods after they are baked. *Slicing-machine operators* slice bread, cakes, and other items and place them on conveyors to be packaged. *Chocolate temperers* ready chocolate for *enrobing-machine operators* to use in coating or spraying of baked products such as cookies, snack cakes, and crackers. *Cake decorators*, *decorators*, and *icers* put glazes, icings, and decorations on baked goods by hand, while *machine icers* use machines to coat baked products with premixed icing. *Depositing-machine operators* put filling on cookies or crackers, and *filling-machine tenders* insert cream filling into snack cakes.

Bakery helpers and *bakery workers* have more general duties. Helpers grease pans, move supplies, measure dump materials, and clean equipment. Bakery workers sit at benches or conveyors belts, where they may fill, enrobe, slice, package, seal, stack, or count baked goods.

To learn to be a skilled baker, one must work as a *baker's apprentice* for several years.

When baked goods are ready for delivery and sale, *checkers* prorate and distribute baked goods to *route-sales drivers*, who deliver products to stores or other customers and try to drum up new or increased business along their routes. (*See also* the separate article titled "Route sales drivers" elsewhere in this volume.) Bakeries also employ *bakery-machine mechanics* to keep the many mixers, ovens, and other machines in good order.

Requirements

Learning to become a skilled bakery worker takes several years. Workers may acquire skills through education in technical schools or in the armed forces, but they must finish learning on the job.

Most workers begin as bakery helpers, who usually need a high-school diploma. Some move into apprenticeships. Workers with baking education may begin as apprentices. Apprenticeship consists of classroom and on-the-job instruction and lasts between three and four years.

Some chef training schools have bakery programs for students interested in learning diverse baking skills from basic bread to gourmet pastries.

Apprenticeships for maintenance workers and mechanics are available at some companies. Most sales route drivers need high-school diplomas.

Bakery workers must pass physical examinations and receive certificates stating they are free from contagious diseases. They must remain in good health.

Special requirements

In most states, route-sales drivers need a chauffeur's license to drive a truck. Some restaurants require culinary school training.

A bakery products worker packages coconut cakes topped with pineapple slices for retailers throughout the community.

Opportunities for experience and exploration

Persons who attend baking schools will gain hands-on experience in working in bakeries. High-school students may be able to obtain part-time or summer employment as bakery helpers. They may also be able to arrange to tour a local bakery and talk with a worker or two to find out more about the field.

Related occupations

Other careers that might be of interest include confectionery industry workers, cooks, chefs, and bakers.

Methods of entering

Aspiring bakers should apply directly to bakeries for jobs as helpers or apprentices, from which they may move into machine-operator positions. Placement offices at baking schools may help students find jobs or apprenticeships. State employment offices and newspapers may also provide leads.

Advancement

Helpers who learn machine-operator skills may move into these skilled positions, but usually only after years of experience. Because bakeries use many different kinds of machines and processes, versatile workers are the most likely to be promoted. Apprentices are taught as many skills as possible.

Skilled machine operators can move into supervisory slots or become all-round bakers. These bakers may also move into work in hotels, restaurants, or retail bakeries. They may even open their own bakeries and bake their goods by hand.

Bakery workers may work their way into management as they gain experience. The recent trend among bakeries, however, is to have people with college degrees in management or other business fields to fill management slots. Route sales drivers may work into sales manager positions or become route supervisors.

Employment outlook

Approximately 48,000 people were employed in production bakeries in the early 1990s. The U.S. Department of Labor predicts that growth in bakery employment will change little through 1995, although other experts predict a slow decline due to improved automation. Thousands of jobs, however, will open every year as workers retire or change jobs. Jobs for truck drivers and maintenance workers should also be in good supply.

Earnings

In the early 1990s, bakery workers earned an average of about $20,000 a year. They are often paid time and a half for overtime and premium pay for Sunday work. Route sales workers often work on commission, receiving base pay and a percentage of their sales. Apprentice positions are normally paid less than the full wages of experienced employees. Once finished with training, their wages are increased.

Conditions of work

Bakery workers usually work forty hours a week, some on night and evening shifts. The ability to freeze baked goods until they are needed has cut down on the number of plants operating around the clock. Employees receive paid vacations, paid holidays, and insurance and pension plans.

Bakery plants vary in terms of comfort. Some are air-conditioned. All are clean, since bakeries must meet state and federal standards. Workers are protected by local, state, and federal safety laws.

Bakery employees wear uniforms and caps or hairnets for sanitary reasons. Machines can be noisy, and working near ovens can be hot. Some jobs are strenuous, requiring heavy lifting.

Many bakery workers belong to unions. A major union is the Bakery, Confectionery, and Tobacco Workers International. Truck drivers often belong to the International Brotherhood of Teamsters, Chauffeurs, Warehousemen, and Helpers of America. Union-shop bakeries offer union-company pension plans, paid for by the bakers.

Social and psychological factors

Workers in all food preparation occupations must be aware that they can directly affect the health and safety of people who eat their products. Therefore, bakery workers must be responsible, careful individuals. Not only could carelessness affect consumer health, but it could damage machinery, hold up carefully timed processes, and result in poor products that could hurt the company financially. For this reason, skilled bakers can take a lot of pride in their well-done work.

GOE: 06.02.15; SIC: 205; SOC: 8725

◇ **SOURCES FOR ADDITIONAL INFORMATION**

American Bakers Association
1111 14th Street, NW, Suite 300
Washington, DC 20005

American Institute of Baking
1213 Bakers Way
Manhattan, KS 66502

For information on employers and employment opportunities, contact:

American Society of Bakery Engineers
2 North Riverside Plaza, Room 1733
Chicago, IL 60606

Bakery, Confectionery, and Tobacco Workers International Union
10401 Connecticut Avenue
Kensington, MD 20895

Canning and preserving industry workers

Definition

Canning and preserving industry workers are employed in plants that can, preserve, and quick-freeze such foods as vegetables, fruits, frozen dinners, jams, jellies, preserves, pickles, and soups. They also process and preserve seafood, including shrimp, oysters, crab, clams, and fish.

History

As people learned to grow and harvest food, they faced a problem—keeping food from spoiling so they could make it last until the next harvest. Centuries ago, people discovered that salting, drying, and pickling could preserve many meats, fruits, and vegetables. In America's first century, most of this preserving was done in the home. Families grew and canned their own fruits and vegetables to make them last through the winter months. With the industrial revolution, however, came advances in agriculture, refrigeration, sanitation, and automation that have all but completely transferred the business of preserving food to large factories. Very few people in America still grow and preserve large quantities of their own food. But factory-preserved fruits, fish, soup, and vegetables are found in almost every refrigerator and kitchen cupboard in the nation.

Nature of the work

Before food can be preserved, a factory must find a supply of food. Therefore, many workers in the canning and preserving industry work outside the factory. *Field contractors* negotiate with farmers to grow food for processing. They work with farmers to decide what type of food to plant, how to plant and grow it, and when to harvest it. They reach agreements concerning price quantity, and quality. *Purchasing agents* purchase raw materials and other goods for processing. (*See also* the separate article titled "Purchasing agents" in Volume 2.) When crops arrive at the factory, *graders*, including *fruit-buying graders,* examine produce and record its quality, or grade, and mark it for separation by class, size, color, and condition.

Wharf-laborers unload catches of fish for processing from the wharf and transport them to the processing plant's storage area. *Fish-bin tenders* sort fish according to species and size.

At the plant, the *superintendent* coordinates processing activities to coincide with crop harvesting. The *plant manager* hires workers, contacts buyers, and coordinates maintenance and operation of plant machinery.

Most processing of food is done with automatic machines. *Dumping-machine operators* run machines that grip, tilt, and dump boxes of produce onto conveyor belts leading to washing vats. Workers then wash food and inspect it, removing damaged or spoiled items before they can be processed.

Sieve-grader tenders and *sorting-machine operators* tend machines that sort vegetables, shrimp, and pickles according to size. Many foods are bathed in brine, a solution of salt and water. Brine begins preserving food and also separates ripe produce from unripe produce and tender, young peas and lima beans from mature vegetables. *Brine makers* measure ingredients for the solution and boil it in a steam cooker for a specified amount of time. They test the solution's salinity with a hydrometer and pump it to a processing vat. Some *brine makers* operate vats that bathe foods in brine. They are also responsible for emptying and cleaning these machines.

Plants that process fish and shellfish must often kill, shell, and clean food before processing. *Crab butchers* butcher live crabs before canning. *Fish cleaners* and *fish-cleaning-machine operators* scale, slice open, and eviscerate fish. Using a shucking knife, *shellfish shuckers* pry open oyster, clam, and scallop shells and remove the meat. Shrimp, however, are often shelled by machines, operated by workers who must make adjustments according to the size of the shrimp. Later *separator operators* remove any sand or remaining shell particles from shellfish meats using water or air agitating machines. Alternatively, *bone pickers* look for shell particles by placing shellfish meats under ultraviolet light and pick shell out by hand. Some workers operate machines that wash, steam, brine, and peel shellfish.

Often, only part of a fruit or vegetable is wanted for processing, and many workers operate machines that peel or extract elements from produce. *Finisher operators* run machines that separate skin and seeds from tomatoes used in sauces and catsup. *Lye-peel operators* run machines that use lye and water to remove skins of fruits and vegetables. *Fruit-press operators* run power presses to extract juice from fruit for flavorings and syrup, and *extractor-machine operators* extract juice from citrus fruits.

Food must then be cut into the proper size and shape for preserving. *Meat blenders* grind meat for use in baby food. Many workers operate machines that cut or chop produce, and *fish butchers* and *choppers* cut fish into pieces and lengths for freezing or canning.

Next, many foods are cooked. Some are cooked before and others after they are sealed in packages. Many vegetables are blanched (scalded with hot water or steam) before packaging, by *blanching-machine operators*. *Kettle cooks* and their *helpers* cook other fish, fruits, and vegetables in large kettles before packaging. These workers must measure and load water and produce into the kettles; stir, monitor, and test foods as they cook; and remove cooked food from the kettles. Other workers cook fish, meat, and vegetables by deep-fat frying before freezing. *Vacuum-kettle cooks* vacuum-cook fruits and berries for jam and jelly.

Other foods, including many vegetables, are processed after they have been sealed in cans. Packers fill cans or jars with food to specified volume and weight. Other workers operate closing machines to put an airtight seal on the containers. Containers are then taken to retort chambers. The retort is a huge steam pressure cooker which heats containers to temperatures between 240°F and 260°F. *Retort operators* load, start, and stop these machines according to specifications. Food is then quickly cooled to stop cooking. *Pasteurizers* kill bacteria in bottles or canned foods or beverages using hot water spray or steam.

Some food is preserved using brine. *Picklers* mix ingredients for pickling vegetables, fruits, fish, and meat and soak these foods for a specified period of time. *Briners* immerse fresh fish fillets in brine to condition them for freezing. *Brineyard supervisors* coordinate activities of brining workers.

Some cooked food is prepared for canning by evaporating it, and some fish is smoked to preserve it. *Fish smokers* put fish on the burner, and turn a valve to admit smoke into the chamber. Many foods are frozen fresh or after blanching. *Freezing-room workers* move racks of packaged food in and out of freezing rooms. They keep track of the amount of time food remains in the freezing room and remove food when it is frozen for transportation to the frozen food warehouse or delivery trucks. *Freezer-tunnel operators* quick-freeze food.

Other foods, especially fruits, are preserved by drying. *Dehydrator tenders* bleach and dehydrate fruit, while other workers dry eggs, milk, and potatoes for processing into powders and flour.

Once food has been canned, it is labeled, tested, and inspected. *Vacuum testers* tap can lids with sticks to make sure they are vacuum sealed. *Can inspectors* check seams of closed foods and beverage cans by cutting and measuring seams of sample cans. *X-ray inspectors* X ray jars of baby food to ensure they contain no foreign materials. *Canned food reconditioning inspectors* smell opened cans of food as they pass on conveyors belts to detect spoilage.

Workers are also employed to clean cooking kettles and other equipment. *Production helpers* perform a variety of unskilled tasks in canning and preserving plants. Workers may also be designated according to the food they prepare—*steak sauce makers*, *mincemeat makers*, *relish blenders*, and *horseradish makers*, for example.

Cook room supervisors and *preparation supervisors* monitor and coordinate the activities of workers in preparing and canning foods. *Fish processing supervisors* also train new workers and inspect fish.

Other workers in this industry include *food technologists* and *horticulturists.* Food technologists research and develop new ways to treat, use, package, and assure the quality of foods. Horticulturists research and develop new ways to grow produce and new hybrids for processing.

In large plants, a worker may perform one specific task. In smaller plants, a worker may perform all the tasks necessary to preserve one particular food.

Canning workers weigh cans of tuna and add extras chunks to those that are under the required weight.

Requirements

Processing workers usually need a high-school diploma for employment. They usually need no special training and quickly learn their jobs by doing them. A knowledge of chemistry may be helpful in securing a more highly paid position. Many plants provide orientation sessions for new workers and programs on safety and sanitation.

Manual dexterity and mechanical aptitude are important qualifications for processing workers, as are reliability and willingness to learn.

Horticulturists and food technologists need college degrees. Food technologists take courses in preserving, packaging, and marketing foods, while horticulturists take botany, biology, agriculture, and other courses.

Special requirements

Skilled and technical food processing staff in some states must by licensed. In addition, retort room supervisors are required by the federal Food and Drug Administration (FDA) to pass an instruction program in retort operation.

Opportunities for experience and exploration

Because processing work is seasonal, part-time opportunities are limited. Persons interested in this field, however, may be able to obtain positions as cooks or production helpers to learn more about this work. An introduction to the principles of canning may be offered in high-school home economics courses.

Related occupations

Other workers involved in the processing or preparing of food include bakery products workers, bakers, cooks, chefs, confectionery industry workers, and macaroni and related products industry workers.

Methods of entering

Applying to canneries and freezing plants is the most direct way to look for a work in this area. College students may learn of openings through their college placement offices, and some firms recruit on college campuses.

Advancement

Workers with chemistry and other science backgrounds may enter the field as technicians, testing products and recording the results. Others become helpers to quality control inspectors or other technicians. Many firms, however, hire persons with two-year college degrees for this work. People who want to advance into more technical work must obtain more education.

Most workers with little education start as unskilled workers: sorters, helpers, and so on. Advancement opportunities are limited, but in time such workers may become machine tenders, machine operators, inspectors, or work crew leaders. Experienced workers may move into field contractor positions.

Horticulturists and food technologists generally start as researchers. They may advance to supervisory and management positions or go into sales.

Employment outlook

Approximately 80,000 people worked in the canning industry in the early 1990s. This number was expected to decline through 1995. However, according to the U.S. Department of Commerce, the outlook for food processing as a whole is good, so employment in this entire industry may increase, especially in frozen foods, which are expected to grown three times faster than canned products. On the other hand, almost 90 percent of the industry's employees are processing workers whose jobs may be threatened by automation. The largest increase will be for researchers and technicians, fed by advances in biotechnology and research in new freezing techniques. In areas of seasonal canning, such as the fish canneries in Alaska, employment is completely dependent on crops and weather and varies from year to year.

Earnings

Food processing production work is largely seasonal, although some kinds of products can be processed year-round. Information about earnings for these workers is limited, but in the early 1990s the average worker working forty hours a week in canning and preserving earned about $12,000 per year. Inspectors and technicians earned closer to $14,500 per year. Wages depended greatly on the geographic location and size of the plant and the time of year at which it operated.

Professional salaries are much higher, but depend on education, type of position, and experience. Beginning professionals with bachelor's degrees—food technologists and horticulturists, for example—earned about $26,000, to $30,000 annually in the early 1990s. Those with master's degrees earned as much as $32,000 to start. Researchers and scientists with doctorates started at salaries ranging from $30,500 to $36,300. After fifteen years of employment these workers earn up to $42,000 a year.

Conditions of work

Canning and preserving plants are located all over the country. Many are in the Pacific Northwest, along the eastern seaboard, and around the Great Lakes. The work is mostly seasonal, as plants operate only when a crop is harvested or during a season when seafood is caught. Most plants are close to the supply source and are staffed by local people who often hold other jobs as farmers, homemakers, and so on. During harvest season, plants often operate twenty-four hours a day, working three shifts.

Conditions in freezing plants are usually clean and pleasant, although some workers spend much time in temperatures of about 0°F. These workers are provided special clothing and receive warm-up breaks several times during the day. Canneries, on the other hand, may be damp, noisy, and odorous.

Professional technical workers often work in clean, modern, pleasant laboratories and offices. Because many large food processors own plants and acreage across the country, these workers may move from place to place during their careers. Workers such as field contractors and horticulturists may work outdoors.

Social and psychological factors

Processing work is repetitive and offers little advancement opportunity. People generally do not stay in this work for their whole lives. Those who do not tire of repetition, however, may enjoy production work.

Professional workers with ambition and inquiring minds are well suited to this type of work. Researchers must be able to work independently and imaginatively. Because they may be involved in developing new products, their work can offer much satisfaction.

GOE: 06.03.02; SIC: 2033; SOC: 7759

 SOURCES OF ADDITIONAL INFORMATION

American Farm Bureau Federation
225 Tough Avenue
Park Ridge, IL 60068

Food Processors Institute
1401 New York Avenue, NW, Suite 400
Washington, DC 20005

National Food Processors Association
1401 New York Avenue, NW, 4th Floor
Washington, DC 20005

National Frozen Foods Association
604 West Derry Road
PO Box 398
Hershey, PA 17033

**International Jelly and Preserve
Association**
5775 Peachtree-Dunwoody Road, Suite 500-D
Atlanta, GA 30342

American Frozen Food Institute
1764 Old Meadow Lane, Suite 350
McLean, VA 22102

Institute of Food Technologists
221 North La Salle Street, Suite 2120
Chicago, IL 60601

◇ **RELATED ARTICLES**

Volume 1: Baking; Food Processing
Volume 2: Dietitians; Food technologists
Volume 3: See Processing occupations
Volume 4: Dietetic technicians

Confectionery industry workers

Definition

Confectionery industry workers manufacture and package sweets: bonbons, hard and soft candy, stuffed dates, popcorn balls, and other types of confections.

History

People all over the world love sweets. Confections have been made since ancient times. The word "sugar" comes from the ancient Indian language Sanskrit. The cacao bean, from which chocolate is made, originated in Brazil at least 4,000 years ago. Spanish explorers imported the bean to West Africa, making it a huge growing center.

European confectioners have the reputation for making the world's best confections, but most candies Americans consume today are mass produced in American factories, most of them small and employing fewer than twenty workers.

Nature of the work

Confectionery workers use machines to mix and cook candy ingredients, to form candy mix-tures into shapes, and to package them for sale. Many different machines are used to make the molded, filled, pulled, whipped, and coated candies Americans eat. Many candy-making jobs are also done by hand.

Pantry workers assemble, weigh, and measure candy ingredients such as sugar, egg whites, and butter, following a fixed formula. To each batch of ingredients they attach a card denoting the formula used, so the next workers will know which candy is to be made from that batch.

Confectionery cookers cook candy mixtures according to formula, using open-fire or steam-jacketed kettles or pressure cookers. They load ingredients into the machine and start the machine's agitator to mix them. They then set controls regulating the temperature and pressure at which the candy will be cooked and turn valves to admit steam or other heat. They may be responsible for checking the consistency of the batch and adjusting the sugar content if necessary. When the cooking is done they empty the batch onto slabs or cooling belts or into beaters.

Chocolate temperers melt chocolate using water-jacketed tempering kettles that alternately heat and cool the chocolate until it is the proper consistency. The workers who operate these machines regulate the temperature applied, mix and agitate the chocolate in the tank, and test the chocolate's viscosity, adding cocoa butter, or lecithin as needed. This chocolate is used in molded candies or as a coating.

After the candy mixture is cooked, it is formed. Some candy is kneaded on slabs and cut into pieces. *Rollers* knead soft candy into rolls, which are cut into slices and shaped to form bonbon centers. *Rolling-machine operators* roll slabs of candy to specified thicknesses before cutting. *Candy spreaders* pour and spread batches of cooked candy, such as fudge, caramel, and toffee, onto slabs or into trays before cutting and decorating. The cutting is sometimes done by a machine. The *operator* must select and install cutting disks according to the size and shape of candy pieces required. *Hand candy cutters* do this manually.

Other kinds of candy must be spun or pulled into rope-like strands before cutting. *Spinners* and *candy pullers* perform these tasks. A *center-machine operator* runs a machine that makes soft-candy centers for bonbons and chocolates. Other machines make different shapes. *Ball-machine operators* operate rolling machines that form candy balls and disks, and *lozenge makers* run machines that roll dough into sheets and then emboss and cut it into candy lozenges. Other *operators* make lollipops.

Many kinds of candy are made using molds. *Starch-makers* operate machines that make starch molds in which gum or jelly candy is formed. *Molding-machine operators* mold these candies using a mold-printing board. These operators' *helpers* feed the candy-filled starch molds onto conveyors or racks of machines that empty the molds, remove any starch from the candies, and deposit candies in trays. *Hand candy-molders* pour liquid candy into chilled molds to form solid figures such as animals, people, and Christmas trees. Another kind of hand molder is a *kiss setter*, who forms candy kisses using a spatula. *Deposit-machine operators* operate machines that deposit metered amounts of fluid candy into molds or directly onto conveyors. They must check the temperature and flow of the fluid and weigh formed candy samples to assure they meet specifications. *Fruit-bar makers* grind dried fruit and shape it into bars.

Candy that is made to be a center must then be coated, or enrobed. *Enrobing-machine feeders* arrange candy centers in a specified pattern on a conveyor, removing any malformed items. *Enrobing-machine operators* run machines that coat candy with melted chocolate or other coating. They adjust the flow of coating mixture and allow coated candies to cool before further processing. In some plants, candy is dipped by *hand workers*, who scoop coating materials onto slabs and swirl centers, fruits, or nuts with finger or fork and remove them. In other factories, workers called *enrobing-machine corders* mark tops of machine-coated candies to simulate a hand-dipped appearance. They dip their finger in semi-liquid chocolate and draw a line or bead on the top of a newly enrobed piece of candy.

Other workers do similar tasks. *Sanding-machine operators* sugar-coat gumdrops and orange slices. *Coating-machine operators* coat candy and nuts with syrup, coloring, or other materials to glaze or polish them.

Popcorn balls and flavored popcorn are also consider confections. *Corn poppers* operate gas ovens that pop corn. They measure the corn, oil, and salt into the popper and remove the corn when it has popped. *Popcorn-candy makers* measure ingredients for and cook flavored syrup and coat popcorn with it. *Cheese sprayers* spray a mixture of cheese and coconut oil onto popcorn, salt it, and take it to the packing room.

Some workers, including *decorators* and *garnishers*, use icing or nuts to decorate candy. Others make candy that is used to decorate other edibles; *marzipan mixers* mix almond paste for marzipan cake decorations, which are formed by *marzipan molders*. *Casting-machine operators* form sugar decorations for cakes by forcing a sugar paste through a die to form a decoration and deposit it on a paper sheet.

Many plants employ *inspectors* who check and weigh products to make sure they meet company standards.

In smaller plants, a candy maker may be responsible for developing, mixing, cooking, and forming a type of candy. *Candy-maker helpers* help candy makers by tending machines, mixing ingredients, washing equipment, and performing other tasks. In large plants, however, these jobs are often performed by different workers, under the direction of *candy supervisors*. Candy-making plants also employ *factor helpers*, who move trays from machine to machine and help confectionery workers in many other ways.

After candy is formed, it is packaged, usually by machine, after which it is delivered to stores and other establishments in time for Valentine's Day, Mothers Day, Christmas, and Easter—peak candy-buying periods.

Requirements

Most confectionery workers need a high-school diploma to gain employment. Production skills are usually learned on the job. Workers who wish to become candy makers need a background in chemistry and mechanics and a solid knowledge of the industry. High-school courses in chemistry, biology, and shop are useful, but expertise is gained only through experience.

Confectionery workers should have good mechanical skills, be mentally alert, and be in good health.

Special requirements

Confectionery workers, like workers in many food industries, must pass physical examinations before they can begin work at a plant.

Opportunities for experience and exploration

High-school students may be able to obtain part-time or summer employment at large candy-making factories to learn more about this work. Some local plants may offer tours, and students may also write industry associations for more information.

Related occupations

Food processing is an enormous industry in the United States and offers many occupational opportunities. Some others that may be of interest include canning and preserving industry workers, bakery products workers, meat packing products workers, macaroni and pasta products industry workers, and food technologists.

Methods of entering

Job seekers should apply directly to local plants for employment. Newspaper want ads and state employment offices are good sources for leads. In addition, the Bakery, Confectionery, and Tobacco Workers International Union, to which many workers belong, may provide information about local openings.

Advancement

Workers who are willing to learn all aspects of confectionery making can advance to positions as candy makers or supervisors. The more skills, ambition, and education a worker has,

A plant supervisor inspects the size of Hershey chocolates as they come out of an assembly line. Measurement inspection is an important part of quality control.

the greater the chance for advancement. The size of the plant and the employment turnover also affect promotion opportunities.

Employment outlook

Candy sales in the United States have been steady for the past several years, declines occurring only when increases in the price of raw materials led to increased candy prices. In general, however, candy sales are expected to increase, which means employment growth in the industry.

Most opportunities will be in wholesale confectionery companies. The U.S. Department of Labor expects the confectionery industry to thrive through the early 1990s.

Earnings

Confectionery workers' wages depend on their skills and the size and location of the plant. Beginning workers earn less, and workers on the

Pacific Coast earn more, than other workers. The average annual salary for an experienced production worker in the early 1990s was about $23,400. Skilled candy makers can earn more, often starting at a salary as high as $18,720. Mechanics earn comparable wages.

Most confectionery workers earn time and a half for overtime work and receive such fringe benefits as paid vacations, holiday, sick days, and insurance and pension plans.

Conditions of work

Most workers work in large candy-making factories, although about a third of the nation's 700 confectionery plants employ fewer than twenty workers. Most plants are modern, clean, and well lighted. Workers who tend heating machines must exercise caution, but safety conditions are generally good. Workers are often provided clean uniforms to wear at work.

Confectionery workers generally work thirty-eight to forty hours a week at plants located all over the country—in Illinois, California, New York, Ohio, and Pennsylvania, especially. Many belong to unions, particularly the Bakery, Confectionery, and Tobacco Workers International.

The work is not usually physically demanding. Disabled workers may be suited for positions as packers, sorters, and others.

Social and psychological factors

Confectionery work can offer stability and advancement, but it seldom offers variety. As in most production work, work in this industry can be repetitive and dull since most workers perform only one or two tasks.

On the other hand, in smaller plants candy makers may be responsible for developing or modifying recipes and making confections from start to finish. Workers who move into these positions may find them challenging and rewarding.

GOE: 06.04.15; SIC: 2064; SOC: 7664, 7755, 8769

◇ **SOURCES OF ADDITIONAL INFORMATION**

National Confectioners Association of the United States
7900 Westpark Drive, Suite A-320
McLean, VA 22102

Bakery, Confectionery, and Tobacco Workers International Union
10401 Connecticut Avenue
Kensington, MD 20895

◇ **RELATED ARTICLES**

Volume 1: Baking; Food Processing
Volume 2: Dietitians; Food technologists
Volume 3: See Processing Occupations
Volume 4: Dietetic technicians

Coremakers

Definition

Coremakers and related workers in the foundry industry prepare cores, usually made of sand, that form the molds used to make metal castings. Poured metal solidifies around the core and when the core is removed, the desired cavity or contour remains. Cores are made in different sizes and shapes depend-ing upon the eventual size and shape of hole or cavity desired in the final casting. Cores may be made either by hand or machine.

Cores are used to cast items that require hollow centers. Pipes, tubes, and other metal pieces are manufactured by casting around a core that is removed after the cast has set. The core establishes the open area.

History

Coremaking has been an essential part of foundry work since metalworking developed the techniques to make articles of metal that had holes and indentations and were made from molds. Some of these early cores were made of wood, others of metals. Both would be considered crude by today's standards. The 1800s were a period of great expansion in the use of metal. The period following the Civil War saw the full flowering of the Industrial Revolution in the United States. This revolution introduced many types of machines, and coremaking, along with other foundry work, expanded greatly. The twentieth century has been a time of increased production of metal articles and machinery. Automobiles, airplanes, farm machinery, mining machinery, furnaces, stoves, refrigerators, air-conditioners, and armaments, as well as machine parts, are made with the help of coremakers.

Nature of the work

Coremakers begin their work by cleaning the core box, a block of wood or metal hollowed out to the shape of the desired core, with blasts of compressed air. Parting sand is then dusted over the interior of the core box so that removal of the finished core may be facilitated. The box is then partially filled with sand either by mechanical or manual means. Sand is then tamped in the box by hand, mallet, or other tamping tools. Periodically, when the core sand reaches certain levels in the box, wires are bent to the proper shape and inserted in the sand to add strength to the core. Special care is taken to ram the sand solidly and compactly into the core box so there will be no air pockets or other weaknesses in the finished core.

The *machine coremaker* who operates a turn-over-draw machine fastens the core box to the machine and jogs it up and down so as to pack the sand tightly in the box. The operator then turns the box over by using a lever, after it has been filled, and jolts the core out on a table. The raw core is then ready for baking and finishing. Other *machine coremakers* operate machines that form cores by forcing sand through a tube, while still others run a machine that blows the sand into the core box.

The basic operations for making a core are more or less standard. There are, however, various degrees of specialization. A hand coremaker, for example, makes cores by hand rather than with machines. This worker may make small cores at a bench or large cores that require floor space in the foundry. Machine coremakers are usually found in large factories where a great many identical parts must be made. They generally set up, adjust, and operate machines that make sand cores by forcing sand into specially shaped hollow forms.

The *pipe coremaker* makes clay cores around which pipes are cast. This is a bench worker who mixes mud, loam, and sand together with molasses and smooths this mixture in a rod held in a vise. This core is partially baked to dry it out, removed from the oven, coated again to the desired diameter, and returned to the oven for the final baking.

Core checkers use various tools to make sure that the cores that have been produced are of the correct size and shape.

A *core-oven tender* puts the green cores into the oven and raises the heat to the proper temperature to harden and strengthen the cores. This worker must know how to regulate the fire so that the temperature will be maintained at the exact place required. The tender then removes the baked cores, allows them to cool, and delivers them to the finishers.

A *core setter* positions the finished core in the sand mold.

Coreroom foundry laborers assist coremakers in various ways, such as hauling sand, fastening sections of cores together, applying a graphite solution to give cores a smooth finish, transporting cores to and from the ovens, and so on.

Requirements

An eighth-grade education is sometimes accepted as a minimum educational requirement for helpers' jobs in the coremaking operations. A few months of training will usually qualify workers for making simple cores and operating core ovens. To become an all-around, fully qualified coremaker, a four-year apprenticeship is usually required. During these four years, apprentice coremakers are the teachers in an on-the-job program that takes the apprentice through all phases of the work. They learn simple bench hand coremaking, floor work, oven tending, machine coremaking, core finishing, core assembling, and other skills necessary for intricate multiple-part coremaking. On-the-job training is supplemented by classroom instruction where stress is placed on learning the different qualities of various metals and on arithmetic. In many cases, companies require apprentices to be high-school graduates.

Because working conditions are usually quite demanding, coremakers must be in ro-

Coremakers
Processing Occupations

A coremaker assembles small, intricate cores that will be used in castings for aerospace equipment.

bust health. Floor coremakers engage in heavy work, and physical strength is necessary. Small cores can be made at benches and do not require much physical strength.

Special requirements

Some types of hand coremaking require a high degree of manual dexterity.

Opportunities for experience and exploration

The young person interested in this kind of work may seek employment as a helper. It is sometimes possible to visit foundries, observe the work in progress, and ask questions about it on an individual basis or as a member of a school group. Arrangements with the foundry management should be made before such trips are undertaken.

Related occupations

Other occupations that require similar interests and aptitudes include machinists, job setters, die setters, numerical-control machine-tool operators, and patternmakers.

Methods of entering

A common method of getting a job as coremaker is by direct application to the company. The new employee, however, usually must work as a helper to learn the basic skills of coremaking. Jobs may also be secured at employment agencies and offices. Because a large number of the workers in foundries are members of unions, it may be a good idea to apply at the union hiring hall.

Advancement

The helpers may advance to coremakers if they can prove themselves able to do the work. The maker of simple cores may achieve the skills needed to make the complex cores. The journey worker with the necessary leadership qualifications may become a shop supervisor. Advancement may sometimes be in the form of transfer from foundry work dealing with one kind of metal to work dealing with a different metal.

Employment outlook

All present signs point to little or no change in the number of coremakers needed in the next few years. In the early 1990s, there were about 22,000 coremakers and mold makers. Any expansion in the need for cores will probably be balanced by the increased productivity of the individual worker. Increased use of machines in coremaking will be the reason for this. Some new workers will be required to replace workers who transfer to other jobs, retire, or die.

The outlook for jobs varies from place to place. Some areas have a much greater concentration of foundry work than others do. Coremakers, along with molders and patternmakers, are the most highly skilled of the workers in foundries, and they will be in more demand than unskilled workers.

Earnings

Coremakers working in foundries have higher average wages than workers in manufacturing as a whole. Production workers in iron and steel foundries made an average of $8.50 an hour in the early 1990s, while the same workers in nonferrous foundries averaged $7.80 an hour. Production workers in all manufacturing industries made slightly less. More than some other occupations in manufacturing, however, coremaking is sensitive to changes in business conditions, and opportunities are fewer when business is uncertain or in a period of recession.

Conditions of work

Many of the newer foundries have improved working conditions, but the traditional foundry is an extremely noisy, hot, and smoky place to work. Concrete floors may make the jobs hard on the feet. Fumes from the many foundry operations are unpleasant and hard on the lungs. Among foundry workers, coremakers have the lowest injury record. But that rate is somewhat higher than the average for all manufacturing.

Because most coremakers belong to unions, hours of work, overtime pay, health plans, and other benefits are arranged by contract between the unions and the companies. Among the unions that represent coremakers are the International Molders' and Allied Workers' Union of North America; the United Steelworkers of America; the International Union, Automobile, Aerospace and Agricultural Implement Union of America; and the International Union of Electrical, Radio and Machine Workers.

Social and psychological factors

Metal shaping methods have been shifting toward the least expensive of these methods, that of casting. So coremaking, which is one of the processes necessary to casting, is becoming more basic in the production of many things necessary to twentieth-century living. Cores are used in making airplane and missile parts, automobile bodies and engine components, tractor wheels and hay balers, water mains and water faucets, barbers' clippers and bathtubs, as well as thousands of other articles used in industry and the home.

The potential danger involved in working in a foundry and the generally unpleasant working conditions in many of the plants require strength to fill these jobs. People who can stand up under these conditions can be proud of their achievement, can be assured of good pay, and will have a sense of satisfaction in doing an essential job.

GOE: 06.04.08; SIC: 3543; SOC: 7542

◇ **SOURCES FOR ADDITIONAL INFORMATION**

Glass Molders, Pottery, Plastics, and Allied Workers Union
608 East Baltimore Pike
PO Box 607
Media, PA 19063

American Cast Metals Association
455 State Street
Des Plaines, IL 60016

Non-Ferrous Founders Society
455 State Street
Des Plaines, IL 60016

◇ **RELATED ARTICLES**

Volume 1: Metals
Volume 3: Forge shop occupations; Iron and steel industry workers; Machinists; Molders; Tool makers and die makers

Dairy products manufacturing workers

Definition

Dairy products manufacturing workers set up, operate, and tend continuous flow or vat-type equipment to process milk, cream, butter, cheese, ice cream, and other dairy products following specified methods and formulas.

History

Dairy products are a common and important part of our diet. A good source of nutrients and protein, dairy products include milk and various products made from milk such as cheese, butter, cream, ice cream, and yogurt. About 90 percent of the dairy products in the world, and almost all the dairy products in this country, come from cow's milk; the rest is made from the milk of goats, sheep, reindeer, yaks, and other animals. About one-third of the milk produced in this country is sold as milk, about one-third goes into the making of butter, and one-third into the production of cheese and other dairy products.

Since animals were first domesticated, mankind has kept cattle for meat and milk. For centuries, farms of every type kept a few cows to stay self-sufficient in milk and butter. Because fresh milk spoils easily if it is not kept cold, any surplus milk that was not made into butter or cheese would turn sour and need to be thrown out. Before the invention of refrigeration, cheese was the only dairy product that could be shipped from one region or country to another. Over the years, many distinctive types of hard cheeses were developed and became associated with various regions, for example, Cheddar from England, Edam and Gouda from Holland, Gruyere from Switzerland, and Parmesan and Provolone from Italy.

A real dairy products industry has developed only in the last century, with the invention of such specialized machines as the cream separator, experiments in refrigeration, and the scientific study of cattle breeding. The rise in urban populations also gave an extra impetus to the growth of the dairy industry, as more and more people moved from farms to the city. Another important development was the introduction of pasteurization, named for the noted French chemist Louis Pasteur. Many harmful bacteria live in fresh milk, and a number of digestive diseases and disorders are a direct re-

sult of them. In the 1860s, Pasteur developed (but did not discover) the process of pasteurization, which involves heating a foodstuff to a certain temperature to kill bacteria, then cooling the food again. In modern dairy pasteurization, the milk is heated to about 145°F for thirty minutes, then cooled rapidly. Sanitation is extremely important in dairy production, and today it is monitored carefully by government health inspectors.

The dairy industry is now a $45 billion-a-year business, as sales of cheeses, ice cream, and low-fat milk products continue to soar. U.S. dairy farms are located in the Northeast, Great Lakes, Corn Belt, Appalachian, and Southern Plains regions, and in California and Washington. Dairy processing plants are usually located near dairy farms to keep transportation costs down and ensure the quality of the product. America's dairy farms are so productive that the federal government by statute intervenes in the dairy industry to support the farm price of milk. With no mandated ceiling on milk output, the federal government must buy, at a given price, all surplus milk. Because fresh milk is highly perishable, the government instead acquires manufactured products such as butter, cheese, and nonfat dry milk.

Nature of the work

Dairy products manufacturing workers handle a wide variety of machines that process milk, manufacture other dairy products, and ready the dairy products for shipping. Workers are usually classified by the type of machine they operate, and workers at some plants handle more than one type of machine. For every type of machine, pipeline, or holding vat, it is essential that it be kept clean and free from contamination.

Whole milk is delivered to the dairy processing plant from farms in large containers or in special tank trucks. The milk is stored in large vats until the *dairy-processing-equipment operator* is ready to use it. First, the operator will connect the vats to the processing equipment with pipes, assembling the valves, bowls, plates, disk, impeller shaft, and whatever else is needed to prepare for operation. The operator then turns valves to pump a sterilizing solution and rinsing water through the pipes and equipment. While keeping an eye on temperature and pressure gauges, the worker opens the valves to pump the whole milk into a centrifuge, where the spinning separates the cream from the skim milk. The milk is also pumped through a homogenizer to produce a specified emulsion (consistency as a result of the distribution of fat through the milk) and through a filter to remove any sediment. All this is done through continuous flow machines.

The next step in processing is pasteurization, or the killing of harmful bacteria that exist in the milk. The milk is heated by coils through which steam and hot water are pumped. After it reaches a specific temperature, the milk is cooled as refrigerant is pumped through other coils. Once the milk has been pasteurized, it is either bottled in glass, paper, or plastic containers, or it is pumped to other storage tanks for further processing. The dairy-processing-equipment operator may also add to the milk specified amounts of liquid or powdered ingredients, such as skim milk, lactic culture, stabilizer, neutralizer, and vitamins, to make products such as buttermilk, chocolate milk, or ice cream mix. The batch of milk is tested for acidity at various stages of this initial process. The worker records the specified time, temperature, pressure, and volume readings for this batch of milk. The tanks may need to be cleaned again before the next batch of whole milk is processed.

A good portion of the country's processed milk is nonfat dry milk, which is easier to ship, export, and store than fresh milk. Dry milk is made in a gas-fired drier or oven tended by the *drier operator*. The operator first activates the drier, vacuum pump, and circulating fan, and adjusts the dampers of the drier. Once the proper drier temperature is reached, the pump sprays the liquid milk into the heated vacuum chamber where the milk droplets are dried to powder and fall to the bottom of the chamber. The operator will test this dried powder for the proper moisture content when it is conveyed out of the chamber, and will check the chamber walls for burnt scale, which indicates excessive temperatures and will appear as sediment when the milk is reconstituted. Any necessary adjustments to the drier are then made. *Milk-powder grinders* operate equipment that mills and sifts the milk powder, ensuring a uniform texture.

For centuries, butter was made by hand in butter churns, in which ripened cream was agitated with a plunger until pieces of butter congealed and separated from the buttermilk. Modern butter-making machines perform the same operation on a much larger scale. After sterilizing the equipment, the *butter maker* will start a pump that admits a measured amount of

A dairy products worker distributes fresh cottage cheese into containers covered with cheese cloth. The containers collect whey as the cottage cheese is drained.

pasteurized cream into the churn. The butter maker activates the churn and, as the cream is agitated by paddles, observes the gradual separation of the butter from the buttermilk. Once the process is complete, the buttermilk is pumped out and stored, and the butter is sprayed with chlorinated water to remove excess buttermilk. With a testing apparatus, the butter maker then tests the butter for moisture and salt content, and achieves the desired consistency by adding or removing water. Finally, the butter maker examines, smells, and tastes the butter to grade it according to a predetermined standard.

In addition to this churn method, butter can also be made by the butter chilling method. In this process, the butter maker will pasteurize and separate cream to obtain butter oil. The butter oil is then tested in a standardizing vat for its levels of butter fat, moisture, salt content, and acidity. The butter maker adds certain amounts of water, alkali, and coloring to the butter oil and starts the agitator to mix the ingredients. This mix is then chilled in a vat at a specified temperature and congeals into butter.

Cheese makers cook milk and other specified ingredients according to formula to make cheese. The cheese maker fills a cooking vat with milk of a prescribed butterfat content, heats the milk to a specified temperature, and dumps measured amounts of dye and starter culture into the milk. The mixture is agitated and tested for acidity, because the level of acid-

405

ity will effect the rate at which the enzymes will be able to coagulate the milk proteins to make the cheese. When a certain level of acidity has been reached, a measured amount of rennet (the lining membrane of an animal stomach which serves to curdle the milk) is dumped in. The milk is then left alone to coagulate into curd, the thick, protein-rich part of the milk used to make cheese. The cheese maker later pulls curd knives through the curd or separates the curd with a hand scoop to release whey, the watery serum portion of the milk. The curd is then agitated in the vat and cooked for a period of time, with the cheese maker squeezing and stretching samples of curd with the fingers and adjusting the cooking time to achieve the desired firmness or texture. Once this is done, the cheese maker or his or her helpers drains the whey from the curd, adds ingredients such as seasonings, and then molds, packs, cuts, piles, mills, dumps, or presses the curd into specified shapes. To make certain types of cheese, the curd may be immersed in brine, rolled in dry salt, pierced or smeared with a cultured wash to develop mold growth, or placed on shelves to be cured. Later, the cheese maker will sample a plug of the cheese for its taste, smell, look, and feel. Sampling and grading is also done by the *cheese grader*, an expert in cheeses who is required to have a state or federal license.

The distinctive qualities of various kinds of cheeses depend on a number of factors, including the kind and condition of the milk, the cheese making processes, and the method and extent of curing. For example, cottage cheese is made in the method described above. However, the *cottage cheese maker* at the last cooking stage will start the temperature low and slowly increase it to cook the whey. This accounts for this cheese's very loose consistency. Cottage cheese and other soft cheeses are not cured like hard cheeses and are meant for immediate consumption.

Process cheese products are made by blending and cooking different cheeses, cheese curd, or other ingredients, such as cream, vegetable shortening, sodium citrate, and disodium phosphate. The *process-cheese cooker* dumps these various ingredients into a vat and cooks them at a prescribed temperature. When the mixture reaches a certain consistency, the process cheese cooker pulls a lever to drain the cheese into a hopper or bucket. The process cheese may be pumped through a viscolizer to achieve a finer texture. Unheated cheese or curd may be mixed with other ingredients to make cold pack cheese or cream cheese. Other cheese workers include *casting-machine operators,* who tend the machines that form, cool,

and cut the process cheese into slices of a specified size and weight, and *grated-cheese makers,* who handle the grinding, drying, and cooling equipment that makes grated cheese.

Ice cream is made from milk fat, nonfat milk solids, sweeteners, stabilizer (usually gelatin), and various flavorings such as syrup, nuts, and fruit. Ice cream can either be made in individual batches by *batch freezers* or in continuous-mix equipment by *freezer operators.* In the second method, the operator measures the dry and liquid ingredients, such as the milk, coloring, flavoring, or fruit puree, and dumps them into the flavor vat. The mix is then agitated, pumped into freezer barrels, and injected with air. In the freezer barrel, the mix is agitated with beater, scraper, and expeller blades to mix the contents with air and to keep the mix from clinging to the freezer walls while it slowly hardens. The operator then releases the ice cream through a valve outlet which ripples the ice cream and which can inject flavored syrup for rippled ice cream. The ice cream is then transferred to a filling machine that pumps it into cartons, cones, cups, or molds for pies, rolls, and tarts. Other workers may process the ice cream into its various types, such as cones, vari-colored packs, and special shapes. These workers include *decorators, novelty makers I and II, flavor room workers,* and *sandwich-machine operators.*

New workers usually start out as *dairy helpers, cheese maker helpers,* or *cheese making laborers.* Beginning workers may do any of a number of support tasks: scrubbing and sterilizing bottles and equipment, attaching pipes and fittings to machines, packing cartons, weighing containers, and moving stock. If they prove to be reliable workers, they may be given more responsibility and assigned tasks such as filling tanks with milk or ingredients, examining canned milk for dirt or odor, monitoring machinery, cutting and wrapping butter and cheese, or filling cartons or bags with powdered milk. In time, they may be trained to operate and repair any of the specialized processing machines found in the factory.

Requirements

Most dairy manufacturing workers learn their skills from training sessions and on-the-job experience. Employers prefer to hire workers with at least a high school education. Courses that can be useful in this field include mathematics, biology, and chemistry. Machine shop classes can also be useful for the experience gained in handling and repairing heavy machinery.

Special requirements

Because of the importance of consumers' safety when buying dairy products, most dairy products manufacturing workers need to be licensed by either a state board of health or other local government unit. Licenses are intended to guarantee workers' knowledge of health laws, skills in handling equipment, and ability to grade the quality of various goods according to generally established standards. Cheese graders may need to be licensed by the federal government as well.

Opportunities for experience and exploration

Those who are interested in a job at a dairy processing plant may want to look for summer jobs as helpers in such plants. By assisting equipment operators, cheese makers, butter makers, and other workers, students should be able to understand the nature of these jobs and gauge their interest in this field.

Related occupations

Other workers in the food processing industry that have many of the same interests, skills, and aptitudes as those working in the dairy products manufacturing industry are bakery products workers, canning and preserving industry workers, confectionery industry workers, and macaroni and related products industry workers.

Methods of entering

For those who wish to enter the dairy processing industry, the best place to look for information about job openings may be the personnel offices of local dairy plants. Other sources of information include newspaper want ads and state employment offices.

Advancement

With enough experience, dairy-products manufacturing workers may advance to a position as a shift supervisor or production supervisor. With more school experience, they may also move up to a position as plant manager, plant engineer, or laboratory technician.

Those workers who wish to change industries may find that their plant skills can be transferred to other types of food processing. With more higher education, they might also be able to find work as a dairy plant inspector or lab technician for local or state health departments.

Employment outlook

Consumption of milk and dairy products in the United States continues to remain high, and an increasing specialized international market system will also keep demand high for U.S. dairy products. Products that have grown in demand include cheese, ice cream, and lowfat milk, which takes more whole milk to produce.

Despite this demand, however, employment in the dairy processing industry is expected to decline in the future. Improvements in technology and automation are two factors in this. In the early 1990s approximately 16,000 dairy workers were employed in factories nationwide. The demand for laboratory technicians and plant managers is expected to remain strong.

Earnings

In the early 1990s, the average hourly wage for dairy production workers was estimated to be $10.26. In the early 1990s, it is projected that most dairy products workers will earn between $15,000 and $20,000 per year. Overtime pay is common for those who work more than a forty-hour week. Plant engineers, plant managers, and production supervisors can earn $30,000 per year or more.

Conditions

Because of the strict health codes and sanitary standards to which they must adhere, dairy plants are generally clean, well-ventilated workplaces, equipped with modern and well maintained machines. When workplace safety rules are followed, dairy processing plants are not hazardous places to work.

Dairy products manufacturing workers tend to stand for most of their workday. Although the milk itself is generally transported from tank to tank via pipelines, workers may have to lift and carry other heavy items, such as cartons of flavoring, emulsifier, chemical additives, and finished products like cheese. To clean vats and other equipment, workers may have to get inside storage tanks and spray the walls with hot water, chemicals, or live steam.

Social and psychological factors

Like other jobs in food processing factories, the work of dairy products manufacturing workers has the potential to become repetitive. The dairy processing worker, however, must continue to perform carefully and meticulously, because the health of a great many people depends on scrupulous attention to sanitary regulations. Managers may be able to keep workers alert by assigning them to different machines.

GOE: 06.02.15; SIC: 202; SOC: 7476

◇ SOURCES OF ADDITIONAL INFORMATION

American Dairy Science Association
309 West Clark Street
Champaign, IL 61820

International Association of Ice Cream Manufacturers
888 16th Street, NW
Washington, DC 20006

International Dairy-Deli Association
PO Box 5528
313 Price Place, Suite 202
Madison, WI 53705

Milk Industry Foundation
888 16th Street, NW
Washington, DC 20006

National Cheese Institute
699 Prince Street
PO Box 20047
Alexandria, VA 22320

National Milk Producers Federation
1840 Wilson Boulevard
Arlington, VA 22201

◇ RELATED ARTICLES

Volume 1: Agriculture; Food Processing
Volume 2: Food technologists
Volume 3: Bakery products workers; Canning and preserving industry workers; Confectionery industry workers; Dairy farmers; Macaroni and related products industry workers; Meat packing production workers
Volume 4: Agribusiness technicians; Animal production technicians; Laboratory technicians

Electroplating workers

Definition

Electroplating is that process by which articles as diverse as automobile bumpers and electronic components are given a protective or necessary surface or a more attractive appearance with a layer of chromium, nickel, silver, gold, or other metal, by using a plating solution and an electric current (electrolysis). The skilled workers who do this job are known as *electroplaters* or *platers*; they may have other job titles depending on the specific processes they perform or the equipment they operate.

History

Electroplating was originally developed in 1840 by G. R. and H. Elkington who introduced the use of "electro-deposition" to plate base metals such as copper, brass, or German silver with silver or gold. They found an immediate market in the rising middle classes who wanted luxury goods that appeared much more valuable than they actually were.

Nature of the work

Electroplating is an intricate process. The platers must first study specifications to determine which parts of the product are to be plated, which type of plating is to be used, and how thick the metal is to be applied. They then mix a compound of the plating metal with chemicals to prepare the plating solution. They determine the amount of electric current necessary to carry the metal particles through the plating solution, and the length of time it will take to reach the desired thickness. At times they must design special racks to hold the product in the plating tank.

The platers must prepare the product for the plating process. They clean it first, using cleansing solutions or by scouring, and then cover with lacquer, rubber, or plastic tape any sections that are not to be plated. Then the article is placed in the tank for the specified time for the plating to reach a desired thickness. The article is suspended from the cathode rod, a negative terminal. A stick or piece of the plating metal is suspended from the anode, a positive terminal. As the plater moves the controls on the rectifier, the electric current flows from the anode to the cathode, causing the metal at the anode to decompose and that free metal then to be deposited on the object attached to the cathode.

The article is then removed from the tank, rinsed, and dried. When the article is finished, the plater must examine it for any defects, and must check the thickness of the plating. The plater may use micrometers, calipers, or electronic devices to check the thickness of plating. This examination may be done by specialized *plating inspectors.*

Some platers have special titles. *Barrel platers* operate an apparatus that consists of a perforated or mesh barrel that is loaded with objects to be plated and then immersed in the plating solution. *Electrogalvanizing-machine operators* and *zinc-plating-machine operators* run and maintain special machines that coat steel strips or wires with zinc. *Production platers* operate and maintain automatic plating equipment. When the objects to be plated do not conduct electricity—as when baby shoes are bronzed—

Electroplaters immerse jewelry in a solution, electroclean the jewelry, and then plate it with a protective metal.

electroformers prepare the objects for plating by coating them with a conductive solution.

The duties of a plater vary according to the size of the shop. In some large shops the major plating decisions are made by chemists and chemical engineers, and the platers do routine plating work. In other shops, the plater is solely responsible for the whole process, ordering the chemicals and other supplies, preparing and maintaining a constant solution, following the plans, plating the products, and completing the job. Under these circumstances the plater often has helpers to supervise and may be called a *plater supervisor.* Platers may be assisted in standardized tasks by *electroplating laborers.*

Requirements

Most electroplaters are hired as helpers and learn the trade by working with skilled platers. It usually takes a minimum of four years to become a skilled plater this way. Many employers limit the plater to one or two metals because less time is required for this. This may prove to be unfortunate for the plater, because as a specialist one may find it difficult to transfer to other shops where other metals are used, if an opportunity should arise. Another method of fulfilling the requirements of the electroplating trade is through an apprenticeship program. Not too many young people have been trained this way, although this training provides a better all-around preparation for the job. It usually includes classroom instruction in the properties of metals, chemistry, and electricity as applied to plating along with regular on-the-job training. The apprentice is taken step-by-step through each phase of the plating process, and by the end of three or four years of training the apprentice does cleaning and plating without supervision, makes solutions, examines results. The worker has become a fully qualified plater and is prepared to do one or all operations in the plating process or may qualify as a supervisor.

Special requirements

There are no special requirements for the electroplating trade, but as the whole plating process becomes more complex, the greater use of precision plating will require platers with a high degree of technical training and education. Some platers are members of the Metal Polishers, Buffers, Platers and Helpers International Union. Others have been organized by the International Union, United Automobile, Aerospace, and Agricultural Implement Workers of America, and the International Association of Machinists.

Opportunities for experience and exploration

High-school courses in chemistry, electricity, physics, mathematics, and blueprint reading will provide a good background for a person who is interested in becoming an electroplater. A one- to two-year course in the principles and practices of electroplating is offered by some colleges and vocational schools. Many branches of the American Electroplaters Society conduct courses in the fundamentals of electroplating. Part-time or summer employment in a job shop or in a plant that has a plating department may offer a person an opportunity to observe the work of the electroplater.

Related occupations

Other occupations that involve many of the same skills and aptitudes as those of electroplaters include tool and die makers, job setters, coremakers, machinists, and mechanics.

Methods of entering

Ordinarily it is the practice for a person to enter this trade by working as a helper and learning the trade from a skilled plater. Newspaper want ads can give leads to job openings, and vocational training programs will probably have replacement services.

Advancement

There are some advancement possibilities for the electroplater. When properly qualified, the plater may advance to supervisor. If experienced in work with a variety of metals, the plater may transfer to other shops that offer a promotion or higher pay or both. With some additional training, an electroplater may qualify in one of the newer methods of finishing metals, such as anodizing, which is increasing in importance in much manufacturing.

Employment outlook

In the early 1990s, about 40,000 persons were employed as electroplaters throughout the country. Most of them worked in the Midwest or Northeast near the centers of the metalworking industry. About two out of every three worked in independent job shops specializing in metal plating and polishing for other manufacturers and for individuals. The remaining platers were employed in the plating departments of large manufacturing firms. These plants manufacture such products as plumbing fixtures, electric appliances, radio and television products, automobiles, kitchen utensils, wire products, mechanical measuring instruments, hardware items, and many other kinds of metal products.

The growth of this occupation through the late 1990s is expected to provide some job openings in addition to those that are normally available because of death, retirement, and transfers to other jobs. Two factors are expected to influence the growth in employment in this field. One is the expansion in the machinery and metalworking industries, and the other is the technical developments in the use of other metals and metal alloys in the electroplating process. Therefore, during the next decade, the number of electroplaters is expected to increase, even considering the effect of mechanization on the industry and other related processes requiring electroplaters.

Earnings

Information available in this field indicates a wide range of earnings for electroplaters, depending on experience, the type of work being done, and location. Apprentice workers start at minimum wage and receive raises at regular intervals throughout their training. The average yearly earnings of platers in the early 1990s were $18,480. Experienced electroplaters were making as much as $30,000.

Working conditions

Conditions are generally good for platers today. Ventilating systems have reduced the odor and humidity problems in most plants and many plants are completely modernized. Although there are some hazards from working with acids and other chemicals, protective clothes and other safety precautions have reduced the dangers. There may be some lifting, but in most cases, mechanical devices are employed to do the heavy work.

Some platers are members of the Metal Polishers, Buffers, Platers and Helpers International Union; United Automobile, Aerospace and Agricultural Implement Workers of America; and the International Association of Machinists and Aerospace Workers. Some of these unions offer health insurance and other benefits.

Social and psychological factors

This type of work often taxes the ingenuity and originality of the worker. It is an exacting trade that requires precise and careful work. There is a variety of steps in the process, and in many cases a variety of products so that the work rarely is dull. Geographic locations are not as limited as they are in some fields, since electroplaters are employed in almost every part of the country.

GOE: 06.02.21; SIC: 3471; SOC: 7343

◇ **SOURCES FOR ADDITIONAL INFORMATION**

National Association of Metal Finishers
111 East Wacker Drive
Chicago, IL 60601

American Electroplaters' and Surface Finishers Society
12644 Research Parkway
Orlando, FL 32826

◇ **RELATED ARTICLES**

Volume 1: Automotives; Machining and Machinery
Volume 3: Automobile body repairers; Electrotypers and stereotypers; Forge shop occupations; Iron and steel industry workers
Volume 4: Chemical technicians; Metallurgical technicians

Glass manufacturing workers

Definition

Glass manufacturing workers perform a series of tasks to produce blown or pressed glassware. *Blow-pipe workers* use blow-pipes, pincers, forks, and paddles to manipulate, remove, and carry hot glass pieces to cooling areas. *Pressworkers* set and monitor heating controls and timers on furnaces, glazing machines, or lehrs. Glass manufacturer workers remove excess glass by using a hand cutter, flame, or saw. Workers make a variety of products including windshields, tableware, and art objects. Much of the glass manufactured is done with machines, but artists are also used to make, decorate, and finish glassware.

Glass manufacturing workers
Processing Occupations

History

From the time of colonization, when Captain John Smith set up the first glass factory at Jamestown, Virginia, in 1608, glass has been a valuable commodity. This rather common material was used for trade currency, jewelry and art objects, lamps, and some of the finest tableware—crystal goblets, vases, and platters. Glassmakers from around the world, particularly Germany, Holland, and Poland, have come to work in this country, imparting their artistry and craftsmanship, helping us to develop our many uses for this material as well as the quality of its production.

While glass is no longer traded or used for acquisition purposes, it is no less valuable in its many uses. Scientific laboratories, the automobile industry, and construction companies utilize glass products for such items as test tubes, windshields, and glass block and windows. Offices and private homes are also filled with glass items of a functional as well as a decorative nature. Glass may be considered one of our most common materials, but its function and value are expansive.

Nature of the work

Glass is comprised of soda ash, limestone, silica sand, and other raw materials. The heating and forming processes performed by glass workers utilize its malleable quality.

Machine operators and tenders comprise the majority of glass manufacturer workers. The industry has become increasingly more reliant on automatization to be able to meet the demand for glass products. The workers are categorized primarily by the machines they operate: *forming machine operators, furnace operators,* and *lehr tenders,* who monitor special ovens that heat and cool glass.

Forming machine operators often manufacture items such as glass containers and tableware, products that are primarily made from molding or formation processes. Glass containers such as bottles are made through the blow molding process. Gobs of molten glass, called "gather," are dropped on spindles of a machine that works similarly to a carousel. The spindles are attached to a center hub, and gather is placed on each spindle. The machine shoots a puff of air through the spindle into the gather, forming the bottle shape. The final forming is accomplished through heating the objects. When the finished bottle has cooled, it is released from the spindle and the process is repeated. Forming machine operators control and monitor the entire process of feeding the gather, controlling the heat and release of the formed bottle.

Similarly, press molding utilizes a related process, where gobs of glass are manipulated by plungers that imprint and form the gather into specific shapes. Many common items are manufactured through this process, such as auto headlights, ashtrays, and certain glass cookware.

Molding glass has increased the varieties of shapes and designs, as well as assisting productivity. Machines that form glass tubing can dispense hot glass from the furnace at high speeds; the float glass process, used for flat glass, can dispense a ribbon of glass up to ten or twelve feet wide at the rate of 1,500 feet per hour.

The float glass process utilizes parallel, fire-finished surfaces, which form the smooth exteriors of products such as windows, windshields, and mirrors. The ovens and furnaces are monitored by furnace and lehr operators. These workers monitor heating and speed controls as well as controls for cooling the glass. The float process begins with molten glass flowing into a tank holding molten tin from the furnace. The speed the glass is allowed to flow and natural gravity produce the desired thickness of the glass pane. When the glass has hardened it becomes loosened from the molten tin and is left to cool in a lehr.

Although glass factories produce the majority of products quickly and rather efficiently, *glass blowers* still do their work by hand and create unique tableware and art objects. Glass blowers set a gob of glass on a charred woodblock and begin to shape it. They then blow into the glass with a blowpipe refining the final shape and contour to each piece. Glassblowers usually require more intense training than factory workers.

Requirements

Working in glass manufacturing requires many skills: workers must operate and closely monitor the furnaces and lehrs, as well as the press mold machines. They may also be required to control the flow of the molten glass. These duties require concentration, manipulation, and confidence. Physical endurance is a plus, as sometimes employees have to stand for their entire shift, and overtime work is fairly commonplace in this industry. Though a considerable portion of this industry is machine-oriented, that does not diminish the need for

412

clear-thinking, capable performance on the part of the workers.

Special requirements

Apprentice programs are most highly recommended for this field. Because many glass manufacturer workers have good union representation, it may be best to apply for apprenticeship through one such organization. The American Flint Glass Workers Union and the Aluminum, Brick, and Glassworkers International Union represent glassworkers and can supply information about training programs and requirements. Some large manufacturers may also have independent apprentice training programs. Training may vary depending on the specific area of work an apprentice takes on; most, however, will combine laboratory work and practical experience with classroom instruction.

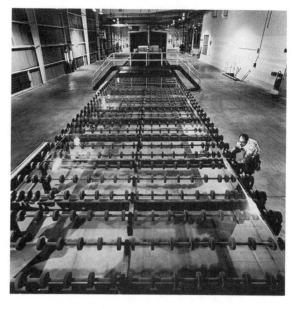

A glass manufacturing worker visually inspects a continuous sheet of glass as it is conveyed through the cooling section of the plant.

Opportunities for experience and exploration

Students interested in becoming a glass worker should contact union branches in their area and request information regarding training and application requirements. Many organizations will be listed in the telephone book in the Yellow Pages section. Large local manufacturing companies will also be listed in that section. Personnel and human resource departments may also be able to supply information on job prerequisites.

Students still in school may consider taking art classes or shop courses to develop their manual dexterity and become familiar with working with similar materials. Classes in glass blowing and molding are frequently offered by community art centers. Stained-glass construction is also a course commonly offered.

Related occupations

Other similar manufacturing occupations include industrial chemicals workers, leather tanning and finishing workers, plastics products manufacturing workers, and paper processing workers.

Methods of entering

Many times employment opportunities are listed in the want-ads sections of local newspapers. Some larger factories, however, may prefer to display a "help wanted" sign on their outside directory. Personnel departments will most likely have the most current listing of availabilities though.

Applying for apprenticeship positions with a supporting union is also a path in establishing contact. Some shops only hire union workers, a fact that might be something for applicants to remember. Work may be obtained by the apprentice at the company where he or she has trained. Placement may also be assisted by union agents.

Advancement

Glassworkers may advance by changing shifts or by learning a new machine. As there are a few different types of glass manufacturing, the ability to develop knowledge and skill can sometimes mean better pay or hours. Some workers may choose to advance by moving to a larger shop or joining a union.

Supervisory and management positions may be available as well, but can sometimes require additional education.

Glass manufacturing workers
Processing Occupations

Employment outlook

The glass manufacturing trade seems to be experiencing different growth paths. The glass container industry projects a decrease in opportunities for the next several years. A contributing factor to this hinges on recycling efforts by private citizens and environmental groups, as well as the increasing use of aluminum containers.

The market for flat glass, however, should continue to grow through the continued usage by larger companies and industry related projects. Research in both areas will continue to develop better glass products and explore additional uses.

Earnings

Glass manufacturer workers usually put in a forty-hour week. While many factory-based occupations experience high-production seasons that require overtime hours, many glass workers put in overtime hours on a fairly regular basis.

Straight time for flat glass workers can amount to almost $700 per week, with an hourly rate of approximately $16. Pressed or blown glass workers may earn almost $500, with an hourly rate of about $12.

The shifts in glass factories run all night long, and the later shifts most often guarantee higher wages for those employees. In addition, time and a half and double time pay is many times given for shifts of more than eight hours and for holiday pay.

The union support of glass factories can provide excellent health insurance and retirement benefits. Because of the nature of the work and its importance in the private and commercial areas, however, factories that do not share union support may also provide fine benefits packages to their workers.

Conditions of work

Factory conditions for glass production have greatly improved over the years. Technological advancement has created ovens and furnaces that do not generate as much exterior heat as previously. Health and safety department standards have also contributed to improved conditions as well.

Glass factories are busy shops. Often, they operate around the clock, and there may be a significant noise level. Sometimes, however, the work is strenuous and the hours can be long.

Social and psychological factors

Glass workers have challenging jobs, enjoy a high productivity rate, and have good potential for earning. They can take satisfaction in knowing they have an important skill and contribute much to society through the kinds of goods they make. Glass manufacturer workers are in an industry that provides employee support and the opportunity to advance and gain more knowledge.

GOE: 06.04; SIC: 321, 322; SOC: 76

◇ **SOURCES OF ADDITIONAL INFORMATION**

The American Flint Glass Workers Union
1440 South Byrne Road
Toledo, OH 43614

Glass Workers International Union
Aluminum, Brick, and Glass Workers
International Union
3362 Hollenberg Drive
Bridgeton, MO 63044

National Glass Association
8200 Greensboro Drive
Suite 302
McLean, VA 22102

◇ **RELATED ARTICLES**

Volume 1: Glass
Volume 3: See Processing Occupations

Heat treaters

Definition

Heat treaters subject metal to heat, cold, and chemicals to change their properties to make them harder, stronger, less brittle, and more flexible.

History

When people in the Middle East learned to make bronze in about 3800 B.C., they became some of the world's first heat treaters. By mixing together copper and tin and heating it, they found they had a metal that was harder and stronger than copper and could be hammered to a sharper edge than copper alone. By 1500 B.C., iron was being widely used near the Black Sea, and its alloy steel was in use in India by 1000 B.C.

Since about A.D. 800, Japanese sword makers have been perfecting the heat treating of metals in the art of sword making. By heating and hammering steel into blades with as many as 30,000 layers of metal, they have created sword blades of amazing flexibility and strength.

Today's heat treaters use computerized ovens and sophisticated timing and temperature data to heat-treat metals in many different ways for many different purposes. The image of the Herculean worker thrusting tongs into fiery furnaces is now only a memory.

Nature of the work

The time and temperature of a heat treatment depends on the metal of alloy being treated and the qualities desired in the finished product. Different treatments are needed for making flexible sheet metal, copper wire, and hard ball bearings. Some processes use temperatures as low as 250° Fahrenheit, some as high as 2,450° Fahrenheit, in furnaces using metal belts or wire baskets to hold the heated pieces. Some qualities can only be achieved by subjecting the metal to temperatures hundreds of degrees below zero.

Heating or annealing metal softens it, refines its grain, and removes inner stress points. Tempering it (reheating it after it was cooled) makes it tough and flexible. In carburizing, heat treaters use gas, carbon, or chemical baths to harden the surface of steel objects.

Heat treaters must also know exactly how long to heat an object and how to cool it. Cooling is called "quenching" and may be done by immersing the object in liquids, by cooling in the furnace, or by cooling in the air. The rates of cooling greatly affects the properties of the finished product.

Thus, heat treaters must use their knowledge of metals, heating and cooling processes, and the desired qualities of the end product to determine how to heat and cool an object and for how long. Some heat treaters are in charge of both making these determinations and operating the furnace and quenching equipment needed to carry out the processes. They control temperature and times to harden, temper, anneal, and carburize (or case harden) material. They decide whether to quench the object in water, oil, or air. And they load objects into and remove them from heat treating equipment. Workers designated as *heat treaters II* treat objects using instructions devised by more skilled or experienced heat treaters. Workers may begin as *heat treater apprentices*. Heat treaters usually work under the direction of a *heat-treater supervisor*.

Many workers specialize in one phase of heat-treating. *Heat-treat inspectors* check parts before and after treatment to make sure they meet standards and specifications. *Annealers* control furnaces to heat metal objects. They load the objects into boxes or tubes for annealing and during the process control heating and cooling to prevent oxidation. *Flame-annealing-machine setters* operate machines that anneal the sidewalls of metal cartridges and shell cases before further processing. *Flame-hardening-machine setters*, using their knowledge of heat-treating methods and metal properties, set up flame-hardening machines to harden material to specification. *Flame-hardening-machine operators* follow setters' instructions in operating hardening machinery.

Case-hardeners put steel objects in wire baskets and immerse them in baths of heated chemicals, such as sodium cyanide, to harden them. Alternatively, they pack the objects in boxes with a carbonaceous material and heat them in the furnace, or put them in a furnace suffused with a carbon-rich gas such as methane. They then remove and quench the objects.

Temperers reheat heated, quenched, and hardened metal and requench it in water, oil,

A heat treater checks the gauges on a computerized machine that controls the timing devices and the temperature of the furnace.

Heat treaters may work in commercial heat-treating plants, which heat treat objects on contract for other firms. Or they may work in the heat-treating department of a company that produces metal objects.

Requirements

Most employers require beginning heat treaters to have high-school diplomas. High-school courses that heat treaters may find valuable include machine shop, mathematics, chemistry, and drafting.

Heat treaters must be able to learn and understand the principles of heat treating and must be able to follow detailed instructions exactly. Manual dexterity and quick reflexes are also important. In addition, good eyesight, good health, strength, and endurance will help heat treaters succeed in their work.

Special requirements

There are no special requirements for this type of work.

Opportunities for experience and exploration

Many workers enter the heat-treating field through apprenticeships. Most of these apprenticeships last four years and consist of classroom study and on-the-job training. The U.S. Department of Labor's Bureau of Apprenticeship and Training coordinates the establishment of apprenticeship programs with heat-treating employers.

Related occupations

Other occupations of interest to young people looking at heat treating as a career include die and tool makers, job setters, machinists, electroplating occupations, coremakers, and molders. Industrial engineers, chemists, and metallurgists develop the science behind the heat processing-system, establishing improved metals.

brine, or molten lead to remove stains and brittleness. *Induction-machine operators* change the properties of metal using electricity. Following set procedures, they attach the object to a coil in an electronic induction machine. Electricity flows through the coil, and thus through the object, for a specified period of time.

Special kinds of heat treaters include *heat-treating bluers,* who heat gun parts with bone chips and whale oil to rust-proof them and give them a decorative blue finish. *Rivet heaters* heat-treat rivets, and *hardeners* treat watch parts. Other heat treaters work on jewelry and ammunition components. *Production hardeners* case-harden mass-produced items such as buckles and screws.

Heat treaters also use unskilled helpers. *Heat-treater helpers* clean rust, grease, and scale from treated parts; hang parts on racks or load them onto conveyors; put parts in furnaces; quench parts; pack carbon materials around objects to be carburized; and mark identification symbols on parts. *Furnace helpers* load and unload pieces from processing in furnaces. They may also feed metal into straighteners and break sludge from furnace parts.

After objects are treated, a *hardness inspector* tests objects to assure they have reached the desired degree of hardness.

Methods of entering

Job seekers can learn of heat-treating openings by canvassing local commercial heat treaters and manufacturers of metal objects such as engines, automobiles, and farm machinery. These manufacturers often have their own heat treating plants as part of their factory. Newspaper ads may announce openings, and state employment agencies have information about apprenticeships and how to apply for them.

Advancement

As heat treaters become more skilled and experienced, they may move into positions such as inspectors or supervisors. Advancement to positions involved with metallurgy usually require more education, as advancement to management may. Employees who are hardworking and display interest in their jobs and willingness to learn have the greatest chance for advancement.

Employment outlook

Heat treaters currently work in plants all over the United States, with areas of metal manufacturing concentrated around Lake Michigan and in California, Pennsylvania, and New York. The outlook for workers in this field will always depend on the market for manufactured metal products, which in turn depends on the strength of the economy. Through the early 1990s, competition for heat treating positions will be keen. Skilled heat treaters, however, should be able to find work relatively easily.

Earnings

Heat treaters earn hourly wages, with those working second and third shifts often earning higher wages than first-shift workers. In the early 1990s, most heat treaters earned between $17,000 and $23,000, depending on their skill and experience.

Conditions of work

Conditions for heat treaters have been steadily improving. Employers and unions have become more conscious of safety practices. Machinery has reduced health hazards caused by fumes, smoke, and heat. Heat treaters, however, often suffer burns, cuts, and bruises from handling hot metal parts. In large plants the work may be repetitive.

Many, but not all, heat treaters belong to the International Molders and Allied Workers' Union. Most heat treaters receive paid holidays, sick days, vacations, health insurance, and pension plans.

Social and psychological factors

Heat treaters can become very interested in their work. As they become more skillful, they may have responsibility for determining how best to treat objects, a task that can be a rewarding challenge.

On the other hand, beginning jobs can be repetitious. Workers who do not tire of much repetition and who have the strength and endurance to work with hot, heavy metals may enjoy heat treating work.

GOE: 06.02.10; SIC: 3398; SOC: 7544

◇ **SOURCES OF ADDITIONAL INFORMATION**

ASM International
Career Guidance Department
Metals Park, OH 44073

Metal Treating Institute
302 3rd Street
Suite 1
Neptune, FL 32233

U.S. Department of Labor
Bureau of Apprenticeship and Training
Room N–4469
Frances Perkins Building
Third Street and Constitution Avenue
Washington, DC 20210

◇ **RELATED ARTICLES**

Volume 1: Metals
Volume 3: See Processing occupations

Industrial chemicals workers

Definition

Industrial chemicals workers operate the machinery and regulate the processes that turn raw materials into chemicals useful to industry, or that use processed chemicals to manufacture complete products.

History

Thousands of things that Americans use every day, such as clothing, equipment, and some food products, are created from or processed by industrial chemicals. And every day, more new uses for chemicals are being developed.

Because general consumers only see the end result, they probably don't realize how many chemicals and industrial processes are required to make familiar products. Often an organic substance, such as wood, or an inorganic substance, such as ore or crude petroleum, is broken down into chemicals called "intermediates," which are later processed with other materials or chemicals to produce an item. For example, crude petroleum can be broken down into petrochemicals that are later processed into plastics, synthetic fibers, solvents, and asphalt. Many chemicals can go into the manufacture of a consumer or industrial product, either as an ingredient, a processing agent, or a catalyst.

Many times a large manufacturing company will have its own chemical department or division that identifies and produces the industrial chemicals it will use in its operations. At other times, a company will purchase the chemicals it needs from firms that specialize in making the chemicals alone. No single company produces all the industrial chemicals the country needs. Thousands of small- and medium-sized firms across the country specialize in one certain type of chemical that can be used in a variety of products, such as dyes, acids, phosphates, varnishes, adhesives, solvents, rubber, drugs, cosmetics, explosives, and fertilizers.

Nature of the work

Very few unskilled production jobs exist in the industrial chemicals industry. Because of the huge variety of chemicals produced and chem-ical processes involved, literally hundreds of different job titles exist. Most work responsibilities are learned on-the-job, after the employee has gained some experience in industrial work. Most of the jobs in the industrial chemicals field, however, have quite a bit in common. The major differences are in the type of chemical being made and the type of machine being operated.

Industrial chemicals workers routinely measure ingredients and prepare batches accordingly to preset formulas. They set the controls on their machines to regulate temperature, pressure, time, and material flow. They monitor gauges to observe the progress of the operation and use measuring devices to test the quality of the product being made. They keep records of what they do throughout the day and try to stay within production quotas and quality standards. They may take samples of what they are making and send them to be tested in the company laboratory. Once they are finished processing a batch of chemicals, they send them on to the next phase of production and prepare a new batch for processing. They keep their machinery operating smoothly and notify their managers if any problems arise.

Perhaps the best way to examine the types of jobs in this field in more detail is to classify them into groups according to the types of machines that employees operate. The U.S. Department of Labor uses a system that groups workers who operate machines that perform the following functions: mixing and blending; filtering, straining, and separating; distilling; heating, baking, drying, seasoning, and melting; coating, calendaring, laminating, and finishing; grinding and crushing; reacting; and processing.

Workers in mixing and blending occupations operate machines that combine, mingle, or completely fuse materials into a single mass or compound. This may be done with a mixing machine, agitator tank, blender, kettle, steam cooker, or simple vat and paddle. Into one of these types of containers, the worker will pour two or more raw ingredients by opening sluices from other storage vats, by emptying cars from overhead conveyors, by dumping the contents of a barrel or drum, or by manually scooping or shoveling materials from a hopper, box, or other container. The worker measures the exact amount of ingredients each time according to a preset formula, then activates the mixing machine, keeping an eye on the gauges and controls that monitor such variables as pressure, temperature, speed, and time. When the mixture has reached the desired texture, consistency, color, or other characteristic, the mixing worker will stop the machine, possibly taking a sample for testing. The worker then readies the mixture for transport to its next destination, either by opening pipes to pump it to a new storage bin or processing machine, by emptying it into drums or portable vats, or by sending it down a conveyor belt.

The chemical mixture can be in one of several states: a liquid solution, a paste, a soupy mixture called a "slurry," or a dry powder of particles ground to a specific size. The worker records the amount and condition of the mixture in a log, and readies the mixing bin or machine for the next batch. Many products are mixed from raw ingredients in this way, including glue, fertilizers, paints, acids, perfumes, paper and pulp solutions, raw plastics, cement, and dry explosives.

In processing, a chemical product may need to have impurities removed, catalytic agents recaptured, water and moisture extracted, or particles of a certain size separated. Workers in the filtering, straining, and separating occupations tend machines that separate desirable materials from waste by means of filtering, precipitating, straining, sifting, squeezing, centrifugal force, or agitating devices. Separation can also be done by boiling or by freezing. This cleansing and separating can be performed on dry mixtures, liquid and semi-liquid compounds, and even gases.

Press filters and centrifugal driers are often used to separate slurry into liquid and solid parts. The *filter-press operator* sets up the press by covering the plates used in the filter with cloth, canvas, or paper. After the plates are in place, the slurry is pumped from the mixing tank through the filter plate press, and impurities and moisture are removed. After the process, the plates are removed. If the filtering was done to produce a liquid product, the plates are cleaned of solid material using scrapers, water, steam, or condensed air; if the filtering was done to produce a solid product, the operator cuts the solid mixture from the plates with a knife and loads it on drying trays. The *centrifuge operator* works in much the same way when separating slurry with a centrifuge, a machine that spins the slurry like a washing machine in the spin cycle. Centrifuges can be used when the end product is either solid or liquid. If it is liquid, the centrifuge operator discards the solid waste in the machine; if the end product is a solid, the operator discards the liquid that the centrifuge removes.

Industrial chemical workers operate a propylene refrigeration unit in Houston, Texas.

Certain products, including turpentine, alcohol, and liquid oxygen and nitrogen, are distilled from their raw ingredients or elements. Workers in the distilling occupations operate machinery that distills products by heating mixtures to vaporize their more volatile ingredients and separate them from the less volatile parts. This vapor is then cooled and condensed so that a nearly pure or refined substance is produced in liquid form. The responsibilities of *batch-still operators*, *extractor operators*, and other distilling workers include pumping material into the distilling tank, setting controls to regulate temperature and pressure according to formula, monitoring the condensation of the distillate, and testing the distillate or drawing off samples.

Often a chemical product or mixture will need to be heated or dried before it can be used as intended. Workers in the heating, baking, drying, seasoning, melting, and heat-treating occupations treat chemicals with machines such as kilns, vacuum driers, rotary or tunnel furnaces, centrifuges, spray driers, and autoclaves (high-pressure tanks). In this way, liquids and slurries can be turned into dry or paste form through baking or evaporation; gases used in processing can be removed from products; and solid products such as rocket fuel cores can be cured. The work of *drier operators, evaporator operators, autoclave operators, pot firers,* and others in this field is generally similar: following preset guidelines on temperatures, times, and pressures to use, the worker loads the material to be dried into furnace hoppers or onto conveyor belts, or opens pipelines from storage tanks; loads a preset amount of material into the heating unit; monitors temperature and pressure gauges; tests the material to see that it has been dried to the desired degree; unloads the heating unit by scooping, scraping, or shaking; and sends the product to its next processing station.

Giving materials a uniform thickness or a desired finish is the concern of workers in the coating, calendaring, laminating, and finishing occupations. To accomplish this, they operate machines such as press rollers, laminating machines, and coating machines. *Dyers* mix coloring solutions in a tank or kettle, and dye pearl or plastic buttons to match the color of a standard button or sample of fabric. *Cathode makers* tend tanks and operate equipment that coats cathode screens with asbestos for use in electrolytic cells. *Coating-and-baking operators* tend machines that automatically apply and bake enamel, lacquer, or other coatings onto fabricated steel parts. Similar to other chemical occupations, the coating-and-baking operator mixes the solution in a vat, monitors the steel parts that are dipped into the solution via a conveyor belt, and sets controls for the heating unit at a specified temperature to impart the desired finish.

Some dry chemicals need to crushed, smashed, pulverized, or reduced in size by some other method before they can be used. Workers in the grinding and crushing occupations tend machines that reduce materials to smaller sizes, such as granules, grits, powder, or paste. A good example of this type of worker is the *grinder operator,* who first installs screens in the grinding machine that will make sure the particles will be the proper size when they are discharged. The operator then starts a feed conveyor or shovels materials into the machine hopper; activates the grinder; and observes the ground product for lumps, impurities, and improperly sized pieces as it is discharged onto a conveyor belt or into containers.

Raw elements are often mixed together to activate a chemical reaction. Workers in the reacting occupations operate and monitor machines that combine liquids and/or gases or that heat materials to produce a distinct chemical change in their makeup. For example, sulfuric acid and phosphate rock are combined by the *phosphoric-acid operator* to produce phosphoric acid. The chemical reaction may take place on its own, or it may need to be facilitated by heat, electricity, pressure, or other variable. *Kettle operators* control heated reaction kettles in which a liquid chemical is heated to dissolve a solid compound. The chemical reactions are carefully monitored to ensure the correct temperature, pressure, concentration, and other factors that are crucial to a successful reaction.

At other times, a chemical reaction can be initiated by a catalyst, which is a chemical that causes another chemical to undergo a reaction while remaining relatively unchanged itself. In the chemical industry, this can be accomplished in a chamber or container called a catalytic converter, which is staffed by a *catalytic-converter operator.* According to preset formulas, the operator turns valves and starts pumps to admit the feed stock of the chemical to be changed into the converter units, where it mixes with the catalyst that is already present. The operator regulates the temperatures, pressures, and reaction times for the most efficient and effective processing, then pumps the reacted chemical either to storage tanks or, if needed, through auxiliary equipment such as scrubbers, compressors, or filters. The catalyst remains in the converter and may need to be replaced or replenished periodically.

The final group of chemical workers are employed in processing. Chemicals may need to be processed in many ways: stored, shipped, mixed, or changed in form so that it can be used when needed. Among workers in this category are *gasoline catalyst operators,* who operate machines to combine the raw chemical ingredients to make high-octane gas; *tank-farm attendants,* who tend the spheres or tanks that store or distribute liquid chemicals; *casting-and-curing operators,* who control equipment that cures rocket fuel and fills rocket motor cases with rocket fuel; *briquetter operators,* who run machines that form ore mixture or chemical compounds into briquettes; *crystallizer operators,* who tend crystallizers that process chemical solutions into crystalline form; and *flaker operators,* who handle drum-flaking machines that solidify and convert chemical compounds into flakes before they are shipped or further processed. Also included in this group are *pilot-control operators,* who set up and operate chemical production equipment on a small scale to test production methods and chemical processes and to conduct product research under laboratory conditions.

These are just a sampling of the hundreds of occupations involved in the production of industrial chemicals. As specialized as the job titles are, workers in these occupations do have a few characteristics in common: They operate their machinery with accuracy and care; they continually monitor the conditions under which the chemicals are processed; and they follow the guidelines set by the chemists, supervisors, and other decision-makers in the company.

Requirements

Most of the machinery in the chemical industry is automated or computer-controlled. Although most of the jobs in this industry are skilled or semiskilled, no special training or experience is usually required for plant work. Because most of the work is highly specialized according to the particular machine or type of process, most beginning workers learn their responsibilities through on-the-job training lasting from several days to several months. Some apprenticeships that combine classroom study with work experience are available.

Because of the increasingly complicated machinery used in chemical processing, employers prefer to hire workers with at least a high school diploma. Knowledge of basic mathematics and science are essential for those wishing to enter this profession, and computer skills and machine shop are also useful. More advanced knowledge of chemistry and physics are important for those who wish to advance to technical and managerial positions.

Special requirements

Industrial chemical workers are represented by two major unions: the International Chemical Workers Union and the Oil, Chemical, and Atomic Workers International Union. Industrial chemical companies work to further the interests of the business through the Chemical Manufacturers Association. In business and governmental concerns, the thousands of small manufacturers of processed and consumer chemical products are represented by more than sixty different trade associations.

Opportunities for experience and exploration

Some community colleges have programs that allow students to combine classroom work with on-the-job experience. These programs are designed in cooperation with chemical manufacturers to allow students to experience life at the factory and to advance their skills before they take full-time jobs.

Related occupations

Other workers do work similar to that performed by industrial chemical workers. Some of these include paint and coating industry workers, petroleum refining workers, and plastics products manufacturing workers.

Methods of entering

Students interested in a job in the industrial chemicals industry should look for information on job openings through classified ads and employment agencies. Information on jobs can also be had by contacting the personnel offices of individual chemical plants and union offices. Information on apprenticeship programs can be found through state apprenticeship and employment bureaus.

Advancement

Promotion is the most common form of advancement for skilled chemical industry workers. Many start out as laborers or unskilled helpers, then move up to positions as chemical operators and skilled operators of complex processes. With more education, a worker may be able to move up the technical ladder to a position with the company's laboratory or sales force. Skilled process workers from other types of industrial plants are rarely hired by the chemicals industry. The principal means of advancement for production workers are plant expansion, employee turnover, and retirements.

Employment outlook

Many outside factors are currently operating on the industrial chemical industry. Forces such as the price of fuel, government pollution controls, environmental concerns, and increasing competition with overseas chemical manufacturers have combined to cloud the prospects of future growth for the domestic chemical industry. The demand for industrial chemicals, however, has not decreased, and advancements in technology are making new production processes possible. While these complicated processes will create new jobs for technical workers, most jobs will continue to be for production workers.

Earnings

Earnings for chemical production workers in the early 1990s were about $435.00 per week, or $10.89 per hour. Workers are usually paid more for overtime. Some workers can earn $500.00 or more each week. Hourly rates for each production job are often set by union contract.

Fringe benefits include group, hospital, and life insurance, paid holidays and vacations, and pension plans. Many workers can qualify for tuition aid for college study from their companies.

Conditions

An eight-hour day, forty-hour week is common among chemical workers. Most chemical plants operate around the clock, which means that workers are needed on all three shifts. Those who work the night or weekend shift usually earn more per hour.

The working conditions for chemical workers vary depending on the specific job, the type and condition of the equipment, and the size and age of the plant. While chemical processing jobs used to be dangerous, messy, and uncomfortable, working conditions have improved greatly over the years. Technical advances, government regulation, and improved safety methods have improved the working conditions in plants. Some workers are required to wear protective clothing and equipment such as respirators. Few jobs in this industry are strenuous, and following established safety procedures can reduce the possibility of accidents greatly.

Social and psychological factors

Production workers in the chemical industry must be able to perform repetitive tasks and

still pay attention to detail. They must be able to follow instructions exactly and precisely. They should be able to work without direct supervision and pay careful attention to safety rules and emergency procedures.

GOE: 06.04.11; SIC: 28; SOC: 7676

◇ **SOURCES OF ADDITIONAL INFORMATION**

American Chemical Society
1155 East 16th Street, NW
Washington, DC 20036

American Institute of Chemical Engineers
345 East 47th Street
New York, NY 10017

Chemical Coaters Association
PO Box 241
Wheaton, IL 60189

Chemical Manufacturers Association
2501 M Street, NW
Washington, DC 20037

Chemical Specialties Manufacturers Association
1001 Connecticut Avenue, NW
Washington, DC 20036

National Institute for Chemical Studies
Environmental Research
2300 MacCorkle Avenue, SE
Charleston, WV 25304

◇ **RELATED ARTICLES**

Volume 1: Chemistry; Chemicals and Drugs; Metals; Plastics; Rubber
Volume 3: See Processing Occupations
Volume 4: Chemical technicians; Drug technicians; Metallurgical technicians; Petroleum technicians; Plastics technicians

Iron and steel industry workers

Definition

Iron and steel industry workers melt, mold, and form iron ore and other materials to make the iron and steel used in countless products. These workers operate furnaces, molding equipment, and rolling and finishing machines to make iron pipes, grates, and other objects, and steel slabs, bars, billets, sheets, rods, wires, and plates. Iron and steel products range from carpentry nails to building girders, from cars to guitar strings.

History

Civilization changed forever when people first learned to heat and hammer iron ore into iron objects about 3,000 years ago. The first raw iron used was probably that found in meteorites on the surface of the earth. Smelting of iron ore from under the earth's surface came later. People already knew how to make metal alloys (bronze, an alloy of copper and tin, had been in use since 3800 B.C.) and about 500 years after iron became widely used, steel was being made in India. Until modern times, however, steel was fairly rare. Now steel is one of the most ubiquitous substances in our civilization. Modern blast furnaces duplicate many of the processes used by the ancients, but in quantities they never could have dreamed of.

Nature of the work

Today most molten iron goes into steel. Elements such as chromium, nickel, and manganese are added to the iron. The material is then tempered—heated and cooled to make it hard and tough. Forged steel—hammered or squeezed—is strong and dense. To make iron and steel, the iron is first melted in huge blast furnaces, often more than ten stories tall. These furnaces are water-cooled steel cylinders heated by blasts from other, dome-topped cylinders that heat air for melting ore. *Skip operators* fill railroad cars with raw materials such as iron ore, coke, or limestone, work controls that hoist the cars up to the top of the furnace, and dump the contents in layers into the furnace. *Stove tenders* heat air in the domed cylinders (or stoves) until it is the correct temperature and

open valves to blast the heated air into the furnace. At temperatures exceeding 3,000°F, the materials burn and melt. The limestone purifies the iron, and pure molten iron collects at the bottom of the furnace, while the limestone and impurities float on the top as slag.

Blast furnace keepers and *helpers* then tap the furnace to remove the molten metal. They drill tap holes in the furnace's firebrick lining and allow the slag to run out of the furnace. The liquid iron flows through a taphole drilled lower, into torpedo or bottle cars that keep the iron heated. Keepers and helpers then shoot clay into the tapholes to plug them. One furnace can make as many as 8,000 tons of iron per day.

Pure molten iron may be cast into molded forms called "pigs," which are used to make engine blocks and other items. *Pig-machine operators* and their *helpers,* under the direction of *pig-machine supervisors,* run machines that position molds under ladles holding the molten iron. By moving controls, they tilt the ladles and allow the iron to flow into the molds. *Workers* spray the molds with lime to keep iron from sticking.

Most iron is made into steel, however, in one of three kinds of furnaces: the basic oxygen furnace, the open hearth furnace, and the electric furnace. To make steel, kiln operators heat minerals such as lime, chromium, or manganese before they are mixed with iron. *Mixer operators* transfer molten iron from bottle cars to mixers and mix the iron and other elements together. *Furnace operators* regulate the temperature and flow of coolant in furnaces, into which *charging-machine operators* dump loads of iron and other elements using controls that move mechanical arms to pick up boxes of materials and rotate them to spill the contents into the furnace. *Open-hearth furnace helpers* perform a variety of tasks to help run, load tap, and clean steel making furnaces. *Melter supervisors* coordinate the activities of these workers and test the molten steel for color and temperature.

When the steel is ready, the furnace is tilted or tapped to allow the molten metal to run into ladles. Next, the steel is formed by pouring it into molds to make ingots. *Hot-metal crane operators* control cranes that pick up the ladles and hold them above molds. *Steel pourers* and their *helpers* assemble the stoppers used to plug these ladles. Other workers maintain the molds. *Hot-top liners and helpers* line the mold covers with firebrick and mortar. *Mold workers* remove the

423

A steel worker operates the computer controls at a forging press.

ingots from the molds and clean and coat the molds for the next casting.

The steel ingots then go to soaking pits for further processing. In the soaking pits, the ingots are reheated so that they may be rolled. *Charger-operators* and their *helpers* move steel through soaking-pit furnaces, where they stay heated at temperatures of up to 2,450°F for as long as fourteen hours. They are then ready for rolling, or shaping into billets, blooms, and slabs. Bottom makers reline the bottom of the soaking pits with coke dust to keep oxide scale from forming on ingots. The soaking pits are then ready for more ingots.

Rail-tractor operators transport hot ingots and slabs from soaking pits to conveyors that take them to rolling mills. There, massive steel rollers squeeze the hot ingots into specified shapes. In five minutes, a twenty-five by twenty-seven inch ingot can be rolled into a bloom with a nine-by-nine inch cross section or into a four-inch billet. *Roll builders* and *mill utility workers* set up rollers for steel to pass through. *Guide setters* adjust rollers according to the type of shape required. *Mill recorders* control the scheduling of rolling ingots and record production data. *Manipulators* operate mechanisms that guide the ingots into the rolling mills. *Primary mill rollers* and *rolling attendants* operate machines that perform the first rolling operations. *Roll-tube setters* adjust machines that roll ingots into shapes for pipes and tubing.

Some rolled steel goes to foundries to be made into tools, heavy equipment, and machine gears. Most, however, goes to finishing mills to be made into sheet steel, piping, wire, and other types of steel. *Hot mill tin rollers* run machines that roll slabs into sheets and strips. *Roller-leveler operators* run machines that remove wrinkles from sheets. *Roughers, rougher operators, speed operators, screwdown operators,* and *table operators* set up and operate mills that reduce billets, blooms, and slabs to various shapes, de-

pending on requirements. Some finishing operators make seamless tubing by piercing steel billets lengthwise and rolling them into tubing. *Reeling-machine operators* then round out and burnish the inner and outer surfaces of these tubes. As steel strips are made, *coiler operators* wind them into coils, checking for defects and cutting them into specified lengths. *Tubing-machine operators* roll metal ribbon into tubes and solder the seams to form conduit. *Finishers* roll strips, sheets, and bars to specified gauges, shapes, and finishes.

Most rods and tubes and other solid and hollow objects are formed through extruding and drawing hot metal through a die. *Draw-bench operators* and their *helpers*, under the guidance of their *supervisors*, adjust dies to specified dimensions and draw hot metal rods through them to give them a specified shape and diameter. *Tube drawers* do the same in forming steel tubes.

Other workers process metal that is recovered in powder form from other iron and steel making processes. Much of this powder comes from dust in furnace flues. *Batch makers* tend equipment that recovers powdered metal and separates it from impurities. *Mixers* blend batches of powdered metal, and *sinter workers* make sinter cake, a mass of powdered metal formed without melting. This powder is processed by *press setters* and *operators* to make bearings, gears, filters, and rings.

Steel production is recorded by workers to assure that procedures are carried out correctly. *Inspectors* and *assorters* check steel products to make sure they meet customers' specifications. Other workers test samples of metal to measure their strength, hardness, or ductility.

The industry also employs various mechanics and construction workers, including *brick-layers* who line furnaces with firebrick and refractory tile and repair cracked or broken linings. *General and hoisting laborers* are employed to feed, unload, and clean machines; to move supplies and raw materials; to hoist materials for processing; and to perform a variety of other unskilled tasks. Other workers bale scrap metal or strap coils.

Many other workers supervise employees in iron and steel making departments.

Requirements

Most iron and steel workers learn their skills on the job, some through apprenticeship. While many employers prefer high-school graduates, they also hire workers without diplomas. Apprenticeships are open to workers age eighteen and over, and they teach skills through four- or five-year programs of classroom lectures and on-the-job training.

Some employers also pay for workers to take courses in subjects they can use on the job: chemistry, management, and metallurgy, for example. Other education is available through home-study courses, night high school classes, technical schools, and colleges.

Special requirements

There are no special requirements for this type of work.

Opportunities for experience and exploration

Union and industry representatives may be willing to speak with high school students about careers in the iron and steel industry. Local mills may offer tours. Workers in apprenticeships have the opportunity to see how they like the work as they learn their skills.

Related occupations

Other workers in processing occupations who employ skills and aptitudes similar to those of iron and steel industry workers are molders, heat treaters, coremakers, machinists, paint and coatings industry workers, and industrial chemicals workers.

Methods of entering

Newspaper want ads and state employment agencies sometimes list openings in iron and steel mills. Job seekers should also apply directly at mills' personnel offices. Workers who would like to begin as apprentices should contact a union local or a state apprenticeship bureau.

College students who are about to graduate with degrees in business, management, engineering, or metallurgy may find that steel companies recruit on campus for people to fill professional positions. They can learn about recruitment schedules from their school placement offices.

Advancement

Beginning iron and steel workers and those new to a plant may start in a pool of unskilled laborers. Because iron and steel workers have a strong union, advancement is often dependent on seniority. As workers gain skills and seniority they may move into more difficult, higher paying jobs. Workers may take five years to learn the work of supervisors or rollers but then wait much longer for openings to occur. With further education and training, workers may advance into management positions.

Employment outlook

The iron and steel industry is highly dependent on the health of the national economy. Auto sales and building construction largely dictate the amount of steel that mills can sell; if Americans cannot afford to buy new cars or build new buildings, steel production decreases. In the 1980s, newspaper headlines reported heavy layoffs for steel workers as the economy slumped and more and more steel was imported from other countries at prices American mills could not match. Automation has also decreased the number of workers needed. Increases in defense spending and steady economic recovery could help the iron and steel industry to become healthy again, but growth in employment is not expected during the early 1990s. However, some jobs will be available as workers retire, die, or change careers. The more skills a worker has, the greater the chance for employment.

Earnings

Iron and steel mills operate twenty-four hours a day. Workers work one of three shifts: day, night, or graveyard (11 P.M. to 7 A.M.). Late-shift workers receive premium pay, as do those who work overtime (more than forty hours per week), Sundays, and holidays.

In 1988, iron and steel workers earned an average salary of about $28,000 a year. Apprentices earn about half the weekly wages of experienced workers. Workers receive paid vacations, sick leave, pension plans, health and life insurance, and other fringe benefits—benefits that surpass those of almost all other American workers.

425

Conditions of work

Most mills are located in Illinois, Indiana, Pennsylvania, Ohio, and Texas. Most workers in these mills belong to the United Steelworkers of America Union.

Safety is a great concern in iron and steel mills. Furnaces create incredibly high temperatures, and machines handle mountains of materials. Yet the iron and steel industry is one of the safest in America. While steel workers of the past worked in searing, dangerous conditions, today's workers often work in air-conditioned spaces and come no closer to machinery than pressing a button. Those who work in close proximity to machines and molten metal wear safety clothing and equipment (hard hats, safety glasses, and so on) provided by the company. Still, some workers are exposed to heat and great amounts of noise. The industry spends a great deal of money and effort making mills as safe as possible for these and other workers.

Social and psychological factors

Physical strength and endurance are still important for iron and steel workers, despite advances in automation. Workers who can work well in team situations, who have mechanical aptitude, and who are dependable, careful, and willing to learn may enjoy this work and perform it successfully.

GOE: 06.02.24; SIC: 332; SOC: 77

◇ **SOURCES OF ADDITIONAL INFORMATION**

United Steelworkers of America
Five Gateway Center
Pittsburgh, PA 15222

American Iron and Steel Institute
113 15th Street, NW
Washington, DC 20005

◇ **RELATED ARTICLES**

Volume 1: Metals
Volume 2: Engineers
Volume 3: See Processing occupations
Volume 4: Metallurgical technicians

Leather tanning and finishing workers

Definition

Leather tanning and finishing workers make leather out of hides and skins and by cleaning, tanning, currying, and finishing them. The leather they make is later used to manufacture shoes, belts, luggage, gloves, saddles, and many other products.

History

Ever since people began to use animals for food, they have used animal skins to make clothing, coverings, and containers. Primitive hunters clothed themselves in hides, communicated with each other using hide-covered drums, and moved down waterways in hide canoes. Ancients wore leather sandals and went to war bearing hide shields and many-layered leather armor. Valued for beauty, strength, and durability, leather has remained one of the world's most popular materials. Modern processing has given us leathers of increased softness, strength, and flexibility.

Nature of the work

Leather is made by curing, shaving, treating, and finishing the hides of sheep, goats, deer, pigs, cows, horses, and elk. Different kinds of leathers are called cowhide, horsehide, sheepskin, capeskin, kid, and chamois.

Workers in slaughterhouses remove hides from animals and cure them with salt to prevent decay. They then tie them in bundles and ship them to tanneries.

At the tannery, workers untie the bundles and begin to process them. *Hide inspectors* examine the shipments and check to see if they meet specifications of type, weight, and grade. They also check for defects and record these data. Drum attendants tend machines filled with wetting agents and disinfectants, into which the cured hides are put and agitated to remoisturize them and completely wash out the curing salts. Hides may soak in these machines for as many as twenty hours.

After the hides are removed from soaking, workers remove the flesh, fat, and hair. *Wool pullers* remove wools from sheep pelts, while *fleshing-machine operators* tend machines that scrape flesh and hair from hides. Hides are then de-limed and rinsed in chemicals and water to completely prepare them for tanning. Workers called *beaming inspectors* examine hides for remnants of hair and flesh. Incompletely cleaned hides then go through reprocessing. The rest go on the tanning operations.

In tanning, the hides are preserved and turned to leather. Lightweight leathers are tanned with the chrome-tanning process, while heavy leathers are tanned with tannins. In chrome-tanning, hides are soaked for a few hours in chemical solutions. Tannins are made from trees and plants, and hides may soak in them for several weeks. *Tanning-drum operators* load large vats with tanning agents and hides and regulate temperatures. *Continuous-process, rotary-drum tanning-machine operators* operate machines that de-hair, de-flesh, and tan leathers in one machine.

After leathers are tanned, *wringer-machine operators* wring out the moisture left in the hides. *Hide splitters* and *splitting-machine feeders* cut leather to specified thicknesses. Split leathers are then colored or otherwise finished. *Color matchers* mix pigments used to dye leathers, and *hides and skins colorers* dye leathers by pulling them through trays or immersing them in drums filled with coloring and softening agents.

Trimmers cut leathers to specified shapes. After leather is trimmed, it is finished to make it soft and pliable. *Stakers* put leather in a machine that flexes and stretches it to make it pliable. Some leather is buffed smooth in buffing machines by *machine buffers*. *Sprayers* finish the surface of leather pieces by spraying them with solutions that make them resistant to scuffs and stains. *Leather coaters* apply grease or lacquer to waterproof leather. *Roller-machine operators* tend roller machines that smooth or glaze the surface

A leather tanning worker pulls sheets of leather out of a tanning drum. From there the hides will get softened and colored.

of leathers and accentuate their natural grain. *Embossers* may then operate machines that print designs on the leather.

After processing, *measuring-machine operators* measure each piece of leather and write the measurements on the piece. *Inspectors and sorters* then examine the pieces for defects and thickness and sort them according to quality, color, and other properties. Workers then wrap them in bundles and label them. The leather is sold to companies that make the leather products Americans use every day.

Leather manufacturers also employ general laborers, who apply solutions to hide pieces, move hides and supplies from one processing machine to another, and perform many other tasks. *Frame makers* construct and maintain the frames over which leather is stretched after tanning, and *roll fillers* install and replace the blades and rollers in rolling machines.

In addition, supervisors coordinate the work of employees in many leather manufacturing departments, such as the *pelting room*, the *finishing room*, the *split and drum room*, the *split-leather department*, the *tan room*, the *beam department* (in which hides are de-haired, fleshed, and washed), the *vat house*, and the *hide house*.

Requirements

Leather tanning and finishing workers most easily find work if they have high-school diplomas or their equivalents. Because workers generally learn their skills on the job, however, employers do not usually require experience. Most workers begin as laborers and learn to operate tanning and finishing machines over time.

High-school courses in shop and chemistry may help prepare students for this type of work. Workers must be healthy and should have a fair amount of physical strength.

Special requirements

There are no special requirements for this type of work.

Opportunities for experience and exploration

High-school students who are interested in this field may wish to contact leather workers' unions to receive information or speak to persons working in the industry. Trade journals such as *The Leather Manufacturer*, published in Massachusetts, may help would-be leather workers learn more about the trade. Students who live near tanneries may try to arrange a tour of the plant to observe leather processes firsthand.

Related occupations

The work done by people is very similar to the work done by others employed in processing industries. These include electroplating workers, heat treaters, petroleum refining workers, rubber goods production workers, and glass manufacturing workers.

Methods of entering

While state employment offices and school placement centers may help job seekers find work in the leather industry, the most common way of obtaining a position is by applying directly to tanneries. Labor unions and apprenticeship committees may also help applicants get started in this industry.

Advancement

Workers almost always start as laborers in this field. With experience, however, they can move into machine operators' jobs. As their knowledge of leather increases, they may become graders, inspectors, or, with further

education, supervisors, buyers, or sales representatives.

Employment outlook

In the early 1990s, about 19,000 people were employed in U.S. tanneries in Illinois, Wisconsin, California, Pennsylvania, the East Coast, and other areas. Automation and synthetic replacements for leather have slowed the growth of positions in the leather industry. Leather production, however, has remained fairly steady. and technically skilled workers should have little trouble finding jobs.

Earnings

According to limited available information, tanning and finishing workers earn average annual salaries of about $13,520 for forty-hour work weeks, plus extra pay for overtime, weekend, and holiday work. Most workers have good fringe benefits that include life and health insurance, paid vacations, paid holidays, and often pension plans.

Conditions of work

Most tanning workers belong to one of two unions: the United Food and Commercial Workers International or the Leather Workers International Union of America. Tanners work indoors and are employed twelve months a year.

Tannery processes are often accompanied by unpleasant odors, and many workers must also get used to lifting heavy objects such as soaked hides. These workers, and those involved in chemical processes, may wear protective boots and clothing. Other leather work, however, is clean and dry and may be performed sitting down.

Social and psychological factors

As with many production jobs, this work can be repetitive. It also requires some teamwork, so the ability to work well with others is very important. While many tannery jobs are appropriate only for those who can handle and enjoy heavy physical labor, others require only a certain amount of dexterity and patience and may be successfully performed by persons with physical disabilities.

GOE: None; SIC: 3111, SOC: 7657

◇ **SOURCES OF ADDITIONAL INFORMATION**

Leather Workers International Union of America
PO Box 32
11 Peabody Square
Peabody, MA 01960

U.S. Hide, Skin and Leather Association
1707 N Street, NW
Washington, DC 20036

American Leather Chemists Association
University of Cincinnati
Location 14
Cincinnati, OH 45221

Leather Industry Workers of America
2501 M Street, NW, Suite 550
Washington, DC 20037

◇ **RELATED ARTICLES**

Volume 1: Apparel
Volume 3: See Processing Occupations

Macaroni and related products industry workers

Definition

Macaroni and related products industry workers operate the machinery that mixes, shapes, cuts and dries all types of pasta, including macaroni, spaghetti, lasagna, and egg noodles.

History

Macaroni and other types of pasta noodles are most often associated with Italy and Italian food, but according to legend, pasta was invented by the Chinese and brought to Italy by the adventurer Marco Polo in the late thirteenth century. This claim has been, of course, hotly contested by Italians, who say that they had been making pasta for some twenty to eighty years before Polo's journeys. Whatever its source, pasta remains one of the world's most popular foods. Italian immigrants introduced pasta on a large scale to America during the period of heavy immigration from 1880 to 1920, and today pasta is a staple in the diets of most Americans.

Macaroni, spaghetti, lasagna, manicotti, linguini, and the letters in a bowl of alphabet soup are all examples of pasta. Pasta is made from water and coarse, yellow flour called "semolina," which is made from hard durum wheat. Pasta is described as noodles when eggs are used in place of some or all of the water. The different kinds of pasta are determined by the various sizes and shapes in which it comes. More than 150 different types of pasta are made from a few basic ingredients, and all are created in practically the same manner.

Nature of the work

The settings where pasta is made can range from an average home kitchen to a busy restaurant to a giant factory. Whatever the setting, however, the manufacturing process is basically the same, a simple process of mixing dough, kneading it dense and flat, and cutting it into noodles. While the dough is most often made of semolina and water, many pasta chefs have their own special ingredients to add, and manufacturers are branching out into more ex-

429

Macaroni and related products industry workers
Processing Occupations

otic forms of pasta. Among these specialties are whole wheat pasta and pasta made with spinach, tomato, pepper, carrots, beets, or eggs.

Hundreds of small pasta factories operate across the country, and many have been in the hands of the same family for generations. They are often part of a restaurant operation, in which case the pasta may or may not be for sale to the public. If the pasta is made to be served in the restaurant, it will usually be kept soft and fresh, not dried like the kind found in supermarkets. Depending on the scope of operations of one of these small plants, one person can handle all the work of making pasta, or two or three people can work in shifts. Quite often, these workers, who are known as *noodle makers* or *noodle-press operators*, handle other cooking and kitchen chores as well.

The first step in making pasta is measuring out the proper amounts of flour and warm water, together with whatever other special ingredients are to be included. The ingredients are dumped into a large, stainless steel mixing bowl, and stirred and kneaded by an electric mixer into a smooth, thick dough. When several batches of dough have been mixed, they are laid out on a flat stainless steel or marble surface covered with flour. The pasta is kneaded a few times by hand and shaped into sections that are about two feet long, a foot wide, and two inches thick. The tray of dough is then placed in a cold room for several hours to cool. After it has been sufficiently chilled to be workable, the sections of pasta dough are rolled through a machine and flattened to a thickness of an eighth of an inch. The dough is then passed through a cutting machine that slices it into thin strips about an eighth of an inch wide. The pasta worker cuts these strips into two-foot lengths, sprinkles and tosses them with flour to separate the strips, and returns the pasta to the cold room. After sufficient chilling, the pasta is ready to be cooked and served.

Pasta is also made in large factories for regional or national distribution. In these settings, workers are generally limited to operating and monitoring the complex, automated machines that do most of the work. These machines are usually controlled by computers, and workers are responsible for one task only.

At large pasta factories, flour is usually brought in on railroad cars and removed by machinery operated by the *conveyor operator*. The flour is extracted from the railroad cars by pneumatic hoses, transferred to sifting and weighing stations, and put into storage bins. The conveyor operator monitors the transfer process by switches and gauges on a control panel, and records the details of the shipment, such as the amount and type of flour and the name of the supplier.

Mixing the ingredients and sending the dough through kneading and pressing machines is the job of the *press tender*. From a control panel, the press tender can operate the chutes that carry the flour and other ingredients to the mixing compartments, where they are added to water and kneaded into dough. The press tender then operates the valves that push the pasta dough through the dies, or pierced metal plates, that produce the various types of pasta. For example, dies with small round holes produce long strands of spaghetti, dies with flat slots turn out lasagna noodles, and dies with large holes with needles in the center and a notch in one side produce elbow macaroni. Depending on the production schedule for the different types of noodles, the press tender installs these various dies using hand tools. As the pasta is squeezed through the dies, the press tender operates the machine that cuts the pasta into certain lengths and hangs it over rods to dry. For macaroni, pasta shells, and other small goods, the cutting machines operate more quickly. Press tenders are responsible for the quality of the pasta, from the mixing through the extrusion process. They watch the color of the pasta and test its texture to make certain that it meets the standards of the company.

After the pasta is cut, it needs to be dried. This is a crucial and precise process. If the pasta is dried too fast, it becomes brittle and easily breakable, but if it is dried too slowly, spoilage or mold may occur. *Drier operators* control the equipment that dries the pasta according to the specifications of the company's laboratory. From the dials on the panel board, the drier operator can open steam valves that regulate the temperature, humidity and drying time in the preliminary, secondary, and final drying chambers. Because current weather conditions have an effect on the drying of the pasta, the drier operator takes them into account. Like the press operator, the drier operator inspects and feels the pasta to tell whether it meets established quality standards. Once the pasta has been properly dried, the *machine stripper-cutter* uses machinery equipped with guillotine knives or band saws to cut the pasta into lengths suitable for packaging.

There is very little waste in a pasta factory. Any sort of scraps from the press, processing or drying operations is collected by the *scrap separator* and sorted according to size and condition. Scraps are then either thrown away, remilled, or sold as hog or poultry feed. The maintenance of pasta dies is the job of the *die cleaner*, who removes the dies from the pressing machines, washes them and inspects them for any damage.

Requirements

There are no special education or practical requirements for working in a pasta factory because most of the tasks are learned on the job. Workers usually start as general helpers or laborers, assisting the scrap separator or die cleaner, for example, and are later trained for more skilled work. As pasta plants become more and more automated, however, employers will be looking for more technical skills among new workers.

A high-school diploma or a GED certificate is definitely an advantage, especially if a worker wants to advance to a higher position such as manager. Machine shop classes and work at other jobs that demonstrate skills in operating and repairing machinery are also a plus. Other types of job experience, such as kitchen work, may be helpful as well, because it shows responsibility, reliability, and the willingness to work.

Special requirements

Pasta workers employed in mid-size or large factories may be members of the Bakery and Confectioners Union, while workers in smaller establishments generally are not represented by unions. In certain areas of the country, such as the Northeast and Midwest, support for unions is stronger and membership more widespread than in other regions.

Opportunities for experience and exploration

Students who wish to learn more about work in a pasta factory should apply for part-time or summer jobs, either at a large plant or at a restaurant that makes its own noodles. Depending on the size of the operation, they may advance quickly to a position of mixing, making, or drying the pasta, under the supervision of a more skilled worker. One of the easiest ways to develop skills is to make pasta at home. Although methods are different, the materials and end result are the same.

A pasta worker pulls out fresh linguini as it is being sliced by a machine. She will then lay the strips of linguini on a rack to dry.

Related occupations

Other workers who have similar skills and aptitudes in food processing include confectionery industry workers, canning and preserving industry workers, and bakery products workers. Bakers, chefs, and cooks work with food preparation. Caterers work with food preparation and presentation.

Methods of entering

Jobs in pasta plants are often advertised in the want ads of the local paper. Job seekers can answer these ads, or apply for work at the personnel office of a local pasta plant. Another good source for leads is friends who work in a plant and hear about job openings.

Advancement

Work experience and skill are the keys to advancement for pasta makers. After a time as a general helper, an employee may be promoted to a more demanding job such as handling the complicated machinery. A worker may advance to become a group leader or shift supervisor. For those who work in a factory that makes other food products, such as pasta sauces or soups, they may be able to advance to another division of the company. Those workers with an entrepreneurial inclination may wish to take their experience and start their own small pasta plant or restaurant.

Macaroni and related products industry workers
Processing Occupations

Employment outlook

More and more people are eating pasta across the U.S.—in traditional dishes, in salads, in casseroles, and in many other ways. Concerns about health are partially responsible for this demand; the American Heart Association has approved pasta and other grain products as complex carbohydrates that are low in fat. For this and other reasons, the demand for pasta is growing at a phenomenal 5% per year. Sales of pasta have doubled in the past 20 years, and experts predict that they will double again in the next decade.

Pasta production companies are expanding their line of pasta to include noodles made with spinach, whole wheat, tomato, and other nutritive substances. There has also been a major increase in the sale of freshly-made pasta noodles. The companies that produce these products tend to be small businesses, shipping to limited regional areas, much as a bakery operates.

About 10,000 workers are employed nationwide by the large pasta manufacturers, and many thousands more work in the smaller plants and restaurants that operate with staffs of 20 workers or less. Demand for pasta workers is expected to remain high, although as factories equip themselves with more complex machinery, workers with technical or mechanical skills will be more sought after than unskilled workers.

Earnings

Workers who are employed in large factories, which are usually located in large metropolitan areas, earn more than workers in small or mid-size plants. In small plants with 20 or fewer workers, employees earn around $6.00 an hour. In mid-size plants with 20 to 100 employees, wages range from $5.00 to $9.00 an hour for weighers, packers and cleaners, while press tenders earn from $5.85 to $9.29 an hour.

In large pasta factories with more than 100 workers, workers in most jobs earn between $9.00 and $10.00 an hour. General helpers start at around $5.45, while experienced workers earn up to $11.15. These large factories usually operate around the clock, and have employees work in eight-hour shifts. Workers on the evening and night shifts generally earn from $0.15 to $0.25 more per hour than workers on the day shift.

After one year of service, workers in large plants generally enjoy two or three weeks of paid vacation, along with pension plans and life, health, and hospital insurance. About 40 percent of large and mid-size plants also offer sick leave. These types of benefits are generally not available in small plants and restaurants.

Conditions

Most pasta plants are clean, sanitary and well ventilated work places. The machinery is more modern in some than in others, but most are generally safe places that are carefully watched to meet health codes. This is true of both large manufacturing plants and smaller, family-owned businesses.

Pasta workers are on their feet most of the day, although they generally get morning and afternoon breaks in addition to their lunch breaks. Workers in smaller plants that are not heavily automated may be required to lift heavy sacks of flour or trays of dough or noodles.

The atmosphere in small, family operations is generally more informal and friendly than that found in large factories. Workers in small plants can trade jobs or work shifts with other employees without much trouble. Many work part-time and enjoy close relationships with other workers. The atmosphere in larger plants generally is more impersonal and businesslike. Workers remain at their assigned stations and follow the rules set down by the company.

Social and psychological conditions

For the most part, pasta making is repetitive, assembly line work. Workers must be able to be able to perform the same routine tasks without becoming careless or bored. Pasta factories prize employees who are dependable and hard-working, and who are concerned with the quality of the pasta they are making. While little prestige is connected with making pasta, some people find other rewards in their work, especially if it is a small operation where family pride is important. There are many opportunities to establish strong ties with co-workers as well, such as bowling leagues and company picnics. Successful companies also know the value of letting good employees know how much they are valued by listening to their suggestions or by giving an award to the employee of the month.

GOE: None; SIC: 2098; SOC: None

◇ **SOURCES OF ADDITIONAL INFORMATION**

Bakery, Confectioners and Tobacco Workers International Union
10401 Connecticut Avenue
Kensington, MD 20895

National Pasta Association
1901 North Fort Myer Drive
Suite 1000
Arlington, VA 22209

◇ **RELATED ARTICLES**

Volume 1: Baking; Food Processing; Food Service
Volume 2: Food technologists
Volume 3: Cooks, chefs and bakers; Food service workers; Bakery products workers; Canning and preserving industry workers; Confectionery industry workers; Dairy products manufacturing workers; Meat packing production workers; Tobacco products industry workers

Meat packing production workers

Definition

Meat packing production workers slaughter, clean, cut, process, and package cattle, hogs, sheep, and poultry. They also process parts of animals for production into meat by-products such as margarine, lard, hides, wool, soap, feed, and fertilizer.

History

Europeans who settled New England in the early seventeenth century raised their own livestock, mostly pigs. In the fall, they slaughtered the animals and packed the meat in barrels full of salt or lard to preserve it for the winter. Settlers who packed more than they could eat sold it to ships, crews, and others who could not raise their own livestock. After the American Revolution, when people began to live in cities, an entire culture of people who could not raise their own food was born, and the meat packing industry was born along with it.

During the next century, when settlers began to populate the western half of the country, stockyards, and meat packing plants sprang up near railroads. Ranchers drove their cattle hundreds of miles form the ranges where they grazed to the yards where they were sold. Until recently, large stockyards in cities near many types of transportation, Chicago in particular, packed most of the country's meat. Advances in transportation and refrigeration, however, have made it easier to transport meat than livestock, and packing houses have begun to operate closer to the places where cattle are bred and grazed—especially Iowa, Kansas, Nebraska, Missouri, Texas, Minnesota, and California.

Nature of the work

The type of work meat packing production workers perform depends on their skill level and the size of the plant in which they work. Skilled workers kill, dress, cut, and cure meats. In small plants workers may perform a variety of tasks, while in large plants jobs are more specialized.

First, workers must kill or slaughter the animals. They use humane methods that do not cause the animals pain; these methods must meet federal standards established by the 1958 Humane Slaughter Act. To begin, workers called *stunners* admit a certain number of animals from a large yard into a pen, where they use electric prods, carbon dioxide, sledge hammers, or cartridge-firing devices to quickly knock the animals unconscious. *Shacklers* then chain the animals' hind legs to hoists or conveyors that suspend them above killing floors for slaughtering. *Animal stickers* then cut the unconscious animals' carotid arteries and let the blood drain from the carcasses. Poultry is killed in almost the same way. *Poultry hangers* shackle and suspend live poultry from conveyors, and *poultry killers* sever the birds' jugular veins with a knife as they pass on the conveyors overhead.

Before butchering, workers remove the hair, hide, or feathers from the animals. *Steamers* spray steam on suspended hog carcasses to remove hair and dirt, and *de-hairing-machine tenders* do the same thing with scalding hot water. *Singers* use torches to singe hair from hog carcasses. *Shavers* use knives and scrapers to remove dirt and hair from hog carcasses and to prepare them for further processing. *Skinners* remove the hides of cattle, hog, and sheep carcasses using knives, and *hide pullers* remove hides using machines.

Poultry-picking machine operators run machines that remove the feathers of slaughtered poultry, scald the birds, wash them, and prepare them for butchering. *Poultry dressers* ready chickens for marketing.

After hides are removed, *hide trimmers* trim off any fat, viscera, or ragged edges. *Depilatory painters* paint sheep skins with chemicals to loosen wool. *Wool pullers* remove wool from pelts; sort the wool into bins according to color, texture, and length; and scrape the hides until they are free from hair.

Gambrelers and their helpers use what are called gamb sticks to spread the legs of animal carcasses and hang the carcasses on an overhead rail to prepare them for dressing.

Next, *carcass splitters* use saws, cleavers, and knives to dismember and cut animal carcasses into large pieces before further processing. *Eviscerators* then remove the intestines, internal organs, and other viscera from the carcasses and deposit the viscera in bins for further processing. *Offal separators* separate edible viscera parts from waste portions. Some glands are purchased by agricultural and pharmaceutical companies to make chemicals or drugs. *Casing cleaners* clean, cure, and soak intestines for use as sausage casings. *Casing splitters* split cured casings and press them flat so they may be made into surgical sutures, violin strings, and strings for tennis rackets.

Butchers and their *apprentices* cut the heads off carcasses and trim off bruises and blemishes. Carcasses go to cooling rooms where they hang for one or two days. Then butchers cut the sides into meat cuts, using knives, cleavers, and power saws. Meat trimmers trim fat, skin, tendons, tissues, and ragged edges from meat cuts. *Meat machine peelers* and *head trimmers* trim meat and other parts from animal heads using machines or knives. *Band saw operators* tend electric band saws that cut portions from hams to prepare them for curing or smoking.

Some meat is boned. *Meat boners* cut bones from standard cuts of meat—chucks, loins, rounds, and so on—to prepare them for packing and marketing. *Poultry boners* bone cooked poultry before it is processed.

Meat that is not sold fresh must be preserved. Meats are pickled, dry-cured, and smoked, and some are cooked and canned. *Pickling-solution makers* mix phosphate, nitrate, and brine solutions together to cure meat. *Picklers* immerse meats in vats of pickling solutions to cure them before they are smoked. And *pickle-pumpers* inject meats with curing solution using a machine that pumps the solution into the meat through needles. *Dry curers* pack pork, ham, bacon, or casings into boxes or vats with dry-curing agents such as sugar, sodium nitrate, and salt. *Smoked-meat preparers* soak and clean meats to be smoked and then hang them on conveyors to be carried to the smoke room. *Smokers* load racks and cages with meat and push them into the smokehouse for smoking. They ignite sawdust in the smokehouse burner and start fans to blow the smoke into the chamber. They regulate temperatures, humidity, and time of smoking. They determine when smoking is done and remove meats to the chill room. *Cooks* bake, boil, and deep-fat fry meats such as ham, beef, sausage, and tripe to prepare them for further processing.

Many kinds of meat are ground, chopped, or formed to make sausages and other products. To make sausages, *casing-running-machine tenders* tend machines that gather casings into stuffing-machine nozzles, ready to be stuffed. *Sausage-meat trimmers* trim meat from bones and dice it; *meat grinders* grind it; *seasoning mixers* weigh and mix seasonings to flavor it; then *chopping-machine operators* tend machines that chop and mix ground meat with seasonings to make emulsion for sausages and other products like bologna, meat loaves, and wieners. *Sausage makers* and *mixers* may also perform these tasks. Then *stuffers* run machines that force meat emulsion into casings to make sausages and similar products. *Linkers* twist and tie sausage-filled casings to make sausage links of specified lengths. *Linking-machine operators* do this by machine. Later, *sausage inspectors* make sure sausages are of uniform length and firmness.

Other meats are pressed or otherwise formed by *meat press operators, meat molders, pork-cutlet makers,* and *turkey-roll makers*. *Ham-rolling-machine operators* run machines that wind binding around hams, and *tiers* roll and tie cuts of meat to form roasts.

By-products such as lard and animal feed are processed by meat packing industry workers. *Lard bleachers* and *refiners* cook and filter animal fat. *Hasher operators* and *rendering-equipment tenders* process waste for use as animal feed.

The industry also employs a variety of graders and inspectors, who grade meat, skins, pelts, and hides, according to sales value, quality, size and type,

After meat is processed, *scaler-packers* and *hand packagers* package meat for shipment or sale.

Workers with several years of experience supervise other workers in various departments. Opportunities for unskilled workers include *laborers,* who load and unload racks of meat, clean equipment, and perform various other duties as needed; and *order runners,* who take smoked meats out of bins and racks and put them on conveyors leading to packing rooms. Because meat packing plants must meet stringent sanitation requirements, cleaning workers are also important. They include *box-truck washers* and *equipment cleaners.*

In addition, kosher meats must be killed according to directions in Jewish law. *Shactos* are special butchers licensed by rabbinical authority. They and their helpers inspect and kill animals so the meat may be sold as kosher.

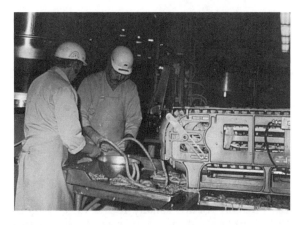

Linking machine operators in a sausage factory ensure that the sausages are of uniform length and size.

Requirements

Most meat packing production workers learn their skills on the job. Therefore, even though they may progress to be semiskilled workers, those entering the industry usually need no more education than a high-school diploma and no special training. Some employers will hire individuals with eighth-grade educations to perform some tasks. High-school courses in agriculture and shop may help workers find jobs.

For workers required to use sharp instruments such as axes, knives, and other blades, good eyesight with strong depth perception are exceedingly important to avoid injury on the job. Manual skills are also important for those cutting the meat.

Workers who want to advance or find good jobs may want to investigate home-study courses offered by the American Meat Institute Center for Continuing Education. This program acquaints students with the business and technology of meat packing.

Special requirements

There are no special requirements for this type of work.

Opportunities for experience and exploration

Trade journals such as *Meat Industry,* published in California, and *Meat Plant Magazine,* published in Missouri, are valuable sources of information for the worker who wants to explore the meat packing industry. Employees at local meat packing plants may also be willing to speak with persons interested in this type of work. Beginning workers may start out in apprenticeships, learning to cut meat and perform other semiskilled tasks.

Related occupations

The work of meat packing workers is similar to the work done by these workers: dairy products manufacturing workers, macaroni and related products industry workers, confectionery industry workers, and bakery products workers.

Methods of entering

The best way to find work in meat packing is to apply directly to local plants. State employment agencies may also know of openings.

Advancement

Entry-level workers generally start as laborers on the killing floor, helpers in sausage kitchens, hide workers, or meat cutting apprentices. As they become more skilled they advance to more difficult jobs. Skilled, dependable workers have the best chance of advancement, but they must usually wait until openings occur. Some may become supervisors, and those with seniority and a great deal of experience may take jobs in the management of the plant.

Employment outlook

Automation in meat packing plants has cut down on the need for production workers. Displaced workers are usually found other jobs in the plant, so entering the industry as an unskilled worker has become more difficult, despite the increasing demand for meat. Because turnover is fairly high, however, there are jobs available for some entry-level workers. As they become more skilled, it may be easier for workers to find work at different plants. Competition for positions, however, has clearly given the edge to high-school graduates.

Earnings

In the early 1990s, meat packing production workers working thirty-six to forty hours per week plus occasional overtime earned average annual salaries of between $18,900 and $21,700. Skilled workers earned more. In union plants, beginners earned about $15,780. Workers receive time and a half for overtime and Saturdays and may receive double pay for working Sundays and holidays. They generally receive good fringe benefits, including paid vacations, sick leave, pension plans, paid holidays, and life and health insurance. These benefits may depend on the union contract in effect at the plant.

Conditions of work

Working conditions for meat packers have improved since the introduction of unions in the first half of the century. About half of the country's meat packing workers belong to either an independent union or to the United Food and Commercial Workers International Union, AFL-CIO. Still, meat packing can be dangerous, unpleasant work. Some workers have trouble coping with the sights, sounds, and smells of slaughtering and butchering animals. Floors may be wet and slippery. Some plant areas are hot; others are cold. However, Occupational

Safety and Health Administration (OSHA) rules and federal sanitation requirements control the safety and cleanliness of plants. Workers wear protective clothing to minimize the danger of cuts, slips, falls, and burns.

Social and psychological factors

Workers who cannot get used to working in the surroundings of the meat packing industry will have trouble coping with this type of work. On the other hand, strong, careful, mechanically apt workers who are not sensitive to such conditions can succeed in this industry if they are willing to work hard.

GOE: 06.04.15; SIC: 2011; SOC: 5217

◇ **SOURCES OF ADDITIONAL INFORMATION**

American Association of Meat Processors
PO Box 269
Elizabethtown, PA 17022

American Meat Institute
PO Box 3556
Washington, DC 20007

International Association of Meat Processors
Box 35880
Tucson, AZ 85740

United Food and Commercial Workers International Union
1775 K Street, NW
Washington, DC 20006

Western States Meat Association
PO Box 12944
Oakland, CA 94604

◇ **RELATED ARTICLES**

Volume 1: Food Processing
Volume 2: Dietitians; Food technologists
Volume 3: See Processing occupations
Volume 4: Dietetic technicians

Molders

Definition

Molders and related workers form sand molds for use in the production of metal castings. Using a two-part box called a flask, they pack specially prepared sand around a pattern of the object that is to be cast. Then the pattern is removed and molten metal is poured into the cavity, where it solidifies as it cools and forms the casting.

History

Because of the disappearance of many historical artifacts it is difficult to say precisely when molding began. Considering the great versatility of the molding process, however, it can be assumed that its origins go thousands of years back in time.

It is known that Solomon placed two brass pillars before the entrance of his temple, demonstrating to the world a highly developed knowledge of the art of molding. If one considers the use of iron to date from the crude uses of iron made by the Egyptians and Chinese as early as 3000 B.C. the antiquity of the molder's art is apparent.

Its greatest impetus, however, came during the Industrial Revolution. Prior to that time, molders were really craft workers who used the molding technique to produce their wares. When the idea of the production line was introduced, the work of the molder began to be more similar to the job as it is today. Today's perfected techniques and technologically advanced molding machines have made metal casting one of the fastest, most economical, and most versatile ways to produce metal products.

Nature of the work

Molders work in foundries that produce castings from iron, steel, and the nonferrous metals (alloys containing no appreciable amounts of iron). Castings are the basic parts of all kinds of metal products, from heavy machinery to automobile engines to household appliances. The casting begins with a mold, which the molder prepares from specially treated sand. In green sand molding, the most common method because it is the least expensive, molders pack and ram a mixture of sand, clay, and chemicals around a pattern (a model of the object to be duplicated) in a molding box called a flask. Flasks are usually made in two parts which can be separated to allow removal of the pattern by the molder without damaging the mold cavity.

The entire operation is handled in a specific series of steps. After positioning the drag (lower) half of the pattern and flask, molders sprinkle or spray them with a parting agent and place reinforcing wire in the flask. Sand is sifted over the pattern and pressed into its contours. Then the molders shovel sand into the flask and pack it in place with hand ramming tools or a pneumatic hammer. With this completed, the molders position the cope (top) half of the pattern and flask on the drag half and repeat the procedure. Then the halves are separated and the pattern removed. The molders cut a hole in the mold through which the liquid metal will be poured. They position a core in the cavity left by the pattern (to produce a hollow casting), reassemble the flask, and pour molten metal into the mold. When the metal cools and solidifies, the casting is removed and the mold cleaned. Some of these final steps may be performed by *mold closers*.

In a molding process called the "sweep method," the mold is hollowed out to the desired shape by a rotating board instead of a stationary pattern. The molders in this process are called *sweep molders*. The special processes for casting copper are performed by workers called *mold makers*.

A few foundries still construct molds using the traditional hand methods, but most molds today are made by machines that pack and ram the sand mechanically. This advanced technology makes it possible to turn out large quantities of identical sand molds quickly, simply, and more economically. Workers who operate these machines are called *machine molders,* and it is their job to set up the machine, to control the pressure applied to the sand by working the pedals and levers, and to cut pouring spouts in the mold. They also assemble the flask and pattern on the machine table and fill the flask with the prepared sand mixture. The workers who operate the machines that pack the sand into the flask are called *sand-slinger operators.* Those who operate machines that make shell molds are called *shell molders.*

In the foundries that still use manual methods, hand molders compact the sand around the pattern with hand tools such as trowels and

437

The formation of giant molds involves the use of cranes to carefully arrange individual sections.

hand rammers and with power tools such as pneumatic rammers and squeeze plates. Molds for small castings, such as jewelry, are usually made on a workbench by *bench molders*, while those for large, bulky castings are made on the foundry floor by floor molders. Some molders are capable of making many different kinds of molds; others, with less skill, may specialize in a few simple types.

The work of a molder calls into play a knowledge of such variables as metal characteristics, molding sand, contours of patterns, and pouring procedures. It is a physically active occupation requiring standing, walking, crouching, kneeling, stooping, lifting, carrying, and handling, in either a job or production foundry. A job foundry generally specializes in specific items for a production foundry, which produces a larger item from parts manufactured by various job foundries.

Other workers with an important role in the foundry metal casting process are coremakers, who prepare the cores that are placed in molds to form the hollow sections in castings, and patternmakers, who construct precise patterns, or models, for the products being cast.

Requirements

An eighth-grade education is the minimum requirement for a molder apprentice, particularly for one going into the less-skilled hand molding work. A high-school education is valuable for the apprentice aspiring to more skilled foundry jobs such as coremaker, patternmaker, and various supervisory occupations. In high school, it is important to take subjects such as mathematics, drafting, and various shop courses which teach the use of hand tools.

To become a skilled hand molder, workers need to complete a two-to-four-year apprenticeship or acquire a comparable amount of on-the-job experience. A shorter training period is generally required to become a qualified machine molder.

Apprenticeship programs are usually co-sponsored by the employer and the International Molders and Allied Workers Union. Apprentices work under the close supervision of experienced molders. At first they are given simple tasks to perform, such as shoveling sand; then they are gradually moved up to more difficult and responsible jobs, such as ramming molds, removing patterns, and setting cores. They also learn how to operate various molding machines, and eventually to make complete molds. Apprentices may be put to work in various departments to gain an all-round knowledge of foundry methods and practices. They also receive at least 144 hours of classroom instruction a year in subjects such as shop mathematics, metallurgy, and shop drawing.

Hand molders who do repetitive work that does not require much skill usually learn their jobs during a brief training period. As trainees they work alongside an experienced molder to make a particular kind of mold, and after two to six months they are usually able to make a similar mold without help. Most machine molders also acquire their skills with on-the-job training which may take only a few months. The length of time varies depending on the individual worker and the foundry, but in general it is less than the time required for hand molders.

The molder needs a high degree of manual dexterity and good eye-hand coordination, as well as above-average strength. Persons in this occupation stand while working, must move about a great deal to do accurate work, and must be competent in using such molding tools as shovels and rammers.

There are more jobs, of course, in large industrial cities such as Detroit, where foundries exist for the sole purpose of supplying parts for new automobiles. For maximum opportunity of continued employment, then, it is necessary for the molder to live in or near large industrial areas. There are, however, some small production companies and factories that employ molders all across the country.

Special requirements

There are no special requirements for this occupation.

Opportunities for experience and exploration

It is a well-recognized fact that a high-school education does not guarantee a person a job. If there is a limited number of jobs available, it makes sense that an employer will favor an applicant with satisfactory job experience of some sort, whether in molding or some similar work. Therefore, students prior to high-school graduation can prepare for a full-time job as a molder by applying for work during vacations and in the summer in foundries. Even if the part-time work is no more than sweeping up the floor, the students are gaining some foundry experience. The temporary workers who are interested in the molder's work ask questions, offer suggestions, and become well acquainted with a molder are on their way toward learning whether or not this is the kind of permanent work they want.

Most foundry employers who see this kind of interest in part-time workers will sometimes let them work at different jobs so they can gain varied work experiences as well as information about molding. Foundries are therefore very suitable places to obtain part-time or summer employment.

Related occupations

Other workers who have similar skills and aptitudes include coremakers, heat treaters, rubber goods production workers, and plastics products manufacturing workers.

Methods of entering

As in many skilled and semiskilled occupations in which almost all workers are members of a union, beginning molders must serve an apprenticeship of two to four years. Working with a journeyman, the apprentices have the opportunity to learn by doing, first shoveling and ramming sand and later drawing patterns and setting cores. Later they begin to do much of the complete molding operation and learn other jobs in the foundry as well. In addition to a complete all-around job experience, the apprentice molders receive classroom instruction in shop arithmetic, metallurgy, and shop drawing.

Of course, molders may also learn the job in a more informal manner by simply observing experienced molders at work and helping them as the opportunity arises. The value of the more formal apprenticeship is that the management of the foundry and the union know that the apprentices are preparing themselves for the job of molder, which often speeds up the process of becoming a journey worker molder.

The state employment office is always a good place to contact for foundry work. Of course, one may also go directly to the foundry's personnel office to fill out an application form. Because molding is often a job where union membership may benefit the worker, it is possible to find available openings through a local of the International Molders and Allied Workers Union.

Advancement

Molders who are qualified and have the necessary seniority may advance to the position of all-around molders. They will then work with different types of molding operations from beginning to end rather than repeat the same operation on one casting. Some foundries have molding supervisors who supervise a group of molders.

Molders who have worked in various departments of the foundry as part of their apprenticeship are in an excellent position to obtain a departmental supervisory position or even advance to foundry superintendent, providing a thorough knowledge of the various jobs, skill in working with people, and a general high level of interest are all present. Further formal training through trade or technical schools may enable employees to make themselves continually valuable to an employer.

Employment outlook

Approximately 24,000 persons are employed as molders in plants that make and sell castings in the early 1990s. Most of these foundries are small operations, with fewer than 250 workers. The largest concentration of foundries may be found in areas that have easy access to raw materials, most notably the Great Lakes states, the West Coast, and Alabama.

There are relatively few new workers going into molding today, and those who are entering this field are mainly replacing approximately 1,000 workers who annually retire, die, or move into other occupations.

Little increase in the total number of molders is expected during the early 1990s despite the expected sizable increase in foundry production. This is because of the continued trend toward more machine molding and less hand molding.

The amount of work available for those who enter this occupation may fluctuate greatly from year to year, because the market for certain foundry products is affected by changes in the economy. During a recession, for example, as the demand for farm machinery and motor vehicles drops, so does the demand for the metal castings used in their manufacture. The result is that foundry workers may be laid off or put on short workweeks.

Earnings

Average annual earnings for floor molders in the early 1990s ranged from about $16,220 in nonferrous plants (those that pour alloys containing no appreciable amounts of iron) to $17,225 in iron and steel foundries. Bench molders earned somewhat less, averaging about $14,230 in iron foundries and $15,225 in steel and nonferrous foundries. The pay for most workers in this occupation was lower than the average for production workers in all manufacturing industries, which was $18,150. Molders who were paid on an incentive basis generally had higher earnings.

Conditions of work

Foundry work is hazardous, and the injury rate is higher than the average for all manufacturing industries. Molders risk burns from the hot metal, as well as cuts and bruises from handling metal parts, molds, and power tools. Many foundries, however, have introduced safety programs and the use of safety equipment that have helped reduce injuries.

The foundry is a noisy place to work, and molders are exposed to dust, dirt, fumes, heat, and sudden temperature changes when the molten metal is being poured into the molds. These conditions could cause rheumatism, colds, pleurisy, and other lung ailments. Many plants have installed improved ventilating and air-conditioning equipment to reduce these health hazards, but they still exist in some older foundries.

Molders work inside and with others. Molding is mostly day work and based on a forty-hour workweek. The work is strenuous and requires standing, stooping, and moving around, and lifting and carrying.

Social and psychological factors

Molders may suffer the loss of some intrinsic value of their art as machines continue to replace hand molding. This is to say that they may not feel so creative about their work as more and more of it is done by machines. They may compare it unfavorably with the time when molding was largely a hand operation requiring an individual talent.

In any repetitious work there is danger of boredom and the possible increase in accidents. As the molders expand their work to all-around molding, they will find increasing satisfaction through the knowledge that molding is exacting work, requiring knowledge, skill, and manual dexterity, and that it contributes to an essential and necessary occupation.

GOE: 06.01.04; SIC: 3544; SOC: 76

◇ SOURCES OF ADDITIONAL INFORMATION

Information about training programs for molders may be obtained from local foundries, the local offices of the state employment service, the nearest office of the state apprenticeship agency, or the Bureau of Apprenticeship and Training, United States Department of Labor, and also from:

Glass, Molders, Potters, and Allied Workers International Union
608 East Baltimore Pike
PO Box 607
Media, PA 19063

For additional career guidance material (sent free when requested on stationery with a school letterhead), write to:

American Foundrymen's Society/Cast Metals Institute
Golf and Wolf Roads
Des Plaines, IL 60016

For apprenticeship information, contact:

International Molders and Allied Workers Union
Apprenticeship Programs
608 East Baltimore Pike
PO Box 107
Medra, PA 19063

◇ **RELATED ARTICLES**

Volume 1: Metals
Volume 3: Coremakers; Forge shop occupations; Iron and steel industry workers; Tool makers and die makers

Paint and coatings industry workers

Definition

Workers in the paint and coatings industry produce paints in paste form, ready-to-use paint, varnishes, lacquers, putty, enamel, stain, shellac, and other coatings. They operate machines that mix, color, and otherwise process these substances.

History

When two young boys found paleolithic paintings in the cave of Lascaux in France, the paint—tens of thousands of years old—was still wet. The drawings of horses and men appeared in bright, earthy colors, displaying the painter's materials—crushed minerals, soil, clay, and plant matter. Since prehistoric times, people have mixed colored substances with liquids to form paints for protecting and beautifying structures and implements, for decorating themselves, for creating art. As time passed, people developed more and more colors for paints, more and more subtle shades. They learned which materials would last longest, retain their color, best seal out water and weather. Adding egg white to pigment was found to give a relatively permanent, glossy finish. Plants, such as indigo, were cultivated for their ability to cast color.

Today's technology demands many sophisticated types of coatings, from the hard, shiny gloss on a sports car to spacecraft paint able to withstand incredible extremes of heat and cold. Housepaint, artists' watercolors, the sparkling lacquer on pianos and furniture, sign paint, wood stains, and many, many others are now developed in the laboratories of American paint companies and manufactured by paint and coatings industry workers.

Nature of the work

In the laboratories of the nation's paint companies, *researchers, chemists,* and *lab technicians* develop new finishes and coatings to meet the demands of consumers. They develop formulas and mix and test new paints, subjecting them to detergents, pressure, heat, cold, gases, and light to see if they will protect and preserve surfaces. Most coatings are now synthetic, including acrylic, epoxy, and urethane finishes.

In the laboratory, *formula figurers* translate formulas from the lab to formulas for production. *Paint-sample clerks* keep files on coatings samples and their characteristics. *Sample-color makers* mix different kinds of pigments, keep track of substances used, and paint samples of the mixtures on paper to compare color characteristics and ensure color conformity in products.

When paint is ready for production, workers following formulas weigh and measure raw ingredients to be ground into paste. Raw ingredients include pigments, latex, germ killer, driers, fire retardants, wetting agents, and others. *Mill operators* operate machines equipped with rollers, stones, or sand to grind ingredients into paste. They adjust the grinding elements, regulate cooling and heating, feed ingredients into the mill, and test the ground paste for consistency.

Some paint pastes are sold in that form. Others are mixed with other agents to form liquid coatings. *Mixers* mix paint products with oils, solvents, and resins to thin paint, varnish, and stain. To make lacquer (a glossy paint made from nitrocellulose combined with plasticizers, pigments, and solvents) *lacquer makers* operate machines that grind, mix, heat, and separate ingredients. *Varnish makers* and their *helpers* control equipment that melts, cooks,

A paint production supervisor checks the color consistency of paint in a vat and notes his observations. Such inspections must be made at regular intervals throughout the day.

and mixes the gums, oils, naphtha, turpentine, and pigments that go into varnishes.

The pigments that go into paints and coatings are also made by production workers. *Pigment processors* operate various kinds of equipment, including reaction, bleach, and wash tanks; filters; driers; furnaces; and mills. They operate controls to feed materials into these machines, which make such pigments as barites, iron oxide, titanium, and bentonite. Some pigments are baked to heighten their color. *Calcine-furnace loaders* load dry pigments into clay containers and use hydraulic lifts and forklifts to load the containers into the kiln. *Calcine-furnace tenders* regulate the heat in these kilns. Pigments made with lead and oxides into read-lead oxides used in paint are loaded into ovens by *red-lead burners.* They control temperatures and ensure that materials are uniformly heated. Other pigments are boiled, including cadmium liquor, which is made by *cadmium liquor makers* from cadmium moss. Glass is also heated in ovens to make flux for enamel.

Tinters operate machines that mix pigments with base materials to form colored paints, putty, lacquer, and enamel. *Centrifuge operators* filter varnishes and lacquers to remove impurities.

The paint and coatings industry also employs a variety of people to maintain equipment and perform general tasks. *Tank cleaners* use pneumatic chisels, hand scrapers, and other tools to scrap caked materials from paint production machines. *Laborers* clean work areas, haul and dump materials, and perform other duties to keep the plant clean and running smoothly.

Many workers supervise others in paint production. These workers select formulas, coordinate workers' activities, plan production schedules, and assure product quality. *Varnish*

inspectors also assure quality by testing sample varnish lots for clarity, cracking, crystallization, and drying speed.

Other paint production workers package products. Some help marketing efforts by producing the sample color chips that are glued onto color-card display sheets or folders, from which customers select colors for purchase.

Requirements

While most paint and coatings industry employers prefer to hire workers with high-school diplomas, standards vary from firm to firm. Many prefer workers with mechanical backgrounds, but most workers receive the bulk of their training on the job. Depending on the type of job a worker is hired to do, on-the-job training can last from two to twenty-four weeks.

Workers in paint laboratories may need somewhat more education. Lab technicians may have a better opportunity for employment if they have completed a two-year college course in chemistry and paint technology.

High-school students preparing for paint production jobs will benefit from taking courses in chemistry, physics, math, and business. Computer skills may also be useful. At some firms, ambitious workers may receive tuition to take college night classes in paint technology.

Special requirements

This type of work requires no special qualifications.

Opportunities for experience and exploration

Students in paint technology programs will have plenty of opportunities to explore paint and coatings production work. Others may try to obtain part-time or summer work at local plants or at least arrange to speak with plant employees about their work. Paint technology trade journals are other sources of information that can help prospective workers learn more about the field.

Related occupations

Other processing occupations that require similar interests and skills include industrial chemical workers, glass manufacturing occupations, paint and coatings industry workers, and rubber goods production workers.

Methods of entering

Persons interested in paint and coatings production work should apply directly to local plants and paint laboratories. However, state employment agencies and school guidance counselors may also know of openings. Jobs may also be found through newspaper advertisements.

Advancement

The number of different departments and positions in paint labs and plants makes movement possible. With experience and increasing skills, workers may move into supervisor positions. Lab technicians who work hard and obtain some college training may be able to move into chemists' jobs. Movement is not limited as much as education as it is by motivation, experience, and talent.

Employment outlook

Because housepaint makes up some 40 percent of the paint business and auto paints account for another significant share of the field, the industry is somewhat sensitive to the fortunes of the construction and auto businesses. The fortunes of these two industries have been poor in recent years. Demand for new kinds of paints, new colors, and improved paint protection, however, have held the industry at a fairly steady level. Industrial coatings are also an important part of the industry, and demand for them continually increases.

Automation is replacing some production workers, however, and college graduates and others with technical backgrounds have the best chances for employment. There will be some production jobs available to replace the thousands who leave the profession each year through death, retirement, or career change.

Earnings

In the early 1990s, paint and coatings production workers earned an average of about $17,250 a year. These earnings were based on a thirty-nine-hour average workweek and were highly dependent on geographic location, experience, and type of job. Lab technicians earn more than production workers, but less than chemists with bachelors' degrees, who in the early 1990s entered the field at salaries of about $22,000 a year.

Most employees receive insurance, paid vacations and holidays, and pension plans. All union workers receive these benefits, plus opportunities to participate in savings plans and credit unions.

Automotive painters and other industry painters earn hourly salaries of $17 or higher. Entry level positions may earn only half the experienced workers salary. For individuals who are paid on commission or on a work-for-hire basis, there is normally a fee for the full job. The faster worker will be able to complete more jobs and thus gain a higher salary.

Conditions of work

The great amount of automation in the paint and coatings industry makes paint production work fairly light. In labs and processing rooms fumes and odors disappear through modern ventilation systems. Workers also wear protective clothing to prevent injury from heat and chemicals. Many workers control or observe machines. This work may require a good deal of standing.

Paint and coatings workers worked an average of thirty-nine hours a week. Plants are located throughout the United States, especially California, Illinois, Ohio, New Jersey, and Michigan.

Social and psychological factors

Mechanical aptitude is important for paint production workers, as is the ability to work with their hands. Production work can be repetitive, but workers who are willing to learn a variety of skills can make their work challenging and rewarding. Good eyesight, coordination, and patience with details will also help workers succeed in the paint and coatings industry.

GOE: 06.02.11; SIC: 285; SOC: 7664

Paper processing occupations

Definition

The process by which wood is transformed into paper involves the use of highly complicated machinery and employs many skilled and semiskilled production workers, as well as scientific and technical personnel.

History

The word "paper" is derived from *papyrus,* the reeds from which the ancient Egyptians made their writing material, but wood-based paper as we know it today was invented in China about A.D. 100. The art of papermaking spread to the Middle East and, eventually, as a result of the Crusades, to Europe. Until the Industrial Revolution, all paper was made by hand in a laborious process. The invention, in the eighteenth and nineteenth centuries, of machines for crushing and grinding pulpwood and pressing pulp into paper made possible the mass-production of paper on a giant scale and the development of pulp and paper processing into a major industry.

Nature of the work

The U.S. Department of Labor has catalogued nearly 250 distinct job titles for the skilled and semiskilled workers who operate pulp and paper processing machinery. These workers perform a variety of duties, many of them requiring precise coordination and judgment. Those whose titles reflect the major stages in paper manufacturing are discussed here; many workers with closely defined tasks may be involved in any stage.

The *barker operator* controls the movement of cut logs into and out of a machine that cleans and strips the bark from them. Several types of machines may be used in this step of the papermaking process, but all operate on the same principle. The logs are fed into the barker on a conveyor belt. In the barker, they are tumbled against a revolving drum that strips off the bark, while a jet of water, controlled by the barker operator, washes off dirt and impurities. If logs become jammed in a machine, the barker operator breaks up the jam with a pike pole and chain hoist. The cleaned and stripped logs are carried on a conveyor belt to the chipping machine.

The *chipper* operates a machine that cuts logs into one-inch-square chips in preparation for their conversion into pulp. The logs are carried down a conveyor chute and pushed into the chipper disk, which cuts them into the required size. The chipper operates controls that regulate the flow of the logs according to their size.

The pulpwood chips are then conveyed to the stationary or rotary steam digesters, where they are cooked with soda ash, acid, or other chemicals. The *digester operator,* a skilled worker who supervises one or more helpers, operates controls that regulate the temperature and pressure inside the digesters and the flow of steam into the digesters. This worker tests samples of the digester liquid to determine when the pulp has been cooked to the proper degree. When the process is completed, the pulp, which now has the consistency of wet cotton, is blown or dumped into a pit, where it is washed to remove traces of chemicals and other impurities.

The *beater engineer* controls the process that mixes the pulp with sizing, fillers, and dyes to produce furnish, or liquid pulp solution, the last step before finished paper. One starts the pumps of the beater engines and regulates the flow of pulp into the vat by means of valves. After the furnish has been mixed, the beater draws samples of it for testing in the lab and examines it visually to make sure the desired consistency and fiber size have been reached.

The *paper-machine operator* is largely responsible for the quality of the finished paper. (Since almost all paper plants in the United States use the Fourdrinier machine method, this worker may also be called a *Fourdrinier-machine tender* or *Fourdrinier operator*.) As the furnish enters the "wet end" of the huge Fourdrinier machine, it flows over a continuously vibrating belt of fine wire screen, which causes the fibers to adhere and form a thin sheet of paper as the liquid from the pulp drains out. The paper-machine operator regulates the flow of pulp and of speed and pitch of the wire belt to produce paper of a desired thickness, width, and strength. This operator checks the quality of the paper being produced visually and by drawing samples to be sent to the laboratory. This person also supervises the workers who prepare the machine for operation and install the wire belts.

Backtenders work at the "dry end" of the Fourdrinier machine, usually under the supervision of the paper-machine operator. They operate the machines that dry, calendar (smooth), and finish the paper, and wind it onto rolls. They control the temperature of the drying and calendaring rolls, adjust the tension of the rolls, and control the speed of the continuous sheet of paper. They inspect the paper for spots, holes, and wrinkles, and mark defective sections for removal. The backtender also operates the machinery that cuts the rolls of paper into smaller rolls for shipment.

Pulp-and-paper-testers use standard testing equipment and chemical analyses to control the quality of paper products. In some plants, this is a separate occupation; in others, a paper-machine operator may also perform the duties of a pulp-and-paper tester. Testers determine the liquid content of cooked pulp and measure its acidity with a pH meter. Using a wire screen, press, and drying oven similar to those used in the days when all paper was made by hand, they make a single sheet of paper from the pulp. They then examine it under a microscope and count the number of dirt specks in a unit area. They test the sample sheet for bursting, tearing, and folding strength on apparatus specially developed for this purpose. These tests are also performed on samples of paper from the huge rolls produced by the Fourdrinier machine. The pulp-and-paper tester also tests paper samples for brightness, using a reflectance meter; and for weight, thickness, and

A pulp and paper tester takes a sample of pulp at various stages in the manufacturing process and examines their contents.

bulk, using scales and a micrometer. All test data are recorded and reported to the machine operators, with instructions to correct variations from standard. Here is a partial list of the many other paper processing occupations: *coating-mixer supervisors, beater room supervisors, wood room supervisors, calendaring supervisors, paper coating supervisors, wet room supervisors, paper machine supervisors, pulp plant supervisors, repulping supervisors, paper testing supervisors, paper testing supervisors, rag room supervisors, pulp-refiner operators, wood grinder operators, evaporator operators, moisture-conditioner operators, Blow-pit operators, decker operators, save-all operators, air-drier-machine operators, coating-machine operators, combiner operators, supercalendar operators, dampener operators, oiling-machine operators, pump press operators, rag-cutting-machine tenders, coating mixer tenders, matrix-drier tenders, cooker tenders, pulp- press tenders, screen tenders, chips screen tenders, screen tenders, molding-machine tenders, plate workers, rag-cutting-machine feeders, beater-and-pulper feeders, trasher feeders, paper final inspectors, color developers, head wood grinders, synthetic soil blocks pulpers, pulpers, magazine grinder loaders, bleach-boiler fillers, water-quality testers, chip testers, weight testers, screen handlers, wet-machine handlers, wet machine cutters, winder helpers.*

For more information on the manufacturing of paper, see Volume 1: Wood. For information on the use of paper in production, see the articles "Printing," and "Pulp and Paper" in Volume 1.

This researcher is employed by a paper company to study tree growth in various climates. She will determine the best conditions for maximal growth of several tree species.

Requirements

Paper companies generally prefer to hire high-school graduates for jobs as skilled and semi-skilled production workers. Those with degrees from junior colleges or technical institutes may be hired as laboratory technicians. High-school courses in chemistry, physics, and mathematics are valuable. Workers who install, set up, and repair paper-processing machinery will benefit from courses in shop, mechanical drawing, and blueprint reading.

Courses in machinery and machine repair also are helpful for those workers interested in machine maintenance of the numerous types used in this industry.

Because of the highly automated machinery in pulp and paper plants, few production jobs in this field require great physical strength. Manual dexterity, mental alertness, and good vision and hearing are very important for the skilled workers who tend complicated control panels and check the quality of the product.

Special requirements

There are no special requirements for paper processing occupations in addition to those already mentioned.

Opportunities for experience and exploration

Students who have had summer job experience on logging crews in forests owned by paper companies can often transfer their knowledge and skills to jobs in the company's plant. Summer jobs in plant maintenance and as machine helpers are also sometimes available.

Related occupations

The publishing, printing, and papermaking industries offer many occupational opportunities. Other positions might include editor, press operator, prepress workers, binding line workers, editorial production workers, art directors, engravers, typesetters, and photographers.

Methods of entering

Paper production workers usually begin as laborers or helpers and move up to more skilled jobs as they gain experience and skill. Some companies have on-the-job training programs for production and maintenance workers.

Advancement

Job progress in pulp and paper plants is from routine, unskilled jobs to positions requiring considerable technical skill and independent judgment, such as paper-machine operator. Those with unusual competence and supervisory ability may become supervisors of plant sections or of an entire phase of operations.

It should be noted that advancement routes in this field are usually limited to specific work areas, so that a digester operator, for instance, who wished to transfer to the Fourdrinier machine area would have to start at the bottom in the new assignment.

Production workers who continue their educations and receive degrees in science may obtain positions as laboratory and testing technicians or engineers.

Employment outlook

In the early 1990s, about 730,000 people were employed in the paper and allied products industries. Most of the production workers involved in the papermaking process are employed in large plants that perform the entire paper conversion operation from cut logs to finished paper. Sometimes these plants are located in forests, where the raw material is immediately available, but more often they are located in or near towns and cities, where transportation facilities are convenient. Traditionally, pulp and paper plants have been situated on the banks of rivers downstream from large forests, so logs could be floated down to their doors.

The demand for paper products should increase substantially in the next decade, but because of increasing automation of paper processing machinery, production jobs in this field are expected to show a very moderate increase. Employees with scientific or technical backgrounds will be in demand to fill research positions.

Earnings

In the early 1990s, production workers in the paper processing industry earned an average of $17,750 a year. Earnings ranged from $13,200 to more than $27,600 for experienced machine operators.

Conditions of work

Most pulp and paper plants operate twenty-four hours a day, seven days a week. The day is divided into three shifts. Production workers with seniority usually are assigned to the day shift, but may sometimes have to work nights and weekends.

Few jobs in this field require hard physical labor. Some areas of the plant, however, may be hot, humid, and noisy. The strong odors of the chemicals used in papermaking can be very unpleasant.

Social and psychological factors

Paper production workers in skilled jobs exercise a great deal of control over the production process and are responsible for the quality of the finished product. Watching raw materials being transformed into an essential commodity of civilization before one's eyes can be a source of great satisfaction.

GOE: 06.04.14; SIC: 262; SOC: 76

◇ **SOURCES OF ADDITIONAL INFORMATION**

American Paper Institute
260 Madison Avenue
New York, NY 10016

Paper Industry Management Association
2400 East Oakton Street
Arlington Heights, IL 60005

◇ **RELATED ARTICLES**

Petroleum refining workers

Definition

Petroleum refining workers operate machines that refine crude petroleum into gasoline, kerosene, fuel and lubricating oils, gases, solvents, asphalts, waxes, greases, and petroleum coke. They use several different heating and treating processes to make oil into these products. Refining involves purifying, filtering, heating and pressurizing as some methods of treatment.

History

Before the nineteenth century, many people used whale oil to light lamps. No engines were yet in use; electricity had not yet been discovered. But whale oil was not easy to get, and people began to drill oil wells to find a replacement. Crude oil has few uses, but people learned to boil it to obtain kerosene. The rest of the oil they threw away—this part contained gasoline. With the Industrial Revolution, however, many different fuels and lubricants became necessary, and many were developed from petroleum. Today, petroleum products run our cars, make up our faces, clothe our bodies, fuel our jet planes, and fulfill thousands of other functions.

Nature of the work

Petroleum is refined in many ways to make many products. First, however, it is heated in pipes in a huge furnace. The heated oils produce vapors, which pass into tall fractionating tanks, where they condense into fractions, or different parts. Pipes set at different levels draw off the fractions, including gasoline, kerosene, diesel and jet fuels, fuel oils, waxes, asphalt, coke, and lubricants.

Some of these products are ready for use. Others are processed further to purify or alter them. In cracking, heat and pressure turn heavy oils into high-octane gasoline. Other fractions go to petrochemical plants, where they are made into plastics, fabrics, synthetics, medicines, cosmetics, detergents, and thousands of other products.

The petroleum refining industry employs workers in four broad categories: operations, maintenance, engineering, and scientific support. Operations workers run the vast array of machines that refine petroleum, usually from control panels far removed from the actual machinery. *Control-panel operators* operate controls that regulate the temperature, pressure, rate of flow, and tank level in petroleum-refining and petrochemical-processing units. They observe and regulate meters and instruments to process petroleum under specified conditions. *Furnace operators* pump the crude petroleum or refined products through the processing, storage, and shipping departments of refineries. After fractionating, *treaters* and their *helpers* control equipment that removes impurities and improves the quality of gasoline, kerosene, and lubricants, using steam, clay, hydrogen, solvents, and chemicals. *Clay roasters* use a kiln to clean and treat for reuse clay that has been used to treat oil.

Certain refined oils are blended to achieve specific qualities or make specific fuels. *Compounders* and their *helpers* add antioxidants, corrosion inhibitors, detergents, and other additives to enhance lubricating oils for autos, industry, and other uses. *Blenders* blend gasoline with chemicals, lead, or distilled crude oil to make specified commercial fuel. *Grease makers* heat oils with fat, soda, water, dye, and mineral oils to produce various grades of lubricating grease.

In the operation of petrochemical-processing plants, *paraffin-plant operators* operate filter presses to separate oil of paraffin distillate from paraffin wax. *Paraffin-plant-sweater operators* operate sweater tanks (tanks that heat and cool substances) to separate liquid from processed paraffin distillate. *Lead recoverers* at naphtha-treating plants operate centrifuge machines that separate lead compound from naphtha-treating solution. This compound is used to treat gasoline.

Other operations workers include *oil-recovery-unit operators,* who separate recoverable oil from refinery sewage systems, and *refinery laborers,* who prepare work sites, load and unload equipment, dump ingredients for mixing into machines, and perform many other tasks. In addition, the industry employs workers to drive trucks to deliver products to customers and workers to gauge and load these products into the tank trucks.

Maintenance workers make up more than half of all refineries' employees. They keep the machinery running and the workplaces safe. *Fire marshals* at refineries coordinate fire fighters' activities, inspect equipment and workplaces to make sure they meet fire regulations, order fire drills, and direct fire fighting and rescues in the event of a refinery fire. *Mechanical inspectors* inspect tanks, pipes, pipe fittings, stills, towers, and pumps for defects and report need for repairs. They use specialized instruments and formulas to measure thicknesses of walls and pipes and to determine rates of corrosion and decay. *Line walkers* patrol pipelines to look for leaks. *Salvagers* and their *helpers* then fix defective valves and pipe fittings using hand and power tools.

Other maintenance workers include *gas-regulator repairers,* who fix and install equipment that controls the pressure of gases used in petroleum refining. *Meter testers* make sure the meters showing the flow and pressure of gases, steam, and water function correctly. In addition, *electrical repairers* repair and maintain refineries' electrical systems, including motors, transformers, wiring, switches, and alarms.

Other workers, including *tube cleaners*, keep equipment clean so it will perform at required standards. *Tankcar inspectors* examine the wheels, bearings, brakes, and safety equipment of refining tank cars to prevent catastrophic accidents. *Construction and maintenance inspectors* inspect petroleum-dispensing equipment at distributing plants.

Scientists and engineers plan refining plants; devise ways to treat and improve products; and develop, improve, and test refinery processes. Refineries employ *chemical engineering technicians* to help chemical engineers plan, design, and test refining plants. *Drafters* draw plans for layout, operation, and construction of petroleum refining equipment. Others test sample products in laboratories and in engines to make sure they meet company specifications and perform well in engines. These are just a few of the many scientific support workers who help refine petroleum.

Also working in refineries are a variety of managers and supervisors. *Contract managers* negotiate purchase and delivery of crude oil for refining and sale of refineries' products. Title clerks process paperwork to grant oil companies right to lease or purchase land for oil drilling. Bulk plant managers manage storage and distribution facilities for petroleum products. *Dispatchers* regulate the flow of products through refineries' processing, treating, and shipping departments. In addition, all processes at refineries are headed by supervisors, who coordinate workers' activities, plan production schedules, and oversee processes.

Requirements

Petroleum refining operators may need only a high-school diploma. Engineers and scientists need advanced degrees. Maintenance workers may need some special training in repairing certain kinds of equipment.

Production workers learn most of their skills on the job. Courses in physics, chemistry, mathematics, and computer science, however, may help them learn these skills more readily.

Apprenticeships are also available to teach workers specialized maintenance jobs. These programs may take as many as five years to complete.

Research jobs require college work—some may require a master's degree or doctorate. High-school students preparing for such college study should take math, chemistry, science, drafting, English, and biology.

A mechanical inspector of an oil refinery checks the pipe and pipe fittings for defects. Leakage can be a serious fire hazard at a refinery.

Special requirements

Engineers in all industries may undergo certification processes. See the separate article in Volume 2 title "Engineers" for more information on engineering requirements.

Opportunities for experience and exploration

Workers in apprenticeship programs learn about refining through classroom and hands-on training. Others interested in the work may apply for summer jobs in refineries. Because refineries run twenty-four hours a day, late-shift work may also be available to those exploring the industry. Industry unions, to which most refinery workers belong, are also good sources of information about this type of work.

Related occupations

Other processing jobs that might be of interest include industrial chemicals workers, pharmaceutical industry workers, paints and coatings industry workers, and plastics products manufacturing workers.

Methods of entering

Job seekers should go directly to the employment offices of local refineries and fill out applications. Unions and state employment offices may know of openings, as well.

College and university students may interview on campus with companies that have recruitment programs. College placement offices may also list available positions.

Advancement

Advancement in the petroleum refining industry depends on experience, judgment, and type of position. Operators may move to more responsible, higher-paying machine-operating positions, or to supervisory jobs. Engineers may be promoted to department heads, supervising many workers and taking charge of whole refining processes. Workers able to think fast, act effectively in emergencies, and learn new skills when necessary should be in a good position to receive promotions as they become available.

Employment outlook

Demand for petroleum products has been fairly steady, and employment should remain so for the foreseeable future. Thousands of jobs to replace workers who leave the industry are available every year.

Growth for jobs related to exploration of new petroleum sources is declining, however. Domestic companies have cut back on land exploration, and the United States Congress has restricted many locations for off-shore drilling. The restrictions will hold until the year 2000, when the government position will be reevaluated.

Automation and computerization, however, are changing the face of the refinery employment population. Unskilled workers are becoming less important than those with computer, chemistry, engineering, and mechanical backgrounds. While automation is also decreasing the number of workers in plants, jobs should be available for repair personnel, pipefitters, electricians, and machinists.

Earnings

In the early 1990s, refinery workers earned an average of about $27,000 a year, although salary is greatly dependant on job type and experience. Higher salaries are earned by chemists and engineers, who can earn from $30,000 to $60,000 a year, depending on experience. Workers receive premium pay for evening and night shifts. They also usually receive paid vacations and holidays, and pension and health plans.

Conditions of work

Most workers belong to unions. The largest is the Oil, Chemical and Atomic Workers International Union (AFL-CIO). Most refineries are near oil fields, deep-water ports, or major cities. Seventy percent of the nation's 300 refineries are in California, Illinois, Indiana, Louisiana, New Jersey, Pennsylvania, and Texas.

Some operations may be in fairly remote areas. Conditions in locations such as Alaska and the North Sea can be quite rugged during winter months. The most difficult, though, are normally encountered on drilling platforms.

Refinery operators work forty hours a week plus occasional overtime. Because plants operate all the time, operators may work nights, evenings, weekends, or holidays, depending on seniority.

Refinery work may take workers outside to check equipment. Inside workers at control panels work in clean, modern conditions.

Social and psychological factors

Maintenance workers need physical strength, but operators mainly need to be alert and able to make quick decisions. In the laboratory, care and judgment are essential attributes.

For those stationed in small towns or remote locations, boredom may be a problem during nonworking hours.

GOE: 06.01.03; SIC: 291; SOC: 4525

◇ **SOURCES OF ADDITIONAL INFORMATION**

American Association of Petroleum Landmen
4100 Fossil Creek Boulevard
Fort Worth, TX 76137

American Petroleum Institute
1220 L Street, NW
Washington, DC 20037

International Federation of Petroleum and Chemical Workers
PO Box 6565
Denver, CO 80206

National Petroleum Refiners Association
1899 L Street, NW
Suite 1000
Washington, DC 20036

**Oil, Chemical and Atomic Workers
International Union**
PO Box 2812
Denver, CO 80201

Society of Petroleum Engineers of AIME
PO Box 833836
Richardson, TX 75083

◇ **RELATED ARTICLES**

Volume 1: Energy
Volume 2: Engineers; Geologists
Volume 3: Petroleum drilling occupations;
See Processing Occupations
Volume 4: Petroleum technicians

Pharmaceutical industry workers

Definition

Pharmaceutical industry workers perform a variety of duties to invent and manufacture health products and service the field. Employees in research and development may study, invent, or improve remedies or nutritional supplements. Pharmaceutical operators work machines that fill capsules or tubes and form tablets or pills. Operators may also prepare powdered or granulated products as well as inspect quality and weight of goods. Sales representatives sell remedies and/or distribute products for usage on a trial basis or to introduce new items to pharmacists, retail stores, or medical practitioners.

History

Our earliest remedies for injury and sickness came from the earth in the form of herbs and tree leaves, barks and roots. The process to heal an injury may have been by trial and error, or have resulted from a sequence of planned treatments to relieve pain or discomfort. And while medical research has invented numerous cures for ailments and diseases, sometimes the ingredients found in these treatments still come from simple, natural sources. Burns are treated with lotion derived from aloe plants, and sometimes cough remedies contain eucalyptus essences.

Today, however, scientists do not limit themselves to any one form of remedy. Chemical compounds and mixtures are made into some remarkable drugs. The discovery of penicillin, morphine, and vaccines have cured sickness, disease and helped people live longer and in better health. The pharmaceutical industry is

one that actively works to improve the quality of our health, and subsequently, our lives.

Nature of the work

The pharmaceutical, or drug, industry has many branches that in composition serve the nation by providing remedies and pain relievers, nutritional supplements, and electronic and diagnostic equipment. The branch for research and development concentrates on improving existing products, running tests and experiments to invent new ones, as well as evaluating products from other markets and countries. Pharmacists, research assistants, and laboratory assistants comprise the research and development branch. To varying degrees their work is experimental and reflects the process of discovery. These workers may run laboratory tests, record data, and write lab reports and take care of lab equipment. Pharmacists may direct projects and duties to research assistants, who are then aided by the laboratory assistants.

The products that the research and development branch produces are manufactured by pharmaceutical operators. Many of these employees work on production lines tending equipment that measures, weighs, mixes, or granulates ingredients that forms, fills, coats, or compresses pills and capsules. Often these employees inspect the goods, looking for broken tablets, or unfilled capsules. Specific positions that help comprise this area of the industry include *capsule filling machine operator, ampule fillers and examiners*, and *fermenter and granulator machine operators*. Capsule machine tenders put medicine into a filling hopper and empty capsules into a loading hopper. The machine then

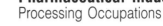

Due to sanitation requirements, pharmaceutical industry workers must keep minimal parts of their body exposed.

fills the capsules with that specific medicine. This process may be used for certain antihistamines, vitamins, or general pain relievers.

Ampule fillers and examiners work with glass tubes that are filled with medicine and then sealed. The process for filling is quite similar to that of the capsule filler. The operator, however, must adjust the gas flames to the appropriate temperature so that the tubes are completely sealed. Inspection of the product also takes place upon completion of this process. Once filled, the examiners check for cracks, leaks, or other damages with magnifying glasses or hold the tube next to a clear light for a closer look.

Operators for the granulator use machines that are equipped with fine blades that mix ingredients and then crush or mill them into powdered form so that they may ultimately be formed into pills. In addition to the actual medical ingredients, gelatins or starch pastes may be added to help the pill keep its form. Again, inspection and evaluation is made to check for appropriate hardness, size, weight, and dryness.

The third branch of this industry is comprised of administration and labor positions. Production managers may direct workers in the manufacturing field by scheduling projects, deadlines, and time necessary for completion. These employees may oversee the factories and enforce safety and health regulations, monitor efficiency, and make work assignments. They may also direct and schedule the shipping department that packs and loads the products for distribution.

Service representatives supply hospitals, independent medical practitioners, pharmacists, and retail stores with products, remedies, and equipment. Sales reps may sometimes be pharmacists as well as trained sales agents.

Telephone calls and office visits allow the representatives to keep in good contact with buyers, monitor supplies, and needs, as well as introduce new products for a trial basis. Often, reps supplement any free samples of new products with printed literature, when available. Sales reps may promote vitamins and other nutritional supplements, pain relievers, treatments for burns or insect bites, and general health care supplies.

The pharmaceutical industry has two distinct environments of activity: the laboratory and the business world. This field has many possibilities for employment for it is a crucial profession that people and medical practitioners have come to count on to provide remedies and educated guidance.

Requirements

Workers in the pharmaceutical industry must be alert, pay attention to detail, have precise and consistent work habits, and understand the scope and purpose of the field they are in, regardless of their specific position. Some positions may require more developed dexterity, while others may need problem-solving and planning skills.

Special requirements

Most positions in this industry require some training and education. It is also likely for certain labor positions to command a higher wage if the employee has some strong high-school training or education in their background. Some pharmaceutical companies offer on-the-job training to nonprofessional workers. Employees in sales may be required to have sufficient training or background in pharmacology, while certain areas of administration may prefer course work in liberal arts, data processing, or business and marketing.

College training may consist of pre-pharmacy training, with such courses as mathematics, English, various areas of the sciences—chemistry, biology and physics—as well as business and communications studies. Completion of a four-year bachelor's degree in biology, chemistry, or pharmacy is often a prerequisite for some positions in this field. The American Council on Pharmaceutical Education lists accredited pharmacy programs that take five years of post-high-school education.

Master's degrees and doctorates are often required for positions in the branch of research and development. Areas of study may include pharmacology, microbiology, or chemistry.

Opportunities for experience and exploration

Classes in physics, chemistry, biology, and other related course work is a reasonable way to explore the level of interest in science, as well as pharmacology. Students may write to colleges for information on science majors, schools that have professional or prepharmacology programs, as well as hospitals and pharmaceutical companies for information on job opportunities. Science-related clubs and social organizations often hold meetings or lectures from professionals in various fields and offer career guidance as well.

Related occupations

Other processing occupations similar to pharmaceutical industry workers include industrial chemical workers, paint and coatings industry workers, petroleum refining workers, and plastics products manufacturing workers.

Methods of entering

College trained applicants may send resumes and cover letters to pharmaceutical companies listed in their area Yellow Pages, or through school contacts with professional organizations or placement and employment services of their universities.

Newspapers and professional publications list job opportunities of many kinds and many levels. Nonprofessional workers might check newspapers or contact firms in the telephone book requesting a job application.

Advancement

There are many outlets for advancement in the field of the pharmaceutical industry. Laboratory assistant and research assistants may prepare for advancement with additional education and be promoted to new research projects or duties. Production workers may advance to managerial positions or learn how to operate more sophisticated machinery. Administrators

may become supervisors, executives, sales representatives, or marketing executives. There are many possibilities for advancement in the industry for employees who are willing to develop new skills and take on more responsibilities; some positions, however, require additional, formal training, as well as job development.

Employment outlook

Many pharmaceutical manufacturing companies are investigating growth in related areas, such as cosmetics, and this growth may require more employees to run machines and mix chemicals, as well as train sales and marketing personnel to educate buyers on these new products. Researchers may test and evaluate new products and be in need of assistance to handle these new departments.

Earnings

Production employees may work eight hours per shift; at some pharmaceutical firms, however, those shifts may run around the clock. Most other employees work days, their shifts lasting from eight to ten hours.

Production workers average almost $12 per hour, though the salary range for these employees is broad, having to do with the size of the firm, shift worked, years at the company, and the geographical location of the plant. Overtime compensation however is time and a half or double time.

Professional employees are paid on salary. An entry level position may pay as much as $18,000 per year. Workers who mix the medicines and chemicals may earn over $32,000 annually, and scientists and administrators can earn more than $58,000. Work schedules for these employees do not always adhere to strict eight hour schedules. Scientists may work weekends or put in very long days if they are conducting a specific test or experiment. Administrators often bring work home with them or have late meetings with staff.

Conditions of work

Administrators work in office environments that are often modern, neat, and have good lighting and ample work spaces. Scientists perform most of their duties in their laboratories, which are clean and organized and modernly equipped.

Production workers and laborers often work in the factories which are well ventilated and offer good lighting, but may be noisy and crowded. Workers may have to package products and load them onto trucks or docks by hand or with forklifts. Safety equipment may be required for some tasks.

Social and psychological factors

Professional positions in the pharmaceutical industry require concentration, motivation, and problem solving skills. Researchers may work long hours and perform exacting experiments. These positions can be challenging as well as rewarding.

Machine operators must be precise, know how to follow very specific instructions, and be perceptive. Their hours are more set, and the range of their duties may be fixed; however, there is not much diversity and the sameness of the work could become taxing.

GOE: 06.02.11; SIC: 283; SOC: 694

◇ SOURCES OF ADDITIONAL INFORMATION

American Council on Pharmaceutical Education
311 West Superior Street
Chicago, IL 60610

Pharmaceutical Manufacturers Association
110 15th Street, NW
Washington, DC 20005

◇ RELATED ARTICLES

Volume 1: Chemicals and Drugs
Volume 2: Pharmacists; Pharmacologists; Toxicologists
Volume 3: See Processing Occupations
Volume 4: Pharmacy technicians

Plastics products manufacturing workers

Definition

Plastics products manufacturing workers mold, cast, and assemble products made of plastics materials. The objects they make are almost without number. They include dishes, signs, toys, insulation, appliance parts, automobile parts, combs, gears bearings, and many, many others.

History

Thermoplastics, plastics that soften with heat and harden when cooled, were discovered in France in 1828. Forty years later, in the United States, John and Isaiah Hyatt first made cellulose nitrate. Not until 1909, however, was the first synthetic plastic produced by L.H. Baekeland.

Since then, plastics have revolutionized the world. They are used in countless products, and research constantly finds more uses for them.

Nature of the work

Plastics are usually made by a process called "polymerization," in which many molecules of the same kind are combined to make networks of giant particles. All plastics can be formed or shaped; some become pliable under heat, some at elevated room temperatures. When treated, some plastics become hard, some incredibly strong, some soft like putty.

Plastic objects are formed using several different methods. In compression molding, plastics compounds are compressed and treated inside a mold to form them. In injection molding, liquid plastic is injected into a mold and hardened. Blow molding is like glass blowing—air is forced into plastic to make it expand to the inner surface of a mold. In extrusion, hot plastic is continuously forced through a die to make products like tubing. Laminated items are made of resin-soaked sheets fused together, while the calendar process forms sheets by forcing hot plastics between rollers. Finally, in fabrication, workers make items out of solid plastic pieces by heating, sawing, and drilling.

While plastics compounds may be mixed in plastics materials plants, plastics fabricators may employ *blenders* or *color mixers* and their *helpers* to measure, heat, and mix materials to produce or color plastic materials. *Grinding-machine operators* run machines that grind particles of plastics into smaller pieces for processing. *Pilling-machine operators* take plastics powder and compress it into pellets or biscuits for further processing. Other workers are responsible for making the molds (*plaster form makers*) and patterns (*plastics pattern makers*) that are used to determine the shape of the finished plastics items. *Foam-machine operators* spray thermoplastic resins into conveyor belts to form plastic foam.

Many plastics products plants make good according to clients specifications. When this is the case, *job setters*, using their knowledge of plastics and their properties, adjust molding machines to clients' instructions. For example, they change the die through which the plastic flows, adjust the speed of the flow, and replace worn cutting tools when necessary. Then the machine is ready to accept the plastic and produce the object.

Injection molders run machines that liquify plastic powders or pellets, inject liquid plastic into a mold, and eject a molded product. Phonograph records, typewriter keys, and many other common products are made by injection molding. Injection workers set and observe gauges to determine the temperature of the plastic and examine ejected objects for defects.

Many objects are made from a compound called "polystyrene," which when molded using heat and pressure makes cast foam products such as balls, coolers, and packing nests. *Polystyrene-bead molders* operate machines that expand these beads and mold them into sheets of bead board. *Polystyrene-molding-machine tenders* run machines that mold pre-expanded beads into objects. At the end of the molding cycle, they lift the cast objects from the molds and press a button to start the machine again.

Extruder operators and their *helpers* set up and run machines that extrude thermoplastics to form tubes, rods, and film. They adjust the dies and machine screws through which the hot plastic is drawn, adjust the machine's cooling system, weigh and mix plastics materials, empty them into the machine, set the temperature and speed of the machine, and start it.

Blow-molding-machine operators run machines that mold objects such as bleach bottles and milk bottles by puffing air into plastic to expand it. *Compression-molding-machine operators* and *tenders* run machines that mold thermosetting plastics into hard plastic objects. *Casters* make similar molded products by hand. *Strippers* remove molded items from molds and clean the molds. Some molded products must be vacuum cured. *Baggers* run machines that perform this task.

Plastic sheeting is formed by *calendar operators*, who adjust the temperature, speed, and roller position of machines that draw plastic between rollers to produce sheets of specified thickness. *Stretch-machine operators* stretch plastic sheets to specified dimensions. *Preforms laminators* press fiberglass and resin-coated fabrics over plaster, steel, or wooden forms to make plastic parts for boats, cars, and airplanes.

Other common plastic products are fiberglass poles and dowels. *Fiberglass-dowel-drawing-machine operators* mount dies on machines, mix and pour plastics compounds, draw fiberglass through the die, and soak, cool, cure, and cut dowels. *Fiberglass tube molders* make tubing used in fishing rods and golf club shafts.

Plastics that are not molded may be cut into shapes. *Shaping-machine operators* cut spheres, cones, blocks, and other shapes from plastic foam blocks. *Pad cutters* slice foam rubber blocks to specified thicknesses for such objects as seat cushions and ironing board pads.

Many products undergo further processing to finish them. *Foam-gun operators* reinforce and insulate plastic products such as bathtubs and auto body parts by spraying them with plastic foam. *Plaster-sheet cutters* use power shears to cut sheets, following patterns glued to sheets by *pattern hands*. *Sawyers* cut rods, tubes, and sheets to specified dimensions. *Trimmers* trim plastic parts to size using a template and power saw. *Machine finishers* smooth and polish the surface of plastic sheets. And *plastics heat welders* use hot-air guns to fuse together plastic sheets.

Hand finishers trim and smooth products using hand tools and sandpaper. *Buffers* remove ridges and rough edges form fiberglass or plastic castings. *Sponge buffers* machine-buff the edges of plastic sponges to round them, and

A worker at a plastics factory installs a pressure gauge onto a vat of materials that are used in the production process.

pointing-machine operators round the points on the teeth of plastic combs. And *edge grinders* tend machines that square and smooth edges of plastic floor tile.

Some *plastics workers (assemblers)* and *laminated plastics assemblers-and-gluers* assemble pieces to form certain products. These may include skylights (*skylight assemblers*) and wet suits (*wet suit gluers*). Other workers are *lacquerers, embossers, printers, carvers,* or *design inserters. Inspectors* inspect and test finished products for strength, size, uniformity, and conformity to specifications.

Experienced workers supervise plastics-making departments, and the industry also employs unskilled workers such as *laborers* to help haul, clean, and assemble plastics materials, equipment, and products.

Requirements

Plastics industry workers must have a high-school diploma to enter the field. They learn most of their skills on the job. In extrusion plants, trainees can become Class I extruders after about three months.

Applicants with some knowledge of chemistry, mathematics, physics, drafting, industrial technology, or computer science have a better chance of being hired. Some colleges offer associate or bachelor's degrees in plastics technology. Job seekers with these degrees have a definite competitive edge and may also advance more quickly.

Plastics workers all need the ability to work well with tools. They need mechanical aptitude and manual dexterity. Lifting equipment and materials takes some strength, and workers who operate machines must stand much of the time.

Special requirements

There are no special requirements for this type of work.

Opportunities for experience and exploration

College students in plastics technology courses will have the opportunity to get hands-on experience in plastics making. For others, apprenticeships provide experience and a chance to explore the field. Apprenticeships in tool and die making for plastics last 4 or 5 years and teach skills through classroom instruction and on-the-job training. A high-school education is normally a prerequisite for an apprenticeship.

Related occupations

Other associated occupations include industrial chemicals workers, rubber goods production workers, molders, coremakers, and petroleum refining workers.

Methods of entering

Job seekers should apply directly to the personnel departments of plastics plants in the area in which they wish to work. Newspaper want ads may list openings in the industry, and state employment agencies may also provide leads.

Advancement

In the plastics industry, advancement comes with experience, skill, and education. Because plants like to teach workers their own methods, and because skilled plastics workers are scarce, most plastics companies promote workers from within to fill more responsible and higher paying jobs.

Workers who pursue bachelor's or associate's degrees in plastics technology have the best chances for advancement. In time, they may move into supervisory or management positions.

Apprenticeships as tool-and-die makers may also lead to more highly paid production work.

Earnings

Wages for plastics workers vary with the type of process used, the plant's geographic location, and the size of the company. New workers may receive minimum wage in extrusion plants, while more experienced workers and supervisors can earn more than three times that. In the early 1990s, extrusion plant supervisors earned as much as $31,000 a year.

Fabrication plant workers earned somewhat less than injection workers. The annual earnings for fabricators ranged from $12,700 to $16,600. Fabrication supervisors received about $21,000 a year.

Wages in injection molding plants are highly dependent on the type of job performed. While mold designers earned $41,600 to $52,000 a year, supervisors earned about $11,440. While toolmakers and mold makers earned about $29,000 and $31,200 respectively, operators earned about $9,260 a year. New injection workers are usually paid minimum wage plus ten percent. Production workers also usually receive time and half for overtime.

Most plastics workers receive paid holidays, sick leave, and vacations, and health and life insurance. They may also be able to participate in profit-sharing plans.

Conditions of work

Plastics industry workers work forty hours per week. Because plants operate on three shifts, beginning workers may work nights and move to day shifts as they gain experience and authority.

Plastics plants are generally safe, well lighted, well ventilated, and modern. Workers must observe safety precautions when working around hot machines and plastics, sharp machine parts, and electrical wiring, and when sawing, cutting, or drilling plastic parts.

Plastics work, however, is not usually strenuous. Workers use machines to lift heavy dies and other equipment.

Social and psychological factors

As with most production work, jobs in the plastics industry often demand a fair amount of repetition. Workers who need great variety may not enjoy production work. Plastics plants tend to be smaller than many other types of factories so a sense of teamwork often develops among the small-sized staff. Such camaraderie can lead to increased job satisfaction and enjoyment.

GOE: 06.04.13; SIC: 282; SOC: 71

◇ SOURCES OF ADDITIONAL INFORMATION

Plastics Institute of America
Stevens Institute of Technology
Castle Point State
Hoboken, NJ 07030

Society of the Plastics Industry
1274 K Street, NW, Suite 400
Washington, DC 20005

United Rubber, Cork, Linoleum, and Plastic Workers of America
887 South High Street
Akron, OH 44308

◇ RELATED ARTICLES

Volume 1: Plastics
Volume 3: See Processing occupations
Volume 4: Plastics technicians

Rubber goods production workers

Definition

Workers in the rubber goods industry make products from natural and synthetic rubber materials. They soften, mold, form, cure, and otherwise treat rubber to make thousands of different products.

History

Natural rubber is a pliable, stretchy material made from the milky juice of various tropical plants. It is called "rubber" because it is used to make erasers—at one time called "rubbers" because they rubbed out mistakes.

Until World War I, most rubber used in U.S. products was imported from South America. From then until World War II, most rubber came from Southeast Asia. When this supply was cut off by war, scientists developed a synthetic material that could be used in rubber's place. Today, both natural and synthetic rubber are found in countless objects, from shoes to conveyor belts, baby bottles to mammoth storage containers, rubber balls to gaskets on spacecraft. About 60 percent of the rubber used in the United States is made into tires for automobiles, trucks, and other vehicles.

Nature of the work

Rubber goods are formed from natural or synthetic rubber materials. Different products go through different processes, but generally all rubber is heated, shaped, and finished. Most of this work is done by machine.

The first step in rubber goods production is breaking up and mixing the crude rubber. *Rubber cutters* cut bales of crude rubber into pieces, moving levers on a large hydraulic cutter. *Rubber-mill tenders* mix, blend, knead, or refine crude rubber by running it through a mill with corrugated rolls that break it apart and soften it. Plasticator machines also grind and soften rubber. Rubber is then mixed with chemicals to keep it from spoiling in light, heat, or air. *Production weighers* use balances or floor scales to weigh the correct amount of chemicals for mixing. *Formula weighers* operate tram cars on monorails beneath storage bins to collect and weigh ingredients. Rubber is mixed with zinc oxide, sulphur, acid, or fillers in mixing machines called banbury mixers. Chemists and others decide which chemicals to use, and test samples of the mix before processing. *Foam rubber mixers, frothing-machine mixers,* and *cement mixers* tend special machines that mix materials into foam rubber and rubber cement.

Mixed and heated rubber is then shaped in one of several ways. It may be rolled into sheets, molded in shapes, or extruded into tubing or other forms. *Calendar operators* run machines that pull rubber sheets of specified thickness. *Sponge-press operators* run machines that roll and cure sponge rubber into sheeting for gaskets, insulation, and carpet padding. *Dusting-and-brushing-machines operators* then dust the sheets with talc to keep them from sticking together before further processing. Other workers build up rubber layers using thin piles of sheet rubber to make machine cores (*rail builders*), airplane fuel tanks (*self-sealing-fuel-tanks builders*), rubber belts (*belt builders; sectional-belt-mold assemblers; v-belt builders; belt-builder helpers*), expansion joints (*expansion-joint builders*), and other products.

Some rubber is formed by molding. *Pourers* fill curing molds with latex using a hose or a machine lever on a conveyor-belt machine. Some rubber products are formed by injection, in which a machine operated by an *injection-molding-machine tender* injects hot rubber into a mold and ejects a molded product. Products such as balloons and rubber gloves are formed by *dippers*, who dip molds into liquid rubber to coat them. Most other molded rubber products, including tires, are pressed and heated in molds. *Foam-rubber molders* make foam cushions this way. *Press tenders* make hard objects such as golf and bowling balls. *Arch-cushion press operators* heat-press sponge rubber into arch cushions for rubber shoes and boots, and *thermal molders* mold rubber floor mats. Other molding is done by spraying. *Foam dispensers* spray liquid foam rubber into molds to make padded dashboards and car-door panels. *Skin formers* form plastic sheeting into skins for these products. *Strippers* remove molded items from molds and prepare molds for further use. *Mold cleaners* clean, store, and distribute these molds.

The final method of forming rubber is called extrusion. In this method, liquid rubber is drawn through dies to form continuous shaped rubber products such as tubes and strips. *Tuber-machine operators* and their *helpers* set up and run extrusion machines. They select the proper die and install it on the machine, feed rubber stock into the machine, and set the speed at which the rubber is to be drawn through the die. *Extruder tenders* regulate and run machines that extrude rubber into strands for elastic yarn. In shoe and boot making, *wink-cutter operators* extrude and cut rubber strips for rubber soles.

Much rubber is used to back fabric for rugs and other goods. *Four-roll calendar operators* use calendar machines to coat fabric with rubber. *Calendar-let-off operators* run machines to cure and dry coated fabrics. *Calendar-wind-up tenders* accumulate the coated fabric into rolls of specified size. Other workers (*roofing-machine operators; calendar feeders; calendar-let-off helpers; calendar operator helpers; calendar-wind-up helpers*) help calendar workers in these tasks. Finally, *fabric normalizers* shrink rubberized fabric to increase its strength.

Although much rubber is cured while forming, curing is sometimes done in a separate step. In curing, rubber is subjected to heat and pressure to increase its hardness, durability, stability, and elasticity. One curing process is called vulcanization. Foam-rubber sheeting is formed by *foam-rubber curers* who roll a latex mixture into curing ovens. Rubber belts are cured in presses (*belt-press operators I; v-belt curers; belt-press operators II; automatic vulcanizing load operators*). Weatherstripping is also made by vulcanizing sponge-rubber beading (*weather-strip operators*).

Rubber sheets, strips, and tubing must then be cut into specified lengths and shapes to form products of specified types and sizes. *Rubber-goods cutter-finishers* and *machine cutters* use machines to cut rubber; they then verify the sizes of goods, using rulers, calipers, gauges, and templates. *Tube-machine cutters* cut extruded rubber into lengths. *Die cutters* stamp out rubber shapes using machines with sharp dies. *Roll cutters* use a lathe to cut rolls of rubber or rubberized fabric. *Rubber-cutting-machine tenders* use a guillotine to cut rubber slabs. *Molded-rubber-goods cutters* use dies to trim molded articles. Other workers are more specialized. *Strap-cutting-machine operators* cut straps; *band cutters* and *band-machine operators* make rubber bands; *hose cutters* cut tubing into hose lengths by machine or by hand.

Mat punchers punch automobile floor mats from sheeting, and other workers cut rubber into footwear parts. *Splitting-machine-operators* cut scrap tires or rubber sheets into pieces for reclamation.

Rubber items made of a single piece of rubber are then finished to form products or ready them for assembly. They may be buffed to smooth and polish them (*buffers*) or coated with

A rubber goods worker installs some rubber tubing to an engine. The pliability of rubber allows for a more compact design to structures such as engines.

vinyl (*dippers*). Workers called *openers* pull weather stripping through a machine to force apart sides stuck together during curing. *Machine skivers* bevel edges of shoe parts to prepare them for cementing or stitching. Other workers cover with fabric (*v-belt coverers*); notch, measure, and brand (*v-belt finishers*); and cut and shape the edges (*v-belt skivers*) of belts. *Padded-products finishers* repair defects in padded automobile parts by injecting wrinkles and gaps with liquid rubber foam.

Tubing can be spliced (*rubber-tubing splicers*) for use as sealant, or cut and sealed for use in catheters (*catheter builders*). Buckle straps may be coated and wound (*buckle-strap-drum operators*) or folded (*strap-folding-machine operators*) according to specifications. Some workers roll rings on the mouths of balloons (*ring-rolling-machine operators*); some form tubes by cementing rubber sheets into cylindrical shapes (*tube-building-machine operators*); and some (*tumbler-machine operators*) operate tumblers that smooth molded objects by breaking off flash—rough edges caused by rubber seeping into the joins of the mold. Other workers finish combs (*pointing-machine operators*) or press watertight seams on shoes (*pressers*). *Crimpers* fold and press edges of articles to reinforce them, and

Rubber goods production workers
Processing Occupations

braiding-machine tenders and *wire-winding-machine tenders* cement cord or wire around hoses for reinforcement.

Rubber goods made from several pieces must be assembled. Workers position and cement or stitch pieces to make inflatable buildings (*laminators; stripers and tapers*), footwear (*fitter-placers; wader-boot-top assemblers; hand boot makers*, shock absorbers for airplane gas tanks (*airplane-gas-tank-liner assemblers*), hoses (*dual-hose cementers; hose coupling joiners; hose makers*), pneumatic airplane deicers (*tube-and-manifold builders*) inflatable animals and figures for parades (*balloon makers*), and many other types of rubber goods (*rubber-goods assemblers*).

Some rubber goods are decorated. Balloons are dipped into dye and soap to color and polish them (*balloon dippers*) and sometimes printed with designs or lettering (*balloon design printers*). *Branding-machine tenders* print brand names on rubber hoses. *Rubber-printing-machine operators* print decorative designs on rubber sheets that will be made into footwear.

Workers also inspect finished goods to make sure they meet standards and often repair defects (*self-sealing-fuel-tank repairers; rubber-goods inspector-testers; hose inspectors and patchers; rubber testers*). Workers called *classifiers* examine rejected footwear to determine whether it can be sold as seconds or whether it must be cut up into scrap.

Different rubber processes are managed by various *supervisors*, and the rubber goods industry also employs a variety of miscellaneous workers, including *general laborers*, repairers (*braider setters; mat repairers; shoe sticks repairers*), and workers that grind scrap rubber for reuse (*pulverizer-moll operators; grinders.*).

Requirements

Because most rubber goods production workers learn their skills on the job, a high-school diploma is often the only necessary qualification. Apprenticeship programs and special training are offered to some workers to help them develop specialized skills.

Workers need college degrees, however, if they plan to pursue chemistry, engineering, or research jobs in the rubber goods industry.

Production workers must be in good enough health to stand much of the day and must have some aptitude for working with machines and other tools. Those who work as inspectors must have good eyesight and be able to make quick decisions.

Special requirements

There are no special requirements for this type of work.

Opportunities for experience and exploration

Students in college programs may be able to obtain summer jobs in rubber goods plants. This way they can decide whether they like the work and obtain experience that may help them gain full-time employment when they graduate. Other job seekers may also be able to obtain temporary work, or may enroll in apprenticeship programs that can teach them specialized production skills. Also, local rubber goods plants may allow groups to tour their facilities.

Related occupations

Other occupations that are similar in nature and skills to rubber goods production workers include plastics products manufacturing workers, industrial chemicals workers, and pharmaceutical workers.

Methods of entering

Direct application to the personnel offices at rubber goods plants is the best way to look for work in this industry. The United Rubber Workers of America union and state employment agencies may also know of openings.

Advancement

Most beginning workers enter the industry with little or no skill. They learn rubber goods production by doing it. As they learn, they can advance to more highly paid, more skilled, more responsible positions. Workers in skilled positions usually have several years' experience.

Because skills may also be learned in technical schools or colleges, education also helps workers advance.

Some rubber goods workers eventually enter the tire-retreading industry as machine tenders, managers, or technicians.

460

Employment outlook

While demand for rubber is expected to grow, production jobs will increase more slowly, largely because of automation and advances in technology that make rubber goods last longer. Rubber goods production is also highly dependent on the fortunes of the auto industry. The first half of the 1980s saw a great slump in auto sales, and some tire-making plants were forced to close.

As synthetic rubber is developed further, the uses for rubber will continue to expand. The reliance of rubber sales on the sales of the automotive industry will begin to decline proportionally to the expansion elsewhere. The production of specialized rubber materials will also shift the industry away from the mass production of general purpose rubber.

Workers in plants that make other rubber goods, however, are less likely to fall victim to automation. In addition, modern building construction has created new demands for rubber noise-control pads, rubber-like paints, and waterproofings. The industry will need workers to produce these goods. And if the auto industry resurges, the outlook for rubber goods workers may improve.

Earnings

Although rubber goods production salaries vary with the worker's skill level, experience, and seniority, they are generally very good for production work. In the early 1990s workers made about $24,000 a year. In other plants, workers made about $13,800 a year. Night shift workers are paid more.

Rubber goods workers generally receive paid vacations, holidays, sick leave, life and health insurance, and pension plans.

Conditions of work

The rubber goods industry has one of the best safety ratings in the production field. Protective parts on machinery and walkways prevent accidents, and special ventilation systems take heat, fumes, and dust out of the plant. Most plants have adequate lighting and heating and cooling systems.

Most of the 500 rubber goods plants in the United States are located in Ohio, although new plants are springing up in the South. Most workers at these plants work around forty hours per week. Many belong to unions.

Social and psychological factors

Like most production work, rubber goods jobs often involve repetitive tasks. Workers who do not mind repetitive activities may enjoy rubber goods work. Working with hot presses, sharp tools, and heavy machinery takes steady nerves and mechanical aptitude. In small plants, a sense of teamwork can greatly contribute to job satisfaction.

GOE: 06.04.28; SIC: 30; SOC: 76

◇ SOURCES OF ADDITIONAL INFORMATION

International Institute of Synthetic Rubber Producers
2077 South Gessner Road
Suite 133
Houston, TX 77063

Rubber Manufacturers Association
1400 K Street, NW
Washington, DC 20005

United Rubber, Cork, Linoleum, and Plastic Workers of America
87 South High Street
Akron, OH 44308

◇ RELATED ARTICLES

Volume 1: Rubber
Volume 3: See Processing Occupations

Tobacco products industry workers

Definition

Tobacco industry workers manufacture cigars, cigarettes, chewing tobacco, smoking tobacco, and snuff from leaf tobacco. They dry, cure, age, cut, roll, form, and package tobacco to make products used by millions of Americans.

History

The word tobacco is probably derived from the word "taino," a roll of tobacco leaves the Indians of the West Indies smoked at the time Columbus discovered the New World. Explorers of North and South America found natives cultivating this indigenous plant, which when smoked or chewed acted as a mild stimulant. In America's early days tobacco became a large and economically important industry. Today, tobacco production employs a huge number of workers in the country's southern states and automation has made many processes easier and faster. About 85 percent of the tobacco grown in America goes into cigarettes, and the entire tobacco growing, producing, shipping, warehousing, and sales industry makes many billions of dollars each year.

Nature of the work

Tobacco production begins with harvesting the tobacco and ends with packaging products for consumers to use. Harvested tobacco is first cured. Bright tobacco, grown in the Southeast, is flue-cured—dried in an enclosed space by heating it. Burly tobacco, grown in the South Central region, is air cured.

Cured tobacco is then purchased by tobacco production manufacturers. The first step in manufacturing is separating the tobacco leaf from stems and foreign matter. A variety of workers are employed in threshing and stemming tobacco leaves before further processing. Some workers feed tobacco into machines to perform this task; others separate elements by hand. After this process is complete, the tobacco must be dried again. *Redrying-machine operators* perform this task, using machines with hot air and fans.

After redrying, the tobacco is ready to be aged. Various workers add moisture to the dry tobacco to ready it for packing. They sprinkle or immerse tobacco leaves, using water. The tobacco is then prized, or packed, into hogsheads (barrels). Hogsheads can hold about 1,000 pounds of tobacco. Various workers, including *bulkers, prizers,* and others pack these containers, which then go to warehouses for aging. *Hydraulic-press operators* pack hogsheads using scales, electric hoists, and hydraulic presses.

The aging process takes about two years, during which the tobacco acquires its aroma and flavor. Workers then take the tobacco to factories, where others remove it from the hogsheads.

The tobacco is then conditioned by again adding moisture and blended by *blenders,* who select various grades and kinds of tobacco to produce a blend with specific characteristics. *Blending laborers* replenish supplies of these different tobaccos on the blending line. Some blending workers blend tobacco for specific products, including cigars and snuff. *Blending-line attendants* tend the conveyors and machines that produce the specified blends.

Some tobacco is also flavored using what is called "casing fluid." *Casing-material weighers, casing-machine operators, wringer operators, casing cookers,* and *casing-fluid tenders* all participate in this flavoring process by preparing the casing material, saturating the tobacco with it, and removing excess fluid before further processing.

Flavored tobacco is then ready to be cut. Filler tobacco is shredded and cleaned in shredding machines, operated by *filler-shredder feeders, machine-filler shredders,* and their *helpers. Snuff grinders and screeners* tend machines that pulverize chopped tobacco into snuff and sift it through screens to remove oversized particles. *Riddler operators* tend screening devices to separate coarse pieces of tobacco from cut tobacco.

Cut tobacco is then ready to be made into tobacco products. Cigarettes are made by machines that wrap shredded tobacco and filter with papers. Various workers feed these machines, make the filters, and run the machines, which also print the company's name and insignia on the rolling papers.

Cigar making is similar, except the filler tobacco is wrapped in a tobacco leaf instead of paper. Various workers are responsible for sorting and counting appropriate wrapper leaves for cigars. Binder leaves are also cut to hold tobacco together before wrapping. Then filler tobacco and binder leaves are rolled into bunches by hand or by machine. Bunches are pressed into cigar-shaped molds, and *bunch trimmers* trim excess tobacco from the molds before the bunches are wrapped. Machine-made cigars are the products of workers who feed filler tobacco into a machine, and *auto rollers* and *wrapper layers,* who wrap bunches with sheet tobacco or wrapper leaves. Other workers perform the tasks of wrapping bunches by hand. *Cigar-head piercers* then use machines to pierce draft holes in the cigar ends. Some cigars are pressed into a square shape by *tray fillers* and *press-machine feeders* before they are packaged in cigar bands and cellophane. *Patch workers* repair defective or damaged cigars by patching holes with out pieces of wrapper leaf.

Some tobacco is formed into other products, such as plugs, lumps, and twists. These products are chewed instead of smoked. Twists and some plugs are made by hand, while most plugs and lumps are made by machine. These machines slice, mold, press, and wrap these items, and workers are responsible for feeding, regulating, and cleaning the machines.

Many workers are employed in packaging the manufactured tobacco products. *Cigar packers, hand banders,* and *machine banders and cellophaners* package cigars. *Cigar banders* stamp trademarks on cigar wrappers. *Cigarette-packing-machine operators* then pack the packs into cartons. *Case packers and sealers* pack the cartons into cases and seal them. *Packers* pack other tobacco products into cartons or packs. Other workers pack snuff, chewing tobacco, and other products into tins and other packages. *Snuff-box finishers* glue covers and labels on boxes of snuff.

Product inspectors examine packages; weigh and remove waste from products; make sure tobacco used is the correct grade and quality; and inspect cigars, cigarettes, and cigarette filters for quality. The industry also employs a variety of workers to maintain equipment; load, unload, and distribute materials; separate, arrange, and prepare loads of tobacco for different processing stages; salvage defective items for reclamation; and maintain records of tobacco bought and sold.

Requirements

Most tobacco production workers can obtain jobs with an eighth-grade education or a couple of years of high school. They learn their skills on the job.

Maintenance and mechanical workers may need high-school diplomas and machine maintenance experience or skills. These workers may also learn on the job, however. Mechanical

Workers at a tobacco factory separate a load of tobacco leaves from stems and other foreign matter that may have been mistakenly harvested.

aptitude and good eyesight are essential for both production and maintenance jobs.

Special requirements

There are no special requirements for this type of work.

Opportunities for experience and exploration

Part-time and seasonal tobacco production work may be available for persons interested in exploring the field. If not, local plants may agree to provide opportunities for students to tour the plant and speak with employees about their work. The Bakery, Confectionery and Tobacco Workers' International Union, to which most tobacco production workers belong, is also a good source of information for persons interested in learning more about tobacco production positions.

Related occupations

Other occupations that have similar aptitudes and skills include canning and preserving industry workers, leather tanning and finishing workers, and meat packing production workers.

Methods of entering

The best, and often only, way to obtain a tobacco production job is to apply directly to local tobacco products plants. State employment offices and union locals may also provide leads on available positions. Newspapers sometimes also advertise openings.

Advancement

In the tobacco products industry, advancement comes with increased skills. Machine operators may advance to more complex machinery or to supervisory positions. Ambitious workers may learn to become tobacco buyers or graders.

Employment outlook

Employment in the tobacco industry has rapidly decreased in the past twenty years. In the early 1990s fewer than 50,000 workers were employed. This decline was mainly a result of automation, but may worsen if Americans continue to change their smoking habits. Sales will continue to decrease if Americans further cut down on or give up smoking. Machine-tending mechanics, and supervisory jobs will continue to be available, however, and a certain number of workers each year will be needed to replace those who die, retire, or leave the industry.

Earnings

Unions have kept tobacco production wages higher than most other producers of consumable goods. In the early 1990s, cigarette makers earned about $23,400 a year. Pay depended on plant size and location and on the worker's skill level. Cigar workers earned less. Skilled workers earned more. Tobacco products workers usually receive health and life insurance, paid holidays and vacations, pension plans, and disability benefits.

Conditions of work

Most tobacco factories are in North Carolina and Virginia. Some are in Louisville, Kentucky. A number of cigar factories are in Florida and Pennsylvania. Conditions in these factories are good. Because most work is automated, plants are clean, well-lighted, and cool. Safety is a prime concern, and workers are well protected and comfortable. Workers work forty-hour weeks and often receive rest breaks and low-cost meals.

On the other hand, tobacco smells strong and the stemming process fills the air with tobacco particles and dust. Workers who find the smell offensive will not enjoy tobacco work.

Social and psychological factors

The main drawback to production work, including tobacco production, may be the repetitive nature of the tasks. Workers who do not mind monotony may do well in tobacco work. Others may find that the pay and pleasant conditions make up for the repetition. Still others may find challenges in striving to learn new processes and in the operation of new machines.

GOE: 06.04.28; SIC: 21; SOC: 76

◇ **SOURCES OF ADDITIONAL INFORMATION**

Cigar Association of America
1100 Seventeenth Street, NW, Suite 1202
Washington, DC 20036

Tobacco Growers' Information Committee
PO Box 18089
Raleigh, NC 27619

Tobacco Institute
1875 I Street, NW, Suite 800
Washington, DC 20006

Bakery, Confectionery, and Tobacco Workers International Union
1401 Connecticut Avenue
Kensington, MD 20895

◇ **RELATED ARTICLES**

Volume 1: Agriculture
Volume 3: See Processing Occupations

Machine Trades Occupations

The backbone of a technological society is the machine trades worker who makes the models, tools, dies, machines, and equipment that are necessary to modern industry. The mechanic and maintenance person who maintains and services factory machinery, airplanes, automobiles, and other major equipment is essential to the smooth functioning of our economy.

Machining occupations include instrument makers, tool-and-die makers, patternmakers, millwrights, farm-equipment mechanics, diesel mechanics, and others. In the early 1990s, approximately 1.1 million people were employed in these machining occupations.

As with other skilled occupations, individuals interested in the machine trades are increasingly required to have a high-school diploma. They should also possess mechanical ability and manual dexterity.

The activities of this field also require the employee to understand basic machine functions, blueprints, and specification interpretations.

Apprenticeship programs are the primary means for entering and training in any of the occupations in this group, although it is possible to work up to a skilled position through experience and supervised on-the-job training.

Workers in this group can advance to such positions as blue-collar worker supervisors, machine programmers, instrument technicians, service managers, and maintenance managers. A good number own their own businesses.

Employment opportunities in the machine trades will vary depending on the degree of automation possible within each area. For example, the space program requires complex machinery needed for space exploration. But automated production operations and new industrial materials and processes will cut down on the numbers of workers needed in this and some of the other machining occupations, such as machine tool operator. The number of jobs available for mechanics and repairers is expected to increase greatly as industrial production rises, causing greater mechanization and higher levels of personal income. It is expected that there will be thousands of jobs available each year just from retirements, transfers, or deaths.

The earnings of this group compare favorably with those of skilled workers in other trades, and union and management contracts generally provide for a full complement of insurance, pension, and tuition payment benefits.

Air-conditioning, refrigeration, and heating mechanics

Definition

Air-conditioning, refrigeration, and heating mechanics install, repair, and service the machinery used to cool or heat interior environments. They may specialize in installation as *domestic air-conditioning installers* or service (maintenance and repair) or in a particular type of equipment, such as gas furnaces or commercial refrigerators as *refrigeration mechanics*. Some work with all three systems—cooling, refrigeration, and heating.

History

In their search for ways to make their environment more comfortable and convenient, people have come a long way from the fireplaces that used to warm their homes and from the little ice houses where they used to store their food and liquids. In the 1920s, the production of synthetic coolants such as Freon established relatively inexpensive, effective refrigeration systems. By the 1950s, the same systems were used to cool air in home air-conditioning units. Vapor compression is still used today to run cooling systems.

Air-conditioning and heating systems today are often referred to as environmental control systems. They control not only the temperature but the humidity and even the cleanliness of the air in homes, offices, stores, factories, schools, and other buildings. With modern refrigeration, foods, drugs, and other perishable items may be stored safely for longer periods of time, and improved techniques for freezing foods have made home freezers or combination refrigerator-freezers standard equipment in most U.S. kitchens.

With the ever-increasing use of refrigerators, freezers, and climate control equipment, the need for skilled mechanics in this field has, likewise, grown and now provides many different job opportunities.

In the early 1990s, there were approximately 185,000 air-conditioning, refrigeration, and heating mechanics employed in the United States. Most of the air-conditioning and refrigeration mechanics and furnace installers worked for cooling and heating contractors.

Most of the oil burner mechanics were employed by fuel oil dealers, and most gas burner mechanics by gas utility companies. The balance worked for supermarket chains, school systems, manufacturers, and other organizations with large air-conditioning, refrigeration, or heating systems. About one-fifth of the total number of mechanics were self-employed.

Nature of the work

Air-conditioning, refrigeration, and heating are complex systems involving more than one machine. Central air-conditioning, for example, uses fans, compressors, condensers, and evaporators to cool and dehumidify the air. Then the treated air is distributed throughout a building by metal ducts or special piping. To do a thorough, competent job, a mechanic must understand the entire system and be able to work with ducts and pipes, as well as with the machinery.

Some mechanics specialize in installation or service (maintenance and repair) or in certain types of equipment, while others may handle it all—both installation and service of cooling, heating, and refrigeration equipment. *Window unit air-conditioning installer-servicers*, for example, install, repair, and service window units only.

Air-conditioning and refrigeration mechanics install and service central air-conditioning systems and a variety of refrigeration equipment. The installation may range from small wall units, either water- or air-cooled, to large central plant systems. Moreover, the mechanics may work on commercial refrigeration fixtures used in supermarkets, hotels, and restaurants, such as display cases, walk-in coolers, and frozen-food units. Installations in locker plants and at frozen-food plants are also covered in this line of work.

The job may take mechanics to private homes, office buildings, stores, factories, hotels, and restaurants. At times they may have to go to new construction sites. In the installation of new air-conditioning or refrigeration equipment, the mechanics follow blueprints, design specifications, and manufacturers' recommended procedures to install motors, condensers, evaporators, and other components. They must be good welders, solderers, and pipe fitters to be able to connect the equipment to the duct work, refrigerant lines, and electric power source. After completing the installation, the mechanics must check their work, using various testing devices.

In maintenance work, these mechanics inspect and examine the various parts of the system to detect leaks and other faults. They must adjust compressors and motors, as well as thermostatic controls to keep temperatures at specified levels.

The repair work of the air-conditioning and refrigeration mechanics commences with the diagnosis of the cause of breakdown. In so doing, they often disassemble brushes, valves, springs, and connections to inspect their condition. After the trouble is located, the reassembly may include the installation of such things as new piping, packing, valves, and pipe couplings, or the complete overhauling of a pump or a compressor, which will put the equipment into working order.

Furnace installers are also known as *heating-equipment installers*. Following blueprints or other specifications, they install oil, gas, electric, solid-fuel (such as coal), and multi-fuel heating systems. They set the furnace in place and install fuel supply lines, air ducts, pumps, and other components. Then they connect the electrical wiring and thermostatic controls, and, finally, they check the unit for proper operation. Maintenance and repair of the oil- or gas-burning equipment is handled by specialized mechanics.

Oil-burner mechanics maintain and repair oil-fueled heating systems to keep them in good operating condition. If the system is not working properly during the fall and winter, the seasons of heaviest use, the oil-burner mechanics check the thermostat, burner nozzles, controls, and other parts to locate the problem, then correct it by adjusting or replacing parts. The more extensive maintenance work is done in the summer, when the heating system can be shut down. During this season the mechanics replace oil and air filters and vacuum-cleaning vents, ducts, and other parts that accumulate soot and ash.

Gas-burner mechanics, also called *gas-appliance servicers*, have duties similar to those of oil burner mechanics, except that they maintain and repair gas-fueled heating systems. Their work also changes with the season. During the winter they make repairs and adjustments to correct any malfunctions. In the summer they inspect and clean the system to get it ready for the heating season. Gas-burner me-

An air-conditioning refrigeration mechanic inspects the safety features of an air-conditioning system in an industrial plant.

chanics may also repair cooking stoves, clothes dryers, water heaters, outdoor lights and grills.

Other specialists include *evaporative cooler installers, hot-air furnace installers-and-repairers, solar-energy system installers and helpers,* and *air and hydronic balancing technicians.*

The tools used by air-conditioning, refrigeration, and heating mechanics to work with refrigerant lines and air ducts include hammers, wrenches, metal snips, electric drills, pipe cutters and benders, and acetylene torches. To check electrical circuits, burners, and other components, the mechanics work with volt-ohmmeters, manometers, and other testing devices.

The installation and repair of cooling and heating systems may sometimes be performed by other craft workers. This is often true on very large jobs, especially where workers are covered by union contract. To install a large air-conditioning system, for example, the duct work might be done by sheet-metal workers, the electrical work by electricians, and the installation of piping, condensers, and other components by pipe fitters. Room air conditioners and home refrigerators are serviced by appliance repairers.

Requirements

High-school graduation is fast becoming a prerequisite for training in this field. The student's preparation should at least include courses in mathematics, physics, mechanical drawing, electricity, and blueprint reading.

Many high schools, private vocational schools, and junior colleges now offer programs in air-conditioning, refrigeration, and heating. Courses cover such subjects as air-conditioning, refrigeration, and heating theory; design and construction of equipment; and the basics of installation, maintenance, and repair. Completion of such a program is not mandatory, but graduates may receive preference when applying for employment, because they will not need as much on-the-job training.

Mechanical aptitude is a necessity for these mechanics, and good physical condition is required to lift and move heavy equipment.

To qualify as an air-conditioning, refrigeration, and heating mechanic, a person must complete either an apprenticeship or an on-the-job training program. Apprenticeship programs are run by unions and air-conditioning, refrigeration, and heating contractors. To be considered for the program, an individual must be a high-school graduate and pass a mechanical aptitude test. Apprenticeships last four years and combine varied work experience under qualified supervision with 144 hours of classroom study a year in related subjects, such as the use and care of tools, safety practices, blueprint reading, and air-conditioning theory.

As the concerns over the cooling gas, chlorofluorocarbons (CFCs), grows, the training in efficient containment of CFCs grows. In repairs, it is increasingly important to contain the gas, and it is equally important to avoid leaks in appliances.

Most mechanics, however, acquire their skills in on-the-job training programs that consist of working several years under the guidance of experienced mechanics. Trainees usually begin as helpers and do simple jobs such as carrying materials, insulating refrigerant lines, and cleaning furnaces. As they acquire more skill and knowledge, they are given more difficult tasks, such as cutting and soldering pipes and sheet metal, and checking electrical circuits. After four or five years, new mechanics are able to do all types of repairs and installations.

Experienced mechanics may keep up with changes in technology and expand their skills by taking courses offered by associations such as the Refrigeration Service Engineers Society, the Petroleum Marketing Education Foundation, and the Air-Conditioning Contractors of America.

Special requirements

Many mechanics are members of the United Association of Journeymen and Apprentices of the Plumbing and Pipefitting Industry or the Sheet Metal Workers International Association. Union membership, however, is not required by some contractors or service shops.

Opportunities for experience and exploration

High-school students may test their interest in the occupation through courses in physics, mathematics, mechanical drawing, and shop work. A dislike for the theoretical aspects of science will handicap an individual because a trainee is required to know some of the theory of air-conditioning, refrigeration, and heating.

Work experience for high-school students is difficult because most lack the skills or strength needed. Field trips to construction sites, service shops, and technical schools, however, will give an overall view of the nature of the work done.

Refrigeration, air-conditioning, and heating work in the armed forces is an excellent method for acquiring some technique and firsthand experience.

Related occupations

Many other occupations are available to those people with mechanical interests and aptitudes. These include motorcycle mechanics, general mechanics, aviation mechanics, and automobile mechanics.

Methods of entering

There are two ways individuals can enter the occupation of air-conditioning, refrigeration, and heating mechanic—as apprentices or as on-the-job trainees.

If they wish to become apprentices, the applicants usually contact air-conditioning, refrigeration, or heating equipment manufacturers or contractors; the state employment service; or the appropriate union headquarters (United Association of Journeymen and Apprentices of the Plumbing and Pipefitting Industry or the Sheet Metal Workers International Association). They must have the approval of the joint apprenticeship committee by this method.

If the apprenticeship program is filled, the applicants may wish to enter the field as on-the-job trainees. In this case they usually contact either the employer or the state employment service.

Advancement

Successful completion of the training program is necessary to be a qualified air-conditioning, refrigeration, and heating mechanic. Several opportunities for advancement are open to experienced mechanics. If they are able to get along well with people and have good judgment and planning skills, they may advance to lead man or foreman.

To advance to the job of estimator, who estimates the final cost of installation of the equipment, mechanics must be personable and have good judgment, excellent knowledge of the trade, and a knack for arithmetic.

In some regions of the country an air-conditioning, refrigeration, and heating mechanic may become a city or county inspector of work done by contractors. Another advancement is to that of a manufacturer's service specialist. Some mechanics eventually go into business for themselves by operating a repair shop or contracting business.

Employment outlook

The job prospects for air-conditioning, refrigeration, and heating mechanics are expected to increase about as fast as the average for all occupations throughout the next decade as more residential, commercial, and industrial buildings are constructed. Employment will also increase along with the installation of new energy-saving heating and cooling systems in existing homes and buildings. In addition, the greater use of a variety of frozen foods has increased the need for home freezers and plants for the manufacturing and storing of frozen products. Refrigeration also is becoming increasingly important in the manufacture of drugs, medicines, high-test gasoline, and synthetic rubber. Finally, many openings will occur as older, experienced mechanics retire, die, or transfer to other occupations.

Beginning mechanics, however, may find the competition heavy for jobs as helpers or apprentices because these trades have attracted so many people. Preference will usually be given

to graduates of training programs that emphasize hands-on experience.

Because people and businesses depend on air-conditioning, refrigeration, and heating systems, poor economic conditions do not have much effect on the employment of mechanics in this field. Even when new construction slows up, mechanics are kept busy installing new, more efficient equipment or doing maintenance and repair work on systems already present in existing buildings.

Earnings

The hourly wage rate for air-conditioning, refrigeration, and heating mechanics varies according to the type of equipment installed or serviced. Those who install large commercial units usually make more than those working with small home systems. The median annual pay for qualified mechanics working under union contracts in the early 1990s was $23,000, although many experienced workers made $37,400 and more. Mechanic apprentices earn about 40 percent of the regular mechanic's wage at the beginning of their training, increasing to about 85 percent during the fourth year. Mechanics who worked on both air-conditioning and heating equipment generally earned more than those who limited their work to only one or the other.

Mechanics often work extra hours during busy seasons, for which they receive overtime pay. Employment in businesses that service both air-conditioning and heating equipment is fairly steady year-round, but some employers may temporarily reduce hours or lay off some mechanics when seasonal peaks end. Mechanics usually receive fringe benefits such as health insurance, retirement pay, and paid vacations.

Conditions of work

Most air-conditioning, refrigeration, and heating mechanics have a forty-hour workweek, except during seasonal peaks, when they must work overtime or irregular hours. Mechanics may sometimes work reduced hours or face temporary layoff between busy seasons, although most employers try to provide a full workweek throughout the year. Independent mechanics will also be affected by the seasonal aspect of the work and have to budget their business finances and schedules accordingly.

In this occupation mechanics work in a variety of places and situations. They may work in a well-ventilated repair shop one day, on customers' premises the next, and the following week at a new office building. They usually are required to lift heavy objects as well as to stoop, crawl, or crouch when making repairs and installations.

Some of the hazards of the trade are burns, electric shocks, falls, exposure to refrigerants, and dangers associated with lifting heavy objects.

Some of this work calls for the instructing of the customer in the use and care of equipment.

Social and psychological factors

One of the characteristics of the work of the air-conditioning, refrigeration, and heating mechanic is the variety of duties and frequent changes in the place of work. Some days they must cooperate with other types of skilled craftsmen when making installations. On other days, they may make service calls to private homes and work independently. On these calls they must be tactful, courteous, and neat; they should try to answer all questions and to instruct the customer in the care and operation of the equipment. Workers in other occupations who have skills similar to those of air-conditioning, refrigeration, and heating mechanics include boilermakers, electrical appliance servicers, electricians, pipe fitters, plumbers, and sheet-metal workers.

GOE: 05.05.09; SIC: 1711; SOC: 6111

◇ SOURCES OF ADDITIONAL INFORMATION

Information about employment and training opportunities may be obtained from individual air-conditioning, refrigeration, and heating contractors; local offices of the United Association of Journeymen and Apprentices of the Plumbing and Pipefitting Industry or the Sheet Metal Workers International Association; local joint union-management apprenticeship committees; or local offices of the state employment service or state apprenticeship agency.

The national office of the union is:

United Association of Journeymen and Apprentices of the Plumbing and Pipefitting Industry of the U.S. and Canada
PO Box 37800
Washington, DC 20013

Pamphlets on career opportunities and training are available from:

Air-Conditioning and Refrigeration Institute
1501 Wilson Boulevard
6th Floor
Arlington, VA 22209

National Association of Plumbing-Heating-Cooling Contractors
180 South Washington Street
PO Box 6808
Falls Church, VA 22046

For information about training in oil heating systems, contact:

Petroleum Marketing Education Foundation
101 North Alfred Street
Alexandria, VA 22314

◇ RELATED ARTICLES

Volume 1: Construction; Engineering
Volume 2: Engineers; Industrial designers
Volume 3: See Machine Trades Occupations
Volume 4: Air conditioning, heating, and refrigeration technicians; Automotive cooling system diagnostic technicians; Electromechanical technicians; Tap-and-die-maker technicians; Welding technicians

Aircraft mechanics and engine specialists

Definition

Aircraft mechanics and engine specialists examine, service, repair, and overhaul aircraft and aircraft engines. They also repair, replace, and assemble parts of the airframe (all parts of the plane other than the power plant or engine).

History

On December 17, 1903, the first successfully powered flight was recorded by the airplane designed and built by Wilbur and Orville Wright. Since that day, advances in the development of aircraft and air transportation have been enormous, and improvements are continually being made. The complexity of aircraft design and development, and thus in service and maintenance, has made the job of aircraft mechanic a very necessary and important one. With the growth and development of both commercial airlines and military aircraft, the work of the skilled aircraft mechanic has become vital to both our national economy and defense.

Nature of the work

The work of *airframe and power-plant mechanics* employed by scheduled airlines varies according to whether they are line maintenance mechanics or overhaul mechanics.

Line maintenance mechanics are all-around craft workers who must be able to make repairs on all parts of the plane. Working at the airport, they make emergency and other necessary repairs after aircraft land and before they take off. They may be directed by the pilot, flight engineer, or head mechanic as to the repairs to make; or they may inspect the plane thoroughly themselves for oil leaks and cuts or dents in the surface and tires, and test the operation of radio, radar, and light equipment. In addition, changing oil, cleaning spark plugs, and replenishing the hydraulic and oxygen systems are line maintenance mechanics' duties. They work as fast as safety permits so the aircraft can be put back into service quickly.

To keep aircraft in top operating condition, overhaul mechanics perform scheduled maintenance, make repairs, and complete inspections required by the FAA. Scheduled maintenance programs are based on the number of hours flown, calendar days, or a combination of these factors.

Overhaul mechanics work at the airline's main overhaul base on either or both of the two major parts of the aircraft: the airframe, which includes wings, fuselage, tail assembly, landing gear, control cables, propeller assembly, and fuel and oil tanks; or the power plant, which may be radial, turbo jet, turbo prop, or rocket engine.

Working on parts of the aircraft other than the engine, the airframe mechanics inspect the various components of the airframe for worn or defective parts. They may check the sheet-metal surfaces, measure the tension of control cables, or check for rust, distortion, and cracks in the fuselage and wings. They consult manufacturers' manuals and the airline's maintenance manual for specifications, and to determine whether repair or replacement is needed to correct the malfunction. Airframe mechanics repair, replace, and assemble parts using a variety of tools, including power shears, sheet-metal breakers, arc and acetylene welding equipment, rivet guns, and air or electric drills.

Concentrating on the engine, aircraft power-plant mechanics inspect, service, repair, and overhaul this part of the plane. Looking through specially designed openings while working from ladders or scaffolds, they examine the external appearance of an engine for such problems as cracked cylinders, oil leaks, or cracks or breaks in the turbine blades. They also listen to the engine in operation to detect sounds of malfunctioning, such as sticking or burnt valves. The test equipment used to check the operation of an engine includes ignition analyzers, compression checkers, distributor timers, and ammeters.

If necessary, the mechanics remove the engine from the aircraft, using a hoist or a forklift truck, and take the engine apart. They use sensitive instruments to measure parts for wear and use X-ray and magnetic inspection equipment to check for invisible cracks. Worn or damaged parts, such as carburetors, superchargers, and magnetos, are replaced or re-

Aircraft mechanics must be knowledgeable in many aspects of airplane maintenance. On a given day, they may be asked to repair anything from serious engine problems to simple door jams.

paired; then the mechanics reassemble and install the engine.

Aircraft mechanics adjust and repair electrical wiring systems and aircraft accessories and instruments; inspect, service, and repair pneumatic and hydraulic systems; and handle various servicing tasks, such as flushing crankcases, cleaning screens, greasing moving parts, and checking brakes.

Mechanics may work on only one type of aircraft or on many different types, such as jets, propeller-driven planes, and helicopters. For greater efficiency, some may even specialize in one section of a particular type of aircraft, such as the engine or electrical system. Among other specialists, there are *air-conditioning, pressure sealer-and-testers, experimental, field and service, flight-test shop, aircraft accessories, pneumatic, experimental-aircraft, aircraft rigging and controls,* and *plumbing and hydraulics, mechanics, aircraft body,* and *bonded structures, repairers* such as *burnishers and bumpers, airplane electricians,* and *reclamation workers.*

Mechanics who work for businesses that own their own aircraft usually handle all repair and maintenance work. The planes, however, are generally smaller and less complex. In small, independent repair shops, mechanics must inspect and repair many different types of aircraft. The airplanes include small commuter planes, usually run by an aviation company, private company planes and jets, and private individually-owned aircraft. The airport may also have planes on hand for flying instructors.

Requirements

The first prerequisite for prospective aircraft mechanics is a high-school diploma. Courses in mathematics, physics, chemistry, and mechanical drawing are particularly helpful because they teach the principles involved in the operation of an aircraft, and this knowledge is often necessary to make the repairs. Machine shop, auto mechanics, or electric shop courses might be desirable to test the student's mechanical aptitudes.

Licensing by the FAA may also be a requirement for aircraft mechanics. Most of the mechanics who work on civilian aircraft have FAA licenses as airframe mechanics, power-plant mechanics, or aircraft inspectors. Airframe mechanics are qualified to work on the fuselage, wings, landing gear, and other structural parts of the aircraft; power-plant mechanics are qualified for work on the engine. Mechanics may qualify for both airframe and power-plant licensing, allowing them to work on any part of the plane. Combination airframe and power-plant mechanics with an inspector's license are permitted to certify inspection work done by other mechanics. Mechanics without licenses must be supervised by those who are licensed.

FAA licenses are granted only to aircraft mechanics with previous work experience: eighteen months for an airframe or power-plant license, thirty months working with both engines and airframes for a combination license. To qualify for an inspector's license, mechanics must have held a combined airframe and power-plant license for at least three years. In addition, all applicants for licenses must pass written and oral tests and demonstrate their ability to do the work authorized by the license.

At one time, mechanics were able to acquire their skills through on-the-job training. This is rare today. Now most mechanics learn the job either in the armed forces or in trade schools certified by the FAA. The trade schools provide training with the necessary tools and equipment in a program that ranges from eighteen months to two years. The FAA will sometimes accept successful completion of such schooling in lieu of work experience, but the schools do not guarantee an FAA license, or jobs for that matter.

The experience acquired by aircraft mechanics in the armed forces is sometimes general enough to satisfy the work requirements for FAA licensing, and such veterans may be able to pass the exam with a limited amount of additional study. Jobs in the military service, however, are usually too specialized to satisfy the FAA requirement for broad work experience. In that case, the mechanics will have to complete the training program at a trade school. The school will occasionally give some credit for material learned in the service. Nevertheless, aircraft mechanics with military experience will find it an asset when seeking employment, because employers consider trade school graduates with this experience to be the most desirable applicants.

Aircraft mechanics must be able to work with precision and meet rigid standards. Their physical condition is also important. They need more than average strength to lift heavy parts and tools, as well as the agility required for reaching and climbing. And they must not be afraid of heights, since they work on top of the wings and fuselages of large jet planes.

An airplane mechanic presents problems in the hydraulic system of the landing gear to the captain.

Special requirements

In addition to education and licensing, union membership may be a requirement, particularly for aircraft mechanics employed by major airlines. The principal unions organizing aircraft mechanics are the International Association of Machinists and Aerospace Workers and the Transport Workers Union of America. In addition, some mechanics are represented by the International Brotherhood of Teamsters, Chauffeurs, Warehousemen and Helpers of America.

Opportunities for experience and exploration

To test their ability and interest in the work of the aircraft mechanic, students should take mathematics, physics, and shop courses. Working with electronic kits, tinkering with automobile engines, and assembling model airplanes give invaluable opportunity for exploration.

A guided tour of an airfield will give a brief overall view of the work done in this industry. Even better would be a part-time or summer job as a helper on the flight line or in the baggage department. Small airports may also offer some job opportunities as part-time, summer, or replacement worker in several areas. Mechanical training, usually from classroom experience, is essential for mechanics' positions.

In addition, experience with aircraft in the Armed Forces or the Civil Air Patrol is an excellent method for acquiring some technical knowledge plus a feel for the occupation.

Related occupations

Other occupations in this field include general mechanics, automobile mechanics, motorcycle mechanics, small engine mechanics, and appliance repairers.

Methods of entering

High-school graduates who wish to become aircraft mechanics may enter this field by enrolling in an FAA-certified trade school. These schools generally have placement services available for their graduates.

Another method is to make direct application to the employment offices of individual airlines or the local offices of the state employment service. The field may also be entered through enlistment in the armed forces.

Advancement

The type of promotion depends in part on the size of the organization for which an aircraft mechanic works. The initial promotion is usually based on merit and comes in the form of a salary increase. To advance further, many companies require the mechanic to have a combined airframe and power-plant license, as well as an aircraft inspector's license.

Advancement may take the following route: journey mechanic, head mechanic or crew chief, inspector, head inspector, and shop supervisor. With additional training, a mechanic may advance to engineering, administrative, or executive positions. With business training, some mechanics open their own repair shops.

Employment outlook

About 111,000 aircraft mechanics were employed in the early 1990s, more than 10 percent of which worked for aircraft assembly firms. About 40 percent worked for scheduled airlines, and more than 25 percent worked for the federal government. Most of the rest were general aviation mechanics who worked in independent repair shops or for certificated supplemental airlines, crop-dusting and air-taxi firms, and businesses using their own planes for employee or cargo transportation.

The largest number of aircraft mechanics work near large cities that are the airlines' main stops. Many of those who work for the federal government are civilians employed at military aviation installations. Others work for the Federal Aviation Administration (FAA), mainly in their headquarters in Oklahoma City. The mechanics employed by independent repair shops are located at airports in every part of the country.

Overall, the outlook for aircraft mechanics is good for the next decade. An increased number of jobs is expected as a result of growth in the industry, with more and more planes flying passengers and freight. In addition, many openings will occur through the transfer, retirement, or death of mechanics presently working. The opportunities for jobs, however, will differ in general aviation, airline companies, and the federal government.

Qualified mechanics, particularly if they are willing to relocate, should find plenty of opportunities in general aviation. Rapid growth is expected in the number of smaller planes owned by private individuals as well as by companies that use them for executive transportation. Because wages paid by small companies are usually low, there will not be as much competition for these jobs as for those with airlines and large private companies. As a matter of fact, many of the openings that occur will be the result of experienced mechanics' leaving for better-paying jobs in the larger companies.

Additional airline jobs may be created to fill the demand for airline transportation by a population that earns more and travels more frequently. The airline jobs, however, will be much more difficult to obtain because the high wages they pay attract a larger number of qualified applicants than there are jobs available.

The number of mechanics employed by the federal government is expected to increase. These jobs are affected by changes in defense spending, and the number of openings will fluctuate depending on whether there is a reduction or an increase in the defense budget.

During a recession, when people have less money for travel, airlines usually cut the number of flights they operate. As a result, fewer mechanics are needed for maintenance. This means that mechanics may face layoffs when economic conditions are poor.

Earnings

In the early 1990s, aircraft mechanics were paid an average of about $30,000 per year. Some skilled, experienced mechanics made about $48,000.

Most major airlines are covered by union agreements. Their mechanics generally earned more than those working for other employers.

An attractive fringe benefit for airline mechanics and their immediate families is reduced fares on their own and most other airlines.

Conditions of work

Most aircraft mechanics work a five-day, forty-hour week. Their working hours, however, often include nights, weekends, and holidays, because airline schedules call for three eight-hour shifts around the clock.

Each airline usually has one main overhaul base, where more than half of its mechanics are employed. These are found in the larger cities or on the main airline routes, such as New York, Chicago, Los Angeles, Atlanta, San Francisco, and Miami.

When doing overhauling and major inspection work, aircraft mechanics generally work in hangars with adequate heat, ventilation, and light. If the hangars are full, however, or if repairs must be made quickly, they may work outdoors, sometimes in unpleasant weather. Outdoor work is frequent for line maintenance mechanics, who work at airports, because they must make minor repairs and preflight checks at the terminal to save time. To maintain flight schedules, or to keep from inconveniencing customers in general aviation, the mechanics often have to work under pressure.

The work is physically strenuous and demanding. Mechanics often have to lift or pull as much as fifty pounds of weight. They may stand, lie, or kneel in awkward positions, sometimes in precarious positions on a scaffold or ladder. Further, noise and vibration are common when testing engines. Regardless of the stresses and strains, aircraft mechanics are expected to work quickly and with great precision.

Although the power tools and test equipment are provided by the employer, mechanics may be expected to furnish their own hand tools.

Social and psychological factors

The lives of thousands of passengers, not to mention huge monetary investments in aircraft, depend in large part on the work done by aircraft mechanics. It is a tribute to their skill and dependability that traveling in a plane is safer than riding in an automobile. Most passengers today have such confidence in aircraft that they fly thousands of feet above the ground and hundreds of miles an hour without even thinking twice about it.

One of the advantages to be derived from working in this occupation is that mechanics and their immediate families are entitled to a limited amount of free or reduced-fare transportation on their companies' flights, depending upon length of service. In addition, they may fly at greatly reduced rates with other airlines.

Because airlines operate flights at all hours of the day and night and extra flights during holidays, the work schedule of the mechanics is often irregular. Yet these workers have the security of knowing that they receive paid sick leaves and that retirement, insurance, and hospitalization benefits are included in their contracts.

GOE: 05.05.09, 06.01.04; SIC: 4581; SOC: 61

◇ SOURCES OF ADDITIONAL INFORMATION

Aviation Maintenance Foundation
PO Box 2826
Redmond, WA 98073

For information about jobs in a particular airline, write to the personnel manager of the individual company. A list of airline companies and their addresses may be obtained from:

Air Transport Association of America
1709 New York Avenue, NW
Washington, DC 20006

Information on jobs in a particular area may be obtained by contacting employers at local airports or local offices of the state employment service.

◇ RELATED ARTICLES

Volume 1: Aerospace Manufacturing; Transportation
Volume 2: Automotive body repairers; Automobile mechanics; Electrical repairers; Electricians; Farm equipment mechanics; Flight engineers; Telephone and PBX installers and repairers
Volume 4: Aeronautical and aerospace technicians; Automotive, diesel, and gas turbine technicians; Avionics technicians; Electrical technicians; Electromechanical technicians

Automobile-body repairers

Definition

Automobile-body repairers repair damaged bodies and body parts, whether metal or plastic, of automotive vehicles such as automobiles, buses, and light trucks. Following repair manuals and using hand tools and power tools, they straighten bent frames and body sections, remove and replace badly damaged body parts, and smooth out less-serious dents and creases.

In small shops, body repairers may also paint body surfaces or replace safety glass.

Some specialize in fiberglass bodies. In large shops, body repairers may specialize in one type of repair, such as frame straightening, fender repairing, or glass installation. Supervisors generally examine the damaged vehicles and estimate the cost of repairs.

History

Toward the end of the nineteenth century, an invention was introduced that would revolutionize transportation and become one of the major industries in the United States. It was the automobile. Steam-powered vehicles had been in existence since about 1770, when Nicolas-Joseph Cugnot, a Frenchman, adapted a steam engine to drive an artillery tractor, but it was not until after the development of the internal-combustion engine that the manufacture of automobiles became feasible. The first gasoline-fueled automobile in North America was produced in 1892 by the Duryea brothers, J. Frank and Charles Edgar. Henry Ford built his first car in 1893. The horseless carriage captured the interest and excitement of Americans, but few could afford them. Cars had to be made to order, and the cost was high. At the turn of the century, fewer than 8,000 automobiles had been produced.

To solve the problem of building an automobile at a reasonable price, Ransom Eli Olds adopted an idea that had been used in industries manufacturing watches, sewing machines, and revolvers. He contracted independent machinists to make standard components, which were shipped to his plant for assembly. In 1908, Henry Ford made improvements on the assembly-line technique to mass-produce cars that the average person could afford. By 1913, Ford was able to assemble a Model-T in only twelve and one-half hours.

The automobile quickly replaced the horse for local travel and began to compete with the railroads for longer trips. A federal highway-building program opened up unlimited horizons, and the demand for automobiles boomed, until today the annual output of personal vehicles numbers in the millions. Americans drive everywhere—to work, to school, to the shopping center, to vacation areas. When on the road there are vehicles such as trucks and buses, all traveling at speeds that were unforeseen little more than a century ago, it is not surprising that thousands of traffic accidents occur each day. Cars are designed to withstand some impact, and fold to avoid occupant injury in other collisions.

Nature of the work

When a motor vehicle has been damaged in a traffic accident, it is the job of body repairers to restore the body and body parts to like-new condition. Most repairers work only on cars and small trucks, although they usually are able to fix any kind of vehicle. A few repairers work mainly on large trucks, buses, or tractor trailers. Specialists include *used-car renovators, truck-body builders and apprentices, automobile-bumper straighteners, service mechanics, squeak, rattle and leak repairers,* and *automobile-body customizers.*

The first person to examine a damaged vehicle brought into a shop is generally a *shop supervisor* or *estimator,* who determines the extent of the damage and estimates how long the repairs will take and how much they will cost. The estimate is submitted to the owner of the vehicle for approval before any work is done. Then the vehicle is turned over to the body repairers with instructions as to what needs to be done and how much time it should take.

Car and truck bodies today may be made of metal or plastic. The repair techniques used may vary accordingly. Repairers work with both materials, although a few of them specialize in fiberglass bodies.

To gain access to the body and fenders, the automobile body repairers may remove upholstery, accessories, electrical and hydraulic window- and seat-operating equipment, or trim. If the frame or a body section of the vehicle has been bent or twisted, *frame repairers and straighteners* can restore it to its original shape and position by chaining or clamping it to an alignment machine that usually uses hydraulic pressure to pull the damaged metal into alignment.

Dents in metal bodies are removed in several ways, depending on how deep they are. If fenders, sections of body panels, or grills are too badly damaged to repair, the body repairers remove them with wrenches and a pneumatic metal-cutting gun or acetylene torch, and new parts are bolted or welded into place with wrenches and welding equipment. Less serious dents are pushed out with a hydraulic jack or hand prying bar, or the repairers knock them out with hand tools or pneumatic hammers. To smooth out small dents and creases, the repairers position a small anvil, or dolly block, against one side of the dented area and beat the opposite side with a hammer. Small pits and dimples are removed with pick hammers and punches. Dents that cannot be corrected with this treatment may be filled with solder or plastic. After the filler hardens, the repairers file, grind, or sand the surface to prepare it for painting. In most shops the final sanding and painting are done by other specialists, designated automobile painters.

An increasing number of new vehicles have plastic bodies, which are more difficult to repair and more often require complete replacement of parts. Body repairers remove the damaged panels and, if the dents can be repaired, begin by determining the type of plastic the parts are made of. In most cases, the repairers can use a hot-air welding gun or immerse the part in hot water to soften the plastic so they can press it back into its original shape by hand. Dents that cannot be worked out this way may be filled with new plastic material and smoothed out.

Body repairers often aim headlights, align wheels, and "bleed" hydraulic brake systems. In many shops, particularly small ones, they may do both body repairing and painting, while in large shops they may specialize in just one type of repair, such as frame straightening or door and fender repairing.

Automobile body repairers generally work by themselves with minimal supervision beyond the original general directions. In large, busy shops, however, they may be assisted by helpers or apprentices.

Requirements

A high-school diploma is not a requirement to become an automobile-body repairer, but, as is true in many trades, employers often prefer to hire high-school graduates. Courses of particular benefit in preparing for this work are automobile body repair and automobile mechanics, which are offered by many high schools, vocational schools, and private trade schools. Persons who are interested in entering this occupation should know how to use tools and should be in good physical condition, with the strength to handle heavy body parts.

Automobile body repairers acquire their skills in three or four years of on-the-job training. In an apprenticeship program this training is combined with a study program. While apprentices spend most of their time gaining experience on the job, they also attend classes in mathematics, job safety procedures, business management, and other related subjects. Training authorities consider this the best method for learning the job, but there are very few apprenticeship programs available.

Most body repairers learn the trade simply by working at it. They begin as helpers, working alongside more experienced workers, and learn to do the simple tasks first, such as removing damaged parts and installing repaired or replacement parts. Then they are trained to

Automobile-body repairers prepare a damaged car for body work. Parts of the car are removed so that the frame can be realigned.

remove small dents and to make minor repairs. Gradually they progress to the major tasks, such as straightening frames. After several years they should have the skills to handle all aspects of body repair.

A recognized standard of achievement in this field is certification by the National Institute for Automotive Service Excellence. Certification is voluntary. To qualify, body repairers must pass a written examination and have at least two years of work experience. (Completion of a high school, vocational school, or trade school program in automobile body repair may be substituted for one year of experience.) To remain certified, it is necessary to take the examination again at least every five years.

Automobile body repairers are expected to furnish their own tools, although employers may provide power tools. Tools are an investment. Trainees usually accumulate them as they gain experience; after a number of years in the business, experienced workers may have a collection of tools worth hundreds of dollars.

Special requirements

While union membership is not a requirement for all automobile-body repairers, many of them belong to the International Association of Machinists and Aerospace Workers; or the International Union, United Automobile, Aerospace and Agricultural Implement Workers of America; or the Sheet Metal Workers International Association; or the International Brotherhood of Teamsters, Chauffeurs, Warehousemen and Helpers of America (Ind.). Most of the body repairers who are union members work for large automobile dealers, trucking companies, and bus lines.

Opportunities for experience and exploration

High-school students may evaluate their interest in and begin to prepare for this occupation by taking shop courses. Many high schools, along with vocational schools and private trade schools, offer courses directly related to automobile body repairing. Studying automobile mechanics also provides useful experience. Subjects in the areas of mathematics and business help provide a broad foundation for the technical skills that are of primary importance.

To get a practical viewpoint, students may seek permission to visit local repair shops to observe and talk to the body repairers employed there.

Part-time and summer jobs in gasoline service stations and automotive supply houses will give the students an opportunity to acquire a familiarity with the language of the occupation and with the kinds of problems and equipment they will encounter when they enter it.

In addition, many young persons test their mechanical aptitudes by building model cars or buying an old car to repair and refinish.

Related occupations

Many other kinds of mechanics' jobs are available to people who find the work described in this article interesting. Other occupations that might be of interest include aircraft mechanics, small appliance repairs, service station owners or managers, motorcycle mechanics, or motorboat mechanics.

Methods of entering

Persons wishing to become automobile body repairers must begin as trainees, either in an apprenticeship or in an on-the-job training program.

Information about apprenticeships and other training programs, as well as details about work opportunities, may be obtained from locals of the unions mentioned previously or from local offices of the state employment service. Prospective body repairers, however, usually apply directly to employers, such as au-

tomobile dealers and body-repair shops. Job leads may be found in newspaper want ads or through school placement offices or private employment agencies.

Advancement

Advancement in this occupation often takes the form of salary increases. With experience and managerial ability, however, a body repairer may advance to shop supervisor. Many workers go into business for themselves, and a few become automobile damage appraisers for insurance companies.

Employment outlook

In the early 1990s, there were more than 196,000 automobile-body repairers throughout the country, in towns and cities of every size. Most of them worked in shops specializing in body repairs and painting, or for car and truck dealers. Some were employed in businesses that maintained their own motor vehicles, and a few worked for car and truck manufacturers. A large group—almost 25 percent—of body repairers were self-employed, usually operating their own shops. Compared with all other occupations, automobile-body repairers may expect an above average increase in employment throughout the next decade. The number of traffic accidents will grow along with the number of motor vehicles, although the rate of increase may not be as rapid because of better highways, driver training courses, and improved bumpers and safety features on the newer vehicles. Many openings, of course, will occur as older, experienced workers retire, die, or change occupations.

The automobile repair business is not greatly affected by changes in economic conditions. Major body damages must be repaired to keep a vehicle in safe operating condition. The lighter weight design used in both foreign and domestic cars to increase fuel efficiency allows cars to be damaged easier. During a downswing, however, people often postpone minor repairs, such as dents and crumpled fenders, until their budgets can accommodate the expense. Nevertheless, body repairers are rarely laid off. Instead, when business is bad, employers hire fewer new workers. During recessions, inexperienced beginners face strong competition for jobs.

Earnings

According to automobile dealers in twenty-four large cities, automobile body repairers earned an average of $35,190 to $43,700 in the early 1990s. Helpers and trainees are generally paid 30 to 60 percent of the wages earned by skilled workers.

In automobile dealers and repair shops, many body repairers work on commission. That is, they receive a percentage—usually 50 percent—of the labor costs charged to customers. The total amount they earn varies, then, depending on how many repair jobs need to be done and how fast the repairers can work. Employees often guarantee a minimum weekly salary in addition to the commission. Helpers and trainees are paid an hourly rate until they become skilled enough to work on commission. Hourly wages are also paid to body repairers who work for trucking companies, bus lines, and other businesses that maintain their own vehicles.

Conditions of work

Body repairers usually work forty to forty-eight hours a week. The condition of the shops they work in varies depending on size and age. Most of them are well ventilated, but—new or old—they are often dusty and smell of paint, and they are usually noisy places because of the constant hammering on metal and the whine of power tools.

The work is strenuous and dirty, and it often must be done while standing or crouching in awkward and cramped positions. Body repairers have to be careful to guard against cuts from sharp metal edges, burns from torches and heated metal, and injuries from power tools.

Social and psychological factors

This occupation will appeal to persons who enjoy working with their hands, who do not mind getting dirty, and who are resourceful in working out solutions to a variety of problems. Like a jigsaw puzzle, each damaged vehicle presents a unique challenge. Body repairers depend on a thorough knowledge of automobile construction and repair techniques to help them develop appropriate methods for each job. Being able to turn a wrecked car into one that looks like new provides a real sense of accomplishment.

Self-reliance is an important characteristic, because body repairers usually work by themselves with only general instructions from the shop supervisor.

GOE: 05.05.06; SIC: 7532; SOC: 6115

◇ SOURCES OF ADDITIONAL INFORMATION

Automotive Service Association
1901 Airport Freeway
Suite 100
PO Box 929
Bedford, TX 76095

Automotive Service Industry Association
444 North Michigan Avenue
Chicago, IL 60611

National Institute for Automotive Service Excellence
1920 Association Drive
Reston, VA 22091

◇ RELATED ARTICLES

Volume 1: Automotives
Volume 3: Aircraft mechanics and engine specialists; Automobile mechanics; Automobile-repair-service estimators; Automotive painters; Farm-equipment mechanics; Forge shop occupations; Machine tool operators
Volume 4: Automotive cooling systems technicians; Automotive, diesel, and gas turbine technicians; Automotive exhaust technicians; Mechanical technicians; Tire technicians; Welding technicians

Automobile mechanics

Definition

Automobile mechanics repair and service the mechanical and electrical parts of passenger cars, trucks, buses, and other automotive vehicles. After making the necessary inspection and tests to determine the cause of faulty operation, the mechanics repair or replace defective parts to restore the vehicle to proper operating condition.

For a thorough inspection, they may raise the vehicle using a hydraulic jack or hoist to work on the underside or remove and disassemble the engine or faulty unit. Besides repairing and replacing minor components, automobile mechanics overhaul or replace major parts such as carburetors and generators and rebuild such items as crankshafts and cylinder blocks. They also rewire electrical systems, adjust brakes, align front ends, replace shock absorbers, repair radiator leaks, adjust headlights, install and repair accessories, and mend dented fenders and other body parts.

Some workers in this occupation specialize in a type of vehicle and are known as bus, truck, motorcycle, or foreign-car mechanics. Others specialize in a type of repair, such as automatic transmissions, tune-ups, automobile air-conditioning, front-end alignment, brakes, automobile radiators, or automobile electrical systems.

History

The history of the occupation of automobile mechanic parallels the development and widespread use of the automobile. Although many men were working on its invention, the present-day car had its beginning in the three-wheeled steam automobile, built in France in about 1770 by Nicolas-Joseph Cugnot. In the United States, the first patent for a steam automobile was granted in 1784 to Oliver Evans.

In the late nineteenth century, automotive transportation was revolutionized by the development of the internal combustion engine by Gottlieb Daimler in Germany. The first motor vehicle using such a gasoline engine, driven by Carl Benz in Germany in 1885, was shown at the Chicago World's Fair in 1893. That year also saw the first successful U.S. car, which was designed and operated by the Duryea brothers, Charles Edgar and J. Frank. The beginning of the automobile industry in the United States occurred with the sale of the Winton automobile in 1898.

Yet all these automobiles were produced in small numbers because of limited manufacturing facilities and small consumer demand. Not until the federal highway building program in 1916 gave impetus to the use of more cars did mass production of automobiles begin.

Since World War I, the development of the automobile has become more complex, from its design and construction to its servicing. And as the automobile grew in complexity, the need for skilled automobile mechanics likewise grew, since car owners could no longer make all the necessary repairs themselves.

Nature of the work

The skilled automobile mechanic can perform a wide variety of jobs on many different makes and kinds of vehicles.

Prior to the sale of an automobile, the dealer's mechanics adjust and check various parts of the car to ensure proper operation. After the purchase of the automobile, periodic checkups are necessary to keep the vehicle performing at its designed level. Wear, abuse, and deterioration require the replacement or repair of parts of the automobile. Qualified mechanics can do almost any type of adjustment or repair job. Their duties include disassembling and overhauling engines, transmissions, clutches, and other parts of the car, as well as grinding valves, adjusting brakes, and aligning the front wheels.

The mechanics' chief skill is the ability to find the cause of faulty operation. The first thing they do is get a description of the mechanical or electrical difficulties from the owner of the car or, in a dealership, from the repair service estimator who wrote the repair order. Then they may test-drive the car or use testing devices, such as motor analyzers, spark-plug testers, or compression gauges, to locate the defect. For example, the customer may state that his engine seems to lack power. Mechanics will listen to and look at the engine to locate the difficulty. They will look for defects in the ignition or fuel system, check to see if the proper weight of oil is being used, check to see if the exhaust system is clogged, check the action of the valves, and the like. In each check they will pick up clues that will enable them to diagnose the trouble.

After finding the cause of the problem, the mechanics make adjustments or repairs. If a part is too badly damaged or worn to be repaired, or if it cannot be repaired at a reasonable cost, the mechanics replace it.

Mechanics who work in small shops may be required to prepare estimates of the cost of repairs, including materials and labor, before starting the job. In larger repair shops, a repair service estimator generally prepares the estimate.

Because the automobile is a complex machine, there are a number of mechanics who specialize in the repair or service of specific parts. These specialists usually work in larger shops with different departments, in car diagnostic centers, or in small shops that concentrate on a particular type of repair work.

Tune-up mechanics often use scientific test equipment to help them locate malfunctions in the fuel, ignition, and emissions-control systems. They adjust the ignition timing and valves, and adjust or replace spark plugs, distributor points, and other parts to bring engine performance up to efficiency standards.

Brake repairers work on the hydraulic and power-brake systems, adjusting, removing, repairing, and reinstalling such items as brake linings, drums, shoes, wheel and master cylinders, and diaphragms. Some mechanics specialize in both brake and front-end work.

Transmission mechanics adjust, repair, and maintain gear trains, couplings, hydraulic pumps, and other parts of the automatic transmission system. Repair of these complex mechanisms requires considerable experience and training, including a knowledge of hydraulics.

Front-end mechanics are concerned with suspension and steering systems. They align and balance wheels, often using special alignment equipment and wheel-balancing machines, and make necessary repairs to the systems.

Automotive electricians adjust, repair, overhaul, and install voltage regulators, generators, starters, and other components of the electrical or ignition system. They may use electricians' hand tools to repair or replace defective wiring and rebuild electrical units. To locate electrical system malfunctions, they often use ammeters, ohmmeters, and voltmeters.

Air-conditioning mechanics install, maintain, and service air conditioners and service components, such as compressors and condensers, in automobiles.

Automobile radiator mechanics clean radiators, using caustic solutions. They locate and solder leaks and install new radiator cores. Some radiator mechanics also repair car heaters and air

An automobile mechanic gives a car its annual inspection.

conditioners and may solder leaks in the gas tanks.

There are also *wheelwrights, muffler installers, automobile-accessories installers, spring floor service workers, motor dynamometer testers, motorcycle mechanics, bus inspectors, vehicle-fuel-systems converters, brake adjusters, clutch rebuilders, hand spring repairers, heavy repairers, motorcycle subassembly repairers, automotive-generator-and-starter repairers,* and *automatic-window-seat-and-top-lift repairers.*

As a part of preventive maintenance, automobile mechanics check parts and adjust, repair, or replace them before they break down. They usually follow a checklist to be sure they do not overlook any important parts, such as belts, hoses, steering systems, spark plugs, brake systems, carburetor, wheel bearings, and other possible trouble spots.

Many different tools are used by the automobile mechanic, ranging from inexpensive simple hand tools to complicated and expensive equipment. Mechanics usually must furnish their own hand tools. Beginners are expected to accumulate tools as they gain experience. After a number of years, mechanics may have hundreds of dollars invested in tools. Employers furnish the power tools, engine analyzers, and other test equipment.

To maintain and increase their skills and to keep up with new technology, automobile mechanics must regularly read service and repair manuals, shop bulletins, and other publications, and possibly take part in new or advanced training programs.

Requirements

Most employers prefer to hire high-school graduates with mechanical aptitude and some understanding of automobile construction and operation. The students' preparation should include courses in physics, chemistry, and mathematics to help them better understand how an automobile operates, as well as English and business arithmetic, which are of value to mechanics who deal with the public and calculate the cost of repairs. The courses in automobile repair work offered by many high schools, vocational schools, community and junior colleges, and private trade schools are very desirable, particularly when combined with work experience related to automotive service.

To qualify as an automobile mechanic, however, persons interested in this occupation must complete either an apprenticeship or on-the-job training program. Apprenticeship programs are offered through many auto dealers and independent repair shops and may consist of three or four years of training. A typical four-year program may require about 8,000 hours of practical shop experience, working on brakes, chassis, transmissions, engines, electrical systems, exhaust emission controls, and other components, including at least 576 hours of formal instruction about these subjects, as well as topics such as motor theory, use of blueprints and shop manuals, and safety.

Although training authorities generally recommend a formal apprenticeship program, most automobile mechanics learn the trade on the job. The on-the-job training program consists of working for approximately three or four years under the guidance of experienced mechanics. Usually the trainees begin as helpers, lubrication workers, or gasoline station attendants until they acquire the skill and knowledge necessary for more difficult tasks. While the beginners may be able to make simple repairs after only a few months' experience, it usually takes one to two years to become a service mechanic able to make the more difficult types of routine service and repairs. Another year or two are then required to reach the journey level and become familiar with all types of repairs. After reaching the journey level, mechanics who specialize need an additional one or two years to learn a difficult specialty such as automatic-transmission repair. On the other hand, radiator mechanics and brake specialists do not need an all-round knowledge of automobile repair and may learn their jobs in about two years.

Special or additional training is sometimes made available through the cooperation of employers and automobile manufacturers. Automobile dealers may send promising beginners to factory-sponsored mechanic training programs; factory representatives may come to repair shops to conduct short training sessions; and experienced mechanics may be sent to factory training centers to learn to repair new models or to receive special training in automatic transmissions or air-conditioning repair.

Certification by the National Institute for Automotive Service Excellence is not a requirement, but it is a widely recognized standard of achievement for automobile mechanics. Mechanics may voluntarily apply for certificates in one or more of eight different service areas, such as tune-ups, brake and front-end work, or electrical system repair. General automobile mechanics are certified in all eight specialized areas. To qualify for certification in each area, mechanics must have at least two years' experience and pass a written examination. (Completion of an auto mechanics program in high school, vocational or trade school, or community or junior college may be substituted for one year of experience.) To renew their certification, mechanics must take the examination every five years.

Special requirements

Membership in a labor union may be a requirement for some mechanics. The unions organizing automobile mechanics include the International Association of Machinists and Aerospace Workers; the International Union, United Automobile, Aerospace and Agricultural Implement Workers of America; the Sheet Metal Workers International Association; and the International Brotherhood of Teamsters, Chauffeurs, Warehousemen and Helpers of America (Ind.).

Opportunities for experience and exploration

Automobile mechanics' work is one of the few occupational fields that offers a wide range of opportunities for experience and exploration.

In high-school shop courses, individuals can appraise their mechanical ability and interest in this work. Tinkering with cars as a hobby provides valuable firsthand experience with the work of a mechanic. In addition, part-time work in a gasoline service station will give a feel for the kind of problems they will face in this field.

Experience with automotive repair work in the armed forces is another method for acquiring some technique and firsthand experience.

Related occupations

Other occupations that have similar aptitude and skill requirements as those of automobile mechanics include diesel mechanics, general maintenance mechanics, motorcycle mechanics, and small appliance repairers.

Methods of entering

Persons who wish to become automobile mechanics have two avenues of entrance into the occupation: the apprenticeship or the on-the-job training program.

If they wish to become *apprentices,* the prospective automobile mechanics usually contact either employers, the state employment service, or the appropriate local union headquarters. Apprentices usually work for a lower wage than experienced employees. They may be given classes while on the job, while they work under a trainer who provides practical experience.

If applicants wish to enter the field as on-the-job trainees, they usually contact an employer directly from an advertisement in the newspaper or go to a local employment agency for a lead.

Graduates of a technical or vocational school offering automobile shop training may find a job from the school's placement office.

Advancement

Successful completion of the training program is necessary before an individual can become a qualified automobile mechanic. After increasing their efficiency and skill for several years, and with additional training, all-around automobile mechanics may become specialists in some segment of automobile repair work and thus receive a higher salary than that of regular mechanics.

If they have certain personal characteristics, such as the ability to deal with people, good judgment, and planning skills, mechanics may advance to positions such as shop supervisor, service sales worker, service manager, or repair service estimator. Another possible advancement is for the mechanic to become a car or truck sales worker or to manage a dealer's parts department. Some mechanics eventually go into business for themselves, operating a repair shop or a gasoline service station.

Employment outlook

In the early 1990s, more than 998,000 automobile mechanics were employed throughout the country. Most of them worked for automobile dealers, automobile repair shops, gasoline service stations, and department stores with automotive service facilities. Others were employed by federal, state, and local governments, taxi-cab and automobile leasing companies, and other organizations that repair their own vehicles. In automobile manufacturing plants, mechanics are employed to adjust and repair cars that come off the assembly lines. Most automobile mechanics work in small shops employing no more than five mechanics, but some of the larger shops may have more than 100 employees. Automobile dealers generally have a larger staff of mechanics than the independent shops. Employment opportunities for automobile mechanics are expected to increase rapidly during the next decade. There are several reasons for this excellent outlook. The number of car registrations is expected to increase due to increases in population, new families, consumer buying power, and multicar ownership. Also more new cars will be equipped with power equipment, pollution-control and safety devices, and other features that will increase maintenance requirements. Because of the complexity of parts, motorists will be forced to turn to a skilled mechanic to make repairs and adjustments rather than do it themselves. In addition, warranty conditions on many new cars demand servicing at periodic times by qualified mechanics. Gas-powered farm equipment, such as tractors, is expected to be used by many more farmers than previously.

In addition to a greater demand for automobile mechanics because of growth in the industry, thousands of job openings will occur to replace experienced mechanics who retire, die, or change jobs.

Fluctuations in economic conditions have little effect on employment in this field; mechanics generally enjoy the security of steady work. Beginners may find it more difficult getting a job during an economic slump, however, when employers may be more reluctant to take on inexperienced workers.

Earnings

The earnings of the automobile mechanic vary according to the type of employer and the section of the country. In the early 1990s, highly skilled journey mechanics employed by automobile dealers in twenty-four cities earned an average of about $27,450 annually. Yearly salaries actually ranged from about $14,400 to about $42,000.

In automobile dealer repair shops and in independent repair shops, many experienced mechanics are paid a percentage of the labor costs charged to the customer. This commission is usually paid in addition to a guaranteed minimum weekly salary. Total weekly earnings in this case depend on the amount of work the mechanic is able to complete; mechanics who can complete repairs in less than the average time are able to earn considerably more money.

Conditions of work

Most automobile mechanics have a forty to forty-eight-hour workweek, although some may work longer hours. For the most part, the mechanic's work is performed indoors in a repair shop. Some older repair shops may be cold and drafty in the winter and hot in the summer. The new ones are well ventilated and heated, however, with special devices to remove fumes from the air. These repair shops are often noisy from running engines and body repair work, and the threat of fire is continually present due to oil and gasoline. Most shops have strict safety procedures because of this.

In the performance of their duties, automobile mechanics are required to stoop, bend, crawl, and lift heavy objects. Tripping over crawlers or jack handles is a common accident, as are cuts from broken parts of tools, burns, and allergic reactions to solvents or oils. The biggest complaint is not about the hazards, however, but about the grime and grease ever present in various automobile parts.

Social and psychological factors

A qualified mechanic is always able to secure a job. Because changes are always taking place in the automobile industry, mechanics must keep up to date with all innovations and refinements that are made each year. They must read with understanding the various technical and service manuals as part of their work, and they may

participate in employer- and factory-sponsored training programs.

In addition to the mechanical work, the mechanic must be able to tolerate a certain amount of questions and criticism, for some customers have high levels of curiosity and expectation.

GOE: 05.05.09; SIC: 7538; SOC: 6111

◇ **SOURCES OF ADDITIONAL INFORMATION**

Automotive Service Association
1901 Airport Freeway, Suite 100
PO Box 929
Bedford, TX 76095

Automotive Service Industry Association
444 North Michigan Avenue
Chicago, IL 60611

National Automobile Dealers Association
8400 Westpark Drive
McLean, VA 22102

For information about becoming a certified automobile mechanic, write to:

National Institute for Automotive Service Excellence
1920 Association Drive
Reston, VA 22091

◇ **RELATED ARTICLES**

Volume 1: Automotives
Volume 3: Aircraft mechanics; Automotive body repairers; Automobile repair service estimators; Diesel mechanics; Electrical repairers; Farm equipment mechanics
Volume 4: Aeronautical and aerospace technicians; Automotive cooling system technicians; Electromechanical technicians; Mechanical technicians

Automobile-repair-service estimators

Definition

Automobile-repair-service testers and *estimators* act as the link between car owners seeking repair or maintenance on their vehicles and the mechanics who perform the work. They inspect cars and trucks to determine the need for repairs and their costs. To ascertain what repairs are needed, service estimators question the customer, visually inspect the vehicle and machine as well as road test it. They may perform such minor tasks as replacement of battery cables, lubrication of hinges, and adjustment of brakes. Additionally, they may act in a supervisory capacity over the mechanics.

History

The twentieth century is the age of the automobile. The gas-powered motor vehicle has evolved from a curiosity of the 1893 Chicago World's Fair into an integral aspect of life. The commitment by federal, state, and local governments to provide a comprehensive network of roads has enhanced the status of the automobile and its role in everyday life. In the year 1900, there were fewer than 8,000 cars on the road. By the 1990s nearly 10 million were being produced annually. With the passing of time, auto manufacture has become a highly competitive, international industry. Cars made in Sweden, Japan, Germany, Italy, Yugoslavia, Spain, Canada, Korea, Australia, the U.S.S.R., and the United Kingdom and France, as well as the United States, can be found on American roads. They have become more stylistically diverse and technologically complex. The Model T of the early 1900s little resembles the computerized, accessory laden, and aerodynamically designed vehicle of today.

Throughout its long history, one aspect of car use has remained the same: periodic repair and maintenance is required. As cars have become more numerous so the demand and the need for car repair facilities and qualified personnel has grown. It is in the larger shops, with more than twenty employees, that the division of labor requires that an automobile repair service estimator be employed. With the proliferation of automobile insurance, companies pay for the damages to a client's car. If repair costs exceed the car's value, they may now choose not to have repairs done.

Nature of the work

Being a service estimator involves more than just filling out an itemized list of the costs of parts and labor, and arranging for the work to be done. It is a multifaceted job that includes aspects of problem-solving with technological know-how, public relations, and sales skills. Above all, to be successful a service estimator must be a good communicator.

There are two general types of repair estimating done. Cars brought in for routine maintenance are scheduled for service according to manufacturer guidelines. In this instance, the auto-repair-service estimator simply fills out a repair order containing the necessary information—owner name and address, make and year of car, mileage, and description of work to be done.

It is when a car is brought in for repairs beyond normal maintenance that various facets of the estimator's job can come into play. If a vague description of the problem is given, the service estimator must correctly question the customer to discover the specific problem. It may be necessary to visually inspect the vehicle and, perhaps, road test it to make a correct diagnosis.

The estimator also figures out the cost of repairs and estimates how long it will take to perform the necessary work, explaining to the customer just what is wrong and why sometimes expensive repairs are needed. Often service estimators must impress upon wary motorists that the work to be done will improve performance of the vehicle, make it safer, and prevent more serious—and more expensive—problems. It is in these situations that the service estimator assumes sales, public relations, and educational functions.

In large dealerships, the work load is routed by a shop dispatcher; in smaller shops, it is the responsibility of the service estimator. In either case, the auto-repair-service estimator continues to act as the link between the customer and the mechanic, answering customer questions regarding the work being done and relaying additional information from the mechanic to the car owner. Following the completion of repairs, service estimators often road test the car to make sure it is running properly. When the customer comes to pick up the vehicle, the service estimator answers all questions about the work done, settling any complaints

A service estimator must consult several manuals before quoting a price for repairs.

about the quality of workmanship and the repair costs. If any errors have been made on the bill or if any grievance regarding workmanship is found to be justifiable, the service estimator may adjust the charges accordingly, following the approval of the service manager.

Requirements

Automobile-repair-service estimators should be interested in automobile technology and they should want to work with people. They should understand how and why a car works and possess the ability to transmit this knowledge to people who may or may not be familiar with the operation of motor vehicles in a technical sense. This is a public-oriented, service job where having a pleasing, even-tempered personality is a must.

Most service estimators receive on-the-job training from experienced estimators and the service manager. In many instances, the trainees assist the shop dispatcher, helping route work to mechanics and estimating the time needed for repairs as well as their costs. The training period is usually from one to two years and some service estimators enroll in automobile manufacturer-sponsored training programs.

To be accepted into a service estimator training program, the applicant should be twenty-one years old, possess a high-school diploma, and have some junior college or trade or vocational school experience. Prospective service estimators should take courses in motor vehicle repair or automotive training to learn the "technical" side of the business. Also ben-

eficial are courses in speech, English, commercial arithmetic, and sales. Many times, mechanic trainees and parts-counter trainees are promoted to this position; or experienced mechanics may be hired to fill it.

Special requirements

The nature of the job, the fact that the service estimator often is the shop's only contact with the public, means that employers look for individuals who can build confidence in customers to gain repeat business. The only special requirement for this job, then, concerns personality and appearance. Service estimators must be neat and courteous, even-tempered, and able to both listen well and communicate effectively.

Opportunities for experience and exploration

The best way to explore the opportunities available for this work is to secure employment in an auto repair shop. In this way, familiarity with the operation of a repair shop or an auto dealership can be gained. It also is possible to interview auto repair service estimators about the work they do.

Related occupations

The automobile industry, and in particular the service section, have a number of other occupations that might be of interest. These include automobile-body repairers, automobile mechanics, motorcycle mechanics, and diesel mechanics.

Methods of entering

Employment can be secured by applying directly to the repair facility or answering an advertisement in the "help wanted" section of a newspaper. The local office of the U.S. Employment Service also can provide information on job openings. Frequently, service estimators are recruited from the work force of the auto repair shop.

Advancement

The opportunities for advancement are good. Individuals demonstrating leadership abilities can rise to shop supervisor or service manager. Many go into their own business, opening gas service stations or auto repair shops.

Employment outlook

This is a small occupation with the potential for substantial growth. In the early 1990s, about 18,000 people were working as service estimators, primarily in metropolitan areas. During the next decade, as the number of automobiles on the road increases, the growth rate for service estimators is expected to outstrip the national average for all occupations. In addition to increased demand, attrition through death, retirement, or just leaving the profession will create even greater opportunities.

Because of the nature of the auto repair business, service estimators can expect steady employment with little fluctuation. They are not significantly affected by shifts in the economy. Even in tight times, most auto repairs cannot be put off. The risk of an accident or incurring even greater expense for repair jobs, make most motorists employ a normal maintenance schedule. In addition, during recessions, the tendency is to fix up old cars rather than to purchase new ones. Geographically, most jobs are available in metropolitan areas where the demand for auto repairs is high.

Earnings

In the early 1990s, auto-repair-service estimators earned, on the average, 25 percent more than all other nonsupervisory workers in industry, save for those in farming. Statistics gathered from twenty-four large cities indicate that the average annual wage was about $24,000. Payment to service estimators follows two tracks. Some work on a combined salary/commission basis, receiving a basic wage plus a percentage of the total for repairs and parts purchased by their customers. Others work on a straight commission basis.

Conditions of work

The job of a service estimator is not physically exhausting, though it might be emotionally so.

It requires standing on one's feet all day. There are extremely busy times, like in the morning when customers bring their cars in for repairs and in the evenings when they come to pick them up. Service estimators usually work from forty to forty-eight hours a week. The job involves heavy public interaction.

There is little outside work in inclement weather. Mostly, service estimators work in clean, well-lighted, and well-heated shops.

Social and psychological factors

Service estimators possess many employment advantages. Their work brings them into close contact with many new and interesting people. It allows them to offer a valuable service to customers when such aid is really needed. It also keeps them informed about the current state-of-the-art auto technology, both in terms of manufacture and repair. Most important, the work is steady, secure, and relatively high-paid.

There are, however, some disadvantages to the job. Service estimators spend long hours on their feet and their workday is broken up into extremely busy and relatively quiet periods. As the shop link with the public, the service estimator occasionally has to deal with irate, dissatisfied customers. The drawbacks, however, are outweighed by the benefits, particularly when the wide opportunities for advancement in the auto repair business are taken into account.

Though membership is not mandatory, some service estimators belong to the following unions: the International Brotherhood of Teamsters, Chauffeurs, Warehousemen and Helpers of America (Ind.); the Sheet Metal Workers International Association; or the International Association of Machinists and Aerospace Workers.

GOE: 05.07.02; SIC: 7538; SOC: 6881

 SOURCES OF ADDITIONAL INFORMATION

Automotive Service Industry Association
444 North Michigan Avenue
Chicago, IL 60611

National Institute for Automotive Service Excellence
1920 Association Drive
Reston, VA 22091

National Automobile Dealers Association
8400 Westpark Drive
McLean, VA 22102

◇ **RELATED ARTICLES**

Volume 1: Automotives
Volume 3: Automobile sales workers; Automotive body repairers; Automobile mechanics
Volume 4: Automotive diesel, and gas turbine technicians; Electromechanical technicians

Bicycle mechanics

Definition

Bicycle mechanics repair and service all types of bicycles using hand tools and power tools.

History

The bicycle first appeared in Scotland around the year 1839. For many years the bicycle was designed with a very large front wheel that was pedaled and steered, with a smaller wheel in back for balance. Over the years many advances in design and technology were made, such as hollow steel frames, ball bearings, metal wheel spokes and rubber-rimmed wheels. It wasn't until 1885 that the first bicycle with a sprocket-chain drive and equal-sized front and rear wheels—the style of modern bikes—was introduced in England. The pneumatic tire was invented in Scotland four years later. Bicycle riding was very popular in America during this time, reaching its peak of popularity around the year 1900. For many decades later in this country, bicycles were considered children's toys, but the 1960s saw a resurgence in their popularity among adults of all ages, a popularity that has continued to this day.

Nature of the work

Repairing bicycles takes mechanical skill and attention to detail. Many repairs such as replacing brake cables are relatively simple, while others can be very complicated. Mechanics use a variety of tools to repair and maintain bikes, including wrenches, screwdrivers, drills, vises

and specialized tools. Further complicating their job are the increasing number of brands of bikes, both domestic and foreign, each of which has its own unique qualities and mechanical problems.

Bike mechanics work on both new and used bicycles. They work on bikes that customers bring in for emergency work or "tune ups." They also repair used bikes which their dealership buys from the public or takes in trade from customers for resale later. Many times new bikes will come from the manufacturer in need of assembly, and the bike shop will put them together and see how well they run. Many department stores and discount houses contract out this type of work to bike shops, and it can be very profitable.

While some of the repairs made to bikes could easily be done by the bike owner, others are more complicated. Customers without the time or inclination to learn how to service their bikes take them to professional bike mechanics. Fixing a flat tire is one example. Leaks in clincher tires (those with a separate inner tube) can be done at home or given to the bicycle mechanic. Repair of sew-up tires (which have no inner tubes) is a more complicated process that requires a mechanic. Mechanics can also build wheels, replace and tighten spokes, and "true," or align, the wheels. When a wheel is built, the spokes are laced between the rim and the hub of the wheel, then tightened individually with a special wrench until the wheel spins without wobbling. Mechanics can also use a truing machine to test how balanced the wheel is spinning.

The gear mechanism on multiple-speed bikes is also a common concern for bicycle mechanics. Bikers shift gears by means of a mechanism called a derailleur, which can be located on the back wheel hub or at the bottom bracket assembly where the pedals and chain meet. The derailleur needs adjustment often. The mechanic aligns the front and rear gears of the derailleur to reduce wear on both the chain and the gear teeth, and adjusts the mechanism to keep the pressure on the chain constant. The gear mechanisms can differ greatly among different makes of bicycle, and the mechanic has to stay abreast of the latest models and trends.

Bicycle mechanics have to be able to spot trouble in a bike and know how to respond. They may have to straighten a bent bike frame using a special vise and a heavy steel rod. They can adjust or replace the braking mechanism so that the force on the brakes is correct. They may also take apart, clean, grease, and reassemble the headset, or front hub, and the bottom bracket that houses the axle of the pedal crank.

Mechanics who work in a bike shop may also work as salespeople, advising customers on their bike purchases and handling sales of biking accessories, such as horns, clothing, and bike locks. In some shops, especially those located in resort areas, the bike mechanic may also work as a *bicycle-rental clerk*. In cold-weather areas where biking is seasonal, bike mechanics may also work on other recreational equipment such as camping gear, snowmobiles or small engines.

Bicycle mechanics are busiest in the spring and summer months when bicyclers do the most damage to their bikes.

Some people work as mechanics with the dream of one day opening their own bike shop. These people would find it very helpful to take high-school or college courses in accounting, finance and small business management.

Requirements

A high-school diploma or other formal education is not required for a job as a bicycle mechanic, although classes in shop and physics can prove useful. Bicycle maintenance courses are offered at some technical schools, and three states—Oregon, Colorado, and Massachusetts—currently have schools for bicycle mechanics. The Schwinn Bicycle Company also offers factory instruction to the mechanics of their authorized dealers.

For the most part, however, bike mechanics learn on the job. At least two years of hands-on training is required to become a thoroughly skilled mechanic, but because of the constant introduction of new makes and models of bikes, there are always new things to learn. Many times, when a new model of bike is introduced, bike mechanics have to show that they can service the new model before getting authorization from the bike's manufacturer or distributor. Once the bike distributor visits the bike mechanics on the job and is satisfied that their work is competent, then the shop can be authorized to sell and service that new brand.

Special requirements

There are no special requirements for people working as bicycle mechanics.

Opportunities for experience and exploration

Part-time or summer jobs as a bicycle mechanic are relatively easy to come by for anyone who is good with tools and knows the basics of bike construction. Students should contact local bike dealerships, the names of which can be found in the yellow pages, in person and ask about any possible job openings. If there are no immediate openings, the manager or owner of the dealership may be able to direct the hopeful applicant to someplace that is hiring. The other area of experience is maintaining and repairing one's own bike.

Related occupations

Other workers perform work that is similar in skill and aptitude requirements as the work done by bicycle mechanics. These workers include automobile mechanics, diesel mechanics, general maintenance mechanics, and motorcycle mechanics.

Methods of entering

Once a mechanic has a part-time job, he or she may be able to turn it into a full-time job, if the shop has enough business. Otherwise, he or she can take their experience and try to find a job with another bike shop. For those without experience, the best way to find a job is the one described above: personally contacting local bike shops to find one that is willing to hire a new trainee. If one has all the tools needed, independent repair work is possible using ads and referrals.

Advancement

For those who like to service and work on bikes, advancement opportunities are limited. After a few years of service, a bicycle mechanic may take over managing the bike shop in which he or she works. A mechanic may also move on to a job with the bicycle department of a large department or sporting goods store, and from there move up to department manager or regional sales manager. Another possibility is to work as a sales representative for a bicycle manufacturer or distributor.

Bicycle mechanics may also wish to own and operate their own bike stores. They can work a few years to gain experience, save or borrow enough money, and then go into business either alone or with a partner. To start a business that specializes strictly in repair in a small town might require about $1,000 worth of starting capital. To open a store in a larger city and offer bikes for sale and repair might take $10,000 or more. Operating a successful small business requires long hours, sometimes ten or twelve hours a day, six days a week, and the risk of failure is always high. It takes time, money, and hard work to establish a successful business. To advance from a job as a bicycle mechanic in any of these ways, it is very advisable to take college courses in business, management, and accounting.

Employment outlook

The popularity of cycling continues to grow and shows no signs of slowing down. People are bicycling because they are concerned about fitness. They also care about the environment, because bikes do not burn gas or pollute the atmosphere. As long as bikes remain popular, bicycle mechanics will be in demand.

Bicycle repair is relatively immune to fluctuations in the economy. In times of economic boom, people buy more new bikes and mechanics are kept busy by assembling, selling and servicing them. During economic recessions, people bring their old bikes to mechanics for repair.

Earnings

Bicycle mechanics generally work a five-day, forty-hour week, although they may work overtime in the spring when people bring their old bikes out of storage. Novice mechanics may start at $3.35 to $4.50 per hour, but as they gain more experience and skill, they could earn $10.00 per hour or more. Wages vary depending on the area of the country and the size of the city or town, but in general bike shop owners and customers are both willing to pay for skilled and dependable mechanics.

Conditions

The work bench and area where a bicycle mechanic performs can vary from spacious to cramped, depending on the individual store. Working with grease and oil, mechanics usually get their hands and clothing dirty, but the work in general is not strenuous. Very large bike and specialty shops are the only places where heavy work such as painting, brazing, or frame straightening takes place.

Mechanics work by themselves as they service each bike. Dealing well with the public and other co-workers, however, is important. The atmosphere around a bike shop can be very hectic, especially during peak seasons and in shops where mechanics also work as clerks or store owners.

Social and psychological factors

Bicycle mechanics must be detail-minded and enjoy tackling a new challenge, because every bike presents a unique problem to be analyzed and fixed. It is essential that they be mechanically inclined and enjoy working with their hands. Some bicycle parts like derailleurs and multispeed hubs are like puzzles to take apart and put back together, so a mechanic should be exacting and dedicated enough to repair them skillfully. A personal interest in cycling is also a valuable advantage.

Opportunities for advancement and high pay are relatively few for the person who remains a bicycle mechanic. It can be a good way, however, to earn money for college. In addition, people tend to respect mechanics and others who work well with their hands. Reliable craftsmanship is a disappearing commodity, and good bicycle mechanics have unique skills. Because they can see the immediate result of their work, bicycle mechanics can take pride in their work and in the respect others give them.

GOE: 05.10.02; SIC: 7699; SOC: 6129

◇ **SOURCES OF ADDITIONAL INFORMATION**

Bicycle Institute of America
1818 R Street, NW
Washington, DC 20009

National Bicycle Dealers Association
129 Cabrillo Street, Suite 201
Costa Mesa, CA 92627

◇ **RELATED ARTICLES**

Volume 1: Machining and Machinery; Recreation and Park Services; Retailing
Volume 3: Diesel mechanics; General maintenance mechanics

Bindery workers

Definition

Binding is the final step in the production of books and magazines. *Bindery workers* take the printed pages of books, pamphlets, catalogs, and magazines, and fold, cut, sew, staple, or glue them together to produce finished reading materials.

History

Bookbinding is an ancient and honored craft. As early as the third century A.D., when books were still written on papyrus and animal skins, the parchment manuscripts were kept stored between two boards. During the Middle Ages, bookbinding was developed into a fine art by monks in monasteries who decorated the board covers of sacred books with costly bindings made of elaborately worked metal, jewels, ivory, and enamel.

Around the year 900, the English introduced the use of leather to cover the boards and soon became leaders in this field. English kings employed official binders responsible for decorating the books in the royal library. Nobles and other powerful figures followed their monarchs' lead and also established libraries of luxuriously bound volumes. The fine bindings made for royal or noble patrons were usually decorated with coats of arms or family crests. In this way, the bookbinder became highly regarded as an artist.

With the invention of the printing press in the fifteenth century, the way was opened for an ever-increasing number of books. Because of the growing demand for books among ordinary citizens, the making and binding of books was transferred from the monasteries and palaces to the shops of printers and binders. Soon the names, initials, or emblems of printers and binders were stamped onto the book covers they made.

Today, most bookbinding is done in a routine manner by automated machines, but it is still possible to secure richly bound books, crafted by highly skilled workers, at prices from several hundred to several thousand dollars. These may be special printings of limited editions, or the restoration of old or damaged

While many of the binding processes are mechanized, bindery workers must ensure that the machines are running smoothly.

books. The average modern book, however, is simply bound in paper, cloth, or a composite material that can be purchased inexpensively. The art of bookbinding, together with the skills of the hand bookbinder, is rapidly becoming a thing of the past.

Nature of the work

Although originally a handicraft, modern bookbinding operations are practically all mechanized. The average bookbinder today is a highly skilled machine operator who knows little or nothing about hand bookbinding. This bookbinder sets up and operates folding, gathering, sewing, stitching, trimming, casemaking, and covering machines.

The average bookbinder may work at several different kinds of binderies: edition or pamphlet binderies that specialize in large numbers (or "runs") of books, magazines, and pamphlets; trade or job binderies that produce smaller quantities on a contract basis for printers and publishers; or manifold or loose-leaf binderies that bind blank pages into ledgers, notebooks, checkbooks, diaries, and notepads. In addition, some bookbinders are employed in large libraries where they concentrate on repairing old, worn, or damaged bindings.

Bindery work can consist of one or more steps. Some binding jobs, such as preparing leaflets or newspaper inserts, require only a single step, in this case folding. The most complicated binding work is that of edition binding, or the production of books from large printed sheets of paper. Book pages are usually not produced individually, but are printed on a large sheet of paper six or eight at a time. These large sheets are folded by machine into units

called "signatures," and these signatures are joined together in the proper order to make a complete book. Full-page illustrations are usually printed separately on different paper stock and inserted into the signature either by hand or by machine. The signatures are then assembled into the proper order by a gathering machine and sewed or glued together to make what is called a "book block." After gathering, the book blocks are compressed in a machine to ensure compactness and uniform thickness, trimmed to the proper size, and reinforced with glued fabric strips along the spine. The covers for the book are created separately and are pasted or glued to the book block by machine. The books may undergo a variety of finishing operations, such as gilding the edges of pages and the insertion of paper dust jackets, and finally they are inspected and packed for shipment.

These same operations, or operations that are very similar, are also used in the binding of magazines, catalogs, and directories. In large binderies, they are usually done in an assembly-line fashion by bindery workers who are trained in only one or two procedures. Some workers specialize in operating specific equipment such as folding or gathering machines, while others specialize in adjusting and preparing equipment to perform a particular job. In many shops, much of the work is done by bindery workers who are trained to perform tasks assigned by an experienced worker or bookbinder. For example, semiskilled bindery workers perform such tasks as punching holes into sheets, stamping numbers on sheets, fastening sheets or signatures together using a machine stapler, and feeding covers and signatures into various machines for stitching, folding, ruling, or gluing.

Bindery workers are often referred to by the name of the particular machine they operate: for example, *folding*, *saddle-stitching*, *automatic gluing*, *book-sewing*, *covering*, *rounding and backing*, and *case-making machine operators*. Other specialists include *book trimmers*, *forwarders*, *inkers*, *casers*, *book repairers*, and *pressers*.

In spite of machines and technology, a small number of *bookbinders* still work in hand binderies. These highly skilled workers design original or special bindings for limited editions or restore and rebind rare or damaged books for private collections and museums. This hand work requires creative ability, knowledge of materials, and a thorough background in the history of binding. Hand bookbinding is perhaps the only kind of binding work that gives the individual the opportunity to work at a variety of bindery jobs.

Requirements

Most bindery workers, both skilled and semi-skilled, learn their craft through on-the-job training. Inexperienced workers usually start by doing simple tasks such as moving paper from cutting machines to folding machines. As workers gain experience, they advance to more difficult tasks and may learn how to operate one or more pieces of equipment. A one- to three-month training period is generally required to learn how to operate a new piece of equipment.

As in most occupations, employers prefer to hire experienced people, so those individuals with some knowledge of binding operations are likely to have an advantage in being accepted for employer-provided training. High-school students interested in bindery careers can gain some exposure to the industry by taking shop courses or attending a vocational-technical high school. Occupational skill centers also provide an introduction to the industry.

Formal apprenticeships, while not as common as they used to be, are still available. They enable workers to acquire the high levels of specialization and skill needed for some jobs. A four-year apprenticeship usually is necessary to teach bookbinders how to restore rare books and to produce valuable collectors' editions. Rare and old book restoration now includes the costly and delicate procedure of de-acidifying the paper. Several techniques are available and all require special equipment and training. The acid-laden paper crumbles easily and requires great skill to handle properly. A two-year apprenticeship program is usually required of bindery workers whose occupations are less complicated. Most union shops require an apprenticeship program to combine on-the-job training with some formal classroom instruction. Four-year college programs are recommended for those who want to own or manage their own bindery shops.

Accuracy, neatness, patience, and good eyesight are among the qualities needed for this occupation. Finger dexterity is essential for those who count, insert, paste, and fold, while mechanical aptitude is required of individuals operating newer automated equipment. Artistic ability and imagination are required for hand bookbinding. Employers look for individuals with basic language and mathematics skills.

Special requirements

There are no special requirements for these occupations.

Opportunities for experience and exploration

There are several ways to explore the occupations of bookbinders and bindery workers. A young person may learn firsthand about bindery work through summer employment in a local bindery. By observing actual job situations and by talking with full-time employees, the interested student can both learn and earn.

In addition, many trade and vocational schools offer courses in bookbinding in which the rudiments of the trade may be learned. Some schools even have work-study arrangements with trade or job binderies that enable their learners to broaden their experience in the field. Contacts made during this training period may be useful in securing full-time employment after graduation. Often, too, experience gained in a trade school will result in the shortening of the regular apprenticeship period.

Related occupations

Other book and magazine industry occupations that might be of interest include printing press operators, photoengravers, typesetters, art directors, book designers, illustrators, photographers, and editors and writers.

Methods of entering

For those who plan to become bookbinders, the best way to enter the trade is to apply for a place in the apprenticeship program at the state employment service bureau, a bindery, or the appropriate union headquarters, such as the International Brotherhood of Bookbinders. Those seeking bindery worker jobs may enter the two-year apprenticeship program in the same way.

If applicants wish to enter the field as on-the-job trainees, they should contact the employer directly by answering want ads or go to the state employment service bureau, especially when work is sought in one of the small non-union binderies. Graduates of trade schools may find a job through the school's placement service.

Advancement

Advancement may come faster for those who have completed the apprenticeship program than for those who attempt to learn the trade solely through on-the-job training. Once training is successfully completed, however, bookbinder status is achieved.

Skilled workers who possess certain personal characteristics, such as interpersonal skills, good judgment, and planning skills, may advance to a position as bookbinding inspector, supervisor, or shop superintendent. Opportunities for this type of advancement are limited to large binderies. For those who possess the necessary business knowledge and adequate capital, another form of advancement is to open up their own bindery business.

Employment outlook

In the early 1990s, approximately 85,000 people worked as bookbinders. Of these, 11,000 were full bookbinders and more than 74,000 were bindery machine operators, setters, and setup operators.

Anticipated growth in the printing industries should result in a promising future for bindery occupations. Commercial printers are expected to hire more bindery workers as the volume of printed material grows because of economic expansion and increased reliance on catalogs, newspaper inserts, and direct mail advertising to spur consumer demand. Increased demand for books and magazines is also expected, as the general population ages and has more time for leisure reading.

Accompanying this growth, however, will be an emphasis on improving productivity and more complex automated equipment. The binding process is becoming increasingly mechanized, as new equipment is introduced that performs a number of operations in sequence and permits shorter periods of preparation and faster production speeds. As a result, labor requirements have been reduced, and the jobs of many semiskilled bindery workers who once assisted skilled bookbinders have already been eliminated. As in other occupations, most job openings will result from the need to replace experienced workers who change jobs or leave the labor force.

Earnings

Bindery workers' salaries vary according to the type of work they do and the region of the country in which they live. Skilled bookbinders' earnings are below the average wages paid to other printing craft workers. In the early 1990s, the wages for union workers ranged from $18,500 to $26,000 per year.

Apprenticeship pay starts at about 40 percent to 50 percent of the bookbinder's rate and grows to about 85 percent of the rate toward the end of the training period. Wages are generally higher in unionized plants than in nonunion shops. Most union contracts provide for time-and-a-half pay for overtime, and double time for Sunday and holiday work.

Conditions of work

The average workweek for bookbinders and bindery workers ranges from thirty-five to forty hours. Modern binderies are usually well lighted and well ventilated but often noisy. Although bindery workers are subject to few dangers, they must be careful to prevent injury while operating stitching machines, stapling machines, and power cutters. Certain jobs can be very tiring to arms and legs because of long periods of standing and continuous reaching and stretching while feeding materials into the machines. The jobs of some workers can be fairly strenuous and require considerable lifting, stooping, kneeling, and carrying. Because much of the work is done in an assembly-line manner, it is often repetitive and may become monotonous.

Social and psychological factors

Because books are basic to education, and education is the foundation on which our democracy and way of life are built, it is easy to appreciate the importance of the work of those who help make books. The products of the bookbinders' and bindery workers' skills provide millions of readers with pleasure, information, and entertainment. Businesses and industry also rely on the binding profession for producing important documents and keeping records. Through the medium of bound magazines, millions of dollars worth of America's business advertising is brought to the public.

Those who are interested in bindery worker occupations should realize that the job calls for a personality that can adapt to routine, not for one that requires variety. Hand bookbinding is perhaps the most satisfying of the occupations in this field because it requires creativity and a knowledge of many different processes; however, opportunities for these workers are limited by the small number of establishments that do this highly specialized work.

GOE: 06.04.04; SIC: 2789; SOC: 76

Printing Industries of America
1730 North Lynn Street
Arlington, VA 22209

◇ **SOURCES OF ADDITIONAL INFORMATION**

Binding Industries of America
70 East Lake Street
Chicago, IL 60601

Graphic Communications International Union
1900 L Street, NW
Washington, DC 20036

Graphic Arts Technical Foundation
4615 Forbes Avenue
Pittsburgh, PA 15213

Compositors and typesetters

Definition

Compositors and *typesetters* set type, arrange the type with cuts and photoengravings, and compose and prepare preliminary printing plates. Though they work today primarily with photocomposition, some still set type by hand or use linotype or monotype machines. Computer-generated typesetting and electronic page makeup systems are transforming the industry.

History

The history of modern printing began soon after 1440 with the invention of movable type. In Germany, Johannes Gutenberg printed the Bible as the first book to be composed in the new way. For several centuries before that, some books had been printed from carved wooden blocks. But most of the books of ancient and medieval times were laboriously copied by hand. They were so expensive that they were chained so they could not be stolen.

Gutenberg's movable type made it possible to use the same letters over and over. Also, the letters themselves, because they were individual, were cheaper to make. Thus the cost of the composition of books was greatly reduced, and books became more plentiful.

Benjamin Franklin, a great American of the 1700s, was a leader in the establishment of schools in Pennsylvania and at the same time was a printer. He began as an apprentice printer and later occupied many exalted positions. Yet in the beginning of his will, written at the age of 86, he identified himself as a printer. Peter Zenger, the ardent eighteenth century printer who fought for freedom of the press, is another example of a printer who realized the power and privilege of his craft.

Ottmar Mergenthaler, a German immigrant to the United States, invented the Linotype machine in 1886. Linotype allowed the typesetter to set type from a keyboard which used a circulating matrix to set letters in place. Before this invention, printers were setting type by hand, one letter at a time, picking up each letter individually from their typecases as they had been doing for more than 400 years. At about the same time, Tolbert Lanston invented the Monotype. Suddenly printers were able to multiply over and again the results of each compositor's work. Newspapers advanced from the small two-page weekly of Franklin's time to the huge editions of today's metropolitan daily press. More periodicals, advertisements, books, and other printed matter have resulted.

Compositors and typesetters
Machine Trades Occupations

Nature of the work

It is the function of the composing room to set type and assemble it with cuts for the press workers to use in printing. There is a great variety of duties and skills involved in composing room occupations.

Compositors set type by hand or machine for articles, headings, and other printed matter. They select the type style and size according to instructions for the job to be done. When *compositors* or *compositors apprentices* set copy by hand, which is rarely done anymore, they select one letter or character at a time, putting it in a tray called a "composing stick." They insert lead, brass, or copper to even out the line; they may later insert lead slugs or lines of quads to adjust the length of the whole setup. When the stick is full, the type is dumped from the stick to another tray called a "galley." In the galley, the type is fastened tightly together, inked, and then paper is pressed against it by *galley strippers*. This sample of the printed article is called a proof, and is examined for mistakes by *proof sheet correctors* so that the compositor may correct them. When the job is finished, the type is cleaned and returned to its storage case till it is used again.

The ad compositor gets together the type and cuts needed for an advertisement. This worker spaces the materials in a galley according to a predetermined plan furnished in the copy prepared by the customer. The ad may ultimately be stereotyped, electrotyped, and printed from type, engraved, or proofed for photographic reproduction.

The *Linotype operator* operates a semiautomatic machine that has a keyboard, consisting of small, or lowercase, letters and numbers, and large, or uppercase, capital letters. The keyboard is operated to form a line of type, hence the name of the machine. The operator starts the machine, reading from copy clipped to his or her copy board, strikes the keyboard and activates the proper matrices that form a line. This makes a slug of metal with raised letters on it. This slug is of the length desired for the length of a line of type in the finished printed material. By operating a lever, the compositor causes the slug to be deposited in a metal tray called a "galley" that is on one side of the machine. After the proof is made, the galley is returned to the operator for corrections. The Linotype operator has the duty of seeing that solid pieces of lead, called "pigs," are added to the melting pot when needed. Nearly all newspaper plants, large commercial shops, and typesetting shops once used these machines and operators to set type, but Lino-

type machines in most instances have been replaced by computerized typesetting machines.

The *Monotype operator* operates a machine that perforates ribbons of paper. The machine has a keyboard with 270 keys. The operator selects the keys of the desired size and style, loads a roll of paper on a spindle, threads it through the machine, sets the scales for the control of length of line and space between the words. By striking the keys, the operator causes the paper to be perforated. When the operator comes to the end of the copy on the copyholder from which he or she has been working, the operator tears the tape from the supply roll, puts typecasting instructions on the reel, and sends it to the Monotype caster. The big advantage of this machine was that corrections could be made by hand without setting an entire line, but it too is being replaced.

Today, the most active of the machine compositors is the *phototypesetting operator*. This worker's machine sometimes has the appearance of other typesetting machines, but its operation results in a film or photographic paper print. The operator must be familiar with photographic processes to develop the films. This person must also be familiar with electronics, because much of the equipment has electronic controls. The product of such typesetting machines may be called "cold type," for no hot metal casting is involved. This occupation includes typewriter style typesetting, too.

Proofreaders have the responsibility of cross-checking trial proofs before the final printing is made. They check for grammatical, typographical, and composition errors, by reading the original copy against the proof. A special proofreader's code of marks is used for indicating errors. Marked-up proofs are returned to the compositor for corrections, additions, or deletions in the copy.

Specialists include *phototypesetting equipment monitors, typesetting-machine tender, veritype, photocomposing-perforator-machine, photocomposition-keyboard, magnetic-tape-composer, terminal-system, electronic-typesetting-machine, terminal makeup, typesetter perforator, casting-machine, type-casting machine, paste-up copy-camera, photocomposing-machine operators, copy cutters, type-proof reproducers,* and *job printers and apprentices.*

Requirements

A high-school education is usually a requirement for entering composing room occupations. It is necessary for compositors to have a good knowledge of spelling, grammar, and arithmetic. Courses in printing and typewriting are also good preparation for apprenticeship in printing.

Most composing room workers learn their trades as helpers or as apprentices. Apprenticeships usually cover a period of six years, but it may be shortened by two or more years for those apprentices who have had previous experience or schooling. The apprentice begins with the simplest and most routine tasks and gradually advances through the more complicated aspects of composition.

In small shops and in small communities, especially where the shops are not unionized, new workers gain their knowledge and skills as helpers. Trade school work is helpful in such cases. The helpers pick up their skills in the general course of the performance of their work. There is no formal obligation on the part of the employer, as in the apprenticeship programs, to give definitely planned and scheduled instruction.

Typesetters use computers to compose text and set it into type. With the aid of software, much of this work can be done in-house.

Special requirements

There are no special requirements for composing room occupations; most print shops, however, are unionized and union membership may be required.

Opportunities for experience and exploration

The chances for exploration in the composing room occupations are plentiful. There are printing establishments in all communities. Most will admit visitors with appointments, and most of them welcome any young person who wants to investigate printing as an occupational possibility by touring their facilities.

Part-time employment offers good opportunities to observe and experience the requirements, duties, and benefits of such work. Valuable experience and insights can be gained in printing and graphic arts classes at many junior and senior high schools.

Related occupations

Other occupations that might appeal to persons with the skills and aptitudes for compositing and typesetting work may also be in other publishing and printing jobs. These include edi-

tors, writers, printing press operators, prepress workers, art directors, lithographic workers, photoengravers, and book designers.

Methods of entering

Entering the printing trades is often done through jobs as helpers. In union shops, apprentices are usually chosen from among the helpers.

In small towns, direct application to the local printing shop or newspaper is a good way to enter the trade. Contacting the proper official of the appropriate local union is another avenue toward employment. School publications, particularly at the college level, may do their own typesetting.

Advancement

There are more than sixty-five occupations in the printing field, so there are many avenues for advancement for a young person. From a job as a helper or directly from high school or trade school, one may enter an apprenticeship. The degree of advancement depends on ability, desire to learn, willingness to work, and opportunities open at a particular time and in a particular place.

One common ambition of printers is to have shops of their own. While a great majority of people in printing work are employed by others, many of the printing establishments in this country are "one-person" shops operated by their owners.

Compositors and typesetters
Machine Trades Occupations

Employment outlook

In the early 1990s, there were approximately 94,000 jobs in the field, about 37 percent of them in newspaper plants and 23 percent in commercial printing plants. Employers tended to cluster in the large printing centers of Chicago, Dallas, Los Angeles, New York, Philadelphia, and Washington, D.C.

There are declining opportunities for employment in most composing room occupations in most areas. Automation has replaced many workers in the past twenty years. Opportunities may open up in smaller towns or cities more readily than in larger cities, where computerized phototypesetting is now the rule. Many jobs are open for keyboard operators in computerized phototypesetting.

Earnings

In all parts of the country, composing room workers earn higher wages than skilled workers generally. There is considerable variation in wages from shop to shop, from city to city, and from state to state.

Wages are usually higher in union shops than in nonunion shops. Those who work night shifts are often paid a higher hourly rate than daytime workers. Time-and-a-half pay for overtime is frequent; sometimes double- or even triple-time pay is required by union contracts.

In the early 1990s, experienced union compositors made an average annual salary of about $27,350. Compositors who worked on night shifts for newspapers received extra pay. Wages for helpers, apprentices, and computer typists were considerably lower.

Conditions of work

At newspapers and in small shops, the usual workweek is forty hours. Often in job shops, it is three-and-one-half–hours, and in some it is thirty-five hours, and there are pressures for an even further reduction. More than half the printing trades workers are under pension, welfare, and health insurance plans. It is common practice to allow two-week paid vacations after a year of service, on up to a possibility of four weeks after forty years. A number of compositors are members of the International Typographical Union.

Most composing rooms are quite noisy. In many shops, the noise of the Linotype machines is made worse by the noises of presses. Pungent smells of ink, hot lead, and a variety of chemicals are often present. Often the workers perform their duties under bright artificial lights. Some of the modern plants are air conditioned; many of the older ones are too hot in the summer and not warm enough in the winter. Proofreaders and machine operators sit for prolonged periods at their positions. Hands may become soiled and often special clothes are worn so that street clothes will not be damaged. In some of the jobs, it is necessary to take special precautions for the protection of health. Young people with handicaps such as deafness have been able to enter the field and work satisfactorily.

Social and psychological factors

The social significance of the work of the printers is realized when the importance of printing is considered. A world without newspapers, books, advertisements, business forms, even scorecards and calendars would be hard to imagine. Business and commerce depend on printing; schools and other educational institutions rely on it; world communication is aided by the power of printed words.

The composing room workers, then, along with their fellow craft workers, have a sound basis for pride in their occupations. They may take great satisfaction from seeing the results of their work in the finished products.

GOE: 05.05.13; SIC: 2791; SOC: 6841

◇ **SOURCES OF ADDITIONAL INFORMATION**

Book Manufacturers Institute
111 Prospect
Stamford, CT 06901

Graphic Arts Technical Foundation
4615 Forbes Avenue
Pittsburgh, PA 15213

Printing, Publishing, and Media Workers sector of the CWA
Communications Workers of America
1925 K Street, NW, 4th Floor
Washington, DC 20006

Printing Industries of America
1730 North Lynn Street
Arlington, VA 22209

Typographers International Association
2262 Hall Place, NW
Washington, DC 20007

◇ **RELATED ARTICLES**

Volume 1: Printing
Volume 3: Electrotypers and stereotypers;
Lithographic occupations; Photoengravers; Printing press operators; Typists

Diesel mechanics

Definition

Diesel mechanics repair and maintain diesel engines that power such machines as buses, ships, automobiles, trucks, railroad trains, generators, construction machinery, and farm and highway equipment.

History

The diesel engine, an internal combustion engine, was patented by Rudolph Diesel in 1892. There are certain basic differences between gasoline and diesel engines. In the gasoline engine, the fuel and air are mixed in the carburetor before entering the engine. When this mixture enters the cylinder, it is compressed and an electric spark ignites the mixture. In the diesel engine, the fuel is sprayed or injected into the cylinder where the heat of compression ignites the mixture. The diesel engine tends to be more efficient than the gasoline engine because it has more air than needed to burn the fuel. It is also more economical to operate because it uses less fuel in delivering the same power as a gasoline engine and also uses cheaper fuel.

The initial use of diesel engines was in stationary power-plant applications. By 1908, however, a diesel engine was used to power a Russian tanker. In 1910, the English used a diesel engine to power a submarine. Ten years later the first diesel-powered bus and locomotive were developed. A diesel-powered airplane made its first flight in 1931. In the same year a diesel-powered racer competed at Indianapolis. The first commercial trucks with diesel engines appeared in 1932. The switch by railroads from steam to diesel engines began in 1934, when a passenger diesel locomotive made a record run between Chicago and Denver.

To date, the diesel engine is an important source of power. In some areas of work it goes unchallenged as a provider of power. A conservative estimate shows that the rate of increase of diesel engines is ten million horsepower per year.

Nature of the work

The work of diesel mechanics will vary depending on whether they service automotive engines, industrial power engines, marine engines, stationary engines, or railway engines. Even though each type of diesel engine is based on the same theoretical principles, the equipment they power may vary in terms of transmission, gear systems, and accessory items. As a result of these differences, sometimes it is difficult for the diesel mechanic to transfer from one type of equipment to another. Specialists include *diesel-engine testers*, *fuel-injection servicers*, *industrial truck mechanics*, *tractor mechanics*, and *diesel-engine erectors*, who assemble, analyze, repair, and disassemble diesel engines and turbines.

The work of a diesel mechanic can be divided into maintenance, repair, and rebuilding. Maintenance work is primarily done to keep the engine in proper operation. This includes such procedures as checking lubricating oil levels; clearing air and oil filters; removing and checking injectors, fuel pumps, and nozzles; and checking the water cooling system.

In spite of using proper maintenance, scheduled parts of the diesel engine can wear out or become defective. The diesel mechanic removes, replaces, and adjusts such items as

499

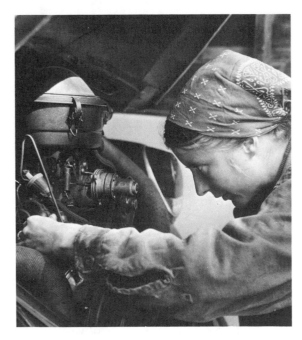

Annual tune-ups and routine maintenance often comprise the bulk of a diesel mechanic's schedule.

fuel pumps, injectors, piston rods, crankshafts, and bearings. A frequent repair job is the reseating or regrinding of exhaust, intake, and air valves.

To rebuild an engine a diesel mechanic takes the whole engine apart. This is usually scheduled at regular intervals such as 18 months or 100,000 miles. The mechanic uses various instruments to check each part and either reconditions or replaces it if it shows wear or is defective. This calls for an ability to measure accurately. For example, rod alignment must be accurate to within .001 of an inch. The task of rebuilding an engine may be done by a single mechanic, or a number of mechanics may work on separate parts of the engine.

Because the diesel engine has wide uses, the mechanic has to have some special training to be capable of performing certain jobs. For example, in diesel locomotives one may be required to inspect air-brake compressors, electric generators, and fuel systems.

In this work, the diesel mechanic will use hand tools, surface gauges, pressure gauges, feelers, and micrometers to check the wear of parts. The mechanic will also use ring spreaders, liner pullers, and on occasion a lathe when he rebuilds an engine. It is customary for the mechanic to own most of the hand tools. Most mechanics buy their own tools. Experienced mechanics often invest hundreds of dollars in tools.

Requirements

The qualifications for diesel mechanics vary because the type of engine they repair and service can be simple or complex or may have a number of auxiliary parts. Generally speaking, diesel mechanics should be of average intelligence and have a degree of mechanical aptitude. Their background should show satisfactory performance in high-school courses in shop work, mathematics, and science. It is essential to be able to read with understanding, for a considerable amount of time is spent reading service manuals. Completion of a U.S. Navy course in diesel engines is often considered proper experience.

Some diesel mechanic jobs are very strenuous. As a result, the individual may be required to lift up to one hundred pounds.

Training for the occupation will vary from on-the-job to formal classroom work. The person who has proper training will have the best chances for employment.

An apprenticeship program provides the best means of becoming a proficient diesel mechanic. The age range for apprentices is between eighteen and twenty-five. A satisfactory performance on tests given by the state employment bureau is one of the prerequisites for consideration. Some experience in a filling station or auto shop is also desirable.

The length of the apprenticeship will vary from three to four years. For example, the apprenticeship program with diesel engine manufacturers generally lasts four years. Trainees get a combination of classroom training and practical experience in fixing types of engines, blueprint reading, hydraulics, welding, and other subjects. They also learn about valves, bearings, injection systems, starting systems, cooling systems, and other parts.

Many young people who become diesel mechanics first work on gasoline engines.

An individual who is a mechanic's helper may be upgraded to mechanic by means of on-the-job training. As the need arises and skills develop, the mechanic's helper moves from such simple tasks as cleaning air filters and checking starting batteries to the more complex tasks of overhauling fuel pumps and nozzles. To become a proficient mechanic, the helper must supplement experience with correspondence or technical school courses. When employed by firms that use or repair diesel engines, the helper usually will be given an additional six to eighteen months of training.

There are a number of private, public, and vocational schools that give formal training in diesel equipment. The training consists of both theory and practice of maintenance, repair, and rebuilding of diesel equipment. There are no rigorous entrance requirements to these schools. Some employers prefer to hire a person trained in this manner because they feel that the graduate can keep up with the rapid changes in diesel equipment.

Special requirements

There are no special requirements to become a diesel mechanic. Most of these workers, however, do belong to the union that is most appropriate for their particular work in this field. Marine engineers, who are diesel engineers on ships, must be licensed by the U.S. Coast Guard.

Opportunities for experience and exploration

The best way to explore one's interest and aptitude is through tinkering with engines found in automobiles, motorcycles, go-carts, and lawn mowers. A job in a filling station will point up the routine found in maintenance work. A field trip to a truck maintenance shop, railroad roundhouse, or merchant ship will show the variety of places of employment. A course in combustion engines in a technical or vocational school will demonstrate some of the technical knowledge a diesel mechanic is expected to know. Experience in a military service school such as the Navy's diesel mechanic school or the Army's heavy equipment school will test the individual's interest rigorously.

Related occupations

Other mechanical occupations that may be of interest include bicycle mechanics, automotive mechanics, automobile-body repairers, general maintenance mechanics, and motorcycle mechanics.

Methods of entering

An individual can become a diesel mechanic by transferring from gasoline engine mechanic; by apprenticeship training or on-the-job training; or by attending technical schools. Some gasoline engine mechanics transfer over to diesel

engines for a variety of reasons. For example, a bus or truck company may change from gasoline- to diesel-powered vehicles. Another mechanic who is a specialist in power steering or electrical systems may be asked to switch to diesel work. Some skills, like the reboring of cylinders, transfer over. Other skills, however, especially those associated with the fuel system, must be learned.

Advancement

There are several lines of advancement open in this occupational field to a highly skilled diesel mechanic. The type of advancement will vary with the industry. Those who work for a large trucking company, bus line, or any company using automotive-type diesels have the following promotional possibilities: master mechanic, assistant service manager, and service manager. In working with locomotive or stationary engines, their line of advancement would be supervisor or plant superintendent. If they work for a manufacturer of diesel equipment, they may become a field representative, a training specialist, or a salesperson. If they work aboard a ship, they can become a licensed marine engineer with the proper training and experience.

To be considered for an administrative position one must be able to deal with people, express oneself well, work under stress, and influence others.

Employment outlook

In the early 1990s, there were approximately 218,000 persons employed as diesel mechanics. They worked in the service departments of distributors and dealers that sold diesel-powered farm and construction equipment and trucks. They also worked for bus lines, construction or trucking companies, shipping lines, electric power plants, and federal, state, and local governments.

There has been a steady increase in diesel power use in commerce, agriculture, and industry. During the last three decades, the number of buses and trucks using diesel engines has more than doubled. Farm mechanization will continue to increase, resulting in more diesel tractors, harvesters, and other machines. New superhighways and federal redevelopment programs have required large numbers of cranes, bulldozers, trucks, and other equipment. Increased petroleum production de-

Diesel mechanics
Machine Trades Occupations

mands additional equipment for drilling operations. Moderate growth has taken place in railroad, marine, and mining industries. Diesel taxicabs are expected to be used on a larger scale in the future.

Increased use of diesel equipment has produced a demand for mechanics to maintain, repair, and overhaul such equipment. A qualified mechanic is hard to find. Diesel power will be the predominant source of power in spite of increased use of atomic reactors and gas turbines.

Earnings

The hourly rate for diesel mechanics varies with the industries. Wage data collected from employers of workers who repair trucks, buses, construction equipment, and stationary engines indicate that the average annual earnings for diesel mechanics in the early 1990s were $29,950 (with a forty-hour week). Some skilled experienced workers made $43,630 and more. Most diesel mechanics work on an hourly pay scale. The average hourly wage is between $12 and $13. Mechanics employed by transportation firms receive the highest average wage at almost $14 an hour.

Apprentices make about half the wages of experienced employees, with raises every six months until training is completed.

Some of the fringe benefits were time-and-a-half for overtime, paid vacations and holidays, and health and life insurance. Those working for railroads received free travel passes.

Conditions of work

The work of a diesel mechanic is usually performed inside a garage, shop, or ship. Some jobs require a high degree of strength and stamina. The heaviest equipment is moved by cranes or hoists. The mechanic must handle greasy and dirty motors, and some of the work is carried out in awkward or cramped positions.

If a diesel mechanic works for a bus or construction company, some repair work is done on the job site. This type of work calls for improvisation and ingenuity, because key equipment or parts may be lacking to make the appropriate repair.

There are many hazards in this occupation. Heavy lifting may cause various injuries. One may receive a burn while steam cleaning an engine or touching a hot engine. Slipping on a greasy floor is another hazard. Most places of employment have adequate safety procedures to minimize the dangers, however.

Some of the industries, like construction or transportation, may have seasonal variations of employment. The work in a shipyard is dependent in part on government contracts. A diesel mechanic usually works a forty-hour week, though in some shops, because of the need for emergency repairs, overtime is frequent. Some shops may have round-the-clock shifts. Extra pay is given for night work.

Some of the unions to which diesel mechanics belong are the International Association of Machinists and Aerospace Workers; the Amalgamated Transit Union; the Sheet Metal Workers' International Association; the International Union, United Automobile, Aerospace and Agricultural Implement Workers of America; and the International Brotherhood of Electrical Workers.

Social and psychological factors

Diesel mechanics must be dependable and accurate. Their development of a knack for repair work is indispensable. They know the work in this field is important, for without the power and propulsion supplied by diesel engines the many conveniences and production of certain products would not be possible. The work is challenging because of the variety of problems that occur that require intelligence and mechanical aptitude to solve.

GOE: 05.05.09; SIC: 7538; SOC: 6112

◇ **SOURCES OF ADDITIONAL INFORMATION**

Amalgamated Transit Union
5025 Wisconsin Avenue, NW
Washington, DC 20016

International Association of Machinists and Aerospace Workers
1300 Connecticut Avenue, NW
Washington, DC 20036

International Brotherhood of Electrical Workers
1125 15th Street, NW
Washington, DC 20005

International Union, United Automobile, Aerospace and Agricultural Implement Workers of America
8000 East Jefferson Avenue
Detroit, MI 48214

Sheet Metal Workers International Association
1750 New York Avenue, NW
Washington, DC 20006

◇ **RELATED ARTICLES**

Volume 1: Automotives
Volume 2: Engineers
Volume 3: Automobile mechanics; Farm-equipment mechanics; Industrial machinery mechanics
Volume 4: Automotive, diesel, and gas turbine technicians; Mechanical technicians

Farm-equipment mechanics

Definition

Farm-equipment mechanics work on farms or in farm equipment repair shops, where they repair, overhaul, and perform preventive maintenance on farm machinery, equipment, and vehicles, such as tractors, tilling equipment, harvesters, pumps, trucks, and other mechanized, electrically powered, or motor-driven equipment.

History

Not much is known about the methods used by prehistoric farmers, but, like the primitive peoples in some parts of the world today, they probably loosened and turned the soil with sturdy, pointed sticks or blades of stone or hard wood attached to crude handles. The first plows were rough contrivances that were pulled by humans until someone conceived the idea of tying them to cows, bulls, or oxen. Early reaping knives or sickles were fashioned from sharp, polished flint fastened to handles of wood or bone. To thresh grain, farmers spread it on a hard floor and drove oxen or pulled a flint-studded sledge back and forth over it.

Although wood and stone were eventually replaced by metals, farming methods remained simple for centuries. Farmers repaired their own tools or brought them to the local blacksmith to have the metal parts rejoined. Even the early models of tractors were un-complicated machines that farmers could usually repair themselves.

In the last third of the century, however, farm equipment has grown so large and complex that it requires a specialist to service and repair it. Agriculture today is a large-scale business that depends on a variety of specialized machines to do the work quickly, efficiently, and economically. It is not uncommon to find on a farm both diesel and gasoline tractors, some with 300-horsepower engines, along with harvesting combines, hay balers, corn pickers, crop dryers, and elevators. Even if farmers had the mechanical skills to repair their own equipment, their time is too valuable to do so. One piece of machinery might require several days to take apart, correct the malfunction, then reassemble the parts. Farm-equipment mechanics are skilled workers who are familiar with the equipment, can diagnose the cause of malfunctions, and have the knowledge of mechanical, electrical, and hydraulic systems necessary to correct the problems.

Because of the complexity of modern farm machinery, most farm-equipment dealers employ mechanics to assemble, service, and repair the equipment sold to farmers.

Nature of the work

The efficient operation of a farm depends on the proper performance of many large, complex machines, including tractors, tilling equipment, harvesters, combines, silo fillers, plows, balers,

A farmer discusses the maintenance of his harvesting equipment with a mechanic who specializes in farm equipment repairs.

crometers and torque wrenches, they may use welding equipment, grinders, saws, and other power tools. In addition, they sometimes perform major repairs with machine tools, such as the drill press, lathe, and milling and woodworking machines. They do most of their work in a shop, but during planting or harvesting seasons they may have to make emergency repairs at the farm to prevent any critical delays.

If farmers bring their equipment in periodically for preventive maintenance, the job is made easier for the mechanics, and the farmers are generally assured that the equipment will be in working order when needed. This simply involves a regular schedule of testing, adjusting, cleaning parts, and tuning engines to prevent trouble before it occurs.

The nature of the mechanics' work in a large shop is often specialized. Some of them only overhaul gasoline or diesel engines or repair clutches or transmissions. Others only repair air-conditioning units in the cabs of combines and large tractors or repair certain types of equipment, such as hay balers or harvesters. Some farm equipment mechanics who work for dealers and wholesalers specialize in supervisory, inspection, or bodywork. *Sprinkler-irrigation-equipment mechanics* install and maintain self-propelled circle-irrigation systems; *assembly repairers* fix defects in agricultural equipment; *dairy equipment repairers* inspect and repair dairy equipment; *farm-equipment mechanics* and *greasers* service machinery and vehicles; and *farm-machinery set-up mechanics* uncrate, assemble, adjust, and often deliver machinery to farm locations.

Mechanics who work on farms may install and repair wiring and motors to maintain farm electrical systems, build and repair plumbing and irrigation systems, or construct and maintain buildings and other farm structures.

pumps, trucks, and automobiles. It is the responsibility of farm-equipment mechanics to keep them in working order and to repair or overhaul them when they break down.

When a piece of equipment is not working properly, the farmer may be able to give some indication as to its past performance, but the mechanic has several testing devices to help diagnose the problem. A compression tester, for example, can determine whether cylinder valves leak or piston rings are worn, and a dynamometer is used to measure engine performance. The mechanics also make a visual examination of the machinery and observe and listen to motors and engines in operation, looking for clues to the difficulty. The defective units are dismantled; broken, worn-out, or faulty parts are either repaired or replaced, depending on the extent of the damage; then the machine or piece of equipment is reassembled, adjusted, lubricated, and tested to be sure it is operating efficiently.

Farm-equipment mechanics use a great many tools in their work. Besides hand tools such as wrenches, pliers, hammers, and screwdrivers, and precision instruments such as mi-

Requirements

Most employers prefer to hire high-school graduates, but they also look for an aptitude for mechanical work and consider a farm background desirable, because persons who grow up on a farm usually are familiar with farm equipment and may have had some experience with its repair. Job applicants who will have an advantage are those with previous experience or training in diesel and gasoline engines, the maintenance and repair of hydraulic systems, and welding. Many high schools and vocational schools offer courses in these subjects.

Farm-equipment mechanics may also be required to read circuit diagrams and blueprints

to make complex repairs to electrical and other systems. In fact, technical training is becoming increasingly important as more complicated farm machinery is developed. Some employers are beginning to require one or two years of vocational training in agricultural mechanics, including electronics.

Most mechanics learn their trade on the job. They are hired as helpers and receive their training from experienced mechanics. Trainees begin by helping with simple tasks and gradually move up to more difficult ones. How fast they progress depends on their attitude and prior experience, but it usually takes at least two years before a mechanic is qualified to handle almost any type of repair work. Highly specialized repair and overhaul work requires additional training and experience.

Another way to learn the trade is through an apprenticeship program, which combines three or four years of on-the-job training with classroom study related to farm equipment repair and maintenance. The few farm-equipment mechanics who enter the occupation as apprentices are usually selected from shop helpers. Some mechanics enter the field from related occupations, such as farmers, farm laborers, heavy-equipment mechanics, automobile mechanics, or air-conditioning mechanics. Persons with this related experience may also begin as helpers, but their training period could be considerably shorter.

To keep up to date on the latest farm-equipment, mechanics and trainees may take special short-term courses conducted by equipment manufacturers. In these programs, which may last a few days, company service representatives explain the design and function of new models and teach the mechanics how to maintain and repair them. Some dealers help broaden their mechanics' skills by sending them to local vocational schools for special intensive courses in subjects such as air-conditioning repair or hydraulics.

Farm machinery is usually large and heavy. Mechanics need the strength to lift transmissions and other heavy machine parts. At the same time, they need manual dexterity to be able to handle tools and very small components.

Special requirements

Other than those mentioned above, there are no special requirements for this occupation.

Few farm-equipment mechanics are members of a labor union. Those who choose to join belong to the International Association of Ma-

chinists and Aerospace Workers; the International Union, United Automobile, Aerospace, and Agricultural Implement Workers of America; or the International Brotherhood of Teamsters, Chauffeurs, Warehousemen and Helpers of America (Ind.).

Opportunities for experience and exploration

High-school students may test their mechanical aptitude by taking shop and machine courses, welding, mechanical drawing, auto mechanics, and related courses. School guidance counselors and shop teachers are sources of advice in this area. Vocational schools may offer a great variety of subjects of particular interest to would-be farm-equipment mechanics.

A knowledge of how farm machines work is definitely necessary to the farm-equipment mechanic. Living or working on a farm after school hours, on weekends, or during the summer could provide valuable experience. If working on a farm is not feasible, part-time and summer jobs in gasoline service stations, automobile repair shops, or automotive supply houses may be considered. While not directly related to farm equipment, they would at least impart a familiarity with the language and tools of mechanics.

Related occupations

Other jobs that might be of interest include farm equipment technicians, farm extension workers, diesel mechanics, general maintenance mechanics, and automotive mechanics.

Method of entering

Persons interested in becoming farm-equipment mechanics usually apply directly to local farm-equipment dealers or to local offices of the state employment service. Graduates of a vocational school may obtain job leads from the school placement service.

Most beginners start out as helpers and become qualified mechanics after at least two years of on-the-job training. There are a few apprenticeship programs available, lasting from three to four years. Apprentices are generally chosen from among shop helpers.

Advancement

There are several advancement possibilities for farm-equipment mechanics. While working for a farm-equipment dealer, mechanics with experience and managerial ability may be promoted to shop supervisor or manager. It is also possible to become self-employed and open a repair shop. To advance to service representative for farm-equipment manufacturers, a few mechanics earn two-year associate degrees in agricultural mechanics.

Farm-equipment mechanics may advance and broaden their knowledge and skills by keeping abreast of recent developments in farm equipment. Manufacturers frequently sponsor training demonstrations and conduct programs lasting several days at which new models of machines are explained along with maintenance and repair methods.

Employment outlook

There were approximately 20,000 farm-equipment mechanics employed in the early 1990s. Most of them worked in dealers' service departments; others in independent repair shops, on large farms, or in farm equipment wholesale and manufacturing establishments; and a few were self-employed. Most of the repair shops employ fewer than five mechanics, while dealers often have ten or more on their payroll. Farm-equipment mechanics are employed throughout the country, with the greatest concentration in small cities and towns.

Because of the development of more technically advanced farm machinery, there will be a greater demand for farm-equipment mechanics during the next decade. This increase is expected to keep pace with the average for all occupations. The complexity of the new equipment demands greater maintenance. At the same time, it has become difficult, if not impossible, for farmers to make their own repairs. They are forced to rely on skilled mechanics. For example, many tractors being manufactured today have much larger engines, with transmissions that have as many as twenty-four speeds. And more complex electrical systems operate the many gauges and warning devices that tell the operator when brakes are wearing out, when the oil pressure is low in the transmission, or when there is not enough coolant in the radiator. Skilled mechanics are also needed to service the air-conditioning systems that are built into the cabs for the comfort of the operator.

Another reason there will be a greater demand for mechanics is because most large manufacturers of farm equipment now also produce a line of small tractors and lawn and garden equipment for home use. Sales of the smaller equipment have increased tremendously in the last ten years or so and are expected to continue. Dealers will need more mechanics to service the equipment. Because some type of farming is done in every part of the United States, farm-equipment mechanics are employed throughout the country, mostly in or near small cities and towns. Opportunities will be best for applicants who have lived or worked on farms and already know how to operate farm machinery and make small repairs.

Agriculture is a seasonal industry. Therefore, the demand for mechanics is always greatest when the planting or harvesting is being done. Mechanics may work six or seven days a week, ten or twelve hours a day, during these busy periods. In the winter, however, when the work slows down, they may work fewer than forty hours a week, and some workers may be laid off.

Earnings

In the early 1990s, mechanics who worked for farm-equipment dealers were paid an average annual wage of about $18,200. Workers with the most experience and those who performed the most complicated repairs earned up to about twice that amount. Salaries were also greater in heavily agricultural areas, where there is keen competition for highly skilled mechanics.

During planting and harvesting seasons, farm-equipment mechanics often have to work overtime, for which they are paid time-and-a-half. During the winter, however, they may work short hours or even be laid off.

Conditions of work

Farm-equipment mechanics generally work indoors, repairing, adjusting, and overhauling machinery and equipment that has been brought into the shop. During the busy planting and harvesting seasons, however, when delays in farm operations would be critical, mechanics may have to travel many miles to a farm and perform emergency repairs in the field in any kind of weather.

Conditions in the repair shops vary. Most modern shops are well ventilated, lighted, and heated, but some older shops may have fewer comforts and conveniences. Regardless of the shop, repairing machinery is dirty work; mechanics have to contend with grease, gasoline, rust, and dirt. Working with heavy equipment can be dangerous. Care must be taken with large parts supported on jacks or by hoists, because there is always the chance they may slip. Other hazards to be guarded against are burns from hot engines and cuts from sharp edges of metal. Physical injury may also result from careless handling of tools.

Social and psychological factors

This is a particularly attractive career for persons who prefer life in rural surroundings. At the same time, there are opportunities in the fringe areas of many metropolitan cities for those who also want the advantages of urban life.

Farm-equipment mechanics usually work independently, with little supervision. It is important that they be self-reliant and have the ability to solve problems and work under pressure. When a farm machine breaks down, it can be very expensive for the farmer in terms of lost time. The mechanics must diagnose the problem quickly and perform the repairs without delay.

GOE: 05.05.09; SIC: 7699; SOC: 6118

◇ **SOURCES OF ADDITIONAL INFORMATION**

Farm and Industrial Equipment Institute
410 North Michigan Avenue
Chicago, IL 60611

North American Equipment Dealers Association
10877 Watson Road
St. Louis, MO 63126

◇ **RELATED ARTICLES**

Volume 1: Agriculture; Automotives
Volume 3: Air conditioning, refrigeration, and heating mechanics; Automobile mechanics; Diesel mechanics; Electrical repairers; Machine tool operators
Volume 4: Agricultural equipment technicians; Automotive, diesel, and gas turbine technicians; Electromechanical technicians; Mechanical technicians

Flight engineers

Definition

Flight engineers monitor the operation of various mechanical and electrical devices aboard an airplane. They are concerned with the condition and the performance of the plane before, during, and after the flight.

History

Roger Bacon, an English scientist and writer who lived in the fourteenth century, was one of the first people to study seriously the problem of flying. After him came Leonardo da Vinci, who drew pictures of wings he thought could

be attached to human arms and legs; the Montgolfier brothers, Joseph-Michele and Jacques-Etienne, who built the first successful balloon with a basket suspended below for passengers; Henri Giffard, who built and flew the first successful engine-powered airship; and the Wright brothers, Orville and Wilbur, who built and flew the first successful gasoline-powered airplane.

The need for flight engineers arose as planes became more complex. Ordinary jet airliners, for example, may have several hundred devices and instruments, many of which need to be checked frequently. There are also gauges to indicate pressures, fuels, and temperatures. Pilots of such planes need the assistance of flight engineers to watch all these indicators.

A flight engineer conducts preflight tests to detect any mechanical difficulties. Without his expertise, a flight could be in jeopardy.

Many aircraft being designed with today's advanced technology, however, no longer require such monitoring.

Nature of the work

Before takeoff, a flight engineer inspects the outside of the plane—tires, fuel tanks—and inside the plane assists the pilot and the copilot in making preflight tests of instruments and equipment. During the flight, the engineer watches and operates many instruments and devices to check the performance of the engines and the air-conditioning, pressurizing, and electrical systems. The engineer also keeps records of engine performance and fuel consumption. This person reports any mechanical difficulties to the pilot and, if possible, makes emergency repairs. After the plane has landed, the engineer makes certain that any necessary repairs to the plane are done by a mechanic.

Requirements

The age range for flight engineers is from twenty-one to thirty-five years. Airlines require the applicant to be in excellent physical condition, and to meet a height requirement. A high-school education is required, and at least two or more years of college would be desired. Young people who have a flight engineer certificate are more readily hired, although a person who has a commercial pilot's license may be hired and

then given additional training. One can qualify for a flight engineer's certificate with two years of training or three years of work experience in the maintenance, repair, and overhaul of aircraft and engines, including a minimum of six months' training or one year's experience on four-engine piston and jet planes. At least 200 hours of flight time as a captain of a four-engine piston or jet plane, or 100 hours of experience as flight engineer in the armed forces will also qualify you for airlines work. The completion of the Federal Aviation Agency (FAA) approved course of ground and flight instruction is another way to qualify.

An applicant for a license must also pass a written test on flight theory, engine and aircraft performance, fuel requirements, weather, and maintenance procedures. In addition, the applicant must pass a rigid in-flight test on normal and emergency duties and procedures and be able to pass a rigorous yearly physical examination.

In a practical flight test on a four-engine plane, one must demonstrate knowledge of preflight duties and procedures.

Special requirements

All flight engineers must be licensed by the FAA. Some airlines give flight engineers training to qualify for a commercial pilot's license or an airline transport pilot's license.

Opportunities for experience and exploration

The nature of this work affords little opportunity for experience and exploration. A young person with a definite interest in planes, engines, and related technological areas, however, should find reading material that will give him or her additional insight into this occupation. It may be possible to obtain experience at small airports, working with engines, or in some schools that offer air-cadet programs.

Related occupations

Other aviation and aerospace jobs that might be of interest include pilots, flight attendants, avionics technicians, aeronautical and aerospace technicians, aviation engineers, and aircraft mechanics and engine specialists.

Methods of entering

After gaining the necessary experience, the best way to become a flight engineer is by direct application to an airline. To gain experience, it may be necessary to work in maintenance or repair and then transfer when an opening is available as flight engineer.

Advancement

A flight engineer can become a chief flight engineer for an airline. Seniority, which allows one to select choice routes and schedules, is the usual road to advancement. The person who qualifies as a pilot can be promoted from flight engineer to copilot and may then follow the regular line of advancement open to other copilots.

Employment outlook

In the early 1990s, fewer than 7,500 workers were employed as flight engineers. Most of them worked for the major scheduled airlines and were stationed in or near large cities.

Employment of flight engineers is expected to decrease in the next decade because of the rise in the number of computerized flight engineering systems being installed.

Earnings

Starting salaries for flight engineers averaged about $19,200 a year in the early 1990s. Their later earnings depended on size, speed, and type of plane; hours and miles flown; length of service; and type of flight—domestic or international. They are guaranteed minimum monthly wages. Most flight engineers belong to a union and receive retirement, health, and insurance benefits.

Conditions of work

Flight time for flight engineers is restricted by the FAA to eighty-five hours a month. In international operations, they are limited to flying 100 hours a month, 300 or 350 hours every 90 days, depending on the size of the flight crew. In general, the working conditions in airline work are very good. There are many benefits to the individual in this field. For instance, employees and their immediate family get free or limited amounts of free transportation on their company's planes. When flight engineers are away from home, about a third of the time, the company usually pays their expenses.

Social and psychological factors

The flight engineer has a position of responsibility. The work requires skill and training and the ability to act under a variety of circumstances. A person must be able to function well with the flight crew and the ground crew. Much time must be spent away from home in this occupation, and in some instances there may be mental stress.

GOE: 05.03.06; SIC: 4512; SOC: 825

◇ **SOURCES OF ADDITIONAL INFORMATION**

Flight Engineers' International Association
905 16th Street, NW
Washington, DC 20006

Future Aviation Professionals of America
4959 Massachusetts Boulevard
Atlanta, GA 30337

General Aviation Manufacturers Association
1400 K Street, NW, Suite 801
Washington, DC 20005

◇ **RELATED ARTICLES**

Volume 1: Engineering; Transportation
Volume 2: Engineers, aerospace; Pilots
Volume 3: Aircraft mechanics; Automobile mechanics
Volume 4: Aeronautical and aerospace technicians; Avionics technicians; Electromechanical technicians; Instrumentation technicians

Forge shop occupations

Definition

Forging is a process of shaping metal by heating it, placing it between two metal dies attached to power hammers or presses, then pounding or squeezing it into the desired shape. There are two basic kinds of dies: the open die and the impression, or closed, die. The open die is flat, similar to a blacksmith's hammer; the impression die has a cavity shaped like the piece being produced.

History

Forging is a process of making metal objects by pounding or squeezing the metal into the desired shapes. It is an ancient art, older than recorded history, probably dating back to the discovery of metals. Primitive humans no doubt used rocks as anvils and hammers to fashion weapons and tools.

Very large metal objects were beyond the strength of the early blacksmiths. Then, in the thirteenth century, the use of water power increased their lifting capability to nearly a thousand pounds. The size and production of forgings were further increased with the introduction of the steam engine early in the eighteenth century and again with the invention of direct-acting piston hammers in about 1840.

These forging machines were equipped with a flat, stationary die on which the metal was placed and a second die that was moved vertically to pound the metal into shape. The forgings produced by this method lacked uniformity; superficially the pieces may have looked alike, but each had minute differences. It was the demand for identical gun parts during the Civil War that hastened the evolution of the closed-contour, or impression, die. The metal was placed between two dies containing a cavity shaped exactly like the piece being produced, and force was applied to turn out quantities of exact duplicates.

These basic techniques are still in use today. However, modern forging hammers weigh as much as 50,000 pounds, and forging presses are capable of exerting thousands of tons of force. Five workers using today's heavy power equipment and dies can turn out more forgings in an hour than five old-fashioned blacksmiths could make in a year.

Before the advent of the automobile early in the twentieth century, most forges manufactured machine parts. Now about two-thirds of forging production goes to the automotive industry.

Nature of the work

Metal parts that are shaped by the forging method are exceptionally strong when subjected to constant stress and pressure. Forge shops produce many items that must withstand heavy wear, such as wrenches, drill bits, and parts for automobiles and aircraft.

The metal used for forging is usually steel, although forges also work with aluminum, copper, brass, bronze, and other nonferrous metals (metals containing no iron). Nonferrous forgings resist corrosion and have a lighter weight-to-strength ratio, making them ideal for such uses as in aircraft landing gear.

Forged products are commonly found in our everyday life, and they range in size from a tiny key that can be carried in a pocket to a bulky piece of industrial machinery weighing many tons. Regardless of size, the techniques used to shape the metal are basically the same: The metal is first heated to a very high temperature in a furnace, or forge, until it is workable. Then it is placed between two metal dies and pounded or squeezed into shape by power hammers or presses that exert a tremendous force. Finally, the excess metal and rough edges are trimmed or ground away; the forgings are heat-treated to harden and temper the metal, smoothed, polished, and otherwise finished; and they are inspected to ensure that they meet all specifications.

The equipment of a forge shop includes various types of hammers, presses, dies, upsetters (presses that produce nails, screws, bolts, and other headed items), and furnaces. The workers also use hand tools, such as hammers, tongs, and punches to mold and shape forgings. Finished products are inspected with measuring devices such as rules, scales, and calipers. Some of the major forge-shop production occupations are described below.

Hammer smiths operate or direct the operation of power hammers equipped with open dies. They may head a crew of four or more workers, including a hammer driver or hammer runner, a crane operator, a heater, and one or two helpers. Hammer smiths draw on their knowledge of forging and the physical properties of metal and follow blueprints, diagrams, and work orders to shape heated metal stock into forgings that meet exact specifications. After determining how the metal is to be positioned under the hammer and which tools will be needed to produce the curves and angles for the finished product, they align and bolt the dies into the ram and anvil of the machine, using rules, squares, and hand tools. The metal is heated in furnaces regulated by workers called *heaters*. When the color of the metal indicates that it has reached the proper temperature for forging, the hammer smiths signal the heater to remove the metal from the furnace and direct the crane operator to place it in position under the hammer. They determine how much hammer force is needed and instruct the *hammer driver*, or *hammer runner*, who regulates the action of the machine. The hammer smiths decide if and when the metal has to be reheated during the operation and verify the dimensions of the forging with the use of rules and calipers.

Hammer operators have duties similar to those of hammer smiths, described above, and are assisted by heaters and helpers. The major difference is that hammer operators forge metal parts with impression-die, rather than open-die, hammers. It takes a highly skilled operator to turn out the intricate forgings that these closed-die hammers are capable of producing. Hammer operators regulate the action of the machine, causing the ram to strike the metal repeatedly, forcing it into the shape of the impression in the die. By moving the workpiece through a series of dies, the operator attains progressively finer detail.

Press operators set up and operate power presses that use hydraulic pressure to slowly squeeze metal forgings into shape, unlike the power hammers that create forgings by pounding the metal. Using skills similar to those of hammer smiths and hammer operators, the press operators set the dies with rules, squares, shims, feelers, and hand tools; determine when the metal has reached forging temperature; operate the controls that regulate machine pressure; and move the hot metal between the dies.

Upsetters operate still another type of closed-die forging machine. It is equipped with a horizontal ram and a gripping die and is used to produce headed items, such as nails, screws, and bolts. After setting the dies and cams and determining that the metal stock has been heated to the proper temperature, the upsetters position the metal so that it extends beyond the gripping dies. The metal is then upset, or headed, by the ram, which squeezes the metal

A worker in a Santa Fe railroad shop dries a bearing with an air gun.

into the gripping-die cavity. Upsetters may be assisted by heaters and several helpers.

Heaters control the furnaces that heat the metal stock, such as bars, billets, plates, and rods, to proper temperatures for forging. The furnaces may operate on gas, oil, or electricity and are equipped with dials, gauges, and regulating knobs so that the heaters are able to verify and maintain specific temperatures. The heaters use tongs or a chain hoist to position the metal in the furnace and to transfer the heated metal to the hammers or presses. They determine when the stock is ready for forging by observing the color of the metal or reading the pyrometer. Heaters generally work as members of a hammer, press, or upsetter crew.

Inspectors examine completed forgings for accuracy, size, and quality and determine causes of any defects. They measure the parts with instruments such as calipers, micrometers, gauges, and rules and may test strength and hardness with special machines and electronic devices. Internal flaws may be detected using ultrasonic inspection equipment. A visual examination of the parts may reveal surface defects, such as scale, laps, and cracks. Inspectors report defects and causes to a supervisor and may shut down production to revise the heating temperature, modify the force of the hammer, or realign the dies.

Die sinkers are skilled workers who make the impression dies for the forging hammers and presses. They begin by studying blueprints or drawings, then outlining the item to be forged on two matching steel die blocks. They use a variety of machine tools, such as milling machines, EDM (electrical discharge machinery), and ECM (electrical chemical machinery), to form the impression cavities in the die blocks. The impressions are contoured and finished to specifications with tools that include power grinders, scrapers, files, and emery cloths. Die sinkers inspect the finished die cavities, using templates and measuring instruments, such as calipers, micrometers, and height gauges, and make a sample forging to check against specifications.

Cleaning and finishing forgings require many workers. Occupations in this group include the following:

Trimmers operate power presses equipped with trimming dies to remove excess metal from forgings and may inspect parts visually or with set gauges.

Grinders remove rough edges and smooth contoured surfaces of forgings and forging dies, using a variety of abrasive tools, including files, stones, emery cloths, and power grinders and buffers. Inspection for flaws and smoothness is done both visually and by touch.

Sandblasters or *shotblasters* clean and polish forgings with blasts of compressed air mixed with abrasives, such as sand, grit, or metal shot. Large parts are loaded on racks in an enclosed room and the abrasive directed over the surfaces by nozzle. Small parts may be cleaned in a tumbling barrel or in an abrasive cabinet equipped with glove-fitted openings through which the blasters insert their arms to manipulate the parts under a nozzle. Sandblasters wear protective equipment, such as helmet, suit, gloves, and hoods, to protect themselves against injury.

Picklers control equipment that cleans the forgings chemically. Surface scale is removed by immersing the parts in a series of acid baths and rinses. Picklers are responsible for draining, cleaning, and refilling the tanks and for maintaining the consistency of the cleaning solutions.

Heat treaters harden and temper metal by first heating, then cooling the forged objects. They load the furnaces and regulate the heat. After the prescribed time, they quench the metal parts in water, oil, or other bath or allow them to cool either in the furnace or in the air.

Requirements

Applicants with a high-school diploma will have an advantage over those with less education, particularly if they have taken such courses as mechanical drawing, blueprint reading, graphics, mathematics (especially geometry), machine shop and other shop courses.

Forge shop workers generally acquire their skills through on-the-job training. Most of them start out as helpers or heaters on hammer or press crews and work alongside more experienced employees. As they prove their abilities, they are given more responsibility and are gradually advanced to more complicated jobs. To become a qualified hammer smith, for example, may require several years of training and experience.

Another way to learn the job is by serving an apprenticeship. Some forge shops offer programs lasting four to six years for skilled occupations such as hammer smith, hammer operator, press operator, die sinker, and heat treater. Apprentices acquire practical experience along with classroom training in metal properties, power hammer and furnace operation, hand-tool use, and blueprint reading.

The training period for inspectors varies depending on the complexity of the forgings and the examination they require. Inspectors who examine simple forgings visually or with uncomplicated gauges may need only a few weeks of on-the-job training. Those who must ensure that forgings conform to complex, detailed specifications usually require several months' training in blueprint reading and mathematics.

Workers in this occupational group should be in good physical condition. They need stamina to endure the heat and noise of a forge shop and must be strong enough to lift heavy dies and forgings.

Special requirements

Union membership may be a requirement for some forge shop workers. Many of them belong to the International Brotherhood of Boilermakers, Iron Shipbuilders, and Blacksmiths, while others are members of the United Steelworkers of America; the International Union, United Automobile, Aerospace and Agricultural Implement Workers of America; the International Association of Machinists and Aerospace Workers; and the International Die Sinkers Conference (Ind.).

Opportunities for experience and exploration

High-school and vocational school courses that offer training in machining and other shop work are valuable in terms of testing one's interest in metalworking, as well as gaining some practical experience. Guidance counselors may offer additional suggestions or set up a tour of a local forge shop.

Older students may be able to find part-time or summer jobs as helpers in forge shops or other metalworking establishments.

Related occupations

Other workers who are involved in machining and metal work include machinists, machine tool operators, forge shop occupations, and tool makers and die makers.

Methods of entering

The usual way to enter this occupation is to apply directly to the personnel departments of forge shops. Job leads and information about apprenticeships may be obtained by contacting local offices of the state employment service or locals of the labor unions mentioned earlier. Applicants who are hired generally begin as helpers or heaters. More advanced jobs require several years of training.

Advancement

Forge shop production workers come up through the ranks, starting out as helpers or heaters. As they acquire skills over several years of training, they may be advanced to more complicated jobs. One measure of success is to become a hammer smith, for example, and direct a crew of four or more workers. Advancement may also take the form of salary increases.

Employment outlook

In the early 1990s, the forging industry employed approximately 52,000 production workers.

The demand for forgings is expected to grow along with the expansion of the aerospace and energy-related industries. Oil drilling and coal mining operations, for example, will require many drill bits and other forged products. This increased production, however, will not mean the employment of many more forge shop workers, because improvements in equip-

Press operators at a forging plant monitor the operation of a large automatic molding line that makes diesel engine blocks.

ment and techniques will result in a greater output per worker. Although some new jobs will be created to meet the increased demand for forged products, most openings will occur as older, experienced workers retire, die, or change occupations.

Forge shops are located throughout the country, but most of them will be found near centers that produce the steel for forgings or near plants that are large users of forged products. Thus, employment for production workers in this field will be best in and around cities such as Detroit, Chicago, Cleveland, Los Angeles, Houston, and Pittsburgh.

Fluctuations in the economy affect some forge shops. For example, many forged parts are used in the manufacture of automobiles. In an economic downswing, the sale of new cars drops considerably, resulting in a reduced demand for parts. Forge shops that supply the parts to the automobile manufacturers, then, will have fewer jobs until car sales go up again.

513

General maintenance mechanics
Machine Trades Occupations

During periods when production is slow, forge shop workers may work short weeks or be laid off.

Earnings

In the early 1990s, production workers in iron and steel forging plants were paid an average of about $24,000 annually. This was somewhat higher than the average for all manufacturing production workers.

Conditions of work

Because of the nature of the work, forge shops are noisy, hot, and dirty, and they present more hazards than most manufacturing plants. Labor and management, however, cooperate to minimize the discomfort and danger. Heat deflectors and ventilating fans may be installed to reduce heat and smoke. Improved machinery and shop practices help cut down the noise and vibration from the hammers. Workers are given safety training and use protective equipment, such as face shields, ear plugs and muffs, safety glasses, safety shoes, and helmets; and machines are equipped with safety guards.

Cranes are used to move very large objects, but workers may still be required to lift and move heavy forgings and dies. The heat, the noise, and the heavy work require greater than average stamina, endurance, and strength.

Social and psychological factors

Being able to work as part of a team is an important characteristic for workers in this occu-

pation, and those who direct the operations must be able to motivate the team members to cooperate for maximum efficiency. Great care must be exercised in every aspect of production to turn out forgings of high quality that match specifications precisely.

An even temperament will help the forge shop worker to tolerate the noise and heat. In fact, a certain amount of satisfaction may be derived from controlling large, powerful machinery used to create useful metal objects.

GOE: 06.02.02; SIC: 3312, 3462, 3463, 3483; SOC: 73,75

◇ **SOURCES OF ADDITIONAL INFORMATION**

Forging Industry Association
Landmark Office Tower, Suite 300-LTV
25 Prospect Avenue, West
Cleveland, OH 44115

◇ **RELATED ARTICLES**

Volume 1: Machining and Machinery; Metals
Volume 2: Engineers
Volume 3: Heat treaters; Machine tool operators; Machinists; Patternmakers; Tool makers and die makers
Volume 4: Metallurgical technicians; Tap-and-die maker technicians; welding technicians

General maintenance mechanics

Definition

General maintenance mechanics repair and maintain machines, mechanical equipment, and buildings, and work on plumbing, electrical, and air-conditioning and heating systems. They

also do minor construction work and any necessary type of routine or preventive maintenance to keep businesses, schools, factories, and apartment buildings running and in good condition. They usually are skilled in electrical, wood, and metal work.

History

For the greater part of the history of human labor, workers needed to know how to perform many different tasks in their line of work. Blacksmiths, for example, had to know about metalworking, horseshoeing, decorative metalwork, and many other aspects of their trade. Carriage makers had to know carpentry, metalworking, wheel-making, upholstery, and design. With the advent of the Industrial Revolution, however, workers became more and more specialized. This was due in part to different methods of production, such as the assembly line, and to the fact that the knowledge in each field grew as time went on.

General maintenance mechanics, on the other hand, cannot specialize in any one field. To keep the buildings and machines for which they are responsible in top working order, they must be skilled to a reasonable degree in a variety of fields—construction, electrical work, carpentry, plumbing, machining, and heating and cooling technology, to name a few. At the same time, these "jacks of all trades" must remain adaptable, knowledgeable, and perceptive to be able to diagnose problems quickly and solve them properly. Without their maintenance and problem-solving skills, buildings and machinery would deteriorate rapidly, resulting in billions of dollars lost and many human lives endangered.

Nature of the work

General maintenance mechanics perform almost any job that may be required to maintain a building or the equipment in it. At various times, they may be called on to replace faulty electrical switches; fix air-conditioning motors; install water lines; build partitions; make plaster or drywall repairs; open clogged drains; dismantle, clean, and oil machinery; paint windows, doors, and woodwork; and many other different operations. Because of the diverse nature of the responsibilities of maintenance mechanics, they have to be skilled in the use of most hand tools and power tools, or realize when a more specialized repair person has to be called.

General maintenance mechanics work in almost any kind of setting. They work on the machinery and buildings of factories, hospitals, schools, hotels, offices, stores, malls, gas and electric companies, government agencies, and apartment buildings.

Those in small establishments, where they are the only person working in maintenance,

do all repairs except for very large or difficult jobs. In larger establishments, their duties may be limited to specialized tasks; for example, one mechanic may be in charge of installing and setting up new equipment, while another is in charge of the heating and ventilation systems. Those mechanics who are in charge of keeping machinery in top working order are usually classified as *factory* or *mill maintenance repairers*, while those who work more on the maintenance of the physical structure are called *building maintenance repairers*.

One of the most important aspects of maintaining buildings and machinery is knowing when and how to fix problems. Very often it pays to plan ahead. General maintenance mechanics often do routine preventive maintenance to correct defects before a piece of machinery breaks down or a building begins to deteriorate. Some types of machines are inspected regularly— daily, weekly, monthly, or quarterly—because they endure much abuse or would endanger people's lives if they were in disrepair. Regular maintenance checks can also prevent a small problem from growing into a huge, expensive mess. Maintenance mechanics may follow a checklist, inspecting belts, checking fluid levels, replacing filters, oiling moving parts, and so forth. They are careful to keep records of the type and extent of repairs they do and the date when something was last inspected or repaired. These types of records are often important for such things as insurance requirements and government safety regulations.

Once a problem or defect has been identified and diagnosed, the maintenance mechanic must plan how the repairs will be done. The mechanic often consults blueprints, repair manuals, and parts catalogs to determine what to do. Supplies and new parts are obtained from distributors or storage rooms, and the mechanic replaces worn or broken parts where necessary. They may do this with common hand tools or power tools, as well as specialized equipment and electronic test devices. In remote locations or in emergencies, an old part may need to be fixed or a new part fabricated on site. At these times, the factory maintenance repairer may need to set up and operate machines, such as a lathe or a milling machine, to make the new part, or operate gas- or arc-welding equipment to join metal parts together.

Requirements

Graduation from high school is preferred, but not always required, for entry into this occupa-

A general maintenance mechanic shaves a metal piece on an assembly machine so that the manufacturing process may continue smoothly.

tion. High-school courses in mechanical drawing, electricity, woodworking, blueprint reading, science, and mathematics are useful. Shop courses are a good way to learn about mechanics and machinery, as are courses at trade or vocational schools. Mechanical aptitude, manual dexterity, and the ability to use shop math are important for general maintenance mechanics. Good physical health is also necessary because the job involves much walking, standing, reaching, and heavy lifting. Difficult or complicated jobs require the ability to solve problems, and many positions require the ability to work without direct supervision.

Special requirements

Some general maintenance mechanics are represented by labor unions such as the United Automobile Workers and the American Federation of State, County, and Municipal Employees. Mandatory union membership depends on the employer.

Opportunities for experience and exploration

Shop classes can give students a good indication of their mechanical aptitude and their enjoyment for maintenance work. Another way to learn about the job of general maintenance mechanics is to apply for a summer or part-time job as a mechanic's helper. Such work can usually be found in factories, apartment complexes, retirement homes, hospitals, and utility companies. Demand for such helpers is not seasonal, as maintenance work has to be done year-round.

Related occupations

Other occupations that may interest young people with the aptitudes and skills for general maintenance mechanics include janitor, cleaners, automobile mechanics, diesel mechanics, and industrial machinery mechanics.

Methods of entering

Most general maintenance mechanics learn their skills informally while on the job. They start as helpers, watching and learning from skilled maintenance workers. After a time, they will begin with simple maintenance jobs like fixing leaky faucets and replacing light bulbs, and gradually progress to more difficult tasks such as overhauling machinery or building walls.

Information on job openings for mechanic's helpers can be found in newspaper want ads, school placement offices, and government employment agencies. For those enrolled in trade or vocational schools, the outplacement office is a good source for referrals and information. In addition, job seekers can contact the employment offices of companies they would like to work for to learn about openings. Union offices are sometimes a good place to learn about training and apprenticeship programs, although these are usually more specific to a certain trade such as electrical work or carpentry than to general maintenance. However, some general mechanics learn their skills by working as helpers to other repair or construction workers such as carpenters, electricians, machinery repairers, or automobile mechanics, and then move into general maintenance. It generally takes from one to four years of on-the-job training or school, or a combination of both, to become a fully qualified general maintenance mechanic, depending on the skill level required.

Advancement

Some general maintenance mechanics who are employed in large companies or organizations can advance to a position as maintenance supervisor. In smaller organizations, promotion opportunities are limited.

The general maintenance mechanic can also take the skills learned on the job and apply them to apprenticeships in one of the traditional trades. Wages for carpenters, electricians, plumbers, and other trades people can be higher than those for maintenance mechanics. Those with the technical knowledge and business sense may also want to go into business for themselves by starting companies that, for example, install heating and cooling or electrical systems.

Employment outlook

The job outlook for general maintenance mechanics is good. The Department of Labor predicts that employment for these workers will grow about as fast as the average for all other occupations through the year 2000. This is because jobs for maintenance mechanics are related to the number of buildings and the amount of equipment that needs maintenance and repair. As the number of office and apartment buildings, stores, hospitals, hotels and factories increases, the number of people employed as general maintenance mechanics should increase as well. In addition to the jobs created by construction and industrial expansion, many more openings will arise as experienced workers transfer to other occupations and leave the work force.

Nearly one million general maintenance mechanics were employed in the early 1990s, in almost every industry. About one-quarter of general maintenance mechanics worked for manufacturing and industrial companies. For these workers, any recession in their respective industries may mean the possibility of layoffs. Most mechanics, however, work in more stable environments and are not usually subject to layoffs because their buildings must be properly maintained regardless of overall economic conditions.

Earnings

Earnings for general maintenance mechanics vary widely, depending on the industry and geographic area. In the early 1990s, their earnings ranged from less than $11,000 per year to more than $36,000 per year. Wages are generally paid on an hourly basis, with a range from $6 to $13 an hour. Wages are generally highest in transportation companies and public utilities, and generally lowest in service firms. On average, workers in the Midwest and Northeast earn more than their counterparts in the West and South. Mechanics who work more than forty hours per week earn overtime pay.

Conditions

Most general maintenance mechanics work a forty-hour week. Some work evening or night shifts or on weekend shifts. They may also be on call for emergency repairs.

In the course of a single workday, maintenance mechanics will be called on to perform a variety of tasks, generally at a number of locations in a building or even in several different buildings. It is a strenuous job, and working conditions will usually vary with each assignment. Mechanics may have to stand for long periods of time, lift heavy objects, and work in places that are uncomfortably hot or cold. Like other maintenance craft workers, they may have to work in awkward and cramped positions or on ladders. On the job, they are subject to electrical shocks, burns, falls, and cuts and bruises. It is very important for them to follow safety regulations and use tools properly to minimize the risks of hazard to them and to other people.

Those employed in small establishments, where they may be the only maintenance worker, often operate with little or no direct supervision. Those who work in larger establishments usually report to a maintenance supervisor who will assign responsibilities and oversee repairs.

Social and psychological factors

While the work of a general maintenance mechanic can be grueling, it does hold advantages for certain types of people. Those who enjoy tackling a variety of different responsibilities on the job and who can work well with their hands may find this occupation rewarding. It calls for a person with scrupulous work habits who can take personal initiative to get the job done. This occupation also calls for certain problem-solving skills in different mechanical areas and the ability to spot trouble and fix it before it gets out of hand.

GOE: 05.05.09; SIC: Any industry; SOC: 613   **517**

Gunsmiths

Definition

Gunsmiths use machines and hand tools to build, repair, and modify firearms of all sorts to meet blueprint and customer specifications.

History

Gunpowder is believed to have been invented in the ninth century by the Chinese, who used it mainly for rockets and firecrackers. When gunpowder was introduced to Europe in the fourteenth century, the face of warfare was changed forever. It is still used today, from large field artillery to small handguns.

When first devised, firearms were basically small, hand-held cannons fired by igniting gunpowder through a touchhole by a small flame. This basic idea was refined in later guns such as the matchlock, wheel lock and flintlock, which used a spark-producing mechanism to ignite the powder charge. In the fifteenth century, the rifle was invented. The rifle gets its name from the fact that the interior of its barrel is "rifled" or cut with spiralling grooves, which puts a spin on the bullet and thus improves the accuracy of the shooter. Rifles were first widely used by the American colonists, and today all firearms, with the exception of the shotgun, are made with rifled bores.

Handguns have almost as much history as long guns. The most important breakthrough in its development came with the invention of the modern revolver by Samuel Colt in 1835. A crude version of a "revolving pistol" was invented in the late 1500s, but Colt's design, which allowed a gun to fire six bullets before reloading, set new standards for automatic firearms for many years.

Today firearms are very popular in America, among sports enthusiasts, collectors and law enforcement agents. But assembly lines are not suited to the manufacture of quality firearms. The work of the gunsmith is part craft and part art. Despite its long history, gunsmithing is a profession with a low profile. Often the skills needed for the trade are kept within a family and passed on from generation to generation.

Nature of the work

Both long guns and handguns consist of three basic elements: the barrel, the stock, and the action or firing mechanism. The gunsmith assembles these parts according to blueprint orders or to customer specifications. The pieces are usually made by parts manufacturers, but for special custom-made guns or for the restoration of antique guns, the gunsmith may make the piece.

The gunsmith first takes the stock of the gun and attaches the barrel and the action to it. Then the parts are aligned properly. The gunsmith may also attach equipment such as metallic or optical sights for aiming the gun, pistol grips, decorative pieces and recoil pads to cushion the impact of the blast to the shooter.

Gun stocks may be either machine made or cut by hand. Those that come from factories may be only partially completed, so the gunsmith can carve it to a perfect fit for the action and barrel being attached. The firing and accuracy of the gun will be affected if all the pieces are not expertly put together. One popular method of attaching the pieces is called glass bedding, in which the gunsmith pours a liquid compound such as fiberglass into the hollow part of the stock. The action and barrel are then attached and the compound is allowed to harden, which ensures a tight fit. The gunsmith may finish or polish the gun stock with lacquers, oils, resins or other finishing material. Hardwoods such as walnut and maple are most often used for stocks because of their beauty and durability. Often a gun owner will have the stock decorated and carved with designs, such as outdoor scenes or a simple diamond pattern to improve the grip. Sometimes the action and stock are also engraved.

Gunsmiths also treat and protect the metal parts of the firearm by a process called "bluing." The first step in the process is to strip the old finish from the action and the barrel, then the metal parts are immersed in a bluing salt bath. This gives the metal a rust-resistant surface and also imparts a bluish color to the metal. Certain gunsmiths become experts in this, and other gunsmiths may send their bluing work to them. Specialization in other aspects of the gunsmithing process is fairly common among practitioners.

Other gunsmithing tasks include the reboring of barrels to enlarge the caliber of the bore and cutting new rifling into the barrels of small firearms with a broaching machine. Gunsmiths also can install choke devices onto shotgun barrels to allow more control of the shot pattern.

Custom work on firearms gives gunsmiths the chance to display their special skills. Often a hunter will come in with plans for a specially hand-made rifle, and the gunsmith will make the rifle from blank factory pieces. Gunsmiths can also adapt a firearm for special use, such as converting a military rifle to a hunting rifle. To do this, they might rechamber the action to accept nonmilitary cartridge cases. The barrel might also be rebedded or replaced, the trigger mechanism modified, and recoil pads and butt plates added. Gunsmiths are often asked to re-

A gunsmith carves the wooden handle of a rifle. Hand-crafted guns are a rarity.

pair antique guns that have historic or sentimental value. They will take the mechanism apart and replace any worn or broken pieces. If these pieces are not still manufactured, the gunsmith may have to make it or contract another tradesperson to make it.

After assembling or repairing firearms, the gunsmith may test-fire the pieces with proof loads to determine their strength, alignment and proper assembly. Expert gunsmiths with an aptitude for machining and physics may design new guns by laying out plans on paper and calculating bullet-flight arcs, sight positioning and other details. Many gunsmiths operate firing ranges or gun and hunting supply stores in addition to their gunsmithing business. They may also work for sporting goods stores or manufacturers and distributors of firearms and hunting products.

Requirements

To become a skilled gunsmith, a person needs a strong background in metallurgy, ballistics, welding, machining, chemistry, woodworking, and electronics. Classes that can help high-school students prepare for this career include mechanical drawing, blueprint reading, metal-work, woodworking, shop math, physics, and chemistry. Practical application of mathematics, including decimals, fractions, and the metric system, is also very important.

Some people learn the trade of gunsmithing through apprenticeships in a gunsmith's shop or in a firearms factory. This can take up to four years of study. Another method of training is to take classes at one of eight gunsmithing schools around the nation. These schools, located in Arizona, Colorado, Oklahoma, and Pennsylvania, may have entrance requirements and even entrance exams for prospective students. Some of these schools have a two-year degree program, while others award diplomas after completion of 2,500 to 2,800 hours of classes and shop work. Some of the subjects taught at these schools include algebra, trigonometry, metallurgy, drafting, machining, ballistics, and technical report writing. In shop classes students learn welding, brazing, soldering, barrel fitting, small-parts design, custom stock-making, and heat treatment. A list of accredited gunsmithing and gun repair schools is published by the National Association of Trade and Technical Schools.

Special requirements

A few professional associations exist to further the interests of gunsmiths, gun manufacturers, and gun enthusiasts. The largest and most well known of these is the National Rifle Association. Others include the National Shooting Sports Foundation and the Sporting Arms and Ammunition Manufacturers' Institute.

Opportunities for experience and exploration

It is essential for gunsmiths to have an interest in the proper use and care of firearms. Students can expose themselves to proper gun handling through classes offered by the National Rifle Association, YMCA, 4-H Club, or local hunting club or sporting goods store.

If they know any independent gunsmiths, students might be able to get a part-time or summer job helping them around their shops. Another possible source of experience is a job at a sporting goods store or shooting range. Students with mechanical aptitude or an interest in machining might get jobs as machinists or tool and die makers, and then apply the skills learned at these jobs to gunsmithing.

The Armed Forces gives basic training in arms maintenance and trains specialists as well.

Related occupations

Many other occupations might appeal to those who have the skills and aptitudes necessary to be a gunsmith. These include forge shop occupations, patternmakers, tool makers, die makers, machinists, and machine tool operators.

Methods of entering

Gun shops and other employers prefer to hire skilled gunsmiths. Job seekers might gain experience in gunsmithing or machining through the methods described above, or by graduating from a gunsmithing school or serving an apprenticeship with a gun manufacturer. With this experience, the job seeker can approach a gun shop owner directly. Openings are scarce, however, because most shops employ only a handful of people, usually no more than two or three.

Advancement

Advancement is not as applicable a concept in gunsmithing as it is in some other professions. After many years of study, a gunsmith may learn the many different aspects of the trade and be able to call himself or herself a master gunsmith. However, because the staffs of most gun shops are small, there are very few chances for promotion. Advancement for most gunsmiths means establishing their own businesses, but this is often a risky undertaking. Independent gunsmiths need to know not only their trade but also sound business methods. Demand for skilled gunsmiths is usually high, however, so those who can get and keep customers may do well and even hire assistants or apprentices.

Employment outlook

There is a shortage of skilled gunsmiths in America. Fewer than 2,500 gunsmiths were employed full-time in the early 1990s. Hunting and shooting are growing in popularity across the country, however, so the demand for gunsmiths is likely to increase.

Many people turn to friends or amateur gunsmiths to repair their guns for nominal fees or free of charge. These amateurs cannot, however, match the skills of expert gunsmiths.

Earnings

The wages of expert gunsmiths can range from $7 to $14 per hour or more. Apprentices usually earn between $5 and $8 per hour. Earnings can vary with each individual employer and with the region of the country. At some gun shops, gunsmiths are paid a percentage of the receipts for work they complete.

Considering the degree of skill required for the work, gunsmiths are relatively underpaid. Workers who perform related jobs in machining and tool and die making can earn much more. Gunsmiths who are in business for themselves usually earn more, but they also have to pay for machines, equipment, and parts. Those gunsmiths who work for others are generally expected to supply their own hand tools, a full set of which costs around $500.

Conditions

Gun shops and gunsmithing operations are usually clean, compact, and efficient. Heavy machinery may be very noisy, and firing ranges certainly are, but following general industrial safety precautions will reduce this nuisance. Misfiring or exploding guns are also an occupational hazard that must be watched for.

Gunsmiths usually work a five-day, forty-hour week. They are on their feet most of the day, moving from their workbenches to different machines. Self-employed gunsmiths can set their own working hours. The busiest time of the year for gunsmiths is just before and during hunting season, when hunters bring in their firearms for cleaning and repair.

Social and psychological factors

Gunsmiths must have good eyesight, manual dexterity and mechanical ability. Because every firearm is a unique instrument, and because of the great amount of work put into customizing guns, gunsmiths should also be creative problem solvers. Patience and an attention to detail

are also essential traits. Although they earn less than other workers in the machine trades, gunsmiths are willing to make the sacrifice because they enjoy working with firearms and take pride in a well-crafted piece of machinery. At some level the work is that of an artisan.

GOE: 05.05.07; SIC: 348; SOC: 6129

◇ SOURCES OF ADDITIONAL INFORMATION

National Rifle Association of America
1600 Rhode Island Avenue, NW
Washington, DC 20036

National Shooting Sports Foundation
555 Danbury Road
Wilton, CT 06897

Students interested in military training for gunsmithy and weapons technicians should contact local recruiters or:

U.S. Army Recruiting Command
Fort Sheridan, IL 60037

Navy Recruiting Command
4015 Wilson Boulevard
Arlington, VA 22203

Director of Personnel Procurement Division
HG U.S. Marine Corps (MC-MR)
Washington, DC 20380

◇ RELATED ARTICLES

Volume 1: Machining and Machinery; Metals
Volume 3: Assemblers; Forge shop occupations; Job and die setters; Machine tool operators; Machinists; Millwrights; Tool makers and die makers; Sporting goods production workers

Industrial machinery mechanics

Definition

The workers who inspect, maintain, repair, and adjust machinery and equipment to ensure its proper operation in the various industries are known as *industrial machinery mechanics*. They are often called *maintenance mechanics* or *industrial machinery repairers*.

History

All machines are based on six types of "simple" machines: lever, wheel and axle, pulley, inclined plane, wedge, and screw. By combining these, people through the ages have improved their standard of living by making machines that could do more work in less time than humans or animals could do.

Before 1750, the beginning of the Industrial Revolution in Europe, work was done by hand and usually in the home. Families grew their food, wove their cloth, and bought or traded very little. Gradually economic life changed. Factories appeared where before piecework was done in homes. Inventors developed crude new machines for mass producing earthenware, iron skillets, bricks, and other much-needed commodities. The spinning jenny was one of the first machines of the Industrial Revolution. After it came the long procession of inventions and developments, including the steam engine, wrought iron, power loom, cotton gin, the steamboat, locomotive, telegraph, and Bessemer converter. Today there are electric typewriters, dynamos, automobiles—an endless parade of machines, even computers that can activate other machines.

The Industrial Revolution continues even today, although now it is known as the age of automation, and as machines become more numerous, and more complex, the job of the mechanic becomes more necessary.

Nature of the work

Preventive maintenance is a major part of this job. Mechanics inspect the equipment, oil and grease the machines, and clean and repair parts. Thus they prevent trouble that could cause costly breakdowns and delays. They keep maintenance records of the equipment they service.

When breakdowns occur, mechanics may partially or completely disassemble a machine to make the necessary repairs. After the machine is reassembled, they may have to make adjustments.

They may have to follow blueprints, lubrication charts, and engineering specifications in maintaining equipment. They may also use parts catalogs, or may even have to sketch defective parts.

Many types of new machinery have programmed internal evaluation systems that check equipment accuracy and condition. This assists the mechanic's job, but he or she then also becomes responsible for maintaining the check-up system.

The types of machinery on which industrial machinery mechanics work are as varied as the types of industries in operation in this country today. Their tools include wrenches, screwdrivers, pliers, and portable power tools.

Requirements

In the past, most industrial machinery mechanics have learned the skills of the trade informally by spending several years as helpers in a particular factory. In the future, as machinery becomes more complex, formal apprenticeship programs will become more important. This training usually lasts four years and includes both on-the-job and related classroom training. Apprentices learn the use and care of the tools, and the operation, lubrication, and adjustment of the machinery and equipment they will maintain. In class they learn shop mathematics, blueprint reading, safety, hydraulics, welding, and other subjects related to the trade.

Students interested in this field should have mechanical aptitude and manual dexterity.

Special requirements

There are no special requirements for industrial machinery mechanics other than those already mentioned. Most of the workers in this occupation belong to a union.

Opportunities for experience and exploration

Repairing home appliances gives a good opportunity to explore this field, as does tinkering with the engine of an old car. Part-time work or a summer job may be obtained in an industrial plant that would give a student interested in this field an opportunity to observe repair work being done.

Related occupations

Many other specialized mechanics positions might be of interest to people with the aptitudes for industrial machinery mechanics. These jobs include automobile mechanics, motorcycle mechanics, bicycle mechanics, general maintenance mechanics, and motorboat mechanics.

Methods of entering

Jobs can be obtained either by direct application to one of the many industries using industrial equipment or machinery, or with the direction of a vocational counselor.

Advancement

Industrial machinery mechanics advance from helper to apprentice to fully qualified mechanics.

Employment outlook

About 430,000 industrial machinery mechanics were employed in the early 1990s primarily by the industries that manufactured food and kindred products, primary metals, machinery, chemicals, fabricated metal products, transportation equipment, paper, rubber, and textiles.

The job outlook in this field is somewhat poorer than the average for the next decade. With the widespread use of automatic equipment with lower maintenance requirements, less repair work will be needed.

An industrial machinery mechanic disassembles and repairs a high-speed cylinder.

Earnings

Average straight-time hourly earnings of industrial machinery mechanics employed by a wide variety of industries across the country in the early 1990s averaged about $32,000 annually. These workers are not usually affected by seasonal changes in production, because much repair work and major overhaul is done during this time.

Conditions of work

Common shop injuries are to be expected in this field, but accidents are being reduced or eliminated by the many safety devices found in most factories today. In general, working conditions are good. But because the machinery is not always readily accessible, mechanics may work in stooped or cramped positions or on high ladders.

Most industrial machinery mechanics covered by union-management contracts are provided with fringe benefits such as paid holidays and vacations, health insurance, life insurance, and retirement pensions.

Social and psychological factors

These workers are responsible for valuable equipment. They are often called upon to exercise considerable independent judgment. They must know their trade and have the manual dexterity to perform the job. It is a vital job in the production line and offers a secure position to the person who qualifies.

GOE: 05.05.09; SIC: Any industry; SOC: 6112

◇ **SOURCES OF ADDITIONAL INFORMATION**

International Association of Machinists and Aerospace Workers
1300 Connecticut Avenue, NW
Washington, DC 20036

International Union of Electronic, Electrical, Salaried, Machine, and Furniture Workers
1126 16th Street, NW
Washington, DC 20036

International Union, United Automobile, Aerospace and Agricultural Implement Workers of America
8000 East Jefferson Avenue
Detroit, MI 48214

United Steelworkers of America
Five Gateway Center
Pittsburgh, PA 15222

◇ **RELATED ARTICLES**

Volume 1: Machining and Machinery; or see Table of Contents for areas of related interest
Volume 3: Automobile mechanics; Farm equipment mechanics; Forge shop occupations; Iron and steel industry workers; Job and die setters; Machinists; Millwrights
Volume 4: Mechanical technicians

Instrument makers

Definition

An *instrument maker*, also called an *experimental machinist and model maker*, fabricates, modifies, or repairs mechanical instruments, or mechanical assemblies of electrical or electronic instruments, such as chronometric timing devices, barographs, seismographs, and so forth. Workers do this by following blueprints and engineering sketches and using machine tools, welding and heat treating equipment, precision measuring instruments, and hand tools.

Experimental machinists assemble prototype, or original, equipment that will be used to test design specifications.

History

Instrument making closely parallels the birth of metalworking machines in the United States. One of the first Americans to use machinery to work metal in a mass production process was Eli Whitney, who was commissioned in 1798 to manufacture 10,000 rifles. He was followed by Oliver Evans, who developed the automatic sequence, in the early 1800s. Later, the Civil War created a vast labor shortage and forced a change to mechanization wherever possible.

A new stage in the development of mechanization was marked by the early work done by Frederick Taylor, who introduced scientific management. Taylor's work in the early 1900s made possible the synchronization of people and machines in the form of assembly-line production. The automated production lines of today's plants are the logical descendants of Taylor's early work in this field.

Even though each of the preceding developments has had a profound effect upon instrument making, growth and development of basic research, new atomic energy applications, and the need for developing smaller instruments are having an even greater effect. Each new scientific development has forced the instrument maker to do more exacting work with greater accuracy than ever before.

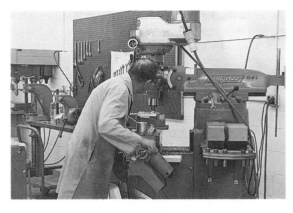

An instrument maker refines a piece of equipment by shaving the metal.

Nature of the work

Because instrument makers often work on their own, and their job calls for highly developed manual skills and reasoning abilities, they have considerable prestige among their fellow employees. Instrument makers must be familiar with the use of instruments in production, research, and testing work in government and industry. They must also be familiar with the various tools and machines used, such as lathes, drills, grinders, and milling machines.

Instrument makers often work closely with engineers and scientists in the development of ideas and designs into experimental models, special laboratory equipment, and special-purpose instruments. Experimental devices made by these crafts workers are used, for example, to regulate heat, measure distance, record earthquakes, and control industrial processes.

These skilled crafts workers often work from rough sketches, verbal instructions, or ideas rather than from detailed blueprints. Thus, in making parts, they frequently have to use considerable imagination and ingenuity. Instrument makers sometimes work on parts that must not vary from specifications more than one ten-millionth of an inch. To meet these standards, instrument makers commonly use micrometers, standard measuring instruments, and special equipment or precision devices, such as the electronic height gauge. They often work with a variety of materials, and it is not unusual to find them working with steel, plastics, ivory, or platinum.

Often an instrument maker is called upon to design, build, and test the finished instruments for proper operation. In large shops or where other different operations are involved, the instrument maker works with other specialists, each making a part of the instrument.

Although instrument makers, regardless of what they are working on, have similar basic duties, they may be known by a special title. The jeweler, for example, is usually located in firms making instruments and apparatus and works on delicate and highly sensitive instruments and apparatus, such as barographs, thermographs, chronometers, photographic recording instruments, and balance mechanisms, which demand high-level precision work. A parts mechanic is usually found in the light, heat, and power industries making jigs, dies, and other special tools for use in the construction and repair of electrical instruments. The precision-instrument tool maker is usually employed in the communications and research laboratory, making and assembling scientific tools, instruments, and apparatus for experimental projects. The job may involve laying out cutting lines of such structural parts as brackets and housings on such stock as silver, steel, and plastic, using square, rule, and scribe. This worker will also cut and shape parts, using machine tools such as lathes, presses, milling machines, and so forth.

The main centers of instrument making are located in and around a few large cities, particularly New York, Chicago, Los Angeles, and Washington.

Requirements

Because of the nature of the work, people who are interested in becoming instrument makers should have a strong interest in mechanical subjects and a superior ability to work with their hands. Because instrument makers often work alone or with little supervision, they must be resourceful people who can take initiative. They often must study the individual parts of the instrument and visualize their relationship to the completed instrument; because of this, they should have a better-than-average spatial relations ability. Instrument makers must understand how the instrument is used and the principles involved in its operation. Instrument makers take considerable pride in their creative, yet mechanical, work.

Employers generally prefer applicants for entry jobs as instrument makers to be high-school graduates with courses in algebra, geometry, trigonometry, science, and machine shop work. In addition, technical schooling in electricity and electronics is considered desirable in this field.

Most instrument makers come from the ranks of machinists or skilled machine tool operators. These craft workers must work one or two years under close supervision on relatively simple tasks before qualifying as instrument makers.

Other instrument makers learn their trade in a four- to five-year apprenticeship training program. A typical four-year program includes approximately 8,000 hours of shop training and 576 hours of related classroom instruction. Shop training emphasizes the use of machine tools, hand tools, measuring instruments, and the working properties of various materials. Classroom instruction usually covers such related technical subjects as mathematics, physics, and blueprint reading. Persons interested in this field usually take a battery of psychological tests that include such areas as spatial visualization, mechanical aptitude, manual dexterity, and other important skills.

Special requirements

Those interested in qualifying as instrument makers usually must pass an oral or written examination, or both, and be able to demonstrate their ability by performing the various tasks involved in instrument making. The examination is usually practical in nature.

Opportunities for experience and exploration

High-school students may explore this occupational field by visiting shops and laboratories where instrument makers are employed. Courses in machine shop and mechanical drawing may give the young high-school student an opportunity to explore, firsthand, many of the necessary skills related to instrument making.

Related occupations

Other occupations that may hold interest to young people with the skills for instrument makers include gunsmiths, contact lens manufacturing workers, and patternmakers.

Methods of entering

Major means of entrance are through advancing from jobs as machinists or skilled machine tool operators and apprenticeship training programs. Aspirants who have completed high school can apply for apprenticeship training directly to personnel offices of shops and laboratories known to hire instrument makers. State and private employment agencies frequently know of firms seeking persons who have been trained in this field.

Advancement

Promotion opportunities in this occupation are available to instrument makers, depending upon their training and special abilities. As their skill increases and their knowledge broadens, they may advance to increasingly responsible positions. Approximately ten years of experience are needed to rise to the highest level of skill involved in instrument making. Additional training beyond high school in physics and machine design enables some instrument makers to advance to the job of technician. Others may become supervisors of less skilled instrument makers and assist in training them on the job or at technical schools.

Employment outlook

In the early 1990s, there were about 4,500 people employed as instrument makers.

Employment in this relatively small occupation is expected to increase modestly through the next decade. The following factors point to this increased need: more instrument makers will be needed to make models of new instruments to be mass-produced in the future; custom or special-purpose instruments needed in limited numbers will have to be devised; the expanding fields of atomic energy, guided missiles, and industrial automation will need additional instrument makers; many new precision instruments will emerge from growing research and development programs of universities, government agencies, private laboratories, and manufacturing firms; and there will be openings as a result of promotions, transfers, retirements, and deaths.

Earnings

Earnings of instrument makers compare favorably with those of other highly skilled metalworkers. In the early 1990s, instrument makers generally earned a median salary of about $24,400 annually.

Companies employing instrument makers usually provide paid holidays and paid vacations in addition to life insurance, hospitalization, medical and surgical insurance, sickness and accident insurance, and pensions.

Many instrument makers are members of unions and enjoy the benefits won by these unions. Among the labor organizations in this field are the International Association of Machinists and Aerospace Workers; the International Union, United Automobile, Aerospace and Agricultural Implement Workers of America; the International Union of Electrical Workers; the United Steelworkers of America; and the Mechanics Educational Society of America.

Conditions of work

The majority of instrument shops are clean, well lighted, and free from dust. Because they work with high-speed machine tools and sharp cutting tools, workers in this occupation need good safety habits, and safety instructions are an important part of job training. Safety rules generally require special glasses, aprons, and tightly fitting clothes. The work is not physically strenuous; however, the need to watch controls closely, to check the accuracy of the work carefully, and the great attention paid to details may prove mentally fatiguing to some.

Social and psychological factors

An instrument maker should possess strong mechanical ability, manual dexterity, aptitude,

and interest in working with machinery. Because it is important to make precise measurements and read blueprints accurately, good eyesight is essential. Ability to express oneself orally, and in writing, is important because instrument makers are often required to prepare written and verbal reports for their superiors. Instrument makers must possess intelligence and creativity because they must often develop original solutions to the problems they encounter.

GOE: 05.05.11; SIC: 34, 35, 38; SOC: 6813

◇ SOURCES OF ADDITIONAL INFORMATION

International Association of Machinists and Aerospace Workers
1300 Connecticut Avenue, NW
Washington, DC 20036

International Union, United Automobile, Aerospace and Agricultural Implement Workers of America
8000 East Jefferson Avenue
Detroit, MI 48214

NMTBA—Association for Manufacturing Technology
7901 Westpark Drive
McLean, VA 22102

For students interested in industrial arts and technology, the following organization is for elementary through high school students:

Technology Student Association
1914 Association Drive
Keston, VA 22091

◇ RELATED ARTICLES

Volume 1: Machining and Machinery
Volume 2: Engineers
Volume 3: Industrial machinery mechanics; Machine tool operators; Machinists; Millwrights; Patternmakers; Tool makers and die makers
Volume 4: Electromechanical technicians; Instrumentation technicians

Job and die setters

Definition

Job setters and *die setters* prepare machine tools and production tools for others to use. They set up jigs, fixtures, molds, and dies on machines for the making of everything from food processors and cameras to automobiles and yachts.

History

The need for setup workers evolved out of the Industrial Revolution. As machines were invented, and as they became more numerous and more complex, there was a need for workers to ready or adjust them for operation. James Watt began experiments with steam engines in 1736, and as he perfected his experiments he needed more perfect tools. In 1775, John Wilkinson invented the boring machine, which smoothed holes, and thus steam was not lost from the steam engine.

Later, lathes were invented, screw-cutting machines, shapers, steam hammers, and other machine tools. Today our highly industrial society could not function without the many inventions in this field and the specialized setters who make certain that they perform as intended.

Nature of the work

Setters get the equipment ready for their co-workers, the machine operators, who run machine tools. They set up the fixtures that hold the pieces being worked on, and they adjust the sequence, speed, and flow. They set cutting bits to shave off the exact amount of material. They set up planers, mills, grinders, presses, turret lathes, and automatic machine centers. After set up, they test the machine by running off several pieces to make certain that their settings are accurate.

Setup workers demonstrate, show, or tell operators how to run the machines. They warn them about potential difficulties and explain how to avoid them. During a job run, setters make adjustments when necessary, and they change cutting tools and adjust specifications if needed.

Setters may work on only one type of machine or on most of the machines in any one plant or factory; they may work with only one metal, alloy, or plastic, or with several—and they may work on only one product, or on a variety. Specialists include *buffing-line set-up workers; thread tool grinder set-up operators; trim-machine adjusters; slitter service and setters; honing; spline-rolling machine; job setters;* and *punch-press, machine, spring coiling machine, threading-machine, grinder machine, molding-and-coremaking machines, machine try-out; automatic-spinning lathe, mold,* and *shear setters.*

Requirements

Employers usually prefer to hire high-school graduates who have taken algebra, geometry, and trigonometry—as well as metal or machine shop. Though trade schools teach shop math and machine trades, apprenticeships are generally thought to be the best way into this field.

Special requirements

There are no special requirements for this work. Most setters, however, do belong to one of the unions related to the trade.

Opportunities for experience and exploration

Machine shop courses in high school or technical school provide one way of gaining some experience in this work. Summer jobs in unskilled work are sometimes available in manufacturing plants that have large machine shops, as may be found in the aircraft industry. Working with the skilled workers in such a plant will provide the student with a beginning knowledge of machine tools and the work of setup operators.

Related occupations

Other occupations that might be of interest to those with the skills and aptitudes for job and die setters include machinists, millwrights, forge shop occupations, patternmakers, and machine tool operators.

Methods of entering

Job applicants should ask for help from high-school counselors and the local state employment office. They should also apply at machine shops or factories.

Beginners usually take four-year apprenticeships in order to become journeyworker all-round machinists. They may work as machinists for several years before becoming setters.

Advancement

Promotion from setter to shop supervisor is considered a natural step by most employees. Skilled setup operators may also open their own shop, for which they should prepare by acquiring business skills.

Employment outlook

In the early 1990s about 93,000 setup operators worked in U.S. factories that make automobiles, trucks, planes, farm equipment, and other types of machinery. Most of them worked in factories that also employ many semiskilled machine tool operators. Setup operators work in every state, but primarily in large industrial centers.

While the overall outlook for job and die setters is positive, more and more businesses will be turning to automatic numerical control technology during the next decade. Electronic controls will replace many manual operations previously done by setters, but, at the same time, the need for programmers and inspectors will increase.

Earnings

In the early 1990s in the larger cities, setters had a median annual salary of about $27,450. Apprentices started at about 50 or 60 percent of journeyworkers' wages, which in turn was lower than that of master machinists.

In most work situations, setters have a forty-hour workweek. Some plants pay double time for weekend work, and many pay time and a half for more than eight hours per shift,

more than forty hours per week, and all sixth or seventh day work. Night or early morning shifts sometimes pay more, and many employers give incentive, or piecework, pay.

Conditions of work

Overall working conditions for setters are good. Machine shops are not too noisy and are usually well lighted and ventilated. Most are air-conditioned during the summer months.

Setters spend much of their workdays on their feet, but they do not have to do anything strenuous because cranes do most of the lifting. Safety measures, including machine guards and safety glasses, and rules are usually enforced.

Social and psychological factors

Most job and die setters work much of their time alone and are totally responsible for the accuracy of their settings. They are also responsible for directing the work of the machine operators, however, so must also like being with and supervising others.

Setters work with a large number of different machines and tools, programming them to produce a wide variety of products. They gain much satisfaction in this highly skilled work, which produces fine quality articles with care and precision.

GOE: 06.01.02; SIC: 3544; SOC: 7329

◇ **SOURCES OF ADDITIONAL INFORMATION**

International Association of Machinists and Aerospace Workers
1300 Connecticut Avenue, NW
Washington, DC 20036

International Union, United Automobile, Aerospace and Agricultural Implement Workers of America
8000 East Jefferson Avenue
Detroit, MI 48214

International Brotherhood of Electrical Workers
1125 15th Street, NW
Washington, DC 20005

International Union of Electronic, Electrical, Salaried, Machine, and Furniture Workers
1126 16th Street, NW
Washington, DC 20036

NMTBA—Association for Manufacturing Technology
7901 Westpark Drive
McLean, VA 22102

◇ **RELATED ARTICLES**

Volume 1: Machining and Machinery
Volume 3: Industrial machinery mechanics; Machine tool operators; Machinists
Volume 4: Electromechanical technicians; Mechanical technicians

Knit goods industry workers

Definition

Knit goods industry workers are men and women who set up, operate, and repair the machines that knit various products, such as sweaters, socks, hats, sweatshirts, undergarments, lace, and other garments. The work is distinct from weaving, in that knitting consists of drawing one strand of yarn through the loops of another with needles, while weaving builds fabric by interlocking threads at right angles to each other.

History

Although we may not stop to think about it, knitting and weaving are two distinct and separate crafts. Weaving is quite ancient, while knitting was not introduced to Europe until sometime in the 1400s. The first knitting machine was invented in England in 1589. Other well known forms of knitting include lace making and crocheting.

Although some people still knit special gifts and articles of clothing at home, a large knitting industry powered by automatic machinery has grown to satisfy the need for all types of knitted goods. While there are knitting mills in every state in the union, nearly 60 percent of all those employed in the textile industry work in North Carolina, South Carolina, and Georgia. Historically, because cotton was and is produced primarily in the southern states, heavy industry such as knitting and textile mills was situated near the cotton, which was cheaper than shipping the cotton to mills in the north.

Many regional specialties, however, have arisen over time. Mills in the northeast produce most of the country's sweaters, while those in the southeast produce most of our knit shirts. Most of the country's underwear is produced in the southeast and eastern Pennsylvania, while most of our socks and stockings come from North Carolina, which has 80 percent of the nation's hosiery mills.

Nature of the work

Two different methods can be used in the manufacture of knit goods: the cut-and-sew method and the full-fashioned method. While both of these employ some of the same types of machine operators, they also have certain employees that are unique to each.

With the cut-and-sew method, the various parts of the knit product, such as sleeves, body, and collar, are made separately, dyed, trimmed, and then sewn together. The first step is to adjust the knitting machine to produce the type and pattern of knit that the product requires. Automatic knitting looms are controlled in a number of ways, usually by metal plates, cards, tapes, or chains that control the operation of the needles. On a Jacquard, or Jacquard loom machine (named after its French inventor), the knit pattern is controlled by holes punched in metal plates. The *Jacquard-plate maker* will snap small covers over particular holes in a pattern plate, then link plates together to form a continuous chain. The Jacquard-plate maker and the *knitter mechanic* then work together to install the plates in the knitting machine and start a trial run to determine that the specified knit pattern is being produced. While the needles are controlled in this manner, the guide bars (flat metal bars on which yarn guides are attached) are controlled by pattern chains assembled by the *pattern assembler*. Patterns can also be dictated by pattern wheels that control the operation of the needles in circular knitting machines. Needle jacks are inserted in notches in the pattern wheel by the *pattern wheel maker*, who sometimes marks the top of the pattern wheel to indicate where the pattern begins.

After the patterns are installed, the *knitting-machine operator* tends the machine as it turns yarn into the basic parts for garments. Often an operator will tend more than one machine. Spools of yarn are placed on the creel (spindles for holding bobbins) of the machine, and the yarn is threaded through the needles, yarn guides, tension springs, and carriers using a hook. The operator then ties the new yarn to the ends of the old yarn still in place, and activates the machine to knit a small piece of cloth, or a false start, to thread the new yarn into the machine. The operator laps this false start around a take-up roller, adjusts the counters on the machine to produce a certain number of pieces, and activates the machine. While the machine is working, the operator checks to be sure there are no flaws in the knitting and that the yarn threads don't break or run out.

Knitted sections are collected on the take-up roller or are folded and stacked into bundles as they come out of the machine. After a certain number, the operator will take a roll or bundle and attach a tag that specifies the lot number, size, color, and number of pieces. The bundles are then weighed, bundled, or packed into sacks, and sent to the laundry or dye house. The operator then resets the knitting machine and inspects it for routine maintenance before starting a new lot. Routine maintenance can include replacing broken needles, emptying waste oil, refilling oil cups, and greasing machine parts.

In larger plants, regular maintenance of the machines is the job of the *knitting-machine fixer*, who can also set up a machine to produce a certain fabric pattern like the knitter mechanic. The fixer will observe the machine in operation, and turn set screws and handwheels to adjust the gears and cams of the machine. The fixer also repairs or replaces broken machine parts; aligns and straightens needles, sinkers, and dividers; and cleans and oils the machine.

After knitting, the garment parts must be cleaned and softened. The *knit-goods washer* runs the knitted tubular cloth through a ma-

A worker at a hosiery factory inspects the nylons for defects. Such work requires keen eyesight.

chine that washes it with detergent and treats it with fabric-softening chemicals. If the cloth is made of undyed yarn, it must be cleaned and specially treated before it is dyed. The cloth is again bundled into sacks, cleaned, and bleached if the garment is to be white or pastel colors. The bags are then taken to be dyed by the *dye-tub operator*. The operator fills the dye machine with water and steam to a specified level; pours in the dye, cleaning agent, or finishing chemicals; sets the temperature and dyeing time, according to the formula; places the cloth into the compartments of the machine; and submerges the cloth into the dye. After the specified dyeing time, the tubs are drained and then refilled for a second scouring cycle to remove excess dye from the material. Fabric softeners and finishing chemicals are then added in the final rinse. The dyed fabric is then sent to *drying-machine operators* who tumble dry it in machines and send it to the people who assemble the pieces into whole garments. The cloth may also be brushed to impart a certain nap or feel.

On their way from the dye house, the *garment steamer* removes wrinkles from the fabric pieces with a machine that emits steam and hot air. The knit cloth at this stage is still in long tubular form. Most often the cloth needs to be slit open, laid flat, cut into the proper pieces, and then sewn together. The *tubular-splitting-machine tender* cuts the fabric to flatten it out, watching carefully for defective splitting. The fabric is then laid out in layers so the *pattern marker* can examine the fabric and mark the material for cutting the garment pieces. Next, *machine cutters* use round knives or band knives to cut the pieces that will be sewn together to make the finished garment.

The pieces are bundled together according to lot and sent to the *overedge sewer,* who puts them through a sewing machine equipped with a rotary cutter to trim the raw cuts and loose threads. At the same time, the machine sews the edges with an overedge stitch for decoration and for the prevention of unraveling. The garment pieces are then taken to the *sewing-machine operator* to be sewn together. Finally, labels, buttons, and any other small items are sewn to the garment, which is then inspected and packed for shipment.

The second method of manufacturing knit goods—the full-fashioned method—produces items that are knitted in one piece, such as fancy sweaters, socks, hats, and scarves. A few special steps are required in this method, which can be described using a sweater as an example. The bottom edge and cuffs of the sweater are first made on flat knitting machines. The *topper* loops the stitches of these ribbed sweater parts onto the points of a transfer bar, which makes it easy to transfer the part to the needles of the knitting machine. The transfer bar will hold several ribbed parts, separated by lengths of loose yarn that is not knitted, so that several sweaters can be knitted in succession. The *full-fashioned garment knitter* takes the transfer bar, positions it over the needle bed of the knitting machine, and pushes the stitches from transfer points onto the machine needles. The transfer bar can then be removed. The knitter operates the knitting machine, which is specially programmed to increase or decrease stitching at specified points in the garment. For example, stitching starts low at the point where the sweater hooks up with its linked bottom, increases in the body of the sweater, and then decreases at the shoulders and sleeves to narrow the sweater. This can happen automatically or by the action of the knitter. The sweater is then taken off the machine and another is started.

The sweater is sent to the *looper* who operates a looping machine to attach the collar and to shape the sweater further. The needles of the machine can impart a chain stitch along the shoulders, armholes, sleeves, and collar of the sweater that sharpens the contours and shape of the sweater, making it look more like a cut-and-sewn sweater. The sweater is then cleaned, dyed, softened, and finished in the same manner as described for the cut-and-sew method.

Requirements

Most of the production jobs in the knit goods industry are learned on the job, although the basic skills involved can be learned in high school or technical school. Although most employers prefer to hire high-school graduates, it is not absolutely required. Technology is increasing in the knitting industry and other textile industries, and this will create a demand for employees with solid educational backgrounds. The machines may be computer controlled that perform stitch-making and assembly. Color patterns for garments can also be computer controlled. See Volume 4: CAD/CAM technicians, for further information.

Programs in textile design and textile technology are offered at many technical schools and two-year colleges. There, cutters can learn pattern making, cutting, and pattern grading.

Training periods vary significantly from job to job and from mill to mill. Training may be as short as a few days for a cleaner or as long as several months for a machine tender. For certain occupations such as sewing machine operators and steamers, piecework pay is used as an incentive so that, once the employee has mastered the job, he or she is motivated to work swiftly.

Apprenticeships for knitters and other craftspeople in the knitting industry are generally available. Students interested in preparing for these apprenticeships should pursue a high-school curriculum that includes blueprint reading and drawing, basic mathematics, shop math, and machine shop practice. Information on apprenticeships can be obtained from the regional offices of the U.S. Bureau of Apprenticeship and Training and state employment offices, as well as contacting textile and apparel companies directly.

Special requirements

Many workers in the knit goods industry belong to unions that represent the interests of the entire textile industry. These unions include the International Ladies' Garment Workers' Union, which has 283,000 members; the Amalgamated Clothing and Textile Workers Union, with 303,000 members; and the United Garment Workers of America, with 25,000 members. These unions also represent workers in the textile, weaving, and manmade fibers industries. Some knit goods plants are nonunion shops.

Opportunities for experience and exploration

Some state employment agencies operate programs that give students the chance to take high-school courses and participate in on-the-job training in various occupations in the knit goods industry. Students should contact their state agencies for information on these types of programs and other part-time or summer jobs available. Unions are also a good source of information on jobs in the industry.

Related occupations

Other occupations that perform work similar to knit goods industry workers include apparel industry workers, textile technicians, fashion designers, and art directors.

Methods of entering

People with production jobs in the knit goods industry start from the bottom as helpers and apprentices and work their way up. Technical school or college graduates may be able to find work through school placement offices. To find out about job openings and apprenticeship programs, job seekers can contact the knitting mills directly or find out more through a state employment agency or union office.

Advancement

After an apprenticeship period, workers can move up through the ranks of their job, for example, moving from an apprentice knitter to an assistant knitter to a skilled knitter. Workers can also move from their present job to one that offers more skilled or higher paying work. For example, a floor worker who moves material between the areas of the mill can train for and move into a job as a sewing machine operator.

Workers who have proven themselves with their machinery can advance in several ways. Some become instructors and train new employees. Others advance by taking positions requiring more skills and greater responsibility. Because machine operators and setup crews are the most highly skilled production workers, first-line management positions are usually filled from their ranks. Most companies have training programs to help interested employees

advance; many pay all or part of the tuition for work-related courses.

Employment outlook

The entire textile industry, of which the knit goods industry is a part, employed approximately 309,000 workers in the early 1990s. Employment prospects for knit goods workers and other textile workers are expected to decline in the next decade. While the demand for knit goods has increased along with population growth, automation, and competition from overseas have combined to keep the demand for knit goods workers down.

The continuing growth of imports can be expected to prompt greater industry specialization. Companies will concentrate on manufacturing products in which they have a competitive advantage. Labor-saving, computerized machinery has increased productivity. Job prospects look best for skilled engineers, technicians, computer personnel, and others who know how to operate and service complex knitting machinery.

Earnings

The earnings of knitting mill workers vary according to the mill they work in and the goods they produce. Knitting mill workers are the lowest paid of all textile workers, earning an average weekly salary of $252 in the early 1990s, or $6.30 an hour. Union shops pay more than nonunion shops.

Women's hosiery workers earn an average of $6.11 an hour. Those who work in circular knit fabric mills earn $6.75 an hour. Knit outerwear mills pay workers $6.08 an hour, while knit underwear mills pay an average of $5.79 an hour. Production workers may work for a flat daily wage or for an incentive wage that pays them more when they produce more pieces. Apprentices are normally paid wages somewhat lower than experienced employees.

Benefits, like wages, can vary depending on the mill and the union contract. They usually include paid holidays and vacations, health and life insurance, retirement plans, sick and funeral leave, and educational reimbursement. Additionally, most companies operate company stores in which employees can get discounts on the goods the company produces.

533

Conditions of work

Working conditions depend on the age of the mill and its degree of modernization. Newer buildings have better ventilation and temperature control equipment that reduces some of the problems caused by dust and fumes. Workers in areas with high levels of dust or fumes use protective glasses and masks that cover their nose and mouth. Although some of the newer knitting machinery has reduced the level of noise in mills, workers in some areas still must wear earplugs.

The usual workweek in a knitting mill is from thirty-five to forty hours long. Knitters usually work longer shifts, however, sometimes up to sixty hours a week. Workers may be laid off during slow seasons.

Because these workers are performing the same tasks throughout their shifts, their work can be very repetitious. Physical stamina is required because machine operators are on their feet much of the time. Knitters must have good eyesight to spot dropped stitches and broken threads, and the agility and alertness to tend many machines at once.

Although there are safety features on all new machinery, the knit goods industry worker needs to pay continual attention to the job. With steamers, cutters, and dye tubs, the equipment can inflict harm when used improperly.

The conditions of work for cottage industry (small family-run businesses) workers can be quiet, friendly environments, with most of the knitting done by hand. The work can be difficult, though and the pay is usually quite low. Most hand made garments come from foreign countries now.

Social and psychological factors

The work in knitting mills is usually routine and repetitious. People interested in this type of work must be able to perform the same tasks over and over without letting the quality of their work suffer.

GOE: 06.02.06; SIC: 225; SOC: 7652

◇ **SOURCES OF ADDITIONAL INFORMATION**

Amalgamated Clothing and Textile Workers Union
15 Union Square
New York, NY 10003

American Textile Manufacturers Institute
1801 K Street, NW, Suite 900
Washington, DC 20006

Man-Made Fiber Producers Association
1150 17th Street, NW
Washington, DC 20036

National Knitwear Manufacturers Association
365 South Street
Morristown, NJ 07960

International Ladies' Garment Workers' Union
1710 Broadway
New York, NY 10019

United Garment Workers of America
4207 Lebanon Road
Hermitage, TN 37076

◇ **RELATED ARTICLES**

Volume 1: Apparel; Textiles
Volume 3: Industrial machinery mechanics; Textile manufacturing occupations
Volume 4: Textile technicians

Machine tool operators

Definition

Machine tool operators shape metal and plastic to precise dimensions by using machine tools. They are usually known by the machine they operate, such as engine lathe operator, turret lathe set-up operator, or milling machine set-up operator. The *setup operators* are machinists who specialize in readying the necessary equipment and instructing in its use.

History

The history of machine tools is relatively recent. When James Watt experimented with steam engines, he could not find anyone who could drill a perfect hole; thus his engines leaked steam. In 1775, John Wilkinson invented the boring machine.

Just twenty-five years later Matthew Murray, Joseph Clement, and Richard Murray developed the planer. Thus holes and flat surfaces could be smoothed to necessary degrees.

Lathes have been known since ancient times, and are probably a variation of the potters wheel. In 1800, Henry Maudslay invented the first good screw-cutting lathe. James Nasmyth invented the shaper, and also the steam hammer and other machine tools.

The growth of machine tools is partly responsible for the mass production methods found in the United States. The most rapid spurt in their development has come since World Wars I and II. It was necessary to build tanks, planes, jeeps, ships, and guns rapidly and accurately, so machines had to be devised that would turn out the thousands of pieces required. Since that time there has also been a steady increase in the amount of goods that Americans desire, so production methods learned for war have been converted and improved to make the countless products America manufactures today.

Nature of the work

The work of the machine tool operator differs from that of the all-around machinist, or production machine operator, in that machine tool operators do not have the diversified knowledge necessary to set up and operate most machines in a machine shop. The machine tool operator can generally do only the work connected with one particular specialty. In other words, a machinist knows about specialized machines such as grinders, shapers, honers, reamers, chippers, and planers, while the machine tool operator is limited to a single machine, usually does little or no hand fitting or assembly work, and depends on a setup machinist to ready, adjust, and maintain the equipment.

The machine tool operator receives a daily assignment, which, if the job is a large one, may last all day or for a number of days. The machine is preset so far as the speed and the amount of cutting, reaming, or drilling is concerned. This means that, in the case of a drill press, the machine is set to drill only so far and no more into the metal stock. No matter how much pressure is exerted on the handle, the drill will go no deeper than the preset stop will allow. If this stop loosens, the machine tool operator will generally call the setup machinist to remeasure the distance the drill should travel, and relock it into place.

The typical operators push a starting button to start the drill, pick up a piece of metal stock, insert it into the guide that holds it during machining, pull down the lever of the drill press until the piece is drilled the prescribed distance, and release the lever. They remove the stock from the machine and place it in a bin for completed parts.

From time to time during the drilling, they squirt oil from an oilcan against the drill. Because the drill easily overheats from friction, it is necessary to cool the drill in this way.

Except in cases of machinery breakdown, or while new stock is being brought up for machining, the machine tool operator repeats the same process until the job is completed.

With other machines the process is similar: that of lifting, placing the part into the machine, doing the machining, and removing the finished piece.

Skilled setup operators use micrometers and other gauges to set up their machines and possibly the machines of other workers in the shop. During the course of the day, they will replace worn and broken belts, change cutting tools on their machines, check measurements on their work to ensure their continued accuracy. If a major repair or replacement is needed, they may call a repairer, or do the re-

A machine tool operator uses several control panels to shape a piece of metal. He must form the piece using precise dimensions.

pairs themselves if they are working in a small shop that has no repairer available.

Many shops make no distinction between skilled machine tool operators and machine tool operators as far as job title is concerned, but the work generally differs because of the greater ability of the skilled worker.

Requirements

As in the case of most other semiskilled and some skilled occupations, there are no special educational requirements for the job of machine operator. A student interested in this work should have better than average mechanical aptitude, an interest in machines, and some school or job experience in blueprint reading, shop mathematics, and use of simple hand tools. Also helpful are such subjects as algebra, geometry, trigonometry, English, and drafting or mechanical drawing.

Although a high-school diploma is not required, it is a major asset in employment and is considered for promotions.

Special requirements

Most machine tool operators belong to one of the unions open to workers in this field.

Opportunities for experience and exploration

A young person may be hired for summer or part-time work, particularly if the shop has seasonal work or a large contract needing additional work. Such part-time work is affected by general employment conditions. Working with as many different machine tools as possible at home and at school will also afford opportunities to explore interests and aptitudes in this field.

Related occupations

Other occupations that require interests, skills, and aptitudes similar to machine tool operators include patternmakers, machinists, tool makers, die makers, and forge shop occupations.

Methods of entering

Application for work should be made directly to the personnel office of the machine shop. A young person may start doing a wide variety of jobs around the shop. Most machine tool operators learn their skills on the job in a machine shop, observing a skilled operator at work. Then they have an opportunity to work under supervision until they are completely familiar with the work. This training usually lasts one and one-half to two years.

Some machine tool operators learn their trade through a union apprenticeship program, and some companies have a formal training course for machine operators.

Advancement

The machine tool operator who knows how to read blueprints and use tools such as micrometers and gauges, and who is willing to try new methods, is more likely to be moved into supervisory jobs with more responsibility, or to more varied and versatile positions such as programmer, who assists in planning the jobs. The operator may also advance to all-around machinist and tool-and-die maker.

Employment outlook

Approximately 1,060,000 machine tool operators and setup operators were employed in the early 1990s. Many of these worked in metalworking industries, such as plants that manufacture machinery and transportation equipment such as automobiles and aircraft. Many others worked in plants manufacturing electrical machinery and equipment, or fabricated metal and plastic products, or in factories that make textiles, paper, glass, or chemicals. A few machine tool operators worked in industrial research laboratories and shops that fabricate models of new products.

There has been much written in the last few years about automation. It would seem that the demand for machine operators would increase along with the increase in machines. Many of the new machines, however, are self-operating and more efficient. Machine operators will be needed to replace those people who retire, die, or change jobs. Employment in this field is expected to increase about as fast as the average for all occupations through the next decade.

New techniques in manufacturing are responsible for the slow growth of employment in this field. Faster and more versatile automatic machine tools, the increasingly widespread use of numerically controlled machine tools, chemical milling, electrical milling, electrical discharge and ultrasonic machining, as well as machining by electron beams and lasers, are all contributing factors in the gradual increase of machine tool operators.

The young person who keeps an open mind, wants to learn, and is willing to be retrained in these new methods will be able to change jobs if necessary with a minimum of effort.

Earnings

Machine tool operators are paid either an hourly rate or on an incentive basis, or a combination of both. In addition, they are rated according to experience and skill at their trade with Class A being the most highly skilled. In the early 1990s, straight-time annual wages averaged about $20,280. Set-up workers usually made an extra dollar or more per hour. It is generally an occupation requiring forty work hours per week, with time and a half for overtime.

Many machine tool firms have retirement plans to which the employer as well as the employees contribute. Most operators are also eligible for Social Security as well as group hospitalization insurance.

In many manufacturing operations, the plant closes down during the year for changes in machinery necessary to make new models. The worker is seldom paid for this "downtime" for retooling. Machine tool operators must consider these layoffs when figuring or estimating their yearly salary.

Conditions of work

This is inside work that is free from outdoor fluctuations of temperature and moisture. It is somewhat dangerous because of the high speeds and pressures at which these machines operate. Safety equipment must be used and safety rules must be observed. There are some hazards, as well, in skin irritations resulting from oils used on the cutting or drilling machines. These jobs are less hazardous than they once were, partly because of the increased emphasis on safety. Most operators must wear goggles and avoid loose clothing. Machinery is now designed with operator safety in mind. Older machines can be more dangerous, but all machines must be operated with great care.

Machine shops vary considerably in heat, ventilation, and lighting, as well as in being dusty and noisy. There are still many old and outdated machine shops in existence.

Social and psychological factors

The repetition of the eye and hand movements required to turn out piece after piece of identical parts is boring for some people, causing them to turn their attention to other things, which can result in accidents. As workers become involved in planning the jobs to be done, and as they become more skilled through greater knowledge of more than one machine, their work has more variety. They will have much more satisfaction in their work when they are skilled and conscientious workers.

International Association of Machinists and Aerospace Workers
1300 Connecticut Avenue, NW
Washington, DC 20036

International Union, United Automobile, Aerospace and
Agricultural Implement Workers of America
8000 East Jefferson Avenue
Detroit, MI 48214

International Brotherhood of Electrical Workers
1125 15th Street, NW
Washington, DC 20005

International Union of Electronic, Electrical, Salaried, Machine, and Furniture Workers
1126 16th Street, NW
Washington, DC 20036

NMTBA—Association for Manufacturing Technology
7901 Westpark Drive
McLean, VA 22102

◇ **RELATED ARTICLES**

Volume 1: Machining and Machinery; Metals
Volume 3: Industrial machinery mechanics;
Job and die setters; Machinists; Millwrights
Volume 4: Electromechanical technicians;
Mechanical technicians

Machinists

Definition

Machinists, also called *production machine operators* and *all-around machinists*, are skilled workers who can operate all kinds of machine tools and use machinist's hand tools to cut, drill, grind, or otherwise form a piece of metal into a desired shape and size, usually with an extremely high degree of accuracy.

History

Machine tools to form and shape metal have their antecedents in the tools used to make weapons, especially guns. But the modern era of metalworking equipment to make metal parts accurately according to specifications began with the development of the steam engine by James Watt and others in the latter part of the eighteenth century. John Wilkinson invented the boring machine to make steam engine cylinders more nearly round. A lathe to cut screw threads was developed by Henry Maudslay in 1800.

The Industrial Revolution opened up a new method of production. The ability to use metal molds and energy-powered engines to produce items that were originally only hand-crafted lowered costs and speeded up production time.

In the United States at about the same time, Eli Whitney was using tools and machines to make parts for guns with such accuracy that a quantity of parts could be made and assembled interchangeably. The interchangeability of parts produced by machines became the basis of modern mass production methods. Throughout the nineteenth century, more specialized and refined machines for metalworking were designed, and the electric motor as a source of power made further improvements possible.

By 1888, there were enough machinists in various industries to organize a machinists' union. The growth of the automobile industry in the twentieth century was probably the largest single force in developing metalworking machinery and in increasing the demand for machinists.

Nature of the work

The machinist can operate most types of machine tools. These tools can be described as power-driven machines that firmly hold both the piece of metal to be shaped and a cutting instrument. When these machines are in operation, the piece of metal is cut, shaved, ground, or drilled according to specifications.

With a working knowledge of the operation and uses of the various machine tools, together with an understanding of the properties of steel, cast iron, aluminum, brass, and other metals, the machinist is able to shape metal into parts of precise dimensions.

The work done by machine tools can be classified into one of the following categories: drilling, boring, turning (lathe), milling, planing (shaper, slotter, broach), and grinding.

Among the machinists' duties are the planning and the selecting of tools and material, the cutting, and the finishing operations required for each job, according to blueprint or written specifications. They first read the blueprints to set up the proper machine. They then select the proper cutting tools and set the speed and feed controls, according to the type of metal to be used in the product.

At times machinists may produce a number of identical machined products by working at a single machine. At other times they may produce one item by working on a variety of machines. After completing these machining operations, they may finish the work by hand, using files and scrapers, and then assemble the finished parts with wrenches and screwdrivers.

A high degree of accuracy is required in all machinists' work. Some specifications call for accuracy of one ten-thousandth of an inch or greater. To achieve this precision they must use instruments such as scribers, micrometers, calipers, verniers, scales, and gauges.

The machinist may find employment in three types of machine shops: a production shop where large quantities of identical items are produced; a job shop where a relatively few of each kind of item are produced; or a maintenance shop where parts are repaired or new ones are produced. The kind of machines one will use, the type of metal used, and the product to be produced will depend on the place of employment. For example, for the highly precise, expensive equipment used for science, specialized shops are used.

Machinists specialize as *electrical-discharge-machine setup operators*; *lay-out* and *propeller lay-out workers*; *rocket-engine mechanics*; *firearms model* and *fixture makers*; and *automotive, experimental, maintenance, fluid-power,* and *motion-picture equipment machinists*.

A production machine operator repairs a massive generator rotor on a 120-inch lathe.

Requirements

A machinist must be mechanically inclined and temperamentally suited to do highly accurate work requiring concentration and physical effort. One must have good vision (corrections allowed), superior judgment of depth and distance, and a high degree of finger and arm dexterity. For trainee or apprentice jobs, most companies prefer high-school or vocational school graduates. Student preparation should include algebra, geometry, physics, mechanical drawing, and machine shop. Courses in electronics and hydraulics may also be helpful.

To qualify as a machinist, a person must complete either an apprenticeship or on-the-job training program. The apprenticeship program consists of four years of carefully planned activity combining approximately 8,000 hours of shop training with 570 hours of related classroom instruction.

The on-the-job training program consists of working for four or more years under the supervision of experienced machinists, progressing from one machine to another. Trainees usually begin as a machine operator and as they show necessary aptitude they are given additional training in the machine they are operating. Further instruction in the more technical

A machinist operates a milling machine with great precision. Such machines can perform many functions using only one setting of the core box.

aspects of machine shop work is obtained through the studying of manuals and occasionally, classroom instruction. The amount of progress made is dependent on the vacancies in the shop and on the skill of the individual.

Special requirements

There are no special requirements for the occupation of machinist.

Opportunities for experience and exploration

In high school a student has several avenues open for exploring the occupation of machinist. Courses in machine shop and mechanical drawing will test one's accuracy, patience, and ability in this type of work, while courses in algebra and geometry will gauge one's skill in shop mathematics. Hobbies such as building

model airplanes and tinkering with automobiles provide a valuable firsthand experience with the workings of mechanical things.

To observe the machinist at work, field trips to machine shops can be arranged by the school counselor. An excellent opportunity for exploring this occupation would be a part-time job in a machine shop.

Related occupations

Other occupations require many of the same aptitudes and interests as those asked of machinists. Some of these include machine tool operators, patternmakers, numerical-control machine-tool operators, tool makers, and die makers.

Methods of entering

There are two ways an individual can enter the occupation of production machine operator: as an apprentice, or as an on-the-job trainee.

Those who wish to become an apprentice usually contact either employers, the state employment service bureau, or the appropriate union headquarters (International Association of Machinists or the United Automobile, Aerospace and Agricultural Implement Workers). They must, however, have the approval of the joint apprenticeship committee before they can enter the occupation as an apprentice.

If the apprenticeship program is filled, the applicant may wish to enter the field as an on-the-job trainee. In this case, one usually contacts the employer and begins work as a machine tool operator.

The Bureau of Apprenticeship and Training, U.S. Department of Labor, as well as the state employment office (which is a source of information about the Manpower and Development Training Act), are good places to contact for information.

Advancement

Successful completion of the training program is necessary before workers can become qualified machinists. After increasing their efficiency and skill for several years, and with additional training, many promotional opportunities are open to them. They may specialize as a tool-and-die maker or as an instrument maker. In a large production shop they may become a setup operator or a layout worker.

Those who have the ability to deal with people, good judgment, and planning skills, may progress to such supervisory positions as shop supervisor and superintendent of the shop.

Another possible advancement for the exceptionally well-qualified machinist who has had additional training at a technical school is into experimental and design work, process planning, and estimating. Some machinists eventually go into business for themselves.

Employment outlook

Employment opportunities for machinists are expected to increase moderately in the next two decades. There are several reasons for this outlook. The metalworking industry is expanding, and there will be many openings resulting from deaths and retirements.

Automation poses no immediate threat to machinists. Because they have the ability to work with a variety of machine tools, they can always be transferred to nonautomated machinery. Also, the new automated equipment requires a skilled machinist to set up, operate, and maintain it. In highly mechanized plants production machinery is linked together so that a breakdown in one machine can cause a general work stoppage. Maintenance machinists are needed to prevent and repair such costly breakdowns.

Earnings

Although earnings of production machine operators vary according to the section of the country, their average earnings compare favorably with those of other skilled factory workers.

The average annual pay for machinists in the early 1990s was more than $27,450 for a forty-hour week. Some machinists work on an incentive piecemeal basis, rather than for an hourly wage.

Conditions of work

Most machinists have a forty-hour workweek with extra pay for overtime. They work indoors in machine shops that usually are fairly clean, properly lighted, and well ventilated but at times quite noisy.

Although machining work is not physically strenuous, because the machines do the actual work, the machinist must stand on the job most of the day. Often one must wear special shoes to reduce foot fatigue. In addition, safety glasses are required since cutting tools, moving machine parts, and flying metal chips could cause injury to the eyes.

Paid holidays and vacations; life, medical, and accident insurance; and pension plans are usually available to all machinists.

Social and psychological factors

Probably the most interesting thing about the work of machinists is the variety of things they are able to do. Because they can set up and operate almost every machine in the shop, their work may vary with the production needs of the company. Their intelligence and ingenuity is often challenged by the needs of each job, and their accuracy and patience is tested by the precise demands of production. Production machine operators play an important role in the world of complex machinery and must have pride in their workmanship.

GOE: 05.05.07; SIC: Any industry; SOC: 6813

◇ **SOURCES OF ADDITIONAL INFORMATION**

International Association of Machinists and Aerospace Workers
1300 Connecticut Avenue, NW
Washington, DC 20036

International Union, United Automobile, Aerospace and Agricultural Implement Workers of America
8000 East Jefferson Avenue
Detroit, MI 48214

The National Tooling and Machining Association
9300 Livingstone Road
Fort Washington, MD 20744

The Tooling and Manufacturing Association
1177 South Dee Road
Park Ridge, IL 60068

Millwrights
Machine Trades Occupations

For information on apprenticeships in general and specialty machine work, contact:

Bureau of Apprenticeship and Training
Department of Labor
Room N–4649
Francis Perkins Building
Third Street and Constitution Avenue
Washington, DC 20210

◇ **RELATED ARTICLES**

Volume 1: Machining and Machinery
Volume 3: Forge shop occupations; Instrument makers; Iron and steel industry workers; Machine tool operators; Patternmakers; Tool makers and die makers
Volume 4: Electromechanical technicians

Millwrights

Definition

Millwrights move and install heavy industrial machinery and other equipment, including the construction of any necessary foundation. They may also find it necessary to dismantle, operate, repair, or lubricate this machinery. To do this, millwrights must be skilled in the use of basic tools and machinery, and they must be able to read blueprints and schematic diagrams.

History

The history of the millwright dates back to the Industrial Revolution, with the introduction of machinery too complicated for the average worker to understand. It became necessary to assign workers to handle and repair the machines. With the growth of industrial establishments and the increasing complexity of machines, the millwright became an integral part of the labor force.

Nature of the work

Millwrights are highly skilled workers. Basically, their job is to install heavy machinery. To do this they must be skilled in the use of hand and power tools, such as hoists, cranes, electric drills, and welding equipment. They read blueprints to determine where machinery will be placed and to determine whether a foundation is necessary. If so, they must construct it. They

must also be able to read schematic diagrams to handle the electric connections, if any. Millwrights must also be proficient in the use of such measuring instruments as micrometers, calipers, plumb bobs, and levels.

Because installation and removal of heavy machinery demands a great deal of time, the millwright must do a variety of jobs, such as chiseling out a place in the concrete wall of a factory where a beam can be placed to hold a pulley, or working up high, or in cramped, hot places bolting machinery to the floor.

In accordance with the trend toward specialization, workers in one of the larger plants will usually be responsible for a particular phase of the machinery. Once it is installed, they may be called upon to do repairs or perform preventive maintenance. Millwrights may also be responsible for oiling and greasing the machinery. They also sometimes work with pipefitters and machinery repairers in keeping a production line in operating condition. *Manufacturer's service representatives* work for the manufacturer of the machinery and oversee its installation and start-up. *Machinery erectors* specialize as heavy machinery assemblers and dismantlers.

Requirements

Usually the millwright serves from six to eight years as an apprentice. Others choose formal four-year apprenticeships that combine on-the-job training and related classroom instruction.

One interested in this occupation should be between the ages of eighteen and twenty-six, be above average in size and strength, be in good health and have a high-school diploma, although a high-school education is not specifically required. An above-average mechanical aptitude also benefits the apprentice millwright. High-school courses of value are those generally taught in most industrial education courses: shop mathematics, blueprint reading, hydraulics, electricity, use of basic tools, and job safety. It is certainly required also that the millwright learn to use the square and level and have experience at working with wood, steel, concrete, and other building materials. The majority of job openings, of course, are in the large industrial areas of the steel, machinery, automobile, paper, woodworking, chemical, and construction industries.

Two millwrights test the quality standards of a large machine part at the Bethlehem Steel Industries.

Special requirements

Union membership may be considered a special requirement of this job.

Opportunities for experience and exploration

Because the millwright has a crew of helpers, it is possible summer work may be available to students who do not mind hard work. This would be true if a neighboring plant is in the middle of a change-over, just beginning, or closing down, because these three operations require that machinery be moved. Working directly with a millwright may help students decide whether they might be interested in doing this kind of work after graduation from high school. In addition, the summer worker may learn many valuable things about work in general, such as responsibility for the best use of time, how it feels to be really tired at the end of a day's work, and one's reaction to working under supervision and with others in this field.

Related occupations

Other occupations that are similar in interest and skill levels include machine tool operators, numerical-control machine-tool operators, job and die setters, industrial machinery mechanics, diesel mechanics, and tool-and-die makers.

Methods of entering

Most young people are first hired for unskilled or semiskilled work in a company. The company posts on a board the job openings such as millwright apprentice, and those interested and qualified may bid for the jobs. Openings are filled from lists of those who bid by selecting the millwrights most qualified as to experience and seniority.

Advancement

One way of advancement is through the millwright apprenticeship, which is a combination of on-the-job experience as a helper, and night school, where practical courses that apply directly to the daily work are taught by experienced people in the various fields. In addition, employees can qualify for jobs with greater responsibility by attending trade and technical schools on their own.

With the proper training, skill, and seniority, one can move up in the plant to a job as millwright supervisor. Skilled, experienced employees may also work as trainers for the apprentices.

Employment outlook

In the early 1990s, there were about 87,000 millwrights employed. The outlook for the foreseeable future is slow for the employment of millwrights as competition from abroad is hurting the manufacturing industries somewhat. Machines continue to be employed in greater numbers, however, and millwrights are needed to dismantle old machinery and install and maintain the modern, automated replacements. The paper and pulp industry is a good example of this expected expansion and mechanization. In addition, there will be some openings for people to replace millwrights who die, retire, or change jobs. Millwrights work in all states, with approximately half of them in the heavily industrialized states of Michigan, Ohio, Pennsylvania, Illinois, New York, and Indiana.

Earnings

Median annual wages for an experienced millwright in the early 1990s were about $30,000. Millwrights employed by construction companies usually earned more than those employed in manufacturing industries.

Wages, of course, vary from city to city and depend, in part, upon the general living costs of that area. Employer–union contracts usually include benefits such as paid vacations, hospitalizations, medical and surgical insurance, and retirement pensions. Apprentices generally start at 50 percent of the millwright's salary and progress to the full rate by the end of the training period.

Conditions of work

The work of the millwright is generally indoors, out of the elements, but it is not by any means comfortable, relaxed work. The work is often hard, physical labor, in surroundings made unpleasant by heat, noise, and confinement. In addition, it is often hazardous, although protective devices and emphasis on safety have reduced the number of accidents in recent years.

Millwrights may be called to work at unusual hours because of emergencies because of a breakdown in machinery or when a model change is to be made.

Social and psychological factors

Many millwrights enjoy their job because it is challenging. They get satisfaction from correcting the faults of a machine that is not working properly. It is not repetitious for the most part, as each problem calls for a different solution.

GOE: 05.05.06; SIC: 1796; SOC: 6178

◇ **SOURCES OF ADDITIONAL INFORMATION**

International Association of Machinists and Aerospace Workers
1300 Connecticut Avenue, NW
Washington, DC 20036

International Union of Electronic, Electrical, Salaried, Machine, and Furniture Workers
1126 16th Street, NW
Washington, DC 20036

International Union, United Automobile, Aerospace and Agricultural Implement Workers of America
8000 East Jefferson Avenue
Detroit, MI 48214

United Brotherhood of Carpenters and Joiners of America
101 Constitution Avenue, NW
Washington, DC 20001

United Steelworkers of America
Five Gateway Center
Pittsburgh, PA 15222

◇ **RELATED ARTICLES**

Volume 1: Machining and Machinery; or *see* Table of Contents for areas of specific interest
Volume 3: Industrial machinery mechanics; Job and die setters; Machine tool operators; Machinists
Volume 4: Electromechanical technicians; Mechanical technicians

Office-machine servicers

Definition

Office-machine servicers, or *service technicians*, inspect, adjust, clean, and repair all types of office machines such as typewriters, computers, adding and calculating machines, cash registers, posting and mailing equipment, and so forth. They may be able to tell what is wrong with certain machines by operating them and listening for unusual sounds, or they may take the machines apart and examine the parts to detect wear or other cause of malfunctioning.

History

Business machines have become an indispensable part of the modern-day business world. Their growth from crude beginnings in the nineteenth century, with its simple machines, to the complex electronic equipment of the offices of today, is one of the fascinating stories of the industrial age. Without the modern business machine and the people who keep them in operation, the whole structure of office procedure on which all of today's business is based would be impossible.

The servicing of the early machines required relatively simple mechanical ability. As the needs of business have grown, many of the machines have become so intricate that the skills for their care have made more and more extensive periods of training necessary. For some servicers, a knowledge of electricity, electronics, and photography is now required.

Nature of the work

A great portion of the work of servicers is done in the offices of the businesses using the machines and is often specialized. Two specialized typewriter servicers are the *aligner* and the *repairer* or *adjustor*. These servicers, who are the most numerous, specialize in the maintenance and care of electric typewriters.

Other specialists include *mail-processing-equipment* and *scale mechanics* and *cash-register, dictating-transcribing-machine,* and *statistical-machine servicers*. All of these servicers have the same basic duties, which are to install, maintain, and if necessary, repair the machines that they service.

When major repair or overhaul is necessary, the equipment is often taken to repair shops where there is room and facility for dismantling and reassembling it. During this process new parts are installed where needed. Most manufacturers of office machines have their own service departments. Sometimes servicers set up their own shops and operate independently of the manufacturers. At times these independent servicers specialize in one or two types of machines. In areas where there are too few machines of special types to make servicing them profitable, the independent office-machine servicers take care of several kinds of machines. At times these shops sell machines and supplies. Some of the independent dealers employ a dozen or more workers and some only one or two. In some of the smaller communities and in some of the smaller businesses, servicing is combined with sales. Sometimes the servicers sell supplies for use with the machines as well as the machines themselves. It is usual, in addition to repairing and servicing machines, for servicers to maintain a regular schedule of inspection trips to keep the machines running properly and to catch any small defects preventing them from causing severe and expensive breakdowns.

Tools used by business machine servicers vary from simple hand tools like pliers, screwdrivers, and wrenches to calipers, meters, voltmeters, gauges, and other instruments used in servicing the newer kinds of electric and electronic devices.

Requirements

The education and training needed to enter the field of business machine service covers a wide range. Often, in the smaller shops, no special training is required to service the simplest machines. At the other extreme, it is necessary to have an understanding of the fundamentals of electricity, electronics, and photographic processes. A high-school education is usually a minimum requirement for a job in this field.

Superior mechanical aptitude is required. Any experience in the electrical or mechanical areas is also useful. Post–high-school mechanics or electronics training of at least a year and sometimes more, is usually required to qualify for trainee jobs to service the intricate electro-mechanical and electronic equipment or to at-

Office-machine servicers
Machine Trades Occupations

An office-machine servicer consults a readout to determine the extent of repairs needed. Servicers must travel with an assortment of equipment to handle several types of mechanical problems.

tain supervisory positions. This training is often available in colleges, city trade schools, state technical training institutions, or privately sponsored schools. Young veterans who have had electronics training in the armed forces are specially desired by employers in this field.

Since so much of the work is done in the offices of and in association with office employees, it is desirable that servicers be neat in appearance and have a pleasant and cooperative personality.

The amount of time it takes to learn the business machine service trade ranges from one to five or more years. One to two years are necessary to learn to repair the simplest machines such as manual typewriters and adding machines. Accounting-bookkeeping machines take at least three to four years of practice and training to learn. Two-and-a-half to three-and-a-half years are necessary to become an expert cash register servicer. One needs frequent refresher courses to keep up with new developments in the complex data-processing and computing machines. The employee's company may provide retraining as technology changes and equipment is updated. Many repair workers may choose training that allows them to specialize.

It is not often that any unusual strength is required in this trade. Sometimes, however, it is necessary to lift machines or move them to hand trucks when they have to be taken to the shop for repairs.

Special requirements

Applicants for trainee jobs are frequently tested on their mechanical aptitude, knowledge of basic electricity or electronic fundamentals, manual dexterity, general intelligence, and abstract reasoning abilities.

Opportunities for experience and exploration

Office-machine service may be observed in offices where machines are used. In public and private schools, servicers periodically service duplicating machines, typewriters, and such machines as are used in business courses. Arrangements may be made for interested pupils to observe the work.

In towns that have repair shops or branch offices, school counselors may plan field trips for the purpose of learning about the work. It may be possible sometimes for a pupil to get a summer or weekend job at a repair or sales shop.

In technical schools, students sometimes gain experience in school-work programs. The armed forces, too, offer opportunities for training and experience.

Related occupations

Other occupations that require manual dexterity and skill with hand tools include appliance repairers, automobile mechanics, instrument makers, gunsmiths, and bicycle mechanics.

Methods of entering

The usual way of entering the occupation is through on-the-job training. Employers look for young people who are pleasant and cooperative. Some of the large manufacturing firms conduct formal apprenticeship programs of two, three, or four years. On-the-job training is combined with work experience, and courses in manufacturers' schools are also utilized.

When young people are hired by independent shops, they often do not receive much formal training. But when they are employed as trainees in manufacturers' branch offices, they are usually sent to company schools for courses varying in length from several weeks to several months. After factory training, they return to branch offices for on-the-job training before they are accepted as fully skilled workers.

Independent shops look for servicers who have had training in factory schools. Some mechanics from the independent shops that have dealers' contracts with manufacturers are sent to factory schools to learn how to service those companies' particular lines of machines.

Advancement

The usual line of advancement in this field is from servicing the least complicated machines, where the fundamentals are learned, to learning the more complex ones. When the servicers have learned the machines thoroughly, they sometimes become part-time or full-time salespersons, or they may become supervisors. Some open shops of their own and employ repairers, while others obtain higher positions in the organization of the various manufacturing companies concerned. Some companies conduct classes of their own for the upgrading of their employees. Others pay part or full tuition at technical schools for their employees, or encourage their taking home-study courses that are related to the servicer's job. This school work is frequently done by the business machine servicers on their own time.

Employment outlook

The rapidly growing business machine industry will provide many thousands of jobs for servicers through the next decade. Job opportunities will also occur to replace experienced workers who transfer to other fields, retire, or die. The number of persons working in the business machine industry as servicers has more than tripled since 1955, reaching about 60,000 persons in the early 1990s.

Expansion of the need for clerical records and services in modern business is the basis for a rapidly expanding need for business machine servicers. Many records are required for tax purposes. Research and accounting projects are also primary causes for the increase. The number and variety of computerized machines continues to grow.

A majority of the workers will continue to be hired by the service departments of the manufacturers to take care of their own particular line of equipment. Sometimes large insurance companies, huge business corporations, and government agencies maintain their own ser-

vicing staffs. Sales agencies also will employ workers to service the machines they sell.

It is probable that chances for steady employment in this field will be available for those who establish themselves in it. In periods of business prosperity, the sale of increasing numbers of machines will necessitate more servicers. If business slows down and less equipment is sold, it is probable that more service will be required on existing machines as they get older.

Earnings

The length of service and the type of machine being serviced enter into the amount of pay earned. In the early 1990s, the median annual wage was $24,500. Repairers of electronic business machines, especially computers, were generally the highest paid. Servicers sometimes supplement their wages by earning commissions on sales of machines and supplies. Workers employed by the government or by large corporations are under retirement and group insurance plans.

Conditions of work

Business machine repairers usually have regular year-round work. Most of the time a servicer's work is performed in clean, well-lighted, and well-ventilated offices or shops. The work is cleaner than that of most mechanics and repairers, and there is less lifting than in most other repair service jobs. There is little danger of accident. Servicers usually work in the offices where the machines are used and themselves dress much like office workers. Some workers do all their work in one shop or in one town. But many of those who work for manufacturers travel extensively in caring for the machines in a district for which they are responsible.

Social and psychological factors

Some people get great satisfaction from being able to determine what is wrong with a mechanical device and then fix it so it will function smoothly. Some enjoy planning a system of mechanical operations to meet the needs of bookkeeping or data processing plans, just as servicers of electronic equipment are often called on to do. Much of the work in this field is done on an individual basis. Therefore, business machine repairers must be prepared to work alone.

GOE: 05.05.09; SIC: 7629; SOC: 6174

 SOURCES OF ADDITIONAL INFORMATION

Computer and Business Equipment Manufacturers Association
311 First Street, NW, Suite 500
Washington, DC 20001

National Office Machine Dealers Association
12411 Wornall
Kansas City, MO 64145

◇ **RELATED ARTICLES**

Volume 1: See Table of Contents for areas of specific interest
Volume 3: Aircraft mechanics; Appliance installers and repairers; Automobile mechanics; Industrial machinery mechanics; Vending machine mechanics
Volume 4: Automatic equipment technicians; Data processing technicians; Electrical technicians; Electromechanical technicians; Electronics technicians

---

Patternmakers

Definition

A *patternmaker* builds the patterns used to make the molds in which foundry castings are formed. Patternmakers work from blueprints prepared by the engineering department of the foundry. They prepare the patterns from metal stock, or, more commonly, from rough castings made from an original wood pattern, and must be familiar with such metalworking machines as lathes, drill presses, and shapers. Patternmakers may also construct a pattern from wax, ceramics, or wood.

History

There are examples of molding in ancient times. Earthenware, sand, or metal molds were used to make duplicate ceramic vessels and metal utensils and jewelry. Shapes hollowed out in sand pits allowed for the heated liquid metal to cool quickly, and for the shape to be reused. These techniques were refined and, with the impetus supplied by the Industrial Revolution, became an integral part of foundry operation.

Nature of the work

Precision or accuracy is the keynote of the patternmakers' job whether they are making a small pattern on a workbench by hand or a large pattern made by machine to be used in floor molding. Theirs are the guiding hands that determine whether each molding made from the pattern will be smooth and flawless and of the proper dimension, or whether there will be inaccuracies in the many finished parts formed by the mold.

Patternmakers begin by studying a blueprint of the part to be cast. From this they compute the dimensions and plan the sequence of operations.

The *wood patternmaker* selects the appropriate wood stock, lays out the pattern, marks the design for each section on the proper piece of wood, and saws each piece roughly to size. This worker then shapes the rough pieces into final form, using various woodworking machines, such as lathes, planers, handsaws, and sanders, as well as many small hand tools. Finally, the wood patternmaker assembles the pattern segments by hand. The *metal patternmaker* follows the basic sequence of operation using metal stock and the proper metal tools. Other specialists include *spring* and *sample patternmakers* and *last-pattern graders.*

Much of the patternmaker's work consists of checking dimensions with extremely accurate tools so that the work will always be according to specification. From the patternmaker, the pattern passes to the coremaker and molders for the actual production of castings.

Requirements

The basic requirement for the would-be patternmaker is a high degree of mechanical aptitude. In addition, he or she must have an aptitude to readily see spatial relationships. Tests are often given in junior or senior high school that measure both mechanical aptitude and skill in perceiving spatial relationships.

While a high-school education is not required, the nature of the job of patternmaker is such that certain industrial education or shop courses, or the equivalent experiences of a good trade school, are helpful. A person interested in becoming a patternmaker should take mechanical drawing, geometry, and any other courses that provide practice in exact measurement and construction of items such as are found in machine and woodworking shops. Along with this experience comes the important experience in working with hand tools and power-driven equipment. While not all this experience is required, it does assist young people in appraising their aptitude for work of this kind.

It is required that a patternmaker, during an apprenticeship, work closely under the supervision of an experienced worker so that the prospective apprentice learns to follow orders exactly as they are given.

Special requirements

Because of the skill necessary for this occupation, a union-management apprenticeship of four or five years is required, along with about 144 hours of classroom instruction during each of those years.

Opportunities for experience and exploration

Foundries are factories in which both skilled and unskilled workers are required. It is often possible for a high-school student of working

This patternmaker is operating a rigid hydraulic duplicator. He uses a plastic-faced aluminum-backed model for machining a cast iron core.

age to obtain summertime work as a laborer, doing whatever the supervisor asks to be done. The value of such work, no matter how menial, should not be minimized by the young person. Any working experience whatsoever in a foundry provides knowledge of the world of work which is important to the individual applying for the job of patternmaker after high-school graduation.

In addition, a young person who is inquisitive and not afraid of asking questions can probably find a patternmaker who will be pleased to take the time and effort to show the student-worker what is involved. The knowledge gained may help the young person who is interested get a permanent job after graduation.

Methods of entering

It is difficult to take a job in a foundry hoping to informally learn the trade of patternmaker. Even those machinists who have worked closely with patternmakers and who have been able to transfer to patternmaking need additional on-the-job training. The prospective patternmaker generally applies for an apprentice program either through a foundry or the union. This program includes a minimum of

144 hours a year of classroom work in subjects related to the job, as well as the job training, working in all phases of the occupation with a journeyman patternmaker.

On the job, the apprentice begins with routine duties. The responsibility is gradually increased, along with a reduction of close supervision as the worker's skill increases.

Advancement

Because of the time involved in the apprenticeship program to become a patternmaker, and because of the satisfaction of the job resulting from the creative aspect of it, there are few patternmakers who look for further advancement. Those who spend many years in the accomplishment of a difficult skill often want to spend the remainder of their working life developing this skill. In the same vein, the foundry management hesitates to advance to another job employees who are capable and satisfied in a position that would be difficult to fill.

In large foundries, however, patternmakers may become supervisors. Employers will generally promote those whose ability to supervise others seems more valuable to the foundry than the patternmaker's skill in this one trade alone.

Employment outlook

Employment of foundry patternmakers is expected to grow slowly, if at all, during the next decade. The trend toward the production of large numbers of identical castings will result in greater use of metal and plastic rather than wood patterns. As the more durable metal patterns can be used many times in the making of identical molds, the number of individual patterns required for a given number of castings has declined.

Replacement needs will provide some job opportunities for new workers to be trained as patternmakers. It is estimated that a few hundred new patternmakers will be needed annually to replace workers who transfer to other fields, retire, or die. Most of the job openings will be in metal patternmaking.

Because patternmakers learn either basic metalworking or woodworking skills, they can find jobs in related fields when patternmaking employment is not available. Wood patternmakers can qualify for skilled woodworking jobs, such as cabinetmaker, and metal patternmakers can transfer their skills to machining occupations such as machinist or layout artist.

Earnings

Patternmakers have higher than average earnings for manufacturing occupations. In the early 1990s, workers in iron and steel foundries averaged from $22,464 to $32,450 annually, and those in nonferrous foundries made $21,200. Metal patternmakers generally received higher average hourly wages than wood patternmakers. There was some opportunity for overtime, which was reimbursed at the rate of one-and-a-half times the regular rate.

Many patternmakers become eligible for retirement programs; most are eligible for group hospitalization.

Conditions of work

The job is not strenuous in that it does not require great strength for lifting or physical endurance. It does, however, require standing the majority of the time. A foundry is generally a noisy place and sometimes dusty. Heat is another factor objectionable to many workers.

Most foundry jobs are located in large, highly industrial areas, which often means that the worker must commute a long way to and from home through busy traffic.

Social and psychological factors

Patternmakers are skilled workers. This means that they are fairly independent of close supervision on the job. At the same time they must accept the responsibility of having a pattern ready in accordance with the plant production schedule. The patternmaker receives a greater intrinsic value from this job than many workers whose hours are filled with much repetition.

GOE: 05.05.07; SIC: Any industry; SOC: 68

◇ **SOURCES OF ADDITIONAL INFORMATION**

American Foundrymen's Society
Golf and Wolf Roads
Des Plaines, IL 60016

Glass Molders, Pottery, Plastics, and Allied Workers International Union
608 East Baltimore Pike
PO Box 607
Media, PA 19063

American Cast Metals Association
455 State Street
Des Plaines, IL 60016

◇ **RELATED ARTICLES**

Volume 1: Machining and Machinery; Metals
Volume 2: Carpenters; Forge shop occupations; Machinists; Molders; Tool makers and die makers
Volume 4: Drafting and design technicians; Metallurgical technicians

Pinsetter mechanics

Definition

Pinsetter mechanics maintain, adjust, and repair automatic pinsetting machines in bowling centers. They observe and test the operation of the machine to determine the cause of a malfunction, disassemble and repair or replace mechanical or electrical components, and clean and lubricate the machine. They also may direct assistants; paint and recondition bowling pins, alleys, and bowling-center furnishings; and maintain an inventory of parts.

Mechanics who work for pinsetter manufacturers install automatic pinsetters in bowling centers, and service machines in centers that do not have their own mechanic.

History

Bowling has been practiced by various peoples throughout the world since ancient times. Researchers have discovered evidence of its existence as early as 5200 B.C. Variations of the game were developed in areas as far apart as Egypt and Polynesia.

In medieval Germany, a form of bowling was practiced in the cloisters of churches. Parishioners would stand at one end of the cloister and throw a stone or other object at a bottle-shaped club, or *Kegel,* placed at the opposite end. Hitting the *Kegel* was considered a sign that the contestant was living a pure life. The rite soon became popular as a sport among the populace. It was played with anywhere from three to seventeen pins in different sections of Germany and the Low Countries. Historians

also report that bowling tournaments were a pastime in twelfth-century England.

Early forms of the game were played with ball-shaped boulders and wooden pins on outdoor alleys covered with clay or cinders or both. The first record of an indoor alley dates back to 1455. Before that, bowling was generally an outdoor game, but by the nineteenth century it had become almost exclusively an indoor activity.

Today's game, using ten pins, is probably descended from ninepins, which was played by the Germans, Dutch, and Swiss. Ninepins was introduced to America by the Dutch in the seventeenth century, and it soon attracted a wide following. By 1875 a tenth pin had been added, and bowling was so popular that organizations were formed to govern the uniformity of playing areas and rules.

The first automatic pinsetting machine was installed in August 1952 in a bowling alley in Brooklyn. Prior to that time, pins had to be collected and set up by hand, and the balls returned, by human pinspotters located in the area behind the pins. Not only was this a time-consuming task, but the pinspotters ran the risk of being hit by flying pins.

With the automatic machines came the need for mechanics to service them for efficient operation and to repair them in case of breakdown.

Nature of the work

The automatic pinsetter in a bowling center is a complex machine that retrieves bowling pins knocked down by a player, resets the pins at

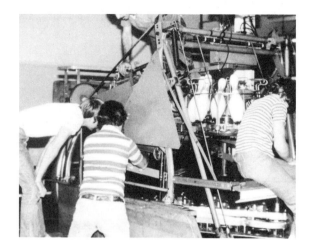

Pinsetter mechanics must have general maintenance and electronics skills in order to keep the machines in working order.

the end of the lane, and returns the ball to the player. Normally, the operation proceeds quickly and smoothly; but when the machinery breaks down or does not function up to standard, games are held up and the bowlers are inconvenienced. Because the success of a bowling center depends on the satisfaction of its customers, it is important to keep the pinsetter running properly. This is the job of the pinsetter mechanic.

To prevent breakdowns, pinsetter manufacturers recommend a regular schedule of maintenance. Periodically, the mechanics clean the pinsetters, lubricate the gears and other moving parts, and adjust the motors. They inspect the many mechanical and electrical parts that are crucial to the normal operation of the machine. Electrical relays, solenoids, transformers, motors, and wiring may be tested with ohmmeters, voltmeters, and other testing devices.

When a malfunction occurs, pinsetter mechanics refer to maintenance manuals and diagrams of electrical circuits to help determine the cause of the difficulty. Their diagnosis, however, often depends on a thorough knowledge of the machinery, acquired through years of experience. Faulty parts, such as gears, bearings, coils, armatures, wiring, and motors, are either repaired, replaced, or adjusted, using many different types of hand and power tools, including wrenches, screwdrivers, soldering irons, and portable hoists.

Mechanics may train and supervise one or more assistant mechanics or pin chasers. These workers learn how the pinsetter operates and how to make minor repairs, such as releasing jammed pins and balls, so they can maintain the machine when the mechanic is off duty.

In some bowling centers, mechanics perform other maintenance tasks, such as conditioning lanes, cleaning and painting bowling pins, and repairing seats and tables. They also maintain a perpetual inventory and order replacements for spare parts, and may keep records of malfunctions and estimate maintenance costs.

Some mechanics are employed by pinsetter manufacturers. They travel to the various bowling centers in their area and install automatic pinsetters. They may also service machines for those centers that do not have a full-time mechanic.

Requirements

There are no education requirements for this occupation. Applicants, however, who are high-school graduates and have completed courses in electricity, machine repair, blueprint reading, and shop math are favored by some employers. Having experience in some type of machine repair is also an advantage.

Pinsetter mechanics usually start out as assistant mechanics and acquire their skills through on-the-job training. The head mechanics explain the operation of the machine, demonstrate how to maintain it and make repairs, and supervise the work of the assistants. Trainees first learn to do the simpler tasks, such as lubricating and cleaning the pinsetter and performing other preventive maintenance, then progress to increasingly more complicated repair jobs. After one or two years of training and experience, mechanics are able to diagnose and repair all types of mechanical and electrical breakdowns.

Another way for mechanic trainees to learn their job is to take courses offered by pinsetter manufacturers to persons already employed by a bowling center. The employers usually pay the tuition. The courses last two to four weeks and combine classroom lectures with shop work on demonstration machines. Mechanic trainees learn about the structure and operation of the manufacturers' machines and how to locate the sources of typical troubles. They also learn preventive maintenance methods, how to read wiring diagrams, and how to work with the tools of the trade.

Mechanical aptitude is an important consideration for pinsetter mechanics. The work requires good eyesight (with normal color vision), as well as good eye-hand coordination. Mechanics often work in awkward positions; however, only average physical strength is needed.

Special requirements

There are no special requirements for this occupation, except to stress one of the points made above. Good eyesight must include normal color vision.

Opportunities for experience and exploration

To prepare for a career as a pinsetter mechanic, high-school students may take courses in electricity, machine repair, blueprint reading, and shop math.

Experience in repairing any type of machinery may influence future employers favorably, so students would be wise to seek part-time and summer employment as helpers in machine and electrical repair shops.

Related occupations

There are many types of mechanics that provide occupational opportunities similar to those of the pinsetter mechanics. These include general maintenance mechanics, aircraft mechanics, automobile mechanics, motorcycle mechanics, diesel mechanics, and industrial machinery mechanics.

Methods of entering

Persons interested in becoming pinsetter mechanics may apply directly to bowling centers or inquire about job opportunities at the local bowling proprietors' association. In addition, local offices of the state employment service may be able to provide information about employment and training.

Advancement

Some pinsetter mechanics who work for large bowling-center chains or pinsetter manufacturers advance to maintenance supervisor, and a few mechanics eventually become assistant managers or managers of bowling establishments. Otherwise, there are very few opportunities for advancement in this occupation, except in terms of salary increases.

Employment outlook

In the early 1990s, there were about 6,500 pinsetter mechanics employed in the United States, almost all of them in bowling centers. Manufacturers of automatic pinsetters employ a few mechanics to install machines and service those in bowling centers that do not have full-time mechanics. Pinsetter mechanics may be found in every state, although jobs are more plentiful in heavily populated areas that have many bowling centers.

As the population increases, there will be a greater demand for bowling facilities. This growth, however, will be somewhat offset by the high cost of constructing bowling centers. Overall, little or no change is expected in the employment of pinsetter mechanics throughout the next decade. This is a small occupational group, and job opportunities are limited, except for those openings that normally occur when experienced mechanics retire, die, or change occupations.

Fluctuations in the economy have little effect on the employment of pinsetter mechanics. Even though bowling centers may lose business in a recession, they still need mechanics to service and repair their equipment. Another reason employers are reluctant to lay off skilled mechanics is that the workers may find jobs in other bowling centers and then be unavailable when business picks up again.

Earnings

Wages vary greatly depending on where the bowling center is located and how much experience the mechanic has. In the early 1990s, head mechanics had average annual earnings of about $24,400, while mechanic trainees averaged less than $12,000.

Conditions of work

The automatic pinsetters are located at the ends of bowling lanes. Mechanics do much of their work in the long, narrow corridors behind the machinery. To make their repairs and adjustments, they have to stoop, kneel, crouch, and crawl around the machines and often must climb and balance on the work platform of the pinsetter.

Many bowling centers also have larger workrooms where mechanics keep supplies and tools and may do some kinds of repairs. These rooms are usually well lighted and ventilated, but they are often quite noisy when the pinsetters are operating.

Mechanics who work for pinsetter manufacturers travel to bowling centers in their areas to install and repair machines.

If pinsetter mechanics are not careful, they may suffer the usual hazards of shop workers—cuts, falls, bruises, electric shock—but their job is not otherwise dangerous.

Social and psychological factors

This is one of the many mechanics' jobs that appeal to persons who like to work with their hands. Because there are few opportunities for advancement, mechanics must derive most of their satisfaction from their skills in maintaining smoothly running machinery and troubleshooting breakdowns, knowing that the successful operation of the bowling center depends on their abilities. On the other hand, this possible drawback is balanced by the security of knowing that the job is relatively safe from economic downswings.

GOE: 05.10.04; SIC: 3949; SOC: 6179

◇ **SOURCES OF ADDITIONAL INFORMATION**

Information about job opportunities may be obtained from potential employers or the local bowling proprietors' association. For information about employment and training, contact local offices of the state employment service.

◇ **RELATED ARTICLES**

Volume 1: Recreation and Park Services; Sports
Volume 3: Electrical repairers; Office machine servicers; Vending machine mechanics
Volume 4: Electrical technicians; Electromechanical technicians; Robotics technicians

Printing press operators and assistants

Definition

Printing press operators and their *assistants* "make-ready" (prepare) type forms and press plates, set up, operate, clean, and maintain presses, including feeding, loading and unloading paper; controlling ink flow; and matching colors.

History

The first printing presses were developed in Germany after Johannes Gutenberg invented movable type in 1440. Movable type made it possible for a great variety of material to be set up for printing with fair speed. Each letter is cast in its own metal body and thus can be easily set, or arranged and locked into a form for the press. The first presses consisted of two flat surfaces; the type was inked by running a roller dipped in ink over it, a sheet of paper placed on it, and a lever turned to force the type down on the paper. Two people working together could print about 300 pages per day.

Printing in the United States began in Cambridge, Massachusetts, in 1639. Boston, New York, and Philadelphia soon became the principal centers of printing in the country.

In about 1814, Friedrich Koenig, another German, developed the first practical cylinder press. This was later improved for use in printing newspapers. The first web press, by which both sides of the paper were printed, was developed in 1865 by William Bullock, an American. Ten years later a device was added to fold the paper after printing.

Today, the large web rotary presses can produce a 100,000 newspapers an hour.

Nature of the work

A description of the different types of presses is necessary for a clear understanding of a press operator's work. There are three basic types of presses—platen, cylinder, and rotary—that are, in turn, controlled by *platen-*, *cylinder-*, and *rotogravure-press operators.* Each type of press is designed for a different kind of work and is different in size and complexity. There is, of course, an overlap in the uses and sizes. Platen presses are used for small jobs that will take paper only up to fourteen by twenty-four inches. The printing and impression surfaces are both flat. Rollers distribute ink over the type surface and paper is then pressed to the face of the type form. Paper is either inserted by hand or automatically fed into the press.

Cylinder presses are used for books, magazines, and pamphlets. They can handle large sheets of paper up to seventy-two inches wide. In this type of press, the printing surface is flat and the impression surface is a cylinder. The type form is locked into place on the "flat-bed" of the press and paper is fed automatically or by hand onto the cylinder, which is then imprinted as it rolls over the type form.

Web presses, also called "rotary presses," are used to print newspapers, magazines, and books. These presses are the largest, fastest, and most complex in use today. Both surfaces are cylinders, and paper is automatically fed between them from a roll. For this press, a curved metal cast, made from the type form, is mounted on the cylinder. The web press prints on both sides of the paper, folds, cuts, and assembles the pages.

The work of press operators and their assistants differs according to the size of the printing plant. Generally, press operators receive the press plates and prepare and operate the printing presses. They prepare them by inspecting and oiling moving parts, cleaning and adjusting ink rollers, and cleaning the ink fountains. When the type form arrives from the compositor, they lock it into place on the platen or cylinder press. Then they make adjustments so that the paper will be in the exact position to take the impression of the type. They mix and match ink, if necessary. They fill the ink fountain and adjust the ink flow. They pack the cylinder or platen with layers of paper to make a hard surface. Then they run off a trial sheet and

submit it for approval. When the "press sheet" is approved, they run off another sheet and check the light and dark parts, and, to make the printing even, use "overlay," usually pieces of tissue paper, to build up the parts of the cylinder or platen where the low type will strike. This is called "makeready"; it is the most delicate and difficult part of the press operator's work, and requires much skill to make the impression neither too dark nor too light. When the printing is even, an automatic counter is set and the press started. During the "run," press operators must constantly check the printed matter to see that it is clear, lined up straight, and that ink is not offsetting (blotting) onto other sheets; in color work, they must make certain that the colors line up properly. On a web press, they must rethread paper through the press if the web breaks, and must load supply rolls of paper in the press. On a platen or cylinder press, they may feed paper into the press by hand.

In small shops, the press operators oil and clean the presses and make minor repairs; the presses are generally small and relatively simple, and paper is fed by hand. In larger shops, press operators have assistants and helpers and the large web presses are watched and operated by a large crew under the supervision of a press operator-in-charge. Assistants who feed paper into presses by hand are called press feeders.

The many specialists of the industry include *strippers*; *steel-die, plastic, tip, bag, balloon design, wallpaper, box, binding, ink,* and other printers; *web, engraving, lithograph tab-card, offset, proof, flexographic,* and *assistant press operators*; *transfer* and *print line operators*; and *offset-duplicating, rubber-printing, tape rules printing, cutting-and-printing,* and *wad-printing machine operators.*

Requirements

A high-school education is usually required to enter an apprenticeship program. Increased importance, however, is placed on having had specialized courses in high school, such as art, print shop, mathematics, chemistry, and physics.

A five-year apprenticeship is the usual requirement to become a newspaper press operator on a web press; specialized technical education or experience in a print shop is counted toward the five years. The length of apprenticeship also varies according to the kind of press: in commercial shops, there is a two-year apprenticeship leading to press assistant, or

Modern printing techniques use computers extensively. Thus, pressroom operators must be able to work with computerized controls.

four years to press operator; in newspaper and other shops using web presses, the required time is five years. The training on the job includes learning to take care of the equipment, to "makeready," to run the presses, to clean and maintain a press, and to become familiar with various types of inks and papers. The apprentice participates in related classroom or correspondence courses at the same time.

Special requirements

There are no special requirements for press operators, although almost all of them belong to a union.

Opportunities for experience and exploration

Most high schools offer a number of opportunities for exploring the occupation of printing press operator. Taking a print shop class is the most direct experience available. Working on the high-school newspaper or yearbook is another way to gain some familiarity with printing processes. Delivering material for printing to a print shop, or just making a visit alone or in a group to a local printing plant, provides the opportunity to see presses in action and to get the feeling of the atmosphere in which a press operator works. Part-time, temporary, and summer jobs may sometimes be available as cleanup workers and press feeders in printing plants.

Related occupations

The printing and publishing industries offer many occupational opportunities. These include photoengravers, lithographic workers, writers, editors, prepress workers, and bindery workers.

Methods of entering

A press operator starts as an apprentice, or sometimes as a helper. High-school vocational counselors can guide students into apprenticeship programs. Some printers choose their apprentices from among press assistants and others employed in the plant. Therefore, a young person may work in a printing establishment for years before becoming an apprentice.

Advancement

Generally, in large print shops, the line of promotion is from press helper to press assistant, press operator, press operator-in-charge, print shop supervisor, and superintendent. A press operator who is interested and able in other aspects of the printing business may find advancement by transferring into the sales or purchasing departments. Those with business ability may do well in their own shops.

Employment outlook

In the early 1990s, about 228,000 press operators and assistants were employed in the printing industry. The number of openings for press operators is expected to be modest in the foreseeable future. Some jobs are made available through retirements and deaths; and the continuing rise in quantity of printed material will create new jobs, although much of the additional work will be done by larger and more efficient machines.

Earnings

In the early 1990s, the basic annual wage rate for letterpress operators in unionized firms was about $33,390. For lithographic press operators on a single color nineteen by twenty-five-inch press, it was about $36,966. Higher rates are, of course, paid for night shifts and overtime work; work outside of the regular day hours is fairly common.

Apprentices are paid about 40 to 50 percent of an experienced press operator's wage rate. They receive pay increases regularly, usually every six months, and, in the last year of an apprenticeship, they are receiving 80 to 95 percent of the press operator's rate.

Press operators, as well as other craft workers in the printing industry, are among the highest paid production workers in all of the manufacturing industries.

Conditions of work

Many print shops are small, with about five employees, but the largest ones will have from 250 to 1,000 employees. The pressroom is a busy, noisy place; there is a great deal of noise and vibration when presses are running. There are frequent deadlines to meet, and tension and pressure are part of the atmosphere. The press operator's errors are serious as they may require a complete job to be rerun, doubling the cost and delaying the finish time.

There is considerable contact with ink and cleaning fluids; there may also be some discomfort from the heat and temperature, as these are set according to the demands of the paper stock.

The work is fairly strenuous, including lifting of ink rollers and type forms.

Social and psychological factors

Printing crafts workers generally have high regard for their specialized skills and take pride in producing quality work. Press operators are involved in the final processing and must exercise great care in preparing the press and in watching the operation. They know they are, in fact, responsible for the correct printing of material.

GOE: 05.05.13; SIC: 27; SOC: 76

◇ **SOURCES OF ADDITIONAL INFORMATION**

Graphic Communications International Union
1900 L Street, NW
Washington, DC 20036

Printing Industries of America
1730 North Lynn Street
Arlington, VA 22209

◇ **RELATED ARTICLES**

Textile manufacturing occupations

Definition

The textile industry is one of the largest and most diversified in the United States, employing about 2 million workers in production, design, research, management, and marketing. The process by which natural and man-made fibers are converted into yarn and then woven into cloth is highly complex and involves many categories of production workers.

Manufacturing covers all phases of cloth processing from just after the harvesting of raw materials or the processing of synthetic materials, to the dyeing, weaving, and storing of cloth.

History

People began weaving the four basic natural fibers (cotton, linen, wool, and silk) into cloth as early as the late Stone Age. Pieces of woven cloth dating from about 4,000 B.C. have been found at archaeological sites in Europe, Asia, the Middle East, and South America. Silkworm culture began in China about 2600 B.C. and spread to the Mediterranean world in the sixth century A.D.

In the late eighteenth and early nineteenth centuries, the invention of several machines revolutionized textile production, changing it from a cottage industry to a large-volume, mass production industry. Among these inventions were the spinning jenny, the power loom, the cotton gin, and the sewing machine. Cotton, linen, wool, and silk remained virtually the only sources of textile products until 1855, when the first artificial fiber, nitrocellulose rayon, was invented. Since then, hundreds of synthetic fibers have been developed from such sources as coal, wood, ammonia, and proteins.

Of the textile material produced by the nearly 7,000 textile plants in the United States today, only about half is used for wearing apparel. The rest is used for household products (towels, sheets, upholstery) and in industry (conveyor belts, tire cords, parachutes).

Nature of the work

Most textile production workers are employed either in spinning and weaving plants that produce "gray goods," such as, raw, undyed, and unfinished fabric, or in finishing plants, where the gray goods are dyed, bleached, printed, or glazed. Some large textile companies combine these two segments of the manufacturing process under one roof.

The *staple cutters* perform one of the first steps in the transformation of raw fiber into cloth. They place bales of raw stock or cans of sliver (combed, untwisted strands of fiber) at the feed end of the cutting machine, and break open the bales. They then guide the raw stock or sliver onto a conveyor belt or feed rolls, which pull it against the cutting blades. They examine the cut fibers as they fall from the blades and measure them to make sure they are the required length.

The *frame spinner*, also called *frame operator* or *spinning-frame tender*, tends machines that draw out and twist the sliver into yarn. These workers patrol the spinning-machine area to ensure that the machines have a continuous supply of sliver or roving (a soft, slightly twisted strand of fiber made from sliver). They replace nearly empty packages of roving or sliver with full ones. If they detect a break in the yarn being spun, or in the roving or sliver being fed into the spinning frame, they stop the machine and repair the break. They are responsible for keeping a continuous length of material threaded through the spinning frame while the machine is operating.

The *spinning supervisors* supervise and coordinate the activities of the spinning workers. From the production schedule, they obtain the necessary information about the quantity and texture of yarn to be spun, and the type of fiber to be used. They then determine the proper spacing of the drafting rollers and the size of the twist gears to be used to produce the type of yarn desired, using mathematical formulas and tables and their knowledge of spinning machine processes. As the spun yarn leaves the spinning frame, they examine it to detect variations.

The *beam-wrapper tenders* work at a high-speed machine that winds yarn onto beams preparatory to weaving. A creel, or rack of yarn spools, is positioned at the feed end of the machine. Beam-warper tenders examine the creel to make sure that the size, color, number, and arrangement of the yarn spools correspond to specifications. They then thread the machine with the yarn from the spools, pulling the yarn through drop wires and tension, spreading, and measuring devices, and fastening the yarn to the empty warp beam. After setting a counter to record the amount of yarn wound, they start the machine. If a strand of yarn breaks during warping, stopping the machine they locate and tie the broken ends. When the specified amount of yarn has been wound on the beam, they stop the machine, cut the yarn strands, and tape the cut ends.

The *weavers* or *loom operators* operate a battery of automatic looms that weave the yarn into cloth. They observe the process carefully to detect flaws in the cloth, breaks in warp or filling (cross) threads, or mechanical defects. Weaving defects are repaired by cutting and pulling out the filling threads in the defective area. Thread breaks are repaired by attaching new yarn at the broken end and threading it through the appropriate part of the loom.

The *dye-range operators* control the feed end of a dyeing range, in which widths of cloth are spread on a dye pad and then dried. The operators position a roll of cloth at the feed end, and machine-sew the end of it to the lead cloth already in the machine. They turn valves to admit dye to the dye pad from the mixing tank and regulate the temperature of the dye mixture and of the air in the drying box. They record the amount of yardage dyed, the lot numbers, and the machine running time.

The *laboratory testers* take samples of fibers and yarn at various stages in the manufacturing process and test them for conformance to standards. They make visual tests, such as a count of the number of twists per inch in yarn; tests for strength, using a break tester; weight tests, to determine evenness and moisture content; and chemical tests, to determine the amount of oil or size in a yarn sample. After recording the results of these tests, they report any variations from standard to the supervisor.

The *cloth testers* perform similar tests on gray goods and finished cloth samples. They count the number of warp and filling threads in a sample, test its tensile strength in a tearing machine, and crease it to determine the degree of resiliency. They may also test for such characteristics as abrasion resistance, heat transmission, and water repellency, depending on the type of cloth.

A textile production worker adjusts the tension on one of the rapier weaving machines.

Requirements

For most textile production jobs, a high-school education is desirable, although not absolutely required. Courses in English, chemistry, physics, and mathematics will prove helpful. Laboratory testers should have at least an associate degree from a two-year college or vocational-technical institute.

The textile worker should have good manual dexterity, mental alertness, and the ability to comprehend the workings of often complicated machines, and to follow directions. A laboratory worker should have scientific aptitude, good vision and dexterity, and, if the job entails writing reports, the ability to express one's thoughts clearly and concisely.

Special requirements

There are no special requirements for textile industry jobs, although many production workers belong to a union.

Opportunities for experience and exploration

High-school courses in chemistry, shop and mechanical drawing, and hobbies involving chemistry, model building, or working with machinery are good preparation for production or laboratory jobs in the textile field. Summer employment in textile plants is sometimes available for high school students.

Related occupations

Textile industry workers are required to have good eye-hand dexterity, stamina, and an ability to enjoy repetitious activities. Other jobs that ask the same include knit goods industry workers, contact lens manufacturing workers, job and die setters, and patternmakers.

Methods of entering

Most textile production workers obtain their jobs by answering newspaper advertisements or by applying directly to the personnel office of a textile plant. A new worker usually receives between a week and several months of on-the-job training, depending on the complexity of the job.

Graduates of textile technology programs in colleges and technical institutes are notified of job openings through the school's placement office. Often, positions are obtained before graduation. Sometimes a student may be sponsored in a textile program by a textile company

Textile manufacturing occupations
Machine Trades Occupations

While much of the textile industry is mechanized, people are needed to supervise and adjust the machines. This worker oversees the production of spools at the American Textile Manufacturing Institute.

in the area; upon graduation, the student goes to work for the sponsoring company.

Advancement

The production worker who shows above-average competence, good judgment, and leadership ability has a good chance of being promoted to a supervisory position, as a supervisor in charge of a bank of machines or of a stage in the production process.

Laboratory workers may advance to supervisory positions in the lab, or, if their educational background includes courses in industrial engineering, safety, and quality control, they may move up to management jobs exercising control over the production process.

Employment outlook

In the early 1990s, about 2.7 million employees worked for about 7,000 textile plants in 47 states or for related industries.

The demand for textile products for fashion, home, and industrial uses is constantly increasing. The employment outlook in this field, especially for those with scientific and technical training, is expected to remain good through the next decade.

Earnings

Textile industry workers generally earn lower salaries than production workers in other manufacturing industries. In the early 1990s, wages ranged from $12,600 annually in yarn and thread mills to $14,980 in textile finishing plants. Wages varied by location, being generally higher in the North than in the South. The median salaries of professional workers in the textile industry averaged more than $14,600 in the early 1990s.

Conditions of work

Modern textile plants are clean, well-lighted, air-conditioned, and humidity-controlled. Most plants operate twenty-four hours a day, with three shifts a day. Some machine-tending production jobs involve much repetition. Workers in these jobs need to be both patient and alert, so that they are not bored or distracted by the routine and can immediately detect any breakdown or change in the machine's rhythm. Most textile work is not strenuous, but it does require other abilities.

Social and psychological factors

Some textile production jobs are routine and repetitive, so those who like mobility and a variety of duties are not well-suited for them. Many higher-level production jobs, however, call for precise discrimination and individual judgment in such areas as mixing dyes, setting up looms, and testing samples of cloth and yarn. Textile workers can be proud of their role in fulfilling one of the basic needs of all people.

GOE: 06.02; SIC: 22; SOC: 75,76

◇ **SOURCES OF ADDITIONAL INFORMATION**

American Association of Textile Chemists and Colorists
PO Box 12215
Research Triangle Park, NC 27709

American Textile Manufacturers Institute
1801 K Street, NW, Suite 900
Washington, DC 20006

Institute of Textile Technology
PO Box 391
Charlottesville, VA 22902

National Council for Textile Education
Education Program Information
PO Box 391
Charlottesville, VA 22902

◇ **RELATED ARTICLES**

Tool makers and die makers

Definition

Tool-and-die makers are highly skilled workers who produce the fittings needed for mass production of metal parts. *Tool makers* specialize in producing jigs and fixtures to hold metal that is being shaved, drilled, or stamped. They also make gauges and other measuring devices for manufacturing precision metal parts. *Die makers* construct metal forms, or dies, for stamping or forging operations to shape metal or plastics. They may also design and repair dies, jigs, and tools. Tool-and-die makers have a broad knowledge of machining operations, shop practices, mathematics, and blueprint reading. They use most types of machine tools and precision-measuring instruments.

History

One of the earliest tools used by humans was the stone chip used to skin animals. A number of hand tools made of copper or iron were used by the Egyptians. Leonardo da Vinci developed a crude pole lathe. The first machine tool with a high degree of precision was the screw-cutting lathe developed by Henry Maudslay in 1800. Most of the products turned out by these machine tools were tailor-made at the request of a customer.

In 1798, Eli Whitney received an order from the U.S. government to make 10,000 rifles. Because of the rigid time limits in which he had to complete the order, Whitney developed new work methods. The essential idea was the standardization of parts. One part could fit any gun rather than one gun. Jigs and fixtures were used to ensure identical parts. To cut the metal,

he improved the milling machine invented earlier. The era of mass production was born.

The increase of technical knowledge has developed a need for new and ever more precise tools and methods.

Nature of the work

Tool-and-die makers are highly skilled machinists who make fixtures, dies, jigs, and gauges. Although not production workers, they make mass production possible. The key to mass production is the standardization of parts. Cars, airplanes, and refrigerators, to function effectively, must have parts that fit properly. Some of the devices made by tool-and-die makers reduce the cost of production by replacing a machinist with a semiskilled person like a machine operator or tender. These semiskilled persons are aided in their production process by gauges made by tool-and-die makers.

The tool-and-die maker may make many devices or specialize in one item. A jig maker makes devices that hold the metal and automatically guide the required tool so that it produces identical parts. A fixture maker makes a device that is attached to a machine tool to hold the work. Often jigs and fixtures are combined in the same task to cut the cost of production. To ensure that the jig or fixture is in proper alignment or that the machined part meets job specifications, a gauge maker creates the necessary precision instruments.

The work done by tool-and-die makers of necessity has to be precise. They are expert in the use of all tools. They use standard machine tools that have been finely adjusted such as the lathe, milling machine, and internal grinder

A die maker assembles a metal stamp that will be installed on another machine. Such work requires great precision and concentration.

and some special ones such as the jig borer. They also use such hand tools as files, chisels, and scrapes. To lay out their work, they must have an excellent knowledge of shop mathematics and blueprint reading. They must be able to use various measuring devices and gauges to check the accuracy of their work. Die makers make dies (metal forms) that shape material. These devices are used to stamp or forge various metals. They can also make metal molds that are used in molding plastics and die casting. Because most of these devices are used to mass produce a part, the die maker must use measuring tools to work with accuracy greater than .0001 of an inch.

One of the unique features of the work of tool-and-die makers is that they usually do all the work needed to make a device. They may begin by analyzing a variety of specifications such as blueprints, sketches, and models in order to visualize the finished product. Once that is done, they compute the dimensions, decide on the necessary machining, and plan layout and assembly operations. They then lay out the metal stock and set up and operate machine tools. While work is in operation, tool-and-die makers are required to keep a close check on dimensions through the use of such measuring instruments as dial indicators, gauge blocks, and micrometers. Satisfied that all parts are correctly machined, they then fit the pieces together to obtain the finished product. The end result is an item helpful in the production of parts essential to a manufacturing process.

Tool-and-die makers work in automobile, aircraft, missile, and other metalworking industries. Die makers find work in forge shops, punch shops, and plastic product companies. They may also work in a job shop where tools

and dies are tailor-made for a variety of manufacturers. Specialists include *stamping die-try-out workers, carbide operators, die finishers, plastic-fixture builders; saw, bench tool, plastic tool, extrusion die template,* and *die-casting and plastic molding mold makers;* and *trim, wire drawing, electronic, paper goods,* and *jewelry die makers.*

Requirements

Because tool-and-die makers work independently on a task demanding a high degree of accuracy, they must be above average in intelligence, numerical ability, spatial perception, and mechanical aptitude. They must have an excellent background in mathematics (especially trigonometry and geometry) and principles of mechanics. Previous experience in drafting or mechanical drawing is also helpful.

Those considering tool-and-die making as an occupation should also be above average in the manipulation of small objects with their fingers, and should be able to move their hands easily and skillfully. They should have good eyesight, though correction is permitted. Though they sit part of the time, they should be able to bend, stoop, and lift moderately heavy objects. Most employers demand a high-school diploma of tool-and-die maker trainees. Very often some shop training or some work experience in a machine shop is required. An entering apprentice should display patience and a knack for following progressively more complex directions.

Special requirements

There are no special requirements for tool-and-die makers other than those already mentioned.

Opportunities for experience and exploration

There are several ways to prepare for this occupation. Such high-school courses as geometry, trigonometry, physics, mechanical drawing, and shop work should be taken. Hobbies such as automobile tinkering, model making, and electronic kit assembling may also be helpful. The essential point of these activities is to find out the degree of patience, accuracy, and mechanical interest an individual possesses.

Those careless in their work habits will find it difficult to become tool-and-die makers, for the work requires precision work. A field trip to a machine shop may give an overall view of the type of work done in this field. At times, part-time work may be obtained in a machine shop after school or during the summer time. This type of experience usually consists of sweeping floors and clearing out the machine tools, but it is valuable for it gives a firsthand experience as to the type of work done in a machine shop.

Related occupations

Other work that requires manual dexterity, numerical ability, and stamina includes pattern-makers, job-and-die setters, and numerical-control machine-tool operators.

Methods of entering

There are several ways by which workers can become tool-and-die makers. First, they can work their way up from a semiskilled job in the machine shop. If they have average intelligence, the necessary mechanical aptitude, and dexterity, they are given additional training. As openings occur in other types of machine tools, they work and train on them. Their shop work is supplemented by training in blueprint reading, layout work, instrument reading, and shop mathematics. The amount of time required to become a tool-and-die maker by this method varies with the ability of the individual and the need for additional skilled help by the employer; however, it may take many years.

It is also possible for a trained machinist to become a tool-and-die maker with additional training. This training would include layout work, advanced shop mathematics, heat treating, and being able to work with precision tools, and may be obtained through vocational and correspondence schools.

The best way to become a tool-and-die maker, however, is through an apprenticeship program. Some manufacturing concerns have apprenticeship training in tool or die making, while other companies have only on-the-job training. To become an apprentice, the applicant must meet educational requirements, must then perform satisfactorily on tests given by the state employment service, and must have the approval of the joint (labor-management) apprenticeship committee. Some experience in a machine shop prior to the time of application is also helpful. The apprenticeship program usu-ally lasts four years. Because tool-and-die makers are essentially skilled machinists, apprentices learn how to set up and operate various machine tools such as the lathe, milling machine, grinders, jig borer, and the like. They learn how to use various hand tools to finish and assemble the various devices they make. Because of the high degree of precision required in the work, they are taught how to use precision measuring devices. In addition to shop training, they will receive about 500 hours of classroom instruction. Some of the subjects they will study are blueprint reading, shop mathematics, heat treating, properties of various metals, and design. After apprenticeship, several years' experience are usually required to learn more difficult tool-and-die work.

Advancement

It takes a number of years after completing training before workers can become topflight tool-and-die makers. This results from the fact that it takes a considerable amount of time to make a device such as a jig, fixture, or die. Once they have acquired the necessary experience, several avenues of advancement are open to tool-and-die makers. If they have suitable personal characteristics, they may become a supervisor or a superintendent. This would include basic management skills: overseeing employees' work; interviewing, hiring, and firing staff; and delegating responsibility for tasks.

Some tool-and-die makers are upgraded to do experimental work with tools and dies. Others become tool designers. These positions call for people who have a high degree of ingenuity and can apply their past work experience to the development of a new tool.

Another field open to tool-and-die makers is that of tool inspector. In some areas, such as the electronic and space industries, a high degree of accuracy is needed in the production of component parts. Consequently, some companies use tool-and-die makers to inspect jigs, fixtures, gauges, and other aids to production. Their broad background in machine tools and skill in using various measuring devices make them ideal tool inspectors.

A small number of tool-and-die makers who can obtain the necessary money can open their own tool-and-die shop. This type of enterprise (a job shop) is continually in demand because some manufacturing concerns, such as the makers of plastic products, do not maintain their own tool-and-die making department.

Tool makers and die makers
Machine Trades Occupations

Employment outlook

About 165,000 tool-and-die makers were employed in the early 1990s. The demand for tool-and-die makers will increase little during the foreseeable future because of increased automation. It is estimated that some openings will occur each year because of death and retirement, however.

In some industries, the number of devices made by tool-and-die makers has been reduced because of electronically controlled machine tools. Some industries, however, still require the designing and development of more and more precise tools and instruments. Some of the younger tool-and-die makers are receiving training in electronics to understand and develop devices for the newer machine tools.

Earnings

The median annual salary in the early 1990s for tool-and-die makers was $27,150. Actual salaries varied widely according to location, hours and shifts worked, and experience. The usual fringe benefits such as health insurance, paid vacations, and pension plans are available to most tool-and-die makers.

Conditions of work

Tool-and-die makers usually work in well-lighted and ventilated rooms where noise and other distractions are kept to a minimum. Conditions may vary slightly because manufacturing concerns such as forges and stamping mills of necessity make a lot of noise. Safety procedures keep injuries to a minimum. One unfavorable aspect of the job is that an allergic reaction may result from oil, grease, or coolants used in the machining process. Even though tool-and-die makers may sit during part of the work day, they do stoop, bend, push, and lift objects that may weigh about fifty pounds.

Social and psychological factors

Tool-and-die makers need patience, good work habits, and the ability to perceive pertinent detail in objects. They must be able to work in situations where high standards and measurement tolerances are demanded. Because they make various types of devices, their work is full of change rather than routine, and often they do the entire job of making the device with a minimum of supervision. They obtain a great deal of personal satisfaction from the various devices they make. If they advance to a supervisory position, they must have such personal traits as tact, poise, ability to deal with people, and good oral and written expression.

GOE: 05.05.07; SIC: 34; SOC: 6811

◇ SOURCES OF ADDITIONAL INFORMATION

International Association of Machinists and Aerospace Workers
1300 Connecticut Avenue, NW
Washington, DC 20036

International Union of Electronic, Electrical, Salaried, and Machine, and Furniture Workers
1126 16th Street, NW
Washington, DC 20036

International Union, United Automobile, Aerospace and Agricultural Implement Workers of America
8000 East Jefferson Avenue
Detroit, MI 48214

NMTBA—Association for Manufacturing Technology
7901 Westpark Drive
McLean, VA 22102

◇ RELATED ARTICLES

Volume 1: Machining and Machinery
Volume 3: Instrument makers; Machinists; Patternmakers
Volume 4: Instrumentation technicians; Mechanical technicians; Tap-and-die-maker technicians

Vending-machine mechanics

Definition

Vending-machine mechanics install, maintain, and repair coin-operated vending machines placed in establishments on a concession basis. They test new machines to be sure they are working properly; install them in factories, offices, public places, and various places of business; check, clean, and adjust machines periodically; and examine malfunctioning machines, diagnose the problem, and repair or replace parts.

History

Vending machines are not a product of contemporary times. Citizens of Egypt in about the third century B.C. dropped coins into a simple device that dispensed holy water. Coin-operated machines sold pencils in China in A.D. 1076 and pipe tobacco in England in the 1700s. In the 1880s the first vending machines appeared in North America and dispensed chewing gum and postcards.

Today these machines are found everywhere—in stores, offices, factories, institutions, airports, public places, and businesses of all kinds. The items available by dropping money into a machine are almost unlimited—cold soft drinks, hot soups and beverages, candy, snacks, sandwiches, nuts, cigarettes, newspapers, toys, notions, and much more. Services are provided by coin-operated machines, too, such as storage lockers, laundry equipment, and railroad station and airport luggage carts.

Vending machines vary in size and complexity from the small penny peanut machines to the large machines that may have hot or cold food storage compartments, may accept coins or paper money (rejecting counterfeits) and return change, or may be set to brew coffee automatically. Electronic monitors allow the machines to "read" paper money.

The popularity of these machines may be attributed to the ever-growing trend toward self-service. Not only do they save time for the consumer, but they make many products available more economically because no sales attendants are necessary. To provide satisfactory service, however, route service personnel carefully maintain the machines and collect the money.

Nature of the work

It is a rare commercial or industrial building nowadays that does not have a vending-machine installation. In office buildings, factories, and recreational centers, machines dispense coffee, tea, milk, hot chocolate, candy, gum, sandwiches, salads, and a variety of snacks and soft drinks; in restaurants and bars, cigarettes; in public washrooms, articles of hygiene; and in apartment buildings, newspapers and laundry facilities. The list is endless. These machines are generally placed in establishments on a concession basis, and it is the job of vending machine mechanics to keep them in good working order.

Before installing new machines, mechanics test them to be sure they are operating properly. Most vending machines today have extensive electronic components for coin handling as well as for the operation of the machine, including the way the coffee is brewed, the way soft-drink cups are manufactured, and the way refrigerated food is dispensed. The complicated electrical and electronic machines require involved inspection. A beverage dispenser, for example, has various systems, which include ice-making, refrigeration, and carbonation for soft drinks or heating units for coffee and hot beverages. The mechanics make sure that the drinks are mixed properly with the right proportion of ingredients, that the dispenser does not overfill or underfill the cups, that the liquids are maintained at the right temperature, and that the coin-activated mechanism and the change-making system work.

At the location where the vending machines are to be used, the mechanics connect them to electrical and water sources, referring to diagrams or other specifications, if necessary, to complete the assembly. Then they fill the machines with ingredients or products and test their operation once more.

A major part of the mechanics' job is preventive maintenance. They check the machines on a regular schedule to prevent trouble before it occurs: clean electrical contact points, lubricate mechanical parts, test the operation, and make whatever adjustments are necessary so that the items are dispensed properly.

If a machine breaks down, the mechanics make a service call to diagnose and correct the malfunction. Problems such as loose wires, leaks, or faulty mechanisms are easy to spot, and the electronic circuit boards of the newer

Vending machine mechanics must keep track of each machine's supplies and compare the number of items sold with the amount of money collected. If there is a discrepancy, then they must find the problem and fix it.

machines make it possible to troubleshoot the more complicated malfunctions electronically, exchanging components that are not working properly with replacements, and returning defective parts to the shop or supplier.

Vending-machine mechanics use a variety of tools in their repair and maintenance work. Hand tools include hammers, screwdrivers, wrenches, pipe cutters, and soldering irons. Power tools include grinding wheels, saws, and drills.

Mechanics often must do some clerical work, such as writing reports, preparing cost estimates for repairs, and ordering parts. Those who work for small vending companies may be combination "mechanic–route workers." In addition to repair and maintenance work, they also stock the machines with merchandise, collect the money, fill the coin and currency changers, and keep daily records.

Requirements

A high-school education is an asset for beginning mechanics, even though employers may not require a diploma. Preparation should include high-school or vocational school courses in electricity, refrigeration, and machine repair. Currently there are about ten high schools and junior colleges in the country that offer one- to two-year programs specifically designed for vending machine mechanics.

Mechanics may receive their training either informally on the job or through an authorized apprenticeship program. Most new workers learn by observing experienced mechanics, re-

ceiving instruction from them, and doing work under their supervision. Entry-level jobs are usually for general shop helpers or route drivers. Beginners are first given simple tasks to perform—cleaning, painting, or refurbishing machines. Gradually, they are taught to rebuild machines—removing and repairing faulty parts, adjusting and testing machines. Then they begin to accompany an experienced mechanic on service calls. When they are sufficiently skilled, they are permitted to go out alone, knowing that the more experienced mechanics are available whenever necessary to lend their expertise to a particularly complex problem. Completion of this on-the-job training may take as little as six months or as long as three years, depending on ability, previous education, and the quality of instruction.

A three-year apprenticeship program established by the National Automatic Merchandising Association (NAMA) to help employers train new workers combines guaranteed periods of training in various skills with 144 hours of classroom instruction in subjects such as basic electricity, blueprint reading, customer relations, and safety. The NAMA program awards a certificate to mechanics who complete the apprenticeship training and pass performance and written tests.

Manufacturers periodically sponsor training sessions in repair shops or in their own service facilities so that mechanics can learn to maintain and service new types of vending machines. Employers usually pay wages and expenses for mechanics attending these sessions. Employers also encourage mechanics, both beginners and experienced workers, to take evening courses in such job-related subjects as basic electricity or refrigeration, and often pay at least part of the tuition and book expenses for those mechanics who successfully complete the courses.

Vending machine mechanics must have mechanical ability. If job applicants cannot demonstrate this through previous work experience, they may be required to score well on mechanical aptitude tests. Employers also look for honesty and a respect for the law, since they must trust their mechanics with thousands of dollars' worth of merchandise and cash. A pleasant manner and tact are important qualities so that mechanics can deal effectively with many different people in the businesses and other establishments where the machines are located.

High-school students should study metal shop, mechanics, and basic math and science for a background education that will assist them in training.

Special requirements

A commercial driver's license and a good driving record are mandatory for most mechanics who must drive to the various machine locations.

Because vending machines dispense food, mechanics must have a knowledge of state public health and sanitation standards and be familiar with local electrical and plumbing codes. It is also essential that they know and follow safety procedures, especially when working with electricity and gas or when lifting heavy objects.

While union membership is not a requirement for everyone, many vending machine mechanics who work for large companies belong to various trade unions.

Opportunities for experience and exploration

High-school students may test their interest in and aptitude for this kind of work and prepare for a career as a vending-machine mechanic by taking shop courses in electricity and machine repair and, if available, in refrigeration, blueprint reading, and electronics.

Future employers will be impressed by previous experience as a measure of an individual's aptitude for mechanical repair work. Part-time and summer employment as helper in any kind of electrical or mechanical repair shop will provide good credentials for the beginning mechanic.

Related occupations

The variety of careers available to people with the skill, interest, and aptitude for work as mechanics is wide. Other positions might include general maintenance mechanics, industrial machinery mechanics, automobile mechanics, motorcycle mechanics, and office-machine servicers.

Methods of entering

High schools and vocational schools often have placement services available for graduates. Persons interested in this occupation may also obtain information on job openings from the personnel offices of individual vending machine companies or from local offices of the state employment or apprenticeship service.

Advancement

Trainees generally begin as shop helpers or route drivers and become fully qualified mechanics in three years or less. For apprentices, the duration of the training program is three years. After that, with experience and managerial ability, some mechanics are promoted to supervisory positions. Those who have the ability and motivation may, with some investment capital, open their own vending companies.

Employment outlook

In the early 1990s, there were about 35,000 vending machine servicers and repairers employed in the United States to maintain and repair more than 5 million machines. Most of them worked for vending companies that sell food and a variety of other items through machines. Some were employed by soft-drink bottling companies that have their own coin-operated machines. Mechanics are distributed throughout the country, although greater numbers of them are concentrated in large population centers where vending machines are plentiful.

There will be some growth in the vending machine industry through the next decade, although it will be slower than the average for all occupations. Additional jobs will be created because of two main factors. First, more coin-operated machines will be installed to meet the demand for fast-food service. This will be especially true as an increasing number of industrial plants, hospitals, and stores move to suburban areas where there may not be many restaurants close-by. Second, vending companies will be selling a greater variety of products through the machines. In addition, normal job openings will occur as older, experienced mechanics retire, die, or change occupations.

Vending-machine mechanics are employed throughout the country, but jobs are more easily available in metropolitan areas, where many machines are needed to serve a large population. Job opportunities will be best for mechanics with previous experience repairing coin-operated machines. Those with training or experience in electronics will have the advantage as manufacturers use more electronic components in their vending machines. Untrained, inexperienced workers generally will have weaker prospects, unless they live in an area where there is a shortage of skilled mechanics. In that case, vending-machine companies that need more mechanics may well promote qualified route drivers or hire inexperienced people who proved their mechanical aptitude in high school by taking shop and electricity courses.

Experienced mechanics are rarely laid off even when economic conditions are poor, because employers are afraid they may not be available for rehire when business picks up again.

Earnings

Vending-machine mechanics in the early 1990s earned between $7,350 and $37,440 annually, though most made between $13,728 and $21,220. Starting apprentices are paid 50 percent of the experienced mechanics' rate.

The workweek is usually five days, or forty hours, with premium pay for overtime. Some union contracts guarantee workers extra pay for night work or for emergency calls on weekends or holidays.

Conditions of work

Some mechanics work only in company repair shops and some work only in the field, but most mechanics do both. They drive to machine locations in a service truck, for which they need a commercial driver's license. The shops are usually quiet, well-lighted, and well-ventilated places, with plenty of space for making repairs.

Because many vending machines are in operation twenty-four hours a day, seven days a week, mechanics may have to make emergency service calls at night or on weekends or holidays. If machines are maintained on a regular schedule, this may not happen frequently. In any case, mechanics who work more than forty hours a week are generally paid overtime.

Vending-machine repair work is not especially hazardous. Mechanics who are careless may suffer minor electrical shocks or cuts from sharp tools and metal objects. They usually learn, however, to observe safety procedures during their training periods, especially when working with electricity and gas. Vending machines can be quite large, and mechanics sometimes must lift heavy parts or move the machines to get at the mechanisms.

Social and psychological factors

Millions of people depend on coin-operated machines for countless products and services. Keeping those machines working properly despite their hard use—and abuse—by customers is an important responsibility.

There are many trades that call for mechanical ability, but several factors make the occupation of vending machine mechanics appealing. The work is relatively clean and gives mechanics the opportunity to work in a number of different places and meet a variety of people.

GOE: 05.10.02; SIC: 7359; SOC: 772

◇ **SOURCES OF ADDITIONAL INFORMATION**

General information on vending-machine mechanics and a list of schools offering courses for this occupation may be obtained from:

National Automatic Merchandising Association
20 North Wacker Drive
Chicago, IL 60606

◇ **RELATED ARTICLES**

Volume 3: Industrial machinery mechanics; Office machine servicers; Pinsetter mechanics
Volume 4: Electromechanical technicians

Bench Work Occupations

According to the *Dictionary of Occupational Titles*, this category includes occupations in which workers use hands and fingers, hand tools, and bench machines, to fit, grind, carve, assemble, and repair relatively small objects and materials such as televisions, toasters, and other appliances. The work is usually performed at a set position in a plant, shop, and at a bench, worktable, or conveyor. At the more complex levels, workers frequently read blueprints, follow patterns, use a variety of hand tools, and assume responsibility for meeting standards. Workers at the less complex levels are required to follow standardized procedures.

This category also includes artisan crafts such as jewelers, pottery makers, and instrument repairers. Such jobs require manual dexterity and artistic craftsmanship. It is the type of work that is difficult to replace with automated equipment. The quality and desirability of hand-crafted products remains high.

Nearly 1.5 million persons are engaged in the servicing and repair of the thousands of small industrial and commercial items that are the mainstay of our society. Entry into this field is generally through training programs, with experience being gained through on-the-job training under supervision. Training can be acquired through company programs, combined technical school-job programs, or formal apprenticeship programs that provide thorough training.

Workers in this occupation can advance to positions such as supervisor or service manager; can switch to sales positions; or can operate their own sales and service businesses.

Employment possibilities in this occupational group are not as great as in some of the other trades. While there will be several thousands of job openings each year because of retirement, transfers, or deaths, the actual increase in the numbers of jobs available will be moderate to negligible. This is because the costs of producing many consumer goods have gone down and it is frequently simpler to replace a watch or a television set, and so forth, than to have it repaired. For the craftmen, however, there will continue to be demand for handmade and hand tooled items. Although the demand may not be as strong, a market will remain for these products for some time to come.

Appliance repairers

Definition

The *appliance repairer* installs and services all types of major electrical and gas appliances, such as washing machines, refrigerators, kitchen ranges, and vacuum cleaners, in a customer's home or business establishment.

History

Though some small home appliances, such as the iron and the coffee percolator, were patented before the twentieth century, the general use of appliances did not take place until the end of World War I. Several factors contributed

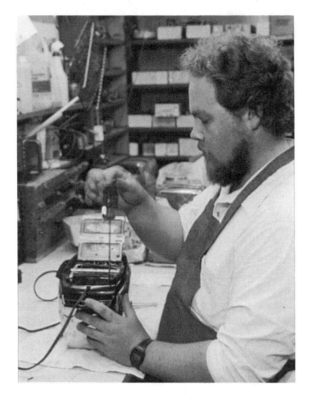

An appliance repairer disassembles the bottom of a toaster to replace some damaged parts.

to the rise of the use of home appliances: the development of efficient, compact electric motors; the ability of electric utilities to generate more power; and the difficulty in employing reliable household help.

With one or two people in a family doing most of the domestic chores, efficiency was needed to get those chores done. Machines that reduced or eliminated the time needed by the worker were in great demand.

Since the end of World War II, there has been a tremendous growth in the use and production of home appliances. This increase is a result of the rapid growth of the population and a higher standard of living. In addition, the development of new products, such as dishwashers, electric can openers, room air conditioners, and food waste disposers, as well as the improved efficiency of the older types of products and the advanced marketing skills of manufacturers, has increased the use and demand for home appliances. In recent years there has also been an upsurge in the establishment of coin-operated washing and drying machine laundry establishments and coin-operated dry-cleaning businesses.

Because of this increased use of appliances, the need to install, repair, and service them has grown rapidly.

Nature of the work

Appliance repairers must utilize the human senses as well as tools in their work. They look for frayed electrical cords, cracked hoses, and broken connections; listen for loud humming or grinding noises; check for gas fumes or burning materials; and turn gears or other moving parts to see if they are jammed or too tight. The repairer also finds other causes of trouble by using special tools or testing devices. They must be able to combine all their observations into a diagnosis to repair the particular appliance.

Appliance repairers must make service calls to homes and answer customers' questions and complaints about their appliances. They will often advise customers about the care and use of their appliances, especially when installing them. They must be able to order parts from a catalog, record time spent, parts used, and applicability of warranty on each repair job, give estimates on the cost of repairs, and sometimes sell new or used appliances. Most repairers drive light trucks or automobiles, some of which are equipped with two-way radios.

Although many appliance repairers service, maintain, and repair most appliances, there are also some who specialize in one kind, or even one brand, or in a number of appliances. *Window unit air-conditioning installer-servicers*, for example, work only with portable window units, while *domestic air-conditioning installers* handle both window and central systems.

Household-appliance installers specialize in the installation of refrigerators and freezers, washing machines and clothes dryers, and electric ranges and ovens; *electrical-appliance servicers* maintain and repair those common kitchen units.

Small electric-appliance repairers handle portable household electrical appliances such as toasters, percolators, lamps, heaters, fans, food processors, and irons. In this case, the customer usually takes the particular appliance to the repair shop for any servicing that is needed, such as replacing worn or defective parts.

The *gas-appliance repairer* installs, repairs, and cleans all types of gas appliances such as gas ranges or stoves, heaters, and gas furnaces, and also advises the customer on proper, efficient, and economical use of gas.

Requirements

The appliance repairer must be able to work independently and at times supervise the work of others: for example, in the installation of heavy-duty laundry equipment. Some of the personal requirements needed are mechanical aptitude, dexterity, normal eyesight and hearing (correction permitted), patience, strength, and the ability to meet and deal with people effectively. Lacking some of the personal qualities may not necessarily prevent individuals from entering this occupation, as they may become bench workers and do all their work in the repair shop.

It is usually necessary that an applicant for an appliance repairer's job be a high-school graduate with some knowledge of physics and electricity (especially wiring diagrams).

Applicants are usually hired as helpers and acquire their skills and work experience through on-the-job training. Some companies will assign a helper to accompany an appliance repairer on work assignments to aid in the installation of new appliances in customers' homes. They will also observe and eventually assist experienced repairers in diagnosing and correcting problems with home appliances. Other companies assign helpers to work in the shop where they learn to rebuild used parts and work on simple repair jobs.

By the end of six to twelve months, the trainee possesses enough knowledge of appliances to make all but the most complex repairs alone. Often a trainee is sent on service calls alone, which would necessitate having a driver's license. An additional year or two is required to make trainees fully qualified. During this period, they may attend service schools sponsored by various appliance manufacturers or local distributors (often on company time) to gain information about the technical aspects of the work. They should also study service manuals to familiarize themselves with new appliances and how to repair them. This aspect of training—attending courses updating information, and reading manuals—is a continual part of a repairer's job.

There are some public and private technical and vocational schools that provide formal classroom and laboratory experiences in the service and repair of appliances. The length of the course varies from one to two years. Repair of some of the small appliances may be learned through correspondence courses. In addition, basic facts about electric motors, machinery and other related factors may be learned by this method.

Special requirements

There are no special requirements for this job.

Opportunities for experience and exploration

One may explore the appliance servicing field by visiting local appliance repair shops, appliance dealers, gas and electric utility companies, and appliance manufacturers, where part-time or summer jobs may be available. Personal aptitude and interest for this type of work can be measured by success or failure in such efforts as assembling electronic kits, repairing model racers or bicycles, and experiments in physics.

Related occupations

Other occupations that require skills and aptitudes similar to those of appliance repairers include locksmiths, watch repairers, jewelers and jewelry repairers, and instrument repairers.

Methods of entering

A typical way of entering the occupation is to become a helper in some repair shop. If one has the necessary qualifications, the employer may select the individual for on-the-job training. Another way is to take some courses in appliance repair work at a vocational or technical school. As a result the individual may develop sufficient skill to become acceptable to an employer.

Advancement

The kind of advancements that are made in this occupation depend mainly on the place of employment. In a small repair shop of three to five persons, advancement would be slow because the owner would be likely to do most of the administrative work. Working for a large retailer, a factory service center, or a gas or electric utility company, however, one could progress from repairer to supervisor, assistant service manager, and service manager.

A second possibility for advancement is through the factory service training school. A repairer who is proficient, knows the product, and can speak effectively, can conduct classes in the training of other repairers. Another outlet for a teaching interest in this area is a technical or vocational school that offers courses in appliance repair work.

A third type of advancement is for the repairer to open an appliance repair shop. This step requires the individual to have the money to buy the necessary tools, parts, tables, trucks, and any other equipment.

A repairer who works for an appliance manufacturer can advance to such higher paying jobs as writing service manuals or teaching other repairers to service new models of appliances. This may involve being trained in writing or reading skills. Sometimes repairers advance to the position of selling appliances.

Employment outlook

In the early 1990s, there were about 100,000 appliance repairers employed throughout the country. A large number worked in independent repair shops, sometimes owned and operated by other appliance repairers. The rest were employed by appliance dealers, department stores, gas and utility companies, appliance manufacturers, and various firms that service coin-operated washing machines and coin-operated dry-cleaning machines.

It is expected that employment opportunities for appliance repairers will grow throughout the early 1990s. The reasons for this prediction are numerous.

The number of appliances in U.S. homes has been steadily increasing. For example, a few years ago automatic washers and dryers were considered luxuries and now are standard equipment in many homes. Other items such as dishwashers, dehumidifiers, air conditioners, and hair dryers are being bought at an increasing rate for home, commercial, and industrial use.

Some appliances have become so complex that they require expert servicing. For example, some washing machines are designed to automatically dispense soap and bleaching and water conditioners at set times during the washing cycle. Adjustment of these controls requires technical know-how.

The demand for appliances will also be stimulated by the growing population and the increasing numbers of young married couples who spend large amounts of their incomes on home furnishings. Rising incomes and living standards will also stimulate employment through a demand for more and better appliances throughout the next decade.

There will be thousands of opportunities of employment in this field each year because of promotion, transfer, death, or retirement.

Earnings

In the early 1990s, the wage rates for some experienced appliance repairers in unionized shops ranged from less than $11,400 to more than $34,800 annually. The median was $21,840. Apprentices may earn less during their training period. The difference in pay was a result of geographical location, nature of the employing establishment, and other factors. Workers employed by gas and electric utility companies generally have a higher hourly wage range. In addition, many workers employed by large utilities, manufacturers' service centers, or other employers receive paid vacations and sick leave, health insurance, and other benefits, as well as credit toward retirement pensions. Some of these companies sponsor employee savings funds and contribute money to the accounts of employees who participate. Opportunities for overtime pay are especially favorable for repairers of major appliances.

Conditions of work

Appliance repairers generally work a forty-hour week. The conditions of work may vary according to the size of appliance being installed or repaired. Repairers who fix small appliances work indoors at a bench and seldom have to handle heavy objects. Repair shops are generally quiet, well lighted, properly ventilated, and provide the necessary tools.

Repairers who work on major appliances (stove, refrigerator, washing machine) work in a variety of situations. Because they normally work in the customer's home, they may encounter variable lighting conditions, limited space to work in, and an accumulation of debris, for the appliances normally are "dirt catchers." In addition, they may have to crawl, bend, stoop, crouch, or lie down to carry out some of the repairs. The repairer may have to shove, push, or lift the appliance to remove a panel housing.

Although appliance repair work is usually safe, accidents are possible while the repairer is driving, handling electric wires or parts, or lifting heavy appliances. Beginners, however, are always carefully instructed in the simple precautions necessary to prevent electric shock, and in the safe use of tools.

There is no seasonal fluctuation of employment in this occupation since repairs on electric or gas appliances are needed at all times of the year and the work is done indoors.

Social and psychological factors

The appliance repairer will find the work interesting and challenging because of the variety and complexity of situations to be encountered. A balky appliance presents a problem where patience, intelligence, and mechanical ingenuity are required for its solution. One factor that appeals to many repairers is that they work with a minimum of supervision or alone.

GOE: 05.10.03; SIC: 762; SOC: 6156

◇ **SOURCES OF ADDITIONAL INFORMATION**

Gas Appliance Manufacturers Association
1901 North Moore Street, Suite 1100
Arlington, VA 22209

National Association of Retail Dealers of America
10 East 22nd Street
Lombard, IL 60148

◇ **RELATED ARTICLES**

Volume 1: Energy
Volume 3: Air-conditioning, refrigeration, and heating mechanics; Electric-sign repairers; Electricians; Line installers and cable splicers; Office machine servicers; Telephone and PBX installers and repairers; Vending machine mechanics; see also Bench work occupations
Volume 4: Electrical technicians; Electromechanical technicians; Mechanical technicians

Assemblers

Definition

An *assembler* puts together parts of a product during the various steps of the manufacturing process and during the final assembly of the product. There are two basic kinds of assemblers—floor assemblers and bench assemblers. *Floor assemblers* work with large or heavy equipment on shop floors. *Bench assemblers* put together small materials while working at a bench.

History

Many of the technological developments in our society have resulted from the needs of an increased and expanded population. As items such as radios and television sets were developed, it became profitable to produce them on a mass basis. Many people were able to afford such items and, thus, have increasingly come to expect them as an essential part of a comfortable existence. To produce consumer goods on a mass basis required the services of many people to perform relatively isolated activities at some point in the production process. Recent developments in the aircraft industry also require that large numbers of individuals assemble given portions of what will eventually be a completed plane or missile.

Nature of the work

All assemblers put together parts of finished products. Specific details of their jobs vary widely in terms of the products with which they deal and the industry in which they work. Assembling jobs in different industries range from those requiring a great deal of skill to others that can be learned in a few hours. Most assemblers are found in the aircraft industry, the automobile industry, and the electronics industry. Semiskilled assemblers work under close supervision and follow simple instructions to do what is essentially repetitive work. These assemblers use, as a rule, pliers, screwdrivers, soldering irons, power drills, and wrenches.

Electrical accessories assemblers put together mechanical parts of such electrical

573

Aided by computers, these assemblers put together electronic parts at a Honeywell plant.

Requirements

Applicants for assembly jobs should have aptitude for mechanical work. They should be dependable and physically capable of doing the work assigned to them, and should be able to do routine work at a steady, rapid pace. Workers should also be able to learn the tasks required of them in a brief period of time. Assemblers must be careful in the performance of routine tasks and must be able to get along well with their fellow employees. Hand-eye coordination is also important.

There are no special educational requirements for work as an assembler, but a high-school education would prove valuable as a means of advancing to a more responsible position as a skilled assembler. High-school courses in mechanical and industrial arts, including work in blueprint reading and electronics, should prove helpful.

Special requirements

Some precision assembly jobs do have special requirements. For example, some assembly workers in the electronics industry are required to take tests for color blindness. This requirement is necessary because these workers deal with products containing a great many wires and other materials of different colors. Other assembly jobs have comparable requirements.

Opportunities for experience and exploration

The most common method of gaining experience as an assembler is to accept a summer position in a factory that employs assemblers. Another means of gaining experience is to enroll in electronics courses or other courses in high school that require students to gain a knowledge of the manner in which certain products are constructed and assembled. Some people can gain high-level assembly skills in the armed forces. The least that an interested person can do is to visit a factory and watch assemblers at work.

Related occupations

Other workers who need eye-hand coordination and skills such as assemblers have included

equipment as light sockets, switches, and plugs. They fit together, by hand, many small parts, such as plastic socket bases, shafts, contacts, springs, washers, and terminals, in a prearranged sequence by using a screwdriver. They test the operation of moving parts and remove faulty parts.

Precision assemblers put together items that, as the name implies, require great accuracy. Aerospace, electronics, and medical equipment industries all need machines that are extremely accurate. Precision assemblers build these machines.

A *hand assembler* in a paper goods factory fits together and secures fabricated parts of paper containers, such as spout-type salt containers or powder-puff boxes.

The *hypodermic needle assembler* drives hypodermic needles into needle hubs with a mallet to complete hypodermic needle assemblies and inspects assemblies for defects, such as bent or rough needles, incorrect length, bevel, or points on needles, and loosely fitted parts, by using gauges and hand tools.

Other assemblers work in the jewelry, leather, tire, boat building, and many other industries.

jewelers, jewelry repairers, locksmiths, opticians, and watch repairers.

About 353,000 of them were classified as precision assemblers.

Methods of entering

The most common way to enter this line of work is to apply directly to a factory that employs assemblers. Advertisements for assemblers will appear in the "help wanted" section of a local newspaper. Inexperienced workers are hired and trained on the job to do semiskilled assembling work. The training period lasts only a few hours or at most a few weeks. Once trainees acquire sufficient speed and efficiency in the work they are expected to do, they become personally responsible for the quality of the work they produce. Because factories have their own training programs, officials often prefer trainees who have had no experience in the work to be done. They prefer to train applicants to use the employer's assembly methods.

Advancement

In assembly work, the possibilities for advancement are limited. A few assemblers do manage to become skilled inspectors or supervisors. Other assemblers who know how to read blueprints and who have had training in shop mathematics can acquire positions as skilled assemblers. Some assemblers may take courses in evening schools or technical institutes and eventually advance to jobs as technicians, junior engineers, or, in a small number of cases, professional engineers.

Employment outlook

The employment outlook is generally favorable, although the need for assemblers will vary greatly by industry. Technological developments may decrease the need for hand assemblers in some industries. There is also a relationship between the number of assembly jobs and such factors as general business conditions and the defense needs of the nation. Adverse conditions generally result in layoffs. Nevertheless, it is expected that there will be a moderate job increase in the need for assemblers in the foreseeable future, especially in those industries that produce electrical and electronic products. In the early 1990s, more than 1 million people earned their livelihoods as assemblers.

Earnings

There are wide variations in the earnings of semiskilled assembly workers. The earnings of assemblers are related to the kind of skill involved in the assembly process, the type of product assembled, the size and location of the plant in which they are employed, and the way in which they are paid. It should be noted that assemblers are paid in two major ways: a straight hourly wage, or by piecework; that is, pay is determined by the number of items assembled. It is often possible for adept assemblers on piecework to make more money than those assemblers who receive a straight hourly wage.

Earnings of assemblers vary widely throughout the country. In the early 1990s, the median annual salary was about $18,150. Assemblers who work in manufacturing industries generally enjoy a number of fringe benefits, which include holiday and vacation pay, health insurance, life insurance, and retirement pensions.

Conditions of work

Most assemblers work a standard forty-hour week, although they are expected to work longer during rush periods. Because there are so many kinds of assemblers, it is difficult to describe working conditions that apply to all of them. For example, some assemblers work in clean and well-lighted rooms. Other assemblers work in rooms where there is much oil and grease. Again, some assemblers must work with heavy equipment and are subject to physical strain. Others work with tiny equipment, and eyestrain is a frequent complaint. Assembly line workers are often under pressure to complete a task in a given amount of time. They must complete an assembly task as items move by their work stations on a conveyor belt. Many assemblers must stand to perform their work.

Social and psychological factors

Assemblers must have patience and must be able to work under pressure. Because of these requirements, many employers have found that young people who are school dropouts have difficulty with assembly work. It is also necessary that assemblers relate well with their fellow workers—since they spend much of their workday in working quarters close to each other.

Two other psychological factors should be mentioned. First, most assemblers will spend their lives doing assembly work. There is little opportunity for advancement. Therefore, assemblers must be able to tolerate routine work and expect to do it for the rest of their lives. Second, assemblers are subject to lengthy layoffs in periods of economic recession. Such situations may interfere with long-range plans they have made that require steady financial outlays.

A number of assemblers belong to labor unions, especially those assemblers who work in manufacturing industries. Unions in which assemblers hold membership include the International Association of Machinists; the International Union of Electrical, Radio, and Machine Workers; and the International Union, United Automobile, Aircraft and Agricultural Implement Workers of America.

GOE: 06.04; SIC: Any industry; SOC: 772

◇ **SOURCES OF ADDITIONAL INFORMATION**

Motor Vehicle Manufacturers Association of the United States
7430 Second Avenue, Suite 300
Detroit, MI 48202

National Association of Manufacturers
1331 Pennsylvania Avenue, NW, Suite 1500N
Washington, DC 20004

◇ **RELATED ARTICLES**

Volume 1: Aviation and Aerospace; Automotives; Electronics; Plastics
Volume 3: Aircraft mechanics; Automobile mechanics; Electrical repairers; Plastic products manufacturing workers; see also Bench work occupations
Volume 4: Aeronautical and aerospace technicians; Automotive, diesel, and gas turbine technicians; Electronics technicians; Plastics technicians

Furniture manufacturing occupations

Definition

The manufacture of high-grade wooden furniture requires the services of a number of skilled artisans, including *cabinetmakers, hand carvers, furniture finishers,* and *finished-stock inspectors.*

History

The use of furniture for comfort and decoration goes back to the beginnings of human civilization. Over the centuries, furniture has been made in many styles, from classically simple to heavy and ornately carved pieces. Until quite recently, wood was the basic material for almost all tables, chairs, beds, chests, and other items of household furniture. Modern designers have produced innovative and exciting furniture in metal and plastics. There is still, however, a great demand for quality furniture in traditional styles, for which wood is still the indispensable and inimitable material.

The furniture industry in the United States began with the first colonists. The simple, utilitarian wooden articles produced at first soon gave way to more elegant products, as skilled craft workers emigrated from Europe and began producing copies and variations on English and French designs. As tools and skills improved so did the ornamentation on furniture.

Furniture production remained a handicraft in the United States until the 1820s, when woodworking machinery was introduced. Furniture factories were built near sources of wood and water power, especially in the Midwest. Grand Rapids, Michigan, was one of the early centers of furniture manufacturing, and is still often referred to as the "furniture capital of America." In recent years, North Carolina has become the leading state in the country in the manufacture of wooden furniture.

Nature of the work

Cabinetmakers construct articles of furniture, using blueprints or drawings as guides. They select lumber of the proper color, grain, and texture for the furniture piece and draw the outlines of the parts on it. They use a power saw to cut out the separate parts of the piece. The parts are trimmed and shaped with a plane and wood chisel so they will fit together smoothly. The cabinetmaker glues or nails the parts of the piece together or bores holes for the insertion of dowels. When the piece is fully assembled, it is sanded and scraped before it is sent to the finisher. The sanding and scraping phase is surface preparation. This precedes staining, coloring, or waxing. Cabinetmakers or finishers may do the preparation. Hardware, such as hinges, doorknobs, and drawer pulls, may also be installed.

Hand carvers carve ornamental designs, such as scrolls and stylized leaves and flowers, in furniture parts. They may create and sketch the design or work from a sketch furnished by an architect, furniture designer, or customer. They draw the design to scale and transfer the outline to the furniture part by tracing over the drawing and a piece of carbon paper with a stylus. They clamp the part in a vise and rough out the design, using a chisel, mallet, jig saw, and router. The rough design is then refined and trimmed, using precise hand tools.

Furniture finishers use sandpaper or a power sander to smooth the surface of raw wood furniture prior to finishing. They select and mix the ingredients that will produce the specified finish. After removing or masking hardware and other parts not intended to be finished, they brush or spray coats of stain, varnish, shellac, or paint on the piece, then, after the coating is dry, polish and wax the piece and replace any parts that were removed during finishing. Some finishers specialize in antiquing, which produces highlights and shadings on a wood surface by rubbing with cloth or abrasives after staining.

Finished-stock inspectors examine completed articles of furniture to ensure that they meet specifications. If they detect a minor defect, such as a slight roughness in a drawer edge, they may smooth it with sandpaper or a plane. Minor defects in the finish are repaired with a heated blade and sticks of wax and lacquer.

An aspiring cabinetmaker receives guidance from his instructor. He may work as an apprentice for several years before he is considered an expert in cabinetry.

Requirements

Skilled furniture craft workers are creative artists in wood, producing items of aesthetic beauty and usefulness with their hands. Manual dexterity, good eyesight, a sense of proportion and balance, and the ability to visualize written specifications and drawings in terms of three-dimensional objects are important attributes for the cabinetmaker and hand carver.

High-school graduation is desirable but not essential for jobs in furniture manufacturing. Courses in woodworking, shop, blueprint reading, mathematics, and English are helpful.

Special requirements

There are no special requirements for furniture manufacturing occupations.

Opportunities for experience and exploration

An interest in whittling and woodworking as a hobby provides a valuable background for a prospective furniture craft worker. Summer jobs in furniture factories are often available for students. These jobs may not require much skill, but at least the student will have the opportunity to watch skilled artisans at work.

Many vocational schools and adult education programs offer courses in furniture making.

Related occupations

Other workers who are involved with furniture and textiles include furniture upholsterers, textile manufacturing workers, and furniture movers.

Methods of entering

Most furniture workers begin as helpers or apprentices. Several years of apprenticeship or on-the-job training are usually required for a furniture craft worker to become proficient in a chosen area of skill. Some furniture repair shops also offer a chance to learn construction skills.

Advancement

Furniture craft workers can expect regular salary increases as they gain experience and proficiency. Those with above-average skills and organizational ability may become supervisors of projects.

Employment outlook

In the early 1990s, more than 165,000 people were employed in the manufacture of wooden furniture in the United States, producing articles made entirely of wood (tables, chests of drawers) and the wooden frames for upholstered furniture (sofas, easy chairs).

During that period, there was a shortage of skilled furniture craft workers in the United States, especially in the South. Vocational programs were instituted in many areas to meet this need. The outlook for furniture manufacturing jobs is expected to remain favorable through the next decade.

Earnings

The average annual earnings of all furniture manufacturing workers in the early 1900s was more than $12,500. Skilled artisans with several years' experience could expect to earn considerably more.

Conditions of work

Furniture factories and workshops are usually clean and well-lighted. The sawdust and wood shavings that accumulate are not serious irritants, especially if they are kept moist. Workers who use power tools to cut wood are usually required to wear safety glasses. Attention must be paid while operating dangerous equipment.

Some of the jobs in this field require prolonged standing and stooping. Workers may also have to lift and turn heavy pieces of furniture.

Social and psychological factors

Furniture craft workers should enjoy working with their hands to create a product that bears the stamp of individuality. Patience, good judgment, and meticulous care are essential qualities for jobs in this field. There can be great satisfaction in working with wood, a natural substance that is pleasing to both the eye and the hand.

GOE: 05.03, 05.05; SIC: 251, 252; SOC: 772

◇ **SOURCES OF ADDITIONAL INFORMATION**

American Furniture Manufacturers Association
PO Box HP-7
High Point, NC 27261

American Association of Furniture Designers
PO Box 2688
High Point, NC 27261

◇ **RELATED ARTICLES**

Volume 1: Furniture
Volume 3: Carpenters; Furniture upholsterers

Furniture upholsterers

Definition

A *furniture upholsterer* restores old or worn upholstered furniture. Repairing frames, replacing the fabric, and replacing the springs and webbing are some of the steps taken in the upholstery process.

History

Before the 1400s, chairs and couches were made comfortable by putting loose cushions against the back and on the seat of the furniture. Later, during the Italian Renaissance, it became the style to attach the cushions to the frames of the furniture.

Nature of the work

The upholsterer first removes the worn fabric and, if necessary, any materials covering the springs. Any broken or bent springs must then be replaced. If the webbing that holds the springs is worn it must be ripped out. The frame is now exposed and if it appears loose some regluing may be needed. Webbing strips are stretched lengthwise and crosswise on the frame, interlacing where they cross. The number of strips is determined by the number of springs used. Tacks are used to hold the strips in place on the underside of the furniture. The springs are then placed in position and tied with twine. Diagonal twines offer double security. Burlap is used to form a covering for the stuffing that pads the springs. Curled horsehair and foam rubber are examples of materials used for padding. The upholsterer then cuts the fabric, sews it where necessary, and fits it smoothly on to the prepared padding. Specific types of workers include inside *upholsterers,* who do mostly work with padding, and *upholstery repairers,* who will repair worn upholstery but not necessarily replace it.

Upholsterers use few tools in their work. Hammers, scissors, tacks, staples, and pliers are some of the small hand tools used in the upholstery process. A special tool, a webbing stretcher, is used to do the tight stretching of the webbing and the fabrics. Upholsterer needles and a sewing machine are used in the final stage.

An upholsterer employed in a small shop lays out the pattern and cuts the fabrics. Upholsterers employed in a larger shop might do only one of these. A small shop usually employs ten or fewer employees. In the early 1990s, more than three-fourths of the upholsterers were employed in small shops. Other places of employment are chain operations such as motels, hotels, and theaters. Department stores and furniture stores frequently have their own upholstery departments. Most upholsterers are employed in larger cities.

Requirements

Some tools are used in the upholstery process, and coordination is needed, especially with the stretching of fabric and webbing. Upholsterers must know how to figure yardage of fabric needed and the correct way to cut fabric.

A strong back is necessary, as frequently the upholsterer lifts and moves heavy pieces of furniture. The constant pulling and stretching of fabrics is a strain on the back, also.

Special requirements

There are no special requirements other than those already mentioned.

Opportunities for experience and exploration

Some high-school students are hired for summers or after-school hours and Saturday work. Students are given tasks to do in the shop according to the ability and skill that they display. Upholsterers usually have a small van or truck to pick up furniture for upholstery, and frequently hire students to help in the pick up and delivery of the furniture.

High schools and vocational schools sometimes offer courses in upholstery. A brief course is frequently offered in evening adult education programs.

Furniture upholsterers must be able to hand-sew sections of fabric in awkward places that machines cannot reach. In addition, they must have the strength to tug padding and fabric into place.

Related occupations

Other workers with similar talents and skills include seamstresses and tailors, apparel industry workers, and furniture manufacturing occupations.

Methods of entering

Becoming an upholsterer aid or helper is one way to learn the trade. During the training a helper will begin by removing old fabric, padding, or springs from furniture. As experience is gained, the helper moves on to more difficult tasks. The on-the-job training could be mastered in two to three years if the helper learns quickly and has initiative. Assistant positions may be available in furniture production houses and factories. Some small reupholstery and furniture repair businesses may also hire beginners to train.

There are formal apprenticeship programs that take from three to four years, including classroom instruction and laboratory work.

Advancement

An upholsterer who has extensive on-the-job training and has shown competence will be able to expect a higher salary and in some shops promotion. The experienced upholsterer with management skills can also open a shop or become the manager of the upholstery department in a furniture store.

Employment outlook

In the early 1990s, nearly half of the estimated 63,000 upholsterers were employed in New York, California, Pennsylvania, Texas, Illinois, and Ohio.

Little change is expected in the employment of upholsterers through the next decade. Most of the job openings each year occur because of death or retirement, and these figures are not expected to change remarkably.

Earnings

There is no available national basis figure on earnings. Some sources indicate that experienced upholsterers receive about $19,900 to $30,000 annually. Occasionally, upholsterers are paid on a piecework basis. The salary for upholsterers is determined by experience, length of time with present employer, and the location where employed. Upholsterers working in the North, West, and East can usually expect a higher salary than in the South.

Conditions of work

Because most of the upholsterer's work is indoors, the shop is usually large enough to give the upholsterer space to move around. The shops are generally well ventilated, because there is some dust caused by removing old stuffing.

Back strain is common with upholsterers, as they must frequently stand or bend in awkward positions while working. The furniture is moved several times during the upholstery process, and this moving of furniture can also entail strenuous physical labor.

The workweek is normally forty hours a week, with some overtime at peak times of the year. In most shops it is possible to receive paid vacations and sick leave. Some shops provide a health insurance plan.

The upholsterer who works in an upholstery department of a department store receives a discount on all purchases.

Social and psychological factors

The tools an upholsterer works with are not dangerous. An experienced upholsterer has little difficulty in handling the tools of the trade. There is a labor union.

GOE: 05.05.15; SIC: 7641; SOC: 6853

◇ **SOURCES OF ADDITIONAL INFORMATION**

National Association of Professional Upholsterers
PO Box 2754
200 South Main
High Point, NC 27261

International Institute of Carpentry and Upholstery Certification
3715 East Mill Plain
Vancouver, WA 98661

For information on the general field of furniture manufacturing, contact:

American Society of Furniture Designers
PO Box 2688
High Point, NC 27261

◇ **RELATED ARTICLES**

Volume 1: Furniture
Volume 3: Furniture manufacturing occupations

Instrument repairers

Definition

Instrument repairers inspect, test, repair, and adjust the many instruments, gauges, meters, and indicators that monitor industrial operations and flow of materials through equipment and engines.

History

The term "instrument" is a broad name for a large variety of mechanisms that monitor and measure physical characteristics. Some familiar everyday instruments include the electric meter on a house, a car's speedometer and tachometer, a thermostat control, a boat's compass and barometer, and scales of all types. Instruments are used even more widely in industry, especially manufacturing, refining and power generating. Among the physical characteristics that instruments measure are temperature, pressure, combustion, liquid flow and level, acidity and alkalinity, weight and distance.

Over the years, as many human activities in industry were taken over by automation, the accuracy of instruments became increasingly crucial. In keeping these mechanisms working properly, instrument repairers have a very great responsibility. Defective instruments in hospitals could endanger people's health. In power plants, meters that don't function could result in millions of dollars lost to the power company. Passengers' safety in airplanes and trains depends on accurate instrumentation. Instrument repairers perform a vital service in literally hundreds of fields of endeavor.

Nature of the work

Instrument repairers can work in many different types of environments. Some *instrument repairers* work in auto repair shops, fixing speed-

581

An instrument repairer is shaving off uneven sections of a damaged machine.

ometers and odometers. *Meter repairers* work for utility companies and spend time at people's homes testing, cleaning, and repairing their gas and water meters. Other repairers work in heavy industry. *Scale balancers* inspect and adjust the mechanisms of scales to ensure their accuracy and proper balance. *Gas-regulator repairers* work on relief valves, gas regulators (governors), and other equipment to control gas pressure in city gas mains, pipelines, in-plant gas systems, and petroleum refineries. As manufacturing plants became more and more automated, the instruments that monitor the condition of products and materials have grown more complex. *Electromechanical inspectors* inspect and test many of the devices that are used in automated production, using very precise measuring and testing devices. Among the instruments regularly repaired are voltmeters, ammeters, ohmmeters, barometers, altimeters, position indicators, and pressure and steam gauges.

At times it is obvious that an instrument needs to be repaired, because what it is measuring is readily observable. At other times, the instrument must be kept on a regular maintenance schedule to perform with the best results. The instrument repairer is usually well versed in the design of most of the instruments that need to be tested. The repairer, however, still needs to consult references often, including blueprints, manufacturer's instructions, diagrams, and troubleshooting manuals.

The repairer is often forced to remove the instrument to inspect it. This is usually done with basic hand tools such as wrenches and screwdrivers. The instrument repairer may disassemble the entire apparatus, remove deposits and debris with a wire brush, clean it using solvents, lubricate it if necessary, and replace any parts that may be worn or defective. Hand tools

that may be used here include soldering irons, calipers, and micrometers.

The instrument repairer then calibrates the instrument to a specified standard and tests it to make sure it is working. To "calibrate" an instrument is to mark it so that it can be used to measure something meaningfully; a thermometer, for example, is calibrated to show degrees of temperature. Calibration and testing often take place simultaneously. The repairer will usually hook up some sort of testing device or meter to determine if the instrument is working properly. For example, on a natural gas pipeline, the instrument repairer may use a testing device to see how many cubic feet of gas are currently travelling through the pipe, then calibrate the permanent instrument to equal this amount.

After reinstalling the instrument, the instrument repairer will record in a notebook the date of repair, the problem, and the steps taken to fix it. Some instrument repairers work for the instrument's manufacturer and visit the factories that use the instrument. They show the factory workers how the instrument operates and how to make adjustments and minor repairs to prevent major breakdowns. Other instrument repairers are employed full time at a power plant, refinery, manufacturing plant, airport, or other site, and have a regular schedule of instruments to maintain and repair.

Requirements

A high-school diploma is a must for instrument repairers, especially as instruments become more complex. Math and physics classes are important. English and social studies are also important, because instrument repairers must be able to read and follow instructions carefully and express themselves clearly in both speech and report writing. Machine and electrical shop classes will expose students to many relevant electrical and mechanical properties and equipment, and mechanical drawing classes will give students experience in reading blueprints and visualizing components and their mechanical relationships from diagrams.

Most firms prefer to hire workers who have some training beyond high school and experience in the industries that use the instruments in question. Two-year programs in electrical, mechanical, or instrument technology are offered at many community colleges and technical institutes. Students in these programs study courses in physics, electronics, electricity and mathematics that have direct relevance to a career as an instrument repairer. Instrument repair can also be learned from technical training in the armed forces, which can be helpful in getting a job after discharge from the service.

Another way to learn the skills of instrument repair is through apprenticeship programs offered by some manufacturers. An apprenticeship usually lasts from two to four years, and can consist of on-the-job training and classroom study. Sometimes instrument manufacturers offer training courses to the employees of their customers, where they learn about the maintenance and repair of newly purchased instruments.

Special requirements

There are no special requirements for this occupation.

Opportunities for experience and exploration

People who already work in industries that rely on instruments may get some exposure to how instruments are handled and maintained. For example, an airline mechanic may use a voltmeter to test the output of a plane's batteries, and may become interested enough in instrumentation to take additional classes in instrument repair.

Related occupations

Other workers employ many of the same skills and aptitudes in their work as do instrument repairers. These include instrument makers, musical instrument repairers and tuners, jewelers and jewelry repairers, and appliance repairers.

Methods of entering

High-school graduates should contact the personnel departments of the industries that construct, use, or repair instrument systems. There they can get information about job and training opportunities and apprenticeship programs. Want ads in the newspaper and job listings with public and private job services can give job seekers an idea of where the greatest number of opportunities are.

Many community colleges and technical schools have placement offices to help their new graduates find jobs. Graduates may contact these firms in person or send out resumes.

Advancement

With enough experience, an instrument repairer may be promoted to the position of *instrument maintenance supervisor*. These supervisors oversee and coordinate the work of the instrument repairers in a department, occasionally trouble-shooting in difficult situations. Instrument repairers may also go to work as sales or service representatives for the firms that manufacture instruments.

As instruments become more and more complex, instrument repairers are well advised to continue with their education while employed. This will enable them to be ready when technical advances affect their work. With enough education, instrument repairers may advance to higher paying positions such as engineering assistant, engineering technician or electronics engineer.

Employment outlook

Through the early 1990s, experts forecast a slight increase in the demand for instrument repairers. This will be a result, in part, of the increase in automated manufacturing and the demand for more utility services such as electricity and telephone service. The health care industry will also need more instrument repairers as diagnostic and therapeutic machinery becomes more advanced.

Earnings

Instrument repairers are generally paid on the same scale as other skilled maintenance workers. While rates vary among industries and with the job performed, instrument repairers were paid an average weekly wage of between $413 and $523 in the early 1990s. Overtime and night or weekend work usually pays more. Those instrument repairers who travel to distant locations on service calls are usually given an expense account to compensate for on-the-job costs and travel expenses. Instrument repairers also receive benefits such as paid vacations, cost of living allowances, health and hospital insurance, and pension plans.

Conditions

Instrument repairers work in various conditions depending on their job assignments. Those who inspect newly manufactured instruments usually work in clean, comfortable surroundings, often using their own workbench and tools. Because of the precision the work involves, the environment is usually quiet and well equipped. When an instrument repairer has to inspect instruments on site, conditions can vary widely. The instrument may be located in a loud, dirty factory, in a remote area, in an airplane hangar, or in a hospital.

Instrument repairers generally work a forty-hour, five-day week. Some may be called in emergencies to troubleshoot a problem. They may be on call during evenings and weekends, and have to respond quickly to problems that arise. In large factories that have instrument repairers on the payroll, repairers may be needed on each shift the plant operates.

Social and psychological factors

Mechanical skills, manual dexterity, and a keen mind are essential for instrument repairers. When confronted by an unexplained problem with an instrument, the instrument repairer needs to apply all of his or her technical knowledge until the problem is solved. This can take a great deal of patience and ingenuity. With the rapid advances of technology in this field, however, there will always be challenges for the ambitious instrument repairer and many exciting opportunities to take advantage of.

GOE: 05.05.10; SIC: Any industry; SOC: 6151

◇ RELATED ARTICLES

Volume 1: Computer Hardware; Computer Software; Electronics; Engineering
Volume 2: Biomedical engineers; Engineers; Medical technologists; Nuclear medicine technologists; Numerical control tool programmers
Volume 3: Air-conditioning, refrigeration, and heating mechanics; Aircraft mechanics and engine specialists; Appliance repairers; Automobile mechanics; Flight engineers; Industrial machinery mechanics; Instrument makers; Office machine servicers
Volume 4: Calibration technicians; Electronics test technicians; Instrumentation technicians; Nuclear instrumentation technicians; Test technicians

Jewelers and jewelry repairers

Definition

Jewelers fabricate, either from their own design or one by a design specialist, rings, necklaces, bracelets, and other precious jewelry out of gold, silver, or platinum. They also make repairs, alter ring sizes, reset stones, and refashion old jewelry. Restringing beads and stones, resetting clasp and hinges, and mending breaks in ceramic and metal pieces are other aspects of the *jewelry repairer's* job.

A few jewelers are also *gemologists*, who examine, grade, and evaluate gems, or *gem cutters*, who cut, shape, and polish gemstones.

History

There is not a time known when people have not worn adornments of some type. Beads have been found in the graves of prehistoric peoples. During the Iron Age, jewelry was made of ivory, wood, or metal. Precious stones were being bought and sold at least 4,000 years ago in ancient Babylon, and there was also widespread trade in jewelry by the Phoenicians and others in the Mediterranean and Asia Minor.

The art of jewelry making was known in ancient Egypt and Greece as well as in the Indian civilizations of North and South America. The jeweler's art reached a high level of skill during the Renaissance.

Although jewelry is used primarily for decorative purposes, it has also been used by primitive peoples as protection against evil spirits and by nobility as a sign of rank. It is also a form of wealth, with fabulous sums being paid for expensive gems.

In earlier societies, jewelry was made by hand, and skillful jewelers still employ this means today. Costume jewelry and synthetic gems, however, are machine-made.

Once a piece of jewelry is sketched on paper, the jeweler then creates a wax model that will then be cast into a precious metal.

Nature of the work

The materials of the jeweler and the jewelry repairer are usually precious and semiprecious or synthetic stones and gold, silver, and platinum. The jeweler begins by forming an article in wax or metal with carving tools and then places the wax model in a casting ring and pours plaster into the ring to form a mold. The mold is then inserted in a furnace to melt the wax. A metal model is then cast from the plaster mold. The jeweler pours the precious molten metal into the mold or uses a centrifugal casting machine to cast the article. Final touches, such as cutting, filing, and polishing, complete the work.

Jewelers do most of their work sitting down. They are constantly using their eyes and fingers. Small hand and machine tools such as drills, files, saws, soldering irons, and jewelers' lathes are used to make the jewelry. Jewelers' work must be done with extreme precision and patience because of the expensive nature of the materials that they use. They often wear an eye "loupe," or magnifying glass.

Jewelers usually specialize in creating or making certain kinds of jewelry, or in a particular operation such as making, polishing, or stone-setting models and tools. Specialists include *stone setters, fancy-wire drawers,* and *locket, ring, hand chain makers,* and *sample makers.*

Experienced jewelers may become qualified to make and repair any kind of jewelry. Assembly-line methods employing factory workers are used to produce costume jewelry and some types of precious jewelry, but the models and tools needed for factory production must be made by highly skilled jewelers. Costume jewelry is often made by a die stamping process.

Jewelers and jewelry repairers are both self-employed and employed by manufacturing and retail establishments. Although some jewelers operate their own retail stores, an increasing number of jewelry stores are owned or managed by business persons who are not jewelers. In such instances, a jeweler or jewelry repairer may be employed by the owner, or the store may send its repairs to a trade shop operated by a jeweler who specializes in repair work. Jewelers who operate their own stores sell jewelry, watches, and, frequently, such merchandise as silverware, china, and glassware. Most retail jewelry stores are located in or near large cities, with the eastern section of the nation providing most of the employment in jewelry manufacturing.

Requirements

Extreme patience and skill are needed by the jeweler to handle the expensive materials of the trade. Although the physically handicapped may find employment in this field, superior eye-hand coordination is essential. Basic mechanical skills such as filing, sawing, and drilling are vital to the jewelry repairer. Jewelers who work from their own designs need to have artistic ability, as well as good eyesight and finger dexterity. Retail jewelers, and those who operate or own trade shops and manufacturing establishments, must possess the ability to deal with other people and a knowledge of business management and practices.

A high-school education is normally necessary for persons desiring to enter the jewelry trade. High-school courses in chemistry, physics, mechanical drawing, and art are especially useful. Jewelry repair courses are offered by some trade schools that teach watchmaking and watch repairing. The work of the jeweler and jewelry repairer may also be learned through an apprenticeship or by informal on-the-job training. On-the-job training will often include instruction in design, quality of precious stones, and chemistry of metals. The apprentice becomes a jeweler upon the successful completion of a three- to four-year apprenticeship. Also, the apprentice is usually required to pass written and oral tests covering the trade. The apprenticeship generally involves three levels or steps.

Special requirements

Because of the expensive nature of the jeweler's materials, many employers require jewelers and jewelry repairers to be bonded. The companies that do the bonding normally look into the applicant's background for information about his honesty and trustworthiness.

Opportunities for experience and exploration

It is possible to explore jewelry as a career while still in high school by visiting retail stores and shops where jewelry is repaired and made, as well as jewelry factories. One may observe the jeweler's routine and become acquainted with jewelry terminology by securing part-time employment during the school year or summers as a clerk or salesperson in a retail jewelry store. Many trade shops where jewelry is made and repaired are one- and two-person operations, and their size restricts the possibilities for experience and exploration in this area. Interested students may interview local jewelers for additional information and personal observations.

Related occupations

Other workers who have skills and interests similar to jewelers include instrument makers, instrument repairers, silverware industry workers, and assemblers.

Methods of entering

The best method of entering this line of work is to obtain employment in jewelry manufacturing establishments in major production centers. A trainee is thus able to acquire the many skills needed in the jewelry trade. The number of trainees accepted in this manner, however, is relatively small. Persons desiring to establish their own retail business will find it helpful to first obtain employment with an established jeweler or a manufacturing plant. Considerable financial investment is required to open a retail jewelry store, and jewelers in such establishments find it to their advantage to be able to do repair work on watches as well as the usual jeweler's work. Less financial investment is needed to open a trade shop. These shops generally tend to be more successful in or near large population centers where they can take advantage of the large volume of jewelry business. Both of these establishments (retail stores and trade shops) are required to meet local and state business laws and regulations.

Advancement

Advancement in this field depends on individual skill and initiative and, if one works for a manufacturing establishment, the promotion policies of a given company. The most usual avenue of advancement is from employee in a factory, shop, or store to owner or manager of a trade shop or retail store. Owning and operating one's own shop is also possible.

Employment outlook

Approximately 38,000 jewelers and jewelry repairers were employed in the early 1990s.

The employment outlook is about average for this occupation. An expanding population should require more jewelers than have been employed in the past. In addition, it is estimated that several hundred jewelers are needed each year to replace those who leave the trade because of death, retirement, or transfer to other occupations. Both skilled all-around jewelers and specialists should have no problem in obtaining employment in jewelry factories, whereas employment in retail stores is limited to those stores large enough to employ a trained staff of jewelers and jewelry repairers.

Earnings

In the early 1990s, full-time jewelry store sales employees received a median annual wage of about $18,700. Those dealing with diamonds averaged $21,600. Skilled manufacturing workers made from $17,470 to $45,000. Store managers averaged about $30,000, and owners, $42,000 or more.

Conditions of work

The working conditions of the retail jeweler are similar to those of skilled workers who operate or work in other retail establishments. They usually work a forty- to forty-eight-hour week, with some seasonal variation at Christmas and Easter. The production worker in New York City is under contract for a thirty-five-hour week and is paid time and a half for all time in excess of the thirty-five hours. Seasonal variations also affect the hours of the production workers and those who work in trade shops. Normally there is some unemployment following seasonal peaks.

Social and psychological factors

Jewelers and jewelry repairers must be able to engage in painstaking, concentrated work. While the work is not physically strenuous, it requires an interest in detailed and exacting activity. The necessity for better than average finger and hand dexterity and eye-hand coordination can be a source of frustration to anyone who lacks these skills. The precision instruments of the jeweler can also result in numerous cuts and scratches of the fingers. Jewelers employed in New York in jewelry manufacturing companies are members of the Service Employees International Union.

GOE: 01.06.02; SIC: 3911, 7631; SOC: 6822

◇ **SOURCES OF ADDITIONAL INFORMATION**

Jewelers of America
1271 Avenue of the Americas
New York, NY 10020

Manufacturing Jewelers and Silversmiths of America
The Biltmore Plaza Hotel
3rd Floor
Kennedy Plaza
Providence, RI 02903

◇ **RELATED ARTICLES**

Volume 1: Design; Retailing
Volume 2: Designers; Fashion designers

Locksmiths

Definition

Locksmiths, or *lock experts,* install, repair, and replace locks, door and window closers, and exit devices. They disassemble locks both to make repairs and to revise combinations. They open locks that have missing keys, cut new keys, or make duplicate keys.

Some locksmiths specialize in designing and making locks. *Locksmith apprentices* aid the locksmiths they work with, while learning, practicing, and finally mastering their chosen craft.

History

The desire to guard and protect families, residences, and possessions is ancient and probably universal. The earliest known lock and key, about 4,000 years old and quite large in size, were found in the ruins of Khorsabad palace near the biblical city of Nineveh. They were of the wooden pin-tumbler type—later widely used in Egypt and even found in Japan, Norway, and the Faeroe Islands—that eventually developed into the steel Yale lock. The Romans introduced metal locks (primarily iron and bronze), padlocks, warded locks, and, most importantly, small locks—with even smaller keys. Elaborate and intricate decorative surface design introduced in Germany and France during the Middle Ages, transformed locks into works of art, but were little improved in safety or security.

Then, in England in 1778, Robert Barron patented a lever lock with double-acting tumblers, and just forty years later his countryman Jeremiah Chubb improved on its reliability by incorporating a detector in its mechanism. Meanwhile, Joseph Bramah, also from England, introduced his innovative Bramah lock and key in 1784 (it remained unpicked for more than fifty years). In 1851, Robert Newell of New York exhibited his Parautoptic lock (which supposedly remains unpicked to this day) at the Crystal Palace in London. The American Linus Yale had patented a pin-tumbler lock in 1848 from which his son Linus Yale, Jr., evolved the Yale cylinder lock during the 1860s. In 1873 James Sargent of Rochester, New York, adapted an earlier Scots patent for a lock that incorporated a clock, which allowed vaults or safes to be opened only at preset times. Others experimented with the "letter-lock," which was being used in England on trick boxes and toy padlocks, until the keyless combination lock, since used by banks, was perfected. Many other specialized locks were devised for specific purposes—but most of today's locks, at least the best thought of and the most commonly used, are but the improved direct descendants of the original Yale lever, Bramah, and combination devices. Security-conscious citizenry demands complicated, sophisticated locks, which, in turn, need knowledgeable care: locksmiths have never had it so good.

Nature of the work

Locksmiths install locks in homes, offices, and factories. They then spend part of their working day aiding those who have locked themselves out of their houses, places of work, or vehicles. If keys are locked inside, locksmiths can pick the lock, or if keys are lost, locksmiths can make new ones. Locksmiths repair locks by taking them apart to find out what is wrong; they examine, clean, file, and adjust the cylinders and tumblers—or they may just replace them.

Locksmiths may open a safe if its combination lock doesn't work smoothly, first by listening for vibrations when rotating the dial carefully and listening for the interior mechanism to indicate a change in direction—or then, if it does not open, by drilling. Manufacturing plants, banks, schools, hospitals, and other large institutions periodically contract locksmiths to rekey all of their locks. To rekey locks, components are changed.

Locksmiths do most of their work in shops. While working there, on such portable items as padlocks and luggage locks, they may explain and recommend to their customers specialty locks, safety doors, or other new protective products. Locksmiths who own their own businesses usually have to keep books and tax records, prepare statements, take mail to and from post offices, order merchandise, and inventory, display, and price goods.

Locksmiths find work in any community large enough to need their services, but there are always more jobs available in large metropolitan areas. Most locksmiths work in locksmith shops for other locksmiths, but many open their own businesses. Some locksmiths work for governmental veterans' hospitals, housing developments, military bases, and federal agencies. Others work for large hardware or department stores. Industrial complexes and huge factories employ locksmiths to install and maintain complete security systems. School systems, hotels and motels, and military compounds employ locksmiths to regularly install or change locks.

Requirements

Locksmiths must be able to plan and schedule jobs and to use the right tools, techniques, and materials for each. They should have good vision, especially for spatial perception, and good hearing, which is necessary when working with combination locks. Eye-hand coordination is essential when working with tiny locks and their intricate interiors. And, of course, all locksmiths must have tact and patience when dealing with their public.

Special requirements

Although there are no other individual requirements than those already mentioned, it is well to remember that many U.S. cities and counties require locksmiths to be licensed, and for that they must be fingerprinted and pay local fees. The trade has no labor union.

Opportunities for experience and exploration

Prospective locksmiths should take machine shop in high school to gain experience in using a variety of hand tools. Mathematics, mechanical drawing, and electronics would also be of use. The U.S. Department of Labor's Bureau of Apprenticeship and Training helps set up apprentice programs that often require up to four years of training. After a three-month probationary period, trainees become apprentices. Then they take 144 hours or more of formal classroom work for each year they stay in the program.

Initiates can also begin a locksmithing career by taking a correspondence course, in which they receive instructions, assignments, tools, and model locks and keys. Lessons can be supplemented with supervised on-the-job training when a master locksmith who will agree to do so is found.

Related occupations

Other workers with similar interests and skills include jewelers, jewelry repairers, musical instrument repairers, and watch repairers.

Methods of entering

Beginners should either apply at locksmith shops directly or check with state employment offices for business and industry listings of openings for locksmiths. On-the-job training usually begins under the supervision of journeyworker locksmiths or supervisors. Some students begin working by serving as helpers to locksmiths after school or during the summer, and some find correspondence courses helpful in getting their first jobs.

Advancement

Because most locksmiths regard their work as lifetime professions, they keep abreast of new developments in the field so that they can increase both their skills and earnings. Industrial locksmiths advance from apprentice to journeymen to master locksmith to any of several kinds of supervisory or managerial positions. They might also become any one of a number of specialists. One of the most promising recent specialty growth areas is that of electronic security. Such safety devices and systems are becoming standard equipment for banks, hotels, and many industries—and further growth is predicted.

Employment outlook

The locksmith employment outlook is excellent for the next decade. Population growth and an expanding public awareness of the need for preventive measures against home, business, and car burglary is creating a need for more security. Many individuals and firms are replacing older lock and alarm systems with the latest developments in computerized equipment. Industrial expansion and renewed home building are projected for the next decade. The occupation itself has remained a fairly stable one, and locksmiths with an extensive knowledge of their trade need rarely be unemployed.

Earnings

Locksmiths who are self-employed often work up to sixty hours a week. Apprentices and locksmiths working in industries and institutions usually work forty hours a week. In the early 1990s, experienced locksmiths earned an average of about $48,000 annually. Exact wages depend on the type of business, location, and number of out-of-shop calls. Self-employed locksmiths may be small business operators who earn less than some salaried employees, or they may head a large operation and earn much more through contracts with large businesses.

Conditions of work

Locksmiths stand much of their working time, but they also crouch, bend, stoop, and kneel while working. Sometimes they have to lift heavy gates, doors, and other objects when dealing with safes, strong rooms, or lock fittings, and they must also have stamina and patience. Locksmiths' workshops are usually well lit, well heated, and well ventilated. Some shops, particularly the mobile ones, however, may be so crowded and small that workers must move carefully around fixtures and stock. Some locksmiths must work outside installing or repairing protective or warning devices, and some do a lot of driving on assignments away from the shop. Some work alone much of the time, but many work at stores, banks, factories, or schools where there are usually people about. Physical injuries are not common, but minor ones can occur from soldering irons, welding equipment, electric shocks, flying bits from grinders, and sharp lock or key edges.

Social and psychological factors

Locksmiths must be reliable, accurate, and, most importantly, honest. They know that sat-isfied customers have to be assured of their skill, dependability, and integrity—and they derive personal satisfaction from knowing that they earn aural and visual thanks, trust, and confidence from clients.

This field of endeavor will appeal to persons who enjoy working with their hands, who are resourceful solving a variety of problems, and who like to deal with a wide range of customers in a number of settings. Each lost key, broken lock, or security problem is a unique challenge—so the job is never really repetitious or boring. The craft requires skill and training and a great deal of responsibility—not only for the valuable contents of safes and vaults and the shops' merchandise, but for every customer's peace of mind.

GOE: 05.05.09; SIC: 7699; SOC: 6173

◇ **SOURCES OF ADDITIONAL INFORMATION**

Associated Locksmiths of America
3003 Live Oak Street
Dallas, TX 75204

Locksmith Security Association
32630 Concord Drive
Madison Heights, MI 48071

National Locksmith Suppliers Association
1800 Arch Street
Philadelphia, PA 19103

◇ **RELATED ARTICLES**

Volume 3: Instrument makers; *see also*
Bench work occupations
Volume 4: Electromechanical technicians;
Mechanical technicians

Musical instrument repairers and tuners

Definition

There are a variety of musical instrument tuners and repairers, but the general responsibility of all of them is to maintain instruments so that they perform properly. The most numerous of these professionals are the *piano tuners* and the *pipe-organ tuners and repairers.*

History

The world's first musical instrument was the human body. Paleolithic dancers clapped, stamped, and chanted, and slapped their bodies to mark rhythm. Gourd rattles, bone whistles, scrapers, hollow branch and conch shell "trumpets," wooden rhythm pounders and knockers, and bullroarers followed. By the early Neolithic times, drums that produced two or more pitches and pottery and cane flutes that gave several notes were developed. The musical bow, a primitive stringed instrument and forerunner of the Jew's harp, preceded the bow-shaped harp (about 3000 B.C.) and the long-necked lute (about 2000 B.C.).

Just before the Christian era, the pipe organ—the first keyboard instrument—was invented in Alexandria. It utilized water power to send a stream of air through its pipes. A few centuries later, organs were built in Byzantium that used bellows to produce the air. From that time until about A.D. 1500, all the features of the modern pipe organ were developed.

The first fiddle, played by scraping a taut bow across several stretched strings, appeared in early medieval Europe and was followed by the harpsichord, whose strings were plucked. It was a Florentine harpsichord maker, Bartolommeo Cristofori, who in about 1709 first published a diagram and description of a pianoforte, which made music when its strings were struck. Although he built several of the instruments, Italian interest in them faded fast. Experimentation continued in Germany, however, and in about 1730 Gottfried Silberman perfected the type of pianoforte that was popularized by Wolfgang Amadeus Mozart and his contemporaries. Silberman's instrument was used on the European continent into the early nineteenth century. In the meantime, the English continued to make improvements—adding pedals, expanding the keyboard, and installing heavier action—until in 1830 the instrument reached a form similar to today's piano.

Contemporary orchestral instruments include percussion, woodwind, brass, and string families. All of them require some care and maintenance.

Nature of the work

People do not have to be musicians to recognize a flat note. Their pleasure in music, whether classical or rock, can be ruined by a poorly tuned instrument. It is the work of tuners and repairers to keep the instruments performing properly—an important job when you consider the millions of people who depend on music for entertainment.

Piano tuners, using a tuning hammer and fork, adjust piano strings so that they will be in proper pitch. When a piano key is pressed, it causes a felt-covered wooden hammer to strike a string to produce a note. The number of times a string vibrates per second is called its pitch. For a piano to be in tune, all the strings must be set at the right pitch.

The piano tuners remove the board from the front of an upright piano to expose the strings. They use felt or rubber strips to mute the sound of strings adjacent to the one they are testing. Beginning with "A" or the "C" string, they strike the key and compare the pitch to that of a standard tuning fork. If it does not match, they use a tuning hammer (sometimes called a "tuning lever" or "wrench") to turn the steel pin that tightens or loosens the string. When the tension of the string has been properly adjusted, its pitch will match that of the tuning fork. Then the tuners test the remaining strings and set them in relation to the "A" or the "C" string. It takes about an hour and a half to tune the 230 strings of a standard eighty-eight-key piano.

Most piano tuners work in repair shops or in homes or establishments where the instruments are located, but some may work in piano factories, making the initial adjustments.

icate sound from one pipe or music as complex and as loud (especially in the largest organs) as that of a symphony orchestra.

Pipe-organ tuners and repairers and *organ-pipe voicers* service organs that make music by forcing air through two kinds of pipes: flue pipes and reed pipes. The flue pipe produces a note when a current of air strikes the metal lip of an opening on the side of the pipe. The note is determined by the length of the pipe. A reed pipe sounds when air vibrates a slender brass reed inside the pipe. The length of the reed, along with the size and length of the pipe, determines the note.

To tune a flue pipe, a slide is moved that increases or decreases the length of the "speaking" (note-producing) part of the pipe, varying its pitch. A reed pipe is tuned by varying the length of the brass reed inside the pipe.

To tune an organ, the "A" pipes are first tuned by matching their pitch with that of a tuning fork. The other pipes are then adjusted with reference to the tuned pipes. Tuning may require a day or more for a moderate-sized organ, and much longer for a giant, concert organ.

Pipe-organ repairers also diagnose, locate, and correct problems in the operating parts of the organ. This involves working with the electric wind-generating equipment and with the slides, valves, keys, air channels, and other equipment that enable the organist to produce the music desired. They also perform preventive maintenance, such as cleaning pipes, on a regular basis.

Occasionally a new organ is installed in a new or existing church or auditorium. The largest organs are designed and installed by the manufacturer. Each is unique, and its construction and installation are carefully supervised by the designer. Moderate-sized organs, usually installed in churches, are also often individually designed for the structure in which they will be played. *Pipe-organ installers* are sometimes employed to assemble organs by following the designer's blueprints closely during installation. The work involves assembling and connecting premanufactured components, such as the air chest, blowers, air ducts, and pipes, using a variety of hand and power tools. Installers may work in teams, especially with the largest pipes of the organ. An installation job may take weeks or even months, depending on the size of the organ.

Violin repairers specialize in maintaining bowed instruments (violins, violas, and cellos), inspecting them for broken or defective parts, playing them to detect poor sound, and adjusting and repairing them when necessary. *Bow rehairers* maintain the quality of the taut, vibrat-

Concentrating on his craft, a musical instrument repairer tunes a snare drum.

Because pianos and organs work differently, repairers rarely work on both instruments. Furthermore, organ repairers themselves fall into two groups, specializing in either pipe organs or *electronic organs.*

A pipe organ consists of three major parts: a source of a stream of air (in modern organs, usually an electric motor and fan or compressor), a series of keyboards to regulate the flow of air into the various pipes, and the pipes themselves, arranged in ranks (rows).

A large pipe organ may contain as many as 5,000 separate pipes; a small organ usually has about 200 pipes. These pipes range in size from seven inches in length and one-quarter inch in diameter to 30 feet in length and more than a foot in diameter. The largest organs may have as many as six keyboards to enable the organist to combine the sounds of as many of the pipes as possible.

As the organist plays, air is directed into the various ranks of pipes, and from there into individual pipes. The combination of the various sounds of different pipes blends in the final musical effect. A pipe organ can produce a deling horsehair string that is stretched from end to end of the resilient wooden bow. *Wind-instrument repairers* are authorities on both brass and woodwind instruments (clarinets, tubas, trumpets, flutes, cornets, and saxophones), examining mechanical parts, cleaning both interiors and exteriors, removing dents in metal and cracks in wood, and regulating all mechanisms. There are also *percussion tuners* and *repairers*, who work on drums, bells, cymbals, and castanets; *accordion tuners* and *repairers*, who work on the free-reed portable accordion, the piano accordion, the bandoneon, and the related concertina, harmonium, and harmonica; *fretted-instrument repairers*; *harp regulators*; *trombone-slide assemblers*; *metal-reed tuners*; *tone regulators*; and *chip tuners*.

Requirements

For beginning jobs servicing musical instrument employers prefer high-school graduates. It is not essential that they be able to play the instruments, but general music courses will help them develop an ear for tonal quality. Courses in woodworking will prove useful when repairing the many moving parts that are made of wood in pianos and pipe organs.

Most tuners and repairers acquire their skills through on-the-job training. Inexperienced applicants are hired as trainees by music stores, large repair shops, or self-employed technicians. They handle routine tasks, do general cleanup work, and help move and install instruments. Working under the close supervision of experienced workers, they learn to tune and repair instruments. Four or five years of training are generally required to become a qualified piano or pipe-organ repairer.

Personal qualifications for persons in this occupational group include keen hearing, mechanical aptitude, stamina, and manual dexterity. A neat appearance and pleasant personality are important when technicians must repair instruments in customers' homes.

Experienced instrument tuners and repairers expand their knowledge by studying trade magazines and manufacturers' service manuals related to new developments in their field. They may improve their skills in training programs and at regional and national seminars.

Special requirements

There are no special requirements for this occupational group.

Opportunities for experience and exploration

Courses in music will develop the students' ear for tonal quality, and lessons in playing one or more instruments will acquaint them with their mechanisms. The music department of the high school or a nearby college can be an excellent source of information. Interviews with and demonstrations by instrument tuners and technicians may be arranged through school vocational counselors or church organists. Most craft workers are willing to share an hour or so of conversation about their craft and can in a short time acquaint an interested person with the essential nature of the work they do.

Part-time and summer jobs that are closely related to this occupation may be difficult to obtain, because full-time trainees usually handle the routine tasks of a helper; nevertheless, it is worth applying for such work at music stores and repair shops in case they have no need for full-time trainees. General clerical jobs in stores that sell musical instruments may help familiarize students with the language of the field and may offer the opportunity to observe technicians at work. Persons interested in electronic-organ repair may find work related to electronics in television and radio repair shops. Others may learn electronics in the armed forces.

Related occupations

The work done by musical instrument repairers and tuners is similar to the work done by instrument repairers, instrument makers, and jewelers and jewelry repairers.

Methods of entering

Almost all musical instrument tuners and repairers enter the field by applying directly to local instrument dealers and repair shops and training for several years.

Advancement

Tuners and repairers may advance their skills by participating in training programs. A few tuners and repairers who work for large dealers or repair shops may work into supervisory positions.

Musical instrument repairers and tuners
Bench Work Occupations

Opening a repair business requires only a small investment in tools. Before doing this, however, the worker should have adequate training to survive the strong competition that exists in the tuning and repair business. It is probably wiser to continue working another job until a clientele becomes large enough to support a full-time business. Self-employed tuners generally operate out of their homes.

Employment outlook

In the early 1990s, there were approximately 9,200 musical instrument tuners and repairers employed in the United States, most of whom worked on pianos. About 80 percent of the total were employed by music stores, and most of the others worked in repair shops or for instrument manufacturers. About 40 percent of them were self-employed.

Little or no change is expected in employment throughout the next decade. The few job openings that occur will be the result of experienced workers' retiring, dying, or leaving the occupation.

Untrained workers will find it especially hard to obtain jobs, despite the fact that the number of musical instruments will increase as the population grows and people have more leisure time. There will be a demand for tuning and repair work for these instruments plus the millions already in use; but training requires time, and most music-store owners and self-employed tuners and repairers find it more profitable to spend that time doing the work themselves or giving it to their experienced workers. Individuals with some familiarity with the trade or those who have taken classes in musical instrument repair technology may have more success getting a trainee job.

It is a luxury for most owners to have their instruments tuned and repaired, and they tend to postpone these services when money is scarce. Therefore, tuners and repairers may lose income during an economic downturn. In addition, few trainees are hired when business is slow. The field of pipe-organ repair is not as sensitive to fluctuations in the economy as those that are more consumer-oriented, because most pipe organs are owned by churches and musical organizations, which are less affected by the economy than individuals are.

The best opportunities for musical instrument tuners and repairers are in cities and states with large populations, or extensive musical programs in schools or performance groups.

Earnings

Wages vary depending on area and the skill of the worker. In the early 1990s, experienced workers earned between $25,000 and $42,000 per year, while apprentices received from $8,600 to $10,000. Once they are promoted beyond the status of apprentice, repairers and tuners make between $12,000 and $18,000 annually. Some helpers work for the training and receive no pay.

Conditions of work

Tuners and repairers work in shops, homes, churches, and other public buildings, where working conditions are usually good. They may work more than forty hours a week during the fall and winter, when people spend more time indoors playing musical instruments. Self-employed tuners and repairers often work evenings and weekends, when it is more convenient for the customer.

Installing a huge pipe organ requires considerable physical work. Tuning and repairing involve little physical strain but may mean working in cramped locations for some length of time. The work does not present any dangers other than small cuts and bruises when making repairs.

Some musical instrument repairers develop a reputation for being the finest in the field and world-class musicians will fly those repairers to their performances to be sure their instruments will be in the best working order. This is particularly true for piano tuners.

Social and psychological factors

Musical instrument tuners and repairers usually work alone. Tuning an instrument can often take more than a day, which can be tedious and tiring. Patience and an attention to detail are good qualities for workers in this field.

Because many tuners and repairers work for themselves, they must present themselves to their potential clients as being competent, cooperative, and pleasant to work with, which involves being able to meet and work with others.

GOE: 06.02.03; SIC: 7699; SOC: 722

◇ **SOURCES OF ADDITIONAL INFORMATION**

For information about piano technicians and a list of schools offering courses in piano technology, write:

Piano Technicians Guild
4510 Belleview, Suite 100
Kansas City, MO 64111

For general material on instrument repair, write:

National Association of Professional Band and Instrument Repair Technicians
8 Ardith Drive
PO Box 51
Normal, IL 61761

◇ **RELATED ARTICLES**

Volume 3: Musical occupations; see also Bench Work Occupations
Volume 4: Electronic-organ technicians; Piano technicians; Pipe organ technicians

Opticians and optical mechanics

Definition

Opticians fit eyeglasses and adjust them to the client's comfort; they may also make up the eyeglasses following the prescription of an ophthalmologist or optometrist. In some cases, they function only as dispensing opticians who fit the eyeglasses, while the optical mechanics fabricate the eyeglasses.

History

Even though the discovery of glass can be traced back to early Egyptian and Syrian civilizations, it was not until the thirteenth century that the use of glass to correct visual defects was invented by Salvino d'Armate. The secret of his invention was not made known to the existing world until long after his death. His colleagues traveled through the various countries of the known world and trained court attaches to grind lenses for the proper correction of the wearer's vision. Eventually, all European countries had men who were craft workers in this field. By the seventeenth century these craft workers had banded together into a union, called a "guild."

Further development of eyeglasses was made by Benjamin Franklin, who invented the bifocal lens in the eighteenth century. Thomas Young, in 1801, discovered the eye condition of astigmatism, and in 1827, cylindrical and compound lenses were invented to correct this condition.

In 1887 a Swiss physician, A. E. Fick, made the first contact lens. These first lenses were made of heavy glass and exerted an uncomfortable pressure on the eyeball, as well as being difficult to fit. In the late 1930s a light plastic was developed that could be easily molded to shape. In 1950 a lens that floated on the wearer's tears was introduced; and today, an even smaller corneal lens, covering only the cornea, is in widespread use.

Nature of the work

Dispensing opticians and optical mechanics do nearly all of the work involved with making and fitting eyeglasses to patients. The tasks performed by the dispensing optician include making certain that the glasses follow the prescription, determining exactly where the lenses should be placed in relation to the pupils of the eyes, assisting the customer in selecting the proper eyeglass frame, preparing work orders for the optical laboratory mechanic, adjusting the frame of the eyeglasses to the contours of

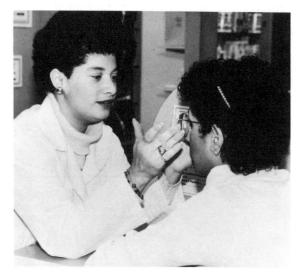

A dispensing optician adjusts the frame of a customer's eyeglasses. For proper vision, it is important that eyeglasses fit the contours of a person's face.

the customer's face (using small hand tools and precision instruments), and selling optical goods.

Dispensing opticians must exercise great precision, skill, and patience in fitting contact lenses. They must measure the curvature of the cornea, and then, following the optometrist's prescription, prepare complete specifications to be followed by an optical mechanic or a firm specializing in the manufacture of these lenses. They must then teach the customer how to remove, adjust to, and care for the lenses, a process that sometimes takes several weeks.

The tasks performed by the optical mechanic would include grinding and polishing the surfaces of eyeglass lenses, checking to see if ground lenses conform to the prescription requirements, marking and cutting ground and polished lenses, using precision measuring instruments, assembling lenses and frames, and repairing broken or damaged eyeglasses. In small optical shops, the mechanic performs all such duties, although the mechanic does not make contact lenses. In larger optical shops specialists might include *lens mounters, lens-mold setters, lens-inserters, lens-matchers,* and *lens-fabricating-machine tenders; bench workers, embossers, eyeglass-frame truers, spindle frame carvers, washers, clip coaters, contact-lens-flashing punchers, machine sizers, contact lens lathe operators, hand grinders,* and *eyeglass-lens cutters; precision-lens generators, polishers,* and *centerers and edgers; eyeglass frames* and *hand lens polishers;* and *gold frame, molded frame, multifocal lens,,* and *final assemblers.*

Dispensing opticians and optical mechanics are viewed as skilled workers and generally have to meet certain specified standards. They must be familiar with many of the methods, materials, and operations employed in the optical industry. This is especially true of the dispensing optician who, in small shops or laboratories, often has to perform all of the tasks involved in fabricating and fitting eyeglasses.

Opticians and mechanics are employed by retail optical shops, prescription departments of wholesale optical laboratories, special prescription shops in large ophthalmic factories, and ophthalmologists. Most dispensing opticians and optical mechanics are located in large cities and industrial areas.

Requirements

Finger dexterity, eye-hand coordination, special discrimination of spatial relations, muscular and touch requirements, and, in some cases, sharp color discrimination are some of the more important physical qualifications for this work. Because of the nature of the work, physically handicapped persons who have full use of their eyes and hands and can do sedentary work can perform many of the more specialized jobs in the larger laboratories.

Employers generally prefer applicants for entry jobs as dispensing opticians and optical mechanics to be high-school graduates who have had courses in the basic sciences. A knowledge of physics, algebra, geometry, and mechanical drawing is particularly valuable in acquiring the basic skills for these occupations.

As a general rule, optical mechanics are required to serve a four-year apprenticeship training program before qualifying as skilled workers. Dispensing opticians usually serve from four to five years in apprenticeship programs.

Within recent years there has been a trend toward a more formal type of technical training program for dispensing opticians. Employers prefer to hire graduates of two-year college programs in opticianry. These associate degree holders are also able to advance more rapidly than apprentices.

In a two-year optician program, the student can expect to take general college courses such as communication skills, sociology, and mathematics, as well as technical subjects such as mechanical optics, geometric optics, ophthalmic dispensing procedures, contact lens practice, anatomy and physiology of the eye, and business concepts. The two-year program also includes considerable laboratory work in grinding, polishing, and other procedures.

The ability to get along well with others, patience, accuracy, and a pleasing personality are important assets for opticians.

Special requirements

In the early 1990s, more than twenty states (and Puerto Rico) had licensing requirements governing dispensing opticians: Alaska, Arizona, Arkansas, California, Connecticut, Florida, Georgia, Hawaii, Kentucky, Massachusetts, Nevada, New Jersey, New York, North Carolina, Ohio, Rhode Island, South Carolina, Tennessee, Vermont, Virginia, and Washington. Iowa had a voluntary certification bill. Some of these states also require licenses for optical mechanics employed in retail optical shops or for the optical shop itself. Some states may permit dispensing opticians to fit contact lenses, providing they have had additional training. To obtain a license, the applicant must generally meet certain minimum standards of education and training and must also be able to pass an oral or written examination, or both, for certification. Usually, the examination is practical in nature. For more specific information on the licensing procedure, the licensing boards of the individual states should be consulted.

Opportunities for experience and exploration

A student may explore the optical field while in high school by visiting the shops and laboratories where dispensing opticians and optical mechanics are employed. Part-time or full-time summer employment in an optical shop as a messenger or stock clerk may give the high-school student an opportunity to observe, first-hand, the skills needed in this occupation.

Related occupations

Other workers who are involved in eye care include ophthalmologists, dispensing opticians, contact lens manufacturing workers, ophthalmic laboratory technicians, optometric technicians, and optics technicians.

Methods of entering

One method of entering this field is through a formal, technical training program; however, the usual means is through on-the-job experience and an apprenticeship program. Aspirants who have completed high-school can apply for apprenticeship training directly to the personnel offices of retail shops or optical laboratories known to hire dispensing opticians and optical mechanics. They might also try large ophthalmic goods factories. State and private employment agencies frequently know of firms seeking interested persons in this field.

Advancement

Promotion opportunities in this occupation are available to both the dispensing optician and the optical mechanic, depending upon training and special abilities of the worker. Upon completion of the apprenticeship program, the workers may advance to surface-room mechanic or to bench-room mechanic. With equal ability in all phases of preparing prescription lenses plus additional training, the optical mechanic can advance to the job of dispensing optician. Optical mechanics can also become supervisors, foremen, and managers.

Many dispensing opticians, after additional experience, open their own shops. The number of proprietors of retail optical establishments has increased substantially in recent years. A few dispensing opticians, with additional college training, become optometrists. The amount of training that the dispensing optician needs to become an optometrist depends upon the individual's formal educational background. Dispensing opticians usually advance to supervisor, sales, or manager positions.

Employment outlook

In the early 1990s, about 50,000 dispensing opticians were employed in the United States.

Within the past decade, there has been a noticeable increase in the number of dispensing opticians. This increase is expected to continue. The following factors point to this increased need: good vision is being increasingly emphasized in the home, school, factory, and office; the wide variety in design of eyeglass frames, including many different styles and colors, has increased the number of pairs of eyeglasses purchased by individuals; the rapid growth in the purchase of contact lenses in recent years is expected to increase, providing more work in the future years; and the increasing size, literacy, and educational level of the population has considerably expanded the market for eyeglasses. The population shift to suburban areas will offer dispensing opticians more opportunities to work in, manage, or establish optical stores.

As in the past, many technological developments affecting employment needs will continue to be made in the manufacture of eyeglasses, and in the equipment used by optical laboratories to fabricate lenses to prescription specifications. In spite of these more efficient methods of production, there will be some growth in the employment of optical mechanics. It should be noted that the total number of people currently employed as opticians and optical mechanics is relatively small and employment opportunities may be limited.

Earnings

The starting annual salary for newly licensed dispensing opticians in New York ranged from $18,700 to $22,460 for qualified optical laboratory mechanics in the early 1990s. Dispensing opticians received a median of about $26,000. Opticians who have their own business establishments may earn $36,000 and more. Supervisors earn up to 20 percent more than skilled workers, depending upon such factors as experience, skill, and responsibilities. Apprentices usually start at about 60 percent of the skilled worker's rate, and their earnings increase periodically upon completion of the apprenticeship program. Workers in the optical occupations usually have steady, year-round employment.

Conditions of work

The work of the dispensing optician requires little physical exertion and is usually performed in pleasant, well-lighted, and well-ventilated business establishments. The optical mechanic will usually work in a shop that is also well lighted and well ventilated; however, a shop of any size is often noisy, because of the grinding and polishing machines used. Although safety measures have eliminated the major hazards often encountered in shops, the optical mechanic is still subject to accidents while using hand tools or operating optical machines.

Social and psychological factors

The ability to use precision instruments and small hand tools, such as lens cutters, chippers, optical pliers, files, protractors, and diamond-point glass drills, calls for a strong interest in, and an exceptional ability to do, the precision work that is essential in performing the tasks called for in these occupations. Tasks involving superior finger dexterity and eye-hand coordination can become extremely frustrating to those persons who are lacking this fundamental skill. In addition to these traits, the dispensing optician must also have a pleasing personality to deal successfully with members of the public.

Some of these craft workers hold membership in the International Union of Electrical, Radio and Machine Workers.

GOE: 05.05.11; SIC: 5995; SOC: 6864

◇ **SOURCES OF ADDITIONAL INFORMATION**

American Board of Opticianry
10341 Democracy Lane
Fairfax, VA 22030

National Academy of Opticianry
10111 Martin Luther King Jr. Highway, Suite 112
Bowie, MD 20716

◇ **RELATED ARTICLES**

Volume 1: Health Care
Volume 3: Instrument makers; Optometrists
Volume 4: Ophthalmic technicians; Optics technicians; Optometric technicians

Shoe industry workers

Definition

Shoe industry workers are crafts workers and machinists who turn the raw materials of leather, rubber, and plastic into finished shoes and boots. Most of this work is done by cutting and stitching machines, but skilled workers are still needed to run the machines, keep production levels high, and handle the special problems that arise from working with a natural material like leather.

History

In the early days of our nation, every good-sized village could count a cobbler (shoemaker) among its artisans. Using the basic raw materials of leather, wood, thread, glue, and nails, the cobbler could construct a pair of shoes from start to finish, to the size and specifications of every customer. The cobbler could also make and repair a variety of other leather goods.

Over the course of the Industrial Revolution, hand-made shoes gradually were replaced by factory-made footwear. Machinery could produce more shoes faster with fewer people. The work of cobblers was narrowed to custom-made shoes, special orthopedic shoes, and the repair of worn-out footwear. Today, Americans buy more pairs of shoes than ever—on average, between four and five pairs each year. Most of these shoes, however, are made overseas, in Taiwan, China, Korea, Brazil, and other countries where the cost of labor is cheaper. Some domestic companies have found a niche for themselves in specialty footwear, such as cowboy boots, work shoes, and quality athletic shoes. The United States, however, imports 85 percent of its shoes from overseas, which means that fewer and fewer people in this country are employed in the manufacture of footwear.

Nature of the work

Even with increased competition from imports, shoe factories in America still produce more than 200 million pairs of shoes in more than 10,000 styles every year. Most of this work is done on more than 300 different kinds of machines, although some work is done by hand.

A single pair of shoes may consist of up to 280 different parts and sections and require 150 different machine steps. Shoes are made in batches, not in individual pairs. These batches may consist of a dozen or more pairs of shoes, and are kept together through the entire manufacturing process to ensure that the shoes are consistent in color, texture, size, and pattern.

The leather in a pair of shoes starts out from tanned animal hides that a shoe manufacturer purchases and keeps in storage. Keeping track of these hides is the job of the *upper-leather sorter*, who sorts, grades, and issues the hides that will be cut into shoe uppers (as opposed to shoe soles). The leather is spread out under a cutting machine, which stamps down and cuts the leather into the various sections used for the shoe. This machine, manned by the *cut-out-and-marking-machine operator*, also marks patterns for stitching, beveling, and punching holes and eyelets. Care must be taken to avoid the natural imperfections that are in each hide and to cut the leather against the grain strategically to minimize stretching when the shoes are worn.

Next, the lining, tongue, toe, and other parts of the shoe are sewn together by machines operated by *standard machine stitchers*. Shoe parts can also be fastened by glue, nails, staples, and slugs applied by machine. Other workers taper leather edges, trim linings, flatten seams, and attach buckles or eyelets. The throat of the shoe is then laced together by the *lacer*.

At this point the shoe upper is still mostly flat and is missing its insole, outsole, and heel. Before these are added, the shoe needs to be shaped and made into the proper shoe size. This is done using individually sized molds called lasts, which are made of wood or plastic and are shaped like feet. The shoe upper and lining are steamed to soften the leather, and then are secured to the lasts and stretched to conform to shape. This can be done either by hand by the *hand laster* or by a lasting machine operated by the *bed laster*.

While this is being done, workers in the sole rooms have been preparing the insoles, outsoles, and heels that will be attached to the shoe uppers. The *stock fitter* stamps out the rough forms for the soles out of tanned hides, while the *rounder* trims the soles to the proper size for the style and size of the shoe. Meanwhile, the heel of the shoe is cut out of wood, leather, or fiberboard by the *groover and turner*.

Two shoe industry workers inspect the craftsmanship of some loafers. Uniformity in color, size, and quality is essential.

Leather strips are then glued to the heel and trimmed.

The insole is the first piece that is attached to the shoe upper. It can be glued on or sewn on by the *thread laster*. Next, foam filling is usually inserted by the *bottom filler* between the insole and outsole to provide a cushion for the ball of the foot and an even surface for attaching the outsole. The outsole is then stitched to the shoe by the welt, or lip of leather, that runs along the outside of the shoe. Now the shoe can be removed from the last and made ready for finishing. The heel is nailed to the shoe by the *heel-nailing-machine operator*, and any excess leather or glue is removed by the *machine trimmer*. The *inker* applies ink, stain, color, glaze, or wax to the shoe parts and along the seams to color and protect the shoe, after which the *brusher* holds and turns the shoe against revolving brushes to clean and polish them. After inspection, the shoes are ready to pack and ship to stores. If shoes have come out of the manufacturing process damaged or unfit for sale, they are sent to a *cobbler*, who uses hand tools and machines to fix or rebuild any defects.

For shoes made of rubber, plastic, fabric, or other material, the manufacturing process is roughly the same. The die that cuts out the basic shoe pieces, however, is usually heated. Many layers of material can be cut at once because, unlike leather, the layers are uniform in color, texture, and thickness. Also, cementing and heating are used more often to join the pieces of nonleather shoes.

Custom shoe makers may assemble shoes by hand individually, or they may modify shoes for special needs and handicaps.

Requirements

Shoe production workers are usually trained on the job. This does not mean, however, that these workers do not need to complete their formal education. As more workers apply for a shrinking number of jobs, employers are more likely to hire people who have high school diplomas and a certain amount of machine skills.

High-school courses in shop and sewing may come in handy when looking for a job in this field. Some thirteen technical and vocational schools also offer training courses in the different aspects of shoe and boot making, lasting from six months to one year. Completion of such a course of study may lead to new job opportunities and higher beginning wages.

Special requirements

Approximately half of the workers in the shoe industry are represented by a union. The largest is the United Food & Commercial Workers International Union of the AFL-CIO, which has about 20,000 members. A smaller, independent union, the Brotherhood of Shoe and Allied Craftsmen, has about 200 members.

Opportunities for experience and exploration

Students may be able to find summer or part-time jobs in the shoe industry, as helpers to craft workers and maintenance workers. Its current depressed state, however, makes it unlikely that many jobs will open up for inexperienced people or people who only want to work part-time.

Related occupations

Other workers deal with leather and with making wearing apparel. These include leather tanning and finishing workers, fashion designers, textile manufacturing occupations, and sporting goods production workers.

Methods of entering

Shoe manufacturing companies generally hire their own workers. Job notices may be found in the want ads or with a state employment agency. Because jobs are scarce, however, the best route for the job seeker to take would be to apply to the shoe factories in person.

Advancement

In the shoe industry, advancement is a matter of learning new jobs and handling more complex machines. It can take anywhere from six weeks to six months to learn how to operate some processing machines completely. Skill in cutting shoe uppers may take up to two years on the job. Higher wages usually accompany a move to a more complex machine. Some skilled workers may work their way up to become *supervisors* of the shoe factory, who usually are made salaried employees.

Employment outlook

In the early 1990s, approximately 65,000 production workers were employed in the shoe industry in about 325 domestic plants. Job prospects for workers in the shoe industry are not good. The domestic shoe industry has been hurt badly by competition from overseas; 207 American shoe factories were closed between 1981 and 1985. The low cost of labor overseas has made it impossible for many American companies to compete. In fact, the United States now exports raw materials for shoes to other countries, who make the shoes and then market them here.

Some technological innovations have been introduced to the shoe manufacturing process, such as the use of computers, robotics, and laser cutting. Most of these new methods, however, will be automated and will not translate into more jobs. Most job openings in this field will only come as other workers die, retire, or change jobs.

For workers who make custom-built shoes or modify shoes for special needs, the job outlook is better. As the general population ages, orthopedic needs should increase.

Earnings

Most new workers in the shoe industry start at a very low wage, which increases after gaining experience on the job, usually after two to six months. After this time, they can work fast enough to be given piecework pay rates. In the early 1990s, the average hourly wage was $5.59, or $196.77 a week. Among the highest paid production workers are cutters, who can earn up to $8.00 an hour. Most production workers are paid a piecework rate, meaning that part of their pay depends on their ability to meet and exceed minimum production quotas.

Most shoe industry workers also enjoy benefits such as health insurance, pensions, paid vacations, and profit sharing, depending on the contract their union or shop has negotiated.

Conditions

Shoe production workers work a thirty-five-hour week on average. The work requires stamina, because employees stand much of the time and because of the swift pace that piecework pay rates require. The work, however, is not strenuous and hazards are few if safety precautions are followed.

The atmosphere in the factory will vary from employer to employer. In most, the facilities are relatively clean and well lit. Because of the heavy use of machinery, plants can get very noisy.

Social and psychological factors

Workers in the shoe industry should be able to do repetitive tasks with speed and accuracy. They should also have good hand-eye coordination and like to work with their hands. The depressed state of this industry, however, lessens the possibility of job security for most workers. Advancement and lifetime employment in this industry is becoming less and less likely for all but a small number of workers.

GOE: 05, 06; SIC: 314; SOC: 8769

◇ **SOURCES OF ADDITIONAL INFORMATION**

Shoe Service Institute of America
5024-R Campbell Boulevard
Baltimore, MD 21236

Brotherhood of Shoe and Allied Craftsmen
PO Box 390
East Bridgewater, MA 02333

Footwear Industries of America
1420 K Street, NW
Suite 600
Washington, DC 20005

Prescription Footwear Association
9861 Broken Land Parkway
Columbia, MO 21046

◇ **RELATED ARTICLES**

Volume 1: Apparel; Design; Textiles
Volume 2: Designers; Fashion designers
Volume 3: Leather tanning and finishing
workers: Rubber goods production workers;
Sporting goods production workers

Silverware industry workers

Definition

Silverware industry workers are designers and artisans who take ideas for eating utensils, platters, teapots, and other types of silverware from the drafting table, through the machining of the metals, to the finished product.

History

The ways people eat, and the utensils they eat with, have changed dramatically from prehistoric times to the present. Spoons, forks, and knives have been made from a variety of different materials, including wood, bone, shells, and various metals, including bronze, gold, pewter, tin and silver. Designs have changed as well, from simple utilitarian shapes to beautifully crafted works of art.

In the mid-1700s, the silverware industry was revolutionized by the introduction of an electrolytic process for plating less expensive metals with silver, which resulted in a type of metal known as Sheffield plate. This led to a huge growth in the silver plating industry in both England and the United States. Silversmithing was an important industry in colonial America, and the pieces produced during that time are valued highly by collectors. One of our most famous colonial silversmiths was the patriot Paul Revere.

Silverware consists of two different classes of utensils: flatware and hollowware. Flatware is the name given to the knives, spoons, forks, and other utensils with which people eat. Hollowware consists of such items as teapots,

pitchers, sugar bowls, creamers, cups, and trays. Everyday dining requires only a few basic pieces of silverware, but in formal dining, place settings can have a great number of utensils and other objects. At the height of formal dining one hundred years ago, a complete dining service for twelve might consist of 300 to 500 pieces of flatware and hollowware.

Despite the general name "silverware," many different types of metals are commonly used today in the manufacture of eating utensils. These include sterling silver, pewter, nickel silver, silver plate, gold electroplate, and stainless steel, which is an alloy of steel, chromium, nickel, and other metals. Regardless of the type of metal used, the steps in silverware manufacturing are basically the same.

Nature of the work

Manufacturing silverware requires the cooperation of more than 60 different types of artisans and workers. The process begins with the *designer* who, after considering current market trends and the products offered by competitors, sketches preliminary styles and patterns for a new line of utensils. If the designs are approved by company management, they are then taken to the *model maker*, who will make full-size models by hand by sculpting or carving in clay, plastic, or plaster. Once it is seen in a three-dimensional model, the design may undergo some alterations. The model maker then prepares a model of the final version which is used as a pattern for the molds and dies that will be used to stamp out the actual silverware.

Dies, which are tools that can stamp, shape, or cut metal, are then constructed by *tool makers* and *die makers.*

Forks, spoons, knives, and other flatware start out in flat sheets of stainless steel, sterling silver, nickel silver, or brass. The *flatware maker* takes these sheets and feeds them into the presses which die-cut the metal into flat blanks roughly the same size and shape as the finished utensils. The flatware maker then inserts the blank into the drop press and drops the ram of that press onto the blank to form the bowl or fork end and curve the handles of the flatware. Between these two stampings, the metal is heated, or annealed, to make it easier to work with; this can be done by the flatware maker or the *annealer.* The flatware is then immersed in a specified chemical solution to cool and clean the metal.

The *trimmer* takes these pieces and, using an emery wheel or bench grinding machine, removes any burrs, flash, or press marks from each and rounds off the edges according to the design. This can also be done with a hand file. Finally, the flatware is shined and polished to a bright finish by the *mirror-finishing-machine operator* or the *polishing machine operator.*

Making knives involves a slightly different process. Many knives with large handles are first stamped into two halves and then joined together by *solderers* or *hollow handle bench workers.* The handle can be hollow or weighted, and the knife blade is attached last by the *hollow-handle-knife assembler.*

Many more people are necessary to manufacture hollowware such as teapots, trays and sugar bowls, because these pieces are very unique and can be very ornate and beautiful. The base metal for most hollowware is brass, which is later electroplated with some precious metal. The brass comes in rolls and is cut into sheets. The *machine operator* molds the brass into shapes using large presses. To this standard shape are added other sections to complete the piece such as spouts, handles, borders, and legs. These other sections are cast in molds using molten Britannia metal, which is a high grade of pewter, and are then wired on and soldered by the *silverware assembler.* When the pieces need trimming after being molded or assembled, the *profile-saw operator* or the *profile trimmer* use a variety of saws to do the job. A lathe can be used to create such objects as candlesticks and goblets; this work is done by *spinners.*

A person who uses a hammer to shape and design metal is called a "smith." *Silversmiths* and *hammersmiths* work with hollowware. Silversmiths assemble and repair all types of hollowware in the manner described above. They

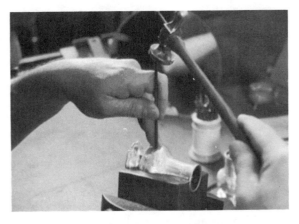

A silver worker chisels a decorative pattern on a candlestick. Such a task requires steady hands.

also repair damaged or deformed pieces using hammers, tongs, pliers, dollies, anvils and tracing punches. Silversmiths can create beautiful designs in silver with hammers and other tools by engraving, embossing, and chasing patterns on the piece. Hammersmiths generally limit themselves to repairing hollowware.

The final step in manufacturing flatware and hollowware is electroplating, a process of putting a layer or many layers of metal on the piece using electricity. A utensil can be coated with a precious metal such as gold, silver, or platinum, or with a less-expensive alloy. A person known as a *plater* oversees this process and operates the machinery.

The pieces of hollowware and flatware are first put on a conveyer which takes them through a series of cleaning vats. The pieces are then given a nickel or copper "strike," or coating, that allows the precious metal to attach to the baser metal in the piece. Each piece is then suspended from a cathode rod (negative pole) and immersed in the plating solution. A rod, or piece of the plating metal, is attached to the anode (positive pole) and immersed in the solution. An electric current, regulated by the plater, is then put through the solution and causes atoms of the plating metal to attach themselves to the utensil. The plater adjusts the voltage and amperage based on job specifications to deposit the proper amount of the precious metal on the piece, creating a beautiful piece of silverware.

Requirements

For most artisan jobs in silverware manufacturing, employers look for workers who have a high school diploma. First and foremost, they look for employees with mechanical skills and command of an art or craft. There is always a demand for graduates of technical schools who have skills useful for this industry. Those who wish to pursue a job as a toolmaker, die cutter, machinist, or bench worker need to have solid backgrounds in mathematics, drafting, sketching, and shop. For the more skilled trades, workers generally serve an apprenticeship of a certain period, during which they study the trade under more experienced workers and attend classes.

Silverware designers need more advanced training in the fine and applied arts. They should have at least a bachelor's degree in industrial or applied design or a similar major, along with classes in art, design and the properties of metal. Some high-school and community art courses are offered in jewelry making. This gives the student an opportunity to work with precious metal designing. High-school classes in drafting, art, plane geometry, and mathematics are a good preparation for this field of study. Designers can also pursue their studies at design schools or earn an associate's degree from a two-year college. A few colleges across the country offer degrees in silversmithing. It is also possible for a production or craft worker, after some years on the job, to move up to the position of designer.

Special requirements

There are no special requirements for silverware production workers.

Opportunities for experience and exploration

Students who may be interested in a career in silverware manufacturing should try to get a part-time or summer job in a silverware factory. This may be more difficult than it sounds, because there are only 200 or so plants in the United States, most of them located in New England. These also tend to be small operations with fewer than twenty workers each. Because employers usually look for new workers who already have experience in the machine trades, it might be a good idea for students to find a part-time job with any type of metal manufacturing or machining company, and then take that experience with them when looking for a job in silverware manufacturing.

Related occupations

Other occupations with similar skill requirements include jewelers, jewelry repairers, instrument repairers, instrument makers, and watch repairers. Artisan trades such as glassmaking, woodworking, and ceramics also offer the same use of skills as silverware artisans.

Methods of entering

The best method for entering this profession for both designers and craftspeople is to contact the hiring office of a silverware plant directly, in person, or in writing. Designers may also learn of openings through the placement office of their school or college. Another source of job information is state employment offices.

Most crafts worker start off in unskilled jobs and work as buffers, trimmers, edgers, or assemblers. They might also start as apprentices and work their way up. Designers may also be assigned less demanding tasks at first, such as drafting.

Advancement

High quality work and consistent efforts are the keys to advancement in silverware manufacturing for both skilled and semiskilled jobs. Unskilled workers can sometimes apply for apprenticeship programs and learn skills such as smithing, soft soldering, spinning, engraving, and toolmaking. Those in skilled positions may move up to jobs as technicians or supervisors.

Employment outlook

Jobs in the silverware industry are not as plentiful as in the past. Recent years have seen greater competition from silverware manufacturers in Europe and Asia, higher prices for silver and steel, and a decreased demand for expensive gifts such as flatware settings and tea services. The past decade has seen a tripling of imports, which has lowered the number of U.S. silverware workers from 12,600 to around 8,000. Most job openings in this field will come as a result of workers retiring or leaving the industry.

Earnings

Most production workers are paid an hourly rate, but may also earn piecework or incentive rates. Wages vary according to the job and the level of skill. Unskilled workers usually start work earning between $5.50 to $7.00 an hour. The average pay for workers in this industry in 1986 was $8.23 an hour. Skilled pieceworkers may earn more than $9.00 an hour. Wages for toolmakers and die makers are even higher, up to $12.00 an hour or more. Salaries for designers can range from $15,000 to $20,000 a year or more. Workers usually receive benefits such as medical and life insurance, pensions, paid holidays and vacations. They also can often buy company products at a discount.

Conditions of work

Unlike some other factories, silverware factories are usually clean, open, and pleasant. The machines are comparatively small, but they can be noisy. The work is not physically strenuous, but some jobs, such as operating a punch press, can become repetitious.

Social and psychological factors

The most important qualities a person can bring to a job in this field are patience, attention to detail, and pride in his or her work. Employees must be careful to do an excellent job with each piece they work on. Good eyesight and manual dexterity are important for both production workers and designers. Designers must also be original and creative. They should have the ability to take an idea and see it through to becoming a finished product. For people with the proper skills and work habits, silverware manufacturing can be rewarding both technically and artistically.

GOE: 06.04.23; SIC: 3914; SOC: 772

◇ **SOURCES OF ADDITIONAL INFORMATION**

Jewelers of America
1271 Avenue of the Americas
New York, NY 10020

National Tooling and Machining Association
9300 Livingston Road
Fort Washington, MD 20744

◇ **RELATED ARTICLES**

Volume 1: Design; Machining and Machinery; Metals
Volume 2: Industrial designers
Volume 3: Assemblers; Electroplating workers; Jewelers and jewelry repairers; Molders; Job and die setters; Lathers; Machine tool operators; Machinists; Millwrights; Tool makers and die makers; Watch repairers
Volume 4: Metallurgical technicians; Profile-grinder technicians; Tap-and-die-maker technicians

Sporting goods production workers

Definition

Sporting goods production workers are involved in all stages of manufacturing, assembling, and finishing sporting goods equipment such as golf clubs, fishing tackle, basketballs, footballs, skis, and baseball equipment. The tasks range from operating machines to fine hand crafting.

History

Throughout human history, every society and culture has developed games and sports for relaxation and competition. Bowling, for example, has been around for centuries; a stone ball and nine stone pins have been found in the ancient tomb of an Egyptian child. Polo is believed to have originated in Asia, and was brought back to England and America by British officers returning from India in the 1800s. Native American tribes played lacrosse with webbed sticks and hard wooden balls centuries ago. Soccer, arguably the world's most popular sport, was invented in England, where the first recorded game was played in 217 A.D.

Some of the most popular games in America have a relatively recent history. Basketball was invented in 1891 by Dr. James Naismith in Springfield, Massachusetts; its popularity grew so fast that it became an Olympic event in 1936. Hockey as we know it was invented in Canada in the 1870s, and it, too, became popular quickly in northern countries and was inaugurated as an Olympic sport in 1920. In the 1870s football started as a college sport that mixed elements of soccer and rugby and soon developed its own unique set of rules. Although folklore attributes the invention of baseball to Abner Doubleday in 1839, it had, in fact, been played for many years previous to that.

Some games, both ancient and modern, have changed little from the time they were first played. Soccer, for instance, has remained popular in part because of its simplicity: All a person needs to play it is a ball. Other games have grown more complex, including the amount and type of equipment used. Modern technology has been applied to many aspects of sport and given us such things as lighter tennis rackets, livelier baseballs, and stronger golf balls. Computers have even been used to improve the design and composition of sports gear. The equipment used in each sport is unique in design and manufacture, and is put together by skilled specialists.

Nature of the work

Each piece of sports equipment is more or less unique. While basketballs and volleyballs are made by the same process, they are made by a different process than footballs and baseballs. The manufacture of sports equipment, however, is not that much different from the manufacture of other types of products and generally require the same types of labor.

Like in the manufacture of other products, machine operators control large machine tools such as presses, and smaller tools such as saws and sewing machines. The product of their work is often passed on to assemblers for completion of the final product. There are different types of assemblers: *Floor assemblers* operate large machines and power tools; *bench assemblers* work with smaller machines to complete a product and often test it; *precision assemblers* perform highly skilled assembly work, often working closely with design engineers and technicians to develop and test new products and designs. These categories can be applied to most of the occupations involved in sports manufacturing, although the names change to reflect the different aspects of each sport.

Take for example the manufacture of golf equipment. The shaft and the head, or club end, of a club are made separately and then assembled, weighted, and balanced. Much of the work is done by the *golf-club assembler*, who, according to the model of club being made, will cut the shaft of the club to a specified length using a bench mounted circular saw. Meanwhile, the precast head of the club is hammered to the desired angle by the *golf-club head former*. One of these workers will then glue the club head onto the shaft and secure it by drilling a small hole through both and inserting a pin. Wooden clubs are glued together the same way except that, once this assembly has dried, the weight of the club is checked and adjusted for the model type. Adjustments can be made by the assembler or the *golf-club weighter* by drilling a hole into the head and then adding molten lead or threaded cylindrical metal weights.

Finally, the handle of the club is attached by the *grip wrapper*, who inserts the club in a rotating machine, brushes adhesive on the shaft, attaches a leather strap and carefully spins the shaft to cover it tightly with the leather strap. When finished, excess leather is trimmed and the grip is fastened with tape or a sleeve. When an iron is completed, the club is examined by a *golf club head inspector and adjuster* to verify conformance with specifications.

The manufacture of fishing equipment, like the making of golf equipment, is a good example of how people work in an assembly line fashion using machine tools to develop a finished product. The *fishing-rod marker* first marks on the rod blank where to place the line guides and decorative marking for the particular style of rod. The *fishing-rod assembler* then takes a rod blank and, using liquid cement, attaches the hardware to the rod, such as the reel seat, handle, and line guides. Line guides can also be attached with thread by the *guide winder*, who decorates the rod by winding thread around it at intervals. While this is being done, the *fishing-reel assembler* assembles the intricate mechanism of the reel and tests it. The reel is then attached to the rod.

The manufacture of some sports products involves straightforward, familiar industrial processes, such as the lathing of baseball bats or the vulcanizing of hockey pucks. Other methods are more complicated and unique. For example, to manufacture basketballs, volleyballs, and soccer balls, the *ball assembler* cements panels of rubberized fabric onto a hollow, spherical frame made of wax. A door opening is left in the ball carcass so that the wax frame can be broken and removed piece by piece. Once this is done, the bladder is inserted into the ball and inflated to a specific pressure. The flaps of the door opening are then aligned with the other seams of the ball and cemented onto the bladder, and the ball is complete.

Over the past decades baseball equipment has changed only slightly, but it stills needs to be made by hand. Baseballs themselves are assembled by *hand baseball sewers*, who cement the leather hide of the ball to the core and sew the hide together using a harness needle and waxed linen thread. For baseball gloves, the cut pieces of leather are sewn together by a *lacer*, but the mitt is inside out. After the lining is put in place by the *lining inserter*, the mitt is taken by the *reverser* and turned right-side out on a series of posts. This basic mitt is then taken by the *baseball glove shaper*, who uses a heated, hand-shaped form to open and stretch the finger linings and, with various rubber mallets, hammers the seams smooth and forms the glove pocket. As a final test, the baseball glove shaper then tries the mitt on and pounds the pocket with his or her fist to make sure its a comfortable fit.

These few examples are meant to show some of the basic industrial processes that go into making sports equipment, but all these processes and many others are adapted to suit the needs of the sport, from skiing to table tennis. Within the limits of safety and economical operation, sporting goods manufacturers are constantly improving designs and changing manufacturing processes to make balls that last longer, mitts that perform better, and equipment that will not hinder an athlete from performing to the best of his or her ability.

Requirements

While a high-school diploma is preferred for workers in this industry, it is usually not a requirement. Employers look for workers who can do accurate, high-quality work at a fast pace. Most employees in the industry learn their trade through on-the-job training. Apprenticeships are also available to learn the more skilled trades.

Electronics are being used more and more in sports for such purposes as timing skiers and runners. As more applications for electronics

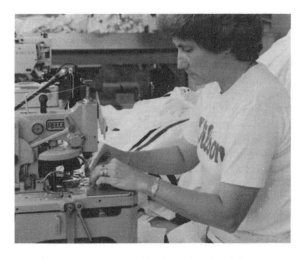

A sporting industry worker assembles jerseys for a baseball team.

are considered, those workers who assemble and manufacture this equipment will need the sort of technical knowledge that they can get at technical schools. Computers are also being increasingly used in both the design and the production of sports gear. Workers who learn about computers from a two- or four-year college or adult education center may have better prospects for holding a job and possibly advancing from production to design work.

In high school, students will find that shop and sewing classes, as well as basic mathematics, will give them a sound basis for working in this industry. These classes will train them to read and follow instructions, diagrams and blueprints.

Special requirements

Some sporting goods production workers belong to a union that represents workers who do similar work with similar materials. One such union is the Amalgamated Clothing and Textile Workers Union, which represents workers who make shoes, caps, hats, uniforms, ski suits, golf gloves, leotards, and other apparel. Other unions include the United Garment Workers of America; the International Leather Goods, Plastics and Novelty Workers Union; the Leather Workers International Union; the Laborers International Union of North America; the International Brotherhood of Electrical Workers; and the International Brotherhood of Boilermakers, Iron Shipbuilders, Blacksmiths, Forgers and Helpers.

Opportunities for experience and exploration

To learn what the work is like in sporting goods production, students could try to get a summer job working in a sports equipment factory. It is unlikely that they will be able to work anyplace but the warehouse or in custodial services, but they will be able to see first-hand what the work involves and talk with employees about their jobs. It also gives them the chance to prove their dependability and good work habits to employers who may want to hire them for more advanced work.

Related occupations

Other occupations that require similar skills and interests include toy industry workers, jewelers and jewelry repairers, musical instrument repairers and tuners, and instrument repairers.

Methods of entering

Those who want to find employment as a sporting goods production worker should look for classified ads in the local newspaper and check for listings of job openings at state employment agencies. School counselors may also be a good source of information about companies looking for workers and who to contact for a job application.

Another method is to contact the personnel office of the manufacturing plant directly. By talking with the right people, job seekers can learn whether any jobs are open or whether to look for work at another plant.

Advancement

Those who do get jobs in a sporting goods factory will usually start on basic tasks and then be trained on-the-job for more advanced work. Some tasks can be mastered relatively quickly, while more complicated work may take months to learn adequately and even longer to master. As mentioned earlier, some manufacturers train employees through an apprenticeship program which combines classroom work with on-site training. Usually an apprentice will sign a contract that specifies the training and wages

agreed upon and the results and minimum length of service that the company expects.

Skilled workers who are able to meet production quotas usually have many options for advancement. They may move on to work on more demanding and higher paying production jobs. Many manufacturers are large and diversified enough to reassign workers to different divisions. Qualified workers may also move to positions of product inspector or supervisor. Moving further up in management usually requires more experience, training, and education in business skills.

If workers have a new product idea or the urge to be their own boss, they may decide to start their own company. Going into business for oneself in any field, however, is a risky venture. Those who are interested must carefully examine costs and the realities of the market before taking this kind of step.

Employment outlook

Sports and other means of fitness are increasing in popularity among health-conscious Americans, and the market for sporting goods is expected to increase as well. Exports of sporting goods have risen during the late 1980s and are expected to continue to do so through the early 1990s.

This does not mean, however, that the number of production jobs will grow. The manufacture of sports gear is very labor-intensive, and to keep their costs down, many manufacturers have moved some of their operations to plants overseas where workers can be paid a lower wage. In addition, advances in automation, robotics, and computer-aided manufacturing are allowing companies to phase out certain production jobs. In the future, the need will be for employees who can program machines, supervise production, and manage resources. More workers will also be needed to test product safety and quality.

Approximately 1,500 sports equipment companies operate about 1,600 manufacturing plants in the United States. About 60 percent of these plants have fewer than twenty workers. Sporting equipment production workers numbered about 35,200 nationwide in the early 1990s. The sporting goods manufacturing industry is generally a solid but not expanding business. Job turnover is fairly high among production and assembly workers, so most new workers will be hired to replace those leaving the industry.

Earnings

Workers can be paid either by an hourly wage, by the number of pieces they produce, or by some combination of both. Beginning workers can earn between $5 to $8.50 per hour. Wages for assemblers range from $4 to $9 an hour, while wages are higher for skilled machine operators. Across the industry, the average wage is around $7 an hour. Most workers also get health insurance, paid holidays and vacations, and pension plans. Some firms also offer stock purchase plans to employees.

Conditions of work

Working conditions will differ according to the plant and the type of work being performed. Some plants are modern and have well-equipped, well-lit work stations for employees. Other plants, however, may have conditions that are less than ideal.

For some jobs, workers might have to sit or stand in one place for the entire work shift, while other jobs demand heavy lifting, hammering, and other physical strains. The work of assemblers may become repetitive over a period of time, and they may be kept under pressure to keep up with production if they work on an assembly line. Almost all workers have production quotas which they must meet.

Heat, noise, dust, and strong odors are unavoidable in many production tasks. Those who operate presses, molds, and other heavy machinery may have to load and remove heavy workpieces made of leather, metal, fiberglass, plastic, and other materials. To shape and form equipment like baseball gloves requires some physical strength. In certain jobs, employees need to wear safety glasses, hard hats, earplugs, or other protective clothing.

Sports equipment production workers usually work an eight-hour day and a forty-hour week. Many factories operate two or three shifts a day, so employees may work days, evenings, nights, or on weekends.

Social and psychological factors

Sports equipment production workers need good eyesight, mechanical skills, and manual dexterity. They should also be able to work at a repetitive task and not let the quality of their work suffer. Workers may also find a knowledge of certain sports helpful in upholding the quality of their work; for example, workers who know and play baseball will be able to tell whether a new glove has the proper fit.

Many workers get satisfaction from producing a high quality piece of equipment that will be used and appreciated by players. Working in a factory, especially one that is close to home, gives many people a sense of belonging, both within the company and within the community. There can be pressure on the job, however, in trying to meet production quotas and quality standards. Some people work better under such demanding conditions, while others dislike the pressure. For those who like to work with their hands or with machinery and who enjoy seeing and taking pride in their finished product, a job in manufacturing sporting goods can be a fulfilling profession.

GOE: None; SIC: 3949; SOC: 772

◇ **SOURCES OF ADDITIONAL INFORMATION**

National Sporting Goods Association
Lake Center Plaza Building
1699 Wall Street
Mt. Prospect, IL 60056

Sporting Goods Manufacturers Association
200 Castlewood Drive
North Palm Beach, FL 33408

◇ **RELATED ARTICLES**

Volume 1: Apparel; Machining and Machinery; Recreation and Park Service; Sports; Toys and Games
Volume 3: Assemblers; Gunsmiths; Knit goods industry workers; Machinists; Machine tool operators; Plastics products manufacturing workers; Rubber goods production workers; Shoe industry workers; Shoe and leather workers and repairers; Textile manufacturing occupations; Toy industry workers

Toy industry workers

Definition

Toy industry workers are employed in all the wide-ranging aspects of inventing, making, and selling children's toys and games. They include workers in research and development, who invent the toy or game; workers in engineering, who determine how to build it and what materials to use; workers in sales and marketing, who figure out how to sell the toy; and workers in assembly, who actually make and build the toy.

History

Children's toys and games go far back in humanity's history. Dolls and figurines have been found among the artifacts of the earliest civilizations, where they were used both as playthings by children and as religious and symbolic figures by adults. Other types of recreation also have roots in ancient cultures. Backgammon is considered one of the most ancient board games, and the Egyptians played a primitive version of chess called "Jackals and Hounds."

Dolls have a long and illustrious history. Many European kings and noblemen gave elaborate dolls in fancy costumes as gifts. Many fashion styles were spread through other regions and countries in this way. Some cities, such as Paris and Sonneberg, Germany, became famous for the manufacture of beautiful, innovative, and well-made dolls. Over the years dolls have been made of wood, clay, china, papier-mache, wax, and hard rubber, and they have been collected and admired by many adults as well as children.

Other types of toys were usually made by hand at home. The mass production of toys began in the nineteenth century during the Industrial Revolution. One of the first and most popular toy fads was the teddy bear, which was named after President Theodore Roosevelt. Toy companies generally devise their own products or adapt them from perennial favorites, but they occasionally buy ideas for new toys and games from outsiders. One famous example of this was a board game devised during the Depression by an out-of-work man in his kitchen. He drew a playing board on his tablecloth and, using the names of streets in his hometown of Atlantic City, devised a game that

let him act out his fantasies of being a real estate and business tycoon. He called the game "Monopoly," and it became one of the most popular games of all time.

The popularity of certain toys rises and falls over time. Some toys maintain their popularity with successive generations of children or experience a comeback after a few years. Computer and video games have boomed in the past decade and will likely become more complex and realistic as technology advances. Still, it is impossible to predict which new toys will become popular, which adds some excitement and pressure to the industry.

Nature of the work

Taking a toy from the idea stage to the store shelf is a long and complex operation, sometimes taking one to two years from start to finish. Ideas for a new toy or game can come from many sources. Large companies may have their own marketing and research and development departments that consider what kind of toys are currently being sold on the market and devise new toys to meet a perceived demand. Companies also get ideas from professional inventors and free-lance designers, and from average people, including children, who write to companies to describe new toys they have devised.

Many toy ideas are considered for production but are eventually scrapped. A toy company has two considerations when it decides whether to produce a toy: how much children will want to play with it and whether it can be profitably manufactured. Only after these two questions are answered will a company make plans to mass produce a game or toy.

A toy must be fun to play with, but there are other measures of a toy's worth other than amusement. Some toys are designed to teach or enhance a child's motor skills, excite their curiosity about the natural world, or let them express their feelings in a healthy way. Often toys are made into prototypes by *model makers* and the marketing research department will organize test groups of children or toddlers to allow them to play with the toys and test their reactions. If the test group enjoys a toy and comes back to play with it more than a few times, then the toy has passed a major milestone.

The company also has to ask itself some important technical and commercial questions: Is the toy safe and durable? Is it similar to any other toys on the market? Does it have a potentially large appeal? Can it be mass produced and still have a low enough cost per unit that it can be made profitably? These types of questions are the responsibility of the research and development department, which draws up detailed designs for new toys, determines what materials should be used, and devises methods to make the toy economically. After the research and development employees have completed their work, the project is passed on to various engineers to get production started.

Electronic toys, video games, and computer games have skyrocketed in popularity in the past decade. These are developed by computer engineers, technicians, and software programmers. Technical development engineers work on these toys, as well as toys that involve advanced mechanical or acoustical technology. Plastics engineers work on plans for plastic toys. They design tools and molds for making plastic toy parts, and determine the type of molding process and plastic that are best for the job. Plastics engineers who work for large firms can design and build 150 or more new molds each year.

To determine the best ways to manufacture the toy, *manufacturing engineers* study the blueprints for the new product and figure out what type of machinery will be needed. These engineers may build this machinery from what the company already owns, or decide to purchase new machinery. At all stages of the engineering process, it is important to keep the costs of equipment and labor down while still maintaining quality.

Once the manufacturing engineers have assembled the machinery to be used in production, *industrial engineers* must design the operations of manufacturing: the layout of the plant, the work hours each step in the process should take, the number of workers needed, how to measure performance, and so on. They often teach supervisors and assembly workers how to operate the machinery and assemble the new toy. They work with shift supervisors to relay what sort of production levels the company expects. Industrial engineers can also be responsible for the system of packaging and shipping the completed toys.

As toys are being built on the assembly line, they are thoroughly inspected by *quality control engineers* for their safety and durability. Most toy companies adhere to the quality standards outlined in ASTM F963-86, a set of voluntary guidelines the toy industry has developed for itself. The toy industry is also monitored by the Consumer Products Safety Commission and must adhere to various federal laws and standards that cover the safety of a toy under normal use and any foreseeable abuse. Finally, getting the toys from the factory to the store shelf is the responsibility of the marketing, sales, and merchandising department. These employees stay in contact with toy stores and retail outlets and can arrange toy displays and in-store product promotions.

In large toy firms, many different people can be employed in the professions described above. Occasionally they are grouped in teams, such as the research and development team, and they see and make decisions on every toy the company makes. In smaller firms, job distinctions may not be so precise and separate, and a small group of employees may work together to develop and sell a toy from beginning to end. The fewer employees in a firm, the more hats they have to wear.

Practically all toys and games are mass-produced by factory workers on assembly lines. Each manufacturing process can be as unique as the toy itself. Many plastic toys need to be cast in injection molds first and then assembled. Wooden and metal toys have to be machined, then assembled, finished, or painted. Board games are made by many of the same printing and binding processes used for books: The playing surface is printed on a piece of paper, then glued to the properly sized piece of cardboard, and the two halves of the board are taped together by bookbinding equipment.

Toy assemblers put together the various plastic, wood, metal, or fabric pieces to make a completed toy. They sometimes sit at a conveyor belt or workbench, and work with hand tools like pliers, hammers, or small power tools to fasten the pieces together. Other times they may operate larger machines such as drill presses, reamers, flanging presses, and punch presses. Some toys like wagons are made on assembly lines, and assemblers only work on a single part like attaching axles or tires. Other toys may be completely assembled by one assembler; for instance, action figures may have their heads, arms, and legs all attached by one person at one station on an assembly line.

The manufacture of dolls provides a good example of the various manual and mechanical operations that can go into the making of a single toy. The head, torso, arms, and legs of the doll are first made in plastic-injection molds by the *plastic dolls mold filler*, cured, trimmed, and sent off on a conveyor belt. The doll's head goes to a *rooter operator*, who operates a large machine that roots or stitches a specific quantity of synthetic hair onto the head. When hair is attached in a wig, the *doll wigs hackler* combs

A toy industry worker constructs several backgammon sets at once. She must fit the materials in place and glue them onto the main board.

and softens synthetic hair by pulling it through the bristles of a hackle, then the *finisher* sets the hair in the specified style by combing, brushing, and cutting. The parts of the doll are then assembled by a toy assembler, and the *hand finisher* completes the doll by dressing it in premade clothes, shoes, ribbons, and bracelets. Once the doll is inspected, it is sent down the assembly line to be packaged and made ready for shipment.

Requirements

The type of skills a person needs to bring to a job in the toy industry depends on the position he or she seeks. A college education is important for those wishing to be managers or engineers. Because of the wide range of activities in the toy business, many degrees can find their place—art, electronics, architecture, psychology, business, the sciences. Many people succeed with skills other than those learned in college classrooms, because of their sales and marketing skills, troubleshooting ideas, management ability, or skill at inventing. The toy industry needs creative and innovative people in all phases of operation, so that toys that kids want to play with can be made, distributed, and sold in the most efficient and profitable way. Because the team approach is used in many toy companies, people can make the most of the special skills of their fellow employ-

ees and learn about different aspects of the business.

No advanced education is needed for those people who work in assembling toys, although experience in work with machinery can be a plus. Most assembling skills are learned on the job from experienced workers.

Special requirements

Licenses and certifications are not required for toy industry workers. The Toy Manufacturers of America (TMA) is a trade group to which most toy companies belong. Members of this group account for 90 percent of the total toy sales across the country. TMA also runs annual trade shows, handles public relations with the media for the industry, and encourages companies to follow voluntary safety and quality standards. Toy inventors, free-lance designers, and toy testing laboratories can hold associate memberships in TMA. To protect their interests regarding wages and hours, workers in toy factories may join labor unions, such as the Amalgamated Toy and Novelty Workers of the AFL-CIO.

Opportunities for experience and exploration

To discover what the toy industry is like, students may apply for summer or part-time jobs with local manufacturers. The most likely areas to find jobs are in assembly work, sales, and marketing. Toy manufacture is a very seasonal business because the majority of toys are still sold around the holiday season. This means that toy makers are usually most busy from March through September.

Related occupations

Other workers who perform similar work include sporting goods production workers, silverware industry workers, shoe industry workers, and watch repairers.

Methods of entering

For an entry-level job in the toy industry, students must contact the personnel offices of the toy manufacturers. This is true for all positions at a factory—engineers, management, marketers, and factory workers. While professional degrees can be helpful for people looking for jobs in engineering or marketing, an open and creative mind is the only prerequisite for a job in this industry.

Advancement

Advancement to better jobs and higher pay will come to both management staff and factory personnel as they acquire skills and seniority. Production workers can advance by learning how to operate different and more complex machinery.

Employment outlook

The overall job outlook for both management and factory personnel is quite good. There are more than 500 toy companies in America, and, while some manufacturing jobs have moved overseas to take advantage of cheaper labor, most companies still employ a high percentage of American workers. The Bureau of Labor Statistics estimates that 50,000 people are employed in the toy industry in this country, with three-quarters of these in production jobs.

The demand for toys, games, and various other amusements continues to grow among both children and adults. In the past, most toys appeared in department stores in the weeks before Christmas. Today, the toy industry operates and supplies its products year-round. While 60 percent of toy sales still take place toward the end of the year, people exchange toys and novelty items on birthdays, graduations, housewarmings, showers, and many different holidays.

Another factor in the strong employment outlook for production workers is the high amount of job turnover. Because of the low pay, monotonous work, and seasonal workloads that toy assemblers endure, many quit after a time to find more stable employment. This means that most manufacturers are continually on the lookout for new production workers.

Earnings

When first hired, factory workers generally earn the minimum wage or slightly more. As they gain experience, they may reach a wage level of $6 an hour or more. Many workers are paid at a piecework or other incentive rate, and machine operators are paid more than those assemblers who work by hand. Generally the union and the toy manufacturer agree to a wage scale and conditions for salary increases. Factory workers are paid overtime when they work longer shifts during the peak production season from July to September.

Management and engineers, on the other hand, are paid a straight salary. Salaries vary widely from company to company and among the different job types. For example, research and development employees can start at about $25,000 per year and rise to $150,000 or more annually. Salary levels for white collar workers depend on their experience, seniority, and quality of work.

Conditions

Most toy factories are simply large rooms in which hundreds of workers perform routine tasks. Some people work at machines, while others sit at tables or assembly lines. Factory workers generally work a five-day, forty-hour week, but during the peak season from July to September or when industry trade shows are upcoming, they may work overtime. At other times of the year, their hours may be cut or the workers may be laid off. They often have to meet production schedules and quotas.

Management and other professional employees work year round. They may need to put in overtime during peak seasons or before trade shows, but they do not earn overtime. Many times managers and executives need to travel, both around the country and to other countries, to finalize contracts, oversee plant operations, attend trade shows, and sell their product lines.

Social and psychological factors

The toy industry is exciting, but it is also fiercely competitive. The great pressure to come up with successful, popular toys every year can drain a person's energy and creativity. No matter how much market research and careful planning is done, the success of any new toy is still a gamble. While this is challenging, it can also be frustrating.

People in this industry possess a unique combination of artistic, technological, and business skills. Those who are interested in the toy

613

industry on both the management and the production sides should be versatile and creative problem-solvers. They must also be able to work well with other people, because getting an idea for a toy from the drawing board to the store shelf is a team effort with a great many players.

GOE: 06.04.23; SIC: 394; SOC: 772

◇ **SOURCES OF ADDITIONAL INFORMATION**

Toy Manufacturers of America
200 Fifth Avenue
New York, NY 10017

International Union of Allied Novelty and Production Workers
147 East 26th Street
New York, NY 10010

Toy Wholesalers Association of America
66 East Main Street
Moorestown, NY 08057

National Association of Doll and Stuffed Toy Manufacturers
200 East Post Road
White Plains, NY 10601

◇ **RELATED ARTICLES**

Volume 1: Toys and Games
Volume 2: Buyers, wholesale and retail; Engineers; Industrial designers; Industrial traffic managers; Marketing, advertising, and public relations managers; Marketing research personnel
Volume 3: Assemblers; Plastics products manufacturing workers; Sporting goods production workers

Watch repairers

Definition

Watch repairers or *watchmakers* repair, adjust, clean, and regulate watches, clocks, chronometers, electromechanical and other kinds of timepieces.

History

Ancient civilizations used various devices as timepieces. These included sundials, sand clocks, water clocks, and candles. The basic clock mechanism was developed by Henry de Vich in the early 1300s. The earliest mechanical turret clocks were large weight-driven machines that had no dials nor hands. In 1335, however, a public clock was installed in Milan, Italy, that struck the hours.

The first really portable clocks, developed in the early 1500s, were cylindrical in shape and ran by means of moving weights. These "watches" were so heavy they were carried in the hand or tied to the waist. Development of

the mainspring and the hair spring made possible the reduction of their size. The flat, round watch appeared on the scene in about 1600, and the first wristwatch was made for Empress Josephine of France in 1807.

A patent for a self-winding pocketwatch was granted in 1780. In 1924, a patent was granted for a self-winding wristwatch. The electronic watch was developed in 1953.

Nature of the work

The watch is a complex machine with many small parts, and to repair one requires precision and delicacy. The ability to locate and correct defects in the watch is an important skill for a watch repairer to have. A set routine provides the watch repairer with means of tracing the defect in a systematic manner. Asking a customer for the past history of a watch may provide information regarding previous repairs. At times, the defect comes from incorrect replacement or improper fitting of parts. Pushing, pulling, and turning the winding stem may show binding, or dirty hands of the watch, or looseness that may permit dust to enter the mechanical parts.

The next step requires the opening of the case and the removal of the dial so that the mechanism can be examined with the aid of a magnifying eyeglass, or loupe. Watch repairers check for defective parts or signs of fouling and inspect springs for rust and alignment of parts. During the process, they may repair or replace such parts as the mainspring, hairspring, jewels or pivots, and escapements. With older watches, they may have to make a part for the watch to function properly. They may clean the watch by means of cleaning solution or, in the larger repair shops, with supersonic sound waves. Oiling of parts requires a delicate touch, for excessive amounts of oil or oil in the wrong spots cause the watch to operate improperly. The watch must be reassembled so that parts fit properly.

The watch repairer uses several devices to assist in the work. A timing machine is used to check the accuracy of the watch. If the watch is inaccurate, appropriate adjustments are made. A watch showing erratic time-keeping is checked for magnetism and demagnetized in a demagnetizer. When repairing electric or electronic watches, various electric meters or oscilloscopes may be used by watch repairers to make repairs or adjustments. They must also be able to use various tools such as pliers, pilar files, pin vises, tweezers, turns, and lathes.

In addition to repair work, many watch repairers do jewelry repair work and sell various items like clocks, watches, jewelry, china, and silverware. This is especially true if they are self-employed or work in a retail store. In large stores or shops, they may have managerial or supervisory duties. If self-employed, they will order parts and merchandise, keep accounts, arrange for advertising, and perform tasks required to maintain an efficient and profitable business.

Requirements

Watch repairers must be able to work independently with a high degree of precision and care. They must be able to make visual comparisons and discriminations and have the ability to perceive pertinent details in objects. They must work with their hands in placing and turning motions. They must make judgments, using set standards, and have the ability to feel and finger objects with deftness. Clarity of oral expression, orderly work habits, and good vision are

Watch repairers must wear special magnifiers on their glasses so that they can easily focus on the piece they are replacing.

also desirable. The owner of a shop must be able to manage other employees, be able to deal with the public, and have a basic business background.

A high-school student's preparations for watchmaking should include mastery of arithmetical and numerical concepts found in mathematics or accounting. This skill is important for those who will be self-employed. Skill in the use of various tools can be obtained in shop courses. Speech and English courses will be of help in meeting the public.

The best way to become a watch repairer is to acquire training at a watch repair school. The typical training period is about one to three years. Training in engraving, jewel repair, and stone setting may add an additional ten months of school to the basic course work. The course of study contains work in disassembling and reassembling, cleaning and oiling, and replacing or repairing parts in various kinds of timepieces. The student receives instruction on the use of such devices as demagnetizers, watchmaker's lathe, and electronic timing equipment. Additional training may be obtained in servicing electronic watches, calendars, chronometers, and timers. A student is usually required to purchase a set of hand tools. Refresher courses are offered as new products come on the market.

On-the-job training is not used too frequently as a method of preparing a watch repairer. More often than not, it is restricted to preparing the relatives of the watchmaker. The use of a formal apprenticeship program to train an individual in watch repair work is rare.

Special requirements

The following states require a watch repairer to be licensed before working at his trade: Indiana, Iowa, Kentucky, Louisiana, Minnesota, and North Dakota. For licensure, the individual must pass a test on the fundamentals of watch repair. The American Watchmakers Institute has provisions for certifying qualified watch repairers. Successful performance on a written examination and a practical test of watch repair is required. The titles of Certified Watchmaker, Certified Master Watchmaker, and Certified Electronic Watch Specialist are awarded to those who successfully pass the qualifying examinations.

Opportunities for experience and exploration

A high-school student can investigate this occupational field by securing a part-time job in a shop where watches and jewelry are repaired and sold. Various shop courses or hobbies where dexterity and patience are needed in using hand tools can be used to analyze one's manual skill. The military service provides an indirect opportunity for training in repairing various precision instruments, although this type of training does not qualify a person for watch repair work. Many jewelry shops hire high-school and college students to work part-time during the holiday seasons.

Related occupations

Other workers are also involved in the making and repairing of jewelry. Other related occupations include jewelers, jewelry makers, jewelry repairers, silverware industry production workers, and instrument repairers.

Methods of entering

Methods of entering this occupational field are rather restricted. Upon completion of a watch-repair school program, the individual may secure help in finding a job from the school's placement department, and may also secure help in finding a job from the American Watch-makers Institute. Because on-the-job training is uncommon, there is only limited opportunity for a person to be upgraded from some other position in the store or shop. In areas where apprenticeship programs in watchmaking exist, an agreement for indenture must be made with an employer and supervised by a state agency.

Advancement

Watch repairers who work in a store or repair shop have only limited opportunities for advancement. In an organization employing a number of repairers, they may be promoted to supervisor or service manager. The typical advancement is to become self-employed after acquiring sufficient experience in repairing various types of watches. An investment of at least $5,000 is needed to buy the necessary equipment and parts to open a watch repair shop. Additional money is required to make the shop a retail jewelry store.

Employment outlook

More than 12,000 watch repairers were employed in the United States in the early 1990s. It is expected that the employment opportunities for watch repairers will be below average during the next decade. As in other occupational fields, an experienced and skilled repairer will always be in demand.

Production of watches should increase because of population expansion. The sales of inexpensive watches will, however, generate less work for repairers. Consumers tend to discard cheaper watches. The person who owns a good watch, however, will usually continue to have it repaired.

With additional training, some of the repairers can work on many types of miniaturized items such as hearing aids, transistorized radios, and the like. Some of the companies that manufacture missile parts or computers require skillful people in assembling the required miniaturized equipment.

Earnings

In the early 1990s, annual salaries for beginning watch repairers ranged from about $10,900 to $17,500. The annual salary for experienced workers ranged from $18,700 to more than $32,500. Service managers and supervisors in large repair shops or stores earned considerably more. In some stores, the repairers receive a commission on the various items they sell. The earnings of self-employed watchmakers ranged between $18,000 and $27,600 a year. Those who sold watches, jewelry, and other items often earned up to about $48,000 a year.

Conditions of work

The watch repairer can work at home or in a department store, a shopping center, a jewelry store, or a repair shop. The work requires proper lighting and ventilation and a considerable amount of sitting. As a result, many physically handicapped people have entered this occupation. Some persons experience eyestrain in the initial phase of training, but by following proper procedures the work can be performed with a minimum of strain.

The basic workweek is forty hours, but repairers ordinarily work between forty-five to forty-eight hours a week. A self-employed person may work longer hours. Repairers usually work one or two evenings a week and Saturdays.

Some repairers belong to the International Jewelry Workers Union or the American Watch Workers Union.

Social and psychological factors

Watch repairers must be able to work well without supervision. Because in many cases they deal directly with the customer, they must be neat in appearance, courteous, and able to speak well. If self-employed, they must be able to carry out many functions associated with operating a business. They should take pride in their skill, because a reputation for quality work enhances their business. A person who likes to work under conditions demanding precision, dexterity, and patience will be comfortable in watch repair work.

GOE: 05.05.11; SIC: 7631; SOC: 6171

◇ **SOURCES OF ADDITIONAL INFORMATION**

American Watchmakers Institute
3700 Harrison Avenue
Cincinnati, OH 45211

Jewelers of America
1271 Avenue of the Americas
New York, NY 10020

◇ **RELATED ARTICLES**

Volume 3: Assemblers; Instrument makers; Jewelers and jewelry repairers; Locksmiths
Volume 4: Electromechanical technicians; Mechanical technicians

Structural Work Occupations

The structural worker builds homes, buildings, highways, and bridges. Numbering about 4 million people, this occupational group constitutes the largest skilled work force in the United States. This group handles every aspect of construction, maintenance, and repair of the major structures built. From the beginning of construction with the laying of the foundation through the wiring, plumbing, and roofing, to the final architectural details and decorations, structural workers are the cornerstone of any structure.

Structural workers include carpenters, painters, plumbers, bricklayers, stonemasons, electricians, roofers, insulation workers, and related workers. Carpenters represent nearly one-third of the total number of people employed in this group. The wide variety of trades points out clearly the high degree of specialization to be found in structural work.

Manual dexterity is a must for any individual interested in the skilled trades discussed in this section; and a high-school education is increasingly required. Vocational and trade schools offer many of the preparatory courses helpful in this field, and informal training can be had by working as a laborer or tender on a construction site. For those seriously interested in one or more of the trades, there are apprenticeship programs available that will provide a broad training background and the experience needed to become a skilled worker.

To become an apprentice, an individual usually must have the approval of a joint (labor-management) committee that evaluates a person's educational background, experience, and performance on apprentice examinations. The apprenticeship program varies in length from three to six years, depending upon the specific trade involved. The number of vacancies available each year, however, tends to be somewhat limited.

Advancements in the structural work occupations depend largely on experience. The workers may become supervisors in charge of a construction crew; they may also prepare estimates for a contractor; they may supervise large building projects; or they may start their own construction business.

The greatest number of job opportunities occur in the construction industry, working for contractors. Other job possibilities lie in the area of maintenance and repair work and in employment by governmental agencies.

The employment trend in the United States for the next decade is expected to be moderately good. Among the factors contributing to an increase in job opportunities are an increasing population, with its need for more homes; renovation of existing homes and office buildings; better highways to handle the growing mobility of the nation; and larger industrial complexes to handle the rising demands of production. This occupational group, however, is closely affected by the state of the economy, and any recession or tightening of money limits the number of jobs available.

Asphalt paving machine operators

Definition

Asphalt paving machine operators operate machines that spread and level hot-mix asphalt paving material on the subgrade of highways, streets, and parking lots.

History

The greatest road builders in history were the ancient Romans. For military and economic reasons, they constructed durable roads with layers of stone, concrete and pebbles to all corners of their empire. Parts of many of these roads are still in use today.

Today roads and highways are also built in layers, but science has made changes in the materials they are made of. Many laboratories study the properties of various road building materials to discover a workable compromise between materials that are durable but also economical. Streets and highways today are paved mainly with asphalt cement. It is made of asphalt, which is an oil product that occurs naturally or can be derived from the refining of petroleum, and aggregate, which can be gravel, sand, crushed stone, or even recycled paving material. The asphalt binds the aggregate into a solid mass that makes a long-lasting and tenacious building material. This mix may be applied cold or hot, but for large paving jobs hot mix asphalt (HMA) is always applied by large paving machines.

Nature of the work

Although the different makes of asphalt paving machines each have their own unique features, the basic processes they perform are the same. They are propelled by a tractor mechanism and are designed to move in a straight path, sometimes by following a preset guide wire. In a receiving hopper, they carry the paving material, or HMA, and keep it warm and workable. Depending on the job, HMA may be mixed at the job site by a portable pugmill or mixed in a factory and trucked to the job site. The HMA is carried on conveyor belts through flow control gates and onto the ground, where it is smoothed and tamped down by a heavy, floating metal plate called a "screed." The screed can be widened to accommodate any width of road; some of the largest asphalt paving machines can lay HMA up to thirty-six feet wide in a single pass. The screed often has heaters and vibrators built in which can be adjusted to ensure uniform paving.

These huge machines are run by asphalt paving machine operators, sometimes called power operators. On some machines, a second employee, the *screed operator*, rides or walks alongside the back of the machine to monitor the application of HMA and to adjust the screed when necessary.

Automatic controls on the machine regulate most of the paving, but the operator can override these controls if necessary. The operator must keep a careful eye on the whole paving process. For example, there must be a steady flow of HMA to the screed, so the operator adjusts the flow control gates. The operator must also make sure there is an adequate supply of HMA in the machine, because stopping to reload and then restarting the machine will make the pavement uneven. The speed of the machine must also be kept constant to ensure even coverage.

Screed operators play an important role in a good paving job. They can adjust the screed to set the thickness of the HMA layer and control the cross slope of the pavement surface. They make sure the screed's leveling mechanism maintains an even surface when the machine hits a hump or a depression in the subgrade or base pavement. If the base pavement changes thickness while new HMA is being added, the screed operator will activate the vibrators or tamper bars in the screed which will compress the HMA and give it a uniform thickness. Screed operators can keep the screed clear of any sticking HMA by adjusting the screed's heaters.

Paving machine operators must be able to tell when the HMA has been improperly mixed from its appearance and workability. For example, blue smoke rising from the mix means there is too much heat, while stiffness may mean it has cooled too much. If the mix slumps, it may contain too much asphalt, but if it is dry and dull-looking, it may not have enough asphalt to cover the aggregate. If steam rises from the pavement, the mix may contain too much moisture. Many variables can affect the suitability of the HMA during the day, so it is checked regularly for density, temperature

It takes several asphalt pavers to operate and manage a paving machine.

and composition by the machine operator and by the *asphalt paving supervisor.*

Paving machine operators inspect their machines at the beginning of the workday and also at day's end. In the morning, they check to make sure all moving parts (screed plate, conveyors, flow control gates and vibrators) are in good working order. They double check the tire pressure or, if the paving machine runs on tracks, make certain that the tracks are fitting tightly. Operators clean their machines when the workday is over and remove any accumulated materials while it is still warm and pliable.

Asphalt paving machine operators work all over the country, laying pavement for streets, highways, airport runways, parking lots, railway roadbeds, and even the linings for sanitary landfills and water treatment plants. Because of budget considerations and the nation's already extensive highway system, more time today is spent repaving old roads than working on new ones. Roads are often laid in multiple layers of pavement which, when packed down, can be up to sixteen-inches thick.

Requirements

A high-school diploma is not necessary for this occupation. A knowledge of machinery, however, which can be acquired in shop classes or in vocational school, is a definite advantage.

Asphalt paving machine operators learn their trade on the job. Some do this through apprenticeships, which require about 432 hours of classroom study and 6,000 hours of on-site training. Trade associations and equipment manufacturers often hold seminars and training sessions for machine operators to learn how to operate new machinery or stay abreast of new industry developments.

Asphalt paving machine operators can also enhance their value to employers by learning how to operate other heavy machinery such as bulldozers, loaders, dump trucks, cranes, and cherry pickers. If a developer or contractor needs someone to run a bulldozer now, there is a good chance a paving machine operator may be needed soon after, and a person who can operate both will have a better chance at regular employment.

Special requirements

Membership in a union is an option for asphalt paving machine operators, but it is not required. The International Union of Operating Engineers is the principal union representing these workers.

A number of professional societies also serve the asphalt industry and can be an important source of information and training for operators. These groups include the American Road and Transportation Association, the Asphalt Institute, the National Asphalt Pavement Association, and the Associated Builders and Contractors.

Opportunities for experience and exploration

Students may learn about paving machines by getting a summer job on a road or construction crew. They may be assigned to strictly physical labor, but they will be able to see if working with this type of machinery and under these conditions interests them.

Related occupations

There are many other occupations that require large equipment handling skills. Some of these include construction machinery equipment operators, such as bulldozers, front-end loaders, and backhoes, bus drivers, semitrailer truck drivers, route drivers, and industrial-truck operators.

Methods of entering

Job seekers should contact developers and contractors directly and express their interest in operating asphalt paving machines. The names of these firms can be found in the telephone directory or from state employment agencies. Because experience is the best way to get a job in this area, job seekers should show a ready eagerness to work. Employers may not have an immediate opening for a paving machine operator, and wouldn't allow inexperienced workers to run these expensive and complicated machines, but they may offer some other type of road or construction work that can be a stepping stone. Once in a job, it will be easier to convince the employer to put a person through the training necessary to operate a paving machine. Another way to gain an apprenticeship is to join a union and apply for training through it.

Advancement

Experienced paving machine operators who show they are dependable and skilled will become well known among contractors, who will in turn hire these operators for their important jobs. With this demand usually comes the possibility of higher pay. Skilled operators who stay with the same employer may be given higher pay or be promoted to a supervisory field position or a job in the office.

Employment outlook

Work for paving machine operators depends for the most part on the availability of public funds, because state and local governments supply paving contractors with most of their business. While a city may have many miles of roads it would like to repave, tight fiscal budgets limit the amount of paving that can be done and the amount of work available for paving machine operators. Concern has been rising, however, in both the federal and state legislatures over the deterioration of the nation's roads and highways, and this may translate into more funds being allotted to restoration and paving work.

In general, job turnover is low among paving machine operators. Many operators stay at their jobs for fifteen or twenty years, and this may limit the opportunities for those wishing to enter the field. Successful, growing companies, however, may be in need of pavers and other operators of heavy machinery. Those who can operate other heavy vehicles such as bulldozers or dump trucks will have the best chance of finding work.

Earnings

In the early 1990s, those paving machine operators who were members of the International Union of Operating Engineers earned approximately $17.25 an hour in wages and $5.45 an hour in fringe benefits, for a total of $22.70 an hour. Those operators working overtime received time and a half.

This is about the same wage that contractors offer their nonunion workers, although those workers with experience and superior skills may earn more. Some contractors offer health care, pension plans and other fringe benefits, but this varies from company to company.

Conditions of work

Asphalt paving machine operators work when the weather is warm, with temperatures higher than 40° F. In some parts of the country, this work can be conducted year-round, but in the colder climates the work is seasonal. In winter climates, contractors begin to get their equipment ready in the beginning of March so that they can begin work as soon as the weather is warm enough. They usually can work until around the middle of October. Workers in the northern regions can take the winter off, while those in warmer climates work all year.

In any climate, paving machine operators work long hours and are on their feet most of the day. In order to complete a job on time, operators can be expected to work ten to fourteen hours a day, six or seven days a week. The searing summer heat working on a roadbed can make the day seem even longer.

Around paving and construction machinery, workers need to protect themselves from hot splashes of asphalt, falling objects and other hazards. Operators protect themselves by wearing hard hats, gloves, safety goggles, steel-toed shoes, and long-sleeved shirts. The smell of heated tar and asphalt can be almost overwhelming at times but frequent exposure can immunize one from noticing the odor. Operators sometimes attach an umbrella to their machine to protect them from the hot sun. To work at particular sites, paving machine operators may have to travel a long distance from home. Some commute, while others stay at motels or with friends until the job is done. Other paving machine operators may choose not to accept such assignments and wait for jobs that are nearer to home.

Social and psychological factors

Important qualities for paving machine operators include dependability and a conscientious attitude toward work. It is also important to be able to get along with people, including the other members of the work crew, contractors, supervisors, engineers, inspectors, and city and state employees. Solid working relationships with these people are the best guarantee to steady employment. Pavers should also possess agility and good balance, and a large amount of stamina.

Because paving work is seasonal and depends on the strength of the local economy and the availability of public funds, the livelihood of a paving machine operator can be tenuous. This seasonality appeals to some people, however. Pavers can also take pride in doing a job well that serves the community.

GOE: 05.11.01; SIC: 1611; SOC: 6466

◇ **SOURCES OF ADDITIONAL INFORMATION**

Asphalt Institute
Asphalt Institute Building
College Park, MD 20740

Associated Builders and Contractors
729 15th Street, NW
Washington, DC 20036

Associated General Contractors of America
1957 E Street, NW
Washington, DC 20006

National Asphalt Pavement Association
6811 Kenilworth Avenue
Riverdale, MD 20737

Association of Asphalt Paving Technologists
1404 Concordia Avenue
St. Paul, MN 55104

◇ **RELATED ARTICLES**

Volume 1: Construction; Engineering; Machining and Machinery
Volume 3: Construction workers; Operating engineers (construction machinery operators); Industrial truck operators
Volume 4: Parking engineering technicians

Automotive painters

Definition

Automotive painters are skilled tradespeople who refinish automotive exteriors. On both old and damaged vehicles, they employ hand and spray methods to recapture the sheen of the original paint. The job involves removing old paint, masking or covering surfaces not to be painted such as the chrome trim, preparing the surface for new paint, and then applying and finishing the required coats, as well as polishing the car's surface. If necessary, they may also remove chrome, windshields, mirrors, and other accessories.

In most cases, they are assisted by on-the-job trainees known as automotive painter helpers. These individuals perform the same tasks,

beginning with the simplest, and taking on more difficult ones with the passage of time.

In either job, auto painters either perform minor touch-ups or repaint an entire car.

History

The skill of applying paint to beautify, protect, or cover a surface is one of man's oldest accomplishments. More than 10,000 years ago, cave dwellers covered the walls of their caves with paintings. As civilization progressed, so did the use of paint. It has been employed for religious, educational, artistic, and utilitarian purposes.

Paint is a universal medium that is highly valued though often taken for granted.

In modern times, the expansion of the painting profession has been tied to technological developments. These have both made paint available in large quantities and opened up new opportunities for those in the trade. In the mid- and late nineteenth century, the invention of new machines allowed manufacturers to mass produce paint. The introduction of the automobile around the turn of the twentieth century created the automobile painter occupation.

Nature of the work

Auto painting is a highly skilled, labor intensive job that requires a fine eye and an attention to detail. Jobs are available in auto repair shops, dealerships, or with organizations that maintain and repair their own motor vehicle fleets.

There are two general types of auto painting. Both can employ the use of a brush and/or a paint sprayer. Touch-up work or a job that requires that less than the whole car be painted usually involves the painter in mixing pigments to match the original color.

Whether in touch-ups or in the painting of a whole automobile, the first step is to hand and power sand the surface to remove any original paint and rust. Any small nicks or scratches are filled with body putty. Parts that are not to be painted, like chrome trim, windows, headlights, and mirrors, are removed or masked by the painter or a helper.

Once the car is prepared for painting, several coats of primer are applied with a sprayer. Vehicles with metal bodies require lacquer; those with plastic ones are sprayed with acrylic enamel. In either case, the auto painter must fine-tune the spraying nozzle, adjusting it for the kind of paint used. The air-pressure regulator also must be correctly adjusted. If the paint is not applied properly, it may run or spread too thickly.

Between each coat of primer, the car is dried. Usually this takes place in a special infrared oven or under heat lamps to speed the process. After drying, auto painters sand the surface to remove any irregularities. This also helps the next coat to adhere better. Lacquer primers are final sanded by hand with a fine grade sandpaper. Final sanding is not necessary for acrylic enamel primers. After the last coat of paint has dried, the auto painter or a helper may polish the vehicle.

The perfect application of paint on an automobile requires the use of a finely-tuned spraying nozzle and an air pressure regulator.

Requirements

Good health, keen eyesight, a steady hand, and a good sense of color are needed by auto painters. A high-school diploma is an advantage but is not required. At the high-school, vocational school, and junior or community college levels, courses in automobile body repair, auto painting, and refinishing should be taken by prospective painters.

On-the-job training is the prime requisite for becoming an auto painter. Usually applicants start as helpers working with experienced painters. Over a period of three to four years, helpers undertake tasks of increasing complexity until they become painters in their own right.

Apprenticeships are also available and are three years in duration. In addition to learning painting skills, participants are taught shop safety practices, color blending, and the proper use of equipment.

Either preparation track—on-the-job training or an apprenticeship program—is an acceptable method of meeting the requirements for becoming an automotive painter.

Special requirements

Though voluntary, certification by the National Institute for Automobile Service Excellence is regarded as the standard of achievement by the trade. To qualify for certification, the applicant must possess two years' field experience, for which one year of schooling may be substituted, and pass a written exam. To maintain certification, the exam must be successfully passed again every five years.

Opportunities for experience and exploration

Prospective auto painters can learn about the trade through taking pertinent courses in school or by working as a helper in a shop. It also is possible to visit a shop and interview auto painters about the work they do.

Related occupations

Other jobs that require skills with automobiles include automobile-body repairers, automobile mechanics, automobile-repair-service estimators, diesel mechanics, motorcycle mechanics, and automobile assembly workers.

Methods of entering

The trade can be entered either through securing a job as a helper or enrolling in an apprenticeship program and getting a job after its conclusion. Information about apprenticeship programs is available from the local office of the state employment service, from auto repair shops and dealers, or from locals of unions who include auto painters in their memberships.

On-the-job training primarily comes about from contacting an employer about a job opening.

Advancement

Both within and outside the shop, auto painters have significant opportunities for advancement. If they demonstrate supervisory capability they can rise to shop supervisor. Many painters, however, try to secure the necessary capital to open their own shops.

Employment outlook

The increasing popularity of the automobile expanded the need for trained personnel who could repaint older cars and those damaged in traffic accidents. In the early 1990s, approximately 60,000 people were employed as transportation equipment painters, the majority of which were auto painters. Most work in heavily populated areas where the number of cars on the road is great.

The employment outlook for automotive painters is connected to the number of motor vehicles damaged in traffic accidents. As the accident rate is expected to increase throughout the next decade, the employment of auto painters is expected to rise faster than the national average for all occupations.

Jobs also will be created through attrition by death, retirement, and the transfer to other occupations. Heavily populated areas will offer the best opportunity for employment.

Because they are not truly affected by economic fluctuations, experienced painters can expect steady, secure employment. No matter what the condition of the economy, cars involved in accidents or suffering from age will continue to need repair and repainting. Persons seeking to enter the trade, however, will find fewer job openings during recessions.

Earnings

In the early 1990s, a survey in twenty-four large cities disclosed that the estimated earnings of experienced automotive painters was more than $35,000 annually. Beginning apprentices receive about half this, with their wages increasing as their competence grows. Eventually, apprentices earn a salary approaching that of experienced auto painters. Helpers start at lower salaries. Automotive painters are paid either on a salary/commission basis or receive a straight salary. Where they work determines how they are paid.

Those working in dealerships or in repair shops receive a minimum weekly guaranteed wage. They also receive a commission based upon the labor cost of the work they do. How much auto painters earn in this type of employment is dependent upon the speed of their work. Helpers and apprentices usually start out at a straight hourly wage until their skills become proficient enough to merit switching to commissions.

Auto painters who work for trucking companies, bus lines, and other businesses that maintain their own vehicles are paid on an hourly basis, without commission.

In either case, auto painters work from forty to forty-five hours per week.

Conditions of work

The work of repainting autos is done inside, mostly in specially ventilated booths. The work involves much bending and stooping and is potentially dangerous. To obviate exposure to dangerous fumes from paint and paint-mixing ingredients, painters wear masks and respirators for protection.

Social and psychological factors

Auto painting is a skilled trade that requires patience, attention to detail, and manual dexterity. The work is not so much physically strenuous as mentally exhausting. Each coat of primer or paint must be applied carefully to achieve the desired effects.

Often the painter works independently, aided by a helper. Because this is a teacher/pupil relationship, the auto painter must be able to communicate well and have the patience to calmly deal with mistakes made by less experienced helpers. At the same time, the painter must be able to instruct helpers while working fast enough to earn commissions.

Painters who work for companies or organizations that maintain their own vehicles, or for large auto dealers often belong to one of the following unions: the International Brotherhood of Teamsters, Chauffeurs, Warehousemen and Helpers of America (Ind.); the International Union, United Automobile, Aerospace and Agricultural Implement Workers of America; the Sheet Metal Workers' International Association; and the International Association of Machinists and Aerospace Workers.

GOE: 05.10.07; SIC: 7532; SOC: 6115

◇ SOURCES OF ADDITIONAL INFORMATION

Automotive Service Association
1901 Airport Freeway
Suite 100
Bedford, TX 76095

Automotive Service Industry Association
444 North Michigan Avenue
Chicago, IL 60611

National Automobile Dealers Association
8400 Westpark Drive
McLean, VA 22102

Regarding certification, contact:

National Institute for Automotive Service Excellence
1920 Association Drive
Reston, VA 22091

◇ RELATED ARTICLES

Volume 1: Automotives
Volume 3: Automobile mechanics; Automotive body repairers

Boilermaking occupations

Definition

There are three main crafts especially connected with boilermaking: *boilermaker*, *layout worker*, and *fitter*. Boilermakers assemble and put into place the prefabricated sections and fittings of boilers, tanks, vats, and similar equipment. Layout workers, using blueprints, mark off dimensions on the metal plate from which the boiler sections will be formed. Fitters check the accuracy of the size and shape of the various parts of the boiler, tank, or other vessel, after they have been cut or otherwise shaped, by assembling the parts in a temporary fashion to see if all parts fit together according to the required specifications.

After the boiler is assembled and installed by the boilermaker, continued maintenance of the heater is also done by the boilermaker. They handle repairs and inspections.

625

Boilermaking occupations
Structural Work Occupations

History

The development of the boilermaking occupations is closely related to the expansion of the Industrial Revolution; throughout the nineteenth century great progress was made in the use of boilers in industry. The use of boilermaking trade products has expanded tremendously, both in total amount and in variety, in the twentieth century. The number of boilermakers (including layout workers and fitters) has increased to meet the huge demands for power and storage by U.S. industry. Naval shipyards and other federal installations, the construction industry, steel manufacturing, petroleum refineries, railroads, the chemical industry, and the gas and electric companies have become frequent users of the boilermakers' skills.

Boilers are often operated at very high pressures. Faulty construction, repair, or operation can therefore be sources of great danger. During the latter part of the nineteenth century, attempts were made through local regulations to prevent accidents caused through careless construction. But it was not until 1908 that a code of such rules and regulations was developed to apply to any sizeable area. Massachusetts created a Board of Boiler Rules in that year, and Ohio followed in 1911. By 1934, nineteen states and fifteen cities had such codes. Today, as a result of the combined efforts of industry, labor unions, and government, safety codes are practically universal. The American Society of Mechanical Engineers has led in the promotion and enforcement of the codes of safe manufacture and maintenance.

Nature of the work

Boilermakers work at the site where the boiler, tank, or vat is to be installed and put into use. Such sites include petroleum-producing areas where storage tanks are to be filled and refineries where gasoline is made, schools and other institutions requiring large heating boilers, factories where boilers are used to generate power to run machines, and atomic energy plants where installations must withstand the high pressures.

Boilermakers may also do repair work at the site. The installation must be checked to identify the specific source of weakness or trouble. It may be necessary to dismantle the boiler or other units and repair or replace worn or defective parts. Occasionally, joints or supports require strengthening. Both repair and installation must be done in compliance with state and local safety codes.

Boilermakers must be skilled in using many types of tools and equipment in installation and repair. Power shears, power rolls, power presses, and oxyacetylene torches are used for cutting and bending metal plates to specifications. Welding equipment and riveting machines are used. Some installation jobs require complete knowledge of the use of rigging equipment such as hoists, jacks, framing, and rollers.

Boilermakers find much work in the ship and boat building industry. They repair hulls, bulkheads, and decks and remove damaged parts by drilling out rivets and cutting off the heads with a chipping hammer. They make wooden patterns from the damaged plates or take measurements of them from which to make new plates, as well as installing the new plates. Sometimes similar work is done on ships' boilers, condensers, evaporators, loaders, gratings, and stacks. Boilermakers ream and align rivet holes and then fasten on new plates by driving in rivets.

Boilermaker layout workers and fitters work in the shop or factory where boilers and similar vessels are fabricated.

Both layout and fit-up workers read and interpret blueprints and specifications in their work.

Layout workers prepare metal plates and tubes that are put together to make a boiler; they mark on the plates and tubes all the curves, lines, and dimensions that are necessary as directions to the workers who will cut and shape the parts, using various metal-cutting and metal-shaping techniques and equipment.

Fitters take over after the metal parts have been formed. To check the accuracy and fit of each part, the fitters assemble them into a unit by bolting or tack-welding the pieces together. If there are inaccuracies in cut or shape, they can be corrected.

Boilermaker specialists include *mechanics*, *welders*, and *helpers*.

Requirements

Today, it is customary to require that an applicant to the boilermaking trade possess a high-school diploma. Such a diploma is almost essential for advancement to any supervisory position. Although in the past many persons have become boilermakers, layout workers, and fitters simply by working in this trade, it is strongly recommended now that a specified apprenticeship period be served. Lasting four years, the formal apprenticeship usually provides about 8,000 hours of job experience under the supervision of an experienced boilermaker. This practical work is supplemented by about 600 hours of classroom instruction in the technical aspects of the trade. An individual who has had certain shop courses in a technical high school may already have some of this knowledge. Familiarity with blueprint reading, welding techniques, the physics and chemistry of various metals, and shop mathematics is called for. On-the-job training includes practice in using knowledge acquired in the classroom, development of skills in rigging, use of hoisting equipment, tube installation and care, welding, riveting, and burning.

Mechanical aptitude and manual dexterity are important qualifications. A strong, resilient body is necessary because the work is strenuous, and stamina is needed to meet continuous exertion. Tolerance of odors, noisy surroundings, and heights is required on many jobs, and it is essential that the worker be able to work in close quarters inside boilers.

A fitter at a boilermaking plant welds metal sections together.

Special requirements

There are no special requirements for the boilermaking occupations. Apprentices usually have a broader range of skills than workers trained on the job.

Related occupations

Other workers who possess many of the same interests and skills include tool and die makers, job and die setters, elevator installers and repairers, and structural-steel workers.

Opportunities for experience and exploration

Because so many skills are used in the boilermaking occupations, one frequently finds opportunities to observe some of them. At times it is possible to watch boilermakers at their trade on a construction project or on repair and maintenance jobs. Equipment operators lifting heavy objects with elaborate rigging are working in many communities, as are welders, some of whose problems and techniques can be readily observed.

Safety is crucial to a boilermaker, and the rules of safety must be learned and practiced. Much of the technical aspect of boilermaking, such as reading plans and handling metals, may be learned in high-school courses. Metal shop and metal working classes are also good training grounds.

Methods of entering

Jobs may be found by application through government employment services and sometimes through private employment agencies; direct application may also be successful. The number of apprenticeships is limited by unions and employers to limit the number of new workers to a number that can reasonably expect to find employment in the trade in the near future. Local union offices furnish information on apprenticeship programs. Sometimes want ads in newspapers serve as a means of securing a job, or a worker may begin as a helper in a repair shop and enter a formal apprenticeship later. In some communities, high schools with metal shop courses are able to help their graduates in locating positions when they have organized placement services or are connected organizationally with branches of the U.S. Employment Service.

Advancement

Supervisory positions such as those of supervisor, gang leader, or superintendent, may be attained by workers skilled in interpersonal relations, as well as the technical and practical aspects of the trade. A few boilermakers go into business for themselves.

Employment outlook

The number of boilermakers is decreasing in the railroad industry as newer types of locomotives and repair shop power sources are developed. Some of the same factors are operating in parts of the shipbuilding industry, and in consequence the demand for boilermakers there may also decrease. These decreases, however, will be offset by demands of other industries. The increased number of power plants in many parts of the country points toward a greater demand. Highly skilled boilermakers will probably be needed in greater numbers, too, in the development of atomic energy installations and in the rising number of chemical plants. Other growing industries, such as petroleum, construction, steel, and gas and electric utilities may increase their demand for boilermakers.

Employment as a boilermaker can be found in all parts of the country, with a major concentration of the work being in the industrialized regions of the Middle Atlantic and the East North Central states. Pennsylvania, New York, New Jersey, Ohio, Illinois, Texas, and California are key states.

In the early 1990s, there were an estimated 39,000 boilermakers, layout workers, and fitters in the United States. The expectation is that for the next decade or two there will be hundreds of job openings annually in the boilermaking occupations because of expansion, deaths, retirements, and transfers of journeymen boilermakers to other trades.

Earnings

Skilled boilermakers are among the best paid of all craft workers. There are, however, variations according to the part of the country they work in, which industry employs them, and skill and experience. Pay is generally lower in industrial establishments and higher in the construction industry, although construction workers may not be employed as steadily. Boilermakers doing installation work usually earn more than those in repair and maintenance. A survey in the early 1990s showed the median annual wage for a boilermaker to be $34,900. Generally, layout workers earned more than boilermakers, and fitters earned less. Apprentices usually start at 60 percent of the experienced worker's rate. Most boilermakers' wages are set by union contracts.

Layout and fit-up workers often work indoors, and as a result their work is not as seasonal as that of many installation workers, whose earnings may also be limited by bad weather.

Conditions of work

The work of the boilermaker tends to be more hazardous than many other metalworking crafts. Boilermakers often work close to dangerous equipment, must manage heavy materials, and climb to considerable heights when constructing oil refineries, water storage tanks, and similar installations. Great progress has been made in recent years in decreasing the accident rate by means of the safety programs of employers and unions and by the use of protective equipment, but the rate of injuries in boiler shops remains higher than the average for all manufacturing industries. The work of boilermakers requires physical exertion and must be carried on under extremes of heat, poor ventilation, noise, and dampness. At times it is necessary to work in cramped quarters inside boilers, vats, or tanks. At other times, the workers must handle material and equipment several stories above ground level. When employers secure contracts in the field, installation workers must, in many cases, remain away from home for considerable periods of time.

Union contracts provide fringe benefits for most boilermakers; these include insurance—hospitalization, surgical, accident, sickness, and life-pension plans—and paid vacations. Most workers in this trade belong to the International Brotherhood of Boilermakers, Iron Shipbuilders, Blacksmiths, Forgers and Helpers. Others are members of the Industrial Union of Marine and Shipbuilding Workers of America; the Oil, Chemical, and Atomic Workers International Union; and the United Steelworkers of America. Addresses are included at the end of this article.

Social and psychological factors

The craft of boilermaking is an essential one in U.S. industry. For some, there is a challenge and an exhilaration in the work of the boilermaker. Sometimes this results from their role as a vital part in the creation and repair of large and important machinery and equipment.

GOE: 05.05.06; SIC: 34; SOC: 6814

 SOURCES OF ADDITIONAL INFORMATION

International Brotherhood of Boilermakers, Iron Shipbuilders, Blacksmiths, Forgers and Helpers
8th Avenue at State Avenue
Kansas City, KS 66101

Industrial Union of Marine and Shipbuilding Workers of America
5101 River Road, Suite 110
Bethesda, MD 20816

The Oil, Chemical, and Atomic Workers International Union
PO Box 2812
Denver, CO 80201

 RELATED ARTICLES

Volume 1: Construction; Energy; Machining and Machinery;
Volume 3: Air-conditioning, refrigeration, and heating mechanics; Industrial machinery mechanics; Plumbers and Pipefitters; Welders
Volume 4: Mechanical technicians; Welding technicians

Bricklayers and stonemasons

Definition

The *bricklayer* is a skilled worker who constructs and repairs walls, partitions, arches, fireplaces, chimneys, and other structures from brick, concrete, cinder and gypsum block, or precast panels made of brick, terra-cotta, tile, cement, stone, and marble. The *stonemason* builds the stone exteriors of structures and sets cut stone in hotels, churches, and other public buildings. The *stone repairers* repair them.

History

Sun-baked clay bricks were used in construction work more than 6,000 years ago in Mesopotamia. Along with bricklaying, stonemasonry was used in ancient Egypt to construct numerous structures. The Romans introduced masonry construction to the rest of Europe, making innovations in bricklaying by using mortar and different types of bonds. As the Roman Empire declined, so did the art of bricklaying. During the period of cathedral building in Europe, from about the tenth century to the

seventeenth century, stonemasons formed guilds in various cities and towns. These guilds functioned much as today's unions do. They had the same categories of work: apprentice, journeyman, and master. Not until the great fire of London in 1666 did the English start to use brick again in building. The Chinese also were expert in bricklaying and stonemasonry, the best example being the Great Wall of China. High in the Andes of South America, Incan stoneworkers had perfected their art by the twelfth century.

Although some brick houses made with imported bricks were built in Florida by the Spaniards, the first bricks actually made in the New World were in Virginia in 1612. These were handmade from clay or shale as they were in ancient times. Machines were not used in the manufacturing of bricks until the mid-eighteenth century. Changes in the content of bricks came shortly after. Concrete and cinder blocks were developed as was structural clay tile. The patent for a sand brick, a combination of sand and hydrated lime, was granted at this time too.

The introduction of "face brick" has changed modern construction methods. In ad-

While the work of a bricklayer may look easy, it takes considerable skill to place bricks evenly on mortar.

dition, through the use of iron oxides, iron sulfides, and other materials, various colored bricks can now be made. Thus, by varying the bond and the hue of brick, artistic effects can be produced. These procedures have popularized the use of brick in modern-day construction.

Stone has remained popular, particularly to enhance the appearance of comparatively high-cost structures such as hotels, public buildings, and churches. In modern construction, a thin covering of stone veneer about two inches thick is applied in various patterns to exterior surfaces of the building, anchored and supported on a steel frame. This is usually done by *composition-stone applicators.*

Nature of the work

The initial step in laying brick and stone is to read the blueprint to check the designer's specifications, and the next is to determine an accurate layout. To check the alignment and positioning of the bricks or stones, a dry course is laid out.

In laying bricks, *bricklayers* first spread a layer or "bed" of soft mortar upon which they place the brick, working it into position with their hands. They then cut off excess mortar so that moisture cannot penetrate. Extreme care must be used to build the corner or lead, for it serves as a guide for the rest of the work. The bricklaying is continually checked for horizontal and vertical straightness by means of mason's levels, gauge lines, and plumb lines. Storey poles and gauge strips are also used to facilitate the checking of the work. If two or more thicknesses of brick are being laid, brick-

layers must lay a "bond" course by arranging bricks in a pattern so that vertical joints do not overlap. Stonemasons basically follow the same steps.

A basic skill of the bricklayer is that of properly mixing, and then efficiently spreading, the mortar so that the joints will be properly and accurately spaced. For the structure to have a neat and uniform appearance, extreme care is necessary from the planning stage to the finishing of the mortar joints on the face of the structure.

The tools used by the bricklayer and the stonemason are mostly hand tools, such as trowels, jointers, hammers, rules, chisels, squares, sketches, gauge lines, mallets, brushes, and mason's levels. Stonemasons may also have occasion to use pneumatic drills and abrasive saws.

Some bricklayers specialize in laying one type of masonry material only. They include the gypsum block setter, the cinder block mason, the concrete block mason, the hollow-tile partition erector, and the terra-cotta mason. Other bricklayers work in the steel and glass manufacturing industries, and specialize in the fire brick and refractory brick linings used in furnaces, kilns, steam boilers, cupolas, and other high-temperature equipment. Still others are employed to construct manholes and catch basins in sewer construction.

The stonemason works primarily with two types of stone: natural cut stone, such as marble, granite, limestone, or sandstone; and artificial stone, which is made to order from cement, marble chips, or other masonry materials. With these stones as the raw materials, stonemasons build such structures as piers, walls, arches, abutments, cornices, sills, jambs, steps, mantels, hearths, and floors.

On some of the large structural projects, each stone is numbered for identification, which the stonemason must set according to specifications. A derrick worker or helper assists the stonemason in finding each stone and in setting it in mortar. Heavy stones are lifted by means of hoists and derricks and held in place by grab hooks or lewises.

In a specialized type of masonry, known as alberene stone-setting, the stonemason sets acid-resistant soapstone linings for vats, tanks, and floors. Other specialized workers include *monument setters, patchers,* and *chimney repairers.*

Requirements

Most employers prefer to hire applicants who are at least seventeen years old and in good physical condition. Although a high-school education or its equivalent is not required, it is definitely preferred.

To qualify, however, a person must complete either an apprenticeship or an on-the-job training program. The apprenticeship program consists of three years of carefully planned activity combining about 6,000 hours of work experience with several hundred hours of related classroom instruction.

On-the-job training, on the other hand, consists of learning the trade informally by working for four or more years under the tutelage of experienced supervisors. The trainees usually begin as helpers and progress from simple to more complex jobs as their skill increases.

Special requirements

There are no special requirements for the occupations of bricklayer and stonemason in addition to those already mentioned.

Opportunities for experience and exploration

Because most high-school students lack the necessary skills, opportunities for work experience in this field are limited. Occasionally it is possible for the student to secure summer employment on a construction project. If not, a field trip to a construction site will give an overall view of the type of work done by bricklayers and stonemasons.

Related occupations

Many other trades workers employ the same types of eye-hand skills including carpenters, cement masons, glaziers, marble setters, tile setters, and terrazzo workers.

Methods of entering

The two basic methods for entering these fields are the on-the-job training and the formal apprenticeship programs. The basic difference in the two approaches is that the apprenticeship program is planned and systematic while the other is more haphazard in nature. Those who

wish to work as on-the-job trainees may contact the contractor directly from an advertisement in the newspaper or go to the local employment service bureau.

If they wish to enter as apprentices, applicants may contact the contractor, state employment service bureau, or the appropriate local union headquarters (Bricklayers, Masons and Plasterers' International Union of America).

Advancement

Successful completion of the training program is necessary before an individual can become a bricklayer or stonemason. After acquiring sufficient experience, the worker may advance to the position of supervisor. Some union contracts require a supervisor if three or more are employed on the job.

Supervisors who have a flair for administration and supervision may become superintendents on a large construction site. With additional technical training, they may also become estimators whose job is to look at building plans, obtain quotations on masonry material, and prepare and submit bids. Another possible advancement is to become a city or county inspector who checks to see if the work done by contractors meets local building code regulations. One out of seven bricklayers and stonemasons go into business for themselves as contractors, making valuable use of their skills and experience.

Employment outlook

In the early 1990s, there were an estimated 150,000 bricklayers and stonemasons employed in the United States. Employment opportunities are expected to rise moderately in the next decade because of the anticipated increase in building construction and the growing popularity of ornamental brickwork, brick masonry load-bearing walls, and stonework.

Technological developments in construction techniques, however, will both aid and hinder the job outlook. For example, more bricklayers may be needed to install the precast panels made of various types of masonry material that are being used in construction. Yet the increased use of glass and metal panels in buildings reduces the number of bricklayers needed.

Bricklayers and stonemasons
Structural Work Occupations

Earnings

Annual salaries for bricklayers and stonemasons in the early 1990s averaged $34,000. The pay varies according to locality, with rates highest in the West. The beginning hourly rate for apprentices is about 50 percent of the journeyman's pay. Various fringe benefits such as hospital, accident, and life insurance, pensions, and paid vacations are available to most workers in this field.

Conditions of work

Most bricklayers and stonemasons have a forty-hour workweek with time and a half for overtime and double-time for work on Saturdays, Sundays, and holidays.

Much work is done outdoors in dusty, hot, cold, or damp conditions. Often workers must stand on scaffolds that are high off the ground, and they must stoop to pick up materials. In any case, they must be on their feet most of the working day.

Some of the hazards in this work are falling off a scaffold, being hit by falling material, and other injuries common to lifting and handling heavy material. In most parts of the country, construction work is seasonal, with time lost because of bad weather conditions.

The apprentice and the experienced worker must furnish their own hand tools and measuring devices. The contractor supplies the mixture for mortar, scaffolding, lifts, ladders, and other necessary equipment required in the construction process.

Social and psychological factors

Well-trained bricklayers and stonemasons can find work in all parts of the country, with hourly wages higher than those of most manual workers. Because construction jobs are often of short duration, however, they must spend time finding their next job. Also, because the work is often seasonal, it requires careful planning to live through periods of unemployment. Nevertheless, many persons find the work a challenging and interesting profession because of its diversity and outdoor location.

GOE: 05.05.01; SIC: 1741; SOC: 6412

◇ **SOURCES OF ADDITIONAL INFORMATION**

Associated General Contractors of America
1957 E Street, NW
Washington, DC 20006

Brick Institute of America
11490 Commerce Park Drive
Reston, VA 22091

International Union of Bricklayers and Allied Craftsmen
815 15th Street, NW
Washington, DC 20005

◇ **RELATED ARTICLES**

Volume 1: Construction; Metals
Volume 3: Cement masons; Construction workers; Drywall installers and finishers; Floor covering installers; Marble setters, tile setters, and terrazzo workers; Plasterers
Volume 4: Architectural and building construction technicians; Poured-concrete-wall technicians

Carpenters

Definition

The work performed by *carpenters* covers many fields of industry. A carpenter's job is to perform work entailing the cutting, shaping, and fastening of wood or material such as fiberboard that is treated as wood. Carpenters perform the two principal jobs of construction and repair. Their work includes the erection of wooden building frames; the installation of interior and exterior trim; the building of concrete forms, pouring chutes, and wooden scaffolds; and the laying of floors. Carpenters make up the largest group of building trade workers; almost any building construction activity requires their work. Carpenters' work takes them to a variety of construction sites such as buildings, trestles, docks, and other installations required by a wide variety of industries.

History

In all probability, the first house was a cave. As primitive people traveled after herds of animals to secure their food, they had to devise various tools to make portable shelters. Wood was first used as support posts for reed and straw roofs, sometime around 5000 B.C. The quality of tools depended greatly on the kinds of materials ancient man used. The hammer, axe, and chisel were among the earliest tools developed by humans (normally made of stone), and a combination of wood and mud was used to provide permanent homes. The discovery of copper and iron made it possible to develop various sawing and drilling devices. The art of carpentry came into its own when wood was used in homes, ships, furniture, and the like.

After the fall of the Roman Empire, the use of wood in home construction became common. Before 1850 braced frame construction was used, but the introduction of balloon construction simplified home building. The invention of power tools such as the circular saw (1777), joiner (1783), and band saw (1803) made it possible to improve the quality of millwork. The development of portable electric and pneumatic tools made faster construction possible while increasing the structural accuracy of the work.

Nature of the work

There are two basic types of carpentry work: rough and finish. The versatile carpenter is skilled in both. *Rough carpentry* includes framing (ballooned or braced), boarding, sheathing, and the installation of subflooring, partitions, studding, floor joists, and rafters. Such carpentry also includes the making of concrete forms, scaffolds, chutes, and the like. Finish carpentry (embracing a variety of specialties) includes the installation of finished flooring, stair work, siding, trim, wallboards, doors, windows, and hardware. *Cabinetmaking* may also be a part of finish carpentry. This type of work requires patience, precision, and pride in workmanship. The appearance as well as the structural accuracy of the work must be a concern. In the larger cities, where there is more construction activity, carpenters tend to specialize in some form of activity. These activities can range from *shipwrights, composition weatherboard appliers,* and *sign erector-and-repairers,* to *house repairers.* Other specialists include *joiners; siders; form, beam, tank,* and *wood boat builders;* and *railcar, mold, bridge, ship, prefab,* and *maintenance carpenters.*

Carpenters generally work in one particular field. They may be employed, for example, in building construction, highway construction, industrial or business maintenance, theatrical productions, or a particular industry such as aircraft, railroads, shipping, or mining as *timber framers* who frame mine shafts with wooden beams.

Requirements

The carpenter is required to work with other carpenters in building various structural elements. The work calls for cooperation with other building trade workers in producing a structure that has a neat and uniform appearance. Accuracy and pride in one's skills are essential in this field. Some of the personal qualities sought are ability to comprehend forms in space and understand relationships of plane and solid objects, and ability to move the hand, foot, and eye in coordination.

Carpenters must be able to read blueprints and sketches, do fundamental layout work, and see that their work meets building code requirements. They must be expert in working

Working in a metropolitan area, a carpenter builds a barricade to keep pedestrians away from the construction. Such barricades are not removed until the construction is complete.

graduation or its equivalent, and interest and background experience in carpentry. A state agency registers the formal apprenticeship agreement.

The basic approach in preparing the apprentice is through a systematic and planned four-year on-the-job training program. Initially, one works at such simple tasks as building concrete forms, rough framing, and nailing subflooring. Toward the end of the training the apprentice will work on projects such as finished trim work, hardware fitting, how to hang doors and set windows, stair building, and paneling.

The work experience is supplemented by about 144 hours of classroom instruction per year. Some of this instruction is centered on care, use, and maintenance of tools, properties of construction materials, and building code requirements. The apprentice also studies the principles of layout, blueprint reading, shop mathematics, and sketching. The apprentice also learns the relationship between carpentry and the other building trades.

An individual may acquire carpentry skills without going through a formal apprenticeship program, but most training authorities strongly recommend the all-round training given in apprenticeship programs. Those demonstrating aptitude and interest may be upgraded from one job to another until they have mastered the trade. The training is haphazard and done with a minimum of supervision. Its completeness depends to a large degree upon the number of vacancies and the amount of work done by the contractor. Becoming a carpenter by this method usually takes longer than by completing an apprenticeship program.

with a variety of building materials such as wood, plywood, wallboard, fiberboard, and insulation. They must use the proper procedures in fastening the materials with nails, screws, bolts, or glue. They are assumed to be skillful in using the various hand and power tools, as well as others that make carpenters technically accurate.

The work involves a great deal of activity, but it puts a premium on stamina rather than physical strength. It requires the carpenter to climb, stoop, kneel, crouch, and reach. Normal vision (correction permitted) is needed to check the accuracy and straightness of the work.

The best way to become a carpenter is to complete a four-year apprenticeship. An applicant needs the approval of a local joint labor-management apprenticeship committee for the carpentry trade to become an apprentice. Some of the typical requirements for an apprenticeship are age of at least seventeen, high-school

Special requirements

There are no special requirements for the job of carpenter other than those already mentioned.

Opportunities for experience and exploration

A high-school student may prepare for a career in carpentry by taking courses in mathematics, drafting, and wood shop. Building simple projects such as birdhouses, doghouses, and cabinets will test an individual's aptitude for an interest in the field. Summer employment at a construction site can provide an overview of the kinds of work performed in the construction industry. Some vocational schools provide night or day courses in the fundamentals of the trade, while the armed forces provide training in carpentry, which could be used as an exploratory experience to gauge one's interest.

Related occupations

Other occupations in construction that might be of interest include construction laborers, plumbers, electricians, cement masons, and bricklayers.

Methods of entering

A person may enter this occupational field by completing an apprenticeship program or upgrading from semiskilled jobs associated with carpentry. A carpenter's apprentice undergoes a four-year planned and systematic program to learn the trade. The upgrading method is unplanned and requires a longer period of time to learn the trade. In each case, an individual must contact a contractor, union, or state employment agency to secure a job. In many instances an applicant for apprenticeship is required to make a satisfactory score on a battery of aptitude tests.

Advancement

The first task of a person interested in securing a promotion in the carpentry field is to complete an apprenticeship. After gaining sufficient experience and competence, carpenters can be considered for appointments as supervisors. If workers have, in addition to their technical know-how, a talent for administration and supervision, they can become general construction supervisors. Those who are skillful at mathematical computations and have a good knowledge of the construction business may become estimators. A number of carpenters become self-employed doing repair or minor construction work. Some of the self-employed who have business knowledge and sufficient money to buy equipment may become contractors.

Employment outlook

In the early 1990s, about 980,000 carpenters were employed in the United States. Thou-

sands of openings a year will occur because of death and retirement, and, if construction activity increases, the number of jobs will be greater. Depending on the state of the economy, the construction business should continue to grow during the next decade; if so, many additional carpenters will be needed for maintenance and repair. Although there has been an increase in the use of prefabricated material in building work, thus far it has had only a slight impact on the carpentry field. This is partly because carpenters are used in the prefabrication process. A skilled carpenter can expect to find steady employment in the next decade, especially one who has obtained apprenticeship training.

Earnings

In the early 1990s, the median annual pay rate, with a thirty-five-hour week, for carpenters was nearly $35,500. Starting pay for apprentices is about 50 percent of the experienced worker's pay scale. They receive an increase every six months. In the last phase of training, the pay is 85 to 90 percent of the carpenter's hourly rate. Fringe benefits such as health insurance, pension funds, and paid vacations are available to most workers in this field.

Conditions of work

Carpenters may work either indoors or outdoors. If they are engaged in rough carpentry, they will do most of the work outdoors. They may be required to work on high scaffolding or in a basement making cement forms. The construction site can be noisy, dusty, hot, cold, or muddy. The work requires individuals to be physically active throughout the day. They will be required to stand, stoop, climb, and reach. Some of the hazards of the job are falling objects, falling from a ladder, strain due to lifting, crushed fingers, and cut fingers or hands. Carpenters using proper procedures can minimize these hazards.

Work in the construction industry calls for periodic changes of jobs and layoffs because of poor weather or materials shortage. Workers in this field must be able to arrange their finances to meet the periods of unemployment. A high percentage of carpenters belong to the United Brotherhood of Carpenters and Joiners of America, Inc.

Social and psychological factors

Carpenters must be able to work with others on construction projects. They are required to follow rigorous building codes and practices in their work. The trade demands that they work with speed and efficiency while producing a neat and structurally accurate piece of work. They should be able to translate the plans found on blueprints into structural elements. They work in a variety of environmental conditions and at various height levels, and they are required periodically to change job locations. There may also be periods of unemployment due to job completion or weather conditions. Persons who enjoy change and who take pride in their work will find carpentry a challenging occupation. Many young persons like carpentry because they are able to work outdoors.

GOE: 05.05.02; SIC: 1751; SOC: 6422

◇ **SOURCES OF ADDITIONAL INFORMATION**

Associated General Contractors of America
1957 E Street, NW
Washington, DC 20006

United Brotherhood of Carpenters and Joiners of America
101 Constitution Avenue, NW
Washington, DC 20001

Architectural Woodwork Institute
2310 South Walter Reed Drive
Arlington, VA 22206

Wood Products Manufacturer's Association
52 Racette Avenue
Gardner, MA 01440

American Wood Council
1250 Connecticut Avenue
Suite 230
Washington, DC 20036

◇ **RELATED ARTICLES**

Volume 1: Construction
Volume 2: Painters and sculptors
Volume 3: Construction workers; Drywall installers and finishers; Furniture manufacturing occupations; Lathers; Musical instrument repairers and tuners; Plasterers
Volume 4: Architectural and building construction technicians

Cement masons

Definition

Cement masons are skilled workers who smooth and finish surfaces of concrete on many different kinds of construction projects ranging from floors and sidewalks to highways, dams, and airport runways.

History

The earliest users of cement were the Romans, who initially developed mortar for bricklaying and later developed a cement made from slaked lime and volcanic ash for the building of roads, aqueducts, and bridges. After the collapse of the Roman Empire, the art of making cement was lost.

In the eighteenth century, through the experiments of John Smeaton, "natural cement" was discovered by burning limestone and grinding the slag, or clinkers. This cement was used to build the famous Eddystone Lighthouse, as well as some parts of the Erie Canal.

In 1824, a cement mixture (that resembled the limestone quarried on the Isle of Portland) was developed by Joseph Aspdin in England, and its success led to the building of the first American Portland cement plant in 1871.

However, until recently, cement was not widely used in construction because of its high costs. With the development of reinforced concrete and appropriate machinery, cement is now used for such projects as buildings, swimming pools, patios, sculpture, fence posts, helicopter pads, and missile launching sites.

Nature of the work

The principal work of the cement mason, also known as cement finisher and concrete mason, is to smooth and finish exposed concrete surfaces to specified textures in a variety of different construction projects.

Basic to the quality of the cement mason's work is the knowledge of his materials. He knows which of the various cement and concrete mixtures will speed or slow the setting time and which to use for surfaces of specified strengths. In addition, masons are aware of the effects of heat, cold, and wind on the curing of the cement and are able to recognize these effects by sight and touch.

Together with this understanding of materials, the cement mason also has a familiarity with blueprint reading, trade mathematics, building code regulations, and estimating materials and costs. With this information in the background, masons are ready to begin their work.

The preparation of a site for concrete pouring is very important. Forms for a framework are set up by the mason to hold the poured concrete until it hardens into the desired shape. Then, steel rods or mesh are set into place. Finally, the cement mason pours or directs the pouring of the cement into the forms so that it flows rather than drops. The wet concrete is then spread, leveled, and tamped. Concrete can now be poured year-round, using heated, temporary shelters.

Using a large wooden trowel called a "bull float," cement masons make the first smoothing operation. On driveways, pavements, and similar projects, they finish by brushing the concrete with a wet brush or pull a canvas belt or burlap strip over it to attain specified surface texture. On certain projects where curved edges are necessary, masons may use such tools as a curb edger or a radius tool. On other structural projects such as walls and floors, they may remove rough or defective spots with a chisel and hammer. Afterwards, the concrete must "cure," or harden to its proper strength, which usually takes about a week.

When working with concrete that is exposed (as ceilings and wall panels inside a building or concrete piers or columns outside), the cement mason must leave a smooth finish.

Cement masons smooth the concrete foundation of a house that is part of a low-cost residential development.

To achieve the desired finish, defects and air pockets must be eliminated. To do this, cement masons prepare a surface by rubbing it with silicon carbide to remove any high spots. They then rub in a rich cement mixture using a piece of burlap or a sponge rubber float. This fills in any imperfections, leaving the desired uniform appearance.

Smaller projects, such as sidewalks, patios, or driveways, are usually done by hand. On large-scale projects, such as highways, power-operated floats and finishing machines are used. Though power-operated equipment can perform many services, there are usually corners and other inaccessible areas in most projects that require hand-finishing. *Concrete-stone finishers, finish ornamental and decorative concrete structures,* and *concrete rubbers* put the finishing coat on poured concrete forms.

A variety of tools is used by all cement masons, ranging from simple hand tools such as chisels, hammers, trowels, screens, and edgers to more expensive equipment such as pneumatic chisels, concrete mixing machines, and cement troweling machines.

Requirements

Most employers prefer to hire persons who are in good physical condition and possess manual dexterity. Although a high-school diploma is not required, the applicant must have at least completed the eighth grade and have some understanding of basic mathematics. To qualify as a cement mason, however, a person must com-

637

plete either an apprenticeship or an on-the-job training program.

To enter the apprenticeship program in most parts of the country, applicants first must have their qualifications approved by a joint (labor-management) apprenticeship committee. This program consists of two or three years of carefully planned activity combining work experience in the use and handling of tools, equipment, and materials of the trade; finishing; layout work; and safety techniques with 144 hours of formal classroom instruction each year in such subjects as applied mathematics and related sciences; blueprint reading; architectural drawing; estimating materials and costs; and local building regulations. Most experts agree that this is the best way to learn the trade thoroughly.

The on-the-job training program is the other way to qualify for the position of cement mason. This consists of working for a number of years under the guidance of experienced masons. Usually trainees begin as cement helpers or laborers until they acquire the skills and knowledge necessary for more difficult work. On-the-job training requires more time to become skillful since it depends on chance vacancies for any upgrading to take place.

Special requirements

There are no special requirements for the occupation of cement mason in addition to those already mentioned.

Opportunities for experience and exploration

There is a variety of ways in which an individual can explore the type of work done by the cement mason.

In high school, students can take courses such as geometry, general mathematics, drafting, and shop.

In addition, summer employment as part of a construction crew will provide a valuable firsthand experience, as will military experience in the Army Engineering Corps.

It should be noted here that some vocational schools have evening programs where the fundamentals of cement work are taught. Some home repair and landscaping may also use cement, in projects like patios and porches.

Related occupations

Other construction occupations that might be of interest include carpenters, marble setters, tile setters, terrazzo workers, bricklayers, stonemasons, and construction laborers.

Methods of entering

A person who wishes to become a cement mason has two avenues of entrance into this field: the formal apprenticeship program or on-the-job training.

Those who wish to become apprentices usually contact a cement contractor, the state employment service bureau, or the appropriate union headquarters (Bricklayers, Masons, and Plasterers' International Union of America or Operative Plasterers' and Cement Masons' International Association). The Bureau of Apprenticeship and Training, U.S. Department of Labor, is another possible source to contact.

Those who wish to enter as on-the-job trainees usually contact the contractor directly or go to the local employment agency for leads.

Advancement

Successful completion of the training program is necessary before individuals can become qualified cement masons. After increasing their skill and efficiency for several years, they may advance in a number of ways.

The skilled cement mason may decide to specialize in one phase of the work, as a lip-curb finisher, an expansion joint finisher, or as a concrete-paving-finishing machine operator.

The cement mason with certain personal characteristics, such as the ability to deal with people, good judgment, and planning skills, may advance to supervisor. With an understanding of the fundamental aspects of the other construction trades, one may advance to job superintendent. Cement masons may also become estimators for concrete contractors, calculating material requirements and labor costs.

Employment outlook

Employment opportunities for cement masons—who numbered more than 135,000 in the early 1990s—are expected to increase to as many as 165,000 during the next decade. There are several reasons for this excellent outlook: an anticipated large expansion of construction in general, the greater use of concrete in this construction, and certain technological improvements.

The growth rate of this occupation may be limited slightly by the trend toward using larger and more automatic equipment, measurement and handling devices that will increase the daily output of the individual cement mason.

Earnings

Although the earnings of cement masons vary according to the section of the country, the median annual salary was more than $36,000 in the early 1990s. Nonunion workers generally have lower wage rates.

A starting apprentice has an hourly rate of about 50 to 60 percent of the mason's wage, but receives a raise every six months, so that in the last phase of training, this wage is between 90 and 95 percent of the experienced worker's pay.

Conditions of work

Like that of other skilled building craft workers, the work of cement masons is active and strenuous. They usually work outdoors in a variety of working conditions, sometimes on the ground, sometimes on ladders and scaffolds. Because pushing, lifting, kneeling, bending, and stooping are necessary, masons must have excellent physical stamina. Because they tend to get covered with dust and water, they must wear protective clothing and boots.

Overtime work, at time-and-a-half pay, is common to the cement mason because once the concrete is poured, all the finishing operations must be carried out before it hardens.

Some of the common hazards are falling off ladders, being hit by falling objects, injuries arising from lifting objects, and rough hands from handling wet concrete. Also to be considered is the fact that the worker must move frequently from one construction site to another and may have to travel some distance from home.

Social and psychological factors

Cement masons must cooperate with other building trade workers in the construction of

many different structures and parts of structures. They are required to work with efficiency and speed to hold down the cost of construction. Speed is also important in establishing a strong foundation for the cement. It must be poured quickly and uniformly. Errors may force entire section to be redone. Their layout work must be accurate, for often the entire project is dependent upon its exactness. Due to weather conditions and job completions, most cement masons are periodically unemployed. Planning and budgeting of income are required to meet these nonproductive periods.

GOE: 05.05.01; SIC: 1771; SOC: 6463

◇ SOURCES OF ADDITIONAL INFORMATION

Associated General Contractors of America
1957 East Street, NW
Washington, DC 20006

International Union of Bricklayers and Allied Craftsmen
815 15th Street, NW
Washington, DC 20005

Operative Plasterers and Cement Masons International Association of the United States and Canada
1125 17th Street, NW
Washington, DC 20036

◇ RELATED ARTICLES

Volume 1: Construction
Volume 3: Asphalt paving machine operators; Bricklayers and stonemasons; Construction workers; Drywall installers and finishers; Marble setters, tile setters, and terrazzo workers; Plasterers
Volume 4: Architectural and building construction technicians; Poured-concrete wall technicians

Communications equipment mechanics
Structural Work Occupations

Communications equipment mechanics

Definition

Communications equipment mechanics usually work in telephone company offices or in customers' offices to maintain communications systems.

Central office equipment installers set up the complex equipment that is used to select, connect, and disconnect telephone lines in central offices, and craft workers with various specialties keep the system in working order.

History

In the early days of the telephone industry, lines were strung directly from one user's telephone to another's. Later, the "party line" was common. On this line one could call anyone else by sounding his or her designated ring of a series of "shorts" and "longs" by turning the crank. As the latter part of the nineteenth century wore on, the old system proved inadequate in more and more places. The increased demand for telephone service made it necessary to replace the early rudimentary switchboards. The newer switchboards became more elaborate, and the telephone office moved from one-room establishments to larger quarters, sometimes into many-storied buildings. In the metropolitan areas it became necessary to establish branch offices, or "exchanges," to meet the needs of businesses and householders. With this continuing expansion, there was the resultant need of expansion in the installation trade. As the apparatus increased in volume, it increased in complexity. Thus came the demand for the present-day skilled communications office equipment mechanics to install and maintain the apparatus needed by the many new customers.

Nature of the work

It must be noted that the majority of the equipment installers are employed by the equipment manufacturers, not by the telephone companies. There are a few installers, however, who do work for local telephone companies as *private-branch-exchange installers* or for private firms specializing in installation work.

Complex switching and dialing equipment is found in the central offices of all local telephone companies. The work of the central office equipment installer is to assemble, wire, adjust, and test this equipment, making certain that it conforms to the manufacturers' standards.

Among their duties, central office equipment installers may set up equipment at a new central office, make additions to existing facilities to meet expansion needs, and replace outdated apparatus at existing central offices. In this work the installer must follow diagrams and blueprints and use a variety of hand and power tools.

Each central office equipment installer has an assigned territory, usually covering several states, in which to work. On small installations or replacement jobs the worker will work with only one or two other installers. On large projects in big cities one may work in a crew of several hundred other installers.

The work of the central office craft workers is to keep this mechanical and electronic equipment in functioning condition. They concentrate on locating potential trouble and seeing that it does not develop into breakdowns in any part of the system that would cause an interruption of service.

The *frame wirers* work at the distributing frames or panels where customers' lines come into the central office. Their job is to string wires and cables to these frames, following printed diagrams, and then to solder the connections. They also remake connections to change circuit layouts. In this work they use a soldering iron and other hand tools.

The *central office repairers* analyze defects in, and test and repair, switches and relays used in telephone circuits. They also make fine adjustments on equipment through the use of special tools and gauges. In this work they use telephone switching equipment, wall meters, and capacity meters as well as many hand tools.

The trouble locators, or *transmission testers*, test customers' telephone lines within the central office to find causes and locations of possible malfunctions. They then report the nature of the trouble to inside and outside maintenance crews and direct and coordinate their trouble-clearing activities. In addition, they may contact customers to arrange service calls and then dispatch the repairers. Trouble locators work at a switchboard equipped with audiovisual alarms; they also use electrical testing

640

devices such as voltmeters and resistance meters. If repairs are needed, the trouble locator directs the crews.

Specialists include *office electricians, test desk trouble locators, telegraph equipment installers,* and *telegraph-plant maintainers. Instrument repairers, electronics inspectors, signal maintainers,* who work on railway switching systems, and *public address servicers.* Satellite communications is also opening the field to *radio mechanics, satellite-communications antenna installers,* and *radio electricians.*

Requirements

The basic requirement for all communication equipment mechanics is a high-school or vocational school diploma, with some knowledge of the major principles of electricity. Pre-employment aptitude tests are usually given to check such things as agility and finger dexterity.

Workers with some college education, especially engineering training, are in increasing demand when filling equipment installer positions. Naturally, mechanical aptitude and good physical condition are also important, as is willingness to travel. To qualify as an installer, however, the new employee must successfully complete an eighteen-month program that combines on-the-job training with formal classroom instruction.

When filling central office craft positions, most telephone companies give preference to current employees such as operators, line installers, or clerical workers. Trainees are occasionally hired, however, from outside the company. Telephone companies conduct their own training programs, which include classroom instruction and on-the-job training. Instruction includes courses in electricity and electronics, as well as in the maintenance of the kind of equipment used by the central office.

Sometimes someone is hired who has had applicable training and experience in another trade, in trade schools, or in the armed forces and is then started above the usual entry level.

Special requirements

In addition to the requirements already mentioned, those considering communication equipment mechanics jobs should have perfect color vision. Telephone equipment uses many color-coded wires, and workers must be able to identify each color accurately.

A communications equipment mechanic repairs a large switchboard panel. Such work requires a steady hand.

Opportunities for experience and exploration

There are several ways to explore the type of work done by communication equipment mechanics. Many high schools and vocational schools offer classes where the basic principles of electricity may be learned. In addition, part-time employment during the school year or on vacations in a shop or business engaged in electrical work may provide an opportunity to gain some knowledge of the skills required. Also, some knowledge of and preparation for this kind of work may be gained in certain assignments in the communication sections of the Armed Forces. There are also home building kits that teach basic radio and telephone assembly. Books on home wiring also exist.

School guidance counselors may aid interested students in arranging visits to the central offices of local telephone companies to observe these workers firsthand.

Small power tools are used to connect the complex network of wires that make up the telephone equipment of the central office.

Related occupations

Other workers within the telecommunications industry whose work may be of interest to communications equipment mechanics include telephone operators, PBX operators, cable installers, radio operators, police dispatchers, and telephone repairers.

Methods of entering

Those interested in becoming communications equipment mechanics generally apply directly to the employment office of the local telephone company. Entry positions are usually as frame wirers. Often central office craft workers are recruited from other occupations within the telephone industry itself.

Because most installers work for the manufacturers of central office equipment, high-school graduates should apply directly to those companies. It is also a good practice to consult the state employment service office or the appropriate labor union for possible leads and assistance.

Advancement

Successful completion of the training program is necessary before an individual can qualify as a central office equipment installer. To advance to the position of engineering or technical assistant, the installer must take additional courses either at an engineering college or technical institute; or, if this is not feasible, the individual must enroll in those courses offered by the employing company for the purpose of improving skills and learning new techniques.

Advancement for central office repairers depends upon the successful completion of the basic nine-month training program. Frame wirers progress when they have proven their skill on the job and as openings occur in the next classification. Advancement usually is to the position of central office repairer or trouble locator. Additional training and instruction are usually required, however, for each new job. Promotion to wire chief or central office supervisor must be preceded by further instruction in electricity and electronics, as well as in the maintenance of the particular type of central office equipment used by the company. From supervisor, the former central office craft worker may advance to engineering assistant or administrative staff worker.

As new types of equipment are developed, all communications mechanics are sent back to school for periods long enough for them to learn about the new equipment.

Employment outlook

About 70,000 communication equipment mechanics were employed in the early 1990s, but employment opportunities were expected to decline in the next decade. Installation of long distance dialing equipment will continue at about the current rate in the near future, but eventually the saturation point will be reached. Also, central offices that were established since the 1950s are expected to continue in operation for many years before they need replacement.

Although many new central offices will be constructed and obsolete equipment replaced, much of the new equipment will consist of partially assembled components, which will greatly reduce the time needed for installation. The time required for testing and maintenance will not make up for the time saved. As a result of retirement and death, there will be some job openings each year.

Earnings

Communications equipment mechanics comprise one of the highest paid groups of skilled workers in the telephone industry. The median annual salary in the early 1990s was $28,900.

Conditions of work

Although the forty-hour workweek is most common among all communications mechanics, it must be remembered that the telephone industry is one that gives continuous service. The workers must keep the mechanisms of those offices in operation twenty-four hours a day, every day of the week. It is necessary, therefore, that some workers be on duty at night, and some on weekends and holidays. However, overtime pay is given to those working unusual hours.

Central telephone offices are clean, well-lighted, well-ventilated places to work. The safety record of the telephone industry is among the best. The work involves little dirt or grease, so that craft workers' clothes remain clean.

Work benefits include paid annual vacations, paid holidays, sick leave provisions, group insurance plans, and retirement and disability pensions.

Social and psychological factors

Mechanically inclined individuals may find that equipment installation work can be a great source of personal satisfaction. A sense of well-being can be achieved by watching the smooth functioning of a system that one has helped to build. As a builder of one unit in the complicated pattern that is our vast system of communication, the central office equipment in-

staller performs an important and highly skilled service.

Central office craft workers must be able to work well with others, because there are many contacts with other people in the performance of their work. They must be able to follow instructions and are at times called on to do meticulous work for considerable periods of time. Workers must be able to function well under pressure.

GOE: 05.05.10; SIC: 1731; SOC: None

 SOURCES OF ADDITIONAL INFORMATION

Communications Workers of America
1925 K Street, NW
Washington, DC 20006

International Brotherhood of Electrical Workers
1125 15th Street, NW
Washington, DC 20005

 RELATED ARTICLES

Volume 1: Electronics; Telecommunications
Volume 3: Office machine servicers; Telephone and PBX installers and repairers
Volume 4: Automated equipment technicians; Electromechanical technicians; Electronics technicians

Construction workers

Definition

Construction workers labor on all types of building construction, loading and unloading construction materials. They stack materials, including small units of machines and equipment, and carry them to building craft workers as needed. Construction laborers per-

form many other duties, depending upon the particular type of construction project, and their activities can range from working with brooms to working with explosives. Pipe layers are construction laborers who put in place sewer and other large, nonmetal pipes and seal the connections where the pipes join. Other workers may specialize in different areas.

A construction worker steadies and guides a section of flooring as a crane places it on top of a construction site.

History

People have always attempted to improve upon their environment by seeking to develop newer and more efficient types of shelter.

As skills developed people broadened their construction to include temples and houses of worship. There are examples of wonderful achievements by people who lived centuries ago—the Egyptian pyramids, the Roman amphitheaters, and the Mayan Temples. The earliest people built their homes by themselves, but, as society developed and the means of building improved, some individuals became specialists at certain kinds of construction. The work of skilled workers became highly specialized, and they required assistance with their materials and with the preparation of work sites. Craftsmen specialized in metal work, woodwork, pottery, and other trades over 2000 years ago. Smiths were the common name for skilled tradesmen. The individuals who aid skilled workers are called *helpers* or *laborers*. The work they do does not require great skill, but it is essential to the total performance of the skilled workers. As the need for construction has increased with our expanding population, there has been a large increase in the need for skilled workers and for the people who help them.

Nature of the work

Construction workers are employed on all kinds of construction jobs, such as bridges, viaducts, and piers; office and apartment buildings; highways and streets; pipelines; railroads; river and harbor projects; and sewers, tunnels, and waterworks. They are also engaged in remodeling and repair work. They perform a variety of tasks, which include loading and unloading construction materials; erecting and dismantling scaffolding; cleaning up rubble; wrecking old buildings; pouring, spreading, and spading concrete; preparing forms for cement; and carrying materials to building craft workers.

Construction workers are viewed as unskilled laborers, but they must be familiar with many of the methods, materials, and operations employed in construction work. Some laborers do work that requires a considerable amount of know-how. This is especially true of those who work with the explosives used to prepare foundations and to blast rocks before construction can begin. They must be aware of the effects of different explosives under varying rock conditions to avoid injury or property damage. In the construction of tunnels and dam and bridge foundations, laborers must have a specialized knowledge of the operations involved. In tunnel work, laborers are required to do all the operations in the pressurized area. This know-how is generally gained from on-the-job instruction provided by supervisors.

Workers are employed by contractors who undertake all types of construction work. Many of these workers are also employed by state and local governments on public works, by public utility companies, and in road repairing and maintenance.

Requirements

It is obvious from the nature of the work to be done that construction workers must be in fine physical condition and able to do much lifting and carrying. These workers must usually be at least eighteen years old and must be able to follow simple instructions given by supervisors. Because these laborers climb ladders and walk along scaffolding, they must have good coordination. Another important characteristic needed by these workers is the ability to tolerate different kinds of weather; much construction is done outdoors, both in cold weather and in extreme heat.

No formal training is necessary to become a construction worker. High-school graduates, however, have better opportunities to eventually become apprentices and skilled workers than other laborers do.

Special requirements

There are no special requirements for entering this kind of work. Some employers, however, require applicants to demonstrate that they can do the kind of work to be assigned to them.

Opportunities for experience and exploration

It is often possible for individuals interested in construction work to gain summer jobs as laborers. This is the best kind of experience students can have to help them evaluate their interest and potential in the construction industry. Interested students can also interview local construction contractors or officials of appropriate unions to learn of other ways in which experience and information might be gained in the construction industry.

Related occupations

Other construction personnel whose work might be of interest include drywall installers and finishers, electricians, carpenters, layout workers, painters, paperhangers, roofers, and sheet-metal workers. Basic construction jobs include bricklayers, stone-masons, and cement masons.

Methods of entering

The most common method of entering this line of work is to apply directly to a construction contractor or to the local office of the Laborers' International Union of North America. Local offices of the U.S. Employment Service and "help wanted" advertisements in local newspapers are other sources for people interested in securing this kind of employment. At first, laborers are assigned the simplest tasks, but, with experience, they are assigned more difficult work.

Advancement

There is little opportunity for advancement in this field of work, although some construction workers do become supervisors. An even smaller number are admitted to apprenticeship programs and eventually become skilled workers. Those interested in work as laborers must be prepared to spend the remainder of their working days as a laborer, with little chance for advancement.

Employment outlook

Of the more than four million construction workers employed in the early 1990s, most were located in highly populated and industrialized sections of the country.

A moderate increase in the volume of construction activity is predicted for the next decade. Some technological developments, such as more efficient grading machinery and new mechanical lifting devices, may limit the need for construction laborers; but the replacement needs in the construction industry through retirement and death will be such that there will be many yearly openings, mainly in connection with large projects.

Earnings

Construction workers often receive substantial hourly wages, which, however, are frequently poor indicators of annual wages. The seasonal nature of construction work and time lost because of other factors play havoc with the annual earnings of construction workers. There is also a great discrepancy in the wages paid to construction laborers in different parts of the country. In the early 1990s, the median annual income of all construction workers was $34,900.

Conditions of work

Construction work is heavy work. Construction laborers must engage in activity that is physically strenuous. Much of the work they do is performed outdoors, and they are subject to whatever climatic conditions prevail.

The major advantage to construction work is that young persons with little formal education can receive better wages in construction work than they can receive in most other kinds of manual labor. Construction industry workers, however, are subject to sharp drops in employment. They must also be willing to change job sites frequently, and some of these sites can be inconveniently located.

Economic recessions, inclement weather, strikes, moves to new construction sites, and other factors greatly reduce the amount of time that construction laborers work.

It should also be noted that construction work is dangerous work. Workers must be careful not to fall off scaffolding and must be wary of falling construction material or possible collapses in unfinished structures. Safety precautions, however, can overcome the danger from many of these possible sources of injury.

Social and psychological factors

Construction workers must be able to engage in strenuous physical activity, must be careful if they are to avoid injury, and must be able to work more than a forty-hour week when necessary.

They must also be able to tolerate the sharp changes in the wages they receive due to the seasonal nature of construction work and other factors and be aware of the small possibilities of advancement.

Many construction workers belong to unions. The union in which many of these workers hold membership is the Laborers' International Union of North America.

GOE: 05.10.01; SIC: 15; SOC: 6479

◇ **SOURCES OF ADDITIONAL INFORMATION**

Associated General Contractors of America
1957 E Street, NW
Washington, DC 20006

American Council for Construction Education
1015 15th Street, NW, Suite 700
Washington, DC 20005

◇ **RELATED ARTICLES**

Volume 1: Construction
Volume 2: Bricklayers and stonemasons; Carpenters; Cement masons; Lathers; Plasterers; Stevedoring occupations
Volume 3: Architectural and building construction technicians

---

Drywall installers and finishers

Definition

Drywall installers and finishers plan, erect, and complete the installation of drywall panels (sometimes known as wallboard or plasterboard) to structural surfaces.

Drywall installers plan the installation of drywall panels; erect the metal framework to which the panels will be fastened; and measure, cut, and install the drywall to cover the walls and ceilings in residential, commercial, and industrial buildings.

Drywall finishers seal the joints between drywall panels, using a paste-like sealing compound and paper tape, to prepare the wall surfaces for painting or wallpapering.

History

Even before humans knew how to write, they were using trowels to spread clay over the walls of their crude shelters in an attempt to keep out the wind and the rain. When the Great Pyramid of Cheops was built nearly 5,000 years ago, the Egyptians used lime for the mortar between the stones and made a gypsum plaster to artistically decorate the interior passages and crypts. Plaster made from lime took a long time to prepare and harden, while gypsum hardened before it could be properly applied; yet it was many centuries before any improvements were made in these materials. Not until after 1900 did developments take place leading to present-day plastering techniques. Once the setting time of gypsum could be controlled by using additives, lime was eliminated as a plastering material except for the finish coat.

Most of the plaster today is mixed by machine and applied in spray form. Nevertheless, its use in the construction of the interior walls of houses and other buildings is expensive and time-consuming compared to the more modern method of installing large drywall panels, which consist of a thin layer of plaster between two sheets of heavy paper. The widespread use of drywall created a need for workers skilled in its installation.

A drywall finisher patches up marks and dents on newly-installed drywall. Afterwards the wall will be covered with paint.

Nature of the work

Drywall is a substitute for wet plaster and is used for the walls and ceilings in the construction of residential, commercial, and industrial buildings. The large panels are sometimes referred to as wallboard or plasterboard. Because it is cheaper, faster, and easier, drywall has almost replaced plaster as a construction material for new houses. Installing the panels and preparing them for painting are the occupations of drywall installers and drywall finishers.

Drywall panels are manufactured in large standard sizes, such as four feet by twelve feet, and have to be cut to fit the various-sized walls, ceilings, soffits, shafts, and partitions, including the small spaces such as above or below the windows. Installers measure the areas carefully and mark the panels accordingly. Using a straight edge and a utility knife, they score the board along the cutting lines and break off the excess. With a keyhole saw, they cut openings for electrical outlets, vents, air-conditioning units, and plumbing fixtures. Then they fit the pieces into place, attach them to the wooden framework with adhesive, and nail them down. Installers generally need a helper to assist with the more cumbersome pieces, and large ceiling panels may have to be raised with a special lift. After the drywall is in place, the installers usually measure, cut, assemble, and install the metal frames and decorative trim for windows, doorways, and vents.

In large buildings, such as offices and schools, the drywall is attached to a metal framework. Specialized installers study blueprints and other specifications to plan work procedures and determine what they will require in terms of material, tools, and additional help. They measure, mark, and cut metal runners and studs and bolt them together to make floor-to-ceiling frames. Furring channels are at-

tached to the ceiling to form rectangular spaces for the ceiling panels. Then the drywall, which has been cut to size, is fitted into place and screwed to the framework.

Drywall finishers must seal and conceal the joints where drywall panels come together and prepare the walls for painting or papering. They mix a quick-drying sealing compound either by hand or with an electric mixer, then spread the paste into and over the joints with a special trowel or spatula. While the paste is still wet, the finishers press perforated paper tape over the joint and press it down to imbed it in the sealer. On large commercial projects, this pasting-and-taping operation is accomplished in one step with an automatic applicator. When the sealer is dry, the finishers spread a cementing material over the tape and blend it into the wall to conceal the joint. Any cracks or holes in the walls or ceiling are also filled with sealer, and nail and screw heads are covered with the compound. With a final sanding of the patched areas, the surfaces are ready to be painted or papered. Some finishers apply textured surfaces to walls and ceilings with trowels, brushes, rollers, or spray guns. Workers in this occupation may specialize as *drywall applicators* or *sprayers* or as *sheetrock applicators*.

Requirements

Most employers prefer applicants with a high-school education, although graduation is not mandatory. High-school or trade school courses in carpentry provide a good background for drywall work. In addition, installers need to be skilled at simple arithmetic to calculate the number of panels a job requires and to plan the cutting and fitting to eliminate

647

waste. Drywall workers should be in good physical condition, able to spend most of the day on their feet, and able to lift and move the heavy panels.

Drywall installers and finishers are trained on the job, beginning as helpers to experienced workers. Installer helpers start out carrying materials, holding panels, and cleaning up. In a few weeks, they are taught to measure, cut, and install panels. Finisher helpers start out taping joints and sealing nail holes and scratches. In a short time, they are taught to install corner guards and to conceal openings around pipes. To complete their training, after they have become skilled workers, both kinds of helpers learn how to estimate the costs of installing and finishing drywall.

Another way of learning this trade is through apprenticeship programs, which combine classroom study with on-the-job training. The United Brotherhood of Carpenters and Joiners of America, in cooperation with local contractors, offers a four-year program in carpentry that includes instruction in drywall installation. A similar four-year program for non-union workers is conducted by local affiliates of Associated Builders and Contractors, Inc. A two-year apprenticeship program for finishers is made available by the International Brotherhood of Painters and Allied Trades.

Special requirements

While union membership is not a requirement for all drywall workers, some installers belong to the United Brotherhood of Carpenters and Joiners of America, and some finishers are members of the International Brotherhood of Painters and Allied Trades.

Opportunities for experience and exploration

Carpentry courses and mathematics are most helpful for high-school or trade school students interested in becoming drywall workers. Field trips to construction sites offer an overview of the industry and may provide the opportunity to observe installers and finishers at work.

Practical experience may be gained through part-time and summer employment as helpers to drywall workers, carpenters, or painters or as laborers on construction jobs.

Related occupations

Other occupations in construction that require similar skills and interests as those of drywall installers or finishers include carpenters, plumbers, cement masons, terrazzo workers, glaziers, insulation workers, and electricians.

Methods of entering

Individuals may enter this field as apprentices or as on-the-job trainees. Those wishing to apply for apprenticeships may contact local contractors or locals of the appropriate unions. Others may apply directly to the personnel offices of individual contractors for jobs as helpers.

Advancement

Opportunities for advancement in this trade are rather limited. Experienced drywall workers with managerial ability may be promoted to supervisory positions, or they may choose to operate their own drywall contracting business.

Employment outlook

Drywall installers and finishers numbered about 85,000 in the early 1990s. Most of them worked for drywall contractors, while others were employed by general contractors.

Because drywall continues to replace plaster as a building material, the outlook for installers and finishers is favorable, and it is estimated that there will be more than 100,000 U.S. drywall workers in another decade.

Opportunities will exist throughout the country, both from increased employment and from vacancies that arise when experienced workers retire, die, or change occupations, although jobs will be more plentiful in metropolitan areas, where contractors have enough business to hire full-time drywall workers. In small towns, carpenters often handle drywall installation, and painters do the finishing.

Because drywall installation and finishing is indoor work, it can be done year-round in any kind of weather. Unlike some other construction occupations, drywall workers seldom lose time because of adverse weather conditions.

Earnings

In the early 1990s, the annual salaries of drywall workers ranged from $19,950 to $49,900. Installer and finisher trainees generally receive about half the rate earned by experienced workers.

The standard workweek for drywall workers runs forty hours. Installers and finishers sometimes work longer, for which they receive overtime pay.

Some contractors pay their installers and finishers on the basis of the amount of work completed. For example, they may pay five to six cents per square foot of panel installed a day. The average worker is capable of installing thirty-five to forty panels a day, each panel measuring four feet by twelve feet.

Conditions of work

Drywall installation is strenuous work. The large panels are heavy and awkward and often require more than one person to maneuver them into position. Ceiling panels are particularly difficult to handle and may have to be raised with special lifting devices. Long hours are spent standing, bending, stooping, and squatting to measure, fit, and fasten the pieces into place. Possible hazards include falls from ladders and injury from power tools. Because sanding creates a lot of dust, finishers sometimes wear protective masks.

Social and psychological factors

This occupation will appeal to persons who enjoy working with their hands and building things. A sense of accomplishment can be derived from two sources: solving the "puzzle" of fitting the pieces of panel together to fill a wall that may be pierced by windows, doorways, and other openings; and seeing the wall grow piece by piece to create a finished room.

The higher-than-average wage earned by drywall workers provides a level of security not enjoyed by many other production workers.

GOE: 05.05, 05.10; SIC: 15; SOC: 6424

◇ **SOURCES OF ADDITIONAL INFORMATION**

Information about job qualifications and training programs may be obtained from:

Associated Builders and Contractors
729 15th Street, NW
Washington, DC 20005

National Joint Painting, Decorating, and Drywall Apprenticeship and Training Committee
1750 New York Avenue, NW, Lower Level
Washington, DC 20006

◇ **RELATED ARTICLES**

Volume 1: Construction
Volume 3: Bricklayers and stonemasons; Carpenters; Cement masons; Lathers; Painters and paperhangers; Plasterers
Volume 4: Architectural and building construction technicians; Poured-concrete-wall technicians

Electric-sign repairers

Definition

Electric-sign repairers examine, maintain, and repair neon and illuminated signs. Minor repairs are performed at the site; major repairs are made in a shop. Repairers test the signs' operation, replace defective parts, repair transformers and structural damage, and may even install new signs.

Neon signs combine electric power with gases that are sealed into hollow tubing that illuminate as different colors.

History

Electric signs have long been used by many different types of businesses as an attention-getting device to advertise products and services. The early signs were often merely painted wooden panels topped or surrounded by naked light bulbs. Today's signs are much more sophisticated, colorful, and attractive, and display an unlimited number of styles and designs. They may be relatively simple, made from plastic and illuminated from within, or they may be complex animated signs formed from neon tubing bent into appropriate shapes and filled with rare (inert) gases. The most familiar of these gases is neon, which was discovered in 1898 and which produces a reddish-orange light. Other colors are produced by argon, krypton, xenon, helium, distilled mercury, and blue gas. The term "neon lights" is used to include all of these.

Because the purpose of electric signs is to attract favorable attention, it is important that their appearance be maintained at a high level. Malfunctioning signs create a poor impression and must be repaired promptly. This is the responsibility of electric-sign repairers.

Nature of the work

Many shops, restaurants, and other businesses depend on electric signs to advertise their products or services. A sign that does not function properly cannot appeal to customers and may even result in a loss of revenue. Whether the defect is simply a burned-out bulb or a major breakdown, a service call is made to an electric-sign repair shop for prompt attention.

Repairers drive to the location in trucks equipped with ladders and boom cranes that can reach tall signs or those placed high above the ground. They carry a supply of replacement parts, a variety of hand and power tools, such as screwdrivers, pliers, saws, and drills, and electric testing devices, including ammeters and voltmeters. The repairers inspect and test the sign to determine the cause of the malfunction. Many of the repairs are made at the site. Burned-out bulbs and transformers are replaced, defective parts removed, new ones installed, and the sign rewired. Major repairs, such as broken neon tubing, must be made in the shop; in such cases, the repairers may have to remove the entire sign. To replace some burned-out parts, such as lamps or flashers in illuminated plastic signs, repairers may have to refer to wiring diagrams and charts.

When the job is completed, repairers usually have to fill out a report that includes the date, location, and nature of the service call. They sometimes estimate the cost of service calls and may sell maintenance contracts to sign owners.

Electric signs are often covered by service contracts. To prevent breakdowns and to keep the signs operating at peak efficiency, repairers inspect them on a regular schedule. They clear away any debris or water that may have accumulated; tighten or weld parts that the wind may have loosened; and check, adjust, and lubricate motors, gears, bearings, and other parts of revolving signs. They also repaint beams, columns, or other framework, and they may repaint portions of the neon tubing to make the signs more readable.

In some large cities, *night-patrol inspectors* drive a scheduled route in a company car to check out the appearance and operation of illuminated and animated signs that their company has under service contract. They may make minor repairs, such as changing light bulbs, but generally they report faults to the service department so repairers may be sent out the next day to correct the problems.

Repairers who work for sign manufacturers may help assemble signs when there are few service calls to make, and some repairers also install signs. Workers in large sign companies may specialize in one type of repair and be designated as sign electricians, neon-tube benders, sign sheet-metal workers, or plastics fabricators.

Neon-tube pumpers are the specialists who charge illuminated sign tubing with inert gases. They attach the tubing to a vacuum pump unit to remove air, then bombard the tubing with high-voltage electric current to eliminate any gaseous impurities. After the tubing has been properly prepared, the pumpers connect it to gas bottles and fill it with neon, argon, helium, krypton, xenon, distilled mercury, or blue gas, depending on the color desired. Finally, they test the sign and seal the tubing. Pumpers may also paint or tape parts of the tubing to separate the letters, words, or symbols that make up the sign.

Requirements

Although sign repair, like many other trades, does not have high educational requirements, employers generally prefer to hire high-school or vocational-school graduates. Courses most helpful to students planning to enter this occupation include mathematics, science, electronics, and blueprint reading.

Electric-sign repairers may learn their trade in one of two ways: through informal on-the-job training or through apprenticeship programs. Most repairers start as trainees, performing basic tasks under the guidance of experienced workers. Beginners work in the shop learning to cut and assemble metal and plastic signs, mount neon tubing, wire signs, and install electric parts. Only after mastering sign construction are they permitted to accompany skilled repairers on service calls and learn repair and maintenance techniques. To become a fully qualified repairer takes at least four years of training and experience.

Apprenticeship programs also usually last four years. Sign repairer or electrician apprenticeships are conducted by union locals and sign manufacturing shops. The programs combine on-the-job training with classroom instruction in such subjects as electricity theory and blueprint reading. To be eligible for apprenticeships, individuals must be at least eighteen years of age and have a high-school diploma. Many of these requirements are the same as the requirements to become a general electrician. Through efforts of the unions and the National Electric Sign Association, more apprenticeship programs should become available in the future for young people interested in this type of training.

Good color vision is mandatory for sign repairers, because electric wires are frequently identified by color. Handling tools requires manual dexterity, and lifting transformers and other heavy equipment calls for physical strength. Repairers must not be afraid of heights, because they do much of their work while standing on ladders or from the baskets of boom trucks.

An electric sign repairer replaces the burned-out bulbs on a clock.

Opportunities for experience and exploration

Students can best prepare for this occupation by taking high-school or vocational school courses in mathematics, science, electronics, and blueprint reading. Any other courses or workshops related to electricity would be a plus. A field trip to a local sign manufacturing shop would be informative and might be arranged through the school guidance counselor.

Working with electronic kits can be helpful in testing a person's aptitude for this work. Of even more value is part-time and summer employment in any shop or business engaged in electrical work.

Related occupations

Several other occupations require electrical skills and interests. These include electricians, electrical repairers, electrical technicians, electromechanical technicians, and electronics technicians.

Methods of entering

Recent graduates may obtain job leads from school placement offices or may apply directly to the personnel offices of individual sign manufacturing shops. Information about employ-

Special requirements

All electric-sign repairers must have a knowledge of the National Electric Codes. In addition, many states require that repairers be licensed. To obtain a license, they must pass an examination in local electric codes and in electric theory and application.

Many electric-sign repairers are members of a union. Unions covering this occupation are the International Brotherhood of Electrical Workers, the Sheet Metal Workers International Association, and the International Brotherhood of Painters and Allied Trades.

ment opportunities and apprenticeship programs is also available from local offices of the state employment service or locals of the appropriate unions. Newspaper want ads are another possible source.

Advancement

Besides advancement in the form of salary increases, opportunities for promotion are not very numerous for electric-sign repairers. Highly skilled repairers with managerial ability may become supervisors, and those also experienced in dealing with customers may become sales representatives for sign manufacturers. Otherwise, with sufficient capital, repairers may establish and operate their own sign manufacturing or repair shops.

Employment outlook

In the early 1990s, there were about 18,000 persons employed in this occupation. Most of them worked for small shops that custombuild, install, and service electric signs and advertising displays. Others worked either for manufacturers, making but not servicing signs, or for businesses that specialize in installation and maintenance.

The outlook for electric-sign repairers should be favorable throughout the next decade. As a result of an increase in the use of signs and advertising displays, employment of these workers is expected to rise as fast as the average for all occupations. More signs will be installed by the many shops and other businesses that will open in the next few years, as well as by existing businesses that will expand and modernize to keep up with the competition. These new signs and all the signs already in use will need regular maintenance if they are to remain functional and appealing. In fact, many state and local governments regulate the appearance of signs and advertising displays. Besides new jobs created to handle the additional demand for repairers, some openings will occur as experienced workers retire, die, or change occupations. Job opportunities exist throughout the country but are best in large metropolitan areas, where electric signs are more plentiful.

Although this industry is sensitive to changes in the economy, sign repairers rarely suffer major layoffs. When new business declines during a downswing, sign companies usually make a greater effort to obtain mainte-

nance work and are thus able to keep their workers employed.

Earnings

A survey of union wages and fringe benefits indicates that electric-sign repairers have earnings that compare favorably with those of other skilled workers. In the early 1990s, experienced repairers were paid an average of about $27,000 annually.

Repairers generally work a five-day, forty-hour week and are paid extra for overtime. In addition, they may receive premium pay if they work at heights above thirty feet.

Conditions of work

Most signs are situated outdoors and must be serviced in any kind of weather. Emergency repairs may have to be made at night or on weekends or holidays. Repairers spend a lot of time traveling to the various locations. In some large cities, inspectors patrol scheduled routes at night to locate and fix or report signs that are not working properly.

As in all occupations engaged in electrical work, there is the possible hazard of shock and burns. In addition, because most of the signs are installed in high places, there is the danger of falling. Such accidents do not happen frequently, however, because employers have instituted training programs to make their repairers aware of safety practices. Special equipment, such as baskets on boom trucks, has been developed that allows easier, safer access to signs.

Social and psychological factors

Some of the work of electric-sign repairers may be routine, such as inspection and maintenance, but there is the variety of working in many locations and meeting different kinds of people. There is also the challenge of being called out on an emergency and having to diagnose the cause of a breakdown and restore a sign to proper operation as quickly as possible. The businesses depend on the promptness and efficiency of their sign repairers.

Individuals who do not enjoy spending long hours indoors will find the mobility of this job appealing. To repeat a point made earlier, however, a fear of heights may disqualify some persons.

GOE: 06.02.22; SIC: 5046; SOC: 772

◇ **SOURCES OF ADDITIONAL INFORMATION**

International Brotherhood of Electrical Workers
1125 15th Street, NW
Washington, DC 20005

National Electric Sign Association
801 North Fairfax Street
Alexandria, VA 22314

Sheet Metal Workers International Association
1750 New York Avenue, NW
Washington, DC 20006

World Sign Associates
200 Fillmore Street, Suite 407
Denver, CO 80206

◇ **RELATED ARTICLES**

Volume 1: Electronics
Volume 3: Electrical repairers; Electricians
Volume 4: Electrical technicians; Electronics technicians; Light technicians

---

Electrical repairers

Definition

Electrical repairers, also called *maintenance electricians,* keep many different types of electrical equipment in good working order, principally by detecting and repairing defective equipment before a breakdown occurs.

History

More than 2,500 years ago Thales, a Greek philosopher, supposedly discovered static electricity by rubbing a piece of amber with a cloth. The amber then picked up feathers. In China, it was discovered that certain stones had the power to lift pieces of iron.

In the sixteenth century, an Englishman, William Gilbert, discovered the principles of magnetism by observing that amber lifted only light objects but loadstone attracted iron. In 1729, Stephen Gray discovered that some substances "conduct" electricity and others do not, thus discovering the principle of conductors and nonconductors.

In 1745 and 1746, the Leyden jar was invented by two scientists independently. This is a device in which charges of static electricity can be built up and stored. From this discovery, interest and development of the application of

electricity developed rapidly. Other people who made key discoveries in the history of electricity are Benjamin Franklin, Luigi Galvani, Andre Marie Ampere, Alessandro Volta, Georg Simon Ohm, Michael Faraday, and Thomas A. Edison.

As inventions have caused an increased application of electricity, the equipment used in electrical circuits required maintaining. Thus the need for the maintenance electrician has evolved.

Nature of the work

The actual work of maintenance electricians depends upon whether they are employed by a large industry, where they probably specialize on particular electrical equipment, or by a small manufacturing plant, commercial business, or public institution, where they are probably called to do a greater variety of tasks. In either case, maintenance electricians may read blueprints of wiring, make mathematical calculations, and splice, solder, cut, bend, measure, and install wire and conduit. They may repair or replace wiring, fuses, transformers, coils, or switches.

In addition to using pliers, wrenches, screwdrivers, knives, drills, and other hand

A maintenance electrician rewires a prefabricated locomotive electrical cabinet for Santa Fe Railways.

tools for installation and repair work, maintenance electricians use test lamps, ammeters, volt-ohm meters, and oscilloscopes to test equipment.

Because of the importance of electricity to industries, as well as to public and commercial establishments, electricians can save costly expenses by eliminating the breakdown of equipment and by making prompt repairs as malfunctions occur. When a major overhaul or replacement of equipment is necessary, however, they are qualified to do this work as well. This occupation also includes the modernization of electrical machinery.

Requirements

A young person interested in becoming a maintenance electrician needs good health, and particularly good color vision to identify different colored wires. Manual dexterity and good mechanical aptitude are also important.

At least a high-school education is necessary. Courses such as algebra and trigonometry, physics, electricity, and basic science courses are valuable. Blueprint reading is important also. Because advances are constantly being made within the field of electrical work, it is also important that the maintenance electrician keep up by acquiring additional formal training periodically.

A young person desiring work in this field should have a keen sense of responsibility since there is always the element of danger in working carelessly with electricity. Because these workers often work alone they should have self-reliance and confidence. They should be inventive and be able to figure out the best way of making an installation.

Special requirements

All maintenance electricians should be familiar with the National Electric Code. Often the electrician needs to know local building codes. In addition, a growing list of cities require that these workers be licensed. Maintenance electrician licenses, where required, can be obtained by passing a comprehensive examination that tests general knowledge of electricity.

In many areas, maintenance electricians belong to the International Brotherhood of Electrical Workers.

Opportunities for experience and exploration

While a person is attending school, there is little opportunity for part-time work in this occupation unless one is fortunate enough to know an electrician who needs a helper. It may be possible, however, to find employment during summer vacations in this field. If such opportunities arise, it is important for the individual to remember that the experience is worth much more than the wages that might be paid. An employer looks favorably upon an applicant who has had part-time work helping an electrician, regardless of the work performed. Other opportunities for exploration may be found in a high-school shop club, on field trips, and by talking with an employed electrician.

Related occupations

Other workers who also use a knowledge of electricity and eye-hand coordination include electricians, electrical technicians, electric-sign repairers, electromechanical technicians, and electronics test technicians.

Methods of entering

Most maintenance electricians apply for apprenticeships through a union or through a local firm that employs maintenance electricians.

The Bureau of Apprenticeship and Training, U.S. Department of Labor, as well as your state employment office, may also be good places to contact for information about training opportunities.

Some in this field learn the trade more informally on the job. The apprenticeship offers many advantages since it covers all the important fields allied to the electrician's work, including classroom instruction and on-the-job training over a four-year period. It is difficult to get accepted into this program, as the number of apprentices is limited to a proportion of the number of skilled workers employed by a union shop.

Advancement

If maintenance electricians have been able to take advantage of the apprenticeship program, and if they are well qualified technically for advancement, they may advance to become construction electricians or supervisors overseeing other maintenance electricians. Occasionally, an outstanding person may advance to a supervisory position such as plant maintenance superintendent. It must be remembered that advancement within a craft, or from craft to craft, depends to a large degree on openings and on seniority within a union.

Employment outlook

About 300,000 maintenance electricians were employed throughout the country in the early 1990s. The greatest number worked in manufacturing plants, especially of metal products, transportation equipment, chemical and allied products, electrical and nonelectrical machinery. Others worked in the transportation industry, communications and public utilities, mines, and wholesale and retail trade establishments. Although repairers are employed in every state, large numbers of them are concentrated in the heavily industrialized states of California, New York, Pennsylvania, Illinois, and Ohio.

There is an increase in jobs expected in this field through the next decade, primarily a result of the expected increase in industrial activity, the number of new homes to be built, and the continual increase in the number of electrical devices. Many new jobs will occur in the primary metal, fabricated metal, machinery, and chemical industries. In addition, many new openings will occur because of the normal

changes caused by death, retirement, and advancement of journeymen electricians.

Earnings

The median annual wage for electrical repairers, as reported by the U.S. Department of Labor in the early 1990s, was about $26,500. Apprentices start at about 60 percent of the skilled worker's wages and range up to 90 percent during the last year of the apprenticeship.

Many maintenance electricians are eligible for retirement funds and also have group hospitalization plans.

Conditions of work

Maintenance electricians spend most of their forty-hour workweek indoors, but in a variety of conditions they range from a clean, carpeted office to a noisy, drafty industrial plant (although such plants are disappearing and being replaced by those that are clean, noise-deadened, and sometimes air conditioned). The work may include climbing ladders, making repairs in cramped quarters, or working in spacious, comfortable surroundings.

There is little room for error in this occupation from the standpoint of safety, and the expense of having necessary equipment "down" for repair. All well-trained electricians are safety-conscious. This and the increased use of protective equipment have reduced accidents considerably in recent years.

The maintenance electrician may work at night or over the weekend during periods when the plant or store is closed in order to have all electrical circuits in good order for the beginning of the new workweek.

Social and psychological factors

The work of maintenance electricians is not considered mainly routine. They are often called upon to "troubleshoot" when breakdowns occur in electrical systems or units. They are also called upon to renovate old systems or create new ones from time to time. They are thus confronted with a variety of problems and new situations. Of course, there are aspects of work that require merely checking or inspecting to see that systems or electrical units will continue to function properly or to maintain safety standards. Because maintenance electricians do not usually work in any one location for any length of time, they come in contact with a variety of people working in different capacities in various places of employment.

GOE: 05.10.03; SIC: Any industry; SOC: 6159

◇ **SOURCES OF ADDITIONAL INFORMATION**

Electrical Apparatus Service Association
1331 Baur Boulevard
St. Louis, MO 63132

National Electrical Manufacturers Association
2101 L Street, NW
Washington, DC 20037

International Association of Electrical Inspectors
930 Busse Highway
Park Ridge, IL 60068

◇ **RELATED ARTICLES**

Volume 1: Construction; Energy
Volume 2: Engineers, electrical
Volume 3: Communications equipment mechanics; Electric-sign repairers; Electricians; General maintenance mechanics; Line installers and cable splicers; Telephone and PBX installers and repairers
Volume 4: Automated equipment technicians; Automatic equipment technicians; Electrical technicians

Electricians

Definition

Electricians design, lay out, assemble, install, test, and maintain electrical fixtures, apparatus, and wiring used in electrical systems that provide light, heat, refrigeration, air conditioning, and power.

History

Electrical phenomena attracted some attention by the sixteenth century, but it was not until the telephone and incandescent lamp were developed in the nineteenth century that its basic laws were formulated. The wireless telegraph, the radio, the vacuum tube, the semiconductor, and the transistor each led to additional discoveries and new products, all stimulating the need for ever more skilled electricians.

Following the early work of Danish scientist Hans Christian Orsted, the English physicist Michael Faraday had build a primitive electric motor in 1821. By the early 1870s, the Belgian-born engineer Zenobe Theophile Gramme produced the first commercially viable electric motor. A battery-powered electric car

was built in the mid-1880s, and in 1888 Nikola Tesla invented the first alternating-current induction motor, the prototype of the modern electric motor.

Electricity led to, and operates, a host of increasingly complex mechanical devices. Computers, radar, sonar, and worldwide communications via satellite have resulted.

The American Institute of Electrical Engineers was founded in 1884, the Institute of Radio Engineers in 1912, and the Institute of Electrical and Electronics Engineers in 1963.

Nature of the work

Electricians usually specialize in construction or maintenance. Most construction electricians are employed by electrical contractors or, in some cases, by builders or general contractors. A substantial number are self-employed. The remainder work on "force account" construction for large industrial plants, public utilities, state and county highway commissions, or for any large organization that employs workers directly to repair their property, remodel, or make improvements.

Many maintenance electricians work in large factories, office buildings, and small plants. Most work in such manufacturing industries as those producing automobiles, airplanes, ships, iron and steel, chemicals, and machinery. Some maintain their own shops, and some work for municipalities, housing complexes, and shopping centers.

Some skilled electricians specialize in installations for power plants, huge mills, and other establishments where unusually high electrical power is required. Specialists include *voltage testers; electric-distribution checkers; mechanical electrical plumbing, protective signal,* and *wind-generating-electric power installers;* and *locomotive, water transportation, airport, prefab home, power-house, substation,* and *maintenance electricians;* and *street-light* and *protective signal repairers;* and *trouble shooters, switch inspectors,* and *street-light servicers electricians.*

Following blueprints and specifications, construction electricians install many types of switches, conduits, controls, circuit breakers, wires, lights, signal devices, and other electrical parts. If there are no specific drawings, they may follow a general blueprint for the job, or they may be told verbally what to do.

When there is no electrical drawing, electricians terminate the incoming electrical service into a central load center and install interior circuits and outlets according to an estimate of the amount of electrical current to be used in various sections of the buildings. They must protect incoming service and interior circuits by fuses or circuit breakers to prevent overheating of wires, appliances, and motors.

In installing wiring, electricians use a mechanical or hydraulic bender to shape conduit (pipe or tubing) so that the conduit will fit the contours of the surface to which it is attached. They then pull the insulated wires or cables through the conduit. The wires or cables must then be connected to circuit breakers, switchgear motors, transformers, or other components. Electricians then test the entire circuit to see if it is grounded, the connections are properly made, and the circuits are not overloaded. Wires are spliced by soldering or other methods.

Maintenance electricians practice preventive maintenance—the use of periodic inspections to find and fix problems before they actually occur. They repair all sorts of electrical equipment—motors, electronic controls, and telephone wiring. They fix or change defective fuses, switches, circuit breakers, and wiring and keep management informed on the reliability of old equipment and the necessity for replacements.

A worker connects hundreds of electrical wires, creating a "harness" that will be installed in a rebuilt train car.

Although an electrician may work for the same employer for several years, job transfers are fairly common. During a single year, an electrician may work for an electrical contractor in the construction of new homes or office buildings, for a manufacturing firm in remodeling its plant or offices, or for homeowners or business firms in making minor electrical repairs. Employment is usually concentrated in the highly industrialized and populated areas.

Requirements

A young person who is interested in this type of work should be in good health and must have good eyesight with normal color vision to distinguish color codes on wires. This type of work requires above-average finger dexterity and mechanical aptitude.

Although some people have learned the trade informally by working for many years as helpers to skilled craft workers, or have gained some knowledge through correspondence or other courses, or through special training while in the armed forces, most agree that the apprenticeship program is the best way to learn all the aspects of the trade. Apprenticeship applicants generally are required to be between the ages of eighteen and twenty-four. A high-school education or its equivalent is desirable. Applicants are required to take tests to determine their aptitude for the trade. The apprentice is protected by a signed agreement with the local joint union-management apprenticeship committee. This committee establishes minimum apprenticeship standards and pay. Most programs are designed to give apprentices all-around training by having them work for several electrical contractors who engage in particular types of work. The International Brotherhood of Electrical Workers and the National Electrical Contractors Association have jointly developed an extensive apprenticeship program. These programs usually require four years of on-the-job training in addition to a minimum of 144 hours of related classroom instruction each year. In a typical four-year program apprentices learn to use, care for, and handle safely the tools, equipment, and materials commonly used in the trade; do residential, commercial, and industrial electrical installations; and maintain and repair installations. In addition, apprentices receive classroom instruction in such subjects as drafting and electrical layout, blueprint reading, mathematics, and electrical theory, including electronics. Many electricians find that to keep abreast of the rapidly changing developments in their field, they must enroll in union-sponsored courses in advanced electronics.

Special requirements

Most cities require electricians to be licensed. To obtain a license, the electrician must pass an examination that requires a thorough knowledge of the craft and of state, county, and municipal building codes. About 95 percent of electricians belong to a union, and those who do not are usually found in smaller communities throughout the country.

Electricians are required to furnish their own tools such as pliers, screwdrivers, brace and bit, and hacksaw. The employer usually supplies power tools and other heavy equipment.

Opportunities for experience and exploration

A person who is interested in repairing and building radios, working with model electric trains, or fixing electrical appliances for the home will probably do well as a construction electrician. The courses taken in high school are also an important indication of the person's aptitude. Such subjects as mathematics, drafting, physics—especially that dealing with electricity—and wood and metal shop would indicate that the student might enjoy working as an electrician.

Related occupations

People who have skills with electricity and an interest in construction or repair might also want to explore the work of the following: electric-sign repairers, electrical repairers, electromechanical technicians, electrical technicians, electrical engineers, electronics technicians, and electronics test technicians.

Methods of entering

There are several ways that people may enter this field. They may contact the local union of the International Brotherhood of Electrical Workers or the joint union-management apprenticeship committee. In some areas, it is possible to become an apprentice to a local electrical contractor by applying directly. Sometimes the state employment service administers tests and arranges interviews for the applicant. The state apprenticeship agency or the Bureau of Apprenticeship and Training, U.S. Department of Labor, may also offer information.

Advancement

In a regular apprenticeship program a person who qualifies progresses to the status of skilled electrician. These craft workers then can become supervisors, superintendents, or estimators for electrical contractors. Some go into business for themselves, and, as their activities expand, they may become contractors. However, a master electrician's license is required for contracting in most large urban areas. An electrician in the building trades can also transfer easily to electrical jobs in the shipbuilding, automobile, or aircraft industry. This worker can also transfer to maintenance electrical work.

Employment outlook

In a period of less than a century and a half, this phase of industry has made such rapid growth that about 590,000 persons were employed as electricians in the early 1990s.

Over the next decade, the number of electricians is expected to rise at a normal rate. Factors that are expected to contribute to the growth of this trade are an increase in construction, greater requirements for electric outlets, switches, and wiring in homes to accommodate the increasing use of appliances and air-conditioning systems, and the extensive wiring needed for the installation of electronic data-processing equipment and electrical control devices being used in commerce and industry. Technological developments, however, such as factory-assembled electrical devices, will affect employment growth in this field. Many additional job opportunities will result from the need to replace experienced electricians who transfer to other types of work, retire, or die.

Earnings

In the early 1990s, a national survey showed that the union annual wage rates for electricians averaged about $33,700. Because electricians are less affected by seasonal changes than most other construction workers, their annual earnings are generally higher, also.

Hourly wage rates of apprentices often start at about 40 to 50 percent of the skilled worker's rate and increase by 5 percent in each six-month period until 80 or 85 percent of the skilled worker's rate is reached during the last period of the apprenticeship.

Conditions of work

Electricians may work indoors or outdoors, often in an uncompleted building. They may be subjected to noise and dirt and variable weather conditions. Most of their work is done standing or walking, sometimes on ladders or scaffolds, or in awkward and difficult places. The job is not considered hazardous, but workers may be subject to burns, electrical shock, or falls. This work provides year-round employment with regular hours—which sometimes includes overtime with pay. Union-management agreements often provide health, vacation, and other benefits and usually provide for employer contribution to some kind of pension plan for the workers.

Social and psychological factors

A construction electrician must be able to adapt to new surroundings and new personalities, because job transfers are frequent. A person who gets along well with most people will find this an asset in this career, as the electrical work is a part of the entire construction. The variety of job locations makes this field a stimulating and challenging one.

GOE: 05.05.05; SIC: 173; SOC: 6432

◇ **SOURCES OF ADDITIONAL INFORMATION**

International Brotherhood of Electrical Workers
1125 15th Street, NW
Washington, DC 20005

National Electrical Contractors Association
7315 Wisconsin Avenue
Bethesda, MD 20814

◇ **RELATED ARTICLES**

Volume 1: Construction; Energy
Volume 3: Communications equipment mechanics; Electric-sign repairers; Electrical repairers; Telephone and PBX installers and repairers
Volume 4: Automated equipment technicians; Automatic equipment technicians; Electrical technicians; Electronics technicians

---

Elevator installers and repairers

Definition

Elevator constructors, also called *elevator mechanics*, are highly skilled craft workers who assemble, install, and repair elevators, escalators, dumbwaiters, and similar equipment.

History

Elevator frameworks were found in the ruins of the palaces of Roman emperors. It was not until the seventeenth century, however, that a crude passenger elevator, known as the "flying chair," was invented by the French builder, Velayer. These early elevators were generally operated by hand, animal, or water power.

A steam-driven freight elevator was built in the United States in 1850. But not until certain safety features were developed by Elisha G. Otis did the elevator industry (and the occupation of elevator constructor) really begin operations in 1857 with the first steam-driven passenger elevator.

About twenty-five years later the steam driven elevator was supplanted by the hydraulic elevator, invented by Cyrus W. Baldwin. Then in 1887 the first U.S.-built electric elevator ushered in their commercial use. With further improvements in construction and design, and with increased speed and reliability, elevators made it possible to construct taller buildings in large industrial cities.

The principle of the escalator, or moving stairway, was invented in 1891 by Jesse W. Reno of the United States and received its name in 1900.

Today, it is rare indeed to find a new commercial, industrial, or apartment building constructed without elevators and frequently escalators. It is the work of elevator constructors to assemble and install these modern conveniences.

Nature of the work

For elevator constructors to be able to assemble, install, and repair modern elevators, most of which are electronically controlled, they must have a working knowledge of electricity, electronics, and hydraulics. Before any installation begins, they must determine the layout of framework, guide rails, motor pump, cylinder and plunger foundations, as well as electrical connections from the builders' blueprints.

Once the layout is understood, the elevator constructor directs a crew in the installation of the guide rails of the car, the hoisting machine, the car frame and platform, the counterweight, the elevator chassis, and the control apparatus. Next, the car frame is connected to the counterweight with cables, the cab body and roof are installed, and the control system is wired. Finally, the entire system is checked, adjusted, and tested.

All elevator installations are inspected and adjusted regularly by elevator constructors who specialize in maintenance and repair work as *elevator examiners and adjusters* and *elevator repairers*. Because of the rapid rate of improvement and innovation in elevator engineering, alteration work is similar to new installation because most of the equipment is usually replaced.

A variety of tools is used by elevator constructors, including hand tools, power tools, and testing meters and gauges.

Requirements

Most employers prefer to hire high-school graduates, at least eighteen years of age, in good physical condition, with some advanced technical training. Mechanical aptitude is an important asset as is an interest in machines.

The high-school student's preparation should include courses in mathematics, physics, and machine shop. Additional courses in electronics and hydraulics will be very helpful.

To qualify as a skilled elevator constructor, however, one must complete a six-month, on-the-job training program at the factory of a major elevator firm, as well as work as a helper-trainee for a period of two to four years. If one has not taken courses in electrical and electronic theory, the trainee must attend classes in these subjects at a trade or technical school.

Special requirements

There are no special requirements for the occupation of elevator constructor in addition to those already mentioned.

Opportunities for experience and exploration

The high-school student should take courses in mathematics, physics, and electrical shop, which are fundamental to the trade. In addition, part-time or summer employment on commercial building sites will give an overall view of the kind of work done, as well as the working conditions.

A visit to an elevator manufacturing firm or to the local union headquarters of the International Union of Elevator Constructors will also be helpful.

Related occupations

Other construction work that might be of interest to elevator installers and repairers include electricians, line installers and cable splicers, operating engineers, roofers, sheet-metal workers, welders, and floor-covering workers.

Methods of entering

To enter the profession, a prospective elevator constructor should contact either elevator manufacturers, local contractors who specialize in elevator maintenance and repair work, or the local office of the International Union of Elevator Constructors.

In addition, the local office of the state employment service bureau may also supply necessary leads and information.

Advancement

After increasing their efficiency and skill for several years, and with additional training, a variety of promotional opportunities are open to elevator constructors.

If they are able to deal with people, and have good judgment and planning skills, they may advance to such supervisory positions as supervisor, estimator, and superintendent. If they have a knack for selling, they can advance to a sales position for an elevator manufacturer.

Some elevator constructors attend engineering college at night to work toward an engineering degree and thus advance to engineering work.

An elevator constructor installs guide rails in a new elevator shaft.

Employment outlook

Most of the estimated 18,200 elevator constructors employed in the early 1990s worked for elevator manufacturers.

Employment opportunities for elevator constructors are expected to increase about as fast as the average for all occupations during the 1990s and beyond. Several hundred new jobs are anticipated annually in this relatively small occupation. There are two reasons for this good outlook: an expansion in new industrial, commercial, and large residential building is expected, and new technological developments may spur the replacement of older elevator installations.

Earnings

Annual salaries for elevator constructors in the early 1990s averaged $37,400. Trainees generally start at 50 percent and helpers 70 percent, with periodic raises, of the rates paid to experienced elevator constructors.

Conditions of work

Most elevator constructors have a forty-hour workweek, with extra pay for overtime. They work indoors in buildings under construction or in those buildings already completed.

Some of the work involves lifting and carrying of heavy equipment and parts. Much of the work is done in cramped or awkward positions.

Elevator constructors lose less work time because of seasonal factors than do most other building trades workers.

Social and psychological factors

Because most of the work is done by small crews, it is essential that the elevator constructor work well with others. This is a skilled trade that requires attention to detail and precise work. While technological developments will contribute to the need for more elevator mechanics, these workers will need to have higher skills and more extensive training in electronics. All skilled elevator constructors must keep up to date with each innovation in the field.

GOE: 05.05.05, 05.05.06; SIC: 1796; SOC: 6176

◇ **SOURCES OF ADDITIONAL INFORMATION**

National Elevator Industry, Inc.
630 Third Avenue
New York, NY 10017

International Union of Elevator Constructors
3530 Clark Building
Suite 530
5565 Sterrett Place
Columbia, MD 21044

◇ **RELATED ARTICLES**

Volume 1: Construction
Volume 3: Electrical repairers; Electricians; Line installers and cable splicers
Volume 4: Automatic equipment technicians; Electrical technicians; Electronics technicians

Floor covering installers

Definition

Floor covering installers include *resilient floor layers*, who install, replace, and repair resilient tile and sheet vinyl on floors of public buildings and private homes, and *carpet layers*, who put down carpets and rugs.

History

The need for floor covering installers was evident by the middle of the nineteenth century. Shortly after the power loom was invented in 1839 and perfected two years later by Erastus Bigelow, the first wall-to-wall carpeting was installed. Sometime thereafter, an early type of linoleum, later called battleship linoleum, was first used on the decks of warships.

It was not until after World War II, however, that a great variety of floor coverings of many kinds was made in great quantities and became widely popular. The industry developed many synthetic materials that were durable for household and commercial use and perfected production processes for various other kinds of flooring.

Nature of the work

The installers' work depends upon whether they specialize in the installation of resilient floor coverings, such as asphalt tile or sheet vinyl, or carpets. Some installers do both types of coverings.

In either case, however, preparation of the floor to be covered is important: it must be firm, dry, smooth, and free of loose dust or dirt. The installer may have to sweep, scrape, sand, or chip dirt and other irregularities from the floor, as well as fill cracks with a filler material. Sometimes the floor must be resurfaced with plywood, hardboard, or mastic cement before any floor covering can be installed. If the floor surface is not smooth, it can cause bumps, cracks, and unevenness on the covering, particularly in vinyls and tiles.

Installers must be able to gauge the moisture content of the subfloor and decide whether conditions are suitable for installing the covering. They should also have a good knowledge of the various types of adhesives and floor coverings available and know which is most suitable for each particular floor condition.

Once the floor is prepared, the installation of the sheet vinyl covering or tile can begin. Installers carefully measure and mark off the floor, according to blueprints or sketches, indicating where the tile joints or seams will be.

When the layout is completed, the installers, often assisted by an apprentice or helper, apply the proper adhesive and lay the floor covering. They must be careful in cutting, matching, and fitting, particularly at door openings and around permanent floor fixtures, such as pipes or posts. After the covering is laid, a roller is often run over it to smooth it and ensure good adhesion to the floor.

In the installation of wall-to-wall carpeting, installers must plan a layout, also, allowing for expected foot-traffic patterns so that the best appearance and longest wear will be obtained. They also must place seams where they will be least noticed.

Once the layout is completed, installers begin to lay "tackless strip" with adhesive or nails along the border of the floor. Next, they cut and place the padding within the framework of the strips. Finally, they place the carpet in position. If the carpet has not been precut and seamed in the floor covering firm's workroom, the installers must do this before stretching and fastening it into place. Some carpeting is tacked directly to certain kinds of flooring. Specialists include *carpet cutters* and *diagrammers and seamers.*

The tools used by all installers include hammers, pry bars, knives, shears, and other cutting devices; measuring and marking tools, such as tape measures, straight edges, chalk and chalk lines; and a variety of special tools, such as stretching devices, notched adhesive trowels, and floor rollers.

A floor covering installer applies adhesive to a surface before placing the sheet vinyl on top of it.

Requirements

Most employers prefer to hire applicants with manual abilities and a high-school education or the equivalent.

Because the installer works on the premises of the customer, an additional requirement is a neat appearance and a pleasant manner.

The high-school student's preparation should include shop courses, as well as general mathematics and geometry.

To become a qualified installer, a person must complete either an apprenticeship or an on-the-job training program. The apprenticeship program consists of three to four years of carefully planned activity combining work experience with related classroom instruction.

The on-the-job training program consists of working for three or more years under the supervision of experienced installers. In this informal training program, trainees begin as helpers or laborers and progress from simple to more complicated jobs as they acquire the necessary skills and as openings occur. Further instruction in floor covering work is obtained by attending trade school or floor covering manufacturers' training courses or taking a home-study program.

Special requirements

There are no special requirements for the occupation of installer in addition to those already mentioned.

Opportunities for experience and exploration

Various opportunities are available to those interested in exploring the work of an installer. In high school, shop courses will test students' accuracy and ability to do skilled work, while geometry will gauge their skill in using mathematics for various layout work.

In addition, helping to install linoleum or tiles at home will give the prospective installer invaluable firsthand experience with the work. Of course, a summer job as a helper or assistant to an experienced installer would be the ideal way to learn about the profession and might help one get a full-time job after high school.

Related occupations

Other workers also install flooring or perform work that requires similar skills. These include terrazzo workers, marble setters, tile setters, and cement masons.

Methods of entering

There are two ways to enter this occupation: as an apprentice or as an on-the-job trainee.

If applicants wish to become apprentices, they usually contact either employers, such as floor covering contractors, retailers, or department stores, the state employment service bureau, or the appropriate union headquarters (United Brotherhood of Carpenters and Joiners of America or the Brotherhood of Painters, Decorators and Paperhangers of America).

If the apprenticeship program is filled, applicants may wish to enter as on-the-job trainees. In this case, they should speak with several employers about training programs before accepting work as trainees.

Advancement

After increasing their skill and efficiency, installers can advance in several ways.

Advancement can be to the position of a supervisor who supervises a group of installers, but this kind of promotion is rare, because most contractors do not have large enough organizations to need supervisors. Occasionally, installers who get along well with people, can communicate effectively, and who know their

business, are promoted to sales. Not only must sales workers know how to sell, but they must measure the floor and know the amount of time and material that each job will require.

Another possible form of advancement is to work for the manufacturer of floor covering material, which, of course, is a large corporation, with many different kinds of jobs available. Still another possibility for advancement is to go into business for oneself, and then employ other installers.

Employment outlook

In the early 1990s, more than 115,000 floor layers were employed in the United States, about 74,000 of them specializing in carpets. Employment opportunities are expected to increase throughout the next decade. There are several reasons for this outlook. Building construction is expected to grow, and with it the greater use of resilient floor coverings and wall-to-wall carpeting because of more versatile materials, patterns, and color range. Renovation of existing buildings is also on the rise. In buildings that were constructed with cement or plywood floors, covering the floor with a protective surface is essential.

In addition, hundreds of job openings will arise yearly from the need to replace experienced floor layers who retire, die, or transfer to other types of work. This occupation is one of the skilled service areas that is not expected to be greatly affected by automation in the future.

Earnings

Although earnings of installers vary according to the section of the country and levels of skill and degree of work specialization, experienced workers were paid an average of $24,900 annually in the early 1990s, though the annual median for carpet layers was somewhat lower, $18,700. About 10 percent of the entire field made about $40,500 a year.

Starting wages for apprentice and other trainees are usually about one-half the rate for experienced workers.

Almost all installers are paid on an hourly basis, although a few workers who are very proficient prefer to be paid by the amount of floor covering they install. Such an incentive plan sometimes works out well for both contractor and layer.

Conditions of work

Most installers have a regular forty-hour work-week with extra pay for overtime. The work is generally done in the daytime, and, since it is inside work, it is not as subject to seasonal lay-offs as some construction work. Nor is there as much dirt or strenuous activity as in most other building trades.

Job hazards are not numerous but include knee injuries, because most work requires a great deal of kneeling, and occasional back injuries from twisting and lifting on the job.

Installers may have to talk to customers while they work, while maintaining pace and efficiency; they must be able to concentrate well to do so.

Social and psychological factors

To like their work, installers should enjoy frequent moves from one job location to another. Those engaged primarily in floor covering in private homes have an opportunity to meet and talk with many customers as they practice their craft. They will have to please not only their employer in terms of quickly performing their duties with a minimum of waste but also the homeowners, who may at times be unreason-

able in their demands and expectations concerning the finished product. Successful installers must always be painstaking and take pride in the quality of their work.

GOE: 05.10.01; SIC: 1752; SOC: 6462

◇ **SOURCES OF ADDITIONAL INFORMATION**

Carpet and Rug Institute
PO Box 2048
Dalton, GA 30722

Resilient Floor Covering Institute
966 Hungerford Drive, Suite 12-B
Rockville, MD 20850

◇ **RELATED ARTICLES**

Volume 1: Construction; Glass
Volume 3: Drywall installers and finishers; Glaziers; Marble setters, tile setters, and terrazzo workers

---

Glaziers

Definition

Glaziers cut, fit, and install plate glass, ordinary window glass, mirrors, and special items such as preassembled stained glass or leaded glass panels for homes, storefronts, interior walls, and ceilings. They also replace glass in automobiles.

History

Although the history of glassmaking dates back to about 2500 B.C. it was not until the Middle Ages that glass was used for windows and mirrors. The work of glaziers began during the twelfth and thirteenth centuries, when stained-

glass windows were first created for churches and cathedrals in Europe. After the sixteenth century, stained-glass windows lost much of their popularity, and the use of such windows fell off almost completely until the 1800s. Since that time, however, stained-glass windows have been used a great deal.

From the fourteenth century, handmade crown glass (which had a bull's eye at the center and concentric ripple lines around that) was in demand for window panes. In 1674, lead glass was made in England, and in 1688, the first plate glass was produced by Louis Lucas in France. This discovery led to the wide use of mirrors. By the late 1700s in the United States, there was a great demand for crown glass, which was produced in Boston from 1793 to about 1827. By the mid-1800s, however, plate

A glazier places an adhesive around the edges of a newly cut piece of glass to prevent contact with the sharp sides.

glass was becoming popular and the demand for trained glaziers to cut and install it was increasing rapidly. After 1890, the development and use of glass made great strides. Along with new and revolutionary methods of making glass came new methods of cutting, welding, sealing, and tempering.

Nature of the work

Glaziers perform a wide variety of jobs in which glass is used. They install mirrors, structural glass, store fronts, walls, doors, ceilings, tables, skylights, showcases, automobile windows, shower doors, tub enclosures, and so forth.

In the process of installing glass, glaziers either use precut glass or cut the glass to size, breaking off the excess by hand or with a notched tool. In installing windows, they then put a bed of putty into the wood or metal sash and press the glass into place, fastening it with

wire clips or triangular metal points. Another strip of putty is applied on the outside edges to seal the glass into place permanently and make it moisture-proof.

When a storefront is being installed, glaziers cut not only the glass but also the metal drain and the metal face moldings to fit the opening. They then screw the drain molding into position and place the plate glass into the metal molding. Finally, they bolt the face molding around the edges and the metal corner pieces to the molding.

Specialists include *stained glass, refrigerator,* and *metal furniture glaziers* and *auto, safety glass,* and *mirror glass installers.*

The tools used by the glazier range from hand tools such as glass cutters and putty knives to power cutting tools and grinders.

Requirements

Most employers prefer to hire applicants with a high-school diploma or its equivalent.

To qualify as a glazier, however, a person must complete either an apprenticeship or an on-the-job training program. The apprenticeship program consists of three years of carefully planned activity combining about 6,000 hours of shop training with 144 hours yearly of formal classroom instruction.

The on-the-job training program consists of working for four or more years under the supervision of experienced glaziers. Trainees usually begin as helpers and progress from simple to more complicated jobs as they increase their skills and knowledge of the trade, and as openings occur.

Special requirements

There are no special requirements for the occupation of glazier in addition to those already mentioned. Most glaziers, however, belong to a union.

Opportunities for experience and exploration

Several opportunities are available to explore the work of a glazier. In high school, shop courses and mathematics will test the person's ability to do this kind of skilled work. Hobbies that require manual dexterity, handiness with tools, patience, and attention to details will also provide good experience for the potential glazier.

In addition, part-time or summer work with a construction company will offer an individual the opportunity to get an overall view as well as some direct experience with the varied work of the glazier.

Related occupations

Other jobs with similar skill requirements that might be of interest include automobile mechanics, drywall installers, construction workers, plumbers, electricians, roofers, and floor covering installers.

Methods of entering

There are two main ways an individual can enter the occupation of glazier: as an apprentice or on-the-job trainee. Some persons enter this work through experience in the armed forces.

Those who wish to become apprentices usually contact glazing contractors, the state apprenticeship agency, or the appropriate union headquarters (International Brotherhood of Painters and Allied Trades). They must get the approval, however, of the joint apprenticeship committee (labor-management) before they can enter the occupation by this method. The Bureau of Apprenticeship and Training, U.S. Department of Labor, as well as the state employment office, are also good places to contact for information.

If the apprenticeship program is filled, applicants may wish to enter the field as on-the-job trainees. In this case, they usually contact the contractor directly and begin work as helpers.

Advancement

After increasing their efficiency and skill for several years, various promotional opportunities are available to glaziers. They can advance to the position of supervisor or job superintendent, who supervises a group of glaziers either for a contractor, or in a factory where glass is installed in sashes, doors, or mirror frames. If they have the necessary business and capital, they can become glazing contractors.

Employment outlook

Approximately 42,000 construction glaziers were employed in the early 1990s, most of them working for glazing contractors. An additional number worked outside the construction industry.

Although this is a relatively small field, an increase to about 60,000 is anticipated through the next decade. There are several reasons for this good outlook. Building construction is expected to increase, as is the use of glass in construction. Also, replacement and modernization work will provide even more job opportunities.

Earnings

Although earnings of glaziers vary in different areas of the country, salaries averaged from about $19,960 to $39,900 annually in the early 1990s.

Wages for apprentices usually start at 50 percent of the skilled glazier's rate and increase periodically until training is completed.

Conditions of work

Most glaziers have a forty-hour workweek, with extra pay for overtime. They work outside at a building site or indoors, often on scaffolds at great heights.

Glaziers may be employed by a construction company, a glass supplier, or a glazing contractor. Sometimes they are required to drive a truck that carries the glass and tools to the job. Other jobs available to glaziers are in factories where they assemble windows or other products that require glass installation. Working conditions vary in these factories according to the size and type of the establishment.

There are risks in this trade, but they are minimal with the use of safety devices.

Social and psychological factors

Glaziers must be able to work well on their own or with others, depending upon where they are employed. This trade requires careful, patient workers who have the aptitude and a willingness to develop the skills necessary to master their craft.

GOE: 06.04.30; SIC: 1793; SOC: 6464, 7759

◇ **SOURCES OF ADDITIONAL INFORMATION**

International Brotherhood of Painters and Allied Trades
United Nations Building
1750 New York Avenue, NW
Washington, DC 20006

◇ **RELATED ARTICLES**

Volume 1: Construction; Glass
Volume 3: Bricklayers and stonemasons; Cement masons; Drywall installers and finishers; Floor covering installers; Marble setters, tile setters, and terrazzo workers; Plasterers

Lathers

Definition

Lathers install the support base on ceilings, walls, and building partitions on which plaster, fireproofing, or acoustical materials are applied.

History

Although the idea of placing a support base or backing on inside walls of buildings to retain warmth is an old one, it was not until the latter part of the nineteenth century that the lather's craft came into being.

By the early part of the twentieth century, construction of large commercial buildings and apartment houses provided lathers with many opportunities to use their craft. Since that time new and improved materials and methods for covering the metal framework of buildings have rapidly developed.

Nature of the work

Wherever there is building construction, lathers may be found installing metal lath (strips of sheet metal "slitted" to form a diamond-shaped pattern) or large pieces of gypsum lath as supporting backings for interior or exterior walls.

The metal lath process includes three steps. First, the lather builds a light metal framework called furring that is fastened securely to the framework of the building. Then the laths are attached to this furring with nails, wires, clips, or staples. Third, the lather cuts openings in the laths for heating and ventilating pipes, and ducts for electrical outlets.

The gypsum board lath process is similar except that this board comes in large sheets and must be cut by the lather to fit small and odd-shaped areas.

In addition to installing lath as support backings for walls, lathers also install corner beads (metal reinforcements used as corner protection and as guides for plasterers) and the wire mesh around steel beams to which plaster is applied for fireproofing. Sometimes their work includes installing wooden backings for acoustical ceilings and wall tiles.

The lather uses many tools, including measuring rules and tapes, drills, hammers, chisels, hacksaws, shears, wire cutters, bolt cutters, pliers, hatchets, stapling machines, and wood and metal drills.

Requirements

Most employers prefer to hire high-school graduates in good physical condition and with a high degree of manual dexterity.

The high-school student's preparation should include courses in geometry and applied mathematics as well as shop courses.

To qualify as a skilled lather, however, a person must complete either an apprenticeship or an on-the-job training program. The apprenticeship program consists of two years of carefully planned activity combining work experience with formal classroom instruction. After each six-month period, apprentices must pass additional examinations.

The on-the-job training program consists of working informally for four or five years under the guidance of experienced lathers. Trainees usually begin as helpers until they acquire the necessary skills and knowledge necessary for more difficult tasks. Frequently, they must take additional courses in night school.

Special requirements

There are no special requirements for the occupation of lather in addition to those already mentioned.

Opportunities for experience and exploration

In high school, students have several avenues open for exploring the occupation of lather. Courses in metal shop, wood shop, and mechanical drawing will test their ability and aptitude for this kind of work, while courses in geometry and mathematics will gauge their skill in estimating and applied mathematics. Furthermore, hobbies requiring work with hand tools such as carpentry will provide a valuable firsthand experience with this work.

To observe the lather at work, field trips to construction sites can be arranged by the school counselor, or students may make such arrangements on their own. An excellent opportunity for exploring this occupation would be a part-time or summer job as a helper or assistant to a skilled lather.

Related occupations

Other construction workers who have skills similar to lathers include drywall installers, drywall finishers, plasterers, and painters and paperhangers.

Methods of entering

There are two ways an individual can enter the occupation of lather: as an apprentice or as an on-the-job trainee.

Those who wish to become apprentices usually contact employers, such as lathing and plastering contractors, the state apprenticeship agency, or the appropriate union headquarters. Applicants must have the approval of the joint apprenticeship committee, however, before they can enter the occupation by this method. The Bureau of Apprenticeship and Training, U.S. Department of Labor, as well as the state employment office, are also good places to contact for information.

If the apprentice program is filled, applicants may wish to enter the field as on-the-job trainees. In this case, they usually contact the employer directly and begin work as helpers.

Advancement

After increasing their skill and efficiency for several years, various promotional opportunities are open to lathers.

They may specialize in working with a specific lath and thus become a metal lather, rock board lather, or wood lather.

If they have certain personal characteristics such as the ability to deal with people, good judgment, and planning skills, lathers may progress to such supervisory positions as supervisor, job superintendent, or job estimator.

Some lathers with enough capital and business knowledge eventually go into business for themselves.

Employment outlook

In the early 1990s, there were about 25,000 lathers employed, the majority of whom worked for lathing and plastering contractors on new residential, commercial, or industrial construction.

Little growth in the employment of lathers is expected through the next decade. Even though some jobs will result from the need to replace workers who retire, die, or leave the occupation for other reasons, the number of lathers is small and there will be relatively few job openings annually.

While population and business growth will stimulate the construction of new buildings and the renovation of old ones, it is expected to have little impact on the demand for lath and lathers. Some lathers will be needed to construct more expensive new buildings, to renovate older buildings, and to provide lath for curved surfaces. However, drywall—a good substitute for, and less expensive than, lath and plaster—has been growing rapidly in popularity as a wall-covering material. As a result, the demand for drywall installers has increased while the demand for lathers has declined.

Earnings

Although the earnings of experienced lathers vary according to the section of the country, the average hourly wage rates compare favorably with others in the skilled building trades. In the early 1990s, the average annual wages of union lathers in metropolitan areas were about $37,400. Apprentices receive about 50 percent of the rate paid to experienced lathers, with periodic increases. Lathers are paid hourly and receive extra compensation for overtime work.

Conditions of work

Most lathers have a regular forty-hour workweek with extra pay for overtime. The work is performed both indoors and outdoors in all kinds of weather on construction sites, which are generally not heated. As in many of the building trades, lathers are subject to seasonal layoffs.

Much of the lathers' workday is spent on their feet, often on ladders and scaffolds. Possible hazards of the trade include cuts, falls, and strains from lifting heavy objects.

Union contracts often include health and life insurance, pension, and other benefits, financed either entirely by the employers or jointly by the workers and the employers. Contract conditions differ among unions.

Social and psychological factors

Lathers have to be able to work well on their own as well as with others. Patience, accuracy, and attention to detail are essential for success in this work. Those who enjoy working with their hands and who are stimulated by outdoor activity will most likely find this job satisfying.

GOE: 05.10.01; SIC: 1742; SOC: 6424

◇ **SOURCES OF ADDITIONAL INFORMATION**

Association of the Wall and Ceiling Industries International
1600 Cameron Street, Suite 200
Alexandria, VA 22314

International Institute for Lath and Plaster
795 Raymond Avenue
St. Paul, MN 55114

United Brotherhood of Carpenters and Joiners of America
101 Constitution Avenue, NW
Washington, DC 20001

◇ **RELATED ARTICLES**

Volume 1: Construction
Volume 3: Bricklayers and stonemasons; Carpenters; Cement masons; Drywall installers and finishers; Plasterers; Sheet metal workers
Volume 4: Poured-concrete-wall technicians

Layout workers

Definition

The *layout worker* is a highly skilled specialist who marks metal castings, forgings, or metal stock to indicate where and how much machining is needed. These workers' markings enable all-around machinists and machine operators to use machine tools simply by following his lines, points, and other instructions. Machinists will then cut, shave, drill, or otherwise shape the metal into the desired specifications. Layout workers plan not only what points on the metal will be shaped, but in what order they will be worked.

History

The history of the occupation of layout workers, as well as other machinists, is bound up with the history of the development of machine tools.

The modern machine tool can be traced to the gun production industry of the sixteenth century. But it was not until the development of the steam engine by James Watt that the demand for refinement of the early crude machines occurred. John Wilkinson then developed the boring machine in order to make steam engine cylinders more nearly round. This was followed by the screw-cutting lathe, developed by Henry Maudslay in 1810. Most of the other early machines were derived from the lathe, including the drilling, milling, sawing, and grinding machines.

The use of mass production methods in the manufacturing of rifles by Eli Whitney resulted in the improvement of existing machines as well as in the invention of new ones. James Nasmyth invented the nut-shaping machine and the steam hammer during the 1830s. Then with the introduction of the micrometer caliper in the 1860s, precision machining became feasible. Finally, the electric motor as a source of power made it possible to further improve machine tools.

In the United States the demands of the automobile manufacturers in the 1920s required a great number and variety of specially developed machines. It was at this time that machine tools and their operators took a permanent place in modern metalworking industries.

Today the work done by these machines forms the basis of all modern industrial production, for they are necessary to the manufacture of every kind of engine, mechanism, and manufactured product. Such diverse items as textiles, metal goods, foodstuffs, building materials, and scientific instruments must be made either on a machine tool or on another machine that is constructed using machine tools.

Nature of the work

Machining is that process by which metal is formed into the desired shape and size with great accuracy. Power-driven machines are used to cut, shave, grind, or drill the metal so that the separate pieces may be easily assembled into the complete product. Before these machines can be set to work, the metal must be marked with machining directions so that a machinist or a machine operator can perform the proper machining operations. This important preliminary work is the task of the layout worker.

To perform this job, layout workers must have a complete knowledge of the operation and the features of a variety of standard machine tools. They must be aware of the sequence of machining operations, the nature of shop practice, and the working properties of many metals, such as steel, cast iron, aluminum, and other metals and metal alloys. After studying blueprints or other specifications, layout workers indicate machining points with a variety of different instruments. These instruments include: the scriber, to mark lines on the surface of the metal; the center punch, to mark the centers on the ends of metal pieces to be drilled or machined; the key seat or box rule, to draw lines and lay off distances on curved surfaces; dividers, for transferring and comparing distances; L or T squares, for determining right angles; and calipers and micrometers, for accurate measurement. High degrees of accuracy are required for all this work, since some specifications call for tolerances as close as .001 of an inch.

Requirements

Because the position of layout worker is usually obtained as a promotion from that of all-around machinist, the basic requirements for this occupation are the same as those for the occupation of machinist and will be found under "Machine tool operators" elsewhere in this encyclopedia.

In addition to completing the four-year machinist apprenticeship program or the equivalent, the layout worker needs from two to six years' further training and experience to develop the necessary skill for this occupation.

Special requirements

There are no special requirements for the occupation of layout worker in addition to those already mentioned.

Opportunities for experience and exploration

A high-school student will find it difficult to explore the work done in this occupation. Courses in machine shop and mechanical drawing, however, will test one's accuracy,

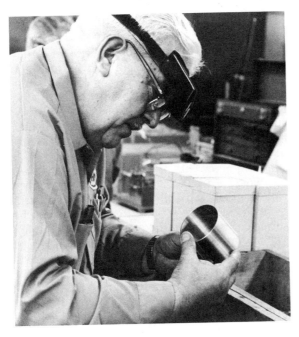

This layout worker is examining a metal cylinder before marking it for a machinist. Good judgment, accuracy, and patience are necessary skills of a layout worker.

patience, and ability, while courses in algebra and geometry will gauge skills in shop mathematics. Students constructing their own metal objects must measure and mark the pieces as a layout worker would.

To observe layout workers in action, field trips to a metalworking industrial plant may be arranged by a school counselor.

Related occupations

Other workers who engage in work with metals include machinists, tool-and-die makers, job-and-die setters, pipe fitters and steam fitters, structural-steel workers, and sheet-metal workers.

Methods of entering

In most companies, positions in the layout department are filled from within the firm by promotion or reassignment. This is because the work requires a solid foundation in all the aspects of the machining operation. Skilled machinists with additional training often qualify for layout work.

Advancement

Several advancement opportunities are open to layout workers with the proper qualifications. If they have certain personal characteristics such as ability to deal with people, good judgment, and planning skills, layout workers may progress to such supervisory positions as shop supervisor or superintendent of the shop. Another possibility for the person with some training at a technical school is to go into experimental and design work, process planning, or estimating. In addition, layout workers can easily transfer to other work such as machine programming, which will become more important with further technological development. Then, of course, there are always some layout workers who open machine shops of their own.

Employment outlook

Employment of layout workers is expected to show little or no change during the next decade.

Adverse effects of automation and technological developments in this field, such as the use of numerically controlled machine tools, are expected to limit employment growth in this occupation. The correct positioning of metal stock and tools, however, will continue to be important, and layout workers will be needed to mark reference points.

Earnings

Although earnings of layout workers vary according to the section of the country, their averages compare favorably with those of other skilled factory workers.

In the early 1990s, average straight-time annual earnings of layout workers were between $19,200 and $30,000 annually.

Conditions of work

Most layout workers have a forty-hour work-week with extra pay for overtime. They work indoors in machine shops that—though fairly clean, properly lighted, and well ventilated—can at times be very noisy.

Although layout work is not physically strenuous, workers must stand at their jobs most of the day. Often they must wear special shoes to reduce foot fatigue. In addition, safety glasses are required since cutting tools, moving machine parts, and flying metal chips could cause injury to the eyes.

Paid holidays and vacations, life, medical, and accident insurance, and pension plans are usually available to layout workers.

Social and psychological factors

The layout workers' job challenges their intelligence and ingenuity and tests their accuracy, precision, and powers of concentration. This work provides satisfaction and a rewarding experience to skilled artisans who take pride in the complexities of their trade and the results of their work.

GOE: 05.05.07; SIC: Any industry; SOC: 6821

◇ SOURCES OF ADDITIONAL INFORMATION

International Association of Machinists and Aerospace Workers
1300 Connecticut Avenue, NW
Washington, DC 20036

International Union of Electronic, Electrical, Salaried, Machine, and Furniture Workers
1126 16th Street, NW
Washington, DC 20036

International Union, United Automobile, Aerospace and Agricultural Implement Workers of America
8000 East Jefferson Avenue
Detroit, MI 48214

NMTBA—Association for Manufacturing Technology
7901 Westpark Drive
McLean, VA 22102

◇ RELATED ARTICLES

Volume 1: Machining and Machinery
Volume 3: Forge shop occupations; Instrument makers; Machinists; Patternmakers; Tool makers and die makers
Volume 4: Instrumentation technicians; Profile-grinder technicians; Proof technicians

Line installers and cable splicers

Definition

Line installers and *cable splicers* construct, maintain, and repair the vast network of wires and cables that connect telephone central offices to the millions of telephones and switchboards in customers' homes and buildings. The work of the line installer and the cable splicer complement each other, whether they are installing, maintaining, or repairing lines.

History

The occupation of line installers and cable splicers came into being in the 1880s, when the telephone was first put to commercial use. As the need developed for more and more telephone lines to connect distant points around the country, line installers and cable splicers were trained and employed to construct and maintain these lines.

Nature of the work

In the construction of new telephone lines, line installers first must dig holes and erect the telephone poles or towers that are used to support the cables. They then climb the erected poles and install the equipment and the cables, usually leaving the ends free for the cable splicers to connect later. To join sections of power line and to conduct transformers and electrical ac-

673

A telephone repairer makes a routine check on a telephone line. Many rural areas still use wooden telephone poles to carry wires.

cessories, line installers splice, solder, and insulate the conductors and related wiring. In some areas where telephone lines are underground, line installers place the cables in underground conduits. Construction line installers usually work in crews of two to five persons, with a supervisor directing the work of several of these crews.

Repairing and maintaining existing lines occupy a major part of the line installer's time. When wires or cables break or a pole is knocked down, the line installer is sent immediately to make emergency repairs. The line crew supervisor is notified when there is a break in a line and is directed to the trouble spot by the trouble locator, who keeps a check on the condition of all lines in a given area. During the course of routine periodical inspection, the line installer also makes minor repairs and line changes.

When construction line installers have completed the installation of poles, wires, and cables or underground conduits, cable splicers complete the line connections. The splicers may do their work on aerial platforms, in manholes, or in underground vaults where the cables are located. Sometimes they may work on board a marine craft when splicing underwater cables.

To join the individual wires within the cable, splicers must cut the lead sheath and insulation from the cables. They then test or phase out each conductor to identify corre-

sponding conductors in adjoining cable sections according to electrical diagrams and specifications. At each splice, they either wrap insulation around the wires and seal the joint with a lead sleeve or cover the splice with some other type of closure. Sometimes they fill the sheathing with gas under pressure to keep out moisture.

Preventive maintenance and repair work are also an important part of the cable splicers' job. Workers often use electric and gas pressure tests to detect possible trouble.

Specialists include *line maintainers, street railway line installers, line repairers, cable splicers, cable testers, construction checkers, line,* and *tower erectors,* and *cable* and *line installers and repairers.* Other types of related workers include *troubleshooters, television cable* and *steel-post installers, radio interference investigators,* and *electric power line examiners.*

Requirements

For positions of both line installer and cable splicer, most telephone companies prefer to hire inexperienced applicants with a high-school or vocational-school education. Applicants must be in excellent physical condition, with manual dexterity and the ability to distinguish colors. Some knowledge of the basic principles of electricity is helpful, too.

Pre-employment tests to determine aptitudes and physical examinations are given to all applicants. Once hired, the new employee becomes a helper and must successfully complete a training program combining classroom instruction with supervised on-the-job training.

Special requirements

There are no special requirements for the positions of line installer or cable splicer in addition to those already mentioned.

Opportunities for experience and exploration

In high school or vocational school, students may test their ability and interest in the occupations of line installer and cable splicer through courses in mathematics, electricity, and machine shop. Hobbies that involve a knowledge of and experience with electricity will also provide a valuable kind of experience.

To observe line installers and cable splicers at work, it may be possible to have a school counselor arrange a field trip by calling the public relations office of the local telephone company.

Direct training and experience in telephone work may be gained in the armed forces. Frequently those who have received such training are given preference for job openings and may be hired in positions above the entry level.

Related occupations

Other occupations that require similar skills and interests include telephone installers, PBX repairers, electronics technicians, radio operators, telephone and electrical repairers.

Methods of entering

The person interested in becoming either a line installer or a cable splicer who meets the basic requirements may enter the occupation by contacting the personnel office of the local telephone company directly.

After successfully completing the training program, the new employee will be assigned either as a line crew member under the guidance of a line supervisor or as a cable splicer's helper under the guidance of experienced splicers. Cable splicer's helpers advance to positions of qualified cable splicers after three or four years of working experience.

Advancement

Both the line installer and the cable splicer must continue to receive training throughout their careers, not only to qualify for advancement but to keep up with the constant technological changes that occur in the telephone industry.

Usually it takes line installers six years to reach top pay for their job, and cable splicers, five to seven years. After reaching the top in the field, and with the proper qualifications, there are many advancement opportunities in the telephone industry. For instance, if line installers have certain personal characteristics, such as the ability to deal with people, good judgment, and planning skills, they may progress to line crew supervisors. With some additional training, the line installer or the cable splicer may advance to telephone installer, telephone repairer, or another higher-rated position.

It should be noted that many line installers and cable splicers transfer to other positions by the time they reach their mid-50s because of the strenuous nature of their work.

Employment outlook

There were about 210,000 line installers and cable splicers in the United States in the early 1990s. Employment opportunities for installers and splicers are expected to increase at a moderately slow rate, despite the fact that the telephone companies will continue to extend lines and cables into suburban areas at about the same rate as at present.

The reason for this outlook is mainly a result of redesigned equipment and various new devices that enable the companies to provide an increasing amount of efficient service with fewer line installers and cable splicers. Satellites may carry an increasing amount of telephone traffic. In spite of this trend, there will be hundreds of new workers needed in this field during the next few decades.

Earnings

Although earnings for both line installers and cable splicers vary according to the section of the country and length of service, their median annual salary was $29,250 in the early 1990s.

Conditions of work

Most line installers and cable splicers have a regular forty-hour workweek, with extra pay for overtime and Sunday work.

Both occupations require that workers perform their jobs outdoors, often in severe weather conditions since telephone lines are sometimes severely damaged by weather. However, when emergencies arise and overtime is necessary during unscheduled hours, workers are guaranteed a minimum of pay at the basic hourly rate, with travel to and from the job being considered work time.

There is a great deal of climbing in these occupations, and some underground work must be done in stooped and cramped conditions. Cable splicers may also do their work on board a marine craft if they are connected with an underwater cable crew.

The hazards of this work have been greatly reduced by the concerted efforts of both the telephone companies and the labor unions to establish safety standards. However, the work is strenuous, and sometimes it is necessary for workers to transfer to other jobs because of the great physical demands.

Telephone companies provide the worker with many benefits. Workers have annual vacations with pay. Usually contracts provide for a one-week vacation for six months to one year of service, two weeks for one to six years, three weeks for seven to fourteen years, four weeks for fifteen to twenty-four years of service, and five weeks for twenty-five years and over. Paid holidays range from eight to eleven days, depending on the area. Payments for sick leave up to seven days for workers with two years of service is a typical plan. In addition, most companies have group insurance plans that provide additional benefits.

Social and psychological factors

Telephone companies provide security and steady employment in both small and large communities across the country. This phase of the industry, line construction and cable splicing, is a vital part of the communications system. Those who are in good physical condition and who like to work outdoors would probably find this job rewarding. In this work, one must be able to get along well with other members of the crew and at times impart knowledge and skill to trainees. This craft is satisfying in itself for the worker who is qualified, and it has the additional advantage of offering ample opportunities for advancement to those workers who are so inclined.

GOE: 05.05.05; SIC: 481; SOC: 6157

◇ **SOURCES OF ADDITIONAL INFORMATION**

Communications Workers of America
1925 K Street, NW
Washington, DC 20006

International Brotherhood of Electrical Workers
1125 15th Street, NW
Washington, DC 20005

◇ **RELATED ARTICLES**

Volume 1: Telecommunications
Volume 3: Electrical repairers; Electricians; Telephone and PBX installers and repairers
Volume 4: Electrical technicians; Submarine cable equipment technicians

---

Marble setters, tile setters, and terrazzo workers

Definition

Marble setters, tile setters, and *terrazzo workers* cover interior or exterior walls, floors, or other surfaces with marble, tile, or terrazzo. Craft workers in each of these trades work primarily with the material indicated by their title. Terrazzo is a mosaic, usually made of polished marble, granite, or ceramic pieces. Tiles are made of stone, concrete or baked, glazed clay.

History

The temples of Greece and the ruins of Rome are testimony to the fact that marble and granite have been used as building materials for thousands of years. It has been difficult through the years to find a longer lasting material than marble, which, at the same time, is soft enough to be cut to size. For this reason sculptors have used marble for busts and statues. Marble, a limestone, is quarried or mined in many countries of the world.

Products such as steel and concrete are replacing marble as a building material to some extent, although marble will continue to be used on interiors and to some extent on the exteriors of commercial, governmental, and institutional buildings. There is, in the minds of many people, a feeling about marble buildings that speaks of a timeless quality of strength and security. There are still enough architects in America with these precise feelings so that the future history of marble as an exterior construction material is assured, however reduced in use it may be.

Terrazzo—small pieces of broken stone set in mortar and polished in place—is used mostly for flooring. It was developed as a building material by the Venetians in the 1500s.

Nature of the work

Half builder, half artist, these craft workers work on newly constructed or remodeled buildings. Generally, the material to be used is delivered ready to be applied on the job. Little cutting and polishing is required of the applicators. Picking up and carrying is generally done by helpers, as well as the mixing of cement and mortar, leaving the applicators free to concentrate on their work. If one has ever seen a wall improperly laid (where the joint lines do not run true), one can realize the importance of accuracy for these workers. Where color is used, the appearance of the whole job can be ruined by an improper blending of hues.

Tile and terrazzo are used mainly on interior building surfaces, while marble is used primarily as exterior facing. Machine hoists aid in the lifting of large marble blocks.

When setting marble, the workers first lay out the job. Then they apply a special plaster mixture to the backing material and set the marble pieces in place. These pieces may have to be braced until they are firmly in place. Special grout is packed into the joints between the marble pieces, and the joints are slightly indented. This indenting is known as "pointing up."

Tile setters attach tile (thin slabs of clay or stone) to either vertical or horizontal surfaces with mortar or specially prepared tile cement. Some tile now comes in strips made by fastening a number of tiles to a special backing of paper so that they do not have to be set individually. Vitreous tile is used primarily for floors, and nonvitreous, for walls.

Terrazzo workers lay a base (first course) of fine, dry concrete, leveling this with a straightedge. They then place metal strips wherever there is to be a joint or where design or color delineations are to be made. This metal stripping is embedded in the first course of concrete. Then the terrazzo workers pour the top course of concrete, a mortar containing marble or granite chips, and roll and level it. Different colored stone chips are used to color whatever pattern has been planned for the finished floor. In a few days, after the concrete has hardened, the floor is ground smooth and polished.

Requirements

The workers in these three trades should be at least seventeen years of age to qualify for the labor-management apprenticeship programs and have a high-school education or its equivalent with some courses in using hand tools, reading blueprints, art, and making precise measurements. Art courses increase the knowledge and perception of colors, and many vocational courses stress the need for manual dexterity. Good physical condition is a necessity.

It is, of course, desirable that the marble, tile, or terrazzo worker live in a locality affording the maximum opportunity for employment such as the larger urban areas. Terrazzo is particularly popular in Florida and California. Most workers in these trades are members of unions.

The apprenticeship programs in each of these trades usually consist of about 6,000 hours or three years of on-the-job training and related classroom instruction. During this time the apprentices learn how to use the tools of their particular trade plus blueprint reading, layout work, basic mathematics, and shop practice.

Special requirements

Other than those already mentioned, there are no special requirements for these trades.

Opportunities for experience and exploration

Young people still in school may obtain work as laborers. The work includes mixing mortar, carrying, lifting, and cleanup work. It is unwise to

A tile installer carefully places a complex pattern of tiles onto a treated surface. When he is satisfied with the pattern, he will fill in the spaces with a special grout.

assume that nothing can be gained by such summer work. By working with master craft workers, asking questions, and making suggestions, one begins to learn the trade.

If students' part-time work is satisfactory, this experience will mean something to them after they graduate from high school and are competing with other young people for a full-time job.

Related occupations

There are other occupations that require similar skills and interests as those of marble setters. These include floor covering installers, bricklayers, stone masons, cement masons, and plasterers.

Methods of entering

Although there is a formal three-year apprenticeship established in these trades, a large percentage of workers learn the work informally by working a certain number of years as a helper, learning the work firsthand from an experienced craft worker.

The person interested in this work should first contact a prospective employer. In addi-

tion, the local office of the state employment service may be a source of information about the Manpower and Development Training Act, apprenticeship, and other programs. After being accepted for a job, the new employee is referred for clearance to the union and, after a period of time working, is made a helper. When an opening occurs for a skilled worker, the best qualified person with the most seniority is recommended for the position.

Advancement

Skilled tile, terrazzo, or marble setters may become supervisors and manage crews of workers for large contractors. They can also become self-employed and do contracting on their own.

The self-employed contractor must know not only the skills of the trade but also the principles of business. These include sales, figuring bids, bookkeeping, the ways to make and keep a business on a firm financial footing, and how to supervise workers.

For those persons interested in advancement, it might be well to consider the advantages of trade and technical schools to keep abreast of any advances in the tools being used and the methods of work being utilized.

Employment outlook

Employment for marble setters, tile setters, and terrazzo workers will probably increase at an average rate over the next decade. These are comparatively small vocational groups, and new jobs will come primarily from natural attrition.

Earnings

Median annual wage rates in the early 1990s for tile setters was about $46,800. Marble setters made about $33,000 and terrazzo workers about $31,200. These wages vary with geographic locations, the higher rates pertaining to the larger cities.

Many opportunities for overtime are available, and under these conditions workers may earn one-and-a-half times the regular hourly wage. Most workers are union members and are eligible for the retirement and hospital insurance benefits of the union.

Apprentices in these trades start at about 50 to 60 percent of the skilled worker's salary and increase periodically up to 95 percent during the final stage of the training.

GOE: 05.05.01; SIC: 1743; SOC: 6413

Conditions of work

Tile setters work mostly inside, while marble and terrazzo workers work both indoors and outside. Helpers do most of the heavy work, so the work is generally lighter and cleaner than the work in most occupations in the construction trades.

Social and psychological factors

These occupations provide the opportunity to be relatively free from routine. There generally is no immediate supervision of the marble setter, tile setter, or terrazzo worker. These workers manage their own time, schedule their work, and have the responsibility of doing whatever is necessary to provide the best possible job.

Individuals in these occupations need a sense of order and neatness, and they should be able to work easily with precise measurements.

Because these workers have an opportunity to plan the job, see that the material is delivered on time, and follow the work through the cleanup phase, they often feel a greater sense of satisfaction from the completed job than would a construction worker who does only one part of the total job.

There is an opportunity to plan and supervise the work of one or two helpers, because most application crews on this type of work are small.

Successful workers, particularly if they also contract their own jobs, must be able to meet and talk with the public.

◇ **RELATED ARTICLES**

Volume 1: Construction
Volume 3: Bricklayers and stonemasons; Cement masons; Drywall installers and finishers; Floor covering installers; Glaziers; Painters and paperhangers; Plasterers

Operating engineers (construction machinery operators)

Definition

Operating engineers operate various types of power-driven construction machines such as shovels, cranes, tractors, pile drivers, concrete mixers, and pumps. *Bulldozer operators* operate the familiar bulldozer, a tractor-like vehicle with a large blade across the front for moving rocks, trees, earth, and other obstacles from construction sites.

History

Although it is not understood precisely how it was accomplished, the Egyptians used some hoisting system to place the giant stone blocks of the pyramids in place. The early Romans constructed roads and bridges of lasting quality. The Great Wall of China remains an amazing architectural feat when one considers there were no machines at that time to aid the builders. It was not until the Industrial Revolution and the invention of the steam engine, however, that Western Europe and America made rapid progress in constructing buildings, roads, and water and sewerage systems.

Construction has always played an important role in history and at present many people measure progress by the increase in new construction in a town or city.

Nature of the work

Operating engineers work for contractors, building highways, dams, airports, and other large-scale projects. They also work in building construction, excavating, grading, landscaping, and hoisting materials. Others work for utility companies, manufacturers, and other firms that do their own construction work. Many work for state and local public works and highway departments. Others work in factories, mines, and steel mills.

Whatever the company, the operating engineers run power shovels, cranes, derricks, hoists, pile drivers, concrete mixers, paving machines, trench excavators, bulldozers, trac-

tors, and pumps. They are often identified by the machines they operate.

In their work, the operating engineers use various pedals and levers to rotate the crane on its chassis, or to raise or lower the boom. They also must be able to use various attachments to the boom such as buckets, pile drivers, or a heavy wrecking ball.

The range of skills of the operating engineer is broader than in most building trades, because the machines themselves differ in the ways they operate and the jobs they do.

Requirements

A high-school education or the equivalent technical training is valuable for the operating engineer and is a requirement for apprenticeship training. It is important that the operator have excellent mechanical aptitude and skillful coordination of eye, hand, and foot movements. In addition, someone who is not skillful can be dangerous to the other workers, so it is necessary to have a good sense of responsibility and seriousness on the job.

The operating engineer should be healthy and strong and have the temperament to withstand dirt and noise as well as changing weather conditions. For application to an apprenticeship program, a candidate generally must be between the ages of eighteen and thirty.

Special requirements

Most operating engineers belong to one of the construction unions, so membership in a union might be considered a special requirement.

Opportunities for experience and exploration

A young person can sometimes gain practical experience by operating machines or at least in observing them in action in the summers, as a laborer or machine operators' helper in construction work. Such jobs may be available on local, state, and federal highway and building construction programs.

Related occupations

Other workers who also are involved in occupations with similar skills as those required in construction and the operation of construction equipment include industrial-truck operators, construction workers, and truck drivers.

Methods of entering

There are two ways to become an operating engineer: through the union apprentice program or through on-the-job training. The apprenticeship, lasting at least three years, has advantages in that the instruction is more complete and in that both labor and management know that the apprentice is training to be a machine operator. When openings occur the qualified apprentice with the most seniority has the best chance for the job. The apprentice, besides learning on the job, also receives some classroom instruction in grade plans reading, elements of electricity, physics, welding, and lubrication services. It must be remembered that most apprenticeship programs are difficult to get into because the number of apprentices is limited to the numbers of skilled workers who are already in the field.

Two good sources to contact for information on apprenticeship programs are the Bureau of Apprenticeship and Training, U.S. Department of Labor, and the local office of the state employment agency.

Other ways to enter this occupation are by direct application to manufacturers, utilities, or contractors who employ operating engineers and by contacting a union.

A power shovel operator uses special hoists to lift the front end of the machine off the ground. He can gain better leverage that way.

Employment outlook

Approximately 230,000 operating engineers were employed in the early 1990s in construction work.

As construction in this country increases, as it is expected to do, jobs for operating engineers will increase. As new machinery is introduced, these machines will need new operators. There is currently an increase in the use of earth movers and other construction equipment outside of construction uses as well as an increase in the mechanization of materials movement in factories and mines.

Advancement

Some operating engineers, generally those with above-average ability and interest, as well as good working habits, advance to job supervisor and occasionally construction supervisor. Some qualify for higher pay by training themselves to operate more complicated machines.

Earnings

The median annual salary for all operating engineers in the early 1990s was about $23,400. Rates vary according to the area of the country and also according to the machine being operated. The wage scale is further complicated by the experience of the operator and the purpose for which the machine is being used. Total yearly salaries are dependent to some extent on weather and climate in the area.

Conditions of work

Operating engineers consider dirt and noise as part of the job. Some of the machines on which they work constantly shake and jolt them. This constant movement, along with the active, outdoor, strenuous nature of the work, make this a physically tiring job. The work is almost entirely done outdoors in almost any kind of weather, and operating engineers must be willing to work under conditions that are often unpleasant.

Social and psychological factors

Operating engineers may have to travel and be away from home frequently. Weather and climate can make their work very pleasant or extremely uncomfortable. For some persons there is much satisfaction in the manipulation of large machinery and equipment, and some take pleasure in the observable progress of the work

completed each day.

GOE: 05.11.01; SIC: 16; SOC: 8312

◇ **SOURCES OF ADDITIONAL INFORMATION**

Associated General Contractors of America
1957 E Street, NW
Washington, DC 20006

International Union of Operating Engineers
1125 17th Street, NW
Washington, DC 20036

◇ **RELATED ARTICLES**

Volume 1: Construction
Volume 3: Boilermaking occupations; Carpenters; Farm equipment mechanics
Volume 4: Architectural and building construction technicians; Mechanical technicians

Painters and paperhangers

Definition

Although painting and paperhanging are two separate skills, many building trades craft workers do both types of work. *Painters* apply coats of paint, varnish, stain, enamel, or lacquer to decorate and protect interior and exterior surfaces of buildings and structures. *Paperhangers* cover room interiors with decorative wallpaper, fabric, vinyls, or other materials.

History

Wall decorations in ancient Rome consisted of mosaics and murals. Used originally to depict scenes, they eventually portrayed architectural

elements and finally geometric and decorative patterns.

The history of the skilled house painter's occupation began in the eighteenth century, when there were few people in the business of manufacturing paint in Europe, and American colonists made their own paints for use on their homes. In 1867, manufacturers made available the first prepared paints. After this, new machines were invented to enable paint manufacturers to produce large amounts of paint.

The history of the paperhanging occupation began in the sixteenth century. Although the Chinese invented decorative paper, it was the Europeans who first used it to cover walls. The poor were the first to use wallpaper in their homes, an inexpensive imitation of the wealthy, who decorated their walls with tapestries and velvet hangings.

Both paperhangers and painters came into great demand as building construction developed on a large scale in the early part of the twentieth century. Since World War II, there have been great advancements in the materials and techniques used by these skilled trades.

Nature of the work

While it must be noted that there is some overlapping in the work done by painters and paperhangers, each trade has its own characteristic skills.

Painters must be able to apply paint thoroughly, uniformly, and rapidly to any type of surface. To do this, they must be skilled in handling brushes and other painting tools and have a working knowledge of the characteristics of paints and finishes from the standpoint of durability, suitability, and ease of handling and application.

Preparation of the surface to be painted is an important duty of painters, especially in repainting. They first smooth the surface, removing old loose paint with a scraper, paint remover, a wire brush, or a blowtorch. If necessary, they must also remove grease and fill nail holes, cracks, and joints with putty, plaster, or some other filler. Many times, a prime coat or a sealer is applied to further smooth the surface and make the finished coat level and well blended in color.

Once the surface is prepared, painters select premixed paints or prepare paint themselves by mixing required portions of pigment, oil, and thinning and drying substances. They then paint the surfaces using a brush, spray gun, or roller. Spray guns are generally used for large surfaces or objects that do not lend themselves to brush work, such as lattices, cinder and concrete block, and radiators.

In paperhanging, the first task is also to prepare the surface to be covered. Rough spots must be smoothed, holes and cracks must be filled, and old paint, varnish, and grease must be removed from the surface. In some cases, old wallpaper must be removed by soaking or steaming. In new work, the paperhangers apply "sizing," a prepared material that makes the plaster less porous and assures better sticking of the paper to the surface.

After setting up the pasteboard and erecting any necessary scaffolding, the paperhangers cut the paper to size, mix the paste, and apply it to the back of the paper. The paste-coated paper is then placed on the wall or ceil-

ing and smoothed into place with brushes or rollers. In placing the paper on the wall, paperhangers must make sure that they match the adjacent edges of strips of figured paper, cut overlapping ends, and smooth the seams between each strip.

Requirements

The basic requirements for the occupations of painter and paperhanger are the same. Most employers prefer to hire applicants in good physical condition, with manual dexterity and a good color sense. Although a high-school education is not essential, it is preferred. An additional requirement is that the applicant not be allergic to paint fumes or other materials used in the trade.

To qualify as a skilled painter or paperhanger, however, a person must also complete either an apprenticeship or an on-the-job training program.

The apprenticeship program, which often combines painting and paperhanging, consists of three years of carefully planned activity including work experience with related classroom instruction. During this period the apprentice becomes familiar with all aspects of the craft.

The on-the-job training program consists of learning the trade informally while working for four or five years under the guidance of experienced painters and/or paperhangers. The trainees usually begin as helpers until they acquire the necessary skills and knowledge for more difficult jobs. Workers without formal apprenticeship training are more easily accepted in these crafts than in most of the other building trades.

Special requirements

There are no special requirements for the occupations of painter and paperhanger in addition to those already mentioned.

Opportunities for experience and exploration

In high school or vocational school there are several ways to explore the skills of the painter and/or paperhanger. Courses in art, industrial arts, and wood shop will test students' interest and ability in this type of work, while courses

683

Professional painters must often work in precarious positions in order to cover all surfaces.

in chemistry and mathematics will gauge their skill in estimating and applied mathematics.

Certainly, painting and paperhanging in one's home or apartment will provide a valuable firsthand experience, often impossible to obtain with other crafts.

Even more valuable, however, would be to get a part-time or summer job as a helper to a painter and/or paperhanger. A person who has done satisfactory part-time work can sometimes go to work full-time for the same employer after graduation.

Related occupations

Other workers employ similar skills and interests in their work. Some of these include lathers, plasterers, floor covering installers, marble setters, and drywall installers and finishers.

Methods of entering

There are two ways that individuals can enter the trade of painter and/or paperhanger: as apprentices or as on-the-job trainees.

If they wish to become apprentices, the applicants usually contact employers, such as painting and paperhanging contractors, the state employment service bureau, the state apprenticeship agency, or the appropriate union headquarters (International Brotherhood of Painters and Allied Trades). They must, however, have the approval of the joint labor-management apprenticeship committee before they can enter the occupation by this method.

If the apprentice program is filled, applicants may wish to enter the trade as on-the-job trainees. In this case, they usually contact employers directly and begin work as helpers.

Advancement

Successful completion of the training program is necessary before individuals can become qualified, skilled painters and/or paperhangers.

If they have management ability and good planning skills, and if they work for a large contracting firm, they may advance to the following positions: supervisor, who supervises and coordinates activities of other painters and/or paperhangers; estimator for a painting and decorating contractor, who computes material requirements and labor costs; and superintendent on a large contract painting job.

Some painters and/or paperhangers, once they have acquired enough capital and business experience, go into business for themselves as painting and decorating contractors.

Employment outlook

In the early 1990s, there were about 389,000 painters and paperhangers employed.

Employment of painters and paperhangers will grow about as fast as the average for all occupations through the next decade. Most job openings will occur as other workers retire, die, or transfer to other occupations. Openings for paperhangers will be fewer, however, because this is a smaller trade.

Increased construction will generate a need for more painters to work on new buildings and industrial structures. Even though newer types of paint have made it easier for inexperienced persons to do their own painting, most painters and paperhangers work on industrial and commercial projects and are not dependent on residential repair and repapering.

Earnings

The average annual salary for painters working a thirty-five-hour week in a metropolitan area in the early 1990s, who were not self-employed, was about $30,576. Wages varied according to the section of the country, however.

Conditions of work

Most painters and/or paperhangers have a regular forty-hour workweek with extra pay for overtime. Their work requires them to stand for long periods of time, to climb, and to bend. Because much of the work is done directly overhead, the painter and/or paperhanger must have strong arms. There is some danger of falling from ladders, although the number of accidents is less than for many jobs in the construction field. Paperhangers, because their hands are often immersed in water, may suffer from arthritis.

It must be noted here that the painter and/or paperhanger will sometimes find it difficult to work in homes when the owner of the house is present, because some owners may want to supervise the job. In this case, the craft worker must be able to work steadily while answering questions about how the work is done and why it is done one way rather than another. The customer will not want costs to increase for the sake of conversation, and the worker must bear this in mind.

Social and psychological factors

Painters and paperhangers more often than not work by themselves, without direct supervi-sion. While this factor may seem desirable to many, it must be remembered that these craft workers have to accept total responsibility for a job that is not done to the satisfaction of the customer.

Persons in these occupations should be able to plan their work on a daily as well as on a job basis. They should be able to estimate fairly the cost of a job and not charge excessively. Due to the fact that much of the work is done in private homes, painters and paperhangers should be neat, orderly, and conscious of caring for the customers' furniture and floors.

GOE: 05.10.07; SIC: 1721; SOC: 6442, 6443

◇ **SOURCES OF ADDITIONAL INFORMATION**

International Brotherhood of Painters and Allied Trades
United Unions Building
1750 New York Avenue, NW
Washington, DC 20006

Painting and Decorating Contractors of America
5913 Old Lee Highway, Suite 338
Fairfax, VA 22030

◇ **RELATED ARTICLES**

Volume 1: Construction
Volume 3: Cement masons; Drywall installers and finishers; Lathers; Marble setters, tile setters, and terrazzo workers; Plasterers
Volume 4: Poured-concrete-wall technicians

Pipe fitters and steam fitters

Definition

Pipe fitters and *steam fitters* design, install and maintain the piping systems for steam, hot water, heating, cooling, lubricating, sprinkling, and industrial processing systems.

History

The Industrial Revolution marked the emergence of pipe fitting as an independent trade. Prior to this period, general plumbers handled the construction and maintenance of piping systems. Additionally, indoor plumbing and municipal water systems were not as widespread as they are today, so regular plumbers could handle the work load.

This all changed with the Industrial Revolution. Factories and other buildings were being erected, cities were expanding, and new homes were being built. All this development called for more indoor plumbing. The expansion of industry also brought about new uses for piping, such as the conveyance of steam, oil, chemicals, heat, natural gas, and compressed air in manufacturing processes. All of this building and expansion required larger and more varied piping systems, and pipe fitting gradually became a profession in its own right.

Nature of the work

Pipe systems do not carry only water. In power plants, they carry live steam to the turbines to create electricity. At oil refineries, pipes carry raw crude oil to processing tanks, then transport the finished products, such as petroleum, kerosene, and natural gas, to storage areas. In some manufacturing plants, pneumatic (air) pipe systems are used to monitor and adjust the industrial processes in the plant. Naval ships, submarines, aircraft, food processing plants, refrigerated warehouses, nuclear power plants, and office buildings are just a few of the many things that are heavily dependent on pipe systems for their operation. Pipe systems are also needed in the home for such things as natural gas, hot and cold water, and sewage.

Pipe fitters are the tradespeople who design, install, and maintain all of these different pipe systems. Steam fitters construct pipe systems that must withstand high amounts of pressure. It is a skilled and demanding line of work, because careless or incomplete work could cost people's lives.

Pipe fitters can work both in existing buildings and buildings under construction. When working in an old building, such as installing a sprinkler system, a pipe fitter sometimes receives nothing more than verbal instructions of the job to complete. The pipe fitter then examines the blueprints of the building, makes the necessary measurements, and draws a layout for how the system is to be installed. Installing a new pipe system in an old building is trickier than in a new one because the system must adapt to the existing construction, and care must be taken that any modifications made to accommodate the pipe system does not weaken the building's structure or interfere with its other operations. Pipe fitters also frequently are called on to fix and repair the pipes in old buildings.

When installing pipe systems in buildings under construction, the pipe fitter usually works under the supervision of the general contractor for the project. The blueprints for the piping are usually drawn up by the architect and the contractor, and show the type of piping needed, what kind of fixtures are required, and where valves and connectors should be placed. With these instructions, the job of the pipe fitter is to use the proper materials to do the best job possible.

Pipe fitters and steam fitters work with pipes made of many different types of materials, including steel, cast iron, copper, lead, glass, and plastic. As they study the blueprints, the pipe fitters decide what types of materials they'll need and how much they'll use. The first step in preparing the pipes is cutting them to the proper length. If pipes need to be screwed together, the pipe fitter will cut threads into the ends of the pipe using a pipe threader, which is attached to the end and rotated to cut a slowly spiralling groove into the pipe. To remove any metal burrs after the thread is cut, the pipe fitter will clean it out using a pipe reamer. Pipes may also need to be bent to the proper angle, which is done with a bending device that can be either manually or electrically powered.

Once the pipes are sized and cut, they are put into position, and the pipe fitter can determine what needs to be done to support or give access to the pipes. Occasionally holes may need to be cut through ceilings, floors, or walls, or the pipes may need to be bracketed to ceiling joists or along walls. Then the pipes are fitted together. This may be done by screwing the pipes into couplers, elbow joints, connectors, or special valves. Very large pipes such as sewer pipes have flat flanges that are bolted together when joined. At this stage, the pipe fitter installs special mechanisms such as pressure gauges or meters.

Finally, the connections between the pipes are sealed and made air tight. Depending on the material the pipe is made of, this is done by soldering, caulking, brazing, fusing, or cementing the joints of the pipes together. The pipe system is then tested to make certain it is completely sealed. Water, air, or gas is pumped into the system at a high pressure and leaks are checked either personally by the pipe fitter or an apprentice or mechanically by means of gauges attached to the pipes. Proper and complete sealing is extremely important. Leaks will affect the performance of the entire system, and in certain cases, such as high-pressure steam pipes or pipes carrying noxious chemicals, leaks can be deadly.

A pipefitter solders two pipes together. To prevent leakage, the soldering process must be done thoroughly.

Requirements

Pipe fitters and steam fitters learn their occupations through apprenticeship programs. These programs take five years to complete, coupling on-the-job training with a minimum of 216 hours of related classroom instruction each year. To apply for apprenticeship programs, persons must be at least eighteen years of age, be in good physical condition, and have earned a high-school diploma or equivalent. Apprentice applicants are expected to have taken high-school courses in shop, drafting, mathematics, physics, chemistry and blueprint reading. Course work from vocational schools and correspondence schools can also supplement an apprentice's training. To measure their mechanical readiness for this profession, apprentice applicants also must take mechanical aptitude tests.

Apprentices sign a written agreement with the local apprenticeship committee, which is made up of members from both union and management. This committee sets the standards for work and training that ensures apprentices gain a broad range of experience through employment with several different contractors. In their training period, they learn to cut, bend, fit, solder, and weld pipes. They also learn the proper use and care of tools and equipment, materials handling, workplace op-

erations and safety (including the regulations of the Occupational Safety and Health Administration), and how to make cost estimates.

Pipe fitters and steam fitters also learn related construction techniques, such as installing gas furnaces, boilers, pumps, oil burners, and radiators. They study and work on various heating and cooling systems, hot water systems, and solar and radiant heat systems. They explore industrial applications such as pneumatic control systems and instrumentation. Classroom work for apprentices includes subjects such as drafting, blueprint reading, applied math and physics, and local building codes and regulations.

Special requirements

Union membership is a requirement for most pipe fitters and steam fitters. The main union representing this trade is the United Association of Journeymen and Apprentices of the Plumbing and Pipe Fitting Industry of the United States and Canada. Another union, the Mechanical Contractors Association of America, represents the construction contractors who hire pipe fitters. Two other unions in the industry are the National Association of Plumbing-Heating-Cooling Contractors and the National Fire Sprinkler Association. In certain industries such as the aerospace or petroleum

Pipe fitters and steam fitters
Structural Work Occupations

industries, pipe fitters and steam fitters may belong to other unions as well.

In some cities, pipe fitters, steam fitters, and sprinkler fitters must be licensed. This requires passing a written test and offering proof of training and skills in the trade.

Opportunities for experience and exploration

To get an idea of the type of work done by pipe fitters and steam fitters, students can look for jobs as construction helpers to these trades. This does not involve the commitment of an apprenticeship, and it is a good vantage point from which to consider whether one is interested in the type of work pipe fitters do and the amount of training that the profession requires. A job as a helper is also a very good stepping stone to apprenticeship programs.

Related occupations

The work of the pipe fitter and steam fitter is similar to other work in the construction field. Some of these include plumbers, sheet-metal workers, electricians, and boilermakers. These workers either work with blueprints and construction or work with assembling or shaping metal.

Methods of entering

After completing high school, those interested in a career as a pipe fitter should seek out information on the various apprenticeship programs available. To do this, job seekers should visit the nearest plumbing and pipe fitting union local or nearby construction contractors to learn the details of apprenticeship programs and how to apply.

Another source for this information is the state employment service office of the U.S. Department of Labor, Bureau of Apprenticeship and Training. Applicants may have to take an aptitude test for admittance to apprenticeship programs.

For those who do not want to commit to an apprenticeship program, they should contact local unions and contractors for work as helpers to pipe fitters and steam fitters.

Advancement

After their training, apprentice pipe fitters become journeyworkers, which means more money and more employment opportunities. They may continue to work for the same contractor or move on to a new employer. If they gain experience in all the skills of the trade, they may rise to the position of supervisor. Some pipe fitters and steam fitters decide to go into business for themselves as independent contractors, lining up job contracts and hiring their own employees. According to the Department of Labor, one out of every seven pipe fitters is self-employed.

Employment outlook

Employment prospects are good for pipe fitters, steam fitters and sprinkler fitters in the next few years. According to the Department of Labor, about 61,000 job openings will occur by the year 1995. Those pipe fitters who work in construction can sometimes experience layoffs when there are lulls in construction activity, while those who maintain existing pipe systems have more steady work. Pipe fitters and steam fitters are less sensitive to swings in the economy than other construction trades.

Expansion of certain industries, such as chemical and food-processing factories and others that rely on automated production, will be an important source of work for pipe fitters. In office and home construction, air conditioning and refrigeration systems will keep pipe fitters busy, as will legislation requiring sprinkler systems in older buildings. Keeping existing pipe systems in good repair will employ many workers in the trade.

Earnings

Although pay rates vary somewhat in different areas of the country, earnings for pipe fitters and steam fitters are among the highest in the construction trades. Union plumbers, pipe fitters and steam fitters earned an average weekly wage of $789 in the early 1990s. Apprentices typically earn from 30 to 50 percent of a journeyworker's wage at the beginning of their training. If their work remains satisfactory, their wages are raised at regular intervals, usually six months, as stipulated in their apprenticeship agreements. Those applicants with some relevant training or experience may receive a higher wage when they begin their apprenticeship. Pipe fitters and steam fitters also enjoy a variety of benefits from their employer or union, including health insurance, pension plans, paid vacations and training opportunities.

Conditions

Like other construction and maintenance work, pipe fitting is hard, dirty, and active work. Much of their work is done in cramped quarters and in uncomfortable positions. Lifting, joining, and installing heavy pipe work and operating large machinery can cause fatigue and muscle strain. Other hazards include cuts from sharp tools, burns from hot pipes and welding material, and related construction injuries. The injury rate for pipe fitters and steam fitters, however, is the same as the average for most construction employees.

Most pipe fitters and steam fitters are employed by building contractors and perform their work at different sites every day. They may work for a few hours at one work site and then travel to another. The construction of a large housing or industrial complex, however, may keep pipe fitters at the same site for several months. Pipe fitters work a regular forty-hour week, although they may work overtime to meet deadlines or complete assignments. Those pipe fitters who are on the maintenance staff of a large processing plant generally work from thirty-five to forty hours a week.

Social and psychological factors

Pipe fitting and steam fitting are demanding trades. Aside from the physical strain the work requires, pipe fitters must also perform very careful, conscientious, and exacting work. Flaws in their work could lead to damage to property and injury to others. They must be able to follow exacting instructions, but also apply their judgment and experience to make decisions and direct other workers when necessary.

Pipe fitters and steam fitters invest a lot of time into their training for the profession, so relatively few of them leave the field to move into other lines of work. Work is available in every part of the country, and the pay is above average. Pipe fitters and steam fitters also can enjoy the prestige and satisfaction of working in one of the skilled construction trades.

GOE: 05.05.03; SIC: 1799; SOC: 645

◇ **SOURCES OF ADDITIONAL INFORMATION**

Associated Builders and Contractors
729 15th Street, NW
Washington, DC 20005

Mechanical Contractors Association of America
5410 Grosvenor Lane, Suite 120
Bethesda, MD 20814

National Association of Plumbing-Heating-Cooling Contractors
PO Box 6808
180 South Washington Street
Falls Church, VA 22046

National Fire Sprinkler Association
Robin Hill Corporate Bank
PO Box 1000
Patterson, NJ 12563

United Association of Journeymen and Apprentices of the Plumbing and Pipe Fitting Industry of the U.S. and Canada
PO Box 38700
Washington, DC 20013

◇ **RELATED ARTICLES**

Volume 1: Construction; Engineering; Machining and Machinery; Public Utilities; Waste Management
Volume 3: Air-conditioning, refrigeration, and heating mechanics; Boilermaking occupations; Construction workers; Industrial chemicals workers; Petroleum drilling occupations; Petroleum refining workers; Plumbers; Power plant occupations; Wastewater treatment plant operators; Welders
Volume 4: Air-conditioning, heating, and refrigeration technicians; Architectural and building construction technicians; Fire control and safety technicians; Fluid-power technicians; Industrial engineering technicians; Instrumentation technicians; Nuclear instrumentation technicians; Petroleum technicians; Pollution-control technicians; Water and wastewater treatment technicians

Plasterers

Definition

Plasterers apply coats of plaster to interior walls, ceilings, and partitions of buildings to produce fire-resistant and relatively soundproof surfaces. They also may work on exterior building surfaces or do ornamental forming and casting work.

History

Plastering is one of the most ancient crafts in the building trades. The trade, however, has evolved in the last fifty years or so into a highly skilled type of work through the development and use of many new and improved materials and techniques.

Nature of the work

Plasterers work on building interiors and exteriors. They apply plaster directly to masonry, wire, wood, or metal or to lath, all designed to hold the plaster in position until it dries. After checking the specifications and plans on interior three-coat work over metal lath, plasterers begin by putting a border of plaster of the desired thickness on the top and bottom of the wall. After this border has hardened sufficiently, they fill in the remaining portion of the wall with two coats of plaster. The surface of the wall area is then leveled and smoothed with a straight-edged tool and a darby (long flat tool used for smoothing). They then apply the third or finishing coat of plaster, which is the last operation before painting or paperhanging. This coat may be finished to an almost velvet smoothness or into one of a variety of decorative textures that are used in place of papering or other finishes.

The plasterer sometimes works with plasterboard or sheetrock, types of wallboard that come ready for installation. When working with such wallboard, the plasterer cuts and fits the wallboard to the studding and joists of ceilings and interior walls. When installing ceilings, workers perform as a team.

Plasterers who specialize in exterior plastering work on buildings are known as *stucco masons.* They apply a weather resistive decorative covering of Portland cement plaster to lath in a similar manner as in interior plastering or with the use of a spray gun. In exterior work, however, the finish coat usually consists of a mixture of white cement and sand, or a patented finish material which may be applied in a variety of colors and textures.

Decorative and ornamental plastering is the specialty of highly skilled *molding plasterers.* This work includes the molding or forming and installing of ornamental plaster panels and trim as well as the casting of intricate cornices and the recesses used for indirect lighting. Such work is little used today because of the great degree of skill involved and the high cost.

In recent years, most plasterers have been making use of machines which spray plaster on walls, ceilings, and structural sections of buildings. Machines that mix plaster have been in general use for many years.

Requirements

Most employers prefer to hire applicants at least seventeen years old, in good physical condition, and with a high degree of manual dexterity. Although a high-school or trade school education is not mandatory, it is highly recommended.

To qualify as a journeyman plasterer, however, a person must complete either an apprenticeship or on-the-job training program.

The apprenticeship program consists of three to four years of carefully planned activity combining from about 6,000 to about 8,000 hours of work experience with an annual 144 hours of related classroom instruction.

On-the-job training consists of working for four or more years under the supervision of experienced plasterers. The trainee usually begins as a helper or laborer and learns the trade informally by observing or by being taught by other plasterers.

Special requirements

There are no special requirements for the position of plasterer in addition to those already mentioned.

Opportunities for experience and exploration

In high school or vocational school, students have several avenues open for exploring the occupation of plasterer. Mechanical drawing, drafting, woodwork, and other shop courses will test their ability and aptitude for this type of work, while courses in mathematics will gauge their skill in the applied mathematics of layout work.

To observe the plasterer at work, field trips to construction sites can be arranged by the school counselor, or students may make such arrangements on their own by telephone or letter.

An excellent firsthand experience in this trade would be to obtain a part-time or summer job as a plasterer's helper or laborer.

Related occupations

Plasterers have good eye-hand coordination and good construction skills. Other occupations that might also be appealing include lathers, painters, paperhangers, terrazzo workers, marble setters, and drywall installers.

Methods of entering

There are two ways individuals can enter the occupation of plasterer: as apprentices or as on-the-job trainees.

Those who wish to become apprentices usually contact local plastering contractors, the state employment service bureau, or the appropriate union headquarters. The Bureau of Apprenticeship and Training, U.S. Department of Labor, as well as the state employment office, are also good places to contact for information.

If the apprenticeship program is filled, applicants may wish to enter the field as on-the-job trainees. In this case, they usually contact a plastering contractor directly and begin work as helpers or laborers.

Advancement

Successful completion of a training program is necessary before individuals can become qualified plasterers. After increasing their skill and efficiency for a few years, several promotional opportunities are open to them.

The plasterer uses his trowel to smooth mortar on a ceiling. This is the first of three coats of plaster.

They may decide to specialize in one area of plastering. For example, they may apply only one particular coat of plaster and become finish plasterers or rough coat plasterers; or they may concentrate on the spray gun technique and become spray gun plasterers.

With additional training they may specialize in exterior work as stucco masons or in ornamental plastering as molding plasterers.

If they have certain personal characteristics such as the ability to deal with people, good judgment, and planning skills, plasterers may progress to supervisors or job estimators.

Many plasterers become self-employed, and some eventually may become contractors themselves.

Employment outlook

There were approximately 23,000 plasterers employed in the early 1990s. Employment opportunities for plasterers are expected to increase slowly during the remainder of the decade and beyond, due to the trend toward wider use of drywall construction.

Recent improvements in both plastering materials and methods of application, however, are expected to increase the scope of the craft and create more job opportunities. To name a few such developments: more lightweight plasters are being used because of excellent sound-proofing, acoustical, and fireproofing qualities; machine plastering, insulating, and fireproofing are becoming more widespread; also, the use of "plaster veneer" or "high density" plaster in creating a finished surface is being used increasingly in new buildings.

Earnings

The median annual salary for plasterers in the early 1990s was about $29,300. However, the minimum wage rate varied considerably according to the section of the country.

Conditions of work

Most plasterers have a regular forty-hour work-week, with occasional overtime when it is necessary to meet a contract deadline. Overtime work is compensated at the rate of one-and-a-half times the regular hourly wage.

The work is performed both indoors, plastering walls, ceilings, and forming and casting ornamental designs, and outdoors, doing stucco work. Plasterers must do a considerable amount of standing, stooping, and lifting. They often get plaster on their work clothes and dust in their eyes and noses.

Most plasterers are members of unions, either the Operative Plasterers' and Cement Masons' International Association of the United States and Canada or the Bricklayers and Allied Craftsmen International Union.

Social and psychological factors

Plasterers can take pride in seeing the results of their work—something they have helped to build that will last a long time. Their satisfaction with progress on the job day by day may be a great deal more than in those jobs where the worker never sees the completed work or where the results are not so obvious.

As highly skilled workers, plasterers have higher earnings, better chances for promotion,

and more opportunity to go into business for themselves than workers with lesser skills. They also can usually find jobs in almost any part of the United States.

GOE: 05.05.04; SIC: 1742; SOC: 6444

◇ **SOURCES OF ADDITIONAL INFORMATION**

Foundation of the Wall and Ceiling Industry
1600 Cameron Street
Alexandria, VA 22314

International Institute for Lath and Plaster
795 Raymond Avenue
St. Paul, MN 55114

International Union of Bricklayers and Allied Craftsmen
815 15th Street, NW
Washington, DC 20005

Operative Plasterers and Cement Masons International Association of the United States and Canada
1125 17th Street, NW
Washington, DC 20036

◇ **RELATED ARTICLES**

Volume 1: Construction
Volume 3: Bricklayers and stonemasons; Carpenters; Cement masons; Drywall installers and finishers; Lathers; Marble setters, tile setters, and terrazzo workers; Painters and paperhangers
Volume 4: Poured-concrete-wall technicians

Plumbers

Definition

Plumbers assemble, install, alter, and repair pipes and pipe systems that carry water, steam, air, or other liquids and gases for sanitation and industrial and other uses. They also install plumbing fixtures, appliances, and heating and refrigerating units.

History

The plumber's occupation is an ancient one. The early Egyptians are known to have used lead pipes to carry water and drainage into and out of buildings. But the use of plumbing in a citywide system was an achievement of plumbers in Rome in the days of the Empire.

In Renaissance times, the techniques of plumbing were revived and used in some of the great castles and monasteries. The greatest advances in plumbing, however, were made in the nineteenth century, when towns grew into cities and the need for adequate public sanitation was recognized.

Nature of the work

Because there is little difference between the work of the plumber and the pipe fitter in most cases, it is often considered to be one trade. Many craft workers do specialize in one field or the other, especially in large cities.

The work of pipe fitters differs from that of plumbers mainly in its location and in the variety and size of the pipes used. Plumbers work mainly in residential and commercial buildings; pipe fitters are generally employed by a large industry such as an oil refinery, refrigeration plant, or defense establishment where more complex systems of piping are used. (*See also* the separate article titled *Pipe fitters and steam fitters* elsewhere in this volume.)

Plumbers assemble, install, and repair heating, water, and drainage systems, especially those that must be connected to public utility systems. Some of their jobs include mending burst pipes, installing and repairing sinks, bathtubs, water heaters, hot water tanks, garbage disposal units, dishwashers, and water softeners. They may also work on septic tanks, cesspools, and sewers. During the final con-

struction stages, plumbers install heating and air-conditioning units, and connect radiators, water heaters, and plumbing fixtures.

Plumbers follow procedures in their work. After inspecting the installation site to determine pipe location, they cut and thread pipes, bend them to required angles by hand or with machines, and then join them by means of welded, brazed, caulked, soldered, or threaded joints. To test for leaks in the system, they fill the pipes with water or air.

Specialists include *diesel engine pipe fitters, ship and boat building coppersmiths, industrial-gas fitters, gas-main fitters, prefab plumbers,* and *pipe cutters.*

A variety of tools are used by plumbers in their work. These include hand tools, such as wrenches, reamers, drills, braces and bits, hammers, chisels, and saws; power machines which cut, bend, and thread pipes; and gas or gasoline torches, welding, soldering, and brazing equipment.

Requirements

Most employers prefer to hire applicants at least eighteen years old, in good physical condition, and with a high degree of mechanical aptitude. Although a high-school education is not required, it is generally preferred.

The student's preparation should include courses in mathematics, chemistry, and physics, as well as the usual shop courses.

To qualify as a plumber, however, a person must complete either a formal apprenticeship or an informal on-the-job training program. To be considered for the apprenticeship program, individuals must pass an examination administered by the state employment agency and have their qualifications approved by the local joint labor-management apprenticeship committee.

The apprenticeship program for plumbers consists of four years of carefully planned activity combining direct training with at least 216 hours of formal classroom instruction. The program is designed to give the apprentices diversified training by having them work for several different plumbing or pipe fitting contractors.

On-the-job training, on the other hand, usually consists of working for five or more years under the guidance of one kind of experienced craft worker. The trainees begin as helpers until they acquire the necessary skills

A plumber installs heavy metal pipes on top of a high-rise that is under construction.

and knowledge for more difficult jobs. Frequently, they must supplement this practical training by taking trade or correspondence school courses.

Special requirements

A license is required for plumbers in many localities. To obtain this license, persons must pass a special examination to demonstrate their knowledge of local building codes as well as their all-around knowledge of the trade. The licensing procedure is a function of the local government and those interested in details of the licensing requirements should contact the city manager's office or licensing office.

To become a plumbing contractor in most localities, a master plumber's license must be obtained.

Opportunities for experience and exploration

Although opportunities for direct experience in this occupation are rare for those in high school, there are ways to explore the field.

Courses in chemistry, physics, mechanical drawing, and mathematics are all necessary to the work of the plumber and pipe fitter. By taking these courses in high school, students will test their ability and aptitude in the theoretical aspects of the trade.

Related occupations

Other occupations that might be of interest include boilermakers, steam fitters, electricians, and sheet-metal workers.

Methods of entering

There are two ways individuals can enter the occupations of plumber: as apprentices or as on-the-job trainees.

Applicants who wish to become apprentices usually contact local plumbing, heating, and air-conditioning contractors who employ plumbers; the state employment service bureau; or the local branch of the United Association of Journeymen and Apprentices of the Plumbing and Pipe Fitting Industry of the United States and Canada. Before they can become apprentices, however, they must have the approval of the joint labor-management apprenticeship committee. The Bureau of Apprenticeship and Training, U.S. Department of Labor, as well as the state employment office, are also good places to contact for information.

If they cannot gain acceptance or if the apprenticeship program is filled, applicants may wish to enter the field as on-the-job trainees.

Advancement

Successful completion of a training program is necessary before an individual can become a qualified journeyman plumber. In some cases, an individual must have a plumber's license.

If plumbers have certain personal characteristics, such as the ability to deal with people, good judgment, and planning skills, they may progress to such supervisory positions as supervisor or job estimator for plumbing or pipe fitting contractors; or, if they work for a large industrial concern, they may advance to the position of job superintendent.

Many plumbers go into business for themselves. Eventually they may expand their activities and become contractors, employing other workers.

Employment outlook

Approximately 200,000 plumbers were employed in the early 1990s. Employment opportunities for plumbers are expected to increase moderately during the next decade, rising to about 225,000 by the year 2000.

There are several reasons for this outlook. First and most important is the anticipated increase in construction activity. Second, plumbing and heating work in new homes is expected to include the installation of more bathrooms per house, washing machines, waste disposals, air-conditioning equipment, and solar heating devices. Third, because pipe work is becoming more important in large industries, more artisans will be needed for installation and maintenance work, especially where refrigeration and air-conditioning equipment are used. Fourth, the need to replace those who transfer to other fields, retire, or die will provide thousands of job openings each year.

Earnings

The annual median salary for non–self-employed plumbers in the early 1990s was $28,900. Wages varied, however, according to location. Hourly pay rates for apprentices usually start at 50 percent of the experienced worker's rate, and increase by 5 percent every six months until a rate of 95 percent is reached.

Conditions of work

Most plumbers have a regular forty-hour work-week with extra pay for overtime.

Unlike most of the other building trades, this field is little affected by seasonal factors. Annual earnings of plumbers and pipefitters are among the highest in the construction trades.

The work of the plumber is active and strenuous. Standing for prolonged periods and working in cramped or uncomfortable positions are often necessary. Possible risks include falls from ladders, cuts from sharp tools, and burns from hot pipes or steam.

Social and psychological factors

Those who would be successful and contented plumbers should like to solve a variety of problems and should not object to being called on during evenings, weekends, or holidays to perform emergency repairs.

As in most service occupations, plumbers should be able to get along well with all kinds of people, because they will be dealing with persons who occasionally will ask questions and make their jobs more difficult.

The plumber should be a person who works well alone or who can perhaps direct the work of helpers and who likes the company of those in the other construction trades.

GOE: 05.05.03; SIC: 1711; SOC: 645

◇ **SOURCES OF ADDITIONAL INFORMATION**

National Association of Plumbing-Heating-Cooling Contractors
PO Box 6808
180 South Washington Street
Falls Church, VA 22042

National Fire Sprinkler Association
Robin Hill Corporate Bank
PO Box 1000
Patterson, NY 12563

United Association of Journeymen and Apprentices of the Plumbing and Pipe Fitting Industry of the United States and Canada
PO Box 37800
Washington, DC 20013

◇ **RELATED ARTICLES**

Volume 1: Construction
Volume 3: Air-conditioning, refrigeration, and heating mechanics; Appliance installers and repairers
Volume 4: Air-conditioning, heating, and refrigeration technicians

Roofers

Definition

Roofers apply composition roofing and other materials such as tile and slate shingles to the roofs of buildings. They also waterproof and damp-proof walls, swimming pools, and many other building surfaces.

History

The occupation of roofer developed as the building and construction fields expanded and as various kinds of modern roofing materials and tools were developed.

Nature of the work

There are several different kinds of roofing materials, each with its own method of application. Although roofers usually are trained to apply most kinds of roofing, they usually specialize in either composition roofing or in tile and slate roofing.

In the most common type of composition roofing, the roofers place overlapping strips of asphalt or tar-coated felt over the entire roof. They then spread a coating of coal tar pitch or hot asphalt over this. Layers of roofing paper and hot asphalt are alternately placed until the required thickness is attained. Finally, a top coat of coal tar pitch and gravel or a smooth surface of asphalt is applied. Sometimes these roofs are covered by applying only one layer of hot asphalt and then raking pebbles over it.

In the application of other composition roofing materials, such as roll roofing or asphalt shingles, the roofer overlaps the material and then fastens it to the roof base with nails or asphalt cement. Sometimes, the material must be cut to fit around corners, pipes, and chimneys. Strips of felt or metal are then nailed along the edge of these intersections to make them watertight.

The more expensive types of roofing, tile, and slate shingles, are installed differently. First, roofing felt is applied over the wood base. Next, the roofer punches holes in the slate or tile pieces so that nails can be inserted, then nails down the shingles, placing each row to overlap the preceding row. Lastly, the exposed nail heads are covered with roofing cement to prevent rusting and water leakage.

Metal roofing is done by special metal roofers or by sheet-metal workers. This type of roof is constructed by soldering metal sheets together and nailing them to the wood sheathing.

Some roofers do waterproofing and damp proofing of walls, swimming pools, tanks, and structures other than roofs. To prepare surfaces for waterproofing, the worker smooths the very rough surfaces and roughs the glazed surfaces. The roofer then brushes or sprays waterproofing fabric to the surface. Damp proofing, a similar kind of work, is done by spraying a coating of tar or asphalt onto interior or exterior surfaces to prevent moisture from penetrating. *Roof applicators* are specialists who spray roofs or other surfaces with urethane or polyurethane foam to insulate, soundproof, or seal them.

Various hand tools are used by roofers in their work, including hammers, roofing knives, mops, pincers, and caulking guns.

Requirements

Most employers prefer to hire applicants who are at least eighteen years of age, in good physical condition, with a good sense of balance. Although a high-school education or its equivalent is not required, it is preferred in most cases.

To qualify as a roofer, however, a person must complete either an apprenticeship or on-the-job training program.

The apprenticeship program consists of three years of carefully planned activity combining a minimum of 1,400 hours annually of work experience with an additional 144 hours of formal classroom instruction.

On-the-job training consists of working informally for four or five years under the guidance and supervision of experienced roofers. The trainees usually begin as helpers to gain the necessary skills and knowledge for more difficult tasks.

Special requirements

There are no requirements for the occupation of roofer in addition to those already mentioned.

Opportunities for experience and exploration

Although direct opportunities for experience in this occupation are difficult to find while in high school or vocational school, there are some preliminary ways to explore the field.

Shop courses will test students' aptitude and ability for doing the work, while mathematics will gauge their skill in estimating and in applied mathematics.

To observe the roofer at work, visits to construction sites may be arranged. But opportunities for a close look at roofers in action will be difficult, due to the heights at which most of their work is performed.

A part-time or summer job as a roofer's helper would be an excellent way to obtain firsthand experience with this work.

Related occupations

Other construction work is similar in nature and skill requirements. Some of these include carpenters, drywall installers, flooring installation workers, construction workers, and plasterers.

Methods of entering

There are two ways an individual can enter the occupation of roofer: as an apprentice or as an on-the-job trainee.

To become an apprentice, the applicant usually contacts employers, such as roofing contractors, the state employment service bureau, or the local office of the United Slate, Tile and Composition Roofers, Damp and Waterproof Workers Association. The Bureau of Apprenticeship and Training, U.S. Department of Labor, as well as the state employment office, are also good places to contact for information.

If the apprenticeship program is filled, the applicant may wish to enter as an on-the-job trainee. In this case, the individual usually contacts a roofing contractor directly and begins work as a helper.

Advancement

Successful completion of a training program is necessary before an individual can become a qualified roofer. Once this status is attained,

Roofers spread hot tar before placing the roofing material. The tar serves as a sealant.

one may specialize in one kind of roofing and become either a composition roofer, slate and tile roofer, or an aluminum or metal shingle roofer.

A roofer who has certain personal characteristics such as the ability to deal with people, good judgment, and planning skills may progress to supervisor or superintendent for a roofing contractor.

Some roofers eventually go into business for themselves.

Employment outlook

About 140,000 roofers were employed in the early 1990s. Employment opportunities for roofers should increase through the next decade.

There are several reasons for this outlook. As building construction activity is expected to remain at a steady level for a number of years, the demand for all building workers, including roofers, will continue. Because roofer skills are required to maintain and repair existing structures, much of their work will continue, even with a letup in new construction. Also, damp proofing and waterproofing are expected to provide an increasing proportion of the roofer's work. Lastly, more than a thousand job openings are available each year because of retirements, deaths, and the transfers of workers to other related fields.

Earnings

The median annual salary for roofers in the early 1990s was $21,200. Actual wages varied according to the section of the country.

Hourly wage rates for apprentices usually start at 55 percent of the skilled worker's rate and increase periodically until, in the last six months of the apprenticeship, the pay is up to 90 percent of the full rate.

Conditions of work

Most roofers have a regular forty-hour workweek, with extra pay for overtime. The work involves physically strenuous activity that is performed outdoors in all kinds of weather. Prolonged standing, climbing, bending, and squatting are all part of the job. Roofers must work while standing on surfaces that may be steep and quite high; they risk injuries from falls while working on a ladder, scaffold, or roof.

Social and psychological factors

Any of the building trades may be satisfying to young persons who enjoy physical exercise and working with their hands. Because the roofers' trade is concerned with finishing work, they can take great pride in the appearance of their completed job.

GOE: 05.10.01; SIC: 1761; SOC: 6468

◇ **SOURCES OF ADDITIONAL INFORMATION**

National Roofing Contractors Association
6250 River Road
Rosemont, IL 60018

United Union of Roofers, Waterproofers and Allied Workers
1125 17th Street, NW
Washington, DC 20036

◇ **RELATED ARTICLES**

Volume 1: Construction
Volume 3: Construction workers; Floor covering installers; Lathers; Marble setters, tile setters, and terrazzo workers; Sheet-metal workers

Roustabouts

Definition

Roustabouts perform the routine physical labor and maintenance around oil wells, drilling fields, and pipelines. They clean the derrick floors, clean pipes, and help maintain operational facilities. Roustabouts do much of the manual labor required on an oil well.

Roustabouts are also used during the construction of rigs and wells. Roustabout is usually a beginning position on oil wells.

History

Ever since the first oil wells were dug in Pennsylvania in the 1860s, science has developed new and more ingenious ways to use the products of crude oil. In that time, the public's demand for oil products has also continued to grow. Oil is a nonrenewable energy source, however, and once the easily accessible supplies of oil are consumed, other supplies have to be discovered and made available. Society's appetite for oil has forced oil companies to search for oil supplies in such far-flung places as the Gulf of Mexico, the north slope of Alaska and the North Sea between Scotland and Denmark. The tools for this work are becoming more and more sophisticated every year, but the job of drilling and extracting the oil supplies continues to be difficult and often dangerous. One of the key players in the drilling and extracting work is the roustabout.

Roustabouts adjust the overthrust belt on a drilling rig.

Nature of the work

Roustabouts perform much of the routine physical labor and maintenance in and around oil fields, pipelines and offshore drilling platforms. Because oil exploration can take place on different types of terrain, roustabouts do much of the work in building a solid foundation for drilling platforms, such as clearing trees and brush, digging ditches, and pouring concrete. They may have to build road beds leading to the platform and be sure drainage is adequate. Once the drilling site has been constructed, roustabouts often stay and help in its operation by loading and unloading trucks and boats, connecting pipes and hydraulic hoses, and painting equipment. They also may assemble and repair oil field machinery and equipment, such as pumps, boilers, valves and steam engines. As more mechanized equipment has been introduced to the job, roustabouts now operate motorized lifts, power tools, and electronic sensors and testers. The time they save in this way is applied to other maintenance duties.

Most roustabouts work with crews around existing oil wells. Others work for companies engaged in drilling wells, almost all of which is done by specialized companies known as drilling contractors. Roustabouts frequently assist skilled workers such as welders, electricians, and mechanics. They generally work under the supervision of a maintenance supervisor.

Requirements

Little or no formal education or training is needed to get a job as a roustabout. More people, however, are applying for jobs than there are job openings, which allows employers to be more selective in the people they hire as roustabouts. More and more of the people being hired have previous experience as roustabouts or other oil workers. Many others have earned an associate's degree in petroleum technology,

which demonstrates their knowledge of oil field operations and familiarity with automated equipment. Generally, technical training, specialized courses, and other pertinent experience can distinguish a person from the crowd of applicants and give a leg up in securing a job. Specialized training can also come in handy when a roustabout begins to seek promotion to more responsible jobs.

Special requirements

Roustabouts must be physically fit, with good coordination, agility, and eyesight. Many employers require that roustabouts pass a physical examination before hiring. Aptitude tests may also be used to determine a person's mechanical ability and other job-related considerations. This sort of work can be very strenuous physically, and even dangerous, especially for those working on open-sea drilling platforms. Because of this, employers need to determine something about an applicant's personality before hiring them and training them.

Roustabouts rarely belong to organized unions. The biggest unions for oil field workers include the International federation of Petroleum and Chemical Workers, the International Union of Petroleum and Industrial Workers, and the Oil, Chemical, and Atomic Workers International Union.

Opportunities for experience and exploration

Persons interested in a job as a roustabout may be able to find summer jobs in an oil field, and be able to learn something about oil field operations, machine maintenance, and safety.

Related occupations

Other work that might be of interest to people looking into the work of roustabouts includes petroleum technicians, petroleum engineers, petroleum refining workers, petroleum drilling workers, and mining workers.

Methods of entering

To be considered for a job as a roustabout, interested persons should contact oil companies and drilling contractors directly. This is the quickest way to find out which firms are hiring. News of job openings can also be gathered from state employment agencies and from school guidance counselors. Roustabouts are usually hired in the field by the maintenance superintendent or by a local company representative. Companies generally prefer to hire workers who live near the work site.

New employees without any experience or specialized training in oil field work are trained on the job by more experienced workers on operations, safety, and machine maintenance. Their first assignments are usually confined to basic labor such as unloading trucks and digging ditches. The turnover rate among roustabouts, like those for other entry-level jobs, is relatively high. For this reason, employers are generally reluctant to invest much time and effort in specialized training. Some employers, however, offer workers the opportunity to enroll in self-study courses offered by the American Petroleum Institute or by various junior colleges. Educational assistance programs are in place at certain companies and reimburse the expenses for job-related courses that employees take on their own time.

Advancement

Many paths for advancement exist for the roustabout who has learned the basic operations of the oil field and shown an aptitude for more difficult work. Advancement opportunities, however, greatly depend on the current economic climate. Recessions in the oil industry, such as the one which occurred in the mid-1980s, severely curtail the number of new jobs and opportunities for advancement in the field.

Roustabouts often move up in the ranks of the area in which they work. Those on drilling crews may take more specialized jobs in operating drilling and extracting equipment, such as roughneck, floor hand, or rotary helper. From these positions, roustabouts can advance to become derrick operators, drillers and tool pushers. Those on maintenance and operation crews can move to jobs such as switcher, gauger, pumper, lease operator or, for those who demonstrate leadership qualities, to chief operator or maintenance superintendent. (For a complete description of these job titles, turn to the article titled "Petroleum Drilling Occupations" elsewhere in this volume.) They might also move into related fields such as oil refining or natural gas processing.

Successful completion of petroleum technology programs can open doors to positions as an engineering technician and related jobs. Some companies run company training schools where roustabouts can learn a trade and possibly take a position as a carpenter, welder or electrician.

Employment outlook

Very little growth in the number of roustabout jobs is expected in the next decade. This is a result of the declining amount of oil exploration and production among American oil companies. Oil production in the U.S. was declining at a rate of 2 to 3 percent in the middle 1980s, and the number of operating wells dropped almost 75 percent during the course of the decade. The current worldwide oil surplus and increased production of countries in the Middle East and the North Sea, along with increased energy conservation measures, will continue to keep the demand for U.S. oil low, and reduce the incentive of oil companies to explore and drill new wells. Other factors affecting oil production include restrictions on land and sea production for ecological reasons and renewed concern about global warming from pollution which may discourage petroleum use.

Few, if any, new roustabout jobs are expected in the foreseeable future. Replacing current workers will account for virtually all job openings, and employers will continue to be selective in their hiring. Job opportunities will be best for persons who have previous experience as a roustabout or formal training in petroleum technology. Job opportunities are also expected to be better on offshore drilling rigs than at on-shore oil fields.

Earnings

The salaries of roustabouts vary according to many factors, including the region of the country, the type of work performed, workers' experience and the current health of the oil industry. Beginning salaries for roustabouts average $8.50 per hour, while the average for all roustabouts was $11.14 an hour in the early 1990s, according to the Department of Labor. Those working on offshore rigs had an hourly rate of $13.41, while on-shore workers earned $11.69 an hour. Roustabouts who worked for contract drilling firms averaged $9.21.

Roustabouts generally receive such benefits as paid vacations, pensions and health insurance. Economic problems in the oil industry, however, may force roustabouts to give up certain benefits, take salary cuts or even accept layoffs.

Conditions

Out in the oil field or on the drilling platform, roustabouts work in all types of weather. Roustabouts on offshore rigs and platforms can experience strong ocean currents, tides, violent storms, and bitterly cold winds. Those who work in oil fields on-shore can experience dust storms, thunderstorms, and extremely hot weather. The biggest physical threat to the safety of oil well and rig workers is fire. Platform fires are not common, and the preventative measures in design and practice are well enforced. When fire does break out, though, it can be deadly.

Because roustabouts work around heavy materials and equipment, their work is strenuous and requires frequent bending, stooping, climbing, and heavy lifting. They are also subject to falls from rigs or derricks, injuries from falling objects, cuts and scrapes from various equipment, and sore or strained muscles from heavy lifting. Fire is always a danger around oil fields, so roustabouts and other workers must be trained and ready to respond to emergencies and handle fire fighting equipment.

Roustabouts who work on offshore drilling rigs generally work a twelve-hour day, seven days a week, after which they are given seven days off. Some offshore crews may be required to work from two to four weeks, with a corresponding amount of time off. These workers generally live on the drilling platform during their work shifts and return to shore via helicopter or crew boat. While on-shore roustabouts may live very near the oil field, offshore workers may live hundreds of miles from the drilling rig.

In on-shore oil fields, roustabouts generally work a five-day, forty-hour week. Many drilling operations work around the clock until oil is discovered or the location is abandoned as a dry hole. This requires three eight-hour shifts of workers every day of the week.

Even though they are initially hired to work fields close to home, roustabouts working with drilling crews should expect to move from place to place, since their work at a particular drilling site may be completed in a few weeks or months. If they are working on a well that is producing oil, roustabouts usually remain at the same location for longer periods of time.

Social and psychological factors

The work of a roustabout requires a person with some unique personal characteristics. Roustabouts must enjoy working outdoors and be ready to pitch in with extra work when the situation requires it. They must be able to work well both on their own and under direct supervision as part of a work crew. Cooperation with other workers is extremely important, especially when everyone must work quickly and operate as a single unit. For those working on offshore platforms, getting along with others is especially important because they live with the same people they work with for extended periods of time.

Roustabouts are also characterized by a taste for adventure. They prefer tackling different jobs in their work, rather than the same job over and over. Travelling to distant cities for their work and moving from work site to work site appeal to roustabouts. They do not typically think of this as a career; they look at it as a way to gain experience, to earn money for things such as college, or to move up to a better paying job in the oil field or with the oil company.

On the negative side, the unusual working conditions of a roustabout may be an impediment to relationships in his or her personal life. Work sites are often far removed from cities and towns, so roustabouts often are forced to find ways to entertain themselves. Establishing a regular home life can be difficult when the possibility of relocation is always present. Marriages and families can also suffer from the long hours that roustabouts, especially those on offshore rigs, spend away from home.

GOE: 05.10.01; SIC: 131; SOC: 656

◇ **SOURCES OF ADDITIONAL INFORMATION**

American Association of Petroleum Landmen
4100 Fossil Creek Boulevard
Fort Worth, TX 76137

American Petroleum Institute
1220 L Street, NW
Washington, DC 20005

Association of Oilwell Servicing Contractors
6060 North Central Expressway, Suite 428
Dallas, TX 75206

Drillsite Supervisors Association
PO Box 133
League City, TX 77573

Gas Research Institute
8600 West Bryn Mawr Avenue
Chicago, IL 60631

Independent Petroleum Association of America
1101 16th Street, NW
Washington, DC 20036

International Association of Drilling Contractors
PO Box 4287
Houston, TX 77210

International Federation of Petroleum and Chemical Workers
PO Box 6565
Denver, CO 80206

International Union of Petroleum and Industrial Workers
8131 East Rosecrans Avenue
Paramount, CA 90723

◇ **RELATED ARTICLES**

Sheet-metal workers

Definition

Sheet-metal workers make, install, repair, and alter ducts used for ventilating, air conditioning, and heating systems, as well as other articles of light sheet-metal, including roofing and siding, stainless steel kitchen equipment, gutters and downspouts, partitions, metal framework, and chutes. These artisans are not to be confused with assembly-line factory workers who also make sheet-metal products but are trained in only a few specific operations.

History

The occupation of sheet-metal worker stems from the ever-increasing development of steel products in the form of sheets and strips, which has depended upon the development of mills and processes to roll steel into thin, strong, flat pieces. Heating, ventilating, and air-conditioning systems for all kinds of buildings—residential, commercial, industrial—provide the major source of employment for sheet-metal workers.

Nature of the work

The job of the sheet-metal worker can be divided into two separate operations: the fabrication or repair of sheet-metal articles and their installation or alteration. While the majority of these articles are the ducts used in heating and air-conditioning systems, some sheet-metal workers do work on metal roofing and siding, gutters and downspouts, as well as specialty products such as custom kitchen equipment.

Before any job is begun, sheet-metal workers must first determine the size and type of sheet-metal to be used. First, they lay out the work, usually from blueprints or drawings, make measurements, and determine angles. Next, the pattern is marked on the metal and cut out with hand or power shears; the metal is then shaped and curved by a band or machine brake. After the holes are drilled or punched, the parts are assembled by welding, soldering, bolting, or riveting them together. Once the rough areas are smoothed with a file or a grinding wheel, metalworkers install the completed unit by welding, bolting, screwing, or nailing it into place.

In some cases, the ducts are fabricated by the sheet-metal worker only if factory-fabricated ducts are not available. Although these factory-made ducts are in standard sizes, there is always the need to tailor them to meet a wide variety of structural conditions before they can be installed.

While some sheet-metal workers specialize either in shop work or in on-site installations, the skilled worker must know all the different aspects of the trade.

Sheet-metal workers are employed by a variety of firms, most of which are involved in the fabrication and installation of air-conditioning, heating, and refrigeration equipment. Contractors involved in residential, commercial, and industrial buildings also employ a large percentage of these workers. Roofing contractors, the federal government, and businesses that do their own alteration and construction work employ sheet-metal workers. The workers may be engaged in work that is done in the sheet-metal shop, or they may do their work on the installation site.

In addition, there are thousands of sheet-metal workers who are employed in non-construction activities, such as the shipbuilding or aircraft industries, or in shops that manufacture specialty products such as food products machinery or electrical generating and distributing equipment.

A sheet-metal worker measures the height of a duct that will be used in a ventilating system.

an apprenticeship or an on-the-job training program.

The apprenticeship program consists of four years of carefully planned activity combining about 8,000 hours of work experience with related classroom instruction. Training includes developing skills in blueprint reading, blueprint drawing, mechanical drawing, and computer skills. Other training is on sheet-metal manipulation by cutting, molding, and shaping.

On-the-job training consists of learning the trade informally by working for four or five years under the guidance of experienced sheet-metal workers. The trainee usually begins as a helper to acquire the necessary skills and knowledge for more difficult tasks. Frequently, one must supplement this working experience with correspondence or trade school courses.

Requirements

Most employers prefer to hire applicants who are mechanically inclined, at least eighteen years old, and in good physical condition. A high-school or vocational school education or its equivalent is required.

To qualify as a sheet-metal worker, however, a young person must complete either

Special requirements

There are no requirements for the trade of sheet-metal worker in addition to those already mentioned.

Sheet-metal workers
Structural Work Occupations

Opportunities for experience and exploration

A high-school student has several avenues open for exploring the occupation of sheet-metal worker. Courses in metal shop and mechanical drawing will test his ability and aptitude for this kind of work, while courses in mathematics will gauge his skill in the theoretical aspects of the trade.

To observe the sheet-metal worker on the job, trips to construction sites can be arranged by the school counselor, or interested students may make such arrangements on their own.

An excellent opportunity for exploring this occupation would be to obtain a part-time or summer job as a helper to a sheet-metal worker.

Related occupations

Other workers who have similar skills and interests include structural steel workers (iron workers), pipe fitters, steam fitters, plumbers, layout workers, machinists, and welders.

Workers who work with metal making and refining include foundry workers, forge shop workers and molders.

Methods of entering

There are two ways an individual can enter the occupation of sheet-metal worker—as an apprentice or as an on-the-job trainee.

The applicant who wishes to become an apprentice should contact employers, such as heating, refrigeration, or air-conditioning contractors or sheet-metal contractors; the state apprenticeship agency; or the local office of the Sheet-Metal Workers' International Association. There must be an opening and the applicant must have the approval of the joint apprenticeship committee, however, before an individual can enter the field by this method. The Bureau of Apprenticeship and Training, U.S. Department of Labor, as well as the state employment office, are also good places to contact for information.

If the apprenticeship program is filled, the applicant may wish to enter the field as an on-the-job trainee. In this case, one usually contacts a contractor directly, and begins work as a helper.

Advancement

Successful completion of a training program is necessary before an individual can become a qualified sheet-metal worker.

With further experience and development of skills, sheet-metal workers have great mobility because they can transfer from the construction field to the metal manufacturing industry and back again.

In addition, these workers may advance to become specialists in design and layout work or in estimating the cost of installations. Other promotional opportunities are to the jobs of supervisor and job superintendent.

Some workers eventually go into business for themselves as sheet-metal contractors.

Employment outlook

Employment opportunities for sheet-metal workers are expected to increase through the next decade. There were about 120,000 sheet-metal workers in the early 1990s, and that number has been projected to reach 150,000 by 2000.

There are several reasons for the excellent employment outlook in this field. First and most important, a large expansion in construction is expected, with an increasingly widespread use of permanently installed central air-conditioning systems in commercial, industrial, and residential buildings. In addition, the manufacturing industries that employ sheet-metal workers also have favorable long-range prospects. Sheet-metal work should also result from growth in the number of large refrigeration systems for home and commercial use.

Prefabrication and improved machinery will make some of the work easier but will not cut down on the need for sheet-metal workers since much work must be made to order.

Earnings

The median annual salary for all sheet-metal workers in the early 1990s was $42,400. Salaries varied considerably throughout the country and were highest in industrial areas.

Apprentices earn 45 percent of the rate paid to experienced workers at the beginning, and receive periodic increases until 80 percent of the full rate is reached during the last six months of training.

Conditions of work

GOE: 05.05.06; SIC: 3444; SOC: 6824

Most sheet-metal workers have a regular forty-hour workweek with extra pay for overtime. Their work is performed indoors in shops and outdoors on construction sites, depending upon which phase of the work they are doing.

The sheet-metal fabrication shops are usually properly heated, lighted, and well ventilated, but at times quite noisy. Construction work is done, of course, outdoors in all kinds of weather. Workers may have to install gutters and roofs high above ground level or ventilation systems inside buildings in awkward, stooped, and cramped positions.

Possible hazards of the trade include cuts and burns from machinery and equipment, as well as falls from ladders.

Social and psychological factors

Sheet-metal workers are skilled artisans who may derive considerable satisfaction from both making an article with their own hands and then installing it and seeing it work.

Unlike most construction workers, seasonal employment is not an important factor, because many skilled persons work in manufacturing plants when construction work cannot be obtained.

◇ SOURCES OF ADDITIONAL INFORMATION

Sheet Metal and Air Conditioning Contractors' National Association
PO Box 70
Merrifield, VA 22116

Sheet Metal Workers' International Association
1750 New York Avenue, NW
Washington, DC 20006

◇ RELATED ARTICLES

Volume 1: Construction; Machining and Machinery
Volume 3: Air-conditioning, refrigeration, and heating mechanics; Appliance repairers; Lathers; Pipe fitters and steam fitters; Plumbers; Roofers
Volume 4: Air-conditioning, heating, and refrigeration technicians

Signal mechanics

Definition

Signal mechanics perform a job that is basic to the signal department of the railroad. They keep wires, switches, and other devices in good operating order.

History

The first steam locomotive was built by Richard Trevithick, an Englishman, in 1804. Although several English locomotives were imported to the United States prior to 1829, "Tom Thumb," built by Peter Cooper, was the first American-built locomotive. It hauled two cars containing a total of forty passengers for about ten miles in the summer of 1830. The Newcastle and Frenchtown Railroad was among the first to use a signal system. A series of raised balls indicated that the track ahead was clear. In 1864, the Pennsylvania Railroad installed the manual block system near Trenton, New Jersey. In this system a train was cleared to enter a "block" (a section of track) by having a telegraph operator wire ahead for permission. The closed electric circuit was developed in 1871. In this system, signaling was accomplished by breaking or shunting the electricity flowing through the rails by means of the locomotive's wheels. The automatic motor-operated semaphore was introduced in 1893. Automatic train control stops became mandatory in 1922, although one of the

Two workers adjust the dish on a microwave tower that forms part of the communications system for a railroad.

creased rail traffic, however, made the system obsolete. The invention of block signaling, semaphore, and coded track circuits enabled the railroads to develop interlocking switches, automatic stops, and centralized traffic control.

The main task of the railroad signal department is to install, maintain, and service the signaling system of a railroad. Signal mechanics ride a railroad track in a motorcar or speeder, within a division, inspecting and repairing signals along the route. They check batteries, refilling them with water or replacing them with fresh ones; clean lenses of the signal lamps; repair defective signals; and submit a written report of their investigation and repair work.

Requirements

The work of the skilled members of the signal department does not require great physical strength or stamina. Some of the semiskilled or unskilled workers are required to be active throughout the day. Because the signal mechanics are required to climb, they should have agility and a sense of balance. They must be able to stoop, kneel, crouch, and reach.

Applicants for entry into this work should be at least eighteen years old and have a high-school education or its equivalent. Knowledge of electricity and mechanical skills is helpful.

Prospective signal department workers obtain their training on the job. In the initial phase, beginning workers do unskilled work under the supervision of experienced workers. Beginners may be upgraded in about a year to the job of assistant if they have shown ability and interest. This job is semiskilled in nature. The individual is promoted to signal maintainer according to seniority and proficiency.

Special requirements

There are no special requirements. Most workers, however, in the field belong to a union.

Opportunities for experience and exploration

High-school students can test their interest and aptitude in this field by taking courses in mathematics, chemistry, physics, and shop. If possible, the shop course should be in electricity, for a knowledge of its fundamentals is neces-

first inventions of this type dates back to 1880. Devices by which an engineer could be signaled in the cab were developed as early as 1872. Coded circuits and cab signals were in operation in the late 1920s. These devices plus others made it possible to develop the "centralized train control" system. After World War II, many trains were equipped with shortwave radio equipment. Currently, closed-circuit television is used to classify and inspect freight cars.

Nature of the work

The basic purpose of railroad signaling is to increase the efficiency and movement of a train without sacrificing any of the safety factors. Initially, the "time-interval system" was used to control rail movement. Timetables and train orders regulated the distance and speed a train could travel. Emergency situations and in-

sary for this work. Assembling electronic kits will enable students to test their finger dexterity and ability to follow schematic drawings. A field trip to a railroad station will give an overview of the importance of the work done in this occupation. The military services provide numerous opportunities for individuals to explore and evaluate their interests in the electric and electronic fields.

Related occupations

There are several occupations related to *signal mechanics*. Please refer to the listing at the end of this article.

Methods of entering

The basic method of entering this occupational field is to start as unskilled workers. If applicants have appropriate experience and knowledge of the fundamentals of electricity, they may start as assistants. Approximately four years are required before a person can be advanced to the position of signal mechanic.

Advancement

Once workers become signal mechanics, they can be advanced to the position of inspector or tester. If they have leadership ability and an excellent grasp of the job, they can be promoted to supervisor, leading signaler, or leading signal mechanic. Individuals who have an excellent technical background and administrative talent can be advanced to the position of assistant supervisor or signal engineer.

Employment outlook

In the early 1990s, approximately 13,000 workers were employed in signal departments by class I line-haul railroads, the large railroad companies. Approximately 10,000 were signal mechanics; about 1,500 were semiskilled workers; and about 900 were unskilled. Several hundred were also employed by the short-line railways and by switching and terminal companies.

The general outlook for this occupational field is somewhat unfavorable, though there will be some opportunities for new workers to obtain jobs. The number of new job openings each year, however, will be limited. This general decline is forecast to continue throughout the next decade. Although passenger traffic will decrease, freight traffic is expected to increase because of such innovations as improved car design, "piggy-backing," and improved handling procedures. Improved signaling and communications systems, however, require less maintenance and repair. Most job opportunities will arise because of the need to replace workers who retire, die, or transfer to other fields.

Earnings

The annual salary for signal mechanics in the early 1990s was about $19,712. The semiskilled assistant signal mechanics had an annual rate of pay average of about $21,450. The unskilled helpers had an annual earnings average of about $17,975. Each works a basic eight-hour day, five days a week. Time-and-a-half is paid for all overtime work. Fringe benefits include health and retirement insurance, paid vacations, and travel passes.

Conditions of work

The work performed by the signal department workers is done outdoors in a variety of weather conditions. The signal mechanics must repair faulty signals at any time or place. Signal maintainers live at home, for they service small areas of track. Some of the hazards are falling from ladders or signal towers, electric shock, injuries common to lifting, and being hit by falling objects. A high percentage of workers belong to a union, the Brotherhood of Railroad Signalmen.

Social and psychological factors

Signal department workers must work as a team outdoors in a variety of working and weather conditions. They must be able to withstand pressures generated by emergency situations. Although workers are promoted on the basis of ability and initiative, a large portion of upgrading is done on the basis of seniority.

GOE: 05.05.05; SIC: 4013; SOC: 6151

Structural-steel workers

Definition

Structural-steel workers, also called *iron workers,* erect, assemble, or install fabricated structural metal products in the construction of industrial, commercial, and large residential buildings. This is a skilled trade.

History

The first iron bridge was built in England in the latter part of the eighteenth century. Improvements in the smelting process of iron ore and discovery of a method to roll steel led to the increased use of iron and steel products. The development of the I-beam and plates made it possible for the first all-steel bridge to be built over the Missouri River in 1878.

Another invention, seemingly unrelated, proved to be an extremely important factor in the use of steel as a building material. Prior to the invention of the elevator in 1859, a building's height had been limited by the number of stairs that the average person would climb. The removal of this factor by the invention of the elevator, along with the fact that weight-bearing walls constructed of stone were sometimes five feet thick, led to ready acceptance of steel construction when it was introduced.

In 1883, framing was used in building a ten-story building in Chicago. The Eiffel Tower was built in 1885 from steel girders. The world's first steel-domed building was built in 1894. The Empire State Building, for twenty-three years the tallest skyscraper in the world, was

dedicated in 1931. The use of welding and high-tensile bolts represents some of the newer developments in steel construction.

Nature of the work

A building is constructed of different combinations and forms of walls, beams, frames, columns, arches, trusses, and ties. It is the task of the structural-steel workers or iron workers to install, assemble, or erect structural metal elements. These building-trades workers are proficient in many phases of structural work.

The structural-steel workers join the steel elements by riveting, bolting, or welding. They work on such diverse construction projects as buildings perhaps as *metal building assemblers,* bridges as *reinforcing-metal workers,* metal storage tanks as *tank setters,* and overhead crane runways. Because of the weight of the steel girders, columns, and beams, they work as a team in raising, positioning, and joining these prefabricated pieces into a skeleton.

There are four steps in the process of erecting the framing: layout, rigging, temporary bolting, and permanent fastening. Using blueprints, sketches, or work orders, the structural-iron worker lays out the work. Truck cranes, crawler cranes, or guy derricks are used to hoist the various structural elements into position. Drift pins and temporary unfinished bolts are used to hold the steel elements in position. Vertical and horizontal alignment of the steel pieces is then checked with plumb bob and level, and the necessary corrections are made.

The final fastening is made by means of bolts tightened by torque wrenches, welding, or riveting. The latter process is generally being replaced by the other two methods of joining the structural elements.

Riggers and machine movers set up and rig hoisting equipment for erecting and dismantling structural-steel frames and for moving heavy construction machinery and equipment. They study the object to be moved and select the best method of moving it. They then attach the lifting device to both the hoisting equipment and the item to be moved and direct the load into position. In some instances, special rigging equipment must be built on the job to move or lift materials or machines having unusual shapes. Riggers must have thorough knowledge of both the uses and limitations of their equipment.

The ornamental ironworkers usually do not build the steel skeleton, but they do assemble or install a variety of metal products needed in the construction of a building. Some of the prefabricated products they work with are metal stairways, ladders, catwalks, metal window sash and doors, metal cabinets, and steel elements used by banks or other businesses to safeguard money and merchandise. They may also install iron fences, gates, lamp-posts, and ornamental ironwork found in homes or apartment buildings. The installation is made by fastening the metal product to some structural element by means of bolts, welding, or setting in concrete.

Reinforcing metalworkers set steel mesh or rods into forms before the concrete is poured. Steel rods or mesh are required to reinforce the concrete because it is weak in tensile strength. In constructing reinforced columns the workers place the rods or bars according to specifications to form one of the following types: tied, spiral, composite, or combination. Their task in framing a reinforced concrete building is to set the reinforcing steel according to blueprints, specifications, or verbal instructions so that it stays in place with the aid of chairs and spacers. Other structural elements on which they do work are domes, arches, slabs, walls, and floors. Workers use pliers and hammers to tie or place the rods or mesh. Occasionally the material must be cut or bent into the desired size or shape, especially mesh, which must be premeasured, cut, positioned, and hammered into place.

The structural-steel workers must be able to work with others in the construction of various buildings, bridges, piers, and the like. These construction workers must work cooperatively in the erection of structural elements that must be precisely aligned and meet rigid building code specifications. Some of the personal qualities required are the ability to use one's hands easily and skillfully; an ability to coordinate hand and foot movements; an ability to visualize objects in two or three dimensions; an ability to change from one task to another; a willingness to take risks; a good sense of balance; and no fear of heights.

The work requires these workers to have physical stamina, for it involves constant activity. Although heavy materials are moved with the aid of hoists and cranes, lifting, pushing, and shoving of parts is required at times. The work does call for the ability to climb, reach, stoop, kneel, and crouch. Normal vision (correction allowable in some cases) is needed to use the various devices for checking the work.

According to the experts, the best way to become a structural-steel worker is to complete a three-year apprenticeship program. The apprentices acquire their trade through on-the-job training under the supervision of a skilled worker. The program is planned systematically to cover all phases of the trade. This includes experience in ornamental iron and steel work, steel reinforcing, structural work, and welding. The apprentice receives at least 144 hours of formal classroom instruction per year, including blueprint reading, welding, use of tools, layout work, and the like.

To secure an apprenticeship, one should contact the International Association of Bridge, Structural and Ornamental Iron Workers.

Special requirements

There are no requirements for the profession of structural-steel worker or ironworkers in addition to those already mentioned.

Opportunities for experience and exploration

High-school students can test their interest for this occupational field by taking courses in mathematics, mechanical drawing, blueprint reading, and shop. Because the trade requires the worker to have some skill in welding, students could profit by taking some basic welding courses. Work experience during the summer is difficult to acquire because of various safety requirements that have to be met. A field trip to a construction site will provide an excellent overview of the work done in this occupation. Military experience may not only be used for

A structural-steel worker welds a girder that will become part of the foundation for a future bridge.

exploratory purposes but, when appropriate, can be applied toward the reduction of time needed to complete an apprenticeship program.

Related occupations

Other workers in construction employ similar skills as those of the structural steel worker. These include sheet-metal workers, construction workers, pipe fitters, steam fitters, and welders.

Methods of entering

The chief method of entering this occupational field is completing an apprenticeship program. An applicant should contact the International Association of Bridge, Structural and Ornamental Iron Workers to gain admittance to this program. The address can be found at the end of this article.

The Bureau of Apprenticeship and Training, U.S. Department of Labor, and the state employment office are good places to contact for information. In addition, local general contractors or the nearest office of the state apprenticeship agency may be able to answer inquiries about apprenticeship programs and training opportunities.

Advancement

After becoming a skilled structural-steel worker, a person needs several years of additional experience to be considered for the position of supervisor. Some of the traits needed to become a supervisor are leadership ability, good oral and written expression, excellent knowledge of the trade, an understanding of the other construction trades, and the ability to make good judgments. Additional education in some technical aspects of engineering are required before a person can become a job superintendent.

Employment outlook

There were about 97,000 persons employed in this field in the early 1990s. The expected general increase in the volume of industrial and commercial building and highway construction during the next decade will create a continual demand for these workers. In addition, it is estimated that approximately 1,300 job openings will be available annually because of death and retirement. The increased use of structural steel in smaller buildings, ornamental panelings in apartment buildings, and exterior glass requiring metal framing will offset any loss of employment because of technological improvements. For example, the development of a compact squirt-welding machine has greatly reduced the time needed for field welding. The general outlook for this occupational field, however, is good because of an anticipated increase in construction work.

Earnings

The average annual salary for structural-steel workers or ironworkers in the early 1990s was about $26,800. The pay for ornamental ironworkers was about the same. The overtime rate was usually double the hourly rate. The beginning apprentice is paid 60 to 70 percent of the skilled worker's rate.

Conditions of work

Structural-steel workers generally work outdoors. They may work below the ground or at heights greater than 500 feet. Agility, balance, and no fear of heights are three basic traits that these craft workers need. Safety nets, scaffolding, and other safety devices have greatly reduced the number of injuries because of falling. Other hazards are injuries caused by falling objects or from lifting heavy objects. The work in many regions of the country is seasonal. In addition, the workers may find themselves unemployed when a project is completed, and many workers travel from city to city to be employed steadily.

Social and psychological factors

Structural-steel workers must be able to work as a team in constructing various building elements. Each worker must be willing to follow rigid rules regarding welding, safety, bolting, and the like. Physical strength and stamina are required, for the work calls for handling heavy and bulky items most of the day. Because the work is usually seasonal, careful planning is required to budget one's money during periods of unemployment. Although the work appears

to be hazardous, the safety record in this occupational field is better than the average for the building trades.

GOE: 05.05.06; SIC: 1791; SOC: 6473

◇ **SOURCES OF ADDITIONAL INFORMATION**

Associated General Contractors of America
1957 E Street, NW
Washington, DC 20006

International Association of Bridge, Structural and Ornamental Iron Workers
1750 New York Avenue, NW
Washington, DC 20006

◇ **RELATED ARTICLES**

Volume 1: Construction; Metals
Volume 3: Cement masons; Elevator constructors; Forge shop occupations; Iron and steel industry workers; Operating engineers; Welders
Volume 4: Architectural and building construction technicians; Welding technicians

---

Swimming pool servicers

Definition

Swimming pool servicers clean, adjust, and perform minor repairs to swimming pools, hot tubs, and their auxiliary equipment.

History

Swimming has always been one of people's favorite pastimes, and in the recent resurgence in health and fitness, it has become more popular

than ever. Swimming pools can be found in numerous settings, including schools, community centers, retirement communities, health clubs, apartment complexes, hotels, and private homes. Hot tubs and whirlpools have also grown in popularity in the past twenty years as places to relax and entertain.

Aside from recreation, swimming pools and spas also have therapeutic value as well. Since early times, the medicinal value of mineral hot springs has attracted people with various ailments to the resorts that were founded around them. In fact, many famous cities, including Saratoga Springs, N.Y., and Bath in England, were founded at the sites of natural hot springs. Today hospitals, rehabilitation centers, and mental health facilities use pools and hot tubs as integral parts of therapy.

Because swimming pools are generally static bodies of water, they must be cleaned and maintained regularly to stay clean, clear, and safe. Otherwise, algae and bacteria would grow and make the water unsafe for swimming. Technology has made advances that make this a relatively simple procedure; some pools have automatic cleaners and many people who own pools can conduct this maintenance themselves. At other times, this work is left up to swimming pool maintenance companies, who employ expert swimming pool servicers to clean customers' pools and troubleshoot any problems.

Nature of the work

Pool servicers are usually employed by firms that construct and/or maintain pools, or they may work for such entities as the park district or city department of recreation. They often work on a route visiting two or three pools a day, or they may only be responsible for one pool and work on it every day. However they work, pool servicers are charged with keeping pools clean and operating. A pool that is maintained regularly and properly can avoid large and expensive problems from developing.

Routine cleaning is one of the pool servicer's regular duties. Leaves and other debris need to be scooped off the surface of the water with a net on a long pole. To clean under the water, servicers use a special vacuum cleaner on the pool floor and walls. With stainless steel or nylon brushes, the servicers scrub pool walls and the tiles and gutters around the pool's edge to remove the layer of grit and scum that collects at the water line. The servicers also hose down the pool deck and unclog the strainers that cover the drains.

After cleaning, the swimming pool servicer will test the cleanliness of the water and the ph balance (the measurement between acidity and alkalinity in the water). While the test is simple and takes only a few minutes, it is very important. The pool servicer takes a sample of the pool water in a jar and adds a few drops of testing chemical to it. This chemical causes the water to turn a certain color, which reveals the chemical content of the pool water. The pool servicer can then determine the proper amounts of chlorine or other chemicals to add to make the water safe and clean. These chem-

icals can be poured directly into the pool or added through a feeder in the circulation system. The chemical makeup of every pool is different and can change daily or even hourly. Home pools usually have their water tested a few times a week, but large public pools are tested hourly. The chemicals are intended to kill algae and bacteria, but too much of the chemicals can cause eye and skin irritation. The pool servicer must wear gloves and be careful when adding these chemicals because they are dangerous and give off harmful fumes in high concentrations. The pool servicer must follow the proper procedures for applying these chemicals every time, and keep records of what was added to the pool.

The pool servicer is also responsible for the routine maintenance of the pool. The pool's circulation system, including the filter, pumps and heater are inspected regularly. To clean the filter, they may force water backwards through it to dislodge any dirt and debris that has accumulated. They make sure there are no leaks in the pipes, gaskets, connections or some other part of the pool. If a drain or pipe is clogged, they will use a steel snake, plunger or other plumber's tools to clear it. They adjust the thermostats, pressure gauges, and other controls to make the pool water enjoyable. They may make minor repairs to the pool's equipment, fixing or replacing small components. They will inform the owner of any major repairs they might think are necessary before doing any work on them.

Closing outdoor pools for the winter and opening them again in the spring are major tasks for swimming pool servicers and keep them very busy during those times of the year. In the fall, servicers will drain the water out of the pool and its auxiliary equipment. Openings into the pool are plugged and all the pool gear, such as diving boards, ladders, and pumps, are removed, inspected, and stored. The pool is then covered with a tarp that is lashed or weighted in place. In climates where it is warm enough so water does not freeze, a pool is usually kept full and treated with special chemicals through the winter.

A lot of work is required when pools are opened in the spring as well. After the pool is uncovered and the tank and pool deck are swept clean, the pool servicer will inspect the pool for any cracks, leaks, loose tiles, and broken lamps. They will repair any items they can and recommend any major maintenance to the owner. The interior of the tank may need to be painted. The servicer will clean and install the equipment removed in the fall, such as ladders and diving boards. The circulation and heating systems are tested to make sure they are operating properly, and then water is added to the pool. Once the pool is filled, the pool servicer again tests the water and adds the proper chemicals to make it safe.

Pool servicers keep careful records of whatever maintenance they perform, both for the company and for the customer. Many pool owners like to do their own pool maintenance, and new methods of cleaning and adding chemicals are making this easier. Complex advancements in pool technology such as automatic chemical dispensers and solar heaters, and the convenience and security of having the work done by outside experts, make it likely that pool servicers will continue to be in demand.

A swimming pool servicer cleans the surface of a pool with a net. Many servicers of private pools make visits to homes several times a week.

Requirements

No formal education requirements exist for swimming pool servicers, but a high-school diploma and a responsible work record are important to employers. A background in the building trades is also a plus.

Classes that are helpful for high-school students wishing to enter this profession include mathematics, biology, chemistry, physics, bookkeeping, and accounting. Shop classes, including pipe fitting, machine shop, electricity, and ceramics, are also an advantage.

Pool servicers who want to advance to the position of shop supervisor or perhaps start their own businesses should take some college courses. Useful studies would include small business management, sales, psychology, and business law, math and English. Another option is to take the Certified Pool/Spa Operators course offered by the National Spa & Pool Institute.

Special requirements

Aside from a valid driver's license, there are no special requirements for swimming pool servicers.

Opportunities for experience and exploration

To learn more about swimming pool maintenance, high-school students might look for summer jobs on the pool maintenance staff of their school, park district, community center,

or local health club. Hotels, motels, apartment buildings, and condominium complexes also frequently have pools and saunas that require maintenance. Students can gain useful experience in cleaning and maintaining pools, testing the water and adding chemicals. This experience may help them get a full-time job with a pool maintenance company. The pool maintenance staff may also be able to give students the names of local companies that hire servicers.

Related occupations

Other occupations that might be of interest include plumbers, boilermakers, pipe fitters, steam fitters, and welders.

Methods of entering

Most pool servicing jobs are with companies that sell, build, and install swimming pools and hot tubs. These companies may advertise for pool servicers in the classified section of the newspaper. Job seekers may look for jobs by answering want ads or by contacting the firms directly, either in person or in writing. New pool servicers receive two to eight weeks of on-the-job training from an experienced servicer.

Even if there are no immediate openings for pool service trainees, a company may have other jobs open, such as sales staff, office workers, stock clerks, or construction workers. By working responsibly and showing enthusiasm in one of these jobs, workers may be assigned to the pool maintenance staff when an opening arises.

713

Swimming pool servicers
Structural Work Occupations

Advancement

Responsible and hard-working swimming pool servicers can advance in a number of ways. They may take on more pools to service, be given better routes, or be allowed to set their own hours and work schedules. They might advance to crew supervisor and assign other servicers to jobs.

Some pool servicers with ambition, experience, and people skills may move on to start their own pool maintenance service. They might also move into related areas, such as building pools, selling pools for a builder, distributing pool care products, or establishing a franchise for a manufacturer of pools and pool equipment.

Employment outlook

Pools and hot tubs are more popular than ever, and the nation's continued concern with personal fitness means that health clubs will continue to operate successfully. Additionally, the health departments in certain cities are urging more inspections of private pools to monitor bacterial growth. These and other factors will combine and translate into more work for swimming pool servicers.

The occupation, however, is still a seasonal one in most parts of the country. Swimming pool servicers have to look for other sources of income in the winter months. Some find jobs servicing indoor pools, while some get other seasonal work or move into other occupations. Turnover is relatively high, especially from one spring to the next, so new job seekers generally have little trouble finding work.

Earnings

During their training, new swimming pool servicers generally earn from $90 to $100 a week. After this training period, they start at a weekly base pay of about $160 in the early 1990s. Workers who are quick and efficient can earn $225 a week or more. Those servicers who can service more than the average number of pools or who become expert troubleshooters and repairers can sometimes demand higher pay. Pool assignments and pay, however, can diminish for servicers who do an inadequate job or are not dependable.

Pool servicers who use their own cars to make their rounds may receive a mileage allowance. They may also receive a uniform allowance to keep their work clothes clean. Some firms may offer pool servicers some form of group insurance and allow workers to take a few sick days during the season, but other benefits are uncommon. Those servicers who work year-round may receive one or two weeks of paid or unpaid vacation, in addition to insurance coverage.

Conditions of work

Swimming pool servicers generally work alone and adhere to a schedule set by their supervisor. They drive their own car or a company van to each pool assignment, usually servicing three pools a day, or more if they are located in the same area or need only a light cleaning. Large public pools need daily cleaning that is often done when the pool is closed at night. It may take two pool servicers most of an eight-hour shift to clean a large public pool.

Regular swimming pool servicing is generally not difficult, strenuous, or dirty. While they may work both indoors and outdoors, they do not usually work on outdoor pools in bad weather. They generally work five to five and a half days a week. Pool servicers have to stretch, bend, kneel, and do some lifting, but the work does not require great physical strength. When they handle pool chemicals, they wear rubber gloves and are very careful not to spill on their skin or breathe any fumes.

Social and psychological factors

Pool servicing work can be an excellent way for students and others to earn money during their summer vacation. They have the chance to enjoy the summer weather and not be cooped up in an office or a factory. Good mechanical skills and an aptitude for tools are important, as are skills in painting, carpentry, machine repair and cement work. While it is not a full-fledged trade like plumbing or pipe fitting, it does offer the chance to learn the basic skills of these and other construction trades.

Because they work under minimal supervision throughout the day, swimming pool servicers should have self-discipline and a responsible attitude. They have to be accurate when testing pool water, handling chemicals, and keeping records. Good customer relations are essential to the survival of the pool service company, so it is very important for pool servicers to be neat in appearance, courteous, and determined to do their job well.

714

GOE: 05.10.04; SIC: 7389; SOC: 6179

◇ **RELATED ARTICLES**

Volume 1: Construction; Recreation and Park Services
Volume 2: Recreation workers
Volume 3: Appliance repairers; Carpenters; Cement masons; Construction workers; General maintenance mechanics; Janitors and cleaners; Marble setters, tile setters, and terrazzo workers; Plasterers; Plumbers

Telephone and PBX installers and repairers

Definition

Telephone and private branch exchange (PBX) installers and *repairers* place, service, and repair telephone and private branch exchange systems in homes and offices. This includes the telephone installer, who installs and removes telephones in homes and places of business; the telephone repairer, who tests, diagnoses, locates, and repairs trouble on customers' telephones to restore service; the telephone installer-repairer, who combines the duties of the installer and repairer; the PBX installer, who installs telephone switchboards and other specialized communication equipment on customers' premises: the PBX repairer, who diagnoses and repairs the trouble on private branch exchange telephone systems and other specialized communication systems; the PBX installer-repairer, who combines the jobs of the PBX installer and PBX repairer.

History

Alexander Graham Bell, working with Thomas Watson, invented the telephone in 1875. Bell, a speech teacher who had made the study of electricity a hobby, wanted to develop a harmonic telegraph so that two or more telegraphic messages could be sent over a single wire at the same time. By chance, the essential principles of the telephone were discovered.

The telephone gained popular attention when it was demonstrated at the Philadelphia Centennial in 1876. By 1892, Chicago and New York were linked by long-distance telephone lines, and by 1915 it was possible to make a telephone call between New York and San Francisco. Although the dial telephone was introduced during the 1930s, the basic patent for it had been granted in 1879. The development of the coaxial cable in 1935 greatly improved long-distance telephone transmission.

Since the end of World War II, there have been a number of improvements in the telephone communication process. The use of TASI (Time Assignment Speech Interpolation) makes it possible to shift conversations along a transmission line automatically. The "data phone" has made it possible for computers in different cities to "talk" to one another. The most outstanding recent development has been the use of satellites for overseas telephone calls.

Nature of the work

A telephone call from the home of one person to another usually goes through a telephone office that houses automatic switching equipment. In hotels, apartment buildings, and busi-

A telephone installer inspects a new phone system, making sure that it is working properly.

ness concerns, an incoming call is taken by a PBX (private branch exchange) operator before it is placed with the appropriate person. For these telephone conversations to take place, a proper combination of wires, cables, electricity, switches, transformers, and other equipment must be erected and installed. This work is done by the central office craft workers, cable splicers, and line repairers. The servicing of the telephone and PBX system on the customers' premises is done by telephone and PBX installers and repairers.

When customers request a new telephone, wish to add an extension, or replace an old wall telephone, station installers and repairers do all the necessary work. They travel to the customer's home or office in a truck that contains all of the needed equipment. If no existing connection is present, they usually climb a pole to attach the incoming wire to the service line. After installing the terminal box, they make all of the required connections. On some jobs, they will bore through walls and floors to do the necessary wiring. Telephone installers also install telephone booths, coin collectors, and switching key equipment, in addition to private or business phones.

Wear and deterioration of wires and parts may cause the telephone to function improperly. It is the job of the telephone repairer to find and repair the difficulty with the assistance of the test-board worker in the central office. Occasionally, the job of telephone installer and telephone repairer are combined and the worker is called a telephone installer-repairer.

Some stores, business concerns, and hotels have a single telephone number. To channel the large number of incoming and outgoing calls, however, they use a switchboard system. In effect, they have their own private telephone system within the building. The PBX installer sets up the necessary wiring and switchboard equipment to make the system function. Some PBX installers also set up teletypewriters, mobile radiotelephones, and equipment for television and radio broadcasting. These workers usually work as part of a crew since the equipment is heavy and bulky, and the wiring is complex.

The PBX repairer, with the assistance of the test-board worker, locates the trouble in and then repairs PBX systems. The PBX repairer also may maintain some of the auxiliary equipment, such as power plants, batteries, and relays. Some PBX repairers service and repair teletypewriters, mobile radiotelephones, and television and radio broadcasting equipment.

Requirements

Telephone companies prefer to hire inexperienced persons and train them for telephone and PBX installation and repair jobs.

Persons interested in these occupations must be high-school or vocational school graduates with mechanical ability and manual dexterity. Applicants with a neat appearance and pleasant personality are preferred.

Once hired, the new workers must successfully complete a training program combining on-the-job work experience with formal classroom instruction. Before new workers can do telephone installation work, they must complete a seven-month training program. During this time, new workers practice making connections and do installation work in a classroom that simulates actual working conditions. They also accompany skilled workers and watch them perform their work.

After workers have become qualified telephone installers, additional training is necessary before they can become telephone repairers, PBX installers, or PBX repairers.

Special requirements

There are no additional requirements for the positions of telephone installer, telephone repairer, PBX installer, or PBX repairer in addition to those already mentioned.

Opportunities for experience and exploration

High-school courses in mathematics, physics, speech, and shop work provide a test of the individual's aptitude, interest, and temperament for these occupations. Building electronic kits or assembling model airplanes or cars are ways in which individuals can test their manual dexterity, mechanical inclinations, and ability to follow drawings and plans.

Because there are no direct work experiences available to high-school students, a field trip to a telephone company can give an overall view of the work done. Direct experience and training in these occupational fields can also be obtained in the armed forces.

Related occupations

Other workers in telecommunications include telephone installers, telephone repairers, switchboard operators, telephone operators, and cable and line splicers.

Methods of entering

Young people who wish to become telephone and PBX installers and repairers should contact the employment office of their local telephone companies. Occasionally, tests will be given to determine the individual's aptitudes for the job. If applicants have the necessary qualifications, they will be assigned to the training program for telephone installers unless they have had some prior experience with this type of work.

If applicants pass all tests but there are no openings at the time, they may be assigned to some other type of job until openings occur. It is a common practice to transfer to installation and repair work from another job classification such as that of line installer or cable splicer.

Advancement

To qualify for more difficult and responsible work, telephone installers and repairers must continue their training throughout their careers. Many promotional opportunities are available to well-qualified workers.

A telephone installer who has worked for a few years may, with additional training, ad-

vance to the higher paying job of PBX installer. In a similar way, the telephone repairer may be promoted to PBX repairer, one of the highest paying craft jobs. Another advancement possibility is to become a telephone installer-repairer or a PBX installer-repairer.

If the installer and repairer have certain other personal characteristics, such as the ability to deal with people, good judgment, and planning skills, they may progress to supervisory positions also.

Employment outlook

In the early 1990s, there were about 120,000 telephone and PBX installers and repairers.

Young people will find many opportunities for steady employment as telephone and PBX installers and repairers throughout the 1990s. Most job openings will result from industry growth, but retirements and deaths will also provide many hundreds of jobs annually. Some jobs will be filled by workers who transfer in from other telephone crafts jobs, such as cable splicers and line installers, but there will be many jobs open to new employees. The volume of service is expected to increase due to the expanding number of telephones to be serviced and repaired, the growing popularity of extension phones, the increased use of specialized types of phone equipment, and the development of improved but more complex equipment.

Employment will be limited, however, because of recent technological changes that have increased the efficiency of repairers. Also, more and more residential customers have modular telephone jacks in their houses or apartments. When these customers move, they simply carry their phones to the new location and plug them into the jacks there. Residential customers are now asked, also, to bring their phones in for repair service if they have a model that can be unplugged.

Earnings

The pay rates for these craft workers vary according to the specific job, the region of the country, and the length of service with the particular company.

In the early 1990s, the average annual rate for telephone and PBX installers and repairers was about $32,450. Earnings increased considerably with length of service.

Conditions of work

Telephone and PBX installers usually have a regular forty-hour workweek, with extra pay for overtime.

Workers engaged in telephone installation and repair jobs work independently, with a minimum of supervision. They must be able to drive a truck in a variety of weather conditions. Because these workers deal with the public, they must have a neat appearance and a courteous, pleasant personality. In addition, they have to speak clearly, for part of their job is to instruct the customer in the use of the telephone. Their work is performed both indoors and outdoors; during emergency situations, they must work at various times of the day and night, on weekends, and on holidays. The installer and repairer often work from a telephone pole outdoors and in stooped, crouched, and cramped positions indoors.

PBX installers and repairers usually work in teams, inasmuch as their work requires more complex equipment and wiring. Most of the work is done indoors, often stooping or crawling.

Fringe benefits for all these workers usually include paid vacations, holidays, sick leave, group insurance, and retirement and disability pensions.

Social and psychological factors

The craft workers in this area are required to follow rigid rules and regulations since failure to do so may result in improper functioning of the equipment. Although their work does not demand the precision of the machinists, the in-stallers and repairers must connect the parts in the appropriate manner and be able to withstand the pressures of emergency situations. To be successful workers in this field, individuals must be willing to continue their technical education indefinitely. Promotions are based on skill and technical knowledge as well as length of service with the company.

GOE: 05.05.05; SIC: 4813; SOC: 4649

◇ **SOURCES OF ADDITIONAL INFORMATION**

Communications Workers of America
1925 K Street, NW
Washington, DC 20006

International Brotherhood of Electrical Workers
1125 15th Street, NW
Washington, DC 20005

◇ **RELATED ARTICLES**

Volume 1: Telecommunications
Volume 3: Communications equipment mechanics; Electrical repairers; Electricians; Line installers and cable splicers; Signal mechanics
Volume 4: Automated equipment technicians; Automatic equipment technicians; Electrical technicians; Electronics technicians

Welders

Definition

Welding is any of a number of methods of joining metals by heating the different pieces that are to be connected. Workers who perform these welding processes include the *arc welder,* who fabricates or repairs metal using electric arc welding equipment; the *gas* or *acetylene welder,* who fabricates and repairs metal objects using gas welding equipment such as an oxy-acetylene torch; the *welding machine operator,* or the arc welding machine operator, who operates a machine that joins metal parts with the use of gas; the *atomic welder,* who fabricates or repairs metal parts using an atomic hydrogen arc welding process; and the *combination welder,* who uses a combination of both gas and arc welding.

The semiskilled workers include the *resistance machine welder*, who operates machines that fuse metal parts by bringing them together under heat and pressure; the oxygen cutter, who uses a gas torch to cut or trim metals; and the *arc cutter*, who uses an electric arc torch to cut or trim metals.

History

The art of welding is an ancient one. Stone carvings depicting forge welding have been found in ancient ruins. Resistance welding, a process similar to forge welding using electricity rather than a hammer, was developed in the laboratory by James Prescott Joule in 1857 but was not perfected until 1886 because of the lack of sufficient electric power.

Thermite welding, which fuses two pieces of metal by means of thermite, a mixture of aluminum and iron oxide, was first used by 1900. Arc welding, a process of fusing metal by means of heat generated from an electric arc, was developed experimentally in 1881 and used commercially in 1889. Various improvements and innovations have been made in welding during the twentieth century. One of the newer processes is cold welding, where ductile metals are joined by pressure rather than a hammer or electricity. Lasers are now also used for welding.

A flame was first used by ancient Egyptians both to join and separate precious metals. A blowpipe and an alcohol flame were used in this process. Although oxygen was discovered in 1774 and acetylene in 1836, the effects of joining the two gases were not observed until 1895, when improved methods of commercial production of acetylene (from calcium carbide) and oxygen (from liquid air) were made. The year 1903 marked the beginning of the commercial use of the oxyacetylene process in welding and cutting. As in arc welding, many improvements in the processes have been made since then.

Nature of the work

The job of the welder and welding machine operator is to join (weld) two pieces of metal by applying intense heat, pressure, or both to melt the edges of the metal so that they fuse permanently. During this process, the worker can use various types of devices to obtain the necessary heat, with or without the aid of pressure, to melt the edges of the metal in a controlled fashion.

These welding procedures are used in the manufacturing and repair of many different products ranging from water faucets, refrigerators, cars, and trains to electronic equipment, airplanes, ships, and missiles.

Because there are several different sources of heat and various methods of controlling and focusing them, more than forty different welding processes have been developed. These various procedures, however, can be grouped into three categories. The arc welding process obtains heat from an electric arc and maintains it between two electrodes or between an electrode and the work. The gas welding process obtains heat in the form of a flame through the mixture of oxygen and some other combustible gas, usually acetylene. The resistance welding process obtains heat from resistance by the workpiece to an electric current and from pressure.

Two of the processes that are used to weld metal—the arc and gas methods—can also be used to cut, scrape, or finish metal.

The work of skilled all-around welders, whether arc, gas, atomic, or combination, begins with the planning and laying out of work from drawings, blueprints, or other specifications. With a working knowledge of the welding properties of steel, stainless steel, cast iron, bronze, aluminum, nickel, and other metals and alloys, the welder then determines the proper sequence of work operations for each job. Although some welders (combination welders) know both arc and gas welding techniques, most specialize in one of the following procedures.

In the most commonly used of the manual arc welding processes, the arc welder obtains a suitable electrode and adjusts the electric current. The welder then strikes an arc (creates an electric current) by touching the metal with an electrode. Next, the welder guides the electrode along the seams of the metal to be welded, allowing sufficient time for the heat of the arc to melt the metal. The molten metal from the electrode is deposited in the joint and together with the molten metal edges solidifies to form a solid connection. The electrode used in the production of the arc is selected by the welder according to job specifications. Occasionally, the welder may use a metal filler and a flux to make the weld.

In gas welding, the process used in almost all of metalworking because of its flexibility, the welder applies an intensely hot flame (obtained from the combustion of fuel gas—most commonly acetylene and oxygen) from a gas welding torch to the metal edges. After obtaining the proper types of welding rods and torch tips, and adjusting the regulators on the oxy-

Welders must have steady hands, good eyesight, and physical strength to perform well on the job.

gen and acetylene cylinders, the welder lights the torch. To obtain the proper size and quality of flame, the welder must adjust the oxygen and acetylene valves on the torch, then hold the flame against the metal to be welded until it melts. The welding rod is then applied to the molten metal to supply the excess metal needed to form the weld.

The atomic welding process introduces hydrogen gas into the electric arc and around the electrodes. This process increases the arc temperature and shields the weld area to prevent oxidation. The atomic welder must first select and insert electrodes and then connect hoses from the hydrogen tank to the electrode holder. After adjusting the gas pressure and the electric current, the welder strikes an arc and does the welding. This process is now being used in welding such materials as aluminum, stainless steel, magnesium, and titanium.

Semiskilled manual welders usually perform repetitive production work that generally does not involve critical safety and strength requirements. The surfaces that they weld are primarily in only one position.

Maintenance welders are skilled workers who travel to construction sites, utility installations, and the like to make repairs in metalwork on site. They generally use a portable gas torch to make their corrective welding.

The work of the semiskilled welding operators varies according to the position involved. Resistance welding is a machine process used in the mass production of parts requiring similar welding operations. The weld is made by heat generated by the resistance of the workpieces to the flow of electricity at the intended location and fused together by the pressure of contacting electrodes. The welding machine operator makes the necessary adjustments in the machine to control the current and the pressure and then feeds and aligns the work. After the welding operation is completed, the operator removes the work from the machine. Some types of resistance welding are spot, projection, flash, and upset welding.

The cutting of metal is done by oxygen cutters or arc cutters by means of oxygen or electric energy. The oxygen cutters (flame or thermal cutters) may use hand-guided torches or machine-mounted torches to cut or trim metals. They direct the flame of oxygen and fuel gas on the area to be cut until it melts. Then an additional stream of oxygen is released from the torch, which cuts the metal along previously marked lines. The arc cutters follow a similar procedure in their work, except that they use an electric arc as the original source of heat. As in oxygen cutting, an additional stream of gas may be released when cutting the metal.

Requirements

Requirements for the positions of arc and gas welders, machine resistance welding operators, and oxygen and arc cutters differ according to the degree of skill involved.

For all welding positions, most employers prefer to hire young people in good physical condition with manual dexterity, steady hands, and good eyesight. For skilled jobs, a minimum of two years of high school or vocational school is necessary, although high-school graduates are preferred.

The high-school student's preparation should include courses in mathematics, mechanical drawing, physics, and shop work. If possible, the shop courses should feature some welding and principles of electricity.

To become proficient in any of the welding trades, however, a person must usually complete an on-the-job training program. The length of training time varies from several weeks for most semiskilled jobs to a period of from one to three years for the skilled jobs.

Because the positions of resistance welding operator and oxygen and arc cutter require little skill, the training period usually only lasts several weeks. During this time, the worker is taught how to operate the particular machine or torch to be used.

Skilled arc or gas welders undergo a one- to three-year period of training. The trainees usually begin as helpers to experienced welders, and in this capacity perform simple, repetitive work that does not involve critical safety. As trainees show ability and promise, they are given more difficult and challenging work. Before becoming qualified welders, they must obtain further instruction in the more technical aspects of the trade through vocational or trade school courses.

Although a formal apprenticeship is generally not required for the occupation of welder, a few large companies do offer such programs. Also, the U.S. Department of the Navy conducts a four-year apprenticeship program for its civilian employees.

Special requirements

In some welding work where the strength of the weld is a highly critical factor (such as certain types of construction work, high pressure pipe systems, atomic energy, and missile manufacturing), the welder may be required to pass a qualifying examination or a certification test or obtain a license. These examinations are given either by employers, a municipal agency, a naval facility, or a private agency designated by local government inspection authorities.

Opportunities for experience and exploration

In high school a student has several avenues open for exploring the welding occupations. Shop courses often offer some welding, as well as instruction in basic principles of electricity, drafting, and blueprint reading. General science, mathematics, physics, and chemistry courses offer good background experience for this trade.

To observe welders or welding machine operators at work, the student may arrange to take a field trip to a manufacturing company that uses various welding processes to get an overall view of working conditions and the types of work performed.

Direct welding experience may also be obtained in the armed forces.

Related occupations

Other construction trades workers perform work similar to the welder's. These workers include structural-steel workers, pipe fitters, steam fitters, boiler makers and installers, elevator installers, plumbers, and layout workers.

Methods of entering

To enter the welding trade as a semiskilled welding machine operator, an oxygen or arc cutter, or a skilled welder, applicants should contact a manufacturing plant, the state employment service bureau, or the local branch of the appropriate union. Classified advertisements in newspapers may also provide leads.

Training programs have been operating in many cities in the United States since 1962 under the provisions of the Manpower and Development Training Act. The training, which may be in the classroom or on the job, stresses the fundamentals of welding and may last from several weeks to one year. The state employment agency can provide information on these programs.

Graduates from approved vocational or training schools may obtain jobs through the school's placement bureau. Vacancies are usually posted as they occur.

Advancement

Successful completion of a training program is necessary before an individual can become a qualified member of the welding trade. Because most workers usually begin as helpers or trainees for simple repetitive jobs, advancement depends on the individual's aptitude, ability, and willingness to undergo additional training.

The welder's helper may be upgraded to oxygen and arc cutting jobs. With some additional training, the next step would be to a position of skilled welder. Once this position has been attained, the all-around welder may specialize in one of the types of gas or arc welding or become a combination welder.

The welder who has the appropriate personal traits and technical knowledge, may advance to positions of supervisor, welding inspector, or welding instructor. With two years'

Welders
Structural Work Occupations

additional training at a vocational school or technical institute, the welder may qualify to become a welding technician.

A small number of experienced welders go into business for themselves and open welding and repair shops.

Employment outlook

In the early 1990s, there were approximately 323,000 welders and oxygen and arc cutters employed in the United States. About two-thirds of these were in manufacturing industries. The number of welding jobs will increase rapidly during the next decade and beyond as a result of the favorable outlook for the metalworking industries and the increased use of the various welding processes.

Qualified welders will be used in increasing numbers in the construction field, as well as for repair and maintenance work in the growing metalworking industries.

The oxygen and arc cutters will show only a small rise because of the increased reliance on machine processes for their work. Many welding machine operators will be phased out, however, and replaced by robot-operated machines.

Earnings

Average hourly earnings of workers in the welding trades depend on the skill of the job, as well as on the industry or activity in which the welder is employed.

Earnings of highly skilled welders compare favorably with those of other skilled metalworking occupations. Average annual pay rates for welders in the early 1990s ranged from about $24,950 to $44,900.

Conditions of work

Since welding work is performed in a variety of industries, only a general picture of the working conditions can be given. Most workers, however, have a regular forty-hour workweek, with extra pay for overtime.

The welder may work inside in a well ventilated and well lighted shop, outside on a construction site, or in the confined space of an underground tunnel. The work requires considerable standing, stooping, reaching, and climbing. The worker is often in contact with

rust, grease, paint, and other elements found on the metal parts to be welded.

The various trade and safety organizations have developed a series of rules and requirements regulating various welding procedures, safety measures, and health precautions. Welders usually wear protective garments such as goggles for eye protection, hardhats for head and skull protection, and face shields for protection of the skin against heat and burns. The hazards arising from electric shock, toxic gases and fumes, explosions, and fire have been minimized through the proper installation of equipment, eye protecting devices, protective clothing, and ventilation requirements.

Operations of resistance welding machine workers are largely free from the hazards associated with welding by hand.

Welders and cutters usually belong to unions representing a given industry. Labor-management contracts provide most employees with paid holidays and vacations; hospitalization, accident, sickness, and life insurance plans; and retirement pensions.

Social and psychological factors

The welding trade is versatile. The widespread use of the welding and cutting processes in industry enables welders and cutters to find jobs in every state. It offers employment in practically any industry: shipbuilding, automotive, aircraft, missiles, nuclear energy, railroads, radio, television, and appliances. Even department stores and food processing plants need the welder's skill.

Skilled welders usually work independently on jobs requiring conformance to rigid standards. Certain jobs require them to be certified by means of an examination, for their finished work involves the safety of others. Production welders may have to become accustomed to jobs that require them to repeat the same process over a considerable length of time. Many jobs require excellent hand-eye coordination, a steady hand, and the ability to produce quality work. Because of the hazards arising from the use of electricity or combustible gas, the welder must be willing to follow set safety procedures. Careless workers are a danger to themselves and to others. As in other skilled areas, they should be willing to keep up to date on the improvements in the field by reading trade journals and service manuals.

GOE: 05.05.06; SIC: 1799; SOC: 7714

722

◇ **SOURCES OF ADDITIONAL INFORMATION**

American Welding Society
PO Box 351040
550 Le Jeune Road, NW
Miami, FL 33135

**International Association of Machinists
and Aerospace Workers**
1300 Connecticut Avenue, NW
Washington, DC 20036

**International Brotherhood of Boilermakers,
Iron Shipbuilders, Blacksmiths, Forgers
and Helpers**
8th Avenue at State
Kansas City, KS 66101

**International Union, United Automobile,
Aerospace and Agricultural Implement
Workers of America**
8000 East Jefferson Avenue
Detroit, MI 48214

**United Association of Journeymen and
Apprentices of the Plumbing and Pipe
Fitting Industry of the U.S. and Canada**
PO Box 37800
Washington, DC 20013

◇ **RELATED ARTICLES**

Volume 1: Construction; Machining and Machinery; metals
Volume 3: Aircraft mechanics; Automobile mechanics; Automotive body repairers; Boiler-making occupations; Forge shop occupations; Pipe fitters and Steam fitters; Sheet-metal workers; Structural-steel workers
Volume 4: Welding technicians

Miscellaneous Occupations

The occupations covered in this section are grouped here because the U.S. Department of Labor's *Dictionary of Occupational Titles* combines the following fields: transportation; packaging; utilities; amusement, recreation, and motion pictures; and graphic arts.

In the early 1990s about 5 million people were employed in the miscellaneous skilled and semiskilled occupations described in this section. The transportation industries have the greatest total number of employees, with air, water, and surface methods represented. Truck drivers make up the largest single group, numbering well more than 2 million, while those in the printing occupations amount to less than 1 million.

To qualify for any one of the jobs in this diversified group, an individual must have the appropriate education, intelligence, aptitude, and interest. Young persons who acquire a good basic education (including courses in mathematics and the sciences), as well as thorough job training, will be better able to compete for the higher paying jobs than applicants without this training.

Although many of the jobs, such as truck driving and public transport, require the individual to be at least average in intelligence, there are some occupations, particularly in printing, that require an intelligence level equal to that of a college graduate, since the work involves complex machinery and design. Mechanical aptitude, manual dexterity, and motor coordination are important factors for these occupations. A sense of responsibility is also important, as many of these occupations can lead to management careers.

There are several ways in which an individual can prepare for one of these occupations. These include apprenticeship programs (particularly in the printing occupations), on-the-job training, and vocational or technical schooling. Apprenticeship programs provide broad training through a combination of work experience and classroom instruction. On-the-job training is an informal method by which the worker can progress from simple to more complex jobs under the supervision of a foreman or other trained worker. Vocational or technical school attendance is usually required in those jobs where the worker must have a good technical background. For example, stationary engineers must have complete knowledge of the function and operation of various heating and power generating equipment.

The next decade is expected to bring a continuing rise in the employment of truck and bus drivers because of the increased use of commercial vehicles for freight and public transportation. On the other hand, employment in the railroad industry is expected to decline because of increased use of electronic equipment.

In general, these occupations offer a rewarding life to those individuals with the necessary aptitudes and educational background.

Airplane dispatchers

Definition

Airplane dispatchers authorize and direct commercial air flights. They read radio reports from the airplane captains during flights and study weather reports to determine any necessary change in flight direction or altitude. They send instructions by radio to the airplane captains during heavy storms, fog, periods of engine failure, or various other emergencies. The airline dispatcher is sometimes called a flight superintendent.

History

The history of the work of airplane dispatchers is, of course, closely related to the history of air transportation in general.

The airplane, although adapted for military use by the United States in 1909, was still used mainly as a novelty until 1914 when the first passenger service was organized. The operation provided air transportation from Tampa to St. Petersburg, Florida, a distance of twenty-three miles. Although the service lasted only three months, it was a history-making venture.

In March of 1917 the U.S. Post Office Department received a grant of $100,000 to experiment with airmail service. By 1920, the service was in operation from coast to coast, and in 1924 it was expanded to include both day and night flights. This development provided the backbone for commercial airlines in the United States.

Although the first scheduled airmail service was begun in 1918, the public did not become enthusiastic about air travel possibilities until Charles Lindbergh made his historic flight across the Atlantic in 1927.

Aviation grew rapidly during World War II, mainly because of the need for new and different types of airplanes to be used in the war effort. Since the war, the growth has been slower and more deliberate.

During the earlier days of aviation, the airplane dispatcher served in a number of capacities, including that of station manager, meteorologist, radio operator, and even mechanic. Oftentimes the dispatchers were pilots pressed into service because of their knowledge of weather and of the needs of the captain making the flight.

Although dispatchers had been used prior to 1938, it was not until then that the federal government's licensing of them came into effect.

Since that time, their work has become more involved and complicated, and the airline industry has relied on them extensively to make a major contribution to the safety of commercial air travel.

Nature of the work

The air dispatchers have control of the movement of planes and are responsible for their safety and efficiency and for making certain that they are operating on a profit-making basis. Their work, however, is not related to that of the air traffic controller who is an employee of the federal government.

Air dispatchers are responsible for determining operation probability, with their judgments based on data received from a number of different sources. They must take into consideration terminal and en route weather, official weather forecasts, wind information, and a number of other factors in their efforts to make certain that each flight will end successfully. They must answer such questions as whether the airplane crew should be asked to report to the field or whether the reservations desk should begin the time-consuming job of notifying passengers that their flight has been delayed or canceled. They may also have to determine whether an alternate route must be used by the pilot, either to include another stop for passengers or to avoid certain weather conditions.

Upon reporting to the field, the captain of the plane will confer with the dispatcher and determine the best route to use, the amount of fuel to be placed aboard the aircraft, the altitude at which the flight will be flown, and the approximate flying time. Both must agree on the conditions of the flight and either has the prerogative of canceling should that person feel the conditions too hazardous to ensure a safe trip.

The dispatchers may also be responsible for maintaining records and determining the weight and balance of the aircraft after loading. They must be certain that every piece of available cargo is hauled aboard each of the appropriate flights. They must be certain that every

725

Prior to flight, pilots check the dispatchers' reports regarding weather, routes, and flight specifications.

one of their decisions, including those about the cargo to be carried, is in keeping with all the safety regulations of the Federal Aviation Agency (FAA) as well as with those of their own airline.

Once in the air, the pilots keep in contact with the dispatcher who will keep the crew informed as to the type of weather they will encounter. This is done through a company-owned radio network, enabling each company to keep in constant contact with each of its planes. Dispatchers also keep records on the various en route positions reported by the plane, and they may have as many as ten or twelve flights under their control at any one time. Should an emergency occur, dispatchers coordinate all action until such time as the emergency has passed.

Following each flight, the pilot will check with the dispatcher for a debriefing. During the debriefing, the pilot brings the dispatcher up to date as to the exact weather encountered and various other conditions involved so that the dispatcher will have this information available for use in scheduling subsequent flights.

Judgment is the prime tool of airplane dispatchers, and they must be able to make instant, workable, and realistic decisions. Because of this, the strains and tensions are often great, especially when a number of flights are in the air or when an emergency is involved.

In the larger airlines, a certain degree of specialization is expected in the office of the dispatcher. An assistant dispatcher may work with the chief dispatcher and have the major responsibility for one particular phase, while a senior dispatcher may be designated to take care of another phase such as the economics of each flight.

Requirements

Airplane dispatchers must be approved by the Federal Aviation Administration (FAA) and may qualify for the examination in one of several different ways. They may work at least one year in a dispatching office under a certified dispatcher, complete an FAA-approved airline dispatcher's course at a specialized school or training center, or show that they have spent two of the previous three years in air traffic control work or some related job.

Upon meeting these preliminary requirements, candidates must pass an examination covering such subjects as civil air regulations, radio procedures, airport and airway traffic procedures, weather analysis, and air-navigation facilities. In addition to this written test, they must pass an oral examination covering the interpretation of weather information, landing and cruising speeds of various aircraft, airline routes, navigation facilities, and operational characteristics of different types of aircraft. They must not only demonstrate a knowledge of these areas to become a certified dispatcher, but also are expected to maintain these skills once certified. Various schools, some of which may be conducted by their employers, will assist them in staying current with new developments in these areas.

Airplane dispatchers are also required to "fly the line" at least once each year as observers over the portion of the system that they service. This requirement enables the dispatchers to maintain familiarity with airline routes and flight operations.

Assistant dispatchers are not always required to be certified. Thus, it may be possible to begin work in a dispatcher's office prior to certification. Most airlines prefer, however, that applicants for dispatchers' jobs have at least two years of college, with preference given to college graduates. Training in mathematics, physics, and meteorology is helpful.

Special requirements

Airline dispatchers must be at least twenty-one years old and in good physical and mental health. Their vision must be normal, although corrective eyeglasses may be used.

Of necessity, they must be able to think rationally and logically under the most trying conditions. Hundreds of lives may be under their guiding hand at any one time, and a poor decision could result in tragedy.

Opportunities for experience and exploration

Other than the course of study mentioned previously, there is little opportunity for an individual to explore this field. Part-time or summer jobs with an airline, however, may offer the interested student an opportunity to observe some of the operations involved in dispatching work. Military service also offers excellent experience, particularly if it has been associated with aircraft or other related areas of work.

Related occupations

Other workers in the air transportation field include pilots, flight engineers, flight attendants, transportation ticket and reservation agents, and air traffic controllers. Related communications work includes radio and telegraph operators, transmitter technicians, and radio dispatchers.

Methods of entering

The occupation is not too easy to enter because of its relatively small size, the special skills required, and the necessary dedication. Few people leave the area once in, thus providing only a few vacancies other than those caused by death or retirement. The nature of the training is such that it cannot be put to use outside of this specific area and, because of this, there is little jumping from one job to another.

Those who are able to break into the field will normally be promoted to assistant dispatchers jobs from related fields. They may come from among the dispatch clerks, meteorologists, radio operators, or those who have been pilots and have retired or been grounded. Obviously, airlines prefer those people who have had a long background in ground-flight operations work. Thus, it is probably wise to plan on starting work in one of these related fields and eventually working into a position as airline dispatcher.

Advancement

The usual line of advancement is from dispatch clerk to assistant dispatcher to dispatcher and then, possibly, to chief flight dispatcher or flight dispatch manager or assistant. It is also possible to become a chief flight supervisor or superintendent of flight control.

The line of advancement will vary depending upon the airline, the size of the facility at which the dispatcher is located, and the number of positions available. At smaller facilities, there may be only two or three different promotional levels available.

Employment outlook

In the early 1990s, there were about 1,000 dispatchers employed by the scheduled airlines and an even smaller number employed by certificated supplemental airlines and private firms. An increase in air traffic may mean a slight increase in the number of air dispatchers needed. However, because of the relatively small size of the field, the employment outlook is not particularly good.

Most of the increase in flights will be compensated for through the use of more automatic equipment, including radio and telephone communication provisions. With the new and improved communications equipment, a single dispatcher will be able to cover a larger area than is currently feasible.

The development of more foreign-flag airlines may provide other job opportunities, but even then the people for these jobs will be found probably among those already employed by the various airlines.

Earnings

In the early 1990s, assistant airline dispatchers averaged between $30,000 and $36,000 annually. Certified dispatchers were earning about $47,000 per year. Flight superintendents made up to about $52,800, and shift chiefs, $64,800.

Conditions of work

Airplane dispatchers are normally stationed at airports near a terminal or hangar and remote from the public. Some airlines operate out of several air dispatch installations, and others use only a single office.

Because airline dispatchers make decisions involving not only thousands of people but also a great deal of money, their offices are often located close to those of management, so that the managers can remain in close contact with the dispatchers. The offices usually operate twenty-four hours per day, with each dispatcher working eight-hour shifts, plus an additional half-hour used in briefing the relief person.

They have at least two weeks of vacation with pay each year, and, in many cases, this may increase to three weeks after ten years and to four weeks after fifteen or twenty years. They are normally covered by group hospitalization and pension plans.

Social and psychological factors

Airline dispatchers must be able to work well either by themselves or with others and must assume responsibility for their decisions. Many lives depend on them each day, and, because of this, there is often a great deal of physical and mental stress involved. In fact, the very nature of the job, that of making unending decisions based on a great deal of information, can cause tension.

There is a great deal of satisfaction, however, in knowing that they are filling one of the most important jobs in any airline. Dispatchers are a vital and indispensable link in the operation.

GOE: 05.03.03; SIC: 4581; SOC: 4752

◇ **SOURCES OF ADDITIONAL INFORMATION**

Future Aviation Professionals of America
4959 Massachusetts Boulevard
Atlanta, GA 30337

Air Traffic Control Association
2020 North 14th Street, Suite 410
Arlington, VA 22201

◇ **RELATED ARTICLES**

Volume 1: Transportation
Volume 4: Audio-control technicians; Radio and telegraph operators; Transmitter technicians

Blue-collar worker supervisors

Definition

Blue-collar worker supervisors act as foremen and forewomen for people employed in manufacturing, retail, and service industries. This is a broad job classification that denotes an individual who serves as the immediate boss for workers who perform any of literally thousands of tasks, from laying bricks and unloading ships, to assembling television sets and servicing automobiles.

There are many designations for this job. In the textile industry blue-collar worker supervisors are called *second-hands*; in shipping, *boatswains*; and in construction, *overseers* or *gang leaders*.

No matter what the title, the job is always similar. Supervisors tell employees what work

is to be done. They oversee the labor to make sure it is being done correctly; and they act as the link between labor and management.

History

There have always been bosses, people whose job it has been to make sure others are doing their work efficiently and properly. As society became more complex, so did the modes of production and distribution. During the Industrial Revolution, the division of labor became more and more pronounced, giving rise to what is known today as first-line management.

Blue-collar worker supervisors occupy the lowest rungs of the management ladder. Originally, their jobs were concentrated in manufacturing where they supervised largely unskilled, immigrant labor. As the U.S. economic system evolved, the employment of such supervisors extended into all areas of government agencies, business, and industry. Today, more than half of the supervisors are employed in manufacturing. Most of the remaining supervisors work in the construction trades, public utilities, transportation, and retail-wholesale trade.

Nature of the work

This is a supervisory position that entails directing the activities of other employees. Often it means ensuring that millions of dollars of equipment and materials are used correctly. This is a multifaceted job that requires strong leadership qualities.

Blue-collar worker supervisors are responsible for work output. They make work schedules, keep production and employee records, and plan job activities. In their planning, such unforeseen problems as machine breakdowns and employee absenteeism must be taken into account. For example, truck terminal loading supervisors assign workers to load the trucks, checking each vehicle to make sure it is loaded correctly and fully. They may mark freight bills as well as record the weight and load of each truck.

Supervisors also teach employees about safe work practices, enforcing safety rules and regulations. They may demonstrate time-saving or labor-saving techniques to workers. In addition, they train new employees.

An important function of the job is acting as the link between labor and management. Blue-collar worker supervisors inform employees of company policies and plans. Where labor unions exist, they meet with union representatives to discuss work problems and grievances. They must be aware of union contracts and run their operations accordingly.

Supervisors recommend productive workers for raises, awards, and promotions. They deal with nonproductive workers by retraining them, issuing warnings, recommending disciplinary action, or suggesting termination.

Requirements

Blue-collar worker supervisors should be skilled, experienced workers familiar with the jobs they oversee. They must possess strong

A supervisor roams past the machinists in his department, overseeing their work and ensuring quality output.

leadership qualities. They also must be able to get along with people so as to motivate their workers, maintain high morale, and command respect.

This job often requires a high-school diploma. One or two years of college or technical school also is desirable. Most supervisors rise through the ranks, gaining valuable experience as well as insight into the job, the people, and the company's management policies. Some are former union representatives familiar with union contracts and grievance procedures. In addition, many companies supplement this job experience by offering training programs to develop supervisory skills.

Today the trend is toward hiring individuals with college or technical school backgrounds, particularly in the technically oriented electrical, petroleum, and aerospace industries. Course work in industrial relations, business administration, mathematics, science, or engineering is preferred. People recruited this way receive on-the-job training until they are able to assume a supervisory position.

Special requirements

The nature of the job defines the special requirements that center on the personality traits already described. Other requirements are related to the industry in which the supervisor works. See specific industry articles for more information.

Blue-collar worker supervisors
Miscellaneous Occupations

Opportunities for experience and exploration

There are several ways to explore this occupation, including visiting places of employment, on-the-job training, and interviewing blue-collar worker supervisors.

Related occupations

Other management occupations include top managers, management trainees, clerical supervisors, bank managers, bank officers, retail managers, restaurant managers, and small business owners.

Methods of entering

There are a number of ways to enter this occupation. Rising through the ranks is the most prevalent. Employment may also be secured through direct application to an employer. One could answer a "help wanted" advertisement in a newspaper. Job information also is available at the local office of the U.S. Employment Service.

Advancement

Opportunities for advancement are good. This is particularly true for individuals with college educations. A supervisor can rise to such higher management positions as department head or manufacturing plant manager. In construction, many gain valuable experience and then open their own businesses.

Employment outlook

In the early 1990s, there were about 1.6 million people employed as blue-collar worker supervisors in the United States.

The number of jobs for blue-collar worker supervisors is expected to increase more slowly than the national average for all occupations. In most cases, expansion is tied to the economy. If incomes rise and demand for goods increases, so do job openings. Retirement, death, and transfer to other occupations will also create opportunities for employment. While most supervisors are employed in production industries, the greatest increases are expected to occur in the trade and service sectors.

Earnings

In the early 1990s, the average full-time, annual salary for supervisors was about $28,800.

This is a salaried position where the wages are often determined by the rates paid to the highest workers supervised. For example, some companies keep supervisor salaries 10 to 30 percent higher than those of their subordinates. Overtime pay is possible.

Conditions of work

While conditions vary from industry to industry, blue-collar worker supervisors generally labor in a normal shop environment. The job entails being on one's feet most of the day overseeing the work of others. It is possible to be subjected to grime and machinery noise.

Social and psychological factors

The job of a blue-collar worker supervisor is somewhat ambivalent. On one side, the job is challenging and multifaceted. Frequently, a worker who has risen through the ranks to occupy this more prestigious position experiences great satisfaction. This individual knows that the job being done is essential to the company's operations and is recognized as such.

Conversely, the supervisor occupies a position between labor and management. He or she may have to oversee the work of friends or relatives. If labor problems arise, the blue-collar worker supervisor is often caught in the middle. In addition, new supervisors recruited from outside may face hostile treatment from workers who thought they were deserving of promotion.

The nature of the job requires an individual who is organized and can work under pressure. The job can be stressful. It may require the supervisor to act as an amateur psychologist to maintain morale and command employee respect. It also brings with it the authority to reward or punish workers, which can prove to be a heavy responsibility.

GOE: Any industry; SIC: Any industry; SOC: 71

◇ **SOURCES OF ADDITIONAL INFORMATION**

American Management Association
135 West 50th Street
New York, NY 10020

National Management Association
2210 Arbor Boulevard
Dayton, OH 45439

◇ **RELATED ARTICLES**

Brake operators, brakers

Definition

The railroad workers called *brakers* do much more than work with brakes as their name would seem to imply. Their titles and responsibilities change depending on whether they are working on passenger trains, freight trains, or in a railroad switching yard. They may be *brakers*, *brake couplers*, *yard couplers*, or *switch tenders*.

History

The work of the braker, along with that of other railroad workers, has a history running back to the second quarter of the nineteenth century. The braker of these early days had to be a rugged person, able to work hard in all kinds of weather and often under dangerous conditions. Traveling was difficult and time-consuming. Threats from outside the train were also a problem, particularly in the Old West.

Until the invention of air brakes by George Westinghouse in 1869, brakes had to be set by hand on each car of the train. In addition, the early flagger had the responsibility of walking ahead of trains that were behind schedule to see that no other trains came upon them unexpectedly around dangerous curves. The increasingly rapid inventions of the last third of the nineteenth century made the job of the braker easier and less dangerous. Further developments in the twentieth century, however, have so improved the efficiency of the braker's work that automation and mechanization are now threatening the existence of many jobs in this field of work.

Nature of the work

The brakers perform a variety of tasks. As flaggers or road freight couplers, they see that proper flags and signal lights are used to ensure the safety of the train. They signal the engineer when to start and when to stop, throw track switches, and couple cars to make trains. Acting as inspectors, the brakers check air brake equipment and see that tools and other equipment are stored in their proper places. In addition, they inspect the train both while it is in motion and during stops, looking for any indication of trouble from sticking brakes to overheated bearings. They make minor adjustments when necessary and report any need for major repairs.

As passenger-train brake couplers, they help passengers on and off trains and open and close outside doors. They often assist the conductor in collecting tickets and looking after the general comfort of the passengers. Further responsibilities for this job include inspecting and operating the air-conditioning, heating, and lighting equipment.

As yard switch tenders, or yard couplers, the brakers work inside the railroad yards performing such jobs as switching, stopping, and distributing cars on proper tracks for the purpose of loading or unloading. They also help make up trains before and after runs.

Requirements

Applicants with a high-school education or its equivalent are preferred by most railroad com-

This switch tender works inside the railroad yard, signaling traffic toward the assigned tracks.

panies for the position of braker. In addition, good physical condition is required, with special emphasis on excellent hearing and eyesight. Color blindness is an absolute bar to employment in this field because of the need to distinguish signals.

Special requirements

There are no special requirements for the job of brake operator other than those mentioned.

Opportunities for experience and exploration

High-school students may learn more about the work by talking to an experienced braker and by arranging to visit a railroad yard. Because the majority of brakers are represented by the United Transportation Union, a visit to the local office of this union may be helpful. Some high schools and vocational schools offer a general course in railroad shop crafts and maintenance work.

Related occupations

Other occupations in train transportation that might be of interest include railroad conductors, railroad engineers, switchyard workers, and railroad clerks.

Methods of entering

Young persons may apply for work as brakers at the local railroad office or at the local branch of the United Transportation Union. Once accepted, new employees are trained on the job by working and receiving instruction from experienced brakers. Before going on the road, the beginning braker must pass a written examination on the rules of railroad operation and the specific regulations of the job. After passing the examination and demonstrating practical ability on trial trips, the new braker's name is placed on the brakers' "extra board" and the new person becomes subject to call for temporary work assignments. One may remain on the extra board for a year or more before obtaining a first assignment.

Advancement

When a braker advances, it is usually to the position of conductor. Two important elements, however, enter into any advancement in this field. First is the matter of seniority: sometimes railroad workers spend ten years as brake operators before advancement. Second, oral and written examinations are required covering such information as timetables, signals, brake systems, and general operating procedure. Thus, while waiting for an opening as a conductor, brakers in freight service often try to transfer to passenger service. This work is considered more desirable because it is less strenuous and often involves shorter hours. Also, some brakers may become baggage handlers rather than conductors.

Employment outlook

The total number of brake operators employed by the railroad industry is expected to decline because of further mechanization of railroad yards and automation of other devices. In the early 1990s, there were about 70,000 brake operators employed by the big railroads. For the next several years, there will probably be some job openings each year as a result of deaths and retirements among the present force.

Earnings

Wages are usually determined by union-management agreements incorporated into contracts. Average earnings per year in the early 1990s were $28,250 for passenger train brake operators. On long-haul freights, they were paid $27,000, and the average wage on local and way freight was $27,200. The yard brake operators averaged $21,100. Pay differentials are given for work on the long-haul trains and for work in mountainous country. Extra pay is also earned for runs of more than 100 miles on freight trains and more than 150 miles on passenger trains.

Conditions of work

Brake operators have a five-day, forty-hour workweek. Time-and-a-half pay is customary for overtime. Because of the nature of the industry, they have to work at night, on weekends, and on holidays. Yard and freight brake operators work in all kinds of weather, in all seasons, and in all parts of the country. The danger of accidents is much greater than among other railroad workers. The passenger brake operators also face accident risks, but not to the degree of those who work on freights and in the yards where activity is much more concentrated.

Railroad workers have been unionized by the railroad brotherhoods and by some independent unions. Brakers are members of the United Transportation Union.

Social and psychological factors

As the number of brakers declines because of automation, it is expected that many workers who do not retire or quit voluntarily will be gradually shifted to other railroad jobs that may require further training, or possibly some examinations. Brakers must have stable personalities to withstand the pressures of the time table.

GOE: 09.01.04; SIC: 4011; SOC: 7317, 7517

◇ SOURCES OF ADDITIONAL INFORMATION

Association of American Railroads
American Railroads Building
50 F Street, NW
Washington, DC 20001

United Transportation Union
14600 Detroit Avenue
Lakewood, OH 44107

◇ RELATED ARTICLES

Volume 1: Transportation
Volume 2: Conductors, railroad; Flight engineers; Locomotive engineers;
Volume 3: Signal mechanics
Volume 4: Automatic equipment technicians

Bus drivers, intercity and local transit

Definition

Bus drivers transport passengers from one place to another, according to definite time schedules and specific routes. Intercity bus drivers drive from city to city collecting passengers, fares, and luggage. Local transit bus drivers take passengers from one place to another within a city.

Some drivers cover special routes and transport special passengers, and may not have a rigid schedule or route to follow. Often aiding the disabled, these drivers work with dispatchers and individual requests.

Local transit bus drivers are responsible for the safety of their passengers.

History

The concept of the modern bus was developed in the late nineteenth century after the introduction of the gasoline engine.

The first bus service was begun around 1905 in New York, the Midwest, and on the West Coast. The first buses were trucks fitted with seats or automobiles lengthened for greater capacity. As roads were improved and better equipment became available, bus systems developed rapidly. They provided service to places that had never had public transportation and thus supplemented the service of the railroad lines.

In the 1930s, the engine-in-rear type of bus was developed and shortly after, buses began to replace the streetcar systems that had been in use in the cities since the early part of the twentieth century.

Nature of the work

The intercity bus driver is in complete charge of the bus. Sometimes drivers take over an already loaded bus mid-route from other drivers. Drivers who start at the terminal, however, inspect the bus carefully before the trip, making sure safety equipment is intact as well as checking oil, gas, water, and tires. After picking up their report blanks, change, express and mail listings, and other necessary items, intercity bus drivers supervise the loading of baggage, pick up the passengers, and collect fares or tickets.

During the trip, drivers must operate the bus carefully, at speeds that will enable them to follow established time schedules and still keep within speed limits. On most runs there are designated stops to make along the route to pick up or discharge passengers, and regular stops for rest and meals. After all such stops, drivers must make certain that all the passengers have returned to the bus.

At the final destination, the intercity driver supervises the unloading of passengers and baggage and then prepares reports on mileage, fares, and time, as required by company rules and the Interstate Commerce Commission (ICC). If an accident or unusual delay occurs, the driver is required to make out a complete written report.

During most runs, the local transit driver makes regular stops every block or two, according to the route and time schedule. As passengers board the bus, the driver notes passes and discount cards; collects fares, tokens, tickets, or transfers; issues other transfers; and makes change. (In most big cities, however, bus drivers do not make change so that the threat of armed robbery might be minimized; passengers then deposit their exact fare or token in a tamper-resistant box, and the driver looks at the fare through a glass viewing window to make sure that the correct amount was paid. Newer, electronic fare boxes count the bills and coins deposited and display the total of each transaction.) Drivers in many cities also check student or senior citizen identification cards to be certain that individuals qualify for discount fares.

Among other duties, local transit drivers must answer questions concerning schedules, routes, transfer points, and street numbers; they must enforce the safety rules and regulations of their company and the city: for example, no smoking.

At the end of the day, local transit drivers turn in trip sheets that include records of fares received, trips made, and any delays or accidents in the course of their schedules.

Bus drivers are also responsible for regulating heating, air conditioning, and lights on their buses.

Requirements

The U.S. Department of Transportation (DOT) specifies these requirements for intercity bus drivers: individuals must be at least twenty-one years old, in good general health, and with good hearing and at least 20/40 vision (corrected). Applicants must speak, read, and write English well enough to fill out reports, read signs, and talk to passengers. Applicants must pass written tests and a driving test in the type of bus they wish to drive.

Some companies set higher requirements for intercity bus drivers, requiring applicants to be at least twenty-five years old and to have 20/20 vision (uncorrected). Many companies prefer applicants with truck or bus driving experience.

Requirements vary by city and state for local bus drivers. Most require that applicants be at least twenty-one years old, have good vision and hearing, and possess a "clean" driving record.

A high-school education or its equivalent is preferred for this occupation. In addition, the prospective bus driver must be able to pass physical examinations given by most employers to test foot, hand, and eye coordination, reflexes, temperament, and emotional stability. Personality and temperament are important because bus drivers must be courteous and tactful in dealing with passengers at all times.

To become qualified bus drivers, new employees must successfully complete a training program lasting several weeks that combines both classroom and driving instruction. Before going on a run, they must pass a written examination on company rules, safety regulations, and record keeping as well as a final driving examination. Intercity drivers must also have instruction in ICC rules.

Once these examinations have been passed, the new drivers are placed on probation from thirty to ninety days, during which time they make regular runs under careful supervision. The new drivers are then placed on the "extra" list for several months to several years until they achieve the necessary seniority to obtain a regular run.

Special requirements

In most states, a trainee for a bus driver's job must have or obtain a chauffeur's license that permits the holder to operate commercial motor vehicles.

Opportunities for experience and exploration

The minimum age of twenty-one for employment as a bus driver gives the high-school graduate an opportunity to gain related employment before being eligible for this occupation. Once a driver's license is obtained, the prospective bus driver can gain valuable and necessary experience in such jobs as truck driving, taxi driving, or even as pickup and delivery driver for any local company or store.

Related occupations

Other transportation workers include airline pilots, cab drivers, route sales drivers, semitrailer truck drivers, and locomotive engineers.

Methods of entering

The person interested in becoming a bus driver who meets the above requirements may enter the occupation by contacting a bus company directly or the local office of the state employment service bureau.

Advancement

To most drivers, advancement means better assignments with higher earnings as their seniority increases. There are, however, limited promotional opportunities for experienced drivers. They may be promoted to dispatcher, supervisor, sales representative, instructor, terminal manager, or regional manager.

Employment outlook

There were a total of about 470,000 bus drivers in the United States in the early 1990s. About 75 percent of them worked for school systems, and about 40 percent of them worked part time.

Employment opportunities for local transit bus drivers are expected to be plentiful in the immediate future as well as in the longer run. There will also be a number of opportunities for new workers to replace drivers who transfer, retire, or die.

Some factors that are expected to improve the long-range outlook for local transit driver employment are federal legislation encouraging the combining of all forms of local public transportation into one coordinated system designed to improve service and reduce fares, the determined effort by many cities to attract people to downtown shopping areas once again through redevelopment, and nationwide efforts to save energy and reduce traffic congestion. Such programs have already proven successful in some cities.

Earnings

The yearly wages of full-time intercity drivers (including "extras") employed by class I intercity bus companies averaged $29,000 in the early 1990s.

Wages of regular intercity drivers are computed on a mileage basis, but short runs may be on an hourly rate. Most regular drivers, however, are guaranteed specified wages in terms of miles or hours per pay period with all extra work meriting extra pay.

Extra intercity drivers are usually paid by the hour when they are on call, but not actually driving, and receive a regular mileage rate when driving. However, most extras receive a weekly or biweekly guarantee either in hours, mileage, or earnings. Trainees are usually paid a flat daily rate. Pay increases from the minimum are usually given every six months to a year, for two years or until the maximum rate is reached.

The earnings of school bus drivers vary according to size of the city, length of service, and type of run. The median hourly rate was $8.70 in the early 1990s.

Local bus drivers are paid by the hour according to a scale worked out by the union and management of the transit system. Drivers on the local transit extra list generally are guaranteed a minimum number of hours of work or a minimum weekly salary.

Nearly all bus drivers are covered by contracts providing for life and health insurance paid solely by the employer and for pension plans financed jointly by workers and employers. Drivers also earn vacations with pay ranging from one to five weeks and usually six or seven paid holidays.

Conditions of work

Most intercity bus drivers have a thirty-two to thirty-six-hour workweek. Work schedules may range from six to ten hours a day and from three-and-one-half to six days a week. The number of hours that bus drivers may work is regulated by the Department of Transportation. Accordingly, they may drive no more than ten consecutive hours, after which they must have at least eight hours off. Intercity drivers are also limited to sixty hours of on-duty time over a seven-day period.

One of the advantages in this type of work is that the driver works without direct supervision and assumes the responsibility for the manner in which the work is executed. Another advantage is the opportunity to travel and to meet the public.

The disadvantages, however, include weekend and holiday work and the necessity of being away from home for varying periods of time. Also, drivers may sometimes be required to report to work on very short notice, for they are always on call. Finally, drivers with little seniority may be laid off when business declines.

Most local transit bus drivers have a forty-hour workweek with time and a half for overtime. The workweek, however, for regular drivers consists of five consecutive days with Saturdays and Sundays counted as regular workdays. Also, because some companies operate on a twenty-four-hour basis, some drivers must work nights.

The runs of regular drivers vary. Some have straight runs that are unbroken except for meal periods, while others drive for several hours, are off for several hours, and then drive again. These are called "swing" shifts.

Although driving a bus is not physically exhausting, bus drivers are exposed to nervous tension that arises from driving a large vehicle on heavily congested streets and from dealing with many types of passengers.

Social and psychological factors

Bus drivers are selected not only for their driving skills but also for their emotional stability and even temperament. Although this is not a job that is physically taxing, it is demanding and requires steady nerves. There is considerable tension when operating a large vehicle in heavy and swiftly moving traffic.

Many drivers enjoy working without direct supervision and take pride in assuming the responsibility for the safety and comfort of the passengers and the bus.

GOE: 09.03.01; SIC: 413; SOC: 8215

◇ **SOURCES OF ADDITIONAL INFORMATION**

American Public Transit Association
1201 New York Avenue, NW, Suite 400
Washington, DC 20005

American Bus Association
1015 15th Street, NW
Washington, DC 20005

Buses International Association
c/o Friendship Publications, Inc.
PO Box 1472
Spokane, WA 99210

◇ **RELATED ARTICLES**

Electrotypers and stereotypers

Definition

As graphic arts technicians, *electrotypers* and *stereotypers* make duplicate plates of type in metal, rubber, or plastic for letterpress printing.

History

The German printer Johannes Gutenberg is regarded as the inventor of movable pieces of type. In 1440, he began using separate metal pieces of type as opposed to a woodcut of a whole page to be printed, and he found that he could disassemble—distribute—the type when finished with a job, save it, and use it again. (Moveable type had been experimented with by the Chinese in earlier centuries, but the number of Chinese characters made the system ineffective.) Shortly afterward, Gutenberg developed a printing press that pressed a sheet of paper against an inked surface.

Printing developed rapidly after Gutenberg published his famous edition of the Bible, and as the need for printed matter increased so did the necessity for more durable type and for faster ways of printing. The speed of production reduced the cost and books became cheaper as technology improved. This increased the demand for books.

By 1500, printing was an established industry in Europe, but it was not until 1725 that English goldsmith William Ged invented the process of stereotyping. Plaster of Paris or clay was originally used to form the matrix or mold.

The New York *Herald* had the first stereotyped plates made to fit the curve of the press cylinder. The process of stereotyping spread rapidly because duplicate plates could be made as required without the need for setting up more type.

In 1839, German physicist Moritz H. Jacobi invented electrotyping. He developed a quick way to produce fine and durable printing surfaces. As the volume of printing increased with daily newspapers, advertising, and book publishing, these two processes increased in importance because printers could make many duplicate plates of the original and thus operate many presses simultaneously.

Nature of the work

Electrotyping and stereotyping are two distinct processes. The first is more intricate and more expensive and produces a finer and more durable plate.

There are several steps in the electrotyping process. First, a wax or plastic mold of the type form is made, coated with a silver nitrate solution or graphite, then suspended in a plating tank of electrolytic solution containing metal. Electrolysis deposits a metallic shell on the coated mold. The shell, which duplicates the original type, is then stripped from the mold, backed with metal or plastic to give it body, and hand-corrected.

In the stereotyping process, molds or mats are made of papier-mache instead of wax or plastic. This involves placing a moist—or a dry for newspaper printing—mat on the type form; adjusting the gauges for time, heat, and pressure; and then running the form under heavy steel rollers to impress type and/or photoengravings on the mat. The impressed mat is placed in a casting box, and molten metal is poured in, producing a stereotype. Some plants use automatic machines to cast stereotypes.

737

Electrotypers and stereotypers
Miscellaneous Occupations

A stereotyper for a newspaper checks a negative produced by a laser machine. All errors must be caught before the negative is placed into the platemaking machine.

Requirements

Nearly all electrotypers and stereotypers learn their trades through an apprenticeship program that covers a four- to six-year period during which all phases of the work are learned. In most plants, however, a particular phase of the work is emphasized and specialists are developed. An applicant for apprenticeship must be at least eighteen years old, with a high-school education or the equivalent. If possible, this education should include mechanical training and chemistry.

The applicant is often given a physical examination and aptitude tests because of the nature of the work. Good eyesight, full use of the arms and hands, and good health are essential personal qualifications. The applicant must also have good hand coordination.

Special requirements

There are no special requirements for electrotypers or stereotypers; however, almost all these workers are members of a union.

Opportunities for experience and exploration

A high-school program that includes chemistry, printing, electrical and metal shop, and mechanical drawing is good experience for a person considering a career in this field. Experience on the staff of a printed school newspaper is also valuable. If possible, it is a good idea to observe workers in printing trade occupations to evaluate the job better.

Related occupations

Other printing occupations that might appeal to people interested in electrotyping and stereotyping include photoengravers, press operators, bookbinders, editors, photographers, writers, and art directors.

Methods of entering

Information on entering this field through an apprenticeship program can be obtained from a local union. High-school vocational counselors can also give interested students information on these occupations.

Advancement

An apprentice advances to being a journeyman electrotyper or a journeyman stereotyper. Because these are separate crafts with separate training, there is little transferring between them. There is little advancing except to become a fully qualified craft worker.

Employment outlook

The total number of workers in these fields is expected to decline in the future as it has in the past ten years. Although there is an anticipated increase in the total volume of printing, this decline in employment will continue because of technological changes. For example, there is an increase in the use of offset printing, automatic plate composition and nonmetallic plates that replace the work done by electrotypers and stereotypers.

Earnings

The average minimum union annual wage rate was about $24,450 for electrotypers and $25,880 for stereotypers in book and job plants in the early 1990s.

Conditions of work

This work is done in a busy, active work area that is usually well lighted and well equipped. There may be some fumes and dust if the plant is not air-conditioned; safety precautions should be taken with chemicals and electricity. Although the field is highly mechanized, workers may still need to lift heavy and hot plates.

Social and psychological factors

These are two of the higher paid printing jobs. The work is repetitious and requires undivided attention. Electrotypers and stereotypers enjoy steady jobs that are both challenging and rewarding.

GOE: 05.05.13; SIC: 2796; SOC: 6849

◇ **SOURCES OF ADDITIONAL INFORMATION**

Graphic Communications International Union
1900 L Street, NW
Washington, DC 20036

Printing Industries of America
1730 North Lynn Street
Arlington, VA 22209

International Prepress Association
7200 France Avenue, South, Suite 327
Edina, MN 55435

◇ **RELATED ARTICLES**

Volume 1: Book Publishing; Newspaper Publishing; Magazine Publishing; Printing
Volume 3: Compositors and typesetters; Electroplating workers; Lithographic occupations; Photoengravers; Printing press operators

Furniture movers

Definition

Furniture movers pack and load couches, tables, dishes, and other items into moving vans for transportation to a different location. They may load and unload the van by hand or by using dollies or hand trucks. Furniture movers prepare inventories of all materials to be transported, noting the condition of each piece. They place items in the new location according to the customer's specifications.

History

Until recently, most people did not change living environments very often, tending to stay in the same area for much of their lives. Maybe a family would move cross-town, but multiple moves were a relatively rare phenomenon.

As transportation improved and job opportunities in distant regions became more and more common, people began to uproot themselves from their homes. This trend began in America at the turn of the century, and it continues to this day.

Now, it is not unusual for people to move every five years, and as our society has become more mobile, furniture movers have kept pace, transporting our beds, carpets, and clothes millions of miles each year.

Furniture movers play a vital role in the relocation of thousands of individuals and families each year. They transport household items and help provide a sense of continuity as people readjust to new surroundings.

Furniture movers
Miscellaneous Occupations

Nature of the work

Furniture movers do more than simply load and unload furniture. Much of their work revolves around planning and preparing for the move. Before any furniture is moved, the head mover (usually the van driver) goes through the household determining in what order the furniture should be loaded. The larger items are usually loaded first so as to avoid stacking heavy items onto smaller items later in the moving process. The movers then make an inventory of all the items, noting the condition of the furniture. During the inventory process, special attention is paid to any damage that may have occurred to the furniture prior to the move so that any later disputes can be avoided. The customer is given a copy of this inventory. The movers then wrap or put in boxes any furniture or other items that the customer has not so packed. The movers then must make sure that all boxes are identified with the name of the owner and appropriately marked according to their contents. This helps in organizing the boxes during the loading and unloading process and also helps if any of the boxes are misplaced.

Depending on the size of the move, anywhere from three to six furniture movers are involved in the loading and unloading process. Their specific responsibilities vary according to the scope of the move and whether it is a local or long-distance move. If it is a local move, the furniture movers load the van and then usually accompany the driver to the specified destination to unload the van. With a long-distance move, the van driver usually drives by himself or herself to the specified destination and is then met by a local team of movers who help unload and set up the furniture.

Van drivers supervise the loading of the furniture into the moving van. They drive the van to specified destinations (in the same city or anywhere in the country) and then supervise the unloading of the furniture, according to the householder's specifications. Van drivers must be skilled in their work. They must be able to back up their huge vans or trailers close to the loading area. Other tasks include inspecting the truck before and after trips, preparing reports on the condition of the truck, and keeping a daily log. They may be expected to make minor mechanical repairs and to keep their trucks in good working order. Van drivers prepare inventories of all items moved and they note the condition of furniture both before and after the move. They secure payment from the customer based on the weight of the furniture, and resolve any difficulties arising from the move.

Van-driver helpers assist van drivers in loading and unloading of the van, wrapping fragile items according to instructions from the driver. They use dollies, hoists, and hand trucks to ensure that the van is loaded safely and properly. The van-driver helpers make sure that the furniture is fastened and packed securely in the van to prevent any damage resulting from movement during the transportation process.

Requirements

Although there are no minimal educational requirements, most employers prefer individuals who have graduated from high school. It is especially important that workers have good oral and written communications skills. All furniture workers must be able to complete and understand an inventory list and be able to follow detailed instructions.

High-school courses should include auto mechanics and other shop courses, English, mathematics, and history.

Furniture movers must be able to lift heavy objects and be physically fit. Experience in driving a truck and loading and unloading heavy material are helpful.

To handle the moving van in an efficient manner, drivers must have excellent coordination and must be able to judge distance and space in an effective manner. The van operator must also be adept at judging the capabilities of their trucks so that they will not overload them. Because van drivers are required to keep records of the material they've moved and logs of the miles they've driven, they must have legible handwriting and be able to do basic arithmetic.

Special requirements

No special licenses or certificates are needed to work as a furniture mover. An appropriate driver's license, usually a commercial driving permit, is needed to drive a moving van. Independent operators may need to get operating permission from the Interstate Commerce Commission to transport furniture and other goods across state lines.

As a means of increasing professional standing, many movers become Certified Moving Consultants by passing an examination given by the National Institute of Moving Consultants. Information on this examination is available from the Institute at the address given at the end of this article.

Movers must usually be twenty-one years of age or older in order to work on interstate moves. Individual moving firms may require their employees to be over twenty-five years of age because of lower insurance premiums for these employees.

Opportunities for experience and exploration

Because summer is a prime moving time, it should not be too difficult to secure a part-time position as a van-driver's helper during this period of the year. Part-time work may also be available at other times of the year as well. Experience in the shipping/receiving department of a large store is another good way of learning about the job responsibilities of a furniture mover. In addition, discussions with professionals already working in the field are another good way of investigating career opportunities.

Furniture movers must be able to handle boxes and other pieces of all shapes and sizes.

Related occupations

Other occupations concerned with handling and transporting heavy materials include truck drivers, refuse collectors, maintenance personnel, and longshoremen.

Methods of entry

Those interested in securing a position as a furniture mover should contact local or national movers directly. The yellow pages of the phone book usually list these moving companies. Moving companies usually require that a van driver have previous truck driving experience as well as a current commercial driving permit. Many moving companies provide van-driver helpers with instruction in packaging procedures to help movers learn how to safely and efficiently pack fragile and bulky furniture. Instructions on filling out inventory lists are also usually provided for all entry-level positions.

Advancement

There are a number of ways in which furniture movers can advance. Experienced van-driver helpers may be promoted to become van drivers or they may secure jobs as dispatchers. Dis-

patchers work in the main office of the moving company and are in constant contact with the various furniture moving teams in the field. Another office position into which a skilled furniture mover can be promoted is the position of estimator. An estimator appraises the household furniture before the actual move and quotes a price of the move to the customer. Movers who have seniority and demonstrate competence in all aspects of the moving industry may become supervisors of a moving operation. A few highly skilled movers with some business ability and sufficient capital go into business for themselves. However, such an enterprise requires sufficient funds to purchase trucks, moving equipment, and other goods.

Employment outlook

As people in the United States continue to move about once every five to seven years, employment opportunities are likely to remain strong through the 1990s. Job opportunities, however, may be somewhat sensitive to the economy. If economic growth slows appreciably, this may limit opportunities somewhat. Employment opportunities figure to be strongest in large metropolitan area because there are more people changing living environments in these locations.

Earnings

Many movers work part-time and they can average anywhere from $6 to $22 an hour, depending on the skill and experience of the worker, the area in which the movers work, and the size of the companies for which they work. Full-time workers should earn anywhere between $11,000 and $21,000 per year depending on the same variables as part-time workers.

Van drivers earn somewhat more than other furniture movers, with salaries ranging between $18,000 and $25,000, depending on skill and experience. Many van drivers are unionized and belong to such unions as the International Brotherhood of Teamsters, Chauffeurs, Warehousemen, and Helpers of America.

All unionized employees receive health insurance, vacation, and other benefits. Most full-time workers who are not members of unions also receive benefits, although they may not receive as substantial a benefits package.

Conditions of work

Most of the moving business takes place in the summer months and therefore these months are the busiest for furniture movers. Movers must be outdoors in all sorts of weather, transporting furniture to and from the moving van. In the summer, excessive heat may be a problem. Cold, rain, and snow are also constant possibilities depending on the geographic region in which the move takes place. The work itself is fairly strenuous, requiring the lifting of couches, pianos, and other heavy or bulky material. A furniture mover might also spend a large amount of time packing and unpacking fragile dishes and other items.

It is not unusual for furniture movers to work over forty hours a week, especially during the busy summer months. Workers are usually paid overtime for any work more than forty per week. It is also common for van drivers to work at least fifty hours a week. Regulations of the Interstate Commerce Commission, however, state that no driver may be on duty for more than sixty hours in any seven-day period. After drivers have driven for ten hours, they must be off duty for at least eight hours before they can drive again.

Interstate furniture movers, especially van drivers, are required to spend a considerable amount of time away from home.

Social and psychological factors

Furniture workers must be diligent, honest, and be able to work as part of a team. They also must be able to work long hours lifting and transporting heavy furniture. There is always the possibility of injury from moving heavy or bulky furniture. Van drivers should be able to drive long distances, sometimes under stressful or tiring conditions. Furniture movers should be sensitive to the fact that customers are often under a lot of pressure because of the emotional and physical demands of relocating. Customers may therefore be argumentative at times. The work of a furniture mover may be tedious at times but many workers enjoy the fact that they do not work in an office or factory environment. Interstate workers get an opportunity to see much of the country. Many workers also get some satisfaction from the fact that their efforts are helping customers through a transition period.

GOE: 05.08.03; SIC: 4213, 4214; SOC: 8213

 SOURCES OF ADDITIONAL INFORMATION

American Movers Conference
2200 Mill Road
Alexandria, VA 22314

Movers' and Warehousemen's Association of America
1952 Gallows Road, Suite 303
Vienna, VA 22180

◇ **RELATED ARTICLES**

Volume 1: Transportation
Volume 3: Industrial-truck operators; Truck drivers, local and over-the-road

Gasoline service station attendants

Definition

Gasoline service station attendants perform duties at full-service automobile service stations as requested by customers. They supply cars or trucks with gasoline or diesel fuel, oil, water, and air; change oil and lubricate vehicles; sell tires, batteries, light bulbs, and other parts; and install such accessories as windshield wipers, rearview mirrors, and spark plugs. They may change and repair tires and may also wash automobiles brought in for service. In smaller self-service stations, they may do little more than accept payments for fuel sold.

History

The first gasoline-powered automobile made in this country appeared in 1893. By 1900, there were fewer than 8,000 automobiles in use. Ever-increasing production, improved internal combustion engines, more and better highways, and an expanding and prosperous population led to the establishment of many new industries and services. The need to service the number of automobiles in the nation was so great that the gasoline service station became a landmark in all of our communities and on all of our highways. Each service station requires at least one attendant; many require several.

Nature of the work

Service station attendants provide appropriate services for drivers of motor vehicles who come to the service station where they work. The duties they perform range widely. They may simply direct people to the nearest motel or they may repair a flat tire for a patron. The duties they perform most often include the following: pumping gasoline, cleaning front windshields, checking the water levels in the radiators and batteries, checking the oil levels in engines and automatic transmissions, checking tires for correct air pressure, and handling cash payments or preparing charge slips for credit-card customers. The service station attendants may also do minor maintenance and repair work; they can usually install accessories, rotate tires, repair flats, replace mufflers, and do lubrication work. They also do maintenance and other

work around the service station, such as cleaning up the service area, setting up displays, and, in some cases, taking inventory. Many attendants are also engaged in providing emergency road service. They drive tow trucks to aid distressed motorists with mechanical problems or to tow their vehicles to the station. Naturally, the attendant uses many kinds of tools in the performance of these duties. Some of these tools are such simple ones as pliers, screwdrivers, and wrenches. More complicated tools and equipment utilized by attendants include power tools, motor analyzers, and wheel alignment machines.

Requirements

As is the case with all other workers who spend much of their time meeting the public, the service station attendant must have a pleasant personality and must demonstrate poise and tact in dealing with the occasional unpleasant customer. Other personal requirements that are assets include the following: mechanical aptitude and ability; a knowledge of simple arithmetic; the ability to speak well and clearly; and physical health sufficiently good for the performance of the job in all kinds of weather. The attendant should be polite in manner and neat in appearance.

It is possible to become a service station attendant without completing high school, but most employers prefer high-school graduates. To qualify for the training programs conducted by many large oil companies, it is almost essential that an applicant be a high-school graduate. The same is also true for the attendant who hopes to advance with any of these oil companies.

Applicants for positions as service station attendants must have a driver's license and some sales ability. Applicants with these qualifications and desirable personal characteristics are generally trained on the job, although, as indicated, many large oil companies have training programs that range from two weeks to two months. These programs emphasize subjects such as simple automobile repairs, sales, and business management.

Successful applicants for positions are generally assigned simple tasks in the first few weeks of employment, and more is usually demanded of them after they have had an oppor-

Gasoline service station attendants
Miscellaneous Occupations

A service station attendant shows a customer the problem with the car's transmission.

tunity to become knowledgeable about the manner in which things are done at a particular service station.

Training programs for service station attendants are also available through the distributive education programs available in many high schools. These programs, usually set up for the last two years of high school, include work in business education, driver education, and actual part-time work experience in service stations. The most basic courses familiarize students with car engines and other components.

Programs with an emphasis on mechanics are also available and are conducted cooperatively by vocational education agencies and local offices of the U.S. Employment Service. This type of training would be especially beneficial to young people interested in becoming mechanic-attendants.

Special requirements

Other than the requirements for gaining admission to and completing the formal training programs described above and the possession of a driver's license, there are no special requirements for becoming a gasoline service station attendant.

Opportunities for experience and exploration

The most desirable means of exploring this area of work are participation in an appropriate distributive education program and gaining part-time summer or holiday employment in a gasoline service station. Interested students can also interview service station attendants personally. But the best means of learning about this work is to apply directly to a service station manager for a part-time job as an attendant.

Related occupations

Some of the other occupations that might be of interest include small business owners, retail managers, automobile mechanics, automobile-body repairers, automobile painters, petroleum refining workers, roustabouts, petroleum engineers, and petroleum drilling occupations.

Methods of entering

Individuals can apply directly to a service station manager for a position, or, if they are high-school graduates, they can apply for one of the training programs conducted by a number of major oil companies. "Help wanted" advertisements in newspapers and the local office of the U.S. Employment Service provide leads on immediate vacancies and the various available training programs.

Advancement

For individuals who demonstrate good management and business ability, there is good opportunity for advancement in this line of work. Many gasoline service station attendants become service station managers and assume more responsibility and receive higher wages. Some attendants acquire mechanical skills through training and experience and become mechanics. With experience, many station managers and automobile mechanics go into business for themselves by leasing a service station from an oil company or by buying their own service station. Attendants who work for oil companies sometimes rise to such positions as salespersons or district managers. This is especially true for the attendants who have taken work in college. Obviously, attendants have many opportunities for advancement open to them.

Employment outlook

In the early 1990s, an estimated 350,000 people were employed full-time as service station attendants and an additional 200,000 station managers and owners were also employed.

A moderate increase in the number of service station attendants needed in the next decade is anticipated. The population shift to the suburbs has made the private automobile the only convenient means of day-to-day transportation for many Americans. Attendants need to service the complex pollution control devices on new automobiles.

In addition to the jobs created by the foregoing factors, there will be some new jobs available each year because of deaths, retirements, or transfers to other kinds of work.

Weighing against these factors, however, is the increasing popularity of self-serve pumps. Motorists saved five cents a gallon or more by pumping their own gas. Still, at least one attendant is needed to take money and to render assistance on request.

Earnings

There are great differences in the wages earned by gasoline service station attendants. Hourly rates vary greatly in terms of the section of the country in which attendants work and the size of the service stations involved. Attendants at large service stations in western and north central states receive the highest wages. About two-thirds of the service station attendants in the country in the early 1990s received about $7,480. In a few large cities, gasoline service station attendants received more than $12,430. Many receive commissions on the accessories they sell and the services they provide.

Conditions of work

The majority of gasoline service station attendants work more than forty hours a week. Many work fifty hours a week or more. These hours include nights, weekends, and holidays in all kinds of weather. Attendants work when others who are relaxing and seeking pleasure require their services.

Many attendants are required to wear uniforms. Some employers pay for these uniforms and their upkeep; others do not. Some employers also provide their employees with such fringe benefits as accident and health insurance and paid vacations. It should be noted, however, that most gasoline service station attendants do not enjoy the extensive fringe benefits provided workers with comparable training in other industries.

Much of the work done by attendants is performed in noisy and grimy surroundings. Gasoline fumes and odors from oil products are also a constant factor in the work of attendants. Burns, cuts, and bruises are hazards for attendants who are not careful in the performance of routine duties.

Social and psychological factors

There are advantages to working as a gasoline service station attendant: There are many opportunities for advancement in this kind of work; the work of service station attendants is steady work; attendants have the opportunity to meet many new and interesting people; and attendants are able to help people when they really need aid.

Negative factors to be considered include the following: attendants work long and irregular hours for relatively little pay; they spend much time on their feet engaged in work that sometimes involves strenuous physical activity; they must work with dirty cars and greasy tools; and they run the risk of injury from pointed tools and hot engines and radiators. Many attendants are willing to put up with these negative factors because they someday hope to own or manage their own service station.

Few service station attendants are members of labor unions. Most of the attendants who are union members belong to the Garage Employees Union.

GOE: 05.10.02; SIC: 5541; SOC: 8319

◇ **SOURCES OF ADDITIONAL INFORMATION**

Automotive Service Association
1901 Airport Freeway, Suite 100
PO Box 929
Bedford, TX 76095

Gasoline and Automotive Service Dealers Association
6338 Avenue N
Brooklyn, NY 11234

American Automobile Association
8111 Gatehouse Road
Falls Church, VA 22047

◇ **RELATED ARTICLES**

Volume 1: Automotives; Energy
Volume 3: Automobile mechanics
Volume 4: Automotive, diesel, and gas turbine technicians

Industrial-truck operators

Definition

An *industrial-truck operator* is also known as an *electric truck operator*. These workers drive small trucks powered by electric batteries to haul heavy materials in and about industrial or other establishments.

History

There has always been a need in factories to move raw materials and products from one place to another. Originally, this work was done by hand. The work required great physical exertion on the part of laborers and was costly to manufacturers in terms of both time and money. Self-powered trucks have changed all of this. It is now possible for workers, with little effort and the use of self-powered trucks, to move and lift huge quantities of material.

Nature of the work

The industrial-truck operator uses a truck to move materials from one section of a factory to another. Some of these trucks have hydraulic lifts, others have scoops attached to them, and still others have tow bars that are used to pull small trailers. The operators of these trucks start and stop the truck, move it forward or backward, and use levers and/or pedals to control the lifting mechanisms, scoops, or other attachments. Operators are sometimes required to service their own trucks and to keep them in working condition. They are also expected to do some manual loading and unloading of the materials they move and to keep records of the material they have moved.

Many industrial-truck operators are found in automobile plants, foundries, and steel mills. In smaller numbers, they are found in all kinds of manufacturing industries. Industrial-truck operators are also employed in warehouses, depots, mines, and, in general, wherever there is a great deal of heavy material to be moved from one place to another. The federal government, including the armed services, employs large numbers of forklift truck operators.

Most industrial-truck operators are employed in states where there is much heavy industry. These states include California, Illinois, Michigan, Ohio, Pennsylvania, and New York.

Requirements

Industrial-truck operators must have excellent coordination and must be able to judge distance and space much better than the average person. These qualifications are essential if the operators are to handle their trucks in an efficient manner without injuring any of their coworkers or damaging the truck or the materials they are carrying. The operators must also be adept at judging the capabilities of their trucks so that they will not overload them or place other unreasonable demands upon them. If they are expected to keep records of the material they move, the operators must also be able to do arithmetic. They must be able to record their loadings accurately and promptly. Although there is no minimal educational requirement, most employers prefer individuals who have graduated from high school.

Most companies have training programs. After applicants have a physical examination, they learn how to operate a self-powered truck in a few days. It takes longer than a few days to learn the layout of the plant and to determine the most efficient way of moving materials from one place to another.

Special requirements

There are no special requirements for work as an industrial-truck operator, although most training programs place particular emphasis on safety instruction.

Opportunities for experience and exploration

A person interested in becoming an industrial-truck operator should visit a plant to observe an operator in action. It is sometimes also possible to secure work as an industrial-truck operator during summer vacations.

Related occupations

Other occupations that require driving and coordination skills include route sales drivers, long-haul truck drivers, bus drivers, heavy construction equipment operators, and operating engineers.

Methods of entering

There are no special methods of entering this field of work. The most common means of entry is to apply for a position in a firm that uses industrial-truck equipment and to go through the on-the-job training program provided by most employers.

Advancement

There is little opportunity for advancement in this line of work. A few industrial-truck operators, however, do become supervisors in charge of the movement of material or of truck operators who do this work.

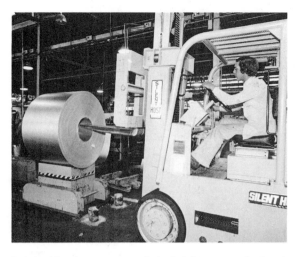

An industrial truck operator uses a hydraulic hoist to move rolls of steel sheets.

Employment outlook

In the early 1990s as many as 389,000 truck operators worked in manufacturing plants.

Many industries that employ industrial-truck operators are expected to increase their use of automated handling systems in the future. Therefore, it is expected that there will be some decrease in the demand for truck operators. Some job openings, however, will be created by deaths, retirements, and transfers.

Earnings

The median annual wage for industrial-truck operators in the early 1990s was $27,760. Without counting overtime pay, the average truck operator (forklift) earned about $27,810. Many truck operators have the opportunity to supplement their regular incomes on occasion by working overtime.

Conditions of work

Some industrial-truck operators work indoors, and others work outdoors. The outdoor operator sometimes works in undesirable weather conditions. Some operators move loose material, which is sometimes dirty and dusty. There are also some hazards associated with moving materials from place to place. Materials can fall and injure the operator and others, and there can also be collisions between vehicles. For these reasons, safety is stressed in the on-the-job training programs.

Social and psychological factors

Industrial-truck operators have to be unusually conscious of safety factors. They must have excellent perception of depth and height and must be constantly on the alert to avoid injuring themselves and their coworkers. Another factor of psychological concern is the relatively scarce opportunities for advancement. Most operators will spend their lives doing this kind of work. The operator, however, will be fairly sure of steady work in the future and will be spared much of the boredom of many factory jobs.

Many industrial-truck operators are members of labor unions. The contracts under which they work generally provide for a number of fringe benefits—paid holidays and vacations, health and medical insurance, life insurance, and retirement pensions.

GOE: 06.04.40; SIC: Any industry; SOC: 8318

◇ SOURCES OF ADDITIONAL INFORMATION

For information about job opportunities and training programs, contact the local office of your state employment service.

◇ RELATED ARTICLES

Volume 1: Automotives; Construction; Metals; Mining
Volume 2: Industrial traffic managers
Volume 3: Operating engineers (construction machinery operators); Stevedoring occupations, Truck drivers, local and over-the-road
Volume 4: Electrical technicians; Electromechanical technicians

Lithographic occupations

Definition

Lithography, also known as offset printing, is one of the basic methods of printing, done on rotary presses from zinc or aluminum plates, using the principle that oil and water do not mix.

A metal plate that has been presensitized with a light-sensitive solution is used. On this plate is photographed the type and design. The image areas on the offset plate are coated with a greasy substance to which the ink will adhere. The plate is then moistened with water so that only the image will take the ink. There is a rubber blanket that transfers the image from the plate to the surface to be printed, and this permits a greater flexibility in the type of paper that can be used.

History

The process of lithography was developed in 1798 by Aloys Senefelder of Germany, who discovered that a certain kind of stone absorbed both oil and water. He drew on the stone with a greasy crayon, dampened it with water, and then applied ink. The oily ink adhered only to the crayon, and he was thus able to press paper against the stone and transfer the image.

Nature of the work

Lithography can be used for all types of printed matter, including books, posters, maps, office forms, and even newspapers. It is an especially satisfactory process for photographs, drawings, and paintings. Many artists use the lithographic technique to create interesting and beautiful prints.

The first step in making lithographic plates is done by the *photographers*, who photograph copy to prepare a positive or negative print. Sometimes they use a screen to break up shadings of copy into dot patterns and color filters. They usually specialize in either black and white or color photography. *Lithographic photographers* are distinguished as *line photographers* (black and white), *half-tone photographers* (black and white), or *color separation photographers*.

It is often necessary to make corrections, reshape or sharpen images, or lighten or darken the negatives when they come from the photographer. This is the job of the *lithographic artists, retouchers,* or *photoengraving retouchers,* whose highly skilled work is performed by hand, using chemicals, dyes, and special tools. Because there are various methods in the retouching process, these artisans may be particularly classified according to the work they do, as dot etchers, retouchers, letterers and so on. Photographic impressions for the lithographic press plates are made from layout sheets called flats or "stripups." These layout sheets are made on paper, glass, or film.

The metal plate used in the lithographic process must be coated with a photosensitive chemical. This work may be completed before the plate reaches the *lithographic platemakers,* or this may be a job for them to do before they continue with their work. The platemaker exposes the sensitized plate through the negative or positive to strong arc lights, usually in a vacuum printing frame. For larger work, a photocomposing machine is used. The plate is then developed and chemically treated to bring out the image. The nonimage areas are now repellent to grease, but the image areas are receptive.

The *lithographic-press operators'* duties include making ready the presses and tending them while they are printing. They install the plate on the press, adjust the pressure for proper printing, adjust the rubber blanket that takes the impression from the plate and transfers it to the paper, adjust water and ink rollers for correct operation, mix ink, and operate the presses. In some cases, in large establishments, the press operator has assistants and helpers. These helpers are usually apprentices.

Other lithographic occupation specialists include *scanner operators, transferrers, photolithographic strippers,* and *laser-beam-color-scanner operators.* Some related occupations are; *strickler attendants,* who mix colors and operate machines that print on hard floor coverings; *stencil machine operators,* who operate machinery that prints on fabric floor coverings; *photoengraving sketch makers,* who prepare fabric design motifs on transparent paper to give to photoengraving photographers; *repeat chiefs,* who inspect the negatives that are used for transfer from one medium to another; *process strippers,* who judge the four color separation negatives against the customer specification; *splicers,* who edit undeveloped film strips together for processing; *paste-up copy-camera operators,* who create negatives from customers copy ready art; *pantographers,* who operate machines that reduce the size of the image and transfer it from zinc

A lithographic worker positions a positive film on a mylar flat before it is exposed onto offset printing plates.

plates to varnished printing rollers; *blueprinting-machine operators,* who operate machines that make industrial-use blueprints; and *leaf stampers,* who tend machines that stamp designs or letters in black, gold or silver onto bindings such as leather, plastic, or canvas. This was originally done in real silver and gold.

Requirements

A person interested in a career in lithography must be at least eighteen years of age, be in good physical condition, and have at least a high-school education or the equivalent. In some instances, mechanical aptitude, good eye-hand coordination, good eyesight, and color perception are also necessary. An artistic sense is an asset, and any knowledge of photography and photographic developing is helpful.

Completion of an apprenticeship program is generally required of all lithographic workers. The usual training period is from four to six years, depending on the job and whether the shop is union or nonunion. The basic lithographic process is taught so that the apprentice becomes familiar with all the aspects of the trade. Emphasis is placed on the area in which the apprentice will work. The program usually includes both classroom and on-the-job training.

Special requirements

There are no special requirements for this field. Most lithographic craft workers, however, belong to one of the unions open to members in this area.

Opportunities for experience and exploration

Some experience in high school or vocational school can be of value to a young person considering lithographic occupations. Some schools have print shops and courses in printing. Art courses, drafting, chemistry, and physics would be helpful. Work with the school newspaper, or a hobby in art or photographic work, may help to develop ability and interest. Summer or part-time work in an offset printing establishment where the various phases of the trade could be observed would be most valuable. If these experiences are impossible, visits to newspapers or printing firms and observation of the work, plus reading about the work, will give some idea of what is involved.

Related occupations

Other occupations that might be of interest include press operators, photoengravers, electrotypers, stereotypers, artists, and bookbinders.

Methods of entering

An apprenticeship is the recommended means of entering the printing occupations and qualifying as a skilled lithographer. Inquiries for this program can be made to local unions or printing shops.

Advancement

Sometimes unskilled workers are taken into the apprenticeship training program and taught a trade. It is possible to advance to supervisor or managerial positions within the firm or to transfer to another firm when an opportunity for a better job arises. For a person with the right combination of business and trade skills, there is the possibility of opening one's own shop.

Employment outlook

It is expected that there will be a moderate growth in the number of lithographic occupations in the next decade. In the early 1990s, there were approximately 65,000 lithographic workers employed. Some openings will be provided by the normal need for replacement of those who retire, die, or transfer to other areas. Offset printing has increased in the last few years, and it should continue to grow because of the increase in the use of photographs, illustrations, and the use of color in printed matter. The anticipated increase may be lessened, however, by technological improvements in some departments.

Earnings

There are many factors that influence wages in the lithographic occupations. Rates vary according to the particular occupation, and even within the occupation, depending upon the degree of skill required and the type and size of the equipment used. Wages also vary from one city to another, and depend on the size of the community and the size of the particular printing establishment.

The annual median salary in the early 1990s for lithographic scanner operators was $43,400.

Conditions of work

Conditions are generally good in printing plants. They are usually well lighted and ventilated. Many of the establishments are air conditioned. The work is not too strenuous; however, conditions do vary according to the occupation in the industry. Some of the work is messy, since oil, grease, and chemicals are used. There are some hazards working around machinery and with sharp tools, but safety precautions reduce the danger.

Social and psychological factors

This craft is one that demands close and routine work and considerable concentration. Its practitioners must be able to cooperate and work well together to turn out accurate, neat work on schedule. There are many advantages in this trade. It offers steady employment under good working conditions and wage rates. There are opportunities for advancement and promotion to higher paying jobs. It is one occupation that seems to be important in all types and sizes of communities and in all parts of the country. For the person with the aptitude and interest, as well as the necessary qualifications, lithography offers a rewarding career and a satisfying future.

GOE: 01.06.01; SIC: 2752; SOC: 6842

◇ **SOURCES OF ADDITIONAL INFORMATION**

National Association of Printers & Lithographers
780 Palisade Avenue
Teaneck, NJ 07666

International Prepress Association
7200 France Avenue, South, Suite 327
Edina, MN 55435

◇ **RELATED ARTICLES**

Volume 1: Book Publishing; Magazine Publishing; Newspaper Publishing; Printing
Volume 3: Bookbinders and related workers; Compositors and typesetters; Electrotypers and stereotypers; Photoengravers; Photographic laboratory occupations; Printing press operators
Volume 4: Darkroom technicians; Film laboratory technicians

Locomotive engineers

Definition

The *locomotive engineer* runs a locomotive on a railroad and is responsible for its safe and efficient operation.

History

Steam locomotives, inaugurated in Wales in 1804, were first tested in the United States in 1825. Their increased use was rapid after the Atlantic and Pacific oceans were joined by rail at Promontory Point, Utah, in 1869.

Electric locomotives were introduced in the late 1800s, and diesel locomotives began operation in Germany in 1932. It is unusual today to see steam locomotives anywhere other than in industrial plant yards or quarries.

The importance of railroads to the growth and rapid expansion of America is impossible to measure.

The romance of railroading is firmly entrenched in American history, and folk songs such as "Casey Jones" have become legendary. The real work of the engineer, however, is not as romantic as it may seem.

Nature of the work

Engineers may work on the road in passenger or freight service, or they may work in a railroad yard. Engineers in passenger service operate the locomotive.

They note their trip orders; inspect the fuel, sand, and water supply; and check the time, gauges, dials in the cab, and signals along the track and those received by train radio. They must know how to reduce speed gradually in order not to disturb the passengers or damage freight.

After their tours of duty, the engineers check on the condition of the locomotive, make minor adjustments, and report any major repairs needed to the repair shops. The yard engineer operates locomotives or switch engines that are used to move freight or passenger cars when trains are being broken up after a run, made up for a run, or when they are being switched for loading or unloading.

Requirements

Vacancies for positions as locomotive engineers are usually filled by firers (apprentice engi-

Locomotive engineers may operate passenger or freight trains. They may also work in a shipyard.

neers) who have the necessary experience. It often takes many years to become an engineer since seniority is very important. To qualify for an engineer's position, a firer must pass comprehensive examinations that deal with the train's mechanical and electrical equipment, fuel economy, safety, timetables, train orders, and operating rules and regulations. Engineers must also be able to operate any kind of locomotive in service on their road.

Mechanical ability, and a knowledge of simple tools, is an asset to engineers. They must keep abreast of mechanical changes in new equipment as it is manufactured, and understand the best way in which engines can be used.

Special requirements

Good health is essential to locomotive engineers, and they are required to take physical examinations at regular intervals. It is particularly important that they have good eyesight and hearing. If at any time they fail to meet the necessary health requirements, they may be restricted to working only in certain types of service. Most engineers belong to a union.

Opportunities for experience and exploration

Because engineers must ride for years as firers in the seat opposite the engineer, they are well-equipped to assume the engineer's duties when their seniority allows them the opportunity for promotion. Students may learn more about this job by arranging an interview with an engineer and by visiting a railroad yard.

Related occupations

Other occupations in the railroad industry include railroad clerks, ticket and reservation agents, yard workers, mechanics, conductors, and managers.

Methods of entering

The only way to become a locomotive engineer is first to become a firer, and then be placed on the "extra board," as an engineer without a regular run, but filling in for regular engineers on vacation and when they are sick. Those who are highest on the extra board when openings occur are promoted to engineers, providing they are otherwise qualified.

Advancement

Because of the seniority rule, it takes many years of working for the railroad in various jobs before becoming a locomotive engineer. There are few young persons in this occupation.

It is possible for an experienced engineer to advance into a supervisory position such as supervisor of engines for the road, but the number of such positions is small.

Employment outlook

In the early 1990s, there were approximately 35,000 engineers employed by class I line-haul railroads. These railroads handled more than 95 percent of the industry's business and employed more than 90 percent of all railroad workers. A few thousand engineers were employed by class II short-line railroads.

The number of job openings in this field will be extremely limited in the near future. Almost all openings will arise from the need to replace workers, and these replacements will be firers. Future employment will also be influenced by union-management negotiations that affect the railroad industry.

Railroad business itself is decreasing; also, there is increasing multiple-unit operation of diesel locomotives. Employment has also been affected by automatically controlled devices for freight car classifying, signal control, and other changes in equipment and operation, all of which have helped to lessen the need for new railroad workers.

Earnings

The earnings of engineers depend on the class of locomotive operated and the kind of service in which the engineer is employed. In the early 1990s, annual earnings of engineers averaged $28,740 in yard service, $34,640 in passenger service, and $36,270 in freight service.

On many roads, the amount a road engineer may earn in a single month is governed by mileage limitations agreed upon by the unions and the railroad companies. Whenever an engineer on one of these roads reaches the top number of miles permitted during a month, another engineer, usually an extra board worker, is assigned to take over for the rest of the month.

Railroads have their own retirement plan to which the employee and employer both contribute. In addition, most employees of the railroads are eligible for group hospitalization and other insurance plans.

Conditions of work

The switch engine operator generally works a standard forty-hour week, and it is not regulated by the number of miles run.

The road engineer, while on the extra board, may work irregular hours. All road engineers are away from home, at their own expense, a certain amount of the time. All railroad engineers may work Sundays, nights, and holidays.

The work is confining, and movement is limited in the cab of the engine.

There is a certain amount of danger in the job from accidents, although modern communications such as train telephones, and better equipment, such as continuously welded rails,

have reduced the number of casualties in recent years.

Social and psychological factors

There is an occupational ladder in railroad operating crews much as in any business. This hierarchy may have an effect on the attitude of young persons toward the occupation. It can be frustrating to workers of ability and ambition to have to wait years for the death or retirement of an engineer before being given a chance at the job. It would seem wise, therefore, for beginners to be interested in the many aspects of railroading, rather than just locomotive engineering, since a large part of their working life may be in occupations other than driving a train.

The engineer, possibly bored by sitting for many miles with nothing to do, may suddenly be called upon to react instantly if an obstruction appears on the track ahead. Such responsibility can be tension-producing without the engineer's even realizing it. On the other hand, being at the throttle of a locomotive and controlling its speed and operating efficiency is a goal prized by many workers in railroading.

GOE: 05.08.02; SIC: 4011; SOC: 8232

◇ SOURCES OF ADDITIONAL INFORMATION

Association of American Railroads
50 F Street, NW
Washington, DC 20001

American Railway Engineering Association
50 F Street, NW, Suite 7702
Washington, DC 20001

◇ RELATED ARTICLES

Volume 1: Transportation
Volume 3: Braker operators, brakers; Conductors, railroad; Diesel mechanics; Signal mechanics
Volume 4: Electromechanical technicians; Mechanical technicians

Motion picture theater workers

Definition

Motion picture theater workers are involved in all aspects of operating a movie theater, from managing the business to running the projector and selling and checking tickets. Although they have various job responsibilities, motion picture theater workers must function as a team to keep the theater running smoothly for the movie-going public.

History

Motions pictures have been a popular form of entertainment since the early 1900s, and theater workers have been involved in operating the equipment and serving the customers since before the first "talkies."

The first motion picture theaters were nickelodeons, mostly storefront buildings converted to theaters by adding chairs, a projector, and a screen. Workers were needed to take the five cent admission price and clean up after the audience had left.

As the motion picture industry expanded after World War I, vaudeville stages became the new theater locations and more workers were needed to serve the larger crowds. With the advent of the talkies in the late 1920s, the motion picture industry began a rise in popularity that has continued largely unabated until today. Employees from theater managers to ticket takers and projectionists are needed to keep "going to the movies" an enjoyable event.

Nature of the work

The specific job responsibilities of theater workers vary largely according to their job titles.

Theater managers are responsible for the overall smooth running of theater operations. All managers should have good marketing, analytical, and people skills. Their duties include supervising other employees, overseeing the maintenance of the physical facilities (both inside and outside the theater), accounting for expenditures and receipts, and maintaining good public relations.

Theater managers select and schedule the films that are to be shown. They are also responsible for planning newspaper advertisements and other promotions concerning current and future films. If the manager works for a large theater chain, these promotional activities may be organized on a nationwide basis, without the theater manager's input.

It is the manager's responsibility to hire employees and then train and assign them job responsibilities. Managers also ensure that the projectors and other equipment are in good working order and that the theater is clean. Managers must also make sure that employees are courteous and attentive to the patrons' needs. They also must keep track of ticket sales, deposit earnings in the bank, and pay employee wages. Managers also often order food and other supplies for the refreshment counter. They must also prepare daily or weekly reports on theater activities for the theater owner.

Managers must be very good at human relations. They are on hand at all film screenings to handle customer concerns and any problems that may occur. They often work with community groups by sponsoring special screenings and other activities to foster good community relations.

Chief projectionists coordinate and direct the training and other activities of those involved with projecting films. In addition to having the job responsibilities of a regular projectionist, chief projectionists ensure that these other projectionists properly fulfill their job responsibilities.

Motion-picture projectionists set up and operate film projection equipment. Working from an elevated booth at the rear of the theater, projectionists operate the movie projection machines, audio equipment, and a film rewinding machine.

For feature-length movies, the projectionists run two projectors to handle seven or more reels of film. After checking the equipment to see that it operates properly, they load the projectors with the first and second reels. The film is threaded through a series of sprockets and guide rollers, with the end attached to the take-up reel. The projectionist then switches on the bulb that provides light for the screen and starts the first projector. When the reel has reached the proper running speed, the projectionist opens a shutter and a picture appears on the screen. Cue marks (small circles on the upper-right hand corner of the screen) signal when the reel is nearly finished. Projectionists then close the shutter on the first projector and simultaneously open the one on the second at the appearance of another series of cue marks.

The projectionists then remove the now full take-up reel and run the film through the rewinding machine. The process is continued until the complete movie has been shown. If the film breaks, the projectionists must work rapidly to rethread it, and they must also be able to perform minor repairs on equipment, such as replacing badly worn projector sprockets that could damage the film.

In many theaters, projectionists are also responsible for turning down the houselights before a film begins and opening the curtains. At the end of the movie, projectionists will reverse this process.

The trend in newer theaters has been to automate projection, along with other operations, so that once the motion picture is running properly, the projectionist is free to undertake other tasks. The result is that a small staff can run a theater, or cluster of theaters, efficiently. Often in small theaters, the theater owner may be the projectionist.

Box office cashiers sell tickets and take money by hand or operate machines that dispense tickets and change. They also answer customer questions concerning the starting and ending times of movies and other similar inquiries. They may also answer telephone inquiries on the same subjects. Cashiers must usually keep very accurate records of numbers of tickets sold and money collected during their work shifts so that end-of-the-day balances can be computed. In some theaters, cashiers prepare the bank deposits for theater managers.

Ticket takers collect tickets from customers as they enter the theater, often tearing the ticket in half and giving one portion to the customer. They also answer customer questions concerning the location of the rest rooms or refreshment counter. After the film begins, ticket takers generally count and record the number of tickets collected and give this information to the theater manager. Ticket takers often have some crowd-control responsibilities during the film. For example, they may ask patrons not to smoke in the theater or help seat late-arrivals.

Ushers have many of the same responsibilities as ticket takers but concentrate on helping customers locate seating. In many theaters, the position of usher is being phased out in favor of ticket takers.

Requirements

Although there are no specific educational requirements for motion picture theater workers,

Workers at movie theater concession stands must be able to fill orders quickly before the movies begin. While the movies are playing, the workers often have little to do.

a high-school diploma is highly recommended, and some college training is desirable, especially for theater managers. High-school students often fill many of the cashier and ticket taker positions in theaters.

Managers should take courses in accounting, business, and marketing. A college degree in business administration is highly advantageous. In addition, managers should have good leadership skills and be able to motivate others.

Projectionists should be at least eighteen years of age, have excellent vision, and good hearing. The job requires a temperament suited to working alone in confined quarters and a certain amount of manual dexterity and mechanical aptitude.

Box office cashiers should possess an aptitude for mathematics and finger dexterity in order to be able to work rapidly. Accuracy and honesty are of great importance.

Ticket takers and ushers should be able to spend long hours standing on their feet interacting with the public. Personal appearance and a good attitude are very important. Tact and diplomacy, accompanied by a smile, are real personal assets.

Special requirements

Most theater workers do not need any special licenses or certificates to work in this profession. Projectionists are required to be licensed in a few states. In most cases projectionists also belong to a local or national union and must serve as an apprentice and pass a competency examination before beginning work. Aspiring projectionists should check with the local chapter of the International Alliance of Theatrical

Stage Employees and Moving Picture Operators for further information.

Opportunities for experience and exploration

There are numerous opportunities for high-school students and other interested people to secure part-time or summer employment in a movie theater, either as a ticket taker, box office cashier, or as a member of the custodial staff. Opportunities for projectionists to explore that occupation are relatively rare as projectionists must join a union. Operating small projectors at home, at school, or in the armed forces will provide some knowledge of the job responsibilities of a projectionist.

Related occupations

Theater managers share many of the job responsibilities as other service-oriented managers, such as hotel managers and apartment house managers. Projectionists share many of the job responsibilities as audiovisual technicians, broadcast technicians, and film editors. Box office cashiers have many of the same responsibilities as bank tellers, food checkers, and game-room supervisors. Ticket takers and ushers have similar job functions as turnstile attendants and amusement park personnel.

Methods of entering

Most entry-level box office cashiers and ticket takers secure positions by applying directly to a specific theater. Often people will hear of these positions through word-of-mouth from friends already working at the theater.

Persons wishing to become a theater manager must usually have some experience working in a theater, although a college degree in business administration or related field may be sufficient.

Those wishing to become a projectionist must complete an apprenticeship program of between one to two years, depending on the policies of the local union. In many cases, projectionists receive little or no pay during this apprenticeship period.

Advancement

Advancement opportunities are directly related to the type of position a theater worker has. A manager may move to a larger theater, with higher pay and more responsibility. If a manager works for a theater chain, there may be an opportunity to manage a number of theaters or, rarely, to be promoted to an executive position at corporate headquarters.

Other theater workers may advance to the position of assistant manager and then manager after exhibiting skill and maturity. An apprentice projectionist should become a full-fledged projectionist after one or two years of training. These projectionists receive higher pay, greater prestige and, with experience, the opportunity to become a chief projectionist. From the position of chief projectionist, they may also become a manager or assistant manager.

Employment outlook

Although more and more motion picture theaters continue to open, job opportunities may decline because of the development of large theater chains that consolidate many job responsibilities and the increasing impact of automation that allows a theater to operate with fewer employees. For example, one manager may be able to supervise a series of multiple-screen theaters. This same series of theaters may be able to operate with only two or three full-time projectionists and a small staff of ticket takers, cashiers, and other employees.

The impact of home video viewing units are not expected to hinder theater growth because people still enjoy the feeling of going out to a show.

Earnings

Managers usually earn between $17,000 to $34,000 per year, depending on the geographic region of the theater and the size of the theater or theater chain. Managers of a series of multiple-screen theaters usually earn more than single-screen theater managers. Benefits usually include health insurance, vacation, and a pension plan. Sometimes managers receive profit-sharing based on the total ticket sales and concession sales of the theater.

Motion picture projectionists usually earn between $10 and $16 an hour, with unionized workers in large cities earning at the upper end of this scale. Unionized workers and most other full-time employees usually receive benefits, such as health insurance, vacation, and, sometimes, a pension plan.

Hourly wages for ticket takers and box office cashiers can vary from between the minimum wage and $7.50 an hour, with experienced workers in large metropolitan areas earning the highest wages. Since many of these workers are employed on a part-time basis, they rarely enjoy health insurance and other benefits, although they may receive some paid vacation.

In general, drive-in theater employees earn less than other theater workers. Drive-in theaters, especially those in colder climates, usually close during the winter months and therefore theater employees at these establishments may have to find other work during these months.

Conditions of work

Movie theaters are usually pleasant, modern buildings, although sometimes a theater may be a bit run down. Many are located in large shopping malls or in downtown areas, easily reachable by public transportation. Specific working conditions may vary, but in general theater employees work long hours and, except for box office cashiers, spend long periods of time on their feet. Most of the work is in the evenings or on weekends.

Managers work between forty and sixty hours a week, spending most of their time either in their offices taking care of administrative responsibilities or in the theater supervising employees and solving any last minute problems. Box office cashiers usually work in an enclosed booth either inside or outside the actual theater. Ticket takers spend most of the work shift on their feet, with a portion of their time at the entrance of the theater checking tickets immediately before a film begins and the rest of the time with various crowd-control responsibilities, such as seating late-arrivals.

Projectionists usually work in projection booths that have adequate lighting, ventilation, and work space. Many of the booths are air-conditioned. The work is relatively free of hazards, but there is danger of electrical shocks and burns if proper safety precautions are not taken. The work itself is not strenuous. The projectionist lifts and handles film reels, but most of these weigh less than thirty-five pounds. Although projectionists are on their feet most of the time, they can sit for short periods while the equipment is in operation.

Many projectionists work evenings, six to eight hours a night, six nights a week. Sometimes they spread their work among several theaters.

Most drive-in employees work indoors in well-lighted environments. Those that work outdoors are usually spared discomfort, at least during the winter months, because the theaters are closed.

Social and psychological factors

Theater employees that interact with the public, such as ticket takers and box office cashiers, should have pleasant, outgoing personalities and be able to smile about the minor frustrations inevitable when working with a large cross section of the population. Managers must be able to think quickly, solve problems effectively, and work long hours under pressure. Managers must also be able to motivate employees and work effectively with various members of the community. They must be able to handle bookkeeping duties and take responsibility for handling large bank deposits.

Projectionists must be able to work alone for long periods of time with little direct supervision and infrequent contact with other theater employees.

All theater workers must be prepared to work nearly every evening and weekend, when friends and family are free, in return for time off during the daylight hours when most people are busy. It may be for this reason that many theater employees enter the profession while young and leave after several years.

Some theater employees enjoy being around the excitement of a first-run performance and enjoy the chance to see films many times. Because of job responsibilities, however, it is unlikely that a theater employee will get a chance to see a film from beginning to end without interruptions.

GOE: 05.10.05; SIC: 783; SOC: 1352, 4364, 5256

◇ **SOURCES OF ADDITIONAL INFORMATION**

For information concerning unions, contact the local chapter of the International Alliance of Theatrical Stage Employees and Moving Picture Machine Operators of the United States and Canada. Career information is available from:

National Association of Theater Owners
4605 Lankershim Boulevard, Suite 340
North Hollywood, CA 91602

Theatre Equipment Association
244 West 49th Street
New York, NY 10019

Petroleum drilling occupations

Definition

Oil companies are constantly searching for new sources of crude oil and natural gas. When a promising site is located, a drilling team goes to work to extract the oil trapped in rock layers far beneath the earth's surface or the ocean floor. The team may include *rig builders, rotary drillers, derrick workers,* and *tool pushers.*

History

Since about 4,000 B.C. people have been using crude oil that seeped through the ground as a fuel and lubricant, but the vast reserves trapped in deep layers of rock were not tapped until the middle of the nineteenth century.

In 1859, a crew under the supervision of Edwin L. Drake, a retired railroad conductor, began drilling for oil near Titusville, Pennsylvania, in an area where numerous oil seeps indicated the presence of a large underground oil deposit. After several months of drilling with a steam-operated drill, Drake's crew struck oil at a depth of seventy feet. The well was soon producing an average of twenty barrels a day.

In the next few years, thousands of wells were sunk in Pennsylvania and adjacent states. Around the beginning of the twentieth century, the vast oil deposits of Kansas, Oklahoma, and Texas began to be tapped. By 1900, American oil wells were producing 64 million barrels a year. About this time, thanks to the increasing popularity of the automobile, gasoline replaced kerosene as the most valuable petroleum derivative. New methods of distilling and refining greatly increased the gasoline yield of a barrel of petroleum.

In the late 1980s, the United States was one of the leading producers of petroleum in the world. People's dependence on petroleum as a source of fuel for transportation and heating, and as an ingredient in the manufacture of many synthetic materials, has made it one of the earth's most critical natural resources.

Nature of the work

After a team of geologists and seismic prospectors has investigated an area and found strong evidence of underground oil deposits, the drilling team is sent in to begin the laborious process of extracting the oil.

First the rig, or derrick, which houses the hoisting equipment, pipes, casing, and other tools, must be built. The *rig builders* fit and bolt together the structural steel parts of the rig, using wrenches and hammers. They also make structural repairs when necessary while the rig is in use. Many rigs used today are portable and can be trucked to another drilling site when they are no longer needed at the original site. For deep drilling, however, permanent rigs are usually built.

The *rotary drillers* usually supervise a crew of three to five helpers. Drilling goes on twenty-four hours a day, seven days a week, so three separate drilling crews work rotating eight-hour shifts on each rig. The rotary drill, powered by a gasoline, electric, or steam engine, is equipped with steel cutting teeth that bore through soil and rock. Sections of pipe are constantly attached behind it as it descends farther into the earth. Mud is pumped down the pipe and out through holes in the drill bit, keeping the bit from overheating. As the mud solidifies, it also serves to strengthen the walls of the drill hole.

The rotary drillers are responsible for selecting the proper drill bit for the type of rock strata to be drilled and for regulating the speed and pressure of the machinery. They take core samples from the drill hole to determine the strata being drilled and decide when to change the drill bit. In addition, they are required to replace drill bits when the bits have become dull. They keep a record of the number of feet drilled each day, the types of strata encountered, and the materials used.

The well service *derrick workers* work on a small platform near the top of the rig. They mix clay with water to make the drilling mud and control the pumps that circulate it through the pipe. When the drill bit must be brought up to the surface, the derrick operators, assisted by "roughnecks," or rotary helpers, disconnect the lengths of pipe as they emerge from the ground and stack the many pipes on a rack next to the platform.

The *tool pushers* are in charge of one or more drilling rigs in an area. They oversee the erection of the rig, the selection of drill bits and operation of drilling machinery, and the mixing of mud. They arrange for the delivery of tools, machinery, fuel, water, and other supplies to the drilling site. If oil or gas is struck, they have a control head put on the well to regulate the flow.

Other specialists include *pipe testers, well pullers, oil-pipe inspectors, clean out,* and *prospecting drillers,* and *technical, formation-testing, oil well service-unit, rotary derrick,* and *mud-plant operators.*

Workers at an offshore drilling platform help place a blowout protector with the use of a crane.

Special requirements

There are no special requirements for petroleum drilling jobs.

Opportunities for experience and exploration

High-school and college students may work part-time and during the summer as members of exploration and drilling crews. These jobs can lead to permanent employment in skilled or professional jobs after graduation.

Related occupations

Other occupations that might be of interest include petroleum refining occupations, roustabouts, petroleum engineers, and petroleum technicians.

Requirements

A high-school education is desirable for drilling crew workers. Courses in shop, mathematics, physics, and blueprint reading are helpful. Because of the strenuous nature of the work, most crew members are vigorous, active people between the ages of twenty and forty, although those in supervisory positions, such as rotary drillers and tool pushers, may be older.

Methods of entering

New members of drilling crews are usually hired in the field by the crew chief or the oil company's representative. They usually begin as laborers, go through a training period of several months, and advance into specialized jobs as they acquire experience.

Petroleum drilling occupations
Miscellaneous Occupations

Advancement

On a drilling crew, the job progression is usually from roughneck or rig builder helper to derrick operator, rotary driller, and tool pusher. Highly skilled workers who continue their educations at a technical institute or college may move up to jobs as petroleum engineers or technicians.

Employment outlook

In the early 1990s, more than 470,000 workers were employed in exploring and drilling for crude oil and natural gas. About half of them were employed by major oil companies; the rest worked for prospecting firms that sold their services to oil companies on a contract basis.

Employment in petroleum drilling occupations is expected to increase substantially through the next decade. In addition, there will probably be a great demand for workers on offshore drilling platforms. Additional workers may join those exploring the Alaskan oil fields.

Earnings

In the early 1990s, nonsupervisory employees in petroleum extraction jobs earned an average of about $24,950 annually. Geologists begin at about $30,500, and seasoned professionals make $60,000 and more. Petroleum engineers and tool pushers also average about $60,000. The rate of pay was somewhat higher for those working on offshore platforms.

Conditions of work

Petroleum drilling crews work outdoors in all kinds of weather, often in extremes of temperature. They may be away from home for weeks and months at a time, living in the field in trailers or tents. Much of the work is strenuous and requires good physical condition, stamina, and quick reflexes. There may be danger of natural gas explosions and fires, but on the whole the work is no more hazardous than many other industrial occupations.

Social and psychological factors

Petroleum drilling occupations are well suited to those who like to work in the open in a job that requires strength, good judgment, and mechanical ability. Those who advance to supervisory positions on drilling crews exercise a good deal of leadership and are responsible for the operation of the well and the safety of the workers under them.

GOE: 05.11; SIC: 13; SOC: 652

◇ SOURCES OF ADDITIONAL INFORMATION

American Petroleum Institute
1220 L Street, NW
Washington, DC 20005

International Association of Drilling Contractors
PO Box 4287
Houston, TX 77210

◇ RELATED ARTICLES

Volume 1: Energy
Volume 3: Coal mining operatives; Industrial machinery mechanics; Operating engineers; Petroleum refining workers
Volume 4: Petroleum technicians

Photoengravers

Definition

Photoengravers, also called *engravers*, *separators*, and *pre-press workers*, make printing plates of illustrations and other copy by photographic means that cannot be set up in type. On these plates the printing surfaces are in relief (letterpress) or intaglio (gravure). Although lithography (offset) is generally replacing photoengraving in many applications, photoengraving is still used.

History

Photoengraving was developed in 1852 by an Englishman, William Henry Fox Talbot, who found that certain solutions hardened when exposed to light, and thus would not dissolve in water. The halftone process for photographs was demonstrated in 1890. Since that time the trade has developed rapidly.

Nature of the work

All phases of photoengraving might be done by one worker, or each phase might be done by a specialist. The whole process is basically the transferring of negative film onto metal plates. The plate is then suspended in an acid bath that eats away areas not to be printed. The plate is then cut, finished, and mounted on a printing block or base.

In detail, the *photographer*, or *camera operator*, takes a picture of the copy to be printed, and the negative is developed. The image is transferred from the negative to a plate that can be used in the printing press. Plates thus made from photographs are called halftone plates. The negative is mounted on a piece of plate glass and blotted to spread and dry evenly.

The *printer* coats one side of a cleaned and polished copper or zinc plate with a photosensitive solution and whirls this plate mechanically over a heater to even out and dry the coating. The glass with the negative on it is placed against the chemically treated plates and exposed to strong lights. This causes the image to be transferred to the printing plates.

The *etcher* develops the plates by placing them in an acid bath. The chemical treatment protects the image area from etching so that when the acid etches or eats away the nonimage area of the plate, the image area is left in relief or standing out from the plate in the same way that type stands out from its base for printing purposes.

Next, the *finisher* touches up any irregularities in the etched plate by using hand-cutting tools; the *router*, or *photoengraver*, further cuts away metal that is not to be printed that the acid did not completely remove; the *blocker* "blocks up" the plate by nailing it to wooden blocks to make it reach the right level for printing, and the *proofer* prints a sample of the photograph or artwork on a proof press. Then, if the duplication is not completely satisfactory, the plate may need to be returned to the finisher or router for additional work.

Other specialists include *photoengraving printers, hand etchers, offset-plate makers, strippers, roller-print tenders, step and request reduction camera operators, stagers, process artists, picture engravers, repeat-photocomposing-machine operators,* and *rubber engravers.*

Photoengraving for gravure is done the same way except the image areas, not the background, are etched away.

Requirements

Those students interested in applying for apprenticeship programs should be at least eighteen years of age and must have high-school educations, with courses in electronics as well as training in art. They should be interested in, and familiar with, photography.

Many employers require a physical examination for prospective photoengravers. An emphasis is placed on good eyesight, since color discrimination and much close work are required. A steady hand is also important.

The apprenticeship program usually covers a four- to six-year period and includes at least 800 hours of related classroom instruction. An apprentice is taught the use of tools, negatives, solutions, and photographic equipment.

Special requirements

There are no special requirements, although most photoengravers belong to a union.

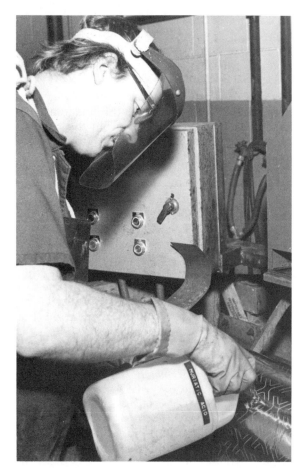

A photoengraver takes chrome off of a rotogravure press cylinder following a press run.

Opportunities for experience and exploration

A young person interested in photoengraving can sometimes work during the summer in plants where such work is done. It is possible to become familiar with the work to some extent by watching and asking questions while employed in some helping capacity. Anybody who is interested in photoengraving can call a local or nearby engraver and ask for a tour of the facilities.

Related occupations

Other printing and publishing occupations that might be of interest include press operators, stereotypers, electrotypers, typesetters, photographers, and art directors.

Methods of entering

The prospective employee usually contacts one of the printing or publishing firms in the area doing separations. They can be either departments of large corporations or small independently owned shops. After employment, the trainee will probably want to make application for an apprenticeship program as the opportunity arises. Each shop is limited as to the number of apprentices it can employ. For instance, in some areas, there can only be one apprentice to every five skilled workers. This, of course, limits the opportunity of entering an apprenticeship program.

Advancement

It takes several years or more to become a skilled scanner operator; therefore, most employees prefer to stay at their trade rather than to move to other departments.

There is one avenue leading to additional responsibility and income, and this is individual ownership of a separating business. As in the ownership of any business, the owner must have knowledge of many things other than the skills necessary to do the work itself. One must be able to promote the service, hold costs down so that a reasonable and fair profit can be realized, supervise employees, and keep records. In addition, the person thinking of beginning a business should have sufficient funds to support personal and business expenses through the difficult establishment phase.

Employment outlook

Fewer than 10,000 photoengravers were employed in the early 1990s, mostly in commercial shops that made plates to be used by others. Newspapers and rotogravure shops employed several thousand. Others worked for the U.S. Government Printing Office and for book and periodical shops. The jobs are usually concentrated in large printing areas, especially New York, Chicago, Philadelphia, and Los Angeles.

In spite of the anticipated continued expansion in printing output, the greater use of photographs and other illustrations, and the increasing use of color, a gradual decline is expected in the present number of photoengravers during the coming years. Wider use of phototypesetting and more rapid and less expensive etching techniques may result in more work for photoengravers, but the introduction of photographically made plates will limit the growth of employment of these workers. On the average, employment growth and replacement needs together probably will result in only a few hundred openings for new workers each year during the next decade.

Earnings

Photoengravers are among the highest paid printing workers. Their average annual salary in the early 1990s was about $38,210. Night-shift workers received extra pay. The usual rate of one and a half times the hourly wage is paid for work beyond thirty-seven-and-one-half–hours a week. Many photoengravers participate in a retirement plan and a group hospitalization program. In addition, unions have secured for their members six paid holidays and two weeks' vacation with pay. Apprentices start at about 40 to 50 percent of the skilled workers' wages and their wages are increased approximately 5 percent per year until they reach the maximum wage.

Conditions of work

The chief disadvantage of the job of photoengraver is the problem of meeting deadlines for publication. The etcher, particularly, must work quickly with no loss of accuracy. There is some pressure on the photoengraver to satisfy the particular demands of advertisers. Many shops stay open at night to fill the orders that come in that day for delivery the next morning. The shops are generally well lighted, heated, and sometimes air-conditioned. The work is not heavy.

Social and psychological factors

This is a stable occupation that is not subject to seasonal layoffs.

GOE: 01.06.01; SIC: 2796; SOC: 6842

◇ **SOURCES OF ADDITIONAL INFORMATION**

Graphic Communications International Union
1900 L Street, NW
Washington, DC 20036

International Prepress Association
7200 France Avenue, South, Suite 327
Edina, MN 55435

Printing Industries of America
1730 North Lynn Street
Arlington, VA 22209

◇ **RELATED ARTICLES**

Volume 1: Printing
Volume 3: Compositors and typesetters; Electrotypers and stereotypers; Photoengravers; Photographic laboratory occupations; Printing press operators
Volume 4: Darkroom technicians; Film laboratory technicians; Photographic equipment technicians

Photographic laboratory occupations

Definition

Photographic laboratory workers develop black-and-white and color film, using chemical baths or printing machines, mount slides, and sort and package finished photographic prints.

History

The first permanent photographs were taken in the early nineteenth century. The size and awkwardness of early cameras and their accessories, the long exposure time needed, and the necessity of developing the photographic plate before the chemical solution on it dried made photography largely the province of professional technicians in its early years. The Kodak camera, introduced in 1888 by George Eastman, brought photography within the reach of amateurs. This hand-held snapshot camera contained a roll of film capable of producing a hundred negatives. The camera with the exposed film in it had to be returned to the Eastman Company in Rochester, New York, for processing.

Further technical developments in photography included the invention of celluloid-based film, light-sensitive photographic paper, and faster methods of developing film. Today, photography has become so popular that there are few U.S. households without at least one camera. Professional photographers are constantly experimenting with new ways of creating interesting pictures. Photographic laboratories have continued to expand their operations to serve this vast number of amateur photographers.

Nature of the work

Developers work mainly in portrait studios, in the photo studios of newspapers, magazines, and advertising agencies, and in commercial laboratories that process the work of professional photographers. They are highly skilled workers who can control the light contrast, surface finish, and other qualities of the photographic print by their mastery of the steps in the developing process.

To develop black-and-white negative film, which accounts for a large percentage of the film used in commercial and art photography, the developer first places the unwound roll of film in a pan of developer solution to bring out the image. The technician then transfers the film to a stop bath to prevent overdevelopment, and to a fixing bath, or hypo solution, to make it insensitive to light. These first three steps are performed in darkness. The developer may vary the immersion time in each solution, depending on the qualities desired in the finished print. After the film is washed with water to remove all traces of chemical solutions, it is placed in a drying cabinet.

The developer may be assisted by a *projection printer*, who uses a projection printer to transfer the image from a negative to photographic paper. Light passing through the negative and a magnifying lens projects an image on the photographic paper. Contrast may be varied or unwanted details blocked out during the printing process.

Most semiskilled workers are employed in large commercial laboratories that process mostly color snapshot and slide film for amateur photographers. Often, they work under the supervision of a developer.

Automatic print developers, tend machines that automatically develop film and fix, wash, and dry prints. These workers attach one end of the film to a leader in the machine; they also attach sensitized paper for the prints. While the machine is running, workers check temperature controls and adjust as needed. The developers check prints coming out of the machine and refer those of doubtful quality to quality control.

The *color-printer operators* control a machine that makes color prints from negatives. Under darkroom conditions, they load the machine with a roll of printing paper. Before loading the negative film, they examine it to determine what machine setting to use to produce the best color print from it. After the photographic paper has been printed, they remove it from the machine and place it in the developer. The processed negatives and finished prints are inserted into an envelope to be returned to the customer.

The *automatic mounter* operates a machine that cuts apart rolls of positive color transparencies and mounts them as slides. After trimming the roll of film, the mounter places it on the cutting machine, takes each cut frame in turn, and places it in a press that joins it to the cardboard mount.

The *photo checkers and assemblers* inspect prints, mounted transparencies, and negatives for color shading, sharpness of image, and accuracy of identifying numbers, using a lighted viewing screen. They mark any defective prints, indicating the corrective action to be taken, and return them with the negatives for reprocessing. Satisfactory prints and negatives are assembled in the proper order, packaged, and labeled for return to the customer.

Labs that specialize in custom work may employ a *retoucher* to alter negatives or prints in order to improve their color, shading, or content. The retoucher uses artists tools to smooth features on faces, for example, or to heighten or eliminate shadows. (Some retouchers work in art studios or advertising agencies; others work as free-lancers for book or magazine publishers.)

Other photographic process specialists include *print controllers, photograph finishers, takedown sorters, black-and-white printer operators, hand mounters, print washers, splicers, cutters, print inspectors, film,* and *automatic developers,* and *photo finishing laboratory* and *film processing utility* workers.

Requirements

High-school graduates are preferred for photographic laboratory jobs. Courses in chemistry and mathematics are recommended. Many two-year colleges and technical institutes offer programs in photographic technology. Graduates of these programs can obtain jobs as developers and supervisors in photo labs.

An interest in photography and an understanding of its basic processes is a natural asset for those applying for jobs in this field. Manual dexterity, good vision with no defects in color perception, and mechanical aptitude are also important.

Special requirements

There are no special requirements for photographic laboratory jobs.

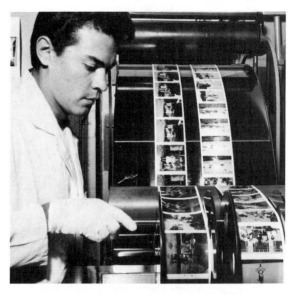

A photographic laboratory worker operates a color printer that prints continuous rolls of proofs from the negatives.

Opportunities for experience and exploration

Many high schools and colleges have photography clubs, which can provide valuable experience for those interested in careers in this field. Evening courses in photography are offered in many technical schools and adult education programs. The armed forces also train personnel as photographic technicians.

Related occupations

Other workers in photography include photoengravers, still photographers, motion picture photographers, photo finishing equipment technicians, photographic equipment technicians, and retail clerks.

Methods of entering

New employees in photographic laboratories begin as helpers to experienced technicians, moving up into specialized jobs, such as printing and developing, as they gain experience. Semiskilled workers usually receive a few months of on-the-job training, while developers may take three or four years to become thoroughly familiar with their jobs.

Advancement

Advancement in this field is usually from technical jobs, such as developer, to supervisory and managerial positions. Semiskilled workers who continue their education in film processing techniques may move up to all-around darkroom (developer) and supervisory jobs.

Aspiring young photographers often take jobs in photo labs to provide themselves with a source of income while they attempt to establish themselves as professionals. There they can learn the most basic techniques in color, black and white, and slide reproduction. Those who accumulate sufficient capital may open their own commercial studios.

Employment outlook

In the early 1990s, about 64,000 people were employed in photographic laboratory occupations. More than half of them were semiskilled workers. The rest were developers, or darkroom technicians.

Employment is expected to increase faster than average in this field through the next decade, both for skilled developers and semiskilled machine operators. The increasing popularity of photography should also provide new job openings in film processing laboratories.

Earnings

In the early 1990s, the median annual salary for photo process workers was about $15,600. Most employees worked a forty-hour week, with premium pay for overtime.

Conditions of work

Photographic laboratories are usually clean, well lighted (except for darkroom areas), and air-conditioned. There is usually no heavy physical labor. Many of the jobs performed by semiskilled workers are limited and repetitive and may become monotonous. Some employees, such as printer operators and photo checkers and assemblers, who must examine small images very closely, may be subject to eyestrain.

Social and psychological factors

Many of the semiskilled jobs in photographic laboratories entail sitting or standing for a considerable amount of time in one place and may be repetitive. Employees in these jobs need patience and ability to concentrate on details.

The work of developers calls for good judgment, ability to apply specialized technical knowledge, and an appreciation of the aesthetic qualities of photography. Their contribution to the clarity and beauty of the finished photograph can be a great source of satisfaction.

GOE: 05.10.05; SIC: 7384; SOC: 4722

◇ SOURCES OF ADDITIONAL INFORMATION

Photo Marketing Association International
3000 Picture Place
Jackson, MI 49201

Professional Photographers of America, Inc.
1090 Executive Way
Des Plaines, IL 60018

Association of Professional Color Laboratories
3000 Picture Place
Jackson, MI 49201

◇ RELATED ARTICLES

Volume 1: Printing
Volume 3: Electrotypers and stereotypers; Photoengravers; Photographers
Volume 4: Darkroom technicians; Film laboratory technicians; Photographic equipment technicians; Photo finishing equipment technicians

---

Power plant occupations

Definition

The key workers in a power plant are the operators who watch, check, control, and keep records of the operation of various kinds of equipment. The basic occupations include boiler, turbine, auxiliary equipment, and switchboard operators.

Other workers in a power plant include maintenance workers and repairers, coal equipment operators and cleaners, and in hydroelectric plants, gate tenders who open and close headgates that control the flow of water to turbines.

History

In 1882, the first electric power plant was set up in London, England, by U.S. inventor Thomas A. Edison, who had invented the electric light. In the fall of that year, the first plant in the United States went into operation in New York.

The demand for electricity spread rapidly, and plant after plant was built to supply communities with electricity. At first, power could only be sent short distances; later, electric plants could transmit current over wide areas. The plants used steam power, supplied by coal, gas, or waterfalls. The plants were owned and operated by the cities.

In the 1930s, the federal government built some large hydroelectric (water-powered) plants. Within the last two decades, nuclear energy has become another source of power for electricity, and a number of nuclear (atomic) energy plants have been built. Most of the electric power today is generated by privately owned companies.

Power plant occupations have changed little over the years; the number of jobs increased greatly at first, but more recently has been increasing only slightly. The work has changed some; coal is used far less than in the past and more control instruments are in use, centralizing the work of the plant.

Nature of the work

A power plant, or generating station, produces electric power for use by the public. The sources of the power are falling water, steam, or internal-combustion engines. Most electricity is produced in steam-powered plants which use coal, gas, oil, or nuclear energy as the fuel that produces the steam. Plants that use falling water for the power supply are called hydroelectric plants and are usually located at dam sites. The kinds of workers vary according to the type of plant. Basically, power plant operators are responsible for watching, checking, controlling, and keeping records of the equipment. They must see that the equipment is working efficiently and notice instantly any trouble that arises.

Boiler operators, sometimes called *firers*, keep the boilers going, regulate the fuel, air, and water supply, and maintain the proper steam pressure. A boiler is the container in which water is converted into steam; it is usually made up of metal shells and tubes. Boiler operators, therefore, are employed only in steam plants. An operator works with one or more boilers and keeps constant watch over them by reading the information shown on control valves, meters, and other instruments.

Turbine operators handle generators as well as turbines. The turbine is an engine that drives the generator, a machine that converts power into electrical energy. This operator starts and shuts down equipment, records the informa-

tion on the gauges, thermometers, and other instruments, such as checking oil pressure at bearings, and keeps the machines running smoothly. In large plants, there are junior operators and helpers to assist the turbine operators; in small plants, the turbine operators handle the turbines alone and may also operate other equipment.

Auxiliary-equipment operators work with many machines such as pumps, fans, blowers, condensers, evaporators, water conditioners, compressors, and coal pulverizers, checking and recording instrument readings. They also watch for trouble and sometimes make their own repairs. This equipment is used only in steam plants.

Switchboard operators regulate the flow of electric power through the plant and onto the outgoing power lines. They do this by reading instrument panels and pulling switches to distribute the power, giving orders to start or stop the generators, and connecting or disconnecting them to power circuits. Switchboard operators regularly read the meters, make frequent tests to check on the amount of current flowing, and keep a running record of what is going on with the equipment. In the smaller plants, all of the plant equipment may be handled by one person in a central control room, by using a closed-television circuit; in such cases, the worker is called a "control-room operator," and there are other workers assigned to do repairs immediately as the equipment needs it. In large plants, there is a chief switchboard operator.

Other specialists include *power-plant* and *power-reactor operators*.

Requirements

Individuals interested in this field should be high-school graduates or have equivalent education. On-the-job training runs from one to three years to become a fully qualified auxiliary equipment operator and from four to eight years to become a fully qualified boiler, turbine, or switchboard operator.

Special requirements

In most large cities, boiler operators who operate high-pressure boilers are required to be licensed, as are turbine operators. Most workers in this field also belong to unions.

Power plant occupations
Miscellaneous Occupations

A switchboard monitor at a power plant continually checks the instrument panels. If necessary, he must make adjustments in power distribution.

Opportunities for experience and exploration

There is an electric power plant in or near every community, and visits to these plants can be arranged for school groups. A visit to a hydroelectric plant is especially interesting as these are located on the edge of a dam overflow or by a natural waterfall.

There is little opportunity for part-time or summer work in power plants, but there may be an occasional opening for a cleanup worker that a high-school student can fill.

Related occupations

Other work that might interest people with skills and aptitudes similar to those of power plant workers include electrical engineers, electrical technicians, electronics technicians, and transmission and distribution workers. Other industries include nuclear and petroleum sciences.

Methods of entering

Beginners in power plant work are hired directly by utility companies and are usually assigned work as cleanup workers. These laborers can then work up from helper to junior operator to auxiliary equipment operator. Another laborer may work from two to six months before becoming a helper and later a boiler operator.

Advancement

Promotions in this field depend greatly on the individual's ability to learn the skills required on each piece of equipment. Boiler or turbine operators can advance to become boiler turbine repairers.

Where a utility system has a number of generating plants of different sizes, operators first get experience in the smaller stations and then are promoted to the larger stations, where conditions are more complex. Some utility companies promote substation operators to switchboard operating jobs. In large plants, switchboard operators can advance to the job of chief switchboard operator.

Employment outlook

With society's dependence on energy, employment opportunities in power plants will exist for a long time. However, the opportunities depend on technological advances. In the early 1990s, more than 585,000 workers were employed in the entire electric power industry.

The number of jobs in power plants is not expected to increase, although there is a continuing need to replace operators who retire, die, or go into other work. Even if electric utility systems increase their production during the next ten years, the use of larger and more efficient equipment will not require an increase in the number of workers. The newer machines are largely automatic and can be operated by far fewer operators; some plants have television screens on which the boiler fires are watched from the control rooms, and one operator, plus repairers, can handle all the equipment. Although atomic energy plants are being built in increasing numbers, these require much the same personnel and so do not alter the employment outlook.

Earnings

Power plant operators' salaries depend on the job itself, the part of the country, and other factors. In the early 1990s, average annual salaries ranged between about $16,670 and $24,360. As power plants are twenty-four-hour operations, there are three shifts of workers, and higher rates are usually paid for night shifts.

Most union contracts provide for vacation benefits ranging from one week the first year to three weeks after ten years. Paid sick leave, hospitalization insurance, and pension plans are usually provided by the employer.

Conditions of work

A power plant is well lighted and ventilated and is clean and orderly. There is considerable noise from the whirring turbines in the turbine room, but other parts of the plant are fairly quiet. The work is not physically strenuous, but most of the assignments require standing up almost constantly. The main exception is, of course, the switchboard operator, who remains seated most of the time. Serious accidents are possible in power plants but are largely prevented by strict observance of safety regulations. The accident rate is much lower in this industry than in most manufacturing industries. Night shifts, weekend work, and emergency overtime are required, but higher rates of pay are provided to workers in all such cases.

Social and psychological factors

Power plant operators have responsibility for their assigned equipment, but they also work as members of a team. They must be able to give as well as follow orders quickly and work under a fair amount of pressure much of the time. The equipment must be watched constantly. An operator, then, must be able to work well alone, and with others in a cooperative effort, knowing that hundreds of people in the community are dependent on a continuous flow of electricity and power.

GOE: 05.06.01, 05.06.02; SIC: 4911; SOC: 6932

◇ **SOURCES OF ADDITIONAL INFORMATION**

U.S. Energy Association
1620 I Street, Suite 615
Washington, DC 20006

International Brotherhood of Electrical Workers
1125 15th Street, NW
Washington, DC 20005

◇ **RELATED ARTICLES**

Volume 1: Energy
Volume 3: Boilermaking occupations; Electrical repairers; Electricians; Industrial machinery mechanics; Stationary firers, boiler tenders; Water and wastewater treatment plant operators
Volume 4: Electrical technicians; Electromechanical technicians; Nuclear reactor operator technicians

---

Refuse collectors

Definition

Refuse collectors pick up garbage and other waste material along designated routes in urban and rural communities and transport it to sanitary landfills or other appropriate locations for disposal. Recently, many refuse collectors have specialized in the types of garbage they collect. This applies to recyclable materials such as glass, newsprint, and aluminum.

They often utilize automated and semi-automated equipment to unload garbage containers, especially in areas where huge amounts of garbage are placed in large dumpsters.

History

Centuries ago, when much of the waste created was food or agricultural material, communities left it pretty much up to individuals to dispose of any waste that could not be reused either as fertilizer or livestock feed. Because there was no overall disposal program, this resulted in individuals often simply dumping unused material in abandoned pits or burning it on their own property. Because there were relatively small numbers of people, this situation was not seen as that problematic.

As populations grew and it was discovered that raw garbage could spread disease, communities began to collect this material and place it in open landfills, away from populated areas. Nondegradable materials, such as glass and metal, were also hauled away. Over the last several decades, the proliferation of paper products and the enactment of local pollution laws accelerated this trend toward community responsibility for waste removal.

In the last few years, many communities have started to implement recycling procedures and other methods to reduce the flow of garbage to the landfills. This, however, has not cut into the demand for qualified refuse collectors to pick up waste material and transport it for appropriate disposal.

Nature of the work

As a general rule, refuse collection teams of two or three people drive along established routes (in alleys or near the curb along side streets) and empty household trash containers into garbage trucks. This garbage is compacted in the truck and later brought to a landfill or other appropriate disposal facility.

Refuse workers collect waste material, such as food waste, paper products, and bottles and plastic containers, from private homes and apartment buildings. In addition, these crews also pick up the refuse from large and small businesses along the route, as well as any discarded furniture or other items left in the proper pick up locations. The work entails continuously hopping on and off the garbage truck and repeatedly lifting heavy trash containers onto the truck. In some locations, the duties of each worker are clearly spelled out, with the driver working in that capacity all day long. In other places, however, the workers alternate between driving and loading and unloading throughout the day.

Refuse workers may work for cities, towns, or privately owned disposal services. These pri-

vately owned companies may provide scavenger service to several communities or work as independent contractors to businesses that have to dispose of their own waste.

Automation has changed the way refuse collectors work. Workers now utilize semi-automated or completely automated systems that lift and empty garbage containers into the truck. This is becoming especially prevalent for servicing large apartment buildings and other locations that have huge dumpsters and other containers that are too heavy to pick up manually. The use of automation, such as a hoist on the back end of the garbage truck, has not only made refuse pick up more efficient but has in some instances led to the need for fewer workers on each refuse truck.

Although the waste is usually taken to a sanitary landfill for disposal, sometimes certain of the waste material is taken to an incinerator for burning. Incineration of certain nontoxic material is sometimes used as a means of generating electricity. Local governments usually enact legislation to determine what portion of the waste is placed in a landfill and what portion is incinerated.

Garbage-collection supervisors direct and coordinate the tasks of the various workers involved in the collecting and transporting of refuse. They make work assignments and monitor and evaluate job performance.

Requirements

Most refuse collectors, especially those in large metropolitan areas, are high-school graduates, and many have completed some college work. Those employed in smaller communities may not need a high-school diploma, but as the industry becomes increasingly automated, more and more cities are beginning to prefer that their employees have a high-school education. Those wishing to advance to a supervisory position will generally need at least a high-school diploma and several years of work experience.

High-school courses should include auto mechanics and other shop courses, English, mathematics, and history.

Refuse workers must be able to lift heavy objects and be physically fit. Sometimes a health examination is required. Experience in driving a truck and loading and unloading heavy material are helpful. Since most refuse is collected in the early morning hours, collectors must enjoy getting up early and working in the mornings.

Special requirements

No special licenses or certificates are needed to work as a refuse collector. An appropriate driver's license is needed to operate the garbage truck. This may involve some training to learn the intricacies of garbage trucks. Most refuse collectors will have to pass a civil service test in order to work for a city or town. Many refuse workers, especially those in metropolitan areas, are required to be members of a union, such as the American Federation of State, County and Municipal Employees (AFSCME). Those who work for private firms may not be unionized.

Opportunities for experience and exploration

It may be helpful to discuss career opportunities with refuse workers already working in the profession. There are some opportunities for summer or part-time work, although people in these positions must meet all the same requirements as full-time employees. Experience as a furniture mover or as a truck driver may be a good way of learning about many of the job responsibilities involved with being a refuse collector.

Related occupations

Other occupations involved with loading and transporting material include baggage-and-mail agents, truck drivers, furniture movers, and delivery personnel. The work of refuse collectors is similar to stevedores and other shipping occupations that load and unload goods.

Methods of entering

Those interested in working for a municipality should contact city government officials in the Department of Sanitation or related office. The federal Office of Personal Management and the local state job service may also list job openings. Sometimes talking to friends involved with city government may lead to employment opportunities. Those interested in working for a private disposal firm should contact that firm directly.

A refuse collector hauls trash into the back of a garbage truck.

Advancement

In some cases, an experienced refuse worker may transfer to a higher paying position in another city department, such as the public works department. In places where refuse workers start off loading and unloading refuse, experienced workers may be promoted to the position of driver and thereby earn a higher salary. A skilled refuse worker may also become a supervisor.

Employment outlook

Employment opportunities are expected to remain strong through the 1990s. Opportunities will be best in heavily populated regions, as these areas generate the largest amount of waste material. Large cities, such as New York, Chicago, Los Angeles, and Miami, will offer good job prospects. Private scavenger firms throughout the country will also offer good employment possibilities.

As communities begin to utilize recycling and other resource recovery techniques as a way of limiting sanitary landfill usage, job responsibilities may change for refuse collectors but employment opportunities should not be adversely affected. In fact, the need for additional pick up service may expand employment opportunities in both the public and private sectors.

Earnings

Earnings vary depending on the geographic location and specific job responsibilities. Beginning refuse collectors who work for a large city and are members of a union earn between $15,000 and $18,000 per year. Nonunionized workers, who are employed by smaller communities or private scavenger services, earn somewhat less and may be paid an hourly rate of between $5.50 and $8.50. Both union and nonunion employees should receive yearly pay increases, but an experienced union worker may receive larger increases than a nonunion worker.

Refuse truck drivers ordinarily get paid a higher salary than those loading and unloading the truck. City workers should average $18,000 to $20,000 to start, with yearly increases following on a fairly regular basis. Their counterparts in smaller communities or the private sector receive somewhat less, with beginning salaries ranging from $6 to $10 per hour. Supervisory personnel generally earn between $21,000 and $24,000 per year.

All unionized workers receive health insurance, vacation, and other benefits. Most full-time workers with private companies also receive benefits, although they may not receive as substantial a benefits package.

Conditions of work

Refuse workers must work outdoors in all types of weather. In many locations, this means daily exposure to cold, rain, or snow. In other climates, excessive heat may be a problem. The work itself is fairly strenuous, requiring the lifting of heavy refuse containers and the operation of hoists and other equipment. Refuse workers often must handle garbage that is smelly or not packed properly. It can be dirty, messy work. Because there is the danger of contamination from raw garbage, refuse workers must wear safety gloves and take other precautions to avoid the spread of disease. There are also the safety concerns involved with driving in urban traffic all day long and working around dangerous equipment. Most workers wear strong work boots to help avoid foot in-

juries that may come from mishandling heavy containers. Various protection measures, such as the wearing of appropriate clothes, are stressed by employers before a worker is allowed to begin work. Other safety precautions are learned from experienced coworkers.

Most refuse workers work a thirty-seven to forty-hour week, and the normal shift is often from 7:00 A.M. to 3:00 P.M. There may be some weekend or evening work, and workers are usually paid extra for working these hours.

Social and psychological factors

Refuse workers are generally part of a refuse collection team, with two or three members on each truck. They must be able to communicate well with each other and an atmosphere of trust among the workers is very important. Because the work can be very strenuous, a positive outlook is vital. Although the occupation can be tedious and somewhat dangerous, it has its advantages, such as relative job security and fairly good salary in regard to other similar occupations. Many refuse workers enjoy the fact that much of their time is spent outdoors.

GOE: 05.12.03; SIC: 4953; SOC: 8722

◇ **SOURCES OF ADDITIONAL INFORMATION**

American Federation of State, County, and Municipal Employees
1625 L Street, NW
Washington, DC 20036

International Brotherhood of Teamsters, Chauffeurs, Warehousemen and Helpers of America
25 Louisiana Avenue, NW
Washington, DC 20001

◇ **RELATED ARTICLES**

Stage production workers

Definition

Stage production workers handle a variety of behind- the-scenes tasks needed to keep a theatrical performance running smoothly. They have such varied responsibilities as costume and set design, prop arrangement, and lighting and sound control. Working together, stage production workers assure the success of a play by adding to the impact of a theatrical performance.

History

Stage production workers have developed as theatrical productions have grown. At first, when theatrical performances were done with little scenery or few props, the production workers would have relatively simple functions. But, as changeable scenery and extravagant costumes came into vogue in eighteenth century Europe, the demands on stagehands became greater. Props had to be placed in the correct location, and stages had to be transformed from "forests" to "deserts," often while the audience looked on.

The development of the curtain removed the stagehands from the limelight, but as larger stages became the norm, lighting, microphones, and other technical concerns became important.

Stage production workers now not only work in theater, but also work on television productions, directing the performances, building and changing sets, and controlling the lighting and sound effects.

Nature of the work

Stage production workers are involved in all aspects of a performance, from designing the costumes and sets, to building, placing, and removing scenery. Specific responsibilities vary according to the job title. In small productions, stage workers must be able to do a variety of tasks, while in larger productions (such as those on Broadway) many have specific technical responsibilities, such as controlling lighting and sound effects. Specific professional responsibilities include the following:

Concert or *lecture hall managers* are responsible for the smooth running of the theater during the performance. They supervise employees, such as the box office cashiers, ticket takers, and ushers, who interact with the audience at the theater. They also oversee the maintenance of the physical facilities (both inside and outside the theater) and ensure that the theater is clean. Managers are often responsible for counting and depositing money from ticket sales and they also usually order food and other supplies for the refreshment counter as well as any other supplies needed for the upkeep of the theater. Managers also often work with the stage director to get any additional crew members of stage materials needed for the performance if needed on short notice. Managers are on hand before and during a performance to answer customer questions and handle any last minute problems.

Stage directors are responsible for coordinating and overseeing all aspects of a theatrical performance. They meet with playwrights or script writers and discuss how to present the play in the most effective manner. Producers, set and costume designers, and stage managers, are then consulted about such issues as selection of actors and actresses, scenery and set design, and a host of other details. Stage directors then formulate a budget, production schedule, and set-design proposals.

Stage directors supervise rehearsals, making sure the play has the right "feel." They instruct actors and actresses on stage positioning and the proper delivery of their parts. Lighting, special effects, and costumes are all scrutinized and decisions are made as to how to best utilize them in the production. Directors refine these decisions during rehearsals and practice performances, and sometimes changes are made based on critical reviews of the actual performances. Stage directors must keep the producer up to date on the status of a show, including a report on any particular problems or concerns and how closely the show is sticking to the projected budget.

Road production general managers oversee and coordinate the business and operational aspects of a theatrical company while it is on tour. They work with local unions to hire stagehands and work with local officials to ensure that the proper performance permits are secured. They also inspect the theater to make sure that scenery and other set design specifications conform to the needs of the performers. Road pro-

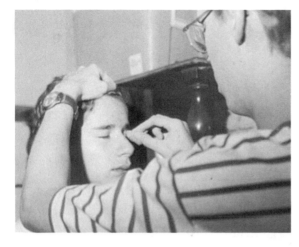

A stage production worker applies makeup to an actor before the performance.

duction general managers have various administrative duties, such as accounting for expenditures and receipts, and arranging accommodations for the cast and crew. They also pay the cast and crew their wages. Road production general managers are responsible for planning newspaper advertisements and other promotional announcements for the production. They maintain good public relations and may work with community groups to promote attendance and otherwise ensure the success of the road production.

Prompters follow the script of the performance and then cue selected performers as to the timing of their lines. Prompters are often used in musical performances and they function as intermediaries between the orchestra and the performers.

Costume designers determine the number and type of costumes needed for a performance, including color patterns and other stylistic matters. They conduct research to design clothes that are historically and stylistically authentic. Costume designers discuss all possible costume configurations with the stage director and then sketch costume designs for the director's approval. The costume designer then checks area stores (including specialized clothing shops) for garments that conform to the desired specifications. If none are found (or those located are too expensive), designers may decide to have the costumes made from scratch. They oversee the purchasing of the fabric and then work with and supervise dressmakers and other experts on the actual creation of the costumes. Costume designers also work with actors and actresses to make sure that the costumes fit properly.

In a large production, a costume designer may supervise several assistants. These assistants help in all aspects of the job, including the locating of such hard-to-find clothing items as hats, wigs, and gloves.

Requirements

Although there are no specific educational requirements for stage production workers, a high-school diploma is usually required and a college degree is highly recommended.

High-school students interested in pursuing careers associated with theatrical productions should take college-preparatory courses such as English, history, and mathematics. In addition, they should take drama courses and participate in school theatrical performances in a variety of capacities, from acting to working on set and helping with promotion.

Concert hall and road production managers should take college courses in accounting, personnel management, business, and marketing. A college degree in business administration or a related field is highly advantageous. In addition, managers should have good leadership skills, be able to motivate others, and be able to attend to details.

Stage directors should pursue an undergraduate or graduate degree in drama, with courses in acting, stage direction, and script writing. In addition, aspiring directors should participate in college theatrical productions and thereby learn through experience.

Costume designers should pursue a graduate degree in design or fine arts. They should have a sense of aesthetics, and have the manual dexterity to work with fabric.

Special requirements

Although stage production workers do not need any special licenses or certificates, some may have to belong to unions. For example, costume designers may belong to the United Scenic Artists; stage directors may belong to the Society of Stage Directors and Choreographers; and prompters may belong to the International Alliance of Theatrical Stage Employees and Moving Picture Machine Operators. These unions may require members to pass a competency test before they can begin work. For specific information on union requirements contact the individual union at a local address or at the address listed at the end of this article.

Opportunities for experience and exploration

Persons interested in pursuing careers in this field should become involved in high-school theatrical performances in any capacity, including acting, stage design, and lighting and special effects technicians. They might also pursue opportunities to volunteer for a community theatrical production in a behind-the-scenes position.

Those interested in management positions should join clubs and seek leadership positions and also part-time jobs in stores or other locations where accounting and supervisory skills are stressed. Those wishing to become stage directors should seek out opportunities to direct high-school productions or at least work as an assistant to a director. Similarly, costume designers should work closely with clothes designers, either within a theatrical operation or perhaps in a private business.

Related occupations

Concert hall or road production managers share many of the organizational and administrative responsibilities as business managers, booking managers, and advance agents. Stage directors share many of the administrative and interpretive responsibilities as drama instructors and actors and actresses. Prompters share many of the job responsibilities as cue selectors and choral directors. Costume designers have similar job functions as clothes designers, interior designers, and set designers.

Methods of entering

Because competition is very keen for all positions associated with theatrical productions, those wishing to pursue a career in this field should get as much experience as possible. It is likely that some people will have to begin in a volunteer capacity or in a position unrelated to the desired occupation. For example, someone wishing to be a stage director probably will have to begin as an assistant to the director or, more likely, as a member of the stage crew. Aspiring costume designers must also work their way up. Those wishing to secure a management position must usually have some experience in theater work, although an undergraduate or graduate degree in business administration may be sufficient. In addition,

those belonging to a union must often pass a competency test in order to begin work.

Because of the great difficulty in securing challenging entry-level positions, many people who want to work in stage production end up in other professions.

Advancement

Advancement opportunities vary according to the type of position the stage worker has. A concert hall manager may move to a larger theater, with higher pay and more responsibility. A road production general manager may similarly move on to provide the same functions for larger shows, with a corresponding increase in salary and prestige.

Many stage directors may move on to direct larger-budget plays or they may become producers. After establishing a good reputation, some theatrical directors may direct productions for television, and thereby receive higher visibility and more money. Some directors may chose to become actors or actresses. (Indeed many successful directors had been actors or actresses before becoming directors.)

Costume designers may also establish a good reputation and fulfill the same job functions for larger, better paying productions. They may also work for television or develop a consulting firm and work for a variety of clients.

Prompters may advance to a more responsible crew position; they may eventually become a stage director or producer, if they have the required education and experience.

It should be noted that advancement opportunities are very competitive, and some very successful theatrical workers may have to be satisfied with a salary increase as the only tangible evidence of a job-well-done.

Employment outlook

Although there are many job opportunities for theatrical workers across the United States, the competition is very keen and qualified applicants may have to be satisfied with part-time or volunteer work. Job prospects are best in large metropolitan areas, but that is also where most of the competition is. Many people start their theatrical careers way off-Broadway and then, after developing skills and a reputation, move to the more competitive, better-paying markets.

Those interested in theatrical work may have to be satisfied with work in sales or restaurants while awaiting an opportunity. Many professionals work part-time in community theater or other amateur environments as a way of gaining experience and exposure. Theatrical workers who can do a variety of tasks stand the best chance of employment. For example, a stage director who will work as a stage manager or other crew member stands a better chance of getting a position than someone who only can, or will, do one type of job.

Many times management personnel do not come directly from the theatrical world but rather gain experience in retail sales or other areas and then move to a theatrical management position when they have sufficient contacts and experience.

Earnings

Earnings vary according to the experience of the worker, specific job responsibilities, the geographic location of the theater, and the budget of the performance.

Concert hall or road production managers can earn anywhere from $500 for a whole season to several thousand dollars a week. These rates obviously depend on the size of the company and the type of theater it is. Broadway or off-Broadway theaters often pay more than other commercial theaters located throughout the country. Sometimes managers receive profit-sharing based on the total ticket sales and concession sales of the theater.

As with managers, stage directors make widely varying salaries, depending on their skill and reputation and the size of the show. A stage director may get only several hundred dollars for a whole series of shows or as much as several thousand dollars a performance. Highly skilled stage directors can literally write their own ticket, earning more than $200,000 a year. Again, Broadway and off-Broadway directors are usually better paid than those in other locations. Stage directors may be paid a commission based on the number of tickets sold for each performance. This serves as a performance incentive as most of the director's work is finished once a play opens. Directors may work only in the summer, when more theater companies are in operation. They can expect to earn anywhere from $200 to $1,000 a week for this seasonal work. Local unions may determine salary scales and the type of health insurance and other benefits provided, and these vary from place to place.

Costume designers are often paid a salary based on the number of costumes designed. Again, these salaries will be highly variable,

with experienced designers working in major markets such as New York and Chicago, earning more than those in other markets. Again, local unions often determine the salary structure. Costume designers who work seasonally should earn between $450 and $650 a week, but those working for community theaters should expect to earn substantially less.

Prompters are often paid hourly and usually earn between $5.50 and $12.00 an hour, again depending on theater location and union regulations. Workers who are not unionized may be paid a straight rate for a whole performance, ranging anywhere from several hundred dollars to several thousand dollars.

Most full-time workers receive health insurance and other benefits. Because workers are hired for a particular time period, vacations are rarely provided. Health insurance and other benefits vary according to the local union contract and the size of the theater.

Because work can be seasonal or temporary, many stage workers have other occupations, either to keep them employed during slow periods or to supplement their income while working at a lower-paying job within the stage worker's profession.

Conditions of work

Stage workers can work in lavish Broadway theaters or in small, marginally equipped community theaters. In most cases, theaters have adequate lighting, ventilation, and work space. Many theaters, however, can be drafty or cold when empty, as they invariably are during rehearsals. Stage production workers can expect to work long hours, especially during rehearsals and actual performances. Touring companies spend much of their time on the road in different theaters and various hotels and motels. Those working behind the scenes, such as prompters, must be aware of lighting and other heavy equipment. Safety precautions must be adhered to and are usually explained by management and reinforced by the stage director.

Stage directors may conduct formal meetings and develop ideas in their offices, but most of their time is spent in the theater either working through the script with the cast or huddled in impromptu meetings with producers or set designers. Most of the stage director's work is accomplished before and during rehearsals. During these periods, the stage director can expect to work between fifty and seventy hours a week, sometimes more. Sleep can be a prized commodity, especially for stage directors handling large shows. Many stage directors have cots stashed away in their offices for late nights or for cat naps during the day.

Costume designers either spend their time in modern design shops sketching or designing costumes, or in the theater fitting performers. They may also spend time in libraries and other locations researching the authenticity of particular modes of dress. Like stage directors, they also spend long hours preparing for a show, with most of their work done before and during rehearsals.

Managers work between forty and sixty hours a week, spending most of their time either in their offices taking care of administrative duties or in the theater supervising employees and solving any last minute problems. Road managers spend much of their time traveling and must be able to adapt to a variety of work situations depending on the type of the theater the company is performing in.

All stage performers work a majority of the time in the evenings or on weekends.

Social and psychological factors

Stage productions are highly exciting events and even though stage workers are usually behind the scenes, they enjoy the pomp and circumstance that surround each performance. This is especially true for large productions, but smaller shows also often attract big audiences and some media attention. The down side of this excitement is that it may be hard to constantly get motivated for each performance. It is vital to treat each show as important.

Stage workers should be able to work closely with a variety of other workers and should be able to handle pressurized situations.

They should be able to handle the disappointment of having a show not run as long as expected, with those in early-closing shows often having to find other jobs on short notice. Those in successful shows must be able to handle completing job responsibilities for longer than expected periods of time.

GOE: 01; SIC: 7922; SOC: 324

◇ **SOURCES OF ADDITIONAL INFORMATION**

United Scenic Artists
575 8th Avenue
New York, NY 10018

International Alliance of Theatrical Stage Employees and Moving Picture Machine Operators of the United States and Canada,
1515 Broadway, Suite 601
New York, NY 10036

Society of Stage Directors and Choreographers
1501 Broadway, 31st Floor
New York, NY 10036

◇ **RELATED ARTICLES**

Volume 1: Performing Arts
Volume 2: Actors and actresses

Stationary engineers

Definition

Stationary engineers operate and maintain stationary equipment that is essential to generate power and to heat, ventilate, dehumidify, and air-condition industrial plants and other buildings. They supervise the staff required to operate industrial plant machinery and they monitor equipment functions.

History

When the Industrial Revolution began to have an impact on industry and commerce, many new occupations were created. Mass production demanded large industrial establishments in which there was adequate heat, power, and ventilation. The same was true of the commercial enterprises housed in large office buildings.

There was a need for individuals to assume responsibility for operating and maintaining heating units, power units, ventilation systems, and other necessities. These individuals were called stationary engineers.

Nature of the work

Although all stationary engineers are primarily concerned with the safe and economical operation of their equipment, their duties are determined to some extent by the size of the plant in which they work and the kind of equipment for which they are responsible. In large plants, stationary engineers might have a supervisory function that is often very demanding. They would be responsible for the operation of the boiler room and all of the personnel employed there. In smaller plants, they may have only one helper, in which event more of their time would be spent in the actual oiling and cleaning of equipment, the greasing of moving parts of equipment, and the cleaning of boiler tubes and walls.

The most important duty of the stationary engineer is constantly to observe meters, gauges, and other instruments to determine the operating condition of the equipment. Other duties include keeping records of amount of fuel used, the temperature and pressure of boilers and repairs made; operating and controlling levers, throttles, switches, and valves to regulate the machinery; repairing equipment if necessary; and constant inspection. All the equipment must be operated in conformity with state and local safety regulations and laws. Occasionally, a stationary engineer may make mechanical changes so that equipment will operate more efficiently or conform to the requirements of a different process.

Specialists include *gas-engine* and *rotary-rig operators, exhauster,* and *refrigerating engineers.*

Requirements

Mechanical aptitude and ability, manual dexterity, and good eye-hand coordination are required by individuals interested in becoming stationary engineers.

Although some individuals become stationary engineers after gaining on-the-job training in lesser but related activities, most employers prefer that individuals go through apprenticeship programs. These apprenticeship programs are jointly developed by representatives of both labor and management and customarily last about four years. Applicants for these apprenticeship programs should be at least eighteen years old and should be graduates of a high school or trade school. Their background should include course work in algebra, geometry, trigonometry, shop mathematics, mechanical drawing, machine-shop practice, physics, and chemistry.

In the apprenticeship program, students learn to operate, maintain, and repair stationary equipment such as blowers, generators, compressors, boilers, motors, and air conditioning and refrigeration machinery. They also learn the use of hand and machine tools including electric grinders, lathes, and drill presses and how to move machinery by hoists, blocks, or other equipment. They may also use precision equipment such as calipers and micrometers.

The on-the-job training aspects of these apprenticeship programs are supplemented by classroom instruction and home study in such technical subjects as practical physics and chemistry, blueprint reading, applied electricity, and theories of refrigeration, ventilation, and air conditioning.

Special requirements

Many states, the District of Columbia, and many cities require stationary engineers to have a license to operate the kind of equipment for which they are responsible. There are three kinds of licenses available to these workers, depending on the steam pressure or horsepower of the equipment. A first-class license permits a person to work with any kind of equipment. The second- and third-class licenses place restrictions on the kind of equipment an individual can operate. Individuals with second- and third-class licenses can operate equipment beyond their license restrictions if they work under the supervision of a stationary engineer with a first-class license.

The requirements for these licenses vary from place to place, but they have in common the following factors: applicants must be at least twenty-one years of age; must have lived for a given period of time in the community in which they plan to work; and must meet the established experience requirements for the license for which they are applying. Individuals who have these qualifications must then pass an examination that is oral, written, or a combination of both. Local government offices can provide detailed information on their specific requirements.

Opportunities for experience and exploration

A student interested in this kind of work should attempt to get a part-time or summer job in a boiler room as a custodian or in another unskilled capacity. Such a job will enable the interested person to observe stationary engineers at work and will provide much information on the working conditions and duties of stationary engineers. Personnel directors at plants employing stationary engineers, counselors at local offices of the U.S. Employment Service, and representatives of appropriate unions can provide information on the part-time positions in boiler rooms available in particular communities. Interested persons can, of course, hold personal interviews with stationary engineers.

Related occupations

Other workers who perform work similar to stationary engineers include boiler tenders, stationary firers, locomotive engineers, and transmission and distribution occupations.

Methods of entering

Although there are several methods of entering this field of work, the preferable method is through the apprenticeship programs described earlier. Individuals who become stationary engineers without having served a formal apprenticeship do so only after many years of experience as assistants to licensed stationary engineers in such jobs as boiler, refrigeration, or turbine operators, supplemented by courses taken in trade schools or through home study.

Advancement

Some stationary engineers advance themselves by working for and receiving higher-grade licenses. Obtaining these licenses, however, does not guarantee advancement. Many first-class stationary firers must work as assistants to other first-class stationary engineers until positions become available. Another means of advancement would be to secure a position in a plant in which the stationary engineer is responsible for larger and more complicated equipment. Other positions to which a station-

The stationary engineer's primary duty is to check the gauges that indicate the equipment's operating condition.

ary engineer might be advanced include plant engineer, building superintendent, and plant superintendent.

Employment outlook

More than 153,000 stationary engineers were employed in the United States in the early 1990s. They worked in factories, power stations, office and apartment buildings, schools, hospitals, hotels, sewage and water treatment plants, and mines. Most stationary engineers are employed in large population centers, such as New York, Texas, California, Illinois, Pennsylvania, Ohio, New Jersey, and Michigan. Some work in rural areas.

The employment outlook in this field of work is below average for all occupations. There may be some stationary engineers needed in the next ten years to replace workers who retire or die. There will also be a need to replace stationary engineers who are promoted or who transfer to other jobs. In addition, new jobs will be created each year during the next decade. These jobs will be the result of the increasing use of large stationary boilers, refrigeration equipment, and air-conditioning facilities in industry, and also the continued growth of pipeline transportation and saline water conversion. The use of automatic equipment may, however, diminish to some extent the number of jobs that could ordinarily be expected to accompany industrial expansion, as will more efficient use of automatic equipment. The trend to use atomic energy more widely to generate power will also be responsible for some new positions in this area of work in the future.

Earnings

There are differences in the earnings of stationary engineers related to the kind of license held and the degree of responsibility of the job. The average annual earnings of stationary engineers of all classes was approximately $31,399 in the early 1990s.

Most stationary engineers are employed in establishments that have union-employer contracts. These contracts generally include such fringe benefits as hospitalization, medical, and surgical insurance, life insurance, sickness and accident insurance, and retirement pensions. Stationary engineers who work in plants that do not have union-employer contracts often receive similar fringe benefits. Among the unions representing these workers are the International Union of Operating Engineers and the International Brotherhood of Firemen and Oilers.

Conditions of work

The work done by stationary engineers is steady work. These employees generally work an eight-hour day for a five- or six-day week. Because many of the establishments in which stationary engineers are employed function twenty-four hours a day, it is common for these workers to work different shifts on a rotating basis. They also take turns at working on Sundays and holidays.

Some of the boiler rooms in which stationary engineers work are clean and well lighted. This is not true, however, of all boiler rooms. Stationary engineers are exposed to the hazardous conditions associated with high temperatures, dirt, oil, smoke, and the disagreeable odors that accompany these elements. While great physical strength is no longer a requisite for stationary engineers, they must have considerable agility and endurance to perform the tasks expected of them. There is some danger attached to working around the boilers and the

electrical and mechanical equipment operated by stationary engineers, but modern safety procedures have greatly reduced the possibility of injury. These workers, nevertheless, must be constantly on the alert to avoid burns, electrical shock, and other possible injuries.

Social and psychological factors

There are many advantages to the work of stationary engineers. The work is steady, and stationary engineers are well paid in both wages and fringe benefits. There are also a number of opportunities for advancement. On the negative side, it should be noted that some of the work involves the performance of tasks in disagreeable positions and circumstances, such as crawling into an overheated boiler on a hot, humid day. The major psychological concern in this field, however, centers around the difficulties that interested young people often have in gaining admission into the long and difficult apprenticeship programs. Competition for admission to apprenticeship programs is keen.

GOE: 05.06.02; SIC: Any industry; SOC: 6931

◇ **SOURCES OF ADDITIONAL INFORMATION**

International Union of Operating Engineers
1125 17th Street, NW
Washington, DC 20036

National Association of Power Engineers
2350 East Devon Avenue, Suite 115
Des Plaines, IL 60018

◇ **RELATED ARTICLES**

Volume 1: Energy; Machining and Machinery
Volume 3: Air-conditioning, refrigeration, and heating mechanics; Boilermaking occupations; Machine tool operators; Stationary firers, boiler tenders; Water and wastewater treatment plant operators
Volume 4: Air-conditioning, heating, and refrigeration technicians; Mechanical technicians

Stationary firers, boiler tenders

Definition

High pressure firers are also known as *boiler tenders, boiler house workers, boiler firers,* and *stokers.* In general, the job is to fire the stationary steam boilers used in a factory, power plant, or other establishment to generate power or to supply steam for industry.

History

Forms of steam boilers were constructed as early as A.D. 78 in Pompeii. It was not until 1698, however, that English engineer Thomas Savery became the first man to employ a steam boiler in useful activity. Many people were impressed with the expansive powers of steam and sought to use steam as a means of solving problems in mining, heating, and cooking. Many of the efforts of those interested in harnessing steam power were successful, and there were significant developments in the design and function of boilers. Boilers played a major role in the Industrial Revolution and were in wide use by the middle of the nineteenth century. As boilers became more complicated, it was necessary to employ individuals who devoted their time and energy to firing and maintaining these boilers in a number of industrial settings.

Nature of the work

Stationary firers are semiskilled workers. They are generally employed in manufacturing plants to take care of the steam boilers that are used to provide power for industrial machinery and to heat industrial plants. Some stationary firers have more responsibilities than others. For example, some of these workers inspect boiler equipment, light boilers, and build up steam pressure. Other stationary firers are simply responsible for keeping boilers in good working order. Some stationary firers are expected to make minor repairs on their equipment. These tenders generally work under the direct supervision of stationary engineers.

Stationary firers are responsible for maintaining proper pressures in steam boilers. To do this, they use mechanical devices to control the flow of air, gas, oil, or powdered coal into the firebox of the boiler. Most of these workers use meters and other equipment to make sure that the boilers are operating properly and in conformity with safety regulations.

Stationary firers work in those sections of the country with great population centers and large industrial plants. Almost half of the stationary firers are employed in the states of Ohio, New York, Pennsylvania, Illinois, Michigan, New Jersey, and California. The following industries employ many stationary firers: lumber, food, iron and steel, paper, chemicals, and transportation equipment.

Requirements

Physical strength is not as important as it was at one time for stationary tenders. Much of the equipment they now use is largely mechanized. Good vision and normal hearing, however, are essential in this line of work. Stationary firers must also have mechanical aptitude and knowledge. They must understand how machinery operates and must be able to do minor repair work. Competent stationary firers can detect trouble in their equipment without relying only on safety devices.

There are no special educational requirements for stationary firers, but high-school graduates are preferred applicants for the on-the-job training programs provided for these workers.

Special requirements

Some large cities, and some states, require that stationary firers have licenses to do their work. The requirements one must meet to acquire these licenses vary from place to place. Most of these requirements, however, include experience and an examination on knowledge of the duties commonly performed by these workers. The licenses required for stationary firers are related to the kinds of boilers to be used in the work done, either high-pressure or low-pressure boiler.

Applicants for the required licenses obtain the knowledge and experience they must have to pass these examinations by working as helpers in boiler rooms at the beginning of their em-

Two stationary firers are performing routine maintenance work on a boiler. They may also control the steam pressure in the boiler.

ployment and by later working under conditional licenses.

Opportunities for experience and exploration

Students interested in a career as stationary firers should have interviews with personnel managers of industrial plants that employ these workers, with representatives of appropriate unions, with counselors at the local office of the U.S. Employment Service, and with practicing stationary firers. There may also be some opportunity for a student to obtain summer or part-time work as a boiler-room helper.

Related occupations

Other workers with similar job responsibilities include stationary engineers, transmission and distribution workers, mechanics, and power plant occupations.

Methods of entering

Prospective firers can enter this field by applying directly to the employment offices of establishments that employ firers for on-the-job training. Most firers start out as helpers in boiler rooms. Information on these jobs can often be secured from local offices of appropriate unions and from offices of the U.S. Employment Service. "Help wanted" advertisements in newspapers also provide leads to jobs.

Advancement

There are two major lines of advancement for stationary firers: some may advance to jobs as maintenance mechanics, and others become stationary engineers. To become stationary engineers, stationary firers add to their on-the-job training by taking such courses as practical chemistry, elementary physics, applied electricity, blueprint reading, heating, ventilation, air conditioning, and refrigeration. These courses can be taken in evening school or from accredited correspondence schools.

Employment outlook

Although boilers are largely mechanized today, there were approximately 82,000 stationary firers employed in the United States in the early 1990s.

Although an increase in the use of stationary boilers and related equipment is expected in the next decade, there will continue to be a decline in the number of stationary firers needed to handle this equipment. Technological developments have resulted in boilers that are controlled automatically from centralized points. Where there is a need for constant observation of boilers, tenders will continue to be needed. In addition, there will be a need to replace some of the firers who die, retire, or transfer to some other kind of work.

Earnings

The earnings of stationary firers are related to the kind of equipment they operate, the industry in which they work, and the section of the country in which they are employed. In the early 1990s, stationary firers in manufacturing plants earned an average annual salary of about $20,400.

Stationary firers enjoy many fringe benefits. These benefits include paid holidays and vacations, hospitalization, medical and surgical insurance, sickness and accident insurance, and retirement pensions.

Conditions of work

Stationary firers do their work in boiler rooms. Some boiler rooms are clean and well lighted; others are not. At times, stationary firers are exposed to much noise, high temperatures, dirt, dust, oil, and grease. They must also tolerate the fumes that come from oil, gas, coal, or smoke. Some of their work is done from such uncomfortable positions as kneeling and crouching. On occasion, stationary firers must also crawl into the boilers for which they are responsible.

The work of stationary firers is not as dangerous today as it was before the introduction of modern equipment and safety procedures. Nevertheless, stationary firers are still subject to burns and falls as well as other injuries from the equipment and machinery with which they must work. There are also dangers related to defective or improperly functioning boilers. Small holes may, for example, release high pressure steam that may injure someone walking by. Explosions are rare, but firers must always be cautious. Some stationary firers are employed in plants in which the boiler rooms are in operation for twenty-four hours a day. Firers in these plants work on one of three shifts and must also take their turns working on Sundays and holidays.

Social and psychological factors

The major concerns of stationary firers center around the downward employment trend. There is reason for some of these workers to be apprehensive that their jobs will give way to increasing mechanization. Also, the employment outlook is other than favorable. These factors would appear to make it difficult for current stationary firers to look forward to promotions and the corresponding increased earnings.

Most stationary firers belong to labor unions. The unions in which they hold membership include the International Brotherhood of Firemen and Oilers and the International Union of Operating Engineers.

GOE: 05.06.02; SIC: Any industry; SOC: 6931

◇ **SOURCES OF ADDITIONAL INFORMATION**

International Union of Operating Engineers
1125 17th Street, NW
Washington, DC 20036

◇ **RELATED ARTICLES**

Volume 1: Energy; Machining and Machinery
Volume 3: Boilermaking occupations; Industrial machinery mechanics; Power plant occupations; Stationary engineers; Water and wastewater treatment plant operators
Volume 4: Mechanical technicians

Stevedoring occupations

Definition

The stevedoring industry handles incoming and outgoing cargoes that travel by water carriers. Longshore workers tie the ships to dock.

The stevedores dock ships, load and discharge cargo from ships that dock, deliver the cargo to truckers, and keep records of all actions. Stevedores oversee the shipworkers while in port.

Stevedoring occupations
Miscellaneous Occupations

History

The history of the stevedoring industry is as old as trade shipping itself. Originally, the crew of a vessel loaded or unloaded its cargo and stores, but as sailing ships gave way to steamships that carried far more cargo, the need arose for more people to handle this increased volume. Also, because shippers paid the highest rates for delivery, it became necessary for shipowners to expedite ships through ports. A demurrage, or large fine, is levied each day for a ship tied up in port. Thus evolved a land labor force to handle cargo for outgoing shipments and to deliver newly arrived cargo into the hands of shippers.

As the need for labor on the waterfront increased, so did the scramble for jobs. Shipowners liked having a large, casual labor force that was hired when ships were working. But when there were no ships working, this labor force found no jobs available. In the 1950s, this situation changed as seniority was introduced in different ways in some ports. Also allowance was made for the increase in mechanization of moving cargo and the modernization of the piers, two changes that began to eliminate many jobs. Early retirement was encouraged, and medical benefits, vacations, and paid holidays were increased. But in certain ports, a hard core of steady workers was developed.

Many other changes have appeared since the days of sailing ships: unions, a Waterfront Commission in New York, port authorities in many cities, and the opening of the St. Lawrence Seaway for oceangoing vessels in the Great Lakes. In the ports along the Great Lakes, shippers are again feeling the need—as the East and West coasts did so many years ago—for a trained labor force for stevedoring work.

Nature of the work

Longshore workers dock ships by tying lines; they move cargo by hand or machine, or serve as porters for passenger luggage. Longshore workers include *dock workers*, or *boat loaders*, who handle cargo on the pier; *hold workers*, who work in the ship's hold, removing cargo from hooks or pallets and stowing it in place; *winch operators*, who operate the various kinds of winches that control the booms to raise or lower cargo movement; *truck loaders*, who assist commercial truck drivers in loading or unloading trucks; *hatch supervisors*, who supervise one gang of workers, consisting of dock workers, hold workers, and forklift drivers; *drivers*, who

operate the rolling stock including forklift trucks, mobile cranes, and pulling trucks; *gear workers*, who maintain and repair and, in some cases, make gear that is used in lifting cargo, and also make the save-all nets which prevent dropped cargo from falling into the water; *mechanics*, who service the industrial equipment and rolling stock; and *carpenters*, who, when required, make braces and other pieces of wood to protect cargo in the hold or on deck.

The *stevedores* are responsible for the stowing of cargo in a vessel and for all the workers on the vessel. They may be responsible for the work and safety of possibly 250 people. They get their instructions from the pier superintendent.

Shipping clerks keep records of all incoming and outgoing cargo. Checkers check over all cargo for quantity, size, condition, destination, and vessel. Cargo going out by truck is checked for identification marks, quantity, consignee, and condition. Incoming cargo must also be recorded by size. A dock boss is responsible for the work of all the checkers. Location workers are checkers who keep records of where cargo is located on the pier. Delivery or receiving clerks keep all records pertinent to the loading or discharge of a vessel, or the receiving or delivery of cargo to or from a trucker.

Timekeepers record time of all union workers on the pier, and their activity time. These records are used for billing purposes as well as payroll.

Pier superintendents operate the entire pier. They study a layout of the ship to know where to stow cargo. Cargo that is to be delivered at the next port must be the last to be loaded. They estimate the number of workers they need, and give orders for hiring. They compute the cost of operations and usually make up bills, at the same time keeping in close touch with the shipping representatives from whom they get directions. On the West Coast, the pier superintendent is often known as a "wharfinger."

Requirements

Those who work in stevedoring should be agile and able-bodied. Their work may be strenuous and sometimes dangerous, depending on weather conditions or type of cargo. They must be able to think clearly and quickly and be able to follow given orders.

The workers in the supervisory occupations, such as stevedores, dock bosses, and pier superintendents, must be able to comprehend the entire operation of loading or discharging a vessel. They must be able to deal with a fluid labor force that changes in number every day and in which inexperienced men are sometimes included.

Special requirements

Occupations for some of the stevedoring jobs require union membership. Furthermore, seniority rights in some ports mean that job openings per day go to the workers who have been working in stevedoring the longest. Thus a newcomer will have to take whatever jobs are left.

Opportunities for experience and exploration

A young person wishing to try various occupations in this field may do so by contacting the local longshore union. Those who wish to work up to be a pier superintendent may explore the possibilities of one of the maritime academies because many graduates take jobs as pier superintendents.

Related occupations

Other occupations that are similar include shipping and receiving clerks, blue collar supervisors, and small business owners.

Methods of entering

The best way of entering this field is to contact the local office of the International Longshoremen's Association.

Advancement

Those who start out on the docks will probably find themselves hold workers or truck loaders. If they are so inclined and seek to learn, they may soon operate a winch or become a forklift driver. Those who are responsible and reliable may move up to hatch supervisor or even stevedore. A clerk may advance to chief clerk. All advancements depend on the individual's ability and the need for other workers at the time.

Longshore workers use cranes to unload heavy steel cargo. Such work requires great strength.

Workers have advanced from the ranks and also from clerks and checkers to be pier superintendents. Some even go on to become steamship representatives.

Employment outlook

In some areas of the country the employment outlook is good. For instance, the Great Lakes area, in which stevedoring as an industry is greatly expanding, needs many trained workers. It has only been in the last three decades that oceangoing vessels could travel the inland lakes; prior to that, the stevedores handled a limited amount of interlakes cargo.

The employment outlook on the coasts is only moderate. Automation in loading, using conveyor belts for instance, and container cargo that is prepacked ready to be put in a ship, have changed the work habits of many piers and in many places have meant a cutback in hiring.

Although a large force of casual labor was used years ago, the trend now is for a full-time, trained hard-core work force.

Earnings

Dock workers on the East Coast in the early 1990s got an annual base wage of at least $30,000. Penalty cargoes such as explosives, damaged cargo, wet hides, and so on, result in a higher wage. Besides their base pay, stevedores are paid overtime for night work. They also have pension funds, paid holidays and vacations, and, usually, extensive medical insurance.

Clerks and checkers average more than $17,160 per year in the early 1990s. Pier superintendents made $25,000 to $42,000 or more per year, depending on the part of the country and the sizes of their piers.

Conditions of work

Piers by their very nature are on the fringes of metropolitan areas, therefore convenient to large cities for shippers, but not necessarily convenient to transportation for their personnel. Parts of all piers are covered by sheds, but most workers are usually outdoors in all kinds of weather. Cargo must be moved on and off piers in all weather because of the high cost of a ship tied up in port. Consequently, when a ship is "working," the hours may be long, starting before 8:00 A.M. and ending anywhere from 8:00 P.M. to midnight, or even on through to the next day.

Most longshore work is strenuous. But clerks and checkers and also timekeepers' work is less physical and more sedentary. Stevedores and pier superintendents, however, must know what is going on all over a pier, which necessitates much walking, running, climbing, and being in the office as much as on deck.

Social and psychological factors

Many young people go into stevedoring as their family members did before them. They love hard work and being out-of-doors and would not want an office job. Though not necessarily impressed by their role in world commerce, they may feel the lure of the sea, as they handle rubber from India, coffee from South America, or cotton goods from Japan.

GOE: 05.11, 05.12; SIC: 4491; SOC: 8313, 8723

 SOURCES OF ADDITIONAL INFORMATION

International Longshoremen's and Warehousemen's Union
1188 Franklin Street
San Francisco, CA 94109

North Atlantic Ports Association
36 Evergreen Road
Reading, MA 01867

Pacific Maritime Association
635 Sacramento Street
PO Box 7861
San Francisco, CA 94120

 RELATED ARTICLES

Volume 1: Transportation
Volume 3: Blue-collar worker supervisors; Industrial truck operators; Operating engineers; Shipping and receiving clerks

Taxi drivers

Definition

Taxi drivers operate motor vehicles to take passengers from one place to another for a specified sum, which is usually based on length of travel and time as recorded on a taximeter.

History

Taxi driving has a long and colorful history. The public hackney coach and the smaller cab appeared in England in the late eighteenth and early nineteenth centuries. These cabs were horse drawn, privately owned vehicles available for public hire and had no fixed routes. The cab was first used in the eastern part of the United States in the nineteenth century. The improvement of roads resulted in a decrease in horseback travel and an increase in carriage and cab traffic. As cities grew larger and more complex, urban transportation problems became more complicated. The result was increased opportunity for cab drivers.

The development of the gasoline engine resulted in the modern taxicab. Company-operated taxi service was an outgrowth of increased private business and adventuresome taxi drivers. The establishment of basic driver requirements and increased labor organization have also contributed to the development of present-day taxi driving.

Nature of the work

Taxicabs are an important part of the transportation system in many cities. Taxicab drivers are often required to do more than simply drive people from one place to another. They also help people with their luggage. Sometimes they pick up and deliver packages. They may also be asked to provide sight-seeing tours for visitors to a community, so it is beneficial if they are familiar with more than one area.

Taxi drivers either own their own cabs, rent cabs, or operate company-owned cabs. If they own their own cab or rent one for a long period of time, they are generally expected to clean their cab. Large companies have cleaners to take care of this task.

Taxi drivers get their passengers (called "fares") in several ways. Most cabs have two-way radio systems through which drivers are notified by a dispatcher as to where to pick up passengers. Other drivers pick up passengers at cab stands to which they return after delivering each passenger. There are also telephones at these cab stands that are used to inform drivers of requests for taxi service. Still other cab drivers park in front of buildings where there are many prospective passengers. These buildings include theaters, hotels, and railroad stations. Drivers also pick up passengers while returning to their stands or stations.

Taxi drivers are generally required to keep accurate records of their activities. They record the time and place at which they picked up passengers and record the same kind of information at the completion of the ride. They also have to keep records on the amount of fares they collect daily.

Taxi drivers are found in almost every town and city in the country, but most are concentrated in large metropolitan areas.

Requirements

Individuals who want to become taxi drivers should have good health, a good driving record, and no criminal record. In general, they should be twenty-one years of age or older. Because drivers do not do heavy repair work on their cars, taxi driving is not physically strenuous. Drivers, however, must have steady nerves. They spend much of their time driving in heavy traffic in all kinds of weather. They must also be able to get along with the many different kinds of people whom they encounter.

Formal education is not generally a requirement for entry into this occupation, but applicants would do well to have at least an eighth-grade education. Such an educational background would help them in the record-keeping phases of their work. High-school courses in driver-training and business arithmetic would also prove helpful to taxi drivers. A good trait is for the driver to be courteous.

In most large cities, taxi drivers must have a special taxicab operator's license in addition to a chauffeur's license. These special licenses are generally issued by police departments, safety departments, or public utilities commissions. To secure these special licenses, taxi drivers must pass rigid examinations including

A taxi driver notes his passenger's destination, place of pickup, and time. These records help the driver run a profitable business.

questions on traffic regulations, accident reports, insurance regulations, and street locations. Some companies help their job applicants prepare for these examinations; other drivers must prepare for these examinations by themselves by studying specially prepared booklets.

Special requirements

Taxi drivers must hold a special license, which is renewed annually and costs a small sum in most places. In some cities (New York is an example), it takes several months to acquire the proper license because of the intensive investigation into the applicant's background.

Opportunities for experience and exploration

There are two major ways to explore this occupation. First, an interested person can observe taxi drivers by riding in a taxi and asking the driver questions about the occupation. Second, an individual can visit the personnel director of a taxicab company. Older students might be able to secure a part-time position as a driver.

Related occupations

Other people working in driving occupations include semitrailer truck drivers, route sales drivers, and local truck drivers.

Methods of entering

The most common way of securing a position as a taxi driver is to apply directly to the employing officer at a taxicab company. Those who have sufficient funds can enter the field by buying their own cabs, provided they can secure a municipal permit to operate it. It may take some time to prepare for and pass the examinations required to obtain a special license to drive a taxi.

Advancement

It is difficult to advance oneself in this field. Some taxi drivers become taxi dispatchers; a small number of others become road supervisors or garage superintendents; and others save enough money to buy a cab of their own. If they are successful, they can then buy more cabs.

Employment outlook

Although comprehensive data are not available, there were approximately 96,000 full-time taxi drivers employed in the early 1990s. There were also many part-time taxi drivers. For example, in New York there were more than 12,000 part-time taxi drivers in the early 1990s.

There is a high turnover rate in this occupation. Therefore, there will always be a large number of openings. There will not, however, be a great increase in the total number of taxi drivers in the near future; more people now own cars, car rental agencies are popular, and people are moving to the suburbs. Each of these factors decreases the need for taxi drivers. There are other factors that make up for these developments. They include the increased difficulty drivers have in locating parking spaces in urban areas, the need for safety at night in urban areas, increases in bus fares, and stronger enforcement of laws against drunk driving.

Earnings

In the early 1990s, full-time taxi drivers averaged, including their tips, between $18,700 and $37,400 annually. Most worked eight to ten hours a day, five days a week. After they had subtracted overhead and driving costs, driver-owners averaged about the same earnings. Earnings fluctuate with the season and the weather. Winter is generally the busiest season, and snow and rain generally produce a busy day.

Most taxi drivers are given a percentage of the fares they collect. Taxicab companies usually pay drivers between 40 and 50 percent of total fares. Other drivers work on a salary plus commission basis. A few drivers are guaranteed minimum daily or weekly wages. Drivers who rent their cabs keep all receipts above the rental price. Tips are an important portion of the earnings of taxi drivers. They generally amount to 15 to 20 percent or more of total fares.

Most taxi drivers do not enjoy the fringe benefits of other workers. They generally do not receive pensions or severance pay.

Conditions of work

Taxi drivers put in long hours of work. Many drivers work nine to ten hours a day for five or six days a week. They do not receive overtime pay. Drivers who work day hours generally start work between 6:00 A.M. and 8:00 A.M. The night shift starts between 3:00 P.M. and 5:00 P.M. Many drivers work Sundays and holidays.

There is a close relationship between general economic conditions and the earnings of taxi drivers. There is more competition for less business when the economy is declining.

Social and psychological factors

Taxi drivers must be able to get along well with all kinds of people. They have to deal with many difficult and trying people without losing their tempers. In addition, they work under a considerable amount of nervous tension. They drive in heavy traffic in all kinds of weather. Often, they are urged to proceed as fast as possible by passengers. Those who comply run the risk of being apprehended for speeding and losing their licenses or of being involved in an automobile accident. Taxi drivers must be able to drive well and safely under constant pressure. For big-city drivers, there is also considerable danger of robbery.

Taxi drivers have little direct supervision. This factor is a desirable aspect of taxi driving. Those who own their cabs have even more freedom. They can set their own hours and decide where they want to work. They must, however, also develop considerable self-discipline, for their earnings are dependent on their fares.

In large cities, a number of taxi drivers belong to labor unions. The main union to which most belong is the International Brotherhood of Teamsters, Chauffeurs, Warehousemen, and Helpers of America (Ind.).

GOE: 09.03.02; SIC: 4121; SOC: 8216

◇ **SOURCES OF ADDITIONAL INFORMATION**

International Taxicab Association
3849 Farragut Avenue
Kensington, MD 20895

Transportation Communications International
3 Research Place
Rockville, MD 20850

◇ **RELATED ARTICLES**

Volume 3: Bus drivers, intercity and local transit; Truck drivers, local and over-the-road

Transmission and distribution occupations

Definition

These workers employed in the electric light and power industry are primarily occupied with getting electric power to the users.

History

The production of electricity started with the discovery of the electric battery by Alessandro Volta in 1800. The development of the dynamo started with the making of electromagnets by William Sturgeon in 1836. Arc lighting, which was first demonstrated by Sir Humphry Davy, was used to provide illumination for lighthouses and streets as early as 1860. This form of lighting was not practical for home use. This was changed with the invention of a practical light bulb by Thomas A. Edison in 1879. Three years later, the first lighting system was installed in New York. In 1887, a power line of about 30 miles in length and carrying more than 8,000 volts was erected in France. In 1895, an electric generating plant was built at Niagara Falls. The development of oil-insulated transformers made it possible to deliver electric power over great distances. In 1914, it was possible to send a current of 150,000 volts over aerial transmission lines. There were problems, however, in the underground transmission of power. Several procedures were tried and dismissed, but the development of lead-sheathed cable made it possible to transmit a current of more than 100,000 volts by 1925. The demand for electricity came when improvements in the design and production methods made it possible to produce a cheap electric light bulb that had a long life. The fluorescent light had its initial start with the invention of the mercury-vapor arc lamp in 1901. However, it was not put on the market until 1938 because of certain basic difficulties in the design.

Nature of the work

One of the basic problems in the distribution of electric power is to carry a continuous and un-interrupted flow of energy that must withstand various atmospheric conditions.

The flow of electric energy is regulated by load dispatchers. They are guided in their work by charts based on previous records and weather conditions. For example, on a hot day when air-conditioning systems, fans, and refrigerators are put to maximum use, additional electricity will be required.

Load dispatchers issue orders by telephone for the production of energy and subsequent release to lines, based on the allocation of load, equipment available for operation, and interaction with the power systems of other companies. Switchboard and substation operators make the necessary adjustments in equipment under their care. The load dispatchers are constantly informed of the state of the transmission system by means of a pilot board. Various meters and recorders tell them how much electricity is flowing and to what area. They constantly keep informed, through master diagrams and panel boards, of the conditions existing throughout the system. They redistribute the loads, direct the switching necessary to isolate the trouble, and make other adjustments to maintain the service in emergency situations, such as fires, storms, or equipment failures. They arrange for the removal of service and restoration of service of lines and equipment requiring repair or maintenance. They keep records of normal and emergency operations performed on their shift and notify proper authorities of the conditions needing attention.

The *substation operators* regulate the flow of electricity through the distribution lines to the consumer by manipulating the switches on a control board. They observe and record readings of switchboard instruments and watt-hour meters to provide data on the amounts of electricity used for the substation operation and amounts distributed from the station. They notify the main generating plant by telephone of the amount of electricity received by the station. These operators connect or break the flow of current by manipulating levers that control circuit breakers. In substations where alternating current is changed to direct current to meet needs of special users, the operator controls converters that perform the necessary changes simultaneously.

The *line installers* erect power lines consisting of poles, cables, and auxiliary equipment, needed to conduct electricity from power plant to the place of use. They instruct and assist the ground helper in erecting the poles; climb and attach the cross arms with lag screws; nail, screw, or bolt insulators, lightning arrestors, transformers, and other auxiliary equipment to the structure or building; and string the cable from pole to pole or building with the assistance of the ground crew, exercising care so that the proper sag is left in the cables to avoid breaking under changing atmospheric conditions. They splice and solder cables for connections and attach the wire from the auxiliary equipment to the power line, using pliers, and wrap insulation tape around the connections.

Ground helpers aid in the setting up of overhead electric lines by digging holes with a shovel and raising poles by means of a hand winch, tamping the dirt around the bottom of each pole to hold it in place. They pass the correct tools and equipment from the ground by tying them to a line and pulling them within the reach of the line repairer. They may also assist (from the ground) in stringing cables.

Troubleshooters are expert line workers who have the technical ability to service transmission or power lines that are not functioning properly. Because they work with energized lines, such as lines with electricity in them, they are required to use rubber gloves, high-voltage flexible jumpers, and safety platforms. By using proper safety procedures, they minimize the danger of an electric shock or burn. Similar procedures are used when repairs or replacements are made on energized lines when the interruption of electricity is regarded as highly impractical or costly.

The troubleshooters examine the power equipment, such as wires and transformers, supplying current to the troubled areas to determine if the broken, hanging, or insufficiently insulated wires or loose connections are causing the trouble. They clear and repair or replace lines that are out of service due to fire, floods, storms, or other causes and replace defective equipment.

In some regions of the country, helicopters are used to inspect transmission lines. This procedure is necessary because lines and equipment deteriorate from vibration, defective insulation, corrosion, and poor original design.

In certain sections of large cities, underground power lines may be used because of the difficulty of erecting poles. A cable splicer working in tunnels does the installation.

The work of *cable splicers* is similar to that of the line repairer's. When cables are installed, cable splicers pull the cable through the conduit

A troubleshooter works on some defective power lines. He is equipped with rubber gloves and high voltage jumpers to avoid electrical shock.

and join cables at connecting points. They spend most of their time in repairing and maintaining cables and changing the layout of the system. They must know the arrangement of the wiring system and must make sure that the conductors do not become mixed up between the substation and the customer's premises.

Requirements

The workers in the distribution occupations learn their trade by on-the-job training. Three to seven years' experience as an assistant or junior operator is needed before an individual can operate a large substation. Seven to ten years of experience as a switchboard or substation operator are needed before an individual can become a load dispatcher. On-the-job training is supplemented with instruction, especially when new devices or equipment are installed.

There are two ways in which an individual can become a line repairer or cable splicer: on-the-job training or apprenticeship program. The apprenticeship training program requires the individual to attend classes to learn blueprint reading, electrical theory, transmission theory, and electrical codes and rules. In each method the trainee initially works as a ground helper and progresses to the more difficult tasks performed by the line repairer. Each program is four years long. Some experts feel that the apprenticeship program is a better way of learning the trade because of the thoroughness of the training.

The training of cable splicers is similar to that of line installers. Workers begin as helpers, and as their knowledge of the job increases they progress to more difficult jobs. The trade is learned in about four years.

Those individuals interested in linework should be in good physical condition since climbing poles and lifting lines and equipment are strenuous work. They must also have steady nerves—as should troubleshooters, especially—and good balance.

Special requirements

There are no special requirements for this work. Most persons in this particular industry belong to a union.

Opportunities for experience and exploration

High-school courses in physics, mathematics, and shop work provide a test of the individual's aptitude, interest, and temperament for these occupations. Shop courses in machines, wood, or electricity are helpful for those who would like to be line workers or cable splicers. Tinkering with cars, building electronic kits, or assembling model airplanes or trains are ways in which students can test their manual dexterity, mechanical inclinations, and ability to follow drawings and plans. Some of the military services provide direct experience and training in these occupational fields. A field trip to a utility or transmission erection site will give an overall view of the variety of work done.

Related occupations

Other workers with similar aptitudes include power plant operators, nuclear energy technicians, electricians, electrical repairers, and electrical technicians.

Methods of entering

Those who wish to enter the transmission and distribution occupations must receive appropriate training before they can become fully qualified. Before individuals are considered for a vacancy, their background, aptitudes, and personal qualities are evaluated. To be placed in one of the few openings available in the apprenticeship program, a person must have the approval of a joint (labor-management) committee. In the distribution occupations, one may start out as an assistant or junior operator.

Advancement

Because the basic method of preparing workers for the transmission and distribution occupations is by means of on-the-job training, the opportunities for advancement are built in. A ground helper who has the necessary aptitudes and interests can become a line repairer or troubleshooter by means of on-the-job training. Line installers or cable splicers who have an excellent knowledge of the technical phases of the work and supervisory ability can become crew chiefs and supervisors. Load dispatchers and substation operators all advance to these positions from other jobs.

Employment outlook

About one-fifth of the total number of workers in the electric power industry are involved in transmission and distribution work. A general increase in the output of electric energy will continue through the next decade. The increase in the number of transmission and distribution workers will only be slight.

There are several factors responsible for this slow rate of gain. The use of power equipment in setting wooden poles has diminished the number of line installers and ground helpers. Currently, many utilities contract for the construction of steel towers rather than building their own. The number of cable splicers has shown a slight increase because of improved methods in making a splice. The use of automatic equipment and telemetric devices has minimized the need for substation operators. Despite the increased use of automated devices, several thousand new workers will be needed each year for the transmission and distribution of electricity.

Earnings

In the early 1990s, the pay for the workers in these occupations varied with the job and region of the country in which they worked. Average salaries of the various trades were between about $20,700 and $27,000. Most utility companies provide extra benefits such as vacations, pension plans, hospitalization, and life insurance. Pay rates for emergency situations vary according to contracts.

Conditions of work

The work of line installers and repairers is done outdoors in a variety of places and weather conditions. They are required to climb poles and towers to attach the lines. At times they are required to work in poor weather conditions to make emergency repairs. Work with energized lines may cause electric shock or burns, although, when proper procedures are used, the danger of getting hurt is rather minute. Other hazards are being hurt by falling objects and injuries from lifting material. Load dispatchers and substation operators work in well-lighted and ventilated buildings. Cable splicers work in confined and sometimes damp spaces underground.

Social and psychological factors

The workers in this field are all part of a large team, some indoors, some out on the lines, and some in underground tunnels. The work can be hard and the hours long, and they know an emergency situation can demand their attention immediately. Thunderstorms and snowstorms can knock power out over a large area. With underground cables this is less of a problem but it is still a regular occurrence. However, they find compensation in their jobs and know that the continuous flow of electricity and power depends on the work of each person on the team.

GOE: 05.06.01; SIC: 4911; SOC: 393

◇ **SOURCES OF ADDITIONAL INFORMATION**

National Electrical Manufacturer's Association
2101 L Street, NW
Washington, DC 20037

International Brotherhood of Electrical Workers
1125 15th Street, NW
Washington, DC 20005

◇ **RELATED ARTICLES**

Volume 1: Energy
Volume 3: Electricians; Electrical repairers; Line installers and cable splicers; Power plant occupations; Telephone and PBX installers and repairers
Volume 4: Automatic equipment technicians; Electrical technicians

Truck drivers, local and over-the-road

Definition

Local truck drivers, or *short haulers,* operate a truck to transport materials, merchandise, or equipment within a limited area. They may load and unload the truck by hand or by using a cable-winch or hoist. They are frequently assisted by truck-driver helpers. They may be expected to make minor mechanical repairs and to keep their trucks in good working order.

Over-the-road truck drivers, or *long haulers*, are also known as *trailer-truck drivers*. They haul goods and materials over long distances in gasoline or diesel powered tractor-trailers, frequently driving at night. Occasionally they load and unload their cargoes and make minor repairs to the vehicles.

History

The trucking industry began early in the twentieth century shortly after the invention of the automobile. Prior to this time, horse-drawn wagons were the major means of local distribution. The diversification of industrial processes and the improvement of highways made it necessary and possible for goods and products to be transported from one section of the country to another. As the design of transport trucks and our superhighways improved rapidly, more trucks were needed to meet the demands of the expanding population in our country. The trucking industry met these demands and has continued to grow.

Nature of the work

The work done by local truck drivers varies with the kind of truck driven and the area in which the work is done. All local drivers, however, must be skilled drivers who can maneuver their vehicles through congested streets without accident. They must be able to pull into tight parking spaces, negotiate narrow alleys, and back up to loading platforms.

Over-the-road truck drivers generally operate gasoline or diesel powered tractor-trailers, which are large and expensive. These drivers generally haul goods and materials over long distances and frequently drive at night. Whereas many other truck drivers spend a considerable portion of their time loading and unloading materials, over-the-road drivers spend most of their working time in actual driving. If, however, deliveries are made in the evening when local loading crews are not available, the drivers are sometimes expected to do their own unloading. Drivers of long-distance moving vans do more loading and unloading work than do other long-haul drivers.

Local drivers of light trucks (under three tons capacity) pick up and deliver light loads. They may load and unload their trucks, but they do not normally make deliveries over an established route. Such drivers are responsible for keeping their trucks in good working con-

dition and for reporting mechanical failures. They may be required to make minor repairs and to change tires. They are also responsible for the contents of the trucks and, in addition, must check the freight bills to ensure accuracy of delivery. They are expected to provide efficient service and to turn in daily records of the transactions they have conducted.

Local drivers of heavy trucks (over three tons capacity) generally have someone to help them with the loading and unloading of their freight and perform duties similar to those of the light-truck driver. Some heavy-truck drivers operate such special trucks as dump trucks and oil trucks and are required to operate mechanical levers, pedals, or other equipment. Drivers of moving vans generally have a crew of helpers to aid in the loading and unloading of household furniture and office equipment.

The transport driver transports new automobiles or trucks from manufacturers to dealers, usually over long distances. The transport driver drives new vehicles onto trailers under their own power and secures them in place with chains and clamps to prevent them from swaying and rolling. The transport driver drives the trailer-truck to its destination and removes the vehicles from the trailer.

Over-the-road drivers must be skilled in their work. They must be able to back up their huge trailers to loading platforms. Other tasks include inspecting the truck before and after trips, preparing reports on the condition of the truck, and keeping a daily log. The skills of over-the-road truck drivers differ from those required for the operation of heavy or light conventional trucks. Trailer-trucks vary in construction, chiefly in the number of wheels and in length, and the operators of one type of truck may be required to undergo a short training period to familiarize themselves with the operation of other types.

Over-the-road and local drivers have two kinds of employers: private carriers and for-hire carriers. Chain food stores or manufacturing plants that transport their own goods are examples of private carriers. There are two kinds of for-hire carriers: trucking companies serving the general public (common carriers) and trucking firms transporting goods under contract to certain companies (contract carriers). Common carriers employ most of the drivers who work on long intercity runs.

Drivers that work independently and own their vehicle usually do all maintenance and repair work. They also find their own customers who need goods transported, through advertisements or personal references. They may establish long-term contracts for shipping with one or two clients.

Requirements

An individual aspiring to a career as a truck driver should have good physical health, at least 20/40 (with or without glasses or lenses) eyesight, and normal depth perception. Local truck drivers should have some mechanical ability, be able to lift heavy objects, and enjoy physical activity and driving.

Over-the-road drivers must be constantly aware of the need to be safe and courteous in their work. Since these drivers spend much of their time alone, they must be able to stay awake under driving conditions that are frequently monotonous.

Minimal qualifications for over-the-road drivers have been established by the Interstate Commerce Commission. These include the following requirements: drivers must be at least twenty-one years of age, able-bodied, with good hearing and vision; they must be able to read and speak English, must have at least one year's driving experience (private automobiles included), and must have good driving records.

Many employers have additional standards. They prefer to employ drivers who are at least twenty-five years old and who have had considerable driving experience. These high standards are necessary because the trucks driven generally cost as much as $60,000 to $80,000, and the freight carried inside them is often worth more than $100,000.

A high-school education is desirable for a truck driver, but many companies employ individuals having only two years of high school and who are twenty-one years of age or older. High-school courses in driver training and in automotive mechanics are undoubtedly helpful. All truck drivers are almost always required to have a commercial driver's license, also called a chauffeur's license.

Special requirements

Special requirements for local truck drivers include driving tests and written examinations on safety regulations as well as intensive physical examinations.

Over-the-road truck drivers might be required to undergo an extensive physical examination as well as written traffic and driving tests. Other tests given by employing companies include tests of sharpness and field of vision, reaction time, the ability to judge speed, and emotional stability. There are also road tests in which applicants are expected to demonstrate that they can handle the kind of vehi-

On long-distance hauls, truck drivers often work during odd hours in order to avoid heavy traffic.

cle they will be operating under a variety of conditions and circumstances.

Opportunities for experience and exploration

High-school students interested in becoming truck drivers might gain some experience as a driver's helper during summer vacations. They should also acquire as much driving experience as possible in both private automobiles and trucks. Many people also gain experience in the armed forces. Students can arrange to have personal interviews with employers of local or over-the-road truck drivers, or with the drivers themselves.

Related occupations

Other driving occupations include industrial-truck operators, taxi drivers, city bus drivers, intercity bus drivers, route sales drivers, and locomotive engineers.

Methods of entering

There are several ways of entering this field of work. Local truck drivers may start as extra drivers and secure experience when regular drivers are ill or on vacation. Promotional events and seasonal demands offer many opportunities for extra drivers. Other local truck drivers secure jobs upon discharge from the armed forces if they have had enough experience with trucks. Many others start out as driver helpers or dock workers.

Jobs are obtained by applying to trucking firms, local and state employment agencies, or by following newspaper ads.

Over-the-road drivers can gain experience as local truck drivers and at a later time apply for entry into the brief training program of a trucking firm that employs long-distance truck drivers. Intercity bus driving is another occupation that many people use as a means of gaining the experience necessary to become an over-the-road truck driver. Most individuals who enter and complete on-the-job training programs make their first few trips with an instructor or an experienced driver. Drivers who work for common carriers generally begin by filling in for regular drivers or helping out when extra trips are necessary. Seniority is the basis for becoming a regular driver with common carriers. Private carriers, on the other hand, are more likely to assign a regular route to beginners.

Advancement

There are a number of ways in which local truck drivers may advance themselves. Some drivers secure jobs as dispatchers or advance to jobs as terminal managers or supervisors when they have seniority and demonstrate competence. Other local truck drivers use their experience to become over-the-road drivers and receive higher wages. Still other local truck drivers with some business ability and sufficient capital organize their own trucking companies and go into business for themselves.

Over-the-road drivers have more limited opportunities for advancement. Some drivers may become safety supervisors, driver supervisors, or dispatchers. The vast majority of over-the-road drivers, however, see advancement as a route that will yield higher earnings.

Employment outlook

Although there is work for local truck drivers in even the smallest towns, most of the 1.7 million local truck drivers employed in the early 1990s were located in and around large metropolitan areas.

There were more than 575,000 over-the-road drivers in the United States in the early 1990s. The companies for which they work usually have their headquarters in much smaller communities.

More jobs for truck drivers become available annually than for almost any other occupation, but so many applicants want to do this work that the field is somewhat hard to enter.

The employment outlook for local truck drivers is moderately favorable. There will be a need for more truck drivers in the foreseeable future because of such factors as the expected increase in freight volume, the continued growth of shopping centers in suburban areas, and the high replacement needs among truck drivers. There are thousands of positions a year created by deaths and retirements alone.

Several factors will also serve to reduce somewhat the number of local truck drivers needed in the next decade. These factors include the trend toward larger deliveries to retail outlets and the introduction of new equipment that will reduce the amount of time required to make deliveries.

There will be an increased need for over-the-road truck drivers as well as local drivers. The increase in industrial activity, continued decentralization of industry, the increase in our suburban population, and improvements in the design of trucks and trailers are all factors supporting this need.

There are also several factors that may restrict the need for over-the-road drivers. Among these are recent changes in methods of transporting goods, such as putting trailers on railroad flat cars (piggyback); better highways, which enable trucks to cover longer distances; and liberalized trucking laws, which enable a truck to carry larger loads. It should also be noted, however, that over-the-road truck drivers are more likely to keep their positions during a recession than many other workers. As businesses reduce their orders during a recession, they will be less likely to order materials by railroad carload.

Earnings

Although some local truck drivers are guaranteed minimum or weekly wages, most of these workers are paid an hourly wage and receive extra compensation for overtime work. Wages vary considerably and are dependent upon the area in which the drivers work, the companies for which they work, the size of truck driven, the kind of product hauled, and the policy and strength of the local union. In the early 1990s hourly salaries for local drivers averaged $12.30 and for all drivers, $15.80.

There is not great variability in the wages received by over-the-road truck drivers. Long-distance truck driving is a highly unionized field, and union-employee contracts are fairly uniform throughout the country. These drivers earned an average of $33,200 per year in the early 1990s, with many making more than $60,000. Drivers for class I firms that had gross operating revenues of more than $1 million earned even more.

Local truck drivers generally belong to unions and enjoy most of the fringe benefits that accompany membership. Health and insurance provisions are contained in labor-management contracts covering most local truck drivers, and pension plans incorporated in these contracts are applicable to more than three-fourths of the local drivers. Paid vacations are also enjoyed by most local drivers. The uniforms worn by local truck drivers are generally provided by the employer.

Conditions of work

Some local drivers work a forty-hour week while others work eight hours a day, six days a week. Some drivers must work at night or very early in the morning. A few drivers are assigned routes when they report to work each day, while others have regular routes.

It is usually common for over-the-road truck drivers to work at least fifty hours a week. However, regulations of the Interstate Commerce Commission state that no driver may be on duty for more than sixty hours in any seven-day period. After drivers have driven for ten hours, they must be off duty for at least eight hours before they can drive again.

Long-distance drivers are required to spend a considerable amount of time away from their homes and families. Many drivers make two or three trips a week. Drivers on this type of run may remain with the truck in some cases for more than one hundred hours. The necessity of sustained driving at night is also fatiguing. Over-the-road truck drivers are involved in an unusually small number of accidents because these drivers have much skill and because of the rigid safety regulations governing their selection and work.

GOE: 05.08.01, 05.12.04; SIC: 421; SOC: 8213, 8214

 SOURCES OF ADDITIONAL INFORMATION

American Trucking Associations
2200 Mill Road
Alexandria, VA 22314

Professional Truck Driver Institute of America
8788 Elk Grove Boulevard, Suite M
Elk Grove, CA 95624

 RELATED ARTICLES

Volume 1: Transportation
Volume 3: Bus drivers, intercity and local transit; Industrial truck operators; Stevedoring occupations; Taxi drivers

Wastewater treatment plant operators

Definition

Wastewater treatment plant operators and *attendants* control and maintain the equipment in sewage treatment plants, removing organic or nonorganic waste materials from water or rendering them harmless. They regulate the flow of sewage into the plant and through the processes of filtering, settling, aeration, and sludge digestion, sometimes collecting samples and performing laboratory tests, and ensure that the water leaving the plant meets government standards of cleanliness. Operators also keep records, make minor repairs to equipment, supervise attendants and other workers, and may operate power-generating equipment.

History

Water purity and the disposal of wastes have been of concern to civilizations since ancient times. The Minoans on the island of Crete built sewers and water lines of terra-cotta around 2500 B.C. The Roman aqueducts were marvelous feats of engineering, and the Cloaca Maxima sewer, built in the third century B.C. to drain the marshy ground around the Forum, is still visited by tourists today. Sanitation methods, however, were limited. Garbage and human wastes were collected from homes and the streets, but little was known about the health hazards of handling such refuse. As cities populations grew, sanitation became a necessity, but modern sanitation engineering dates back only to about 1850 for water supplies and 1870 for sewage.

Today's wastewater treatment plants are highly sophisticated, complex operations, designed to meet increasingly stringent government standards. With the adoption of the Federal Water Pollution Control Act of 1972, a system of uniform controls was put into effect. In accordance with this law, as amended by the Clean Water Act of 1977, it is illegal for industry to discharge any pollutant without a permit. Industries that send wastes to municipal treatment plants must meet minimum standards and pretreat the wastes so they do not damage the treatment facilities. Standards are also imposed on the treatment plants, controlling the quality of the water they discharge.

Nature of the work

Wastewater treatment plants are essential to modern civilization. Without them, domestic and industrial wastes would accumulate, and our water would rapidly become unfit for any use. Disease would spread among the population; fish and wildlife would die off; swimming, boating, and other recreational activities would become unpleasant as well as dangerous; and certain industries would be unable to function. The workers who operate these plants control the equipment and processes that remove the wastes or make them harmless and return the water in sanitary condition, safe for human consumption or other use.

Waste materials from homes, public buildings, and industrial plants are transported by water through sewer pipes to sewage treatment plants. These wastes include both organic and nonorganic solids, some of which may be toxic, such as lead or mercury. Wastewater-treatment-plant operators (sometimes known as sewage plant operators) regulate the flow of incoming sewage by adjusting valves and gates either manually or by remote control, and monitor the various meters and gauges that indicate when the equipment and processes are working properly. They operate and maintain the pumps, engines, and generators that move the raw sewage through the treatment processes of filtration, settling, aeration, and sludge digestion. These workers operate chemical-feeding devices, collect sewage samples and conduct laboratory tests, and maintain the proper level of chlorine in the wastewater. They keep a log of the operations, in which they record the meter and gauge readings, and make minor repairs on valves, pumps, and other equipment, using common hand tools, such as gauges, wrenches, and pliers, as well as special tools. Operators may supervise attendants and helpers who perform routine tasks and maintenance work. Plant operators sometimes have to work under emergency conditions, such as when a heavy rainstorm floods the sewer pipes, exceeding the plant's capacity, or when there is a chlorine gas leak or an oxygen deficiency within the plant.

The duties of plant operators vary considerably depending on the type and size of the plant. In smaller plants, one person may be responsible for the entire operation, including making repairs, keeping records, handling complaints, doing maintenance work, and possibly running and servicing the power-generating equipment for steam and electricity. In larger plants, where duties are specialized, personnel may include *waterworks pump-station* and *water-treatment-plant operators*, chemists, engineers, laboratory technicians, mechanics, helpers, supervisors, and a superintendent.

To meet the elevated standards set by the Federal Water Pollution Control Act of 1972, as amended by the Clean Water Act of 1977, wastewater treatment plant operators are required to operate increasingly more sophisticated systems.

Requirements

In some states the minimum educational requirement for wastewater-treatment-plant operators is a high-school diploma. Even where this is not the case, employers generally prefer applicants with a high-school education or its equivalent. To increase their chances for employment and promotion, some individuals obtain additional, specialized education. There are some two-year programs available leading to an associate degree in wastewater technology. Persons who complete a one-year program are awarded certificates. The programs provide a good general knowledge of water pollution control and prepare students to become operators.

Most beginners, however, acquire their skills on the job. They are hired as attendants or operators-in-training and work under the direction of an experienced operator. The trainees learn by observing the older operator and performing routine tasks, such as recording meter readings, collecting samples of wastewater and sludge, and doing simple maintenance and repair work on pumps, electric motors, and valves. In addition, they do general cleaning and maintenance of plant equipment and property. Some of the larger plants have a formal training program for beginners.

Training courses are offered by most state water pollution control agencies to improve the skills and broaden the knowledge of operators. The courses cover principles of treatment processes and process control, odors and their control, safety, chlorination, sedimentation, biological oxidation, sludge treatment and disposal, and flow measurements. Courses on related subjects are also available by correspondence. Some employers pay part of the tuition for operators who take courses leading to a college degree in science or engineering.

Wastewater-treatment-plant operators need to possess some mechanical aptitude, be competent in basic mathematics, and have the physical agility to climb ladders and move easily around heavy machinery.

A wastewater treatment plant chemist conducts lab tests to determine and monitor the levels of pollutants in wastewater.

Special requirements

A civil service exam may be required for some positions, particularly in large cities and towns. The written exam tests the applicant's mechanical aptitude, math skills, and general intelligence and education.

In forty-four states, certification of supervisors and certain operators is mandatory. Workers who qualify must pass an exam demonstrating their ability to oversee treatment plant operations. In the remaining states, certification is voluntary. Typically, the class of certification depends on the size of the plant. Information or requirements can be obtained by contacting local government offices.

Opportunities for experience and exploration

Machine shop courses offer a good way for students to test their mechanical aptitude for this occupation. Preparation for a career in wastewater treatment should also include courses in mathematics. If a local vocational school or college offers a program in wastewater technology, high-school students may visit the enrollment office to obtain detailed information about requirements and courses. A field trip to a wastewater treatment plant would afford the opportunity to observe the various processes in action and to interview operators about the practical aspects of the work.

Part-time and summer employment as helpers in a wastewater treatment plant offers the best experience, but jobs in any kind of machine shop provide the opportunity to become familiar with handling machinery and common tools.

Related occupations

Waste management and sanitation are growing fields with a number of career opportunities. Other occupations to consider include sanitation engineers, refuse collectors, environmental biologists, and ecologists.

Methods of entering

Graduates of high schools or wastewater technology programs may avail themselves of the services of the school placement office or may obtain information about job opportunities from state or local water pollution control agencies or local offices of the state employment service.

Individuals may also apply for jobs directly at the personnel offices of wastewater treatment plants.

Advancement

Skilled operators with managerial ability may advance to the position of supervisor or superintendent. The qualifications necessary for becoming a superintendent, however, depend on the size and complexity of the plant. In smaller plants, where the superintendent often also serves as an operator, a high-school diploma and increasingly responsible work experience may be sufficient for promotion. In the larger plants being built to meet new water pollution control standards, educational requirements are rising along with the sophistication and complexity of the systems. It is not unusual for superintendents of large plants to have degrees in engineering or science. Operators seeking supervisory positions often must have training in management techniques.

Another route to advancement is to transfer to a related job. A few operators go to work for state water pollution control agencies. As technicians, they monitor and provide technical assistance to plants throughout the state. For these jobs, vocational-technical school or community college training is preferred. Other experienced operators find employment with industrial wastewater treatment plants, companies that sell wastewater treatment equipment and chemicals, engineering consultant firms, or vocational-technical schools.

Employment outlook

In the early 1990s there were approximately 90,000 water and sewage treatment plant operators in the United States. Most of them were employed by local governments; others by the federal government, the utility companies, and sanitary services. Of the almost 2,000 that worked for the federal government, the majority were attached to the armed forces.

Employment is expected to grow about as fast as the average for all occupations throughout the next decade. Some new jobs will be created to handle the limited expansion of wastewater treatment, but most openings will arise when older, experienced workers retire, die, or transfer to other occupations. Operators with formal training will have an advantage when applying for new positions or being considered for promotions.

Workers in wastewater treatment plants are rarely laid off, even during a recession, because treatment of water pollutants is an operation that is essential to the welfare of the country. Employment of operators is distributed throughout the country in proportion to the population, with most jobs in large cities and towns. In small towns, operators may work only part-time or may have to handle other duties as well.

Earnings

Salaries for wastewater-treatment-plant operators vary depending on the size of the plant, the complexity of the job, and the operator's level of certification. In the early 1990s, operators earned an average of $22,440 per year. Trainees were paid about 90 percent as much as operators. Supervisors of treatment plants had average annual salaries of $26,000. Many experienced operators made as much as $32,400 annually, and supervisors of large plants, $36,000 or more.

Conditions of work

Wastewater treatment plants are in continuous operation. Operators work in shifts around the clock, including weekends and holidays, and often work extra hours during emergencies.

Operators work both indoors and out. They must contend with noisy machinery and may have to tolerate unpleasant odors, despite the use of chlorine and other chemicals to minimize the problem. In addition, allergy sufferers may be affected by the dust and other substances in the air.

The job involves stooping, reaching, and climbing. Operators often get their clothes dirty. Safety hazards are presented by such conditions as slippery walkways, dangerous gases, and malfunctioning equipment.

Social and psychological factors

The essential nature of this occupation should be a source of satisfaction, since the entire population depends on clean water. Dealing with the wastes of a society, however, is a job that many people would find unpleasant. Persons entering this field must approach it as a challenge; its problems increase with the population and the ever-stricter government standards.

To compensate for the drawbacks, operators enjoy greater job security than many workers in other fields.

GOE: 05.12.07; SIC: 4952; SOC: 691

◇ SOURCES OF ADDITIONAL INFORMATION

For a copy of Environmental Protection Careers Guidebook, published in 1980 by the U.S. Department of Labor and the U.S. Environmental Protection Agency that contains a list of post-secondary environmental education programs (including wastewater programs), a chapter on water treatment occupations, and other useful information, send $7.50 to:

Superintendent of Documents
U.S. Government Printing Office
Washington, DC 20402

Further information on training is available from:

National Environmental Training Association
8687 Via De Ventura
Suite 214
Scottsdale, AZ 85258

Water Pollution Control Federation
601 Wythe Street
Alexandria, VA 22314

◇ RELATED ARTICLES

Volume 1: Waste Management
Volume 3: Boilermaker occupations; Electricians; Electrical repairers; Industrial machinery mechanics; Stationary engineers; Stationary firers, boiler tenders
Volume 4: Chemical technicians; Electrical technicians; Mechanical technicians

Photographic Credits

Index

Apparel manufacturing
  technicians, **4:** 261
Appliance repairers,
  3: 569-73
Applications programmers,
  4: 32
Applied geophysicists,
  2: 270
Applied Mathematics,
  1: 287
Applied mathematics,
  2: 396
Applied research chemists,
  1: 104
Applied-research
  technicians, **4:** 140
Applied statisticians,
  2: 649
Appointed officials, **1:** 371
Appraisers, **1:** 405, **2:** 44-48
Aquatic biologists, **2:** 64
Aquatic recreation staff,
  1: 416
Arboretum or botanical
  garden supervisors,
  4: 308
Arc welders, **3:** 718
Archaeologists, **2:** 33-37
Architects, **1:** 139, **2:** 37-41
Architect's assistants,
  4: 117-18, 155
Architectural and building
  construction technicians,
  4: 116-22
Architectural drafters,
  2: 179, **4:** 118, 156
Architectural sales
  representatives, **4:** 118
Archivists, **1:** 266, **2:** 41-44,
  296
Armed Forces recreation
  staff, **1:** 411
Armored-car guards and
  drivers, **3:** 308
Arrangers, **2:** 424
Art appraisers, **2:** 46
Art conservators, **2:** 420
  textiles, **1:** 469
Art department staff,
  1: 411
Art designers
  toys and games, **1:** 476
Art directors, **1:** 12, 278,
  2: 22, 122, 166
Art-metal designers, **2:** 166
Art staff
  book, **1:** 79
  broadcasting, **1:** 85
  magazine, **1:** 278
  motion picture, **1:** 321
  newspaper, **1:** 326
  recording, **1:** 411
Art teachers, **2:** 17, 674
Art therapists, **2:** 681
Articles editors, **2:** 706
Artifacts conservators,
  2: 33

Artificial breeding
  technicians, **4:** 291
Artificial breeding
  laboratory technicians,
  4: 291
Artificial insemination
  technicians, **4:** 291
Artist agents, **1:** 412
Artist and repertoire
  managers, **2:** 8
Artist and repertoire staff
  and executives, **1:** 411
Artist and repertoire
  workers, **2:** 574
Artist managers, **1:** 412
Artists, **2:** 454-57, **4:** 347,
  348. *See also* Painters;
  Sculptors
  commercial, **2:** 120-24
  layout, **2:** 121
  performing, **1:** 344-351,
  2: 574
Artists and designers,
  1: 135-141
  ceramics industry, **1:** 98
Artists' managers,
  2: 373-76
Artist's models, **3:** 280
Asphalt paving machine
  operators, **3:** 619-22
Asphalt paving supervisors,
  3: 620
Assayers, **2:** 92
Associate structures
  designers, **4:** 146
Assemblers, **1:** 272,
  3: 573-76, 764
Assembly repairers, **3:** 504
Assessment commissioners,
  2: 45
Assessors, **2:** 44-48
Assignment editors, **2:** 706
Assistant buyers, **2:** 73
Assistant city managers,
  2: 99
Assistant directors
  student personnel,
  2: 116
Assistant field or
  exploration geologists,
  4: 255
Assistant instrumentation-
  design technicians,
  4: 205
Assistant logging
  superintendents, **4:** 303
Assistant principals, **2:** 621
Assistant production
  managers, **4:** 158, 214
Assistant plant engineers,
  4: 118
Associate directors
  associations, **2:** 48
Associate editors
  newspapers, **1:** 326
Associate municipal
  designers, **4:** 146

Association executives,
  2: 48-50
Astronauts, **1:** 43, 46,
  2: 50-55
Astronomers, **1:** 360,
  2: 55-60
Astrophysicists, **2:** 56
Athletes, **1:** 456, **2:** 523-26.
  See also Coaching; Sports
Athletic directors, **2:** 118
Athletics instructors,
  2: 641
Atomic and molecular
  physicists, **1:** 359
Attaches, **1:** 189
Attendance officers, **2:** 288
Attorneys, **2:** 349-54. *See
  also* Law, Lawyers
  criminal, **1:** 253
  district, **1:** 253
  insurance, **1:** 247,
  2: 350
  patent, **1:** 110
  prosecuting, **2:** 350
  tax, **2:** 253, 350
  title, **2:** 253, 351
Auction clerks, **3:** 9
Auctioneers, **3:** 131-34
Audio control technicians,
  4: 326-28
Audiologists, **2:** 637-40
Audiovisual librarians,
  2: 360
Audiovisual program
  productions sales
  representatives, **3:** 179
Audiovisual specialists,
  2: 399-401
Audiovisual technicians,
  4: 328
Audit clerk supervisors,
  3: 5
Audit clerks, **3:** 5
Auditors, **1:** 4, 92, **2:** 2-6
Auto. *See* Automobiles
Autoclave operators,
  3: 420
Automated equipment
  technicians, **4:** 234-35
Automatic-equipment
  technicians, **4:** 104
Automatic mounters,
  3: 764
Automatic print developers,
  3: 764
Automobile body repairers,
  3: 475-79
Automobile bumper
  straighteners, **3:** 476
Automobile club
  information clerks, **3:** 75
Automobile damage
  appraiser, **2:** 324
Automobile mechanics,
  3: 480-84
Automobile radiator
  mechanics, **3:** 481

Automobile rental clerks,
  3: 24
Automobile repair service
  estimators, **3:** 485-88
Automobile sales workers,
  3: 131-36
Automobile testers, **2:** 288
Automotive, diesel, and gas
  turbines
  safety engineers, **4:** 125
  technicians, **4:** 124-30
Automotive cooling system
  technicians, **4:** 123
Automotive design drafters,
  2: 179
Automotive design layout
  drafters, **2:** 179
Automotive electricians,
  3: 481
Automotive engineers,
  1: 38, **2:** 207
Automotive exhaust
  technicians, **4:** 130-31
Automotive field-test
  technicians, **4:** 126
Automotive leasing sales
  representatives, **3:** 179
Automotive painters,
  3: 622-25
Automotive stylists, **1:** 38
Automotive technicians,
  1: 38
Automotives, **1:** 33-40
Auxiliary equipment and
  utility operators, **1:** 334
Auxiliary equipment
  operators, **3:** 767
Aviation, **1:** 41-48
Avionics technicians,
  1: 490, **4:** 7, 131
Baby stroller and
  wheelchair rental clerks,
  3: 24
Babysitters, **3:** 201
Backtenders, **3:** 445
Bacteriologists, **1:** 69
Bacteriology technologists,
  2: 407
Bakers, **1:** 181, **2:** 412,
  3: 204-9
  apprentice, **3:** 391
Bakery helpers, **3:** 391
Bakery machine mechanics,
  3: 391
Bakery products workers,
  3: 389-93
Bakery supervisors, **3:** 390
Bakery workers, **3:** 391
Baking, **1:** 49-53
Ball assemblers, **3:** 606
Ball-machine operators,
  3: 398
Ballet dancers, **2:** 146
Band saw operators,
  3: 434
Bank examiners, **2:** 3
  chief, **2:** 3

812

813

Industrial truck operators,
3: 746-48
Industrial waste inspectors,
2: 287
Infantrymen, **1:** 304-5
Information and education
technicians
forestry, **4:** 300
Information clerk cashiers,
3: 9
Information clerks, **3:** 75
Information officers,
1: 385, **2:** 241
Information scientists,
1: 127, **2:** 361, 658
Information systems
personnel, **1:** 93
Inhalation therapists. *See*
Respiratory therapists
Injection molders, **3:** 455
Injection molding machine
tenders, **1:** 437, **3:** 458
Inorganic chemists, **1:** 109,
2: 92
Inside adjusters, **2:** 324
Inspectors. *See also* Health
and regulatory inspectors
building, **2:** 133
construction, **2:** 133-36
electrical, **2:** 133
machines, **1:** 272
mechanical, **2:** 133
metals, **1:** 297
plumbing, **2:** 133
public utilities, **1:** 392
public works, **2:** 133
quality lens, **4:** 231
Institution librarians,
2: 360
Institutional cleaners,
3: 272
Instrument assemblers,
4: 232
Instrument assistants,
2: 653
Instrument-design
technicians, **4:** 196
Instrument makers, **1:** 272,
3: 524-27
Instrument repairers,
3: 581-84
Instrument-sales
technicians, **4:** 205
Instrumental musicians,
2: 423, 574
Instrumentation chemists,
2: 91
Instrumentation design
technicians, **4:** 205
Instrumentation
maintenance technicians,
4: 205
Instrumentation repair
technicians, **4:** 205
Instrumentation systems
sales representatives,
4: 206

Instrumentation technicians,
1: 152, **4:** 7, 204-9
troubleshooters, **4:** 205
Instrumentation test
technicians, **4:** 56
Insurance, **1:** 243-49
Insurance agents, **1:** 246
Insurance agents and
brokers
life, **3:** 144-49
property and casualty,
3: 149-53
Insurance attorneys,
1: 247, **2:** 350
Insurance checkers, **3:** 53
Insurance claims adjustors,
4: 125
Insurance claims
representatives,
2: 323-26
Insurance clerks, **3:** 37
Insurance firm bookkeeping
and accounting clerks,
3: 5
Insurance physicians,
1: 247
Insurance policy processing
personnel, **3:** 52-55
Intelligence officers, **1:** 305
Intercity bus drivers,
1: 489, **3:** 733-736
Interest clerks, **3:** 37
Interior designers, **1:** 140
Interior designers and
decorators, **2:** 326-331
Interline clerks, **3:** 2, 71
Internal auditors, **2:** 3
Internal Revenue Service
workers, **1:** 4
International affairs
specialists, **1:** 194
International economists,
2: 182
International lawyers,
2: 351
International operations
civil service, **1:** 116
International
representatives, **1:** 482
Internists, **2:** 495
Interpreters, **1:** 194,
2: 331-37, 370
Interpretive dancers,
2: 146
Inventory clerks, **3:** 96
Inventory control
technicians, **4:** 190
Investigators, **2:** 289, **3:** 317
Investment bankers, **1:** 60
Investment counselors,
1: 61
Invoice control clerks, **3:** 2
Iron and steel industry
workers, **3:** 423-26
Ironers, **3:** 303
Ironers and pressers,
3: 227

Jacquard-plate makers,
3: 530
Jailers, **3:** 211
Jammer operators, **3:** 375
Janitorial services, **3:** 272.
See also Building
custodians
Jewelers and jewelry
repairers, **3:** 584-87
Job analysts, **1:** 240, **2:** 463
Job and die setters,
3: 528-30
Job captains, **4:** 120
Job development specialists,
2: 463
Job setters, **1:** 271, **3:** 455
Job study technicians,
4: 263
Job superintendents
construction, **1:** 131
Journalists, **2:** 595-601,
705-6
Judges, **1:** 253, **2:** 349-54
Junior engineers, **4:** 117-18
Junior partners, **2:** 379
Juvenile court workers,
2: 629-30
Keno runners, **3:** 257
Kettle cooks, **3:** 394
Kettle operators, **3:** 420
Keypunch operators, **3:** 30
Kidney machine operators,
4: 387-92
Kiln firers, **2:** 97
Kiln operators, **4:** 302
Kindergarten teachers,
1: 145
Kinesiotherapists,
2: 337-40
Kitchen assistants, **1:** 181
Kitchen clerks, **3:** 96
Kitchen helpers, **3:** 252
Knit goods washers,
3: 531
Knit industry workers,
3: 530-34
Knitter mechanics, **3:** 530
Knitting machine fixers,
3: 531
Knitting machine operators,
3: 531
Lab technicians
paint and coatings
industry, **3:** 441
Labor economists, **2:** 183
Labor relations managers,
1: 240, **2:** 465
Labor union business
agents, **2:** 341-44
Laboratory analysts
plastics, **1:** 365
Laboratory animal care
veterinarians, **2:** 695
Laboratory assistants,
1: 151
Laboratory equipment
cleaners, **3:** 272

Laboratory supervisors,
2: 92
Laboratory technicians,
1: 105, **4:** 23, 209
Laboratory testers, **3:** 559
Laborers, **3:** 442
Lace and textile restorers,
2: 420
Lacers, **3:** 606
Lacquer makers, **3:** 441
Land development
managers, **2:** 528
Land leases-and-rental
managers, **2:** 528
Land leasing examiners,
3: 75
Land surveying managers,
2: 654
Land surveyors, **2:** 654
Landscape architects,
1: 139, **2:** 345-49
Landscape construction
supervisors, **4:** 309-310
Landscape consultants,
4: 310
Landscape contractors,
3: 370, **4:** 309
Landscape development
technicians, **4:** 308
Landscape drafters, **2:** 179,
4: 156
Landscape gardeners,
3: 370, **4:** 309
Landscape laborers, **3:** 370
Landscape maintenance
proprietors, **4:** 309
Landscape maintenance
supervisors, **4:** 309
Landscape planners,
4: 315
Landscapers and grounds
managers, **3:** 369-73
Larder cooks, **3:** 205
Laser technicians, **4:** 47-53
Lasers
research and
development, **4:** 50
Last pattern graders,
3: 549
Lathers, **3:** 668-70
Laundry pricing clerks,
3: 24, 226
Laundry workers, **3:** 225
Law, **1:** 250-55
Law librarians, **1:** 254
Lawn and tree service
spray supervisors, **3:** 370
Lawn service workers,
3: 371
Lawyers, **1:** 250-254,
2: 349-54. *See also*
Attorneys
foreign trade, **1:** 194
Layout artists, commercial
art, **2:** 121
Layout technicians,
4: 209-10, 427

Layout workers, machining, **1:** 271, **3:** 625, 670-73, **4:** 347

Leaf stampers, **3:** 749

Lease buyers, **2:** 528

Leasing real estate agents, **1:** 405

Leather coaters, **3:** 427

Leather stampers, **3:** 311

Leather tanning and finishing, **3:** 426

Legal advisors banking and financial services, **1:** 62

Legal assistants, **2:** 355-58

Legal investigators, **2:** 355-58

Legal secretaries, **3:** 82

Legal staff unions, **1:** 483

Lens blockers, **4:** 230

Lens centerers, **4:** 231

Lens edgers, **4:** 231

Lens finishers, **4:** 427

Lens generators, **4:** 230

Lens graders, **4:** 427

Lens grinders, **4:** 230

Lens molders, **4:** 230

Lens mounters, **3:** 596, **4:** 427

Lens polishers, **4:** 230

Letter and package delivery, **1:** 256-61

Letter carriers, **1:** 259

Letter-of-credit clerks, **3:** 37

Letter-of-credit negotiator, **2:** 232

Letterpress workers, **4:** 347

Liaison technicians, **4:** 7

Librarians, **1:** 265-6, **2:** 358-64
law, **1:** 254
morgue, **3:** 33
music, **1:** 85
tape, **3:** 33
technical, **1:** 109-10

Library administrators, **1:** 265

Library and information science, **1:** 262-68

Library assistants, **2:** 361

Library directors, **2:** 359

Library media specialists, **2:** 399-401

Library technical assistants, **4:** 470-72

Library technicians, **2:** 361, **4:** 470-72

Librettists, **2:** 423

License inspectors, **2:** 289

Licensed land surveyors, **4:** 146, 258

Licensed practical nurses, **1:** 226, **2:** 364-68

Licensed vocational nurses, **2:** 364-68

Life insurance sales agents, **3:** 144-49

Life scientists, **2:** 64

Life studies scientists, **1:** 46

Light technicians, **4:** 351-52

Lighting technicians, **1:** 348

Limnologists, **1:** 69, **2:** 439

Line fishers, **3:** 358

Line installers, **3:** 673-76, 791

Line photographers, **3:** 748

Linen room attendants, **3:** 96

Linen supply load builders, **3:** 226

Linguists, **2:** 368-73

Linotype operators, **3:** 496

Liquor establishment managers, **2:** 304

Literary agents, **1:** 78

Literary agents and artists' managers, **2:** 373-76

Literature researchers, **1:** 266

Lithographers, **1:** 379

Lithographic artists, **1:** 379, **3:** 749

Lithographic occupations, **3:** 748-51

Lithographic photographers, **3:** 748

Livestock inspectors, **2:** 695

Livestock production technicians, **4:** 289

Livestock ranchers, **3:** 346

Load dispatchers, **3:** 790

Loading machine operators, **3:** 335

Loan counselors, **2:** 232

Loan interviewers, **3:** 36

Loan officers, **1:** 60, **2:** 232

Lobbyists, **2:** 549
political, **1:** 370

Local representatives unions, **1:** 482

Location tour guides, **1:** 496

Lock experts, **3:** 588

Locket, ring, hand chain makers, **3:** 585

Locksmith apprentices, **3:** 588

Locksmiths, **3:** 588-590

Lockup workers, **4:** 347

Locomotive engineers, **3:** 751-53

Locomotive lubricating systems clerks, **3:** 71

Log chipper operators, **3:** 374

Log loaders, **3:** 375

Log scalers, **1:** 515

Logging industry workers, **3:** 373-77

Logging-operations inspectors, **2:** 288

Logging superintendents, **3:** 374

Logging supervisors, **3:** 374

Logging tractor operators, **1:** 515, **3:** 374

Logistics engineers, **1:** 168; **2:** 214

Long distance operators, **1:** 463

Longwall mining machine operators, **3:** 334

Loom operators, **1:** 469

Loopers, **3:** 532

Loss control and occupational health consultants, **3:** 293

LPN. *See* Practical nurses, Nurses

Lubrication sales engineering supervisors, **4:** 128

Lubrication sales technicians, **4:** 126

Luggage makers, **3:** 311

Lumber inspectors and/or graders, **4:** 300

Lunch truck drivers, **3:** 172

Lye-peel operators, **3:** 394

Lyricists, **2:** 423

Macaroni and related products industry workers, **3:** 429-33

Machine builders, **1:** 271

Machine coremakers, **3:** 401

Machine cutters, **1:** 437, **3:** 532

Machine designers, **4:** 158, 214
engineers, **1:** 270

Machine drillers, **3:** 334

Machine finishers, **3:** 455

Machine icers, **3:** 390

Machine maintenance employees, **4:** 126

Machine milkers, **3:** 339

Machine molders, **3:** 437

Machine movers, **3:** 708

Machine operators, **4:** 28
textiles, **1:** 468

Machine operators and tenders, **3:** 412
glass manufacturing, **1:** 216

Machine set-up operators, **1:** 271

Machine technicians textiles, **1:** 468

Machine tool operators, **1:** 271, **3:** 535-38

Machine trimmers, **3:** 600

Machines research engineers, **1:** 270

Machining and fabrication technicians lasers, **4:** 50

Machining and machinery, **1:** 269-74

Machining engineers, **1:** 270

Machining workers, **1:** 270, **3:** 270

Machinists, **3:** 538-41

Magazine keepers, **3:** 96

Magazine publishing, **1:** 275-79

Magicians, **2:** 7

Magistrates, **2:** 351

Magnetic tape typewriter operators, **3:** 125

Maids, **3:** 264, 268. *See also* Hotel housekeepers; Housekeepers

Mail and information clerks, **3:** 49

Mail carrier supervisors, **3:** 56

Mail carriers, **3:** 55-59

Mail censors, **3:** 63

Mail clerks, **1:** 259, **3:** 62

Mail handlers, **1:** 259, **3:** 63

Maintainability engineers, **2:** 214

Maintenance and engineering workers, **1:** 234

Maintenance electricians, **3:** 653

Maintenance mechanics, **3:** 522

Maintenance personnel aviation, **1:** 46

Maintenance supervisors, **3:** 272

Maintenance workers baking, **1:** 52
transportation, **1:** 490

Makeup artists, **1:** 348

Mammalogists, **1:** 69

Management foreign trade, **1:** 194

Management accountants, **1:** 3

Management aides, **2:** 312

Management analysts and consultants, **2:** 99, 376-81

Management trainees, **2:** 381-86

Managers, **2:** 256-61
civil service, **1:** 116
newspapers, **1:** 326

Managers of college placement services, **2:** 463

Managers of farm cooperatives, **4:** 297

825